Today's most **popular authors** have collaborated on this exciting new series, which combines **great literature** with remarkably **effective instruction,** bringing real writers and real tools together for real results.

Give your students

Real writers

unprecedented access to award-winning authors (see page T2)

Real tools

remarkably effective tools for differentiated instruction (see page T4)

Real results

built-in benchmarking to guarantee standards mastery and learning success (see page T6)

"This project is what I wish I'd had when I was in school . . . a resource where I could not only read really good writing, but also get a sense about how the authors actually felt!"

—Cornelius Eady
featured unit author

TEACHER'S EDITION CONTENTS

TEACHER'S EDITION

PRENTICE HALL LITERATURE

PENGUIN EDITION

THE AMERICAN EXPERIENCE

VOLUME II

Boston, Massachusetts
Upper Saddle River, New Jersey

ISBN 0-13-131759-8
4 5 6 7 8 9 10 10 09 08 07

CONTRIBUTING AUTHORS

The contributing authors guided the direction and philosophy of *Prentice Hall Literature, Penguin Edition.* Working with the development team, they helped to build the pedagogical integrity of the program and to ensure its relevance for today's teachers and students.

Kate **Kinsella**

Kate Kinsella, Ed.D., is a teacher educator in the Department of Secondary Education at San Francisco State University. She teaches coursework addressing academic language and literacy development in linguistically and culturally diverse classrooms. Dr. Kinsella maintains secondary classroom involvement by teaching an academic literacy class for adolescent English learners through the University's Step to College Program. She publishes and provides consultancy and training nationally, focusing upon responsible instructional practices that provide second language learners and less proficient readers in grades 4–12 with the language and literacy skills vital to educational mobility.

Dr. Kinsella is the program author for *Reading in the Content Areas: Strategies for Reading Success,* published by Pearson Learning, and the lead program author for the 2002 Prentice Hall secondary language arts program *Timeless Voices: Timeless Themes.* She is the co-editor of the *CATESOL Journal* (California Association of Teachers of ESL) and serves on the editorial board for the *California Reader.* A former Fulbright scholar, Dr. Kinsella has received numerous awards, including the prestigious Marcus Foster Memorial Reading Award, offered by the California Reading Association in 2002 to a California educator who has made a significant statewide impact on both policy and pedagogy in the area of literacy.

Sharon **Vaughn**

Sharon Vaughn, Ph.D., is the H.E. Hartfelder/The Southland Corporation Regents Professor at the University of Texas and also director of the Vaughn Gross Center for Reading and Language Arts at the University of Texas (VGCRLA). As director of the VGCRLA, she leads more than five major initiatives, including The Central Regional Reading First Technical Assistance Center; the Three-Tier Reading Research Project; a bilingual-biliteracy (English/Spanish) intervention research study; the Grades 1–4 Teacher Reading Academies that have been used for teacher education throughout Texas and the nation; and the creation of online professional development in reading for teachers and other interested professionals.

Dr. Vaughn has published more than ten books and over one hundred research articles. She is Editor in Chief of the *Journal of Learning Disabilities* and serves on the editorial boards of more than ten research journals, including the *Journal of Educational Psychology,* the *American Educational Research Journal,* and the *Journal of Special Education.*

Kevin **Feldman**

Kevin Feldman, Ed.D., is the Director of Reading and Intervention for the Sonoma County Office of Education and an independent educational consultant. He publishes and provides consultancy and training nationally, focusing upon improving school-wide literacy skills as well as targeted interventions for struggling readers, special needs students, and second language learners. Dr. Feldman is the co-author of the California Special Education Reading Task Force report and the lead program author for the 2002 Prentice Hall secondary language arts program *Timeless Voices: Timeless Themes.* He serves as technical consultant to the California Reading and Literature Project and the CalSTAT State Special Education Improvement Project. Dr. Feldman has taught for nineteen years at the university level in Special Education and Masters' level programs for University of California, Riverside, and Sonoma State University.

Dr. Feldman earned his undergraduate degree in Psychology from Washington State University and has a Master's Degree from UC Riverside in Special Education, Learning Disabilities, and Instructional Design. He has an Ed.D. from the University of San Francisco in Curriculum and Instruction.

Differentiated Instruction Advisor

Don **Deshler**

Don Deshler, Ph.D, is the Director of the Center for Research on Learning (CRL) at the University of Kansas. Dr. Deshler's expertise centers on adolescent literacy, learning strategic instruction, and instructional strategies for teaching content-area classes to academically diverse classes. He is the author of *Teaching Content to All: Evidence-Based Inclusive Practices in Middle and Secondary Schools,* a text which presents the instructional practices that have been tested and validated through his research at CRL.

UNIT AUTHORS

An award-winning contemporary author hosts each unit in each level of *Prentice Hall Literature: Penguin Edition*. In the upper-level courses, some of these authors are renowned scholars or translators, while others are famous for their own contributions to literature. All of these authors serve as guides for your students, helping to introduce the period or culture covered in a unit, discussing the work of a traditional author or their own work or translation, and revealing their own writing processes. Following are the featured unit authors who guide students for *The American Experience*.

Susan **Power (b. 1961)**

Unit 1: A Gathering of Voices (Beginnings to 1750)

Native American novelist Susan Powers is the ideal guide for this unit. She discusses the oral tradition and introduces her own work in relation to traditional Native American selections. Of Dakota Sioux heritage, Ms. Power won the PEN/Hemingway Award for First Novel for *The Grass Dancer*.

William L. **Andrews (b. 1946)**

Unit 2: A Nation Is Born (1750–1800)

Professor William L. Andrews, who studies the links between white and black writers in the formation of American literature, is well suited to introduce this unit and the work of Olaudah Equiano. Holder of a named chair at the University of North Carolina, Professor Andrews is a co-editor of *The Norton Anthology of African American Literature*.

Gretel **Ehrlich (b. 1946)**

Unit 3: A Growing Nation (1800–1870)

Gretel Ehrlich, one of the best essayists writing on nature today, is the perfect choice to introduce this unit and the work of Thoreau. Ehrlich's books have received many prizes, including the Harold D. Vursell Award from the American Academy of Arts and Letters. *Newsday* called her essays in *The Solace of Open Spaces* "stunning."

Charles **Johnson (b. 1948)**

Unit 3: A Growing Nation (1800–1870)

Charles Johnson's versatility and individualism would have delighted Emerson, the author whom he introduces. Johnson, who in high school was influenced by Emerson's essays, is the author of the novel *Middle Passage,* a National Book Award winner, as well as screenplays and works of philosophy.

Nell Irvin **Painter (b. 1942)**

Unit 4: Division, Reconciliation, and Expansion (1850–1914)

Nell Irvin Painter introduces this unit and the work of Sojourner Truth. Her qualifications include her award-winning books *Standing at Armageddon,* which focuses on the time period covered by this unit, and *Sojourner Truth, A Life, A Symbol.* Currently the Edwards Professor of American History at Princeton University, Ms. Painter was the Director of Princeton's Program in African-American Studies from 1997 to 2000.

Tim **O'Brien (b. 1946)**

Unit 5: Disillusion, Defiance, and Discontent (1914–1946)

One of the best novelists writing today, Tim O'Brien pays homage to authors from this unit that he first read in high school. He also introduces his story "Ambush," which builds on the work of early twentieth-century writers as it explores themes arising from wartime experience. Mr. O'Brien's novel *Going After Cacciato* won the National Book Award, and *The Things They Carried,* from which *"Ambush"* comes, was a Pulitzer Prize finalist.

Arthur **Miller (1915–2005)**

Unit 6: Prosperity and Protest (1946–Present)

Arthur Miller, whose play *The Crucible* is a major selection in the unit, introduces both the unit and the play. Widely regarded as a great American playwright, Miller discusses theater's contribution to society and provides personal and historical background on the writing of *The Crucible.* Among other honors, Miller received a Pulitzer Prize for *Death of a Salesman,* a Tony Award for lifetime achievement, and a National Medal of the Arts.

PROGRAM ADVISORS

The program advisors provided ongoing input throughout the development of *Prentice Hall Literature: Penguin Edition*. Their valuable insights ensure that the perspectives of the teachers throughout the country are represented within this literature series.

Sherice Alford
Language Arts Instructor
Cape Fear Senior High School
Fayetteville, North Carolina

Leslie Ballard
State Director
North Central Association CASI
Indiana State University
Terre Haute, Indiana

Heather Barnes
Language Arts Instructor
Central Crossing High School
Grove City, Ohio

Kathryn Shelley-Barnes
District Support Specialist
Traverse City Central High School
Traverse City, Michigan

Karen C. Lilly-Bowyer
Instructional Services Assessment Team
Winston-Salem Forsyth County Schools
Winston-Salem, North Carolina

Lee Bromberger
English Department Chairperson
Mukwonago High School
Mukwonago, Wisconsin

Shawn L. Brumfield
Literacy Coach
Horace Mann Middle School
Los Angeles Unified School District
Local 3
Los Angeles, California

Susanne Buttrey
Librarian
Sycamore Middle School
Pleasant View, Tennessee

Denise Campbell
K-12 Literacy Content Coordinator
Cherry Creek School District
Centennial, Colorado

Patricia A. Cantrowitz
Language Arts Instructor (Retired)
Union-Endicott High School
Endicott, New York

Holly Carr
Language Arts Instructor
Central Crossing High School
Grove City, Ohio

Melody Renee Chalmers
Language Arts Instructor
E. E. Smith High School
Fayetteville, North Carolina

Susan Cisna
Language Arts Instructor
East Prairie Junior High School
Tuscola, Illinois

Barbra Evans-Thompson
English Department Chairperson
Westover High School
Fayetteville, North Carolina

Ebony Forte
Language Arts Instructor
Pine Forest Senior High School
Fayetteville, North Carolina

Linda Fund
Reading Specialist
Ezra L. Nolan Middle School #40
Jersey City, New Jersey

Karen Gibson, Ph.D.
Communication Arts Program Leader
Appleton Area School District
Appleton, Wisconsin

Gail Hacker
Language Arts Instructor (Retired)
North Charleston High School
North Charleston, South Carolina

Kimberly Hartman
Language Arts Instructor
Franklin Heights High School
Columbus, Ohio

Doris Sue Hawkins
Language Arts Instructor
C. W. Otto Middle School
Lansing, Michigan

Darby Holley
Language Arts Instructor
Henry L. Sneed Middle School
Florence, South Carolina

Helen Hudson
Language Arts Instructor
Crawfordsville High School
Crawfordsville, Indiana

Kathleen Keane
English Department Chairperson
Foxborough High School
Foxborough, Massachusetts

John Kiser
English Curriculum Specialist (Retired)
Charlotte-Mecklenburg Schools
Charlotte, North Carolina

Cheryl W. Lee
Language Arts Instructor
Douglas Byrd High School
Fayetteville, North Carolina

Carrie Lichtenberg
Language Arts Instructor
Highlands High School
Ft. Thomas, Kentucky

Catherine Linn
Language Arts Instructor
Palm Springs High School
Palm Desert, California

Agathaniki Locklear
District Technology Resource Teacher
Kenton County Schools
Ft. Wright, Kentucky

John Ludy
Language Arts Instructor
Fremont High School
Fremont, Indiana

Louise R. Matthewson
Language Arts Instructor
Albuquerque Public Schools
Albuquerque, New Mexico

Sherrie McDowell
Language Arts Instructor
Central High School
Cheyenne, Wyoming

Suzanne Mitoraj
English/Language Arts Consultant
Berlin, Connecticut

Nancy Monroe
Language Arts Instructor
Bolton High School
Alexandria, Louisiana

Gail Phelps
Language Arts Instructor
Northwood Middle School
North Little Rock, Arkansas

Matthew Scanlon
K-12 Humanities Supervisor
Hackettstown Public Schools
Hackettstown, New Jersey

John Scott
Language Arts Instructor (Retired)
Hampton City Schools
Hampton City, Virginia

Jean Shope
Language Arts Instructor
Grant Middle School
Albuquerque, New Mexico

Margaret St. Sauver
Staff Development-English/Language Arts
St. Paul Public Schools
St. Paul, Minnesota

Steve Thalheimer
Language Arts Instructor
Lawrenceburg High School
Lawrenceburg, Indiana

Cathy Robbs Turner
Director of Academies
Chattanooga Central High School
Harrison, Tennessee

Sandra VanBelois
Language Arts Instructor
Jack Britt High School
Fayetteville, North Carolina

Martha Lee Wildman
Language Arts Instructor
Lynn Middle School
Las Cruces, New Mexico

Melissa Williams
Language Arts Instructor
Delsea Regional High School
Franklinville, New Jersey

Charles Youngs
HS Language Arts Curriculum Facilitator
Bethel Park High School
Bethel Park, Pennsylvania

CONTENTS IN BRIEF

Unit 1

A Gathering of Voices:
Literature of Early America (Beginnings to 1750)

From the Author's Desk
Susan Power

TEACHING PARTNERS

An award-winning author, scholar, or translator discusses the time period and annotates a literary selection.

Part One Meeting of Cultures

SELECTION GROUPINGS

These groupings allow you to compare a variety of literary works.

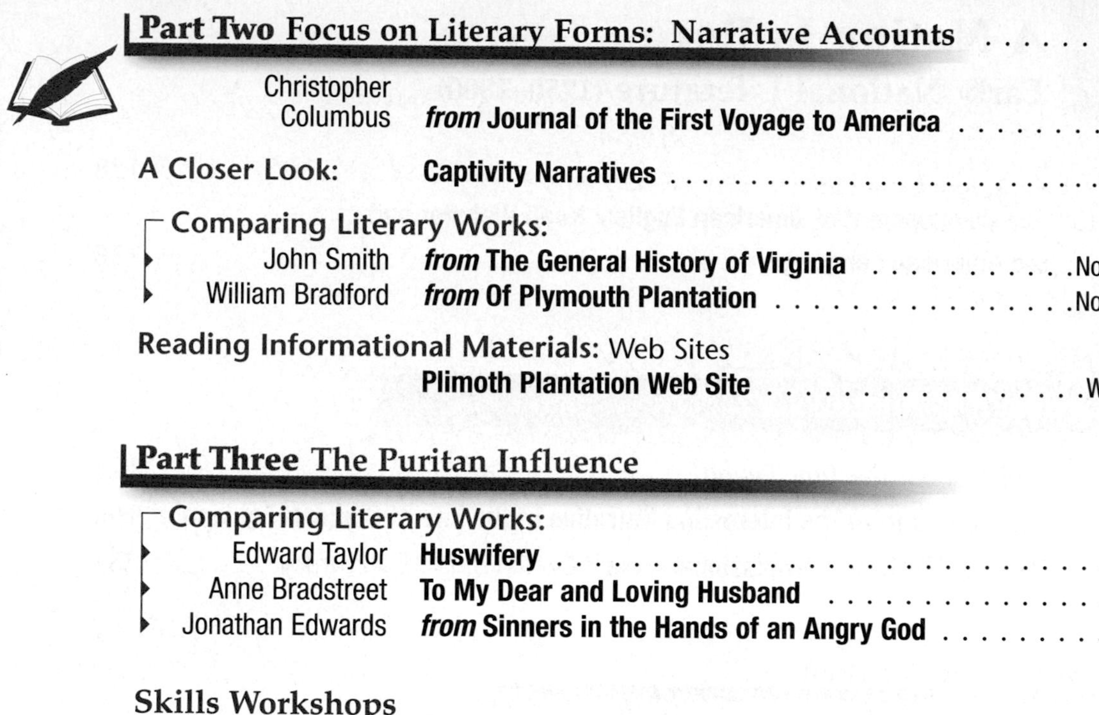

FOCUS ON GENRE
Students focus on a specific genre to enhance understanding and ensure mastery.

Unit 2

A Nation Is Born

Early National Literature (1750–1800)

Unit 3

A Growing Nation

Nineteenth-Century Literature (1800–1870)

From the Scholar's Desk

Gretel Ehrlich

Part One Fireside and Campfire

Part Two Shadows of the Imagination

Unit 4

Division, Reconciliation, and Expansion:

The Age of Realism (1850–1914)

Unit 5

Disillusion, Defiance, and Discontent:
The Modern Age (1914–1946)

From the Author's Desk
Tim O'Brien

Part One Facing Troubled Times

Unit 6

Prosperity and Protest

The Contemporary Period (1946–Present)

INFORMATIONAL TEXTS AND OTHER NONFICTION

Reading Informational Materials—Instructional Workshops

Additional Nonfiction—Selections by Type

Primary Sources: Political Texts and Speeches

Primary Sources: Diaries, Journals, and Letters

Essays:

Narrative Accounts

Autobiography

Historical and Literary Background

INFORMATIONAL TEXTS AND OTHER NONFICTION (continued)

The American Experience—Reading in the Humanities

Literature in Context—Reading in the Content Areas

A Closer Look

Focus on Literary Forms

SKILLS WORKSHOPS

Writing Workshops

SAT® PREP ACT

Vocabulary Workshops

SAT® PREP ACT

Assessment Workshops

SAT® PREP ACT

Communications Workshops

Connections to Literature

Literature Around the World

British Literature

PRENTICE HALL LITERATURE

THE AMERICAN EXPERIENCE

Flag on Orange Field by Jasper Johns (b. 1930) is an example of Johns's use of familiar objects as subject matter. It is this focus that made Johns the "Father of Pop Art and Minimalism," movements that became popular in the 1960s. In this work, painter, sculptor, and printmaker Johns uses *encaustic* paint, paint pigments mixed with hot wax. The material gave his work a sculpture-like appearance. Johns's style has been called "art of assemblage," for its use of ordinary and familiar objects and integration of three-dimensional objects.

PENGUIN  EDITION

Upper Saddle River, New Jersey

Boston, Massachusetts

ISBN 0-13-131719-9

2 3 4 5 6 7 8 9 10   09 08 07 06

Cover: *Flag on Orange Field*, 1957, oil on canvas, Jasper Johns (b. 1930) / Ludwig Museum, Cologne, Germany, Lauros / Giraudon/www.bridgeman.co.uk. Cover art © Jasper Johns/Licensed by VAGA, New York, NY.

Acknowledgments

Grateful acknowledgment is made to the following for copyrighted material:

The James Baldwin Estate "The Rockpile" is collected in *Going to Meet the Man*, (c) 1965 by James Baldwin. Copyright renewed. Published by Vintage Books. Used by arrangement with the James Baldwin Estate. **Susan Bergholz Literary Services** "Antojos" by Julia Alvarez, copyright © 1991 by Julia Alvarez. Later published in slightly different from in *How the Garcia Girls Lost Their Accents*, copyright © 1991 by Julia Alvarez. Published by Plume, an imprint of Dutton Signet, a division of Penguin USA, Inc., and originally in hardcover by Algonquin Books of Chapel Hill. "Straw into Gold: The Metamorphosis of the Everyday" by Sandra Cisneros from *The Texas Observer*. Copyright © 1987 by Sandra Cisneros. First published in *The Texas Observer*, September 1987. Reprinted by permission of Susan Bergholz Literary Services, New York. All rights reserved. **Brooks Permissions** "The Explorer" from *Blacks* by Gwendolyn Brooks. Reprinted by consent of Brooks Permissions. **Toby Cole, Agent for the Pirandello Estate** "War" by Luigi Pirandello from *The Medals and Other Stories*. Used by permission of Toby Cole, Actors & Authors Agency. **Eugenia Collier** "Marigolds" by Eugenia W. Collier, published in *Negro Digest*, November 1969. Used by permission of Eugenia W. Collier. **Sandra Dijkstra Literary Agency** "Mother Tongue" by Amy Tan. Excerpt of *The Joy Luck Club*. Copyright © 1989 by Amy Tan. Used by permission of the author and the Sandra Dijkstra Literary Agency. **Doubleday, a division of Random House, Inc.** "Light Comes Brighter" and "The Adamant" copyright 1938 from *The Collected Poems of Theodore Roethkhe* by Theodore Roethke. Used by permission of Doubleday, a division of Random House, Inc. **Rita Dove** "For the Love of Books" from *Selected Poems*, Pantheon by Rita Dove. Copyright © 1993 by Rita Dove. Reprinted by permission of the author. **The Echo Foundation** "The Echo Foundation Brings Henry Gates, Jr. to Charlotte" by Staff from The Echo Foundation. **Richard Erdoes** "When Grizzlies Walked Upright" by Modoc Indians, retold by Richard Erdoes and Alfonso Ortiz from *American History Customized Reader*. **Faber and Faber Limited** "Mirror" by Sylvia Plath from *Crossing the Water*. Copyright © 1963 by Ted Hughes. **Farrar, Straus & Giroux, LLC** "When in early summer" by Nelly Sachs translated by Matthew & Ruth Mead from *The Seeker And Other Poems*. "Coyote v. Acme" by Ian Frazier from *Coyote Vs. Acme*. "The Death of the Ball Turret Gunner" by Randall Jarrell from *The Complete Poems of Randall Jarrell*. "Losses" by Randall Jarrell from *The Complete Poems of Randall Jarrell*. "The First Seven Years" by Bernard Malamud from *The Magic Barrel*. Copyright © 1950, 1958 and copyright renewed © 1977, 1986 by Bernard Malamud. "Hawthorne" by Robert Lowell from *For the Union Dead*. Copyright © 1964 by Robert Lowell. **Fulcrum Publishing, Inc.** "The Earth on Turtle's Back" by Joseph Bruchac and Michael. J. Caduto from *Keepers of the Earth: Native American Stories and Environmental Activities*. Used by permission of Fulcrum Publishing, Inc. **Graywolf Press** "Traveling through the Dark" copyright 1962, 1998 by the Estate of William Stafford. Reprinted from *The Way It Is: New and Selected Poems* with the permission of Graywolf Press, Saint Paul, Minnesota. **Harcourt, Inc.** "The Life You Save May Be Your Own" by Flannery O'Connor from *A Good Man Is Hard To Find And Other Stories*. Copyright © 1953 by Flannery O'Connor and renewed 1981 by Regina O'Connor. "Everyday Use" by Alice Walker from *In Love And Trouble: Stories Of Black Women*. Copyright © 1973 by Alice Walker. "The Jilting of Granny Weatherall" from *Flowering Judas and Other Stories*, copyright 1930 and renewed 1958 by Katherine Anne Porter. "Grass" and "Chicago" *from Chicago Poems* by Carl Sandburg, copyright 1916 by Holt, Rinehart and Winston and renewed 1944 by Carl Sandburg. Reprinted by permission of Harcourt, Inc. **HarperCollins Publishers, Inc.** "Bidwell Ghost" from *Baptism of Desire* by Louise Erdrich. Copyright © 1990 by Louise Erdrich. "Mirror" from *Crossing the Water* by Sylvia Plath. Copyright © 1963 by Ted Hughes. Originally appeared in The New Yorker. From "Dust Tracks On A Road" by Zora Neale Hurston. Copypright 1942 by Zora Neale Hurston; renewed © 1970 by John C. Hurston. Reprinted by permission of HarperCollins Publishers. **Harvard University Press** "Because I could not stop for Death (#712)" by Emily Dickinson from *The Poems Of Emily Dickinson*, Thomas H. Johnson, ed., Cambridge, Mass.: The Belknap Press of Harvard University Press, Copyright (c) 1951, 1955, 1979 by the Presidents and Fellows of Harvard College. "There's a certain Slant of light (#258)" by Emily Dickinson from *The Poems of Emily Dickinson,* Thomas H. Johnson, ed., Cambridge, Mass.: The Belknap Press of Harvard University Press, Copyright (c) 1951, 1955, 1979 by the Presidents and Fellows of Harvard College. "I heard a Fly buzz—when I died (#465)" by Emily Dickinson from *The Poems Of Emily Dickinson*, Thomas H. Johnson, ed., Cambridge, Mass.: The Belknap Press of Harvard University Press, Copyright (c) 1951, 1955, 1979 by the Presidents and Fellows of Harvard College. "My life closed twice before its close (#1732)" by Emily Dickinson from The Poems of Emily Dickinson, Thomas H. Johnson, ed., Cambridge, Mass.: The Belknap Press of Harvard University Press, Copyright (c) 1951, 1955, 1979 by the Presidents and Fellows of Harvard College. "There is a solitude of space (#1695)" by Emily Dickinson from *The Poems of Emily Dickinson,* Thomas H. Johnson, ed., Cambridge, Mass.: The Belknap Press of Harvard University Press, Copyright (c) 1951, 1955, 1979 by the Presidents and Fellows of Harvard College. "The Soul selects her own Society (#303)" by Emily Dickinson from *The Poems of Emily Dickinson,* Thomas H. Johnson, ed., Cambridge, Mass.: The Belknap Press of Harvard University Press, Copyright (c) 1951, 1955, 1979 by the Presidents and Fellows of Harvard College. Reprinted by permission of the publishers and the Trustees of Amherst College.

(Continued on page R61, which is hereby considered an extension of this copyright page.)

PRENTICE HALL LITERATURE

PENGUIN EDITION

THE AMERICAN EXPERIENCE

VOLUME II

Meeting Your Standards

Students will

1. read American literature selections written between 1914 and 1946.
2. apply strategies for reading poetry that are appropriate for these selections.
3. analyze literary elements.
4. use a variety of strategies to read unfamiliar words and to build vocabulary.
5. learn elements of grammar, usage, and style.
6. use recursive writing processes to write in a variety of forms.
7. develop listening and speaking skills.
8. express and support responses to various types of texts.
9. prepare, organize, and present literary interpretations.

Unit Instructional Resources

In *Unit 5 Resources,* you will find materials to support students in developing and mastering the unit skills and to help you assess their progress.

▶ Vocabulary and Reading

Additional vocabulary and reading support, based on Lexile scores of vocabulary words, is provided for each selection or grouping.

- **Word Lists A and B and Practices A and B** provide vocabulary-building activities for students reading two grades or one grade below level, respectively.
- **Reading Warm-ups A and B**, for students reading two grades or one grade below level, respectively, consist of short readings and activities that provide a context and practice for newly learned vocabulary.

▶ Selection Support

- Reading Strategy
- Literary Analysis
- Vocabulary Builder
- Grammar and Style
- Support for Writing
- Support for Extend Your Learning
- Enrichment

PRENTICE HALL TeacherEXPRESS™ Plan · Teach · Assess You may also access these resources on TeacherExpress.

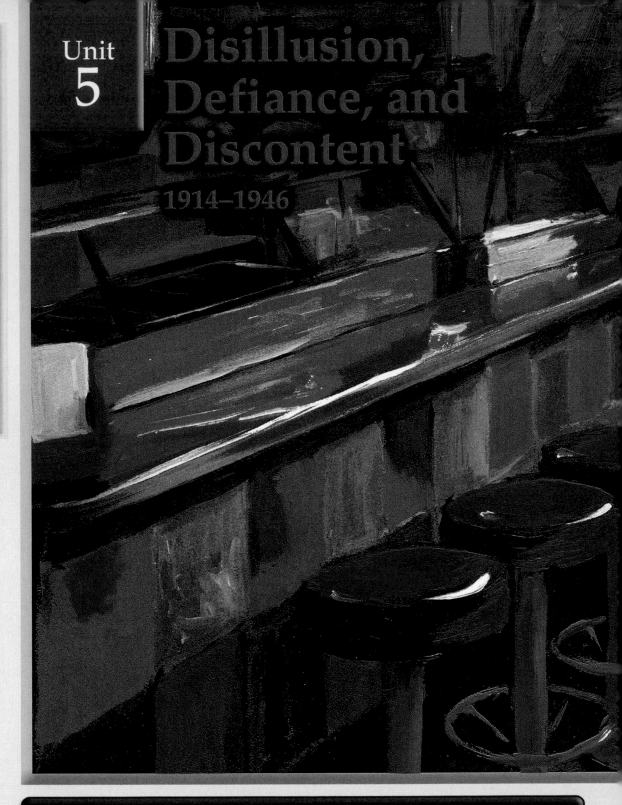

Unit 5 Disillusion, Defiance, and Discontent

1914–1946

Assessment Resources

Listed below are the resources available to assess and measure students' progress in meeting the unit objectives and your state standards.

Skills Assessment

Unit 5 Resources
  Selection Tests A and B

TeacherExpress™
  ExamView® Test Bank Software

Adequate Yearly Progress Assessment

Unit 5 Resources
  Diagnostic Tests 8 and 9
  Benchmark Tests 7 and 8

Standardized Assessment

Standardized Test Preparation Workbook

The Modern Age

"We asked the cyclone to go around our barn but it didn't hear us."

—Carl Sandburg, from *The People, Yes*

This painting, *At the Farmer's Market* by Pam Ingalls, shows a scene of everyday life in the modern world.

Introduce Unit 5

- Direct students' attention to the title and time period of this unit. Have a student read the quotation. **Ask them:** What does this quotation suggest about Americans at this point in their history?
  Possible response: Americans were experiencing hardships and turmoil at this point in their history.
- Have students look at the art. Read the Humanities note to them, and ask the discussion questions.
- Then **ask:** What kinds of literature or themes in literature do you think might come out of this period in American history?
  Possible response: Students may suggest themes of loneliness, disappointment, and hardship. They may suggest that poetry and short fiction would address these themes.

Humanities

At the Farmer's Market, by Pam Ingalls

Pam Ingalls studied at the Accademia Delle Belle Arte in Florence, Italy, and Gonzaga University in Spokane, WA. She also studied under Frederick Frank, Ron Lucas, Richard Schmid, and Burt Silverman. Ingalls creates oil paintings of simple subject matter in the Russian Impressionist tradition. She has won more than 60 prizes and has exhibited her work in over 125 national and international art shows. Use the following items for discussion:

1. What mood does the painting create, and how?
   Possible response: Most students will suggest that despite the vibrant colors the mood is one of isolation.
2. Make up a story about the man sitting alone.
   Possible response: Students' stories should indicate why the person is there and how he feels in the moment.

Unit Features

Tim O'Brien
Each unit features commentary by a contemporary writer or scholar under the heading "From the Author's Desk." Author Tim O'Brien introduces Unit 5 in Setting the Scene, in which he discusses how literature has affected his life. Later in the unit he introduces his own selection, "Ambush." He also contributes his insights in the Writing Workshop.

Connections
Every unit contains a feature that connects the American literature of the period to World Literature. In this unit, students will connect twentieth-century pastoral poetry by Robert Frost and Dylan Thomas.

Use the information and questions on the Connections pages to help students enrich their understanding of the selections in this unit.

Reading Informational Materials
These selections will help students learn to analyze and evaluate informational materials, such as workplace documents, technical directions, and consumer materials. Students will learn the organization and features unique to nonnarrative text.

In this unit, students will read public relations documents from the Museum of Afro-American History.

From the Author's Desk

Introduce Tim O'Brien

- Tim O'Brien introduces the unit and discusses the importance of literature in his life. His story "Ambush" appears later in the unit on pages 834–836.
- Have students read the introductory paragraph about Tim O'Brien. Tell them that O'Brien writes stories that deal with disillusion and discontent. His experiences as a soldier in Vietnam provided sources for many of his works, yet his desire to write had an ultimate connection with his days as a boy in Minnesota.
- Use the *From the Author's Desk DVD* to introduce Tim O'Brien. Show Segment 1 to provide insight into his writing career. After students have watched the segment, **ask** them why people's life-changing experiences, such as fighting in a war, might fuel their desire to write.
  Answer: Life-changing events may lead people to closely examine life, which then prompts them to deal with particular issues and emotions. Writing may help sort those issues and emotions.

Literature As a Magic Carpet

- Have students read Tim O'Brien's discussion about the effects of literature on his life. O'Brien explains that the stories and poetry that he read as a student made him want to become a writer.
  Ask: In what ways has literature been important to Tim O'Brien?
  Possible answer: Literature was a form of escape from an ordinary life, and it inspired him to produce his own literature.
- Tell students that they will also read "Ambush" by Tim O'Brien in Part 3 of this unit. O'Brien will also explain his writing of that piece.

Critical Viewing

Possible response: The man in the picture appears to be focused and involved in what he is reading. His relaxed posture and content expression show his enjoyment of the book.

Setting the Scene

Unit 5 features writing from one of the most innovative periods in American literary history, a period that includes both Modernism and the Harlem Renaissance. The following essay by Tim O'Brien explores his own first encounter with this literature when he was in high school—and its impact on his decision to become a writer. As you read his essay, the unit introduction that follows, and the literature in Unit 5, let yourself experience this exciting time in American history.

From the Author's Desk
Tim O'Brien Talks About the Time Period

Tim O'Brien

Introducing Tim O'Brien (b. 1946) Born in Minnesota, O'Brien was drafted after college to fight in the Vietnam War. Although he has written extensively about the war and its aftermath, he resists being labeled a "Vietnam writer." O'Brien's fiction explores the larger themes of betrayal and loss of faith, as well as the tension between truth and fiction. He has been called "the best American writer of his generation."

Literature As a Magic Carpet

As a boy of fifteen or sixteen, feeling restless and marooned in a small town on the prairies of southern Minnesota, I began using literature as a kind of magic carpet—a way of flying off to more exciting places on the earth, a way of escaping the brutal Minnesota winters and the dull, drowsy, summertime fields of soybeans and alfalfa and corn. I didn't merely read. I was transported. I *lived* inside stories and novels. Just turn a page—that simple—and I was suddenly a soldier in World War I, or a young man in love during the famous Jazz Age, or a grieving parent, or an aging railroad engineer, or an old African American woman trudging down a path through the frozen woods of Mississippi.

Inventing Stories of My Own The word "literature," I'll confess, did not mean much to me. It seemed too fancy, too formidable. Even so, by the time I'd graduated from high school, I had read—mostly on my own, mostly for fun—a good many of the stories and poems that appear in this unit. I remember, for instance, my first encounter with Hemingway's "In Another Country" during the summer between my sophomore and junior years. I remember marveling at the water-clear transparency of the prose, the deceptive simplicity of the plot, the quiet, uncomplaining dignity of the characters, those solid nouns, those invigorating verbs, the unspoken and unspeakable emotional pain that hovered like an invisible vapor just above the surface of each page. More than anything, though, I remember thinking: Wow, I want to try this. I want to invent stories of my own. I want to write fiction someday.

Teaching Resources

The following resources can be used to enrich or extend the instruction for the Unit 5 Introduction.

Unit 5 Resources
- **Names and Terms to Know,** p. 2
- **Focus Questions,** p. 3
- **Listening and Viewing,** p. 144

From the Author's Desk DVD
- **Tim O'Brien,** Segment 1

Poetry As Explosive As Artillery Not much later, in the first months of my junior year in high school, these fantasies about becoming a writer were reinforced by the work of two very dissimilar poets, T. S. Eliot and Robert Frost, both of whom are represented in this unit. Until then, I'd stupidly conceived of poetry as something for English teachers and nearsighted librarians. I hadn't realized that a good poem could be as explosive as any artillery round, as powerful as any rocket lifting off for the moon.

Living the Poem From T. S. Eliot I learned that vivid writing requires vivid imagery, and that vivid imagery requires something unexpected and off the beaten literary path: a patient etherized upon a table; sawdust restaurants; women who come and go, talking of Michelangelo. To this day, Robert Frost's "Stopping by Woods on a Snowy Evening" remains one of my favorite pieces of writing. The words in themselves are ordinary—no need for a dictionary—but the impact of the poem, its pressure on the human spirit, is extraordinary. We feel the cold, snowy dark against our skin. We hear the harness bells, the wind, and the eerie, timeless echo of our own mortality. We don't merely read the poem. We live it. And we come to understand that, one way or another, all of us have promises to keep, and miles to go before we sleep.

Rekindling a Fire My dream of becoming a writer has come true. And yet rereading these stories and poems has rekindled a fire inside me. I'm a teenager again. I want to write a new novel.

▲ **Critical Viewing** In what ways does this young man seem like a reader who uses "literature as a . . . magic carpet," the way Tim O'Brien did? **[Connect]**

Go Online
Author Link

For: An online video
Visit: www.PHSchool.com
Web Code: ere-8501

For: More about Tim O'Brien
Visit: www.PHSchool.com
Web Code: ere-9516

Reading the Unit Introduction

Reading for Information and Insight Use the following terms and questions to guide your reading of the unit introduction on pages 704–711.

Names and Terms to Know
World War I
Lusitania
League of Nations
Prohibition
Great Depression
World War II
Modernism
Imagism
Expatriates

Focus Questions As you read this introduction, use what you learn to answer these questions:
- For what reasons did the United States enter World War I?
- What was the impact of the Great Depression on the government and the people of the United States?
- In what ways did American literature reflect the uncertainty and disillusionment of this period?

Reading the Unit Introduction

Tell students that the terms and questions listed here are the key points in this introductory material. This information provides a context for the selections in the unit. Students should use the terms and questions as a guide to focus their reading of the unit introduction. When students have completed the unit introduction, they should be able to identify or explain each of these terms and answer or discuss the Focus Questions.

To provide students with additional help in reading the Unit 5 introduction, give them pages 2 and 3 from ***Unit 5 Resources.***

Concept Connector

After students have read the unit introduction, return to the Focus Questions to review the main points. For key points, see p. 711.

Go Online Author Link Typing in the Web Codes when prompted will bring students to a video clip and more information on Tim O'Brien.

Using the Timeline

The Timeline can serve a number of instructional purposes, as follows:

Getting an Overview

Use the Timeline to help students get a quick overview of themes and events of the period. This approach will benefit all students but may be especially helpful for Visual/Spatial Learners, English Learners, and Less Proficient Readers. (For strategies in using the Timeline as an overview, see the bottom of this page.)

Thinking Critically

Questions are provided on the facing page. Use these questions to have students review the events, discuss their significance, and examine the *so what* behind the *what happened.*

Connecting to Selections

Have students refer back to the Timeline when they begin to read individual selections. By consulting the Timeline regularly, they will gain a better sense of the period's chronology. In addition, they will appreciate what was occurring in the world that gave rise to these works of literature.

Projects

Students can use the Timeline as a launching pad for projects like these:

- **Focused Timeline** Have students research the events leading up to an item on the timeline and create a smaller, more focused timeline to record them. For example, students can use the biography of T.S. Eliot, as well as other sources, to show the events leading up to the publication of *The Waste Land* in 1922.
- **News Presentation** Have students scan a section of the Timeline, assimilate the information on it, and summarize the important events of this period in a brief oral presentation for their classmates. They can model their presentations on television or radio news reports.

American and World Events

1915 1920 1925

AMERICAN EVENTS

- **1915** Olympic track and field champion Jim Thorpe begins his professional football career. ◀
- **1916** *Chicago Poems* by Carl Sandburg appears.
- **1917** United States enters World War I.
- **1918** President Wilson announces his 14 Points in peace plan.
- **1919** Prohibition becomes law; repealed in 1933.
- **1919** Sherwood Anderson publishes *Winesburg, Ohio.*

- **1920** Nineteenth Amendment to Constitution gives U.S. women the right to vote. ▲
- **1922** T. S. Eliot publishes *The Waste Land.*
- **1923** Wallace Stevens publishes *Harmonium.*

- **1925** F. Scott Fitzgerald publishes *The Great Gatsby.*
- **1926** Langston Hughes publishes *The Weary Blues.*
- **1926** Ernest Hemingway publishes *The Sun Also Rises.*
- **1927** Charles Lindbergh flies solo and nonstop from New York to Paris.
- **1929** Stock market crashes in October, followed by Great Depression of the 1930s. ▶

WORLD EVENTS

- **1915** England: Because of the war in Europe, travelers are cautioned against transatlantic voyages. The *Lusitania* would be sunk despite these warnings.
- **1917** Russia: Bolsheviks seize control of Russia in October Revolution.
- **1918** Worldwide influenza epidemic kills as many as 20 million people.
- **1919** France: Treaty of Versailles ends World War I. ▶

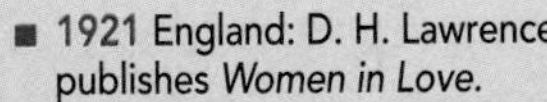

- **1921** England: D. H. Lawrence publishes *Women in Love.*
- **1922** Ireland: James Joyce publishes *Ulysses.*
- **1924** Germany: Thomas Mann publishes *The Magic Mountain.*

- **1925** England: Virginia Woolf publishes *Mrs. Dalloway.*
- **1925** France: French sign Pact of Locarno with Germany, committing both parties to avoid using force to change the boundary line between them.
- **1928** China: Chiang Kai-shek becomes head of Nationalist government.
- **1928** Germany: Kurt Weill and Bertolt Brecht write and produce *The Threepenny Opera.*
- **1929** Japan: Collapse of American silk market hurts workers and farmers.

Getting an Overview of the Period

Introduction To give students an overview of the period, indicate the span of dates in the title of the Timeline.

Next, point out that the Timeline is divided into American Events (on the top) and World Events (on bottom). Have them scan the Timeline, looking both at the American Events and the World Events. Finally, point out that the events in the Timeline often represent beginnings, turning points, and endings (for example, the start of World War II in 1939).

Key Events Have students identify key events related to disillusion, defiance, and discontent. **Possible response:** the stock market crash of 1929 and the start of World War II in 1939.

What adjectives would students use to describe this period of history? **Possible response:** Students may suggest *violent, turbulent, creative,* and *exciting.*

930 1940 1945

- **1933** President Roosevelt closes banks; Congress passes New Deal laws.
- **1939** John Steinbeck publishes *The Grapes of Wrath.*
- **1939** *The Wizard of Oz* and *Gone With the Wind* appear in movie theaters. ▼

. . . we here highly resolve that these dead shall not have died in vain . . .
REMEMBER DEC. 7th!

- **1940** Richard Wright publishes *Native Son.*
- **1940** Civil Aeronautics Board is created to regulate U.S. commercial air traffic.
- **1941** Japanese bomb American naval base at Pearl Harbor, bringing U.S. into World War II. ▲
- **1944** Roosevelt is reelected president for an unprecedented fourth term.

- **1945** Atom bombs dropped on Hiroshima and Nagasaki.
- **1945** Truman declares September 2 V-J Day, or Victory Over Japan Day. World War II ends. ▼

- 1930 India: Mahatma Gandhi leads famous march to the sea to protest British tax on salt.
- 1931 Spain: Salvador Dali paints *The Persistence of Memory.* ▶
- 1933 Germany: Adolf Hitler becomes German chancellor.
- 1936 Spain: Spanish Civil War begins.
- 1939 Poland: German blitzkrieg invasion of Poland sets off World War II.

- 1940 France: French government signs armistice with Germany.
- 1942 France: Albert Camus completes *The Stranger.*

- 1945 Germany: Dresden is hit by Allied firebombing raid. Firestorm virtually destroys city.
- 1945 United Nations Charter signed at end of World War II.

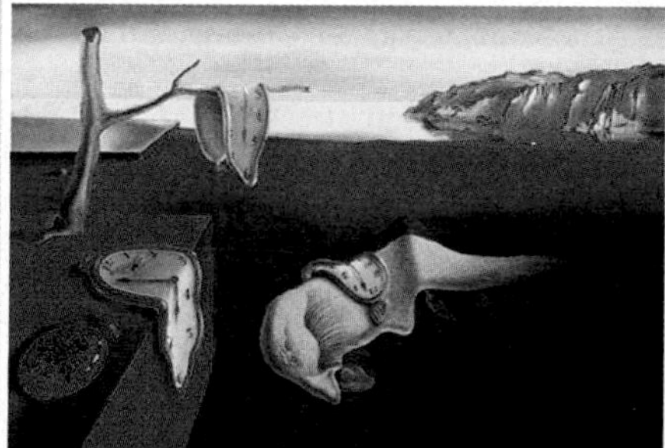

The Persistence of Memory, 1931, Salvador Dali, The Museum of Modern Art, © 2003 Salvador Dali, Gala-Salvador Dali Foundation/ Artists Rights Society (ARS), New York

Analyzing the Timeline

1. (a) When did the United States enter World War I? (b) What does this date of entry suggest about feelings in the United States toward the war?
   Answer: (a) The United States entered World War I in 1917.
   (b) The lateness of this date—the war had been going on for several years—suggests that the United States was reluctant to become involved in a European conflict.
2. (a) Name a feat of flying that occurred in the period 1925–1930.
   (b) What does this event indicate about the development of technology?
   Answer: (a) In 1927, Charles Lindbergh flew solo and nonstop from New York to Paris. (b) It indicates better methods of transportation were shrinking the globe.
3. (a) What is the time span between the end of World War I and the beginning of World War II?
   (b) Judging by this Timeline, how would you characterize the ten years leading up to World War II?
   Answer: (a) The time span is a period of twenty years, from 1919 to 1939. (b) In 1929, the stock market crashed, leading to the Great Depression of the 1930s. This item suggests that the 1930s were a time of economic hardship.
4. (a) When did World War II break out in Europe? When did the United States enter the war?
   (b) What connection can you make between the date the United States entered World War II and its behavior in World War I?
   Answer: (a) World War II broke out in Europe in 1939; the United States entered the war in 1941.
   (b) As in World War I, the United States seemed reluctant to join in the fighting.
5. (a) For how many terms was President Roosevelt elected?
   (b) Judging by events on this Timeline, what might account for this success?
   Answer: (a) In 1944, he won an unprecedented fourth term.
   (b) In 1933, he seems to have dealt decisively with the Depression. Also, people may have wanted to keep a *trusted* leader during a time of crisis such as World War II.

Critical Viewing

1. What does the illustration for the stock market crash of 1929 suggest about the state of the nation? **[Infer]**
   Possible response: It suggests that people who had invested and lost all their money despaired; it also suggests that the wealthiest Americans were resented by many.
2. Compare and contrast the photograph of Dorothy, the scarecrow, and the tin man (1939) with that of the sailor kissing a nurse on V-J day. **[Compare and Contrast]**
   Possible response: Dorothy is in a world of innocent fantasy; the sailor and the nurse, while joyous, are at the end of a long transformative experience.
3. What mood does Salvador Dali's painting (1931) convey? **[Analyze]**
   Possible response: With its limp watches, apparently dead horse, and stretch of open ground, the painting conveys a mood of fear and uncertainty.

Literature of the Period

- Amid the optimism of pre-World War I America, T.S. Eliot was hearing a more melancholy strain and helping to create a new kind of verse. Students can appreciate his achievement by reading "The Love Song of J. Alfred Prufrock," p. 716.
- In Ernest Hemingway's short story "In Another Country," p. 809, students will experience the sense of disillusionment that resulted from World War I.
- As they read F. Scott Fitzgerald's story "Winter Dreams," p. 742, students will come to understand the dreams that tantalized Americans during the 1920s.

Critical Viewing

Possible response: Some students may respond that the poster is corny. Others may feel that its inspirational, patriotic message—with a heroic-looking sailor beckoning toward the flag and liberty hovering at the top—would have been effective.

The Modern Age

The America that entered the twentieth century was a nation achieving world dominance while simultaneously losing some of its youthful innocence and brash confidence. Two world wars, a dizzying decade of prosperity, and a devastating worldwide depression marked this era. With these events came a new age in American literature. The upheavals of the early twentieth century ushered in a period of artistic experimentation and lasting literary achievement.

THE NAVY NEEDS YOU!
DON'T READ AMERICAN HISTORY—
MAKE IT!
U·S·NAVY RECRUITING STATION

▲ **Critical Viewing** Recruiting posters like this one urged Americans to help the war effort during World War I. Why do you think this poster would or would not have been effective in persuading people to enlist? **[Evaluate an Advertisement]**

Historical Background

The years immediately preceding World War I were characterized by an overwhelming sense of optimism. Numerous technological advances occurred, dramatically affecting people's lives and creating a sense of promise for the future. While a number of serious social problems still existed, politicians began to initiate reforms aimed at solving those problems. When World War I broke out in 1914, however, President Woodrow Wilson was forced to turn his attention away from the troubles at home and focus on the events in Europe.

War in Europe World War I was one of the bloodiest and most tragic conflicts ever to occur. It involved a struggle between the Allies (Britain, France, Belgium, Italy, Serbia, Montenegro, Japan, and Russia; later, Russia would drop out of the conflict and the United States would join) and the Central Powers (Germany, Austria-Hungary, and Turkey). When the initial advances of the German forces were halted, the conflict in Europe was transformed into a trench war. The introduction of the machine gun made it virtually impossible for one side to launch a successful attack on its opponents' trenches, however, and the war dragged on for several years, claiming almost an entire generation of European men.

President Wilson wanted the United States to remain neutral in the war, but that proved impossible. In 1915, a German submarine sank the *Lusitania,* pride of the British merchant fleet. More than 1,200 people on board lost their lives, including 128 Americans. After the sinking, American public opinion favored the Allies. When Germany resumed unrestricted submarine warfare two years later, the United States joined the Allied cause.

At first, the reality of war did not sink in. Americans were confident and carefree as the troops set off overseas. That cheerful mood soon passed. A number of famous American writers saw the war firsthand and learned of its horror. E. E. Cummings, Ernest Hemingway, and John Dos Passos served as ambulance drivers. Hemingway later served in the Italian infantry and was seriously wounded. Other, less famous writers fought and died in France. Among them were the poets Joyce Kilmer, who wrote "Trees," and Alan Seeger, who wrote "I Have a Rendezvous with Death."

Enrichment

Ethnic Groups in the U.S. Army

People from every ethnic group enlisted to fight in World War I. About 20,000 Puerto Ricans served in the armed forces. Many Filipinos also served. Scores of soldiers were immigrants who had recently arrived in the United States.

At first, the armed forces did not allow African Americans in combat. When the government changed the rules, more than two million African Americans registered for the draft. Nearly 400,000 were accepted for duty. They were forced into segregated "black-only" units commanded mostly by white officers.

Ask students what the willingness to serve in the army, despite barriers, indicates about the loyalty of ethnic groups.

Possible response: It suggests that ethnic Americans felt a strong commitment to the country and its cause.

Prosperity and Depression The era following the end of the Great War in November 1918 was not a peaceful one for America: President Wilson's dream of seeing the United States join the League of Nations failed, and in the big cities of America, from 1920 to 1933, Prohibition made the sale of liquor illegal, leading to bootlegging, speakeasies, widespread law breaking, and sporadic warfare among competing gangs.

Throughout the 1920s, the nation seemed to be on a binge. After a brief recession in 1920 and 1921, the economy boomed. New buildings rose everywhere, creating new downtown sections in many cities—Omaha, Des Moines, and Minneapolis among them. Radio arrived, and so did jazz. Movies became big business, and spectacular movie palaces sprang up across the country. Fads abounded: raccoon coats, flagpole sitting, and a dance called the Charleston. The great literary interpreter of the Roaring Twenties was F. Scott Fitzgerald. In *This Side of Paradise* and *The Great Gatsby,* Fitzgerald vividly captured the essence of life during this frenzied decade.

Close-up on History

Women Get the Vote

One of the most important events of the immediate postwar period was the passage of the Nineteenth Amendment to the Constitution, giving women the right to vote.

The struggle to grant women the vote, or suffrage, went back many years, but it gathered significant momentum in the early 1900s. Carrie Chapman Catt, a former school principal and reporter, spoke out forcefully for women's suffrage. Catt was also a brilliant organizer, and she devised a state-by-state campaign to win the vote for women. Her campaign succeeded as year by year more states in the West and Midwest gave women the vote, although in most cases, they could exercise this right only in state elections. Gradually, more women called for an amendment to the Constitution to give them a voice in national elections, too.

The suffragist leader Alice Paul and others met with President Wilson soon after he took office in 1913. Although Wilson was not opposed to women's suffrage, he did not support a constitutional amendment. Suffragists became disillusioned after numerous meetings with Wilson and, in January 1917, began to picket at the White House. After several months, police began arresting the protesters. Paul and other arrested women went on a hunger strike, but prison officials force-fed them. Upon their release from prison, Paul and the other women resumed their picketing. They were a determined group.

By early 1918, not long before the end of World War I, the tide began to turn in favor of the suffrage cause. The tireless work of Catt, Paul, and others began to pay off. President Wilson agreed to support the suffrage amendment.

Finally, in 1919, Congress passed the Nineteenth Amendment, and by August 1920, three fourths of the states had ratified it. The amendment doubled the number of eligible voters in the United States and eliminated a long-standing injustice.

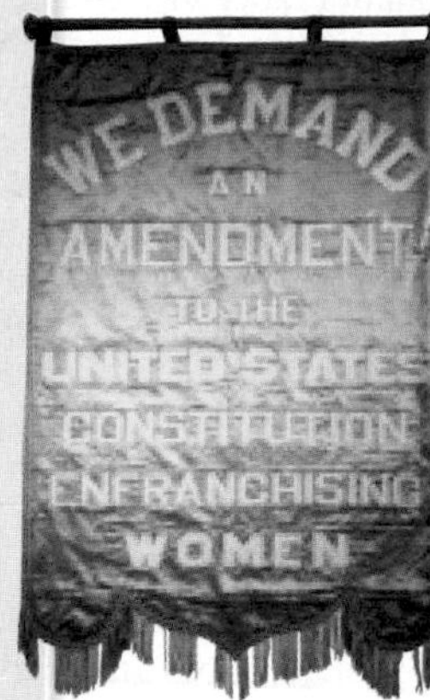

Differentiated Instruction

Solutions for All Learners

Support for Less Proficient Readers
Help these students approach and understand the Historical Background and Literature of the Period by instructing them to focus on the two world wars. What historical causes and effects are associated with the wars? What connections does the essay make between the wars and literature?

Support for English Learners
These students may find the literary concepts associated with Modernism to be particularly challenging. First, explain that World War I was a key influence on these literary movements. Then, have them read through Literature of the Period slowly, pausing to identify words that might reflect that influence.

Enrichment for Advanced Readers
As these students read, encourage them to take notes on how World War I influenced the literature of the period. Then, have them discuss the cultural impact of World War I and speculate on the cultural impact that World War II—which ends this historical period—might have on the era to come.

Background
Economics

The auto industry was the engine of the American economy in the 1920s. Car sales grew rapidly during the decade. The auto boom spurred growth in related fields, such as steel and rubber.

One reason for the auto boom was a drop in prices. By 1924, the cost of a Model T had decreased from $850 to $290. As a result, ordinary Americans—not just the rich—could afford to buy a car. Car prices fell because factories became more efficient. Henry Ford had introduced the assembly line in his factory in 1913. The goal, he said, was to make the cars identical. Before the assembly line, it took 14 hours to put together a Model T. In Ford's new factory, workers could assemble a Model T in 93 minutes!

The assembly line was a key idea in the expansion of manufacturing. It could apply to many industries, ensuring rapid manufacture of less expensive goods. Other companies copied Ford's methods. In 1927, General Motors passed Ford as the top auto maker.

The American Experience
Close-up on History

- Tell students that Carrie Chapman Catt's organizational skills led to her election in 1900 as president of the National American Woman Suffrage Association. She succeeded Susan B. Anthony and held this position until her resignation in 1904. Catt was so dedicated to the cause that she insisted on a prenuptial agreement that allowed her to work exclusively for the movement for four months out of each year.
- Tell students that a new wave of feminism began again in the 1960s and '70s. **Ask** students what they know about this movement.
  Possible response: Students may suggest that women fought for new rights, such as equality in the workplace.

Background
Culture
During the 1920s, artists and writers flocked to Greenwich Village in New York City. Older buildings in the area, including barns, stables, and houses, were converted to studios, nightclubs, theaters, and shops. In 1923, playwright Eugene O'Neill founded the Greenwich Village Theatre, where experimental dramas were performed.

Critical Viewing
Possible response: They probably flourish because people have money to spend and more leisure time in which to enjoy themselves.

Historical Background
Comprehension Check
1. What was the prevailing mood in the years preceding World War I?
   Answer: There was a mood of optimism.
2. What tragic event during World War I turned opinion in America toward the Allies?
   Answer: The event was the sinking of the *Lusitania,* which resulted in 128 American deaths.
3. After World War I, what law caused an outbreak of criminal activity in American cities?
   Answer: In 1919, Prohibition made the sale of liquor illegal, a measure that caused widespread crime as liquor was smuggled into America and sold illegally.
4. How healthy was the economy during most of the 1920s?
   Answer: During most of the 1920s, the economy boomed.
5. Name the event that, in 1929, started the economic downturn known as the Depression.
   Answer: That event was the stock market crash.
6. What caused the United States to enter World War II?
   Answer: The Japanese attack on Pearl Harbor on December 7, 1941, caused the United States to enter the war.

Critical Thinking
1. In what way could you support the assertion that, between 1914 and 1939, the mood of Americans alternated between optimism and pessimism? **[Support]**

Writers flocked to Greenwich Village, in New York City. In 1923, playwright Eugene O'Neill founded the Greenwich Village Theatre, where experimental dramas were performed. Thomas Wolfe taught English at New York University in the Village while writing his novel *Look Homeward, Angel.*

In late October 1929, the stock market crashed, marking the beginning of the Great Depression. By mid-1932, about 12 million people—one quarter of the work force—were out of work. Even as bread lines formed and the numbers of unemployed grew, most business leaders remained optimistic. However, the situation continued to worsen. In the presidential election of 1932, New York's governor Franklin D. Roosevelt defeated incumbent president Herbert Hoover. Roosevelt initiated the New Deal, a package of major economic reforms, to strengthen the economy. Roosevelt's policies helped bring an end to the Depression, and these policies, together with his leadership in World War II, earned him reelection in 1936, 1940, and again in 1944.

▲ **Critical Viewing** The Charleston was a popular dance during the Roaring Twenties. Why do nightclubs featuring music and dance flourish during periods of prosperity? **[Make an Inference]**

World War II Only twenty years after the Treaty of Versailles had ended World War I, the German invasion of Poland touched off World War II. As in the earlier war, most Americans wanted to remain neutral. Even after the fall of France in 1940, the dominant mood in the United States was one of isolationism. However, when the Japanese attacked Pearl Harbor, Hawaii, on December 7, 1941, America could stay neutral no longer. The United States declared war on the Axis powers—Japan, Germany, and Italy.

After years of bitter fighting on two fronts, the Allies—the United States, Great Britain, the Soviet Union, and France—defeated Nazi Germany. Japan surrendered three months later, after the United States had dropped atomic bombs on two Japanese cities. Peace, and the atomic age, had arrived.

Literature of the Period

The Birth of Modernism The devastation of World War I brought about an end to the sense of optimism that had characterized the years immediately preceding the war. Many people were left with a feeling of uncertainty and disillusionment. No longer trusting the ideas and values of the world out of which the war had developed, people sought to find new ideas that better suited twentieth-century life. The quest for new ideas occurred in the world of literature as well, and a major literary movement known as Modernism was born.

Modernists experimented with a wide variety of new approaches and techniques, producing a remarkably diverse body of literature. Yet the Modernists shared a common purpose: They sought to capture the essence of modern life in both the form and content of their work. To reflect the

Critical Thinking continued

Possible response: Before World War I, Americans were optimistic. The war brought Americans face to face with bitter realities. However, the 1920s produced a new optimism as the economy boomed. Then spirits declined as the Depression set in.

2. Judging by what you know about the 1920s, what do you think F. Scott Fitzgerald's stories and novels are like? **[Infer]**
   Possible response: Students may respond that they capture the dazzle, dreams—and perhaps the disillusion—of a fast-moving, showy era.
3. Do the historical events suggest that 1914–1946 would be a time of experimentation in literature? Why or why not? **[Draw Conclusions]**
   Possible response: The rapid changes, dramatic world events, and fluctuations in mood might inspire writers to experiment with new forms and new approaches to language.

fragmentation of the modern world, the Modernists constructed their works out of fragments, omitting the expositions, transitions, resolutions, and explanations used in traditional literature. In poetry, they abandoned traditional forms and meters in favor of free verse, whose rhythms they improvised to suit individual poems. The themes of their works were usually implied, rather than directly stated, creating a sense of uncertainty and forcing readers to draw their own conclusions. In general, Modernist works demanded more from readers than the works of earlier American writers. At the same time, the Modernists helped to earn American literature a place in the world's esteem.

Imagism The Modernist movement was ushered in by a poetic movement known as Imagism. This movement, which lasted from 1909 to 1917, attracted followers in both the United States and England. The Imagists

Point/Counterpoint

Women, Followers—or Cofounders—of Modernism?

Were the female writers and editors who worked alongside men like Pound and Eliot useful followers and helpers of these men, or were they fully contributing cofounders of Modernism? Two scholars disagree about where the credit for founding Imagism should be given.

Women, Followers of Modernism With energy and dispatch, Pound began collecting poetry. . . . He then asked Hilda Doolittle to show him some poems in the tearoom of the British Museum, in the 'rather prissy milieu of some infernal bun shop full of English spinsters,' as Aldington put it. Pound read Hilda's new poems with admiration. According to Aldington, Pound popped his pince-nez, an affectation he had learned from Yeats, when he read her 'Hermes of the Ways,' a poem he immediately cut and changed to make its pristine clarity even more penetrating, and signed the poem 'H.D., Imagiste.' In the space of a few moments Pound had created a literary movement and its first acolytes."

—John Tytell,
Ezra Pound: The Solitary Volcano

Women, Cofounders of Modernism "It is also apparent that a number of women's achievements have been credited to Pound in whole or in part. H.D. made the first real critical comments about the poetry of Marianne Moore, and Moore credited H.D. with suggesting that Moore write prose for the *Dial*—both activities that have been attributed to Pound. Cyrena Pondrom has demonstrated that H.D. also created the poetic style that became known as Imagism. . . . H.D., and especially Amy Lowell, played central roles in disseminating Imagism. . . . Literary histories, however, often give Pound full credit for the development and promotion of Imagism."

—Jayne E. Marek,
Women Editing Modernism

The American Experience
Point/Counterpoint

Underscore that Ezra Pound frequently interacted with other writers and poets, discussing their work and his own. Scholars still debate the degree to which Pound influenced these writers—and possibly deserves credit for the movements they began. Then, **ask** the following questions:

1. What do these two viewpoints have in common?
   Possible response: Both imply that the Modernist period was a time of great literary innovation, and that Pound and H.D. were at the heart of Imagism.
2. In what ways do these viewpoints differ?
   Possible response: They differ on the question of Pound's influence. Tytell believes Pound created Imagism through his influence on H.D., while Marek believes Pound has been credited for other writers' accomplishments.
3. Can you think of contemporary examples of similar debates over who gets credit for a certain development—literary, artistic, or otherwise? Explain.
   Possible response: Students may be able to refer to any number of new forms in the arts or entertainment, such as film genres or formats for television shows. Be sure students are able to identify and explain the debate over credit for any developments they list.

Enrichment

The Movies

Leisure gained a new meaning in the 1920s. Rising wages and labor-saving appliances gave families more time and money, and they looked for new ways to have fun.

In the 1920s, the movie industry came of age and provided Americans with the fun they were seeking. Southern California's warm and sunny climate allowed filming all year round. Soon, Hollywood became the movie capital of the world.

Over the course of the decade, millions of Americans went to the movies. They thrilled to westerns, romances, adventures, and comedies. In small towns, theaters were bare rooms with hard chairs. In cities, they were huge palaces with red velvet seats.

The first movies had no sound. Audiences followed the plot by reading "title cards" that appeared on the screen. A pianist in the theater played music that went with the action.

Critical Thinking

Possible response: Students may respond that the photograph reveals something of the economic hardship of the period, and that the expression of the woman in the photograph conveys the fear and uncertainty many Americans experienced.

rebelled against the sentimentality of nineteenth-century poetry. They demanded instead hard, clear expression, concrete images, and the language of everyday speech. Their models came from Greek and Roman classics, Chinese and Japanese poetry, and the free verse of the French poets of their day. Among the writers associated with the earliest phase of Imagism were H.D. (Hilda Doolittle) and Ezra Pound. When Pound moved on from Imagism, other leaders took over, among them H.D. Amy Lowell, a Massachusetts poet, led the Imagist movement in the United States in its final years.

The Expatriates Postwar disenchantment led a number of American writers to become expatriates, or exiles. Many of these writers settled in Paris, where they were influenced by Gertrude Stein, the writer who coined the phrase "lost generation" to describe those who were disillusioned by World War I. Stein lived in Paris from 1902 until her death in 1946, and her home attracted many major authors, including Sherwood Anderson, F. Scott Fitzgerald, and Ernest Hemingway.

Fitzgerald and Hemingway are the best known of the expatriates, but they are by no means the only ones. Ezra Pound spent most of his adult life in England, France, and Italy. T. S. Eliot, born in St. Louis, went to Europe in 1914, soon settled in England, and lived there until his death in 1965. Some critics have called Eliot's long, despairing poem *The Waste Land* the most important poem of the century.

Most of the "lost generation" saw very little in their civilization to praise or even accept. Archibald MacLeish, an expatriate from 1923 to 1928, wrote several volumes of verse expressing the chaos and hopelessness of those years. MacLeish eventually broke with the expatriates, however. He returned to the United States in the 1930s and became increasingly concerned about the rise of dictatorships. A supporter of President Roosevelt's New Deal, he served as Librarian of Congress during World War II.

New Approaches During the years between the two world wars, writers in both the United States and Europe explored new literary territories. Influenced by developments in modern psychology, writers began using the stream-of-consciousness technique, attempting to re-create the natural flow of a character's thoughts. Drawing its name from the work of psychologist William James, this technique involves the presentation of a series of thoughts, memories, and insights, connected only by a character's natural associations.

▼ Critical Viewing Dorothea Lange took this photograph, which has become a symbol of the Great Depression. What does it "say" about this period? **[Draw a Conclusion]**

Enrichment

Flashes of Wit and Humor

So much of the outstanding writing between the wars echoed disenchantment and despair that the bright, cheery voices of the period tend to be forgotten. The best-known humorist of the time was Will Rogers, the "Cowboy Philosopher" from Oklahoma. He earned that nickname with his homespun humor and wry comments on politics and current events. James Thurber was one of a number of humorous writers associated with *The New Yorker* magazine. Thurber, who was also a cartoonist, showed real psychological insight into odd characters in his works. One of these characters, Walter Mitty, dreams of spectacular achievements while in real life, he is a meek and timid man. Another *New Yorker* writer was E.B. White, a subtle humorist and brilliant stylist. White later wrote *Charlotte's Web, Stuart Little,* and several other classic stories for children.

Ask students to name some of the writers they think are funny and to give examples of their work.

The landmark stream-of-consciousness novel is *Ulysses,* published in 1922 by the Irish writer James Joyce. A number of American novelists soon adopted the technique, most notably William Faulkner in *The Sound and the Fury.* Katherine Anne Porter's short stories and the three novels in John Dos Passos's *U.S.A.* also use stream-of-consciousness narration. The trilogy by Dos Passos includes other devices unusual in a fictional work, such as brief biographies of well-known Americans and quotations from newspapers and magazines.

Poets also sought to stretch the old boundaries. E. E. Cummings's poems attracted special attention because of their wordplay, unique typography, and special punctuation. These devices are more than mere oddities in Cummings's poetry. They are vital to its intent and its meaning.

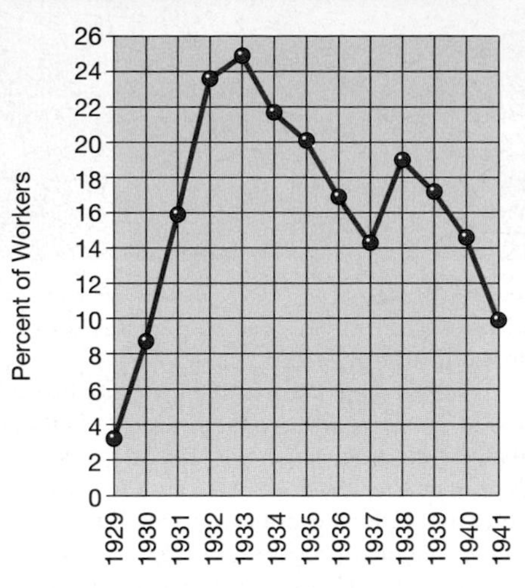

▲ **Critical Viewing** During the Depression, millions of Americans were out of work. According to the graph, what happened to unemployment between 1936 and 1941? **[Interpret a Pattern]**

William Carlos Williams, a New Jersey physician and poet, began by writing poetry like that of John Keats, radically changed his style under the influence of Imagism, and turned an attentive eye on his local world. Unlike the writers who traveled to Europe, Williams sought meaning in American sights and sounds and used informal, conversational speech. His epic poem, *Paterson,* is named for a New Jersey city. He had a great influence on two important poets of the next generation, Allen Ginsberg and A.R. Ammons.

Wallace Stevens, an insurance executive, wrote a more intellectual and self-consciously elegant poetry than that of Williams. Throughout his work, Stevens explored the shifting relationship between reality and the fictions that the imagination creates. His poetry was inspirational for such later poets as James Merrill and John Ashbery.

Marianne Moore is famous for her lines measured by syllable counts, her use of quotations from such real-world texts as "business documents and school books," and her quirky, unforgettable images—in "Poetry," she compares an "immovable critic twitching his skin" to "a horse."

Writers of International Renown The Modernists dramatically altered the complexion of American literature. At the same time, many of these writers earned international acclaim that equaled that of their European literary contemporaries.

Proof of this acclaim is the number of Americans who won the Nobel Prize for Literature. This international award was established in 1901 with funds bequeathed by Alfred Nobel, the Swedish inventor of dynamite. The first American to win the Nobel Prize for Literature was Sinclair Lewis. A native of Sauk Center, Minnesota, Lewis fictionalized his hometown as Gopher Prairie in his first important novel, *Main Street.* Lewis, one of the great satirists of the era, wrote two more classics within the next few years.

Background
Literature

John Dos Passos is still remembered as a radical social critic. After graduating from Harvard University, Dos Passos drove ambulances during World War I and traveled extensively in Europe as a newspaper correspondent. When Italian immigrant Nicola Sacco and Bartolomeo Vanzetti were executed after what many critics declared to be a false conviction, Dos Passos developed the conviction that there were, in fact, two Americas—one for the wealthy and a second for the powerless. The idea of "two nations" within the United States inspired the trilogy *U.S.A.,* in which the author used radical stylistic experimentation to address burning social issues of the day. It is because of *U.S.A.* that Dos Passos is remembered as a critic of American life. Yet the author became disillusioned with the social beliefs behind his great trilogy, and by the end of his life his writing clearly reflected a growing conservativism.

Critical Viewing

Answer: According to the graph, the percentage of unemployed workers fell from 1936 to 1937 (from about 17% to about 14%), rose again from 1937 to 1938 (from 14% to about 19%), and then declined from 1938 to 1941 (from about 19% to 10%).

Critical Viewing

Possible response: In a single panorama, it dramatizes a sequence of events in the history of African Americans. Figures are shown in silhouette, gesturing dramatically, while a rising sun symbolizes hope for the future.

Background

Literature

William Faulkner's Nobel Prize arrived as the writer's career was undergoing a revival. Faulkner's most famous work had been written and published years before, but his reputation in America began to grow with the publication of an anthology, *The Portable Faulkner*, in 1946. The 1949 Nobel Prize, actually presented in 1950, finally solidified Faulkner's place as one of the great American writers. His acceptance speech, which students can read on p. 875, was justly famous. In it, he proclaimed his faith in the human race, even as the world entered the atomic age.

Literature of the Period

Comprehension Check

1. What purpose was shared by Modernist writers?
   Answer: They sought to capture the essence of modern life in the form and content of their work.
2. Name three qualities favored by Imagist poets.
   Answer: They wanted clear expression, concrete images, and the language of everyday speech.
3. (a) What prompted writers to leave the United States and become expatriates in Europe? (b) Which two writers are the best known of the expatriates?
   Answer: (a) Disenchantment stemming from World War I prompted writers to move to Europe. (b) Hemingway and Fitzgerald are the best-known expatriate writers.
4. What is the stream-of-consciousness technique pioneered by writers in this era?
   Answer: It involves the presentation of a series of thoughts, memories, and insights, linked only by a character's natural associations.

Aspects of Negro Life: From Slavery Through Reconstruction, Aaron Douglas, Photographs and Prints Division, Schomburg Center for Research in Black Culture, The New York Public Library, Astor, Lenox, and Tilden Foundations

▲ **Critical Viewing** Aaron Douglas, an African American artist, lived and painted during the Harlem Renaissance. How does his painting "From Slavery Through Reconstruction" communicate the experience of African Americans? **[Analyze Art]**

Babbitt was about an American businessman, while *Arrowsmith* dealt with the medical profession.

Lewis's Nobel Prize in 1930 was the first of many for American writers. In 1936, the prize went to Eugene O'Neill, ranked by most critics as America's greatest playwright. Among his best-known plays are *Desire Under the Elms, The Iceman Cometh,* and *Long Day's Journey Into Night.* O'Neill's plays are sometimes autobiographical, generally tragic, and often experimental. His *Strange Interlude,* produced in 1928, uses stream-of-consciousness asides to reveal the inner feelings of characters. These feelings often contrast with their actual spoken words.

Then, in 1938, the Nobel Prize for Literature went to Pearl S. Buck, an American who spent her early years in China. Buck wrote about that country with understanding and compassion. *The Good Earth* is considered her finest work.

After T. S. Eliot, who had become a British subject, won the award in 1948, William Faulkner won it the following year. Most of Faulkner's novels and short stories are set in mythical Yoknapatawpha County, Mississippi, which closely resembled the region of Mississippi where Faulkner lived. In addition to *The Sound and the Fury,* Faulkner wrote such enduring works as *Light in August* and *The Hamlet.*

Later, Ernest Hemingway and John Steinbeck also won Nobel Prizes for Literature. Hemingway's simple, direct, journalistic style of writing, evident in such novels as *The Sun Also Rises* and *A Farewell to Arms,* influenced a generation of young writers. Much of his best writing focuses on World War I and its aftermath. Many of Steinbeck's works depict the Depression, especially as it affected migrant workers and dust-bowl farmers. Two of Steinbeck's most memorable novels are *Of Mice and Men* and *The Grapes of Wrath.*

The Harlem Renaissance A new literary age was dawning, not only in Greenwich Village and among expatriates in Paris, but also in northern Manhattan, in Harlem. African American writers, mostly newcomers from the South, were creating their own renaissance there. It began in 1921 with the publication of Countee Cullen's "I Have a Rendezvous With Life (with apologies to Alan Seeger)." Another poem by a promising young African American writer—"The Negro Speaks of Rivers," by Langston Hughes—followed six months later.

What occurred thereafter was a burst of creative activity by African American writers, few of whom, other than Cullen, had been born in New York City. Most of them moved to Harlem during the renaissance.

Enrichment

Jazz

The early part of the twentieth century was an era of experimentation and innovation in music and art, as well as literature. Drawing upon the complex rhythms of traditional West African folk music and the harmonies of black folk music of the nineteenth century, African Americans created a vibrant new type of music known as jazz. By the 1920s, listening and dancing to jazz had become a national craze. Due to the success of performers like Duke Ellington (1899–1974) and Fats Waller (1904–1943), Harlem became the nation's jazz center.

If possible, find and play for students a recording of Ellington's "Take the A Train." Ask these questions:

1. Describe this piece of music for someone who has never heard it.
   Possible response: Students may say that the music is free-flowing but focused.
2. How does the music reflect the modern age?
   Possible response: It is quick and innovative, and it has a nervous energy.

Claude McKay, for example, was from Jamaica. His most famous book was *Harlem Shadows*, a collection of poems published in 1922. A year later came Jean Toomer's *Cane*, a collection of stories, verses, and a play.

The Harlem Renaissance was publicly recognized in March 1924, when young African American writers met the literary editors of the city. Carl Van Doren, editor of the *Century*, noted that black writers, long "oppressed and handicapped . . . have gathered stores of emotion and are ready to burst forth with a new eloquence."

The Harlem phenomenon continued throughout the 1920s and into the 1930s. Arna Bontemps, born in Louisiana, published his first novel, *God Sends Sunday*, in 1931. The writers of this renaissance belonged to no single school of literature, but they did form a coherent group. They saw themselves as part of a new and exciting movement. In addition to producing their own exceptional works, they opened the door for the African American writers who would follow them.

A Continuing Tradition World War II did not end the literary revival that had begun after World War I. Many of the older writers continued to produce novels, short stories, plays, and poems. Meanwhile, a new generation of writers arose after World War II to keep American literature at the leading edge of the world's artistic achievement.

Experience — A Writer's Voice

Anne Spencer, Poet of the Harlem Renaissance

Women who participated in the Harlem Renaissance tend to get less attention than the men. That is why it is worth mentioning Anne Spencer (1882–1975), a poet whose work compares favorably with that of her more famous contemporaries: James Weldon Johnson, Langston Hughes, Jean Toomer, and Claude McKay.

Spencer grew up and was educated in Virginia. Her poetry became well known when Johnson selected some of her work to appear in *The Book of American Negro Poetry* (1922). During the Harlem Renaissance, she received visits from such distinguished writers as Johnson, McKay, and W.E.B. Du Bois, author of *The Souls of Black Folk* (1903).

In the following brief poem, Spencer writes in the voice of Paul Laurence Dunbar (1872–1906), an African American poet of the previous generation. Dunbar had written powerful poems like "Douglass" and "We Wear the Mask" (see pages 652 and 654). Here, Spencer indicates the value of his work by having him rank himself with three famous British Romantic poets, all of whom, like Dunbar himself, died young.

Dunbar (1920)

Ah, how poets sing and die!
Make one song and Heaven takes it;
Have one heart and Beauty breaks it;
Chatterton, Shelley, Keats, and I—
Ah, how poets sing and die!

Critical Thinking

1. What qualities of the modern world are reflected in the literary movement known as Modernism? **[Connect]**
   Possible response: Modernism reflects the nervous energy, quick and baffling transitions, and fragmentary qualities of the modern world.
2. What do you think the expatriates were looking for in Europe that they could not find in America? **[Speculate]**
   Possible response: Reasonable answers include: They may have been looking for a chance to cut free from traditional ties and develop their own viewpoints. They may have seen Europe as a place where moral standards were not so rigid.
3. What factors might have brought about the Harlem Renaissance? **[Analyze Causes and Effects]**
   Possible response: Young African Americans from more rural areas may have been inspired by the freedom of the big city and by the loose, free-flowing rhythms of jazz, a form of music newly invented by African Americans.

The American Experience
A Writer's Voice

- Have a student read Spencer's poem aloud to the class. **Ask** students to state what they think the speaker is saying in lines 2–4.
  Possible response: A short life stopped these writers from creating more great poetry.
- **Ask** students how the repetition of words in lines 1 and 5 affects the poem.
  Possible response: Students may suggest that the repetition creates continuity in the poem. It also helps stress the speaker's point of talented poets dying young.

Concept Connector

Have students discuss the Focus Questions on p. 701. Students' discussions should include the following points:

United States's reasons for entering WWI:
- A German submarine bombed the *Lusitania*, which was carrying 128 Americans.
- Germany resumed unrestricted submarine warfare.

Impacts of the Great Depression:
- Many people lost their jobs.
- Franklin D. Roosevelt was elected and initiated the New Deal. His policies helped bring the Depression to an end.

Ways that literature reflected the period:
- A new literary movement called Modernism started after World War I. Writers in this movement abandoned traditional forms and tried to reflect the fragmentation of the modern world.
- Imagist poets rebelled against nineteenth-century sentimentality. They used concrete images and the language of everyday speech.

Critical Thinking

1. Why do you think people use slang? **[Speculate]**
   Possible response: Certain types of slang qualify the user as part of an "in" crowd. Slang may also have an appeal because it is fresh and new.
2. How much slang do you use? **[Relate]**
   Possible response: Give students some methods by which they can evaluate the slang quotient of their own speech, to see whether slang makes up more or less than a fifth of the words they use. For example, they could tape record a brief conversation with a friend and then analyze its slang content.

Answers to the Activity

Encourage students to gather slang words and phrases for their glossaries by keeping small notepads and pencils handy as they go through their school day, and to write down any slang they hear. If they encounter words or expressions with which they are not familiar, they should try to ask about their meanings. Encourage students to develop consistent formats for their glossaries. They may want to include pronunciations as well as definitions. Student glossaries should be as comprehensive as possible.

The Development of American English

Slang As It Is Slung

BY RICHARD LEDERER

Slang is hot and slang is cool. Slang is nifty and slang is wicked. Slang is the bee's knees and the cat's whiskers. Slang is far out, groovy, and outa sight. Slang is fresh, fly, and phat. Slang is bodacious and fantabulous. Slang is ace, awesome, copacetic, the max, and totally tubular.

Those are many ways of saying that, if variety is the spice of life, slang is the spice of language. Slang adds gusto to the feast of words, as long as speakers and writers remember that too much spice can kill the feast of any dish.

Slang has added spice to the feast of American literature as American writers have increasingly written in an American voice, with the words and rhythms of everyday American discourse. Listen to the Harlem Renaissance poet Langston Hughes:

Good morning, daddy!
Ain't you heard
The boogie-woogie rumble
Of a dream deferred?

DEFINING THE "LINGO"

What is slang? In the preface to their *Dictionary of American Slang,* Harold Wentworth and Stuart Berg Flexner define slang as "the body of words and expressions frequently used by or intelligible to a rather large portion of the general American public, but not accepted as good, formal usage by the majority." Slang, then, is seen as a kind of vagabond language that prowls the outskirts of respectable speech, yet few of us can get along without it. Even our statespersons have a hard time getting by without such colloquial or slang expressions as "hit the nail on the head," "team effort," or "pass the buck."

WHAT'S IN THIS NAME?

Nobody is quite sure where the word *slang* comes from. According to H. L. Mencken, the word slang developed in the eighteenth century (it was first recorded in 1756) either from an erroneous past tense of *sling* (*sling-slang-slung*) or from language itself, as in *(thieve)s'lang(uage)* and *(beggar)s'lang(uage).* The second theory makes the point that jargon and slang originate and are used by a particular trade or class group, but slang words come to be slung around to some extent by a whole population.

Slang is a prominent part of our American wordscape. In fact, *The Dictionary of American Slang* estimates that slang makes up perhaps a fifth of the words we use. Many of our most valuable and pungent words have begun their lives keeping company with thieves, vagrants, and hipsters. As Mr. Dooley, a fictional Irish saloon keeper, once observed, "When we Americans get through with the English language, it will look as if it has been run over by a musical comedy."

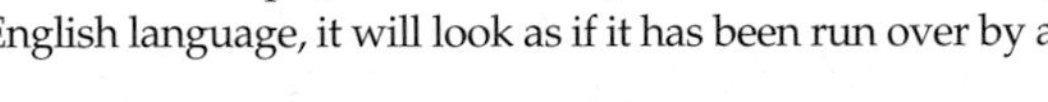

Activity

Student slang is a rich vein of metaphor and word formation. With your classmates, compile a dictionary of the slang used in your school. Provide a sentence or two illustrating the use of each slang term you define.

Enrichment

More on Slang

Point out to students that slang can contribute to the growth of the language. Often, words that we take for granted today were once regarded as outrageous and unacceptable examples of slang.

The following are several slang terms that have gradually become acceptable to most speakers:

joke slump row crank boom fad

Have students list slang terms that they use. Ask them to predict which of their slang terms will have staying power and which will fall away. If possible have them explain their choices.

Possible response: One factor predictive of a word's lasting value may be its ability to describe something better than a more standard word does; another is its ability to describe something for which there is no standard word.

Unit 5 Part 1

Facing Troubled Times

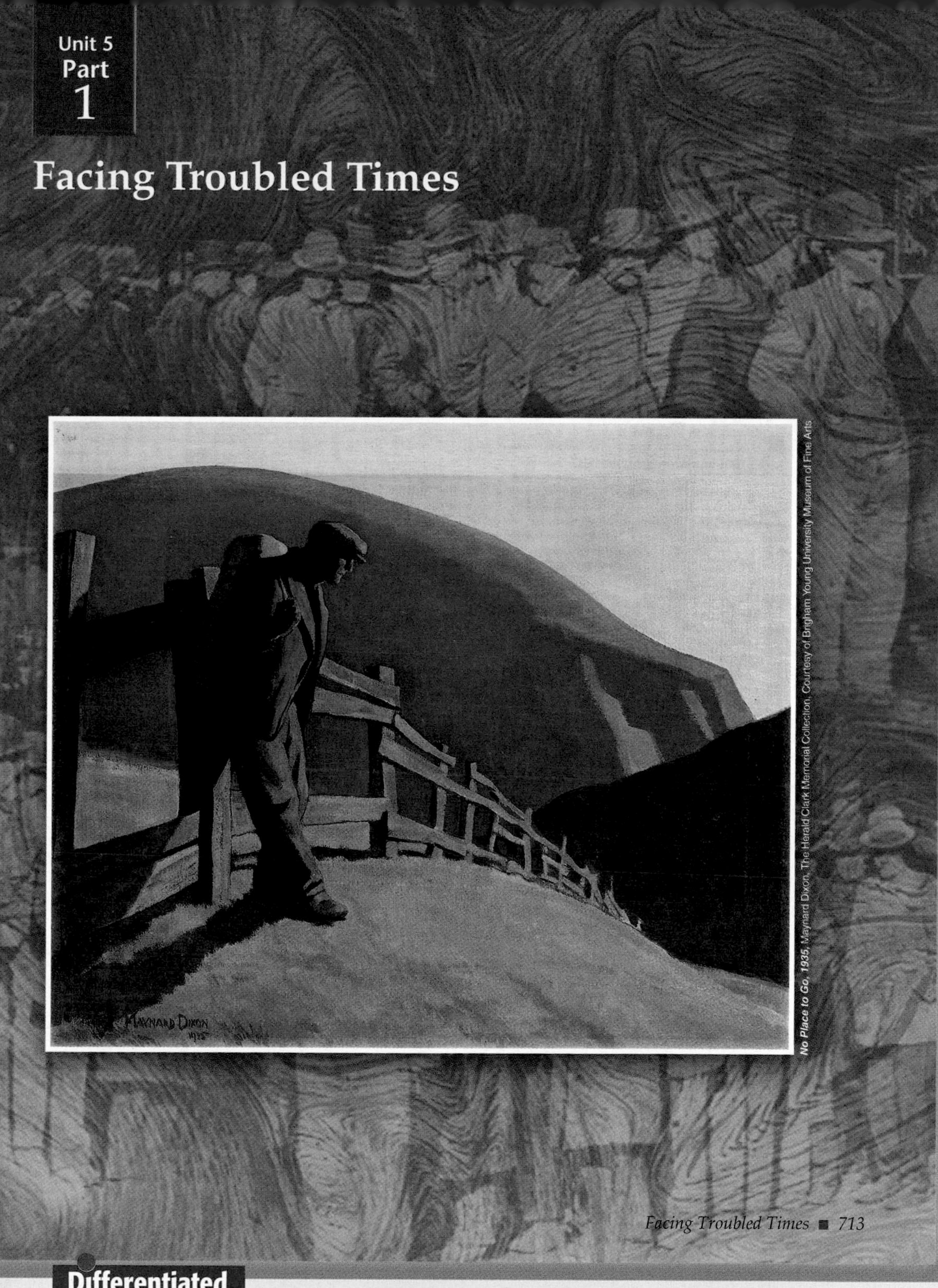

No Place to Go, 1935, Maynard Dixon, The Herald Clark Memorial Collection, Courtesy of Brigham Young University Museum of Fine Arts

Differentiated Instruction Solutions for All Learners

Accessibility at a Glance

More Accessible
In a Station of the Metro

Average
The River Merchant's Wife: A Letter
The Red Wheelbarrow
This Is Just to Say
Pear Tree
Heat
Winter Dreams
The Turtle
The Unknown Citizen

More Challenging
The Love Song of J. Alfred Prufrock
A Few Don'ts
old age sticks
anyone lived in a pretty how town
The Far and the Near
Of Modern Poetry
Anecdote of the Jar
Ars Poetica
Poetry

Selection Planning Guide

The selections in this section reflect the pain and disillusionment Americans felt during the years between the two world wars—a time when many Americans questioned an increasingly complex and impersonal society. "The Love Song of J. Alfred Prufrock" provides students with a glimpse of a troubled individual trapped in conventions. Pound's "In a Station of the Metro" reflects the transient nature of relationships and of society. Similarly, Fitzgerald's short story "Winter Dreams" shows the tentative nature of love in a status-conscious world. "The Unknown Citizen" raises questions about the nature of conformity. This section ends with poems about poetry by Wallace Stevens, Archibald MacLeish, and Marianne Moore.

Humanities

No Place to Go, by Maynard Dixon

Point out that this painting dates from the Great Depression; elicit students' knowledge about that time in American history. Encourage students to relate the content and mood of the painting to historical and social developments of the time period.

Have students link the painting to the focus of this part (Facing Troubled Times) by answering the following question:

- Considering the painting's title, who might the man in it be, and what reasons might he have for traveling on foot in the American West? **Possible response:** He may be a factory worker who has lost his job and is looking for another one. He may be a farmer whose farm has been repossessed and whose quest for an agricultural job has been fruitless.

Benchmark

After students have completed the poems by E.E. Cummings and W. H. Auden, administer **Benchmark Test 7.** If the Benchmark Test reveals that some students need further work, use the **Interpretation Guide** to determine the appropriate reteaching pages in the **Reading Kit** or on **Success Tracker.**

Monitoring Progress

Before students read "The Far and the Near" by Thomas Wolfe, administer **Diagnostic Test 8.** This test will determine students' level of readiness for the reading and vocabulary skills.

The Love Song of J. Alfred Prufrock

Meeting Your Standards

Students will

1. **analyze and respond to literary elements.**
   - Literary Analysis: Dramatic Monologue
2. **read, comprehend, analyze, and critique a poem.**
   - Reading Strategy: Listening
   - Reading Check questions
   - Apply the Skills questions
   - Assessment Practice (ATE)
3. **develop vocabulary.**
   - Vocabulary Lesson: Greek Prefix: *di-*
4. **understand and apply written and oral language conventions.**
   - Spelling Strategy
   - Grammar and Style Lesson: Adjectival Modifiers
5. **develop writing proficiency.**
   - Writing Lesson: Character Analysis
6. **develop appropriate research strategies.**
   - Extend Your Learning: Report
7. **understand and apply listening and speaking strategies.**
   - Extend Your Learning: Role-Play

Block Scheduling: Use one 90-minute class period to preteach the skills and have students read the selection. Use a second 90-minute class period to assess students' mastery of skills, extend their learning, and monitor their progress.

Homework Suggestions

Following are possibilities for homework assignments.

- Support pages from *Unit 5 Resources:*
  Literary Analysis
  Reading Strategy
  Vocabulary Builder
  Grammar and Style
- An Extend Your Learning project and the Writing Lesson for this selection may be completed over several days.

Step-by-Step Teaching Guide	Pacing Guide
PRETEACH	
• Administer Vocabulary and Reading Warm-ups as necessary.	5 min.
• Engage students' interest with the motivation activity.	5 min.
• Read and discuss author and background features. **FT**	10 min.
• Introduce the Literary Analysis Skill: Dramatic Monologue. **FT**	5 min.
• Introduce the Reading Strategy: Listening. **FT**	10 min.
• Prepare students to read by teaching the selection vocabulary. **FT**	
TEACH	
• Informally monitor comprehension while students read independently or in groups. **FT**	30 min.
• Monitor students' comprehension with the Reading Check notes.	as students read
• Reinforce vocabulary with Vocabulary Builder notes.	as students read
• Develop students' understanding of dramatic monologue with the Literary Analysis annotations. **FT**	5 min.
• Develop students' ability to listen with the Reading Strategy annotations. **FT**	5 min.
ASSESS/EXTEND	
• Assess students' comprehension and mastery of the Literary Analysis and Reading Strategy by having them answer the Apply the Skills questions. **FT**	15 min.
• Have students complete the Vocabulary Lesson and the Grammar and Style Lesson. **FT**	15 min.
• Apply students' ability to revise for accuracy by using the Writing Lesson. **FT**	45 min. or homework
• Apply students' understanding by using one or more of the Extend Your Learning activities.	20–90 min. or homework
• Administer Selection Test A or Selection Test B. **FT**	15 min.

Resources

PRINT

Unit 5 Resources

Vocabulary Warm-up Word Lists **[L1, L2, EL]** .... p. 4
Vocabulary Warm-up Practice **[L1, L2, EL]** .... p. 5
Reading Warm-up A **[L1, L2, EL]** .... p. 6
Reading Warm-up B **[L1, L2, L3]** .... p. 7

TRANSPARENCY

Graphic Organizer Transparencies

Literary Analysis Graphic Organizer A **[L3]** .... pp. 149, 151
Literary Analysis Graphic Organizer B **[L1, L2, EL]** .... pp. 150, 152

PRINT

Reader's Notebook [L2]
Reader's Notebook: Adapted Version [L1]
Reader's Notebook: English Learner's Version [EL]

Unit 5 Resources

Literary Analysis **[L3]** .... p. 8
Reading Strategy **[L3]** .... p. 9
Vocabulary Builder **[L3]** .... p. 10

PRINT

Unit 5 Resources

Grammar and Style **[L3]** .... p. 11
Support for Writing Lesson **[L3]** .... p. 12
Support for Extend Your Learning **[L3]** .... p. 13
Enrichment **[L4]** .... p. 14
Selection Test A **[L1, L2, EL]** .... pp. 15–17
Selection Test B **[L3, L4]** .... pp. 18–20

General Resources

Rubrics for Response to Literature **[L3]** .... pp. 65–66
Rubric for Dramatic Performance **[L3]** .... p. 131

TECHNOLOGY

Go Online: Research **[L3]**
Go Online: Self-test **[L3]**
***ExamView®* Test Bank [L3]**

Choosing Resources for Differentiated Instruction

[L1] Special Needs Students
[L2] Below-Level Students
[L3] All Students
[L4] Advanced Students
[EL] English Learners

For Vocabulary and Reading Warm-ups and for Selection Tests, **A** signifies "less challenging" and **B** "more challenging." For Graphic Organizer transparencies, **A** signifies "not filled in" and **B** "filled in."

FT Fast Track Instruction: To move the lesson more quickly, use the strategies and activities identified with **FT**.

Scaffolding for Less Proficient and Advanced Students

The leveled Critical Thinking questions after selections progress in the levels of thinking required to answer them. To address the needs of your different students, you may use the (a) level questions for your less proficient students and the (b) level questions with your on-level and advanced students. The occasional (c) level questions are appropriate for your advanced students.

PRENTICE HALL **TeacherEXPRESS™** Plan · Teach · Assess — Use this complete suite of powerful teaching tools to make lesson planning and testing quicker and easier.

PRENTICE HALL **StudentEXPRESS™** Learn · Study · Succeed — Use the interactive textbook (online and on CD-ROM) to make selections and activities come alive with audio and video support and interactive questions.

Go Online Professional Development — **For:** Information about Lexiles
Visit: www.PHSchool.com
Web Code: eue-1111

PRETEACH

Motivation

This dramatic monologue about a critical turning point in the speaker's life surrounds a theme students will find universal—the challenge of seizing an opportunity for emotional connection and the anguish that results when that opportunity goes unrealized. To get students involved in the theme, ask them to imagine you have invited a much-admired celebrity to visit the class. Ask students to record their feelings about such a visit in a journal. How would they express their admiration? What apprehensions might they have about the visitor's reactions? How might their feelings for the visitor affect their ability to communicate during the visit? Invite volunteers to share their entries.

❶ Background

More About the Author

In some works, including "Prufrock," Eliot and other Modernists used a technique known as stream of consciousness, in which they tried to reproduce the natural tendency of the human mind to jump from association to association. Rather than providing answers, the Modernists most often left it up to readers to draw their own conclusions about the meaning of a work.

Build Skills *Poem*

❶ The Love Song of J. Alfred Prufrock

T. S. Eliot (1888–1965)

Always well-spoken and somberly attired, Thomas Stearns Eliot was outwardly the model of convention. His work, in contrast, was revolutionary in both form and content.

Beginnings Born into a wealthy family in St. Louis, Missouri, Eliot grew up in an environment that promoted his intellectual development. He attended Harvard University, where he published a number of poems in *The Harvard Advocate,* the school's literary magazine. In 1910, the year Eliot received his master's degree in philosophy, he completed "The Love Song of J. Alfred Prufrock."

A Literary Sensation Just before the outbreak of World War I, Eliot moved to England. In 1915, he married Vivien Haigh-Wood, a deeply troubled young woman with whom he had a tumultuous relationship. During this period, he also became acquainted with Ezra Pound, another young American poet. Pound urged Harriet Monroe, the editor of *Poetry* magazine, to publish "Prufrock," thus making Eliot's work available to the public for the first time. Shortly thereafter, Eliot published a collection titled *Prufrock and Other Observations* (1917), which caused a sensation in the literary world. Eliot had used techniques, such as an intentionally fragmented structure, that were utterly new. Focusing on the frustration and despair of modern urban life, the poems in Eliot's first book also set the tone for the other poems he would write during the early stages of his career. These early poems alone earned Eliot a lasting place among the finest writers of the twentieth century.

Facing a New World Eliot made his literary mark against the backdrop of a rapidly changing society. Telephones, radios, automobiles—all were transforming life at an unprecedented pace in the early decades of the twentieth century. Uncertain and disillusioned with the values and ideologies that had produced the devastation of World War I, many people were searching for new ideas and values. Eliot was among a group of such writers and visual artists who called themselves Modernists. Modernist poets sought a break with the literary traditions of the past. They believed that poetry had to reflect the genuine, fractured experience of life in the twentieth century, not a romanticized idea of what life was once like. Eliot's exploration of the uncertainty of modern life struck a chord among readers, who were stunned by his revolutionary poetic imagery.

In 1922, Eliot published *The Waste Land,* his most celebrated work. Although Eliot himself once dismissed *The Waste Land* as "a piece of rhythmical grumbling," most readers saw it as a profound critique of the spiritual barrenness of the modern world. The poem is filled with allusions to classical and world literature and to Eastern culture and religion. It was widely read and had an enormous impact on writers and critics. *The Waste Land* is still considered one of the finest works ever written.

A Return to Tradition In his search for something beyond the "waste land" of modern society, Eliot became a member of the Church of England in 1927. He began to explore religious themes in poems such as "Ash Wednesday" (1930) and *Four Quartets* (1943)—works that suggest that he believed religion could heal the wounds inflicted by society. In later years, he wrote several plays, including *Murder in the Cathedral* (1935) and *The Cocktail Party* (1949), as well as a sizable body of literary criticism. In 1948, Eliot received the Nobel Prize for Literature.

Preview

Connecting to the Literature

You may be able to remember occasions when you have wished you had a different personality. Maybe you would have preferred to be more outgoing or more assertive—the type of person who makes things happen. The character of J. Alfred Prufrock speaks to this feeling in all of us.

❷ Literary Analysis

Dramatic Monologue

A troubled J. Alfred Prufrock invites an unidentified companion—perhaps a part of his own personality—to walk with him as he reflects aloud about his bitter realization that life and love are passing him by. Prufrock's so-called love song is a **dramatic monologue**—a poem or speech in which a character addresses a silent listener. As you read this dramatic monologue, use a chart like the one shown to record Prufrock's observations about life, details of his personality, and internal conflicts.

Prufrock's Observations
Personality Traits
Internal Conflicts

Connecting Literary Elements

Just as you might refer to a movie you once saw or a book you once read, Prufrock refers to people and historical or literary events that hold meaning for him. For example, in this passage, he alludes to Shakespeare:

> No! I am not Prince Hamlet, nor was meant to be;
> Am an attendant lord, one that will do
> To swell a progress, start a scene or two . . .

These references, or **allusions,** form a literary shorthand that paints a picture of Prufrock and his culture. As you read, use footnotes and guided reading questions to help you understand these allusions.

❸ Reading Strategy

Listening

This poem contains some of the most famous and haunting passages in literature. One of the reasons the poem affects readers so intensely is its musicality—the sweep and fall of the lines, the repetition and rhyme, and the sounds of the words. To fully appreciate the poem, you must **listen** to it. Try reading the poem aloud, paying attention to the rhythms and repetitions. Consider how the musicality of the poem contributes to its mood and meaning.

Vocabulary Builder

insidious (in sid′ ē əs) *adj.* secretly treacherous (p. 716)

digress (dī gres′) *v.* depart temporarily from the main subject (p. 718)

malingers (mə liŋ′ gərz) *v.* pretends to be ill (p. 718)

meticulous (mə tik′ yo͞o ləs) *adj.* extremely careful about details (p. 719)

obtuse (äb to͞os′) *adj.* slow to understand or perceive (p. 719)

❷ Literary Analysis

Dramatic Monologue

- Tell students that as they read "The Love Song of J. Alfred Prufrock," they will focus on understanding dramatic monologue, a literary genre in which one character addresses a silent listener.
- Have a volunteer read aloud the first sentence of the Literary Analysis instruction. Call attention to the suggestion that the person that Prufrock addresses may be part of his own personality. Encourage students to keep this possibility in mind as they read.
- Give students a copy of **Literary Analysis Graphic Organizer A,** p. 149 in ***Graphic Organizer Transparencies,*** to point out that students can use Prufrock's allusions to build understanding of his character.
- Review the chart shown and then encourage students to complete a similar one as they read the poem.

❸ Reading Strategy

Listening

- Tell students that this poem contains a conversation—or at least one half of a conversation. As such it should be read aloud. The reading skill of listening can help students access the poem more fully.
- To listen critically, students must focus on many aspects of the poem's sound. Review those discussed in the Reading Strategy instruction and confirm students' understanding of each.
- Remind students to read the poem aloud in order to practice listening.

Vocabulary Builder

- Pronounce each vocabulary word for students and read the definitions as a class. Have students identify any words with which they are already familiar.

Differentiated Instruction

Solutions for All Learners

Support for Special Needs Students
Have students complete the **Preview** and **Build Skills** pages for the selection in the ***Reader's Notebook: Adapted Version.*** These pages provide a selection summary, an abbreviated presentation of the reading and literary skills, and the graphic organizer on the **Build Skills** page in the student book.

Support for Less Proficient Readers
Have students complete the **Preview** and **Build Skills** pages for the selection in the ***Reader's Notebook.*** These pages provide a selection summary, an abbreviated presentation of the reading and literary skills, and the graphic organizer on the **Build Skills** page in the student book.

Support for English Learners
Have students complete the **Preview** and **Build Skills** pages for the selection in the ***Reader's Notebook: English Learner's Version.*** These pages provide a selection summary, an abbreviated presentation of the skills, additional contextual vocabulary, and the graphic organizer on the **Build Skills** page in the student book.

TEACH

Learning Modalities
Bodily/Kinesthetic Learners
Encourage students to consider choreographing a mime or dance performance based on "The Love Song of J. Alfred Prufrock" to be performed outside of class. Students might divide the events in the poem into Act I in the narrow streets mentioned by the speaker, Act II at the party, and Act III on a beach. Encourage students to choose appropriate music to accompany each passage.

❶ About the Selection

This poem invites readers into the mind of its speaker J. Alfred Prufrock, as he agonizes, in a dramatic monologue, over whether and how to declare his love to a woman. Prufrock reviews his superficial personal life, and recognizes his sense of alienation and failure, all the while visualizing a scene of amorous declaration that may take place if he summons the courage. By accompanying Prufrock on his internal journey, the reader recognizes how someone might vacillate over which path to take at a fork in life's road, and how that decision-making process can reveal important facets of character.

❷ Reading Strategy
Listening

- Have a volunteer read aloud lines 1–12. Invite students to point out the repetitions in these lines. Then, have students discuss the rhythm of these lines.
- **Ask** students the Reading Strategy question: In what ways do the rhythms and repetitions of this opening stanza invite readers into the poem?
  Answer: Students may note that the words "Let us go" invite readers to join Prufrock on his journey. In addition, the rhythm of the stanza sounds like footsteps, with a repetition of stressed and unstressed words.

❶ *The Love Song of J. Alfred Prufrock*

T. S. Eliot

Background In this poem, surely one of the strangest "love songs" ever written, J. Alfred Prufrock, a stuffy and inhibited man who is pained by his own passivity, invites the reader, or some unnamed visitor, to join him in a journey. Where Prufrock is and where he is going—to a party, a museum, a tea party, or some other gathering—is open to debate. The most important part of this journey, however, takes place within the inner landscape of Prufrock's emotions, memory, and intellect as he meditates on his life.

S'io credessi che mia risposta fosse
a persona che mai tornasse al mondo,
questa fiamma staria senza più scosse.
Ma per ciò che giammai di questo fondo
non tornò vivo alcun, s'i'odo il vero,
senza tema d'infamia ti rispondo.[1]

❷
Let us go then, you and I,
When the evening is spread out against the sky
Like a patient etherized[2] upon a table;
Let us go, through certain half-deserted streets,
The muttering retreats
Of restless nights in one-night cheap hotels
And sawdust restaurants with oyster-shells:
Streets that follow like a tedious argument
Of insidious intent
To lead you to an overwhelming question . . .
Oh, do not ask, "What is it?"
Let us go and make our visit.

1. ***S'io credessi . . . ti rispondo*** The epigraph is a passage from Dante's *Inferno*, in which one of the damned, upon being requested to tell his story, says: "If I believed my answer were being given to someone who could ever return to the world, this flame (his voice) would shake no more. But since no one has ever returned alive from this depth, if what I hear is true, I will answer you without fear of disgrace."
2. **etherized** (ē′ thə rīzd) *v.* anesthetized with ether.

Reading Strategy
Listening In what ways do the rhythms and repetitions of this opening stanza invite readers into the poem?

Vocabulary Builder
insidious (in sid′ ē əs) *adj.* secretly treacherous

Differentiated Instruction Solutions for All Learners

Accessibility at a Glance

	The Love Song of J. Alfred Prufrock
Context	Modern poetry
Language	Accessible vocabulary; some dialogue
Concept Level	Challenging (lengthy dramatic monologue with allusions)
Literary Merit	Noted author; widely anthologized and important twentieth-century poem
Lexile	NP
Overall Rating	More challenging

3 In the room the women come and go
Talking of Michelangelo.[3]
The yellow fog that rubs its back upon the window-panes,
The yellow smoke that rubs its muzzle on the window-panes,
Licked its tongue into the corners of the evening,
Lingered upon the pools that stand in drains,
Let fall upon its back the soot that falls from chimneys,
Slipped by the terrace, made a sudden leap,
And seeing that it was a soft October night,
Curled once about the house, and fell asleep.

And indeed there will be time[4]
For the yellow smoke that slides along the street
Rubbing its back upon the window-panes;
There will be time, there will be time
To prepare a face to meet the faces that you meet;
There will be time to murder and create,
And time for all the works and days[5] of hands
That lift and drop a question on your plate;
Time for you and time for me,
And time yet for a hundred indecisions,
And for a hundred visions and revisions,
Before the taking of a toast and tea.

In the room the women come and go
Talking of Michelangelo.
And indeed there will be time
To wonder, "Do I dare?" and, "Do I dare?"
Time to turn back and descend the stair,
With a bald spot in the middle of my hair—
(They will say: "How his hair is growing thin!")
4 My morning coat, my collar mounting firmly to the chin,
My necktie rich and modest, but asserted by a simple pin—
(They will say: "But how his arms and legs are thin!")
Do I dare
Disturb the universe?
In a minute there is time
For decisions and revisions which a minute will reverse.

For I have known them all already, known them all—
Have known the evenings, mornings, afternoons,
I have measured out my life with coffee spoons;
I know the voices dying with a dying fall

Literary Analysis
Dramatic Monologue and Allusion What might Prufrock's allusion to Michelangelo suggest about the women at the party?

Literary Analysis
Dramatic Monologue
What emotions does the speaker express in the description of his physical appearance?

5  **Reading Check**
At what time of day is the poem set?

3. **Michelangelo** (mī′ kəl an′ jə lō) a famous Italian artist and sculptor (1475–1564).
4. **there will be time** These words echo the speaker's plea in English poet Andrew Marvell's "To His Coy Mistress": "Had we but world enough and time . . . "
5. **works and days** Ancient Greek poet Hesiod wrote a poem about farming called "Works and Days."

3 Literary Analysis
Dramatic Monologue and Allusion

- Remind students of the definition of an allusion, using the Connecting Literary Elements instruction if necessary.
- Discuss with students what conclusions might be drawn about people who stroll about "talking of Michelangelo."
- Then, **ask** students the Literary Analysis question: What might Prufrock's allusion to Michelangelo suggest about the women at the party?
  Possible response: It could suggest that they are educated and that perhaps they intimidate Prufrock.

4 Literary Analysis
Dramatic Monologue

- Have students close their eyes as you read aloud the bracketed passage. **Ask** them to list the details related to Prufrock's appearance. Then, encourage them to visualize Prufrock using these details.
  Answer: He is thin and balding, wearing a buttoned-up coat with a simple but expensive necktie.
- **Ask** students the second Literary Analysis question: What emotions does the speaker express in the description of his physical appearance?
  Answer: He seems to express some insecurity, focusing largely on negatives in his appearance and on the negative reaction he expects from others about it.

5 Reading Check

Answer: The poem is set in the early evening, at teatime.

Differentiated Instruction
Solutions for All Learners

Strategy for Less Proficient Readers
Students may find Eliot's many cultural references and historical allusions confusing. Encourage students to make full use of the numbered footnotes, many of which explain Eliot's allusions. Invite students' questions about the footnotes, and offer clarification as necessary.

Support for English Learners
Spanish- or Italian-speaking students may be able to help their classmates understand Eliot's reference to Dante's *Inferno*. Invite any students who are able to read the epigraph aloud in Italian. Then, have a native English speaker read footnote 1. After students finish the poem, discuss the meaning of the epigraph as a class.

Enrichment for Advanced Readers
Point out that Eliot's language is filled with cultural references and historical allusions. Have students select a list of these references to share and explain to the class. You might suggest that they use a library or the Internet to find literary criticism that explores Eliot's references.

6 Vocabulary Builder
The Greek Prefix *di-*

- Call students' attention to the word *digress* and its definition. Tell students that the Greek prefix *di-* (or *dis-*) means "apart" or "away."
- Have students suggest words that contain this prefix, and write them on the chalkboard. Possibilities include *divide, differ, diffuse, diverge.*
- Have students locate the etymologies of these words in a dictionary. Ensure that they can distinguish between the prefix *di-* or *dis-* meaning "apart" or "away" and the prefix *di-* or *dia-,* which means "through," as in *diagonal* or *diameter.*

7 Literary Analysis
Dramatic Monologue

- Direct students to consider the surrounding context of Prufrock's remark.
- **Ask** the Literary Analysis question: When he says "I have seen the moment of my greatness flicker," what observation does Prufrock make about himself?
Answer: He acknowledges that he isn't going to express his feelings to the woman he loves. He observes that he lacks the greatness, or courage, to do it.

➤ **Monitor Progress:** Help students complete the Literary Analysis Graphic Organizer with the evidence of the bracketed text. Charts should look similar to the following.

Prufrock's Observations
"I am no prophet—and here's no great matter."
Personality Traits
Highly educated, ironic, uncertain of himself
Internal Conflicts
Desire for love conflicts with fear

Beneath the music from a farther room.
 So how should I presume?

And I have known the eyes already, known them all—
The eyes that fix you in a formulated phrase,
And when I am formulated, sprawling on a pin,
When I am pinned and wriggling on the wall,
Then how should I begin
To spit out all the butt-ends of my days and ways?
 And how should I presume?

And I have known the arms already, known them all—
Arms that are braceleted and white and bare
(But in the lamplight, downed with light brown hair!)
Is it perfume from a dress
That makes me so digress?
Arms that lie along a table, or wrap about a shawl.
 And should I then presume?
 And how should I begin?

. . . . . .

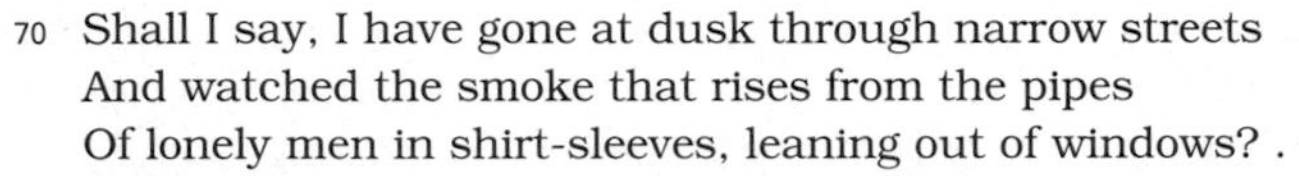

Shall I say, I have gone at dusk through narrow streets
And watched the smoke that rises from the pipes
Of lonely men in shirt-sleeves, leaning out of windows? . . .

I should have been a pair of ragged claws
Scuttling across the floors of silent seas.[6]

. . . . . .

And the afternoon, the evening, sleeps so peacefully!
Smoothed by long fingers,
Asleep . . . tired . . . or it malingers,
Stretched on the floor, here beside you and me.
Should I, after tea and cakes and ices,
Have the strength to force the moment to its crisis?
But though I have wept and fasted, wept and prayed,
Though I have seen my head (grown slightly bald) brought in
 upon a platter,[7]
I am no prophet—and here's no great matter;
7 I have seen the moment of my greatness flicker,
And I have seen the eternal Footman[8] hold my coat, and snicker.
And in short, I was afraid.

6 Vocabulary Builder
digress (dī gres′) *v.* depart temporarily from the main subject

Vocabulary Builder
malingers (mə liŋ′ gərz) *v.* pretends to be ill

Literary Analysis
Dramatic Monologue
When he says "I have seen the moment of my greatness flicker," what observation does Prufrock make about himself?

6. **I should . . . seas** In Shakespeare's *Hamlet,* the hero, Hamlet, mocks the aging Lord Chamberlain, Polonius, saying, "You yourself, sir, should be old as I am, if like a crab you could go backward" (II.ii. 205–206).
7. **head . . . platter** a reference to the prophet John the Baptist, whose head was delivered on a platter to Salome as a reward for her dancing (Matthew 14:1–11).
8. **eternal Footman** death.

Enrichment
The Importance of Tea

Eliot's poem revolves around his observations during an afternoon tea party. In the late nineteenth and early twentieth centuries, afternoon tea parties were social events; people dressed up for the occasion and tables were elegantly set. Small sandwiches and pastries were served in addition to tea. The tea party provided an opportunity for well-born people to "see and be seen." Tea parties were quiet, well-mannered affairs, often, as here, embellished with music and cultural discussions.

Have students compare and contrast Prufrock's party with their own social gatherings. Points of comparison might include:

(1) reasons for the gathering,
(2) social behavior at the gathering,
(3) appropriate dress,
(4) topics of conversation.

And would it have been worth it, after all,
After the cups, the marmalade, the tea,
Among the porcelain, among some talk of you and me,
Would it have been worth while,
To have bitten off the matter with a smile,
To have squeezed the universe into a ball
To roll it towards some overwhelming question,
To say: "I am Lazarus,[9] come from the dead,
Come back to tell you all, I shall tell you all"—
If one, settling a pillow by her head,
Should say: "That is not what I meant at all.
That is not it, at all."

And would it have been worth it, after all,
Would it have been worth while,
After the sunsets and the dooryards and the sprinkled streets,
After the novels, after the teacups, after the skirts that trail along the floor—
And this, and so much more?—
It is impossible to say just what I mean!
8 But as if a magic lantern[10] threw the nerves in patterns on a screen:
Would it have been worth while
If one, settling a pillow or throwing off a shawl,
And turning toward the window, should say:
"That is not it at all,
That is not what I meant, at all."

. . . . . .

No! I am not Prince Hamlet, nor was meant to be;
Am an attendant lord, one that will do
To swell a progress,[11] start a scene or two,
Advise the prince; no doubt, an easy tool,
Deferential, glad to be of use,
Politic, cautious, and meticulous;
Full of high sentence,[12] but a bit obtuse;
At times, indeed, almost ridiculous—
Almost, at times, the Fool.

I grow old . . . I grow old . . .
I shall wear the bottoms of my trousers rolled.

Shall I part my hair behind? Do I dare to eat a peach?
I shall wear white flannel trousers, and walk upon the beach.
I have heard the mermaids singing, each to each.

Reading Strategy
Listening How does the use of rhyme contribute to the effect of this stanza?

Vocabulary Builder
meticulous (mə tik′ yo͞o ləs) *adj.* extremely careful about details

obtuse (äb to͞os′) *adj.* slow to understand or perceive

9  **Reading Check**
What question does Prufrock repeatedly ask himself?

9. **Lazarus** (laz′ ə rəs) Lazarus is resurrected from the dead by Jesus in John 11:1–44.
10. **magic lantern** an early device used to project images on a screen.
11. **To swell a progress** to add to the number of people in a parade or scene from a play.
12. **Full of high sentence** speaking in a very ornate manner, often offering advice.

8 Reading Strategy
Listening

- Invite students to listen as you read aloud the bracketed passage. Then have students read it aloud themselves. Together, identify the rhymes in lines 102–103, 104–105, and 107–110.
- **Ask** students to describe the tone of this stanza and to characterize the poem's speaker based on what they have learned thus far. Then, have students evaluate the relationship between the rhythm of the stanza and its content. What effect does this rhythm have on the content?

Monitor Progress: Ask students the Reading Strategy question: How does the use of rhyme contribute to the effect of this stanza?
Answer: The rhyme gives the stanza a sing-song quality, almost like a nursery rhyme. Some students may observe that this lends a satirical, ironic tone to Prufrock's observations.

9 Reading Check

Answer: Prufrock asks himself, "would it have been worth it, after all?"

Differentiated Instruction
Solutions for All Learners

Support for Special Needs Students
Relate the monologue format to students' own experiences talking or thinking aloud to themselves. Emphasize that the monologue reveals feelings Prufrock cannot share with others. Encourage students to use the Literary Analysis/graphic organizer introduced on the Build Skills page to build a profile of Prufrock from his dramatic monologue. Model how to complete the organizer with Prufrock's views on life and then help students gather information about his personality traits and internal conflicts from the text of the poem.

Support for Less Proficient Readers
Remind students that a dramatic monologue consists of a single individual's speech, either to another person or to him- or herself. Ask students what the purpose of a dramatic monologue might be. Help students understand that it allows the speaker to give voice freely to his or her innermost thoughts and emotions. This is what Prufrock does, saying things that he does not dare speak aloud to others.

ASSESS

Answers

1. (a) and (b) Students' responses should indicate a clear understanding of the poem.
2. (a) He says that because he is damned, he may speak freely because no one ever returns from the dead to share these secrets. (b) It suggests that Eliot intends the reader to see Prufrock as a man living in his own private hell, speaking the truth even if only to himself.
3. (a) He says he has a bald spot and thinning hair, has thin arms and legs, and is dressed elegantly and conservatively. (b) He is likely on the verge of middle age.
4. (a) He describes lower-class neighborhoods, where men as lonely as he lean out of windows, smoking their pipes. (b) They are the streets of the poor, of a crowded urban neighborhood rather than the wider, more spacious streets of Prufrock's cultured society.
5. (a) He uses the image of coffee spoons. (b) He has lived a careful life, with little risk, and he has lived a life filled with trivial, but well-mannered social occasions.
6. (a) Her reaction is to deny whatever interest in him Prufrock may have dared to read into her conversation. (b) He doesn't think they will sing to him. (c) He expects them to reject him.
7. (a) Prufrock sees "the eternal Footman hold my coat, and snicker." (b) Prufrock is afraid both of death and of other people's derision.
8. (a) In the opening stanza, Prufrock prepares to go to a party, which will present the opportunity for him to make a declaration of love. In the closing stanza, he compares the women he admires to mermaids, and his own self-knowledge to death by drowning. (b) The first is hopeful, the second is not.
9. (a) and (b) Students should be able to support their views with specific examples of contemporary behavior.

I do not think that they will sing to me.

I have seen them riding seaward on the waves
Combing the white hair of the waves blown back
When the wind blows the water white and black.

We have lingered in the chambers of the sea
By sea-girls wreathed with seaweed red and brown
Till human voices wake us, and we drown.

Critical Reading

1. **(a) Respond:** What is your primary feeling for Prufrock—pity or irritation? Why? **(b) Respond:** What advice would you give him if he were your friend?
2. **(a) Recall:** What does the speaker say in the opening quotation from Dante's *Inferno*? **(b) Interpret:** What does this quotation suggest about the content of the poem that follows?
3. **(a) Recall:** What details does Prufrock use in lines 36–45 to describe his appearance? **(b) Infer:** At what stage of life is Prufrock?
4. **(a) Recall:** In lines 69–71, what kind of streets does Prufrock describe? **(b) Interpret:** In what ways do these streets differ from those that Prufrock would more customarily visit?
5. **(a) Recall:** In lines 48–53, what image does Prufrock use to describe how he has "measured out" his life? **(b) Analyze:** Judging from this metaphor, how has Prufrock lived?
6. **(a) Recall:** In lines 96–97, what is the woman's reaction to Prufrock? **(b) Recall:** In line 124, how does Prufrock describe the mermaids' reaction to him? **(c) Connect:** How does Prufrock seem to feel about women's interest in him?
7. **(a) Recall:** In line 85, who or what does Prufrock see? **(b) Make a Judgment:** Do you think Prufrock is simply afraid of death, or are his fears more complicated? Explain.
8. **(a) Interpret:** Describe the scenes outlined in the poem's opening and closing stanzas. **(b) Compare and Contrast:** How do the moods of these scenes differ?
9. **(a) Generalize:** Do you think that Prufrock accurately represents many people today? **(b) Relate:** Do we live in a time when it is difficult, even impossible, to be the heroes of our own lives? Explain.

Go Online
Author Link

For: More about T. S. Eliot
Visit: www.PHSchool.com
Web Code: ere-9501

Go Online Author Link For additional information about T. S. Eliot, have students type in the Web Code, then select *E* from the alphabet, and then select T. S. Eliot.

Apply the Skills

The Love Song of J. Alfred Prufrock

Literary Analysis

Dramatic Monologue

1. What do his descriptions of the sky and the city in lines 1–12 suggest about Prufrock's outlook on life?
2. **(a)** How can the first line of this **dramatic monologue** be interpreted to suggest that Prufrock sees himself as divided, both seeking and fearing action? **(b)** At what other points does he express a deeply conflicted sense of self?

Connecting Literary Elements

3. Some of Prufrock's **allusions** paint imaginary portraits that reveal his sense of self. Use a chart like the one shown to examine these allusions and what they suggest about Prufrock's self-image.

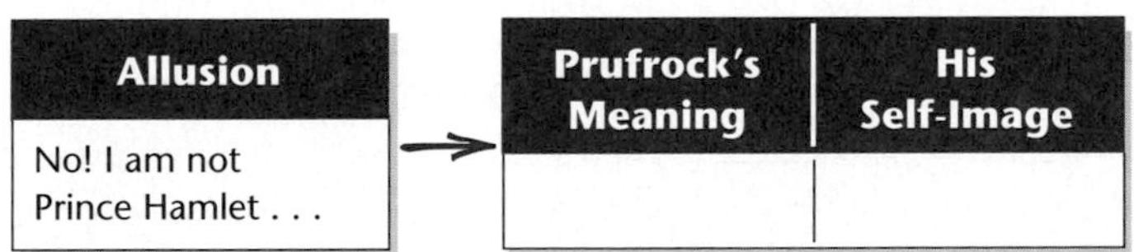

4. **(a)** What is suggested by the repeated reference to Michelangelo? **(b)** In what ways would the portrayal of Prufrock's world be quite different if that reference were to something less refined?

Reading Strategy

Listening

5. In the lines referring to Michelangelo, what is the impact of the use of rhyme?
6. What is the effect of the repetition of "there will be time" in lines 23–34 and again in lines 37–48?
7. What effect do the ellipsis points (three dots used to indicate an elongated pause or an omission) have on the way you hear lines 120–121?

Extend Understanding

8. **Humanities Connection:** Prufrock says there will be time "To prepare a face to meet the faces that you meet." Does this statement accurately describe how people relate to each other? All the time? Sometimes? Explain.

QuickReview

In a **dramatic monologue,** the speaker addresses a silent listener.

Allusions are references to well-known people, historical events, and literary works.

Listen to the music of a poem by reading it aloud and noting sound devices such as rhythm and rhyme.

For: Self-test
Visit: www.PHSchool.com
Web Code: era-6501

Answers

1. The gloomy images, such as those of an etherized patient and of cheap hotels, imply a pessimistic outlook on life.
2. (a) Prufrock refers to himself as "you and I." (b) He refers to himself as divided in line 30 when he says "Time for you and time for me." Also, his vacillation between the desire to speak and his inability to do so suggests deep internal conflict.
3. **Possible response:** Allusion: "No! I am not Prince Hamlet . . ."; Prufrock's Meaning: He is not a heroic figure; His Self-Image: He sees himself as inadequate.

   Another sample answer can be found on **Literary Analysis Graphic Organizer B,** p. 152 in ***Graphic Organizer Transparencies.***
4. (a) **Possible response:** Prufrock suggests that the women are highly cultured and refined. (b) It might make the women seem less intimidating and more accessible.
5. It gives the lines a sing-song quality that make the women seem a bit ridiculous.
6. This repetition heightens the tension as readers wonder whether Prufrock will actually get the job done while there is still time. Also, the repetition conveys Prufrock's anxiety about the task ahead.
7. They make these lines sound wearied and slow, which emphasizes their meaning about growing old.
8. **Possible response:** This line accurately suggests the way people often compose their outward demeanor for the world.

Go Online Assessment Students may use the **Self-test** to prepare for **Selection Test A** or **Selection Test B.**

EXTEND/ASSESS

Answers

❶ Vocabulary Lesson

Word Analysis

1. true
2. false
3. false

Spelling Strategy

1. insidious
2. perfidious
3. invidious

Vocabulary Builder

1. c
2. a
3. a
4. c
5. b

❷ Grammar and Style Lesson

1. modifier: of tea; modifies: cups
2. modifier: talking in the next room; modifies: guests
3. modifier: who secretly disliked each other; modifies: People
4. modifier: to serve tea; modifies: time
5. modifier: crowded with indifferent faces; modifies: drawing room

Writing Application

Paragraphs should describe Prufrock and include at least two correctly used adjectival modifiers.

WG Writing and Grammar, Ruby Level

Students will find further instruction and practice on adjectival modifiers in Chapter 19, Sections 1–3.

Build Language Skills

❶ Vocabulary Lesson

Word Analysis: Greek Prefix *di-*

The Greek prefix *di-* (or *dis-*) means "apart" or "away." The word digress means "to move away from a subject." Each of the following sentences includes a word containing the prefix *di-*. Indicate whether each sentence is true or false.

1. A path *diverges* if it branches off.
2. If you are *diverted,* your focus is sharp.
3. A *diverse* menu features many similar foods.

Spelling Strategy

When you form adjectives by adding the *-ious* suffix to stems ending in *d,* use the spelling *-ious,* as in *studious.* An exception to this rule is the word *hideous.* Add the correctly spelled *-ious* suffix to each stem below.

1. insid_____ **2.** perfid_____ **3.** invid_____

Vocabulary Builder: Synonyms

Review the words from the vocabulary list on page 715. Then, choose the letter of the word that is the best synonym, or word with a similar meaning, for the first word.

1. insidious: **(a)** innocent, **(b)** wealthy, **(c)** dangerous, **(d)** certified
2. digress: **(a)** wander, **(b)** contain, **(c)** hesitate, **(d)** elaborate
3. malingers: **(a)** fakes, **(b)** studies, **(c)** boasts, **(d)** anticipates
4. meticulous: **(a)** messy, **(b)** absurd, **(c)** careful, **(d)** tart
5. obtuse: **(a)** intense, **(b)** stupid, **(c)** friendly, **(d)** prompt

❷ Grammar and Style Lesson

Adjectival Modifiers

Adjectival modifiers, phrases or clauses that modify nouns or pronouns, can have many different grammatical structures. In the examples below, the adjectival modifiers are italicized.

Prepositional Phrase: sawdust restaurants *with oyster shells* (modifies *restaurants*)

Participial Phrase: a patient *etherized upon a table* (modifies *patient*)

Adjective Clause: Streets *that follow like a tedious argument* (modifies *streets*)

Infinitive Phrase: prepare a face *to meet the faces . . .* (modifies *face*)

Practice Copy these sentences. Underline the adjectival modifier, and then circle the noun it modifies in each of the sentences below.

1. The cups of tea sat on the tray.
2. The guests talking in the next room were gossiping about J. Alfred Prufrock.
3. People who secretly disliked each other chatted politely.
4. The hostess said it was time to serve tea.
5. Prufrock entered a drawing room crowded with indifferent faces.

Writing Application Write a brief paragraph describing J. Alfred Prufrock. Include at least two adjectival modifiers in your description.

WG *Prentice Hall Writing and Grammar Connection: Chapter 19, Sections 1–3*

Assessment Practice

Anticipate Missing Words (For more practice, see *Standardized Test Preparation Workbook,* p. 41.)

Many tests ask students to correctly answer sentence-completion questions. Use the following examples to show students how to use context and their prior knowledge to choose the word that would best complete the following passage.

Always somberly attired and well-spoken, Thomas Stearns Eliot was outwardly the model of__________. His work, in contrast, was revolutionary in both form and content.

A rebellion **C** illiteracy
B convention **D** fashion

The context clues "somberly attired" and "well-spoken" provide the key to completing the sentence. In addition, "in contrast" indicates that the word must be the opposite of revolutionary. *B* is the most logical choice.

3 Writing Lesson

Timed Writing: Character Analysis

Ever since Eliot's "Love Song" was published in 1915, J. Alfred Prufrock has fascinated readers. For some, Prufrock is merely a man who fails to achieve his dreams. For others, Prufrock embodies larger failings of the modern age—an absence of heroism or a general weariness. Write an essay analyzing the character of this famous literary creation. ***(40 minutes)***

Prewriting *(10 minutes)* Reread the poem, taking notes about Prufrock's character. Pay attention to details that suggest reasons for Prufrock's passivity and fears, and cite passages to use as support for your point of view.

Drafting *(20 minutes)* Begin by noting the title and author of the work, and stating what you believe about Prufrock's character. Use quotes from the poem and precise language to develop your ideas in each body paragraph.

Revising *(10 minutes)* Review your draft. Highlight any words that seem vague or inaccurate, and replace them with better, more specific word choices.

Model: Revising for Accuracy

Prufrock's lament is ~~big.~~ *sweeping* He ~~talks about~~ *pines for* all that he has lost or that he never had—youth and love. He is keenly aware of, ~~and really upset about~~ *even tormented by,* the passage of time.

Replacing vague words with specific ones makes a piece of writing more accurate and powerful.

WG Prentice Hall Writing and Grammar Connection: Chapter 14, Section 2

Extend Your Learning

Listening and Speaking With a classmate, **role-play** a talk-show host's interview with Prufrock. Explore the reasons for Prufrock's poor self-esteem. Use the following tips:

- Create a list of appropriate interview questions that require in-depth responses.
- Develop Prufrock's responses within the context of his character, using his authentic voice.

Present your role play. **[Group Activity]**

Research and Technology Modernism has had a lasting effect on art, literature, and popular culture. Use print and online sources to research the movement and its impact. If possible, download examples of Modernist art to illustrate your conclusions. Present your findings in a **report.**

For: An additional research activity
Visit: www.PHSchool.com
Web Code: erd-7501

3 Writing Lesson

You may use this Writing Lesson as timed-writing practice, or you may allow students to develop it as a writing assignment over several days.

- To guide students in writing their responses to literature, give them the **Support for Writing Lesson** page (***Unit 5 Resources,*** p. 12).
- Review with students the basic elements of a character analysis: vivid description of the character's appearance, attitudes, and behaviors, along with discussion of reasons for these elements.
- Read through the Writing Lesson steps with students and clarify any confusion.
- Use the Response to Literature Rubrics in ***General Resources,*** pp. 65–66, to evaluate students' analyses.

4 Listening and Speaking

- Before students team up, lead a class discussion about typical features of poor self-esteem. Invite students' comments about this fairly common teenage experience.
- Encourage partners to read both questions and answers aloud before finalizing them. Stress that conversation should sound natural, rather than scripted.
- Provide time for rehearsal so that partners will be prepared to present their role-play without scripts.
- The **Support for Extend Your Learning** page (***Unit 5 Resources,*** p. 13) provides guided note-taking opportunities to help students complete the Extend Your Learning activities.
- Use the rubric for Dramatic Performance, p. 131 in ***General Resources,*** to evaluate students' role-plays.

Go Online Research Have students type in the Web Code for another research activity.

Assessment Resources

The following resources can be used to assess students' knowledge and skills.

Unit 5 Resources
- **Selection Test A,** pp. 15–17
- **Selection Test B,** pp. 18–20

General Resources
- **Rubrics for Response to Literature,** pp. 65–66
- **Rubric for Dramatic Performance,** p. 131

Go Online Assessment Students may use the **Self-test** to prepare for **Selection Test A** or **Selection Test B.**

Meeting Your Standards

Students will

1. **analyze and respond to literary elements.**
   - Literary Analysis: Imagist Poetry
2. **read, comprehend, analyze, and critique nonfiction and poetry.**
   - Reading Strategy: Engaging Your Senses
   - Reading Check questions
   - Apply the Skills questions
   - Assessment Practice (ATE)
3. **develop vocabulary.**
   - Vocabulary Lesson: Forms of *appear*
4. **understand and apply written and oral language conventions.**
   - Spelling Strategy
   - Grammar and Style Lesson: Concrete and Abstract Nouns
5. **develop writing proficiency.**
   - Writing Lesson: An Editor's Review of a Manuscript
6. **develop appropriate research strategies.**
   - Extend Your Learning: Poetry Illustration
7. **understand and apply listening and speaking strategies.**
   - Extend Your Learning: Informal Debate

Block Scheduling: Use one 90-minute class period to preteach the skills and have students read the selection. Use a second 90-minute class period to assess students' mastery of skills, extend their learning, and monitor their progress.

Homework Suggestions

Following are possibilities for homework assignments.

- Support pages from *Unit 5 Resources:*
  Literary Analysis
  Reading Strategy
  Vocabulary Builder
  Grammar and Style
- An Extend Your Learning project and the Writing Lesson for this selection group may be completed over several days.

Step-by-Step Teaching Guide	Pacing Guide
PRETEACH	
• Administer Vocabulary and Reading Warm-ups as necessary.	5 min.
• Engage students' interest with the motivation activity.	5 min.
• Read and discuss author and background features. **FT**	10 min.
• Introduce the Literary Analysis Skill: Imagist Poetry. **FT**	5 min.
• Introduce the Reading Strategy: Engaging Your Senses. **FT**	10 min.
• Prepare students to read by teaching the selection vocabulary. **FT**	
TEACH	
• Informally monitor comprehension while students read independently or in groups. **FT**	30 min.
• Monitor students' comprehension with the Reading Check notes.	as students read
• Reinforce vocabulary with Vocabulary Builder notes.	as students read
• Develop students' understanding of Imagist poetry with the Literary Analysis annotations. **FT**	5 min.
• Develop students' ability to engage their senses with the Reading Strategy annotations. **FT**	5 min.
ASSESS/EXTEND	
• Assess students' comprehension and mastery of the Literary Analysis and Reading Strategy by having them answer the Apply the Skills questions. **FT**	15 min.
• Have students complete the Vocabulary Lesson and the Grammar and Style Lesson. **FT**	15 min.
• Apply students' ability to write briefly and clearly by using the Writing Lesson. **FT**	45 min. or homework
• Apply students' understanding by using one or more of the Extend Your Learning activities.	20–90 min. or homework
• Administer Selection Test A or Selection Test B. **FT**	15 min.

Resources

PRINT

Unit 5 Resources

Vocabulary Warm-up Word Lists **[L1, L2, EL]** .... p. 21
Vocabulary Warm-up Practice **[L1, L2, EL]** .... p. 22
Reading Warm-up A **[L1, L2, EL]** .... p. 23
Reading Warm-up B **[L1, L2, L3]** .... p. 24

TRANSPARENCY

Graphic Organizer Transparencies

Literary Analysis Graphic Organizer A **[L3]** .... p. 155
Literary Analysis Graphic Organizer B **[L1, L2, EL]** .... p. 156
Reading Strategy Graphic Organizer A **[L3]** .... p. 153
Reading Strategy Graphic Organizer B **[L1, L2, EL]** .... p. 154

PRINT

Reader's Notebook [L2]
Reader's Notebook: Adapted Version [L1]
Reader's Notebook: English Learner's Version [EL]

Unit 5 Resources

Literary Analysis **[L3]** .... p. 25
Reading Strategy **[L3]** .... p. 26
Vocabulary Builder **[L3]** .... p. 27

TECHNOLOGY

Listening to Literature Audio CDs [L2, EL]

PRINT

Unit 5 Resources

Grammar and Style **[L3]** .... p. 28
Support for Writing Lesson **[L3]** .... p. 29
Support for Extend Your Learning **[L3]** .... p. 30
Enrichment **[L4]** .... p. 31
Selection Test A **[L1, L2, EL]** .... pp. 32–34
Selection Test B **[L3, L4]** .... pp. 35–37

General Resources

Rubrics for a Critique **[L3]** .... pp. 75–76

TECHNOLOGY

Go Online: Research **[L3]**
Go Online: Self-test **[L3]**
***ExamView*® Test Bank [L3]**

Choosing Resources for Differentiated Instruction

[L1] Special Needs Students
[L2] Below-Level Students
[L3] All Students
[L4] Advanced Students
[EL] English Learners

For Vocabulary and Reading Warm-ups and for Selection Tests, **A** signifies "less challenging" and **B** "more challenging." For Graphic Organizer transparencies, **A** signifies "not filled in" and **B** "filled in."

FT Fast Track Instruction: To move the lesson more quickly, use the strategies and activities identified with **FT**.

Scaffolding for Less Proficient and Advanced Students

The leveled Critical Thinking questions after selections progress in the levels of thinking required to answer them. To address the needs of your different students, you may use the (a) level questions for your less proficient students and the (b) level questions with your on-level and advanced students. The occasional (c) level questions are appropriate for your advanced students.

PRENTICE HALL **TeacherEXPRESS**™ Plan · Teach · Assess — Use this complete suite of powerful teaching tools to make lesson planning and testing quicker and easier.

PRENTICE HALL **StudentEXPRESS**™ Learn · Study · Succeed — Use the interactive textbook (online and on CD-ROM) to make selections and activities come alive with audio and video support and interactive questions.

Go Online Professional Development
For: Information about Lexiles
Visit: www.PHSchool.com
Web Code: eue-1111

PRETEACH

Motivation

When students read Pound's essay and these vivid poems, their senses will stand at attention. To jump-start students' interest in the selections, arrange a variety of sensory stimuli in the classroom: several dramatic photographs; a strongly scented item of food or greenery; textural examples such as carpet or a bowl of dried beans; musical objects or audiotaped sounds. Invite students to tour and interact with the stimuli. Then urge them to free write for a few moments about the images generated by the stimuli. What do they expect to encounter in poetry created under the banner: "It is better to present one Image in a lifetime than to produce voluminous work"?

❶ Background

More About the Authors

Ezra Pound spent most of his life in Europe, where he became a vital part of the Modernist movement. After 1920, Pound focused his efforts on writing *The Cantos,* a long poetic sequence in which he expresses his beliefs, reflects upon history and politics, and alludes to a variety of foreign languages and literatures. In all he produced 116 cantos of varying quality.

Build Skills *Essay • Poems*

❶ The Imagist Poets

Ezra Pound (1885–1972)

As both an editor and a poet, Ezra Pound inspired the dramatic changes in American poetry that characterized the Modern Age. Pound's insistence that writers "make it new" led many poets to discard the forms, techniques, and ideas of the past and to experiment with new approaches to poetry.

Pound influenced the work of the Irish poet William Butler Yeats, as well as that of T. S. Eliot, William Carlos Williams, H. D., Marianne Moore, and Ernest Hemingway—a "who's who" of the literary voices of the age. He is best remembered, however, for his role in the development of Imagism.

Despite his preoccupation with originality and inventiveness, Pound's work often drew upon the poetry of ancient cultures. Many of his poems are filled with literary and historical allusions, which can make the poems difficult to interpret without having the appropriate background information.

Fall From Grace In 1925, Pound settled in Italy. Motivated by the mistaken belief that a country governed by a powerful dictator was the most conducive environment for the creation of art, Pound became an outspoken supporter of Italian dictator Benito Mussolini during World War II. In 1943, the American government indicted Pound for treason; in 1945, he was arrested by American troops and imprisoned. After being flown back to the United States in 1945, he was judged psychologically unfit to stand trial and was confined to a hospital for the criminally insane. There he remained until 1958, when he was released due largely to the efforts of the literary community he had so doggedly supported over the years. He returned to Italy, where he lived until his death.

William Carlos Williams (1883–1963)

Unlike his fellow Imagists, William Carlos Williams spent most of his life in the United States, where he pursued a double career as a poet and a pediatrician in New Jersey. He felt that his experiences as a doctor provided him with inspiration as a poet, and credited medicine for his ability to "gain entrance to . . . the secret gardens of the self."

The child of immigrants, Williams grew up speaking Spanish, French, and British English. Nevertheless, he was enamored of American language and life. He rejected the views of his college friend, Ezra Pound, who believed in using allusions to history, religion, and ancient literature. Williams focused instead on capturing the essence of modern American life by depicting ordinary people, objects, and experiences using current, everyday language.

The Poetry of Daily Life In volumes such as *Spring and All* (1923) and *In the American Grain* (1925), Williams captured the essence of American life and landscape. He avoided offering explanations, remarking that a poet should deal in "No ideas but in things"—concrete images that speak for themselves, evoking emotions and ideas.

In his later work, Williams departed from pure Imagism in order to write more expansively. His five-volume poem *Paterson* (1946–58) explores the idea of a city as a symbol for a man. The poem is based on the real city of Paterson, New Jersey.

Williams continued to write even after his failing health forced him to give up his medical practice. In 1963, he received a Pulitzer Prize for *Pictures from Breughel and Other Poems,* his final volume of poetry.

1

H. D. (Hilda Doolittle) (1886–1961)

In 1913, when Ezra Pound reshaped three of Hilda Doolittle's poems and submitted them to *Poetry* magazine under the name "H. D., Imagiste," the Imagist movement was born. The publication of the poems also served to launch the successful career of the young poet, who continued to publish under the name H. D. throughout her life.

Born in Pennsylvania, Doolittle was only fifteen when she first met Ezra Pound, who was studying at the University of Pennsylvania. In 1911, Doolittle moved to London and renewed her acquaintance with Pound. She married a close friend of his, the English poet Richard Aldington, but the marriage struggled and failed during World War I when Aldington left to fight in France. Doolittle remained a short while in London, where she became a leader of the Imagist group. She returned to the United States and settled in California, where she remained for a year before going back to England. In 1921, she moved to Switzerland, and lived there until her death.

Classically Inspired Like the Greek lyrics that she so greatly admired, H. D.'s early poems were brief, precise, and direct. Often emphasizing light, color, and physical textures, she created vivid, emotive images. Like other Imagist poets, H. D. used everyday speech, carefully and sparingly chosen to evoke an emotional response, to freeze a single moment in time. She also abandoned traditional rhythmical patterns, instead creating innovative musical lines in her poetry. With these unusual techniques, H. D. focused much of her poetry and prose on the issues of her day—World Wars I and II, the growing interest in the human psyche created by Sigmund Freud's work, and the blossoming film medium.

In 1925, almost all of H. D.'s early poems were gathered in *Collected Poems,* a volume that also contained her translations from the *Odyssey* and from the Greek poet Sappho. She also wrote a play—*Hippolytus Temporizes,* which appeared in 1927—and two prose works—*Palimpsest* (1926) and *Hedylus* (1928). During the later stages of her career, she focused on writing longer works, including an epic poem. H. D. is best remembered, however, for her early Imagist poetry.

Background on Imagism

Imagism was a literary movement established in the early 1900s by Ezra Pound and other poets. As the name suggests, the Imagists concentrated on the direct presentation of images, or word pictures. An Imagist poem expressed the essence of an object, person, or incident, without providing explanations. Through the spare, clean presentation of an image, the Imagists hoped to freeze a single moment in time and to capture the emotions of that moment. To accomplish this purpose, the Imagists used the language of everyday speech, carefully choosing each word. They also shied away from traditional poetic patterns, focusing instead on creating new, musical rhythms.

The Imagists were strongly influenced by traditional Chinese and Japanese poetry. Many Imagist poems bear a close resemblance to the Japanese verse forms of haiku and tanka, which generally evoke an emotional response through the presentation of a single image or a pair of contrasting images.

The Imagist movement was short-lived, lasting only until about 1918. However, for many years that followed, the poems of Pound, Williams, H.D. and other Imagists continued to influence the work of other poets, including Wallace Stevens, T.S. Eliot, and Hart Crane.

1 Background

More About the Authors

In his later work, William Carlos Williams departed from pure Imagism in order to write more expansively. His five-volume poem *Paterson* (1946–58) explores the idea of a city as a symbol for a man. The poem is based on the real city of Paterson, New Jersey.

H. D.'s reflections on Sigmund Freud's controversial work of the 1930s grew out of personal experience—she herself underwent psychoanalysis with Freud. Both her reflections on this, *Tribute to Freud* (1956), and the later work, *Bid Me Live* (1960), had autobiographical elements. H. D. spent the World War II years in London, recording those experiences in three long poems: *The Walls Do Not Fall* (1944), *Tribute to the Angels* (1945), and *The Flowering of the Rod* (1946).

Differentiated Instruction

Solutions for All Learners

Support for Special Needs Students

Have students complete the **Preview** and **Build Skills** pages for these selections in the ***Reader's Notebook: Adapted Version.*** These pages provide a selection summary, an abbreviated presentation of the reading and literary skills, and the graphic organizer on the **Build Skills** page in the student book.

Support for Less Proficient Readers

Have students complete the **Preview** and **Build Skills** pages for these selections in the ***Reader's Notebook.*** These pages provide a selection summary, an abbreviated presentation of the reading and literary skills, and the graphic organizer on the **Build Skills** page in the student book.

Support for English Learners

Have students complete the **Preview** and **Build Skills** pages for these selections in the ***Reader's Notebook: English Learner's Version.*** These pages provide a selection summary, an abbreviated presentation of the skills, additional contextual vocabulary, and the graphic organizer on the **Build Skills** page in the student book.

❷ Literary Analysis
Imagist Poetry

- Tell students that as they read the Imagist Poets, they will focus on how the poems reflect the Imagist literary movement and its primary characteristics.
- Discuss the example given in the Literary Analysis instruction. Explain that the words of "In a Station of the Metro" were chosen with extreme precision in order to paint a vivid picture. The poem demands that the reader consider the meaning of each word.

❸ Reading Strategy
Engaging Your Senses

- Tell students that engaging their senses can help them appreciate the vivid images of these poems.
- Invite students to give their own examples of sensory language, perhaps drawing on those they explored in the Motivation activity.
- Discuss the example on the student page, leading students to feel the images H.D.'s language evokes. Point out that H.D. produces her effect on the reader's senses by treating heat as a solid object, capable of being cut, plowed, and turned, like earth.
- Give students a copy of **Reading Strategy Graphic Organizer A,** p. 153 in ***Graphic Organizer Transparencies.*** Model how to use the chart to record sensory images. Direct students to complete similar charts as they read the poetry.

Vocabulary Builder

- Pronounce each vocabulary word for students, and read the definitions as a class. Have students identify any words with which they are already familiar.

Preview

Connecting to the Literature

You may know what it is like to have a song stick in your mind, but have you ever had an image lodge there? The poems you are about to read capture in words some of the striking images that lodged in the minds and emotions of the Imagists.

❷ Literary Analysis

Imagist Poetry

Imagist poems focus on evoking emotion and sparking the imagination through the vivid presentation of a limited number of **images**—words or phrases that appeal to the senses. "In a Station of the Metro," for example, presents just two images and consists of only two lines and fourteen well-chosen words. Few poems have been written that convey so much meaning with such brevity.

Comparing Literary Works

In his essay "A Few Don'ts," Ezra Pound describes the image as something more than a simple word-picture. Instead, he says, it is "that which presents an intellectual and emotional complex in an instant of time."

For Pound, the image brings the reader a new way of seeing—on the physical level through the senses, and on higher levels through the emotions and intellect. As you read these poems, think about which ones best achieve the effect of "that sense of sudden growth" that Pound believed was the highest achievement of art.

❸ Reading Strategy

Engaging Your Senses

These poems are filled with vivid imagery—words or phrases that appeal to the senses. As you encounter each image, **engage your senses** by re-creating in your mind the sights, sounds, smells, tastes, and physical sensations associated with the image. Also note that some images appeal to more than one sense. For example, you can almost see and feel the thickness in the air as H. D. calls on the wind in "Heat":

Cut the heat— / plow through it, / Turning it on either side

Use a chart like the one shown to record the ways in which you engage your senses as you read these poems.

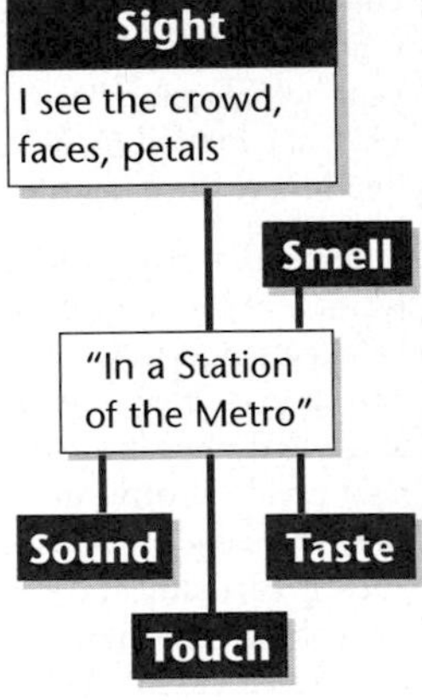

Vocabulary Builder

voluminous (və lo͞om′ ə nəs) *adj.* of enough material to fill volumes (p. 727)

dogma (dôg′ mə) *n.* authoritative doctrines or beliefs (p. 727)

apparition (ap′ ə rish′ ən) *n.* act of appearing or becoming visible (p. 732)

❶ A FEW DON'TS

Ezra Pound

Background Ezra Pound was one of the leading figures in the Imagist movement. As the name suggests, Imagists concentrated on the focused presentation of images, or word-pictures. For example, Pound's original draft of "In a Station of the Metro" consisted of 30 lines. Pound whittled away at the poem until he arrived at a work of only 14 words of great precision and power. In this essay, Pound discusses his beliefs about what poetry should and should not be.

An "Image" is that which presents an intellectual and emotional complex in an instant of time. I use the term "complex" rather in the technical sense employed by the newer psychologists, such as Hart, though we might not agree absolutely in our application.

It is the presentation of such a "complex" instantaneously which gives that sense of sudden liberation; that sense of freedom from time limits and space limits; that sense of sudden growth, which we experience in the presence of the greatest works of art.

It is better to present one Image in a lifetime than to produce voluminous works.

All this, however, some may consider open to debate. The immediate necessity is to tabulate A LIST OF DON'TS for those beginning to write verses. But I can not put all of them into Mosaic negative.[1]

To begin with, consider the three propositions[2] . . . not as dogma—never consider anything as dogma—but as the result of long contemplation, which, even if it is someone else's contemplation, may be worth consideration. . . .

LANGUAGE

Use no superfluous word, no adjective, which does not reveal something.

1. **Mosaic negative** Pound is referring to the Ten Commandments presented by Moses to the Israelites in the Hebrew Bible. Many of the commandments are in the negative and begin with the words "Thou shalt not . . ."
2. **three propositions** Pound is referring to the three rules that English Imagist poet Frank Stuart Flint formulated for the writing of Imagist poetry:
   1. Direct treatment of the "thing," whether subjective or objective.
   2. To use absolutely no word that did not contribute to the presentation.
   3. As regarding rhythm to compose in sequence of the musical phrase, not in sequence of a metronome.

Vocabulary Builder
voluminous (və lo͞om′ ə nəs) *adj.* of enough material to fill volumes

Vocabulary Builder
dogma (dôg′ mə) *n.* authoritative doctrines or beliefs

Reading Check
According to Pound, what is an image?

TEACH

Learning Modalities
Visual/Spatial Learners Point out that Imagist poetry is highly visual. Have students preview the illustrations that accompany the poems. What images and moods do these illustrations evoke?

❶ About the Selection

As one of the founders of Imagism, Ezra Pound helped define its philosophy. In his essay warning Imagist poets against the pitfalls of writing, Pound quickly establishes his essential idea: less is more.

❷ Reading Check

Answer: "An image is that which presents an intellectual and emotional complex in an instant of time." In other words, an image presents an evocative description that speaks to both mind and heart.

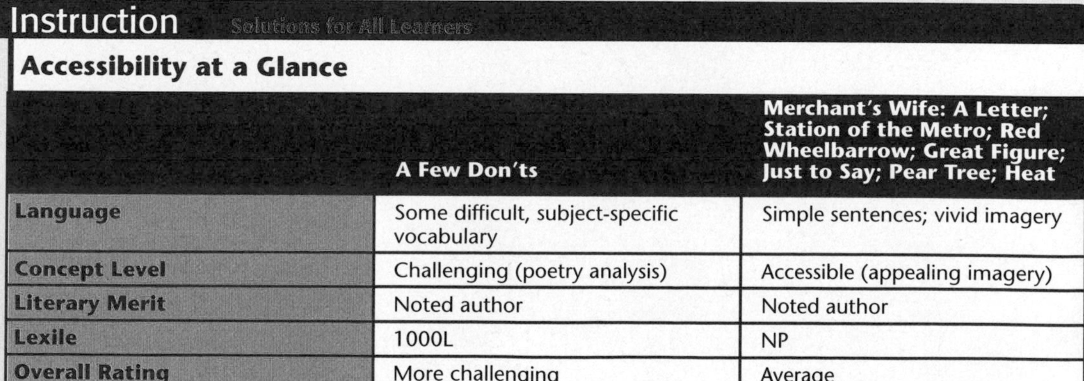

Differentiated Instruction Solutions for All Learners

Accessibility at a Glance

	A Few Don'ts	Merchant's Wife: A Letter; Station of the Metro; Red Wheelbarrow; Great Figure; Just to Say; Pear Tree; Heat
Language	Some difficult, subject-specific vocabulary	Simple sentences; vivid imagery
Concept Level	Challenging (poetry analysis)	Accessible (appealing imagery)
Literary Merit	Noted author	Noted author
Lexile	1000L	NP
Overall Rating	More challenging	Average

❸ Literary Analysis
Imagist Poetry

- Have students paraphrase the bracketed passage. Make sure students clarify the meaning of "Go in fear of abstractions."
- Then, **ask** students the Literary Analysis question: Why is this rule of avoiding abstractions consistent with the goals of Imagist poetry?
  Possible response: Imagist poets sought to evoke specific and vivid images for readers. Abstract ideas do not lend themselves to such specificity.

❹ Humanities

Ezra Pound by Wyndham Lewis

This painting is a portrait of the poet, Ezra Pound, perhaps resting or silently contemplating his work. Use these questions for discussion:

1. How does the painting's style mirror Pound's preference for the "concrete"?
   Answer: The pictured scene is rendered simply and with great clarity.
2. According to Pound, a painter can best describe a landscape. What elements does Lewis incorporate to capture the landscape of his subject?
   Answer: These elements include black clothing, the poet's contemplative and somewhat serious expression, the newspaper, the importance of the figure in the composition. Like a landscape, the portrait includes a wide area around the subject rather than focusing on a face.

❺ Critical Viewing

Possible response: An Imagist poem might emphasize details such as the objects on the table and the expression on the figure's face.

Don't use such an expression as "dim lands *of peace*." It dulls the image. It mixes an abstraction with the concrete. It comes from the writer's not realizing that the natural object is always the *adequate* symbol.

❸ Go in fear of abstractions. Do not retell in mediocre verse what has already been done in good prose. Don't think any intelligent person is going to be deceived when you try to shirk all the difficulties of the unspeakably difficult art of good prose by chopping your composition into line lengths. . . .

Literary Analysis
Imagist Poetry Why is this rule of avoiding abstractions consistent with the goals of Imagist poetry?

Don't imagine that the art of poetry is any simpler than the art of music, or that you can please the expert before you have spent at least as much effort on the art of verse as the average piano teacher spends on the art of music. . . .

RHYTHM AND RHYME

. . . Don't imagine that a thing will "go" in verse just because it's too dull to go in prose.

Don't be "viewy"—leave that to the writers of pretty little philosophic essays. Don't be descriptive; remember that the painter can describe a landscape much better than you can, and that he has to know a deal more about it.

❹

❺ ▲ **Critical Viewing** What key details might be emphasized in an Imagist poem about this portrait of Ezra Pound? **[Synthesize]**

When Shakespeare talks of the "Dawn in russet mantle clad" he presents something which the painter does not present. There is in this line of his nothing that one can call description; he presents. . . .

6 Don't chop your stuff into separate *iambs.*[3] Don't make each line stop dead at the end, and then begin every next line with a heave. Let the beginning of the next line catch the rise of the rhythm wave, unless you want a definite longish pause.

In short, behave as a musician, a good musician, when dealing with that phase of your art which has exact parallels in music. The same laws govern, and you are bound by no others. . . .

A rhyme must have in it some slight element of surprise if it is to give pleasure; it need not be bizarre or curious, but it must be well used if used at all. . . .

Don't mess up the perception of one sense by trying to define it in terms of another. This is usually only the result of being too lazy to find the exact word. To this clause there are possibly exceptions.

The first three simple proscriptions[4] will throw out nine-tenths of all the bad poetry now accepted as standard and classic; and will prevent you from many a crime of production. . . .

---

6. **iambs** (ī′ ambz′) *n.* metrical feet, each consisting of an unaccented syllable followed by an accented one.
7. **The first three simple proscriptions** reference to Flint's three rules outlined in footnote #2.

Critical Reading

1. **Respond:** What is your reaction to Pound's ideas about poetry?
2. **(a) Recall:** What three rules does Pound invite readers to consider? **(b) Define:** What is the difference between dogma and the results of "long contemplation"? **(c) Speculate:** Why does Pound prefer a list of "don'ts" to a list of "do's"?
3. **(a) Recall:** What does Pound consider preferable to abstractions? **(b) Analyze:** Why would the use of abstractions be offensive to an Imagist poet?
4. **(a) Recall:** Does Pound consider Shakespeare's image an example of description or presentation? **(b) Distinguish:** How does presentation differ from description?
5. **(a) Recall:** What rule does Pound suggest should govern the rhythm of a poem? **(b) Interpret:** What does a good musician do that a poet should emulate?
6. **Evaluate:** Do you think following Pound's "don'ts" would make it easier or more difficult to write poetry?

Reading Strategy
Engaging Your Senses
What physical sensations are suggested by the rhythmic wave Pound advocates?

For: More about Ezra Pound
Visit: www.PHSchool.com
Web Code: ere-9502

6 Reading Strategy
Engaging Your Senses

- Read aloud the bracketed text, using hand gestures to convey the physical aspects of the description.
- Encourage students to clarify the meaning of this passage. What exactly is Pound advocating?
- Then, **ask** students the Reading Strategy question: What physical sensations are suggested by the rhythmic wave Pound advocates? **Possible response:** Students may mention a lifting feeling that propels them forward like ocean waves.

ASSESS

Answers

1. **Possible response:** Opinions should be supported by the text.
2. (a) The rules are direct treatment of the topic, use no extra words, use natural musical rhythm. (b) The results of "long contemplation" have been thought out, whereas dogma is mindlessly followed. (c) A list of "do's" might be long; a list of key "don'ts" is manageable.
3. (a) Pound considers the concrete better than the abstract. (b) Imagists seek to capture emotion in spare, concrete images. This doesn't work with abstractions.
4. (a) Pound considers it presentation. (b) Presentation puts forth only the concrete object. Description puts the characteristics of the concrete object at a greater remove from the reader.
5. (a) Pound suggests using the same rules used in composing music. (b) A good musician allows rhythm to rise and fall naturally.
6. Students may say that Pound's rules make it more difficult.

Go Online Author Link For additional information about Ezra Pound, have students type in the Web Code, then select *P* from the alphabet, and then select Ezra Pound.

❼ About the Selections

Ezra Pound's poetry exemplifies the credo he espouses in his essay. In "The River-Merchant's Wife: A Letter," the speaker, who was married as a young girl by the arrangement of her parents, comes gradually to love her husband. By vividly describing her emotions and experiences during his absence, she demonstrates the simple power of human emotion. "In a Station of the Metro" evokes the crowd of a train station in just fourteen words.

❽ Literary Analysis
Imagist Poetry

- **Ask** students the Literary Analysis question: What details in this stanza are most effective in conveying an image?
- Have volunteers take turns reading aloud the bracketed lines. Invite students to suggest details they find especially effective. Then, have students answer the question. **Possible answers:** Effective images include "hair was still cut straight across my forehead," "on bamboo stilts, playing horse," "playing with blue plums."

➤ **Monitor Progress:** Remind students of Imagism's commitment to precision and brevity. Have students evaluate this stanza based on these criteria. Do students find any superfluous words in the stanza?

❼ The River-Merchant's Wife:

Ezra Pound

While my hair was still cut straight across my forehead
I played about the front gate, pulling flowers.
You came by on bamboo stilts, playing horse,
You walked about my seat, playing with blue plums.
And we went on living in the village of Chokan:[1]
Two small people, without dislike or suspicion.

At fourteen I married My Lord you.
I never laughed, being bashful.
Lowering my head, I looked at the wall.
Called to, a thousand times, I never looked back.

At fifteen I stopped scowling,
I desired my dust to be mingled with yours
Forever and forever and forever.
Why should I climb the lookout?

At sixteen you departed,
You went into far Ku-to-yen,[2] by the river of swirling eddies,
And you have been gone five months.
The monkeys make sorrowful noise overhead.

Literary Analysis
Imagist Poetry What details in this stanza are most effective in conveying an image?

1. **Chokan** (chō´ kän´) a suburb of Nanking, a city in the People's Republic of China.
2. **Ku-to-yen** (ko͞o´ tō´ yen´) an island in the Yangtze (yaŋk´ sē) River.

Enrichment

Customs

Pound's poem was adapted from a Chinese poem by Li T'ai Po. At the time that Li T'ai Po was writing, marriages in China were commonly arranged by family leaders rather than by the bride and groom. Love was expected to grow after the marriage. Point out that Pound's poem suggests the system worked, as strong love does grow between the young speaker and her husband.

Acknowledge to students that arranged marriages, while common in Li T'ai Po's time, are more unusual now. Customs such as this one are often unique to a time and culture. Invite students to brainstorm for customs of your community—annual festivals, young people's gathering places, decorated doorways on special holidays. Then urge students to interview longtime residents of the community to learn how these customs originated and changed over time.

You dragged your feet when you went out.
By the gate now, the moss is grown, the different mosses,
Too deep to clear them away!
9 The leaves fall early this autumn, in wind.
The paired butterflies are already yellow with August
Over the grass in the West garden;
They hurt me. I grow older.
If you are coming down through the narrows of the river Kiang,

Please let me know beforehand,
And I will come out to meet you
As far as Cho-fu-Sa.[3]

Literary Analysis
Imagist Poetry What details make this stanza appeal to both the senses and the emotions?

12 **Reading Check**
Who is the speaker in this poem? Whom does she address?

3. **Cho-fu-Sa** (chō´ fo͞o´ sä´) a beach along the Yangtze River, several hundred miles from Nanking.

10

Landscape Album in Various Styles, Ch'a Shih-piao, The Cleveland Museum of Art

11 ▲ **Critical Viewing** In what ways does the mood of this drawing mirror the mood of "The River-Merchant's Wife: A Letter"? **[Analyze]**

Differentiated Instruction
Solutions for All Learners

Support for Less Proficient Readers
To help these students understand the concept of imagery, review the Reading Strategy instruction on p. 726. Model the use of the chart to identify sensory images and monitor students as they complete the chart with images from "The River-Merchant's Wife: A Letter."

Support for Special Needs Students
To help these students experience the vivid images of Pound's poem, focus discussion on a few specific images. For example, you might point out the falling leaves, wind, and colorful butterflies as images that can be felt and heard as well as seen. Help students identify the emotions the images are intended to evoke.

Enrichment for Gifted/Talented Students
Challenge students to create their own Imagist poetry. Direct them to try to capture the essence of an object, person, or incident in a brief Imagist poem. Tell them to use language that is precise and suggestive, and that appeals to the senses with its images.

9 Literary Analysis
Imagist Poetry

- Have students read lines 19–26 several times independently. Discuss the difference between senses and emotions.
- Have students list all the details in this poem that appeal to the senses and the emotions. Encourage them to list these details in two separate columns.
- Then, **ask** them the Literary Analysis question: What details make this stanza appeal to both the senses and the emotions?
  Possible response: Details such as "dragged your feet," "They hurt me. I grow older" appeal to both senses by creating strong visual images and emotions by suggesting the speaker's sadness.

10 Humanities

Landscape Album in Various Styles
by Ch'a Shih-piao

This piece of art depicts a landscape similar to the one described by the river-merchant's wife. Its artist was well-known for somber and melancholy landscapes such as this one. Use this question for discussion:

- How would the setting depicted here make it difficult for the poem's speaker to learn of her husband's progress home?
  Answer: The setting is isolated, making long-distance communication difficult.

11 Critical Viewing

Answer: The mood is somewhat desolate, created by bare trees, an isolated house, and a stark landscape, suggesting the speaker's loneliness for her husband.

12 Reading Check

Answer: The speaker is a young bride. She addresses her husband.

⓭ Vocabulary Builder

Forms of *appear*

- Draw students' attention to the word *apparition* and to its definition.
- Let students know that several common English words are forms of the word *appear,* which means "to come into sight or into being" or "to become understood."
- Invite students to volunteer other forms of the word that they may know.
  Possibilities include: *apparent, appearance*

ASSESS

Answers

1. Encourage students to share their responses.
2. (a) She marries her husband at the age of fourteen. (b) When she first marries, she does not love her husband, but at fifteen she does love him.
3. (a) Her husband goes away. (b) She is unhappy about it.
4. (a) He compares the people's faces with the "petals on a wet, black bough." (b) It creates an intensely vivid image of the train station crowd. (c) One doesn't usually see rain-covered tree branches in a train station.
5. Students should support their opinions with examples from the poetry.

Go Online Author Link For additional information about Ezra Pound, have students type in the Web Code, then select *P* from the alphabet, and then select Ezra Pound.

In a Station of the Metro[1]

Ezra Pound

⓭ The apparition of these faces in the crowd;
Petals on a wet, black bough.

Vocabulary Builder
apparition (ap′ ə rish′ ən) *n.* act of appearing or becoming visible

1. **Metro** the Paris subway.

Critical Reading

1. **Respond:** Of all the images contained in the two poems by Ezra Pound, which did you find the most striking? Why?
2. **(a) Recall:** In "The River-Merchant's Wife," how old is the speaker when she marries? **(b) Compare and Contrast:** In what ways are her feelings for her husband at age fifteen different from those when she first marries?
3. **(a) Recall:** What happens when the river-merchant's wife is sixteen? **(b) Analyze:** How does she feel about this change?
4. **(a) Recall:** In "In a Station of the Metro," what two things does Pound compare? **(b) Interpret:** In what ways does this poem capture the essence of a single moment? **(c) Analyze:** Given the poem's setting, why is the image of "Petals on a wet, black bough" surprising?
5. **Take a Position:** What do you like about Pound's poetry? What do you dislike? Explain.

Go Online
Author Link
For: More about Ezra Pound
Visit: www.PHSchool.com
Web Code: ere-9502

Enrichment

Rail Transportation

"In a Station of the Metro" captures a brief moment inside the Paris Metro, or subway. Subways are rail systems designed to move people around in an urban area. Many are largely underground, though some systems include street level or elevated stations. London built the first subway, known still as the "underground," in 1863. Stations occur at frequent intervals, perhaps as little as a few blocks apart, so that passengers can arrive close to their exact destination. Riders reach underground subway stations by descending stairs to underground platforms. At busy times such as the morning and evening rush hours, crowds of passengers such as Pound describes, cluster on the platform to await trains. Together with commuter trains, subways form the largest part of passenger rail travel in the U.S. today.

⓮ The Red Wheelbarrow

William Carlos Williams

so much depends
upon

a red wheel
barrow

glazed with rain
water

beside the white
chickens.

⓮ The Great Figure

William Carlos Williams

Among the rain
and lights
I saw the figure 5
in gold
on a red
fire truck
moving
tense
unheeded
to gong clangs
siren howls
and wheels rumbling
through the dark city.

⓯ 

The Figure 5 in Gold, Charles Demuth, Metropolitan Museum of Art

⓰ ▶ **Critical Viewing** Artist Charles Demuth created this work of art to accompany his friend Williams's poem. What elements of his painting convey the energy and clamor of the poem? **[Connect]**

⓮ About the Selections

These three poems by William Carlos Williams illustrate the power of strong sensory images to evoke emotions and responses from readers. Whether capturing an everyday farm scene of animals and equipment, freezing in time the tension of a speeding fire engine, or interpreting a letter of apology, the poems use straightforward language to create images that demand attention.

⓯ Humanities

The Figure 5 in Gold by Charles Demuth

This painting evokes many of the images in "The Great Figure" as well as the character of the poet Williams. Point out the artist's inclusion of the nickname Bill at the top of the image, alluding to William Carlos Williams even more deliberately. *The Figure 5 in Gold* captures, as does Williams's poem, the modern world's growing awareness of machines and technology.

Use this question for discussion:

- How does the painting respond to the poem?
  Answer: It distills the poem's topic to its visual core.

⓰ Critical Viewing

Answer: The expanding and repeated "5," which seems to shout at viewers, the fragmented bands of lights that explode from the center of the image, and the bright colors against a dark background all create a mood of urgency and clamor.

Differentiated Instruction Solutions for All Learners

Enrichment for Gifted/Talented Students

Tell students that William Carlos Williams occupies a special place among modern poets. He has been admired for his directness, especially in comparison with poets such as T. S. Eliot, whose poetry features frequent literary references and quotations in foreign languages. According to critic R. P. Blackmur, Williams's poetry grew from everyday life, "the commonplace made unique because violently felt."

Elsewhere Blackmur writes of Williams's basic approach: "He isolates and calls attention to what we are already presently in possession of." Have students respond to these observations in a discussion. Pose the following questions: How are Blackmur's observations illustrated in the poetry on these pages? Do you find anything reflective or spiritual behind Williams's images "isolated" from the commonplace?

17 Reading Strategy
Engaging Your Senses

- **Ask** the following question: What senses are stimulated by the bracketed lines? Direct students to cite specific words from the poem.
- Have students use a sensory details chart to record their responses. Charts should look similar to the following.

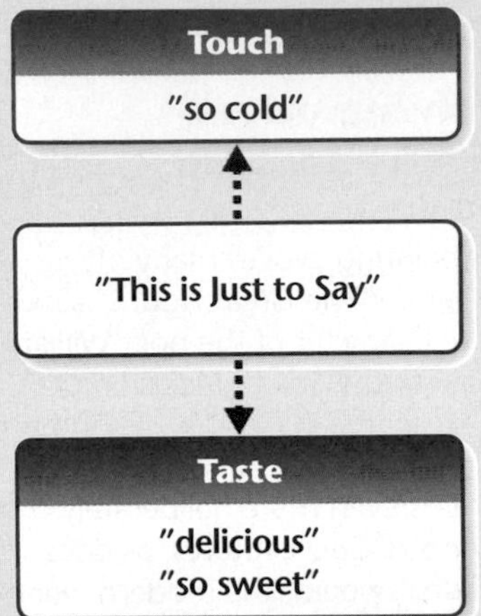

ASSESS
Answers

1. Responses should include citations from the poems.
2. (a) It appeals most to sight. (b) The poem focuses on finite, focused images rather than on reactions to them.
3. (a) He divides *wheelbarrow* and *rainwater.* (b) It forces readers to slow down and take notice.
4. (a) The detail is the figure 5. (b) He may be saying that beauty can be found in unlikely places and that modern life is so hectic and impersonal that people do not notice what is going on around them.
5. (a) The speaker intends to apologize. (b) Details such as "delicious," "sweet," and "cold" suggest that the speaker truly enjoyed the plums and doesn't really regret eating them.
6. Simple moments or images, the subject matter of these poems, suggest interest and pleasure in everyday life.

Go Online Author Link For additional information about William Carlos Williams, have students type in the Web Code, then select *W* from the alphabet, and then select William Carlos Williams.

THIS IS JUST TO SAY

William Carlos Williams

I have eaten
the plums
that were in
the icebox
and which
you were probably
saving
for breakfast

Forgive me
they were delicious
so sweet
and so cold

Critical Reading

1. **Respond:** Which of the three poems by Williams evokes the strongest emotional response in you? Why?
2. **(a) Classify:** In "The Red Wheelbarrow," to what sense does the image appeal most? **(b) Analyze:** In what way does this poem reflect the Imagist emphasis on the concrete?
3. **(a) Recall:** Which words has Williams divided to run on two separate lines? **(b) Analyze:** What is the effect of this arrangement of words?
4. **(a) Recall:** In "The Great Figure," what detail is the focus of the speaker's experience of the fire truck? **(b) Interpret:** In focusing on this detail, what might Williams be saying about beauty and modern life?
5. **(a) Recall:** What is the intention of the speaker in "This Is Just to Say"? **(b) Connect:** Which details in the second stanza challenge the speaker's sincerity?
6. **Evaluate:** Which elements of these poems reflect Williams's interest in portraying—and celebrating—everyday American life?

Go Online Author Link
For: More about William Carlos Williams
Visit: www.PHSchool.com
Web Code: ere-9503

Enrichment

Landscape Painting

H.D.'s poem "Pear Tree" works like a landscape painting to capture the essential image of a fruit tree in full bloom. Describing nature in words or pictures is a long-standing artistic tradition. Many art historians assert that landscape painting in America reached its peak during the nineteenth century when artists of the Hudson River School were active. Characterized by contrast between wilderness and a smaller human element, these landscapes highlighted the magnificence of the American landscape and the relative transience of human occupancy.

Have students view examples of American landscape painting in books or online museum exhibits. Discuss how these images capture the same sense of responsive wonder as does the poem "Pear Tree."

18 PEAR TREE H. D.

19

Silver dust
lifted from the earth,
higher than my arms reach,
you have mounted,
O silver,
higher than my arms reach
you front us with great mass;

no flower ever opened
so staunch a white leaf,
no flower ever parted silver
from such rare silver;

O white pear,
your flower-tufts
thick on the branch
bring summer and ripe fruits
in their purple hearts.

20 ▼ **Critical Viewing**
Which phrases from the poem best describe this image of a pear tree in full flower? **[Evaluate]**

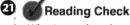

21  **Reading Check**
What image does the poet use to describe the pear tree flowers?

18 About the Selections

These Imagist poems illustrate nature with words so evocative they hardly need accompanying illustrations. In both poems, the poet describes and responds to nature. "Pear Tree" presents H.D.'s rapturous emotional response to a pear tree in bloom, while "Heat" brings the physical experience of a sweltering day into sharp focus for readers. One poem adores nature while the other complains to it, but together they demonstrate the emotional and sensory impact of carefully chosen words.

19 Reading Strategy
Engaging Your Senses

- Have a volunteer read aloud the bracketed stanza. Invite students to close their eyes as they listen, paying attention to the sensory details.
- **Ask** students this question: What sensory experience does the line "higher than my arms reach" create?
  Answer: It creates the experience of stretching up toward the sky.

20 Critical Viewing

Answer: Effective descriptive phrases include "Silver dust/lifted from the earth" and "your flower-tufts/thick on the branch."

21 Reading Check

Answer: She uses the image of silver dust.

Differentiated Instruction
Solutions for All Learners

Support for Less Proficient Readers
Remind students of the admonition that Ezra Pound includes in his essay on Imagist poetry: "Go in fear of abstractions." The opposite of an abstraction is the concrete image, which impresses itself on the senses upon reading.

All the poems included in this grouping should have this effect. Use "Pear Tree" as an example, and ask students for sensory descriptions from it. Ask: what senses are affected by the poem? After students complete the organizer, help them find other poems from the grouping that contain images that appeal to those senses missing from "Pear Tree."

Poem
Sight
Hearing
Smell
Touch
Taste

22 Critical Viewing

Answer: Some students will say the image is effective for its depiction of the thick and hanging air. Others will say it is not, citing the painting's scene as less oppressive than the feelings of the poem.

ASSESS

Answers

1. Encourage students to share their responses. Have them support their answers with specific images and phrases from the poems.
2. (a) The silver dust refers to the leaves and flowers of the pear tree. (b) The pear tree grows upward.
3. (a) It waits for summer and fruit. (b) It is spring.
4. (a) It cannot fall through the thick, hot air. (b) The speaker seems to describe the heat of the sun on a torrid summer day.
5. (a) The speaker uses the words *rend, cut, plow,* and *turn.* (b) They create the impression that the heat is almost a solid substance.
6. The poet feels deeply involved with nature and is also impressed by its power.

Go Online Author Link For additional information about Hilda Doolittle, have students type in the Web Code, then select *D* from the alphabet, and then select Hilda Doolittle.

HEAT

H. D.

O wind, rend open the heat,
cut apart the heat,
rend it to tatters.

Fruit cannot drop
through this thick air—
fruit cannot fall into heat
that presses up and blunts
the points of pears
and rounds the grapes.

Cut the heat—
plow through it,
turning it on either side
of your path.

Overhanging Cloud in July, Charles Burchfield, Whitney Museum of American Art

22 ▲ Critical Viewing
Does this painting capture the oppressive heat of a humid summer day as effectively as the poem does? Explain. **[Evaluate]**

Critical Reading

1. **Respond:** How do these two poems by H. D. make you feel?
2. **(a) Recall:** What is the "silver dust" referred to in the first stanza of "Pear Tree"? **(b) Interpret:** In what sense is the silver dust "lifted from the earth"?
3. **(a) Recall:** What does the pear tree's blossom anticipate? **(b) Infer:** What time of year is the speaker describing?
4. **(a) Recall:** In "Heat," what is the reaction of the fruit to the air? **(b) Interpret:** What specific type of heat is the speaker describing?
5. **(a) Recall:** Which verbs does the speaker use to describe lessening the heat? **(b) Analyze:** What impression of the heat do these verbs create?
6. **Generalize:** Based on these two poems, how would you define the poet's relationship to nature?

Go Online Author Link

For: More about H. D. (Hilda Doolittle)
Visit: www.PHSchool.com
Web Code: ere-9504

Apply the Skills

The Imagist Poets

Literary Analysis

Imagist Poetry

1. Does "The River-Merchant's Wife: A Letter" qualify as a purely **Imagist poem**? Why or why not?
2. **(a)** In "The Red Wheelbarrow," what do you think is the "so much" that depends upon "a red wheel barrow"? **(b)** Would the meaning of this line be different if Williams had used *the* instead of *a*? Explain.

Comparing Literary Works

3. In what ways is Pound's advice to **(a)** avoid abstractions and **(b)** avoid superfluous words evident in all of these poems?
4. **(a)** Use a chart like the one shown to compare and contrast the use of color in the poems by H. D. and Williams. **(b)** What emotions do these uses of color evoke?

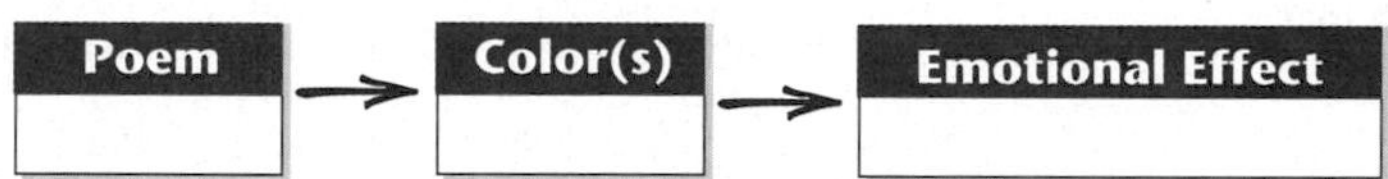

5. Although Pound wrote "the painter can describe a landscape much better than you can," in what ways are these poems like paintings?
6. Which of these poems best exemplifies Pound's idea of the image as "that which presents an intellectual and emotional complex in an instant of time"? Explain your choice.

Reading Strategy

Engaging Your Senses

7. What other **senses,** besides sight, can you engage to re-create the images of "Petals on a wet, black bough"? Explain.
8. Identify two examples of passages in "The River-Merchant's Wife" in which you were able to engage the sense of smell.

Extend Understanding

9. **Literature Connection:** "The River-Merchant's Wife: A Letter" is an adaptation of a poem by the Chinese poet Li Po. What challenges and opportunities face a poet in translating a work of literature from one language and culture to another?

QuickReview

Imagist poetry focuses on evoking emotion and vivid mental associations through the presentation of concise, unadorned images.

By **engaging your senses,** you can fully experience the images in poetry.

For: Self-test
Visit: www.PHSchool.com
Web Code: era-6502

Go Online Assessment Students may use the **Self-test** to prepare for **Selection Test A** or **Selection Test B.**

Answers

1. **Possible responses:** Some students may say that the poem is not a purely Imagist poem because it includes descriptive lines and abstract words. Others may observe that the speaker's descriptions are spare evocations of scenes and images that only suggest, rather than explore, her feelings.
2. (a) **Possible responses:** Some students may say that the "so much" is civilization because a wheelbarrow is a fundamental tool used to build and create. Others may say that "so much" is the poem itself because the image is not complete without the wheelbarrow. (b) **Possible response:** Yes, because the image is of a wheelbarrow, not a specific wheelbarrow.
3. (a) In general, the poems focus on very specific, concrete topics and images. (b) The poems are short and succinct.
4. (a) **Possible responses:** "The Great Figure": Colors: gold, red; Effect: These colors suggest a vibrant, demanding image; "Pear Tree": Colors: silver, white; Effect: These colors suggest a clean, spare, and brilliant image.
   (b) Williams's colors suggest emotions of tension or excitement, while H.D.'s colors suggest emotions of peace, awe, or wonder.
   Another sample answer can be found on **Literary Analysis Graphic Organizer B,** p. 156 in ***Graphic Organizer Transparencies.***
5. They are extremely visual in nature, using imagery to help readers "see" the poems.
6. Students should support their choices with specific examples from the poem.
7. The sense of touch can be engaged to feel the petals and the wet bough. The sense of smell can be engaged to smell the wet bough and the petals.
8. Passages include "I played about the front gate, pulling flowers," and "The paired butterflies are already yellow with August/Over the grass in the West garden."
9. The challenge is to maintain the poem's essential ideas, mood, and cultural context. The opportunity is to evoke an entirely different world for readers, to transport them to another time or place.

Answers

❶ Vocabulary Lesson

Word Analysis

1. appearance
2. apparent
3. apparition

Vocabulary Builder

1. a
2. c
3. b

Spelling Strategy

1. aggressor
2. assign
3. approve

❷ Grammar and Style Lesson

Practice

1. abstract; abstract
2. concrete; concrete
3. concrete; concrete
4. concrete
5. concrete; concrete

Looking at Style

The Imagists believed in evoking concrete images rather than abstract ideas.

Writing and Grammar, Ruby Level

Students will find further instruction and practice on concrete and abstract nouns in Chapter 17, Section 1.

Build Language Skills

❶ Vocabulary Lesson

Word Analysis: Forms of *appear*

Several common English words are forms of the verb *appear,* meaning "to come into sight or into being" or "to become understood."

apparent appearance apparition

Complete each of the following sentences with the correct word from the list above.

1. He made a brief __?__ at the awards dinner—just long enough to pick up his trophy and say a few words.
2. When midnight found the toddlers still running around the house, it became __?__ that the babysitter was no longer in control.
3. The __?__ of a face at the window nearly stopped her heart with fear.

Vocabulary Builder: Synonyms

Select the letter of the best synonym, or word of similar meaning, for the numbered word.

1. dogma: **(a)** doctrine, **(b)** legality, **(c)** statement
2. voluminous: **(a)** loud, **(b)** arrogant, **(c)** comprehensive
3. apparition: **(a)** suspicious, **(b)** vision, **(c)** face

Spelling Strategy

You may need to drop the *d* when adding the prefix *ad-* to a word or word stem beginning with the consonants *p, g, s,* or *c.* If so, you must also double the consonant, as in *appear.* Use this principle to correctly spell the words below.

1. *ad-* + gressor **2.** *ad-* + sign **3.** *ad-* + prove

❷ Grammar and Style Lesson

Concrete and Abstract Nouns

Nouns can be classified according to the item they name. A **concrete noun** names something that can be perceived with one or more of the five senses. Concrete nouns have a physical, tangible reality. An **abstract noun** names something that cannot be seen, heard, smelled, tasted, or touched. These may be qualities, characteristics, emotions, or ideas that are not perceived through the senses.

Concrete: I played about the front *gate,* pulling *flowers.*

Abstract: Two small people, without *dislike* or *suspicion.*

Practice Label the italicized nouns in these sentences as either *concrete* or *abstract.*

1. Don't use such an *expression* as "dim lands of *peace.*"
2. The *leaves* fell early this autumn, in *wind.*
3. I saw the figure 5 in gold on a red firetruck moving tense unheeded to gong *clangs* siren howls and wheels rumbling through the dark *city.*
4. Cut the *heat*—plow through it . . .
5. I have eaten the *plums* that were in the icebox and which you were probably saving for *breakfast.*

Looking at Style Explain why you would expect to find mainly concrete nouns in an Imagist poem.

Prentice Hall Writing and Grammar Connection: Chapter 17, Section 1

Assessment Practice

Anticipate Missing Words **(For more practice, see *Standardized Test Preparation Workbook*, p. 42)**

Many tests ask students to correctly answer sentence-completion questions. Use the following example to show students how to use context and prior knowledge to choose the word that best completes the following passage.

The Imagist poets strove for a spare, clean presentation of an image. To accomplish this purpose, the Imagists carefully avoided using______words.

A easy **C** simple

B everyday **D** unnecessary

The context clues *spare* and *clean* provide the key to completing the sentence. The correct answer will describe words that would prevent something from being spare and clean. *D* is the most logical choice.

❸ Writing Lesson

An Editor's Review of a Manuscript

Imagine that you are a magazine editor who has just received a manuscript from an Imagist poet. Write a letter to the poet explaining why you will or will not publish his or her poems. Be simple, honest, and kind, and include constructive criticism.

Prewriting Choose a poet and reread the poems. Take notes on the strengths and weaknesses of each poem, citing relevant passages.

Drafting Write a letter that explains why you will or will not publish the poems. Discuss strengths, and identify flaws. Select specific words that best convey your meaning.

Revising Review your draft, highlighting any words that are inaccurate or vague. Then, replace those words with better, more specific choices.

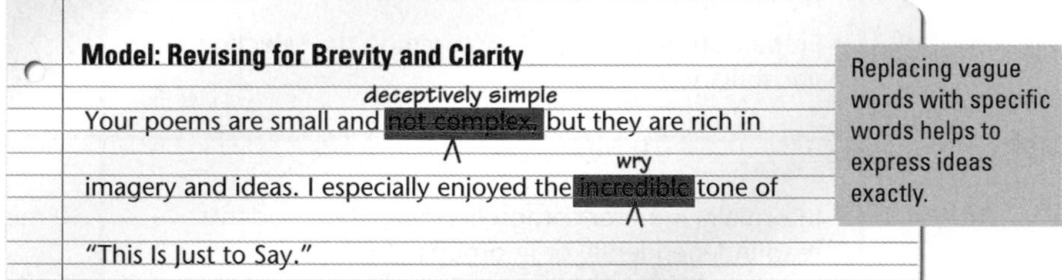

Model: Revising for Brevity and Clarity
deceptively simple
Your poems are small and not complex, but they are rich in
wry
imagery and ideas. I especially enjoyed the incredible tone of
"This Is Just to Say."
Replacing vague words with specific words helps to express ideas exactly.

WG Prentice Hall Writing and Grammar Connection: Chapter 16, Section 1

Extend Your Learning

Listening and Speaking Of "The Red Wheelbarrow," Roy Harvey Pearce writes: "At its worst this is togetherness in a chickenyard. At its best it is an exercise in the creation of the poetic out of the anti-poetic." Which view do you hold? Defend your view in an **informal debate** with classmates. To prepare, keep these tips in mind:

- Find examples to support both positions, and be prepared to argue either side.
- Use examples for the opposing side to develop arguments against that position.

As you debate, stick to agreed-upon time limits. **[Group Activity]**

Research and Technology Select one of the Imagist poems and **illustrate** it, either with artwork of your own or with clippings or printouts from magazines, the Internet, and other sources. If you create your illustration using graphic arts software, you can integrate it in a file with the text of the poem. Then, post your work in the classroom with a brief explanation of your visual interpretation, and use it as the basis for an oral interpretation of the poem.

For: An additional research activity
Visit: www.PHSchool.com
Web Code: erd-7502

❸ Writing Lesson

- To guide students in writing an editor's review, give them the **Support for Writing Lesson** page (*Unit 5 Resources,* p. 29).
- Encourage students to reread Pound's essay for ideas on how to construct a critical analysis of writing. Remind them, however, that they need not adopt Pound's viewpoints.
- After discussing the steps in the Writing Lesson, emphasize the importance of clearly identifying strengths and weaknesses in the poem. Suggest that students use a two-column chart headed "Strengths" and "Weaknesses" as they prewrite.
- Stress that critical writing should remain professional in tone. Students should develop constructive criticism, especially when rejecting a poem for publication.
- Use the rubrics for Critique in *General Resources,* pp. 75–76, to evaluate students' reviews.

❹ Research and Technology

- Help students become familiar with graphic arts software available in your school or local library. You might also lead them in downloading such software from appropriate Internet sources.
- Allow students the alternative of illustrating in a manual medium.
- Encourage students looking for ideas to review the illustrations and photographs that accompany the Imagist poems in the grouping.
- The **Support for Extend Your Learning** page (*Unit 5 Resources,* p. 30) provides guided note-taking opportunities to help students complete the Extend Your Learning activities.

Go Online — Research Have students type in the Web Code for another research activity.

Assessment Resources

The following resources can be used to assess students' knowledge and skills.

Unit 5 Resources
- **Selection Test A,** pp. 32–34
- **Selection Test B,** pp. 35–37

General Resources
- **Rubrics for a Critique,** pp. 75–76

Go Online — Assessment Students may use the **Self-test** to prepare for **Selection Test A** or **Selection Test B.**

Meeting Your Standards

Students will

1. **analyze and respond to literary elements.**
   - Literary Analysis: Characterization
2. **read, comprehend, analyze, and critique a short story.**
   - Reading Strategy: Drawing Conclusions About Characters
   - Reading Check questions
   - Apply the Skills questions
   - Assessment Practice (ATE)
3. **develop vocabulary.**
   - Vocabulary Lesson: Word Analysis: Latin Root: *-somn-*
4. **understand and apply written and oral language conventions.**
   - Spelling Strategy
   - Grammar and Style Lesson: Dashes
5. **develop writing proficiency.**
   - Writing Lesson: Character Analysis
6. **develop appropriate research strategies.**
   - Extend Your Learning: Report
7. **understand and apply listening and speaking strategies.**
   - Extend Your Learning: Presentation

Block Scheduling: Use one 90-minute class period to preteach the skills and have students read the selection. Use a second 90-minute class period to assess students' mastery of skills, extend their learning, and monitor their progress.

Homework Suggestions

Following are possibilities for homework assignments.

- Support pages from *Unit 5 Resources:*
  Literary Analysis
  Reading Strategy
  Vocabulary Builder
  Grammar and Style
- An Extend Your Learning project and the Writing Lesson for this selection may be completed over several days.

Step-by-Step Teaching Guide	Pacing Guide
PRETEACH	
• Administer Vocabulary and Reading Warm-ups as necessary.	5 min.
• Engage students' interest with the motivation activity.	5 min.
• Read and discuss author and background features. **FT**	10 min.
• Introduce the Literary Analysis Skill: Characterization. **FT**	5 min.
• Introduce the Reading Strategy: Drawing Conclusions About Characters. **FT**	10 min.
• Prepare students to read by teaching the selection vocabulary. **FT**	
TEACH	
• Informally monitor comprehension while students read independently or in groups. **FT**	30 min.
• Monitor students' comprehension with the Reading Check notes.	as students read
• Reinforce vocabulary with Vocabulary Builder notes.	as students read
• Develop students' understanding of characterization with the Literary Analysis annotations. **FT**	5 min.
• Develop students' ability to draw conclusions about characters with the Reading Strategy annotations. **FT**	5 min.
ASSESS/EXTEND	
• Assess students' comprehension and mastery of the Literary Analysis and Reading Strategy by having them answer the Apply the Skills questions. **FT**	15 min.
• Have students complete the Vocabulary Lesson and the Grammar and Style Lesson. **FT**	15 min.
• Apply students' ability to elaborate informatively by using the Writing Lesson. **FT**	45 min. or homework
• Apply students' understanding by using one or more of the Extend Your Learning activities.	20–90 min. or homework
• Administer Selection Test A or Selection Test B. **FT**	15 min.

Resources

PRINT

Unit 5 Resources

Vocabulary Warm-up Word Lists **[L1, L2, EL]** ....p. 38
Vocabulary Warm-up Practice **[L1, L2, EL]** ....p. 39
Reading Warm-up A **[L1, L2, EL]** ....p. 40
Reading Warm-up B **[L1, L2, L3]** ....p. 41

TRANSPARENCY

Graphic Organizer Transparencies

Literary Analysis Graphic Organizer A **[L3]** ....p. 159
Literary Analysis Graphic Organizer B **[L1, L2, EL]** ....p. 160
Reading Strategy Graphic Organizer A **[L3]** ....p. 157
Reading Strategy Graphic Organizer B **[L1, L2, EL]** ....p. 158

PRINT

Reader's Notebook [L2]
Reader's Notebook: Adapted Version [L1]
Reader's Notebook: English Learner's Version [EL]

Unit 5 Resources

Literary Analysis **[L3]** ....p. 42
Reading Strategy **[L3]** ....p. 43
Vocabulary Builder **[L3]** ....p. 44

TECHNOLOGY

Listening to Literature Audio CDs [L2, EL]

PRINT

Unit 5 Resources

Grammar and Style **[L3]** ....p. 45
Support for Writing Lesson **[L3]** ....p. 46
Support for Extend Your Learning **[L3]** ....p. 47
Enrichment **[L4]** ....p. 48
Selection Test A **[L1, L2, EL]** ....pp. 49–51
Selection Test B **[L3, L4]** ....pp. 52–54

General Resources

Rubrics for Response to Literature **[L3]** ....pp. 65–66

TECHNOLOGY

Go Online: Research **[L3]**
Go Online: Self-test **[L3]**
ExamView® **Test Bank [L3]**

Choosing Resources for Differentiated Instruction

[L1] Special Needs Students
[L2] Below-Level Students
[L3] All Students
[L4] Advanced Students
[EL] English Learners

For Vocabulary and Reading Warm-ups and for Selection Tests, **A** signifies "less challenging" and **B** "more challenging." For Graphic Organizer transparencies, **A** signifies "not filled in" and **B** "filled in."

FT Fast Track Instruction: To move the lesson more quickly, use the strategies and activities identified with **FT**.

Scaffolding for Less Proficient and Advanced Students

The leveled Critical Thinking questions after selections progress in the levels of thinking required to answer them. To address the needs of your different students, you may use the (a) level questions for your less proficient students and the (b) level questions with your on-level and advanced students. The occasional (c) level questions are appropriate for your advanced students.

PRENTICE HALL **TeacherEXPRESS**™ Plan · Teach · Assess — Use this complete suite of powerful teaching tools to make lesson planning and testing quicker and easier.

PRENTICE HALL **StudentEXPRESS**™ Learn · Study · Succeed — Use the interactive textbook (online and on CD-ROM) to make selections and activities come alive with audio and video support and interactive questions.

Go Online Professional Development
For: Information about Lexiles
Visit: www.PHSchool.com
Web Code: eue-1111

PRETEACH

Motivation

Students may discover that this sad story of obsessive love is reminiscent of many films, books, and real-life experiences. The power of any love story evolves from its characters. Introduce students to Fitzgerald's vividly drawn and alluring centerpiece character—Judy Jones—by reading aloud the following:

> She drew down the corners of her mouth, smiled, glanced furtively around, her eyes in transit falling for an instant on Dexter . . . The smile again—radiant, blatantly artful—convincing."

Have students discuss what this description reveals about Judy. Then, have them predict what might happen when another character falls desperately in love with her. After students have read the story, invite them to discuss their predictions and compare them against the actual plot.

1 Background

More About the Author

People had aspired to wealth long before Fitzgerald's time, but during the 1920s—the decade in which Fritzgerald's fame was at its peak—wealth and status became more accessible than ever. The restricted world of America's wealthy established families had begun to open its doors. Making money—rather than inheriting it—became honorable and admired. Thus, F. Scott Fitzgerald's own desire for wealth became realistic, an achievable goal. Unfortunately, Fitzgerald's wealth and fame were not simple gifts. He struggled with alcoholism, financial and marital problems, and saw the star of his literary success fall into eclipse.

Build Skills *Short Story*

1 Winter Dreams

F. Scott Fitzgerald (1896–1940)

When you open the pages of one of F. Scott Fitzgerald's books, you are transported back in time to the Roaring Twenties, a decade unlike any other in American history. Many Americans lived with reckless abandon, attending wild parties, wearing glamorous clothing, and striving for fulfillment through material wealth. Yet, this quest for pleasure was often accompanied by a sense of inner despair. Fitzgerald was able to successfully capture the paradox of this glittering, materialistic, and often self-destructive lifestyle because he actually lived it. Like many of his characters, he led a fast-paced life and longed to attain the wealth and social status of the upper class. He also experienced the emptiness conveyed in his stories.

A Quick Rise to Fame Francis Scott Key Fitzgerald was born in St. Paul, Minnesota, into a family with high social aspirations but little wealth. The family had a small claim on history: One of their distant relatives was Francis Scott Key, the writer of "The Star Spangled Banner," after whom Fitzgerald was named. As a young man, Fitzgerald was eager to improve his social standing. He entered Princeton University in 1913, where he pursued the type of high-profile social life for which he would later become famous. Fitzgerald failed to graduate, perhaps as a result of his self-indulgent lifestyle, and soon enlisted in the army.

His first novel, *This Side of Paradise* (1920), published shortly after his discharge from the service, was an instant success. With the fame and wealth the novel brought him, Fitzgerald was able to court Zelda Sayre, a southern belle with whom he had fallen in love while in the army. They married in 1920. Together, they blazed an extravagant trail across the societies of both New York and Europe, mingling with rich and famous artists and aristocrats and spending money recklessly.

An American Masterpiece Despite the couple's pleasure-seeking lifestyle, Fitzgerald remained a productive writer, publishing dozens of short stories. In 1925, he published his most successful novel, *The Great Gatsby,* the story of a self-made man whose dreams of love and social acceptance lead to scandal and corruption and ultimately end in tragedy. The novel displayed Fitzgerald's fascination with—and growing distrust of—the wealthy society he had embraced. The book is widely considered to be Fitzgerald's masterpiece, one of the greatest novels in American literature.

Fortunes Turn After the 1929 stock market crash, Fitzgerald's world began to crumble. His wife suffered a series of nervous breakdowns, his reputation as a writer declined, and financial setbacks forced him to seek work as a Hollywood screenwriter. Despite these setbacks, however, he managed to produce many more short stories and a fine second novel, *Tender Is the Night* (1934). Though well-regarded by critics, the book was not a financial success. In the last year of his life, Fitzgerald, who had once been the highest-paid author in the country, earned just $13.13 from his writing.

Fitzgerald was in the midst of writing *The Last Tycoon,* a novel about a Hollywood film mogul, when he died of a heart attack in 1940. His editor approached the novelist John O'Hara about finishing the book, but O'Hara declined. In a letter O'Hara wrote to author John Steinbeck, he explained his refusal, saying that "Fitzgerald was a better just plain writer than all of us put together. Just words writing."

Preview

Connecting to the Literature

Even when you know, deep down, that someone is not right for you, you may continue to long for that person. Such a struggle between reason and emotion forms the heart of this story.

2 Literary Analysis

Characterization

Fitzgerald creates intimate portraits of Dexter and Judy through **characterization**—the revelation of characters' personalities.

- In **direct characterization,** the writer tells the reader what the character is like.
- In **indirect characterization,** characters' traits are revealed through their thoughts, actions, and words, and by what other characters say to or about them.

Fitzgerald brings characters into sharp focus through both methods.

Connecting Literary Elements

Characters' **motivations**—their reasons for acting as they do—may come from internal sources, such as feelings of loneliness, or external sources, such as danger. As you read, identify the characters' motivations for their actions.

3 Reading Strategy

Drawing Conclusions About Characters

Fitzgerald often leaves it up to the reader to draw conclusions about his characters. To **draw conclusions about characters,** combine information from the story with your own experience. Consider this example:

> Dexter stood perfectly still . . . if he moved forward a step his stare would be in her line of vision—if he moved backward he would lose his full view of her face.

If you have ever wanted to hide your interest in someone but could not stop looking, you can conclude that Dexter is enthralled by Judy. Use a chart like the one shown to draw conclusions.

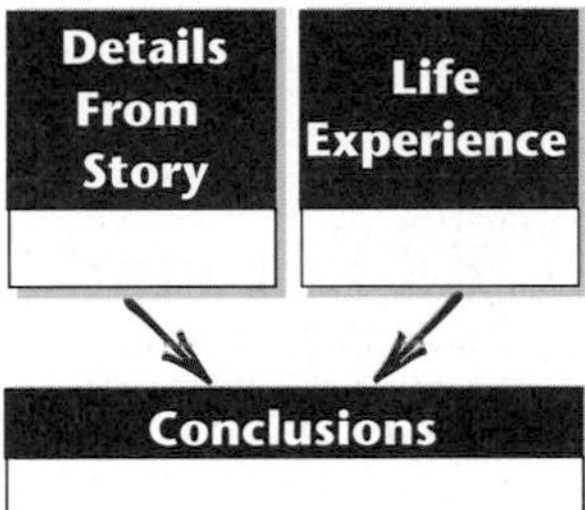

Vocabulary Builder

fallowness (fal′ ō nis) *n.* inactivity (p. 743)

preposterous (prē päs′ tər əs) *adj.* ridiculous (p. 744)

fortuitous (fôr to͞o′ ə təs) *adj.* fortunate (p. 745)

sinuous (sin′ yo͞o əs) *adj.* moving in and out; wavy (p. 749)

mundane (mun′ dān′) *adj.* commonplace; ordinary (p. 750)

poignant (poin′ yənt) *adj.* sharply painful to the feelings (p. 754)

pugilistic (pyo͞o′ jəl is′ tik) *adj.* looking for a fight (p. 756)

somnolent (säm′ nə lənt) *adj.* sleepy; drowsy (p. 757)

2 Literary Analysis

Characterization

- Tell students that as they read "Winter Dreams," they will focus on characterization, the technique authors use to create and develop characters.
- Read the instruction about characterization aloud. Point out the two distinct methods of characterization—direct and indirect—and use these passages to highlight the difference:
  Direct: Whatever Judy wanted, she went after.
  Indirect: She swung her mashie impatiently and without interest.
  Invite students to notice how the second example conveys information by describing a character's behavior, while the first simply states what the character is like.
- Use the Connecting Literary Elements instruction to emphasize that identifying characters' motivations will help students better understand Fitzgerald's characters.

3 Reading Strategy

Drawing Conclusions About Characters

- Remind students that drawing conclusions can help them fully appreciate Fitzgerald's vivid characters.
- To draw conclusions about characters, readers must look carefully at characters' motivations, pay attention to the author's characterization, and consider their own knowledge of human behavior.
- Give students a copy of **Reading Strategy Graphic Organizer A,** p. 157 in ***Graphic Organizer Transparencies.*** Direct students to the chart on the student page. Urge them to record text and life clues that lead them to draw specific conclusions about Dexter and Judy.

Vocabulary Builder

- Pronounce each vocabulary word for students, and read the definitions as a class. Have students identify any words with which they are already familiar.

Differentiated Instruction

Solutions for All Learners

Support for Special Needs Students
Have students complete the **Preview** and **Build Skills** pages for "Winter Dreams" in the ***Reader's Notebook: Adapted Version.*** These pages provide a selection summary, an abbreviated presentation of the reading and literary skills, and the graphic organizer on the **Build Skills** page in the student book.

Support for Less Proficient Readers
Have students complete the **Preview** and **Build Skills** pages for "Winter Dreams" in the ***Reader's Notebook.*** These pages provide a selection summary, an abbreviated presentation of the reading and literary skills, and the graphic organizer on the **Build Skills** page in the student book.

Support for English Learners
Have students complete the **Preview and Build Skills** pages for "Winter Dreams" in the ***Reader's Notebook: English Learner's Version.*** These pages provide a selection summary, an abbreviated presentation of the skills, additional contextual vocabulary, and the graphic organizer on the **Build Skills** page in the student book.

Learning Modalities
Musical/Rhythmic Learners Give students the opportunity to share in Dexter's sensory experiences. Play a recording of the songs noted in the story (p. 748)—available on Jazz Age song collections. Have students identify other sounds in the referenced scene. As they listen to the recording, urge students to imagine all the sounds Dexter hears. Lead students to appreciate how these various sounds might affect Dexter's mood.

❶ About the Selection

This story illustrates the powerful magnetism of love and suggests the extremes to which a person might go in pursuit of it. Dexter Green, an up-and-coming young man, becomes passionately obsessed with capturing Judy Jones and gaining entrance into her wealthy society. No matter how badly Judy behaves, Dexter remains steadfast in his passion, finding her and the glittering life around her both captivating and desirable. As Dexter repeatedly returns to Judy's side to hungrily grasp at her erratic good-will, he demonstrates with poignant force the glory and despair of loving a fantasy—a romantic ideal for which sacrificing all seems worthwhile.

WINTER DREAMS

F. Scott Fitzgerald

Background Written in 1922, this story unfolds against the background of the Jazz Age. Focusing on Dexter Green's obsession with Judy Jones, a beautiful young woman from a prominent wealthy family, Fitzgerald explores the connections between love, money, and social status. Through Dexter, he shows what life was like in the 1920s for an ambitious young man driven by the desire for "glittering things."

I

❶ Some of the caddies were poor as sin and lived in one-room houses with a neurasthenic[1] cow in the front yard, but Dexter Green's father owned the second best grocery store in Black Bear—the best one was "The Hub," patronized by the wealthy people from Sherry Island—and Dexter caddied only for pocket money.

1. **neurasthenic** (no͞or′ əs thĕn′ ik) *adj.* here, weak, tired.

Differentiated Instruction Solutions for All Learners

Accessibility at a Glance

	Winter Dreams
Context	United States in the 1920s; upper-class society
Language	Blend of long and short sentences; dialogue
Concept Level	Accessible (man searching for social status)
Literary Merit	Noted author; popular
Lexile	1090L
Overall Rating	Average

In the fall when the days became crisp and gray, and the long Minnesota winter shut down like the white lid of a box, Dexter's skis moved over the snow that hid the fairways of the golf course. At these times the country gave him a feeling of profound melancholy—it offended him that the links should lie in enforced fallowness, haunted by ragged sparrows for the long season. It was dreary, too, that on the tees where the gay colors fluttered in summer there were now only the desolate sandboxes knee deep in crusted ice. When he crossed the hills the wind blew cold as misery, and if the sun was out he tramped with his eyes squinted up against the hard dimensionless glare.

In April the winter ceased abruptly. The snow ran down into Black Bear Lake scarcely tarrying for the early golfers to brave the season with red and black balls. Without elation, without an interval of moist glory, the cold was gone. Dexter knew that there was something dismal about this Northern spring, just as he knew there was something gorgeous about the fall. Fall made him clinch his hands and tremble and repeat idiotic sentences to himself, and make brisk abrupt gestures of command to imaginary audiences and armies. October filled him with hope which November raised to a sort of ecstatic triumph, and in this mood the fleeting brilliant impressions of the summer at Sherry Island were ready grist to his mill. He became a golf champion and defeated Mr. T. A. Hedrick in a marvelous match played a hundred times over the fairways of his imagination, a match each detail of which he changed about untiringly—sometimes he won with almost laughable ease, sometimes he came up magnificently from behind. Again, stepping from a Pierce-Arrow automobile, like Mr. Mortimer Jones, he strolled frigidly into the lounge of the Sherry Island Golf Club—or perhaps, surrounded by an admiring crowd, he gave an exhibition of fancy diving from the springboard of the club raft. . . . Among those who watched him in open-mouthed wonder was Mr. Mortimer Jones.

And one day it came to pass that Mr. Jones—himself and not his ghost—came up to Dexter with tears in his eyes and said that Dexter was the——best caddy in the club, and wouldn't he decide not to quit if Mr. Jones made it worth his while, because every other——caddy in the club lost one ball a hole for him—regularly——

"No, sir," said Dexter decisively, "I don't want to caddy any more." Then, after a pause: "I'm too old."

"You're not more than fourteen. Why the devil did you decide just this morning that you wanted to quit? You promised that next week you'd go over to the state tournament with me."

"I decided I was too old."

Dexter handed in his "A Class" badge, collected what money was due him from the caddy master, and walked home to Black Bear Village.

"The best——caddy I ever saw," shouted Mr. Mortimer Jones over a drink that afternoon. "Never lost a ball! Willing! Intelligent! Quiet! Honest! Grateful!"

Vocabulary Builder
fallowness (fal´ ō nis) *n.* inactivity

Reading Strategy
Drawing Conclusions About Characters What conclusions do you draw about Dexter's circumstances and desires based on this description of his "winter dreams"?

3 
Reading Check
What does Dexter do for pocket money?

❷ Reading Strategy
Drawing Conclusions About Characters

- Read the bracketed passage aloud to students. **Ask** them to paraphrase it.
  Possible response: Dexter fantasizes about becoming wealthy and then using his golf and diving talents to gain status and show off at the golf club.
- Then, **ask** students the Reading Strategy question: What conclusions do you draw about Dexter's circumstances and desires based on this description of his "winter dreams"?
  Answer: Dexter lacks wealth and status but would like to attain both.

❸ Reading Check
Answer: He caddies at the golf club.

Differentiated Instruction
Solutions for All Learners

Support for Special Needs Students
Tell students that there are two groups of people portrayed in this story—the wealthy members of the golf club, and the workers, people like Dexter Green who serve the wealthy. Help students set up a two-column chart to record information about these two groups as they read.

Vocabulary for English Learners
Walk students through the many names—of places, people, cars, and months—included on pp. 742–743. Make sure students know what each name identifies and demonstrate its correct pronunciation. Then, ask students to name the months of April, October, and November in their home language. Point out these months on a calendar to help students make appropriate seasonal associations with them.

❹ Literary Analysis
Characterization

- Direct students to read the bracketed passage. Remind them to consider elements of both direct and indirect characterization as they answer the Literary Analysis question.
- **Ask** students the Literary Analysis question: What methods of characterization does Fitzgerald use in this passage about Judy Jones?
Answer: He uses indirect characterization, describing Judy through Dexter's perception of her, and direct characterization, describing Judy's physical beauty.

▶ **Monitor Progress:** On the chalkboard, draw a two-column chart like the one shown. Lead students in completing the chart with details from the passage.

Direct	Indirect

4 The little girl who had done this was eleven—beautifully ugly as little girls are apt to be who are destined after a few years to be inexpressibly lovely and bring no end of misery to a great number of men. The spark, however, was perceptible. There was a general ungodliness in the way her lips twisted down at the corners when she smiled, and in the—Heaven help us!—in the almost passionate quality of her eyes. Vitality is born early in such women. It was utterly in evidence now, shining through her thin frame in a sort of glow.

She had come eagerly out on to the course at nine o'clock with a white linen nurse and five small new golf clubs in a white canvas bag which the nurse was carrying. When Dexter first saw her she was standing by the caddy house, rather ill at ease and trying to conceal the fact by engaging her nurse in an obviously unnatural conversation graced by startling and irrelevant grimaces from herself.

"Well, it's certainly a nice day, Hilda," Dexter heard her say. She drew down the corners of her mouth, smiled, and glanced furtively around, her eyes in transit falling for an instant on Dexter.

Then to the nurse:

"Well, I guess there aren't very many people out here this morning, are there?"

The smile again—radiant, blatantly artificial—convincing.

"I don't know what we're supposed to do now," said the nurse looking nowhere in particular.

"Oh, that's all right. I'll fix it up."

Dexter stood perfectly still, his mouth slightly ajar. He knew that if he moved forward a step his stare would be in her line of vision—if he moved backward he would lose his full view of her face. For a moment he had not realized how young she was. Now he remembered having seen her several times the year before—in bloomers.

Suddenly, involuntarily, he laughed, a short abrupt laugh—then, startled by himself, he turned and began to walk quickly away.

"Boy!"

Dexter stopped.

"Boy——"

Beyond question he was addressed. Not only that, but he was treated to that absurd smile, that preposterous smile—the memory of which at least a dozen men were to carry into middle age.

"Boy, do you know where the golf teacher is?"

"He's giving a lesson."

"Well, do you know where the caddy master is?"

"He isn't here yet this morning."

"Oh." For a moment this baffled her. She stood alternately on her right and left foot.

"We'd like to get a caddy," said the nurse. "Mrs. Mortimer Jones sent us out to play golf, and we don't know how without we get a caddy."

Here she was stopped by an ominous glance from Miss Jones, followed immediately by the smile.

Literary Analysis
Characterization What methods of characterization does Fitzgerald use in this passage about Judy Jones?

Vocabulary Builder
preposterous (prē päs′ tər əs) *adj.* ridiculous

Enrichment

The Rising Popularity of Golf

Though golf was once a game played mostly in private clubs reserved for the wealthy and closed to most non-whites, in recent years the game has become more widely accessible and popular in America. As a result, top golfers can now be found among many American cultures and ethnic groups. In 1997, for example, Tiger Woods—whose mother is Southeast Asian and whose father is African American, Native American, and Chinese—won golf's most prestigious prize, the Masters Tournament. At just 21 years of age, Tiger became the youngest Masters champion in history. In the seasons of 2000–2001, Tiger topped this achievement by winning the Masters a second time and becoming the simultaneous titleholder of such major golf tournaments as the U.S. Open, British Open, PGA Championship, and The Players Championship.

"There aren't any caddies here except me," said Dexter to the nurse, "and I got to stay here in charge until the caddy master gets here."

"Oh."

Miss Jones and her retinue now withdrew, and at a proper distance from Dexter became involved in a heated conversation, which was concluded by Miss Jones taking one of the clubs and hitting it on the ground with violence. For further emphasis she raised it again and was about to bring it down smartly upon the nurse's bosom, when the nurse seized the club and twisted it from her hands.

"You little mean old *thing*!" cried Miss Jones wildly.

Another argument ensued. Realizing that the elements of the comedy were implied in the scene, Dexter several times began to laugh, but each time restrained the laugh before it reached audibility. He could not resist the monstrous conviction that the little girl was justified in beating the nurse.

The situation was resolved by the fortuitous appearance of the caddy master, who was appealed to immediately by the nurse.

"Miss Jones is to have a little caddy, and this one says he can't go."

"Mr. McKenna said I was to wait here till you came," said Dexter quickly.

"Well, he's here now." Miss Jones smiled cheerfully at the caddy master. Then she dropped her bag and set off at a haughty mince toward the first tee.

"Well?" The caddy master turned to Dexter.

"What you standing there like a dummy for? Go pick up the young lady's clubs."

"I don't think I'll go out today," said Dexter.

"You don't——"

"I think I'll quit."

The enormity of his decision frightened him. He was a favorite caddy, and the thirty dollars a month he earned through the summer were not to be made elsewhere around the lake. But he had received a strong emotional shock, and his perturbation required a violent and immediate outlet.

It is not so simple as that, either. As so frequently would be the case in the future, Dexter was unconsciously dictated to by his winter dreams.

II

Now, of course, the quality and the seasonability of these winter dreams varied, but the stuff of them remained. They persuaded Dexter several years later to pass up a business course at the State university—his father, prospering now, would have paid his way—for the precarious advantage of attending an older and more famous university in the East, where he was bothered by his scanty funds. But do not get the impression, because his winter dreams happened to be concerned at first with musings on the rich, that there was anything

Literary Analysis
Characterization and Motivation What motivates Judy Jones's behavior in fighting with her nurse?

Vocabulary Builder
fortuitous (fôr to͞o′ ə təs) *adj.* fortunate

6 **Reading Check**
What does Dexter do when told to go out and caddy for Miss Jones?

5 Literary Analysis
Characterization and Motivation

- Have three students act out the scene described in the bracketed passage, in which Dexter observes Judy with her nurse.
- Then, **ask** students the Literary Analysis question: What motivates Judy Jones's behavior in fighting with her nurse?
  Answer: She wants to get her own way and to remind the nurse that she is the boss, despite her youth.

6 Reading Check
Answer: He quits his job as a caddy.

Differentiated Instruction
Solutions for All Learners

Support for Less Proficient Readers
Students may find the link between Dexter's "winter dreams" and his behavior on meeting Judy Jones unclear. Review the paraphrases generated in response to the Reading Strategy question on p. 743. Then, help students summarize Dexter's meeting with Judy. Explain that Dexter doesn't want Judy to view him as a servant.

Strategy for English Learners
Point out the link between Dexter's "winter dreams" (described on p. 743) and his covetous perception of Judy. Note the adjectives, for example "brilliant" and "glow," that Fitzgerald uses to describe both. Explain that these words share similar connotations. Have students look for additional examples of this connection as they read.

Enrichment for Advanced Readers
Challenge students to draw on their knowledge of F. Scott Fitzgerald's life to link his hopes and dreams with those of Dexter Green. Fitzgerald, too, came from a modest background but aspired to wealth and glamour. Given this similarity, how do students think Fitzgerald wanted readers to feel about Dexter?

❼ Humanities

Golf Course–California 1917 by George Wesley Bellows

This picture is a lithograph—an image printed from an inked stone or metal plate. It depicts a golf course much like the one where Dexter and Judy meet in the story. George Wesley Bellows was known for both lithography and painting, especially of sports and action scenes. A serious amateur athlete, Bellows had intimate knowledge of these activities. This image, like a photograph, captures the energy and motion of a golf game in mid-play.

Use these questions for discussion:

1. What do the people depicted here suggest about the manners and expectations of Fitzgerald's characters?
   Answer: They are dressed in almost uniformlike clothing, suggesting a "club" that only some can enter. They appear to be moving slowly and gently, as if they have few cares.
2. How does the golf club and its members depicted here compare with your image of Dexter and Judy at their golf club?
   Answer: Students may say that they envisioned the course as more densely covered in trees making the people less visible to one another.

❽ Critical Viewing

Answer: Students may note that in this private and privileged setting, Dexter would see Judy as somewhat unattainable and more attractive.

❼

merely snobbish in the boy. He wanted not association with glittering things and glittering people—he wanted the glittering things themselves. Often he reached out for the best without knowing why he wanted it—and sometimes he ran up against the mysterious denials and prohibitions in which life indulges. It is with one of those denials and not with his career as a whole that this story deals.

He made money. It was rather amazing. After college he went to the city from which Black Bear Lake draws its wealthy patrons. When he was only twenty-three and had been there not quite two years, there were already people who liked to say: "Now *there's* a boy—" All about him rich men's sons were peddling bonds precariously, or investing patrimonies precariously, or plodding through the two dozen volumes of the "George Washington Commercial Course," but Dexter borrowed a thousand dollars on his college degree and his confident mouth, and bought a partnership in a laundry.

❽ ▲ **Critical Viewing**
Golf was once a game reserved for the wealthy. It is on a golf course like the one in this painting that Dexter meets Judy for the first time. How might this setting have affected Dexter's perception of Judy? **[Analyze]**

It was a small laundry when he went into it, but Dexter made a specialty of learning how the English washed fine woolen golf stockings without shrinking them, and within a year he was catering to the trade that wore knickerbockers. Men were insisting that their Shetland hose and sweaters go to his laundry, just as they had insisted on a caddy who could find golf balls. A little later he was doing their wives' lingerie as well—and running five branches in different parts of the city. Before he was twenty-seven he owned the largest string of laundries in his section of the country. It was then that he sold out and went to New York. But the part of his story that concerns us goes back to the days when he was making his first big success.

When he was twenty-three Mr. Hart—one of the gray-haired men who like to say "Now there's a boy"—gave him a guest card to the Sherry Island Golf Club for a weekend. So he signed his name one day on the register, and that afternoon played golf in a foursome with Mr. Hart and Mr. Sandwood and Mr. T. A. Hedrick. He did not consider it necessary to remark that he had once carried Mr. Hart's bag over this same links, and that he knew every trap and gully with his eyes shut—but he found himself glancing at the four caddies who trailed them, trying to catch a gleam or gesture that would remind him of himself, that would lessen the gap which lay between his present and his past.

It was a curious day, slashed abruptly with fleeting, familiar impressions. One minute he had the sense of being a trespasser—in the next he was impressed by the tremendous superiority he felt toward Mr. T. A. Hedrick, who was a bore and not even a good golfer any more.

Enrichment

Job Search
Review with students the characteristics associated with Judy—vital, beautiful, athletic, superficial, flirtatious, charming, greedy, self-centered. Encourage students to brainstorm for ways that her character and physical qualities could serve Judy in the workplace. For what jobs might she be suited and why? Have students examine the employment ads in a local newspaper or online source to see if they can find a match.

Costume Design
Dexter believes that by donning the costume of the privileged class, he will be able to join it.

Film and theatrical costume designers develop clothing that enables an actor to enter the life and cultural setting of a character. Have interested students read about costume design. Then, invite students to apply costume-design methods to create costumes appropriate to several subgroups in contemporary American culture.

Golf Course—California, 1917, George Wesley Bellows, Cincinnati Art Museum

Then, because of a ball Mr. Hart lost near the fifteenth green, an enormous thing happened. While they were searching the stiff grasses of the rough there was a clear call of "Fore!" from behind a hill in their rear. And as they all turned abruptly from their search a bright new ball sliced abruptly over the hill and caught Mr. T. A. Hedrick in the abdomen.

"By Gad!" cried Mr. T. A. Hedrick, "they ought to put some of these crazy women off the course. It's getting to be outrageous."

A head and a voice came up together over the hill:

"Do you mind if we go through?"

"You hit me in the stomach!" declared Mr. Hedrick wildly.

"Did I?" The girl approached the group of men. "I'm sorry. I yelled 'Fore!'"

Her glance fell casually on each of the men—then scanned the fairway for her ball. 9

"Did I bounce into the rough?"

It was impossible to determine whether this question was ingenuous or malicious. In a moment, however, she left no doubt, for as her partner came up over the hill she called cheerfully:

"Here I am! I'd have gone on the green except that I hit something."

As she took her stance for a short mashie shot, Dexter looked at her closely. She wore a blue gingham dress, rimmed at throat and shoulders with a white edging that accentuated her tan. The quality of exaggeration, of thinness, which had made her passionate eyes and down-turning mouth absurd at eleven, was gone now. She was arrestingly beautiful. The color in her cheeks was centered like the color in a picture—it was not a "high" color, but a sort of fluctuating and feverish warmth, so shaded that it seemed at any moment it would recede and disappear. This color and the mobility of her mouth gave a continual impression of flux, of intense life, of passionate vitality—balanced only partially by the sad luxury of her eyes.

She swung her mashie impatiently and without interest, pitching the ball into a sand pit on the other side of the green. With a quick, insincere smile and a careless "Thank you!" she went on after it.

"That Judy Jones!" remarked Mr. Hedrick on the next tee, as they waited—some moments—for her to play on ahead. "All she needs is to be turned up and spanked for six months and then to be married off to an old-fashioned cavalry captain." 10

"My God, she's good looking!" said Mr. Sandwood, who was just over thirty.

Reading Strategy
Drawing Conclusions About Characters What does Judy's behavior toward the men on the golf course suggest about her character?

 **Reading Check**
What "enormous thing" happens near the fifteenth green?

9 Reading Strategy
Drawing Conclusions About Characters

- Call on a volunteer to read the bracketed passage aloud. Then, help students hear the callous and careless tone in Judy's voice when she speaks.

Monitor Progress: Ask students the Reading Strategy question: What does Judy's behavior toward the men on the golf course suggest about her character?
Answer: It suggests that she is selfish and self-centered, oblivious to other people's concerns. Judy apparently sees herself as entitled to this selfish attitude.

10 Reading Check

Answer: Judy hits another golfer with a ball, but she appears not to care. For Dexter, the "enormous thing" is his seeing Judy Jones again.

Differentiated Instruction
Solutions for All Learners

Support for Less Proficient Readers
Work with students to clarify sentences in which Fitzgerald uses dashes to insert asides or draw attention. For example, you might note this sentence: "Her glance fell casually on each of the men—then scanned the fairway for her ball." Discuss Fitzgerald's use of the dash to emphasize an aspect of Judy's character. By creating a dramatic pause, the dash indicates Judy's perusal of each man as a possible audience for her charms. When she finds each lacking, she moves on.

Support for English Learners
Fitzgerald's creative sentence structure, especially his use of dashes, will likely challenge students. Urge students to read the story in manageable chunks, rephrasing difficult sentences for clarification. You may want to break the story into the numbered sections the author has already provided.

⓫ Literary Analysis
Characterization

- Discuss with students what each man says about Judy in the bracketed passage.
- **Ask** students the Literary Analysis questions: What information about Judy Jones does Fitzgerald provide in this discussion among the golfers?
  Answer: She's pretty, she's immature, she's a pretty good golfer but she doesn't work at it, she has a nice figure, she's a flirt.

▶ **Monitor Progress: Ask** students to identify whether these details about Judy's character are examples of direct or indirect characterization.
Answer: This information is conveyed through the use of dialogue. Therefore, it represents examples of indirect characterization.

"Good looking!" cried Mr. Hedrick contemptuously, "she always looks as if she wanted to be kissed! Turning those big coweyes on every calf in town!"

⓫ It was doubtful if Mr. Hedrick intended a reference to the maternal instinct.

"She'd play pretty good golf if she'd try," said Mr. Sandwood.

"She has no form," said Mr. Hedrick solemnly.

"She has a nice figure," said Mr. Sandwood.

"Better thank the Lord she doesn't drive a swifter ball," said Mr. Hart, winking at Dexter.

Later in the afternoon the sun went down with a riotous swirl of gold and varying blues and scarlets, and left the dry, rustling night of Western summer. Dexter watched from the veranda of the golf club, watched the even overlap of the waters in the little wind, silver molasses under the harvest moon. Then the moon held a finger to her lips and the lake became a clear pool, pale and quiet. Dexter put on his bathing suit and swam out to the farthest raft, where he stretched dripping on the wet canvas of the springboard.

There was a fish jumping and a star shining and the lights around the lake were gleaming. Over on a dark peninsula a piano was playing the songs of last summer and of summers before that—songs from *Chin-Chin* and *The Count of Luxemburg* and *The Chocolate Soldier*[2]—and because the sound of a piano over a stretch of water had always seemed beautiful to Dexter he lay perfectly quiet and listened.

The tune the piano was playing at that moment had been gay and new five years before when Dexter was a sophomore at college. They had played it at a prom once when he could not afford the luxury of proms, and he had stood outside the gymnasium and listened. The sound of the tune precipitated in him a sort of ecstasy and it was with that ecstasy he viewed what happened to him now. It was a mood of intense appreciation, a sense that, for once, he was magnificently attuned to life and that everything about him was radiating a brightness and a glamor he might never know again.

A low, pale oblong detached itself suddenly from the darkness of the Island, spitting forth the reverberate sound of a racing motorboat. Two white streamers of cleft water rolled themselves out behind it and almost immediately the boat was beside him, drowning out the hot tinkle of the piano in the drone of its spray. Dexter raising himself on his arms was aware of a figure standing at the wheel, of two dark eyes regarding him over the lengthening space of water—then the boat had gone by and was sweeping in an immense and purposeless circle of spray round and round in the middle of the lake. With equal eccentricity one of the circles flattened out and headed back toward the raft.

"Who's that?" she called, shutting off her motor. She was so near now that Dexter could see her bathing suit, which consisted apparently of pink rompers.

2. ***Chin-Chin . . . The Chocolate Soldier*** popular operettas of the time.

Literary Analysis
Characterization What information about Judy Jones does Fitzgerald provide in this discussion among the golfers?

Enrichment

Sports Venues

Point out to students that the golf course featured in Dexter's story is a significant physical element in the community. A typical golf course has 18 holes that require walking 7,000 yards (70 football fields) to complete. Most courses are carefully landscaped and may even incorporate natural features such as ponds, streams, or woods. Because they require intensive chemical upkeep to maintain, golf courses sometimes generate ecological problems for the water supplies or wetland areas of surrounding communities. This can cause conflict between golf course owners and residents. Ask students to identify some sports venues—either indoor or outdoor—in your community. How do these facilities affect the community? Have these venues generated any conflicts or controversies? Urge students to consider issues of business activity, traffic flow and parking, visitor density, and the ecological and visual impact of the venues.

The nose of the boat bumped the raft, and as the latter tilted rakishly he was precipitated toward her. With different degrees of interest they recognized each other.

"Aren't you one of those men we played through this afternoon?" she demanded.

He was.

"Well, do you know how to drive a motorboat? Because if you do I wish you'd drive this one so I can ride on the surfboard behind. My name is Judy Jones"—she favored him with an absurd smirk—rather, what tried to be a smirk, for, twist her mouth as she might, it was not grotesque, it was merely beautiful—"and I live in a house over there on the Island, and in that house there is a man waiting for me. When he drove up at the door I drove out of the dock because he says I'm his ideal."

There was a fish jumping and a star shining and the lights around the lake were gleaming. Dexter sat beside Judy Jones and she explained how her boat was driven. Then she was in the water, swimming to the floating surfboard with a sinuous crawl. Watching her was without effort to the eye, watching a branch waving or a sea gull flying. Her arms, burned to butternut, moved sinuously among the dull platinum ripples, elbow appearing first, casting the forearm back with a cadence of falling water, then reaching out and down, stabbing a path ahead.

They moved out into the lake; turning, Dexter saw that she was kneeling on the low rear of the now uptilted surfboard.

"Go faster," she called, "fast as it'll go."

Obediently he jammed the lever forward and the white spray mounted at the bow. When he looked around again the girl was standing up on the rushing board, her arms spread wide, her eyes lifted toward the moon.

"It's awful cold," she shouted. "What's your name?"

He told her.

"Well, why don't you come to dinner tomorrow night?"

His heart turned over like the flywheel of the boat, and, for the second time, her casual whim gave a new direction to his life.

III

Next evening while he waited for her to come downstairs, Dexter peopled the soft deep summer room and the sun porch that opened from it with the men who had already loved Judy Jones. He knew the sort of men they were—the men who when he first went to college had entered from the great prep schools with graceful clothes and the deep tan of healthy summers. He had seen that, in one sense, he was better than these men. He was newer and stronger. Yet in acknowledging to himself that he wished his children to be like them he was admitting that he was but the rough, strong stuff from which they eternally sprang. 13

Literary Analysis
Characterization and Motivation What motivates Judy Jones to get in her boat and approach Dexter?

Vocabulary Builder
sinuous (sin′ yo͞o əs) *adj.* moving in and out; wavy

Reading Check
Where is Dexter when he meets Judy Jones for the third time?

12 Literary Analysis
Characterization and Motivations

- After students read the bracketed passage, direct their attention to the description of Judy's smirk. **Discuss** what such an expression might suggest about Judy's attitude.
  Answer: It suggests a dismissiveness, almost a contempt, on her part.
- Then, **ask** students the Literary Analysis question: What motivates Judy Jones to get in her boat and approach Dexter? Urge students to carefully read the last sentence of the bracketed text before answering.
  Answer: She wants to get away from a man at her house. He has complimented her too much and made himself seem too easy, too accessible.

13 Reading Check
Answer: He is relaxing on a raft in the lake next to the golf club.

Differentiated Instruction
Solutions for All Learners

Strategy for Special Needs Students
A story of this length may challenge the capacity of students to sustain interest over its course. One way to help students meet this challenge is to have them note the importance of the section breaks inserted by the author. Tell students that each break provides a place to pause and reflect on what has passed so far in the story.

Strategy for Less Proficient Readers
Less proficient readers may find the abrupt time shifts in this long story quite confusing. Suggest that they use a timeline to chart the story's events in the sequence in which they occur. If they wish, students can divide their timeline into sections according to those inserted by the author.

Strategy for English Learners
Draw students' attention to the time shift that occurs in Part II. Point out that the events described here take place many years after Dexter's caddying job. Have students note the time shifts on a timeline or sequential record.

⓮ Critical Thinking
Make Inferences

- Read the bracketed passage aloud to students. **Ask** them to summarize the information they learn.
- Then, **ask** students what the information about Dexter's mother's name and her speaking broken English means.
  Answer: Explain that Dexter's reference to his mother's name acknowledges his family's origins in Eastern Europe. His mother spoke broken English because it was not her first language.

⓯ Literary Analysis
Characterization

- Have students read the bracketed passage, taking brief notes about Judy's behavior and apparent feelings. Then, **ask** them how Dexter reacts to Judy.
  Possible response: Judy speaks petulantly, sulks moodily, smiles in a forced manner. She seems unhappy. Dexter reacts with concern and anxiety, but he is also fascinated by her.
- **Ask** students the Literary Analysis question: What does this description reveal about Dexter's and Judy's relationship?
  Possible response: It reveals a one-sided relationship in which Judy's emotional state sets the tone and Dexter is constantly worried that he will not measure up.

14 When the time had come for him to wear good clothes, he had known who were the best tailors in America, and the best tailors in America had made him the suit he wore this evening. He had acquired that particular reserve peculiar to his university, that set it off from other universities. He recognized the value to him of such a mannerism and he had adopted it; he knew that to be careless in dress and manner required more confidence than to be careful. But carelessness was for his children. His mother's name had been Krimelich. She was a Bohemian of the peasant class and she had talked broken English to the end of her days. Her son must keep to the set patterns.

At a little after seven Judy Jones came downstairs. She wore a blue silk afternoon dress, and he was disappointed at first that she had not put on something more elaborate. This feeling was accentuated when, after a brief greeting, she went to the door of a butler's pantry and pushing it open called: "You can serve dinner, Martha." He had rather expected that a butler would announce dinner, that there would be a cocktail. Then he put these thoughts behind him as they sat down side by side on a lounge and looked at each other.

"Father and mother won't be here," she said thoughtfully.

He remembered the last time he had seen her father, and he was glad the parents were not to be here tonight—they might wonder who he was. He had been born in Keeble, a Minnesota village fifty miles farther north, and he always gave Keeble as his home instead of Black Bear Village. Country towns were well enough to come from if they weren't inconveniently in sight and used as footstools by fashionable lakes.

They talked of his university, which she had visited frequently during the past two years, and of the nearby city which supplied Sherry Island with its patrons, and whither Dexter would return next day to his prospering laundries.

15 During dinner she slipped into a moody depression which gave Dexter a feeling of uneasiness. Whatever petulance she uttered in her throaty voice worried him. Whatever she smiled at—at him, at a chicken liver, at nothing—it disturbed him that her smile could have no root in mirth, or even in amusement. When the scarlet corners of her lips curved down, it was less a smile than an invitation to a kiss.

Literary Analysis
Characterization What does this description reveal about Dexter's and Judy's relationship?

Then, after dinner, she led him out on the dark sun porch and deliberately changed the atmosphere.

"Do you mind if I weep a little?" she said.

"I'm afraid I'm boring you," he responded quickly.

"You're not. I like you. But I've just had a terrible afternoon. There was a man I cared about, and this afternoon he told me out of a clear sky that he was poor as a church mouse. He'd never even hinted it before. Does this sound horribly mundane?"

Vocabulary Builder
mundane (mun dān′) *adj.* commonplace; ordinary

"Perhaps he was afraid to tell you."

"Suppose he was," she answered. "He didn't start right. You see, if I'd thought of him as poor—well, I've been mad about loads of poor men, and fully intended to marry them all. But in this case, I hadn't thought of him that way, and my interest in him wasn't strong

Enrichment

The Anatomy of Emotion

As Dexter reacts to Judy Jones's vacillating interest and personal charms, his emotions control his body. Emotions, while they arise from the brain, are associated with the heart. In fact, the heart and other physical elements change in response to emotion. Feelings of love, for example, may result in a faster heart rate, sweaty palms, weak knees, and loss of concentration.

Tell students that as the story progresses and Dexter begins to question his attachment to Judy, his reason battles with his emotions. Reason and decision making are governed by the cerebrum, the largest part of the human brain. The cerebrum has two parts known as the left brain and the right brain, each of which controls the opposite side of the body. Scientists now believe there are important contrasts between the right and left brains of men and women, which contribute to differences in behavior.

Have students use this information to analyze Dexter's reactions to and decisions about Judy.

enough to survive the shock. As if a girl calmly informed her fiancè that she was a widow. He might not object to widows, but——

"Let's start right," she interrupted herself suddenly. "Who are you, anyhow?"

For a moment Dexter hesitated. Then:

"I'm nobody," he announced. "My career is largely a matter of futures."

"Are you poor?"

"No," he said frankly, "I'm probably making more money than any man my age in the Northwest. I know that's an obnoxious remark, but you advised me to start right."

There was a pause. Then she smiled and the corners of her mouth drooped and an almost imperceptible sway brought her closer to him, looking up into his eyes. A lump rose in Dexter's throat, and he waited breathless for the experiment, facing the unpredictable compound that would form mysteriously from the elements of their lips. Then he saw—she communicated her excitement to him, lavishly, deeply, with kisses that were not a promise but a fulfillment. They aroused in him not hunger demanding renewal but surfeit that would demand more surfeit . . . kisses that were like charity, creating want by holding back nothing at all.

It did not take him many hours to decide that he had wanted Judy Jones ever since he was a proud, desirous little boy.

IV

It began like that—and continued, with varying shades of intensity, on such a note right up to the denouement. Dexter surrendered a part of himself to the most direct and unprincipled personality with which he had ever come in contact. Whatever Judy wanted, she went after with the full pressure of her charm. There was no divergence of method, no jockeying for position or premeditation of effects—there was a very little mental side to any of her affairs. She simply made men conscious to the highest degree of her physical loveliness. Dexter had no desire to change her. Her deficiencies were knit up with a passionate energy that transcended and justified them.

When, as Judy's head lay against his shoulder that first night, she whispered, "I don't know what's the matter with me. Last night I thought I was in love with a man and tonight I think I'm in love with you——" it seemed to him a beautiful and romantic thing to say. It was the exquisite excitability that for the moment he controlled and owned. But a week later he was compelled to view this same quality in a different light. She took him in her roadster to a picnic supper, and after supper she disappeared, likewise in her roadster, with another man. Dexter became enormously upset and was scarcely able to be decently civil to the other people present. When she assured him that she had 18
not kissed the other man, he knew she was lying—yet he was glad that she had taken the trouble to lie to him.

Literary Analysis
Characterization What does this conversation reveal about the characters of Dexter and Judy?

Literary Analysis
Characterization and Motivation Why is Dexter so willing to accept Judy's lies?

Reading Check
Where do Dexter and Judy have dinner?

16 Literary Analysis
Characterization

- Invite two students to read aloud the conversation between Dexter and Judy, with you speaking the narrator's text. **Ask** students to explain their reactions to the characters as Fitzgerald portrays them here.
  Possible response: Students will likely react with sympathy for Dexter, and with criticism for Judy's callowness.
- **Ask** students the first Literary Analysis question: What does this conversation reveal about the characters of Dexter and Judy?
  Answer: Dexter is basically honest, sympathetic, and eager to be accepted. Judy is superficial, petty, and coy, but also frank and direct.

17 Literary Analysis
Characterization and Motivation

- **Ask** students if they have ever wished someone would lie to them, perhaps to avoid facing an unpleasant truth.
- Invite a volunteer to read the bracketed text aloud. Have students think about why Dexter might be glad that Judy "had taken the trouble to lie to him."
- Then, **ask** the second Literary Analysis question: Why is Dexter so willing to accept Judy's lies?
  Answer: He wants to believe that Judy cares about him enough to protect his feelings.

18 Reading Check

Answer: They have dinner at Judy's house.

Differentiated Instruction
Solutions for All Learners

Strategy for Special Needs Students
To help students create a word picture of Judy Jones, work with them to pare Dexter's descriptions of her appearance and behavior down to a few essential words. Model this process with the description that begins Section IV. Using these word lists, lead students to see that Judy is inconsistent, indifferent, and insensitive.

Vocabulary for English Learners
Explain that *denouement,* p. 751, is a French word that literally means "untying," but it is used to refer to the final outcome or resolution of a situation. The word has been absorbed into English with its original French spelling intact. Invite any French speakers in the class to pronounce the word and use it in a sentence in French.

Enrichment for Advanced Readers
Have students look up the word *mundane,* which Judy uses to describe her reaction to a suitor's poverty. Discuss the word's connotations with students. Then, ask students to speculate about what effect Fitzgerald was trying to achieve by having Judy use this word. What image of herself is she trying to convey to Dexter?

19 Humanities

The Morning Sun 1920, by Pauline Palmer

This painting shows a young woman much like Judy Jones contemplating herself in the mirror. The artist, Pauline Palmer, was a first-generation American born to German and French parents. She studied in Chicago and Paris, where she became interested in the soft brushwork of Impressionism. Although Palmer is relatively unknown today, in her time she was hugely popular with both critics and collectors.

The Morning Sun is typical of Palmer's work, capturing mood and emotion through the use of light and color.

Use these questions for discussion:

1. If this portrait were of Judy Jones, what might the young woman be thinking at this moment?
   Answer: Judy would likely be thinking about a dress or a man—her thoughts would not be analytical or introspective.
2. How does this painting reflect the privileged world in which Judy Jones lives?
   Answer: The room is furnished with delicate fabrics and decorative objects. The woman wears impractical clothing, as if for a day of lounging and leisure.

20 Critical Viewing

Answer: The painting would show the woman's full face and more movement. It might also depict her interacting with others.

He was, as he found before the summer ended, one of a varying dozen who circulated about her. Each of them had at one time been favored above all others—about half of them still basked in the solace of occasional sentimental revivals. Whenever one showed signs of dropping out through long neglect, she granted him a brief honeyed hour, which encouraged him to tag along for a year or so longer. Judy made these forays upon the helpless and defeated without malice, indeed half unconscious that there was anything mischievous in what she did.

When a new man came to town everyone dropped out—dates were automatically canceled.

The helpless part of trying to do anything about it was that she did it all herself. She was not a girl who could be "won" in the kinetic sense—she was proof against cleverness, she was proof against charm; if any of these assailed her too strongly she would immediately resolve the affair to a physical basis, and under the magic of her physical splendor the strong as well as the brilliant played her game and not their own. She was entertained only by the gratification of her desires and by the direct exercise of her own charm. Perhaps from so much youthful love, so many youthful lovers, she had come, in self-defense, to nourish herself wholly from within.

20 ▼Critical Viewing The mood of this painting is serene. How might this portrait be different if the artist were striving to communicate Judy Jones's energy and magnetic beauty? **[Modify]**

Succeeding Dexter's first exhilaration came restlessness and dissatisfaction. The helpless ecstasy of losing himself in her was opiate rather than tonic. It was fortunate for his work during the winter that those moments of ecstasy came infrequently. Early in their acquaintance it had seemed for a while that there was a deep and spontaneous mutual attraction—that first August, for example—three days of long evenings on her dusky veranda, of strange wan kisses through the late afternoon, in shadowy alcoves or behind the protecting trellises of the garden arbors, of
21 mornings when she was fresh as a dream and almost shy at meeting him in the clarity of the rising day. There was all the ecstasy of an engagement about it, sharpened by his realization that there was no engagement. It was during those three days that, for the first time, he had asked her to marry him. She said "maybe some day," she said "kiss me," she said, "I'd like to marry you," she said "I love you"—she said—nothing.

The three days were interrupted by the arrival of a New York man who visited at her house for half September. To Dexter's agony, rumor engaged them. The man was the son of the president of a great trust company. But at

The Morning Sun, © 1920, Pauline Palmer, Rockford Art Museum

Enrichment

The Grapevine

Because Judy's suitors are obsessed by her, they continually "report" her actions to each other. Even if the information is true, remind students that this method of communication may be considered gossip and could have potentially dangerous results.

Ask students to consider how news and information travel through communities large and small. Beyond the formal channels of television, radio, and print journalism, community leaders such as school principals, police personnel, and the clergy can also distribute news. Point out that students get only a small percentage of their information through such official sources. Students may get their news in the halls between classes or in the other free time they spend with friends.

Link the discussion to the story by asking how Dexter feels about hearing that Judy dates several men. Would he have felt differently if he had *seen* newspaper photos of Judy with the many other men in her life?

the end of a month it was reported that Judy was yawning. At a dance one night she sat all evening in a motorboat with a local beau, while the New Yorker searched the club for her frantically. She told the local beau that she was bored with her visitor, and two days later he left. She was seen with him at the station, and it was reported that he looked very mournful indeed.

On this note the summer ended. Dexter was twenty-four, and he found himself increasingly in a position to do as he wished. He joined two clubs in the city and lived at one of them. Though he was by no means an integral part of the stag lines at these clubs, he managed to be on hand at dances where Judy Jones was likely to appear. He could have gone out socially as much as he liked—he was an eligible young man, now, and popular with downtown fathers. His confessed devotion to Judy Jones had rather solidified his position. But he had no social aspirations and rather despised the dancing men who were always on tap for the Thursday or Saturday parties and who filled in at dinners with the younger married set. Already he was playing with the idea of going East to New York. He wanted to take Judy Jones with him. No disillusion as to the world in which she had grown up could cure his illusion as to her desirability.

Remember that—for only in the light of it can what he did for her be understood.

Eighteen months after he first met Judy Jones he became engaged to another girl. Her name was Irene Scheerer, and her father was one of the men who had always believed in Dexter. Irene was light-haired and sweet and honorable, and a little stout, and she had two suitors whom she pleasantly relinquished when Dexter formally asked her to marry him.

Summer, fall, winter, spring, another summer, another fall—so much he had given of his active life to the incorrigible lips of Judy Jones. She had treated him with interest, with encouragement, with malice, with indifference, with contempt. She had inflicted on him the innumerable little slights and indignities possible in such a case—as if in revenge for having ever cared for him at all. She had beckoned him and yawned at him and beckoned him again and he had responded often with bitterness and narrowed eyes. She had brought him ecstatic happiness and intolerable agony of spirit. She had caused him untold inconvenience and not a little trouble. She had insulted him, and she had ridden over him, and she had played his interest in her against his interest in his work—for fun. She had done everything to him except to criticize him—this she had not done—it seemed to him only because it might have sullied the utter indifference she manifested and sincerely felt toward him.

When autumn had come and gone again it occurred to him that he could not have Judy Jones. He had to beat this into his mind but he convinced himself at last. He lay awake at night for a while and argued it over. He told himself the trouble and the pain she had caused him, he enumerated her glaring deficiencies as a wife. Then he said to himself that he loved her, and after a while he fell asleep. For a week,

Literary Analysis
Characterization What do Judy Jones's varying responses to Dexter's marriage proposals reveal about her feelings for him?

22 
Reading Check
Does Judy have more than one suitor? Explain.

21 Literary Analysis
Characterization

- Have students read the bracketed text aloud. Then, **ask** them to list the several responses Judy makes to Dexter's proposals. Point out the quotation marks that indicate Judy's words.
  Answer: She says "maybe some day," "kiss me," "I'd like to marry you," and "I love you."

➤ **Monitor Progress: Ask** students the Literary Analysis question: What do Judy Jones's varying responses to Dexter's marriage proposals reveal about her feelings for him?
Possible response: They reveal that her feelings change continually, probably as a result of how much control she's feeling over him at that moment. Her responses may also reveal that she's intentionally manipulating him or that she doesn't know her own feelings.

22 Reading Check

Answer: Yes, she has several suitors. Dexter is merely one of them.

Differentiated Instruction
Solutions for All Learners

Strategy for Less Proficient Readers
Have students create a chronology of Dexter's and Judy's relationship. Lead students in constructing the following order: Dexter and Judy meet while he is a caddy (ages 14 and 11); they meet again on the golf course (ages 23 and 20); they date for 18 months; Dexter becomes engaged to Irene Scheerer (age 25).

Vocabulary for English Learners
Review with students English words related to the passage of time. For example, clarify the difference between days, months, and seasons. Encourage students to keep careful track of when various events take place for Dexter and Judy, perhaps adding to the time line they began earlier.

Enrichment for Gifted/Talented Students
Help these students to appreciate the depth of Dexter's tumult. Despite having renounced Judy in favor of sturdy Irene Scheerer, Dexter remains painfully entranced by Judy. Challenge students to look back and read forward to find other examples of Dexter's doomed struggle to stop wanting Judy Jones.

23 Literature in Context

Fitzgerald's Elusive Women Tell students that Fitzgerald once said "Winter Dreams" was a first version of his novel *The Great Gatsby.* This explains the similarity in the characters of Judy Jones and Daisy. The men—Dexter in "Winter Dreams" and Gatsby himself—also follow similar patterns, spending their lives trying to win these elusive women. In the end, however, the fantasy of happiness and success embodied by these women is hollow, and the women merely—and painfully—human.

Connect to the Literature
Encourage students to consider Dexter's character and why he might benefit from Judy's behavior.
Possible response: No, because Judy provides Dexter with a challenge, and her behavior gives him hope that he might get the "glittering things" he desires.

24 Literary Analysis
Characterization and Motivation

- Direct students' attention to the bracketed text. Challenge them to think about times when they felt uninformed or unprepared for a conversation. What kind of image were they trying to project?
- Then, **ask** students the following question: Why does Dexter believe he should know more about books and music when in the company of Irene Scheerer?
Answer: He wants to impress her with his knowledge. Apparently, Irene is quite cultured and well-read. Dexter believes she will see his knowledge of books and music as a sign of his success.

lest he imagined her husky voice over the telephone or her eyes opposite him at lunch, he worked hard and late, and at night he went to his office and plotted out his years.

At the end of a week he went to a dance and cut in on her once. For almost the first time since they had met he did not ask her to sit out with him or tell her that she was lovely. It hurt him that she did not miss these things—that was all. He was not jealous when he saw that there was a new man tonight. He had been hardened against jealousy long before.

24 He stayed late at the dance. He sat for an hour with Irene Scheerer and talked about books and about music. He knew very little about either. But he was beginning to be master of his own time now, and he had a rather priggish[3] notion that he—the young and already fabulously successful Dexter Green—should know more about such things.

That was in October, when he was twenty-five. In January, Dexter and Irene became engaged. It was to be announced in June, and they were to be married three months later.

The Minnesota winter prolonged itself interminably, and it was almost May when the winds came soft and the snow ran down into Black Bear Lake at last. For the first time in over a year Dexter was enjoying a certain tranquillity of spirit. Judy Jones had been in Florida, and afterward in Hot Springs, and somewhere she had been engaged, and somewhere she had broken it off. At first, when Dexter had definitely given her up, it had made him sad that people still linked them together and asked for news of her, but when he began to be placed at dinner next to Irene Scheerer people didn't ask him about her any more—they told him about her. He ceased to be an authority on her.

May at last. Dexter walked the streets at night when the darkness was damp as rain, wondering that so soon, with so little done, so much of ecstasy had gone from him. May one year back had been marked by Judy's poignant, unforgivable, yet forgiven turbulence—it had been one of those rare times when he fancied she had grown to care for him. That old penny's worth of happiness he had spent for this bushel of content. He knew that Irene would be no more than a curtain spread behind him, a hand moving among gleaming teacups, a voice calling to children . . . fire and loveliness were gone, the magic of nights and the wonder of the varying hours and seasons . . . slender lips, down-turning, dropping to his lips and bearing him up into a heaven of eyes . . . The thing was deep in him. He was too strong and alive for it to die lightly.

In the middle of May when the weather balanced for a few days on the thin bridge that led to deep summer he turned in one night

3. **priggish** (prig′ gish) *adj.* excessively proper and smug.

Literature in Context

23 Cultural Connection

Fitzgerald's Elusive Women

From Daisy in *The Great Gatsby* to Judy Jones in "Winter Dreams," F. Scott Fitzgerald's fictional landscape is populated by elusive women. This theme mirrors Fitzgerald's life, which was deeply bound up in that of his wife, Zelda. When they first met, Zelda Sayre was a young Southern society girl, the darling of Montgomery, Alabama. Although Fitzgerald believed himself to be socially inferior to Zelda, he finally won her. The marriage that ensued was troubled and stormy, made more so by Zelda's mental illness. In Fitzgerald's fiction, the lovely, elusive woman becomes not only an object of desire in her own right but a symbol of all that is desirable in life.

Connect to the Literature

Do you think Dexter would be so obsessed with Judy if she had not both "beckoned him and yawned at him"? Explain.

Vocabulary Builder
poignant (poin′ yənt) *adj.* sharply painful to the feelings

at Irene's house. Their engagement was to be announced in a week now—no one would be surprised at it. And tonight they would sit together on the lounge at the University Club and look on for an hour at the dancers. It gave him a sense of solidity to go with her—she was so sturdily popular, so intensely "great."

He mounted the steps of the brownstone house and stepped inside. "Irene," he called.

Mrs. Scheerer came out of the living room to meet him.

"Dexter," she said, "Irene's gone upstairs with a splitting headache. She wanted to go with you but I made her go to bed."

"Nothing serious, I——"

"Oh, no. She's going to play golf with you in the morning. You can spare her for just one night, can't you, Dexter?"

Her smile was kind. She and Dexter liked each other. In the living room he talked for a moment before he said good night.

Returning to the University Club, where he had rooms, he stood in the doorway for a moment and watched the dancers. He leaned against the doorpost, nodded at a man or two—yawned.

"Hello, darling."

The familiar voice at his elbow startled him. Judy Jones had left a man and crossed the room to him—Judy Jones, a slender enameled doll in cloth of gold: gold in a band at her head, gold in two slipper points at her dress's hem. The fragile glow of her face seemed to blossom as she smiled at him. A breeze of warmth and light blew through the room. His hands in the pockets of his dinner jacket tightened spasmodically. He was filled with a sudden excitement.

"When did you get back?" he asked casually.

"Come here and I'll tell you about it."

She turned and he followed her. She had been away—he could have wept at the wonder of her return. She had passed through enchanted streets, doing things that were like provocative music. All mysterious happenings, all fresh and quickening hopes, had gone away with her, come back with her now.

She turned in the doorway.

"Have you a car here? If you haven't, I have."

"I have a coupé."

In then, with a rustle of golden cloth. He slammed the door. Into so many cars she had stepped—like this—like that—her back against the leather, so—her elbow resting on the door—waiting. She would have been soiled long since had there been anything to soil her—except herself—but this was her own self outpouring.

With an effort he forced himself to start the car and back into the street. This was nothing, he must remember. She had done this before, and he had put her behind him, as he would have crossed a bad account from his books.

He drove slowly downtown and, affecting abstraction, traversed the deserted streets of the business section, peopled here and there where a movie was giving out its crowd or where consumptive or

Reading Strategy
Drawing Conclusions About Characters What conclusions about Dexter's feelings for Irene do you draw from this description of "a sense of solidity"?

26 

Reading Check
What is Dexter's relationship to Irene Scheerer?

25 Reading Strategy
Drawing Conclusions About Characters

- Read the bracketed text aloud to students, striving to infuse it with Dexter's longing and sadness. **Ask** students to list the things Dexter describes losing.
  Answer: He describes losing fire, loveliness, magic, wonder, slender lips, a heaven of eyes.
- **Ask** students the Reading Strategy question: What conclusions about Dexter's feelings for Irene do you draw from this description of a "sense of solidity"?
  Answer: His feelings for Irene are not romantic. He sees her as a practical choice for a wife—reliable and trustworthy, but not exciting.

26 Reading Check

Answer: Dexter and Irene are going to announce their engagement in a week.

Differentiated Instruction Solutions for All Learners

Support for English Learners
Point out to students the sentence "That old penny's worth of happiness he had spent for this bushel of content." Help students identify the meaning of unfamiliar words. For example, confirm their understanding that a penny is a small monetary unit. Explain too that a bushel is a unit of dry measure usually reserved for grain or vegetables. It is a fairly large amount when compared to what a penny would buy. With this explanation, help students understand that Dexter has traded a tiny moment of real happiness—with Judy—for a much larger quantity of contentment—with Irene. To emphasize the comparison, help students rank the degree of meaning in "happiness" and "content." Lead them to see that happiness is a much stronger emotion or state than is contentment. Make sure students understand that Dexter feels he has settled for a practical life rather than a passionate one.

27 Reading Strategy
Drawing Conclusions About Characters

- Have students describe Judy as she appears in the passage.
  Answer: She seems pensive, sad, and vulnerable.
- **Ask** students the Reading Strategy question: Given the information Fitzgerald provides in this conversation, what can you conclude about Judy's experiences during her absence?
  Answer: You can conclude that she didn't have a very good time and that her ego was bruised in some way.

pugilistic youth lounged in front of pool halls. The clink of glasses and the slap of hands on the bars issued from saloons, cloisters of glazed glass and dirty yellow light.

She was watching him closely and the silence was embarrassing, yet in this crisis he could find no casual word with which to profane the hour. At a convenient turning he began to zigzag back toward the University Club.

"Have you missed me?" she asked suddenly.

"Everybody missed you."

He wondered if she knew of Irene Scheerer. She had been back only a day—her absence had been almost contemporaneous with his engagement.

"What a remark!" Judy laughed sadly—without sadness. She looked at him searchingly. He became absorbed in the dashboard.

"You're handsomer than you used to be," she said thoughtfully. "Dexter, you have the most rememberable eyes."

He could have laughed at this, but he did not laugh. It was the sort of thing that was said to sophomores. Yet it stabbed at him.

"I'm awfully tired of everything, darling." She called everyone darling, endowing the endearment with careless, individual camaraderie.[4] "I wish you'd marry me."

27 The directness of this confused him. He should have told her now that he was going to marry another girl, but he could not tell her. He could as easily have sworn that he had never loved her.

"I think we'd get along," she continued, on the same note, "unless probably you've forgotten me and fallen in love with another girl."

Her confidence was obviously enormous. She had said, in effect, that she found such a thing impossible to believe, that if it were true he had merely committed a childish indiscretion—and probably to show off. She would forgive him, because it was not a matter of any moment but rather something to be brushed aside lightly.

"Of course you could never love anybody but me," she continued, "I like the way you love me. Oh, Dexter, have you forgotten last year?"

"No, I haven't forgotten."

"Neither have I!"

Was she sincerely moved—or was she carried along by the wave of her own acting?

"I wish we could be like that again," she said, and he forced himself to answer:

"I don't think we can."

"I suppose not. . . . I hear you're giving Irene Scheerer a violent rush."

There was not the faintest emphasis on the name, yet Dexter was suddenly ashamed.

"Oh, take me home," cried Judy suddenly; "I don't want to go back to that idiotic dance—with those children."

Vocabulary Builder
pugilistic (pyōō´ jəl is´ tik) *adj.* looking for a fight

Reading Strategy
Drawing Conclusions About Characters Given the information Fitzgerald provides in this conversation, what can you conclude about Judy's experiences during her absence?

4. **camaraderie** (käm´ ə räd´ ə rē) *n.* warm, friendly feelings.

Enrichment

Marriage Customs

In other times and cultures Dexter would have had little to say about whether he married Judy or Irene. The choice of marriage partner is sometimes severely restricted by cultural and religious beliefs. For example, in cultures such as apartheid South Africa with very distinct ethnic and social groups, intermarriage amongst groups was strongly discouraged. In other cultures—Islam or Orthodox Judaism, for example—marriages might be arranged by parents of the couple. Even in the largely open culture of America, the idea of marrying for love without parental guidance is a fairly recent trend. Marriages have often been influenced by economic reasons, as families seek to expand holdings or shore up finances.

Ask students to contribute information about marriage customs in cultures with which they are familiar. Then, discuss with students which methods they feel are most likely to produce successful marriages.

Then, as he turned up the street that led to the residence district, Judy began to cry quietly to herself. He had never seen her cry before.

The dark street lightened, the dwellings of the rich loomed up around them, he stopped his coupé in front of the great white bulk of the Mortimer Joneses' house, somnolent, gorgeous, drenched with the splendor of the damp moonlight. Its solidity startled him. The strong walls, the steel of the girders, the breadth and beam and pomp of it were there only to bring out the contrast with the young beauty beside him. It was sturdy to accentuate her slightness—as if to show what a breeze could be generated by a butterfly's wing.

He sat perfectly quiet, his nerves in wild clamor, afraid that if he moved he would find her irresistibly in his arms. Two tears had rolled down her wet face and trembled on her upper lip.

"I'm more beautiful than anybody else," she said brokenly, "why can't I be happy?" Her moist eyes tore at his stability—her mouth turned slowly downward with an exquisite sadness: "I'd like to marry you if you'll have me, Dexter. I suppose you think I'm not worth having, but I'll be so beautiful for you, Dexter."

A million phrases of anger, pride, passion, hatred, tenderness fought on his lips. Then a perfect wave of emotion washed over him, carrying off with it a sediment of wisdom, of convention, of doubt, of honor. This was his girl who was speaking, his own, his beautiful, his pride.

"Won't you come in?" He heard her draw in her breath sharply.

Waiting.

"All right," his voice was trembling, "I'll come in."

V

It was strange that neither when it was over nor a long time afterward did he regret that night. Looking at it from the perspective of ten years, the fact that Judy's flare for him endured just one month seemed of little importance. Nor did it matter that by his yielding he subjected himself to a deeper agony in the end and gave serious hurt to Irene Scheerer and to Irene's parents, who had befriended him. There was nothing sufficiently pictorial about Irene's grief to stamp itself on his mind.

Dexter was at bottom hard-minded. The attitude of the city on his action was of no importance to him, not because he was going to leave the city, but because any outside attitude on the situation seemed superficial. He was completely indifferent to popular opinion. Nor, when he had seen that it was no use, that he did not possess in himself the power to move fundamentally or to hold Judy Jones, did he bear any malice toward her. He loved her, and he would love her until the day he was too old for loving—but he could not have her. So he tasted the deep pain that is reserved only for the strong, just as he had tasted for a little while the deep happiness. 30

Even the ultimate falsity of the grounds upon which Judy terminated the engagement that she did not want to "take him away" from

28 **Vocabulary Builder**
somnolent (säm′ nə lənt) *adj.* sleepy; drowsy

Literary Analysis
Characterization
What does this wistful remark about her lack of happiness add to Fitzgerald's portrait of Judy's character?

Reading Check
How long does Dexter's romance with Judy Jones last?

28 Vocabulary Builder

- Draw students' attention to Fitzgerald's use of the word *somnolent,* and read its definition. Then, tell students that the word derives from the Latin root *-somn-*, which means "sleep."
- Read aloud Fitzgerald's sentence containing the word *somnolent.* Invite students to describe the Mortimer Joneses' house in their own words.
- Then, **ask** this question: How does understanding the root of *somnolent* enhance your image of the house?
  Answer: Responses should recognize the house's grandeur and sense of solidity or immobility, and they should reflect students' understanding of the word *somnolent.*

29 Literary Analysis
Characterization

- Refer students to the line near the top of the page: ". . . Judy began to cry quietly to herself. He had never seen her cry before." **Ask** students what they think Judy's crying reveals about her.
  Answer: It suggests that she has had a difficult time, but also that she wants to win Dexter's sympathy.
- Have students read the bracketed text, keeping in mind that Dexter has never seen Judy cry before. Then, **ask** the Literary Analysis question: What does this wistful remark about her lack of happiness add to Fitzgerald's portrait of Judy's character?
  Answer: It adds a dimension of frailty and poignancy to Judy's character, although readers never know for sure whether Judy's unhappiness is genuine or posed.

30 Reading Check

Answer: It lasts one month.

Differentiated Instruction
Solutions for All Learners

Support for Less Proficient Readers
To help students follow the story to its conclusion, have them jot down notes while listening to the story on **Listening to Literature Audio CDs.** Encourage students to listen for Dexter's and Judy's emotions in the different stages of their relationship. Point out how little these really change.

Enrichment for Gifted/Talented Students
Invite students to explore Fitzgerald's descriptive language by rewriting the scene between Dexter and Judy that takes place in the car (pp. 756–757) as a scene from a play. Have students transform Fitzgerald's descriptions into stage directions indicating the physical environment, as well as the actors' body language and vocal inflections.

Strategy for Advanced Readers
Invite students to read back in the story and explore questions about a change in human relationships: In what ways, if any, has the relationship between Dexter and Judy changed? Do the two of them truly know each other? With these questions in mind, how do students anticipate the ending of the story?

㉛ The American Experience

The Jazz Age The Jazz Age was a time of parties and the pursuit of fun. Young men and women became increasingly rebellious, breaking long-held rules about relationships and engaging in casual love affairs without serious commitment. The eager pursuit of wealth and glamour and an increasingly flexible sense of social advancement added to the energy of the decade. When the stock market crash of 1929 ended the economic boom, social mores resumed a more sober tone. It would not be until the 1960s that a strong economy and a powerful youth culture would again challenge the traditional rules of courtship and decorum.

Connect to the Literature
Encourage students to consider each character's lifestyle and motivation. **Possible response:** If the story were set in an earlier time period, each character might not have the same aspirations or social freedoms that are possible during the time period in which the story takes place.

Irene—Judy who had wanted nothing else—did not revolt him. He was beyond any revulsion or any amusement.

He went East in February with the intention of selling out his laundries and settling in New York—but the war came to America in March and changed his plans. He returned to the West, handed over the management of the business to his partner, and went into the first officers' training camp in late April. He was one of those young thousands who greeted the war with a certain amount of relief, welcoming the liberation from webs of tangled emotion.

VI

This story is not his biography, remember, although things creep into it which have nothing to do with those dreams he had when he was young. We are almost done with them and with him now. There is only one more incident to be related here, and it happens seven years farther on.

It took place in New York, where he had done well—so well that there were no barriers too high for him. He was thirty-two years old, and, except for one flying trip immediately after the war, he had not been West in seven years. A man named Devlin from Detroit came into his office to see him in a business way, and then and there this incident occurred, and closed out, so to speak, this particular side of his life.

"So you're from the Middle West," said the man Devlin with careless curiosity. "That's funny—I thought men like you were probably born and raised on Wall Street. You know—wife of one of my best friends in Detroit came from your city. I was an usher at the wedding."

Dexter waited with no apprehension of what was coming.

"Judy Simms," said Devlin with no particular interest; "Judy Jones she was once."

"Yes, I knew her." A dull impatience spread over him. He had heard, of course, that she was married—perhaps deliberately he had heard no more.

"Awfully nice girl," brooded Devlin meaninglessly, "I'm sort of sorry for her."

"Why?" Something in Dexter was alert, receptive, at once.

"Oh, Lud Simms has gone to pieces in a way. I don't mean he ill-uses her, but he drinks and runs around——"

"Doesn't she run around?"

"No. Stays at home with her kids."

"Oh."

"She's a little too old for him," said Devlin.

"Too old!" cried Dexter. "Why, man, she's only twenty-seven."

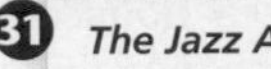

㉛ ***The Jazz Age***

When World War I ended in 1918, Americans were desperate for a good time. They roared into the 1920s at breakneck speed, overthrowing rules about clothing, decorum, and personal style. The flapper, with her short dresses, bobbed hair, and complicated social life became a symbol of the times. She rode in sporty automobiles and danced until dawn to the sounds of jazz, a new kind of music critics blamed for a loosening moral code.

F. Scott Fitzgerald's work and life reflected the gaiety of this time, as well as the emptiness many felt when their pleasure seeking did not prove satisfying. Fitzgerald was not only part of the age, he helped to shape it, naming it the Jazz Age. Through both his life and his fiction, he created some of the decade's most enduring images.

Connect to the Literature

How would this story be different if it were *not* set during the Jazz Age?

He was possessed with a wild notion of rushing out into the streets and taking a train to Detroit. He rose to his feet spasmodically.

"I guess you're busy," Devlin apologized quickly. "I didn't realize——"

"No, I'm not busy," said Dexter, steadying his voice. "I'm not busy at all. Not busy at all. Did you say she was—twenty-seven? No, I said she was twenty-seven."

"Yes, you did," agreed Devlin dryly.

"Go on, then. Go on."

"What do you mean?"

"About Judy Jones."

Devlin looked at him helplessly.

"Well, that's—I told you all there is to it. He treats her like the devil. Oh, they're not going to get divorced or anything. When he's particularly outrageous she forgives him. In fact, I'm inclined to think she loves him. She was a pretty girl when she first came to Detroit."

A pretty girl! The phrase struck Dexter as ludicrous.

"Isn't she—a pretty girl, anymore?"

"Oh, she's all right."

"Look here," said Dexter, sitting down suddenly. "I don't understand. You say she was a 'pretty girl' and now you say she's 'all right.' I don't understand what you mean—Judy Jones wasn't a pretty girl, at all. She was a great beauty. Why, I knew her. I knew her. She was ——"

Devlin laughed pleasantly.

"I'm not trying to start a row," he said. "I think Judy's a nice girl and I like her. I can't understand how a man like Lud Simms could fall madly in love with her, but he did." Then he added: "Most of the women like her."

Dexter looked closely at Devlin, thinking wildly that there must be a reason for this, some insensitivity in the man or some private malice.

"Lots of women fade just like *that*," Devlin snapped his fingers. "You must have seen it happen. Perhaps I've forgotten how pretty she was at her wedding. I've seen her so much since then, you see. She has nice eyes."

A sort of dullness settled down upon Dexter. For the first time in his life he felt like getting very drunk. He knew that he was laughing loudly at something Devlin had said, but he did not know what it was or why it was funny. When, in a few minutes, Devlin went he lay down on his lounge and looked out the window at the New York skyline into which the sun was sinking in dull lovely shades of pink and gold.

He had thought that having nothing else to lose he was invulnerable at last—but he knew that he had just lost something more, as surely as if he had married Judy Jones and seen her fade away before his eyes.

The dream was gone. Something had been taken from him. In a sort of panic he pushed the palms of his hands into his eyes and tried to bring up a picture of the waters lapping on Sherry Island and the moonlit veranda, and gingham on the golf links and the dry sun and the gold color of her neck's soft down. And her mouth damp to his kisses and her eyes plaintive with melancholy and her freshness

Literary Analysis
Characterization and Motivation Why do you think Dexter is "obsessed by a wild notion"? What need drives his behavior?

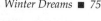

33 

According to Devlin, in what ways has Judy changed since Dexter last saw her?

32 Literary Analysis
Characterization and Motivation

- Have two volunteers act out the entire conversation between Dexter and Devlin. **Discuss** how students think Dexter feels during the conversation.
  Answer: He feels agitated.
- **Ask** students the Literary Analysis questions: Why do you think Dexter is "obsessed by a wild notion"? What need drives his behavior?
  Answer: He is so agitated by the thought of Judy Jones's beauty and spark having been diminished that he wants to go to Detroit and prove Devlin wrong. He needs to believe that Judy Jones, as he recalls her, still exists in the world.

33 Reading Check

Answer: She's become ordinary. She is no longer beautiful, and she no longer captures men's attention everywhere. Women now like her, whereas before they found her threatening.

Differentiated Instruction
Solutions for All Learners

Strategy for Less Proficient Readers
Tell students that one of the qualities that made Fitzgerald a great writer was his capacity to develop characters with psychological depth and realism. His characters can surprise readers, just as real people may do.

Draw a graphic organizer like the one shown to help students draw conclusions about Judy Jones's character: Was she a selfish person in the end? Upon what actions do students base their conclusions? Have students suggest actions to fill out both sides of the organizer. If students have trouble finding unselfish actions, remind them about the final scene of the story.

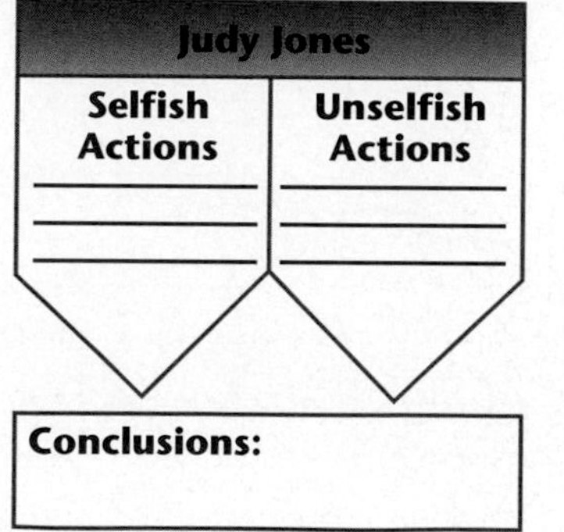

ASSESS

Answers

1. Students should support their answers with clear reasons.
2. (a) In the fall and winter, he feels melancholy but filled with hopeful fantasies. In spring, he feels dismal. (b) Dexter fantasizes about the summer and sees himself achieving success and glamour. (c) Dexter's memories of summer are idealized.
3. (a) He wants the glittering things of wealth. (b) She cares only for pleasure, for the glitter in life. Like wealth and luxury, she is tantalizing but unobtainable.
4. (a) After their first meeting, he quits his job as a caddy. After their second meeting, she becomes his new pursuit, his reason for striving. (b) She causes him to quit his caddying job, and later leads him to break off an engagement.
5. (a) Irene is sweet and honorable, pleasant-looking, and a little stout. (b) It symbolizes his abandoning his pursuit of Judy Jones and settling for a more stable life.
6. (a) He responds by dropping whatever he's doing in order to see her. (b) He is obsessed with her and the ideal that she represents to him.
7. Students may answer that many people in today's world are also obsessed with money and status.

Go Online — Author Link For additional information about F. Scott Fitzgerald, have students type in the Web Code, then select *F* from the alphabet, and then select F. Scott Fitzgerald.

like new fine linen in the morning. Why, these things were no longer in the world! They had existed and they existed no longer.

For the first time in years the tears were streaming down his face. But they were for himself now. He did not care about mouth and eyes and moving hands. He wanted to care, and he could not care. For he had gone away and he could never go back any more. The gates were closed, the sun was gone down, and there was no beauty but the gray beauty of steel that withstands all time. Even the grief he could have borne was left behind in the country of illusion, of youth, of the richness of life, where his winter dreams had flourished.

"Long ago," he said, "long ago, there was something in me, but now that thing is gone. Now that thing is gone, that thing is gone. I cannot cry. I cannot care. That thing will come back no more."

Critical Reading

1. **Respond:** Do you feel sorry for Judy? For Dexter? Explain.
2. **(a) Recall:** What emotions does Dexter feel during the different seasons of the year? **(b) Interpret:** During the winter, how does Dexter reflect upon his summer activities? **(c) Make a Judgment:** Would you say Dexter's memories of the summer are accurate or idealized? Explain.
3. **(a) Recall:** At the beginning of Section II, what does the narrator say Dexter wants? **(b) Interpret:** In what ways does Judy embody Dexter's ambitions?
4. **(a) Recall:** What actions does Dexter take as a result of his first two meetings with Judy? **(b) Connect:** Find two examples in the story that demonstrate the effects of Judy's casual decisions or behavior on Dexter's life.
5. **(a) Interpret:** What is Irene like? Briefly describe her. **(b) Draw Conclusions:** What does the decision to become engaged to Irene symbolize for Dexter?
6. **(a) Interpret:** What is Dexter's response to Judy whenever she reappears in his life? **(b) Analyze:** Why do Dexter's feelings for Judy remain unchanged even after he finally loses her?
7. **Evaluate:** Are Dexter's values and ideals influenced by the times in which he lived, or would his feelings for Judy Jones have been the same in any era? Explain.

For: More about F. Scott Fitzgerald
Visit: www.PHSchool.com
Web Code: ere-9505

Apply the Skills

Winter Dreams

Literary Analysis

Characterization

1. **(a)** Use a chart like the one shown to analyze Fitzgerald's use of **characterization** to portray Judy and Dexter. **(b)** What do you learn about the characters in each example?

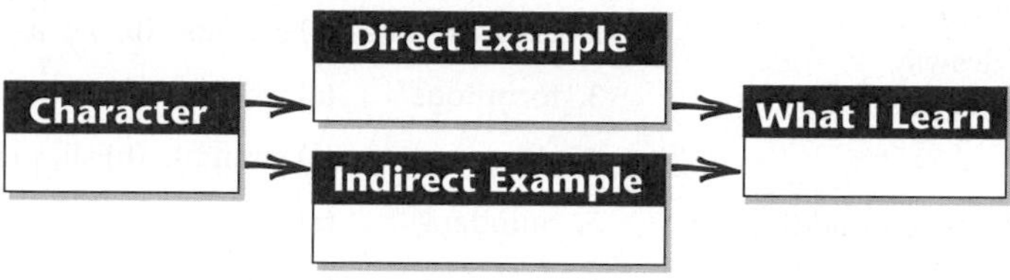

2. Note ways in which both types of characterization work together to create consistent portraits.
3. **(a)** What traits do Dexter and Judy share? **(b)** In what ways are they different? **(c)** Which details of characterization lead you to your answers?

Connecting Literary Elements

4. What details in the story reveal Dexter's **motivation** to be successful?
5. **(a)** What need drives Judy? **(b)** For what does she yearn?
6. Judy tells Dexter that she cannot be happy. In what ways does her behavior throughout the story contribute to her unhappiness?

Reading Strategy

Drawing Conclusions About Characters

7. Demonstrate what you have learned about the characters of Dexter and Judy by writing an account of their last meeting. What did they say and how did they act as their relationship ended?
8. In what ways do the characters of Dexter and Judy reflect Fitzgerald's complex views of material wealth and social status?

Extend Understanding

9. **Social Studies Connection: (a)** How do you think Fitzgerald defines the American Dream? **(b)** Do you agree with critics who have said that Fitzgerald's vision of that dream is conflicted, or divided? Explain.

QuickReview

Writers use both **direct** and **indirect** methods of **characterization** to reveal the personalities of their characters.

A character's **motivations** are the needs and desires that drive his or her behavior, thoughts, feelings, and speech.

To **draw conclusions about characters,** connect clues from the text with your own life experiences.

Go Online Assessment

For: Self-test
Visit: www.PHSchool.com
Web Code: era-6503

Answers

1. (a) and (b) Judy: Direct: Judy Jones was "not a girl who could be 'won' in the kinetic sense . . ."; Indirect: Judy Jones's treatment of Dexter at the beginning of the story; What I Learn: Judy is beautiful, unapproachable, self-centered, and insensitive; Dexter: Direct: Dexter wanted the "glittering things themselves"; Indirect: Dexter's reaction to Judy Jones at the beginning of the story reveals his pride; What I Learn: Dexter is ambitious and proud.

   Another sample answer can be found on **Literary Analysis Graphic Organizer B,** p. 160 in ***Graphic Organizer Transparencies.***
2. Direct characterization allows the author to emphasize particular characteristics or motivations. Indirect characterization makes the characters come alive through their interactions with others.
3. (a) Both are materialistic. (b) Judy comes from a wealthy background, while Dexter does not. (c) Students should use evidence from the text to support their responses.
4. He works as a caddy for extra money and is known as the best caddy at the club, a tribute to his talents and work ethic. He chooses a college for the social advancement it may provide. He works hard at his laundry.
5. (a) Judy appears to need male attention. (b) happiness
6. She continually steps on other people's feelings or needs in order to get her own way and to remain carefree and unattached.
7. Students should be able to create likely scenarios.
8. Judy and Dexter symbolize the forever divided "have's" and "have-not's" that Fitzgerald saw in the world around him. Judy reflects a lifetime of privilege and entitlement. Dexter reflects a lifetime spent striving to enter the inner circle of privilege.
9. (a) **Possible answer:** Fitzgerald saw the American Dream as the achievement of wealth and status. (b) It was conflicted. Fitzgerald saw how people's efforts to realize

Answers continued

the American Dream often resulted in the destruction of their happiness and even their lives.

Students may use the **Self-test** to prepare for **Selection Test A** or **Selection Test B.**

ASSESS/EXTEND

Answers

1 Vocabulary Lesson

Word Analysis

Check to see that students have used each word correctly.

Spelling Strategy

1. antagonistic
2. futuristic
3. angelic

Students should use each word correctly in a meaningful sentence.

Vocabulary Builder

1. a
2. a
3. b
4. a
5. b
6. a
7. b
8. a

2 Grammar and Style Lesson

1. Mr. Hart—one of those golfers who liked to yell *Fore!* at the top of their lungs—gave him a guest card to a prestigious local golf club.
2. He was glad her parents were not there—they might wonder who he was.
3. Whatever she smiled at—at him, at a chicken liver, at nothing—it disturbed him. . . .
4. He had the notion that she—and this was the strange part—actually had feelings for him.
5. "I'd like to marry you," she said "I love you"—she said—nothing.

Writing Application

Check to see that students do not overuse dashes in their descriptions.

WG **Writing and Grammar, Ruby Level**

Students will find further instruction and practice on dashes in Chapter 27, Section 5.

Build Language Skills

1 Vocabulary Lesson

Word Analysis: Latin Root *-somn-*

The word *somnolent* meaning "sleepy," is built on the Latin root *-somn-*, which means "sleep." Using each of the words defined below, write a brief paragraph about a student who keeps nodding off in class.

1. insomnia: *n.* inability to sleep
2. somnolent: *adj.* sleepy; drowsy
3. somniloquist: *n.* one who talks while asleep

Spelling Strategy

Usually, when forming adjectives by adding the suffix *-ic*, do not change the spelling of the base word: *pugilist* becomes *pugilistic.* Add *-ic* to the words below. Then, use each adjective in a sentence.

1. antagonist **2.** futurist **3.** angel

Vocabulary Builder: Antonyms

Review the vocabulary list on page 741. Then, choose the letter of the word that is the better antonym, or word of opposite meaning, for each numbered word.

1. fallowness **(a)** activity, **(b)** emptiness
2. preposterous **(a)** serious, **(b)** sarcastic
3. fortuitous **(a)** wealthy, **(b)** cursed
4. sinuous **(a)** straight, **(b)** slippery
5. mundane **(a)** legal, **(b)** amazing
6. poignant **(a)** dull, **(b)** moving
7. pugilistic **(a)** tough, **(b)** peace-loving
8. somnolent **(a)** alert, **(b)** hard

2 Grammar and Style Lesson

Dashes

Dashes (—) are a form of punctuation that create a longer, more emphatic pause than commas. They signal information that interrupts the flow of text. Dashes can indicate an abrupt change of thought, a dramatic interrupting idea, or a summary statement.

In Fitzgerald's story, dashes draw readers' attention to the information they set off. Look at this example:

Example: When he was twenty-three, Mr. Hart—one of the gray-haired men who liked to say "Now *there's* a boy"—gave him a guest card to the Sherry Island Golf Club for a weekend.

Practice Insert dashes where necessary in the following sentences.

1. Mr. Hart one of those golfers who like to yell *Fore!* at the top of their lungs gave him a guest card to a prestigious local golf club.
2. He was glad her parents were not there they might wonder who he was.
3. Whatever she smiled at him, at a chicken liver, at nothing it disturbed him . . .
4. He had the notion that she and this was the strange part actually had feelings for him.
5. "I'd like to marry you," she said "I love you" she said nothing.

Writing Application Write a brief description of someone you admire. Use dashes to set off a few pieces of information you want readers to notice.

WG *Prentice Hall Writing and Grammar Connection: Chapter 27, Section 5*

Assessment Practice

Analyze Sentence Meaning

On many standardized tests, students are asked to correctly answer sentence-completion questions. Use the following example to show students how to use the meaning of a sentence to choose the word that best completes the passage.

F. Scott Fitzgerald was able to successfully capture the glittering and _______ lifestyle of the Roaring Twenties. Like many of his characters, he longed to attain the wealth and social status of the upper class.

(For more practice, see the *Standardized Test Preparation Workbook*, p. 43)

Select the word that best completes the sentence:

A repressed **C** simplistic
B materialistic **D** frugal

The meaning of the second sentence supports answer *B, materialistic,* as the most logical answer. Answer choices *C* and *D* contradict the second sentence, and choice *A, repressed,* does not fit with the meaning of *glittering.*

❸ Writing Lesson

Timed Writing: Character Analysis

Fitzgerald portrays Dexter Green as a fully rounded character with believable thoughts, feelings, strengths, and weaknesses. Explore Dexter's behavior and motivations in a character analysis. Support your ideas with examples from the story. ***(40 minutes)***

Prewriting *(10 minutes)* Scan the story for examples of Dexter's appearance, words, actions, and motivations. Note how he changes during the story, and then decide whether Dexter's actions are heroic or simply foolish.

Drafting *(20 minutes)* In your introduction, name the author, title, and featured character, and then state your main idea. Describe Dexter's behavior with specific examples and quotations to support your analysis.

Model: Elaborating for Information

Dexter is an outsider looking in on an elegant world. He is so close to it he can almost touch it, and that combination of proximity and distance drives him. As Fitzgerald tells us, "He wanted not association with glittering things and glittering people—he wanted the glittering things themselves."

Direct quotations from the text provide support for the analysis.

Revising *(10 minutes)* Make sure your essay clearly communicates your opinion. Where needed, add quotations or other details to support your points.

WG *Prentice Hall Writing and Grammar Connection: Chapter 14, Section 3*

Extend Your Learning

Listening and Speaking Select a song that might remind Dexter of Judy. Play the song for the class and give a **presentation** about why it is appropriate. Use these tips to guide your work:

- Consider both current music and music from the Jazz Age.
- Speak from notes rather than a script.
- Respond to the audience's questions and feedback about your choice of song.

Conclude by addressing the relationship between music and emotions.

Research and Technology Using a variety of sources, research the lives of F. Scott and Zelda Fitzgerald. Then, write a **report** on their relationship and lifestyle. Incorporate various critical views of the connections between F. Scott's relationship with Zelda and his fiction. Then, take a position to explain which one seems most accurate to you.

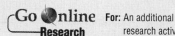

For: An additional research activity
Visit: www.PHSchool.com
Web Code: erd-7503

Assessment Resources

The following resources can be used to assess students' knowledge and skills.

Unit 5 Resources
- **Selection Test A,** pp. 49–51
- **Selection Test B,** pp. 52–54

General Resources
- **Rubrics for Response to Literature,** pp. 65–66

Go Online Assessment Students may use the **Self-test** to prepare for **Selection Test A** or **Selection Test B.**

❸ Writing Lesson

You may use this Writing Lesson as timed-writing practice, or you may allow students to develop it as a writing assignment over several days.

- To guide students in writing their character analyses, give them the **Support for Writing Lesson** page (***Unit 5 Resources,*** p. 46).
- Review the Literary Analysis, Connecting Literary Elements, and Reading Strategy instruction to refresh students' understanding of the elements of literary characters.
- Read through the Writing Lesson steps with students, and clarify any confusion.
- Urge students to focus on developing a central idea about Dexter's character. They can then focus on details that support their main idea.
- Use the Response to Literature Rubrics in ***General Resources,*** pp. 65–66 to evaluate students' analyses.

❹ Listening and Speaking

- Provide, or direct students to sources of Jazz Age music. Point out, however, that students may wish to use contemporary music or music from another time period. Suggest online or local music libraries where students can hear many options.
- Encourage students to play the song in its entirety before they begin speaking and then to play it again in portions as they discuss it.
- The **Support for Extend Your Learning** page (***Unit 5 Resources,*** p. 47) provides guided note-taking opportunities to help students complete the Extend Your Learning activities.

Go Online Research Have students type in the Web Code for another research activity.

Meeting Your Standards

Students will

1. **analyze and respond to literary elements.**
   - Literary Analysis: Theme
2. **read, comprehend, analyze, and critique a short story.**
   - Reading Strategy: Finding Clues to Theme
   - Reading Check questions
   - Apply the Skills questions
   - Assessment Practice (ATE)
3. **develop vocabulary.**
   - Vocabulary Lesson: Latin Prefix: *pro-*
4. **understand and apply written and oral language conventions.**
   - Spelling Strategy
   - Grammar and Style Lesson: Parallel Structure
5. **develop writing proficiency.**
   - Writing Lesson: Essay About Historical Context
6. **develop appropriate research strategies.**
   - Extend Your Learning: Cartoon Strip
7. **understand and apply listening and speaking strategies.**
   - Extend Your Learning: Interview

Block Scheduling: Use one 90-minute class period to preteach the skills and have students read the selection. Use a second 90-minute class period to assess students' mastery of skills, extend their learning, and monitor their progress.

Homework Suggestions

Following are possibilities for homework assignments.

- Support pages from ***Unit 5 Resources:***
  Literary Analysis
  Reading Strategy
  Vocabulary Builder
  Grammar and Style
- An Extend Your Learning project and the Writing Lesson for this selection group may be completed over several days.

Step-by-Step Teaching Guide	Pacing Guide
PRETEACH	
• Administer Vocabulary and Reading Warm-ups as necessary.	5 min.
• Engage students' interest with the motivation activity.	5 min.
• Read and discuss author, and background, features. **FT**	10 min.
• Introduce the Literary Analysis Skill: Theme. **FT**	5 min.
• Introduce the Reading Strategy: Finding Clues to Theme. **FT**	10 min.
• Prepare students to read by teaching the selection vocabulary. **FT**	
TEACH	
• Informally monitor comprehension while students read independently or in groups. **FT**	30 min.
• Monitor students' comprehension with the Reading Check notes.	as students read
• Reinforce vocabulary with Vocabulary Builder notes.	as students read
• Develop students' understanding of theme with the Literary Analysis annotations. **FT**	5 min.
• Develop students' ability to find clues to theme with the Reading Strategy annotations. **FT**	5 min.
ASSESS/EXTEND	
• Assess students' comprehension and mastery of the Literary Analysis and Reading Strategy by having them answer the Apply the Skills questions. **FT**	15 min.
• Have students complete the Vocabulary Lesson and the Grammar and Style Lesson. **FT**	15 min.
• Apply students' ability to provide internal documentation in writing by using the Writing Lesson. **FT**	45 min. or homework
• Apply students' understanding by using one or more of the Extend Your Learning activities.	20–90 min. or homework
• Administer Selection Test A or Selection Test B. **FT**	15 min.

Resources

PRINT

Unit 5 Resources

Vocabulary Warm-up Word Lists **[L1, L2, EL]** .... p. 55
Vocabulary Warm-up Practice **[L1, L2, EL]** .... p. 56
Reading Warm-up A **[L1, L2, EL]** .... p. 57
Reading Warm-up B **[L1, L2, L3]** .... p. 58

TRANSPARENCY

Graphic Organizer Transparencies

Literary Analysis Graphic Organizer A **[L3]** .... p. 163
Literary Analysis Graphic Organizer B **[L1, L2, EL]** .... p. 164
Reading Strategy Graphic Organizer A **[L3]** .... p. 161
Reading Strategy Graphic Organizer B **[L1, L2, EL]** .... p. 162

PRINT

Reader's Notebook [L2]
Reader's Notebook: Adapted Version [L1]
Reader's Notebook: English Learner's Version [EL]

Unit 5 Resources

Literary Analysis **[L3]** .... p. 59
Reading Strategy **[L3]** .... p. 60
Vocabulary Builder **[L3]** .... p. 61

TECHNOLOGY

Listening to Literature Audio CDs [L2, EL]
Reader's Notebook: Adapted Version Audio CD [L1, L2]

PRINT

Unit 5 Resources

Grammar and Style **[L3]** .... p. 62
Support for Writing Lesson **[L3]** .... p. 63
Support for Extend Your Learning **[L3]** .... p. 64
Enrichment **[L4]** .... p. 65
Selection Test A **[L1, L2, EL]** .... pp. 66–68
Selection Test B **[L3, L4]** .... pp. 69–71

General Resources

Rubrics for Research: Research Report **[L3]** .... pp. 49–50

TRANSPARENCY

Graphic Organizer Transparencies

Outline **[L3]** .... p. 309

TECHNOLOGY

Go Online: Research **[L3]**
Go Online: Self-test **[L3]**
***ExamView*® Test Bank [L3]**

Choosing Resources for Differentiated Instruction

[L1] Special Needs Students
[L2] Below-Level Students
[L3] All Students
[L4] Advanced Students
[EL] English Learners

For Vocabulary and Reading Warm-ups and for Selection Tests, **A** signifies "less challenging" and **B** "more challenging." For Graphic Organizer transparencies, **A** signifies "not filled in" and **B** "filled in."

FT Fast Track Instruction: To move the lesson more quickly, use the strategies and activities identified with **FT**.

Scaffolding for Less Proficient and Advanced Students

The leveled Critical Thinking questions after selections progress in the levels of thinking required to answer them. To address the needs of your different students, you may use the (a) level questions for your less proficient students and the (b) level questions with your on-level and advanced students. The occasional (c) level questions are appropriate for your advanced students.

Go Online Professional Development
For: Information about Lexiles
Visit: www.PHSchool.com
Web Code: eue-1111

PRETEACH

Motivation

Students can appreciate this "Little Engine That Could" story on two levels: as a highly detailed and literal account of a turtle's efforts to cross the road and as a thematic statement about the human struggles of the Great Depression. You might engage students' interest in the story by focusing on the first level. Read aloud the following passages:

"As the embankment grew steeper and steeper, the more frantic were the efforts of the land turtle."

"Pushing hind legs strained and slipped. . . ."

"Little by little the shell slid up the embankment . . ."

Ask students whether they think the turtle will succeed in climbing the embankment. Invite students to empathize with the turtle as they read the story.

❶ Background

More About the Author

Steinbeck wrote in many genres. For example, in addition to the novels and short stories for which he is famous, Steinbeck wrote screenplays. His novel *The Grapes of Wrath* was made into a hugely successful film and led to several screenwriting assignments for the author. In particular, Steinbeck received critical praise for his *Viva Zapata!* screenplay. He also developed screenplays for the film adaptations of his stories "The Pearl" and "The Red Pony." In addition, Steinbeck wrote travel sketches, served as a war correspondent in World War II, and wrote nonfiction social commentaries that often formed the basis for his fiction.

Build Skills | Fiction

❶ The Turtle *from* The Grapes of Wrath

John Steinbeck (1902–1968)

No writer captures more vividly than John Steinbeck what it was like to live through the Great Depression of the 1930s.

His stories and novels, many of which are set in the agricultural region of northern California where he grew up, capture the poverty, desperation, and social injustice experienced by many working-class Americans during this bleak period in our nation's history. As in the works of Naturalist writers like Stephen Crane and Jack London, Steinbeck's characters struggle desperately against forces beyond their understanding or control. Many of those characters suffer tragic fates, yet they almost always manage to exhibit bravery and retain a sense of dignity throughout their struggles. Steinbeck's ability to combine harsh critiques of the political and social systems of his times with genuine artistry in his characterization, plot, and language is unique in American literature.

Modest Beginnings Steinbeck was born in Salinas, California, the son of a county official and a schoolteacher. By his late teens, he was already supporting himself by working as a laborer. After graduating from high school, he enrolled at Stanford University. He left before graduating, however, and spent the next five years drifting across the country, working in a variety of odd jobs, including fish hatcher, fruit picker, laboratory assistant, surveyor, apprentice painter, and journalist. Through these experiences, Steinbeck discovered firsthand what it means to survive by manual labor. He also gathered material that he would later use in his books to create authentic portraits of working-class life.

First Success Steinbeck's first three books received little—or negative—attention from critics. However, this changed in 1935 when he published *Tortilla Flat,* his fourth book. The book received the California Commonwealth Club's Gold Medal for best novel by a California author. Two years later, the author earned even greater recognition and acclaim with *Of Mice and Men* (1937). This novel, which portrays two migrant workers whose dream of owning a farm ends in tragedy, became a best-seller and was made into a Broadway play and a movie.

The Great American Novel Steinbeck went on to write what is generally regarded as his finest novel. *The Grapes of Wrath* (1939) is the historically authentic story of the Joad family, Oklahoma farmers dispossessed of their land and forced to become migrant farmers in California. "The Turtle" is an excerpt from the opening pages of this novel, which won the National Book Award and the Pulitzer Prize. The book aroused public sympathy for the plight of migratory farm workers and established Steinbeck as one of the most highly regarded writers of his day.

Steinbeck produced several more successful works during his later years, including *Cannery Row* (1945), *The Pearl* (1947), *East of Eden* (1952), and *The Winter of Our Discontent* (1961). In 1962, he received the Nobel Prize for Literature. In accepting that award, Steinbeck noted his belief that literature can sustain people through hard times. He added that it is the writer's responsibility to celebrate the human "capacity for greatness of heart and spirit—for gallantry in defeat, for courage, compassion and love. In the endless war against weakness and despair, these are the bright rally flags of hope and of emulation." Steinbeck's belief in social justice, and in the human ability to learn from and rise above suffering, infused all his work.

Preview

Connecting to the Literature

Sometimes, a single event can seem to mirror all of life. For example, one long and complicated journey with many detours and wrong turns might be seen as representing the experience of growing up. As you read this selection, think about how the small events it describes could represent something much bigger.

❷ Literary Analysis

Theme

John Steinbeck's narrative about a brief episode in a turtle's life conveys an important **theme,** or insight into life. An author's theme is rarely directly stated. Instead, it is revealed indirectly through these means:

- Characters' comments and actions
- Events in the plot
- The use of literary devices, such as symbols

Sometimes, even small details can serve an important role in conveying a theme, and deserve attention as you read.

Connecting Literary Elements

At first glance, this is just a simple story about a turtle. However, when looked at symbolically, the story grows in power and meaning. Steinbeck's use of **symbols**—people, places, or things that represent something larger than their literal meanings—helps to communicate his theme. To understand the story's symbolism, think about the qualities Steinbeck attributes to each person, place, animal, or object, and how each one might represent some aspect of life.

❸ Reading Strategy

Finding Clues to Theme

To interpret the theme of a story, become a literary detective. Look carefully for **clues to the theme** in the writer's use of symbols, his or her choice of details, and the ways characters react to one another. For example, Steinbeck includes only slight descriptions of how two motorists react when they spot the turtle. As brief as they are, these descriptions provide important clues to the theme. When you encounter such clues, consider the broader or underlying meanings they suggest. Gather clues in a chart like the one shown.

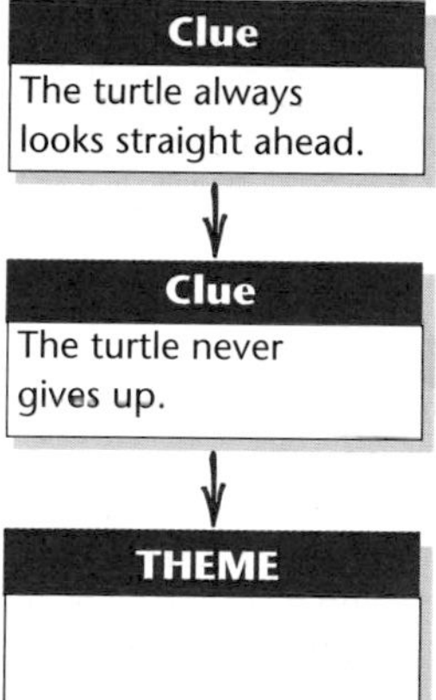

Clue
The turtle always looks straight ahead.
Clue
The turtle never gives up.
THEME

Vocabulary Builder

embankment (em baŋk′ mənt) *n.* mound of earth or stone built to hold back water or support a roadway (p. 767)

protruded (prō tro͞od′ id) *v.* pushed or thrust outward (p. 767)

Differentiated Instruction

Solutions for All Learners

Support for Special Needs Students
Have students read the adapted version of the excerpt from "The Turtle" from *The Grapes of Wrath* in the ***Reader's Notebook: Adapted Version.*** This version provides basic-level instruction in an interactive format with questions and write-on lines. Completing these pages will prepare students to read the selection in the Student Edition.

Support for Less Proficient Readers
Have students read the excerpt from "The Turtle" from *The Grapes of Wrath* in the ***Reader's Notebook.*** This version provides basic-level instruction in an interactive format with questions and write-on lines. After students finish the selection in the ***Reader's Notebook,*** have them complete the questions and activities in the Student Edition.

Support for English Learners
Have students read the excerpt from "The Turtle" from *The Grapes of Wrath* in the ***Reader's Notebook: English Learner's Version.*** This version provides basic-level instruction in an interactive format with questions and write-on lines. Completing these pages will prepare students to read the selection in the Student Edition.

❷ Literary Analysis

Theme

- Tell students that as they read "The Turtle," they will focus on theme, an important insight into life that is usually conveyed indirectly in a literary work.
- Read aloud the instruction on theme. Draw students' attention to the ways in which theme can be implied through various story elements. To emphasize this point, discuss how all the passages students heard in the Motivation activity suggest a theme of struggle.
- Use the instruction for Connecting Literary Elements to help students recognize symbols that may suggest theme. Invite students' ideas about what the turtle might symbolize.

❸ Reading Strategy

Finding Clues to Theme

- Tell students that because writers do not state themes directly, readers must make inferences from clues in the text. Remind students of previous instruction on making inferences and stress that finding clues to theme follows a similar process.
- To find clues to theme, readers must approach each portion of text on multiple levels: literal, figurative, and thematic. Tell students to read the story several times, on each occasion seeking a different level of understanding.
- Give students a copy of **Reading Strategy Graphic Organizer A,** p. 161 in ***Graphic Organizer Transparencies,*** to record thematic clues as they read "The Turtle."

Vocabulary Builder

- Pronounce each vocabulary word for students, and read the definitions as a class. Have students identify any words with which they are already familiar.

❼ Literary Analysis
Theme and Symbol

- Direct students to reread the bracketed passage and to paraphrase the events it describes.
  Answer: The turtle is hit by a truck, rights itself, and continues on.
- Have students offer a definition of *symbol.* Ask students if they think the turtle's actions are symbolic.

▶**Monitor Progress Ask** students the Literary Analysis question: What symbolic meaning might be given to the turtle's actions after it is hit by the truck?
Answer: Even the most difficult of challenges—including the threat of injury or death—can be overcome through patience and persistence.

ASSESS
Answers

1. Students may report that they felt anxious about the turtle's success.
2. (a) The turtle encounters the highway embankment, parapet, the hot surface of the road, and two vehicles. (b) The vehicles are the most dangerous.
3. (a) In the first encounter, the turtle is unharmed though startled into its shell. In the second encounter, the turtle is struck and knocked off the highway. (b) The first driver is careful and kind, swerving to avoid the turtle. The second driver is angry and cruel, and intentionally strikes the turtle.
4. (a) It is crushed by the turtle's shell. (b) The turtle can defend itself well against dangers of certain kinds.
5. (a) The seed is planted.
   (b) **Possible answer:** He is suggesting that different forms of life interact, even helping each other overcome obstacles.
6. **Possible answer:** Yes, the turtle makes a good symbol because he encounters many obstacles yet perseveres and finally succeeds.

tipped to an angle so that the front legs could not reach the level cement plain. But higher and higher the hind legs boosted it, until at last the center of balance was reached, the front tipped down, the front legs scratched at the pavement, and it was up. But the head of wild oats was held by its stem around the front legs.

Now the going was easy, and all the legs worked, and the shell boosted along, waggling from side to side. A sedan driven by a forty-year-old woman approached. She saw the turtle and swung to the right, off the highway, the wheels screamed and a cloud of dust boiled up. Two wheels lifted for a moment and then settled. The car skidded back onto the road, and went on, but more slowly. The turtle had jerked into its shell, but now it hurried on, for the highway was burning hot.

❼ And now a light truck approached, and as it came near, the driver saw the turtle and swerved to hit it. His front wheel struck the edge of the shell, flipped the turtle like a tiddly-wink, spun it like a coin, and rolled it off the highway. The truck went back to its course along the right side. Lying on its back, the turtle was tight in its shell for a long time. But at last its legs waved in the air, reaching for something to pull it over. Its front foot caught a piece of quartz and little by little the shell pulled over and flopped upright. The wild oat head fell out and three of the spearhead seeds stuck in the ground. And as the turtle crawled on down the embankment, its shell dragged dirt over the seeds. The turtle entered a dust road and jerked itself along, drawing a wavy shallow trench in the dust with its shell. The old humorous eyes looked ahead, and the horny beak opened a little. His yellow toe nails slipped a fraction in the dust.

Literary Analysis
Theme and Symbol What symbolic meaning might be given to turtle's actions after it is hit by the truck?

Critical Reading

1. **Respond:** How did you feel as you watched the turtle proceed?
2. **(a) Recall:** What obstacles does the turtle encounter?
   (b) Make a Judgment: Which of these is most dangerous?
3. **(a) Recall:** What happens to the turtle in his encounter with the two drivers? **(b) Compare and Contrast:** Based on their actions, what kinds of people do the two drivers seem to be?
4. **(a) Recall:** What happens to the red ant that slips inside the turtle's shell? **(b) Distinguish:** What does this event suggest about the turtle's capacity to defend itself?
5. **(a) Recall:** What happens to the wild oat head at the end of the story? **(b) Analyze:** What is the author suggesting about the relationships between different forms of life?
6. **Evaluate:** Do you think the turtle makes an effective symbol of the struggles of ordinary people? Explain.

For: More about John Steinbeck
Visit: www.PHSchool.com
Web Code: ere-9506

Go Online Author Link — For additional information about John Steinbeck, have students type in the Web Code, then select *S* from the alphabet, and then select John Steinbeck.

Apply the Skills

The Turtle* from *The Grapes of Wrath

Literary Analysis

Theme

1. What parallels do you see between the experiences of the turtle and human experiences?
2. In what way are the wild oat seeds related to the story's **theme**?
3. What connection do the images from the beginning of the story of "sleeping life waiting to be spread" have to the story's theme?
4. Using your answers to questions 1–3, state the story's theme.

Connecting Literary Elements

5. Knowing that this story served as the introduction to *The Grapes of Wrath,* a novel about a displaced Depression-era farming family seeking a better life, what do you think the turtle **symbolizes**?
6. **(a)** Use a chart like the one shown to examine the turtle's actions at each stage of its journey. **(b)** What does the turtle's journey symbolize?

	Obstacles	Turtle's Reactions	Symbolic Meaning
Climbs Embankment			
Crosses Road			

Reading Strategy

Finding Clues to Theme

7. Steinbeck uses the words *dragging, turning aside for nothing,* and *thrashed slowly* to describe the turtle. **(a)** What effect do these words have on your perception of the turtle? **(b)** How do you think Steinbeck wants readers to respond to the turtle?
8. **(a)** Which characters can be seen as representing nature—or the simple life—and which represent the modern world? Explain. **(b)** Which does Steinbeck likely feel is more important? Explain.

Extend Understanding

9. **Career Connection:** Which of the turtle's personal qualities would be advantageous or disadvantageous in today's business world? Explain.

QuickReview

A story's **theme** is its central message.

Symbols are people, places, or things that represent ideas or qualities larger than their literal meanings.

To **find clues to theme,** consider the details a writer provides and identify their underlying meaning.

For: Self-test
Visit: www.PHSchool.com
Web Code: era-6504

Go Online Assessment Students may use the **Self-test** to prepare for **Selection Test A** or **Selection Test B.**

Answers

1. The turtle faces obstacles that seem almost insurmountable. Life presents people with challenges that are equally daunting.
2. The wild oat seed represents potential life which is surprisingly adaptable and resilient. The turtle's struggle allows the seed to be planted and therefore succeed. This symbolizes the larger theme of success through struggle.
3. These images suggest the latent power and abundance of all forms of life, even those that seem fragile.
4. **Possible answer:** Life is difficult, but obstacles—including those presented by the modern world—can be overcome.
5. **Possible answer:** The turtle symbolizes those who were poor and struggling during the Great Depression.
6. (a) Climbs Embankment: Obstacles: steep sides, the parapet; Turtle's Reactions: stubborn persistence and sheer determination; Symbolic Meaning: determination people summon when facing "uphill" battles; Crosses Road: Obstacles: traffic; Reactions: retreats into shell, then regroups and goes on; Symbolic Meaning: Even when it seems impossible, keep trying (b) The turtle's journey symbolizes the struggles of people facing terrible obstacles during the Great Depression.

   Another sample answer can be found on **Literary Analysis Graphic Organizer B,** p. 164 in ***Graphic Organizer Transparencies.***
7. (a) These words personify the turtle and make readers perceive it as a fighter. (b) He wants them to be sympathetic toward it.
8. (a) The turtle and the woman who swerves to avoid it can be seen as representing nature and the simple life. The truck driver may represent the modern world. (b) Steinbeck probably feels nature is more important.
9. The turtle's persistence would be advantageous in today's complex business world. His slow speed might be seen as a disadvantage.

EXTEND/ASSESS

Answers

❶ Vocabulary Lesson

Word Analysis

1. *Project* means "to plan or look ahead"; We *project* high sales next quarter.
2. *Proceed* means "to continue forward"; *Proceed* to the next corner and turn left.
3. *Progress* means "to move forward"; The turtle *progressed* steadily up the hill.
4. *Prohibit* means "to forbid or keep from moving forward"; Because of the danger they present, we *prohibit* trucks on this road.
5. *Produce* means "to generate"; The turtle's persistence will *produce* success in the end.
6. *Propose* means "to suggest a plan"; I *propose* using the turtle's experience as an example.

Vocabulary Builder

1. False 2. True

Spelling Strategy

1. no 2. no 3. yes

❷ Grammar and Style Lesson

1. for animals; for the wind, for a man's trouser cuff
2. turning; dragging
3. struck the edge; flipped the turtle; spun it; rolled
4. . . .ants and ant lions to set traps; grasshoppers to jump
5. into the shell, into the soft skin

Writing Application

Paragraphs should contain at least three examples of parallel structure. Students should be able to identify these examples in discussion.

Build Language Skills

❶ Vocabulary Lesson

Word Analysis: Latin Prefix *pro-*

In this story, John Steinbeck uses the word *protruded,* which begins with the Latin prefix *pro-*, meaning "forward." Knowing this meaning helps you to define the whole word *protruded,* which means "thrust forward," and other words beginning with the prefix *pro-*.

Add the prefix *pro-* to the word roots below. Then, define each word and use it in a sentence.

1. *-ject*
2. *-ceed*
3. *-gress*
4. *-hibit*
5. *-duce*
6. *-pose*

Vocabulary Builder: True or False?

Use your knowledge of the words from the vocabulary list on page 765 to decide whether these statements are true or false.

1. An *embankment* is at the bottom of a lake.
2. When the cat's paw *protruded,* it stuck out.

Spelling Strategy

In some words, removing the prefix or suffix leaves only a word part. For each of the following words, note whether or not the underlined prefix or suffix can be removed to make a base word.

1. terr<u>ify</u> **2.** aggress<u>or</u> **3.** <u>im</u>possible

❷ Grammar and Style Lesson

Parallel Structure

Parallel structure is the expression of similar ideas using similar grammatical form. Parallel structures can involve the use of adjectives, verbs, phrases, or entire sentences.

The use of parallel structures helps to emphasize key ideas and link similar concepts. In "The Turtle," John Steinbeck uses numerous parallel structures to add sophistication to his writing and to indicate the connection between actions and ideas. Look at these examples.

Adjectives: The concrete highway was edged with a mat of *tangled, broken, dry* grass . . .

Infinitive Phrases: . . . the grass heads were heavy with oat beards *to catch* on a dog's coat, and foxtails *to tangle* in a horse's fetlocks, and clover burrs *to fasten* in sheep's wool . . .

Practice Identify the parallel grammatical elements in each sentence.

1. . . . all waiting for animals and for the wind, for a man's trouser cuff . . .
2. . . . a land turtle crawled, turning aside for nothing, dragging his high-domed shell over the grass.
3. His front wheel struck the edge of the shell, flipped the turtle like a tiddly-wink, spun it like a coin, and rolled it off the highway.
4. . . . ants and ant lions to set traps for them, grasshoppers to jump into the air . . .
5. A red ant ran into the shell, into the soft skin . . .

Writing Application Write a short description of a natural event, like a storm or a flight of geese. Use parallel structure to call attention to the key details in your description.

WG Prentice Hall Writing and Grammar Connection: Chapter 20, Section 6

Assessment Practice

Analyze Sentence Meaning **(For more practice, see *Standardized Test Preparation Workbook*, p.44.)**

Many tests require students to correctly answer sentence-completion questions. Often, more than one choice can complete a sentence. Use the following sample item to show students how to analyze sentence meaning, decide whether it is positive or negative, and eliminate choices that have the opposite sense.

John Steinbeck captured the poverty and desperation experienced by many Americans during the Great Depression, a(n) ________ period in our nation's history.

A comfortable **C** bleak
B inconvenient **D** prosperous

The context of the sentence indicates that the correct answer will have a negative connotation, so *A* and *D* are eliminated. Answer choice *B* is too mild to compare to the words *poverty* and *desperation.* **C** is the best choice.

❸ Writing Lesson

Essay About Historical Context

John Steinbeck wrote "The Turtle" as a prelude for his novel *The Grapes of Wrath*, which portrays the struggles of a Depression-era farm family. Steinbeck intended that readers draw parallels between the prelude and the novel. Write an essay connecting the events described in "The Turtle" to the lives of ordinary people during the Great Depression.

Prewriting Research the Great Depression to learn how people reacted to adverse economic circumstances. Then, review "The Turtle" and draw parallels.

Drafting First, provide information about the Depression. In your body paragraphs, note facts and data and explain parallels you found to "The Turtle." Cite the sources of these facts as you draft.

Model: Providing Internal Documentation

The Great Depression of the 1930s was a time of economic disaster. Stock prices fell 40 percent, 9,000 banks failed, and 9 million savings accounts were wiped out. (*http://www.britannica.com,* Great Depression*)*

When citing sources within the essay, include source information parenthetically.

Revising Review your essay. Make sure that you have provided enough historical context to support your observations. Add information as needed, and provide correct citations about where you found the material.

WG *Prentice Hall Writing and Grammar Connection: Chapter 12, Section 5*

Extend Your Learning

Listening and Speaking After preparing a list of questions, conduct an **interview** with someone who lived through the Great Depression. Share your findings with the class. Use the following tips:

- Come to the interview with a tape recorder and writing materials.
- Request your subject's permission to record the conversation.

Frame your post-interview presentation with an engaging introduction and conclusion.

Research and Technology With a partner, pare "The Turtle" down to its essential thematic message. Write and illustrate a **cartoon strip** conveying that message. If possible, use graphic arts software to lay out and generate your cartoon. **[Group Activity]**

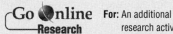

For: An additional research activity
Visit: www.PHSchool.com
Web Code: erd-7504

Assessment Resources

The following resources can be used to assess students' knowledge and skills.

Unit 5 Resources
- **Selection Test A,** pp. 66–68
- **Selection Test B,** pp. 69–71

General Resources
- **Rubrics for Research: Research Report,** pp. 49–50

Go Online Assessment Students may use the **Self-test** to prepare for **Selection Test A** or **Selection Test B.**

❸ Writing Lesson

- Review possible research sources with students, including the use of search engines for online research.
- To guide students in writing their essays about historical context, give them the **Support for Writing Lesson** page (***Unit 5 Resources,*** p. 63).
- Suggest they use the Outline graphic organizer on p. 309 in ***Graphic Organizer Transparencies.***
- Read through the Writing Lesson steps with students and clarify any questions.
- Urge students to use descriptive details to convey information about the Great Depression in a vivid manner.
- Use the Research: Research Report rubrics in ***General Resources,*** pp. 49–50 to evaluate students' essays.

❹ Research and Technology

- Refer students to the Literary Analysis and Reading Strategy instruction for help in identifying the essential thematic message of the story.
- Emphasize that drawing ability will not be evaluated and that students may draw manually or electronically.
- Suggest that students use slideshow software to animate their cartoons.
- The **Support for Extend Your Learning** page (***Unit 5 Resources,*** p. 64) provides guided note-taking opportunities to help students complete the Extend Your Learning activities.

Go Online Research Have students type in the Web Code for another research activity.

Meeting Your Standards

Students will

1. **analyze and respond to literary elements.**
   - Literary Analysis: Satire
2. **read, comprehend, analyze, and critique poetry.**
   - Reading Strategy: Relating Structure to Meaning
   - Reading Check questions
   - Apply the Skills questions
   - Assessment Practice (ATE)
3. **develop vocabulary.**
   - Vocabulary Lesson: Greek Root: *-psych-*
4. **understand and apply written and oral language conventions.**
   - Spelling Strategy
   - Grammar and Style Lesson: Parentheses
5. **develop writing proficiency.**
   - Writing Lesson: Introduction to a Poetry Reading
6. **develop appropriate research strategies.**
   - Extend Your Learning: Written Report
7. **understand and apply listening and speaking strategies.**
   - Extend Your Learning: Group Discussion

Block Scheduling: Use one 90-minute class period to preteach the skills and have students read the selection. Use a second 90-minute class period to assess students' mastery of skills, extend their learning, and monitor their progress.

Homework Suggestions

Following are possibilities for homework assignments.

- Support pages from *Unit 5 Resources:*
  Literary Analysis
  Reading Strategy
  Vocabulary Builder
  Grammar and Style
- An Extend Your Learning project and the Writing Lesson for this selection group may be completed over several days.

Step-by-Step Teaching Guide	Pacing Guide
PRETEACH	
• Administer Vocabulary and Reading Warm-ups as necessary.	5 min.
• Engage students' interest with the motivation activity.	5 min.
• Read and discuss author, and background, features. **FT**	10 min.
• Introduce the Literary Analysis Skill: Satire. **FT**	5 min.
• Introduce the Reading Strategy: Relating Structure to Meaning. **FT**	10 min.
• Prepare students to read by teaching the selection vocabulary. **FT**	
TEACH	
• Informally monitor comprehension while students read independently or in groups. **FT**	30 min.
• Monitor students' comprehension with the Reading Check notes.	as students read
• Reinforce vocabulary with Vocabulary Builder notes.	as students read
• Develop students' understanding of satire with the Literary Analysis annotations. **FT**	5 min.
• Develop students' ability to relate structure to meaning with the Reading Strategy annotations. **FT**	5 min.
ASSESS/EXTEND	
• Assess students' comprehension and mastery of the Literary Analysis and Reading Strategy by having them answer the Apply the Skills questions. **FT**	15 min.
• Have students complete the Vocabulary Lesson and the Grammar and Style Lesson. **FT**	15 min.
• Apply students' ability to use details to support meaning by using the Writing Lesson. **FT**	45 min. or homework
• Apply students' understanding by using one or more of the Extend Your Learning activities.	20–90 min. or homework
• Administer Selection Test A or Selection Test B. **FT**	15 min.

Resources

PRINT

Unit 5 Resources

Vocabulary Warm-up Word Lists **[L1, L2, EL]** . . . . .p. 72
Vocabulary Warm-up Practice **[L1, L2, EL]** . . . . .p. 73
Reading Warm-up A **[L1, L2, EL]** . . . . .p. 74
Reading Warm-up B **[L1, L2, L3]** . . . . .p. 75

TRANSPARENCY

Graphic Organizer Transparencies

Literary Analysis Graphic Organizer A **[L3]** . . . . .p. 167
Literary Analysis Graphic Organizer B **[L1, L2, EL]** . . . . .p. 168
Reading Strategy Graphic Organizer A **[L3]** . . . . .p. 165
Reading Strategy Graphic Organizer B **[L1, L2, EL]** . . . . .p. 166

PRINT

Reader's Notebook [L2]
Reader's Notebook: Adapted Version [L1]
Reader's Notebook: English Learner's Version [EL]

Unit 5 Resources

Literary Analysis **[L3]** . . . . .p. 76
Reading Strategy **[L3]** . . . . .p. 77
Vocabulary Builder **[L3]** . . . . .p. 78

TECHNOLOGY

Listening to Literature Audio CDs [L2, EL]

PRINT

Unit 5 Resources

Grammar and Style **[L3]** . . . . .p. 79
Support for Writing Lesson **[L3]** . . . . .p. 80
Support for Extend Your Learning **[L3]** . . . . .p. 81
Enrichment **[L4]** . . . . .p. 82
Selection Test A **[L1, L2, EL]** . . . . .pp. 83–85
Selection Test B **[L3, L4]** . . . . .pp. 86–88

General Resources

Rubrics for Comparison-and-Contrast Essay **[L3]** . . . . .pp. 69–70

TECHNOLOGY

Go Online: Research **[L3]**
Go Online: Self-test **[L3]**
***ExamView*® Test Bank [L3]**

Choosing Resources for Differentiated Instruction

[L1] Special Needs Students
[L2] Below-Level Students
[L3] All Students
[L4] Advanced Students
[EL] English Learners

For Vocabulary and Reading Warm-ups and for Selection Tests, **A** signifies "less challenging" and **B** "more challenging." For Graphic Organizer transparencies, **A** signifies "not filled in" and **B** "filled in."

FT Fast Track Instruction: To move the lesson more quickly, use the strategies and activities identified with **FT**.

Scaffolding for Less Proficient and Advanced Students

The leveled Critical Thinking questions after selections progress in the levels of thinking required to answer them. To address the needs of your different students, you may use the (a) level questions for your less proficient students and the (b) level questions with your on-level and advanced students. The occasional (c) level questions are appropriate for your advanced students.

PRENTICE HALL **TeacherEXPRESS**™ Plan · Teach · Assess — Use this complete suite of powerful teaching tools to make lesson planning and testing quicker and easier.

PRENTICE HALL **StudentEXPRESS**™ Learn · Study · Succeed — Use the interactive textbook (online and on CD-ROM) to make selections and activities come alive with audio and video support and interactive questions.

Benchmark

After students have completed these poems, administer **Benchmark Test 7** (***Unit 5 Resources***, p. 89). If the Benchmark Test reveals that some students need further work, use the **Interpretation Guide** to determine the appropriate reteaching pages in the **Reading Kit** or on **Success Tracker**.

Go Online Professional Development
For: Information about Lexiles
Visit: www.PHSchool.com
Web Code: eue-1111

PRETEACH

Motivation

Read an excerpt from Jerry Seinfeld's book *Seinlanguage* or a column by Dave Barry, or share a video of the stand-up comedy of Jay Leno or David Letterman to show that no subject is off limits to columnists and comedians who challenge and satirize society and its rituals. Ask students whether they enjoyed the contemporary satire. How do they view the role of writers and artists in analyzing society? Tell them that they're about to encounter a group of poems that comment on society.

❶ Background

More About the Authors

The poems of E.E. Cummings are often instantly recognizable because of their style. In addition, Cummings wrote *concrete poetry*—poetry in which the shape of the poem reinforces its meaning. For example, his poem about a grasshopper, "r-p-o-p-h-e-s-s-a-g-r," forms the shape of a grasshopper hopping and reforming itself.

After leaving Oxford, Auden taught school from 1930 to 1935 and later worked for a government film unit. Auden was the most active of the group of young English poets who, in the late 1920s and early 1930s, saw themselves bringing new techniques and attitudes to English poetry.

Build Skills *Poems*

❶ old age sticks • anyone lived in a pretty how town • The Unknown Citizen

E. E. Cummings (1894–1962)

After working in the French ambulance corps and spending three months behind bars as a political prisoner during World War I, Edward Estlin Cummings studied painting in Paris and subsequently began writing poetry in New York City. A graduate of Harvard University, his first published poems appeared in the *Harvard Monthly.* Though some critics attacked the unconventional style of his poetry, Cummings's work was popular with general readers. People admired his playful use of language, his distinctive use of grammar and punctuation, and his interest in a poem's appearance—a sensitivity that might have stemmed from his talent as a painter. Cummings also became known for his concern for the individual and his ability to recognize life's ironies.

Form vs. Content Although Cummings's poems tend to be unconventional in form and style, they generally express traditional ideas. In his finest poems, Cummings explores the customary poetic terrain of love and nature but makes innovative use of grammar and punctuation to reinforce meaning. Many of his poems also contain comic touches as Cummings addresses the confusing aspects of modern life. Cummings was also a skillful satirist who used his poems to challenge accepted notions and fixed beliefs.

Cummings received a number of awards for his work, including the Boston Fine Arts Poetry Festival Award and the Bollingen Prize in Poetry. In 1968, six years after his death, a volume of his poetry, *The Complete Poems, 1913–1968,* was published. At the time of his death, he was the second most widely read poet in the United States, after Robert Frost.

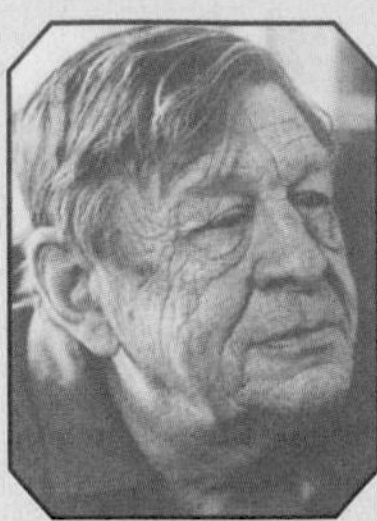

W. H. Auden (1907–1973)

Although he was influenced by the Modernist poets, Wystan Hugh Auden adopted only those aspects of Modernism with which he felt comfortable. At the same time, he maintained many elements of traditional poetry. Throughout his career, he wrote with insight about people struggling to preserve their individuality in an increasingly conformist society.

Auden was born in England and attended Oxford University. At age twenty-three, he both published his first volume of poetry and developed a passionate interest in politics. He spoke out against poverty in England and the rise of Nazism in Germany.

A New Country In 1939, just before World War II, Auden moved from England to the United States. That move was coincident with his rediscovery of his Christian beliefs. His works *The Double Man* (1941) and *For the Time Being* (1944) depict religion as a way of coping with a disjointed modern society. Despite the comfort he found in religion, Auden became disillusioned with modern life in his later years. He used his poetry to explore the responsibilities of the artist in what he saw as a faithless modern age.

Auden earned the Pulitzer Prize in 1948 for his long narrative poem *The Age of Anxiety* (1947), which explores the confusion associated with post-World War II life. He later produced several more volumes of poetry and a large body of literary criticism. He also anthologized others' works and coauthored at least one musical composition—a libretto for the opera *The Rake's Progress.* From 1954 to 1973, Auden served as Chancellor of the Academy of American Poets.

Preview

Connecting to the Literature

Do you ever wonder how you can express your individuality and distinguish yourself from the rest of humanity—or even from your immediate circle of friends? The following poems address this human desire.

2 Literary Analysis

Satire

Satire is writing that ridicules the faults of individuals, groups, institutions, or even humanity in general. Although satire is often humorous, its purpose is not simply to make readers laugh but also to correct the shortcomings that it points out. By poking fun at our flaws, satirists are trying to persuade readers to accept their point of view. As you read, think about the serious point each poet makes through satire.

Comparing Literary Works

Satirical writings vary in **tone**—a quality that reveals a writer's attitude toward his or her subject, characters, or audience. The tone of a satirical work may be tolerant, humorous, bitter, or biting, and is revealed through the writer's choices of words and details. For example, in naming his characters "anyone" and "noone," Cummings suggests the lack of distinction that comes with excessive conformity. His satire is biting, though it is softened by other elements of the poem:

one day anyone died i guess
(and noone stooped to kiss his face)

As you read these poems, compare each poet's tone, and identify the varying kinds of satire that result.

3 Reading Strategy

Relating Structure to Meaning

You can often connect the ideas of poetry with the form the words take:

- **Structure** is the way a poem is put together in words, lines, and stanzas.
- **Meaning** is the central idea the poet wants to convey.

In his poems, Cummings plays typographical games and breaks rules of grammar and syntax. His structure suits his theme: individual challenges to convention. Use a chart like the one shown to link structure to meaning.

"anyone lived in a pretty how town"

Structure	Meaning
Nine stanzas of four lines apiece	The regularity of the stanzas emphasizes the routine of town life.

Vocabulary Builder

statistics (stə tis′ tiks) *n.* science of collecting and arranging facts about a particular subject in the form of numbers (p. 777)

psychology (sī käl′ ə jē) *n.* science dealing with the mind and with mental and emotional processes (p. 778)

2 Literary Analysis

Satire

- Explain to students that in *satire,* an author uses humor for a specific purpose: to ridicule a problem in the world and promote change. Satire can take aim at people, institutions, or societies.
- Explain to students the role of tone in satire. Have students discuss the tone of the lines quoted in Comparing Literary Works. What is Cummings satirizing?
- As students read the selection, have them consider the following questions: What is being ridiculed? What is the tone? What kind of change might the poet be promoting?

3 Reading Strategy

Relating Structure to Meaning

- Read aloud the definitions of *structure* and *meaning* listed in the Reading Strategy instruction. Emphasize to students the difference between the two concepts.
- Explain to students that a poem's structure helps to communicate its meaning. Use the graphic organizer to show a relationship between stanza structure and meaning.
- Give students a copy of **Reading Strategy Graphic Organizer A,** p. 165 in ***Graphic Organizer Transparencies.*** Encourage students to use such a chart to relate the structures of poems to their meanings.

Vocabulary Builder

- Pronounce each vocabulary word for students, and read the definitions as a class. Have students identify any words with which they are already familiar.

Differentiated Instruction Solutions for All Learners

Support for Special Needs Students
Have students complete the **Preview** and **Build Skills** pages for these selections in the ***Reader's Notebook: Adapted Version.*** These pages provide a selection summary, an abbreviated presentation of the reading and literary skills, and the graphic organizer on the **Build Skills** page in the student book.

Support for Less Proficient Readers
Have students complete the **Preview** and **Build Skills** pages for these selections in the ***Reader's Notebook.*** These pages provide a selection summary, an abbreviated presentation of the reading and literary skills, and the graphic organizer on the **Build Skills** page in the student book.

Support for English Learners
Have students complete the **Preview** and **Build Skills** pages for these selections in the ***Reader's Notebook: English Learner's Version.*** These pages provide a selection summary, an abbreviated presentation of the skills, additional contextual vocabulary, and the graphic organizer on the **Build Skills** page in the student book.

TEACH

Learning Modalities Logical/ Mathematical Learners

Explain to these students that some elements of a poem's structure can be measured very precisely. The pattern of stressed and unstressed syllables in a poem is called *meter,* and it is a part of a poem's structure that can contribute to its meaning.

❶ About the Selections

Cummings challenges the way people live in both of these poems. In "old age sticks," Cummings illustrates the cyclical nature of human experience. Youth's liveliness is contrasted with old age's conservatism, but gradually youth becomes old age. "anyone lived in a pretty how town" paints a picture for readers of an anonymous town in which people live routine and unremarkable lives. The seasons pass with regular predictability as the main characters, "anyone" and his wife "noone," do nothing special and are basically unnoticed by the town's other occupants. With their unusual syntax and satirical views, these poems explore the relationship between the individual and society's structure.

❶ old age sticks

E. E. Cummings

old age sticks
up Keep
Off
signs)&

youth yanks them
down(old
age
cries No

Tres)&(pas)
youth laughs
(sing
old age

scolds Forbid
den Stop
Must
n't Don't

&)youth goes
right on
gr
owing old

❷ ***Remember Now the Days of Thy Youth,*** 1950, Paul Starrett Sample, Hood Museum of Art, Dartmouth College, Hanover, NH

❸ ▲ **Critical Viewing** Do you think that the elderly men in this painting could belong to the group that Cummings describes, or are they a different sort? On what details did you base your conclusion? **[Speculate]**

Differentiated Instruction Solutions for All Learners

Accessibility at a Glance

	old age sticks; pretty how town	The Unknown Citizen
Context	Social satire	Social satire
Language	Unconventional punctuation; unusual and complicated syntax	Generally simple syntax
Concept Level	Challenging (satire on routine lives in small towns)	Accessible (shortcomings of bureaucratic institutions)
Literary Merit	Noted author; high interest	Noted author
Lexile	NP	NP
Overall Rating	More challenging	Average

anyone lived in a pretty how town

E. E. Cummings

Background E. E. Cummings's style is among the most distinctive of any American poet. He molded his poems into unconventional shapes by varying line lengths and inserting unusual spaces between letters and lines. Many of his poems contain little punctuation; the few marks that do appear often highlight important ideas. In addition, Cummings rarely uses capital letters, except for emphasis. Another distinguishing mark of his style is his use of the lower-case *i* when his speakers refer to themselves. This small *i* is meant to convey the idea of a self as a small part of mass society and Cummings's belief in the need for modesty.

anyone lived in a pretty how town
(with up so floating many bells down)
spring summer autumn winter
he sang his didn't he danced his did.

Women and men(both little and small)
cared for anyone not at all
they sowed their isn't they reaped their same
sun moon stars rain

children guessed(but only a few
and down they forgot as up they grew
autumn winter spring summer)
that noone loved him more by more

when by now and tree by leaf
she laughed his joy she cried his grief
bird by snow and stir by still
anyone's any was all to her

4 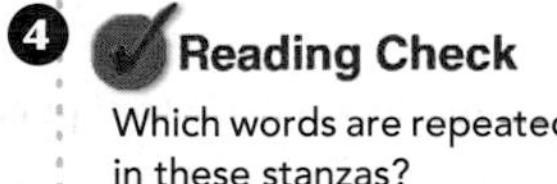

Reading Check

Which words are repeated in these stanzas?

2 Humanities

Remember Now the Days of Thy Youth, by Paul Starrett Sample

American painter Paul Starrett Sample discovered art while convalescing from tuberculosis. While living in Los Angeles and later in New England, Sample painted scenes of American life that made him immensely popular. His work was included in exhibitions such as the 1939 New York World's Fair. Many critics today consider Sample one of America's most important but underrecognized painters. *Remember Now the Days of Thy Youth,* much like Sample's famous *Maple Sugaring in Vermont,* captures an everyday moment in the lives of ordinary people. Ask:

1. How do the figures in the painting represent the contrasting groups in the poem "old age sticks"?
   Answer: The old men on the porch represent "old age"; the mother and baby and the young couple represent "youth."
2. In the world of the poem, how would you expect the young couple depicted here to behave toward "old age" on the porch?
   Possible response: They would either ignore or overrule "old age," perhaps blocking their view.

3 Critical Viewing

Possible response: Students may say that the men are of the "sticks up Keep Off signs" group because they are old, and because they are watching instead of participating. Others may say the men are not interfering with youth as it heads on its way.

4 Reading Check

Answer: The word "anyone" is repeated, as are the names of the seasons: "spring," "summer," "autumn," and "winter."

Differentiated Instruction

Solutions for All Learners

Support for Special Needs Students
These students may find Cummings's interruption of words and sentences in "old age sticks" challenging. Guide students to see that the interruptions illustrate youth's willingness to interrupt and ignore old age.

Support for Less Proficient Readers
These students may be confused by the names "anyone" and "noone" in "anyone lived in a pretty how town." Explain that "anyone" is the poem's main character. If students are confused by line 12, explain that "noone" is his wife. While the poem seems to say that nobody loves "anyone," this is a play on words.

5 Reading Strategy
Relating Structure to Meaning

- Call students' attention to the poem's *stanzas.* Ask students to identify what characteristics the stanzas all share.
  Answer: Each stanza has four lines. Students may also notice internal rhymes and repetition.
- Point out that the common features make stanzas regular. Then, **ask** them the Reading Strategy question: How do the regular stanzas reinforce the ideas of the poem?
  Possible response: The regularity of the stanzas emphasizes the monotonous routine of town life.

ASSESS
Answers

1. **Possible response:** Students may feel that they are scolded by their elders as "youth" is by "old age"; they may also feel that their lives are as routine as those of "anyone" and "noone."
2. (a) Old age "sticks up Keep Off signs," "cries," and "scolds." Youth yanks the signs down and "laughs." (b) **Possible response:** Youth is *carefree* and lively; old age is conservative and authoritarian.
3. (a) Youth is "growing old." (b) **Possible response:** Youth shows no care for old age, yet youth is growing old.
4. (a) He names the male character "anyone" and the female character "noone." (b) **Possible response:** He might view them as unimportant because no one around them notices or cares about them.
5. (a) They "laughed their cryings" and "slept their dreams." (b) **Possible response:** "Laughed their cryings" implies that they hid their feelings. "Slept their dreams" means they lived unimaginative, unfulfilled lives.
6. **Possible response:** Students may respond that the poem criticizes society for stifling and ignoring the individual. Some students may see the love anyone and noone share as an escape from their cold and anonymous world.

someones married their everyones
laughed their cryings and did their dance
(sleep wake hope and then)they
said their nevers they slept their dream

stars rain sun moon
(and only the snow can begin to explain
how children are apt to forget to remember
with up so floating many bells down)

one day anyone died i guess
(and noone stooped to kiss his face)
busy folk buried them side by side
little by little and was by was

all by all and deep by deep
and more by more they dream their sleep
noone and anyone earth by april
wish by spirit and if by yes.

Women and men(both dong and ding)
summer autumn winter spring
reaped their sowing and went their came
sun moon stars rain

Reading Strategy
Relating Structure to Meaning How do the regular stanzas of four lines each reinforce the ideas of the poem?

Critical Reading

1. **Respond:** What parts of your life do you see in these poems? Explain.
2. **(a) Recall:** In "old age sticks," what actions do old age and youth take? **(b) Compare and Contrast:** Explain the differences Cummings points out between youth and old age.
3. **(a) Recall:** In the final stanza of "old age sticks," what does the poem say is happening to youth? **(b) Interpret:** Explain the irony in this final stanza.
4. **(a) Recall:** What does Cummings name the main male and female characters in "anyone lived in a pretty how town"? **(b) Speculate:** What is the poet suggesting in this choice?
5. **(a) Recall:** What does Cummings say the people do with their cryings and their dreams? **(b) Interpret:** What message is the poet conveying about the ideas of individuality and conformity?
6. **Evaluate:** Which poem presents a more positive view of life? Explain.

For: More about E. E. Cummings
Visit: www.PHSchool.com
Web Code: ere-9507

Go Online Author Link For additional information about E. E. Cummings, have students type in the Web Code, then select C from the alphabet, and then select E. E. Cummings.

6 # The Unknown Citizen

W. H. Auden

(To JS/07/M/378 This Marble Monument Is Erected by the State)

7 

The Turret Lathe Operator (J. G. Cherry series), Grant Wood, Cedar Rapids Museum of Art, Cedar Rapids, Iowa. © Estate of Grant Wood/Licensed by VAGA, New York, NY

8 ▲ **Critical Viewing** In what ways does the man in this painting appear to fit Auden's description of "the unknown citizen"? **[Analyze]**

He was found by the Bureau of Statistics to be
One against whom there was no official complaint,
And all the reports on his conduct agree
That, in the modern sense of an old-fashioned word, he was a saint,
For in everything he did he served the Greater Community.
Except for the War till the day he retired
He worked in a factory and never got fired,
But satisfied his employers, Fudge Motors Inc.
Yet he wasn't a scab or odd in his views,
For his Union reports that he paid his dues,
(Our report on his Union shows it was sound)

Vocabulary Builder

statistics (stə tis′ tiks) *n.* science of collecting and arranging facts about a particular subject in the form of numbers

9  **Reading Check**

What makes the subject of the poem "a saint"?

6 About the Selection

This poem highlights how society can become so concerned with recording data that it obliterates individuals and their emotions or beliefs. The poem's central character, the unknown citizen, is documented, analyzed, and studied, yet no one knows anything about his true personal experience of the world.

7 Humanities

Turret Lathe Operator, by Grant Wood

Grant Wood was born and lived much of his life in or near Anamosa, Iowa. There he painted, taught art, and promoted regional art, especially that capturing the unique Midwestern experience. *Turret Lathe Operator* is part of a series commissioned by a dairy equipment manufacturer to show quality craftsmanship in its factory. **Ask:**

- Why might the unknown citizen in the painting or poem not communicate his unhappiness to the world?
  Possible response: He might assume the world is not interested in his opinions.

8 Critical Viewing

Possible response: Students may say he looks like an ordinary man who would not challenge or surprise anyone. In the factory, as long as his machine keeps going, no one will notice him.

9 Reading Check

Answer: He is "a saint" because he appears to have "served the Greater Community" rather than himself.

Differentiated Instruction

Solutions for All Learners

Support for English Learners

Stress that Auden's poem is not meant to be read literally. Help them locate examples of exaggeration, such as lines 14, 15, 19, 24, and 26, and discuss the *tone* these examples convey. Reading along with **Listening to Literature CD** can help students recognize tone.

Enrichment for Gifted/Talented Students

If these students are interested by the parallels between the poems in this selection and the paintings on pp. 774–775 and 777, encourage them to learn more about the artists, Paul Starrett Sample and Grant Wood. Students can deliver presentations on the artists, including reproductions of their paintings.

10 Reading Strategy
Relating Structure to Meaning

- Call students' attention to line 18. Be sure that they recognize the capitalization of "Producers Research" and "High-Grade Living." **Ask** students what these terms describe.
  Answer: They are bureaucratic groups in the Unknown Citizens' society.
- **Ask** the Reading Strategy question: Why do you think Auden capitalizes words in line 18?
  Possible response: Auden implies that these groups are falsely elevating their own status.

  Monitor Progress Encourage students to discuss the meaning of other examples of unusual capitalization in the poem.

ASSESS
Answers

1. **Possible response:** Students who have had interaction with bureaucracies—from government offices to standardized tests—may have experienced this feeling.
2. (a) The state identifies him as JS/07/M/378. (b) **Possible response:** They suggest the impersonal nature of the society; they suggest that he has no true identity.
3. (a) He worked in a factory for most of his life; he paid union dues; he was married and had children. (b) **Possible response:** The state knows nothing about his feelings or concerns. (c) **Possible response:** These are not data that can be easily monitored.
4. (a) The speaker calls the questions "Was he free?" and "Was he happy?" absurd. (b) **Possible response:** Students will probably say that these questions are very important. (c) The final lines are strongly satiric. The speaker cares little and knows less about the citizen's reality. The poet is poking fun at the bureaucratic structure of society.
5. **Possible response:** Our government has a large, bureaucratic system in place like the one described in the poem. However,

And our Social Psychology workers found
That he was popular with his mates and liked a drink.
The Press are convinced that he bought a paper every day
And that his reactions to advertisements were normal in every way.
Policies taken out in his name prove that he was fully insured,
And his Health-card shows he was once in hospital but left it cured.
10 | Both Producers Research and High-Grade Living declare
He was fully sensible to the advantages of the Installment Plan
And had everything necessary to the Modern Man,
A phonograph, a radio, a car and a frigidaire.
Our researchers into Public Opinion are content
That he held the proper opinions for the time of year;
When there was peace, he was for peace; when there was war,
he went.
He was married and added five children to the population.
Which our Eugenist[1] says was the right number for a parent of
his generation,
And our teachers report that he never interfered with their
education.
Was he free? Was he happy? The question is absurd:
Had anything been wrong, we should certainly have heard.

1. **Eugenist** (yo͞o jen′ ist) *n.* a specialist in eugenics, the movement devoted to improving the human species through genetic control.

Vocabulary Builder
psychology (sī käl′ ə jē) *n.* science dealing with the mind and with mental and emotional processes

Reading Strategy
Relating Structure to Meaning Why do you think Auden capitalizes words in line 18?

Critical Reading

1. **Respond:** Have you ever felt as though you have been reduced to a number? Explain your answer.
2. **(a) Recall:** How does the state identify the unknown citizen in the poem's subtitle? **(b) Interpret:** What do these numbers and letters suggest?
3. **(a) Recall:** Identify at least three facts the state knows about the citizen's life. **(b) Interpret:** In what ways is the citizen "unknown" to the state? **(c) Deduce:** Why might the state have heard nothing about these aspects of the citizen's life?
4. **(a) Recall:** What questions does the speaker refer to as "absurd"? **(b) Make a Judgment:** Are these questions actually absurd? Explain. **(c) Analyze:** In what ways do the final two lines clarify the poet's attitude or beliefs?
5. **Apply:** Which aspects of the society in the poem are like contemporary America? Which are different? Explain.
6. **Evaluate:** What types of information about the man do you feel are missing from the poem? Explain.

For: More about W. H. Auden
Visit: www.PHSchool.com
Web Code: ere-9508

Answers continued

the poem exaggerates the idea of bureaucratic control over the individual.

6. **Possible response:** Information about the man's inner life—about his loves, fears, hopes, and dreams—is missing from the poem.

Go Online Author Link For additional information about W. H. Auden, have students type in the Web Code, then select **A** from the alphabet, and then select W. H. Auden.

Apply the Skills

old age sticks • anyone lived in a pretty how town • The Unknown Citizen

Literary Analysis

Satire

1. What changes might E. E. Cummings like to see in the world of "old age sticks"?
2. In "anyone lived in a pretty how town," what small-town qualities and behaviors does Cummings **satirize**?
3. **(a)** Using a chart like the one shown here, name four groups that report on the unknown citizen's activities in W. H. Auden's poem. **(b)** What do the concerns of the state and these groups reveal about society as a whole?

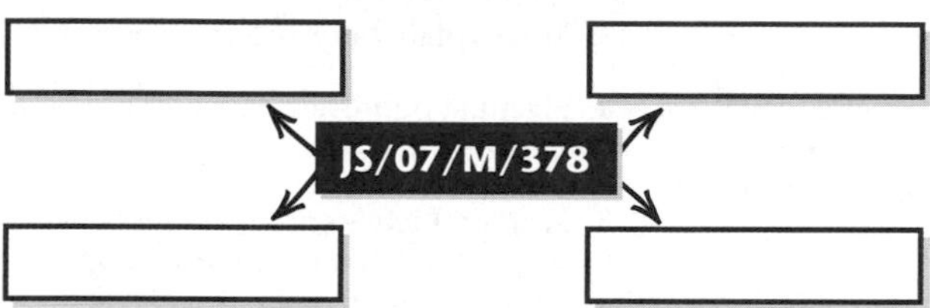

4. **(a)** Based on "The Unknown Citizen," what values do you think Auden holds dear? **(b)** What type of society do you think he supports?

Comparing Literary Works

5. In what way does each of the poems explore the conflict between individuality and conformity to a group?
6. **(a)** Identify the **tone,** or attitude, of each poem. **(b)** Note two details from each poem that reveal the tone. **(c)** Which tone do you find most effective for the purpose of satire? Explain.

Reading Strategy

Relating Structure to Meaning

7. How does the **structure** of "old age sticks" relate to the idea of rules and rule-breaking as it is presented in the poem?
8. Discuss how Auden's style of capitalization affects the **meaning** and tone of his poem.

Extend Understanding

9. **Cultural Connection:** In what way have bureaucracies such as government agencies or corporations affected our sense of individuality and identity? Explain.

QuickReview

Satire is writing that ridicules the flaws of people or society.

Tone is the author's attitude toward his or her subject, characters, or audience.

To **relate structure to meaning,** consider how the arrangement of words, lines, and stanzas might reflect the poem's central ideas.

For: Self-test
Visit: www.PHSchool.com
Web Code: era-6505

Students may use the **Self-test** to prepare for **Selection Test A** or **Selection Test B.**

Answers

1. He might like "old age" to become more tolerant of "youth" and "youth" more attentive toward "old age."
2. He satirizes conformity and coldness with which people treat each other.
3. (a) **Possible response:** his Union; High-Grade Living; Public Opinion researchers; the Eugenist (b) People have little freedom and are controlled by the state.
4. (a) Auden values freedom, individuality, and empathy. (b) He probably supports a society that emphasizes individuality and freedom.
5. **Possible response:** "old age" suggests that young people have more individuality than "old age"; "anyone lived" suggests that individuals can lose their identities in society; "The Unknown Citizen" argues that societies can deny one's identity.
6. (a) **Possible response:** The tone in "old age sticks" is one of resignation; the tone in "anyone lived in a pretty how town" is disdainful; the tone in "The Unknown Citizen" is contemptuous.
(b) Details in "old age sticks" include the description of old age putting up signs and youth tearing them down. Details in "anyone lived" include "cared for anyone not at all" and "children are apt to forget to remember." Details in "The Unknown Citizen" include "The question is absurd" and the last line. (c) **Possible response:** Auden's tone is most effective because it contrasts with the detachment of the speaker.
7. **Possible response:** The regular length of the lines corresponds to old age's tendency toward rules. The other structural elements are nontraditional, in keeping with rule-breaking youth.
8. **Possible response:** Auden capitalizes state and societal institutions, reinforcing their formality and officiality.
9. **Possible response:** American citizens have been depersonalized. For example, people who work for government or corporations must look and behave in similar ways.

EXTEND/ASSESS

Answers

❶ Vocabulary Lesson

Word Analysis

1. *psychiatry:* the branch of medicine concerned with the disorders of the mind. He specialized in *psychiatry* in medical school.
2. *psychosomatic:* a physical disorder originating in or aggravated by the psychic or emotional process. The patient's symptoms are *psychosomatic* because no one could find physical causes for them.
3. *psychotic:* of, or having the nature of, a psychosis. The serial killer was a confirmed *psychotic.*
4. *psychiatrist:* a doctor specializing in disorders of the mind. The *psychiatrist* diagnosed the patient with schizophrenia.

Spelling Strategy

1. *psychopath;* She ranted as if she was a psychopath.
2. *psychic;* He asked the *psychic* what his future would hold.
3. *psoriasis;* His skin showed signs of *psoriasis.*

Vocabulary Builder

1. psychology
2. statistics
3. psychology
4. statistics
5. psychology

❷ Grammar and Style Lesson

1. (at least no sensible person)
2. (except for the love poems)
3. (especially when read by an actor)
4. (I'd guess)
5. (except for their different punctuation styles)

Writing Application

Paragraphs should use parentheses at least twice.

Build Language Skills

❶ Vocabulary Lesson

Word Analysis: Greek Root *-psych-*

The name Psyche—a heroine in a Greek myth—comes from a Greek word meaning "breath" or "soul." The Greek root *-psych-* means "soul" or "mind," and it forms the basis for a number of English words, including *psychology.* Write definitions for the following *-psych-* words. Then, write a sentence using each word.

1. psychiatry
2. psychosomatic
3. psychotic
4. psychiatrist

Spelling Strategy

Some words begin with the *s* sound but are actually spelled *ps: psychology, psalm.* These words derive from the Greek letter *psi,* pronounced *si.* Complete the spelling of the words below. Then, write a sentence for each.

1. __ychopath **2.** __ychic **3.** __oriasis

Vocabulary Builder: Context

The word *psychology* refers to the science dealing with mental and emotional processes. The word *statistics* refers to the science of tabulation or counting. Decide whether each of the following situations relates more closely to psychology or statistics.

1. Teacher assigns class lesson on grieving process.
2. Teacher keeps records of completed assignments.
3. You explain your dream to a friend.
4. Scientist publishes paper on blood diseases in New York State.
5. A star athlete's endorsement boosts product sales in the first two weeks following an advertisement's release.

❷ Grammar and Style Lesson

Parentheses

Parentheses are used to enclose extra information that is interruptive or loosely related to the rest of the sentence but that does not deserve special attention. Use parentheses instead of dashes and commas to set off such information.

Example: My father's new truck (the one he bought last month) has a lot of power.

Practice Rewrite each of the following sentences, adding parentheses to improve the clarity.

1. No person at least no sensible person could accuse Cummings of being a conformist.
2. Cummings's unconventional poetry except for the love poems can be silly, serious, and witty.
3. Auden's poetry especially when read by an actor always affects listeners.
4. Auden's political viewpoints I'd guess were formed over time.
5. The works of two poets except for their different punctuation styles have much in common.

Writing Application Write a paragraph about one of your hobbies, using parentheses at least twice to set off information.

WG *Prentice Hall Writing and Grammar Connection: Chapter 27, Section 5*

Assessment Practice

Try Words in a Sentence **(For more practice, see *Standardized Test Preparation Workbook,* p.45.)**

Many tests require students to correctly answer sentence-completion questions. Use the following sample item to show students that they can often eliminate choices because they are illogical, the wrong part of speech, or inconsistent with the sentence meaning.

Thomas Wolfe's first novel, *Look Homeward, Angel,* was a critical and _____ success and earned Wolfe widespread _____.

A moral; abuse
B financial; recognition
C personal; apathy
D profit; applause

The first word in answer choice *D* is the wrong part of speech. The context of the sentence indicates that the second word will have a positive meaning, eliminating choices *A* and *C.* Answer *B* is the best choice.

3 Writing Lesson

Introduction to a Poetry Reading

Poetry readings—in coffee shops, bookstores, libraries, or community centers—often feature the work of more than one writer. Imagine that you have been asked to organize a reading of Auden's and Cummings's poetry. Write an introduction that welcomes your audience, provides some background information on the poets, and briefly compares their work.

Prewriting Reread the poems. Develop a central idea about similarities and differences in the work of Cummings and Auden. Jot down details or examples from the poems that support this main idea.

Model: Gathering Details of Support

Theme: Cummings uses a highly ordered stanza structure in "anyone lived in a pretty how town."

Structure: In "The Unknown Citizen," Auden explores the effect of a highly organized society on individuals.

Specific references to poetry will strengthen an introduction to the works.

Drafting Keep your remarks brief but informative and well supported with details. Use a conversational writing style suitable to oral delivery.

Revising Make sure you provide enough information to prepare the audience for the poetry they will hear. Revise to ensure that your details are relevant and support your main points.

WG *Prentice Hall Writing and Grammar Connection: Chapter 14, Section 2*

Extend Your Learning

Listening and Speaking The poem "anyone lived in a pretty how town" is set in the country. How might the poem be different if it were set in a city? In a **group discussion,** brainstorm the topic. Consider the following:

- What kinds of lives would people live?
- How would the setting change the activities?
- In what ways might it affect relationships?

After discussing the differences, write a revision based on an urban setting, and share it with the class. **[Group Activity]**

Research and Technology Auden speaks out against totalitarianism—a system in which the government takes control of civil life. Use the Internet to investigate totalitarian governments in Europe after World War I. Compile your findings in a **written report.** Incorporate spreadsheets on the topic in your word-processor document.

For: An additional research activity
Visit: www.PHSchool.com
Web Code: erd-7505

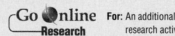

3 Writing Lesson

- To support students in preparing an introduction to a poetry reading, give them the **Support for Writing Lesson** page (***Unit 5 Resources,*** p. 80).
- Explain to students that their introductions should provide background information about each poet. Review the background information provided.
- As students begin drafting, remind them that their introductions are meant to be read aloud. Students should write in a conversational tone.
- Use the Comparison-and-Contrast Essay rubrics in ***General Resources,*** pp. 69–70, to evaluate students' work.

4 Listening and Speaking

- Put students in groups to reread "anyone lived in a pretty how town." Have groups consider the bulleted questions. Encourage students to take notes on their discussions.
- Before students begin to write their poems, remind them to keep Cummings's themes and tone as they change the poem's setting.
- Have students practice reading their poems in groups before presenting them to the class.
- The **Support for Extend Your Learning** page ***(Unit 5 Resources,*** p. 81) provides guided note-taking opportunities to help students complete the Extend Your Learning activities.

Go Online Research Have students type in the Web Code for another research activity.

Assessment Resources

The following resources can be used to assess students' knowledge and skills.

Unit 5 Resources
Selection Test A, pp. 83–85
Selection Test B, pp. 86–88
Benchmark Test 7, pp. 89–94

General Resources
Rubrics for Comparison-and-Contrast Essay, pp. 69–70

Go Online Assessment Students may use the **Self-test** to prepare for **Selection Test A** or **Selection Test B.**

Benchmark

Administer **Benchmark Test 7.** If the Benchmark Test reveals that some students need further work, use the **Interpretation Guide** to determine the appropriate reteaching pages in the **Reading Kit** or on **Success Tracker.**

Meeting Your Standards

Students will

1. **analyze and respond to literary elements.**
   - Literary Analysis: Climax and Anticlimax
2. **read, comprehend, analyze, and critique a short story.**
   - Reading Strategy: Predicting
   - Reading Check questions
   - Apply the Skills questions
   - Assessment Practice (ATE)
3. **develop vocabulary.**
   - Vocabulary Lesson: Latin Root: *-temp-*
4. **understand and apply written and oral language conventions.**
   - Spelling Strategy
   - Grammar and Style Lesson: Restrictive and Nonrestrictive Participial Phrases
5. **develop writing proficiency.**
   - Writing Lesson: Comparison and Contrast Essay
6. **develop appropriate research strategies.**
   - Extend Your Learning: Written Report
7. **understand and apply listening and speaking strategies.**
   - Extend Your Learning: Interview

Block Scheduling: Use one 90-minute class period to preteach the skills and have students read the selection. Use a second 90-minute class period to assess students' mastery of skills, extend their learning, and monitor their progress.

Homework Suggestions

Following are possibilities for homework assignments.

- Support pages from ***Unit 5 Resources:***
  Literary Analysis
  Reading Strategy
  Vocabulary Builder
  Grammar and Style
- An Extend Your Learning project and the Writing Lesson for this selection group may be completed over several days.

Step-by-Step Teaching Guide	Pacing Guide
PRETEACH	
• Administer Vocabulary and Reading Warm-ups as necessary.	5 min.
• Engage students' interest with the motivation activity.	5 min.
• Read and discuss author and background features. **FT**	10 min.
• Introduce the Literary Analysis Skill: Climax and Anticlimax. **FT**	5 min.
• Introduce the Reading Strategy: Predicting. **FT**	10 min
• Prepare students to read by teaching the selection vocabulary. **FT**	
TEACH	
• Informally monitor comprehension while students read independently or in groups. **FT**	30 min.
• Monitor students' comprehension with the Reading Check notes.	as students read
• Reinforce vocabulary with Vocabulary Builder notes.	as students read
• Develop students' understanding of climax and anticlimax with the Literary Analysis annotations. **FT**	5 min.
• Develop students' ability to predict with the Reading Strategy annotations. **FT**	5 min.
ASSESS/EXTEND	
• Assess students' comprehension and mastery of the Literary Analysis and Reading Strategy by having them answer the Apply the Skills questions. **FT**	15 min.
• Have students complete the Vocabulary Lesson and the Grammar and Style Lesson. **FT**	15 min.
• Apply students' ability to build contrast in writing by using the Writing Lesson. **FT**	45 min. or homework
• Apply students' understanding by using one or more of the Extend Your Learning activities.	20–90 min. or homework
• Administer Selection Test A or Selection Test B. **FT**	15 min.

Resources

PRINT
Unit 5 Resources
Vocabulary Warm-up Word Lists **[L1, L2, EL]** .... p. 98
Vocabulary Warm-up Practice **[L1, L2, EL]** .... p. 99
Reading Warm-up A **[L1, L2, EL]** .... p. 100
Reading Warm-up B **[L1, L2, L3]** .... p. 101

TRANSPARENCY
Graphic Organizer Transparencies
Literary Analysis Graphic Organizer A **[L3]** .... p. 171
Literary Analysis Graphic Organizer B **[L1, L2, EL]** .... p. 172
Reading Strategy Graphic Organizer A **[L3]** .... p. 169
Reading Strategy Graphic Organizer B **[L1, L2, EL]** .... p. 170

PRINT
Reader's Notebook [L2]
Reader's Notebook: Adapted Version [L1]
Reader's Notebook: English Learner's Version [EL]
Unit 5 Resources
Literary Analysis **[L3]** .... p. 102
Reading Strategy **[L3]** .... p. 103
Vocabulary Builder **[L3]** .... p. 104

TECHNOLOGY
Listening to Literature Audio CDs [L2, EL]
Reader's Notebook: Adapted Version Audio CD [L1, L2]

PRINT
Unit 5 Resources
Grammar and Style **[L3]** .... p. 105
Support for Writing Lesson **[L3]** .... p. 106
Support for Extend Your Learning **[L3]** .... p. 107
Enrichment **[L4]** .... p. 108
Selection Test A **[L1, L2, EL]** .... pp. 109–111
Selection Test B **[L3, L4]** .... pp. 112–114

General Resources
Rubrics for Comparison-and-Contrast Essay **[L3]** .... pp. 69–70
Rubrics for Research: Research Report **[L6]** .... pp. 49–50

TECHNOLOGY
Go Online: Research **[L3]**
Go Online: Self-test **[L3]**
***ExamView*® Test Bank [L3]**

Choosing Resources for Differentiated Instruction

[L1] Special Needs Students
[L2] Below-Level Students
[L3] All Students
[L4] Advanced Students
[EL] English Learners

For Vocabulary and Reading Warm-ups and for Selection Tests, **A** signifies "less challenging" and **B** "more challenging." For Graphic Organizer transparencies, **A** signifies "not filled in" and **B** "filled in."

FT Fast Track Instruction: To move the lesson more quickly, use the strategies and activities identified with **FT**.

Scaffolding for Less Proficient and Advanced Students

The leveled Critical Thinking questions after selections progress in the levels of thinking required to answer them. To address the needs of your different students, you may use the (a) level questions for your less proficient students and the (b) level questions with your on-level and advanced students. The occasional (c) level questions are appropriate for your advanced students.

PRENTICE HALL **TeacherEXPRESS™** Plan · Teach · Assess Use this complete suite of powerful teaching tools to make lesson planning and testing quicker and easier.

PRENTICE HALL **StudentEXPRESS™** Learn · Study · Succeed Use the interactive textbook (online and on CD-ROM) to make selections and activities come alive with audio and video support and interactive questions.

Monitoring Progress

Before students read "The Far and the Near," administer **Diagnostic Test 8** (***Unit 5 Resources,*** p. 95). This test will determine students' level of readiness for the reading and vocabulary skills.

Go Online Professional Development **For:** Information about Lexiles
Visit: www.PHSchool.com
Web Code: eue-1111

PRETEACH

Motivation

Thomas Wolfe's story juxtaposes two perspectives on life—the far and the near views. As students read, they will discover the sharp contrast between these two perspectives. Engage students' interest in the story by involving them in the following demonstration. Have students describe a distant part of the school, such as the gymnasium or library. Then, visit the identified location as a class. Again, invite students to describe it. How do the two descriptions differ? Challenge students to explain the contrast.

❶ Background

More About the Author

Thomas Wolfe's autobiographical novel *Look Homeward Angel* has become a classic of American literature. Since its publication in 1929, it has never gone out of print. The book describes Wolfe's boyhood in Asheville, North Carolina with such frankness and realism that the town would not permit it to be purchased for the public libraries for over seven years. Today, however, Wolfe is regarded as one of Asheville's most illustrious citizens, and his boyhood home —the house he called "Dixieland" in the novel—has become a site attracting thousands of literary tourists each year.

❶ The Far and the Near

Thomas Wolfe (1900–1938)

A man of tremendous energy, appetites, and size, Thomas Wolfe poured out thousands of pages of fiction during his brief career. Driven by the desire to experience all life had to offer, he pursued variety. He lived in the city and in the country, in America and in Europe, in the North and in the South. He reflected this passion for life in his work—in its sheer volume, in the expanses of time and territory it covers, and in his characters who were symbols of greater humanity.

An Instant Success Born in Asheville, North Carolina, Wolfe grew up in a large, eccentric family whose members later served as models for his fiction. His mother speculated in real estate. His father made tombstones. Shortly before the age of sixteen, Wolfe entered the University of North Carolina. There, he became interested in playwriting, a focus he pursued during and after his postgraduate studies at Harvard. Wolfe eventually moved to New York City, where he taught composition at New York University and wrote plays in his spare time.

Unable to find success as a playwright, Wolfe turned to writing fiction. With the assistance of Maxwell Perkins, the leading editor of the time, Wolfe published his first novel in 1929, the loosely autobiographical *Look Homeward, Angel.* The novel was a critical and financial success and earned Wolfe widespread recognition. In 1930, Wolfe was awarded a Guggenheim fellowship that allowed him to travel extensively in Europe.

A New Direction Inspired by the success of his first novel, Wolfe began working on a sequel. Once again, Perkins helped him shorten and shape the novel, which was published in 1935 as *Of Time and the River.* The novel sold well, yet Wolfe was criticized for basing his work too closely on his own life and for his reliance on Perkins.

A New Direction Stung by the criticism, Wolfe switched publishers and struck out on a new course. He became obsessed with the idea that his duty as a writer was to act as a social historian, to interpret his time and place. Unfortunately, he died of a brain infection before he could finish another novel.

Wolfe did, however, leave several thousand pages of manuscript in the hands of another editor, Edward Aswell. Aswell shaped Wolfe's drafts into two more books, *The Web and the Rock* (1939) and *You Can't Go Home Again* (1940).

Sharp Contrasts The contrasts between Wolfe's early, highly personal writings and his later, more socially focused work can perhaps be traced to the differences between his brooding, ambitious mother and his outgoing but self-indulgent father. Certainly, contrast plays a key role in much of Wolfe's writing.

As if to nurture To develop these differences in his work, Wolfe pursued life with an enormous appetite. He said, "I will go everywhere and see everything. I will meet all the people I can. I will think all the thoughts, feel all the emotions I am able, and I will write, write, write."

Final Assessment Had he not died so young, there is little doubt that Wolfe's literary output would have been great. Despite the criticism that he lacked discipline, his talent was profound. In his novels and short stories he displayed a strong sense of time and place, an ability to create vivid and realistic descriptions, and a deep understanding of the human condition. All of these abilities find expression in Wolfe's story "The Far and the Near," which explores the often painful disparity between imagination and real life.

Preview

Connecting to the Literature

At some time in your life, you have probably looked forward to an experience, only to find that it was not what you had dreamed of. In this story, a man learns the difference between hopes, dreams, and sober reality.

2 Literary Analysis

Climax and Anticlimax

The **climax** of a story is the high point of interest or suspense, the point when the conflict reaches its greatest intensity. Usually something decisive occurs, showing how the conflict will ultimately be resolved. When what happens is unexpectedly disappointing, ridiculous, or trivial, it is called an **anticlimax.** Like a climax, an anticlimax is the key moment in the story, but it is more a low point than a high point in the action. The reader, who has been expecting something important or serious to occur, is suddenly confronted with a letdown. When used effectively, an anticlimax can create a variety of effects, from pathos—sorrow or sympathy—to humor.

Connecting Literary Elements

To keep readers engaged, writers must grab their interest early. Once a story's central conflict is introduced, the events leading up to the climax help build readers' anticipation. These events constitute a story's **rising action.** As you read, identify the elements of the rising action to see how they add to your expectations of the climax.

3 Reading Strategy

Predicting

This story about a train engineer's life is a bit like a real train ride: Signposts guide the way to the final destination. These clues enable you to **predict** upcoming events and outcomes. Watch for signals in the story's details that can help you predict where the action is headed. Consider this passage from the story:

> Every day, a few minutes after two o'clock in the afternoon, the limited express . . . passed this spot.

Because the writer tells you the place is important, you might predict that the story will involve "this spot" in some way. As you read, predict what is to come. Record the information in a chart like the one shown here.

Clues

+

Prior Knowledge, Experience, or Expectations

=

Prediction

Vocabulary Builder

tempo (tem′ pō) *n.* rate of activity of a sound or motion; pace (p. 786)

sallow (sal′ ō) *adj.* sickly; pale yellow (p. 787)

sullen (sul′ ən) *adj.* sulky; glum (p. 788)

timorous (tim′ ər əs) *adj.* full of fear (p. 788)

visage (viz′ ij) *n.* appearance (p. 788)

Differentiated Instruction
Solutions for All Learners

Support for Special Needs Students
Have students read the adapted version of "The Far and the Near" in the ***Reader's Notebook: Adapted Version.*** This version provides basic-level instruction in an interactive format with questions and write-on lines. Completing these pages will prepare students to read the selection in the Student Edition.

Support for Less Proficient Readers
Have students read "The Far and the Near" in the ***Reader's Notebook***. This version provides basic-level instruction in an interactive format with questions and write-on lines. After students finish the selection in the ***Reader's Notebook,*** have them complete the questions and activities in the Student Edition.

Support for English Learners
Have students read "The Far and the Near" in the ***Reader's Notebook: English Learner's Version***. This version provides basic-level instruction in an interactive format with questions and write-on lines. Completing these pages will prepare students to read the selection in the Student Edition.

2 Literary Analysis
Climax and Anticlimax

- Read the instruction on Climax and Anticlimax aloud.
- Invite a volunteer to describe the concepts of climax and anticlimax in his or her own words.
- Then, **ask** one or two students to relate the plot line of a favorite film or TV show. As each student speaks, tell the class to identify the climax—the moment of highest tension or suspense.
- Invite students to suggest examples from movies or television shows of anticlimax —when the viewer's expectations are disappointed in some way, and the story resolves in a trivial or meaningless outcome.
- Urge students as they read this story to pay attention to the ways in which the author builds and then foils their expectations.

3 Reading Strategy
Predicting

- Have a volunteer read the instruction about Predicting aloud.
- Draw students' attention to the idea of signposts or clues provided by the author. Tell students that an author deliberately includes such clues to build readers' expectations.
- Conduct a discussion about the variety of clues given in the passage on this page. **Ask:** What can readers predict about "the limited express" or "the spot" noted in the passage?
  Answer: The story will involve the train and the place in some important way.
- Give students a copy of **Reading Strategy Graphic Organizer A,** p. 169 in ***Graphic Organizer Transparencies***. Tell them to fill in the chart with details that will help them make predictions.

Vocabulary Builder

- Pronounce each vocabulary word for students, and read the definitions as a class. Have students identify any words with which they are already familiar.

TEACH

Learning Modalities
Bodily/Kinesthetic Learners
Students will appreciate the changing perspective best by experiencing it physically. Select an object that is both definite in form and highly detailed. Show students the object from a distance. Invite their observations. Then, show them the object close up. Again, invite their observations. Discuss how the changing proximity affects their responses.

❶ About the Selection

The central character, a train engineer, passes by a house every day for twenty years. A woman and her daughter appear each time and wave. Through the difficulties the engineer endures in his career, the image of the women remains constant. When he retires, he visits them, only to discover that the women are unattractive and unfriendly—nothing like what he had expected. The story underscores the idea that distance and anticipation are often more pleasant than reality.

❷ Humanities

Stone City, Iowa, by Grant Wood

Grant Wood, an American painter, was a lifelong resident of Iowa. He studied painting in Europe before returning to Iowa to embrace the inspiration he found in its familiar people and places.

Stone City, Iowa is a perfect example of Wood's interest in everyday objects and scenes. Although the painting depicts realistic elements, the almost geometric forms give the picture a surrealistic air. Use this question for discussion:

- What elements in the painting underscore the importance of perspective addressed in Wolfe's story? **Possible answer:** The picture's rising foreground and diminishing background frame the town, making it a focal point. In addition, the perspective omits any unpleasant details, making the town seem idyllic. Similarly, in the story, the engineer's distance from the women makes them a focal point for his imagination, and erases the possibilities of their flaws or failings.

❶ The Far and the Near

Thomas Wolfe

❷

Stone City, Iowa, Grant Wood, Joslyn Art Museum, Omaha, Nebraska,

Differentiated Instruction Solutions for All Learners

	The Far and the Near
Context	Early twentieth century
Language	Mixture of short and long sentences with embedded clauses; sophisticated sentence structure
Concept Level	Accessible (juxtaposition of character's changing perspective)
Literary Merit	Noted author; suspenseful
Lexile	1390L
Overall Rating	More challenging

Background With the driving of the "golden spike" on May 10, 1869, at Promontory, Utah, the first transcontinental rail link was completed. Finishing the western half had taken more than six years, the work of thousands, and the lives of many. With its completion, America's love affair with the railways had officially begun. Now, people could travel the width of the young nation in relative comfort; they could strike out for the inexpensive land available to homesteaders; they could return East to visit relatives. In many ways, the nation grew more united. Cities grew at railroad hubs such as Chicago and St. Louis. As the railroad crisscrossed the nation, untamed land and lifestyles, like those of cowboys, disappeared. America became a nation of towns like the one the engineer in "The Far and the Near" observes from his perch in the train engine.

On the outskirts of a little town upon a rise of land that swept back from the railway there was a tidy little cottage of white boards, trimmed vividly with green blinds. To one side of the house there was a garden neatly patterned with plots of growing vegetables, and an arbor for the grapes which ripened late in August. Before the house there were three mighty oaks which sheltered it in their clean and massive shade in summer, and to the other side there was a border of gay flowers. The whole place had an air of tidiness, thrift, and modest comfort.

3 Every day, a few minutes after two o'clock in the afternoon, the limited express between two cities passed this spot. At that moment the great train, having halted for a breathing

Literary Analysis
Climax, Anticlimax, and Rising Action What effect does the routine of "every day" have on your expectations of the story?

5  **Reading Check**
What happens every day a few minutes after two o'clock?

4 ◄ **Critical Viewing** In what ways might this painting reflect the engineer's perspective on the farms and villages he sees along his train route? **[Analyze]**

❸ Literary Analysis
Climax, Anticlimax, and Rising Action

- Remind students that readers' expectations build as the action of a story progresses.
- Have students read the bracketed passage silently. Then, **ask** them to describe the scene depicted in the first paragraph and to note what happens "every day."
  Answer: Every day, the train passes by a tidy cottage on the outskirts of a small town.
- **Ask** students the Literary Analysis question: What effect does the routine of "every day" have on your expectations of the story?
  Possible answer: It suggests that the story will involve the cottage, and perhaps some alteration to the daily routine.

❹ Critical Viewing

Possible answer: Students may note that the painting depicts the town from afar and above in a way that mirrors the engineer's perspective.

❺ Reading Check

Answer: A train traveling between two unnamed cities passes a small cottage.

Differentiated Instruction
Solutions for All Learners

Vocabulary for Less Proficient Readers
Although Wolfe's story is very brief, it covers a time period of twenty years. To ensure that students gain a clear understanding of when events are taking place, urge them to note words and phrases related to time. For example, on this page, draw their attention to the words "Every day."

Strategy for English Learners
Some of Wolfe's sophisticated sentences may challenge students. Help students to rephrase difficult sentences using a simple subject-verb-object construction.

Enrichment for Advanced Readers
This story depicts experiences that fail to live up to a character's expectations. Encourage students to extend their exploration of the story by comparing and contrasting it with other pieces of literature or movies that deal with a similar theme. In what ways do various characters respond to their disappointments?

6 Vocabulary Builder
Latin Word Root *-temp-*

- Draw students' attention to Wolfe's use of the word *tempo,* and read its definition. Then, tell students that the Latin root *-temp-* means "time."
- Have students **suggest** other words that contain this root, and list them on the chalkboard.
  Possible answers: temporary, temporal, contemporary
- Have students look up the meanings of these words in a dictionary.
- Finally, have them write sentences using these words correctly.

7 Reading Strategy
Predicting

- Explain to students that the narrator's description of how the engineer feels about the house and the two women provides clues to what might happen.
- **Ask** students the Reading Strategy question: What do you predict is going to happen to the man's happiness?
  Possible answer: The engineer idealizes the scene and has an unrealistic attachment to it. Such fantasizing will lead to disappointment.

8 Literary Analysis
Climax, Anticlimax, and Rising Action

- Invite a volunteer to read the bracketed passage aloud.
- As students listen, instruct them to pay close attention to the description of the engineer's experiences during his working years. **Ask** students why they think Wolfe elaborates on the circumstances that caused him grief, but provides no details about the joys?
  Possible answer: Wolfe wants the reader to understand that the man has experienced tragedies, even if he witnessed them largely from the distant perspective of the passing train.
- Then, **ask** students the Literary Analysis question: In what ways does this detailed description of the old man's experiences with "grief and joy" add to your expectations of the story?
  Possible answer: The description increases our understanding that the engineer's fantasy of the two women is deeply important to him. It adds to the expectation that the resolution of his conflict will be a moment of high drama.

space at the town nearby, was beginning to lengthen evenly into its stroke, but it had not yet reached the full drive of its terrific speed. It swung into view deliberately, swept past with a powerful swaying motion of the engine, a low smooth rumble of its heavy cars upon pressed steel, and then it vanished in the cut. For a moment the progress of the engine could be marked by heavy bellowing puffs of smoke that burst at spaced intervals above the edges of the meadow grass, and finally nothing could be heard but the solid clacking tempo of the wheels receding into the drowsy stillness of the afternoon.

Vocabulary Builder
tempo (tem′ pō) *n.* rate of activity of a sound or motion; pace

Every day for more than twenty years, as the train had approached this house, the engineer had blown on the whistle, and every day, as soon as she heard this signal, a woman had appeared on the back porch of the little house and waved to him. At first she had a small child clinging to her skirts, and now this child had grown to full womanhood, and every day she, too, came with her mother to the porch and waved.

The engineer had grown old and gray in service. He had driven his great train, loaded with its weight of lives, across the land ten thousand times. His own children had grown up and married, and four times he had seen before him on the tracks the ghastly dot of tragedy converging like a cannon ball to its eclipse of horror at the boiler head[1]—a light spring wagon filled with children, with its clustered row of small stunned faces; a cheap automobile stalled upon the tracks, set with the wooden figures of people paralyzed with fear; a battered hobo walking by the rail, too deaf and old to hear the whistle's warning; and a form flung past his window with a scream—all this the man had seen and known. He had known all the grief, the joy, the peril and the labor such a man could know; he had grown seamed and weathered in his loyal service, and now, schooled by the qualities of faith and courage and humbleness that attended his labor, he had grown old, and had the grandeur and the wisdom these men have.

Literary Analysis
Climax, Anticlimax, and Rising Action In what ways does this detailed description of the old man's experiences with "grief and joy" add to your expections of the story?

But no matter what peril or tragedy he had known, the vision of the little house and the women waving to him with a brave free motion of the arm had become fixed in the mind of the engineer as something beautiful and enduring, something beyond all change and ruin, and something that would always be the same, no matter what mishap, grief or error might break the iron schedule of his days.

The sight of the little house and of these two women gave him the most extraordinary happiness he had ever known. He had seen them in a thousand lights, a hundred weathers. He had seen them through the harsh bare light of wintry gray across the brown and frosted stubble of the earth, and he had seen them again in the green luring sorcery of April.

Reading Strategy
Predicting What do you predict is going to happen to the man's happiness?

He felt for them and for the little house in which they lived such tenderness as a man might feel for his own children, and at length the picture of their lives was carved so sharply in his heart that he

1. **boiler head** the front section of a steam locomotive.

felt that he knew their lives completely, to every hour and moment of the day, and he resolved that one day, when his years of service should be ended, he would go and find these people and speak at last with them whose lives had been so wrought into his own.

That day came. At last the engineer stepped from a train onto the station platform of the town where these two women lived. His years upon the rail had ended. He was a pensioned servant of his company, with no more work to do. The engineer walked slowly through the station and out into the streets of the town. Everything was as strange to him as if he had never seen this town before. As he walked on, his sense of bewilderment and confusion grew. Could this be the town he had passed ten thousand times? Were these the same houses he had seen so often from the high windows of his cab? It was all as unfamiliar, as disquieting as a city in a dream, and the perplexity of his spirit increased as he went on.

Presently the houses thinned into the straggling outposts of the town, and the street faded into a country road—the one on which the women lived. And the man plodded on slowly in the heat and dust. At length he stood before the house he sought. He knew at once that he had found the proper place. He saw the lordly oaks before the house, the flower beds, the garden and the arbor, and farther off, the glint of rails.

Yes, this was the house he sought, the place he had passed so many times, the destination he had longed for with such happiness. But now that he had found it, now that he was here, why did his hand falter on the gate; why had the town, the road, the earth, the very entrance to this place he loved turned unfamiliar as the landscape of some ugly dream? Why did he now feel this sense of confusion, doubt and hopelessness?

At length he entered by the gate, walked slowly up the path and in a moment more had mounted three short steps that led up to the porch, and was knocking at the door. Presently he heard steps in the hall, the door was opened, and a woman stood facing him.

And instantly, with a sense of bitter loss and grief, he was sorry he had come. He knew at once that the woman who stood there looking at him with a mistrustful eye was the same woman who had waved to him so many thousand times. But her face was harsh and pinched and meager; the flesh sagged wearily in sallow folds, and the small eyes peered at him with timid suspicion and uneasy doubt. All the brave freedom, the warmth and the affection that he had read into her gesture, vanished in the moment that he saw her and heard her unfriendly tongue.

And now his own voice sounded unreal and ghastly to him as he tried to explain his presence, to tell her who he was and the reason he had come. But he faltered on, fighting stubbornly against the

9 ***The American Railroad***

The first railroad in America was built in 1826; it ran three miles—from Quincy, Massachusetts, to the Neponset River. Fourteen years later, the first steam locomotive was built in New York, running seventeen miles from Albany to Schenectady. By the late 1800s, a complete network of rail lines linked the nation, opening every corner to settlement and growth. Businesses and towns developed where rail lines crossed. As the railroads expanded, the economy of the country also grew. Freight cars carried coal and other products, while passenger trains helped people resettle or visit relatives in other regions. Thousands of jobs were created, and the United States soon became the greatest industrial nation in the world.

Connect to the Literature

Do you think it is possible to know a place—and its people's lives—by seeing it from a train, as the engineer does? Explain.

Literary Analysis
Climax and Anticlimax
Explain why the woman's appearance is anticlimactic.

Vocabulary Builder
sallow (salʹ ō) *adj.* sickly; pale yellow

11  **Reading Check**
What does the engineer do after retiring from the railroad?

9 The American Experience

The American Railroad

The railroad affected the development of the United States in countless ways. Not only did the railroad spur the growth of American industry, it gave farmers and ranchers in the nation's West access to the markets of the densely populated East. This was, in part, how the nation grew more united, as the note on p. 787 suggests. The railroad also influenced popular culture. Songs and literature about the emerging railroad abounded, including folksongs like "I've Been Working on the Railroad."

Connect to the Literature

Encourage students to consider the reasons why a person might romanticize or idealize other people or places.
Possible response: It is not possible to know people or places from a distance; however, it is possible to know people or places as you believe they are or wish them to be.

10 Literary Analysis

Climax and Anticlimax

- Have students read the bracketed passage. Point out that the engineer is "sorry he had come." Ask students if this moment represents a climax or an anticlimax.
Answer: It is an anticlimax.
- Then, **ask** the Literary Analysis question: Explain why the woman's appearance is anticlimactic.
Answer: The engineer expects her to be "beautiful and enduring." Now he sees that she is ordinary and unattractive. This moment, which the engineer thought would be momentous, is disappointing—an anticlimax.

➤ **Monitor Progress: Ask** students for their reactions to this anticlimactic moment. Encourage them to discuss how they would have reacted if Wolfe had fulfilled the engineer's hopes.

11 Reading Check

Answer: He goes to visit the mother and daughter whose house he had passed every day for twenty years.

Differentiated Instruction

Solutions for All Learners

Strategy for Special Needs Students
Students may have difficulty grasping the subtleties of this challenging story. You can preview the story using the ***Adapted Reader's Notebook.*** Then, guide students through the selection, encouraging them to reread particularly confusing passages.

Strategy for Gifted/Talented Students
Display Transparency 10 in **Fine Art Transparencies, Volume 1**. Discuss Hopper's painting, directing students' attention to the railroad tracks. What might it be like to live in the house and have a train pass by each day? Invite students to write a short story from the point of view of the woman whom the engineer visits.

Enrichment for Advanced Readers
Help students to appreciate how Wolfe crafts the changing mood as the story progresses. Challenge them to compare and contrast his use of language early in the story with his diction at the end. In particular, encourage them to pay close attention to connotative meaning in his word choices.

ASSESS

Answers

1. **Possible answer:** Most students will hope that he will find the "something beautiful and enduring" which he is seeking. Students should offer reasons for their responses.
2. (a) While riding his train, the engineer passes a cottage on the outskirts of a small town and a woman and her daughter wave at him. (b) **Possible answer:** It suggests his life is unchanging, monotonous.
3. (a) He idealizes them. (b) **Possible answer:** It represents companionship, the comforts of a tidy home, a simple way of life.
4. (a) He retires from his career. (b) The town is not as he imagined it; it is ordinary, somewhat squalid. He finds it bewildering. (c) **Possible answer:** He realizes it as soon as he steps off the train.
5. (a) He realizes that his magical vision is gone forever. (b) **Possible answer:** In his imagination, the women had come to represent warmth and beauty. As it turns out, they are unfriendly and unattractive.
6. **Possible answer:** He is suggesting that human longing is extremely powerful.
7. **Possible answer:** Some students may feel that hope and reality are inherently contradictory. Others may be more optimistic. Encourage students to discuss their opinions.

Go Online Author Link For additional information about Thomas Wolfe, have students type in the Web Code, then select *W* from the alphabet, and then select Thomas Wolfe.

horror of regret, confusion, disbelief that surged up in his spirit, drowning all his former joy and making his act of hope and tenderness seem shameful to him.

At length the woman invited him almost unwillingly into the house, and called her daughter in a harsh shrill voice. Then, for a brief agony of time, the man sat in an ugly little parlor, and he tried to talk while the two women stared at him with a dull, bewildered hostility, a sullen, timorous restraint.

And finally, stammering a crude farewell, he departed. He walked away down the path and then along the road toward town, and suddenly he knew that he was an old man. His heart, which had been brave and confident when it looked along the familiar vista of the rails, was now sick with doubt and horror as it saw the strange and unsuspected visage of an earth which had always been within a stone's throw of him, and which he had never seen or known. And he knew that all the magic of that bright lost way, the vista of that shining line, the imagined corner of that small good universe of hope's desire, was gone forever, could never be got back again.

Vocabulary Builder

sullen (sul′ ən) *adj.* sulky; glum

timorous (tim′ ər əs) *adj.* full of fear

visage (viz′ ij) *n.* appearance

Critical Reading

1. **Respond:** As you read about the engineer's approaching visit to the little town, what did you hope he would find?
2. **(a) Recall:** What has been the engineer's daily experience for the last twenty years? **(b) Interpret:** What does this tell you about the engineer's life?
3. **(a) Recall:** How does the engineer feel about the little house and the two women? **(b) Infer:** What do the house and the women represent to him?
4. **(a) Recall:** What event makes the engineer's visit to the town possible? **(b) Recall:** What is the engineer's first impression of the town when he comes to visit? **(c) Connect:** When does he first sense that his experience is unlikely to match his expectations?
5. **(a) Recall:** What realization does the engineer come to at the end of the story? **(b) Contrast:** In what ways do the engineer's observations in the final scene contrast with his expectations?
6. **Analyze:** Considering the title of the story, what do you think Wolfe is saying about human longing?
7. **Apply:** The engineer is crushed when he discovers that his optimism was not based on reality. Is it possible to confront reality and remain hopeful about life at the same time? Explain.

For: More about Thomas Wolfe
Visit: www.PHSchool.com
Web Code: ere-9509

Apply the Skills

The Far and the Near

Literary Analysis

Climax and Anticlimax

1. **(a)** What is the story's **anticlimax**? Support your answer. **(b)** In what way does the anticlimax resolve the story's central conflict?
2. What effect does the anticlimax have on both the engineer and the reader?
3. Why do you suppose Wolfe chose to give this story an anticlimax rather than a **climax**? Explain.
4. If you were to rewrite this story with a climax rather than an anti-climax: **(a)** What details would change? **(b)** How would such a revised story end?

Connecting Literary Elements

5. **(a)** When in the story does the rising action begin? **(b)** Using a chart like the one shown, list three events in the rising action that led to the moment of greatest tension.

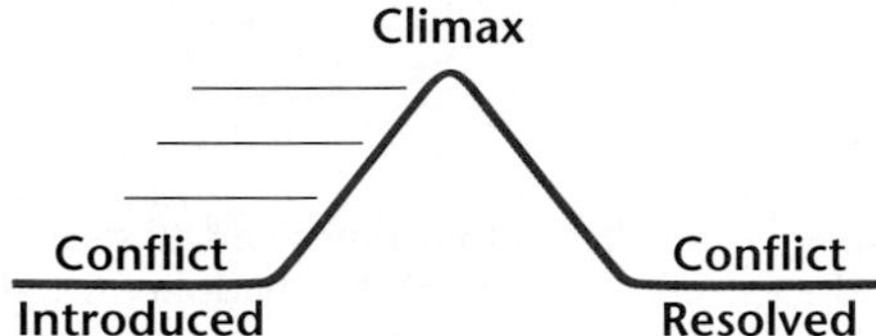

6. How does the repetition of the engineer's attachment to the woman and her house contribute to the tension created in the story's **rising action**?

Reading Strategy

Predicting

7. When you read about the engineer's decision to visit the two women after retiring, what did you **predict** would happen?
8. Based on your own experience, did you predict that the engineer's view of the world would change when he stepped down from the "high windows of his cab"? Explain.

Extend Understanding

9. **Cultural Connection:** In what way does the romantic notion of train travel add to the distortion between the engineer's view of the world from far away and his view up close?

QuickReview

The **climax** is the high point of interest or suspense in a story.

An **anticlimax** is a decisive moment that is unexpectedly disappointing or trivial.

The **rising action** in a story begins when the conflict is introduced and includes the events that create the tension and lead to the climax.

To **predict**, use clues in the story to make educated guesses about upcoming events and outcomes.

For: Self-test
Visit: www.PHSchool.com
Web Code: era-6506

Answers

1. **Possible response:** (a) The anticlimax is the moment when the door is opened and the engineer is "instantly sorry he had come." (b) The engineer's disappointment shatters his idealized vision, unhappily ending the conflict between hope and reality.
2. **Possible response:** It is a disappointment for both the engineer and the reader.
3. **Possible response:** Students should recognize that Wolfe's point that reality cannot match idealized dreams is best made with an anticlimax.
4. **Possible response:** (a) When the engineer arrives in the town, it would be prettier and more welcoming. (b) Such a revised story might end in a love affair between one of the women and the engineer.
5. (a) The rising action begins when the engineer begins to idealize the small house and the women.
(b) **Possible response:**
1. The engineer sees the woman and her daughter. 2. The engineer visits the town. 3. The town seems strange and ugly.

   Another sample answer can be found on **Literary Analysis Graphic Organizer B,** p. 172 in ***Graphic Organizer Transparencies.***
6. **Possible response:** The repetition builds the tension by heightening expectations and making it clear that this dream of the two women is extremely important to the engineer.
7. **Possible response:** Many students will say that they predicted the engineer's disappointment.
8. **Possible response:** Many students will say that they predicted the engineer's disappointment upon leaving the train and getting closer to the real world.
9. **Possible response:** Train travel removed the engineer from the details of the towns he passed through, thus adding to his idealized notions of what he saw.

Go Online Assessment Students may use the **Self-test** to prepare for **Selection Test A** or **Selection Test B.**

EXTEND/ASSESS

Answers

❶ Vocabulary Lesson

Word Analysis

1. fleeting, not lasting
2. of the moment, modern
3. spontaneous, unplanned
4. the rhythm or beat of a musical work

Spelling Strategy

1. edge 2. generous 3. reject

Vocabulary Builder

1. After being bedridden for weeks, the man's complexion had become *sallow*.
2. The child's *timorous* voice revealed her fear of the dentist.
3. Grinning nervously as he made his excuses, the student's *visage* nearly gave him away.
4. The *sullen* girl disliked her school.
5. As everyone struggles to meet the deadlines, the *tempo* of work in an office becomes very fast.

❷ Grammar and Style Lesson

1. *nonrestrictive:* schooled by the humbleness that attended . . . *Comma use:* and now, schooled by the humbleness that attended his labor, he had grown old
2. *restrictive:* converging like a cannon ball to its eclipse . . . ; (no commas needed)
3. *restrictive:* loaded with its weight of lives . . . ; (no commas needed)
4. *restrictive:* receding into the drowsy stillness . . . ; (no commas needed)
5. *nonrestrictive:* trimmed with green blinds. *Comma use:* On the outskirts of a little town was a tidy little cottage, trimmed with green blinds.

Build Language Skills

❶ Vocabulary Lesson

Word Analysis: Latin Root *-temp-*

Built on the Latin root *-temp-*, meaning "time," *tempo* means "pace" or "the rate of activity of a sound or motion." Using this knowledge, define the following words:

1. temporary
2. contemporary
3. extemporaneous
4. tempo

Spelling Strategy

The *j* sound can be spelled in a few ways, including *ge* as in *visage*, or *j* as in *juice*. In your notebook, complete each of the following words using either *j* or *g*.

1. ed__e 2. __enerous 3. re__ect

Vocabulary Builder: Context

For each item, follow the directions by writing a sentence using a word from the vocabulary list on page 783.

1. Describe a man who has been ill for many weeks.
2. Describe how a child might feel before visiting the dentist.
3. Describe a student giving an outrageous excuse for failing a test.
4. Write the first sentence of a story about a girl who is unhappy and angry about her life.
5. Describe an activity in a busy office.

❷ Grammar and Style Lesson

Restrictive and Nonrestrictive Participial Phrases

A **participial phrase** consists of a participle (a form of a verb that acts as an adjective) and its modifiers or complements. The entire phrase acts as an adjective. If the phrase is essential to the sentence's meaning, it is **restrictive** and not set off by commas. If it is not essential, it is **nonrestrictive** and should be set off by commas.

Restrictive: . . . a light spring wagon *filled with children.* (essential)

Nonrestrictive: And finally, *stammering a crude farewell,* he departed. (not essential)

Practice Copy these passages, identifying participial phrases and adding commas as necessary.

1. . . . and now schooled by the humbleness that attended his labor he had grown old . . .
2. . . . four times he had seen before him on the tracks a ghastly dot of tragedy converging like a cannon ball to its eclipse of horror at the boiler head . . .
3. . . . He had driven his great train loaded with its weight of lives across the land ten thousand times.
4. . . . nothing could be heard but the solid clacking tempo of the wheels receding into the drowsy stillness of the afternoon.
5. On the outskirts of a little town was a tidy little cottage trimmed with green blinds.

Looking at Style Explain how each of the participial phrases in the Practice enables Wolfe to insert action into a description.

Writing Application Describe a let down you have experienced, using two participial phrases.

WG *Prentice Hall Writing and Grammar Connection: Chapter 19, Section 2*

Assessment Practice

Try Words in a Sentence **(For more practice, see *Standardized Test Preparation Workbook*, p. 46.)**

Many tests require students to correctly answer sentence-completion questions. Use the following sample item to show students that they can often eliminate choices because they are illogical, the wrong part of speech, or inconsistent with the sentence meaning.

Have you ever felt a conflict between asserting your ______________ and maintaining your ______________ toward society?

A duty; obligation
B uniqueness; separateness
C independence; indifference
D individuality; responsibility

Because the sentence uses the word *conflict*, the correct pair will have somewhat opposite meanings, eliminating *A* and *B*. *C* is illogical. Answer *D* is the best choice.

3 Writing Lesson

Timed Writing: Comparison-and-Contrast Essay

Write an essay in which you compare the two viewpoints suggested by the title "The Far and the Near." Explain how the engineer's view of things depends on distance from or proximity to them. Consider what the story suggests about the dreams we dream from afar. ***(40 minutes)***

Prewriting *(10 minutes)* Reread the story and note passages that reflect the engineer's thoughts and feelings about the world from a distance.

Drafting *(20 minutes)* Address each of the passages you have selected, comparing the engineer's thoughts and reflections while riding the train to the realities he later experiences.

Revising *(10 minutes)* Reread your essay to make sure you have drawn a strong comparison between the engineer's experiences of life from both vantage points. Strengthen your word choices to emphasize contrasts.

Model: Revising to Build Contrast

From a distance, the backyards appear ~~pretty~~ [green and lush] and the ~~houses~~ [tidy little cottages] look like havens of hospitality and warmth. Up close, however, the ~~grass~~, [overgrown weeds,] scattered trash, and ~~siding~~ [peeling clapboard] tell another [cold and neglected] story of a community.

The additional descriptive details make the contrast more striking.

Prentice Hall Writing and Grammar Connection: Chapter 9, Section 2

Extend Your Learning

Speaking and Listening Some people feel that train travel is a magical experience. Conduct an **interview** with someone who has traveled by rail. Start by asking questions like these:

- How did the landscape appear from the train?
- What was romantic or exciting about the journey?
- In what way is rail travel different from auto trips?

Share your findings with the class.

Research and Technology In a group, research the evolution of the railroad and the nation's love affair with it. Devise a research outline. Then, contribute sections to a **written report** explaining the history of the railroad and the changes that have taken place in recent decades. **[Group Activity]**

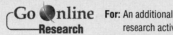

For: An additional research activity
Visit: www.PHSchool.com
Web Code: erd-7506

3 Writing Lesson

You may use this Writing Lesson as timed-writing practice, or you may allow students to develop it as a writing assignment over several days.

- To support students in preparing a comparison-and-contrast essay, give them the **Support for Writing Lesson** page (***Unit 5 Resources,*** p. 106).
- Remind students that their comparison-and-contrast essays should clearly explain—and use supporting details to show—the differences between the engineer's changing perspectives.
- Have students reread the story, marking passages to use in their essays.
- Draw students' attention to the model to help them strengthen their contrasts with concrete detail.
- Use the Comparison-and-Contrast Essay rubrics in ***General Resources,*** pp. 69–70 to evaluate students' work.

4 Research and Technology

- Remind students that their written reports should explain both the history of the railroad and the ways in which it changed American culture.
- Suggest that students assign specific research tasks, such as the building of the railroad, the completion of the transcontinental rails, and so on. Once they have gathered enough material, students can then meet to focus their ideas.
- The **Support for Extend Your Learning** page (***Unit 5 Resources,*** p. 107) provides guided note-taking opportunities to help students complete the Extend Your Learning activities.
- Use the rubrics for Research: Research Report, pp. 49–50 in ***General Resources,*** to evaluate student work.

Go Online Research — Have students type in the Web Code for another research activity.

Assessment Resources

The following resources can be used to assess students' knowledge and skills.

Unit 5 Resources
- **Selection Test A,** pp. 109–111
- **Selection Test B,** pp. 112–114

General Resources
- **Rubrics for Comparison-and-Contrast Essay,** pp. 69–70
- **Rubrics for Research: Research Report,** pp. 49–50

Go Online Assessment — Students may use the **Self-test** to prepare for **Selection Test A** or **Selection Test B.**

Meeting Your Standards

Students will

1. **analyze and respond to literary elements.**
   - Literary Analysis: Simile
2. **read, comprehend, analyze, and critique poetry.**
   - Reading Strategy: Paraphrasing
   - Reading Check questions
   - Apply the Skills questions
   - Assessment Practice (ATE)
3. **develop vocabulary.**
   - Vocabulary Lesson: Latin Root: *-satis-*
4. **understand and apply written and oral language conventions.**
   - Spelling Strategy
   - Grammar and Style Lesson: Subject Complements
5. **develop writing proficiency.**
   - Writing Lesson: Comparison and Contrast Essay
6. **develop appropriate research strategies.**
   - Extend Your Learning: Collection of Poems
7. **understand and apply listening and speaking strategies.**
   - Extend Your Learning: Round-table Discussion

Block Scheduling: Use one 90-minute class period to preteach the skills and have students read the selection. Use a second 90-minute class period to assess students' mastery of skills, extend their learning, and monitor their progress.

Homework Suggestions

Following are possibilities for homework assignments.

- Support pages from *Unit 5 Resources:*
  Literary Analysis
  Reading Strategy
  Vocabulary Builder
  Grammar and Style
- An Extend Your Learning project and the Writing Lesson for this selection group may be completed over several days.

Step-by-Step Teaching Guide	Pacing Guide
PRETEACH	
• Administer Vocabulary and Reading Warm-ups as necessary.	5 min.
• Engage students' interest with the motivation activity.	5 min.
• Read and discuss author and background features. **FT**	10 min.
• Introduce the Literary Analysis Skill: Simile. **FT**	5 min.
• Introduce the Reading Strategy: Paraphrasing. **FT**	10 min.
• Prepare students to read by teaching the selection vocabulary. **FT**	
TEACH	
• Informally monitor comprehension while students read independently or in groups. **FT**	30 min.
• Monitor students' comprehension with the Reading Check notes.	as students read
• Reinforce vocabulary with Vocabulary Builder notes.	as students read
• Develop students' understanding of simile with the Literary Analysis annotations. **FT**	5 min.
• Develop students' ability to paraphrase with the Reading Strategy annotations. **FT**	5 min.
ASSESS/EXTEND	
• Assess students' comprehension and mastery of the Literary Analysis and Reading Strategy by having them answer the Apply the Skills questions. **FT**	15 min.
• Have students complete the Vocabulary Lesson and the Grammar and Style Lesson. **FT**	15 min.
• Apply students' ability to provide necessary background information by using the Writing Lesson. **FT**	45 min. or homework
• Apply students' understanding by using one or more of the Extend Your Learning activities.	20–90 min. or homework
• Administer Selection Test A or Selection Test B. **FT**	15 min.

Resources

PRINT
Unit 5 Resources

Vocabulary Warm-up Word Lists **[L1, L2, EL]** ....p. 115
Vocabulary Warm-up Practice **[L1, L2, EL]** ....p. 116
Reading Warm-up A **[L1, L2, EL]** ....p. 117
Reading Warm-up B **[L1, L2, L3]** ....p. 118

TRANSPARENCY
Graphic Organizer Transparencies

Literary Analysis Graphic Organizer A **[L3]** ....p. 175
Literary Analysis Graphic Organizer B **[L1, L2, EL]** ....p. 176
Reading Strategy Graphic Organizer A **[L3]** ....p. 173
Reading Strategy Graphic Organizer B **[L1, L2, EL]** ....p. 174

PRINT
Reader's Notebook [L2]
Reader's Notebook: Adapted Version [L1]
Reader's Notebook: English Learner's Version [EL]
Unit 5 Resources

Literary Analysis **[L3]** ....p. 119
Reading Strategy **[L3]** ....p. 120
Vocabulary Builder **[L3]** ....p. 121

TECHNOLOGY
Listening to Literature Audio CDs [L2, EL]

PRINT
Unit 5 Resources

Grammar and Style **[L3]** ....p. 122
Support for Writing Lesson **[L3]** ....p. 123
Support for Extend Your Learning **[L3]** ....p. 124
Enrichment **[L4]** ....p. 125
Selection Test A **[L1, L2, EL]** ....pp. 126–128
Selection Test B **[L3, L4]** ....pp. 129–131

General Resources

Rubrics for Comparison-and-Contrast Essay **[L3]** ....pp. 69–70
Rubric for Analyzing Persuasive Techniques **[L3]** ....p. 83

TRANSPARENCY
Graphic Organizer Transparencies

Venn Diagram **[L3]** ....p. 316

TECHNOLOGY
Go Online: Research **[L3]**
Go Online: Self-test **[L3]**
***ExamView*® Test Bank [L3]**

Choosing Resources for Differentiated Instruction

[L1] Special Needs Students
[L2] Below-Level Students
[L3] All Students
[L4] Advanced Students
[EL] English Learners

For Vocabulary and Reading Warm-ups and for Selection Tests, **A** signifies "less challenging" and **B** "more challenging." For Graphic Organizer transparencies, **A** signifies "not filled in" and **B** "filled in."

FT Fast Track Instruction: To move the lesson more quickly, use the strategies and activities identified with **FT**.

Scaffolding for Less Proficient and Advanced Students

The leveled Critical Thinking questions after selections progress in the levels of thinking required to answer them. To address the needs of your different students, you may use the (a) level questions for your less proficient students and the (b) level questions with your on-level and advanced students. The occasional (c) level questions are appropriate for your advanced students.

PRENTICE HALL **TeacherEXPRESS**™ Plan · Teach · Assess Use this complete suite of powerful teaching tools to make lesson planning and testing quicker and easier.

PRENTICE HALL **StudentEXPRESS**™ Learn · Study · Succeed Use the interactive textbook (online and on CD-ROM) to make selections and activities come alive with audio and video support and interactive questions.

Go Online Professional Development **For:** Information about Lexiles
Visit: www.PHSchool.com
Web Code: eue-1111

PRETEACH

Motivation

Use students' interest in music as a hook to motivate them to read these poems. Start with a class activity in which students share the ways in which their favorite music affects them. Write the responses on the chalkboard. Then, have students discuss the role that song lyrics play in eliciting the types of responses they've noted. Using the ideas that have been generated, work as a class to come up with a short definition of what song lyrics are and how they affect people. Then, point out that poetry shares many of the same qualities as song lyrics. Explain to students that they are about to read three poets' definitions of poetry and its importance within a culture. Focus students' reading by having them compare the poets' definitions of poetry with their own definitions of song lyrics.

1 Background

More About the Authors

The three poets represented in this grouping began to publish their poetry in the same period—the decade of the 1920s, when such writers as T.S. Eliot and Ezra Pound dominated modern verse. MacLeish and Moore became active figures in American cultural life, Moore as the editor of *The Dial* and MacLeish as the Librarian of Congress and later as a professor at Harvard University. Stevens, however, continued in his career as an insurance company executive. He was recognized with a Pulitzer Prize in the last years of his life and has since been hailed as one of the most significant poets in American literature.

1 Of Modern Poetry • Anecdote of the Jar • Ars Poetica • Poetry

Wallace Stevens (1879–1955)

Wallace Stevens believed that the goal of poetry was to capture the interaction between fantasy and reality. He spent his career writing poems that delve into the imagination and the ways in which it shapes our perception of the physical world. He uses elaborate imagery and precise words to express his philosophical themes. Stevens depended largely on the natural world for his inspiration because nature, he said, is the only certainty.

Insurance Executive by Day Stevens was born and raised in Reading, Pennsylvania. After completing his education at Harvard University, he took a job at an insurance company in Hartford, Connecticut, and eventually became the company's vice president. He did not publish his first collection of poetry, *Harmonium* (1923), until he was forty-three years old. In *Harmonium* and much of his other work, Stevens uses dazzling imagery to capture the beauty of the physical world while expressing the dependence of that beauty on the perceptions of the observer. Although the book received little public attention, it was praised by critics and launched Stevens's literary career.

Stevens published many volumes of poetry, including *Ideas of Order* (1935), *Parts of a World* (1942), *Transport to Summer* (1947), and *The Auroras of Autumn* (1950). His *Collected Poems* earned him the Pulitzer Prize in 1955. Despite his success as a poet, however, Stevens continued his career in insurance until the end of his life. "It gives a man character as a poet to have this daily contact with a job," he once said. A brilliant and unusual figure, he is now regarded as one of the most important poets of the twentieth century.

Archibald MacLeish (1892–1982)

Archibald MacLeish was born in Glencoe, Illinois. MacLeish was trained as a lawyer but, unlike Stevens, he turned his back on his first career to devote himself completely to poetry. His early poems, such as "Ars Poetica," are experimental in form, reflecting the influence of the Modernists. By contrast, his later poems are more traditional and accessible. As unrest spread throughout the world in the 1930s, MacLeish used poetry to explore political and social issues. Over the course of his career, MacLeish produced more than thirty books and won three Pulitzer Prizes.

Marianne Moore (1887–1972)

Born in Kirkwood, Missouri, Marianne Moore first gained a footing in the literary world as the editor of *The Dial*, a highly regarded literary journal. In that role, she encouraged many new writers by publishing their work. However, she was hesitant to publish her own work, although it had been admired by many noted poets. In fact, her first book, *Poems* (1921), was published without her knowledge.

As a Modernist, Moore wrote poems that were unconventional, precise, inventive, and witty. Unlike most other Modernists, however, she chose not to write about the state of modern civilization. Instead, she explored subjects such as animals and nature. "Poetry," one of her best-known poems, delves into the subject of poetry itself.

Preview

Connecting to the Literature

You probably have your own special way of looking at the subjects you care about most deeply. In these selections, three major poets present their views on a subject about which they are deeply passionate: poetry.

❷ Literary Analysis

Simile

A **simile** is a comparison between two seemingly different things. A connecting word such as *like* or *as* indicates the comparison. For example, the word *like* signals the comparison in the following simile:

The sound of the explosion echoed through the air like thunder.

By comparing the sound of an explosion to thunder, the simile stresses its loud, jarring power. Like poetry itself, similes show us the world in startling new ways. As you read, compare the similes used by each poet.

Comparing Literary Works

The poets whose works appear in these selections devote their attention to the genre of poetry itself. Although the art of writing poetry defies definition, each writer attempts an explanation. The poets use imagery to give body to their ideas. **Imagery** is language that uses **images**—words or phrases that appeal to one or more of the five senses of sight, smell, touch, sound, or taste. Compare the types of images each poet presents and determine the ways in which these images advance each poet's explanation of poetry.

❸ Reading Strategy

Paraphrasing

Because poetry is written in verse and is likely to contain unexpected words and images, it can be difficult to understand. One way to make sure that you grasp what you are reading is to **paraphrase**—to identify key ideas and restate them in your own words. Paraphrasing can remove barriers that make some poems seem too difficult to understand. In a chart like the one shown, list the difficult passages and paraphrase them.

Difficult Passage
"I, too, dislike it: there are things that are more important beyond/all this fiddle."
Paraphrased
I also dislike poetry. It's nonsense, and a lot of other things are more important.

Vocabulary Builder

suffice (sə fīs′) *v.* be adequate; meet the needs of (p. 794)

insatiable (in sā′ shə bəl) *adj.* constantly wanting more (p. 794)

slovenly (sluv′ ən lē) *adj.* untidy (p. 795)

dominion (də min′ yən) *n.* power to rule (p. 795)

palpable (pal′ pə bəl) *adj.* able to be touched, felt, or handled (p. 796)

derivative (də riv′ ə tiv) *adj.* not original; based on something else (p. 798)

literalists (lit′ ər əl ists) *n.* those who take words at their exact meaning (p. 799)

❷ Literary Analysis

Simile

- Explain to students that in a *simile*, an author compares two unlike things using the words "like" or "as." Note that some similes are highly imaginative, while others, like the example on this page, are more ordinary.
- Encourage students to identify and diagram other similes they find in the poems in this grouping.

❸ Reading Strategy

Paraphrasing

- Explain to students that poetry can be especially challenging for readers because it is often dense with meaning.
- Use the difficult passage included in the chart to illustrate the challenge of reading poetry. Encourage students to discuss the meaning of the passage.
- Direct student attention to the paraphrased text in the model chart. Point out that the paraphrase uses more accessible language and makes the passage's meaning easier to understand.
- Give students a copy of **Reading Strategy Graphic Organizer A,** p. 173 in ***Graphic Organizer Transparencies.***
- Encourage students to use paraphrasing to decode difficult passages in the poems.

Vocabulary Builder

- Pronounce each vocabulary word for students, and read the definitions as a class. Have students identify any words with which they are already familiar.

Differentiated Instruction

Solutions for All Learners

Support for Special Needs Students
Have students complete the **Preview** and **Build Skills** pages for these selections in the ***Reader's Notebook: Adapted Version.*** These pages provide a selection summary, an abbreviated presentation of the reading and literary skills, and the graphic organizer on the **Build Skills** page in the student book.

Support for Less Proficient Readers
Have students complete the **Preview** and **Build Skills** pages for these selections in the ***Reader's Notebook.*** These pages provide a selection summary, an abbreviated presentation of the reading and literary skills, and the graphic organizer on the **Build Skills** page in the student book.

Support for English Learners
Have students complete the **Preview** and **Build Skills** pages for these selections in the ***Reader's Notebook: English Learner's Version.*** These pages provide a selection summary, an abbreviated presentation of the skills, additional contextual vocabulary, and the graphic organizer on the **Build Skills** page in the student book.

TEACH

Learning Modalities
Verbal/Linguistic Learners
Pair students with visual/spatial learners to expand their experience of the poem's imagery. Have students read the poem aloud as their visual/spatial partners illustrate its images with original or found visuals.

❶ About the Selections

The poems by Stevens explore the creative process as he defined it. They break down that process into the intimate moments of imagination, inspiration, and painstaking perfectionism that together work to create poetry.

❷ Vocabulary Builder

The Latin Root *-satis-*

- Call students' attention to the word *insatiable* and its definition. Tell students that the Latin word root *-satis-* means "enough."
- Have students **suggest** words and phrases that contain this root, and list them on the chalkboard. **Possible answers:** *satisfy, satisfactory, satiate,* and *satiety.*
- Next, have students look up the meanings of these words in a dictionary.
- Finally, direct students to reread the poem, looking for places where they can replace an existing word or phrase with a word containing the Latin root *-satis-*. Call on volunteers to read their new sentences aloud.

❶ Of Modern Poetry

Wallace Stevens

Background Wallace Stevens's poetry reflects the influence of the Symbolist literary movement. Originating in the last half of the nineteenth century, Symbolist poets believed that ideas and emotions are difficult to communicate because people perceive the world in such personal ways. These poets tried to convey meaning through symbols—people, places, and objects that represent ideas beyond their concrete meaning. As a result, the work of Symbolist poets like Stevens can often be interpreted in many different ways.

The poem of the mind in the act of finding
What will suffice. It has not always had
To find: the scene was set; it repeated what
Was in the script.
Then the theatre was changed
To something else. Its past was a souvenir.

It has to be living, to learn the speech of the place.
It has to face the men of the time and to meet
The women of the time. It has to think about war
And it has to find what will suffice. It has
To construct a new stage. It has to be on that stage
And, like an insatiable actor, slowly and
With meditation, speak words that in the ear,
In the delicatest ear of the mind, repeat,
Exactly, that which it wants to hear, at the sound
Of which, an invisible audience listens,
Not to the play, but to itself, expressed
In an emotion as of two people, as of two
Emotions becoming one. The actor is
A metaphysician[1] in the dark, twanging
An instrument, twanging a wiry string that gives
Sounds passing through sudden rightnesses, wholly
Containing the mind, below which it cannot descend,
Beyond which it has no will to rise.
It must
Be the finding of a satisfaction, and may
Be of a man skating, a woman dancing, a woman
Combing. The poem of the act of the mind.

Vocabulary Builder
suffice (sə fīs′) *v.* be adequate; meet the needs of

Vocabulary Builder
insatiable (in sā′ shə bəl) *adj.* constantly wanting more

Reading Strategy
Paraphrasing Restate the sentence in lines 18–24 in your own words.

1. **metaphysician** (met′ ə fə zish′ ən) *n.* a person versed in philosophy, especially those branches that seek to explain the nature of being or of the universe.

Differentiated Instruction Solutions for All Learners

Accessibility at a Glance

	Of Modern Poetry; Anecdote of the Jar	Ars Poetica; Poetry
Context	The art of poetry	The art of poetry
Language	Difficult vocabulary	Figurative language
Concept Level	Challenging (abstract presentation; symbolic)	Challenging (difficult subject matter)
Literary Merit	Noted author; classic	Noted author; classic
Lexile	NP	NP
Overall Rating	More challenging	More challenging

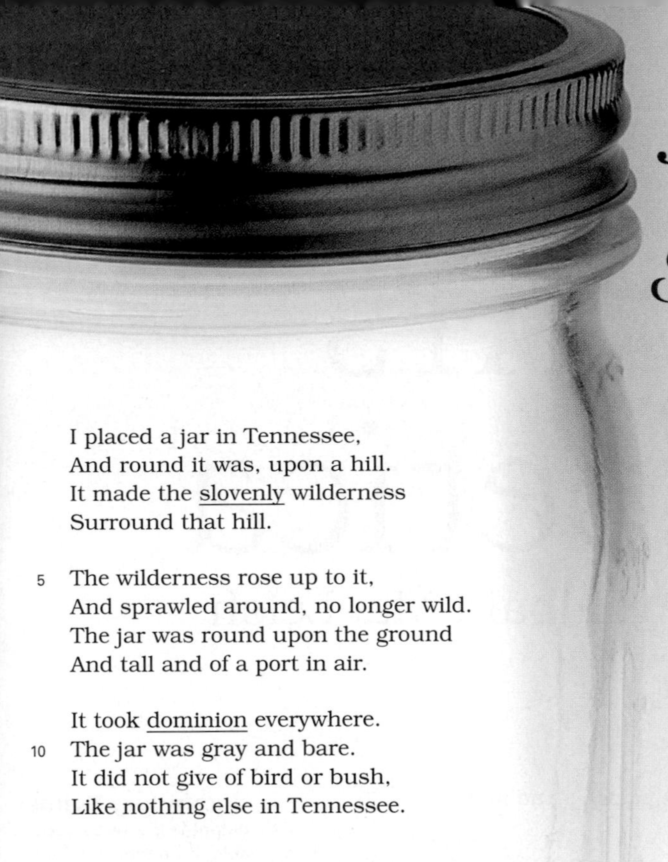

Anecdote of the Jar

Wallace Stevens

I placed a jar in Tennessee,
And round it was, upon a hill.
It made the slovenly wilderness
Surround that hill.

The wilderness rose up to it,
And sprawled around, no longer wild.
The jar was round upon the ground
And tall and of a port in air.

It took dominion everywhere.
The jar was gray and bare.
It did not give of bird or bush,
Like nothing else in Tennessee.

Vocabulary Builder
slovenly (sluv′ ən lē) *adj.* untidy

Vocabulary Builder
dominion (də min′ yən) *n.* power to rule

Critical Reading

1. **(a) Recall:** In the first stanza of "Of Modern Poetry," what does the poet say happened to the theater?
   (b) Interpret: What does "the theatre" represent?
2. **(a) Recall:** What does the poem suggest about the relationship poetry must have with the people of its time? **(b) Analyze:** Does the poet believe the work of poetry to be difficult? Explain.
3. **(a) Recall:** In "Anecdote of the Jar," how does the wilderness receive the jar? **(b) Analyze:** How does the jar affect the wilderness?
4. **(a) Recall:** What words describe the jar in the first and third stanzas?
   (b) Compare and Contrast: How does the image of the jar in the third stanza differ from its depiction in the first?
5. **Evaluate:** Does the jar effectively symbolize the human imagination? Support your answer.

For: More about Wallace Stevens
Visit: www.PHSchool.com
Web Code: ere-9510

❸ Reading Strategy
Paraphrasing

- Point out that paraphrasing—restating a passage in your own words—can make poetry easier to understand.
- **Present** the Reading Strategy task to students: Restate the sentence in lines 18–23 in your own words. Ask students to use a paraphrase chart to develop their responses.
  Possible response: The poet must listen carefully to inspiration, experimenting with different forms and testing each word against an inner, trusted instinct.

➤ **Monitor Progress:** Encourage students to discuss how paraphrasing helps to clarify the poem's meaning.

ASSESS
Answers

1. (a) It "was changed/To something else." (b) **Possible response:** It represents society, which changed dramatically as the modern age began.
2. (a) It has to "face the men of the time" and "meet the women of the time." (b) **Possible response:** The poet does believe it is difficult work; poetry must "learn the speech" of the modern world and "construct a new stage" for itself.
3. (a) The wilderness rises up to the jar and "sprawl[s] around," tamed. (b) **Possible response:** The jar gives order to the wilderness.
4. (a) The words "round," "gray," and "bare" describe the jar. (b) **Possible response:** In the first stanza, the jar is simply part of the landscape. In the third stanza, the jar has taken "dominion everywhere."
5. **Possible response:** Students may respond that it does because it gives order to the wilderness.

Go Online Author Link For additional information about Wallace Stevens, have students type in the Web Code, then select *S* from the alphabet, and then select Wallace Stevens.

4 About the Selection

This poem catalogs in vivid sensory images and figurative language the myriad ways in which poetry can touch the human spirit. MacLeish portrays poetry as a living force, rendering it as the outlet for human emotion expressed through concrete and accessible images.

5 Literary Analysis

Simile

- Remind students that in a *simile*, a writer compares two unlike things using the words *like* or *as*.
- Have students read the bracketed passage. Then, **ask** the Literary Analysis question: Identify the simile in line 5 and explain what two things the speaker compares.
  Answer: The entire stanza is a simile; the speaker compares poetry with a smooth and mossy stone.

▶ **Monitor Progress: Ask** students to explain the effect of this simile. What does the simile communicate to the reader?
Possible response: The comparison stresses that poetry should communicate through its sensory images, not through rhetoric.

6 Critical Viewing

Possible response: Students should identify the images in lines 9–14: the moon climbing, bare trees against a moonlit night, and the moon behind the winter leaves.

4 Ars Poetica[1]

Archibald MacLeish

A poem should be palpable and mute
As a globed fruit.

Dumb
As old medallions to the thumb,

5 Silent as the sleeve-worn stone
Of casement ledges where the moss has grown—

A poem should be wordless
As the flight of birds.

A poem should be motionless in time
As the moon climbs,

Vocabulary Builder
palpable (palʹ pə bəl) *adj.* able to be touched, felt, or handled

Literary Analysis
Simile Identify the simile in line 5 and explain what two things the speaker compares.

1. **Ars Poetica** The title is an allusion to the ancient Roman poet Horace's "Ars Poetica," or "The Art of Poetry," which was composed about 20 B.C.

6 ◀ **Critical Viewing** Which of the poem's images can be found in this photograph? **[Interpret]**

Enrichment

The Moon's Orbit

The moon's climb is not really motionless, of course, just slow enough that the movement is difficult to see. It takes 27 days, 7 hours, and 43 minutes for the moon to complete an orbit around the Earth. Each night the moon appears to rise in the sky, both because it is orbiting around the Earth and because the Earth itself is turning. The moon's light—a reflection of the sun's light—takes different shapes, or phases, as the lit portion of the moon's surface rotates through our path of vision.

Have students work in groups to calculate the moon's rate of movement through the night sky and create an accurate, movable model of the moon and Earth.

Leaving, as the moon releases
Twig by twig the night-entangled trees,

Leaving, as the moon behind the winter leaves.
Memory by memory the mind—

A poem should be motionless in time
As the moon climbs.

A poem should be equal to:
Not true.

❼ For all the history of grief
An empty doorway and a maple leaf.

For love
The leaning grasses and two lights above the sea—

A poem should not mean
But be.

Critical Reading

1. **Respond:** Do you like the way poetry is described in this poem? Why or why not?
2. **(a) Recall:** Identify at least three items the speaker compares to poetry. **(b) Analyze:** What do you think the speaker means by saying that a poem should be "palpable and mute," "wordless," and "motionless in time"?
3. **(a) Recall:** With what images can a poem show the history of grief, as the speaker states? **(b) Recall:** With what images should it show love? **(c) Speculate:** Why do you think MacLeish chose to focus on these emotions?
4. **(a) Interpret:** What contradiction do you see in lines 7–8? **(b) Analyze:** What do you think this contradiction suggests about the subject, poetry?
5. **(a) Interpret:** What contrast does the poet make in the final two lines? **(b) Define:** How would you define the difference between *meaning* and *being?*
6. **Extend:** In what ways do you think poetry can touch the human spirit? Explain.

For: More about Archibald MacLeish
Visit: www.PHSchool.com
Web Code: ere-9511

❼ Critical Thinking

Interpret

- Read the bracketed passage aloud. **Ask** students to explain what the poet is saying in the final stanza. **Possible response:** Poetry should not simply convey ideas but should reach the reader through the emotions and senses.
- Invite students to describe their responses to the final stanza. What does it mean to them? **Possible response:** Students may mention times of grief or love when poetry moved them.

ASSESS

Answers

1. **Possible response:** Students may respond that they like the description of poetry as a concrete living entity. Students should provide a clear explanation of their reactions.
2. (a) The speaker compares a poem to a "globed fruit," "old medallions," "sleeve-worn stone of casement ledges," and "the flight of birds." (b) **Possible response:** Poetry appeals to the sense of touch, expresses meaning through concrete images, and is timeless.
3. (a) A poem shows the history of grief in "an empty doorway and a maple leaf." (b) It shows love in "leaning grasses and two lights above the sea." (c) **Possible response:** They are two of the strongest emotions.
4. (a) Poetry, which is composed of words, cannot be literally "wordless." (b) **Possible response:** It suggests that poetry should rely on images appealing to the senses and emotions rather than the intellect.
5. (a) The poet distinguishes between a poem's *meaning* something and its *being* something. (b) *Meaning* suggests that a poem refers to a subject; it implies distance from an experience. *Being* suggests that the poem is an experience in its own right.
6. **Possible response:** Poetry expresses the deepest human emotions.

Go Online Author Link For additional information about Archibald MacLeish, have students type in the Web Code, then select *M* from the alphabet, and then select Archibald MacLeish.

❽ About the Selection

This poem explains why poetry must be accessible to be effective. The speaker acknowledges, with a self-effacing tone, that poetry is unimportant next to world affairs, but insists nonetheless on its relevance. Poetry can command strong emotional reaction. It can be found in nature and in people. Though imperfect when obscure and unfinished, when expertly rendered, genuine poetry is worthy of interest.

❾ Humanities

Untitled, 1984 by Alexander Calder

This painting is of the modern school, much like Marianne Moore's poetry. The painter, Alexander Calder, was born in Philadelphia into a family of artists. He studied at the Art Students League and later in Paris. Calder is best known for his innovative mobiles in which—as in this painting—geometric shapes play off one another. Use the following questions for discussion:

1. How do you think Moore would have felt about this painting?
   Possible response: She might have felt it was too abstract.
2. What elements of the painting's style reflect the structure of Moore's poem?
   Possible response: Its whimsical shapes remind readers of Moore's creative punctuation and sentence structure.

❿ Critical Viewing

Possible response: Sample sentence: The painting appears to be a random assemblage of shapes, yet as one studies it, a high sense of order, play, and beauty begin to emerge. Explanation: If you are not intimidated by poetry, and regard it with attention, you might find in it something powerful and true.

⓫ Literary Analysis
Simile

- Have students read the bracketed passage in the third stanza. Direct attention to the simile "the immovable critic twitching his skin like/a horse that feels a flea."
- **Ask** students the Literary Analysis question: What does this simile suggest about the speaker's attitude toward critics?
  Possible response: She sees critics as dull and insensitive people who treat the new in poetry as a mere annoyance.

❽

Poetry

Marianne Moore

❾

Untitled, 1984, Alexander Calder, Solomon R. Guggenheim Museum, New York

I, too, dislike it: there are things that are important beyond all this
        fiddle.
  Reading it, however, with a perfect contempt for it, one discovers in
  it after all, a place for the genuine.
      Hands that can grasp, eyes
      that can dilate, hair that can rise
         if it must, these things are important not because a

high-sounding interpretation can be put upon them but because they
        are
  useful. When they become so derivative as to become unintelligible,
  the same thing may be said for all of us, that we
      do not admire what
      we cannot understand: the bat
         holding on upside down or in quest of something to

eat, elephants pushing, a wild horse taking a roll, a tireless wolf under
  a tree, the immovable critic twitching his skin like a horse that feels
      a flea, the base-
  ball fan, the statistician—
      nor is it valid
         to discriminate against "business documents and

❿ **▲ Critical Viewing** Write a sentence describing this painting "with a perfect contempt for it." Explain what the result shows you about Moore's point in lines 2–3. **[Connect]**

Vocabulary Builder
derivative (də riv′ ə tiv) *adj.* not original; based on something else

⓫ **Literary Analysis**
Simile What does the simile comparing a critic to a horse suggest about the speaker's attitude toward critics?

school-books"; all these phenomena are important. One must make a distinction
however: when dragged into prominence by half poets, the result is not poetry,
nor till the poets among us can be
"literalists of
the imagination"—above
insolence and triviality and can present

for inspection, "imaginary gardens with real toads in them," shall we have
it. In the meantime, if you demand on the one hand,
the raw material of poetry in
all its rawness and
that which is on the other hand
genuine, you are interested in poetry.

Vocabulary Builder
literalists (lit′ ər əl ists) *n.* those who take words at their exact meaning

Critical Reading

1. **Respond:** In your opinion, which word or phrase best describes Moore's poem—"fiddle," "derivative," or "genuine"? Explain.
2. **(a) Recall:** What does the speaker say a person discovers when reading poetry "with a perfect contempt for it"? **(b) Interpret:** What type of poetry does the speaker dislike?
3. **(a) Recall:** What does the speaker say happens when poems become derivative? **(b) Synthesize:** What qualities does the speaker believe good poetry should possess?
4. **(a) Interpret:** What apparent contradiction exists in the phrase "literalists of the imagination"? **(b) Analyze:** In what way is the meaning of this phrase furthered by Moore's image of "imaginary gardens with real toads"? **(c) Generalize:** From where is Moore suggesting good poetry derives its power?
5. **Extend:** Do you think that the lyrics of today's popular music meet Moores' criteria for good poetry? Why or why not?

For: More about Marianne Moore
Visit: www.PHSchool.com
Web Code: ere-9512

ASSESS

Answers

1. **Possible response:** Students may feel that Moore's poem deserves her own highest praise—"genuine." Students should provide a clear explanation for their responses.
2. (a) Some of it is good and worthwhile; there is a place in it for the "genuine." (b) **Possible response:** The speaker dislikes poetry that is pretentious or obscure, requiring "high-sounding interpretations."
3. (a) They become "unintelligible" and cannot be admired. (b) **Possible response:** She believes that poems should be accessible and concrete.
4. (a) Literalism suggests a dedication to fact, while imagination suggests the possibility of fancy. (b) Flights of fancy are implied by the idea of "imaginary gardens," but "real toads" suggests a reliance on things ordinary, concrete, and even ugly—the literal. (c) Moore suggests that good poetry derives its power from the concrete objects and experiences of everyday life.
5. **Possible answers:** Students may respond that if song lyrics rely on concrete images and evoke clear emotions Moore might consider them to be poetry.

Go Online Author Link For additional information about Marianne Moore, have students type in the Web Code, then select *M* from the alphabet, and then select Marianne Moore.

Answers

1. **Possible response:** It should approach some ideal, rounded form.
2. **Possible responses:** *Items compared:* a poem and a flight of birds; The simile uses the word as. *Interpretation:* Poetry should convey movement rather than words about movement.
3. **Possible response:** All of the similes combine to create a sense of a poem as an organic, living thing one can experience directly.
4. **Possible response:** Poetry must both absorb and reflect the realities of the modern world.
5. (a) The image is of the moon climbing above the trees in the winter. (b) **Possible response:** The image suggests that poetry must transcend the specific moment that produced it in order to be timeless.
6. (a) They appeal to the sense of sight, but also to touch and physical sensation. (b) **Possible response:** The images allow Moore to suggest the raw, physical energy she believes poetry can—and should—contain.
7. **Possible responses:** (a) Stevens: "It has to be. . . like an insatiable actor"; MacLeish: "A poem should be. . . silent as the sleeve-worn stone"; Moore: "imaginary gardens with real toads in them" (b) All three want poetry to touch people's souls through their senses and to be relevant to people's lives. (c) Steven's ideas are more intellectual and abstract. MacLeish's ideas emphasize the emotional and sensory aspects of poetry. Moore's ideas emphasize the clarity and directness she prizes in poetry.
8. **Possible responses:** (a) The wilderness enveloped the jar and both the landscape and the jar were improved. (b) These things are important because they are practical, not lofty or intellectual.
9. **Possible response:** Students may identify music or theater, and argue for various criteria by which to judge quality work.

Go Online Assessment Students may use the **Self-test** to prepare for **Selection Test A** or **Selection Test B.**

Apply the Skills

Of Modern Poetry • Anecdote of the Jar • Ars Poetica • Poetry

Literary Analysis

Simile

1. In "Ars Poetica," what does the word *globed* suggest about a poem?
2. Find four **similes** in "Ars Poetica" and interpret their meaning. Analyze them in a chart like the one shown.

3. How do all the similes work together in this poem to create a vision of poetry as something that "should not mean / But be"?

Comparing Literary Works

4. Based on "Of Modern Poetry," how would you summarize Steven's definition of poetry?
5. **(a)** Identify the **image** in lines 9–14 in "Ars Poetica." **(b)** How does this image help you understand MacLeish's definition of poetry?
6. **(a)** To what senses do Marianne Moore's images of animal behavior appeal? **(b)** What unites the images in defining poetry for Moore?
7. **(a)** Select one key image from each poem that captures the poet's beliefs about poetry. Explain your choice. **(b)** How do the poets' ideas about poetry compare? **(c)** How do they contrast?

Reading Strategy

Paraphrasing

8. **Paraphrase** the following passages from the poems, giving them straightforward and direct meanings:
   (a) from "Anecdote of the Jar," lines 5–8
   (b) from "Poetry," lines 6–8 ("these things . . . useful.")

Extend Understanding

9. **Career Connection:** These poems express distinct ideas about the characteristics good poems possess. Select another field of artistic endeavor and identify various elements that make for quality work.

QuickReview

A **simile** is a comparison between two seemingly dissimilar things and is indicated by a connecting word such as *like* or *as.*

Imagery is language that appeals to the senses by using **images.**

To **paraphrase,** identify key passages and restate them in your own words.

For: Self-test
Visit: www.PHSchool.com
Web Code: era-6507

Build Language Skills

❶ Vocabulary Lesson

Word Analysis: Latin Root *-satis-*

The word *insatiable* contains the Latin root *-satis-*, which means "enough." Combined with the prefix *in-*, meaning "not," you can determine that *insatiable* will suggest "not enough." Use your knowledge of *-satis-* to define each word below.

1. satisfy
2. satisfactory
3. satiate
4. satiety

Spelling Strategy

When choosing between the suffixes *-able* and *-ible* to form adjectives, opt for *-able* if you are unsure of the spelling. Like *insatiable,* many more adjectives are formed with *-able* than with *-ible.* Add *-able* or *-ible* to each word part below. Then, check your choice in a dictionary.

1. avail__
2. reli__
3. palp__
4. illeg__
5. fall__
6. pli__

Vocabulary Builder: Context

Follow the instructions below to write a sentence for each item, using a word from the vocabulary list on page 793. Use each word once.

1. Describe someone who never exercises imagination.
2. Define the territory governed by a king.
3. Describe the quality of a peach in a beautiful painting.
4. Explain why a friend's room is always such a terrible mess.
5. Criticize a musician whose work lacks originality.
6. Explain why a minimum amount of nutritional food is not enough to maintain one's health.
7. Criticize a sibling who always wants more possessions.

❷ Grammar and Style Lesson

Subject Complements

Subject complements are nouns, pronouns, and adjectives that follow linking verbs (often forms of the word "to be") and identify or describe the subjects.

Sentences containing subject complements are effective when defining something.

S LV SC
Noun: The actor is a *metaphysician . . .*

S LV SC
Pronoun: The poet is she who is a literalist of the imagination.

S LV SC
Adjective: A poem should be *wordless . . .*

Practice Copy each of the following sentences. Underline the subject complement in each one and label it a noun, a pronoun, or an adjective.

1. The winner of this year's poetry prize is you!
2. The subject of the poem was a waterfall.
3. Good poetry should be thrilling.
4. Poets are deep thinkers.
5. The oldest book in the library is a volume of poetry.

Writing Application Write a brief descriptive poem about a familiar person or object. Begin each line with the name of the person or object. Follow it with a linking verb and a subject complement.

WG *Prentice Hall Writing and Grammar Connection: Chapter 18, Section 3*

EXTEND/ASSESS

Answers

❶ Vocabulary Lesson

Word Analysis

1. to fulfill the needs of
2. good enough to fulfill a need
3. to provide with more than enough
4. the state of having had more than enough

Spelling Strategy

1. available
2. reliable
3. palpable
4. illegible
5. fallible
6. pliable

Vocabulary Builder

1. Someone who never uses his or her imagination is a *literalist.*
2. The territory governed by a king is his *dominion.*
3. In a beautiful painting, the peach looks *palpable* and ripe.
4. My friend has *slovenly* habits.
5. The musician's work is very *derivative.*
6. That amount of nutrition will not *suffice* to maintain your health.
7. My sibling has an *insatiable* appetite for possessions.

❷ Grammar and Style Lesson

1. you; pronoun
2. waterfall; noun
3. thrilling; adjective
4. thinkers; noun
5. volume; noun

Writing Application

Students' poems should maintain an appropriate descriptive focus on one person or object; each line should contain a subject complement.

Assessment Practice

Analyze Sentence Meaning **(For more practice, see *Standardized Test Preparation Workbook*, p. 47.)**

Many tests require students to correctly answer sentence-completion questions. Often, more than one choice can complete a sentence. Use the following sample item to show students how to analyze sentence meaning to eliminate incorrect choices.

The Symbolist poets believed that the Modern Age was a time of uncertainty, and that people's ideas and emotions were _____ to communicate.

A easy
B fair
C difficult
D enjoyable

The context of the sentence indicates that the correct answer will have a negative connotation, so *A* and *D* are eliminated. Answer choice *B* does not make sense in the sentence. *C* is the best choice.

❸ Writing Lesson

You may use this Writing Lesson as timed-writing practice, or you may allow students to develop it as a writing assignment over several days.

- To support students in preparing a comparison-and-contrast essay, give them the **Support for Writing Lesson** page (***Unit 5 Resources,*** p. 123).
- Remind students that their essays should clearly explain each poem's main ideas, as well as compare and contrast those ideas.
- Guide students in rereading the poems. You may paraphrase the ideas in all four poems as a class.
- As students draft, be sure that they include necessary background information on each poet's beliefs.
- Use the Comparison-and-Contrast Essay rubrics in ***General Resources,*** pp. 69–70, to evaluate students' work.
- Suggest that students use the Venn Diagram organizer in ***Graphic Organizer Transparencies,*** p. 316.

❹ Listening and Speaking

- Have students create and discuss their own definitions of poetry. Remind them that poetry analysis is highly subjective; they should develop ideas they can support.
- Divide the class into two groups. They should begin by analyzing each poet's views before moving on to the round-table discussion.
- Remind students to remain consistent to the poets' ideas and to adopt appropriate behavior for a discussion, listening and speaking respectfully.
- The **Support for Extend Your Learning** page (***Unit 5 Resources,*** p. 124) provides guided note-taking opportunities to help students complete the Extend Your Learning activities.
- To evaluate students' participation, use the rubric for Analyzing Persuasive Techniques in ***General Resources,*** p. 83.

Go Online Research — Have students type in the Web code for another research activity.

SAT PREP ACT

3 Writing Lesson

Timed Writing: Comparison and Contrast Essay

Stevens, Moore, and MacLeish were not only three of the most important American poets of the twentieth century, they were three of the deepest thinkers about the art of poetry. Write an essay in which you compare and contrast the ideas expressed in two of these poems about poetry. Note the distinct ways in which each poet explains, above all, why poetry is important. ***(40 minutes)***

Prewriting *(10 minutes)* Reread each poem and paraphrase the ideas it presents. Compare and contrast the ideas and determine an organizing principle or main idea to develop in your essay.

Drafting *(20 minutes)* Begin by introducing each poet and providing a general statement about his or her beliefs about poetry. Then, write a brief statement of your main point. Develop your ideas, with quotes from the poems in the body paragraphs.

Model: Providing Necessary Background

Wallace Stevens believed that human beings perceive the world in an entirely subjective way. For Stevens, reality itself was an expression of the imagination. These views come through in his ideas about poetry.

The inclusion of general information about a subject's point of view clarifies the ideas that will follow.

Revising *(10 minutes)* Review your draft, making sure that you have supported your ideas with appropriate quotations from the poem. Replace any less effective quotations with better choices.

WG Prentice Hall Writing and Grammar Connection: Chapter 9, Section 3

4 Extend Your Learning

Listening and Speaking In a small group, analyze different poets' views of poetry. Then, stage a **round-table discussion** on the issue "What Is Poetry?" Each group member should take a poet's position. Use the following tips as a guide:

- Develop a central argument of your view.
- Include logical appeals based on examples.
- Incorporate emotional appeals, such as a poem's impact on you or others.

Share the results of your discussion with the class. **[Group Activity]**

Research and Technology Create a **collection of poems** on another topic, such as sports or nature, that focus on a guiding question. Use print and online poetry reference sources to locate appropriate poems. Include an introduction that explains how the poems relate to one another.

For: An additional research activity
Visit: www.PHSchool.com
Web Code: erd-7507

Assessment Resources

The following resources can be used to assess students' knowledge and skills.

Unit 5 Resources
- **Selection Test A,** pp. 126–128
- **Selection Test B,** pp. 129–131

General Resources
- **Rubrics for Comparison-and-Contrast Essay,** pp. 69–70
- **Rubric for Analyzing Persuasive Techniques,** p. 83

Go Online Assessment — Students may use the **Self-test** to prepare for **Selection Test A** or **Selection Test B.**

Unit 5
Part
2

Focus on Literary Forms: Short Stories

Do It Yourself Landscape, Andy Warhol, Museum Ludwig, Cologne, photo courtesy of Rheinisches Bildarchiv Köln

Differentiated Instruction

Solutions for All Learners

Accessibility at a Glance

More Accessible	Average	More Challenging
The Corn Planting	In Another Country	A Worn Path

Selection Planning Guide

The selections in this section deal with the anxiety and fear felt by many during the modern era, that is, from the period of World War I to the present. "In Another Country" is told through the eyes of a wounded American World-War-I volunteer recuperating in a hospital in Italy. A soldier's fear of death, the fragility of life, the disillusionment with modern technology, and the futility of careful planning are poignantly brought out in this Hemingway story. In "The Corn Planting," an American farm couple, isolated from fast-paced society, cope with the unexpected death of their son by communing with nature through the planting of corn. "A Worn Path" presents an elderly woman with a mission. In spite of her anxiety over making an arduous journey, and over becoming confused at times, a grandmother walks many miles into town to pick up medicine for her injured grandson. She has made this ritualistic journey many times since the young boy swallowed lye long ago.

Humanities

Do It Yourself Landscape, Andy Warhol

Andy Warhol (1930–1987) led the Pop Art movement during the 1960s, making artworks out of commonplace elements of popular culture. In this artwork, Warhol cleverly imitates the look of a partially finished paint-by-number painting, popular during the 1950s and early 1960s. Explain that such a painting would start out like the outlined white spaces on this work, the numbers indicating which color to use within each space.

Ask the following question:

- What seems peculiarly American and twentieth-century about the idea of do-it-yourself art?
  Possible response: Such art is democratic—no one needs to be specially skilled or inspired. It also reflects the techniques of modern mass-production.

Meeting Your Standards

Students will

- **understand the structure and main elements of the short story.**
- **apply knowledge of short stories to identify the conflict and theme.**

1 Elements of a Short Story

- Tell students that the elements of a short story plot primarily concern the conflict. Characterization, setting, mood, tone, and other elements focus on the characters' attempts to resolve conflict.
- Emphasize that the conflict can be any problem that a character in the story faces. Explain that often a character struggles against two or more forces. For example, in Jack London's "To Build a Fire," a man struggles against the cold, an external conflict. He has internal conflicts about his lack of self-assurance and his fear.
- Give students a copy of the Character Wheel graphic organizer, p. 306 in ***Graphic Organizer Transparencies,*** and use it to discuss the elements of a short story. Discuss a story with which students are familiar to identify the elements in the graphic organizer.
- Point out that the protagonist is usually the character that is best developed in a short story. The writer, through direct and indirect characterization, helps the reader see, understand, and sympathize with the character. For example, in Steinbeck's "The Turtle," readers develop sympathy for the turtle, and worry what will happen when the truck swerves to hit it.
- Review briefly the short story "To Build a Fire." **Ask** students how the setting in London's story contributes to the conflict.
Answer: The story's setting is a freezing, remote wilderness. Together the cold and remoteness serve as the antagonist, the problem that the man tries but fails to solve.

Focus on Literary Forms

Defining Short Stories

A **short story** is a brief work of fiction. Short stories have no fixed length, but most are between five hundred words and fifty pages—brief enough to be read in one sitting.

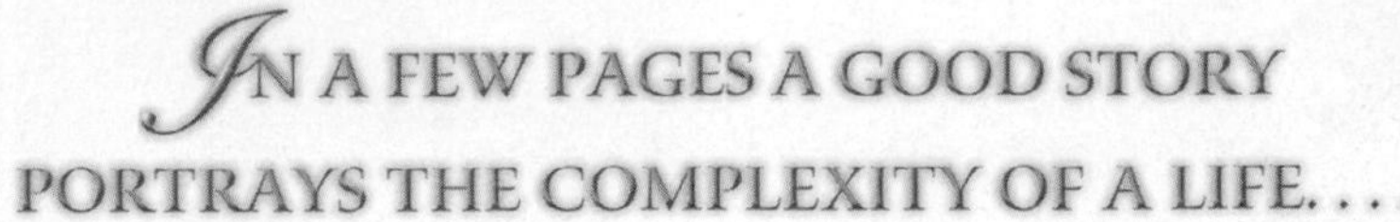

IN A FEW PAGES A GOOD STORY PORTRAYS THE COMPLEXITY OF A LIFE. . . .

—*Bernard Malamud*

1 Elements of a Short Story

A short story typically includes several key elements.

- The **plot** is the sequence of events that makes up a narrative. A short story focuses on a **conflict,** or struggle, that the main character faces, and the plot is structured around the development and resolution of this conflict. An **external conflict** occurs when a character struggles against an outside force, such as another character, nature, or society. An **internal conflict** occurs within a single character who is struggling with opposing feelings, beliefs, needs, or desires.

The Structure of a Plot
The **exposition** introduces the characters, the setting, and the basic situation.
The **rising action** introduces the central conflict, which increases in intensity.
The **climax** is the high point of tension, when the conflict is greatest.
The **falling action** shows the conflict lessening in intensity.
The **resolution,** or **denouement,** resolves the conflict and often shows how the main character has changed.

In some modern stories, the climax occurs so close to the end of the plot that it overlaps with the resolution. Often the resolution is subtle—a character realizes something or simply comes to terms with a problem. Sometimes, there's no real resolution at all.

- The **characters** in a story are the people or animals who participate in the action. A story focuses on the conflict of its main character, or **protagonist**. A writer uses techniques of **characterization** to develop and reveal a character's personality. For example, in "Winter Dreams," page 742,

F. Scott Fitzgerald tells us that Dexter "wanted not association with glittering things and glittering people—he wanted the glittering things themselves."

- **Setting** is the time and place of a story. The setting may simply serve as the background for the action, or it may play a crucial role in the story's plot or conflict, as in Jack London's story "To Build a Fire," page 620.
- **Theme** is the central idea, message, or insight that a story reveals. Because the theme is usually implied, rather than directly stated, the reader may have to piece together different clues to infer the writer's meaning. Often what the protagonist learns or how this character changes is the key to the story's theme. For example, in Tony Earley's "Aliceville," page 1030, the narrator's new self-knowledge and sense of loss at the end of the story is the key to the story's theme.
- **Point of view** is the perspective or vantage point from which a story is told. Point of view is determined by what type of **narrator,** or voice, is telling the story. A writer's choice of narrator is critical because it controls the type of information readers learn about the characters.

2

Characteristics of Fiction Writing

The following elements also play an important role in short stories:

- **Tone** is the writer's attitude toward the characters, the reader, or the subject matter. Tone is closely related to the narrator's voice. In Ernest Hemingway's "In Another Country," the narrator's tone is cool and detached, letting the facts speak for themselves.
- **Mood,** or **atmosphere,** is the feeling that a story evokes in the reader. In the first paragraph of "The Fall of the House of Usher," page 312, Edgar Allan Poe immediately establishes an oppressive, foreboding mood.
- A **symbol** is a person, a place, or an object that has its own meaning but also stands for something larger than itself. For example, in Nathaniel Hawthorne's story "The Minister's Black Veil," page 340, the veil has symbolic meaning that can be interpreted in different ways.

3

Strategies for Reading Short Stories

Use these strategies as you read short stories.

Identify the Conflict Identify the story's conflict, and look for the moment when it reaches a climax. Then, predict how it might resolve.

Interpret the Story's Theme Look for clues that help you interpret the theme of the story. To help you determine the story's messages, pay close attention to the story's ending—particularly the insight the protagonist gains or the way in which this character changes.

Differentiated Instruction

Solutions for All Learners

Strategy for Special Needs Students
Suggest that students keep a character chart (such as the one shown to the right) as they read a short story.

In the left column, they should write the name of the protagonist. In the right column, they should list details about the character as they discover them in the story. Details might include what the main character says or does, and what other characters say about the main character. In the bottom row, they should describe the character's personality, values, and motives.

Character	Details
	1.
	2.
	3.
	4.

Summary of the character:

- Tell students that they can discover themes through the process of making inferences. Review the skill with students; point out that they should identify clues about characters, setting, plot, and symbols. By combining these clues, they can infer the writer's theme.
- Explain that a symbol may have a traditional meaning. For example, a red rose is quickly understood to refer to love. At other times, a symbol will get its meaning from the context in which it is used. Details in Nathaniel Hawthorne's story "The Minister's Black Veil," suggest a symbolic interpretation of the veil. Review briefly "The Minister's Black Veil." **Ask** students what the veil symbolizes.
  Possible response: The veil stands for forbidden acts committed in secret.
- Encourage students to identify and discuss point of view in a story they have read recently. Invite them to speculate on how the story would change if told from a different point of view.

2 Characteristics of Fiction Writing

- Point out that someone can say the same words in two tones of voice and convey two different meanings. Tone in fiction is the written equivalent of tone of voice.
- Tell students that tone is the author's or the speaker's attitude toward the subject; mood is the audience's response to the story.

3 Strategies for Reading Short Stories

- Tell students that a short story is different from a novel because it is meant to be read in a single sitting.
- Encourage students to keep a prediction log as they read short stories. First students should identify the conflict. Then they should list details relating to the conflict and use the details to make predictions. Students should continue finding details and revising predictions as they read.
- Tell students to pause occasionally as they are reading and think generally about the meaning of events. Tell students to ask themselves, "What does this mean? What is the main idea the author is getting at?" Often, the theme will emerge as they respond to these general questions.

Meeting Your Standards

Students will

1. **analyze and respond to literary elements.**
   - Literary Analysis: Point of View
2. **read, comprehend, analyze, and critique short fiction.**
   - Reading Strategy: Identifying With Characters
   - Reading Check questions
   - Apply the Skills questions
   - Assessment Practice (ATE)
3. **develop vocabulary.**
   - Vocabulary Lesson: Latin Root: *-val-*
4. **understand and apply written and oral language conventions.**
   - Spelling Strategy
   - Grammar and Style Lesson: Punctuating Dialogue
5. **develop writing proficiency.**
   - Writing Lesson: Memorial Speech
6. **develop appropriate research strategies.**
   - Extend Your Learning: Research Report
7. **understand and apply listening and speaking strategies.**
   - Extend Your Learning: Sequel

Block Scheduling: Use one 90-minute class period to preteach the skills and have students read the selection. Use a second 90-minute class period to assess students' mastery of skills, extend their learning, and monitor their progress.

Homework Suggestions

Following are possibilities for homework assignments.

- Support pages from *Unit 5 Resources:*
  Literary Analysis
  Reading Strategy
  Vocabulary Builder
  Grammar and Style
- An Extend Your Learning project and the Writing Lesson for this selection group may be completed over several days.

Step-by-Step Teaching Guide	Pacing Guide
PRETEACH	
• Administer Vocabulary and Reading Warm-ups as necessary.	5 min.
• Engage students' interest with the motivation activity.	5 min.
• Read and discuss author and background features. **FT**	10 min.
• Introduce the Literary Analysis Skill: Point of View. **FT**	5 min.
• Introduce the Reading Strategy: Identifying With Characters. **FT**	10 min.
• Prepare students to read by teaching the selection vocabulary. **FT**	
TEACH	
• Informally monitor comprehension while students read independently or in groups. **FT**	30 min.
• Monitor students' comprehension with the Reading Check notes.	as students read
• Reinforce vocabulary with Vocabulary Builder notes.	as students read
• Develop students' understanding of point of view with the Literary Analysis annotations. **FT**	5 min.
• Develop students' ability to identify with characters with the Reading Strategy annotations. **FT**	5 min.
ASSESS/EXTEND	
• Assess students' comprehension and mastery of the Literary Analysis and Reading Strategy by having them answer the Apply the Skills questions. **FT**	15 min.
• Have students complete the Vocabulary Lesson and the Grammar and Style Lesson. **FT**	15 min.
• Apply students' ability to add emotional appeal to writing by using the Writing Lesson. **FT**	45 min. or homework
• Apply students' understanding by using one or more of the Extend Your Learning activities.	20–90 min. or homework
• Administer Selection Test A or Selection Test B. **FT**	15 min.

Resources

PRINT
Unit 5 Resources
- Vocabulary Warm-up Word Lists **[L1, L2, EL]** .... p. 132
- Vocabulary Warm-up Practice **[L1, L2, EL]** .... p. 133
- Reading Warm-up A **[L1, L2, EL]** .... p. 134
- Reading Warm-up B **[L1, L2, L3]** .... p. 135

TRANSPARENCY
Graphic Organizer Transparencies
- Literary Analysis Graphic Organizer A **[L3]** .... p. 177
- Literary Analysis Graphic Organizer B **[L1, L2, EL]** .... p. 178
- Reading Strategy Graphic Organizer A **[L3]** .... p. 179
- Reading Strategy Graphic Organizer B **[L1, L2, EL]** .... p. 180

TECHNOLOGY
From the Author's Desk DVD .... Tim O'Brien, Segment 2

PRINT
Reader's Notebook [L2]
Reader's Notebook: Adapted Version [L1]
Reader's Notebook: English Learner's Version [EL]
Unit 5 Resources
- Literary Analysis **[L3]** .... p. 136
- Reading Strategy **[L3]** .... p. 137
- Vocabulary Builder **[L3]** .... p. 138

TECHNOLOGY
Listening to Literature Audio CDs [L2, EL]
Reader's Notebook: Adapted Version Audio CD [L1, L2]

PRINT
Unit 5 Resources
- Grammar and Style **[L3]** .... p. 139
- Support for Writing Lesson **[L3]** .... p. 140
- Support for Extend Your Learning **[L3]** .... p. 141
- Enrichment **[L4]** .... p. 142
- From the Author's Desk .... p. 143
- Listening and Viewing .... p. 144
- Selection Test A **[L1, L2, EL]** .... pp. 145–147
- Selection Test B **[L3, L4]** .... pp. 148–150

General Resources
- Rubrics for Response to Literature **[L3]** .... pp. 65–66
- Rubrics for Research: Research Report **[L3]** .... pp. 49–50

TRANSPARENCY
Graphic Organizer Transparencies
- Outline **[L3]** .... p. 309

TECHNOLOGY
Go Online: Research **[L3]**
Go Online: Self-test **[L3]**
ExamView® **Test Bank [L3]**

Choosing Resources for Differentiated Instruction

[L1] Special Needs Students
[L2] Below-Level Students
[L3] All Students
[L4] Advanced Students
[EL] English Learners

For Vocabulary and Reading Warm-ups and for Selection Tests, **A** signifies "less challenging" and **B** "more challenging." For Graphic Organizer transparencies, **A** signifies "not filled in" and **B** "filled in."

FT Fast Track Instruction: To move the lesson more quickly, use the strategies and activities identified with **FT**.

Scaffolding for Less Proficient and Advanced Students

The leveled Critical Thinking questions after selections progress in the levels of thinking required to answer them. To address the needs of your different students, you may use the (a) level questions for your less proficient students and the (b) level questions with your on-level and advanced students. The occasional (c) level questions are appropriate for your advanced students.

PRENTICE HALL **TeacherEXPRESS™** Plan · Teach · Assess — Use this complete suite of powerful teaching tools to make lesson planning and testing quicker and easier.

PRENTICE HALL **StudentEXPRESS™** Learn · Study · Succeed — Use the interactive textbook (online and on CD-ROM) to make selections and activities come alive with audio and video support and interactive questions.

Go Online Professional Development
For: Information about Lexiles
Visit: www.PHSchool.com
Web Code: eue-1111

PRETEACH

Motivation

Tell students that it is likely that at some time in their lives they will find themselves in the unenviable position of being the bearer of bad news. Then, divide students into groups. Hand each group an index card with news of an injury, accident, incarceration, dire financial reversal, and so on. Tell them that it is their job to pass on that news to someone who will probably find it very upsetting. Give a different piece of bad news to each group.

Groups can discuss and role-play ways in which to break the news to the people most affected by it. Should they be direct? Should they try to soften the blow? Should they be comforting? Should they deliver the news and then disappear? Have students talk or write about how they think it would feel to give bad news. Students who actually have had that responsibility can volunteer to describe their experiences. Explain to students that each of the stories they're about to read focuses on how people handle difficult situations such as the ones they dealt with in the activity.

Build Skills | Short Stories

1 In Another Country • The Corn Planting • A Worn Path

Ernest Hemingway (1899–1961)

Ernest Hemingway's fiction expressed the sentiments of many members of the post-World War I generation. He wrote about people's struggles to maintain a sense of dignity while living in a sometimes hostile world.

The Red Cross Hemingway, the son of a physician, was born and raised in Oak Park, Illinois, a suburb of Chicago. In high school, he played football and wrote newspaper columns. Eager to serve in World War I, he tried to join the army but was repeatedly turned away due to an eye defect. He joined the Red Cross ambulance corps instead and, in 1918, was sent to the Italian front. Just before his nineteenth birthday, he was severely wounded and spent several months recovering in a hospital in Milan, Italy. His experiences during the war helped shape his view of the world and provide material for his writing.

Expatriates After the war, Hemingway had a difficult time readjusting to life in the United States. To establish himself as a writer, he went to Paris as a foreign correspondent for the *Toronto Star.* In Paris, he befriended Ezra Pound, Gertrude Stein, F. Scott Fitzgerald, and other American writers and artists living overseas. The literary advice of these friends and his work as a journalist helped him develop his concise, concrete, and highly charged writing style.

In 1925, Hemingway published his first major work, *In Our Time,* a series of loosely connected short stories. A year later he published *The Sun Also Rises,* a novel about a group of British and American expatriates trying to overcome the pain and disillusionment of life in the modern world.

Hemingway became as famous for his lifestyle as he was for his writing. Constantly pursuing adventure, he hunted big game in Africa, attended bullfights in Spain, held records for deep-sea fishing in the Caribbean, and participated in amateur boxing.

The full body of Hemingway's work—including *A Farewell to Arms* (1929), *For Whom the Bell Tolls* (1940), and *The Old Man and the Sea* (1952)—earned him the Nobel Prize for Literature in 1954.

Sherwood Anderson (1876–1941)

Sherwood Anderson was one of the most influential American writers of the first half of the twentieth century. The third of seven children, Anderson was raised in a small town in Ohio. His father was a harness maker and house painter who was not always able to earn enough money to support the family. At fourteen, Anderson dropped out of high school to work, taking a variety of unskilled jobs. He eventually joined the army to serve in the Spanish-American War, which ended just before he arrived in Cuba. At the age of twenty-three, after a year of military service, Anderson returned to his hometown and finished high school.

His Best-known Work After, completing highschool, Anderson moved to Chicago to pursue a writing career. He worked as an advertising copywriter and met poets Carl Sandburg and Edgar Lee Masters and novelist Theodore Dreiser. After witnessing the success of Masters's *Spoon River Anthology,* Anderson began his own fictional explorations of life in rural America. Using his boyhood observations and experiences as material, he created his best-known work, *Winesburg, Ohio* (1919), a unified collection of short stories. In this work, Anderson presents small-town life in a strikingly different manner from earlier works of literature. He looks beneath the surface of the characters' lives to construct psychological portraits. He also uses everyday speech to capture the essence of characters, a technique he borrowed from Mark Twain.

In addition to writing, Anderson became a successful businessman heading the Anderson Manufacturing Company, which made paint and roof-pitch. He did not enjoy business, and in his mid-thirties, he abandoned the company to devote himself to writing. Although Anderson's literary reputation rests mainly on *Winesburg, Ohio,* he also published other successful books, including *Windy McPherson's Son* (1916), *The Triumph of the Egg* (1921), *Horses and Men* (1923), and *Death in the Woods and Other Stories* (1933).

Eudora Welty (1909–2001)

Eudora Welty's stories and novels capture life in the deep South, creating images of the landscape and conveying the shared attitudes and values of the people. She often confronts the hardships of life in poor rural areas. Despite her awareness of people's suffering, her writing remains optimistic.

Welty was born in Jackson, Mississippi, where she spent most of her life. She attended Mississippi State College for Women before transferring to the University of Wisconsin, from which she graduated in 1929. Hoping to pursue a career in advertising, she moved to New York and enrolled at Columbia University School of Business. However, because of the worsening economic depression, she was unable to find steady employment and returned to Jackson in 1931.

Writing Fiction After accepting a job as a publicist for a government agency, Welty spent several years traveling throughout Mississippi, taking photographs and interviewing people. Her experiences and observations inspired her to write, and in 1936 her first short story, "Death of a Traveling Salesman," was published.

In her fiction, Welty displays an acute sense of detail and a deep sense of compassion toward her characters. For example, in "A Worn Path," she paints a sympathetic portrait of an old woman whose feelings of love and sense of duty motivate her to make a long, painful journey through the woods.

One of the leading American writers of the twentieth century, Welty published numerous collections of short stories and novels. In 1973, her novel *The Optimist's Daughter* won the Pulitzer Prize.

Background

World War I was the first truly global war, involving nations on every continent but Antarctica. The Great War, as it was also called, began in Europe in 1914, sparked by nationalist pride and systems of alliances among nations. The Central Powers (Germany, Austria, Turkey) fought the Allies (England, France, Russia) with other nations joining one side or the other. Italy, where Hemingway's "In Another Country" takes place, was not strategically important, but it helped the Allies by drawing Central Power troops away from other battle areas.

The war lasted four brutal years. Throughout most of the conflict, a stalemate existed. Both sides were dug into trenches, and took turns rushing one another. Each rush was greeted by a barrage of machine-gun fire, with thousands falling dead. Other soldiers fell to new weapons of killing—inventions such as airplanes, long-range artillery, and poison gas—that many people had hoped would deter aggressors and prevent war. Many of the wounded were saved, however, by advances in medical treatment, such as surgical disinfectants and rehabilitative techniques to strengthen injured limbs.

❶ Background

More About the Authors

In his time, Sherwood Anderson was enormously influential in the world of American literature. *Winesburg, Ohio* appeared just after World War I and can be seen as heralding an important literary moment in the United States. Anderson's experimental use of everyday language directly influenced Ernest Hemingway's style. Anderson's influence worked on other levels, as well. Hemingway owed his first book publication to the older author.

Hemingway became famous with his first novel, *The Sun Also Rises,* and his literary star quickly outshone Anderson's. In 1926, Hemingway published *Torrents of Spring,* a mean-spirited satire of Anderson's work. As Anderson's importance seemed to fade, Hemingway emerged as perhaps the most famous and influential American author of the twentieth century. Tragically, he took his own life in 1961, but he remains a giant literary figure whose influence continues to this day.

Eudora Welty matured as a writer in a literary landscape permanently changed by such authors as Anderson and Hemingway. While her style and immediate subject matter—the people of small-town Mississippi—seem very different from those of the two older writers, her explorations of human relationships travel ground broken by the generation of writers that immediately preceded her generation.

Differentiated Instruction

Solutions for All Learners

Support for Special Needs Students
Have students use the support pages for these selections in the ***Reader's Notebook: Adapted Version.*** Completing these pages will prepare students to read the selections in the Student Edition.

Support for Less Proficient Readers
Have students use the support pages for these selections in the ***Reader's Notebook.*** After students finish the pages in the *Reader's Notebook,* have them complete the questions and activities in the Student Edition.

Support for English Learners
Have students use the support pages for these selections in the ***Reader's Notebook: English Learner's Version.*** Completing these pages will prepare students to read the selections in the Student Edition.

❷ Literary Analysis
Point of View

- Explain that a narrator who is a character and speaks to the reader using the words "I" or "we" is a *first-person narrator.* One who is not a character and describes the actions using "he," "she," and "they" is a *limited third-person narrator.*
- Be sure students understand that different kinds of narrators have different *points of view* on the action in a story.
- Give students a copy of **Literary Analysis Graphic Organlzer A,** p. 177, in ***Graphic Organizer Transparencies*** to use as they read the stories.

❸ Reading Strategy
Identifying With Characters

- Explain to students that by identifying with characters they can appreciate and understand stories more fully.
- As an example, point out that the narrator of the first story is an injured soldier being consoled by a doctor. Readers who have also been injured may know how the narrator feels. Those who have not been physically injured may nonetheless understand the emotional turmoil the soldier experiences.

Vocabulary Builder

- Pronounce each vocabulary word for students, and read the definitions as a class. Have students identify any words with which they are already familiar.

Preview

Connecting to the Literature

In each of these stories, characters undertake journeys that dramatically affect their lives. As you read, notice the ways in which their journeys compare to ones that you have made.

❷ Literary Analysis

Point of View

The **point of view** of a story is the perspective from which it is told.

- In stories told from the **first-person point of view,** the person telling the story participates in the action, uses the pronoun *I,* and shares his or her own thoughts and feelings.
- In stories told from the **limited third-person point of view,** the narrator stands outside the action and does not use the pronoun *I.* However, this narrator sees the world through one character's eyes and reveals only what that character is thinking and feeling.

As you read, use a chart like the one shown to analyze the type of narration each story demonstrates.

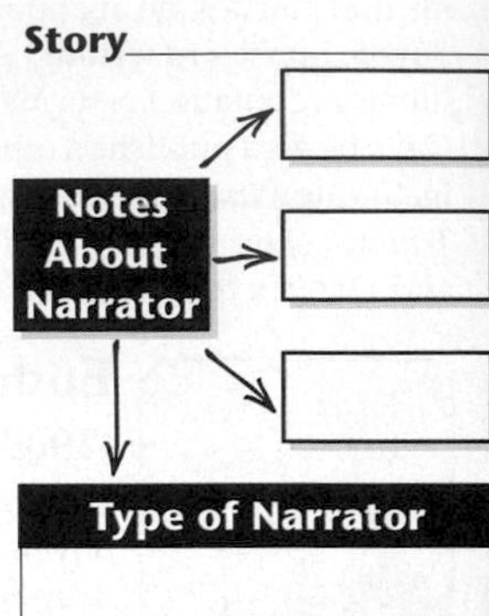

Comparing Literary Works

Each of these stories is told from a different point of view. In each case, the **narrator,** or person telling the story, controls information and directly influences the reader's perceptions. Examine the effects of different points of view by comparing the information each narrator shares. Notice the biases each displays and the level of sympathy or interest each generates. Finally, determine the reasons you think each author chose the narrative point of view he or she did, and how that choice gives a specific shape to the story.

❸ Reading Strategy

Identifying With Characters

Even if your journeys differ from the ones taken by these characters, you might feel as though you know them. When you **identify with characters,** you relate to their thoughts and feelings and connect them with your own experiences. As you read, identify with characters by comparing your life experiences with theirs.

Vocabulary Builder

invalided (in´ və lid´ id) *v.* released because of illness or disability (p. 814)

grave (grāv) *adj.* serious; solemn (p. 821)

limber (lim´ bər) *adj.* flexible (p. 821)

obstinate (äb´ stə nət) *adj.* stubborn (p. 827)

❶ IN ANOTHER COUNTRY

ERNEST HEMINGWAY

In the fall the war[1] was always there, but we did not go to it any more. It was cold in the fall in Milan[2] and the dark came very early. Then the electric lights came on, and it was pleasant along the streets looking in the windows. There was much game hanging outside the shops, and the snow powdered in the fur of the foxes and the wind blew their tails. The deer hung stiff and heavy and empty, and small birds blew in the wind and the wind turned their feathers. It was a cold fall and the wind came down from the mountains.

1. **the war** World War I (1914–1918).
2. **Milan** (mi lan′) a city in northern Italy.

❷ ▲ **Critical Viewing** What mood is conveyed in this image of a hospital serving soldiers during World War I? Which details contribute to the mood? **[Interpret]**

TEACH

Learning Modalities
Bodily/Kinesthetic Learners

Invite students to develop an exercise program for someone like the major or the narrator in the first story in the selection, "In Another Country." Their goal is to strengthen or increase the use of a particular injured limb. Students should assume that the complex scientific equipment that exists today is not available. Students can also consider how their program will be presented to the patients.

❶ About the Selection

True to Hemingway's style, this story of a soldier in a World War I military hospital describes a time, but it does not create and then resolve a single conflict. The narrator, an American serving as an officer in the Italian army during World War I, convalesces after a serious injury to his leg. He befriends other wounded soldiers, but once they decide his medals were awarded because he is an American while theirs were won for acts of valor and self-sacrifice, he feels isolated from them. The narrator is "in another country," both physically and emotionally. It is a place where he feels no connection to anyone else.

❷ Critical Viewing

Possible response: The image conveys a mood of calm, but with trouble and pain close by. Details that add to this mood include the white sheets and the placid expression on the nurse's face combined with the haunted or pained look of the American soldier.

Differentiated Instruction
Solutions for All Learners

Accessibility at a Glance

	In Another Country	The Corn Planting	A Worn Path
Context	WWI	Midwestern farm family	The rural South
Language	Accessible	Accessible (little dialogue)	Accessible
Concept Level	Abstract (alienation)	Abstract (generational alienation)	Abstract (journey, real and spiritual)
Literary Merit	Noted author, widely anthologized	Noted author, interesting character study	Noted author, widely anthologized
Lexile	1050L	910L	780L
Other	No simple conflict, no resolution	Midwestern stoicism and love	Character-driven
Overall Rating	Average	More accessible	More challenging

❸ Literary Analysis
Point of View

- Remind students that *point of view* refers to the narrator's perspective. In first-person point of view, the narrator is a character in the story who speaks to the reader using the words "I" and "we."
- Instruct students to use **Literary Analysis Graphic Organizer A** for "In Another Country."
- Before they fill in the boxes on their charts, **ask** students what type of narrator tells this story.
  Answer: The story has a first-person narrator.
- **Ask** the Literary Analysis question: How can you tell right from the start that the story is told from a first-person point of view?
  Possible response: The narrator uses the words "we" and "I". The narrator is a character in the story.

❸ We were all at the hospital every afternoon, and there were different ways of walking across the town through the dusk to the hospital. Two of the ways were alongside canals, but they were long. Always, though, you crossed a bridge across a canal to enter the hospital. There was a choice of three bridges. On one of them a woman sold roasted chestnuts. It was warm, standing in front of her charcoal fire, and the chestnuts were warm afterward in your pocket. The hospital was very old and very beautiful, and you entered through a gate and walked across a courtyard and out a gate on the other side. There were usually funerals starting from the courtyard. Beyond the old hospital were the new brick pavilions, and there we met every afternoon and were all very polite and interested in what was the matter, and sat in the machines that were to make so much difference.

The doctor came up to the machine where I was sitting and said: "What did you like best to do before the war? Did you practice a sport?"

I said: "Yes, football."

"Good," he said. "You will be able to play football again better than ever."

My knee did not bend and the leg dropped straight from the knee to the ankle without a calf, and the machine was to bend the knee and make it move as in riding a tricycle. But it did not bend yet, and instead the machine lurched when it came to the bending part. The doctor said: "That will all pass. You are a fortunate young man. You will play football again like a champion."

In the next machine was a major who had a little hand like a baby's. He winked at me when the doctor examined his hand, which was between two leather straps that bounced up and down and flapped the stiff fingers, and said: "And will I too play football, captain-doctor?" He had been a very great fencer, and before the war the greatest fencer in Italy.

The doctor went to his office in a back room and brought a photograph which showed a hand that had been withered almost as small as the major's, before it had taken a machine course, and after was a little larger. The major held the photograph with his good hand and looked at it very carefully. "A wound?" he asked.

"An industrial accident," the doctor said.

"Very interesting, very interesting," the major said, and handed it back to the doctor.

"You have confidence?"

"No," said the major.

There were three boys who came each day who were about the same age I was. They were all three from Milan, and one of them was to be a lawyer, and one was to be a painter, and one had intended to be a soldier, and after we were finished with the machines, sometimes we walked back together to the Café Cova, which was next door to the Scala.[3] We walked the short way through the communist quarter

Literary Analysis
Point of View How can you tell right from the start that the story is told from the first-person point of view?

3. **the Scala** (skä′ lä) an opera house in Milan.

Enrichment

Physical Therapy and Therapists

Physical therapy is the treatment of injury or illness by physical means. Physical therapists work with a wide range of patients, from those who have severe injuries and are in need of intensive therapy, to the throngs of Americans suffering from lower back pain. The tools of the physical therapist are exercise, massage, infrared or ultraviolet light, electrotherapy, and heat.

Interested students can research to find out more about the daily activities of physical therapists. Students can learn about how a physical therapist's approach to healing differs from that of chiropractors, psychiatrists, orthopedists, acupuncturists, and other practitioners. Also, students can research the nature of the education and training physical therapists undergo, as well as the necessary licensing requirements.

because we were four together. The people hated us because we were officers, and from a wine-shop someone called out, "A basso gli ufficiali!"[4] as we passed. Another boy who walked with us sometimes and made us five wore a black silk handkerchief across his face because he had no nose then and his face was to be rebuilt. He had gone out to the front from the military academy and been wounded within an hour after he had gone into the front line for the first time. They rebuilt his face, but he came from a very old family and they could never get the nose exactly right. He went to South America and worked in a bank. But this was a long time ago, and then we did not any of us know how it was going to be afterward. We only knew then that there was always the war, but that we were not going to it any more.

We all had the same medals, except the boy with the black silk bandage across his face, and he had not been at the front long enough to get any medals. The tall boy with a very pale face who was to be a lawyer had been a lieutenant of Arditi[5] and had three medals of the sort we each had only one of. He had lived a very long time with death and was a little detached. We were all a little detached, and there was nothing that held us together except that we met every afternoon at the hospital. Although, as we walked to the Cova through the tough part of town, walking in the dark, with light and singing coming out of the wine-shops, and sometimes having to walk into the street when the men and women would crowd together on the sidewalk so that we would have had to jostle them to get by, we felt held together by there being something that had happened that they, the people who disliked us, did not understand.

We ourselves all understood the Cova, where it was rich and warm and not too brightly lighted, and noisy and smoky at certain hours, and there were always girls at the tables and the illustrated papers on a rack on the wall. The girls at the Cova were very patriotic, and I found that the most patriotic people in Italy were the café girls—and I believe they are still patriotic.

The boys at first were very polite about my medals and asked me what I had done to get them. I showed them the papers, which were written in very beautiful language and full of *fratellanza* and *abnegazione*,[6] but which really said, with the adjectives removed, that I had been given the medals

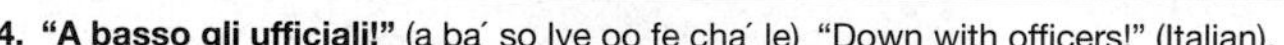

4. **"A basso gli ufficiali!"** (a ba´ so lye oo fe cha´ le) "Down with officers!" (Italian).
5. **Arditi** (är dē´ tē) a select group of soldiers chosen specifically for dangerous campaigns.
6. ***fratellanza*** (frä täl än´ tsä) **and** ***abnegazione*** (äb´ nā gä tzyō´ nā) "brotherhood" and "self-denial" (Italian).

5 Literature in Context

History Connection

"The War to End All Wars"

In this story, the characters struggle courageously against their disillusionment with war and technology. World War I resulted in astonishing destruction and massive death as a result of new technologies such as airplanes, poison gas, and long-range artillery. Many who enlisted did so expecting a swift victory, but the war lasted four grueling years. Up to ten million soldiers died, as well as many civilians. Some people believed that this widespread destruction and loss of life would make World War I "The War to End All Wars," but they were proved wrong.

Connect to the Literature

Do you think the narrator in this story has any expectation of ever fighting again? Explain.

6 **Reading Check**

What do the narrator and the "three boys" have in common?

Differentiated Instruction

Solutions for All Learners

Support for Special Needs Students
If students are confused by the story's setting and do not seem to understand what is happening, preview the story with students and explain its central events.

Strategy for Gifted/Talented Students
After reading about the wounded men walking to the Cova, have these students discuss what it means to feel detached. Ask them to explain why these men are "a little detached" and to offer reasons why people come to feel aloof and indifferent. Then, ask each student to write a short poem about the feeling of detachment.

Strategy for Advanced Readers
Call students' attention to the sentence, "We only knew then that there was always the war, but that we were not going to it anymore." Point out that here the narrator rephrases the opening sentence of the story. Have students discuss the effect of this repetition.

4 Critical Thinking

Infer

- Read the bracketed passage out loud with the class. Discuss with students their impressions of the narrator and the three "boys."
- **Ask** students: How old do you think the narrator and the other "boys" are? Why?
  Possible response: Students may say that the young soldiers are perhaps 18–20 years old because none of them had careers before the war; their plans are for what they are "to be."
- Remind students that wars are fought by soldiers who are mostly their age and slightly older.

5 Literature in Context

"The War to End All Wars" World War I was a nineteenth-century war fought with twentieth-century weapons; the military tactics lagged behind the capabilities of the weaponry. As a result, casualties were staggering and the wounds extraordinary and appalling. Although some soldiers came home with psychological wounds and others with illnesses, some were simply ripped apart. It has been estimated that more than 12 percent of all injured soldiers suffered from facial wounds. Perhaps a third of these unfortunate men were permanently disfigured. Polite society sometimes shunned them. Much of the support the hundreds of decorated veterans received was from their fellow victims. Attempting to dignify their experience, they bonded together to form mutual-aid societies.

Connect to the Literature Ask students whether they know anyone who has been injured in war. Encourage students to explain how that person might feel about fighting again.
Possible answer: Some students may think the narrator is moved by his injuries, his experiences in battle, or the major's suffering so that he will not fight again. Others may say that he is so alienated that he is indifferent to war and its consequences.

6 Reading Check

Answer: They are about the same age, serve in the Italian military, earned similar medals, and have been wounded.

7 Reading Strategy
Identifying With Characters

- Instruct students to pause after reaching the top of this page. Remind them that by identifying with characters they can better understand characters' motivations and behavior.
- Point out that the narrator has revealed that he and his fellow officers are hated in Milan's communist quarter.
- **Ask** students the Reading Strategy question: Have you ever been in a situation where you did not feel fully accepted or part of a group? How did it make you feel?
  Possible response: Students may recall incidents when they have felt antagonized by their classmates. They may be able to identify with the officer's prideful disdain of their detractors.

➤ **Monitor Progress:** Have students discuss how realistic they feel the reactions of the wounded officers are.

8 Background
Literature

Explain to students that this paragraph describes an experience much like Hemingway's own as a Red Cross volunteer during World War I. He didn't take part in the fighting; he was an ambulance driver. During one run he was hit by several fragments from a mortar shell and wounded. For this he received medals and glowing citations.

Encourage students to consider this information as they read. How does this knowledge shape their response to the narrator of "In Another Country"?

9 Critical Viewing

Possible response: The cold metallic appearance of the room would probably have been frightening.

7 because I was an American. After that their manner changed a little toward me, although I was their friend against outsiders. I was a friend, but I was never really one of them after they had read the citations, because it had been different with them and they had done very different things to get their medals. I had been wounded, it was true; but we all knew that being wounded, after all, was really an accident. I was never ashamed of the ribbons, though, and sometimes, after the

8 cocktail hour, I would imagine myself having done all the things they had done to get their medals; but walking home at night through the empty streets with the cold wind and all the shops closed, trying to keep near the street lights, I knew that I would never have done such things, and I was very much afraid to die, and often lay in bed at night by myself, afraid to die and wondering how I would be when I went back to the front again.

The three with the medals were like hunting-hawks; and I was not a hawk, although I might seem a hawk to those who had never hunted; they, the three, knew better and so we drifted apart. But I stayed good friends with the boy who had been wounded his first day at the front, because he would never know now how he would have turned out; so he could never be accepted either, and I liked him because I thought perhaps he would not have turned out to be a hawk either.

The major, who had been the great fencer, did not believe in bravery, and spent much time while we sat in the machines correcting my grammar. He had complimented me on how I spoke Italian, and we talked together very easily. One day I had said that Italian seemed such an easy language to me that I could not take a great interest in it; everything was so easy to say. "Ah yes," the major said. "Why, then, do you not take up the use of grammar?" So we took up the use of grammar, and soon Italian was such a difficult language that I was afraid to talk to him until I had the grammar straight in my mind.

The major came very regularly to the hospital. I do not think he ever missed a day, although I am sure he did not believe in the machines. There was a time when none of us believed in the machines, and one day the major said it was all nonsense. The machines were new then and it was we who were to prove them. It was an idiotic idea, he said, "a theory, like another." I had not learned my grammar, and he said I was a stupid impossible disgrace,

Reading Strategy
Identifying With Characters Have you ever been in a situation like the narrator's where you did not feel fully accepted or part of a group? How did it make you feel?

9 ▼ **Critical Viewing** How might you have reacted to this World War I operating room if you had been a wounded soldier? Explain. **[Relate]**

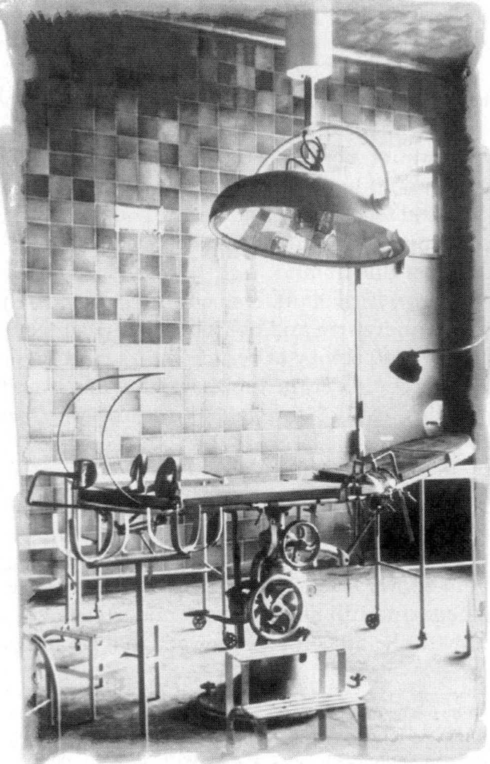

Enrichment

Medical Advances

Advances in medicine and in the treatment of wounds are often the byproduct of war. During the Civil War, for example, nursing care was transformed from a menial service to a genuine profession. That war also introduced the idea of a special ambulance corps to give first aid to the wounded and then transport them from the battlefield. Following World War I, the problem of dealing with the hundreds of thousands of disfigured and mutilated soldiers led to advancements in plastic surgery and the prosthetic arts. Many veterans, whom the French called "the men with the broken faces," endured a series of painful operations meant to correct or minimize disfigurement.

Interested students can do research to learn more about war-related advancements in medical care. For a unique look at several "before-and-after" photos of some of the first reconstructive surgery patients, students can view the PBS series *The Great War* (1996).

and he was a fool to have bothered with me. He was a small man and he sat straight up in his chair with his right hand thrust into the machine and looked straight ahead at the wall while the straps thumped up and down with his fingers in them.

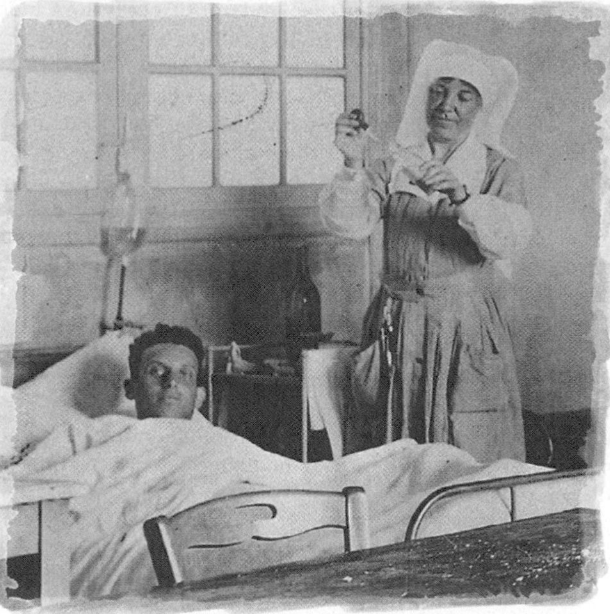

"What will you do when the war is over if it is over?" he asked me. "Speak grammatically!"

"I will go to the States."

"Are you married?"

"No, but I hope to be."

"The more of a fool you are," he said. He seemed very angry. "A man must not marry."

"Why, Signor Maggiore?"[7]

"Don't call me 'Signor Maggiore.'"

"Why must not a man marry?"

"He cannot marry. He cannot marry," he said angrily. "If he is to lose everything, he should not place himself in a position to lose that. He should not place himself in a position to lose. He should find things he cannot lose."

He spoke very angrily and bitterly, and looked straight ahead while he talked.

"But why should he necessarily lose it?"

"He'll lose it," the major said.

He was looking at the wall. Then he looked down at the machine and jerked his little hand out from between the straps and slapped it hard against his thigh. "He'll lose it," he almost shouted. "Don't argue with me!" Then he called to the attendant who ran the machines. "Come and turn this damned thing off."

He went back into the other room for the light treatment and the massage. Then I heard him ask the doctor if he might use his telephone and he shut the door. When he came back into the room, I was sitting in another machine. He was wearing his cape and had his cap on, and he came directly toward my machine and put his arm on my shoulder.

"I am so sorry," he said, and patted me on the shoulder with his good hand. "I would not be rude. My wife has just died. You must forgive me."

"Oh—" I said, feeling sick for him. "I am so sorry."

He stood there biting his lower lip. "It is very difficult," he said. "I cannot resign myself."

7. **Signor Maggiore** (sēn yōr′ mäj jō′ rā) "Mr. Major" (Italian); a respectful way of addressing an officer.

11 ▲ **Critical Viewing**
Does this World War I military hospital compare with the hospital Hemingway describes? Explain. **[Compare and Contrast]**

12  **Reading Check**
Why does the mayor believe "a man must not marry"?

10 Critical Thinking
Interpret

- Have students read the bracketed passage. Encourage students to discuss their reactions to the information the major reveals. Did it surprise them?
- **Ask** students to reread the exchange between the narrator and the major regarding marriage. Guide them to recognize that the major's anger is a response to his wife's death.
- Then, **ask** students: Why did the major respond to learning of his loss by being angry?
  Possible response: Some students might say that anger is a common reaction to tragedy. Others might say that the major has not yet accepted the loss.

11 Critical Viewing

Possible response: Students may say that the place Hemingway has described seems to be a clinic housed in an impressive building. It appears to be full of machines, not crowded with beds filled with badly wounded men.

12 Reading Check

Answer: A man must not marry because "[h]e should not place himself in a position to lose" something as important as a spouse.

Differentiated Instruction
Solutions for All Learners

Support for Less Proficient Readers
Students may find the narrator's conversation with the major on this page to be challenging. Have them read the passage once through for a general impression. Then, have them reread the passage as they listen to it read aloud on **Listening to Literature CDs.** Guide students to understand that the major becomes highly emotional on the subject of marriage. Encourage them to speculate on what might be the cause of the major's anger.

Support for English Learners
You may wish to use the major's thoughts on grammar for discussion. Students can understand that speaking Italian was easy for the narrator when he was unaware of correct grammar. Then, as soon as he tried to speak correctly, Italian became difficult. Ask students learning English if they face the same problem. Discuss whether there is an everyday English that is easy to speak and a "classroom" grammar that is difficult to learn.

13 Vocabulary Builder
The Latin Root *-val-*

- Call students' attention to the word *invalided* and read its definition. Tell students that the Latin root *-val-* means "strength" or "value."
- Have students suggest words and phrases that contain this root, and list them on the chalkboard. **Possible answers:** *equivalent, valor, prevail.*
- Then, have students look up the meanings of these words in a dictionary and write sentences in which they use each word correctly.

ASSESS
Answers

1. **Possible response:** Students may say that the story aroused pity for all the injured men.
2. (a) The narrator was wounded in the leg and is receiving physical therapy to restore muscle activity. (b) **Possible response:** The Italian boys are proud of their accomplishments—and their wounds—because they have fought for their country.
3. (a) He says that they "were to make so much difference," that they are new, and that these men are the first to use them. (b) **Possible response:** His leg does not bend despite the machines.
4. (a) The people hate them just because they are officers. (b) **Possible response:** The abuse creates a stronger bond between the wounded men.
5. (a) The major's wife dies. (b) He reacts with anger. (c) **Possible answer:** It is ironic because the major escaped death in the war, but his wife, protected from such dangers, died after a short illness.
6. **Possible response:** Grammar follows rules; it can be understood and mastered. By contrast, the war is confusing and seems to have no rules.
7. **Possible response:** Advancements in modern technology have brought weapons of destruction that have maimed countless thousands of men like those in the story; constructive uses of technology, represented by the

He looked straight past me and out through the window. Then he began to cry. "I am utterly unable to resign myself," he said and choked. And then crying, his head up looking at nothing, carrying himself straight and soldierly, with tears on both his cheeks and biting his lips, he walked past the machines and out the door.

13 The doctor told me that the major's wife, who was very young and whom he had not married until he was definitely invalided out of the war, had died of pneumonia. She had been sick only a few days. No one expected her to die. The major did not come to the hospital for three days. Then he came at the usual hour, wearing a black band on the sleeve of his uniform. When he came back, there were large framed photographs around the wall of all sorts of wounds before and after they had been cured by the machines. In front of the machine the major used were three photographs of hands like his that were completely restored. I do not know where the doctor got them. I always understood we were the first to use the machines. The photographs did not make much difference to the major because he only looked out of the window.

Vocabulary Builder
invalided (in′ və lid id) *v.* released because of illness or disability

Critical Reading

1. **Respond:** What emotion did this story arouse most strongly in you? Explain.
2. **(a) Recall:** Why does the narrator go to the hospital every day? **(b) Infer:** What type of attitudes would you say he encounters from other patients at the hospital in the same situation? Explain.
3. **(a) Recall:** What does the narrator say about the machines at the hospital? **(b) Interpret:** Why do you think he has developed this attitude toward the machines?
4. **(a) Recall:** How do the people in the communist quarter of the city react to the officers? **(b) Relate:** How do you think these reactions make the officers feel?
5. **(a) Recall:** What happens to the major's wife? **(b) Recall:** How does the major react? **(c) Analyze:** Do you find what happened ironic or surprising? Explain.
6. **Interpret:** Given the setting of the story, a hospital during wartime, what might be the significance of the major's interest in grammar?
7. **Apply:** Do you think this story reflects the sense of disillusionment that arose among writers and artists during World War I? Explain.

For: More about Ernest Hemingway
Visit: www.PHSchool.com
Web Code: ere-9513

Answers continued

rehabilitation machines, seem far less effective than their destructive counterparts. The story seems to be saying that the advance of civilization has created more, not less, suffering, and thus expresses a strong sense of disillusionment.

Go Online Author Link For additional information about Ernest Hemingway, have students type in the Web Code, then select *H* from the alphabet, and then select Hemingway.

14 The Corn PLANTING

SHERWOOD ANDERSON

The farmers who come to our town to trade are a part of the town life. Saturday is the big day. Often the children come to the high school in town.

It is so with Hatch Hutchenson. Although his farm, some three miles from town, is small, it is known to be one of the best-kept and best-worked places in all our section. Hatch is a little gnarled old figure of a man. His place is on the Scratch Gravel Road and there are plenty of poorly kept places out that way.

Hatch's place stands out. The little frame house is always kept painted, the trees in his orchard are whitened with lime halfway up the trunks, and the barn and sheds are in repair, and his fields are always clean-looking.

Hatch is nearly seventy. He got a rather late start in life. His father, who owned the same farm, was a Civil War man and came home badly wounded, so that, although he lived a long time after the war, he couldn't work much. Hatch was the only son and stayed at home, working the place until his father died. Then, when he was nearing fifty, he married a schoolteacher of forty, and they had a son. The schoolteacher was a small one like Hatch. After they married, they both stuck close to the land. They seemed to fit into their farm life as certain people fit into the clothes they wear. I have noticed something about people who make a go of marriage. They grow more and more alike. Then even grow to look alike.

Their one son, Will Hutchenson, was a small but remarkably strong boy. He came to our high school in town and pitched on our town baseball team. He was a fellow always cheerful, bright and alert, and a great favorite with all of us.

For one thing, he began as a young boy to make amusing little drawings. It was a talent. He made drawings of fish and pigs and cows, and they looked like people you knew. I never did know, before, that people could look so much like cows and horses and pigs and fish.

Literary Analysis
Point of View From whose point of view is this story being told? Support your answer.

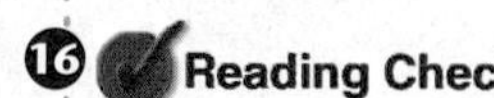
16 **Reading Check**
What is the overall condition of the Hutchenson farm?

14 About the Selection

Told from the point of view of a friend of the family, this story describes the alienation of a son from his parents. The narrator describes the Hutchensons as people who "fit into their farm life." When their son, Will, leaves to study art in Chicago, his parents live for news of his life; he frequently sends letters that they treasure. The Hutchensons claim that they can never visit Chicago because of the demands of the farm. When a friend of the narrator receives a telegraph about Will's death, he and the narrator both go out to the farm to inform his parents. In an eerily silent reaction to the news, the Hutchensons grieve in the only way they know how: they go out into the night to plant corn.

15 Literary Analysis
Point of View

- Remind students that a narrator who speaks to the reader using "I" tells a story from a *first-person point of view.*
- Have students read the bracketed passage. **Ask** them to look for indications as to who is telling the story.
- **Ask** students the Literary Analysis question: From whose point of view is this story being told? Support your answer.
  Answer: The story is told by a first-person narrator who lives in the place he is describing and knows the inhabitants. This point of view is indicated by the narrator's use of "I" and detailed descriptions.

▶ **Monitor Progress:** Encourage students to create Point of View charts for this story, based on the model on p. 808.

16 Reading Check

Answer: The farm is so neat and well-maintained that it stands out from its surroundings.

Differentiated Instruction
Solutions for All Learners

Enrichment for Gifted/Talented Students
As students begin reading "The Corn Planting," have them consider the name "Scratch Gravel Road." Invite them to visualize what a place with that name might look like. Students are likely to envision unproductive, dry, lifeless land with some shacks and other evidence of hard times. Point out that Hatch Hutchenson's farm contrasts with that image. Have students create illustrations of Scratch Gravel Road, including the Hutchensons' farm.

Support for Advanced Readers
Point out that "In Another Country" ends without a resolution, reflecting the Modernist perception of life as being uncertain and confusing. Also, guide students to recognize that this story, like some of those in the previous unit, contains dramatic irony; the major postponed marriage until he was finished with the war and could assure his young bride of his well-being, only to have her die unexpectedly.

17 Critical Viewing

Answer: Corn plays an important part in this story because the Hutchensons grow corn on their farm. You might ask students to consider, given the story's title, what role corn might play in the story's resolution.

When he had finished in the town high school, Will went to Chicago, where his mother had a cousin living, and he became a student in the Art Institute out there. Another young fellow from our town was also in Chicago. He really went two years before Will did. His name was Hal Weyman, and he was a student at the University of Chicago. After he graduated, he came home and got a job as principal of our high school.

17 ▼ **Critical Viewing** In what way does corn play an important part of this story? **[Connect]**

Hal and Will Hutchenson hadn't been close friends before, Hal being several years older than Will, but in Chicago they got together, went together to see plays, and, as Hal later told me, they had a good many long talks.

I got it from Hal that, in Chicago, as at home here when he was a young boy, Will was immediately popular. He was good-looking, so the girls in the art school liked him, and he had a straightforwardness that made him popular with all the young fellows.

Hal told me that Will was out to some party nearly every night, and right away he began to sell some of his amusing little drawings and to make money. The drawings were used in advertisements, and he was well paid.

He even began to send some money home. You see, after Hal came back

Enrichment

Chicago

Chicago was a major city in the Midwest when Will Hutchenson went there to study at the Art Institute. In 1837, when it was incorporated, Chicago had a population of about 4,200. By the time of its Great Fire in 1871, the population had soared to 300,000. By 1893, the city had sufficiently recovered to host the World Columbian Exposition commemorating the 400th anniversary of the European discovery of America. With unlimited opportunities to rebuild after the Great Fire, Chicago provided America's finest architects with an unprecedented boost; the city filled up with decorative and monumental buildings. The Art Institute is one such structure which today houses an impressive collection of artwork. Tell students that Ernest Hemingway grew up in Chicago.

here, he used to go quite often out to the Hutchenson place to see Will's father and mother. He would walk or drive out there in the afternoon or on summer evenings and sit with them. The talk was always of Will.

Hal said it was touching how much the father and mother depended on their one son, how much they talked about him and dreamed of his future. They had never been people who went about much with the town folks or even with their neighbors. They were of the sort who work all the time, from early morning till late in the evenings, and on moonlight nights, Hal said, and after the little old wife had got the supper, they often went out into the fields and worked again.

You see, by this time old Hatch was nearing seventy and his wife would have been ten years younger. Hal said that whenever he went out to the farm they quit work and came to sit with him. They might be in one of the fields, working together, but when they saw him in the road, they came running. They had got a letter from Will. He wrote every week.

The little old mother would come running following the father. "We got another letter, Mr. Weyman," Hatch would cry, and then his wife, quite breathless, would say the same thing, "Mr. Weyman, we got a letter."

The letter would be brought out at once and read aloud. Hal said the letters were always delicious. Will larded them with little sketches. There were humorous drawings of people he had seen or been with, rivers of automobiles on Michigan Avenue in Chicago, a policeman at a street crossing, young stenographers hurrying into office buildings. Neither of the old people had ever been to the city and they were curious and eager. They wanted the drawings explained, and Hal said they were like two children wanting to know every little detail Hal could remember about their son's life in the big city. He was always at them to come there on a visit and they would spend hours talking of that.

"Of course," Hatch said, "we couldn't go."

"How could we?" he said. He had been on that one little farm since he was a boy. When he was a young fellow, his father was an invalid and so Hatch had to run things. A farm, if you run it right, is very exacting. You have to fight weeds all the time. There are the farm animals to take care of. "Who would milk our cows?" Hatch said. The idea of anyone but him or his wife touching one of the Hutchenson cows seemed to hurt him. While he was alive, he didn't want anyone else plowing one of his fields, tending his corn, looking after things about the barn. He felt that way about his farm. It was a thing you couldn't explain, Hal said. He seemed to understand the two old people.

It was a spring night, past midnight, when Hal came to my house and told me the news. In our town we have a night telegraph operator at the railroad station and Hal got a wire. It was really addressed to Hatch Hutchenson, but the operator brought it to Hal. Will Hutchenson was dead, had been killed. It turned out later that he

Literary Analysis
Point of View and Narrator How does the narrator interact with other characters?

20 
Reading Check
How does the narrator describe Hal's relationship to Will?

18 Literary Analysis
Point of View and Narrator

- Remind students that with *first-person point of view,* we learn about the actions of the story through one character, the narrator.
- Have students read the bracketed passage. Be sure they recognize that this information about the Hutchensons was given to the narrator by Hal.
- **Ask** students the Literary Analysis question: How does the narrator interact with other characters?
  Possible response: The narrator appears to be in regular communication with Hal, who tells him what the Hutchensons do and say. Students should recognize that he does not interact directly with the Hutchensons at all.

19 Vocabulary Builder
The Latin Root *-val-*

- Call students' attention to the word "invalid" in this passage. Remind them that the Latin root *-val-* means "strength" or "value."
- **Ask** students to use this fact along with their knowledge of the root *-in-*, which means "not," to construct a definition of "invalid."
  Answer: As it is used here, "invalid" means "a disabled person."

20 Reading Check

Answer: Hal, who is older than Will, knew Will at home but they were not close. They became good friends in Chicago.

Differentiated Instruction
Solutions for All Learners

Support for Less Proficient Readers
Students may wonder why, if they love their son so much and are so curious about his life, the Hutchensons do not visit him in Chicago. Introduce these two possibilities: that their reluctance stems from a powerful sense of responsibility and connection to their land; that it comes from a fear of and disconnection from modern life.

Support for English Learners
Point out to students that it is unconventional to present what two different speakers say in one paragraph. Explain that Anderson puts Hatch and his wife's dialogue in one paragraph because the narrator is relating this information second-hand and Hatch and his wife are essentially saying the same thing.

Support for Advanced Readers
Have students contrast Will's life in Chicago with the farm life his parents knew. Explain that Will and his parents are separated by a period of enormous change. Hal bridges the two generations and serves as a link between Will and his parents. Encourage students to research the differences between Will's generation and his parents'.

㉑ Critical Thinking
Speculate

- Instruct students to pause before reading the bracketed passage. **Ask** them to describe their responses to the Hutchensons' reaction to Hal's news.
  Possible response: Most students will find the Hutchensons' reaction believable, although some will observe that they have not yet fully absorbed the news.
- Have students read the bracketed passage. Then, **ask** them to predict what the Hutchensons are going to do once they emerge from the house.
  Possible response: Students' predictions will vary but may include ideas such as: they will kill themselves; they will begin digging a grave; they will sit somewhere in the field and pray or meditate; they will bury his letters; and so on.

㉒ Reading Strategy
Identifying With Characters

- Remind students that identifying with characters can make it easier to understand them.
- Have students read the bracketed passage. Encourage them to consider carefully the emotions it describes.
- **Ask** the Reading Strategy question: Putting yourself in Hal's place, how do you think he felt telling the Hutchensons about Will's death?
  Possible response: Hal knows how much the Hutchensons loved their son and dreads having to tell them of his death.

▶ **Monitor Progress:** Encourage students to discuss how their responses help them to understand Hal's character.

was at a party with some other young fellows and there might have been some drinking. Anyway, the car was wrecked, and Will Hutchenson was killed. The operator wanted Hal to go out and take the message to Hatch and his wife, and Hal wanted me to go along.

㉑ I offered to take my car, but Hal said no, "Let's walk out," he said. He wanted to put off the moment, I could see that. So we did walk. It was early spring, and I remember every moment of the silent walk we took, the little leaves just coming on the trees, the little streams we crossed, how the moonlight made the water seem alive. We loitered and loitered, not talking, hating to go on.

㉒ Then we got out there, and Hal went to the front door of the farmhouse while I stayed in the road. I heard a dog bark, away off somewhere. I heard a child crying in some distant house. I think that Hal, after he got to the front door of the house, must have stood there for ten minutes, hating to knock.

Then he did knock, and the sound his fist made on the door seemed terrible. It seemed like guns going off. Old Hatch came to the door, and I heard Hal tell him. I know what happened. Hal had been trying, all the way out from town, to think up words to tell the old couple in some gentle way, but when it came to the scratch, he couldn't. He blurted everything right out, right into old Hatch's face.

That was all. Old Hatch didn't say a word. The door was opened, he stood there in the moonlight, wearing a funny long white nightgown, Hal told him, and the door went shut again with a bang, and Hal was left standing there.

He stood for a time, and then came back out into the road to me. "Well," he said, and "Well," I said. We stood in the road looking and listening. There wasn't a sound from the house.

And then—it might have been ten minutes or it might have been a half-hour—we stood silently, listening and watching, not knowing what to do—we couldn't go away——"I guess they are trying to get so they can believe it," Hal whispered to me. I got his notion all right. The two old people must have thought of their son Will always only in terms of life, never of death.

We stood watching and listening, and then, suddenly, after a long time, Hal touched me on the arm. "Look," he whispered. There were two white-clad figures going from the house to the barn. It turned out, you see, that old Hatch had been plowing that day. He had finished plowing and harrowing a field near the barn.

The two figures went into the barn and presently came out. They went into the field, and Hal and I crept across the farmyard to the barn and got to where we could see what was going on without being seen.

It was an incredible thing. The old man had got a hand cornplanter out of the barn and his wife had got a bag of seed corn, and there, in the moonlight, that night, after they got that news, they were planting corn.

It was a thing to curl your hair—it was so ghostly. They were both in their nightgowns. They would do a row across the field, coming

Reading Strategy
Identifying With Characters Putting yourself in Hal's place, how do you think he felt telling the Hutchensons about Will's death?

Enrichment

Corn

Corn, a member of the grass family, was first cultivated in Central America. In the history of the domestication of plants, corn is actually a latecomer, trailing by a thousand years the cultivation of beans and squash. The original wild corn is small. The much larger size and shape of the modern corncob is a result of centuries of selective breeding.

Corn has long been a staple of Native American societies throughout North America, and different groups have celebrated its cultivation in one way or another. For example, the Pueblo people have traditionally honored their Corn Mothers by providing all newborn children with corn fetishes. Mississippian groups like the Muskogee, Chickasaw, Choctaw, and Cherokee have held Green Corn Dances after each summer's harvest. Invite students to learn more about the specifics of the Green Corn Dance or other Native American ceremonies that honor this key crop. They can share their findings with the class.

quite close to us as we stood in the shadow of the barn, and then, at the end of each row, they would kneel side by side by the fence and stay silent for a time. The whole thing went on in silence. It was the first time in my life I ever understood something, and I am far from sure now that I can put down what I understood and felt that night—I mean something about the connection between certain people and the earth—a kind of silent cry, down into the earth, of these two old people, putting corn down into the earth. It was as though they were putting death down into the ground that life might grow again—something like that.

They must have been asking something of the earth, too. But what's the use? What they were up to in connection with the life in their field and the lost life in their son is something you can't very well make clear in words. All I know is that Hal and I stood the sight as long as we could, and then we crept away and went back to town, but Hatch Hutchenson and his wife must have got what they were after that night, because Hal told me that when he went out in the morning to see them and to make the arrangements for bringing their dead son home, they were both curiously quiet and Hal thought in command of themselves. Hal said he thought they had got something. "They have their farm and they have still got Will's letters to read," Hal said.

Critical Reading

1. **Respond:** With which character did you identify the most in this story? Why?
2. **(a) Recall:** Why does Hatch Hutchenson choose not to go off to make his own way in the world? **(b) Interpret:** What does the narrator mean by the statement that Hatch "got a rather late start in life"?
3. **(a) Recall:** What did the Hutchensons always do when Hal came to visit? **(b) Analyze:** Why do you think they did this? **(c) Infer:** Why do you think the Hutchensons spend so much time working in their fields?
4. **(a) Recall:** Why is Hal given the task of taking the bad news to the Hutchensons? **(b) Evaluate:** Do you think Hal does a good job of telling them about Will's death? Why or why not?
5. **(a) Recall:** What do the Hutchensons do after learning their son has died? **(b) Interpret:** How does the narrator explain their reaction? **(c) Evaluate:** Do you agree with his assessment? Explain.
6. **Apply:** What message about life do you think this story conveys? Support your answer.

For: More about Sherwood Anderson
Visit: www.PHSchool.com
Web Code: ere-9514

Differentiated Instruction
Solutions for All Learners

Strategy for Special Needs Students
Students may be confused by the story's conclusion. After they complete the story, ask students to explain what the Hutchensons did in response to their son's death. If they are unsure, have them read pp. 818–819 again.

Support for Less Proficient Readers
If students are challenged by the Hutchensons' response to their son's death, ask them for interpretations of why the elderly couple would grieve in this way. Guide students to recognize that after their son, their farm and their land were the most important things in the Hutchensons' lives.

Strategy for Advanced Readers
Ask students to consider the Hutchensons' response to their son's death. Point out that Hal says, "They must have been asking something of the earth." What were they asking? Did they find it, as Hal believes? Encourage students to write paragraphs interpreting the story's conclusion.

ASSESS

Answers

1. **Possible response:** Students may identify with the narrator, who witnesses powerful emotions without really being a part of them. Student explanations should include details from the story.
2. (a) Hatch has to care for his injured father. (b) **Possible response:** He did not begin an independent life of his own until he was almost fifty, when he finally married.
3. (a) The Hutchensons talked with Hal about their son, Will. (b) **Possible response:** They depend on Will, their only son, to provide them with hope for the future. (c) **Possible response:** They love the farm and the land more than anything except their son. They feel more comfortable working the land than doing anything else.
4. (a) Hal is quite close to the Hutchensons and has always acted as a conduit for information about Will. (b) **Possible response:** Some students will say Hal did a poor job because he blurted the news out without any preamble. Others will say it is a difficult enough task and that his willingness to do it at all makes it a good job.
5. (a) They plant row after row of corn under the moonlight. (b) He describes their behavior as a way of planting death so that life might grow again. (c) **Possible response:** Yes. They seem to turn to the other love in their lives, the land—to gain control of their experience, and to find comfort.
6. **Possible response:** The story conveys the message that life is unpredictable and that tragedy can strike anyone at any time. Student responses should be supported with references to the story.

Go Online Author Link For additional information about Sherwood Anderson, have students type in the Web Code, then select *A* from the alphabet, and then select Anderson.

㉓ Humanities

Miz Emily, by Joseph Holston

This piece of art shows an African American woman pausing to look out into the distance. The dramatic juxtaposition of light and shadow as well as the facial expression and posture of the woman help to bring out her character. Use these questions for discussion:

1. What can you infer about this woman and her life based on her facial expression, her stance, and her clothing?
   Possible response: Students may say that she looks as if she is used to hard work; she wears an apron and a head wrap, which indicate she is some kind of laborer. Her loose sweater indicates that she is old and sensitive to the cold. She grasps a walking stick, suggesting that she is taking a walk. She may be pausing for rest or to take stock of her work for the day.
2. Notice how the light streams in on the woman's face. What might the artist mean by this?
   Possible response: Students may say that the light represents a higher calling, or a gleam of hope in the distance to contrast with the hard life she seems to lead. The light could signify sunrise or sunset, suggesting a change: either a new dawn or an ending.

Miz Emily, Joseph Holston, Courtesy of Joseph Holston

820 ■ *Disillusion, Defiance, and Discontent (1914–1946)*

A Worn Path

Eudora Welty

It was December—a bright frozen day in the early morning. Far out in the country there was an old Negro woman with her head tied in a red rag, coming along a path through the pinewoods. Her name was Phoenix Jackson. She was very old and small and she walked slowly in the dark pine shadows, moving a little from side to side in her steps, with the balanced heaviness and lightness of a pendulum in a grandfather clock. She carried a thin, small cane made from an umbrella, and with this she kept tapping the frozen earth in front of her. This made a grave and persistent noise in the still air, that seemed meditative like the chirping of a solitary little bird.

She wore a dark striped dress reaching down to her shoe tops, and an equally long apron of bleached sugar sacks, with a full pocket all neat and tidy, but every time she took a step she might have fallen over her shoelaces, which dragged from her unlaced shoes. She looked straight ahead. Her eyes were blue with age. Her skin had a pattern all its own of numberless branching wrinkles and as though a whole little tree stood in the middle of her forehead, but a golden color ran underneath, and the two knobs of her cheeks were illumined by a yellow burning under the dark. Under the red rag her hair came down on her neck in the frailest of ringlets, still black, and with an odor like copper.

Now and then there was a quivering in the thicket. Old Phoenix said, "Out of my way, all you foxes, owls, beetles, jack rabbits, coons and wild animals! . . . Keep out from under these feet, little bobwhites[1]. . . . Keep the big wild hogs out of my path. Don't let none of those come running my direction. I got a long way." Under her small black-freckled hand her cane, limber as a buggy whip, would switch at the brush as if to rouse up any hiding things.

On she went. The woods were deep and still. The sun made the pine needles almost too bright to look at, up where the wind rocked. The cones dropped as light as feathers. Down in the hollow was the mourning dove—it was not too late for him.

The path ran up a hill. "Seem like there is chains about my feet, time I get this far," she said, in the voice of argument old people keep to use with themselves. "Something always take a hold of me on this hill—pleads I should stay."

Vocabulary Builder
grave (grāv) *adj.* serious; solemn

Vocabulary Builder
limber (lim′ bər) *adj.* flexible

1. **bobwhites** *n.* partridges.

25 **Critical Viewing** What details in this image suggest Phoenix's strong character? **[Connect]**

26 **Reading Check**
What are some of Phoenix Jackson's distinguishing features?

24 About the Selection

This story is a prose portrait of Phoenix Jackson, an elderly southern black woman who selflessly makes an arduous journey into town to obtain medicine for her ailing grandson. In this errand of "love carried out," she overcomes one real or imagined obstacle after another. Her interactions with the people she meets reveal more of her character—she is at once determined, confused, and tired. When she reaches her destination—where the reader first learns the nature of her mission—she rises to the occasion. She leaves the doctor's office with the medicine, proudly determined to purchase a simple Christmas gift for her grandson despite the nurse's deliberate references to the "charity" status of her grandson's treatment.

25 Critical Viewing

Possible response: Students may say that the determined look on the face of the woman in the picture suggests Phoenix's strong character. The picture may evoke for students the steadfastness with which Phoenix undertakes her journey and the fearlessness with which she deals with obstacles.

26 Reading Check

Answer: Her distinguishing features include her eyes, her wrinkles, the golden color of her skin, the burning in her cheeks, and her still-black hair.

Differentiated Instruction

Solutions for All Learners

Support for English Learners
You can help students to understand the meaning of the dialectical grammar Phoenix uses by supplying missing verbs and helping verbs, pronouns, and inflected endings. If necessary, use the ***Reader's Notebook: English Learner's Version*** to preview the story's plot.

Strategy for Advanced Readers
Explain to students that birds play a key symbolic role in this story. Point out, for example, that the name *Phoenix* refers to the mythological Egyptian bird that rose from the ashes of its own funeral pyre. Suggest that students make note of and interpret this and other references to birds in the story.

27 Reading Strategy
Identifying With Characters

- **Ask** students to pause when they reach the bracketed passage. Guide them to recognize Phoenix's familiarity with the path she is walking.
- Have students read the bracketed passage. Point out Phoenix's running commentary, emphasizing that she uses figurative language to describe the difficult parts of her journey.
- **Ask** students the Reading Strategy question: Why do you suppose Phoenix is talking her way through the woods?
  Possible response: Students may say that the sound of her voice soothes her. By identifying the obstacles she faces, she may eliminate her fear that the woods present an unknown challenge.

Monitor Progress: Encourage students to discuss what they might have in common with Phoenix's feelings about the woods.

28 Literary Analysis
Point of View and Narrator

- Have a volunteer read the bracketed passage aloud. As they listen, tell students to note any information that a passerby would not be able to perceive.
- Then, **ask** the Literary Analysis questions: What private information does the narrator share in the paragraph beginning "But she sat down to rest"? What is the effect?
  Answer: Phoenix's hallucination of a boy offering her cake is entirely private. It allows the reader to understand that Phoenix's grasp of reality is not always firm.

After she got to the top she turned and gave a full, severe look behind her where she had come. "Up through pines," she said at length. "Now down through oaks."

27 Her eyes opened their widest, and she started down gently. But before she got to the bottom of the hill a bush caught her dress.

Her fingers were busy and intent, but her skirts were full and long, so that before she could pull them free in one place they were caught in another. It was not possible to allow the dress to tear. "I in the thorny bush," she said. "Thorns, you doing your appointed work. Never want to let folks pass, no sir. Old eyes thought you was a pretty little *green* bush."

Finally, trembling all over, she stood free, and after a moment dared to stoop for her cane.

"Sun so high!" she cried, leaning back and looking, while the thick tears went over her eyes. "The time getting all gone here."

At the foot of this hill was a place where a log was laid across the creek.

"Now comes the trial," said Phoenix.

Putting her right foot out, she mounted the log and shut her eyes. Lifting her skirt, leveling her cane fiercely before her, like a festival figure in some parade, she began to march across. Then she opened her eyes and she was safe on the other side.

"I wasn't as old as I thought," she said.

28 But she sat down to rest. She spread her skirts on the bank around her and folded her hands over her knees. Up above her was a tree in a pearly cloud of mistletoe. She did not dare to close her eyes, and when a little boy brought her a plate with a slice of marble cake on it she spoke to him. "That would be acceptable," she said. But when she went to take it there was just her own hand in the air.

So she left that tree, and had to go through a barbed-wire fence. There she had to creep and crawl, spreading her knees and stretching her fingers like a baby trying to climb the steps. But she talked loudly to herself: she could not let her dress be torn now, so late in the day, and she could not pay for having her arm or her leg sawed off if she got caught fast where she was.

At last she was safe through the fence and risen up out in the clearing. Big dead trees, like black men with one arm, were standing in the purple stalks of the withered cotton field. There sat a buzzard.

"Who you watching?"

In the furrow she made her way along.

"Glad this not the season for bulls," she said, looking sideways, "and the good Lord made his snakes to curl up and sleep in the winter. A pleasure I don't see no two-headed snake coming around that tree, where it come once. It took a while to get by him, back in the summer."

She passed through the old cotton and went into a field of dead corn. It whispered and shook and was taller than her head. "Through the maze now," she said, for there was no path.

Then there was something tall, black, and skinny there, moving before her.

Reading Strategy
Identifying With Characters Why do you suppose Phoenix is talking her way through the woods?

Literary Analysis
Point of View and Narrator What private information does the narrator share in the paragraph beginning "But she sat down to rest." What is the effect?

Enrichment

The Journey and Egyptian Myths

The journey, with its obstacles and travails, has been a common element in literature for thousands of years. Phoenix Jackson's story parallels Egyptian myths relating the journey of the dead through the twelve gates of Osiris's underworld. The bull and the two-headed snake are two of the many mythical creatures who guard the underworld. That journey ended when the travelers faced the god, who pronounced judgment on them. The dead person's heart was weighed on a balancing scale overseen by Truth. If the person failed the test, he or she was destroyed by a ferocious beast called the Devourer of Souls. If the person passed and was judged worthy of the afterlife, he or she entered eternity, free to pursue the same pleasures enjoyed on earth.

Invite interested students to investigate journey or quest myths of other cultures. For example, they might look into the Buddhist story of Siddhartha, or the Nibelung saga of ancient Teutonic mythology.

29 At first she took it for a man. It could have been a man dancing in the field. But she stood still and listened, and it did not make a sound. It was as silent as a ghost.

"Ghost," she said sharply, "who be you the ghost of? For I have heard of nary death close by."

But there was no answer—only the ragged dancing in the wind.

She shut her eyes, reached out her hand, and touched a sleeve. She found a coat and inside that an emptiness, cold as ice.

"You scarecrow," she said. Her face lighted. "I ought to be shut up for good," she said with laughter. "My senses is gone. I too old. I the oldest people I ever know. Dance, old scarecrow," she said, "while I dancing with you."

She kicked her foot over the furrow, and with mouth drawn down, shook her head once or twice in a little strutting way. Some husks blew down and whirled in streamers about her skirts.

Then she went on, parting her way from side to side with the cane, through the whispering field. At last she came to the end, to a wagon track where the silver grass blew between the red ruts. The quail were walking around like pullets, seeming all dainty and unseen.

"Walk pretty," she said. "This the easy place. This the easy going."

She followed the track, swaying through the quiet bare fields, through the little strings of trees silver in their dead leaves, past cabins silver from weather, with the doors and windows boarded shut, all like old women under a spell sitting there. "I walking in their sleep," she said, nodding her head vigorously.

In a ravine she went where a spring was silently flowing through a hollow log. Old Phoenix bent and drank. "Sweet gum[2] makes the water sweet," she said, and drank more. "Nobody know who made this well, for it was here when I was born."

The track crossed a swampy part where the moss hung as white as lace from every limb. "Sleep on, alligators, and blow your bubbles." Then the track went into the road.

Deep, deep the road went down between the high green-colored banks. Overhead the live-oaks met, and it was as dark as a cave.

A black dog with a lolling tongue came up out of the weeds by the ditch. She was meditating, and not ready, and when he came at her she only hit him a little with her cane. Over she went in the ditch, like a little puff of milkweed.[3]

Down there, her senses drifted away. A dream visited her, and she reached her hand up, but nothing reached down and gave her a pull. So she lay there and presently went to talking. "Old woman," she said to herself, "that black dog come up out of the weeds to stall you off, and now there he sitting on his fine tail, smiling at you."

A white man finally came along and found her—a hunter, a young man, with his dog on a chain.

2. **sweet gum** *n.* a tree that produces a fragrant juice.
3. **milkweed** *n.* a plant with pods that, when ripe, release feathery seeds.

Literary Analysis
Point of View From what point of view is the story being told? How do you know?

30  **Reading Check**
What is Phoenix Jackson's attitude as she walks?

29 Literary Analysis
Point of View

- Remind students that they can determine a story's *point of view* by looking closely at the way the narrator speaks to readers and the information the narrator presents about characters.
- Have students read the bracketed passage.
- Then, **ask** students the Literary Analysis question: From what point of view is the story being told? How do you know?
  Answer: The story is told through the limited third-person point of view, in which events are viewed from the perspective of Phoenix Jackson. Students should note that the story includes both real and imagined events that could only be known by the main character.

30 Reading Check

Answer: She is determined, even as she struggles with obstacles and her own confusion.

Differentiated Instruction
Solutions for All Learners

Support for Special Needs Students
Be sure that students understand that the story describes a journey taken on foot by an old African American woman in the South. If students are confused, have them read along with **Listening to Literature CDs.**

Strategy for Less Proficient Readers
Guide students to distinguish between the story's concrete details that describe Jackson's journey and the imagined details that reveal the daydreams her mind creates. Encourage students to construct charts listing both concrete and imagined details.

Strategy for Advanced Readers
Ghosts are only one of the many images of death in this story. Ask students to identify other words and images the author uses to create a grim atmosphere. Students may mention, in addition to the bull and two-headed snake, "dark pine shadows," "frozen earth," "mourning dove," "big dead trees," and "buzzard."

31 Humanities

Georgia Red Clay, by Nell Choate Jones

This oil painting offers a surreal representation of a dirt road winding through the Georgia countryside. Use these questions for discussion:

1. How would you describe the mood of this painting?
   Possible response: Students may describe it as dark, foreboding, eerie, or dreamlike.
2. This painting depicts a rural scene in Georgia. What elements of this work relate to Welty's story, which is set in Mississippi?
   Possible response: Students may say that the painting depicts a hilly, winding country path, such as the one described in the story. The gnarled trees are foreboding, suggesting Phoenix's frame of mind during parts of her walk. The odd light suggests the haze through which she views events.

32 Critical Viewing

Possible response: Some students may say that the surrealistic nature of the painting mirrors the dreamlike state in which Phoenix seems to exist. Others may say that Phoenix's path lay through dense pine woods, neither passing farmhouses nor hardwood trees, as depicted in the painting.

"Well, Granny!" he laughed. "What are you doing there?"

"Lying on my back like a June bug waiting to be turned over, mister," she said, reaching up her hand.

He lifted her up, gave her a swing in the air, and set her down. "Anything broken, Granny?"

"No sir, them old dead weeds is springy enough," said Phoenix, when she had got her breath. "I thank you for your trouble."

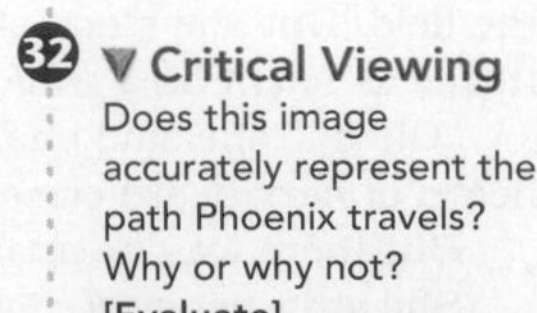

32 ▼ Critical Viewing
Does this image accurately represent the path Phoenix travels? Why or why not? [Evaluate]

31

"Where do you live, Granny?" he asked, while the two dogs were growling at each other.

"Away back yonder, sir, behind the ridge. You can't even see it from here."

"On your way home?"

"No sir, I going to town."

"Why, that's too far! That's as far as I walk when I come out myself, and I get something for my trouble." He patted the stuffed bag he carried, and there hung down a little closed claw. It was one of the bobwhites, with its beak hooked bitterly to show it was dead. "Now you go on home, Granny!"

"I bound to go to town, mister," said Phoenix. "The time come around."

He gave another laugh, filling the whole landscape. "I know you old colored people! Wouldn't miss going to town to see Santa Claus!"

33 But something held old Phoenix very still. The deep lines in her face went into a fierce and different radiation. Without warning, she had seen with her own eyes a flashing nickel fall out of the man's pocket onto the ground.

"How old are you, Granny?" he was saying.

"There is no telling, mister," she said, "no telling."

Then she gave a little cry and clapped her hands and said, "Git on away from here, dog! Look! Look at that dog!" She laughed as if in admiration. "He ain't scared of nobody. He a big black dog." She whispered, "Sic him!"

"Watch me get rid of that cur," said the man. "Sic him, Pete! Sic him!"

34 Phoenix heard the dogs fighting, and heard the man running and throwing sticks. She even heard a gunshot. But she was slowly bending forward by that time, further and further forward, the lids stretched down over her eyes, as if she were doing this in her sleep. Her chin was lowered almost to her knees. The yellow palm of her hand came out from the fold of her apron. Her fingers slid down and along the ground under the piece of money with the grace and care they would have in lifting an egg from under a setting hen. Then she slowly straightened up, she stood erect, and the nickel was in her apron pocket. A bird flew by. Her lips moved. "God watching me the whole time. I come to stealing."

The man came back, and his own dog panted about them. "Well, I scared him off that time," he said, and then he laughed and lifted his gun and pointed it at Phoenix.

She stood straight and faced him.

"Doesn't the gun scare you?" he said, still pointing it.

"No, sir, I seen plenty go off closer by, in my day, and for less than what I done," she said, holding utterly still.

He smiled, and shouldered the gun. "Well, Granny," he said, "you must be a hundred years old, and scared of nothing. I'd

Georgia Red Clay, 1946, Nell Choate Jones, Morris Museum of Art, Augusta, Georgia

Literary Analysis
Point of View What detail in this paragraph reveals the point of view from which the story is told? Explain.

35 

Whom and what does Phoenix encounter on her journey?

33 Literary Analysis
Point of View

- Before students read the bracketed passage, ask them to pause and consider point of view.
- Guide students to recognize that if the story were told from the hunter's viewpoint, they would learn in a more direct way that he considers Phoenix to be inferior. As it is written, the reader infers the hunter's feelings based on his language and behavior.
- Have students read the bracketed passage. Then, **ask** the Literary Analysis question: What detail in this paragraph reveals the point of view from which the story is told? Explain.
  Answer: The nickel that falls from the man's pocket reveals that the story is told from Phoenix's point of view, because she is the only one who sees it.
- Be sure students understand that Phoenix lives in dire poverty at a time when 5 cents was not an insignificant sum; a nickel could mean the difference between eating a meal or going hungry.

34 Reading Strategy
Identifying With Characters

- Have students read the bracketed passage. **Ask** them to pause and consider Phoenix's actions.
- Point out that Phoenix's act of taking the nickel that fell and her awareness that she is stealing show both her poverty and her sense of honor.
- **Ask** students: What does it say about Phoenix that she is used to having a gun pointed at her or near to her? **Possible response:** Students may say that it indicates that she was once a slave and had experienced the bullying of armed overseers or perhaps that she was a poor sharecropper accustomed to harsh treatment by callous landowners.

35 Reading Check

Answer: Phoenix is knocked down by a stray dog and then encounters a hunter with his own dog.

Differentiated Instruction
Solutions for All Learners

Support for Special Needs Students
Have students read the conversation between Phoenix and the hunter once on their own to form a general impression. Then, ask them to describe the encounter. If they are confused about what is happening—Phoenix has fallen over when the white man spots her and helps her up; she tells him she is going to town; she sees he has dropped a nickel, distracts him, and picks it up; he frightens away a stray dog with his gun—use the ***Reader's Notebook: Adapted Version*** to aid comprehension.

Enrichment for Advanced Readers
Explain to students that when this story was first published in 1941, the term *colored people* was commonly used to refer to African Americans. The term is no longer considered acceptable. Encourage students to identify and research other aspects of relations between black and white characters in this story that are no longer accepted today, such as the openly patronizing attitude the hunter displays towards Phoenix.

36 Critical Thinking
Speculate

- Read the bracketed passage out loud for students. Review with them the actions and details the passage describes: Phoenix enters a large building, goes up many stairs, and enters a door marked by a framed document with a gold seal.
- **Ask** students: Why does Welty not identify the building with the gold seal?
  Possible response: Students may suggest that the narrator is describing the building as Phoenix herself sees it.
- Encourage students to keep the narrator's point of view in mind as they read on.

37 Literary Analysis
Point of View

- Remind the class that this story is told from a limited third-person point of view. A third-person narrator describes events from Phoenix's perspective—including events in her mind.
- Have students read the bracketed passage. Guide them to recognize that the attendant's comment reveals her assumptions about Phoenix.
- **Ask** students the Literary Analysis question: What response does this dialogue describing the way others see Phoenix evoke in you? Why?
  Possible response: Students are likely to be empathetic toward Phoenix, who has just made a formidable journey on her grandson's behalf and who is now being treated with coldness and condescension.

▶ **Monitor Progress:** Be sure students understand that point of view can influence readers' sympathies toward characters.

give you a dime if I had any money with me. But you take my advice and stay home, and nothing will happen to you."

"I bound to go on my way, mister," said Phoenix. She inclined her head in the red rag. Then they went in different directions, but she could hear the gun shooting again and again over the hill.

She walked on. The shadows hung from the oak trees to the road like curtains. Then she smelled woodsmoke, and smelled the river, and she saw a steeple and the cabins on their steep steps. Dozens of little black children whirled around her. There ahead was Natchez[4] shining. Bells were ringing. She walked on.

In the paved city it was Christmas time. There were red and green electric lights strung and criss-crossed everywhere, and all turned on in the daytime. Old Phoenix would have been lost if she had not distrusted her eyesight and depended on her feet to know where to take her.

She paused quietly on the sidewalk where people were passing by. A lady came along in the crowd, carrying an armful of red-, green- and silver-wrapped presents; she gave off perfume like the red roses in hot summer, and Phoenix stopped her.

"Please, missy, will you lace up my shoe?" She held up her foot.

"What do you want, Grandma?"

"See my shoe," said Phoenix. "Do all right for out in the country, but wouldn't look right to go in a big building."

"Stand still then, Grandma," said the lady. She put her packages down on the sidewalk beside her and laced and tied both shoes tightly.

"Can't lace em with a cane," said Phoenix. "Thank you, missy. I doesn't mind asking a nice lady to tie up my shoe, when I gets out on the street."

36 Moving slowly and from side to side, she went into the big building, and into a tower of steps, where she walked up and around and around until her feet knew to stop.

She entered a door, and there she saw nailed up on the wall the document that had been stamped with the gold seal and framed in the gold frame, which matched the dream that was hung up in her head.

37 "Here I be," she said. There was a fixed and ceremonial stiffness over her body.

"A charity case, I suppose," said an attendant who sat at the desk before her.

But Phoenix only looked above her head. There was sweat on her face, the wrinkles in her skin shone like a bright net.

"Speak up, Grandma," the woman said. "What's your name? We must have your history, you know. Have you been here before? What seems to be the trouble with you?"

Old Phoenix only gave a twitch to her face as if a fly were bothering her.

"Are you deaf?" cried the attendant.

But then the nurse came in.

Literary Analysis
Point of View What response does this dialogue describing the way others see Phoenix evoke in you? Why?

4. **Natchez** (nach′ iz) a town in southern Mississippi.

Enrichment

Eudora Welty

Eudora Welty uses descriptive adjectives and strong images to create a deeply sympathetic character in Phoenix. Phoenix moves readers because they are able to connect with her emotionally.

Welty has this to say regarding the purpose of fiction: "I don't think literature—I'm talking about fiction now—I don't think it can exhort, or it loses every bit of its reality and value. I think it speaks to what is more deeply within, that is, the personal, and conveys its meaning that way. And then one hopes that a person made alert or aroused to be more sensitive to other human beings would go on to look at things on a larger scale by himself. I wouldn't want to read a work of fiction that I thought had an ulterior motive, to persuade me politically. I automatically react the other way. . . . I think things should be in a column or an editorial or a speech. But perfectly on the up and up. That's because I understand as a person, not as a motto."

"Oh, that's just old Aunt Phoenix," she said. "She doesn't come for herself—she has a little grandson. She makes these trips just as regular as clockwork. She lives away back off the Old Natchez Trace." She bent down. "Well, Aunt Phoenix, why don't you just take a seat? We won't keep you standing after your long trip." She pointed.

The old woman sat down, bolt upright in the chair.

"Now, how is the boy?" asked the nurse.

Old Phoenix did not speak.

"I said, how is the boy?"

But Phoenix only waited and stared straight ahead, her face very solemn and withdrawn into rigidity.

"Is his throat any better?" asked the nurse. "Aunt Phoenix, don't you hear me? Is your grandson's throat any better since the last time you came for the medicine?"

With her hands on her knees, the old woman waited, silent, erect and motionless, just as if she were in armor.

"You mustn't take up our time this way, Aunt Phoenix," the nurse
38 said. "Tell us quickly about your grandson, and get it over. He isn't dead, is he?"

At last there came a flicker and then a flame of comprehension across her face, and she spoke.

"My grandson. It was my memory had left me. There I sat and forgot why I made my long trip."

"Forgot?" The nurse frowned. "After you came so far?"

Then Phoenix was like an old woman begging a dignified forgiveness for waking up frightened in the night. "I never did go to school. I was too old at the Surrender,"[5] she said in a soft voice. "I'm an old woman without an education. It was my memory fail me. My little grandson, he is just the same, and I forgot it in the coming."

"Throat never heals, does it?" said the nurse, speaking in a loud,
39 sure voice to old Phoenix. By now she had a card with something written on it, a little list. "Yes. Swallowed lye. When was it?—January—two-three years ago—"

Phoenix spoke unasked now. "No, missy, he not dead, he just the same. Every little while his throat begin to close up again, and he not able to swallow. He not get his breath. He not able to help himself. So the time come around, and I go on another trip for the soothing medicine."

"All right. The doctor said as long as you came to get it, you could have it," said the nurse. "But it's an obstinate case."

"My little grandson, he sit up there in the house all wrapped up, waiting by himself," Phoenix went on. "We is the only two left in the world. He suffer and it don't seem to put him back at all. He got a sweet look. He going to last. He wear a little patch quilt and peep out holding his mouth open like a little bird. I remembers so plain now. I not going to forget him again, no, the whole enduring time. I could tell him from all the others in creation."

5. **the Surrender** the surrender of the Confederate army, which ended the Civil War.

Literary Analysis
Point of View and Narrator Here, the narrator does not share Phoenix's thoughts. How does this affect you as a reader? Explain.

Vocabulary Builder
obstinate (äb′ stə nət) *adj.* stubborn

40  **Reading Check**

Why is Phoenix at the doctor's office?

Differentiated Instruction
Solutions for All Learners

Support for Less Proficient Readers
Guide students to recognize that the building in town to which Phoenix comes is probably a hospital or a clinic. Evidence includes the presence of a nurse and the fact that Phoenix is asked about her history.

Enrichment for Gifted/Talented Students
Remind students that Eudora Welty is known not only as a writer but also as a photographer. Encourage them to look for Welty's photographs of the South. Students can put together a presentation on Welty's South, displaying photographs and connecting them to "A Worn Path."

Background for Advanced Readers
Explain to students that the Natchez Trace is a road that runs from the city of Natchez diagonally through the entire state of Mississippi. Point out that the name probably derives from the Natchez, an Indian nation of the Southeast, and identifies a hunting or trading route. Encourage them to research the history of the Trace.

38 Literary Analysis
Point of View and Narrator

- Remind students that the point of view of a story is shaped by its narrator and the narrator's perspective.
- Have students read the bracketed passage. Guide them to recognize that while the narrator has previously shared Phoenix's thoughts, here they are not revealed.
- **Ask** students the Literary Analysis question: Here, the narrator does not share Phoenix's thoughts. How does this affect you as a reader? Explain.
  Possible response: Students may note that since Phoenix arrived at the doctor's office, her thoughts have not been revealed; instead, the narrator shows us how she appears from the attendant and nurse's perspective. The change in perspective may make students angry at the attendant and nurse for their patronizing, dismissive attitude.

39 Reading Strategy
Identify With Characters

- Have students read the bracketed passage. Encourage them to consider the emotions that Phoenix reveals here.
- **Ask** students: Can you identify with Phoenix Jackson's feelings in this situation? Explain.
  Possible response: Most students will sympathize with Phoenix, inferring that she has had a hard life and asks little of the attendants at the clinic. Many, however, will say that they have not experienced such a situation and cannot truly identify with her.

40 Reading Check

Answer: She is there to get medicine for her grandson, who suffers the lingering effects of swallowing lye.

"All right." The nurse was trying to hush her now. She brought her a bottle of medicine. "Charity," she said, making a check mark in a book.

Old Phoenix held the bottle close to her eyes, and then carefully put it into her pocket.

"I thank you," she said.

"It's Christmas time, Grandma," said the attendant. "Could I give you a few pennies out of my purse?"

"Five pennies is a nickel," said Phoenix stiffly.

"Here's a nickel," said the attendant.

Phoenix rose carefully and held out her hand. She received the nickel and then fished the other nickel out of her pocket and laid it beside the new one. She stared at her palm closely, with her head on one side.

Then she gave a tap with her cane on the floor.

"This is what come to me to do," she said. "I going to the store and buy my child a little windmill they sells, made out of paper. He going to find it hard to believe there such a thing in the world. I'll march myself back where he is waiting, holding it straight up in this hand."

She lifted her free hand, gave a little nod, turned around, and walked out of the doctor's office. Then her slow step began on the stairs, going down.

Critical Reading

1. **Respond:** Do you think Welty's use of language suits her story, or would you have used language differently? Explain.
2. **(a) Recall:** At what time of year does the story take place? **(b) Interpret:** What is significant about the story taking place at this time?
3. **(a) Recall:** What obstacles does Phoenix encounter on her journey? **(b) Analyze:** How does she deal with each of those obstacles?
4. **(a) Recall:** For what reason does Phoenix make her journey? **(b) Interpret:** What emotions does her journey express?
5. **(a) Recall:** In what way does Phoenix initially respond to the questions asked by the attendant and the nurse? **(b) Infer:** What does their reaction reveal about their attitudes toward her? **(c) Assess:** Do you think Phoenix sees herself as others see her?
6. **Synthesize:** In mythology, the Phoenix is a bird that rises from the ashes. Why do you think the author named the main character of this story Phoenix?
7. **Assess:** In what specific ways do you think Phoenix Jackson's character has been shaped by hardship? Explain.

Go Online — Author Link

For: More about Eudora Welty
Visit: www.PHSchool.com
Web Code: ere-9515

ASSESS

Answers

1. **Possible response:** Welty's use of language suits her story because it not only communicates the action but conveys the subtleties of Phoenix's feelings and thoughts.
2. (a) It takes place in December, near Christmas. (b) **Possible response:** The behavior of the other characters towards Phoenix contrasts with the true Christmas spirit.
3. (a) Obstacles include the distance she must travel on foot, a thorny bush, a log bridge across a creek, barbed-wire fencing, a pathless field, a scarecrow, a dog, a hunter, and a desk attendant. (b) **Possible response:** She deals with the obstacles with steady determination. Although some are more difficult for her than others, no obstacle stops her.
4. (a) Phoenix goes to Natchez to pick up her grandson's medicine. (b) **Possible response:** Phoenix's journey expresses her profound love for her grandson.
5. (a) At first, she fails to respond, saying she momentarily forgot why she came. (b) **Possible response:** The attendant and the nurse regard Phoenix with a mixture of helpfulness, irritation, and wondrous disbelief. (c) **Possible response:** Phoenix sees herself as more physically fit and mentally sharp than others see her.
6. **Possible response:** She is named Phoenix because she rises from every obstacle, and completes her journey.
7. **Possible response:** Phoenix shows perseverance and optimism during her journey. Life in troubled times has made Phoenix a strong person.

Go Online — Author Link For additional information about Eudora Welty, have students type in the Web Code, then select *W* from the alphabet, and then select Welty.

Apply the Skills

In Another Country • The Corn Planting • A Worn Path

Literary Analysis

Point of View

1. **(a)** Identify three details that show Hemingway's story was written using a **first-person point of view.** **(b)** How would the story be different if Hemingway had used a **limited third-person point of view**?
2. **(a)** What point of view does Anderson use in "The Corn Planting"? **(b)** Is the narrator of "The Corn Planting" the best character to tell the story? Why or why not?
3. How would "A Worn Path" be different if Welty had told the story from Phoenix Jackson's first-person point of view?
4. Using a different point of view from the original, rewrite a paragraph from one of the stories. Then, compare the two versions. **(a)** What is gained in your version? **(b)** What is lost?

Comparing Literary Works

5. **(a)** For each selection, identify the type of **narrator** being used. **(b)** Note specific ways in which each narrator allows some information to be revealed and some to be hidden.
6. **(a)** Compare the emotions the narrator evokes in you in each story. **(b)** In what way does the author's choice of a narrator create a different level of emotional involvement in each story?

Reading Strategy

Identifying With Characters

7. Among the three stories, choose the characters with whom you **identify** most and least. Provide reasons for your choices.
8. Did you sympathize with Phoenix Jackson? Why or why not?
9. Using a diagram like the one shown, list one personality trait, interest, or value you might share with a character in each story.

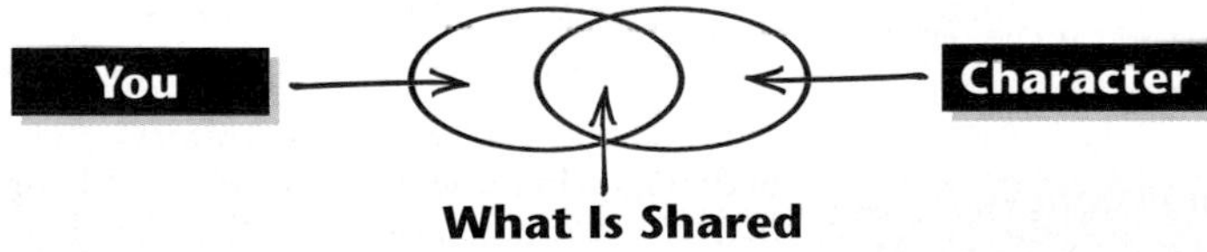

Extend Understanding

10. **Social Studies Connection:** What does Hemingway's story tell you about war that a history textbook might not?

QuickReview

Point of view is the perspective from which a story is told. The **first-person point of view** features a narrator who is a character in the story. In a story using the **limited third-person point of view,** the narrator stands outside the action and conveys the thoughts and feelings of a single character.

The **narrator** is the voice telling the story.

To **identify with characters,** connect their thoughts and feelings with your own experiences.

For: Self-test
Visit: www.PHSchool.com
Web Code: era-6508

Go Online Assessment Students may use the **Self-test** to prepare for **Selection Test A** or **Selection Test B.**

Answers

1. (a) Details include the narrator's use of "I" and "we," presence as the story's central character, and description of his own thoughts and feelings. (b) **Possible response:** The thoughts and feelings of all the characters might have been presented.
2. (a) Anderson uses a first-person point of view, but his narrator is not a part of the main action of the story. (b) The narrator is ideally suited to tell the story; his distance from the events and his close understanding of the people and community allow him to present the story clearly and with great empathy.
3. **Possible response:** It might have focused in greater detail on Phoenix's emotions.
4. Paragraphs must demonstrate an understanding of point of view.
5. (a) "In Another Country": first-person; "A Corn Planting": first-person; "A Worn Path": third-person. (b) Both first-person points of view limit the narrator to his own perceptions. The third-person point of view could convey the perceptions of all characters.
6. **Possible answers:** (a) and (b) Students' responses should be supported by details from the story.
7. **Possible response:** Students may say they identified most with the narrator of "In Another Country," because he is close to their age, and least with the Hutchensons, people from a different generation.
8. **Possible response:** Students may say they sympathize with Phoenix because she undertakes an arduous journey in order to help her grandson.
9. **Possible response** for "In Another Country": **You:** Want to be brave; never served in war **Narrator:** Living in Italy; injured in war **What Is Shared:** Young and uncertain.

   Another sample answer can be found on **Reading Strategy Graphic Organizer B,** p. 180 in ***Graphic Organizer Transparencies.***
10. **Possible answers:** Wounded soldiers felt camaraderie; certain kinds of rehabilitative machines were first used during the war.

EXTEND/ASSESS

Answers

❶ Vocabulary Lesson

Word Analysis

1. Having legal force or power, correct. **Possible response:** Something that is *valid* has the strength of accuracy behind it.
2. Equal in value, amount, or force. **Possible response:** Things which are *equivalent* are of equal value or strength.
3. Strength of mind or spirit, especially in the face of danger. **Possible response:** It takes great strength to have *valor.*
4. To gain the advantage; to be victorious or triumphant. **Possible response:** One must be strong to *prevail.*

Spelling Strategy

1. gnu 2. knife 3. knit 4. gnat

Vocabulary Builder

1. No. Someone who is invalided has been removed from service.
2. No. Grave news is serious.
3. Yes. Athletes need to make their limbs limber before attempting difficult movements.
4. No. An obstinate person is stubborn and uncooperative.

❷ Grammar and Style Lesson

1. "No," said the major.
2. "Well," he said, and "Well," I said.
3. "Don't argue with me!"
4. I offered to take my car, but Hal said "No, let's walk out."
5. "How old are you, Granny?" he was asking.

Looking at Style

Possible response: The reader understands only as much as the narrator does.

Build Language Skills

❶ Vocabulary Lesson

Word Analysis: Latin Root *-val-*

The Latin root *-val-* means "strength" or "value." Use a dictionary to define each of the words below. Then, write a sentence explaining how each word's definition might relate to the meaning of *-val-*.

1. valid
2. equivalent
3. valor
4. prevail

Spelling Strategy

When words begin with the letters *gn* or *kn*, as in *gnarled, gnaw, knee,* and *knock,* the *g* or *k* is silent. In your notebook, complete the spelling of the following words.

1. __nu
2. __nife
3. __nit
4. __nat

Vocabulary Builder: Clarify Word Meaning

Review the words from the vocabulary list on page 808 and notice the way each word is used in the selections. Then, answer yes or no to each question. Explain each of your answers.

1. If a soldier is *invalided,* has he or she been transferred to combat duty?

2. Would someone bringing *grave* news be smiling?

3. Would a gymnast need to be *limber* before performing?

4. Would you want to pair up for a project with someone described as *obstinate*?

❷ Grammar and Style Lesson

Punctuating Dialogue

Dialogue is one of the most effective tools in a writer's toolkit. Dialogue brings characters to life by letting readers "hear" the characters' own words. Because each writer carefully punctuates the dialogue, you can easily tell who is speaking each line.

To correctly punctuate dialogue, always put quotation marks around the speaker's exact words. Place periods, commas, question marks, and exclamation points inside the quotation marks. Use a new paragraph for each new speaker.

Example: "Ghost," she said sharply, "who be you the ghost of? For I have heard of nary death close by."

Practice The punctuation marks in the following pieces of dialogue have been misplaced or omitted. Rewrite each item, using correct punctuation.

1. "No" said the major.

2. "Well, he said, and Well," I said.

3. "Don't argue with me"!

4. I offered to take my car, but Hal said No, Let's walk out.

5. "How old are you, Granny"? he was asking.

Looking at Style When you compare the amount of dialogue in these three stories, you'll notice that "The Corn Planting" has the least. How does this difference affect the way you relate to the characters? Explain.

WG Prentice Hall Writing and Grammar Connection: Chapter 5, Section 4

Assessment Practice

Analyze Sentence Meaning

(For more practice, see *Standardized Test Preparation Workbook*, p. 48.)

Many tests require students to correctly answer sentence-completion questions. Often, more than one choice can complete a sentence. Use the following sample item to show students how to analyze sentence meaning, decide whether it is positive or negative, and eliminate choices that have the opposite sense.

Ironically, despite the devastation of World War I, modern medicine _____ during the period.

A advanced
B declined
C regressed
D changed

The signal words *Ironically* and *despite* indicate the correct answer will have a positive connotation. *B* and *C* can be eliminated. *D* is too mild an answer. *A* is the best choice.

Writing Lesson

Memorial Speech

As Hal Weyman in "The Corn Planting," write the speech you might give at Will's memorial service. In your remarks, acknowledge both Will's family and his dreams. Also include personal traits revealed from the story.

Prewriting Reread the story and note personal details about Will. Look for Hal's opinions about Will's strength, talents, and personality.

Drafting To begin, identify Will Hutchenson, and explain the sad occasion for the speech. Organize your main points in order of importance, noting the memories of greatest significance. Retell anecdotes in a style reflecting Hal's character.

Revising Reread your speech to make sure it reveals Will's personality and expresses his dreams. Highlight and revise vague words and add details that evoke emotion.

Model: Revising to Add Emotional Appeal

person whom I'll never forget because he had endless enthusiasm for life.
Will Hutchenson was a ~~great guy.~~ An only child, he was the source of pride for his parents. ~~He was talented.~~ He dreamed of becoming a successful artist, and he had talent that was too young to die.

Phrases such as *endless enthusiasm for life* and *talent that was too young to die* add emotional appeal.

Prentice Hall Writing and Grammar Connection: Chapter 28, Section 1

Extend Your Learning

Listening and Speaking Write and narrate a **sequel** to Welty's "A Worn Path" that describes what happens when Phoenix Jackson gets home. Use these questions to help you plan:

- Is Phoenix's grandson alive?
- Is anyone else present?
- What does Phoenix feel and do?
- How will your story end?

In an oral presentation, share your story with your class.

Research and Technology Hemingway's story drew upon his service in the Italian army. With a partner, conduct library and Internet research to find information on Italy's role in World War I and Hemingway's participation. Prepare a **research report** on your findings, including maps and charts as visual aids. **[Group activity]**

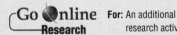

For: An additional research activity
Visit: www.PHSchool.com
Web Code: erd-7508

Assessment Resources

The following resources can be used to assess student's knowledge and skills.

Unit 5 Resources
- **Selection Test A,** pp. 145–147
- **Selection Test B,** pp. 148–150

General Resources
- **Rubrics for Response to Literature,** pp. 65–66
- **Rubrics for Research: Research Report,** pp. 49–50

Go Online Assessment — Students may use the **Self-test** to prepare for **Selection Test A** or **Selection Test B.**

❸ Writing Lesson

- To give students guidance for writing this memorial speech, give them the **Support for Writing Lesson** page from ***Unit 6 Resources,*** p. 140.
- Use the Response to Literature rubrics in ***General Resources,*** pp. 65–66, to evaluate students' work.
- Remind students that their speeches should capture Will's personality, hopes, and ambitions, as well as the strength of the bond in Will's family.
- As students reread, remind them that their speech is from Hal's point of view. They should note Hal's knowledge of Will and feelings for his family.
- Remind students that they should organize their ideas either in order of importance or in chronological order. Use the Outline transparency in the ***Graphic Organizer Transparencies,*** p. 309, as a model.
- When students begin to revise, encourage them to include at least one emotional detail in each paragraph.

❹ Research and Technology

- Remind students to collect information for creating maps and other visuals. Have them use varied resources, including textbooks, encyclopedias, atlases, databases, and the Internet.
- If students have difficulty finding information, tell them to search under "Italian Front in World War I" and "Hemingway."
- After they gather their research materials, have students determine if they have appropriate information to use for maps, charts, and diagrams.
- Adapt the Research: Research Report rubrics in ***General Resources,*** pp. 49–50, to assess students' reports.
- The **Support for Extend Your Learning** page (***Unit 6 Resources,*** p. 141) provides guided note-taking opportunities to help students complete the Extend Your Learning activities.

Go Online Research — Have students type in the Web code for another research activity.

From the Author's Desk

Tim O'Brien

- Tell students that like many writers, Tim O'Brien bases his fiction on real-life events. This gives him the freedom to create purely imagined stories while remaining connected to the events that inspired them.
- Show Segment 2 on O'Brien on the *From the Author's Desk DVD.* Discuss with students how O'Brien's story reflects the issues, topics, and themes introduced by other writers in this unit.

A Short Story That Is Also Part of a Novel

- Have students read about Tim O'Brien's inspiration for "Ambush." **Ask:** Why do you think O'Brien chose to write about such an event?
  Possible answer: This event had a profound effect on him; perhaps he learned something very important during that time and felt that he needed to honor the memory.

From the Author's Desk

Tim O'Brien

Tim O'Brien is an award-winning fiction writer. His novel *Going After Cacciato* won the National Book Award, *The Things They Carried* was a finalist for a Pulitzer Prize, and *In the Lake of the Woods* was named the best novel of the year by *Time* magazine.

Contemporary writer Tim O'Brien grew up reading the twentieth-century writers in Unit 5, including Ernest Hemingway, F. Scott Fitzgerald, Eudora Welty, Thomas Wolfe, Robert Frost, and T. S. Eliot. They fueled his passion to become a writer and helped him develop his ideas about literature. In fact, O'Brien's nonfiction and fiction about the Vietnam War may remind readers of Hemingway's fiction about World War I, such as "In Another Country" (page 809). Like Hemingway, O'Brien explores the psychological and moral effects of war on the soldiers who fought it—yet who may not feel like heroes when the war is over.

As you read O'Brien's essay and the story that follows, think about the ways in which each generation of writers takes what it can from the previous generation but then must face the unique challenges of its own time period.

TIM O'BRIEN INTRODUCES *"Ambush"*

A Short Story That Is Also Part of a Novel

"Ambush" is part of a larger work of fiction, a novel called *The Things They Carried,* but I must quickly add that the story is also meant to stand entirely on its own. It has a beginning, a middle, and an end. It can be understood and appreciated, I hope, with no additional information.

An Invented Character Who Has My Name Although the main character in the story is named Tim, which is my own name, and although many years ago I did in fact serve as an infantryman in Vietnam, "Ambush" is nonetheless a piece of fiction. The events in this story are largely invented. The characters, too, are invented, including the character named Tim. (I don't have a daughter, for example, and until very recently I had no children at all.) As a novelist and short-story writer, I am not limited by what actually happened. In fiction, I am free to write about what did *not* happen. I can write about what almost happened, or what could've happened, or what should've happened.

Fact Versus Fiction While the story is mostly imagined, it is loosely based on a "real life" ambush during the war. The mosquitoes, the trail junction, the dark night, the tension—all that comes from my own experience. In the actual incident, however, I did not throw a hand grenade that killed the young man. As it truly happened, a group of seven or eight of us simultaneously fired our rifles at three shadowy, barely visible enemy soldiers creeping across a rice paddy.

Teaching Resources

The following resources can be used to enrich or extend the instruction for From the Author's Desk.

Unit 5 Resources
From the Author's Desk, p. 143
Listening and Viewing, p. 144

From the Author's Desk DVD
Tim O'Brien, Segment 2

One moment the night was silent, the next moment it exploded—gunfire and screams and yellow-white flashes in the dark. Later, when dawn broke, one of my friends discovered a dead Viet Cong soldier. But I did not inspect the body. I did not so much as glance at it. I certainly did not stand gaping like the character in this story.

▲ **Critical Viewing** This photograph was taken during the Vietnam War. What thoughts and emotions do you imagine these soldiers are experiencing? **[Speculate]**

Confession and Lament I will never know whether a bullet from my own weapon killed that young man. Perhaps so, perhaps not. But in the end, it doesn't matter. I was there that night. I pulled the trigger. And I am therefore responsible. In my view, that's what "Ambush" is finally about: responsibility. Even now, like the protagonist in this story, I still have trouble forgiving myself. I still hear the gunfire and the screams. I still have the sour, fruity taste of terror in my mouth. I still feel the guilt. And I suppose that's why I sat down one day to write "Ambush"—as a kind of confession, as a lament, as a way of acknowledging my full personal responsibility for the death of a fellow human being.

Thinking About the Commentary

1. **(a) Recall:** Why did O'Brien choose to write "Ambush" as fiction? **(b) Speculate:** In what ways do you think fiction is strengthened if it is based on real events?
2. **(a) Recall:** What does O'Brien say that "Ambush" is finally about? **(b) Infer:** What impact do you think writing "Ambush" has had on O'Brien's memories of his own experience?

As You Read *"Ambush"* . . .

3. Compare and contrast the events in the story with the real events that O'Brien describes in this commentary.
4. Think about the ways in which the main character does and does not resemble O'Brien himself.

Critical Viewing

Possible response: The soldiers are feeling fear and anxiety. They are possibly thinking about their plan of attack.

ASSESS

Answers

1. (a) O'Brien chose to write a fictional story because he did not want to be limited by what actually happened. (b) **Possible answer:** In a sense, a story that is based on real events is already complete. It just needs to be told. Real events also provide the seeds of inspiration that grow into a story as a writer creates new interpretations of events.
2. (a) It is a confession; his way of acknowledging his responsibility for the death of another person. (b) **Possible answer:** It surely revived difficult memories, but it may have provided a new perspective, which helped him better understand what happened.
3. In the story, Tim kills a soldier walking alone. In real life, a group of soldiers fire at several enemy soldiers. The character gapes at the dead body, while O'Brien refused to look at the dead soldier. The setting in both stories is similar as is the taste that both men feel in their mouths.
4. The character and O'Brien are similar because both feel guilt about their actions. The character's reaction to the dead body is different than O'Brien's reaction.

TEACH

Learning Modalities
Bodily/Kinesthetic Learners In "Ambush," author Tim O'Brien gives readers vivid descriptions of the postures and movements of soldiers at war. Such descriptions can offer these students a way to enter into the story. Encourage students to prepare, rehearse, and perform a pantomime of the central action of the story. One student should play the narrator, and a second student should play the Viet Cong soldier. Students should capture the body language, movements, and gestures O'Brien describes.

1 About the Selection

Tim O'Brien's memories of the Vietnam War inform this haunting story. Asked by his daughter if he had killed anyone in the war, a Vietnam veteran remembers the Viet Cong soldier he killed on watch one dawn. He then shares the fear and ambivalence he experiences as he balances his struggle to survive with his personal values and respect for life.

2 Tim O'Brien
Author's Insight

- Tell students that although fictional, this story draws on author Tim O'Brien's experiences in Vietnam and after the war. You may wish to encourage discussion of students' expectations for the story.
- Have students read the marked passage. Then, call their attention to the Author's Insight note. Encourage students to discuss O'Brien's statement that it was necessary to have the narrator's daughter pose the question that begins the story.
- Before they continue reading, **ask** students to predict how the narrator will respond to his daughter's questioning.
  Possible response: Students may say the narrator will not answer his daughter directly, or will deny having taken lives. Most students will predict that the question will lead the narrator to recall traumatic experiences he had in Vietnam.

1
AMBUSH

Tim O'Brien

2 When she was nine, my daughter Kathleen asked if I had ever killed anyone. She knew about the war; she knew I'd been a soldier. "You keep writing these war stories," she said, "so I guess you must've killed somebody." It was a difficult moment, but I did what seemed right, which was to say, "Of course not," and then to take her onto my lap and hold her for a while. Someday, I hope, she'll ask again. But here I want to pretend she's a grown-up. I want to tell her exactly what happened, or what I remember happening, and then I want to say to her that as a little girl she was absolutely right. This is why I keep writing war stories:

He was a short, slender young man of about twenty. I was afraid of him—afraid of something—and as he passed me on the trail I threw a grenade that exploded at his feet and killed him.

Or to go back:

Shortly after midnight we moved into the ambush site outside My Khe. The whole platoon was there, spread out in the dense brush along the trail, and for five hours nothing at all happened. We were working in two-man teams—one man on guard while the other slept, switching off every two hours—and I remember it was still dark when Kiowa shook me awake for the final watch. The night was foggy and hot. For the first few moments I felt lost, not sure about directions, groping for my helmet and weapon. I reached out and found three grenades and lined them up in front of me; the pins had already been straightened for quick throwing. And then for maybe half an hour I kneeled there and waited. Very gradually, in tiny slivers, dawn began to break through the fog, and from my position in the brush I could see ten or fifteen meters up the trail. The mosquitoes were fierce. I remember slapping at them, wondering if I should wake up Kiowa and

3 **▲Critical Viewing**
What elements of the landscape shown here suggest the physical challenges soldiers faced in Vietnam? **[Deduce]**

Tim O'Brien
Author's Insight
The character of Kathleen, the narrator's daughter, seemed essential to this story. Adults rarely ask a direct, embarrassing question such as: "Did you ever kill anyone?" But a child of nine might easily ask just such a question.

Vocabulary Builder
ambush (am′ boosh′) *n.* lying in wait to attack by surprise

ask for some repellent, then thinking it was a bad idea, then looking up and seeing the young man come out of the fog. He wore black clothing and rubber sandals and a gray ammunition belt. His shoulders were slightly stooped, his head cocked to the side as if listening for something. He seemed at ease. He carried his weapon in one hand, muzzle down, moving without any hurry up the center of the trail. There was no sound at all—none that I can remember. In a way, it seemed, he was part of the morning fog, or my own imagination, but there was also the reality of what was happening in my stomach. I had already pulled the pin on a grenade. I had come up to a crouch. It was entirely automatic. I did not hate the young man; I did not see him as the enemy; I did not ponder issues of morality or politics or military duty. I crouched and kept my head low. I tried to swallow whatever was rising from my stomach, which tasted like lemonade, something fruity and sour. I was terrified. There were no thoughts about killing. The grenade was to make him go away—just evaporate—and I leaned back and felt my mind go empty and then felt it fill up again. I had already thrown the grenade before telling myself to throw it. The brush was thick and I had to lob it high, not aiming, and I remember the grenade seeming to freeze above me for an instant, as if a camera had clicked, and I remember ducking down and holding my breath and seeing little wisps of fog rise from the earth. The grenade bounced once and rolled across the trail. I did not hear it, but there must've been a sound, because the young man dropped his weapon and began to run, just two or three quick steps, then he hesitated, swiveling to his right, and he glanced down at the grenade and tried to cover his head but never did.

Tim O'Brien
Author's Insight
In these sentences I try to humanize the young enemy soldier—his clothing, his posture, the unhurried and slightly distracted way he walks up the trail.

Vocabulary Builder
ammunition (am′ yo͞o nish′ ən) *n.* anything hurled by a weapon or exploded as a weapon

muzzle (muz′ əl) *n.* front end of a barrel of a gun; the snout of an animal

5  **Reading Check**
What does the speaker do when he sees the young man on the path?

Differentiated Instruction
Solutions for All Learners

Support for Less Proficient Readers
These students may find the lengthy third paragraph and rich sensory details of "Ambush" to be very challenging. Use the first two paragraphs to preview the story for these students. Explain that in the rest of the story, the narrator will revisit the moment he killed an enemy soldier. Then, have students read the long paragraph on pages 834–836 slowly, pausing after every couple of sentences to visualize the scene. At the end of the paragraph, be sure they understand that all that has actually happened was contained in the story's brief second paragraph. Have students write short summaries to show their understanding.

3 Critical Viewing
Possible response: Elements include the water the soldiers must wade in, the dense brush they have to climb through, and the insects and other pests that such an environment would invariably harbor.

4 Tim O'Brien
Author's Insight

- Call students' attention to the short second paragraph on page 834. Point out that this summary is devoid of detail, but is followed by the words "Or to go back." **Ask** students what they think this phrase signals.
  Possible response: The narrator uses these words to bring readers back to Vietnam, to witness rather than just hear about what he experienced.
- Before they read the marked passage, **ask** students to describe what is happening in their own words.
  Possible response: The narrator is in the jungles of Vietnam, part of a two-man team waiting through the night for an ambush. Shortly before dawn, he is woken to keep watch. Frightened and disoriented, his attention is caught by a young man appearing on the trail.
- Have students read the marked passage. Point out that this is a much richer description than the initial mention of "a short, slender young man of about twenty."
- Call students' attention to the Author's Insight note next to the marked passage. Encourage them to discuss whether or not O'Brien succeeds in humanizing the enemy soldier. **Ask** students why he would seek to do this.
  Possible response: Humanizing the enemy soldier is a way for O'Brien to transport readers to the Vietnam he experienced, a situation full of fear and ambiguity.

5 Reading Check
Answer: The speaker pulls the pin on a grenade and throws it at the young man "to make him go away"—in other words, to kill him.

❻ Tim O'Brien
Author's Insight

- Have students read the marked passage. Explain that the narrator is aware that the man he killed posed no threat. Then, call students' attention to the Author's Insight note.
- **Ask** students to explain in their own words the impact of the sentence, "And it will always be that way." **Possible response:** The sentence shows that no one ever escapes the horror and guilt of war, no matter how much time goes by.

❼ Tim O'Brien
Author's Insight

- Have students read the marked passage. **Ask** them to interpret the narrator's vision of the man he killed walking back into the fog. **Possible response:** The vision may suggest the narrator is still haunted by the man he killed.
- Call attention to the Author's Insight note next to the final paragraph. Encourage them to speculate on what kind of life the young man might have had if the narrator had not thrown the grenade and on how the narrator's life might be different.

ASSESS
Answers

1. Some students will argue that a father should be truthful; others will respect his decision to protect his daughter.
2. (a) He says, "There was no real peril." (b) He means that he will never be able to accept that he killed without being in real danger.
3. (a) He is stunned and cannot stop staring at the man's body. (b) Kiowa tells him to accept the realities of war.
4. (a) He fantasizes watching the young man complete his walk down the trail unharmed. (b) It shows readers that the ambivalence, the guilt, and the horror of war stay forever with those who experience it.
5. (a) The first telling is objective, lacking details; the second is much more detailed and describes the narrator's emotions in depth. (b) Students may feel he chose this device to emphasize the complexity of war—there is no simple truth.

It occurred to me then that he was about to die. I wanted to warn him. The grenade made a popping noise—not soft but not loud either—not what I'd expected—and there was a puff of dust and smoke—a small white puff—and the young man seemed to jerk upward as if pulled by invisible wires. He fell on his back. His rubber sandals had been blown off. There was no wind. He lay at the center of the trail, his right leg bent beneath him, his one eye shut, his other eye a huge star-shaped hole.

❻ It was not a matter of live or die. There was no real peril. Almost certainly the young man would have passed by. And it will always be that way.

Later, I remember, Kiowa tried to tell me that the man would've died anyway. He told me that it was a good kill, that I was a soldier and this was a war, that I should shape up and stop staring and ask myself what the dead man would've done if things were reversed.

None of it mattered. The words seemed far too complicated. All I could do was gape at the fact of the young man's body.

Even now I haven't finished sorting it out. Sometimes I forgive myself, other times I don't. In the ordinary hours of life I try not to dwell on it, but now and then, when I'm reading a newspaper or just sitting alone in a room, I'll look up and see the young man coming out of the morning fog. ❼ I'll watch him walk toward me, his shoulders slightly stooped, his head cocked to the side, and he'll pass within a few yards of me and suddenly smile at some secret thought and then continue up the trail to where it bends back into the fog.

Tim O'Brien
Author's Insight
This sentence, for my money, is among the best I have ever written. Only seven very simple words, yet for me the sentence carries the weight of eternity, the permanent and inescapable horror of war.

Tim O'Brien
Author's Insight
As the narrator imagines the young man continuing up the trail to where it bends back into the fog, he is also imagining that the ambush never occurred, that the dead young man has a long and full life ahead of him in a future that will never be.

Critical Reading

1. **Respond:** If you had been the narrator, would you have told your nine-year-old this story? Why or why not?
2. **(a) Recall:** What does the narrator say to describe the degree of danger he faced? **(b) Interpret:** What does he mean when he says "And it will always be that way"?
3. **(a) Deduce:** How does the narrator react to the killing? **(b) Interpret:** In what way does Kiowa respond to the narrator's reaction?
4. **(a) Recall:** At the end of the story, what does the narrator fantasize? **(b) Interpret:** In what ways does this fantasy add to the story's meaning?
5. **(a) Compare and Contrast:** The narrator tells his story twice. Compare and contrast the short and long versions. **(b) Speculate:** Why do you think the author chose this narrative device?
6. **Make a Judgment:** Kiowa uses the expression "a good kill." Is there such a thing? Explain.

For: More about Tim O'Brien
Visit: www.PHSchool.com
Web Code: ere-9516

Answers continued

6. Some students will argue that a killing in wartime is justified. Others will argue that no killing is ever "good."

Go Online Author Link For additional information about Tim O'Brien, have students type in the Web Code, then select *O* from the alphabet, and then select Tim O'Brien.

Unit 5 Part 3

From Every Corner of the Land

The Tower, Charles Demuth, Columbus Museum of Art, Ohio

Differentiated Instruction

Solutions for All Learners

Accessibility at a Glance

More Accessible
Chicago
"Out, Out—"
from Here Is New York

Average
Grass
The Jilting of Granny Weatherall
A Rose for Emily
Nobel Prize Acceptance Speech
Birches
Stopping by Woods on a Snowy Evening
Mending Wall
The Gift Outright
The Night the Ghost Got In
from Dust Tracks on a Road
I, Too
Refugee in America
From the Dark Tower
Storm Ending

More Challenging
Acquainted With the Night
The Negro Speaks of Rivers
Dream Variations
The Tropics in New York
A Black Man Talks of Reaping

Selection Planning Guide

The works in this section reflect the breadth of American literature in the early-to-mid-twentieth century. This literary look at the regional diversity of the United States takes students from Carl Sandburg's rough and ready "Chicago" and E.B. White's dynamic urban portrait in *Here Is New York* to Faulkner's Mississippi in "A Rose for Emily." Katherine Anne Porter uses a stream-of-consciousness style to tell the tale of a rural woman's life in "The Jilting of Granny Weatherall," a story that is likely to both challenge and intrigue students. Frost's poetry, set against a vividly painted New England backdrop, has a depth and power that belie its simple language. The engaging excerpt from Zora Neale Hurston's *Dust Tracks on a Road* introduces a sampling of poetry by the leading writers of the Harlem Renaissance. These poems are rich with images and metaphors that express what it meant to be an African American at a time when memories of both slavery and the Civil War were still fresh in the American consciousness.

Humanities

The Tower, by Charles Demuth, 1920

Sir Christopher Wren (1632–1723), to whom this painting pays tribute, was England's most famous architect. After the Great Fire of London in 1666, he redesigned at least portions of more than half of the churches that had been burnt. His church spires, in particular, are admired for their grace and variety. **Ask:**

- What various facets of America do you see reflected in this painting? **Possible response:** This painting reflects America's New England roots, its combination of past and future, its social variety.

Benchmark

After students have completed the excerpt from "Here Is New York," administer **Benchmark Test 8**. If the Benchmark Test reveals that some students need further work, use the **Interpretation Guide** to determine the appropriate reteaching pages in the **Reading Kit** or on **Success Tracker.**

Monitoring Progress

Before students read the excerpt from *Dust Tracks on a Road* by Zora Neale Hurston, administer **Diagnostic Test 9.** This test will determine students' level of readiness for the reading and vocabulary skills.

Meeting Your Standards

Students will

1. **analyze and respond to literary elements.**
   - Literary Analysis: Apostrophe
2. **read, comprehend, analyze, and critique poetry.**
   - Reading Strategy: Responding
   - Reading Check questions
   - Apply the Skills questions
   - Assessment Practice (ATE)
3. **develop vocabulary.**
   - Vocabulary Lesson: Related Words: *brutal*
4. **understand and apply written and oral language conventions.**
   - Spelling Strategy
   - Grammar and Style Lesson: Sentence Types
5. **develop writing proficiency.**
   - Writing Lesson: Analytical Essay
6. **develop appropriate research strategies.**
   - Extend Your Learning: Report
7. **understand and apply listening and speaking strategies.**
   - Extend Your Learning: Stand-up Comedy Routine

Block Scheduling: Use one 90-minute class period to preteach the skills and have students read the selection. Use a second 90-minute class period to assess students' mastery of skills, extend their learning, and monitor their progress.

Homework Suggestions

Following are possibilities for homework assignments.

- Support pages from ***Unit 5 Resources:***
  Literary Analysis
  Reading Strategy
  Vocabulary Builder
  Grammar and Style
- An Extend Your Learning project and the Writing Lesson for this selection group may be completed over several days.

Step-by-Step Teaching Guide	Pacing Guide
PRETEACH	
• Administer Vocabulary and Reading Warm-ups as necessary.	5 min.
• Engage students' interest with the motivation activity.	5 min.
• Read and discuss author and background features. **FT**	10 min.
• Introduce the Literary Analysis Skill: Apostrophe **FT**	5 min.
• Introduce the Reading Strategy: Responding **FT**	10 min.
• Prepare students to read by teaching the selection vocabulary. **FT**	
TEACH	
• Informally monitor comprehension while students read independently or in groups. **FT**	30 min.
• Monitor students' comprehension with the Reading Check notes.	as students read
• Reinforce vocabulary with Vocabulary Builder notes.	as students read
• Develop students' understanding of apostrophe with the Literary Analysis annotations. **FT**	5 min.
• Develop students' ability to respond with the Reading Strategy annotations. **FT**	5 min.
ASSESS/EXTEND	
• Assess students' comprehension and mastery of the Literary Analysis and Reading Strategy by having them answer the Apply the Skills questions. **FT**	15 min.
• Have students complete the Vocabulary Lesson and the Grammar and Style Lesson. **FT**	15 min.
• Apply students' ability to connect contradictory information by using the Writing Lesson. **FT**	45 min. or homework
• Apply students' understanding by using one or more of the Extend Your Learning activities.	20–90 min. or homework
• Administer Selection Test A or Selection Test B. **FT**	15 min.

Resources

PRINT
Unit 5 Resources
- Vocabulary Warm-up Word Lists **[L1, L2, EL]** ....p. 151
- Vocabulary Warm-up Practice **[L1, L2, EL]** ....p. 152
- Reading Warm-up A **[L1, L2, EL]** ....p. 153
- Reading Warm-up B **[L1, L2, L3]** ....p. 154

TRANSPARENCY
Graphic Organizer Transparencies
- Literary Analysis Graphic Organizer A **[L3]** ....pp. 181, 183
- Literary Analysis Graphic Organizer B **[L1, L2, EL]** ....pp. 182, 184

PRINT
Reader's Notebook [L2]
Reader's Notebook: Adapted Version [L1]
Reader's Notebook: English Learner's Version [EL]
Unit 5 Resources
- Literary Analysis **[L3]** ....p. 155
- Reading Strategy **[L3]** ....p. 156
- Vocabulary Builder **[L3]** ....p. 157

TECHNOLOGY
Listening to Literature Audio CDs [L2, EL]

PRINT
Unit 5 Resources
- Grammar and Style **[L3]** ....p. 158
- Support for Writing Lesson **[L3]** ....p. 159
- Support for Extend Your Learning **[L3]** ....p. 160
- Enrichment **[L4]** ....p. 161
- Selection Test A **[L1, L2, EL]** ....pp. 162–164
- Selection Test B **[L3, L4]** ....pp. 165–167

General Resources
- Rubrics for Response to Literature **[L3]** ....pp. 65–66
- Rubrics for Research: Research Report ....pp. 49–50

TECHNOLOGY
Go Online: Research **[L3]**
Go Online: Self-test **[L3]**
ExamView® **Test Bank [L3]**

Choosing Resources for Differentiated Instruction

[L1] Special Needs Students
[L2] Below-Level Students
[L3] All Students
[L4] Advanced Students
[EL] English Learners

For Vocabulary and Reading Warm-ups and for Selection Tests, **A** signifies "less challenging" and **B** "more challenging." For Graphic Organizer transparencies, **A** signifies "not filled in" and **B** "filled in."

FT Fast Track Instruction: To move the lesson more quickly, use the strategies and activities identified with **FT**.

Scaffolding for Less Proficient and Advanced Students

The leveled Critical Thinking questions after selections progress in the levels of thinking required to answer them. To address the needs of your different students, you may use the (a) level questions for your less proficient students and the (b) level questions with your on-level and advanced students. The occasional (c) level questions are appropriate for your advanced students.

PRENTICE HALL **TeacherEXPRESS™** Plan · Teach · Assess — Use this complete suite of powerful teaching tools to make lesson planning and testing quicker and easier.

PRENTICE HALL **StudentEXPRESS™** Learn · Study · Succeed — Use the interactive textbook (online and on CD-ROM) to make selections and activities come alive with audio and video support and interactive questions.

Go Online Professional Development — **For:** Information about Lexiles **Visit:** www.PHSchool.com **Web Code:** eue-1111

Motivation

Obtain the video of the John Hughes 1986 film *Ferris Bueller's Day Off,* which offers viewers a whirlwind tour of the "City of the Big Shoulders" as it looks in modern times. Play portions of the movie to show scenes in which the teen and his high school friends are in the Loop, at the Board of Trade, at a Cubs game at Wrigley Field, at a parade down Michigan Avenue, and at a posh French restaurant. Ask students to give their impressions of the city. Then, tell students that they are going to read a famous poem about Chicago, written nearly a century ago. Have them keep modern Chicago in mind as they read. Invite them to compare the images from the film with the images Sandburg presents.

❶ Background

More About the Author

Quoting Rudyard Kipling to describe himself, Carl Sandburg once said, "I will be the word of the people. Mine will be the bleeding mouth from which the gag is snatched. I will say everything." Both poems collected here offer profound images of the people or comments on their behalf. In particular, "Grass" speaks out against the human waste of war.

Sandburg was part of a group of writers known as the Chicago School. These men—Sherwood Anderson and Theodore Dreiser, among others—lived and wrote in Chicago in the early 20th century. Sandburg also wrote for children, in his humorous stories *Rootabaga Stories* (1922), *Rootabaga Pigeons* (1923), and *Potato Face* (1930).

❶ Chicago • Grass

Carl Sandburg (1878–1967)

You may enjoy the work of a contemporary poet or songwriter who seems to speak right to you. The poetry of Carl Sandburg seemed to speak directly to many of the people of his time. It celebrated the lives and the vitality of ordinary Americans, and made Sandburg one of the most popular poets of his day.

No writer better captured the spirit of industrial America than did Carl Sandburg, whose poems paint vivid portraits of the working class, capturing its energy and enthusiasm. In his poems about mills and factories, meatpacking houses, and railroads, he paid tribute to the struggles and hopes of the poor.

Modest Beginnings The son of Swedish immigrants, Sandburg was born and raised in Galesburg, Illinois. He was forced to leave school after eighth grade in order to help support his family. As an adolescent, he worked as a laborer, and when he was nineteen, he set out to see the country. He did so by hitching rides on freight trains. In 1898, after spending six years working at a variety of odd jobs, Sandburg enlisted in the army. Though the Spanish-American War was being fought at the time, Sandburg did not see combat. After the war, he attended Lombard College, but dropped out before graduating. He then spent several years traveling around the country, again working at a variety of jobs.

The Bard of Chicago In 1912, Sandburg settled in Chicago, one of the nation's great industrial cities. He made his living as a newspaper reporter and began to publish poetry in *Poetry* magazine, a highly regarded literary journal based in Chicago. His first book, *Chicago Poems,* published in 1916, sold well and was praised for its passion and vigor. Sandburg soon earned widespread recognition and helped establish Chicago as one of the nation's leading literary centers. During the next ten years, he published three more successful collections of poetry: *Cornhuskers* (1918), *Smoke and Steel* (1920), and *Slabs of the Sunburnt West* (1922).

Writing Lincoln's Life While continuing to write poetry, Sandburg began touring the country, delivering lectures on Walt Whitman and Abraham Lincoln—two men whom he greatly admired—and starting a career as a folk singer. He also spent a great deal of time collecting material for a biography of Lincoln, and he prepared an anthology of American folk songs he had heard during his travels. He collected these songs from cowboys, lumberjacks, factory workers, and hobos. *The American Songbag* appeared in 1927. In 1940, Carl Sandburg received a Pulitzer Prize for his multi-volume biography of Lincoln, and in 1951 he received a second Pulitzer Prize for his *Complete Poems.* Sandburg was also awarded the United States Presidential Medal in 1964, and he was asked to address a joint session of Congress on the 150th anniversary of Lincoln's birth.

Power of Positive Thinking Sandburg was an optimist who believed in the power of ordinary Americans to fulfill their dreams. He was not interested in experimenting with complicated syntax or images, as were some other poets of his generation. Instead, he reached out to his readers with poems that were concrete and direct. Sandburg offered a variety of definitions of poetry, among them these two: "Poetry is a search for syllables to shoot at the barriers of the unknown and the unknowable," and "Poetry is the opening and closing of a door, leaving those who look through to guess about what is seen during a moment."

Preview

Connecting to the Literature

If you have ever celebrated the comeback of someone who seemed to have been defeated, then you understand the spirit in which Carl Sandburg wrote. In reading these poems, you will see that Sandburg recognized people's and cities' failures, but he cheered the invincibility of their souls.

Literary Analysis

Apostrophe

Apostrophe is a literary device in which a speaker directly addresses a thing, an abstract concept, or a person who is dead or absent. For example, in "Chicago," Sandburg addresses the city as if it were a person:

They tell me you are wicked and I believe them . . .

And they tell me you are crooked and I answer: Yes . . .

As you read "Chicago," think about the effect of this technique, and identify the reasons that Sandburg chose to speak directly to the city of Chicago.

Comparing Literary Works

These poems concern two very different subjects and evoke distinct emotions. "Chicago" is a celebration of life in an industrial city, while "Grass" is a lament for loss of life in war. In "Chicago," the speaker addresses the city directly; in "Grass," it is the grass itself that speaks. Despite these differences, the poet uses similar techniques to achieve his aims. For example, both poems use **personification,** figurative language in which a non-human subject is given human qualities. As you read, use a chart like the one shown to examine the ways in which Sandburg uses personification, but to different effect in each poem.

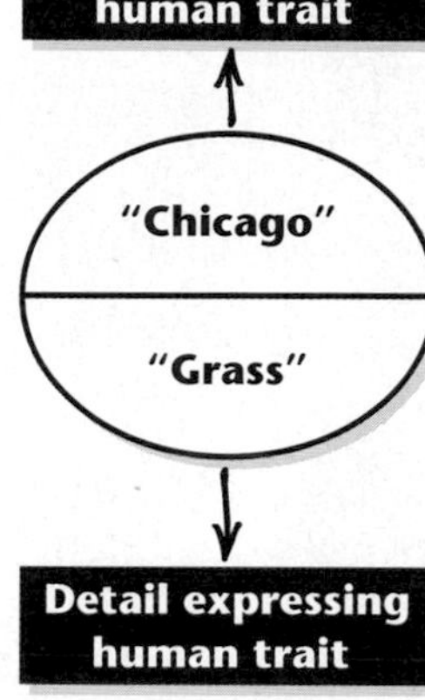

Reading Strategy

Responding

When you **respond** to a poem, you think about the message that the poet has conveyed and reflect on how you feel personally about the topic. You take the time to consider how the poet's message relates to your own life and to the world in which you live, and to think about how you can use or apply what you have learned from the poem. As you read these poems, connect your own experiences to the images and ideas Sandburg presents.

Vocabulary Builder

brutal (brōōt′ əl) *adj.* cruel and without feeling; savage; violent (p. 841)

wanton (wän′ tən) *adj.* senseless; unjustified (p. 841)

cunning (kun′ iŋ) *adj.* skillful in deception; crafty; sly (p. 841)

2 Literary Analysis

Apostrophe

- Tell students that as they read Carl Sandburg's poems, they will focus on *apostrophe,* a literary device in which the poet addresses a person or thing directly.
- Have a volunteer read aloud the excerpts in the Literary Analysis instruction. Point out the specific word ("you") that makes these lines examples of apostrophe.
- Discuss the instruction under Comparing Literary Works, and use it to help students understand how personification and apostrophe work together.
- Give students a copy of **Literary Analysis Graphic Organizer A,** p. 181 in ***Graphic Organizer Transparencies,*** and direct students to complete the chart as they read the poems.

3 Reading Strategy

Responding

- Explain to students that responding includes thoughts, feelings, associations, and any other reactions evoked by a reading.
- Remind students that responding to poetry is at the core of their reading experience. Encourage them to trust their reactions, even when they don't "understand" the poem.

Vocabulary Builder

- Pronounce each vocabulary word for students, and read the definitions as a class. Have students identify any words with which they are already familiar.

Differentiated Instruction

Solutions for All Learners

Support for Special Needs Students
Have students complete the **Preview** and **Build Skills** pages for these selections in the ***Reader's Notebook: Adapted Version.*** These pages provide a selection summary, an abbreviated presentation of the reading and literary skills, and the graphic organizer on the **Build Skills** page in the student book.

Support for Less Proficient Readers
Have students complete the **Preview** and **Build Skills** pages for these selections in the ***Reader's Notebook.*** These pages provide a selection summary, an abbreviated presentation of the reading and literary skills, and the graphic organizer on the **Build Skills** page in the student book.

Support for English Learners
Have students complete the **Preview** and **Build Skills** pages for these selections in the ***Reader's Notebook: English Learner's Version.*** These pages provide a selection summary, an abbreviated presentation of the skills, additional contextual vocabulary, and the graphic organizer on the **Build Skills** page in the student book.

Learning Modalities
Visual/Spatial Learners
Provide photos of the Chicago Sandburg portrays as well as "before and after" photos of Gettysburg and the World War I battlefields. Ask students to think about whether the tone of the poems matches the visual images in these pictures.

❶ About the Selections

Using spirited but simple words and phrases, Sandburg expresses his love and admiration for what he sees as a vital, brawny, sweating giant of a city.

In "Grass," Carl Sandburg observes that today there is only grass where once monumental battles between great armies took place. The serenity of nature obscures the horror and futility of war.

❷ Critical Viewing

Answer: It shows the mosaic of people and activities, the bustle of business and the marketplace, and the vitality and struggle of people to survive.

❶

Carl Sandburg

Differentiated Instruction Solutions for All Learners

Accessibility at a Glance

	Chicago	Grass
Context	Chicago, early 20th century	Nature vs. human destruction
Language	Vivid descriptions; rhythmic language	Simple vocabulary and sentences
Concept Level	Accessible (personification of Chicago)	Accessible (Power of nature; passage of time)
Literary Merit	Classic	Noted author
Lexile	NP	NP
Overall Rating	More accessible	Average

Background

The 1920s was a time of excitement in America. The economy was booming, and jazz was the rage. Sandburg's poems of industrial America celebrate the energy of the times.

Hog Butcher for the World,
Tool Maker, Stacker of Wheat,
Player with Railroads and the Nation's Freight Handler;
Stormy, husky, brawling,
City of the Big Shoulders:

They tell me you are wicked and I believe them, for I have seen
your painted women under the gas lamps luring the farm
boys.
And they tell me you are crooked and I answer: Yes, it is true I
have seen the gunman kill and go free to kill again.
3 And they tell me you are brutal and my reply is: On the faces of
women and children I have seen the marks of wanton hunger.
And having answered so I turn once more to those who sneer at
this my city, and I give them back the sneer and say to them:
Come and show me another city with lifted head singing so proud
4 to be alive and coarse and strong and cunning.
Flinging magnetic curses amid the toil of piling job on job, here is
a tall bold slugger set vivid against the little soft cities;
Fierce as a dog with tongue lapping for action, cunning as a
savage pitted against the wilderness,
Bareheaded,
Shoveling,
Wrecking,
Planning,
Building, breaking, rebuilding,
Under the smoke, dust all over his mouth, laughing with
white teeth,
Under the terrible burden of destiny laughing as a young man
laughs,
Laughing even as an ignorant fighter laughs who has never lost
a battle,
Bragging and laughing that under his wrist is the pulse, and
under his ribs the heart of the people,
Laughing!
Laughing the stormy, husky, brawling laughter of Youth, half-
naked, sweating, proud to be a Hog Butcher, Tool Maker,
Stacker of Wheat, Player with Railroads and Freight Handler
to the Nation.

◄**Critical Viewing** In what ways does this bustling street scene of Chicago reflect Sandburg's poem? **[Connect]**

Vocabulary Builder

brutal (bro͞ot′ əl) *adj.* cruel and without feeling; savage; violent

wanton (wän′ tən) *adj.* senseless; unjustified

cunning (kun′ iŋ) *adj.* skillful in deception; crafty; sly

5 

Reading Check

Who is the "you" the speaker addresses?

3 Vocabulary Builder

Related Words: *brutal*

- Call students' attention to the word *brutal* and its definition. Tell students that there are several words related to *brutal.*
- List the words presented in the Vocabulary Development Lesson in Build Language Skills: *brute, brutality, brutalize,* and *brutish.* Have students look up these words in a dictionary.
- Have students create sentences using these words based on the two Sandburg poems presented here.

4 Literary Analysis

Apostrophe and Personification

- Read aloud lines 10–11 to students. Have students identify the type of figurative language that Sandburg uses in these lines. Lead students to see that Sandburg personifies the city.
- **Ask** students to describe the effect of this personification. What qualities of the city are expressed in these lines?
  Answer: The use of personification makes the city seem a vibrant, loud, and bustling place.

5 Reading Check

Answer: The speaker addresses the city of Chicago as "you."

Differentiated Instruction

Solutions for All Learners

Support for Less Proficient Readers

Guide students to understand that with the rough, robust, and coarse images at the beginning of the poem, Sandburg is celebrating the essence of Chicago, not complaining about the city. Help them to appreciate that to him these images are rich and heroic. Read the poem aloud to convey its gusto.

Support for Special Needs Students

Have students listen to you read the poem aloud. Help them define any words or phrases they do not understand. Then, ask them how the poem makes them feel. Guide them to see the vital personality Sandburg gives his city. Emphasize that this is the most important message of the poem.

Enrichment for Gifted/Talented Students

After reading the poem aloud, invite students to render Sandburg's personified "City of the Big Shoulders" in another medium. Regardless of the medium they choose, they should try to capture the vitality and energy of Sandburg's portrayal.

ASSESS

Answers

1. Students should be prepared to explain their responses.
2. (a) He uses the names "Hog Butcher for the World, Tool Maker, Stacker of Wheat, Player with Railroads, the Nation's Freight Handler, and City of the Big Shoulders." (b) They tell you that the city is full of industry and business, that it is a transportation center, and that it is a busy, vibrant place.
3. (a) The city is wicked, crooked, and brutal. (b) The speaker thinks the city is wonderful despite its faults. If anything, he thinks these faults contribute to the city's vitality.
4. (a) It claims to cover the evidence of war. (b) He is saying that the death and destruction of war are futile, for they will be covered up and forgotten by nature.
5. (a) Responses should show an awareness of regional variations. (b) It is highly varied and unique, yet also similar to Chicago in its vitality.

Go Online **Author Link** For additional information about Carl Sandburg, have students type in the Web Code, then select S from the alphabet, and then select Carl Sandburg.

Grass

Carl Sandburg

Pile the bodies high at Austerlitz and Waterloo.[1]
Shovel them under and let me work—
    I am the grass; I cover all.

And pile them high at Gettysburg
And pile them high at Ypres and Verdun.[2]
Shovel them under and let me work.
Two years, ten years, and passengers ask the conductor:
    What place is this?
    Where are we now?

    I am grass.
    Let me work.

---

1. **Austerlitz** (ôs′ tər lits′) **and Waterloo** sites of battles of the Napoleonic Wars.
2. **Ypres** (ē′ pr) **and Verdun** (vər dun′) sites of battles of World War I.

Critical Reading

1. **Respond:** Unlike some poets, Sandburg tells you what to feel and think. How do you react to his directness? Why?
2. **(a) Recall:** In "Chicago," what names does the speaker use to address the city in the first stanza? **(b) Interpret:** What do these names tell you about the city's economy and atmosphere?
3. **(a) Recall:** What three specific faults concerning his city does the speaker acknowledge? **(b) Interpret:** In what ways do these faults affect the speaker's attitude toward the city?
4. **(a) Recall:** In the first stanza of "Grass," what does the grass claim to be able to do? **(b) Draw Conclusions:** Is Sandburg suggesting that the death and destruction of war can be covered over and easily forgotten? Support your answer.
5. **(a) Distinguish:** In what ways is the city described in "Chicago" similar to and different from other cities with which you are familiar? **(b) Apply:** What do the differences among American cities reveal about the nation's character?

For: More about Carl Sandburg
Visit: www.PHSchool.com
Web Code: ere-9517

Apply the Skills

Chicago • Grass

Literary Analysis

Apostrophe

1. **(a)** In which lines of "Chicago" does Sandburg address the city directly? **(b)** What effect does this use of **apostrophe** create?
2. **(a)** Using a chart like the one shown, contrast the lines in the poem that directly address the city with those that address others. **(b)** Which section contains more positive images?

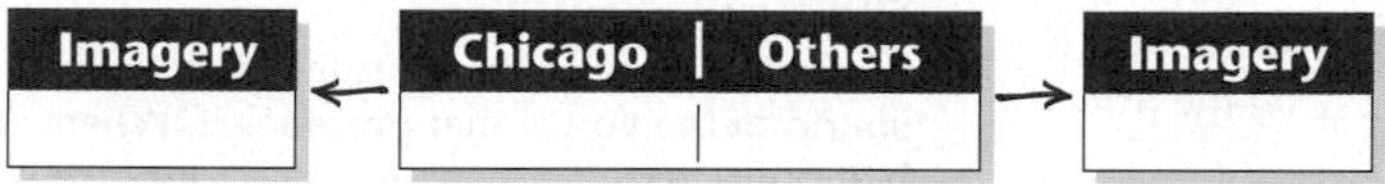

Comparing Literary Works

3. **(a)** Compare and contrast the use of specific details in "Chicago" and "Grass." **(b)** In what ways does the choice and amount of detail suit each poem's subject? **(c)** What distinct moods do these details evoke?
4. **(a)** Identify at least one feeling Sandburg has for Chicago that he might feel toward a friend. Support your answer with examples. **(b)** In "Grass," with what two words does the poet **personify** the grass?
5. In what ways do the uses of personification serve the distinct goals of each of these poems? Explain.

Reading Strategy

Responding

6. Which words or images in "Chicago" were most striking to you? Explain.
7. In what tone of voice do you imagine the grass speaks?
8. What is your **response** to the grass's message?

Extend Understanding

9. **Literature Connection:** Some critics have said that Sandburg opened poetry to new subjects by writing about industry and laborers. Other poets of his day, like T. S. Eliot, wrote about more intellectual subjects. What benefits or harm do you see—for poetry or popular culture—in Sandburg's appeal to the common person?

QuickReview

Apostrophe is a literary device in which a speaker directly addresses a thing, a concept, or a person who is dead or absent.

Personification is a type of figurative language in which a nonhuman subject is given human traits.

To **respond** to a literary work, think about what it says, consider how it makes you feel, and notice the thoughts it triggers in your mind.

For: Self-test
Visit: www.PHSchool.com
Web Code: era-6510

Answers

1. (a) Sandburg uses apostrophe in lines 6–8. (b) They make the city of Chicago seem like a person.
2. Chicago: lines 6–8; Imagery: negative images of the city's problems; Others: balance of poem; Imagery: positive images of the city's vital and spirited essence.

   Another sample answer can be found on **Literary Analysis Graphic Organizer B,** p. 184 in ***Graphic Organizer Transparencies.***
3. (a) "Chicago" has many specific details, while "Grass" is brief and includes few specific details, which are then repeated. (b) The extensive use of details in "Chicago" helps paint a clear picture of the city, while the repetition of a few details in "Grass" helps emphasize the poem's message. (c) In "Chicago," details evoke a mood of vitality and action. In "Grass," the few details evoke a mood of sadness and futility.
4. (a) He feels pride in the city's strength and vitality, as expressed in lines 10–12. (b) He uses the words "I am" to personify the grass.
5. Personification makes Chicago come alive for readers, while it allows Sandburg to speak as the grass in "Grass."
6. Students should be able to explain their choices.
7. **Possible response:** It speaks in a patient and enduring voice.
8. Students should be able to explain their responses.
9. **Possible response:** Students might say that Sandburg helped draw attention to the lives of everyday people by exploring this topic in his poems.

Go Online Assessment Students may use the **Self-test** to prepare for **Selection Test A** or **Selection Test B.**

EXTEND/ASSESS

Answers

❶ Vocabulary Lesson

Related Words

1. brute
2. brutality
3. brutish
4. brutalize

Vocabulary Builder

1. b
2. c
3. c

Spelling Strategy

1. barest
2. piling
3. smokily
4. caring

❷ Grammar and Style Lesson

1. Shovel me under and let me work. (Imperative)
2. I have seen hunger on children's faces. (Declarative)
3. Where are we now? (Interrogative)
4. Show me another city. (Imperative)
5. I am overjoyed by this response! (Exclamatory)

Writing Application

Check to see that students have included and properly punctuated all four types of sentences.

WG Writing and Grammar, Ruby Level

Students will find further instruction and practice on sentence types in Chapter 20, Section 1.

Build Language Skills

❶ Vocabulary Lesson

Related Words: *brutal*

The word *brutal* means "cruel, crude, or harsh." Use this information and your knowledge about parts of speech to complete each sentence using a related word from the list below.

brute brutality brutalize brutish

1. Sam was so rough with my brother that I told him he was behaving like a __?__ and asked him to leave.
2. Many who participated in World War I were stunned by the __?__ on the front lines.
3. Use your knife and fork, and stop that __?__ behavior at once!
4. Those who __?__ innocent animals should receive the harshest punishment.

Vocabulary Builder: Synonyms

Select the letter of the word that is closest in meaning to each of the numbered vocabulary words.

1. brutal: **(a)** unwise, **(b)** violent, **(c)** heavy
2. cunning: **(a)** suspicious, **(b)** diligent, **(c)** crafty
3. wanton: **(a)** rapid, **(b)** kind, **(c)** rash

Spelling Strategy

In the word *brute,* the final *e* marks the long sound of the vowel that precedes it. When a suffix beginning with a vowel is added to such a word, the final *e* is usually dropped: *brute* becomes *brutish.* For each of the following words, create a new word containing the given suffix.

1. bare (add *-est*)
2. pile (add *-ing*)
3. smoke (add *-ily*)
4. care (add *-ing*)

❷ Grammar and Style Lesson

Sentence Types

There are four sentence types. A **declarative** sentence makes a statement and ends with a period. An **interrogative** sentence asks a question and ends with a question mark. An **imperative** sentence is a statement and gives a command or makes a request; it ends with a period. An **exclamatory** sentence expresses a strong emotion and ends with an exclamation point.

Declarative: I am grass.

Interrogative: What place is this?

Imperative: Pile the bodies high.

Exclamatory: Look at that man!

Practice Add the correct end punctuation, and label the sentence type for each of the following examples.

1. Shovel me under and let me work
2. I have seen hunger on children's faces
3. Where are we now
4. Show me another city
5. I am overjoyed by this response

Writing Application Write a paragraph in which you praise and/or criticize your city or town. Use all four types of sentences in your essay.

WG Prentice Hall Writing and Grammar Connection: Chapter 20, Section 1

Assessment Practice

Analyze Sentence Meaning

(For more practice, see *Standardized Test Preparation Workbook*, p. 50.)

Many tests require students to correctly answer sentence-completion questions. Often, more than one choice can complete a sentence. Use the following sample item to show students how to analyze sentence meaning, decide whether it is positive or negative, and eliminate choices that have the opposite sense.

Carl Sandburg's poems focus on the lives of the working classes. By writing about mills and factories, he honored the ________ and hopes of the poor.

A cowardice **C** struggles
B avarice **D** idleness

The context indicates that the missing word will have a positive connotation. *A, B,* and *D* are all negative in this context. *C* is the best choice.

Writing Lesson

Timed Writing: Analytical Essay

Using either "Chicago," or "Grass," write an essay analyzing Sandburg's use of repetition. Explain the ways in which the poet's use of repetition emphasizes particular ideas and heightens specific emotions. ***(40 minutes)***

Prewriting ***(10 minutes)*** Select a poem to analyze, and examine it for examples of repetition. Note which elements—words, phrases, sentence structures, or grammatical forms—are repeated, and consider their effect.

Drafting ***(20 minutes)*** In your introduction, briefly summarize the poem, and state your main point about its use of repetition. Develop your ideas, with quotes from the poem, in the body paragraphs.

Revising ***(10 minutes)*** Review your draft, and make sure that you have explained your ideas in a consistent way. Use contrasting colors to underline any contradictory information. If you cannot connect the contradictions to your main idea, delete them.

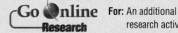

Model: Revising to Connect Contradictory Information

Reading "Chicago" is like riding the rapids on a river; you are swept along in a stream of words and do not stop to examine the validity of the ideas. However, the ideas in a Sandburg poem are important.

Transitional words such as *however* connect contradictory information to a main idea.

 *Prentice Hall Writing and Grammar Connection: Chapter 8, Section 2*

Extend Your Learning

Listening and Speaking Acting as the city of Chicago, deliver a **stand-up comedy routine.** First, research Chicago's history for events you can turn into anecdotes. Then, use these tips to prepare:

- Decide what your attitude will be—tough or sensitive.
- Find body language to fit your attitude.

When presenting your routine, appeal to your audience's experiences, and create a bond that will result in laughter.

Research and Technology Working with a partner, use the Internet and other sources to research the population of Chicago. Collect statistics related to that population, and create a **report** that demonstrates how the population of Chicago today reflects its history. **[Group Activity]**

For: An additional research activity
Visit: www.PHSchool.com
Web Code: erd-7509

❸ Writing Lesson

You may use this Writing Lesson as timed-writing practice, or you may allow students to develop it as a writing assignment over several days.

- To guide students in writing their analyses, give them the **Support for Writing Lesson** page (***Unit 5 Resources,*** p. 159).
- Reread the poems with students, identifying examples of repetition.
- Review the Writing Lesson to guide students in developing their essay.
- Use the Response to Literature rubrics in ***General Resources,*** pp. 65–66, to evaluate students' analyses.

❹ Research and Technology

- If you wish, divide the class into groups to research different time periods in Chicago history.
- Discuss the types of research sources students might use. Suggest almanacs and Web sites such as those created by the City of Chicago.
- Encourage students to include some kind of graphic organizer, such as a chart or graph, in their report.
- Use the Research: Research Report rubrics, pp. 49–50 in ***General Resources,*** to evaluate students' work.
- The **Support for Extend Your Learning** page (***Unit 5 Resources,*** p. 160) provides guided note-taking opportunities to help students complete the Extend Your Learning activities.

Go Online Research Have students type in the Web Code for another research activity.

Assessment Resources

The following resources can be used to assess students' knowledge and skills.

Unit 5 Resources
- Selection Test A, pp. 162–164
- Selection Test B, pp. 165–167

General Resources
- Rubrics for Response to Literature, pp. 65–66
- Rubrics for Research: Research Report, pp. 49–50

Go Online Assessment Students may use the **Self-test** to prepare for **Selection Test A** or **Selection Test B.**

Meeting Your Standards

Students will

1. **analyze and respond to literary elements.**
   - Literary Analysis: Stream of Consciousness
2. **read, comprehend, analyze, and critique a short story.**
   - Reading Strategy: Clarifying Sequence of Events
   - Reading Check questions
   - Apply the Skills questions
   - Assessment Practice (ATE)
3. **develop vocabulary.**
   - Vocabulary Lesson: Greek Prefix: *dys-*
4. **understand and apply written and oral language conventions.**
   - Spelling Strategy
   - Grammar and Style Lesson: Imperative Sentences
5. **develop writing proficiency.**
   - Writing Lesson: Stream-of-Consciousness Monologue
6. **develop appropriate research strategies.**
   - Extend Your Learning: Oral Report on Hospice Care
7. **understand and apply listening and speaking strategies.**
   - Extend Your Learning: Conversation

Block Scheduling: Use one 90-minute class period to preteach the skills and have students read the selection. Use a second 90-minute class period to assess students' mastery of skills, extend their learning, and monitor their progress.

Homework Suggestions

Following are possibilities for homework assignments.

- Support pages from ***Unit 5 Resources:***
  Literary Analysis
  Reading Strategy
  Vocabulary Builder
  Grammar and Style
- An Extend Your Learning project and the Writing Lesson for this selection may be completed over several days.

Step-by-Step Teaching Guide	Pacing Guide
PRETEACH	
• Administer Vocabulary and Reading Warm-ups as necessary.	5 min.
• Engage students' interest with the motivation activity.	5 min.
• Read and discuss author and background features. **FT**	10 min.
• Introduce the Literary Analysis Skill: Stream of Consciousness. **FT**	5 min.
• Introduce the Reading Strategy: Clarifying Sequence of Events. **FT**	10 min.
• Prepare students to read by teaching the selection vocabulary. **FT**	
TEACH	
• Informally monitor comprehension while students read independently or in groups. **FT**	30 min.
• Monitor students' comprehension with the Reading Check notes.	as students read
• Reinforce vocabulary with Vocabulary Builder notes.	as students read
• Develop students' understanding of stream of consciousness with the Literary Analysis annotations. **FT**	5 min.
• Develop students' ability to clarify sequence of events with the Reading Strategy annotations. **FT**	5 min.
ASSESS/EXTEND	
• Assess students' comprehension and mastery of the Literary Analysis and Reading Strategy by having them answer the Apply the Skills questions. **FT**	15 min.
• Have students complete the Vocabulary Lesson and the Grammar and Style Lesson. **FT**	15 min.
• Apply students' ability to create a vivid character by using the Writing Lesson. **FT**	45 min. or homework
• Apply students' understanding by using one or more of the Extend Your Learning activities.	20–90 min. or homework
• Administer Selection Test A or Selection Test B. **FT**	15 min.

Resources

PRINT

Unit 5 Resources

TRANSPARENCY

Graphic Organizer Transparencies

PRINT

Reader's Notebook [L2]

Reader's Notebook: Adapted Version [L1]

Reader's Notebook: English Learner's Version [EL]

Unit 5 Resources

TECHNOLOGY

Listening to Literature Audio CDs [L2, EL]

PRINT

Unit 5 Resources

General Resources

TECHNOLOGY

Go Online: Research **[L3]**

Go Online: Self-test **[L3]**

***ExamView*® Test Bank [L3]**

Choosing Resources for Differentiated Instruction

[L1] Special Needs Students

[L2] Below-Level Students

[L3] All Students

[L4] Advanced Students

[EL] English Learners

For Vocabulary and Reading Warm-ups and for Selection Tests, **A** signifies "less challenging" and **B** "more challenging." For Graphic Organizer transparencies, **A** signifies "not filled in" and **B** "filled in."

FT Fast Track Instruction: To move the lesson more quickly, use the strategies and activities identified with **FT**.

Scaffolding for Less Proficient and Advanced Students

The leveled Critical Thinking questions after selections progress in the levels of thinking required to answer them. To address the needs of your different students, you may use the (a) level questions for your less proficient students and the (b) level questions with your on-level and advanced students. The occasional (c) level questions are appropriate for your advanced students.

PRENTICE HALL **TeacherEXPRESS**™ Plan · Teach · Assess Use this complete suite of powerful teaching tools to make lesson planning and testing quicker and easier.

PRENTICE HALL **StudentEXPRESS**™ Learn · Study · Succeed Use the interactive textbook (online and on CD-ROM) to make selections and activities come alive with audio and video support and interactive questions.

Go Online Professional Development **For:** Information about Lexiles **Visit:** www.PHSchool.com **Web Code:** eue-1111

Motivation

Write the word "granny" on the chalkboard. Ask students to begin with that word and then freewrite their thoughts and associations as they occur. Encourage them to write quickly for about five minutes, without stopping to organize or order their impressions. Have small groups of students share their freewriting, and discuss the associations that led them from one thought to the next. Do they notice any common threads? Tell students that they have just created a piece of stream-of-consciousness writing—the same style used in the short story they are about to read.

❶ Background

More About the Author

Katherine Anne Porter sometimes described her life with a certain measure of creative license. According to some historians, at one time Porter described her childhood as refined and her schooling as in-depth (though this was far from true). She also borrowed from her own life to create her fiction. For example, she based the novel *Ship of Fools* in part on her own 1931 journey from Mexico to Europe.

❶ The Jilting of Granny Weatherall

Katherine Anne Porter (1890–1980)

Katherine Anne Porter's life spanned World War I, the Great Depression, World War II, and the rise of the nuclear age, making her deeply aware of what she called "the heavy threat of world catastrophe." For Porter, her exceptionally well-crafted fiction was an "effort to grasp the meaning of those threats, to trace them to their sources, and to understand the logic of this majestic and terrible failure of the life of man in the Western world." Her stories were often set in the South and featured characters at pivotal moments in their lives, faced with dramatic change, the constricting bonds of family, and the weight of the past.

A descendant of legendary pioneer Daniel Boone, Porter was born in Indian Creek, Texas. She was raised in poverty and haphazardly educated in convent schools. Commenting on her schooling, Porter said that she received a "fragmentary, but strangely useless and ornamental education." Instead, she added, her true education came by reading five writers—American authors Henry James, T. S. Eliot, and Ezra Pound, Irish writer James Joyce, and Irish poet W. B. Yeats.

Beginnings as a Writer Porter began writing at an early age, though she did not publish her first book until she was forty years old. As a young adult, she worked as a journalist. Her work took her to many places, including Mexico City, where she lived for eight years. She became deeply involved in Mexican politics and culture, even writing a study of Mexican crafts. While in Mexico, Porter also developed an interest in writing fiction, and in 1922 she published her first story, "María Concepción," in *Century*, a highly regarded literary magazine. Eight years later, she published her first book, *Flowering Judas* (1930). The book, a collection of six short stories, was praised by critics and earned Porter widespread recognition. *Flowering Judas and Other Stories*, an expanded edition of the book containing ten stories, was published in 1935.

Literary Achievements Katherine Anne Porter went on to produce several other major works, including *Noon Wine* (1937); *Pale Horse, Pale Rider* (1939); *The Leaning Tower and Other Stories* (1944); and *Ship of Fools* (1962)—Porter's only novel. Her last major work, *The Never-Ending Wrong*, a nonfiction account of the trial of Sacco and Vanzetti during the 1920s, was published in 1977. Although her body of work was relatively small in comparison to those of other major writers of her time, her work consistently received high praise from critics and earned her a place among the finest writers of the twentieth century. Her *Collected Stories* (1965) was awarded the Pulitzer Prize and the National Book Award. In addition, her novel, *Ship of Fools*, was made into a popular film.

A First-Rate Artist In his review of *The Leaning Tower and Other Stories*, critic Edmund Wilson tried to account for the "elusive" quality that made Porter an "absolutely first-rate artist." He said, "These stories are not illustrations of anything that is reducible to a moral law or a political or social analysis or even a principle of human behavior. What they show us are human relationships in their constantly shifting phases and in the moments of which their existence is made. There is no place for general reflections; you are to live through the experiences as the characters do." You will discover that Wilson's observations can be applied to "The Jilting of Granny Weatherall," which takes readers on a journey through the various phases of an elderly woman's life in the moments leading up to her death.

Preview

Connecting to the Literature

Think about the drifting thoughts and images that greet you as you fall asleep. If you can remember these semi-conscious thoughts of yours, you may be able to understand Granny Weatherall a little better. The old woman in this story is visited by a host of such images from her past. As you read, try to uncover the meaning of her memories.

Literary Analysis

Stream of Consciousness

People's thoughts do not flow in neat patterns; they proceed in streams of insight, memory, and reflection. During the early 1900s, some writers began using a literary device called **stream of consciousness,** in which they tried to capture the natural flow of thought. These narratives usually

- present sequences of thought as if they were issuing directly from a character's mind.
- omit transitional words and phrases found in ordinary prose.
- connect details only through a character's associations.

Note the way Granny Weatherall's thoughts wander among memories, dream-like images, and accurate perceptions of the present moment.

Connecting Literary Elements

Stream-of-consciousness narratives often involve the use of **flashback,** or interruptions in which an earlier event is described. A flashback may take the form of a character's memory, a story told by a character, a dream or daydream, or a switch by the narrator to a time in the past.

As you read, pay attention to the details that trigger Granny's flashbacks, determine the form of the flashback, and decide how each relates to events in the present. Use a chart like the one shown to link past to present in the story.

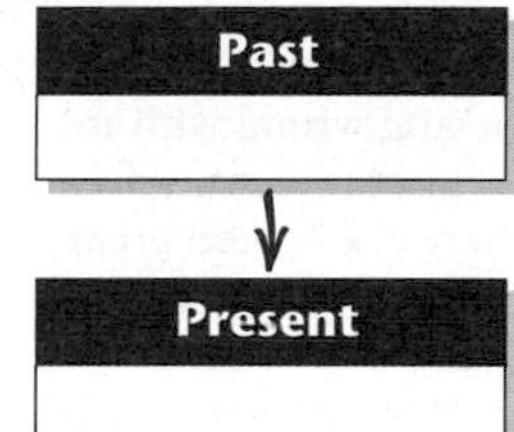

Reading Strategy

Clarifying Sequence of Events

This story evokes an array of different moments spanning eighty years as Granny Weatherall drifts in and out of reality. To stay oriented in this complex narrative, **clarify the sequence of events.** Watch for jumps in Granny's thinking, often signaled by a shift from present-moment dialogue to Granny's inner thoughts.

Vocabulary Builder

piety (pī′ ə tē) *n.* devotion to religious duties (p. 854)

frippery (frip′ ər ē) *n.* showy display of elegance (p. 855)

dyspepsia (dis pep′ shə) *n.* indigestion (p. 856)

2 Literary Analysis

Stream of Consciousness

- Tell students that as they read Porter's story, they will focus on stream of consciousness, a writing style in which the flow of text mirrors the natural streams of human thoughts.
- Read the instruction about stream of consciousness aloud, focusing on the bulleted text.
- Remind students of the Motivation activity from the previous page. Clarify the idea that stream-of-consciousness writing follows similar connecting bridges of associations.
- Use the Connecting Literary Elements instruction to note how stream of consciousness can jump about in time. Urge students to use this instruction to navigate the story's events.
- Give students a copy of **Literary Analysis Graphic Organizer A,** p. 185 in ***Graphic Organizer Transparencies.*** Encourage students to use this chart to record key moments in the narrative.

3 Reading Strategy

Clarifying Sequence of Events

- Tell students that clarifying the sequence of events will enable them to keep track of the story as it jumps about in time.
- To clarify the sequence of events, readers must look for signals that suggest sequence. Mentions of Granny's age or contextual details, for example, can suggest sequence.
- Have students list key moments in Granny's life and then number them in sequence.

Vocabulary Builder

- Pronounce each vocabulary word for students, and read the definitions as a class. Have students identify any words with which they are already familiar.

Differentiated Instruction

Solutions for All Learners

Support for Special Needs Students
Have students complete the **Preview** and **Build Skills** pages for the selection in the ***Reader's Notebook: Adapted Version.*** These pages provide a selection summary, an abbreviated presentation of the reading and literary skills, and the graphic organizer on the **Build Skills** page in the student book.

Support for Less Proficient Readers
Have students complete the **Preview** and **Build Skills** pages for the selection in the ***Reader's Notebook.*** These pages provide a selection summary, an abbreviated presentation of the reading and literary skills, and the graphic organizer on the **Build Skills** page in the student book.

Support for English Learners
Have students complete the **Preview** and **Build Skills** pages for the selection in the ***Reader's Notebook: English Learner's Version.*** These pages provide a selection summary, an abbreviated presentation of the skills, additional contextual vocabulary, and the graphic organizer on the **Build Skills** page in the student book.

Learning Modalities
Interpersonal Learners
As the story progresses, Granny passes in and out of lucidity. When she is lucid, she feels proud and doesn't want her daughter humoring or babying her. Help students recognize that Granny is in Cornelia's home, under her care, and that Cornelia believes that her mother is neither thinking clearly nor capable of caring for herself.

❶ About the Selection

On her deathbed, between visits from her daughter, her doctor, and her priest, old Ellen Weatherall, who is referred to as "Granny," thinks back on her life as she slips in and out of consciousness. She recalls George, who left her standing at the altar on their wedding day, and John, who became her husband but died when their children were still young. She reflects with pleasure and pride on her raising of the children, but remains deeply troubled by the recollection of having been jilted sixty years earlier. Unable to come to terms with the pain of that experience and haunted by the death of her daughter, Hapsy, Ellen suddenly realizes that death has come to claim her. As she is about to die, she suffers one last jilting—her loss of faith—when God fails to provide a sign that would indicate that He is waiting for her with open arms.

❷ Literary Analysis
Stream of Consciousness

- Have students read the bracketed passage. Discuss the doctor's actions as clues to the actual events occurring in the story.
- **Ask** students the Literary Analysis question: While Granny is engaged in a dialogue with the doctor, what is really happening in the room?
Answer: The doctor examines her and then departs.

❶ The Jilting of Granny Weatherall

Katherine Anne Porter

Background Katherine Anne Porter's view of life and the literature she created were shaped by the universal sense of disillusionment resulting from World War I, the despair of the Great Depression, and the World War II horrors of Nazism and nuclear warfare. Sometimes, as in the novel *Ship of Fools*, Porter focused on social and political issues such as Nazism. In contrast, works like "The Jilting of Granny Weatherall" pinpointed the dissolving families and communities of the modern age.

She flicked her wrist neatly out of Doctor Harry's pudgy careful fingers and pulled the sheet up to her chin. The brat ought to be in knee breeches. Doctoring around the country with spectacles on his nose! "Get along now, take your schoolbooks and go. There's nothing wrong with me."

Doctor Harry spread a warm paw like a cushion on her forehead where the forked green vein danced and made her eyelids twitch. "Now, now, be a good girl, and we'll have you up in no time."

"That's no way to speak to a woman nearly eighty years old just because she's down. I'd have you respect your elders, young man."

"Well, Missy, excuse me," Doctor Harry patted her cheek. "But I've got to warn you, haven't I? You're a marvel, but you must be careful or you're going to be good and sorry."

"Don't tell me what I'm going to be. I'm on my feet now, morally speaking. It's Cornelia. I had to go to bed to get rid of her."

❷ Her bones felt loose, and floated around in her skin, and Doctor Harry floated like a balloon around the foot of the bed. He floated and pulled down his waistcoat and swung his glasses on a cord. "Well, stay where you are, it certainly can't hurt you."

"Get along and doctor your sick," said Granny Weatherall. "Leave a well woman alone. I'll call for you when I want you. . . . Where were you forty years ago when I pulled through milk leg[1] and double pneumonia? You weren't even born. Don't let Cornelia lead you on,"

❷ Literary Analysis
Stream of Consciousness
While Granny is engaged in a dialogue with the doctor, what is really happening in the room?

1. **milk leg** painful swelling of the leg.

Differentiated Instruction Solutions for All Learners

Accessibility at a Glance

	The Jilting of Granny Weatherall
Context	An old woman near death
Language	Simple vocabulary; stream of consciousness; dialogue
Concept Level	Accessible (woman looks back at her life)
Literary Merit	Noted author
Lexile	820L
Other	Sequence of events difficult to follow
Overall Rating	Average

3

4 ▲ **Critical Viewing** What elements of this surreal illustration of an old woman in her "garden of memories" might represent Granny Weatherall? **[Connect]**

she shouted, because Doctor Harry appeared to float up to the ceiling and out. "I pay my own bills, and I don't throw my money away on nonsense!"

She meant to wave good-bye, but it was too much trouble. Her eyes closed of themselves, it was like a dark curtain drawn around the bed. The pillow rose and floated under her, pleasant as a hammock in a light wind. She listened to the leaves rustling outside the window.

5 **Reading Check**
Where is Granny Weatherall as she speaks to the doctor?

3 Humanities

Garden of Memories by Charles Burchfield

This picture shows an old woman sitting in a nearly immobile posture. She and the buildings and landscape around her reflect the drooping apathy of extreme old age and the haunting sense of memory and emotion. The artist created this "drooping" effect with his individualistic combination of crayon and watercolor.

Use this question for discussion:

- How would you describe the mood of this piece of art? How does the mood mirror the mood of the story?
Answer: The painting is sinister and filled with strange apparitions and melancholy. Granny also feels strange, sees "apparitions" as she revisits memories, and experiences melancholy.

4 Critical Viewing

Answer: The old woman sunk in a chair and surrouded by apparitions might represent Granny. Also, the drooping, somewhat distorted landscape and buildings could represent Granny's experience of the world around her.

5 Reading Check

Answer: Granny Weatherall is in her bed.

Differentiated Instruction

Solutions for All Learners

Support for Special Needs Students

Students may be confused by the title, which appears at first to have little link to the current events of the story. After defining the word *jilting*, explain that the title refers to an event from long ago in Granny Weatherall's life. Reassure students that they will learn about that event as they read the story.

Support for English Learners

Review the title with students. First, discuss the meaning of *jilting*. Then, explore the implications of the name *Weatherall*. Tell students that the word *weather* can mean "endure." Guide students to see that the name may suggest someone who can weather, or endure, all situations.

Strategy for Gifted/Talented Students

Discuss the story's title with students, pointing out the name *Weatherall* and discussing its implications. Ask students to think about the importance of a name, whether in real or fictional situations. Then, ask students to suggest appropriate names for some of the other characters in the story.

❻ Literature in Context
House Calls

Prior to the 1930s, babies were almost exclusively born at home, people were treated at home, and they almost always died at home rather than in the hospital. In the course of a typical day, a general practitioner might make as many as 15 to 20 house calls, in addition to seeing patients in his or her office.

Connect to the Literature

Be sure students consider the type of medical care Granny Weatherall is used to receiving.

Possible response: Students might say that Granny Weatherall would prefer to stay with Cornelia because she has always been taken care of at home by friends and relatives. Cornelia might feel unburdened and relieved that her mother is getting better care at a hospital.

❼ Reading Strategy
Clarifying Sequence of Events

- Read aloud the bracketed passage to students, pausing slightly at "The box in the attic . . ." to suggest a possible mental bridge.
- **Ask** the following question: Are the images of household items memories of the past or pictures of the present? Direct students to reread the bracketed passage again before answering the question. Point out the word *afterwards* in the passage as a clue to sequence.

  Answer: The images that begin the passage are memories of the past. The discussion of the boxes of letters could be past, present, or both as Granny experiences a passing moment of lucidity in which she realizes that she is dying.

No, somebody was swishing newspapers: no, Cornelia and Doctor Harry were whispering together. She leaped broad awake, thinking they whispered in her ear. ❻

"She was never like this, never like this!" "Well, what can we expect?" "Yes, eighty years old. . . ."

Well, and what if she was? She still had ears. It was like Cornelia to whisper around doors. She always kept things secret in such a public way. She was always being tactful and kind. Cornelia was dutiful; that was the trouble with her. Dutiful and good: "So good and dutiful," said Granny, "that I'd like to spank her." She saw herself spanking Cornelia and making a fine job of it.

"What'd you say, Mother?"

Granny felt her face tying up in hard knots.

"Can't a body think, I'd like to know?"

"I thought you might want something."

"I do. I want a lot of things. First off, go away and don't whisper."

She lay and drowsed, hoping in her sleep that the children would keep out and let her rest a minute. It had been a long day. Not that she was tired. It was always pleasant to snatch a minute now and then. There was always so much to be done, let me see: tomorrow.

Tomorrow was far away and there was nothing to trouble about. Things were finished somehow when the time came; thank God there was always a little margin over for peace: then a person could spread out the plan of life and tuck in the edges orderly. It was good to have everything clean and folded away, with the hair brushes and tonic bottles sitting straight on the white embroidered linen: the day started without fuss and the pantry shelves laid out with rows of jelly glasses and brown jugs and white stone-china jars with blue whirligigs and words painted on them: coffee, tea, sugar, ginger, cinnamon, allspice: and the bronze clock with the lion on top nicely dusted off. ❼ The dust that lion could collect in twenty-four hours! The box in the attic with all those letters tied up, well, she'd have to go through that tomorrow. All those letters—George's letters and John's letters and her letters to them both—lying around for the children to find afterwards made her uneasy. Yes, that would be tomorrow's business. No use to let them know how silly she had been once.

While she was rummaging around she found death in her mind and it felt clammy and unfamiliar. She had spent so much time preparing for death there was no need for bringing it up again. Let it take care of itself now. When she was sixty she had felt very old, finished, and went around making farewell trips to see her children and grandchildren, with a secret in her mind: This is the very last of

Literature in Context

History Connection

House Calls

In this story, eighty-year-old Ellen Weatherall dies at home, having been attended by the family doctor. Up until the 1930s, it was a common practice for doctors to deliver most of their services in the home. Medical technology was simple enough that home treatment was as good as—or better than—hospital treatment. However, after World War II, the field of medicine changed dramatically. New techniques for diagnosis and treatment required special technology and facilities. Economic factors also came into play; house calls were considered wasteful of the doctor's time. Today, except in some rural areas, the house call has faded into memory.

Connect to the Literature

How do you think Granny would react if she were moved to a hospital or nursing home? How would Cornelia feel?

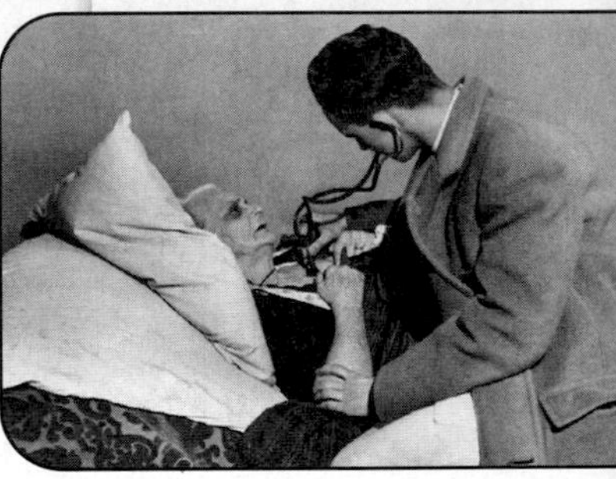

Enrichment

Gerontology

As people today live longer and longer, the care and treatment of older people and issues involving the elderly have grown in prominence. Those interested in the problems facing America's elderly population will find many career opportunities. From jobs in geriatric medicine, dentistry, psychology, social work, and physical and occupational therapy, to work in estate planning and elder law, there are many jobs geared to planning for old age and improving the circumstances of the elderly.

Invite interested students to explore career opportunities in one or more of the aforementioned fields. Ask them to do research to track the changes the field has undergone in recent years and to predict the direction in which it is going. Students can gather their information from the library, by contacting associations like the AARP, and by interviewing people working in the field.

your mother, children! Then she made her will and came down with a long fever. That was all just a notion like a lot of other things, but it was lucky too, for she had once for all got over the idea of dying for a long time. Now she couldn't be worried. She hoped she had better sense now. Her father had lived to be one hundred and two years old and had drunk a noggin of strong hot toddy on his last birthday. He told the reporters it was his daily habit, and he owed his long life to that. He had made quite a scandal and was very pleased about it. She believed she'd just plague Cornelia a little.

"Cornelia! Cornelia!" No footsteps, but a sudden hand on her cheek. "Bless you, where have you been?"

"Here, mother."

"Well, Cornelia, I want a noggin of hot toddy."

"Are you cold, darling?"

"I'm chilly, Cornelia. Lying in bed stops the circulation. I must have told you that a thousand times."

Well, she could just hear Cornelia telling her husband that Mother was getting a little childish and they'd have to humor her. The thing that most annoyed her was that Cornelia thought she was deaf, dumb, and blind. Little hasty glances and tiny gestures tossed around her and over her head saying, "Don't cross her, let her have her way, she's eighty years old," and she sitting there as if she lived in a thin glass cage. Sometimes Granny almost made up her mind to pack up and move back to her own house where nobody could remind her every minute that she was old. Wait, wait, Cornelia, till your own children whisper behind your back!

In her day she had kept a better house and had got more work done. She wasn't too old yet for Lydia to be driving eighty miles for advice when one of the children jumped the track, and Jimmy still dropped in and talked things over: "Now, Mammy, you've a good business head, I want to know what you think of this? . . ." Old. Cornelia couldn't change the furniture around without asking. Little things, little things! They had been so sweet when they were little. Granny wished the old days were back again with the children young and everything to be done over. It had been a hard pull, but not too much for her. When she thought of all the food she had cooked, and all the clothes she had cut and sewed, and all the gardens she had made—well, the children showed it. There they were, made out of her, and they couldn't get away from that. Sometimes she wanted to see John again and point to them and say, Well, I didn't do so badly, did I? But that would have to wait. That was for tomorrow. She used to think of him as a man, but now all the children were older than their father, and he would be a child beside her if she saw him now. It seemed strange and there was something wrong in the idea. Why, he couldn't possibly recognize her. She had fenced in a hundred acres once, digging the post holes herself and clamping the wires with just a negro boy to help. That changed a woman. John would be looking for a young woman with the peaked Spanish comb in her hair and the painted fan.

Literary Analysis
Stream of Consciousness
Notice the path of Granny's thoughts. What are some topics she touches on, and how are they linked in her mind?

9 
Reading Check
What journey did Granny Weatherall take when she was sixty years old? Why?

8 Literary Analysis
Stream of Consciousness

- Have a volunteer read aloud the bracketed text, striving for a natural flow of thoughts.
- **Ask** students the Literary Analysis question: Notice the path of Granny's thoughts. What are some topics she touches on, and how are they linked in her mind?
Answer: Granny's thoughts run back to a time twenty years earlier when she had originally faced her mortality. Then, she thinks of her long-lived father, a hot toddy, and the annoyance of having to live with her daughter.

▶ **Monitor Progress:** Have students begin an organizer like **Literary Analysis Graphic Organizer A,** p. 185 in ***Graphic Organizer Transparencies.*** As you reread the bracketed text, invite students to complete the organizer showing Granny's thoughts and the mental connecting bridges she moves across.

9 Reading Check

Answer: Because she thought she was dying, she made farewell trips to each of her children.

Differentiated Instruction
Solutions for All Learners

Support for Less Proficient Readers
Direct students to the passage at the bottom of the previous page, in which Granny recalls making a trip at age sixty. Help students understand Granny's attitude toward death. Guide them to see that she is resigned to it now, unafraid, having had the experience of facing it twenty years earlier.

Vocabulary for English Learners
Read aloud the passage at the bottom of the previous page, in which Granny recalls a trip she made at age sixty. Confirm that students understand the age "sixty." Then, clarify the meanings of the word *will.* Explain that the word *will* can refer to a document describing a person's wishes concerning the disposal of personal property after death.

Enrichment for Advanced Readers
Challenge students to learn about the concept of a living will, in which a person creates a will describing his or her wishes when ill or infirm. Discuss the kind of living will Granny might have created after her brush with death at age sixty. What might she instruct her children to do should she become terminally ill?

10 Literary Analysis
Stream of Consciousness and Flashback

- Invite students to read the bracketed passage at least twice. Encourage them to visualize the scene Granny recalls and to share their visualizations.
- **Ask** students the Literary Analysis question: What do you learn about Granny from this flashback to a time when her children were small?
  Answer: You learn that she was deeply religious, that her children trusted her, and that they lived in simple surroundings without electricity.

11 Literary Analysis
Stream of Consciousness

- Ask volunteers to read the bracketed passage.
- Then **ask** students the second Literary Analysis question: What memory does Granny try to keep from surfacing? Why?
  Answer: She doesn't want to remember being jilted at the altar. The experience was deeply painful to her.

Digging post holes changed a woman. Riding country roads in the winter when women had their babies was another thing: sitting up nights with sick horses and sick children and hardly ever losing one. John, I hardly ever lost one of them! John would see that in a minute, that would be something he could understand, she wouldn't have to explain anything!

It made her feel like rolling up her sleeves and putting the whole place to rights again. No matter if Cornelia was determined to be everywhere at once, there were a great many things left undone on this place. She would start tomorrow and do them. It was good to be strong enough for everything, even if all you made melted and changed and slipped under your hands, so that by the time you finished you almost forgot what you were working for. What was it I set out to do? she asked herself intently, but she could not remember. A fog rose over the valley, she saw it marching across the creek swallowing the trees and moving up the hill like an army of ghosts. Soon it would be at the near edge of the orchard, and then it was time to go in and light the lamps. Come in, children, don't stay out in the night air.

Lighting the lamps had been beautiful. The children huddled up to her and breathed like little calves waiting at the bars in the twilight. Their eyes followed the match and watched the flame rise and settle in
10 a blue curve, then they moved away from her. The lamp was lit, they didn't have to be scared and hang on to mother any more. Never, never, never more. God, for all my life I thank Thee. Without Thee, my God, I could never have done it. Hail Mary, full of grace.

Literary Analysis
Stream of Consciousness and Flashback What do you learn about Granny from this flashback to a time when her children were small?

I want you to pick all the fruit this year and see that nothing is wasted. There's always someone who can use it. Don't let good things rot for want of using. You waste life when you waste good food. Don't let things get lost. It's bitter to lose things. Now, don't let me get to thinking, not when I am tired and taking a little nap before supper. . . .

The pillow rose about her shoulders and pressed against her heart and the memory was being squeezed out of it: oh, push down the pillow, somebody: it would smother her if she tried to hold it. Such a fresh breeze blowing and such a green day with no threats in it. But he had not come, just the same. What does a woman do when she has put on the white veil and set out the white cake for a man and he doesn't come? She tried to remember. No, I swear he never harmed me but in that. He never harmed me but in that . . . and what if he did? There
 was the day, the day, but a whirl of dark smoke rose and covered it, crept up and over into the bright field where everything was planted so carefully in orderly rows. That was hell, she knew hell when she saw it. For sixty years she had prayed against remembering him and against losing her soul in the deep pit of hell, and now the two things were mingled in one and the thought of him was a smoky cloud from hell that moved and crept in her head when she had just got rid of Doctor Harry and was trying to rest a minute. Wounded vanity, Ellen, said a sharp voice in the top of her mind. Don't let your wounded vanity get the upper hand of you. Plenty of girls get jilted. You were jilted, weren't

Literary Analysis
Stream of Consciousness What memory does Granny try to keep from surfacing? Why?

Enrichment

Rural Women
Rural women, living far from hospitals and medical doctors, often depended on the services of neighbors and midwives in delivering their babies. Students may be surprised at Granny's elation in recalling that she "hardly ever lost one" of the sick children or animals she nursed. Inform them that at that time, infant mortality rates were far higher than they are today; it was not uncommon for children to die of illnesses or diseases that are easily treated with modern medicine.

For example, once-common childhood diseases such as measles, mumps, diphtheria, and whooping cough could be deadly. Today, nearly all American children are vaccinated against these and other diseases. As a result, the incidence of some diseases—for example, polio—has been reduced to almost zero. Such advances in medical care would have made Granny Weatherall's life as a rural woman much, much easier.

you? Then stand up to it. Her eyelids wavered and let in streamers of blue-gray light like tissue paper over her eyes. She must get up and pull the shades down or she'd never sleep. She was in bed again and the shades were not down. How could that happen? Better turn over, hide from the light, sleeping in the light gave you nightmares. "Mother, how do you feel now?" and a stinging wetness on her forehead. But I don't like having my face washed in cold water!

Hapsy? George? Lydia? Jimmy? No, Cornelia, and her features were swollen and full of little puddles. "They're coming, darling, they'll all be here soon." Go wash your face, child, you look funny.

Instead of obeying, Cornelia knelt down and put her head on the pillow. She seemed to be talking but there was no sound. "Well, are you tongue-tied? Whose birthday is it? Are you going to give a party?"

Cornelia's mouth moved urgently in strange shapes. "Don't do that, you bother me, daughter."

"Oh, no, Mother. Oh, no. . . ."

Nonsense. It was strange about children. They disputed your every word. "No what, Cornelia?"

"Here's Doctor Harry."

"I won't see that boy again. He just left five minutes ago."

"That was this morning, Mother. It's night now. Here's the nurse."

"This is Doctor Harry, Mrs. Weatherall. I never saw you look so young and happy!"

"Ah, I'll never be young again—but I'd be happy if they'd let me lie in peace and get rested."

She thought she spoke up loudly, but no one answered. A warm weight on her forehead, a warm bracelet on her wrist, and a breeze went on whispering, trying to tell her something. A shuffle of leaves in the everlasting hand of God, He blew on them and they danced and rattled. "Mother, don't mind, we're going to give you a little hypodermic." "Look here, daughter, how do ants get in this bed? I saw sugar ants yesterday." Did you send for Hapsy too?

It was Hapsy she really wanted. She had to go a long way back through a great many rooms to find Hapsy standing with a baby on her arm. She seemed to herself to be Hapsy also, and the baby on Hapsy's arm was Hapsy and himself and herself, all at once, and there was no surprise in the meeting. Then Hapsy melted from within and turned flimsy as gray gauze and the baby was a gauzy shadow, and Hapsy came up close and said, "I thought you'd never come," and looked at her very searchingly and said, "You haven't changed a bit!" They leaned forward to kiss, when Cornelia began whispering from a long way off, "Oh, is there anything you want to tell me? Is there anything I can do for you?"

Yes, she had changed her mind after sixty years and she would like to see George. I want you to find George. Find him and be sure to tell him I forgot him. I want him to know I had my husband just the same and my children and my house like any other woman. A good house too and a good husband that I loved and fine children out of him. Better

Literary Analysis
Stream of Consciousness
What actual events are taking place in the room, and in what ways do they affect Granny's thoughts?

13 **Reading Check**
What happened to Granny sixty years ago?

12 Literary Analysis
Stream of Consciousness

- Call on a volunteer to read aloud the bracketed passage. Review where Granny is during this sequence of dialogue and description, clarifying if necessary that she is in her bed under the care of her daughter Cornelia.
- **Ask** students the Literary Analysis question: What actual events are taking place in the room, and in what ways do they affect Granny's thoughts?
  Answer: Granny's daughter Cornelia is weeping and talking to her mother. Doctor Harry also returns and examines Granny. Granny's thoughts reflect the physical environment but in distorted ways.

13 Reading Check

Answer: She was jilted at the altar by George.

Differentiated Instruction
Solutions for All Learners

Support for Less Proficient Readers
Make sure students recognize that Granny is drifting in and out of consciousness. Elicit from students that Granny, at the moment, is thinking way back into her past and imagining that Hapsy, her deceased daughter, is there with her now. She barely hears or recognizes Cornelia, who is caring for her.

Vocabulary for English Learners
Explain to students that when Granny recalls the time she "put on the white veil and set out the white cake" and the man didn't come, she is remembering having been jilted, or left standing at the altar, by the man she was supposed to marry.

Strategy for Advanced Readers
Ask students whether they believe Granny has fully recovered from her jilting. Ask them to support their response with evidence from Granny's memories of the event sixty years past. Discuss Granny's prayers to forget that moment and her link to a hellish image of fiery smoke.

14 Literary Analysis
Stream of Consciousness and Flashback

- Direct students' attention to the opening phrase "Since the day the wedding cake was not cut, but thrown out and wasted." Discuss with students what this phrase refers to.
- **Ask** students the Literary Analysis question: What event central to Granny's life do you learn more about in this flashback?
  Answer: Readers learn more detail about the day Granny was jilted at the altar.

than I hoped for even. Tell him I was given back everything he took away and more. Oh, no, oh, God, no, there was something else besides the house and the man and the children. Oh, surely they were not all? What was it? Something not given back. . . . Her breath crowded down under her ribs and grew into a monstrous frightening shape with cutting edges; it bored up into her head, and the agony was unbelievable: Yes, John, get the Doctor now, no more talk, my time has come.

When this one was born it should be the last. The last. It should have been born first, for it was the one she had truly wanted. Everything came in good time. Nothing left out, left over. She was strong, in three days she would be as well as ever. Better. A woman needed milk in her to have her full health.

"Mother, do you hear me?"

"I've been telling you—"

"Mother, Father Connolly's here."

"I went to Holy Communion only last week. Tell him I'm not so sinful as all that."

"Father just wants to speak to you."

He could speak as much as he pleased. It was like him to drop in and inquire about her soul as if it were a teething baby, and then stay on for a cup of tea and a round of cards and gossip. He always had a funny story of some sort, usually about an Irishman who made his little mistakes and confessed them, and the point lay in some absurd thing he would blurt out in the confessional showing his struggles between native piety and original sin. Granny felt easy about her soul. Cornelia, where are your manners? Give Father Connolly a chair. She had her secret comfortable understanding with a few favorite saints who cleared a straight road to God for her. All as surely signed and sealed as the papers for the new Forty Acres. Forever . . . heirs and assigns[2] forever. Since the day the wedding cake was not cut, but thrown out and wasted. The whole bottom dropped out of the world, and there she was blind and sweating with nothing under her feet and the walls falling away. His hand had caught her under the breast, she had not fallen, there was the freshly polished floor with the green rug on it, just as before. He had cursed like a sailor's parrot and said, "I'll kill him for you." Don't lay a hand on him, for my sake leave something to God. "Now, Ellen, you must believe what I tell you. . . ."

So there was nothing, nothing to worry about any more, except sometimes in the night one of the children screamed in a nightmare, and they both hustled out shaking and hunting for the matches and calling, "There, wait a minute, here we are!" John, get the doctor now, Hapsy's time has come. But there was Hapsy standing by the bed in a white cap. "Cornelia, tell Hapsy to take off her cap. I can't see her plain."

Her eyes opened very wide and the room stood out like a picture she had seen somewhere. Dark colors with the shadows rising towards the ceiling in long angles. The tall black dresser gleamed with nothing

Vocabulary Builder
piety (pī´ ə tē) *n.* devotion to religious duties

Literary Analysis
Stream of Consciousness and Flashback What event central to Granny's life do you learn more about in this flashback?

2. **assigns** persons to whom property is transferred.

Differentiated Instruction
Solutions for All Learners

Strategy for Less Proficient Readers
To reteach sequence of events, have students create timelines. Instruct them to write the events of the story on note cards or paper cut into strips. Each event should be stated in a few words. When all the events are noted, students should put the cards or paper strips in chronological order and number them. Then, organize the numbered events into a timeline.

on it but John's picture, enlarged from a little one, with John's eyes very black when they should have been blue. You never saw him, so how do you know how he looked? But the man insisted the copy was perfect, it was very rich and handsome. For a picture, yes, but it's not my husband. The table by the bed had a linen cover and a candle and a crucifix. The light was blue from Cornelia's silk lampshades. No sort of light at all, just frippery. You had to live forty years with kerosene lamps to appreciate honest electricity. She felt very strong and she saw Doctor Harry with a rosy nimbus around him.

"You look like a saint, Doctor Harry, and I vow that's as near as you'll ever come to it."

"She's saying something."

"I heard you, Cornelia. What's all this carrying on?"

"Father Connolly's saying—"

Cornelia's voice staggered and bumped like a cart in a bad road. It rounded corners and turned back again and arrived nowhere. Granny stepped up in the cart very lightly and reached for the reins, but a man sat beside her and she knew him by his hands, driving the cart. She did not look in his face, for she knew without seeing, but looked instead down the road where the trees leaned over and bowed to each other and a thousand birds were singing a Mass. She felt like singing too, but she put her hand in the bosom of her dress and pulled out a rosary, and Father Connolly murmured Latin in a very solemn voice and tickled her feet.[3] My God, will you stop that nonsense? I'm a married woman. What if he did run away and leave me to face the priest by myself? I found another a whole world better. I wouldn't have exchanged my husband for anybody except St. Michael[4] himself, and you may tell him that for me with a thank you in the bargain.

Light flashed on her closed eyelids, and a deep roaring shook her. Cornelia, is that lightning? I hear thunder. There's going to be a storm. Close all the windows. Call the children in. . . . "Mother, here we are, all of us." "Is that you, Hapsy?" "Oh, no, I'm Lydia. We drove as fast as we could." Their faces drifted above her, drifted away. The rosary fell out of her hands and Lydia put it back. Jimmy tried to help, their hands fumbled together, and Granny closed two fingers around Jimmy's thumb. Beads wouldn't do, it must be something alive. She was so amazed her thoughts ran round and round. So, my dear Lord, this is my death and I wasn't even thinking about it. My children have come to see me die. But I can't, it's not time. Oh, I always hated surprises. I wanted to give Cornelia the amethyst set—Cornelia, you're to have the amethyst set, but Hapsy's to wear it when she wants, and, Doctor Harry, do shut up. Nobody sent for you. Oh, my dear Lord, do wait a minute. I meant to do something about the Forty Acres, Jimmy doesn't need it and Lydia will later on, with that worthless husband of hers. I meant to finish the altar cloth and send six bottles of wine to

3. **murmured . . . feet** administered the last rites of the Catholic Church.
4. **St. Michael** one of the archangels.

Vocabulary Builder
frippery (frip´ ər ē) *n.* showy display of elegance

Literary Analysis
Stream of Consciousness
What is the connecting link between Granny's thoughts about her amethyst set, the Forty acres, and the altar cloth?

16 

Reading Check
What does Granny finally realize is happening to her?

15 Literary Analysis
Stream of Consciousness

- After students read the bracketed passage on their own, read it aloud to them to show Granny's increasing agitation.
- **Ask** the Literary Analysis question: What is the connecting link between Granny's thoughts about her amethyst set, the Forty Acres, and the altar cloth?
  Answer: Granny is thinking of all the tasks she intended to accomplish before her death and the items she had intended to give away.

16 Reading Check

Answer: She realizes that she is dying.

Differentiated Instruction
Solutions for All Learners

Strategy for Special Needs Students
A story that skips about in time will likely be highly challenging for students. Help them focus on concrete scenes that can be easily visualized. For example, point out the visit from Father Connolly. Help students visualize the priest sitting at Granny's bedside, administering the last rites to the dying old woman.

Strategy for Less Proficient Readers
Direct students' attention to the conversation between Cornelia, Granny, and Father Connolly, at the top of the previous page. Point out to students that Granny is close to death and that Father Connolly has arrived to administer the last rites of the Catholic Church.

Background for English Learners
Draw students' attention to the presence of Father Connolly at Granny's bedside. Explain that he is a Roman Catholic priest who will perform the last rites—rituals related to dying. Ask students to share rituals linked to dying from their own cultural or religious heritage.

Vocabulary Builder

Word Analysis: Greek Prefix *dys-*

- Draw students' attention to the word *dyspepsia* and invite a volunteer to read aloud its definition.
- Explain that the word includes the Greek prefix *dys-*, meaning "difficult" or "bad." **Ask** the class to brainstorm for other words beginning with this prefix. If necessary, prompt students with ideas from the dictionary.

Possible responses: dysfunctional; dyslexia.

ASSESS

Answers

1. Students might tell Granny that her life has been a success: she married a good man and raised children of whom she is proud.
2. (a) Her daughter Cornelia sits with her. (b) Granny is largely annoyed with Cornelia.
3. (a) Her children are named Hapsy, Lydia, Jimmy, and Cornelia. (b) She longs to see Hapsy. (c) Hapsy is dead.
4. (a) Granny wants to avoid the memory of being jilted at the altar by George, but the memory eventually surfaces. (b) She tries to tell herself that he never meant to harm her, that jilting happens to many girls.
5. (a) Granny's memories of caring for her children and farm, of helping neighbors with sick children and animals, and of enduring both the jilting and her husband's early death suggest her strengths. (b) Granny has weathered many difficult situations during her life.
6. (a) She doesn't feel ready to go because she is waiting for a sign of how to face death. (b) As she faces death, she sees no sign from God of any welcome to the afterlife. She feels jilted by her faith as she once felt jilted by George.
7. Students should offer explanations for their answers.

Go Online **Author Link** For additional information about Katherine Anne Porter, have students type in the Web Code, then select P from the alphabet, and then select Katherine Anne Porter.

17 Sister Borgia for her dyspepsia. I want to send six bottles of wine to Sister Borgia, Father Connolly, now don't let me forget.

Cornelia's voice made short turns and tilted over and crashed. "Oh, Mother, oh, Mother, oh Mother. . . ."

"I'm not going, Cornelia. I'm taken by surprise. I can't go."

You'll see Hapsy again. What about her? "I thought you'd never come." Granny made a long journey outward, looking for Hapsy. What if I don't find her? What then? Her heart sank down and down, there was no bottom to death, she couldn't come to the end of it. The blue light from Cornelia's lampshade drew into a tiny point in the center of her brain, it flickered and winked like an eye, quietly it fluttered and dwindled. Granny lay curled down within herself, amazed and watchful, staring at the point of light that was herself; her body was now only a deeper mass of shadow in an endless darkness and this darkness would curl around the light and swallow it up. God, give a sign!

For the second time there was no sign. Again no bridegroom and the priest in the house. She could not remember any other sorrow because this grief wiped them all away. Oh, no, there's nothing more cruel than this—I'll never forgive it. She stretched herself with a deep breath and blew out the light.

Vocabulary Builder
dyspepsia (dis pep′ shə) *n.* indigestion

Critical Reading

1. **Respond:** If you were at Granny Weatherall's deathbed, what would you say to help comfort her?
2. **(a) Recall:** Who sits with Granny during her final hours?
(b) Analyze: What is Granny's attitude toward this person?
3. **(a) Recall:** What are the names of Granny's children?
(b) Interpret: Which of her children does Granny long to see?
(c) Deduce: Why is she unable to see this child?
4. **(a) Recall:** As she drifts in and out of consciousness, what memory is "squeezed out" of Granny's heart? **(b) Interpret:** How does Granny try to talk herself out of the pain of this memory?
5. **(a) Interpret:** What memories and details suggest Granny's physical and emotional strength? **(b) Analyze:** Why might the author have chosen "Weatherall" as an appropriate surname for Granny?
6. **(a) Infer:** As she nears death, why does Granny say she "can't go"?
(b) Connect: What is the connection between her experience of having been jilted sixty years ago and her experiences in the final paragraph?
7. **Speculate:** In what ways might this story have been different if Granny had confronted George after he jilted her?

For: More about Katherine Anne Porter
Visit: www.PHSchool.com
Web Code: ere-9518

Apply the Skills

The Jilting of Granny Weatherall

Literary Analysis

Stream of Consciousness

1. What effect does the use of **stream of consciousness** have on the reader's perceptions of Granny's children and of Doctor Harry?
2. **(a)** Find two points at which Granny's thoughts drift from one subject to another that is seemingly unrelated. **(b)** What natural associations connect her thoughts in each of these examples?
3. In what ways does the stream-of-consciousness technique allow for ambiguity—the presence of different and even conflicting meanings—for specific events or for the story as a whole?
4. Is stream of consciousness an effective technique for this story? Explain.

Connecting Literary Elements

5. **(a)** What details trigger Granny's **flashback** to lighting the lamps when her children were young? **(b)** What is the connection between this flashback and her experiences in the present?
6. Use a chart like the one shown to analyze three flashbacks in the story. Identify the form each flashback takes (dream, memory, and so on) and note what you learn about Granny's life from each one.

Form	Trigger

→

What we learn

Reading Strategy

Clarifying Sequence of Events

7. **Clarify the sequence of events** presented in this story by rearranging them in chronological order.
8. Does the jumbled sequence of events as they appear in the story create a complete picture of Granny's life? Explain.

Extend Understanding

9. **Psychology Connection:** This story was written around 1930. Do you think a young person's experience of being left at the altar would have a less profound impact on his or her life if it happened today? Explain your answer.

QuickReview

Stream of consciousness is a literary device used in a story to capture the natural flow of people's thoughts.

A **flashback** is an interruption in a narrative that describes an event from the past.

To **clarify the sequence of events**, reorganize events in the order in which they occurred.

For: Self-test
Visit: www.PHSchool.com
Web Code: era-6511

Answers

1. The reader learns snippets of often unrelated information about Granny's children and Doctor Harry. This information is both limited and subjective.
2. (a and b) **Possible response:** Granny thinks of tasks to be done, and her thoughts drift to possessions, then to fears of her children reading her love letters. When the priest arrives, Granny's thoughts drift from thoughts about his personality to his need for a chair, to religious reflections. His religious affiliation spurs her thoughts about God.
3. By keeping readers' grasp of events loose, the stream-of-consciousness format invites readers to bring their own interpretations to Granny's experiences, memories and thoughts.
4. Porter's use of stream of consciousness conveys a sense of the fractured, complex, and emotional experience of death.
5. (a) She recalls darkness falling around the farm. (b) The room seems to be growing darker as Granny slips toward death.
6. Flashback: Fainting in church when George doesn't show up. Trigger: Father Connolly reminds her of being in church. Form: memory; What you learn: That Granny was deeply upset by the experience of being jilted.

   Another sample answer can be found on **Literary Analysis Graphic Organizer B**, p. 188 in ***Graphic Organizer Transparencies.***
7. **Possible response:** As a young woman, Granny is jilted by George. She later marries John and has children, one of whom dies. After John dies, Granny continues to raise her children and run the household alone. At age sixty, she prepares for death and visits her children. She eventually moves into Cornelia's home, and, at age eighty, Granny dies.
8. No, it presents a picture of those moments Granny finds important as she faces death.
9. **Possible response:** In today's world, with marriage one of many options, jilting might be less of a social embarrassment.

Go Online Assessment Students may use the **Self-test** to prepare for **Selection Test A** or **Selection Test B.**

EXTEND/ASSESS

Answers

❶ Vocabulary Lesson

Word Analysis

Possible responses:

1. dysentery: a disturbance or disease of the intestines
2. dysfunctional: not working properly
3. dyslexia: a difficulty with words and reading
4. dyspepsia: a difficulty with digestion
5. dystopia: a place filled with difficulties

Vocabulary Builder

1. piety
2. dyspepsia
3. frippery

Spelling Strategy

1. anxiety
2. illegality
3. creativity

❷ Grammar and Style Lesson

Practice

1. b
2. b
3. b
4. a
5. a

Writing Application

1. Leave a well woman alone.
2. Don't let Cornelia lead you on.
3. Let a body think.

WG **Writing and Grammar, Ruby Level**

Students will find further instruction and practice on imperative sentences in Chapter 20, Section 1.

Build Language Skills

❶ Vocabulary Lesson

Word Analysis: Greek Prefix *dys-*

The Greek prefix *dys-*, which means "difficult" or "bad," can help you unlock the meanings of many challenging words.

Write a definition of each word below by combining the meaning of the prefix *dys-* with the clues in parentheses. After you have finished, check your definitions in a dictionary and revise if necessary.

1. dysentery (*entery* = intestine)
2. dysfunctional (*functional* = working properly)
3. dyslexia (*lexis* = word or speech)
4. dyspepsia (*pepsis* = digestion)
5. dystopia (*topos* = place)

Vocabulary Builder: Sentence Completions

Select the word from the vocabulary list on p. 847 that best completes each sentence.

1. Kelly showed her __?__ by attending religious services daily.
2. Pizza aggravates my __?__.
3. The skaters strutted by, displaying their __?__ for all to admire.

Spelling Strategy

The suffixes *-ety* and *-ity* change an adjective into a noun. The suffix may be accompanied by other spelling changes as well. For example, *pious* becomes *piety*. For each word below, create a new word using the suffix *-ety* or *-ity*.

1. anxious 2. illegal 3. creative

❷ Grammar and Style Lesson

Imperative Sentences

An **imperative sentence** states a request or gives an order. The subject, *you*, is implied and thus is usually not stated. In this example, notice that the sentence contains three verbs and an implied subject:

Example: "Get along now, take your schoolbooks and go." (*The subject* you *is implied.*)

Practice Review each of the following pairs of sentences. In each pair, identify which example is imperative.

1. **(a)** Will you get along and doctor your sick?
   (b) Get along and doctor your sick.
2. **(a)** I want you to stay where you are.
   (b) Stay where you are.
3. **(a)** They shouldn't be whispering.
   (b) Go away and don't whisper.
4. **(a)** Be a good girl, and you'll get well.
   (b) If you are good, you'll get well.
5. **(a)** Don't worry about it.
   (b) You need not worry about it.

Writing Application Rewrite these sentences to make them imperative:

1. Won't you please leave a well woman alone?
2. You shouldn't let Cornelia lead you on.
3. Can't a body think?

WG *Prentice Hall Writing and Grammar Connection: Chapter 20, Section 1*

Assessment Practice

Analyze Sentence Meaning **(For more practice, see *Standardized Test Preparation Workbook*, p. 5.)**

Many tests ask students to correctly answer sentence-completion questions. Often, more than one choice can complete a sentence. Use the following sample item to show students how to analyze sentence meaning, decide whether it is positive or negative, and eliminate choices that have the opposite sense.

Katherine Anne Porter's work reflects the disillusionment of the postwar era. Many of her works examine the drifting and ________ families and communities of the modern age.

A growing **C** reflective
B uniting **D** dissolving

The context clues *disillusionment* and *drifting* indicate the correct answer will have a negative connotation. ***D*** is the best choice.

Writing Lesson

Stream-of-Consciousness Monologue

A monologue is a dramatic form in which only a single character speaks. Create a character, and write a monologue. Like Katherine Anne Porter, incorporate the character's thoughts and memories in a stream-of-consciousness presentation.

Prewriting List descriptive words and phrases you associate with your character. Group these under the headings "Actions," "Feelings," "Comments," and "Attitudes."

Drafting Select several memories around which to organize the monologue. To heighten the stream-of-consciousness effect, write without transitions.

Model: Using Details to Create a Vivid Character

Here's the jetway, a chute, really, can't go back. *Tickets out, please!* Flying alone that night—was I nine, eleven?—daring myself to peer at the tiny lights outside the scratched plastic oval, and the awesome blackness of the lake beyond.

The use of specific images emphasizes the character's feelings.

Revising Read your monologue aloud to hear whether or not it sounds like a genuine and private voice. Add clues to help your audience follow the thought stream and clarify the purpose of the monologue.

WG *Prentice Hall Writing and Grammar Connection: Chapter 5, Section 4*

Extend Your Learning

Listening and Speaking Suppose that Ellen Weatherall (Granny) and George meet ten years after the jilting. With a partner, role-play the **conversation** they have. To prepare, keep these tips in mind:

- Note details about Ellen's life and how it has changed since the jilting.
- Create a story to explain George's behavior and his life since the jilting.

As you role-play, use language to express the characters' feelings and thoughts and to reflect the time and place in which they live. **[Group Activity]**

Research and Technology Hospice care—benevolent care of terminally ill people—is a growing area of medical specialization. Using a variety of sources, including the Internet and community resources, research the growing hospice field. Use your findings to prepare an **oral report** detailing how Granny might have been cared for in a modern hospice.

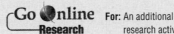

For: An additional research activity
Visit: www.PHSchool.com
Web Code: erd-7510

3 Writing Lesson

- Review the Literary Analysis and Connecting Literary Elements instruction to help students clarify the features of stream-of-consciousness writing.
- To guide students in writing a stream-of-consciousness monologue, give them the **Support for Writing Lesson** page (***Unit 5 Resources,*** p. 176).
- Read through the Writing Lesson steps with students and clarify any confusion.
- Guide students to think about whether their character might be dominated by a particular emotion. If so, urge students to choose memories that explain that emotion.
- Adapt the Narration: Short Story rubrics in ***General Resources,*** pp. 57–58, to evaluate students' monologues.

4 Listening and Speaking

- Invite students to recap events from the story that pertain to Granny and George's relationship. Note these events on the chalkboard for all to see.
- Encourage students to determine the two characters' attitudes toward each other.
- Have students try out their explanatory stories on another team before developing the final script for their role-play.
- The **Support for Extend Your Learning** page (***Unit 5 Resources,*** p. 177) provides guided note-taking opportunities to help students complete the Extend Your Learning activities.

Go Online Research — Have students type in the Web code for another research activity.

Assessment Resources

The following resources can be used to assess students' knowledge and skills.

Unit 5 Resources
- Selection Test A, pp. 179–181
- Selection Test B, pp. 182–184

General Resources
- Rubrics for Narration: Short Story, pp. 57–58

Go Online Assessment — Students may use the **Self-test** to prepare for **Selection Test A** or **Selection Test B.**

Meeting Your Standards

Students will

1. **analyze and respond to literary elements.**
   - Literary Analysis: Conflict and Resolution
2. **read, comprehend, analyze, and critique a short story and a speech.**
   - Reading Strategy: Clarifying Ambiguities
   - Reading Check questions
   - Apply the Skills questions
   - Assessment Practice (ATE)
3. **develop vocabulary.**
   - Vocabulary Lesson: Word Analysis: Latin Prefix: *in-*
4. **understand and apply written and oral language conventions.**
   - Spelling Strategy
   - Grammar and Style Lesson: Semicolons
5. **develop writing proficiency.**
   - Writing Lesson: Critical Review
6. **develop appropriate research strategies.**
   - Extend Your Learning: Oral Report
7. **understand and apply listening and speaking strategies.**
   - Extend Your Learning: Dramatic Scene

Block Scheduling: Use one 90-minute class period to preteach the skills and have students read the selection. Use a second 90-minute class period to assess students' mastery of skills, extend their learning, and monitor their progress.

Homework Suggestions

Following are possibilities for homework assignments.

- Support pages from *Unit 5 Resources:*
  Literary Analysis
  Reading Strategy
  Vocabulary Builder
  Grammar and Style
- An Extend Your Learning project and the Writing Lesson for this selection group may be completed over several days.

Step-by-Step Teaching Guide	Pacing Guide
PRETEACH	
• Administer Vocabulary and Reading Warm-ups as necessary.	5 min.
• Engage students' interest with the motivation activity.	5 min.
• Read and discuss author and background features. **FT**	10 min.
• Introduce the Literary Analysis Skill: Conflict and Resolution. **FT**	5 min.
• Introduce the Reading Strategy: Clarifying Ambiguities. **FT**	10 min.
• Prepare students to read by teaching the selection vocabulary. **FT**	
TEACH	
• Informally monitor comprehension while students read independently or in groups. **FT**	30 min.
• Monitor students' comprehension with the Reading Check notes.	as students read
• Reinforce vocabulary with Vocabulary Builder notes.	as students read
• Develop students' understanding of conflict and resolution with the Literary Analysis annotations. **FT**	5 min.
• Develop students' ability to clarify ambiguities with the Reading Strategy annotations. **FT**	5 min.
ASSESS/EXTEND	
• Assess students' comprehension and mastery of the Literary Analysis and Reading Strategy by having them answer the Apply the Skills questions. **FT**	15 min.
• Have students complete the Vocabulary Lesson and the Grammar and Style Lesson. **FT**	15 min.
• Apply students' ability to elaborate on an idea by using the Writing Lesson. **FT**	45 min. or homework
• Apply students' understanding by using one or more of the Extend Your Learning activities.	20–90 min. or homework
• Administer Selection Test A or Selection Test B. **FT**	15 min.

Resources

PRINT
Unit 5 Resources
Vocabulary Warm-up Word Lists **[L1, L2, EL]** ....p. 185
Vocabulary Warm-up Practice **[L1, L2, EL]** ....p. 186
Reading Warm-up A **[L1, L2, EL]** ....p. 187
Reading Warm-up B **[L1, L2, L3]** ....p. 188

TRANSPARENCY
Graphic Organizer Transparencies
Literary Analysis Graphic Organizer A **[L3]** ....p. 191
Literary Analysis Graphic Organizer B **[L1, L2, EL]** ....p. 192
Reading Strategy Graphic Organizer A **[L3]** ....p. 189
Reading Strategy Graphic Organizer B **[L1, L2, EL]** ....p. 190

PRINT
Reader's Notebook [L2]
Reader's Notebook: Adapted Version [L1]
Reader's Notebook: English Learner's Version [EL]
Unit 5 Resources
Literary Analysis **[L3]** ....p. 189
Reading Strategy **[L3]** ....p. 190
Vocabulary Builder **[L3]** ....p. 191

TECHNOLOGY
Listening to Literature Audio CDs [L2, EL]

PRINT
Unit 5 Resources
Grammar and Style **[L3]** ....p. 192
Support for Writing Lesson **[L3]** ....p. 193
Support for Extend Your Learning **[L3]** ....p. 194
Enrichment **[L4]** ....p. 195
Selection Test A **[L1, L2, EL]** ....pp. 196–198
Selection Test B **[L3, L4]** ....pp. 199–201
General Resources
Rubrics for Response to Literature **[L3]** ....pp. 65–66

TECHNOLOGY
Go Online: Research **[L3]**
Go Online: Self-test **[L3]**
ExamView® **Test Bank [L3]**

Choosing Resources for Differentiated Instruction

[L1] Special Needs Students
[L2] Below-Level Students
[L3] All Students
[L4] Advanced Students
[EL] English Learners

For Vocabulary and Reading Warm-ups and for Selection Tests, **A** signifies "less challenging" and **B** "more challenging." For Graphic Organizer transparencies, **A** signifies "not filled in" and **B** "filled in."

FT Fast Track Instruction: To move the lesson more quickly, use the strategies and activities identified with **FT**.

Scaffolding for Less Proficient and Advanced Students

The leveled Critical Thinking questions after selections progress in the levels of thinking required to answer them. To address the needs of your different students, you may use the (a) level questions for your less proficient students and the (b) level questions with your on-level and advanced students. The occasional (c) level questions are appropriate for your advanced students.

PRENTICE HALL **TeacherEXPRESS™** Plan · Teach · Assess Use this complete suite of powerful teaching tools to make lesson planning and testing quicker and easier.

PRENTICE HALL **StudentEXPRESS™** Learn · Study · Succeed Use the interactive textbook (online and on CD-ROM) to make selections and activities come alive with audio and video support and interactive questions.

Go Online Professional Development **For:** Information about Lexiles **Visit:** www.PHSchool.com **Web Code:** eue-1111

PREETEACH

Motivation

William Faulkner's story tells about a reclusive woman and her fellow townspeople, who regard her with respect and curiosity. Encourage students to think about the people whom they see in their community but about whom they know little. Tell them to select one of those people, and write a quick character sketch based on the few details that they have about that person. Have volunteers share their sketches. Then explain that in Faulkner's tale, the townspeople know little about Miss Emily, but they are determined to know as much as they can about her.

❶ Background

More About the Author

As he notes in his Nobel Prize acceptance speech, William Faulkner felt it was his task as a writer to highlight what he called the "eternal verities." These values—love, honor, pity, pride, compassion, and sacrifice—often appeared in Faulkner's works only in contrast to dark and violent elements in society. Though he was often criticized for the violence and abnormality in his stories, Faulkner felt the contrast helped him accomplish his goal.

Build Skills *Short Story • Speech*

❶ A Rose for Emily • Nobel Prize Acceptance Speech

William Faulkner (1897–1962)

For some writers, the place of their roots is a wellspring of story material. Oxford, Mississippi, was such a place for William Faulkner. It became the basis for the imaginary world of Yoknapatawpha County—the setting of many of his novels and stories.

A Writer's Roots Although Faulkner never finished high school, he read a great deal and developed an interest in writing from an early age. In 1918, he enlisted in the British Royal Flying Corps and was sent to Canada for training. However, World War I ended before he had a chance to see combat, and he returned to Mississippi. A few years later, longing for a change of scene, Faulkner moved to New Orleans. There, he became friends with author Sherwood Anderson, who offered encouragement and helped get Faulkner's first novel, *Soldier's Pay,* published. In 1926, Faulkner returned home to Oxford, Mississippi, to devote himself to his writing.

A Gold Mine of Inspiration In what he called his "own little postage stamp of native soil," Faulkner uncovered a "gold mine" of inspiration. So compelling and complex was this source of inspiration that Faulkner decided to create a "cosmos of my own"—the fictional county of Yoknapatawpha. From Oxford, Faulkner wrote a series of novels about the decay of traditional values as small communities became swept up in the changes of the modern age. He saw immense dramas acted out in his small, rural town, and he used jumbled time sequences, stream-of-consciousness narration, dialect, page-long sentences, and other difficult techniques to show what he called "the human heart in conflict with itself."

A Slow Spread of Recognition For many years, Faulkner was dismissed as an eccentric—an unimportant regional writer. Gradually, however, critics began to take him seriously. Today, Faulkner is generally considered the most innovative American writer of his time.

Experimenting With Narration The novel that first earned him critical acclaim was *The Sound and the Fury* (1929), a complex book exploring the downfall of an old southern family as seen through the eyes of three brothers, one of whom suffers from severe mental retardation. A year later, Faulkner published *As I Lay Dying,* the story of a poor family's six-day journey to bury their mother. Told from fifteen different points of view and exploring people's varying perspectives of death, the novel was a masterpiece of narrative experimentation. Other innovative works followed, including *Absalom, Absalom!* (1936), which is told by four speakers offering different interpretations of events.

Hollywood Years To earn money during the 1930s and 1940s, Faulkner wrote screenplays in Hollywood. Many of the films he worked on—including *Gunga Din* (1939), *To Have and Have Not* (1945), and *The Big Sleep* (1946)—have become classics of the American cinema.

In some of Faulkner's later works, such as *The Unvanquished* (1938) and *The Hamlet* (1940), he returned to a more traditional style. Yet in these novels, Faulkner continued developing the history of Yoknapatawpha County and its people.

Despite the critical success of his fiction, Faulkner did not earn widespread public recognition until 1946, when *The Portable Faulkner* was published. Four years later, he was awarded the Nobel Prize following the publication of *Intruder in the Dust* (1948), a novel in which he confronted the issue of racism. The narrative techniques he pioneered continue to challenge and inspire writers today.

Preview

Connecting to the Literature

There may be a neighbor or someone at school that you see all the time but do not really know well. Faulkner's story suggests that our guesses about such people reflect how little we know one another.

2 Literary Analysis

Conflict and Resolution

A **conflict** is a struggle between opposing forces. It is the engine that drives most narrative and dramatic works. **Internal conflict** occurs within a character who is torn by competing values or needs. **External conflict** occurs between a character and some outside force such as another person, society as a whole, nature, or fate. A conflict achieves **resolution** when the struggle ends and the outcome is revealed. Look beneath the refined surface of "A Rose for Emily" to find the hints of deeper struggles.

Comparing Literary Works

In his Nobel Prize acceptance speech, William Faulkner takes the opportunity to discuss his ideas about each writer's responsibility to write about topics that matter. As you read "A Rose for Emily," think about its portrayal of a bitterly conflicted human heart—and about how the story meets the literary criteria the speech identifies.

3 Reading Strategy

Clarifying Ambiguities

Ambiguity occurs in a literary work when some element of the work can be interpreted in several different ways. To **clarify ambiguity** in fiction, recognize parts of the action, characterization, or description that the writer may have deliberately left open ended or even inconsistent. Then, look for details or clues in the writing that help you make a logical interpretation. In "A Rose for Emily," Faulkner uses these techniques to build questions for his readers:

- subtle hints or open-ended comments by the narrator
- limited information about the true order, or sequence, of events
- vague details about Emily's actions

As you read "A Rose for Emily," use a chart like the one shown to note details that help you clarify these ambiguities.

Ambiguous Event:
Details:
Ambiguous Event:
Details:
Ambiguous Event:
Details:

Vocabulary Builder

encroached (en krōch′ t) *v.* intruded (p. 862)

obliterated (ə blit′ ər ā td′) *v.* wiped out (p. 862)

vanquished (vaŋ′ kwisht) *v.* thoroughly defeated (p. 865)

vindicated (vin′ də kāt′ əd) *v.* cleared from blame (p. 866)

imperviousness (im pʉr′ vē əs nis) *n.* resistance to being affected (p. 869)

divulge (də vulj′) *v.* reveal (p. 870)

circumvent (sʉr′ kəm vent′) *v.* prevent; get around (p. 870)

thwarted (thwôrt əd) *v.* blocked; frustrated (p. 872)

virulent (vir′yoo lənt) *adj.* extremely hurtful or infectious (p. 872)

inextricable (in eks′tri kə bəl) *adj.* unable to be separated or extracted from (p. 874)

2 Literary Analysis

Conflict and Resolution

- Have students speculate on what it would be like to read literature that is devoid of conflict. Lead them to answer that such literature probably would be dull because conflict provides the drama and excitement that make events worth reading about.
- Review internal and external conflict. Have students give examples of each type of conflict from literature that they have read.
- Clarify the meaning of *resolution* in literary works.
- Tell students that they will find internal and external conflicts in "A Rose for Emily."

3 Reading Strategy

Clarifying Ambiguities

- Write "I could not look at him" on the board. **Ask** students to interpret the meaning of this statement. **Possible responses:** The speaker could not see the other person; the speaker was embarrassed to look at the other person; the speaker was angry with the other person.
- Point out that this is an ambiguous statement. Writers often create ambiguity, and they supply hints that will help readers discern meaning.
- Encourage students to watch for ambiguous statements and to find details in the writing that clarify the writer's meaning.
- Provide a copy of **Reading Strategy Graphic Organizer A,** p. 189 in ***Graphic Organizer Transparencies.*** Tell students to note any ambiguous events and then fill in details about each event. Students can sort the details to clarify ambiguities.

Vocabulary Builder

- Pronounce each vocabulary word for students and read the definitions as a class. Have students identify any words with which they are already familiar.

Differentiated Instruction

Solutions for All Learners

Support for Special Needs Students
Have students complete the **Preview** and **Build Skills** pages for "A Rose for Emily" in the ***Reader's Notebook: Adapted Version.*** These pages provide a selection summary, an abbreviated presentation of the reading and literary skills, and the graphic organizer on the **Build Skills** page in the student book.

Support for Less Proficient Readers
Have students complete the **Preview** and **Build Skills** pages for "A Rose for Emily" in the ***Reader's Notebook.*** These pages provide a selection summary, an abbreviated presentation of the reading and literary skills, and the graphic organizer on the **Build Skills** page in the student book.

Support for English Learners
Have students complete the **Preview** and **Build Skills** pages for "A Rose for Emily" in the ***Reader's Notebook: English Learner's Version.*** These pages provide a selection summary, an abbreviated presentation of the reading and literary skills, and the graphic organizer on the **Build Skills** page in the student book.

Learning Modalities

Intrapersonal Learners These students may enjoy trying to understand the world from Emily's point of view. As you read through the story with students, have them reflect on Emily's motivation for her actions.

❶ About the Selection

The selection begins with the funeral of a town recluse, Miss Emily Grierson, and then retells selected episodes from her life. Miss Emily is a privileged character in the town; she does not pay taxes, and even a nuisance smell about her home is dealt with in a circumspect manner. As she ages, she becomes a creature of curiosity in the town, especially with regard to her romance with Homer Barron, a man who the townspeople think is not right for Miss Emily. When Barron disappears mysteriously, Miss Emily keeps to herself even more than before. After her death, the townspeople discover her sinister secret in a bedroom of her home.

❷ Literary Analysis
Conflict and Resolution

- Read aloud the first seven lines of the second paragraph. **Ask:** What attributes does Faulkner give Miss Emily's home?
  Answer: It is in a "heavily lightsome" architectural style; it was once on a "select" street, but the neighborhood is no longer good. It is the last home on a street that is mostly a business district now.
- Clarify with students that the traits of the house show a conflict between what the house once was and what it has become.
- Prepare students to notice details about changes in Miss Emily that parallel changes in her home.

❶

A Rose for Emily

William Faulkner

Background Like many of William Faulkner's works, this story is set in the fictional town of Jefferson in the fictional county of Yoknapatawpha (Yok´ nuh puh TAW´ fuh) in the actual state of Mississippi. Using his real home of Lafayette County, Faulkner created an amazingly detailed world in his fiction, even down to the map of Yoknapatawpha that he included in one novel. "A Rose for Emily" takes place in Jefferson over the course of more than forty years, from around 1875 to 1920, chronicling the life and death of the reclusive Miss Emily Grierson.

I

When Miss Emily Grierson died, our whole town went to her funeral: the men through a sort of respectful affection for a fallen monument, the women mostly out of curiosity to see the inside of her house, which no one save an old manservant—a combined gardener and cook—had seen in at least ten years.

❷ It was a big, squarish frame house that had once been white, decorated with cupolas and spires and scrolled balconies in the heavily lightsome style of the seventies,[1] set on what had once been our most select street. But garages and cotton gins had encroached and obliterated even the august[2] names of that neighborhood; only Miss Emily's house was left, lifting its stubborn and coquettish decay above the cotton wagons and the gasoline pumps—an eyesore among eyesores. And now Miss Emily had gone to join the representatives of those august names where they lay in the cedar-bemused cemetery among the ranked and anonymous graves of Union and Confederate soldiers who fell at the battle of Jefferson.

Vocabulary Builder

encroached (en krōcht´) *v.* intruded

obliterated (ə blit´ ər āt´d) *v.* wiped out

1. **the seventies** the 1870s.
2. **august** (ô gust´) *adj.* dignified; inspiring respect.

Differentiated Instruction Solutions for All Learners

Accessibility at a Glance

	A Rose for Emily	Nobel Prize Acceptance Speech
Context	Small town Mississippi, from 1875 to 1920	Given during Nobel Prize ceremony
Language	Accessible; long sentences	Accessible; long sentences
Concept Level	Challenging (deliberately vague and ambiguous plot)	Accessible (a major problem facing modern writers and society)
Literary Merit	Prize-winning author; regional	Prize-winning author
Lexile	1140L	1140L
Other	Extended flashbacks	
Overall Rating	Average	Average

Alive, Miss Emily had been a tradition, a duty, and a care; a sort of hereditary obligation upon the town, dating from that day in 1894 when Colonel Sartoris, the mayor—he who fathered the edict[3] that no Negro woman should appear on the streets without an apron—remitted her taxes, the dispensation dating from the death of her father on into perpetuity.[4] Not that Miss Emily would have accepted charity. Colonel Sartoris invented an involved tale to the effect that Miss Emily's father had loaned money to the town, which the town, as a matter of business, preferred this way of repaying. Only a man of Colonel Sartoris' generation and thought could have invented it, and only a woman could have believed it.

When the next generation, with its more modern ideas, became mayors and aldermen, this arrangement created some little dissatisfaction. On the first of the year they mailed her a tax notice. February came, and there was no reply. They wrote her a formal letter, asking her to call at the sheriff's office at her convenience. A week later the mayor wrote her himself, offering to call or to send his car for her, and received in reply a note on paper of an archaic shape, in a thin, flowing calligraphy in faded ink, to the effect that she no longer went out at all. The tax notice was also enclosed, without comment.

Literary Analysis
Conflict and Resolution
What is the cause of the conflict described here, and how is it resolved?

They called a special meeting of the Board of Aldermen. A deputation waited upon her, knocked at the door through which no visitor had passed since she ceased giving china-painting lessons eight or ten years earlier. They were admitted by the old Negro into a dim hall from which a stairway mounted into still more shadow. It smelled of dust and disuse—a close, dank smell. The Negro led them into the parlor. It was furnished in heavy, leather-covered furniture. When the Negro opened the blinds of one window, they could see that the leather was cracked; and when they sat down, a faint dust rose sluggishly about their thighs, spinning with slow motes in the single sun-ray. On a tarnished gilt easel before the fireplace stood a crayon portrait of Miss Emily's father.

They rose when she entered—a small, fat woman in black, with a thin gold chain descending to her waist and vanishing into her belt, leaning on an ebony cane with a tarnished gold head. Her skeleton was small and spare; perhaps that was why what would have been merely plumpness in another was obesity in her. She looked bloated, like a body long submerged in motionless water, and of that pallid[5] hue. Her eyes, lost in the fatty ridges of her face, looked like two small pieces of coal pressed into a lump of dough as they moved from one face to another while the visitors stated their errand.

She did not ask them to sit. She just stood in the door and listened quietly until the spokesman came to a stumbling halt. Then they could hear the invisible watch ticking at the end of the gold chain.

5 Reading Check
Why do members of the Board of Aldermen pay a visit to Miss Emily?

3. **edict** (ē′ dikt) *n.* command.
4. **remitted . . . into perpetuity** (pʉr′ pə to͞o ə tē) cancelled Emily's taxes forever after her father's death.
5. **pallid** (pal′ id) *adj.* pale.

3 Reading Strategy
Clarifying Ambiguities

- **Ask** what Faulkner means by saying that Miss Emily was "a tradition, a duty, and a care" for the town.
  Possible response: She has lived in the town for a long time; the town helps her out; the townspeople worry and wonder about her.
- Have students explain how Faulkner shows that the tax arrangement is a special situation for Miss Emily. **Ask:** What does this arrangement show about Colonel Sartoris?
  Possible response: He was thoughtful and found a way to help Miss Emily without injuring her pride.
- Discuss how this trait contrasts with other information about the Colonel— for example, his treatment of African American women. **Ask** how this makes him an ambiguous character.
  Possible response: He is selective about whom he shows politeness and consideration.

4 Literary Analysis
Conflict and Resolution

- Read the marked paragraph aloud to the class. Ask students how the passage of time affects the town's view of Miss Emily's tax bill.
- Have students read to the end of the section. **Ask** students the Literary Analysis question: What is the cause of the conflict described here, and how is it resolved?
  Answer: The cause of the conflict is the town's desire to get the tax money and Miss Emily's refusal to pay it. The resolution is that Miss Emily does not pay the taxes.

5 Reading Check

Answer: Members of the Board of Aldermen visit Miss Emily to tell her that she must pay her taxes.

Differentiated Instruction
Solutions for All Learners

Support for Special Needs Students

Students may understand the story better if they have a chance to preview it. Lead the students on a tour of the story, previewing its structure in five parts, viewing the illustrations and the questions about them. Focus their attention on the Reading Strategy and Literary Analysis questions, vocabulary words, and footnotes. Tell students that they can use these questions as signposts to help them follow the story and to know what is important about it. Help students formulate additional questions about the story using these tools, and encourage them to write the answers to the questions as they read. If appropriate, have them listen to all or portions of "A Rose for Emily" on **the Listening to Literature Audio CD.**

6 Literary Analysis
Conflict and Resolution

- Have volunteers read the parts of Miss Emily and the officials. Encourage them to read the lines expressively.
- **Ask:** What does the exchange reveal about Miss Emily?
  Possible Response: She thinks that she does not owe taxes, and she does not recognize the sheriff. She also is not aware that Colonel Sartoris is dead.
- **Ask:** How does Miss Emily's attitude affect the resolution of this conflict?
  Answer: Her attitude makes it difficult for the officials to argue with her, and Miss Emily sends them away.

7 Critical Viewing

Answer: The house in the photograph is large and rambling and has porches and carvings.

Her voice was dry and cold. "I have no taxes in Jefferson. Colonel Sartoris explained it to me. Perhaps one of you can gain access to the city records and satisfy yourselves."

"But we have. We are the city authorities, Miss Emily. Didn't you get a notice from the sheriff, signed by him?"

"I received a paper, yes," Miss Emily said. "Perhaps he considers himself the sheriff . . . I have no taxes in Jefferson."

6 "But there is nothing on the books to show that, you see We must go by the—"

"See Colonel Sartoris. I have no taxes in Jefferson."

"But, Miss Emily—"

"See Colonel Sartoris." (Colonel Sartoris had been dead almost ten years.) "I have no taxes in Jefferson. Tobe!" The Negro appeared. "Show these gentlemen out."

7 ▼ **Critical Viewing** In what ways does the house in this photograph match the description of Miss Emily's house on page 862? **[Connect]**

Enrichment

Victorian Architecture

The description of the Grierson home is consistent with the Queen Anne style of Victorian architecture. This style of home was popular in the latter half of the nineteenth century and early twentieth century. Queen Anne homes were popular throughout the South. Many of these homes survive into the twenty-first century and are used as offices and small inns as well as for their original purpose: as family homes.

On the outside, these homes featured large porches, gabled roofs, towers, turrets, and bay windows. The wood homes were often painted in dark colors, such as brick red, deep green, or muddy brown. After a time, many of the homes were painted white, as was the Griersons'. In the late twentieth century, many renovators rediscovered the roots of the style and started painting their homes in the deeper colors again.

II

So she vanquished them, horse and foot, just as she had vanquished their fathers thirty years before about the smell. That was two years after her father's death and a short time after her sweetheart—the one we believed would marry her—had deserted her. After her father's death she went out very little; after her sweetheart went away, people hardly saw her at all. A few of the ladies had the temerity[6] to call, but were not received, and the only sign of life about the place was the Negro man—a young man then—going in and out with a market basket.

"Just as if a man—any man—could keep a kitchen properly," the ladies said; so they were not surprised when the smell developed. It was another link between the gross, teeming world and the high and mighty Griersons.

A neighbor, a woman, complained to the mayor, Judge Stevens, eighty years old.

"But what will you have me do about it, madam?" he said.

"Why, send her word to stop it," the woman said. "Isn't there a law?"

"I'm sure that won't be necessary," Judge Stevens said. "It's probably just a snake or a rat that nigger of hers killed in the yard. I'll speak to him about it."

The next day he received two more complaints, one from a man who came in diffident deprecation.[7] "We really must do something about it, Judge. I'd be the last one in the world to bother Miss Emily, but we've got to do something." That night the Board of Aldermen met—three graybeards and one younger man, a member of the rising generation.

"It's simple enough," he said. "Send her word to have her place cleaned up. Give her a certain time to do it in, and if she don't . . ."

"Dammit, sir," Judge Stevens said, "will you accuse a lady to her face of smelling bad?"

So the next night, after midnight, four men crossed Miss Emily's lawn and slunk about the house like burglars, sniffing along the base of the brickwork and at the cellar openings while one of them performed a regular sowing motion with his hand out of a sack slung from his shoulder. They broke open the cellar door and sprinkled lime there, and in all the outbuildings. As they recrossed the lawn, a window that had been dark was lighted and Miss Emily sat in it, the light behind her, and her upright torso motionless as that of an idol. They crept quietly across the lawn and into the shadow of the locusts[8] that lined the street. After a week or two the smell went away.

6. **temerity** (tə mer′ ə tē) *n.* foolish or reckless boldness.
7. **diffident deprecation** (dif′ ədənt dep′rə kā shen) timid disapproval.
8. **locusts** (lō′ kəsts) *n.* large grasshoppers that travel in swarms and eat crops.

Vocabulary Builder
vanquished (vaŋ′ kwisht) *v.* thoroughly defeated

8 ***Two Influential Writers***

William Faulkner and Ernest Hemingway were probably the two most influential American writers of the twentieth century, even though they were near-opposites. Although Faulkner longed for adventure as a young man, he settled in a tiny corner of rural Mississippi. His prose was dense and complex and featured enormously long sentences. Hemingway, on the other hand, lived a life of epic adventure, traveling the world and hunting big game. His prose—precise and unadorned—introduced a new way of writing to American literature.

Both men won the Nobel Prize—Faulkner in 1950 and Hemingway in 1954—and though they shared a grudging respect, they also waged a famous war of words. Hemingway said that Faulkner "wrote like an old grandmother," and Faulkner replied that Hemingway was "afraid to use a word of more than five letters."

Connect to the Literature

In "A Rose for Emily," where does Faulkner use dense, complex language, and where does his prose seem more simple and unadorned?

9  **Reading Check**

Why do the men break open the cellar door?

8 The American Experience

Two Influential Writers

Just as Faulkner had his home in Mississippi, Ernest Hemingway had a special place, too—Walloon Lake, Michigan, where his family spent summers. Despite an apparently happy childhood, Hemingway struggled throughout his larger-than-life adulthood to find peace. Depressed and ill, Hemingway took his own life in 1961.

Connect to the Literature Review the story up to this point, and help students find contrasting passages that illustrate the two types of writing described in the question.
Possible response: On this page, the dialogue between the neighbor woman and the Judge is simple and unadorned, whereas the first full paragraph on this page is more complex.

9 Reading Check

Answer: The men break open the cellar door to sprinkle lime in case the source of the odor is in the cellar.

Differentiated Instruction
Solutions for All Learners

Support for Less Proficient Readers
Read aloud the first paragraph. Then write on the board details about what is happening in the paragraph. Work with students to create a summary of that paragraph. Then, have each student work with a partner and make a list of details about what is happening on the rest of p. 865. Tell them to use these details to create summaries. Encourage students to read their summaries and describe the events that they have included.

Enrichment for Advanced Readers
Students may be interested in finding out why the midnight visitors to the Grierson homestead sprinkle lime in the cellar and around the outbuildings. Have them use library or Internet resources to find out about lime's disinfecting qualities. Students interested in the chemical properties of lime may try to determine which type of lime was the most likely choice for the task. Have students report their findings to the class.

10 Literary Analysis
Conflict and Resolution

- Read aloud the first three sentences in the third paragraph.
- **Ask** students to interpret the meaning of Miss Emily's meeting people at the door rather than inviting them in.
  Possible responses: She does not want to talk to them; she is hiding something; she does not think that she needs help.
- Tell students to finish reading the paragraph. **Ask** the Literary Analysis question: What conflict arises here between Emily and the town, and how is it resolved?
  Answer: The townspeople know that Emily's father is dead and that he should be buried. Emily says that her father is not dead. After three days, "she broke down," so they quickly buried her father.
- Point out that although this is the third conflict between Emily and people in the town, this actually would be the first conflict if the story were told chronologically.
  Ask students how the resolution of this conflict is different from the resolution of the conflicts reported earlier.
  Answer: In this conflict, Miss Emily gives in; in the others, she wins.
- **Ask** students to explain why this conflict ends differently.
  Possible responses: Perhaps Miss Emily realizes that her unburied father would present a health hazard.

That was when people had begun to feel really sorry for her. People in our town, remembering how old lady Wyatt, her great-aunt, had gone completely crazy at last, believed that the Griersons held themselves a little too high for what they really were. None of the young men were quite good enough for Miss Emily and such. We had long thought of them as a tableau, Miss Emily a slender figure in white in the background, her father a spraddled[9] silhouette in the foreground, his back to her and clutching a horsewhip, the two of them framed by the back-flung front door. So when she got to be thirty and was still single, we were not pleased exactly, but vindicated; even with insanity in the family she wouldn't have turned down all of her chances if they had really materialized.

When her father died, it got about that the house was all that was left to her; and in a way, people were glad. At last they could pity Miss Emily. Being left alone, and a pauper, she had become humanized. Now she too would know the old thrill and the old despair of a penny more or less.

The day after his death all the ladies prepared to call at the house and offer condolence and aid, as is our custom. Miss Emily met them at the door, dressed as usual and with no trace of grief on her face.
10 She told them that her father was not dead. She did that for three days, with the ministers calling on her, and the doctors, trying to persuade her to let them dispose of the body. Just as they were about to resort to law and force, she broke down, and they buried her father quickly.

We did not say she was crazy then. We believed she had to do that. We remembered all the young men her father had driven away, and we knew that with nothing left, she would have to cling to that which had robbed her, as people will.

III

She was sick for a long time. When we saw her again, her hair was cut short, making her look like a girl, with a vague resemblance to those angels in colored church windows—sort of tragic and serene.

The town had just let the contracts for paving the sidewalks, and in the summer after her father's death they began the work. The construction company came with niggers and mules and machinery, and a foreman named Homer Barron, a Yankee—a big, dark, ready man, with a big voice and eyes lighter than his face. The little boys would follow in groups to hear him cuss the niggers, and the niggers singing in time to the rise and fall of picks. Pretty soon he knew everybody in town. Whenever you heard a lot of laughing anywhere about the square, Homer Barron would be in the center of the group. Presently we began to see him and Miss Emily on Sunday afternoons driving in the yellow-wheeled buggy and the matched team of bays from the livery stable.

Vocabulary Builder
vindicated (vin′ də kāt′ əd) *v.* cleared from blame

Literary Analysis
Conflict and Resolution What conflict arises here between Emily and the town, and how is it resolved?

9. **spraddled** (sprad′′ ld) *adj.* seated with spread, sprawling legs.

▲ **Critical Viewing** What emotions do you imagine the young woman in this painting is feeling as she looks out the window? **[Speculate]**

⓫ Humanities

Woman by a Window by Gustav Vermehren

Gustav Vermehren (1863–1931) was a Danish painter known for painting landscapes, interior scenes, gardens, and fjords. This painting shows the influence of the Romantic era on Victorian painters. The flowers and view from the window show a love of nature, while the woman's pensiveness alludes to her inner turmoil.

Use these questions for discussion:

1. How do the details of this painting compare with those in the story?
   Possible response: The furnishings and the woman's clothing seem consistent with those of Miss Emily's era. As Miss Emily often did, the woman is looking out of the window.
2. Which details in the painting contribute to its mood?
   Possible response: The filmy curtains, the flowers, and the soft lines create a mellow, pensive mood. The woman's posture may indicate that she is waiting for something to happen.

⓬ Critical Viewing

Possible response: She is feeling anxiety, curiosity, or perhaps impatience.

Differentiated Instruction

Solutions for All Learners

Support for English Learners

To help students understand the narrator's view of the romance between Miss Emily and Homer Barron, explain that Miss Emily is old-fashioned, well-mannered, and from an influential family. Her social position makes Homer an unlikely suitor. Elicit reasons from the students for the town's wariness about Homer Barron. For example, he is a Yankee (a person from the north) and a laborer. He is loud and gregarious. This is why the narrator doesn't trust him or think that he is suitable for Miss Emily.

Strategy for Advanced Readers

Guide students to realize that much of the distinctive style of "A Rose for Miss Emily" comes from the qualities of the small town in which she lives. Have students list the plot elements that could happen only in a close community, including the special arrangement for Miss Emily's taxes, the midnight visit to her property, and so on. As students read, have them list ways in which the story might have been different if it had taken place in another type of community.

⓭ Humanities

Mrs. Thomas Eakins by Thomas Eakins

Thomas Eakins (1844–1916) was interested in both art and science; he studied at the Pennsylvania Academy of the Fine Arts and attended anatomy lectures at a medical school. He also studied painting in France and Spain.

This painting is typical of the highly realistic portraits Eakins painted after retiring from art education. The subject, Susan Macdowell Eakins, was an artist and photographer in her own right.

Use these questions for discussion:

1. What does the woman's frank stare express?
   Possible response: She is familiar with the painter; she appears as though she is waiting for a response from someone.
2. What effect does the black background have on the painting?
   Possible response: The background makes it seem as though the woman's face is floating. This darkness makes the woman's features, especially her eyes, stand out.

⓮ Critical Viewing

Possible response: Yes, because this appears to be a middle-aged woman with some social standing, and the woman in the picture has a look on her face similar to the look Miss Emily gives the druggist.

13

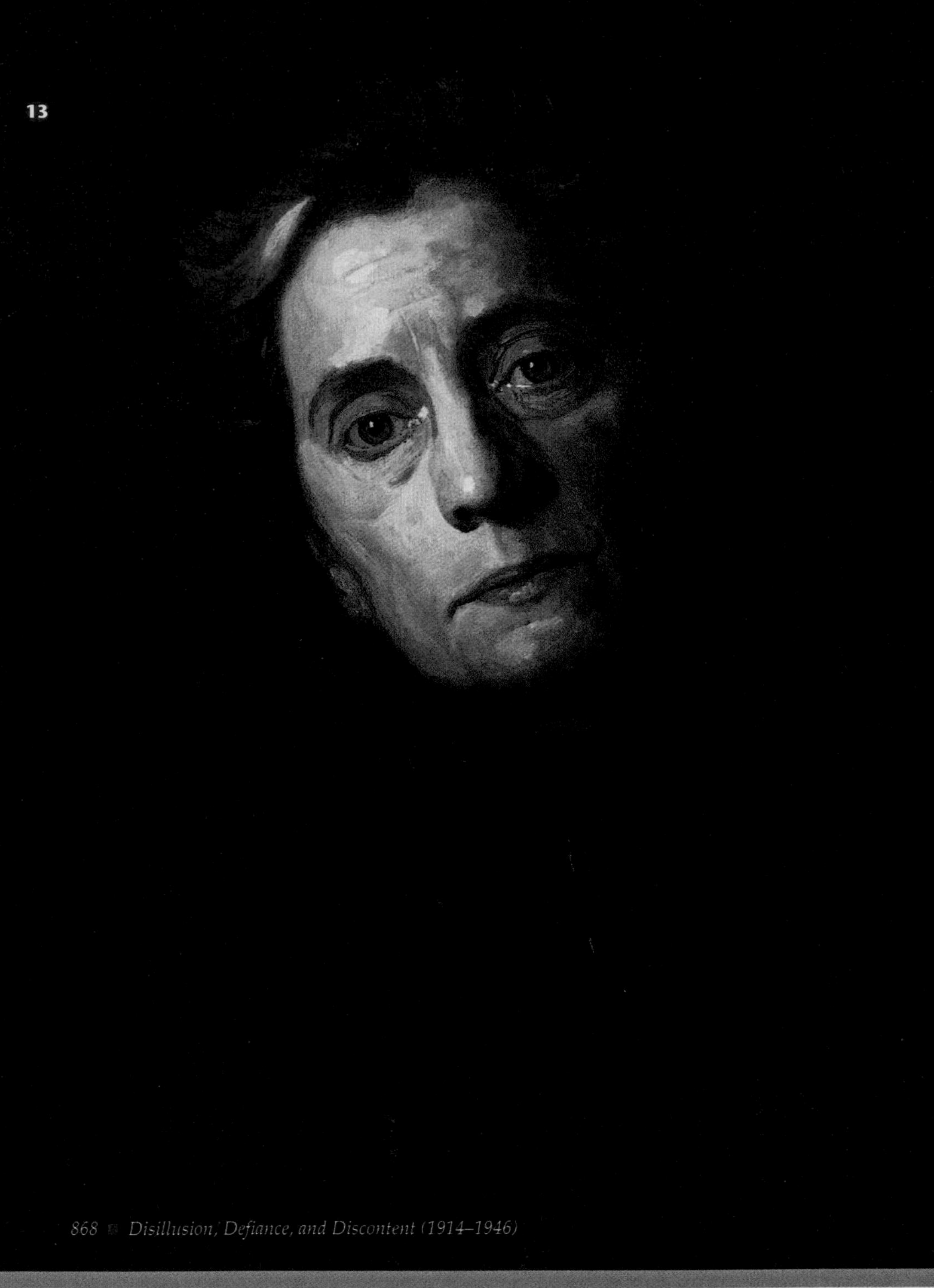

Enrichment

Arsenic in History

Arsenic has been a trusted poison since Roman times. In fact, the Romans of the political class often chose poisoning as a method for removing their enemies. Classical writers have claimed that arsenic was an ideal poison. For one reason, it revealed no color, taste, or odor when mixed with food and drink. Arsenic poisoning also was not easy to recognize because the symptoms matched the symptoms of other disorders, such as food poisoning.

Arsenic poisonings continued into the Middle Ages and beyond. Two of the more famous Renaissance poisoners used arsenic as a secret ingredient in cosmetics. Rumors also continue that Napoleon Bonaparte met his end as a result of a mysterious poisoner.

At first we were glad that Miss Emily would have an interest, because the ladies all said, "Of course a Grierson would not think seriously of a Northerner, a day laborer." But there were still others, older people, who said that even grief could not cause a real lady to forget *noblesse oblige*[10]—without calling it *noblesse oblige.* They just said, "Poor Emily. Her kinsfolk should come to her." She had some kin in Alabama; but years ago her father had fallen out with them over the estate of old lady Wyatt, the crazy woman, and there was no communication between the two families. They had not even been represented at the funeral.

And as soon as the old people said, "Poor Emily," the whispering began. "Do you suppose it's really so?" they said to one another. "Of course it is. What else could . . ." This behind their hands; rustling of craned silk and satin behind jalousies[11] closed upon the sun of Sunday afternoon as the thin, swift clop-clop-clop of the matched team passed: "Poor Emily."

She carried her head high enough—even when we believed that she was fallen. It was as if she demanded more than ever the recognition of her dignity as the last Grierson; as if it had wanted that touch of earthiness to reaffirm her imperviousness. Like when she bought the rat poison, the arsenic. That was over a year after they had begun to say "Poor Emily," and while the two female cousins were visiting her.

"I want some poison," she said to the druggist. She was over thirty then, still a slight woman, though thinner than usual, with cold, haughty black eyes in a face the flesh of which was strained across the temples and about the eyesockets as you imagine a lighthouse-keeper's face ought to look. "I want some poison," she said.

"Yes, Miss Emily. What kind? For rats and such? I'd recom—"

"I want the best you have. I don't care what kind."

The druggist named several. "They'll kill anything up to an elephant. But what you want is—"

"Arsenic," Miss Emily said. "Is that a good one?"

"Is . . . arsenic? Yes, ma'am. But what you want—"

"I want arsenic."

The druggist looked down at her. She looked back at him, erect, her face like a strained flag. "Why, of course," the druggist said. "If that's what you want. But the law requires you to tell what you are going to use it for."

Miss Emily just stared at him, her head tilted back in order to look him eye for eye, until he looked away and went and got the arsenic and

10. ***noblesse oblige*** (nō bles' ō blēzh) *n.* the presumed duty of the upper classes to behave in a noble and generous way (French).
11. **jalousies** (jal' ə sēz) *n.* windows or shades with slats that can be adjusted to let in air and light.

◄ **Critical Viewing** Does this portrait match your mental image of Miss Emily? Why or why not? **[Connect]**

Literary Analysis
Conflict and Resolution
What is the source of the conflict here, and how is it resolved?

Vocabulary Builder
imperviousness (im pur' vē əs nis) *n.* resistance to being affected

17 **Reading Check**
Why do people begin to refer to Miss Emily as "Poor Emily"?

15 Literary Analysis
Conflict and Resolution

- **Ask** a student to summarize what is scandalous about Miss Emily's relationship with Homer Barron.
  Possible response: He is a Yankee and a "day laborer," so he is not a proper boyfriend for her. Although she is poor, she is considered too good for him.
- Read aloud the second paragraph on page 869. **Ask** students the Literary Analysis question: What is the source of the conflict here, and how is it resolved?
  Possible response: The conflict here is between Miss Emily's behavior and what people think that she should be doing. It is resolved by her continuing to do as she wishes.

16 Vocabulary Builder
Latin Prefixes: *in-* and *im-*

- Point out to students that the prefixes *in-* and *im-* mean the same thing.
- Tell students that this prefix can mean "into," "in," "within," "on," or "toward"; it can also mean "no," "not," or "without."
- Point out the word *imperviousness.* Then, define *pervious* and explain its root. (*Pervious* comes from Latin words meaning "way" and "through.")
- Then **ask** students which meaning of the prefix *im-* applies to this word.
  Answer: In *imperviousness, im-* means "not."

17 Reading Check

Possible response: The townspeople begin calling her "Poor Emily" because they feel sorry for her; they know she has very little money; she is not close to any of her relatives.

Differentiated Instruction Solutions for All Learners

Enrichment for Advanced Readers
Students may be unfamiliar with the term *noblesse oblige* that Faulkner uses on this page. Have students research not just the dictionary definition of this term, but its practical meaning in a society that valued manners and a firmly defined social structure as much as Miss Emily's town did. Have students report on the obligations and expectations that *noblesse oblige* imposed on the upper and lower classes, as well as the rights that it granted members of a community. In addition, have them give examples of *noblesse oblige* in a contemporary context, explaining how it is different from and similar to the way it is manifested in "A Rose for Emily."

18 Reading Strategy
Clarifying Ambiguities

- Have a student summarize the events leading up to the last paragraph in Section III.
- Then, read aloud the last paragraph of the section. **Ask** the Reading Strategy question: What is ambiguous about the incident in which Emily buys rat poison?
  Answer: Miss Emily never really tells what she will use the poison for. Even when the druggist says that she must say what she will do with it, she only looks at him.
- Draw a connection between how this conflict ends and how the other conflicts between Miss Emily and townspeople end. Elicit from students that when she refuses to speak, the others just give in to her.

19 Critical Thinking
Infer

- Read aloud the bracketed text. Then, **ask** students why the townspeople have decided that Miss Emily and Homer Barron are married.
  Answer: Miss Emily is doing things that a wife would do for a husband. She buys him an expensive gift, a silver toilet set. She buys clothes for him.
- **Ask** students to explain the statement, "the two female cousins were even more Grierson than Miss Emily had ever been."
  Possible response: The cousins are even stranger than Miss Emily, and the townspeople think that the cousins will leave because Miss Emily is married.

18 wrapped it up. The Negro delivery boy brought her the package; the druggist didn't come back. When she opened the package at home there was written on the box, under the skull and bones: "For rats."

Reading Strategy
Clarifying Ambiguities
What is ambiguous about the incident in which Emily buys rat poison?

IV

So the next day we all said, "She will kill herself"; and we said it would be the best thing. When she had first begun to be seen with Homer Barron, we had said, "She will marry him." Then we said, "She will persuade him yet," because Homer himself had remarked—he liked men, and it was known that he drank with the younger men in the Elks' Club—that he was not a marrying man. Later we said, "Poor Emily" behind the jalousies as they passed on Sunday afternoon in the glittering buggy, Miss Emily with her head high and Homer Barron with his hat cocked and a cigar in his teeth, reins and whip in a yellow glove.

Then some of the ladies began to say that it was a disgrace to the town and a bad example to the young people. The men did not want to interfere, but at last the ladies forced the Baptist minister—Miss Emily's people were Episcopal—to call upon her. He would never divulge what happened during that interview, but he refused to go back again. The next Sunday they again drove about the streets, and the following day the minister's wife wrote to Miss Emily's relations in Alabama.

Vocabulary Builder
divulge (də vulj′) *v.* reveal

19 So she had blood-kin under her roof again and we sat back to watch developments. At first nothing happened. Then we were sure that they were to be married. We learned that Miss Emily had been to the jeweler's and ordered a man's toilet set in silver, with the letters H. B. on each piece. Two days later we learned that she had bought a complete outfit of men's clothing, including a nightshirt, and we said, "They are married." We were really glad. We were glad because the two female cousins were even more Grierson than Miss Emily had ever been.

So we were not surprised when Homer Barron—the streets had been finished some time since—was gone. We were a little disappointed that there was not a public blowing-off, but we believed that he had gone on to prepare for Miss Emily's coming, or to give her a chance to get rid of the cousins. (By that time it was a cabal[12], and we were all Miss Emily's allies to help circumvent the cousins.) Sure enough, after another week they departed. And, as we had expected all along, within three days Homer Barron was back in town. A neighbor saw the Negro man admit him at the kitchen door at dusk one evening.

Vocabulary Builder
circumvent (sur′ kəm vent′) *v.* prevent; get around

And that was the last we saw of Homer Barron. And of Miss Emily for some time. The Negro man went in and out with the market basket, but the front door remained closed. Now and then we would see her at a window for a moment, as the men did that night when they sprinkled

12. **cabal** (kəbäl) *n.* small group of people joined in a secret plot.

20 ▶ **Critical Viewing** What do you predict might be the significance of the staircase in this story? **[Predict]**

Enrichment

Language Development

The acceptable terms for people with African ancestry have changed since Faulkner's time. In Faulkner's era, *Negro* or *colored* were common terms for an African American. Within the context of the story, that is, in the American South of the late nineteenth and early twentieth centuries, *nigger* was also a common term. Today, the word *nigger* is considered an offensive term.

Since Faulkner's time language has changed. In the 1960s, *black* became the preferred term; *African American* later replaced it. A growing racial consciousness in America at that time fueled these changes.

Linguistically, *nigger* and *Negro* are related; both are rooted in the Latin word *niger,* which means "black." Other related words include *Niger,* the name of a river and a country in Africa, and *Nigeria,* another country in Africa.

20 Critical Viewing

Possible response: Perhaps there is a special room on the second floor, or an important event happens in the upper part of the house.

Differentiated Instruction

Solutions for All Learners

Vocabulary for English Learners

Help students with the meanings of some of Faulkner's terms. *Jalousies,* mentioned in the first full paragraph on the page, are blinds or shutters that can be opened to let in light or air. The term is used to show that the townspeople were watching from inside their homes, where Miss Emily and her companion could not see them. *Blood-kin,* which is found two paragraphs later, refers to people who are related by blood and shows that Miss Emily's relations have answered the letter from the minister's wife.

Enrichment for Gifted/Talented Students

A great deal of the atmosphere in this story arises from what Faulkner does *not* say. For example, he does not disclose the encounter between Miss Emily and the Baptist minister or details of Miss Emily's relationship with Homer Barron or her servant. Challenge students to work in groups to select a missing portion of the story and to write what happened. Encourage them to imitate Faulkner's style and apply their observations about the characters as well as to use dialogue that reflects the characters' speech. Invite students to share their work with the class.

21 Critical Thinking

Interpret

- Read aloud the paragraph beginning, "From that time on . . ." After reading, tell students that a number of details in this paragraph require interpretation.
- First, **ask** students why Miss Emily would be giving lessons in china-painting.
  Answer: She needs the money, and she could do the job without leaving her home.
- **Ask** how often her students took classes and which detail reveals that information.
  Answer: They most likely took lessons once a week because that is how often they went to church.

22 Reading Strategy

Clarifying Ambiguity

- Have a volunteer read aloud the bracketed sentence.
- **Ask** what Faulkner means when he says that the front door closed "and remained closed for good."
  Answer: It means that no one else came to visit Miss Emily.

the lime, but for almost six months she did not appear on the streets. Then we knew that this was to be expected too; as if that quality of her father which had thwarted her woman's life so many times had been too virulent and too furious to die.

When we next saw Miss Emily, she had grown fat and her hair was turning gray. During the next few years it grew grayer and grayer until it attained an even pepper-and-salt iron-gray, when it ceased turning. Up to the day of her death at seventy-four it was still that vigorous iron-gray, like the hair of an active man.

From that time on her front door remained closed, save for a period of six or seven years, when she was about forty, during which she gave lessons in china-painting. She fitted up a studio in one of the downstairs rooms, where the daughters and granddaughters of Colonel Sartoris' contemporaries were sent to her with the same regularity and in the same spirit that they were sent to church on Sundays with a twenty-five-cent piece for the collection plate. Meanwhile her taxes had been remitted.

Then the newer generation became the backbone and the spirit of the town, and the painting pupils grew up and fell away and did not send their children to her with boxes of color and tedious brushes and pictures cut from the ladies' magazines. The front door closed upon the last one and remained closed for good.

When the town got free postal delivery, Miss Emily alone refused to let them fasten the metal numbers above her door and attach a mailbox to it. She would not listen to them.

Daily, monthly, yearly we watched the Negro grow grayer and more stooped, going in and out with the market basket. Each December we sent her a tax notice, which would be returned by the post office a week later, unclaimed. Now and then we would see her in one of the downstairs windows—she had evidently shut up the top floor of the house—like the carven torso of an idol in a niche, looking or not looking at us, we could never tell which. Thus she passed from generation to generation—dear, inescapable, impervious, tranquil, and perverse.[13]

And so she died. Fell ill in the house filled with dust and shadows, with only a doddering Negro man to wait on her. We did not even know she was sick; we had long since given up trying to get any information from the Negro. He talked to no one, probably not even to her, for his voice had grown harsh and rusty, as if from disuse.

She died in one of the downstairs rooms, in a heavy walnut bed with a curtain, her gray head propped on a pillow yellow and moldy with age and lack of sunlight.

Vocabulary Builder

thwarted (thwôrt əd) *v.* blocked; frustrated

virulent (vir′ yoo lənt) *v.* extremely hurtful or infectious

---

13. perverse (pər vurs′) *adj.* stubbornly contrary or difficult.

Enrichment

China Painting

Painting on china was a suitable pastime for young ladies of the late nineteenth and early twentieth centuries. Teaching young women this craft would be a genteel way for a woman, such as Miss Emily, to earn money.

China painters bought preformed but undecorated and unglazed ceramic pieces from ceramic shops. These blank pieces could be anything from plates to teapots. Using brushes and special paints, the painters applied designs to the blanks. The decorated wares could then be returned to the shop to be glazed and fired in a kiln.

While there were many professional china painters, the practice was also a burgeoning hobby during this era. Pieces painted by hobbyists were most likely used in their own homes or given away as gifts to friends.

V

The Negro met the first of the ladies at the front door and let them in, with their hushed, sibilant[14] voices and their quick, curious glances, and then he disappeared. He walked right through the house and out the back and was not seen again.

The two female cousins came at once. They held the funeral on the second day, with the town coming to look at Miss Emily beneath a mass of bought flowers, with the crayon face of her father musing profoundly above the bier[15] and the ladies sibilant and macabre[16]; and the very old men—some in their brushed Confederate uniforms—on the porch and the lawn, talking of Miss Emily as if she had been a contemporary of theirs, believing that they had danced with her and courted her perhaps, confusing time with its mathematical progression, as the old do, to whom all the past is not a diminishing road but, instead, a huge meadow which no winter ever quite touches, divided from them now by the narrow bottle-neck of the most recent decade of years.

Already we knew that there was one room in that region above stairs which no one had seen in forty years, and which would have to be forced. They waited until Miss Emily was decently in the ground before they opened it.

The violence of breaking down the door seemed to fill this room with pervading dust. A thin, acrid pall[17] as of the tomb seemed to lie everywhere upon this room decked and furnished as for a bridal: upon the valance curtains of faded rose color, upon the rose-shaded lights, upon the dressing table, upon the delicate array of crystal and

14. sibilant (sib′ ə lənt) *adj.* making a hissing sound with *s* or *sh* sounds.
15. bier (bir) *n.* supporting platform for a coffin.
16. macabre (mə käb′rə) *adj.* gruesome.
17. acrid pall (ak′rid pôl) *n.* bitter and gloomy covering or atmosphere.

24 **Critical Viewing**
Compare and contrast the mood in this painting with the mood of the story. **[Compare and Contrast]**

25 **Reading Check**
Why do people force open the door to an upstairs room in Miss Emily's house?

23 Humanities

Bedroom by Elizabeth Barakah Hodges (b. 1938)

Painting is Elizabeth Barkah Hodges's second career; she holds a doctorate in comparative literature and taught at the university level for two decades before discovering her talent for art. She is from Columbia, South Carolina.

Bedroom is typical of Hodges's work because of its subject; she often paints rooms. Like other works by Hodges, her work shows influences from an earlier artist, the French painter Pierre Bonnard.

Use these questions for discussion:

1. What details in the painting show that this is a more modern work of art than others in the selection?
   Possible response: The odd perspective and the abstract use of flattened shapes are characteristic of a more recent work of art.
2. Would the bedroom in Miss Emily's home have looked like this?
   Possible response: Because this room is orderly, clean, and plain, and the rooms in Miss Emily's home are crowded and dusty, the rooms probably would not be similar.

24 Critical Viewing

Answer: The mood of the painting is peaceful and orderly whereas the mood of the story is one of turmoil and mystery.

25 Reading Check

Possible response: They break open the door because they want to know what is in the mysterious room.

Differentiated Instruction
Solutions for All Learners

Strategy for Less Proficient Readers
In this segment of the story, Faulkner returns the reader to where the story began: the death of Miss Emily. Work with students to help them find clues within the story that show the chronological order of events. For example, on page 863 the narrator mentions that 1894 is the date that her taxes were remitted; on page 865 the narrator mentions the incident during which people noticed a curious smell happened thirty years before Miss Emily refused to pay her taxes, and so on. Even if students cannot find exact dates for events, they will probably find when something happened in relation to another event. Tell them to assemble these clues on a timeline to show the progression of events in the story. Have students refer to the timeline as they reread the story so that they can relate each event to its approximate time in Miss Emily's life.

26 Reading Strategy
Clarifying Ambiguities

- Read the sentence aloud, calmly and deliberately. **Ask** the Reading Strategy question: What is the shocking meaning of the sentence, "The man himself lay in the bed"? **Answer:** A man, either asleep or dead, is lying on the bed; no one expected to find anyone in the room.
- Have students read further to clarify the man's circumstances.

ASSESS
Answers

1. Student may be shocked that Emily kept the body in the house.
2. (a) Emily said that she did not have to pay taxes. (b) Emily had special privileges.
3. (a) The family had been a leading family in the town. (b) She is pitied and patronized because she has fallen on hard times. (c) Emily has become reclusive but refuses to recognize that she receives special privileges.
4. (a) The druggist asks Emily why she needs poison, but she refuses to tell him. (b) The townspeople notice a bad smell. (c) She poisoned Homer Barron.
5. (a) They spent Sunday afternoons together; they were dating. (b) Emily probably poisoned him because he would not marry her.
6. (a) The narrator seems to be someone who lives in the town and was present when many events took place. (b) The narrator first calls her "a tradition, a duty, and a care." In the end, the narrator makes no comment about her, but readers sense that Emily is no longer pitied.
7. (a) Emily values her privacy, as she has only her pupils in her home. She is proud and discreet. She seems possessive of those she loves, even to the point that she cannot give away her father's body or let her boyfriend leave her. (b) Students should explain the reasoning behind their responses.

Go Online — Author Link For additional information about William Faulkner, have students type in the Web Code, then select F from the alphabet, and then select William Faulkner.

the man's toilet things backed with tarnished silver, silver so tarnished that the monogram was obscured. Among them lay a collar and tie, as if they had just been removed, which, lifted, left upon the surface a pale crescent in the dust. Upon a chair hung the suit, carefully folded; beneath it the two mute shoes and the discarded socks.

26 The man himself lay in the bed.

For a long while we just stood there, looking down at the profound and fleshless grin. The body had apparently once lain in the attitude of an embrace, but now the long sleep that outlasts love, that conquers even the grimace of love, had cuckolded[18] him. What was left of him, rotted beneath what was left of the nightshirt, had become inextricable from the bed in which he lay; and upon him and upon the pillow beside him lay that even coating of the patient and biding dust.

Then we noticed that in the second pillow was the indentation of a head. One of us lifted something from it, and leaning forward, that faint and invisible dust dry and acrid in the nostrils, we saw a long strand of iron-gray hair.

Reading Strategy
Clarifying Ambiguities
What is the shocking meaning of the sentence "The man himself lay in the bed"?

Vocabulary Builder
inextricable (in eks′ tri kə bəl) *adj.* unable to be separated or extracted from

18. **cuckolded** (kuk′əld əd) *v.* betrayed by an unfaithful wife or lover.

Critical Reading

1. **Respond:** What was your reaction when you read the final sentences of this story?
2. **(a) Recall:** What happened when the judge tried to get Emily to pay her taxes? **(b) Infer:** What does this incident reveal about Emily's relationship to the town?
3. **(a) Recall:** What had been the position of Emily's family in Jefferson while her father was living? **(b) Infer:** How does her position change over time? **(c) Draw Conclusions:** What seems to be Emily's attitude toward this change?
4. **(a) Recall:** Describe what happens when Emily buys arsenic. **(b) Recall:** What problem do the townspeople notice shortly after that purchase? **(c) Speculate:** What do you think Emily did with the arsenic?
5. **(a) Recall:** What does the story say about Homer Barron and his relationship with Emily? **(b) Infer:** What probably happened to Homer, and why?
6. **(a) Interpret:** The narrator consistently uses the first-person plural pronouns *we, us,* and *our* in discussing Emily's relationship to the town. Who does the narrator seem to be? **(b) Analyze:** Describe the narrator's changing attitude toward Emily, and identify comments from the story that support your opinion.
7. **(a) Generalize:** What values do you think are important to Emily? **(b) Take a Position:** What do you think of Emily's values? Explain.

For: More about William Faulkner
Visit: www.PHSchool.com
Web Code: ere-9519

27 Nobel Prize Acceptance Speech

WILLIAM FAULKNER

Background The Swedish chemist Alfred Nobel earned fame as the inventor of dynamite. Nobel had intended dynamite to be used safely in mining and construction, but disasters often occurred, and his name became associated with tragedy. Nobel eventually succeeded in making dynamite safer. Later, he sought to make the world a better place by establishing a foundation to encourage achievement and diplomacy. The Nobel Prizes, given for achievement in the fields of physics, chemistry, medicine, literature, and world peace, are the result of his efforts. They are the world's most prestigious awards. When William Faulkner received the Nobel Prize for literature in 1950, he gave an acceptance speech that is among the simplest and most moving examples of oratory in our literature.

Stockholm, Sweden
December 10, 1950

I feel that this award was not made to me as a man, but to my work—a life's work in the agony and sweat of the human spirit, not for glory and least of all for profit, but to create out of the materials of the human spirit something which did not exist before. So this award is only mine in trust. It will not be difficult to find a dedication for the money part of it commensurate with the purpose and significance of its origin. But I would like to do the same with the acclaim too, by using this moment as a pinnacle from which I might be listened to by the young men and women already dedicated to the same anguish and travail, among whom is already that one who will some day stand here where I am standing.

Our tragedy today is a general and universal physical fear so long sustained by now that we can even bear it. There are no longer problems of the spirit. There is only the question: When will I be blown up? Because of this, the young man or woman writing today has forgotten the problems of the human heart in conflict with itself which alone can make good writing because only that is worth writing about, worth the agony and the sweat. 28

He must learn them again. He must teach himself that the basest of all things is to be afraid; and, teaching himself that, forget it forever, leaving no room in his workshop for anything but the old verities and truths of the heart, the old universal truths lacking which any story

What does Faulkner believe is the only subject that can yield good writing?

27 About the Selection

In his gracious acceptance speech, Faulkner expresses his concern that the question of physical survival has diverted young writers from dealing with what truly matters in life and literature: love, honor, compassion, and sacrifice. He states his belief that humanity will not only endure, but prevail, because man alone possesses an immortal soul and compassionate spirit. The writer is both obliged and privileged to remind humanity of its nobler capabilities and, thus, can help ensure the success of the human race.

28 Reading Check

Answer: The only subject that can yield good writing is one focused on the problems of the human heart in conflict.

Differentiated Instruction
Solutions for All Learners

Background for Less Proficient Readers

Increase students' access to Faulkner's speech by providing the following information: In 1950 the United States was involved in a Cold War with the Soviet Union. The relationship between the two nations was strained, and the buildup of nuclear weapons in both countries produced a tremendous amount of distrust and fear.

Enrichment for Advanced Readers

Encourage students to explore works of Nobel Prize winners from countries other than the United States. Students can read with the purpose of learning how literature reflects the values and culture of its country of origin. You may wish to have each student select a different Nobel Prize-winning author to research. Students can then share their findings in a series of oral reports. As a whole class, discuss which themes or concerns the authors share in common, despite their different cultural backgrounds. Do students think the works discussed meet Faulkner's criteria for good literature?

ASSESS

Answers

1. Students' responses should reflect an understanding of Faulkner's criteria for good literature.
2. (a) People are too worried about being killed. (b) It is the fear of nuclear destruction.
3. (a) Acccording to Faulkner, the problems of the human heart in conflict are the sole subject of good writing. (b) He sees modern literature as being concerned with trivial or passing emotions and problems rather than with "old universal truths."
4. (a) Humanity will prevail. (b) Enduring is merely continuing to exist, while prevailing expresses the ability to lift the human spirit.
5. (a) It is a writer's duty to write about compassion, courage, honor, hope, pride, pity, and sacrifice. (b) The poet's voice can be a prop or pillar to help people prevail.
6. (a) The use of atom bombs in World War II and Russia's testing of an atom bomb soon afterward led to widespread fear that nuclear war was about to destroy the human race. (b) Responses will vary. Students should be able to support their responses.

Go Online Author Link For additional information about William Faulkner, have students type in the Web Code, then select F from the alphabet, and then select William Faulkner.

is ephemeral and doomed—love and honor and pity and pride and compassion and sacrifice. Until he does so, he labors under a curse. He writes not of love but of lust, of defeats in which nobody loses anything of value, of victories without hope and, worst of all, without pity or compassion. His griefs grieve on no universal bones, leaving no scars. He writes not of the heart but of the glands.

Until he relearns these things, he will write as though he stood among and watched the end of man. I decline to accept the end of man. It is easy enough to say that man is immortal simply because he will endure: that when the last ding-dong of doom has clanged and faded from the last worthless rock hanging tideless in the last red and dying evening, that even then there will still be one more sound: that of his puny inexhaustible voice, still talking. I refuse to accept this. I believe that man will not merely endure: he will prevail. He is immortal, not because he alone among creatures has an inexhaustible voice, but because he has a soul, a spirit capable of compassion and sacrifice and endurance. The poet's, the writer's, duty is to write about these things. It is his privilege to help man endure by lifting his heart, by reminding him of the courage and honor and hope and pride and compassion and pity and sacrifice which have been the glory of his past. The poet's voice need not merely be the record of man, it can be one of the props, the pillars to help him endure and prevail.

Critical Reading

1. **Respond:** Do you agree with Faulkner's definition of good literature? If not, how would you revise it?
2. **(a) Recall:** According to Faulkner, why are there no longer problems of the spirit? **(b) Deduce:** What is the physical fear to which he refers?
3. **(a) Recall:** According to Faulkner, what alone is the subject matter of good writing? **(b) Interpret:** Why does he view most modern literature as ephemeral?
4. **(a) Recall:** According to Faulkner, will humanity endure or prevail? **(b) Define:** In what way does Faulkner define the difference between enduring and prevailing?
5. **(a) Recall:** According to Faulkner, what is a writer's "duty"? **(b) Interpret:** What distinction does he draw about "the poet's voice" in his explanation of how humanity can prevail?
6. **(a) Extend:** What events not long before 1950 gave rise to the fear of which Faulkner speaks? **(b) Hypothesize:** If he were alive today, would he say we have lost or retained that fear? Explain.

For: More about William Faulkner
Visit: www.PHSchool.com
Web Code: ere-9519

Apply the Skills

***A Rose for Emily* • Nobel Prize Acceptance Speech**

Literary Analysis

Conflict and Resolution

1. Complete a chart like the one shown to indicate the various **external** and **internal conflicts** that affect Emily's life. **(a)** How is each conflict **resolved,** if at all?

Conflict	Who vs. Who/What?	Resolution
nonpayment of taxes	Emily vs. town	

(b) What common thread runs through the conflicts that Emily faces?

2. What do Emily's external conflicts with "us"—the people of Jefferson, Mississippi—reveal about Emily? **(b)** What do they reveal about the town of Jefferson?

Comparing Literary Works

3. Identify three literary criteria that Faulkner presents in his Nobel Prize acceptance speech.
4. Judge "A Rose for Emily" by the standards Faulkner sets forth in his Nobel Prize acceptance speech. To what degree does it meet his standards for good literature? Explain.
5. What lessons for humanity might the life of Miss Emily Grierson teach? Explain.

Reading Strategy

Clarifying Ambiguities

6. **(a)** Which event in "A Rose for Emily" did you find most **ambiguous? (b)** What interpretation of this event do you think the text supports? Explain.
7. How does the ambiguity add to the literary quality of "A Rose for Emily"?

Extend Understanding

8. **Media Connection:** Consider the films you have seen recently. Then, using the criteria Faulkner sets down in his Nobel Prize acceptance speech, identify one film that meets these criteria and one that does not. Explain your evaluations.

QuickReview

Conflict is a struggle between opposing forces. Conflict can be classified as **internal** or **external.**

Resolution of a conflict occurs when the struggle ends and the outcome is clear.

Ambiguity occurs in a literary work when some element of that work can be interpreted in different ways.

For: Self-test
Visit: www.PHSchool.com
Web Code: era-6512

Answers

1. (a) **Possible answers:** Conflict—nonpayment of taxes, Emily vs. town, Emily does not pay; Conflict—bad smell at Emily's home, townspeople vs. officials, officials try to get rid of smell; Conflict—Emily's behavior with Homer, Emily vs. minister, minister will not go there again; Conflict—Emily wants poison, Emily vs. druggist, Emily gets the poison without saying why she needs it. (b) Most conflicts are resolved with Emily getting her way. Another sample answer can be found on **Literary Analysis Graphic Organizer B,** p. 192 in ***Graphic Organizer Transparencies.***
2. (a) The external conflicts reveal that she is proud and stubborn. (b) The conflicts reveal that townspeople want to know her business and impose their rules on her.
3. According to Faulkner, good literature is about the problems of the human heart in conflict with itself, the truths of the heart, and lifting the hearts of readers.
4. **Possible response:** Students might say that although Faulkner's story is not a shining example of his standards, it does portray a character that has conflicts of the heart; Miss Emily is a troubled recluse who inspires love, honor, pity, and compassion.
5. **Possible response:**Students may say that people need to be treated with compassion and pity and that many people whom they meet are often not what they appear to be.
6. (a) Students may mention Emily's refusing to pay taxes, the strange smell , her purchase of rat poison, or the opening of the mysterious room. (b) Student responses must be supported by details from the text.
7. Ambiguity adds to the literary quality of the story because it makes readers question what is happening and therefore pay closer attention to the story than they might otherwise do.
8. Students should be able to support their responses.

Go Online Assessment Students may use the **Self-test** to prepare for **Selection Test A** or **Selection Test B.**

❶ Vocabulary Lesson

Word Analysis

1. "cannot be removed"; *in-*; negativity
2. "create a favorable feeling or idea"; *in-*; location
3. "unable to see"; *in-*; negativity
4. "examine something in detail"; *in-*; location

Spelling Strategy

1. courageous 3. continuous
2. cautious

Vocabulary Builder

1. b 5. c 8. c
2. c 6. b 9. c
3. a 7. b 10. a
4. a

❷ Grammar and Style Lesson

1. Yoknapatawpha County is a fictional place; Faulkner set much of his writing there.
2. Faulkner claimed that the name *Yoknapatawpha* was based on two Chickasaw words; no one knows if he was serious.
3. Faulkner created a map of the county; he called himself "Sole Owner & Proprietor."
4. *Yoknapatawpha* is easy to say; follow the same rhythm as "Shave and a haircut . . ."
5. The Sartoris family symbolizes the Old South; Faulkner shows its decline.

Writing Application

Students' paragraphs should reflect correct use of semicolons.

Build Language Skills

❶ Vocabulary Lesson

Word Analysis: Latin Prefix *in-*

The Latin prefix *in-* has two basic meanings:

- a location or direction: "in," "into," "within," "on," or "toward," as in *insert, indent,* and *invade*
- a negative: "no," "not," or "without," as in *inescapable, inseparable,* and *inextricable*

When *in-* is used before a word beginning with *p,* the prefix becomes *im-,* as in *imperviousness.*

Write the meaning of the following words, identifying the prefix and noting whether it indicates location or negativity.

1. indelible
2. impress
3. insensible
4. investigate

Spelling Strategy: *-ious, -eous,* and *-uous*

The spelling of adjectives ending in the suffixes *-ious, -eous,* and *-uous* can be confusing because these endings sound similar. Memorize the spellings of the words in which these suffixes are used, or check the spelling in a dictionary. Make new works by adding *-ious, -eous,* or *-uous* to the following words:

1. courage 2. caution 3. continue

Vocabulary Builder: Analogies

For each item, choose the word that best completes the analogy.

1. encroached : withdrew :: expanded : **(a)** inflated **(b)** collapsed **(c)** magnified
2. obliterated : destruction :: worshipped : **(a)** envy **(b)** deserving **(c)** adoration
3. vanquished : strength :: comprehended : **(a)** intelligence **(b)** fear **(c)** mystery
4. vindicated : blame :: cured : **(a)** illness **(b)** medicine **(c)** physician
5. imperviousness : vulnerability :: animosity : **(a)** anger **(b)** ignorance **(c)** fondness
6. divulge : secret :: correct : **(a)** whisper **(b)** error **(c)** eraser
7. circumvent : disaster :: avoid : **(a)** appearance **(b)** mask **(c)** costume
8. thwarted : frustrating :: encouraged : **(a)** fearing **(b)** reassuring **(c)** praising
9. virulent : disease :: nauseating : **(a)** weakness **(b)** discomfort **(c)** odor
10. inextricable : separate :: invisible : **(a)** see **(b)** hide **(c)** fear

❷ Grammar and Style Lesson

Semicolons

Use a **semicolon** to join two closely related independent clauses or to correct a run-on sentence—an error caused by joining two independent clauses with only a comma.

Combine two related independent clauses:

- My family had fun this summer. We drove cross-country.
- My family had fun this summer; we drove cross-country.

Correct a run-on sentence:

- We laughed and talked a lot, I'll never forget it.
- We laughed and talked a lot; I'll never forget it.

Practice Rewrite the following items, using semicolons to join independent clauses or to correct a run-on sentence.

1. Yoknapatawpha County is a fictional place. Faulkner set much of his writing there.
2. Faulkner claimed that the name *Yoknapatawpha* was based on two Chickasaw words, no one knows if he was serious.
3. Faulkner created a map of the county, he called himself "Sole Owner & Proprietor."
4. *Yoknapatawpha* is easy to say, follow the same rhythm as "Shave and a haircut . . ."
5. The Sartoris family symbolizes the Old South. Faulkner shows its decline.

Writing Application Write a paragraph describing a familiar place. Use at least three semicolons.

WG *Prentice Hall Writing and Grammar Connection: Chapter 27, Section 3*

Assessment Practice

(For more practice, see *Standardized Test Preparation Workbook*, p. 52.)

Anticipate Missing Words

Many tests ask students to correctly answer sentence-completion questions. Use the following example to show students how to use context and their own knowledge to guess a word that would complete the following passage.

Because he wrote about his home in Oxford, Mississippi, William Faulkner was for many years dismissed as an unimportant _________ writer.

A experimental **C** eccentric
B regional **D** untalented

After reading the passage, students might think that the word *local* completes the sentence. *B, regional,* is the best choice.

3 Writing Lesson

Timed Writing: Critical Review

In his Nobel Prize acceptance speech, Faulkner notes that the writer's duty is to help people "endure by lifting their hearts, by reminding them of the courage and honor and hope and pride and compassion and pity and sacrifice which have been the glory of their past." Choose a short story and evaluate it in terms of how well the author fulfills Faulkner's ideal. ***(40 minutes)***

Prewriting *(10 minutes)* Choose a story for analysis, and read it closely. Make notes about whether the author has succeeded or failed, according to Faulkner's standards.

Drafting *(20 minutes)* Start your review with a statement of your position. Then, elaborate by providing details and passages from the story.

Model: Drafting to Elaborate on an Idea

In "The Story of an Hour," Kate Chopin fulfills Faulkner's criteria for writing about "truths of the heart." The core of the tale rests in Mrs. Mallard's thoughts and feelings as she greets the prospect of personal freedom: "Free! Body and soul free!" she exults.

Including specific information elaborates on a basic idea.

Revising *(10 minutes)* Reread your review to confirm you have provided solid supporting evidence for your ideas.

WG *Prentice Hall Writing and Grammar Connection: Chapter 14, Section 3*

Extend Your Learning

Listening and Speaking Working with a partner or a small group, act out a **dramatic scene** based on "A Rose for Emily." Before you rehearse the scene, decide who will play each character. Use these techniques to help you memorize your lines:

- Mark a photocopy of the script, highlighting your lines and noting your movements.
- Make sure you understand what each line means and why you are saying it.
- Record your cues—the words immediately before each of your lines. Leave a blank space on the tape between cues to allow time for you to say your line. **[Group Activity]**

Research and Technology Use print and electronic sources such as library and Internet databases to locate critical articles about "A Rose for Emily." Look for writings that reflect different critical approaches or schools of literary criticism, consulting pages R32–R33 for help identifying types of criticism. Choose the writer whose response is closest to yours, and summarize that article in an **oral report** to the class.

For: An additional research activity
Visit: www.PHSchool.com
Web Code: erd-7511

3 Writing Lesson

- Have student groups brainstorm for possible short stories, discussing those each group member has recently found interesting.
- To guide students in writing a critical review, give them the **Support for Writing Lesson** page (***Unit 5 Resources***, p. 193).
- Read through the Writing Lesson steps with students and clarify any confusion.
- To evaluate students' critical reviews, use the Response to Literature rubrics in ***General Resources***, pp. 65–66.

4 Listening and Speaking

- Students might choose an excerpt from the story rather than the whole text so that their scenes will be of manageable length.
- If possible, choose an extra student to play the role of the narrator.
- Encourage students to adjust the tone, volume, and delivery of their words to accurately reflect the character they are portraying.
- The **Support for Extend Your Learning** page (***Unit 5 Resources***, p. 194) provides guided note-taking opportunities to help students complete the Extend Your Learning activities.

Go Online Research Have students type in the Web code for another research activity.

Assessment Resources

The following resources can be used to assess students' knowledge and skills.

Unit 5 Resources
Selection Test A, pp. 196–198
Selection Test B, pp. 199–201

General Resources
Rubrics for Response to Literature, pp. 65–66

Go Online Assessment Students may use the **Self-test** to prepare for **Selection Test A** or **Selection Test B**.

Meeting Your Standards

Students will

1. **analyze and respond to literary elements.**
   - Literary Analysis: Blank Verse
2. **read, comprehend, analyze, and critique poetry.**
   - Reading Strategy: Reading Blank Verse
   - Reading Check questions
   - Apply the Skills questions
   - Assessment Practice (ATE)
3. **develop vocabulary.**
   - Vocabulary Lesson: Latin Root: *-lum-*
4. **understand and apply written and oral language conventions.**
   - Spelling Strategy
   - Grammar and Style Lesson: Uses of Infinitives
5. **develop writing proficiency.**
   - Writing Lesson: Introduction to an Anthology
6. **develop appropriate research strategies.**
   - Extend Your Learning: Interpretive Presentation
7. **understand and apply listening and speaking strategies.**
   - Extend Your Learning: Eulogy

Block Scheduling: Use one 90-minute class period to preteach the skills and have students read the selection. Use a second 90-minute class period to assess students' mastery of skills, extend their learning, and monitor their progress.

Homework Suggestions

Following are possibilities for homework assignments.

- Support pages from *Unit 5 Resources:*
  Literary Analysis
  Reading Strategy
  Vocabulary Builder
  Grammar and Style
- An Extend Your Learning project and the Writing Lesson for this selection group may be completed over several days.

Step-by-Step Teaching Guide	Pacing Guide
PRETEACH	
• Administer Vocabulary and Reading Warm-ups as necessary.	5 min.
• Engage students' interest with the motivation activity.	5 min.
• Read and discuss author and background features. **FT**	10 min.
• Introduce the Literary Analysis Skill: Blank Verse. **FT**	5 min.
• Introduce the Reading Strategy: Reading Blank Verse. **FT**	10 min.
• Prepare students to read by teaching the selection vocabulary. **FT**	
TEACH	
• Informally monitor comprehension while students read independently or in groups. **FT**	30 min.
• Monitor students' comprehension with the Reading Check notes.	as students read
• Reinforce vocabulary with Vocabulary Builder notes.	as students read
• Develop students' understanding of blank verse with the Literary Analysis annotations. **FT**	5 min.
• Develop students' ability to read blank verse with the Reading Strategy annotations. **FT**	5 min.
ASSESS/EXTEND	
• Assess students' comprehension and mastery of the Literary Analysis and Reading Strategy by having them answer the Apply the Skills questions. **FT**	15 min.
• Have students complete the Vocabulary Lesson and the Grammar and Style Lesson. **FT**	15 min.
• Apply students' ability to use transitions to show examples by using the Writing Lesson. **FT**	45 min. or homework
• Apply students' understanding by using one or more of the Extend Your Learning activities.	20–90 min. or homework
• Administer Selection Test A or Selection Test B. **FT**	15 min.

Resources

PRINT
Unit 5 Resources

TRANSPARENCY
Graphic Organizer Transparencies

PRINT
Reader's Notebook [L2]
Reader's Notebook: Adapted Version [L1]
Reader's Notebook: English Learner's Version [EL]
Unit 5 Resources

TECHNOLOGY
Listening to Literature Audio CDs [L2, EL]
Reader's Notebook: Adapted Version Audio CD [L1, L2]

PRINT
Unit 5 Resources

General Resources

TECHNOLOGY
Go Online: Research **[L3]**
Go Online: Self-test **[L3]**
***ExamView*® Test Bank [L3]**

Choosing Resources for Differentiated Instruction

[L1] Special Needs Students
[L2] Below-Level Students
[L3] All Students
[L4] Advanced Students
[EL] English Learners

For Vocabulary and Reading Warm-ups and for Selection Tests, **A** signifies "less challenging" and **B** "more challenging." For Graphic Organizer transparencies, **A** signifies "not filled in" and **B** "filled in."

FT Fast Track Instruction: To move the lesson more quickly, use the strategies and activities identified with **FT**.

Scaffolding for Less Proficient and Advanced Students

The leveled Critical Thinking questions after selections progress in the levels of thinking required to answer them. To address the needs of your different students, you may use the (a) level questions for your less proficient students and the (b) level questions with your on-level and advanced students. The occasional (c) level questions are appropriate for your advanced students.

PRENTICE HALL
TeacherEXPRESS™ Plan · Teach · Assess
Use this complete suite of powerful teaching tools to make lesson planning and testing quicker and easier.

PRENTICE HALL
StudentEXPRESS™ Learn · Study · Succeed
Use the interactive textbook (online and on CD-ROM) to make selections and activities come alive with audio and video support and interactive questions.

Go Online Professional Development
For: Information about Lexiles
Visit: www.PHSchool.com
Web Code: eue-1111

PRETEACH

Motivation

Before class, set up a low wall down the center of the room, out of boxes, desks, chairs, or masking tape. On either side of the "wall" post a sign that says, "Good fences make good neighbors." As students enter, have them sit on either side of the wall so that about half the class is on each side. Ask students to tell how it feels to be separated from each other. Draw attention to the quotation and ask them to respond to it. Then tell students that they will be reading poems by Robert Frost, one of which explores a response to the line they have discussed.

❶ Background

More About the Author

Despite the apparent insularity of Frost's New England experience, the poetry that resulted from his residence there has been overwhelmingly influential. The scholar Earl J. Wilcox declares that, "between 1915 and 1980 more than three hundred articles focusing on Frost and his poetry appeared in popular journals such as *Reader's Digest* and *The Saturday Evening Post* . . . It has become commonplace during the three decades since his death to see almost daily lines quoted or paraphrased from the poet's most accessible poems in advertisements for computer companies ('Take the road less traveled,' reads one blurb), for sporting goods, for musical events, and an array of other business and cultural events. It seems obvious that Frost remains in the American consciousness in a deep and potent dimension."

Build Skills *Poems*

❶ Robert Frost's Poetry

Robert Frost (1874–1963)

In becoming one of America's most loved and respected poets, Robert Frost displayed the same rugged persistence and determination exhibited by the rural New Englanders he depicted in his poems. Although he eventually received four Pulitzer Prizes and read at a presidential inauguration, Frost's success as a poet did not come overnight or easily. Only after years of rejection by book and magazine publishers did he finally achieve the acceptance for which he had worked so hard.

Early Struggles Frost was born in San Francisco, California. His father died when Frost was eleven, and his mother moved the family to the textile city of Lawrence, Massachusetts. After graduating from high school, Frost briefly attended Dartmouth College. Disliking college life, he left school and spent time working as a farmer, mill hand, journalist, and schoolteacher. During his spare time, he wrote poetry and dreamed of someday being able to support himself solely by writing.

The English Years Frost married and spent ten years farming in New Hampshire. In 1912, unable to get his poems published, he sold the farm and moved his family to England. Once there, he hoped to establish himself as a poet. While living in England, Frost befriended a number of well-known poets, including Ezra Pound, and succeeded in publishing two collections of poetry, *A Boy's Will* (1913) and *North of Boston* (1914). When Frost returned to the United States in 1915, he discovered that his success in England had spread across the Atlantic, and he was on the road to fame.

Critical Acclaim Frost went on to publish several more volumes of poetry, for which he received many awards. He also taught at Amherst College, the University of Michigan, Harvard University, and Dartmouth College and lectured and read at dozens of other schools. Recognition of his poetry did not stop him from farming in Vermont and New Hampshire. In 1960, at John F. Kennedy's invitation, Frost became the first poet to read his work at a presidential inauguration.

New England Life Frost's poetry was popular not only with critics and intellectuals, but also among the general public. He used traditional verse forms and conversational language to paint vivid portraits of the New England landscape and lifestyle. Despite their apparent simplicity, however, his poems are filled with profound meanings, compelling readers to delve beneath the surface to fully appreciate his work.

"Ice on a hot stove" Frost was emphatic about his belief that a poem should reveal its meaning in a continuous process. He wrote: "Like a piece of ice on a hot stove the poem must ride on its own melting. A poem may be worked over since it is in being, but may not be worried into being. Its most precious quality will remain its having run itself and carried away the poet with it. Read it a hundred times: it will forever keep its freshness as a petal keeps its fragrance. It can never lose its sense of a meaning that once unfolded by surprise as it went."

Like his poetry, Frost's personality also had multiple levels. In his public appearances, Frost presented himself as a jovial, folksy farmer who just happened to write poetry. In reality, however, Frost was a deep thinker whose darker, complicated personality sometimes mystified those who knew him.

Preview

Connecting to the Literature

Popular psychology holds that we are, at least in part, products of our environments, suggesting that the way we feel and act on a busy city street will be different from our emotions and behavior when surrounded by nature. In these poems, the setting plays an integral role in creating mood and meaning.

2 Literary Analysis

Blank Verse

Many of Frost's poems do not contain rhyme, but their lines have a regular pattern of stressed and unstressed syllables, or *meter.*

- The basic unit of meter is a *foot*—usually one stressed syllable (´) and one or more unstressed syllables (˘) .
- The most common foot is the *iamb*—one unstressed syllable followed by a stressed syllable (˘ ´).
- A line containing five iambs is written in *iambic pentameter.*
- Verse consisting of unrhymed lines of iambic pentameter is called **blank verse.**

As you read Frost's poems, use a chart like the one shown to identify those that are written in blank verse and those that are written in rhyming iambic pentameter.

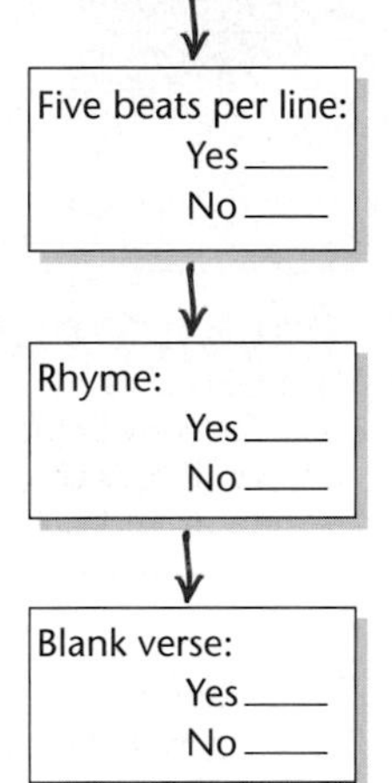

Sample Lines
When I see birches bend to left and right
Across the lines of straighter darker trees.
Five beats per line:
Yes ____
No ____
Rhyme:
Yes ____
No ____
Blank verse:
Yes ____
No ____

Comparing Literary Works

Five of these poems by Frost can be categorized as **pastorals**—poems that deal with rural settings. Traditionally, pastoral poems have presented idealized views of rural life. In Frost's hands, however, rural life is sometimes fraught with ethical lapses, accidents, and even violence. As you read these poems, look closely at how the poet portrays rural life, and examine the differing ways in which the setting contributes to each poem's larger meaning.

3 Reading Strategy

Reading Blank Verse

One way to appreciate **blank verse** is to read it aloud in sentences rather than in poetic lines. Avoid pausing at the end of each line. Instead, follow the punctuation as if you were reading prose: pause briefly after commas, and pause longer after periods. Notice how the flow of blank verse recreates the natural cadences of speech.

Vocabulary Builder

poise (poiz) *n.* balance; stability (p. 883)

rueful (ro͞o′ fəl) *adj.* feeling or showing someone sorrow or pity (p. 889)

luminary (lo͞o′ mə ner′ ē) *adj.* giving off light (p. 892)

2 Literary Analysis

Blank Verse

- Tell students that as they read Robert Frost's poems, they will focus on blank verse—unrhymed iambic pentameter.
- Have volunteers read aloud the bulleted items under Literary Analysis. Then point out the chart on the student page and model its use. Explain that the sample lines are examples of blank verse. Give students a copy of **Literary Analysis Graphic Organizer A,** p. 193 in ***Graphic Organizer Transparencies.*** Urge students to complete a similar chart as they read.
- Discuss the instruction under **Comparing Literary Works.** Urge students to explore why Robert Frost chose to use blank verse in some of his pastoral poems.

3 Reading Strategy

Reading Blank Verse

- Explain that blank verse should be read as sentences, rather than in poetic rhythm.
- Have a volunteer read aloud the Reading Strategy instruction. Model how to read blank verse, using lines 1–9 from "Birches" on the following page.
- Briefly review the pauses indicated by various levels of punctuation, noting, for example, that periods indicate longer pauses than do commas.

Vocabulary Builder

- Pronounce each vocabulary word for students, and read the definitions as a class. Have students identify any words with which they are already familiar.

Differentiated Instruction

Solutions for All Learners

Support for Special Needs Students
Have students use the support pages for these selections in the ***Reader's Notebook: Adapted Version.*** Completing these pages will prepare students to read the selections in the Student Edition.

Support for Less Proficient Readers
Have students use the support pages for these selections in the ***Reader's Notebook.*** After students finish the pages in the *Reader's Notebook*, have them complete the questions and activities in the Student Edition.

Support for English Learners
Have students use the support pages for these selections in the ***Reader's Notebook: English Learner's Version.*** Completing these pages will prepare students to read the selections in the Student Edition.

TEACH

Learning Modalities
Intrapersonal Learners
Although Frost's poetry invokes natural outdoor settings, it also mines the inner landscape of human values and beliefs. Encourage students to compare their own reactions to Frost's ideas. For example, ask students to consider their own views on walls or to respond to "Stopping by Woods on a Snowy Evening."

❶ About the Selection

The speaker, an older man, remembers the childhood pleasure of swinging from birches. He muses about how exploring his environment prepared him for life's greater challenges. Yet, despite preparation, adulthood sometimes feels so burdensome that it helps to recall carefree times as a boy swinging from birches, when his whole life was still ahead of him.

❷ Critical Viewing

Answer: Students should be able to explain their responses with specific details from the photograph.

❶

Birches

Robert Frost

Background Robert Frost spent most of his life in New Hampshire, Vermont, and Massachusetts. Much of his poetry reflects not only the New England landscape, but also its distinctive personalities. Despite Frost's city roots, he was able to gain the acceptance of his country neighbors and to enter their world—a place that was usually closed to outsiders. In so doing, Frost gathered a wealth of material for his poetry.

When I see birches bend to left and right
Across the lines of straighter darker trees,
I like to think some boy's been swinging them.
But swinging doesn't bend them down to stay
As ice storms do. Often you must have seen them
Loaded with ice a sunny winter morning
After a rain. They click upon themselves
As the breeze rises, and turn many-colored
As the stir cracks and crazes their enamel.
Soon the sun's warmth makes them shed crystal shells
Shattering and avalanching on the snow crust—
Such heaps of broken glass to sweep away
You'd think the inner dome of heaven had fallen.
They are dragged to the withered bracken by the load,
And they seem not to break; though once they are bowed

❷ ▲ **Critical Viewing**
Frost's poem is based on his reaction to birch trees. What response does this photograph of birches evoke in you? **[Connect]**

Differentiated Instruction Solutions for All Learners

Accessibility at a Glance

	Out, Out	Birches; Stopping by Woods; Mending Wall; Gift Outright	Acquainted With Night
Language	Simple vocabulary and sentences	Conversational language	Conversational language; repetition
Concept Level	Accessible (death)	Accessible (common life experiences)	Challenging (symbolic representations of loneliness and isolation)
Literary Merit	Noted author	Noted author	Noted author
Lexile	NP	NP	NP
Overall Rating	More accessible	Average	More challenging

So low for long, they never right themselves:
You may see their trunks arching in the woods
Years afterwards, trailing their leaves on the ground
Like girls on hands and knees that throw their hair
Before them over their heads to dry in the sun.
But I was going to say when Truth broke in
With all her matter of fact about the ice storm,
I should prefer to have some boy bend them
As he went out and in to fetch the cows—
Some boy too far from town to learn baseball,
Whose only play was what he found himself,
Summer or winter, and could play alone.
One by one he subdued his father's trees
By riding them down over and over again
Until he took the stiffness out of them,
And not one but hung limp, not one was left
For him to conquer. He learned all there was
To learn about not launching out too soon
And so not carrying the tree away
Clear to the ground. He always kept his poise
To the top branches, climbing carefully

Literary Analysis
Blank Verse and Pastorals What picture of rural life is conveyed in this description of the boy's summer activities?

Vocabulary Builder
poise (poiz) *n.* balance; stability

 **Reading Check**
What does the speaker think of when he sees birches bend to left and right?

Differentiated Instruction
Solutions for All Learners

Strategy for Less Proficient Readers
Poetry should be read many times to help the reader to absorb its meaning and deeper symbolism or significance. Tell students that it is useful, if not essential, to reread lines, stanzas, or whole poems. It can also be helpful to hear the poems several times. Pair students to read aloud to one another.

Strategy for Special Needs Students
To help students build meaning, work in small groups. Read a few lines of each poem aloud, then pause to ask students what they think it means. Guide them in recognizing symbolic meanings, such as his association between climbing a birch and leaving earth and its many demands.

Strategy for Advanced Readers
Robert Frost's poetry, which is full of symbolism, can usually be interpreted on more than one level. Review the meaning of a literary symbol as a person, place, or thing that has meaning in itself and also represents something larger. Encourage students to identify symbols and suggest larger meanings.

3 Literary Analysis
Blank Verse and Pastorals

- Read aloud the bracketed lines for students, emphasizing the blank verse rhythm of the poetry. Invite students to close their eyes and visualize the boy's activities as they listen.
- **Ask** students the Literary Analysis question: What picture of rural life is conveyed in this description of the boy's summer activities?
Possible response: The picture is one of a carefree, if perhaps an isolated summer.

4 Reading Check

Answer: He thinks of times he swung from birches as a boy.

❺ Reading Strategy
Reading Blank Verse

- Invite a volunteer to read aloud lines 43–47 several times until he or she achieves a sentence rhythm. Discuss what students think the lines mean.
  Answer: Adult life is sometimes confusing and hard to navigate.
- **Ask** students the Reading Strategy question: Does reading lines 43–47 as a sentence help to clarify their meaning?
  Answer: Most students will answer yes.

ASSESS
Answers

1. Many students will admit to the occasional need to escape.
2. (a) The ice storm makes the trees bend over. (b) He hopes they are bent because a boy has been playing on them, not because of violent storms. (c) He prefers his version of the facts.
3. (a) The boy is an image of the speaker as a youth. (b) It symbolizes freedom and the experience of learning.
4. (a) He'd like to begin his life over again. (b) He sees the violence in nature and the burdens of daily life, yet still loves Earth and life.
5. **Possible response:** The speaker may be troubled by relationships, responsibilities, or frustrations.

Go Online Author Link For additional information about Robert Frost, have students type in the Web Code, then select F from the alphabet, and then select Robert Frost.

With the same pains you use to fill a cup
Up to the brim, and even above the brim.
Then he flung outward, feet first, with a swish,
Kicking his way down through the air to the ground.
So was I once myself a swinger of birches.
And so I dream of going back to be.
It's when I'm weary of considerations,
And life is too much like a pathless wood

Where your face burns and tickles with the cobwebs
Broken across it, and one eye is weeping
From a twig's having lashed across it open.
I'd like to get away from earth awhile
And then come back to it and begin over.
May no fate willfully misunderstand me
And half grant what I wish and snatch me away
Not to return. Earth's the right place for love:
I don't know where it's likely to go better.
I'd like to go by climbing a birch tree,
And climb black branches up a snow-white trunk
Toward heaven, till the tree could bear no more,
But dipped its top and set me down again.
That would be good both going and coming back.
One could do worse than be a swinger of birches.

Reading Strategy
Reading Blank Verse
Does reading lines 43–47 as a sentence help to clarify its meaning? Explain.

Critical Reading

1. **Respond:** Do you ever yearn to escape from reality for a while? Why or why not?
2. **(a) Recall:** What is the connection between the ice storm and the bent birches? **(b) Recall:** What does the speaker prefer to think when he sees birches "bend to left and right"? **(c) Interpret:** What does the speaker feel about the facts concerning the real causes of the bowed trees?
3. **(a) Recall:** What is the connection between the "swinger of birches" and the speaker? **(b) Interpret:** What does the activity of swinging on birches come to symbolize for the speaker in the poem?
4. **(a) Interpret:** What does the speaker say he'd like to "begin over"? **(b) Analyze:** What aspects of this poem reflect the speaker's conflicting attitudes about life?
5. **Speculate:** What kinds of events, experiences, and feelings in his life might have caused the speaker to make the admission contained in lines 48–49?

For: More about Robert Frost
Visit: www.PHSchool.com
Web Code: ere-9520

Enrichment
Trees as Symbols

Certain trees have come to symbolize a culture or nation. The cedars of Lebanon are included in the nation's flag and have been associated with that country since Biblical times. Unfortunately, few giant cedars remain in Lebanon today; most were cut down in previous centuries to provide wood for building ships and temples. The graceful weeping willow tree, native to China, appears frequently in Chinese art. The American elm has long been part of our nation's heritage. Elms lined many streets in early American villages; to this day most towns and cities still have an Elm Street.

Discuss with students some characteristics that make trees meaningful and enduring symbols. Point out that trees are a visual reference to the cycles of the seasons and therefore to life and death. Note the fact that trees withstand harsh weather and storms and live for many years.

6 Stopping by Woods on a Snowy Evening

Robert Frost

Whose woods these are I think I know.
His house is in the village though;
He will not see me stopping here
To watch his woods fill up with snow.

My little horse must think it queer
To stop without a farmhouse near
Between the woods and frozen lake
The darkest evening of the year.

He gives his harness bells a shake
To ask if there is some mistake.
The only other sound's the sweep
Of easy wind and downy flake.

The woods are lovely, dark and deep,
But I have promises to keep,
And miles to go before I sleep,
And miles to go before I sleep.

7 ▲ Critical Viewing
What elements of this scene differ from the scene the speaker describes? What do the two scenes have in common? **[Compare and Contrast]**

8 Literary Analysis
Blank Verse Is this poem an example of blank verse? Explain.

9 Reading Check
At what exact time of year is this poem set?

Differentiated Instruction
Solutions for All Learners

Background for Less Proficient Readers
To provide background for students as they read this poem, explain that "The darkest evening of the year" refers to the winter solstice. In the Northern Hemisphere this usually falls about December 21st and is the time when either of two points on the ecliptic is at its greatest distance from the celestial equator.

Background for Gifted/Talented Students
Tell students that light is a universal symbol of life, hope, and spiritual connection. Many cultures hold feasts of light during the darkest times of the year, often near the winter solstice. Celebrations may involve candles, lanterns, and wish-making rituals meant to encourage light to return. At the Thai festival of Loy Krathong, people use lotus flowers, banana leaves, or paper to make small boats. They place a lighted candle or piece of burning incense into the boats, which they set sail on a river as they make a wish. If the candle or incense stays lit until the boat sails out of view, the wish is said to come true.

6 About the Selection
The speaker of this poem, on a nighttime journey through a wintry forest, stops to observe the beauty of the scene and to temporarily escape the demands of his life. Although he would like to rest and take in the beauty of the scene, he thinks of the many tasks he must complete. This decision suggests he forestalls death to keep the promises of his life. The poem mines the meaning of life and the things people value most.

7 Critical Viewing
Answer: Students should note that the wooded area in the photo is brightly moonlit, open, and still, rather than dark, windy, and filled with falling snow. Both scenes are peaceful nighttime depictions of snow-covered woods.

8 Literary Analysis
Blank Verse

- Direct students to read the poem silently. Have them count the number of feet in the first two lines and determine the pattern of unstressed and stressed syllables.
- Then, **ask** them the Literary Analysis question: Is this poem an example of blank verse? Explain.
  Answer: Students should note that this poem cannot be an example of blank verse, because it is rhymed.
- Explain to students that poetry using this pattern is an example of iambic tetrameter, as each line has four iambs. Distinguish tetrameter from pentameter, in which each line has five iambs.
- **Ask** students for possible reasons why Frost chose rhymed iambic tetrameter for this poem.
  Possible answer: The quicker rhythm might have suggested the sound of a horse's hooves, evoking the ride through the snowy woods.

9 Reading Check
Answer: It is set "during the darkest evening of the year," the winter solstice.

⑩ About the Selection

The speaker and his neighbor make an annual walk along the fieldstone wall that separates their property to repair the breaks they find. The speaker sees this as an unnecessary act, but the neighbor holds that "Good fences make good neighbors." The speaker suggests that because walls create unnatural separations, natural forces will always work to break them down.

⑪ Literary Analysis
Blank Verse and Pastorals

- Call on a volunteer to read aloud the lines 5–9, stopping after "yelping dogs." Help students **paraphrase** the lines.
  Answer: The speaker has repaired the breaks in the wall created by hunters trying to oust a hiding rabbit.
- **Ask** students the Literary Analysis question: What activities do lines 5–9 suggest are part of rural life?
  Answer: They suggest that rural life includes hunting for rabbits with dogs, and repairing walls.

⑫ Critical Viewing

Answer: Students may respond that weeds have grown right up through the rock wall as if it offered no resistance. Also, some rocks have fallen, due perhaps to frost heaves or animals or people climbing on them.

⑩ Mending Wall

Robert Frost

Something there is that doesn't love a wall,
That sends the frozen-ground-swell under it
And spills the upper boulders in the sun,
And makes gaps even two can pass abreast.
The work of hunters is another thing:
I have come after them and made repair
⑪ Where they have left not one stone on a stone,
But they would have the rabbit out of hiding,
To please the yelping dogs. The gaps I mean,
No one has seen them made or heard them made,
But at spring mending-time we find them there.
I let my neighbor know beyond the hill;
And on a day we meet to walk the line
And set the wall between us once again.
We keep the wall between us as we go.
To each the boulders that have fallen to each.
And some are loaves and some so nearly balls
We have to use a spell to make them balance:
"Stay where you are until our backs are turned!"
We wear our fingers rough with handling them.
Oh, just another kind of outdoor game,
One on a side. It comes to little more:
There where it is we do not need the wall:

Literary Analysis
Blank Verse and Pastorals
What activities do lines 5–9 suggest are part of rural life?

⑫ **▼ Critical Viewing**
What elements of this picture suggest that walls do not belong in the natural world? **[Analyze]**

Enrichment

Surveyor

Boundaries are usually not arbitrary. They have been determined by technical measurements, called surveys, which become part of the legal documentation of land ownership.

Federal surveying of public lands for private purchase began in 1785. Surveyors walked the land, took measurements, recorded their findings, and created fairly accurate maps of most of the privately owned land in America.

Invite interested students to find out more about the process of surveying. For example, what skills or talents are required, which tools are used, and what training and education are needed? Students can investigate what kinds of job opportunities are available. Students might interview a surveyor, or contact a public agency to learn more about the role of surveying to determine or validate property boundaries.

He is all pine and I am apple orchard.
My apple trees will never get across
And eat the cones under his pines, I tell him.
He only says, "Good fences make good neighbors."
Spring is the mischief in me, and I wonder
If I could put a notion in his head:
"*Why* do they make good neighbors? Isn't it
Where there are cows? But here there are no cows.
Before I built a wall I'd ask to know
What I was walling in or walling out,
And to whom I was like to give offense.
Something there is that doesn't love a wall,
That wants it down." I could say "Elves" to him,
But it's not elves exactly, and I'd rather
He said it for himself. I see him there,
Bringing a stone grasped firmly by the top
In each hand, like an old-stone savage armed.
He moves in darkness as it seems to me,
Not of woods only and the shade of trees.
He will not go behind his father's saying,
And he likes having thought of it so well
He says again, "Good fences make good neighbors."

Reading Strategy
Reading Blank Verse
Read lines 28–31 as sentences. In what ways are their meanings clarified?

Critical Reading

1. **Respond:** Which of the poems on pages 885–887 made the strongest impression on you? Explain.
2. **(a) Recall:** In the first stanza of "Stopping by Woods on a Snowy Evening," what two actions does the speaker engage in? **(b) Infer:** What internal conflict do the actions create?
3. **(a) Recall:** What phrase is repeated in the poem's last two lines? **(b) Analyze:** How does this repetition reinforce the theme?
4. **(a) Recall:** In "Mending Wall," what two causes of gaps in walls does the speaker identify? **(b) Speculate:** In what ways are these two causes expressions of a general force the speaker struggles to name? **(c) Interpret:** Why does this force not love a wall?
5. **(a) Recall:** What saying does the neighbor repeat? **(b) Interpret:** What does this saying mean?
6. **(a) Recall:** What image does the speaker use to characterize his neighbor as he repairs the wall? **(b) Interpret:** What is the meaning of the "darkness" in which the man walks?
7. **Make a Judgment:** Are both the neighbor's and the speaker's ideas about the value of walls valid? Explain.

For: More about Robert Frost
Visit: www.PHSchool.com
Web Code: ere-9520

13 Reading Strategy
Reading Blank Verse

- Invite volunteers to take turns reading aloud lines 28–31. Make sure students read the lines as sentences.
- **Ask** students the Reading Strategy question: Read lines 28–31 as sentences. In what ways are their meanings clarified?
Answer: Reading the lines as sentences clarifies the speaker's reasoning: he believes there should be reasons for their existence.

ASSESS
Answers

1. Students should be able to support their responses.
2. (a) He stops in the woods; he watches the snow fall.
(b) He is torn between the desire to enjoy nature's beauty and the awareness that he has commitments to fulfill.
3. (a) The speaker repeats "And miles to go before I sleep."
(b) It creates finality and reinforces the conflict between life's demands and death.
4. (a) The speaker names the freezing and thawing of the earth and the work of hunters. (b) Both reflect natural forces: the seasons and the human thirst for control. (c) It marks territories and claims false ownership.
5. (a) "Good fences make good neighbors." (b) Walls define the boundaries and leave less possibility for conflict.
6. (a) He uses the image of a stone-age "savage." (b) The darkness may be a lack of imagination or thought.
7. **Possible response:** Each view is valid. While walls may be unnecessary in certain circumstances, they may keep the peace between enemies.

Go Online Author Link For additional information about Robert Frost, have students type in the Web Code, then select F from the alphabet, and then select Robert Frost.

Differentiated Instruction
Solutions for All Learners

Strategy for Less Proficient Readers
Brainstorm with the class for reasons not to love a wall, as well as for valid reasons to support putting up walls. You may use the Motivation activity on p. 880 to help students visualize the concept. Encourage students to think metaphorically as well as concretely.

Vocabulary for English Learners
To help these students recognize the poem's meanings about walls, write the saying "Good fences make good neighbors" on the chalkboard. Explain that the phrase is figurative. The fences create the opportunity for good relationships between neighbors, they don't literally make the good neighbors.

Strategy for Advanced Readers
Challenge students to restate the logic the speaker puts forth in lines 28–34 to argue against his neighbor's viewpoint about walls. Invite other students to refute this argument in a debate setting.

14 About the Selection

This shocking, understated poem presents a horrific story of death. Late one ordinary day, a young boy using a power saw to cut wood momentarily loses his concentration and severely cuts his hand. Unfortunately, not only does the boy lose his hand, he loses his life. However, the harsh reality of rural life demands that family members go about their chores because farm life must go on even after a senseless death.

15 Literary Analysis

Blank Verse

- Direct students to read lines 10–12. Then, have a volunteer read aloud the lines, and ask students to describe the meter of the lines.
- Then, **ask** students the Literary Analysis question: Which words or phrases in lines 10–12 capture the rhythms of everyday speech?
  Answer: The phrase "call it a day" sounds in particular like everyday speech, though the entire sentence captures an everyday cadence as well.

➤ **Monitor Progress:** Have students complete the organizer from p. 881 with information about the lines. Students should respond that there is no rhyme scheme and that the poem is written in blank verse.

14

"Out, Out—"

Robert Frost

The buzz saw snarled and rattled in the yard
And made dust and dropped stove-length sticks of wood,
Sweet-scented stuff when the breeze drew across it.
And from there those that lifted eyes could count
Five mountain ranges one behind the other
Under the sunset far into Vermont.
And the saw snarled and rattled, snarled and rattled,
As it ran light, or had to bear a load.
And nothing happened: day was all but done.
Call it a day, I wish they might have said
 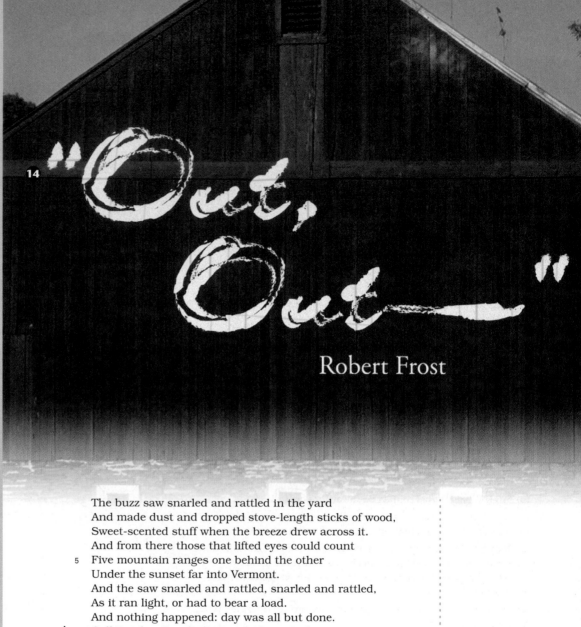
To please the boy by giving him the half hour
That a boy counts so much when saved from work.
His sister stood beside them in her apron
To tell them "Supper." At the word, the saw,
As if to prove saws knew what supper meant,

Literary Analysis
Blank Verse Which words or phrases in lines 10–12 capture the rhythms of everyday speech?

Enrichment

Job Safety

Statistics for fatalities from plane crashes, natural disasters, or epidemic illnesses are widely publicized. However, we rarely hear about the significant number of casualties that occur each year on farms. Nearly one-third of all reported farm accidents involve contact with equipment or machinery.

Brainstorm with the class for different types of farm equipment or machinery that could cause injury, and then for measures workers could take to protect themselves. Have interested students contact the U.S. Labor Department to gather recent statistics on farm-related injuries. Students can present their findings in a chart or graph, and provide a list of safety measures.

Leaped out at the boy's hand, or seemed to leap—
He must have given the hand. However it was,
Neither refused the meeting. But the hand!
The boy's first outcry was a rueful laugh,
As he swung toward them holding up the hand,
Half in appeal, but half as if to keep
The life from spilling. Then the boy saw all—
Since he was old enough to know, big boy
Doing a man's work, though a child at heart—
He saw all spoiled. "Don't let him cut my hand off—
The doctor, when he comes. Don't let him, sister!"
So. But the hand was gone already.
The doctor put him in the dark of ether.[1]
He lay and puffed his lips out with his breath.
And then—the watcher at his pulse took fright.
No one believed. They listened at his heart.
Little—less—nothing!—and that ended it.
No more to build on there. And they, since they
Were not the one dead, turned to their affairs.

1. **ether** (ē′ thər) *n.* chemical compound used as an anesthetic.

Vocabulary Builder
rueful (ro͞o′ fəl) *adj.* feeling or showing someone sorrow or pity

Literary Analysis
Blank Verse and Pastorals
In what ways do lines 19–34 portray a harsh view of rural life?

Critical Reading

1. **Respond:** What do you find more disturbing—the boy's death or the onlookers' reaction to it? Explain.
2. **(a) Recall:** Where is the poem set? **(b) Connect:** In what ways does the description of the setting contrast with the events of the poem?
3. **(a) Recall:** At what time of day does the accident occur? **(b) Support:** What is ironic about the fact that the boy is cut at precisely that moment?
4. **(a) Recall:** What are the boy's first and second responses to the accident? **(b) Interpret:** What does the speaker mean by the expression "the boy saw all" in line 22?
5. **(a) Recall:** In the last line, what is the family's response to the boy's death? **(b) Speculate:** How do you explain this response?
6. **Connect:** The poem's title comes from a scene in William Shakespeare's *Macbeth* in which Macbeth laments the death of his wife with these words: "Out, out, brief candle! / Life's but a walking shadow, a poor player, / That struts and frets his hour upon the stage, / And then is heard no more." What does this quotation reveal about the poem's theme?

For: More about Robert Frost
Visit: www.PHSchool.com
Web Code: ere-9520

16 Literary Analysis
Blank Verse and Pastorals

- After students have read the lines 19–34, **ask** them to describe what has happened.
  Answer: The boy cuts himself badly. The doctor comes to help him, but he dies anyway. His family returns to work.
- Then, **ask** students the Literary Analysis question: In what ways do lines 19–34 portray a harsh view of rural life?
  Answer: They show how easily injury and even death can occur on a farm. They also suggest that the family cannot even take time from the ongoing chores in order to grieve.

ASSESS
Answers

1. Students should support their responses.
2. (a) It is set on a Vermont farm in the summer. (b) The setting is very peaceful, while the events are quite violent.
3. (a) The accident occurs just before supper. (b) The boy was finished with work for the day and—theoretically—out of danger.
4. (a) First he laughs ruefully, then he asks his sister not to let the doctor amputate his hand. (b) **Possible response:** The boy understood the severity of his injury.
5. (a) They go on with their affairs. (b) **Possible response:** They were in shock and unable to process the reality of the death.
6. It conveys the fact that life is short and fragile in nature.

Go Online Author Link For additional information about Robert Frost, have students type in the Web Code, then select F from the alphabet, and then select Robert Frost.

Differentiated Instruction
Solutions for All Learners

Support for Less Proficient Readers
Guide students to recognize the impact Frost creates in lines 14–18 by personifying the saw. Help them understand that Frost describes the saw as though it had a mind and could understand that it was time to be fed, as though the saw "eats" the boy's hand.

Support for English Learners
To help students visualize the tool that plays such a key role in this poem, display pictures of buzz saws or buzz saw blades. Students who have used a buzz saw or have heard one in operation can describe its loud whining sound.

Strategy for Advanced Readers
Ask students to identify words in the opening lines that personify the saw. Discuss how these words, along with those linking dust to death, create an uneasy sense of foreboding. Challenge students to look for other clues in the poem that hint at the tragedy ahead.

17 About the Selections

This poem celebrates the birth of a nation and reminds readers of the human connection to the hope and potential of the landscape. The speaker examines the American colonists' struggle to understand their future on the strange continent. He suggests that—spurred on by a love of the land and high hopes for a future that was as yet unformed—colonists broke free from English rule to form an independent nation.

Drawing on darkness as a time of isolation and loneliness, "Acquainted With the Night" is the city partner of "Stopping by Woods on a Snowy Evening." Here, Frost's speaker views his life as having had times of isolation, loneliness, and despair, but he accepts this as his lot.

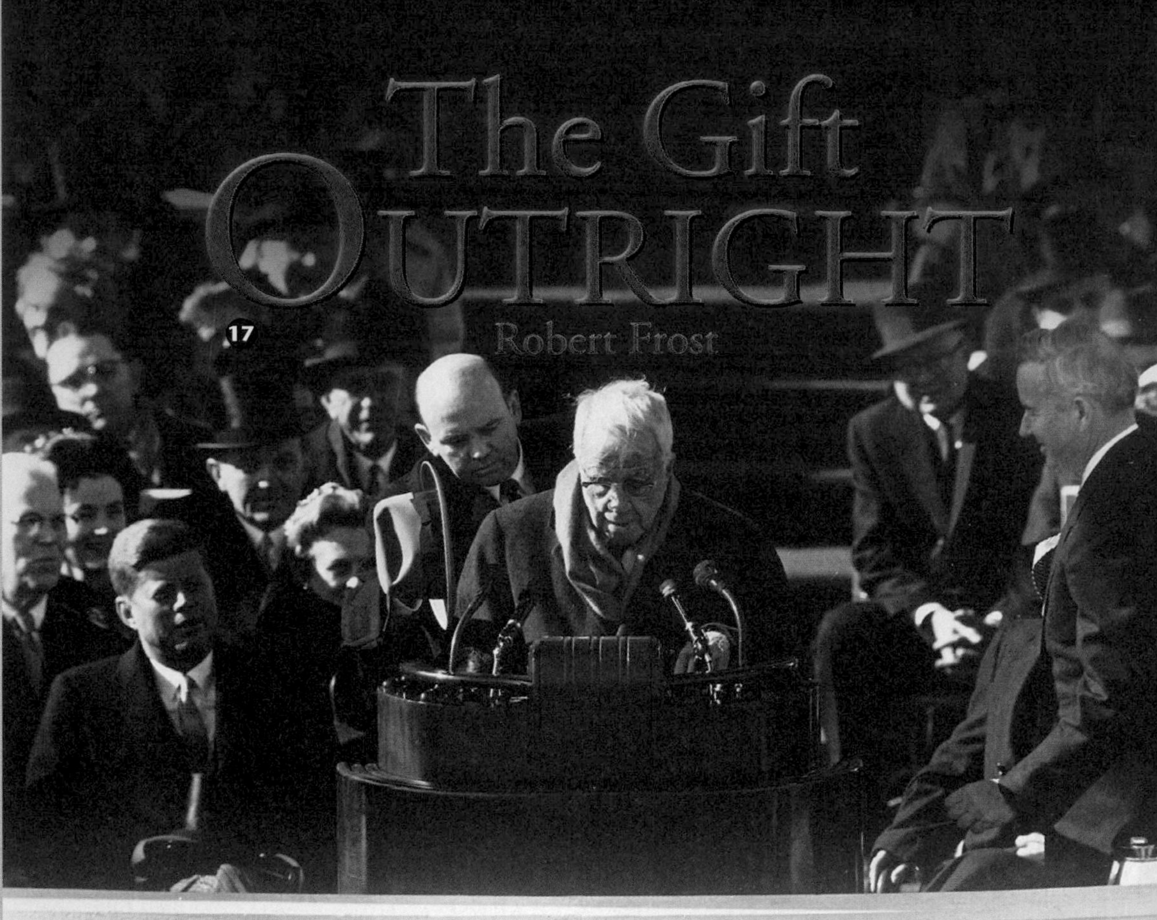

The Gift Outright

Robert Frost

17

Background During the planning stages of John F. Kennedy's presidential inauguration, his staff approached Robert Frost with a request: Would the poet write and recite a poem for the inauguration? Frost declined to write something new but agreed to recite "The Gift Outright." President Kennedy had a second request: Would Frost change the word "would" to "will" in the last line of the poem? The poet agreed. Shortly before the inauguration date, Frost was struck by inspiration and, despite his earlier refusal, drafted a forty-two-line poem, "Dedication," especially for the ceremony. The weather on inauguration day was windy, clear, and sunny. As Frost stood at the podium reading his new poem, the glare of the sun and the whipping wind made it almost impossible for him to see the words on the page. After struggling through the first half of "Dedication," he gave up the effort, and recited "The Gift Outright" from memory.

Differentiated Instruction
Solutions for All Learners

Enrichment for Advanced Readers

Suggest that students read additional works by Robert Frost. Provide students with the titles "North of Boston, "A Boy's Will," and "In the Clearing." You may also wish to use **Authors In Depth,** *The American Experience,* which contains the following selections:

- "The Death of the Hired Man" (poem, p. 143)
- "The Sound of Trees" (poem, p. 148)
- "A Brook in the City" (poem, p. 149)
- "Nothing Gold Can Stay" (poem, p. 150)
- "The Tuft of Flowers" (poem, p. 151)
- "Take Something Like a Star" (poem, p. 152)
- "On 'Choose Something Like a Star' " (nonfiction, p. 153)
- "Fragmentary Blue" (poem, p. 154)
- "Misgiving" (poem, p. 155)
- "For Once, Then, Something" (poem, p. 156)
- from "*Paris Review* Interview with Richard Poirier" (nonfiction, p. 157)

The land was ours before we were the land's.
She was our land more than a hundred years
Before we were her people. She was ours
In Massachusetts, in Virginia,
But we were England's, still colonials,
Possessing what we still were unpossessed by,
Possessed by what we now no more possessed.
Something we were withholding made us weak
Until we found out that it was ourselves
18 We were withholding from our land of living,
And forthwith found salvation in surrender.
Such as we were we gave ourselves outright
(The deed of gift was many deeds of war)
To the land vaguely realizing westward,
But still unstoried, artless, unenhanced,
Such as she was, such as she would become.

Reading Strategy
Reading Blank Verse In what ways does reading this poem aloud as sentences help clarify the poet's meaning?

Critical Reading

1. **Respond:** What does this poem make you feel about America's past and future? Explain.
2. **(a) Recall:** According to the speaker, what was the relationship between the land and the people in colonial America? **(b) Interpret:** What do you think the poet means by the phrase "the land was ours"?
3. **(a) Recall:** According to the speaker, where did the national allegiance of most Americans in colonial America lie? **(b) Interpret:** To where does the speaker say this sense of allegiance shifted?
4. **(a) Recall:** According to the speaker, what were we "withholding" in early America? **(b) Infer:** To what does the speaker suggest earlier generations surrendered in order to become true Americans? **(c) Synthesize:** What does this poem suggest about the meaning of citizenship?
5. **(a) Recall:** In what action did the early Americans find salvation? **(b) Connect:** What is the meaning of the poem's title?
6. **(a) Interpret:** Does the poet suggest there was a price to pay for the "gift outright"? **(b) Analyze:** According to the poet, what was that price, and who paid it?
7. **(a) Generalize:** What picture of American history does this poem create? **(b) Evaluate:** Do you think this poem suggests that American history is a story of continuous progress? Explain.

For: More about Robert Frost
Visit: www.PHSchool.com
Web Code: ere-9520

18 Reading Strategy
Reading Blank Verse

- Have volunteers read lines 5–16 twice, first in poetic fashion and then as sentences. Encourage students to listen carefully for the difference.
- Then, **ask** students the Reading Strategy question: In what ways does reading this poem aloud as sentences help clarify the poet's meaning?
  Answer: It helps listeners organize the long sentences into meaningful ideas.

ASSESS

Answers

1. Students should support their responses.
2. (a) The people took America while still feeling allegiance to England. (b) The speaker means that the colonials lived on it, but did not yet truly possess it.
3. (a) It lay in England. (b) It shifted to the land.
4. (a) We were withholding ourselves. (b) They surrendered to the need to fight and sacrifice for freedom. (c) It suggests that citizenship means a willingness to fight for your country.
5. (a) They found salvation in surrender. (b) It means that Americans should give themselves without reservation.
6. (a) Yes, he does. (b) The deeds of war were the price paid by those who fought for freedom.
7. (a) It creates a picture of heroic sacrifice. (b) Yes, it suggests that the nation had yet to write its history and develop its potential.

Go Online Author Link For additional information about Robert Frost, have students type in the Web Code, then select F from the alphabet, and then select Robert Frost.

Differentiated Instruction
Solutions for All Learners

Strategy for Less Proficient Readers
To help students get meaning from reading blank verse, suggest that they not stop or pause at the end of a line unless there is punctuation. Explain that stopping at the end of each line will produce a choppy effect and will distract from the meaning.

Have students work in groups of two or three to read one of Frost's poems aloud. Ask one person to read aloud, stopping at the end of each complete thought, which usually ends in punctuation. Instruct the others to listen. Then, listeners should briefly state the idea in the lines that were read aloud. Students may exchange roles of reader and listener.

To help students get the rhythm when reading the lines aloud, they can emphasize the stresses in each line as shown here.

Súch as wé were
we gáve oursélves outright

⑲ Literary Analysis
Blank Verse

- Direct students to read the entire poem silently. Then read it aloud together as a class.
- **Ask** students the Literary Analysis question: How do you know that this poem is not an example of blank verse?
  Answer: It contains rhyme.

⑳ Vocabulary Builder
The Latin Word Root *-lum-*

- Draw students' attention to the word *luminary* and its definition. Tell students that the word root *-lum-* derives from the Latin word *lumen,* which means "light."
- Have students **suggest** words that contain this word root, and list them on the chalkboard.
  Possibilities include: *illuminate, luminous, luminescent*
- Have students confirm the meanings of these words in a dictionary.
- Then, ask students to look through the poems, and find places where they might replace an existing word with a word containing the Latin root *-lum-*.

ASSESS
Answers

1. Students should support their responses.
2. (a) He avoids making eye contact. (b) **Possible responses:** He is unwilling to explain his presence.
3. (a) He hears an interrupted cry. (b) He wishes someone would interact with him.
4. (a) The time is neither wrong nor right. (b) A state of lonely acceptance is proclaimed by the final stanza.
5. (a) It might symbolize a feeling of being apart from the human mainstream. (b) The use of repetition draws readers back to the poem's beginning, referring perhaps to the speaker's continual sense of being apart.
6. It uses an everyday setting, a city street, to explore themes such as isolation and loneliness.

Acquainted With the Night
Robert Frost

I have been one acquainted with the night.
I have walked out in rain—and back in rain.
I have outwalked the furthest city light.

I have looked down the saddest city lane.
I have passed by the watchman on his beat
And dropped my eyes, unwilling to explain.

⑲ I have stood still and stopped the sound of feet
When far away an interrupted cry
Came over houses from another street,

But not to call me back or say good-by;
And further still at an unearthly height
One <u>luminary</u> clock against the sky ⑳

Proclaimed the time was neither wrong nor right.
I have been one acquainted with the night.

Literary Analysis
Blank Verse How do you know that this poem is not an example of blank verse?

Vocabulary Builder
luminary (lo͞o′ mə ner′ ē) *adj.* giving off light

Critical Reading

1. **Respond:** How did this poem make you feel? Explain.
2. **(a) Recall:** What is the speaker's reaction when he sees the night watchman? **(b) Interpret:** What is the speaker "unwilling to explain"?
3. **(a) Recall:** What does the speaker hear in the third stanza? **(b) Infer:** From line 10, what does it seem the speaker hoped for?
4. **(a) Recall:** What is proclaimed in the final stanza? **(b) Analyze:** What emotional state is suggested by this proclamation?
5. **(a) Generalize:** What does night symbolize in this poem? **(b) Analyze:** In what ways does Frost's use of repetition heighten the symbolism of the poem?
6. **Evaluate:** How does this poem demonstrate Frost's ability to write poems that seem simple but present deeper meaning?

Go Online
Author Link
For: More about Robert Frost
Visit: www.PHSchool.com
Web Code: ere-9520

Go Online Author Link For additional information about Robert Frost, have students type in the Web Code, then select F from the alphabet, and then select Robert Frost.

Apply the Skills

Robert Frost's Poetry

Literary Analysis

Blank Verse

1. **(a)** Find two instances in "Out, Out—" where Frost deviates from **blank verse.** **(b)** In what ways do these metrical variations emphasize a specific idea or image?
2. **(a)** Identify the two poems presented here that are not written in blank verse. **(b)** What poetic device distinguishes them from the other poems? **(c)** How is the sound of these poems different from those that are written in blank verse?

Comparing Literary Works

3. **(a)** What details of "Out, Out—" and "Mending Wall" present a dark view of rural life? **(b)** What human failings do these poems depict?
4. What ideas about land ownership and boundaries do "Stopping by Woods on a Snowy Evening" and "Mending Wall" express?
5. In "Birches," the speaker expresses ambivalence about life, though he adds "Earth's the right place for love." **(a)** Use a chart like the one shown to determine the nature of his ambivalence. **(b)** Do Frost's other poems express similar ambivalence? Explain.

Reading Strategy

Reading Blank Verse

6. **(a)** Rewrite "The Gift Outright" as five sentences. **(b)** What is the effect of this approach?
7. Read "Out, Out—," pausing at the end of each of the poetic lines. Then, read the poem as a series of sentences. How does each reading affect your understanding of the poem?

Extend Understanding

8. **Psychology Connection:** Pausing to observe nature provides the speaker with a temporary escape from reality in "Stopping by Woods on a Snowy Evening." Why do you think people sometimes need to find this type of temporary escape?

QuickReview

Blank verse is poetry written in unrhymed iambic pentameter.

A **pastoral** is a poem that features rural settings.

Reading blank verse as sentences (rather than as poetic lines) helps you appreciate how blank verse captures the rhythms of everyday speech.

For: Self-test
Visit: www.PHSchool.com
Web Code: era-6513

Go Online Assessment Students may use the **Self-test** to prepare for **Selection Test A** or **Selection Test B.**

Answers

1. (a) While blank verse is frequently not exact, Frost makes clear breaks in lines 27 and 32. (b) The breaks in lines 27 and 32 emphasize the severity of the injury.
2. (a) Neither "Stopping by Woods on a Snowy Evening" nor "Acquainted with the Night" is written in blank verse. (b) The use of rhyme and repetition distinguishes them from the other poems. (c) They have a more regular rhythm than that of the blank verse poems.
3. (a) In "Out, Out" the boy's injury and his family's stoicism in the face of tragedy show a dark side of rural life. In "Mending Wall" the image of hunters and yelping dogs, as well as the closed mind of the neighbor shows a dark side to rural life. (b) "Out, Out" shows indifference; "Mending Wall" shows aggression and self-satisfaction.
4. Both suggest a vision in which land ownership and boundaries are irrelevant.
5. (a) **Negative ideas and images:** heaps of broken glass; withered bracken, bowed [branches], pathless wood; cobwebs broken across it; **Positive ideas and images:** kicking his way through the air, toward heaven, subdued his father's trees, swinger of birches (b) Frost's poems contain hopeful images of people in everyday moments, but also show violent and gloomy moments in life.

   Another sample answer can be found on **Literacy Analysis Graphic Organizer B,** p. 196 in ***Graphic Organizer Transparencies.***
6. (a) Students should write five sentences ending with the periods shown in the poem. (b) Content becomes more accessible.
7. Students may find that reading the poem and pausing at line breaks produces choppiness that interferes with comprehension. Reading blank verse as a series of sentences is a more effective method for retaining meaning.
8. **Possible response:** People find the demands of modern life exhausting. Nature soothes with beauty and the promise of continuity.

EXTEND/ASSESS

Answer

1 Vocabulary Lesson

Word Analysis

1. b
2. a
3. c

Vocabulary Builder

1. luminary
2. poise
3. rueful

Spelling Strategy

1. blissful
2. mournful

2 Grammar and Style Lesson

1. to fetch the cows: adv.
2. to walk the line: adv.
3. to keep, to go: adj.
4. to conquer: adverb
5. to sweep away: adj.

Writing Application

Students' paragraphs should be free of mechanical errors and make proper use of at least three infinitives or infinitive phrases.

WG Writing and Grammar, Ruby Level

Students will find further instruction and practice on uses of infinitives in Chapter 19, Section 2.

Build Language Skills

1 Vocabulary Lesson

Word Analysis: Latin Root *-lum-*

Along with several related English words, including *luminous* and *illuminate,* the word *luminary* (which means "giving off light") is based on the Latin root *-lum-*, meaning "light."

Complete these sentences using the appropriate word from the list below.

a. luminous **b.** illuminate **c.** illumination

1. Is that single bulb enough to __?__ the entire room?
2. The leaves of the linden tree were bathed in __?__ sunlight.
3. The students found __?__ in the wise words of the philosopher.

Vocabulary Builder: Analogies

Complete the following analogies using the words from the vocabulary list on page 881.

1. *Scorching* is to *fire* as __?__ is to *moon.*
2. *Swiftness* is to *runner* as __?__ is to *dancer.*
3. *Joyful* is to *celebrant* as __?__ is to *mourner.*

Spelling Strategy

The one-syllable word *full* is spelled with two *l*'s. However, in words of more than one syllable, such as *rueful* and *stressful,* the suffix *-ful* is spelled with only one *l.* Turn each of the following phrases into a word using a form of the key word and the suffix *-ful.*

1. full of bliss **2.** full of mourning

2 Grammar and Style Lesson

Uses of Infinitives

An **infinitive** is a verb form consisting of the base form of a verb, usually with the word *to.* An **infinitive phrase** consists of an infinitive plus any modifiers or complements, all acting together as a single part of speech. Infinitives and infinitive phrases can be used as adjectives, adverbs, or nouns.

Adverb: But swinging doesn't bend them down *to stay.* (The infinitive acts as an adverb that modifies *bend.*)

Noun: Before I built a wall I'd ask *to know*... (The infinitive acts as a noun serving as the direct object of the verb *ask.*)

Practice For each of the following items, identify the infinitive or infinitive phrase and determine whether it functions as a noun, an adjective, or an adverb.

1. As he went out . . . to fetch the cows— . . .
2. And on a day we meet to walk the line . . .
3. But I have promises to keep, / And miles to go before I sleep . . .
4. Not one was left . . . to conquer.
5. Such heaps of broken glass to sweep away . . .

Writing Application Using at least three infinitives or infinitive phrases, describe an outdoor activity in which you recently participated.

WG Prentice Hall Writing and Grammar Connection: Chapter 19, Section 2

Assessment Practice

Try Words in a Sentence

Use the following item to show students that they can often eliminate choices because they are illogical, the wrong part of speech, or inconsistent with meaning.

Robert Frost moved to England in 1912 hoping to have his poetry accepted, and his strategy worked. He found that his _________ abroad had spread and that he was on the road to _________.

(For more practice, see *Standardized Test Preparation Workbook,* p. 53.)

A failure; ruin
B success; fame
C reputation; despair
D defeat; glory

From the context, students can tell that the correct words should be positive and should have similar meanings. ***B*** is the best choice.

Writing Lesson

Introduction to an Anthology

An anthology is a collection of literature often focused on a specific theme or time period. Anthologies frequently include an introduction that provides an overview of the content and comments on the works. Write an introduction to an anthology that includes poems by Robert Frost.

Prewriting Reread Frost's poems, and make notes about his style and themes. Select the characteristics you will address, and identify poems to cite. Then, sketch out a table of contents.

Drafting Start with a general statement about the poems you chose. Follow by touching on a few key points related to this statement. Focus each paragraph on one key point, supported with passages from the poems.

Revising As you review your work, make sure that you have clearly linked your ideas. Add transitions to introduce examples where necessary.

Model: Revising to Smooth Transitions

Frost's appreciation of beauty is never simple. ~~In~~ For example, in "Stopping by Woods on a Snowy Evening," he reminds us that someone else owns the lovely scene.

Phrases like *for example* provide transitions that improve clarity.

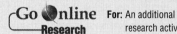

Prentice Hall Writing and Grammar Connection: Chapter 3, Section 2

Extend Your Learning

Listening and Speaking Present a **eulogy** for the boy whose death is described in "Out, Out—." Use these tips to prepare:

- Use clues in the poem to create a sense of the boy's personality.
- Pay tribute to the boy "who did a man's work."
- Address the boy's family in an appropriate manner.

Deliver the eulogy at a "memorial service" in the classroom. **[Group Activity]**

Research and Technology Using a variety of sources, locate recordings of Frost reciting his poems. Select two poems that appeal to you and play the recordings for the class as part of an **interpretive presentation.** Deliver a brief analysis of each poem in which you consider the impressions created by Frost's delivery.

For: An additional research activity
Visit: www.PHSchool.com
Web Code: erd-7512

3 Writing Lesson

- Organize students in groups to discuss characteristics shared by various Frost poems and to brainstorm logical groupings.
- Suggest that students use the **Support for Writing Lesson** page (***Unit 5 Resources,*** p. 210) to plan their introductions.
- Work with students to develop a list of possible transition words.
- Use the Response to Literature Rubrics in ***General Resources,*** pp. 65–66 to evaluate students' analyses.

4 Listening and Speaking

- Suggest that students read some eulogies or share knowledge of eulogies they may have heard. Discuss the key elements of a eulogy.
- Urge students to use their imaginations to extend Frost's description and paint a vivid picture of the boy.
- Encourage students to include appropriate quotes from other works of literature to reflect the boy's circumstances.
- Have students use Peer Assessment: Speech in ***General Resources,*** p. 129.
- The **Support for Extend Your Learning** page (***Unit 5 Resources,*** p. 211) provides guided note-taking opportunities to help students complete the Extend Your Learning activities.

Go Online Research — Have students type in the Web Code for another research activity.

Assessment Resources

The following resources can be used to assess students' knowledge and skills.

Unit 5 Resources
Selection Test A, pp. 213–215
Selection Test B, pp. 216–218

General Resources
Rubrics for Response to Literature, pp. 65–66
Peer Assessment: Speech, p. 129

Go Online Assessment — Students may use the **Self-test** to prepare for **Selection Test A** or **Selection Test B.**

Meeting Your Standards

Students will

1. **analyze and respond to literary elements.**
    - Literary Analysis: Informal Essay
2. **read, comprehend, analyze, and critique nonfiction.**
    - Reading Strategy: Recognizing Hyperbole
    - Reading Check questions
    - Apply the Skills questions
    - Assessment Practice (ATE)
3. **develop vocabulary.**
    - Vocabulary Lesson: Latin Word Root: *-terr-*
4. **understand and apply written and oral language conventions.**
    - Spelling Strategy
    - Grammar and Style Lesson: Commas in Series
5. **develop writing proficiency.**
    - Writing Lesson: Critical Response
6. **develop appropriate research strategies.**
    - Extend Your Learning: Written Report
7. **understand and apply listening and speaking strategies.**
    - Extend Your Learning: Role-Play

Block Scheduling: Use one 90-minute class period to preteach the skills and have students read the selection. Use a second 90-minute class period to assess students' mastery of skills, extend their learning, and monitor their progress.

Homework Suggestions

Following are possibilities for homework assignments.

- Support pages from *Unit 5 Resources:*
    Literary Analysis
    Reading Strategy
    Vocabulary Builder
    Grammar and Style
- An Extend Your Learning project and the Writing Lesson for this selection group may be completed over several days.

Step-by-Step Teaching Guide	Pacing Guide
PRETEACH	
• Administer Vocabulary and Reading Warm-ups as necessary.	5 min.
• Engage students' interest with the motivation activity.	5 min.
• Read and discuss author and background features. **FT**	10 min.
• Introduce the Literary Analysis Skill: Informal Essay. **FT**	5 min.
• Introduce the Reading Strategy: Recognizing Hyperbole. **FT**	10 min.
• Prepare students to read by teaching the selection vocabulary. **FT**	
TEACH	
• Informally monitor comprehension while students read independently or in groups. **FT**	30 min.
• Monitor students' comprehension with the Reading Check notes.	as students read
• Reinforce vocabulary with Vocabulary Builder notes.	as students read
• Develop students' understanding of the informal essay with the Literary Analysis annotations. **FT**	5 min.
• Develop students' ability to recognize hyperbole with the Reading Strategy annotations. **FT**	5 min.
ASSESS/EXTEND	
• Assess students' comprehension and mastery of the Literary Analysis and Reading Strategy by having them answer the Apply the Skills questions. **FT**	15 min.
• Have students complete the Vocabulary Lesson and the Grammar and Style Lesson. **FT**	15 min.
• Apply students' ability to incorporate quotations by using the Writing Lesson. **FT**	45 min. or homework
• Apply students' understanding by using one or more of the Extend Your Learning activities.	20–90 min. or homework
• Administer Selection Test A or Selection Test B. **FT**	15 min.

Resources

PRINT
Unit 5 Resources
Vocabulary Warm-up Word Lists **[L1, L2, EL]** .... p. 219
Vocabulary Warm-up Practice **[L1, L2, EL]** .... p. 220
Reading Warm-up A **[L1, L2, EL]** .... p. 221
Reading Warm-up B **[L1, L2, L3]** .... p. 222

TRANSPARENCY
Graphic Organizer Transparencies
Literary Analysis Graphic Organizer A **[L3]** .... pp. 197, 199
Literary Analysis Graphic Organizer B **[L1, L2, EL]** .... pp. 198, 200

PRINT
Reader's Notebook [L2]
Reader's Notebook: Adapted Version [L1]
Reader's Notebook: English Learner's Version [EL]
Unit 5 Resources
Literary Analysis **[L3]** .... p. 223
Reading Strategy **[L3]** .... p. 224
Vocabulary Builder **[L3]** .... p. 225

TECHNOLOGY
Listening to Literature Audio CDs [L2, EL]

PRINT
Unit 5 Resources
Grammar and Style **[L3]** .... p. 226
Support for Writing Lesson **[L3]** .... p. 227
Support for Extend Your Learning **[L3]** .... p. 228
Enrichment **[L4]** .... p. 229
Selection Test A **[L1, L2, EL]** .... pp. 230–232
Selection Test B **[L3, L4]** .... pp. 233–235
General Resources
Rubrics for Response to Literature **[L3]** .... pp. 65–66
Rubrics for Research: Research Report **[L3]** .... pp. 49–50

TECHNOLOGY
Go Online: Research **[L3]**
Go Online: Self-test **[L3]**
ExamView® **Test Bank [L3]**

Choosing Resources for Differentiated Instruction

[L1] Special Needs Students
[L2] Below-Level Students
[L3] All Students
[L4] Advanced Students
[EL] English Learners

For Vocabulary and Reading Warm-ups and for Selection Tests, **A** signifies "less challenging" and **B** "more challenging." For Graphic Organizer transparencies, **A** signifies "not filled in" and **B** "filled in."

FT Fast Track Instruction: To move the lesson more quickly, use the strategies and activities identified with **FT**.

Scaffolding for Less Proficient and Advanced Students

The leveled Critical Thinking questions after selections progress in the levels of thinking required to answer them. To address the needs of your different students, you may use the (a) level questions for your less proficient students and the (b) level questions with your on-level and advanced students. The occasional (c) level questions are appropriate for your advanced students.

PRENTICE HALL
TeacherEXPRESS™ Plan · Teach · Assess
Use this complete suite of powerful teaching tools to make lesson planning and testing quicker and easier.

PRENTICE HALL
StudentEXPRESS™ Learn · Study · Succeed
Use the interactive textbook (online and on CD-ROM) to make selections and activities come alive with audio and video support and interactive questions.

Benchmark

After students have completed these selections, administer **Benchmark Test 8** (*Unit 5 Resources*, p. 236). If the Benchmark Test reveals that some students need further work, use the **Interpretation Guide** to determine the appropriate reteaching pages in the **Reading Kit** or on **Success Tracker.**

Go Online Professional Development
For: Information about Lexiles
Visit: www.PHSchool.com
Web Code: eue-1111

PRETEACH

Motivation

Bring in a few sample copies of *The New Yorker*—issues from the 1930s and 40s, if these are available from the library—and give students a chance to leaf through them. Explain that both Thurber and White wrote for *The New Yorker* for many years. Thurber also contributed many cartoons to the magazine. Point out *The New Yorker's* distinctive features: its cover illustrations, cartoons and drawings, typeface, and poems. Have students read a paragraph here or a story there to absorb something of the magazine's unique sense of humor. Tell them that they are about to read two essays by writers who helped define the magazine's style.

❶ Background

More About the Authors

Thurber and White met for the first time in 1927. White introduced Thurber to the magazine's editor, Harold Ross, and was thus responsible for Thurber's joining the staff. Thurber's office quickly became conspicuous for the cartoons he drew all over the walls. White urged Thurber to show his drawings to the magazine's art department; when Thurber hesitated, White retrieved some of his friend's cartoons from the trashcan and submitted them for consideration.

Build Skills *Essays*

❶ The Night the Ghost Got In • *from* Here Is New York

James Thurber (1894–1961)

James Thurber's essays, plays, sketches, cartoons, and short stories, such as the well-known "The Secret Life of Walter Mitty," generally evolved from his own experiences. In his humorous autobiographical sketches, Thurber embellishes facts and describes events in an amusing manner. In his short stories, Thurber's characters typically struggle against the unpleasant realities of modern life, often with comical consequences. In his cartoons, Thurber portrays men, women, and a profusion of animals—especially dogs—facing the trials of everyday life.

The New Yorker Thurber was born in Columbus, Ohio. After attending Ohio State University, he joined *The New Yorker* magazine staff in 1927 as managing editor. From there, or so he claimed, he quickly worked his way down to writer. Until the end of his life, Thurber regularly contributed stories, essays, and cartoons to the magazine's pages. He also worked closely with the celebrated writer E. B. White.

Thurber is one of the few humorists whose work is part of the American literary canon. About his comic genius, Thurber was quite modest: "I write humor the way a surgeon operates, because it is a livelihood, because I have a great urge to do it, because many interesting challenges are set up, and because I have the hope it may do some good."

In much of his work, Thurber's humor reveals an edge of unhappiness, especially in his later years when his failing vision caused him much pain and bitterness. Yet he continued to write and draw as well as he could.

Thurber's many published works include *The Owl in the Attic and Other Perplexities* (1931), *The Seal in the Bedroom and Other Predicaments* (1932), *Fables for Our Time* (1940), and the bestselling *My World and Welcome to It* (1942).

E. B. White (1899–1985)

Capturing the interest of adults as well as children, E(lwyn) B(rooks) White established himself as one of the best-loved writers of the twentieth century. His precisely worded essays set a standard against which today's essays can still be judged.

White grew up in Mount Vernon, New York, and studied literature at Cornell University. As an undergraduate, White served as the editor of the *Cornell Daily Sun*. Later, he began a long association with *The New Yorker* magazine. His humorous, topical essays helped to establish *The New Yorker* as one of the nation's most successful general-interest magazines. White produced essays for *The New Yorker* on a weekly basis until 1938. In these essays, many of which are collected in his books *Every Day Is Saturday* (1934) and *Quo Vadimus?* (1939), White used his talents as a humorist to explore numerous social and political themes.

Transcendentalist Influence Influenced by the writings and philosophies of Henry David Thoreau, White believed in simplicity and individualism. These values emerge in nearly everything he wrote. A brilliant observer, he often satirized the complexities of modern life. In fact, in an effort to simplify his own life, in 1939 White bought a farmhouse in Brooklin, Maine, and he and his family began spending most of their time there. White said that the animals in the barn gave him ideas. Some of these ideas took shape in White's work for children.

Two of his children's books—*Stuart Little* (1945) and *Charlotte's Web* (1952)—are among the most beloved children's books of all time. In addition, White's revision of William Strunk, Jr.'s classic style manual, *The Elements of Style*, has become a classic in its own right.

Preview

Connecting to the Literature

Different people are amused by different things. You can discover something about yourself by noting which parts of these essays make you laugh.

2 Literary Analysis

Informal Essay

"The Night the Ghost Got In" and "Here Is New York" are both **informal essays,** brief nonfiction pieces characterized by a relaxed, conversational style and structure. Informal essays usually address a narrow subject, are loosely organized, and include digressions from the main point. Consider this example from "The Night the Ghost Got In":

> Glass tinkled into the bedroom occupied by a retired engraver named Bodwell and his wife. Bodwell had been for some years in rather a bad way and was subject to mild "attacks."

Informal essays give you a glimpse into a writer's personality. As you read these selections, consider what each suggests about its author. Record your findings in a chart like the one shown.

Comparing Literary Works

Although the topics are entirely different, both of these selections are humorous and intended to provoke laughter. Thurber's **humor** revolves around an exaggerated account of a childhood experience, while White's humor satirizes—pokes fun at—New York City. Humor writers must have the ability to perceive the ridiculous, comical, or ludicrous aspects of a personality or situation. Humorists often exaggerate details and embellish facts for comic effect. As you read, compare the elements that make these essays humorous.

3 Reading Strategy

Recognizing Hyperbole

These informal essays draw humor from **hyperbole**, or exaggerations and outrageous overstatements. Examples include bizarre events in Thurber's essay and White's litany of probable disasters. To **recognize hyperbole,** look for details that seem too absurd to be true.

Vocabulary Builder

intuitively (in tōō´ i tiv lē) *adv.* instinctively (p. 899)

blaspheming (blas fēm´ iŋ) *v.* cursing (p. 902)

aspiration (as´ pə rā´ shən) *n.* strong ambition (p. 904)

subterranean (sub´ tə rā´ nē ən) *adj.* underground (p. 904)

claustrophobia (klôs´ trə fō´ bē ə) *n.* fear of being in a confined space (p. 904)

cosmopolitan (käz´ mə päl´ ə tən) *adj.* at ease in all countries or places (p. 904)

Differentiated Instruction

Solutions for All Learners

Support for Special Needs Students
Have students complete the **Preview** and **Build Skills** pages for these selections in the *Reader's Notebook: Adapted Version*. These pages provide a selection summary, an abbreviated presentation of the reading and literary skills, and the graphic organizer on the **Build Skills** page in the student book.

Support for Less Proficient Readers
Have students complete the **Preview** and **Build Skills** pages for these selections in the *Reader's Notebook*. These pages provide a selection summary, an abbreviated presentation of the reading and literary skills, and the graphic organizer on the **Build Skills** page in the student book.

Support for English Learners
Have students complete the **Preview** and **Build Skills** pages for these selections in the *Reader's Notebook: English Learner's Version*. These pages provide a selection summary, an abbreviated presentation of the skills, additional contextual vocabulary, and the graphic organizer on the **Build Skills** page in the student book.

2 Literary Analysis

Informal Essay

- Tell students that essay is from the French verb *essayer* (es • say • YAY), meaning "to try or attempt." An essay is an attempt to share something with the reader—a story, an emotion, or a belief.
- Essayists write for a variety of purposes. An essay can persuade, inform, narrate, or entertain—or it can do some or all of these things at once. As students read these two essays, have them identify each author's purpose in writing.
- Give students a copy of **Literary Analysis Graphic Organizer A,** p. 197 in ***Graphic Organizer Transparencies.*** Tell them to use it to gather information about the writer's style and purpose.

3 Reading Strategy

Recognizing Hyperbole

- Explain that the word *hyperbole* derives from two Greek words literally meaning "to overthrow." In Greek as in English, the compound word *hyperbole* means "excess" or "exaggeration." Compare a verbal exaggeration to an overthrown foul shot in basketball—a shot that goes too far or too high to catch the hoop.
- **Ask** students why a writer would want to use hyperbole. Write the following quotation from "The Notorious Jumping Frog of Calaveras County" (Unit 4) on the chalkboard: *Thish-yere Smiley had a mare—the boys called her the fifteen-minute nag, but that was only in fun, you know, because of course she was faster than that.*

  Point out that "the boys" exaggerate the mare's slowness "for fun."
  Answer: The usual purpose of hyperbole is to add humor to a text.
- As students read the two essays, have them look for examples of hyperbole and think about what this element contributes to each essay.

Vocabulary Builder

- Pronounce each vocabulary word for students, and then read the definitions as a class. Have students identify any words with which they are already familiar.

TEACH

Learning Modalities
Musical/Rhythmic Learners Point out to students that "The Night the Ghost Got In" relies heavily on sound—the footsteps in the dining-room, the smash of the neighbor's window, the New York accents of the policemen, and so on. Have students pay close attention to Thurber's uses of sound and discuss what they contribute to the essay and how they help to draw readers into the story. As an extension, students can apply the same approach to White's essay.

❶ About the Selection

One night, the narrator steps out of the bathtub and is startled to hear footsteps in the dining-room below. He awakens his brother, who also hears the sounds. In turn, the brothers awaken their mother, who breaks a window in the house next door to attract attention and get help. When the police come, they make matters worse by damaging the front doors and arousing the wrath of the narrator's crazy grandfather.

❷ Critical Viewing

Answer: Students may find the facial expressions—the friendly-looking ghost, and the frightened person—comical.

❸ Literary Analysis
Informal Essay

- Have students read the first two paragraphs of the essay. **Ask** them: Why did Thurber write this essay? Which details in the first paragraph lead you to your response?
  Answer: He wants to tell a story; the details include highlights of the plot and a quick preview of the characters. Thurber wants to entertain: the details are funny.
- Then, **ask** the Literary Analysis question: What characteristics of the informal essay does this passage include?
  Answer: The tone is conversational and friendly, like someone sharing a funny story at the dinner table.

❶ The Night the Ghost Got In

James Thurber

The ghost that got into our house on the night of November 17, 1915, raised such a hullabaloo of misunderstandings that I am sorry I didn't just let it keep on walking, and go to bed. Its advent caused my mother to throw a shoe through a window of the house next door and ended up with my grandfather shooting a patrolman. I am sorry, therefore, as I have said, that I ever paid any attention to the footsteps.

❸ They began about a quarter past one o'clock in the morning, a rhythmic, quick-cadenced walking around the dining-room table. My mother was asleep in one room upstairs, my brother Herman in another; grandfather was in the attic, in the old walnut bed which, as you will remember, once fell on my father. I had just stepped out of the bathtub and was busily rubbing myself with a towel when I heard the steps. They were the steps of a man walking rapidly around the dining-room table downstairs. The light from the bathroom shone down the back steps, which dropped directly into the dining-room; I could see the faint shine of plates on the plate-rail; I couldn't see the table. The steps kept going round and round the table; at regular intervals a board creaked, when it was trod upon. I supposed at first that it was my father or my brother Roy, who had gone to Indianapolis but were expected home at any time. I suspected next that it was a burglar. It did not enter my mind until later that it was a ghost.

After the walking had gone on for perhaps three minutes, I tiptoed to Herman's room. "Psst!" I hissed, in the dark, shaking him. "Awp," he said, in the low, hopeless tone of a despondent beagle—he always half suspected that something would "get him" in the night. I told him who I was. "There's something downstairs!" I said. He got up and followed me to the head of the back staircase. We listened together. There was no sound. The steps had ceased. Herman looked at me in some alarm: I had only the bath towel around my waist. He wanted to go back to bed, but I gripped his arm. "There's something down

❷ ▲ **Critical Viewing** The humor in Thurber's drawing echoes the humor in his story. What makes this sketch funny? **[Analyze]**

Literary Analysis
Informal Essay What characteristics of the informal essay does this passage include?

Differentiated Instruction Solutions for All Learners

Accessibility at a Glance

	Ghost Got In	New York
Context	Urban humor	New York City
Language	Complex sentences; dialogue	Informal, descriptive sentences
Concept Level	Accessible (comical situations)	Accessible (description of city neighborhoods)
Literary Merit	Noted author; humorous	Noted author
Lexile	770L	1350L
Overall Rating	Average	More accessible

there!" I said. Instantly the steps began again, circled the dining-room table like a man running, and started up the stairs toward us, heavily, two at a time. The light still shone palely down the stairs; we saw nothing coming; we only heard the steps. Herman rushed to his room and slammed the door. I slammed shut the door at the stairs top and held my knee against it. After a long minute, I slowly opened it again. There was nothing there. There was no sound. None of us ever heard the ghost again.

The slamming of the doors had aroused mother: she peered out of her room. "What on earth are you boys doing?" she demanded. Herman ventured out of his room. "Nothing," he said, gruffly, but he was, in color, a light green. "What was all that running around downstairs?" said mother. So she had heard the steps, too! We just looked at her. "Burglars!" she shouted intuitively. I tried to quiet her by starting lightly downstairs.

"Come on, Herman," I said.

"I'll stay with Mother," he said. "She's all excited."

I stepped back onto the landing.

"Don't either of you go a step," said mother. "We'll call the police." Since the phone was downstairs, I didn't see how we were going to call the police—nor did I want the police—but mother made one of her quick, incomparable decisions. She flung up a window of her bedroom which faced the bedroom windows of the house of a neighbor, picked up a shoe, and whammed it through a pane of glass across the narrow space that separated the two houses. Glass tinkled into the bedroom occupied by a retired engraver named Bodwell and his wife. Bodwell had been for some years in rather a bad way and was subject to mild "attacks." Most everybody we knew or lived near had *some* kind of attacks.

It was now about two o'clock of a moonless night; clouds hung black and low. Bodwell was at the window in a minute, shouting, frothing a little, shaking his fist. "We'll sell the house and go back to Peoria," we could hear Mrs. Bodwell saying. It was some time before mother "got through" to Bodwell. "Burglars!" she shouted. "Burglars in the house!" Herman and I hadn't dared to tell her that it was not burglars but ghosts, for she was even more afraid of ghosts than of burglars. Bodwell at first thought that she meant there were burglars in his house, but finally he quieted down and called the police for us over an extension phone by his bed. After he had disappeared from the window, mother suddenly made as if to throw another shoe, not because there was further need of it, but, as she later explained, because the thrill of heaving a shoe through a window glass had enormously taken her fancy. I prevented her.

The police were on hand in a commendably short time: a Ford sedan full of them, two on motorcycles, and a patrol wagon with about eight in it and a few reporters. They began banging at our front door. Flashlights shot streaks of gleam up and down the walls, across the yard, down the walk between our house and Bodwell's. "Open up!"

Vocabulary Builder
intuitively (in too͞o′ i tiv lē) *adv.* instinctively

Literary Analysis
Informal Essay and Humor What does the humorous digression about the thrill of heaving a shoe reveal about the mother?

5 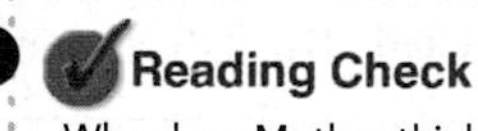

Reading Check
Who does Mother think the intruders are?

4 Literary Analysis
Informal Essay and Humor

- As students read the bracketed passage, have them **consider** why the mother's decision to break the neighbor's window is funny.
  Answer: The mother's decision to break the window is funny because it is so unlikely. Most people would yell for help, dress quickly, and sneak out of the house, or go boldly downstairs. The mother's response is wildly original.
- **Ask** the Literary Analysis question: What does the humorous digression about the thrill of heaving a shoe reveal about the mother?
  Answer: It shows that she is a highly unorthodox person. In spite of her fear of the burglar, she enjoyed the feeling of heaving the shoe.

5 Reading Check
Answer: She thinks the intruders are burglars.

Differentiated Instruction
Solutions for All Learners

Strategy for Special Needs Students
Have students listen to the two essays on the **Listening to Literature Audio CDs,** following along in their textbooks if they wish. While listening, students will naturally laugh at humorous passages. As they do, have them keep a tally of laughs and note what makes each selection funny. Following the readings, invite students to vote on which essay they found funnier. Then, have them explain the reasons for their votes.

Enrichment for Gifted/Talented Students
Invite students to work together to adapt "The Night the Ghost Got In" as a radio play. To translate the essay from prose to drama, students will need to make some changes. For example, the script will need a narrator, who will require guidance on vocal inflection. In addition, the play may call for fewer policemen. Remind students that the essay relies on sound effects; recreating the footsteps, sirens, broken window, and other aural elements will challenge students' ingenuity.

6 Humanities

James Thurber was a cartoonist and illustrator as well as a writer. His pen-and-ink cartoons and drawings frequently appeared in *The New Yorker* as well as in his books.

By the time he was in his mid-50s, Thurber was almost totally blind. He continued drawing, using special tools such as a magnifier, an illuminated board, and a mechanized pencil that produced a glowing neon line. His deteriorating eyesight may explain the lack of detail in his simple drawings. Use these questions for discussion:

1. Which character from the essay appears in the cartoon? How do you know?
   Answer: The cartoon depicts the scene described on the previous page in which the mother throws a shoe at the house next door.
2. In what ways is the cartoon of the policemen on the following page an example of hyperbole?
   Answer: Their puzzlement is exaggerated. There are too many of them looking for clues in a small space.

7 Critical Viewing

Answer: The picture shows just how incongruous and hilarious the mother's actions are.

8 Reading Strategy
Recognizing Hyperbole

- **Ask** students the Reading Strategy question: What details in the paragraph beginning "Downstairs" are examples of hyperbole?
  Answer: Examples of hyperbole are that too many police show up, and they ransack the floor, tearing clothes off hooks and making a mess of the house.
- Then, have students discuss the effect of the hyperbole.
  Answer: The hyperbole adds to the story's humor. It creates a mood like that of a slapstick comedy and creates sympathy for the family.

➤ **Monitor Progress: Ask** students to consider how the policemen's speech is an example of hyperbole.
Answer: The policemen's speech exaggerates a certain street-smart, rough-and-tumble accent.

cried a hoarse voice. "We're men from Headquarters!" I wanted to go down and let them in, since there they were, but mother wouldn't hear of it. "You haven't a stitch on," she pointed out. "You'd catch your death." I wound the towel around me again. Finally the cops put their shoulders to our big heavy front door with its thick beveled glass and broke it in: I could hear a rending of wood and a splash of glass on the floor of the hall. Their lights played all over the living-room and crisscrossed nervously in the dining-room, stabbed into hallways, shot up the front stairs and finally up the back. They caught me standing in my towel at the top. A heavy policeman bounded up the steps. "Who are you?" he demanded. "I live here," I said. "Well, whattsa matta, ya hot?" he asked. I was, as a matter of fact, cold; I went to my room and pulled on some trousers. On my way out, a cop stuck a gun into my ribs. "Whatta you doin' here?" he demanded. "I live here," I said.

6

The Night the Ghost Got In, Copyright 1933, 1961, James Thurber, From *My Life and Hard Times*, published by Harper & Row.

The officer in charge reported to mother. "No sign of nobody, lady," he said. "Musta got away—whatt'd he look like?" "There were two or three of them," mother said, "whooping and carrying on and slamming doors." "Funny," said the cop. "All ya windows and doors was locked on the inside tight as a tick."

8 Downstairs, we could hear the tromping of the other police. Police were all over the place; doors were yanked open, drawers were yanked open, windows were shot up and pulled down, furniture fell with dull thumps. A half-dozen policemen emerged out of the darkness of the front hallway upstairs. They began to ransack the floor: pulled beds away from walls, tore clothes off hooks in the closets, pulled suitcases and boxes off shelves. One of them found an old zither[1] that Roy had won in a pool tournament. "Looky here, Joe," he said, strumming it with a big paw. The cop named Joe took it and turned it over. "What is it?" he asked me. "It's an old zither our guinea pig used to sleep on," I said. It was true that a pet guinea pig we once had would never sleep anywhere except on the zither, but I should never have said so. Joe and the other cop looked at me a long time. They put the zither back on a shelf.

"No sign o' nuthin'," said the cop who had first spoken to mother. "This guy," he explained to the others, jerking a thumb at me, "was nekkid. The lady seems historical." They all nodded, but said nothing;

1. **zither** (zith′ ər) *n.* musical instrument with thirty to forty strings stretched across a flat soundboard and played with the fingers.

7 ▲ **Critical Viewing**
Thurber created this cartoon to accompany "The Night the Ghost Got In." Describe the way in which the illustration adds to the humorous effect of the essay. **[Assess]**

Reading Strategy
Recognizing Hyperbole
What details in the paragraph beginning "Downstairs" are examples of hyperbole?

Differentiated Instruction
Solutions for All Learners

Enrichment for Gifted/Talented Students
Thurber's cartoons inspired Professor Peter Schickele, better known as P.D.Q. Bach, to compose a piece of music entitled *Thurber's Dogs.* Invite students to locate a collection of Thurber's dog cartoons and a recording of the Schickele composition. Students can then browse through the cartoons, listen to the music, and discuss their opinions of Schickele's response to the drawings.

just looked at me. In the small silence we all heard a creaking in the attic. Grandfather was turning over in bed. "What's 'at?" snapped Joe. Five or six cops sprang for the attic door before I could intervene or explain. I realized that it would be bad if they burst in on grandfather unannounced, or even announced. He was going through a phase in which he believed that General Meade's men, under steady hammering by Stonewall Jackson, were beginning to retreat and even desert.

When I got to the attic, things were pretty confused. Grandfather had evidently jumped to the conclusion that the police were deserters from Meade's army, trying to hide away in his attic. He bounded out of bed wearing a long flannel nightgown over long woolen underwear, a nightcap, and a leather jacket around his chest. The cops must have realized at once that the indignant white-haired old man belonged in the house, but they had no chance to say so. "Back, ye cowardly dogs!" roared grandfather. "Back t' the lines, ye yellow, lily-livered cattle!" With that, he fetched the officer who found the zither a flat-handed smack alongside his head that sent him sprawling. The others beat a retreat, but not fast enough; grandfather grabbed Zither's gun from its holster and let fly. The report seemed to crack the rafters; smoke filled the attic. A cop cursed and shot his hand to his shoulder. Somehow, we all finally got downstairs again and locked the door against the old gentleman. He fired once or twice more in the darkness and then went back to bed. "That was grandfather," I explained to Joe, out of breath. "He thinks you're deserters." "I'll say he does," said Joe.

Literary Analysis
Informal Essay Which words in this paragraph reflect a relaxed, conversational style?

10  **Reading Check**
What does grandfather think is happening?

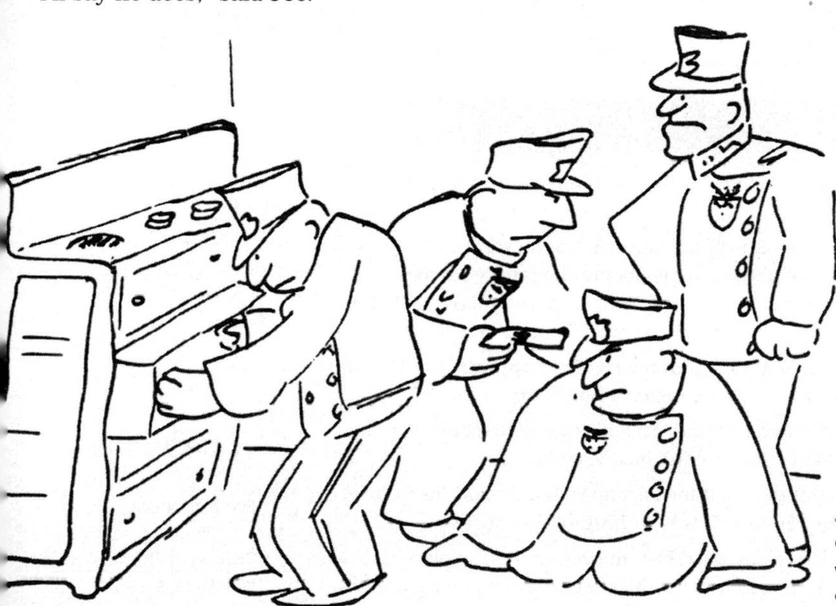

The Night the Ghost Got In, Copyright 1933, 1961, James Thurber, From *My Life and Hard Times*, published by Harper & Row.

◀ **Critical Viewing** 11
Compare this illustration with Thurber's description of the police investigation. What makes each funny? **[Evaluate]**

9 Literary Analysis
Informal Essay

- **Ask** students the Literary Analysis question: Which words in this paragraph reflect a relaxed, conversational style?
  Answer: Examples of conversational diction include "pretty confused," "a smack alongside his head," and "let fly."
- Then, have students **explain** how the informality adds to the humor of the passage.
  Answer: The informality of the language is a funny contrast to the grandfather's rage and belligerence.

▶ **Monitor Progress: Ask** students how the characterization of the grandfather adds to the essay's humor.
Answer: His rage is funny because it is irrational and because the policemen are harmless.

10 Reading Check

Answer: Grandfather thinks the policemen are deserters from the Union army.

11 Critical Viewing

Answer: The cartoon is funny because the policemen are too large and square for the small space, because they are looking all over the place, and because they all appear to be so puzzled. The verbal description is funny because of their accents and their incompetence.

Differentiated Instruction
Solutions for All Learners

Strategy for English Learners

Explain that the policemen speak in heavily accented English that approaches a dialect—for example, "historical" on the previous page is a mispronunciation of "hysterical" and "nekked" means "naked." Likewise, the grandfather's imitation of nineteenth-century military diction is an example of comically exaggerated speech. Have students work with a partner who is fluent in American English to work out these passages of exaggerated speech and to analyze the ways in which they add to the comedy of the essay.

Enrichment for Advanced Readers

Invite students to form a small reading group in which to share and discuss some of Thurber's short stories. Students might consider "The Unicorn in the Garden," "The Secret Life of Walter Mitty," or a selection from *Fables for Our Time,* such as "The Princess and the Tin Box." Have students discuss Thurber's use of hyperbole or other humorous techniques; the balance between fantasy and reality in his stories; and characters and themes that thread throughout his body of work.

ASSESS

Answers

1. Students should support their responses with details from the text.
2. (a) The narrator hears footsteps in the dining-room. (b) The narrator wants to uncover the cause of the noise. Herman wants to hide. The mother wants to call the police. (c) He seems to be the only calm, sane person in the house.
3. (a) The mother breaks the neighbor's window and asks him to call the police. (b) The neighbor's misunderstanding—first thinking that the mother broke their window for fun (which is true, in part), then thinking that they have burglars in their house—is another step in a series of miscommunications and missteps that combine to create humor.
4. (a) He attacks them, grabs one of their guns, and shoots.
   (b) He thinks the policmen are deserters from the Union army.
5. They might have been more frightened.
6. Yes; nothing in the essay suggests that it takes place at a particular time in history or that the situational comedy offers less than a universal appeal.

Go Online Author Link For additional information about James Thurber, have students type in the Web Code, then select T from the alphabet, and then select James Thurber.

The cops were reluctant to leave without getting their hands on somebody besides grandfather; the night had been distinctly a defeat for them. Furthermore, they obviously didn't like the "layout"; something looked—and I can see their viewpoint—phony. They began to poke into things again. A reporter, a thin-faced, wispy man, came up to me. I had put on one of mother's blouses, not being able to find anything else. The reporter looked at me with mingled suspicion and interest. "Just what the heck is the real lowdown here, Bud?" he asked. I decided to be frank with him. "We had ghosts," I said. He gazed at me a long time as if I were a slot machine into which he had, without results, dropped a nickel. Then he walked away. The cops followed him, the one grandfather shot holding his now-bandaged arm, cursing and blaspheming. "I'm gonna get my gun back from that old bird," said the zither-cop. "Yeh," said Joe. "You—and who else?" I told them I would bring it to the station house the next day.

Vocabulary Builder
blaspheming (blas fēm′ iŋ) *v.* cursing

"What was the matter with that one policeman?" mother asked, after they had gone. "Grandfather shot him," I said. "What for?" she demanded. I told her he was a deserter. "Of all things!" said mother. "He was such a nice-looking young man."

Grandfather was fresh as a daisy and full of jokes at breakfast next morning. We thought at first he had forgotten all about what had happened, but he hadn't. Over his third cup of coffee, he glared at Herman and me. "What was the idee of all them cops tarry-hootin' round the house last night?" he demanded. He had us there.

Critical Reading

1. **Respond:** What do you consider the most humorous point in the essay? Why?
2. **(a) Recall:** What event sets off the family's reactions?
   (b) Classify: Describe how each member of the family reacts.
   (c) Distinguish: In what way does Thurber's portrayal of himself in the situation differ from his portrayal of the other characters?
3. **(a) Recall:** Why are the police summoned? **(b) Support:** How does this lack of communication contribute to the humor of the essay?
4. **(a) Recall:** What does grandfather do when the police burst into his room? **(b) Infer:** Why do you think he does this?
5. **Speculate:** In what way might the narrator's family and the police have reacted if they thought it was a ghost in the house?
6. **Take a Position:** This essay describes an event that took place in 1915. Do you think modern readers can still enjoy it? Why or why not?

For: More about James Thurber
Visit: www.PHSchool.com
Web Code: ere-9521

12 *from* HERE IS NEW YORK

E. B. White

Background America has a strong tradition of humor writing. Much of that humor builds on self-ridicule, with people poking fun at their own missteps and failures. Americans seem especially willing to laugh at themselves when they fail to achieve all that they attempt. Although he loves New York City and its energy and excitement, E. B. White still finds plenty to satirize in "Here Is New York."

New York is nothing like Paris; it is nothing like London; and it is not Spokane multiplied by sixty, or Detroit multiplied by four. It is by all odds the loftiest of cities. It even managed to reach the highest point in the sky at the lowest moment of the Depression. The Empire State Building shot 1250 feet into the air when it was madness to put out as much as six inches of new growth. (The building has a mooring mast that no dirigible[1] has ever tied to; it employs a man to flush toilets in slack times; it has been hit by an airplane in a fog, struck countless times by lightning, and been jumped off of by so many unhappy people that pedestrians instinctively quicken step when passing Fifth Avenue and Thirty-fourth Street.)

Manhattan has been compelled to expand skyward because of the absence of any other direction in which to grow. This,

1. **dirigible** (dir′ə jə bəl) *n.* large, long airship.

14 ▶ **Critical Viewing** What objects in this photograph confirm White's attitude about New York? Explain. **[Connect]**

12 About the Selection

E.B. White describes the city of New York, with its soaring buildings, its huge crowds, and its unique inconveniences. He notes that though the city can seem inhospitable and unmanageable to tourists, it is really a huge collection of tiny neighborhoods just like those they left behind.

13 Literary Analysis

Informal Essay

- As students begin to read, **ask** them why they think White wrote this essay. Have students identify details in the opening paragraph to support their answers.
  Answer: White wanted to describe New York. Each detail in the opening paragraph advances his view of the city as a place of extremes. He wants to share his feelings about the city with readers.
- **Ask:** Which aspects of this paragraph suggest that this is an informal essay?
  Answer: Casual language like "shot up into the air,"mention of a man employed to flush toilets, and a humorous reference to pedestrians quickening their step when they pass the Empire State Building add to the essay's sense of informality.

14 Critical Viewing

Answer: White describes New York as the "loftiest" of cities. All the buildings in the photographs, including the Empire State Building shown at far left, are tall.

Differentiated Instruction Solutions for All Learners

Enrichment for Advanced Readers

Point out that New York is the main character in this essay. Have students discuss the ways in which White makes the city a character. Ask them to look for examples of personification and to write brief essays analyzing the city's personality. Finally, have students compare and contrast White's characterization of the city with Thurber's characterizations of the mother, grandfather, and policemen in "The Night the Ghost Got In." Which writer creates more vivid characters? Which literary techniques does each writer use to make characters come alive? Make sure students cite specific details to defend their answers.

⓯ Critical Thinking
Analyzing

- **Ask** students: How does White create a sense of the city as a living, breathing personality, like a character in a story?
  Answer: White anthropomorphizes the city. He describes the challenges it has weathered and uses vivid verbs that suggest the city is responsible for its own success.
- Then, have students **list** words that describe the character of New York City as White depicts it.
  Possible responses: Students might describe the city as brave, enduring, or strong.

⓰ Vocabulary Builder

- Draw students' attention to White's use of the word *subterranean,* and read its definition. Tell them that the word combines the Latin prefix *sub-,* meaning "under," with the root *-terr-,* which means "ground."
- Invite students to **brainstorm** for other words that share the root *-terr-*. Write students' suggestions on the chalkboard. **Possible responses:** terrestrial, terrain, terra-cotta
- Then, have students use each of these *-terr-* words in a sentence describing a city.

⓱ Reading Strategy
Recognizing Hyperbole

- Have a volunteer read aloud the bracketed paragraph. Then, **ask** students how White creates humor in this passage.
  Answer: White uses vivid verbs that help the reader "see" what might have happened to the city. Because the reader knows that the city was not destroyed, he or she enjoys the exaggerated depictions of its demise.
- Then, **ask** the Reading Strategy question: Which details in the passage beginning "Long ago" are examples of hyperbole?
  Answer: White exaggerates the damage that any one of a list of evils might have done to New York.

more than any other thing, is responsible for its physical majesty. It is to the nation what the white church spire is to the village—the visible symbol of aspiration and faith, the white plume saying that the way is up. The summer traveler swings in over Hell Gate Bridge and from the window of his sleeping car as it glides above the pigeon lofts and back yards of Queens looks southwest to where the morning light first strikes the steel peaks of midtown, and he sees its upward thrust unmistakable: the great walls and towers rising, the smoke rising, the heat not yet rising, the hopes and ferments of so many awakening millions rising—this vigorous spear that presses heaven hard.

It is a miracle that New York works at all. The whole thing is implausible. Every time the residents brush their teeth, millions of gallons of water must be drawn from the Catskills and the hills of Westchester. When a young man in Manhattan writes a letter to his girl in Brooklyn, the love message gets blown to her through a pneumatic[2] tube—*pfft*—just like that. The subterranean system of telephone cables, power lines, steam pipes, gas mains, and sewer
16 pipes is reason enough to abandon the island to the gods and the weevils. Every time an incision is made in the pavement, the noisy surgeons expose ganglia[3] that are tangled beyond belief. By rights New York should have destroyed itself long ago, from panic or fire
15 or rioting or failure of some vital supply line in its circulatory system or from some deep labyrinthine short circuit. Long ago the city should have experienced an insoluble traffic snarl at some impossible bottle-neck. It should have perished of hunger when food lines filed for a few days. It should have been wiped out by a plague starting in its slums or carried in by ships' rats. It should have been overwhelmed by the sea that licks at it on every side. The workers in its myriad cells should have succumbed to nerves, from the fearful pall of
17 smoke-fog that drifts over every few days from Jersey, blotting out all light at noon and leaving the high offices suspended, men groping and depressed, and the sense of world's end. It should have been touched in the head by the August heat and gone off its rocker.

Mass hysteria is a terrible force, yet New Yorkers seem always to escape it by some tiny margin: they sit in stalled subways without claustrophobia, they extricate themselves from panic situations by some lucky wisecrack, they meet confusion and congestion with patience and grit—a sort of perpetual muddling through. Every facility is inadequate—the hospitals and schools and the playgrounds are over-crowded, the express highways are feverish, the unimproved highways and bridges are bottlenecks, there is not enough air and not enough light, and there is usually either too much heat or too little. But the city makes up for its hazards and its deficiencies by supplying its citizens with massive doses of a supplementary vitamin: the sense of belonging to something unique, cosmopolitan, mighty, and unparalleled.

Vocabulary Builder
aspiration (as′ pə rā′ shən) *n.* strong ambition

Vocabulary Builder
subterranean (sub′ tə rā′ nē ən) *adj.* underground

Reading Strategy
Recognizing Hyperbole
Which details in the passage beginning "Long ago" are examples of hyperbole?

Vocabulary Builder
claustrophobia (klôs′ trə fō′ bē ə) *n.* fear of being in a confined space

cosmopolitan (käz′ mə päl′ ə tən) *adj.* at ease in all countries or places

2. **pneumatic** (no͞o mat′ ik) *adj.* filled with compressed air.
3. **ganglia** (gaŋ′ glē ə) *n.* mass of nerve cells serving as center of force, energy, activity.

Enrichment

New York, New York

In 1626, the Dutch West India Company established the tiny settlement of New Amsterdam on the southern shore of what was then known as Manna-hata Island. In May of that year, Peter Minuit bought the land from a band of Native Americans, who probably did not own it, for the now infamous price of $24. The tiny village expanded northward, eventually encompassing the entire island. Today, New York City consists of five boroughs—Manhattan Island, Brooklyn, Queens, the Bronx, and Staten Island.

Most of Manhattan is laid out on a grid pattern. Wide north-south avenues are numbered from east to west—First Avenue, Second Avenue, and so on—and narrower east-west cross-streets are numbered from south to north—Fourteenth Street, Fifteenth Street, and so on. Broadway, a former Indian trail and the city's longest and oldest street, runs the full length of Manhattan Island. Its diagonal direction was not altered when the grid plan was instituted.

To an outlander a stay in New York can be and often is a series of small embarrassments and discomforts and disappointments: not understanding the waiter, not being able to distinguish between a sucker joint and a friendly saloon, riding the wrong subway, being slapped down by a bus driver for asking an innocent question, enduring sleepless nights when the street noises fill the bedroom. Tourists make for New York, particularly in summertime—they swarm all over the Statue of Liberty (where many a resident of the town has never set foot), they invade the Automat,[4] visit radio studios, St. Patrick's Cathedral, and they window shop. Mostly they have a pretty good time. But sometimes in New York you run across the disillusioned—a young couple who are obviously visitors, newlyweds perhaps, for whom the bright dream has vanished. The place has been too much for them; they sit languishing in a cheap restaurant over a speechless meal.

Literary Analysis
Informal Essay What does the relaxed, conversational style of this passage reveal about White's attitude toward New York?

The oft-quoted thumbnail sketch of New York is, of course: "It's a wonderful place, but I'd hate to live there." I have an idea that people from villages and small towns, people accustomed to the convenience and the friendliness of neighborhood over-the-fence living, are unaware that life in New York follows the neighborhood pattern. The city is literally a composite of tens of thousands of tiny neighborhood units. There are, of course, the big districts and big units: Chelsea and Murray Hill and Gramercy (which are residential units), . . . Greenwich Village (a unit dedicated to the arts and other matters), and there is Radio City (a commercial development), Peter Cooper Village (a housing unit), the Medical Center (a sickness unit) and many other sections each of which has some distinguishing characteristic. But the curious thing about New York is that each large geographical unit is composed of countless small neighborhoods. Each neighborhood is virtually self-sufficient. Usually it is no more than two or three blocks long and a couple of blocks wide. Each area is a city within a city within a city. Thus, no matter where you live in New York, you will find within a block or two a grocery store, a barbershop, a newsstand and shoeshine shack, an ice-coal-and-wood cellar (where you write your order on a pad outside as you walk by), a dry cleaner, a laundry, a delicatessen (beer and sandwiches delivered at any hour to your door), a flower shop, an undertaker's parlor, a movie house, a radio-repair shop, a stationer, a haberdasher,[5] a tailor, a drugstore, a garage, a tearoom, a saloon, a hardware store, a liquor store, a shoe-repair shop. Every block or two, in most residential sections of New York, is a little main street. A man starts for work in the morning and before he has gone two hundred yards he has completed half a dozen missions: bought a paper, left a pair of shoes to be soled, picked up a pack of cigarettes, . . . written a message to the unseen forces of the wood cellar, and notified the dry cleaner that a pair of trousers awaits call. Homeward-bound 20

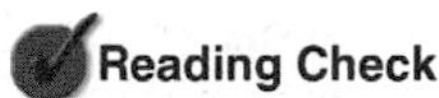

Reading Check
According to the writer, what difficulties might a visitor to New York encounter?

4. **Automat** *n.* restaurant in which patrons get food from small compartments with doors opened by putting coins into slots.
5. **haberdasher** *n.* person whose work is selling men's clothing, such as hats, shirts, neckties, and gloves.

18 Literary Analysis
Informal Essay

- **Ask** students to identify White's purpose in this passage.
  Answer: White explains an outsider's perspective of New York as an overwhelming, noisy, unfriendly place.
- **Ask** students the Literary Analysis question: What does the relaxed, conversational style of this passage reveal about White's attitude toward New York?
  Answer: White regards New York with affection. He understands why some people find it bewildering and why others would never live anywhere else.

19 Critical Thinking
Compare and Contrast

- Have students **compare** this long descriptive paragraph to the paragraph that precedes it. What is the main idea of each paragraph?
  Answer: Shorter paragraph: New York can be intimidating to tourists. Longer paragraph: New York is not so overwhelming; it is simply a big collection of small neighborhoods.
- Then, have students **consider** why White might make these somewhat contradictory points in sequence.
  Answer: White sets up the tourists' point of view only to show that there is far more to the story.

20 Reading Check

Answer: Tourists to New York might encounter unintelligible waiters, "sucker joints," confusing subway maps, rudeness, and noise.

ASSESS

Answers

1. **Possible responses:** No, because he stresses the city's unfriendliness to visitors; yes, because he makes it sound exciting and alive.
2. (a) They make jokes, they don't suffer from claustrophobia, and they exercise patience and grit. (b) It gives them a sense of community and variety.
3. (a) It can be confusing and unwelcoming. (b) Such a person might say that people planning to visit New York should read about the city, get advice from friends who live there, and remain open to adventure instead of being intimidated. They might add that New York is full of beauty and vitality and can offer visitors a wonderful experience.
4. (a) He says that they are tiny villages. (b) They are just like small towns. Just like many small-town dwellers who never move away from home, many New Yorkers never leave their own neighborhoods.
5. (a) It has endurance and strength. (b) It is a marvelous and unique place, and those who live there are lucky.
6. A politician might disagree that the city is challenging for visitors, but would agree that it is a great place to live.

eight hours later, he buys a bunch of pussy willows, a Mazda bulb, a drink, a shine—all between the corner where he steps off the bus and his apartment. So complete is each neighborhood, and so strong the sense of neighborhood, that many a New Yorker spends a lifetime within the confines of an area smaller than a country village. Let him walk two blocks from his corner and he is in a strange land and will feel uneasy till he gets back.

Storekeepers are particularly conscious of neighborhood boundary lines. A woman friend of mine moved recently from one apartment to another, a distance of three blocks. When she turned up, the day after the move, at the same grocer's that she had patronized for years, the proprietor was in ecstasy—almost in tears—at seeing her. "I was afraid," he said, "now that you've moved away I wouldn't be seeing you anymore." To him, *away* was three blocks, or about 750 feet.

I am, at the moment of writing this, living not as a neighborhood man in New York but as a transient, or vagrant, in from the country for a few days. Summertime is a good time to reexamine New York and to receive again the gift of privacy, the jewel of loneliness. In summer the city contains (except for tourists) only die-hards and authentic characters. No casual, spotty dwellers are around, only the real article. And the town has a somewhat relaxed air, and one can lie in a loincloth, gasping and remembering things.

Critical Reading

1. **Respond:** Would you like to visit the New York City of E. B. White's description? Why or why not?
2. **(a) Recall:** According to this essay, what are three ways in which New Yorkers escape mass hysteria? **(b) Connect:** What does New York City offer its citizens in return to help them cope with the city's deficiencies?
3. **(a) Recall:** According to White, what is New York City like for tourists? **(b) Hypothesize:** Describe the way in which someone working in New York City's tourist industry might respond to E. B. White's representation of the city for "outlanders"?
4. **(a) Recall:** What terms does White use to describe New York's neighborhoods? **(b) Compare and Contrast:** In what ways do these neighborhoods compare to small towns?
5. **(a) Draw Conclusions:** What qualities of New York City enable it to function against all odds? **(b) Summarize:** What general conclusions does White's essay reach about the city?
6. **Extend:** How might the city's mayor or a New York State Senator respond to White's description?

Go Online
Author Link
For: More about E. B. White
Visit: www.PHSchool.com
Web Code: ere-9522

Go Online Author Link For additional information about E. B. White, have students type in the Web Code, then select W from the alphabet, and then select E. B. White.

Apply the Skills

The Night the Ghost Got In • from *Here Is New York*

Literary Analysis

Informal Essay

1. Cite an especially strong example of language that reflects the conversational style of Thurber's **informal essay.** Explain your choice.
2. What does "Here Is New York" suggest about White's attitude toward New York and the modern world it symbolizes? Support your answer.
3. What does their calm detachment in the midst of describing chaotic events reveal about the writers' views of the world around them?

Comparing Literary Works

4. **(a)** How would you describe the dominant type of **humor** Thurber uses in his informal essay? **(b)** In what ways does it compare to the humor used by E.B. White?
5. Although White uses humor to make fun of New York, his writing actually reveals some of the city's unique qualities. Using a chart like the one shown, cite three examples of hidden praise.

Humorous Passage	What It Reveals

6. **(a)** What does each author's use of humor add to his exploration of social or political issues? **(b)** Does the presence of humor allow the writer to convey ideas that would otherwise be difficult for readers to accept? Explain.

Reading Strategy

Recognizing Hyperbole

7. Cite an example of **hyperbole** from each essay and explain in what ways it represents an exaggeration.
8. For what purpose does Thurber exaggerate the behavior of his grandfather in his essay?
9. How is White's use of hyperbole appropriate for his subject?

Extend Understanding

10. **Career Connection:** Name three careers in today's world that might provide work for humorists. Explain how humor is used in each case.

QuickReview

An **informal essay** is a brief nonfiction work that is characterized by a relaxed, conversational style and structure.

In literature, **humor** is writing intended to evoke laughter.

To **recognize hyperbole,** look for deliberate exaggeration and outrageous overstatements.

For: Self-test
Visit: www.PHSchool.com
Web Code: era-6514

Answers

1. **Sample answer:** The opening sentence is a blend of the calm and hysteria that make the whole essay so funny.
2. White admires the city as a great achievement of the modern age. He describes it as the modern equivalent of the village church steeple; a symbol of human aspiration.
3. They are amused by the world around them. They observe it even as they participate in it.
4. (a) Thurber's humor rests in the contrast between the narrator's calm behavior and the zaniness with which he is surrounded. (b) Like Thurber's, part of White's humor comes from the author's sense of detached observation. Both write humor that is gentle, not biting.
5. **Possible responses:** The city is exuberant and energetic. The city offers immense variety in foods and consumer goods. The city has spectacular tourist attractions.
6. (a) White uses humor to highlight a cultural divide between residents of New York City and nonresidents. Thurber's use of humor allows him to portray a rather extreme police search in a nonthreatening way. (b) White's use of humor allows him to criticize New York City and to poke fun at tourists without causing offense. Thurber's use of humor allows him to portray family members in a less than flattering light.
7. **Possible response:** Thurber: The number of policemen who come to the house is exaggerated. White: The grocer who nearly cried when his customer who had moved down the street returned is an exaggerated description.
8. Thurber wants to make the reader laugh.
9. New York itself is an example of hyperbole: the buildings are taller, the crowds larger, and the streets noisier than anywhere else.

Answers continued

10. **Possible responses:** A political cartoonist uses humor to expose evils in government. A stand-up comic uses humor to expose problems in society. A teacher uses humor to impart lessons.

Go Online Assessment Students may use the **Self-test** to prepare for **Selection Test A** or **Selection Test B.**

EXTEND/ASSESS

Answers

❶ Vocabulary Lesson

Word Analysis

1. b 2. c

Spelling Strategy

1. photograph 2. symphony

Vocabulary Builder

1. No; an aspiration is a dream.
2. Yes; these pipes are below ground.
3. Yes; blaspheming means cursing.
4. Yes; a cosmopolitan person would feel comfortable anywhere.
5. Yes; it would startle most people.
6. No; it is a small, enclosed space.

❷ Grammar and Style Lesson

1. . . . telephone cables, power lines, steam pipes, gas mains, and . . .
2. . . .began again, circled the dining room table like a man running, and . . .
3. . . . dining-room, stabbed into hallways, shot up the front stairs, and . . .
4. . . . a grocery store, a barbershop, a newsstand, and . . .
5. . . . open, drawers were yanked open, windows were shot up and pulled down, furniture . . .

Writing Application

Have students check one another's paragraphs to make sure they have used two sets of commas in series.

WG Writing and Grammar, Ruby Level

Students will find further instruction and practice on commas in a series in Chapter 27, Section 2.

Build Language Skills

❶ Vocabulary Lesson

Word Analysis: Latin Root *-terr-*

The prefix *sub-* means "under" and the Latin root *-terr-* means "earth" or "land." Therefore, the word *subterranean* means "under Earth's surface." Use the meaning of *-terr-* and context clues to choose the best word for each sentence.

a. terrain **b.** extraterrestrial **c.** terrarium

1. The ___?___ visited from another planet.
2. Put some earth in a glass jar and plant some seeds to make a ___?___ .

Spelling Strategy

Words such as *blaspheme* and *telephone* spell the *f* sound with *ph*. These words derive from Greek and are spelled with the Greek letter *phi* (fī). Write a *ph* word that fits each definition.

1. a portrait taken with a camera
2. a piece of music for an orchestra

Vocabulary Builder: Context

Review the vocabulary list on page 897. Then, answer *yes* or *no* to each question below. Explain your responses.

1. If Susan has an *aspiration* to sail around the world, does she have a vague notion?
2. Must you dig to reach *subterranean* pipes in a city?
3. Would you get in trouble for *blaspheming* in class?
4. Would a *cosmopolitan* person enjoy the streets of Paris?
5. If you heard a very loud bang, would you *intuitively* wince?
6. Would a person suffering from *claustrophobia* enjoy riding in an elevator?

❷ Grammar and Style Lesson

Commas in a Series

Commas in a series are placed between three or more parallel items to link them. Usually, coordinating conjunctions such as *and, or,* or *but* precede the final item. Separate the items in a list with commas.

Example: Bodwell was at the window in a minute, shouting, frothing a little, shaking his fist.

Practice Rewrite these sentences, inserting commas in their appropriate places.

1. The subterranean system of telephone cables power lines steam pipes gas mains and sewer pipes is the reason to . . .
2. Instantly the steps began again circled the dining room table like a man running and started up the stairs toward us . . .
3. Their lights . . . crisscrossed nervously in the dining-room stabbed into hallways shot up the front stairs and finally up the back.
4. You will find within a block or two a grocery store a barbershop a newsstand and shoe-shine rack . . .
5. Doors were yanked open drawers were yanked open windows were shot up and pulled down furniture fell with dull thumps.

Writing Application Write a paragraph, using two sets of commas in series.

WG *Prentice Hall Writing and Grammar Connection: Chapter 27, Section 2*

Assessment Practice

Fill In Missing Words

Many tests require students to complete sentences by choosing from a list of possible words. Use the following sample test item to give students practice at this skill.

Magazines have been important in nurturing American humor. For years *The New Yorker* has __________ the work of cartoonists and humorous writers.

(For more practice, see *Standardized Test Preparation Workbook*, p. 54.)

Which word best fills the blank?

A concealed **C** showcased
B reserved **D** hidden

The second sentence of the passage is intended to illustrate the point made in the first sentence. *The New Yorker* could not nurture artists and writers by concealing, reserving, or hiding their work. Choice **C** is correct.

❸ Writing Lesson

Timed Writing: Critical Response

E. B. White once said, "The most widely appreciated humorists are those who create characters and tell tales . . ." Write an essay responding to this statement. Cite passages from these humorous essays for support. ***(40 minutes)***

Prewriting *(10 minutes)* Review the selections and identify the most humorous characters. Jot down notes about what makes each of them funny. Select the ones you will write about to support your opinions.

Drafting *(20 minutes)* Begin by presenting your response to White's statement. Then, use the examples of humorous characters and passages from the selections to support your position.

Revising *(10 minutes)* Strengthen your essay by incorporating direct quotations that clearly support your opinions.

Model: Incorporating Quotations

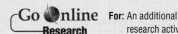

"'Back, ye cowardly dogs! Back t' the lines, ye yellow, lily-livered cattle!'"

Thurber adds even more humor to an already funny and exaggerated essay through the confused character of Grandfather, who yells ~~at the police~~, thinking the police are deserters from Meade's army.

Direct quotations from the text support the critique by showing the humor.

WG Prentice Hall Writing and Grammar Connection: Chapter 14, Section 3

Extend Your Learning

Listening and Speaking With a partner, conduct a **role play** of Thurber and White discussing their essays in the offices of *The New Yorker.* Constructively criticize each other's work, considering the following:

- What makes the essays funny?
- In what ways are they similar?
- In what ways do they differ?
- What would you add or change?

Present your role play to the class.

Research and Technology Thurber and White both worked for *The New Yorker.* Working with a partner, use the Internet and other sources to research "The Algonquin Roundtable," a group of wits associated with *The New Yorker* who met on a regular basis. Deliver your findings in a **written report. [Group Activity]**

For: An additional research activity
Visit: www.PHSchool.com
Web Code: erd-7513

Assessment Resources

The following resources can be used to assess students' knowledge and skills.

Unit 5 Resources
- **Selection Test A,** pp. 230–232
- **Selection Test B,** pp. 233–235
- **Benchmark Test 8,** pp. 236–241

General Resources
- **Rubrics for Response to Literature,** pp. 65–66
- **Rubrics for Research: Research Report,** pp. 49–50

Go Online Assessment — Students may use the **Self-test** to prepare for **Selection Test A** or **Selection Test B.**

Benchmark

Administer **Benchmark Test 8.** If the Benchmark Test reveals that some students need further work, use the **Interpretation Guide** to determine the appropriate reteaching pages in the **Reading Kit** or on **Success Tracker.**

❸ Writing Lesson

You may use this Writing Lesson as timed-writing practice, or you may allow students to develop it as a writing assignment over several days.

- To support students in preparing a response to literature, give them the **Support for Writing Lesson** page (***Unit 5 Resources,*** p. 227).
- Have students choose one of the two essays for this assignment; they need not write about both.
- Remind students to cite specific examples of humor from the text. Since Thurber's illustrations were created specifically for his essay, students may also take those into account in their reviews.
- Remind students that the assignment allows them to criticize the chosen essay for not being funny. If students believe that either White or Thurber has failed to "create characters and tell tales," they are free to defend that point of view.
- Use the Response to Literature rubrics in ***General Resources,*** pp. 65–66, to evaluate students' letters.

❹ Research and Technology

- Tell students that this group of writers is known as the Algonquin Round Table because they met for lunch or cocktails at the large round table in the lounge of the Algonquin Hotel, located on 44th Street near the offices of *The New Yorker.*
- Members of the Algonquin Round Table included short-story writer and poet Dorothy Parker, *The New Yorker* editor Harold Ross, playwright George S. Kaufman, and sportswriter Ring Lardner.
- The **Support for Extend Your Learning** page (***Unit 5 Resources,*** p. 228) provides guided note-taking opportunities to help students complete the Extend Your Learning activities.
- Use the rubrics for Research: Research Report in ***General Resources,*** pp. 49–50, to evaluate students' reports.

Go Online Research — Have students type in the Web Code for another research activity.

Meeting Your Standards

Students will

1. **understand and describe the Harlem Renaissance.**
2. **communicate effectively with others in a cooperative situation.**

Critical Thinking

- Call students' attention to the discussion of the goals of Harlem artists during this period. **Ask:** What kinds of experiences would you expect these artists to have documented?
  Possible response: They may have documented the daily lives of African Americans in the large Northern cities, the experience of moving from rural to urban areas, racism, and the traditions and culture of African Americans.
- Point out that African Americans began the Great Migration to seek greater opportunities and more freedom in the North. Emphasize that it was also a move from mostly rural areas of the South to mostly urban areas of the North. **Ask** how such a radical change in their environment and living conditions may have stimulated the blossoming of African-American creativity.
  Possible response: These radical changes may have reinforced their willingness to challenge old ways of thinking and encouraged them to embrace new ideas.
- **Ask** students why was it important for the writers and artists of the Harlem Renaissance to live and work together in one community.
  Answer: They depended on one another for inspiration and support. These artists all shared a common ancestry and a common culture, and their work flourished in the supportive environment of a creative community.

Critical Viewing

Answer: The picture is busy; there is something to look at in every corner. The picture is full of movement and action. The instruments have prominent positions in the picture, helping the viewer "hear" the music.

A Closer Look

The Harlem Renaissance

Harlem in the 1920s: For some, it conjures images of jazz sessions at hot spots like the Cotton Club, of seedy speakeasies like the Clam Bake and the Hot Feet. For others, it brings to mind the artistic genius of writers like Langston Hughes and Zora Neale Hurston and painters like Aaron Douglas. In the 1920s, the New York City neighborhood of Harlem was home to an unprecedented flowering of African American talent that left an astonishing cultural legacy.

"Known as the Harlem Renaissance, this remarkable period marked the first time that African American artists were taken seriously by the culture at large."

A Celebration of African American Life Known as the Harlem Renaissance, this remarkable period marked the first time that African American artists were taken seriously by the culture at large. "Negro life is seizing its first chances for group expression and self determination," wrote sociologist Alain Locke in 1926. Harlem became what Locke termed "the center of a spiritual coming of age," as its artists celebrated their culture and race.

The artists and writers of the Renaissance did not share a style. Langston Hughes's realistic poems of downtrodden but determined people bear little resemblance to Countee Cullen's elegant sonnets. Instead, these artists shared the urgent need to document the experiences of their people.

The Center of the World In the early 1900s, hundreds of thousands of African Americans embarked on what has come to be called the Great Migration, moving from the rural South to the industrial cities of the North. As more and more African Americans settled in Harlem, it became a meeting ground for writers, musicians, and artists.

The work they produced was unique. Before the Harlem Renaissance, many African American writers had tried to emulate whites. By contrast, the Harlem writers celebrated their racial identity. The goal was to create, as Hughes put it, "an expression of our individual dark-skinned selves."

An Outpouring of Expression From the 1920s through the mid-1930s, sixteen African American writers published more than fifty volumes of poetry and fiction—an astounding amount of work. Other African Americans made their

▼ Critical Viewing In this image of jazz great Duke Ellington leading his band, how do the positioning of the musicians and the use of light and shadow echo the rhythms and energy of jazz music? **[Analyze]**

marks in art, music, and theater. Aaron Douglas incorporated African images into his paintings. Blues singer Bessie Smith performed to packed houses. Musicians Jelly Roll Morton, Louis Armstrong, and Duke Ellington laid the foundations of jazz, a form of music that scholars argue is the only truly American art form.

The movement's most influential advocate may have been Langston Hughes, whose poems combined the rhythms of jazz and blues with stories of Harlem life. Other writers, such as Countee Cullen and Claude McKay, wrote in more classical forms. Novelist Zora Neale Hurston combined African folklore with realistic narratives.

Zora and Langston, Phoebe Beasley

▲ **Critical Viewing**
What elements of the lives and works of Langston Hughes and Zora Neale Hurston are expressed in this image of the two writers? **[Interpret]**

A Powerful Legacy The impact of the Harlem Renaissance has been a subject of debate. Most scholars agree that it opened doors for the acceptance of art and writing by African Americans. However, some say that the Renaissance artists were too interested in seeking the approval of the white establishment. Even Langston Hughes admitted that few African Americans had read his work.

Still, the Harlem Renaissance gave Americans a language with which to begin a discussion of racism. It also broke ground for mid-century African American writers such as Richard Wright, Ralph Ellison, and James Baldwin. Today, Nobel Prize–winner Toni Morrison, novelist and poet Alice Walker, popular mystery writer Walter Mosley, and hundreds of other writers, painters, and musicians owe a debt to the artists of the Harlem Renaissance. For thousands of aspiring writers, artists, and musicians, the Harlem Renaissance was proof that art excludes no one.

Activity

African Americans in Contemporary Arts

Today, African Americans are involved in every area of American culture. With a group, discuss the influence of African Americans on contemporary literature, music, dance, visual art, theater, television, and movies. Use these strategies and questions to guide your discussion:

- Brainstorm for a list of individual African Americans whose artistic accomplishments are helping to shape contemporary culture.
- Without African American creativity, how might our culture be different?
- Do you think African Americans are fairly represented in all the arts? If not, what could be done to improve their representation?

Choose a point person to share your group's conclusions with the class.

Critical Viewing

Answer: This image shows their African American heritage and pride.

Activity

- Direct each group to select a member to take notes as well as a point person who will present the group's conclusions to the class.
- To help students focus their brainstorming, suggest that they list different art categories and brainstorm for names for each category separately.
- Tell students to think about specific kinds of art that have either grown out of the black experience or that are dominated by African Americans, such as jazz, blues, and rap. Have them add to this list and consider how American culture would be different without these art forms.
- After students make their presentations, guide the class in summarizing the groups' conclusions.

Meeting Your Standards

Students will

1. **analyze and respond to literary elements.**
   - Literary Analysis: Social Context in Autobiography
2. **read, comprehend, analyze, and critique nonfiction.**
   - Reading Strategy: Analyzing How a Writer Achieves Purpose
   - Reading Check questions
   - Apply the Skills questions
   - Assessment Practice (ATE)
3. **develop vocabulary.**
   - Vocabulary Lesson: Greek Root: *-graph-*
4. **understand and apply written and oral language conventions.**
   - Spelling Strategy
   - Grammar and Style Lesson: Parallelism in Coordinate Elements
5. **develop writing proficiency.**
   - Writing Lesson: Personal Narrative
6. **develop appropriate research strategies.**
   - Extend Your Learning: Folk-Tale Collection
7. **understand and apply listening and speaking strategies.**
   - Extend Your Learning: Campaign Speech

Block Scheduling: Use one 90-minute class period to preteach the skills and have students read the selection. Use a second 90-minute class period to assess students' mastery of skills, extend their learning, and monitor their progress.

Homework Suggestions

Following are possibilities for homework assignments.

- Support pages from ***Unit 5 Resources:***
  Literary Analysis
  Reading Strategy
  Vocabulary Builder
  Grammar and Style
- An Extend Your Learning project and the Writing Lesson for this selection group may be completed over several days.

Step-by-Step Teaching Guide	Pacing Guide
PRETEACH	
• Administer Vocabulary and Reading Warm-ups as necessary.	5 min.
• Engage students' interest with the motivation activity.	5 min.
• Read and discuss author, and background features. **FT**	10 min.
• Introduce the Literary Analysis Skill: Social Context in Autobiography. **FT**	5 min.
• Introduce the Reading Strategy: Analyzing How a Writer Achieves Purpose. **FT**	10 min.
• Prepare students to read by teaching the selection vocabulary. **FT**	
TEACH	
• Informally monitor comprehension while students read independently or in groups. **FT**	30 min.
• Monitor students' comprehension with the Reading Check notes.	as students read
• Reinforce vocabulary with Vocabulary Builder notes.	as students read
• Develop students' understanding of social context in autobiography with the Literary Analysis annotations. **FT**	5 min.
• Develop students' ability to analyze how a writer achieves purpose with the Reading Strategy annotations. **FT**	5 min.
ASSESS/EXTEND	
• Assess students' comprehension and mastery of the Literary Analysis and Reading Strategy by having them answer the Apply the Skills questions. **FT**	15 min.
• Have students complete the Vocabulary Lesson and the Grammar and Style Lesson. **FT**	15 min.
• Apply students' ability to analyze cause and effect in their writing by using the Writing Lesson. **FT**	45 min. or homework
• Apply students' understanding by using one or more of the Extend Your Learning activities.	20–90 min. or homework
• Administer Selection Test A or Selection Test B. **FT**	15 min.

Resources

PRINT

Unit 5 Resources

Vocabulary Warm-up Word Lists **[L1, L2, EL]** .... p. 245
Vocabulary Warm-up Practice **[L1, L2, EL]** .... p. 246
Reading Warm-up A **[L1, L2, EL]** .... p. 247
Reading Warm-up B **[L1, L2, L3]** .... p. 248

TRANSPARENCY

Graphic Organizer Transparencies

Literary Analysis Graphic Organizer A **[L3]** .... p. 203
Literary Analysis Graphic Organizer B **[L1, L2, EL]** .... p. 204
Reading Strategy Graphic Organizer A **[L3]** .... p. 201
Reading Strategy Graphic Organizer B **[L1, L2, EL]** .... p. 202

PRINT

Reader's Notebook [L2]
Reader's Notebook: Adapted Version [L1]
Reader's Notebook: English Learner's Version [EL]

Unit 5 Resources

Literary Analysis **[L3]** .... p. 249
Reading Strategy **[L3]** .... p. 250
Vocabulary Builder **[L3]** .... p. 251

TECHNOLOGY

Listening to Literature Audio CDs [L2, EL]

PRINT

Unit 5 Resources

Grammar and Style **[L3]** .... p. 252
Support for Writing Lesson **[L3]** .... p. 253
Support for Extend Your Learning **[L3]** .... p. 254
Enrichment **[L4]** .... p. 255
Selection Test A **[L1, L2, EL]** .... pp. 256–258
Selection Test B **[L3, L4]** .... pp. 259–261

General Resources

Rubrics for Narration: Autobiographical Narrative **[L3]** .... pp. 43–44

TECHNOLOGY

Go Online: Research **[L3]**
Go Online: Self-test **[L3]**
***ExamView*® Test Bank [L3]**

Choosing Resources for Differentiated Instruction

[L1] Special Needs Students
[L2] Below-Level Students
[L3] All Students
[L4] Advanced Students
[EL] English Learners

For Vocabulary and Reading Warm-ups and for Selection Tests, **A** signifies "less challenging" and **B** "more challenging." For Graphic Organizer transparencies, **A** signifies "not filled in" and **B** "filled in."

FT Fast Track Instruction: To move the lesson more quickly, use the strategies and activities identified with **FT**.

Scaffolding for Less Proficient and Advanced Students

The leveled Critical Thinking questions after selections progress in the levels of thinking required to answer them. To address the needs of your different students, you may use the (a) level questions for your less proficient students and the (b) level questions with your on-level and advanced students. The occasional (c) level questions are appropriate for your advanced students.

PRENTICE HALL **TeacherEXPRESS™** Plan · Teach · Assess — Use this complete suite of powerful teaching tools to make lesson planning and testing quicker and easier.

PRENTICE HALL **StudentEXPRESS™** Learn · Study · Succeed — Use the interactive textbook (online and on CD-ROM) to make selections and activities come alive with audio and video support and interactive questions.

Monitoring Progress

Before students read the excerpt from *Dust Tracks on a Road,* administer **Diagnostic Test 9** (*Unit 5 Resources,* p. 242). This test will determine students' level of readiness for the reading and vocabulary skills.

Go Online Professional Development
For: Information about Lexiles
Visit: www.PHSchool.com
Web Code: eue-1111

Motivation

Ask students which books were their favorites when they were in fifth or sixth grade. List titles on the board and ask students to bring some of their old books to pass around in class. Have students explain why they liked these books and how the books influenced them. Tell students that they are about to read an autobiographical story of a girl whose love of reading would shape her whole life.

1 More About the Author

Zora Neale Hurston was born in a small hamlet near Tuskegee, Alabama. When she was a child, her family resettled in Eatonville, Florida, the first incorporated African American community in America. Her father served three terms as mayor there. Hurston's Eatonville childhood deeply affected her life. Unlike many—or most—African Americans of her day, Hurston grew up without experiencing the sting of racism. Instead, her community openly expressed pride in African culture, and celebrated its heritage. This environment led the future folkorist to develop a profound self-confidence, as well as a deep appreciation for folklore and literature.

1 *from* Dust Tracks on a Road

Zora Neale Hurston (1891–1960)

Throughout her career as a writer, Zora Neale Hurston was recognized as an influential author and a pioneering force in the documentation of African American culture. Still, she died penniless and was buried in an unmarked grave in a segregated cemetery in Fort Pierce, Florida. Hurston was almost entirely forgotten until author Alice Walker set out on a mission to locate and mark her grave, recording the experience in a 1975 *Ms.* magazine article. Walker's effort restored Hurston to her rightful place in American literature as "the dominant black woman writer" of her time.

Early Influences Hurston was one of the first American writers to recognize that a cultural heritage was valuable in its own right. Her unshakable self-confidence and strong sense of personal worth were fostered by a childhood in Eatonville, Florida, America's first fully incorporated African American township. One of eight children, Hurston was, by her own account, a spirited, curious child who "always wanted to go." Her mother explained this urge to wander by claiming that travel dust had been sprinkled at the door the day Zora was born.

Hurston's childhood abruptly ended when her mother died. Hurston went to live with a series of friends and relatives. By age fourteen, she was supporting herself.

Two Careers Hurston developed an interest in writing while studying at Howard University. In 1925, she moved to New York City, where her gift for storytelling and her outgoing personality helped her to make friends quickly. She soon published a story and a play, firmly establishing herself as one of the bright new talents of the Harlem Renaissance, the blossoming of literature and painting among African Americans in the 1920s, centered in New York. She began attending Barnard College, where her work came to the attention of prominent anthropologist Franz Boas, who convinced Hurston to begin graduate studies in anthropology at Columbia University. With an academic grant, she began a second career as a folklorist.

Preserving a Culture During the Great Migration, when African Americans from the South migrated by the hundreds of thousands to the north—where jobs awaited them in industrial cities like Detroit and Chicago—Hurston moved against the tide. She returned to the South for six years to document the art of "the Negro farthest down." She collected African American folk tales and, in 1935, published *Mules and Men,* the first volume of black American folklore compiled by an African American. Hurston's work helped to document the roots of African American tales in the stories, songs, and myths of Africa. Her second folklore collection, *Tell My Horse* (1938), also provided descriptions of African American cultural beliefs and ritual practices transported from Africa.

The Road to Obscurity Hurston achieved strong critical and popular success during the 1930s and 1940s after publishing the novels *Jonah's Gourd Vine* (1934), *Their Eyes Were Watching God* (1937), and *Moses, Man of the Mountain* (1939). She also wrote numerous short stories, plays, and her prize-winning autobiography, *Dust Tracks on a Road* (1942), which was the most commercially successful of her works.

Unfortunately, controversy and personal scandal led Hurston's career into obscurity. At the time of her death, none of her books were in print. It was not until the 1970s that, with the assistance of Alice Walker, there was a resurgence of interest in Hurston's work. Rescued from the shadows of literary history, she is now generally regarded as one of the important literary figures of the twentieth century.

Preview

Connecting to the Literature

As a child, Zora Neale Hurston was passionate about literature, and that passion led to her success as a writer. As you read, think about an interest of your own that may not only shape your character but also change your life.

❷ Literary Analysis

Social Context in Autobiography

Autobiography is a nonfiction account of a writer's life told in his or her own words. Autobiographical writing documents the writer's feelings about key events and experiences. In addition to personal insights, autobiographies also reveal **social context**—the attitudes and customs of the culture in which the writer lived. The excerpt from Hurston's autobiography recalls an event from her childhood and provides a glimpse of life in her African American community in the South.

Connecting Literary Elements

In this selection, Hurston helps the scenery and settings of her memories come to life through the use of **dialogue.** The words the people speak reflect their culture and reveal their personalities. By showcasing human interaction, dialogue makes literature more conversational, readable, and enjoyable. As you read, notice the ways in which the dialogue adds nuance and color to your understanding of Hurston's experience.

❸ Reading Strategy

Analyzing How a Writer Achieves Purpose

Hurston's **purpose**—to share her personal experience and show the vitality of the African American community—determines her choice of words, details, characters, and events. By linking her choices to her goals, you can analyze her success in achieving her purpose.

As you read, note key words, details, characters, and events in a chart like the one shown. Then review your notes to evaluate how Hurston achieves her purpose.

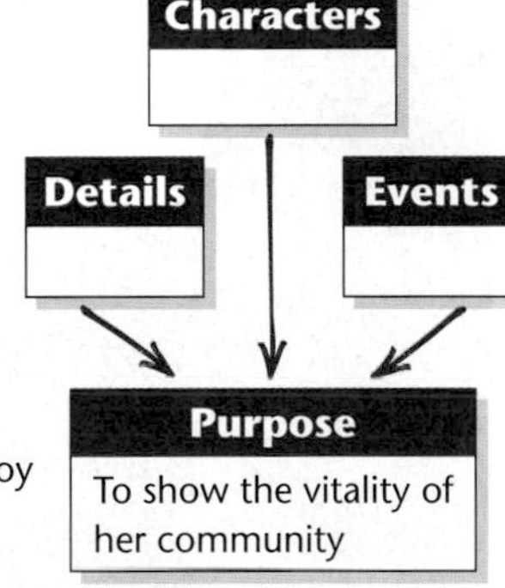

Vocabulary Builder

foreknowledge (fôr′ näl ij) *n.* awareness of something before it happens or exists (p. 915)

brazenness (brā′ zən nis) *n.* shamelessness; boldness; impudence (p. 915)

caper (kā pər) *n.* prank (p. 915)

exalted (eg zôlt′ id) *adj.* filled with joy or pride; elated (p. 916)

geography (jē äg′ rə fē) *n.* study of Earth's surface (p. 917)

avarice (av′ ə ris) *n.* extreme desire for wealth; greed (p. 918)

Differentiated Instruction

Solutions for All Learners

Support for Special Needs Students

Have students complete the **Preview** and **Build Skills** pages for the excerpt from the selection in the ***Reader's Notebook: Adapted Version.*** These pages provide a selection summary, an abbreviated presentation of the reading and literary skills, and the graphic organizer on the **Build Skills** page in the student book.

Support for Less Proficient Readers

Have students complete the **Preview** and **Build Skills** pages for the excerpt from the selection in the ***Reader's Notebook.*** These pages provide a selection summary, an abbreviated presentation of the reading and literary skills, and the graphic organizer on the **Build Skills** page in the student book.

Support for English Learners

Have students complete the **Preview** and **Build Skills** pages for the excerpt from *Dust Tracks on a Road* in the ***Reader's Notebook: English Learner's Version.*** These pages provide a selection summary, an abbreviated presentation of the skills, additional contextual vocabulary, and the graphic organizer on the **Build Skills** page in the student book.

❷ Literary Analysis

Social Context in Autobiography

- Students are familiar with the term "context clues" from their vocabulary studies. Remind them that *context* is a synonym for *setting.* The words and phrases that surround a word form its context. The meaning of a word is shaded and shaped by its context. Likewise, the environment that surrounds and helps to shape a person forms his or her context.
- Have students note the setting—time and place—in which young Zora lives. Encourage them to evaluate all the characters' actions in terms of this setting or social context.

❸ Reading Strategy

Analyzing How a Writer Achieves Purpose

- Review the instruction about author's purpose with students. Remind them that authors often write with more than one purpose. For example, a writer may seek to entertain, inform, or persuade.
- As students read this excerpt, have them pause every few paragraphs to note their reactions. Why might Hurston want to provoke these reactions? How does she do so?
- Give students a copy of **Reading Strategy Graphic Organizer A,** p. 201 in ***Graphic Organizer Transparencies.*** Encourage students to use this chart to record details that they can use to analyze Hurston's methods for achieving her purpose.

Vocabulary Builder

- Pronounce each vocabulary word for students, and read the definitions as a class. Have students identify any words with which they are already familiar.

❻ Literary Analysis
Social Context in Autobiography

- Remind students that social context—the culture in which the writer lives—plays an important role in autobiography.
- **Ask** students: What does Mrs. Calhoun's palmetto switch reveal about the society in which Zora grew up?
Answer: Teachers are permitted to maintain discipline by whipping students.
- Then, **ask** the Literary Analysis question: What social context is revealed in this passage about preparation for visitors?
Answer: The people who run the school want to be sure that they present their students and themselves in the best possible light.

▶ **Monitor Progress:** Have students consider what the warning to wear shoes on the day visitors are expected tells them about the social context.
Answer: If not given the warning, children would go to school barefoot. This suggests that their families can't often afford shoes for them. In order to keep shoes from wearing out too fast, they are probably reserved for church and special occasions.

❼ Humanities

School Bell Time,
by Romare Bearden

Romare Bearden (1914–1988) grew up in Harlem. During the Depression, he became a member of the Harlem Artists' Guild, along with Jacob Lawrence, Aaron Douglas, and others. After World War II, Bearden studied at the Sorbonne in Paris. He was greatly influenced by Cubist painters such as Pablo Picasso. The scraps of fabric and paper cutouts pasted to the canvas make this painting a collage. Use the following questions for discussion:

1. How would you describe the composition of this painting?
Answer: Students may say that it combines abstract and representational elements in a collage-like design with human figures and geometrical patterns.
2. Which figures in the painting are suggestive of characters in Hurston's autobiography?

in the back, with a palmetto switch[5] in her hand as a squelcher. We were all little angels for the duration, because we'd better be. She would cut her eyes and give us a glare that meant trouble, then turn her face towards the visitors and beam as much as to say it was a great privilege and pleasure to teach lovely children like us. They couldn't see that palmetto hickory in her hand behind all those benches, but we knew where our angelic behavior was coming from.

❻ Usually, the visitors gave warning a day ahead and we would be cautioned to put on shoes, comb our heads, and see to ears and fingernails. There was a close inspection of every one of us before we marched in that morning. Knotty heads, dirty ears and fingernails got hauled out of line, strapped and sent home to lick the calf over again.

This particular afternoon, the two young ladies just popped in. Mr. Calhoun was flustered, but he put on the best show he could. He dismissed the class that he was teaching up at the front of the room, then called the fifth grade in reading. That was my class.

So we took our readers and went up front. We stood up in the usual line, and opened to the lesson. It was the story of Pluto and Persephone. It was new and hard to the class in general, and Mr. Calhoun was very uncomfortable as the readers stumbled along, spelling out words with their lips, and in mumbling undertones before they exposed them experimentally to the teacher's ears.

Then it came to me. I was fifth or sixth down the line. The story was not new to me, because I had read my reader through from lid to lid, the first week that Papa had bought it for me.

That is how it was that my eyes were not in the book, working out the paragraph which I knew would be mine by counting the children ahead of me. I was observing our visitors, who held a book between them, following the lesson. They had shiny hair, mostly brownish. One had a looping gold chain around her neck. The other one was dressed all over in black and white with a pretty finger ring on her left hand. But the thing that held my eyes were their fingers. They were long and thin, and very white, except up near the tips. There they were baby pink. I had never seen such hands. It was a fascinating discovery for me. I wondered how they felt. I would have given those hands more attention, but the child before me was almost through. My turn next, so I got on my mark, bringing my eyes back to the book and made sure of my place. Some of the stories I had reread several times, and this Greco-Roman myth was one of my favorites. I was exalted by it, and that is the way I read my paragraph.

"Yes, Jupiter had seen her (Persephone). He had seen the maiden picking flowers in the field. He had seen the chariot of the dark monarch pause by the maiden's side. He had seen him when he seized Persephone. He had seen the black horses leap down Mount Aetna's fiery throat. Persephone was now in Pluto's dark realm and he had made her his wife."

5. **palmetto** (pal met′ ō) **switch** whip made from the fan-shaped leaves of the palmetto, a type of palm tree.

Literary Analysis
Social Context in Autobiography What social context is revealed in this passage about preparation for visitors?

Vocabulary Builder
exalted (eg zôlt′ id) *adj.* filled with joy or pride; elated

Answers continued

Answer: The woman ringing the school bell in the lower right corner may remind students of Mrs. Calhoun, while they may identify the man in the schoolyard as Mr. Calhoun.

School Bell Time, 1978 From the Profile/Part 1: The Twenties series (Mecklenburg County), Romare Bearden, Collection: Kingsborough Community College, The City University of New York; © Romare Bearden Foundation/ Licensed by VAGA, New York, NY

The two women looked at each other and then back to me. Mr. Calhoun broke out with a proud smile beneath his bristly moustache, and instead of the next child taking up where I had ended, he nodded to me to go on. So I read the story to the end, where flying Mercury, the messenger of the Gods, brought Persephone back to the sunlit earth and restored her to the arms of Dame Ceres, her mother, that the world might have springtime and summer flowers, autumn and harvest. But because she had bitten the pomegranate[6] while in Pluto's kingdom, she must return to him for three months of each year, and be his queen. Then the world had winter, until she returned to earth.

The class was dismissed, and the visitors smiled us away and went into a low-voiced conversation with Mr. Calhoun for a few minutes. They glanced my way once or twice and I began to worry. Not only was I barefooted, but my feet and legs were dusty. My hair was more uncombed than usual, and my nails were not shiny clean. Oh, I'm going to catch it now. Those ladies saw me, too. Mr. Calhoun is promising to 'tend to me. So I thought.

Then Mr. Calhoun called me. I went up thinking how awful it was to get a whipping before company. Furthermore, I heard a snicker run over the room. Hennie Clark and Stell Brazzle did it out loud, so I would be sure to hear them. The smart-aleck was going to get it. I slipped one hand behind me and switched my dress tail at them, indicating scorn.

"Come here, Zora Neale," Mr. Calhoun cooed as I reached the desk. He put his hand on my shoulder and gave me little pats. The ladies smiled and held out those flower-looking fingers towards me. I seized the opportunity for a good look.

"Shake hands with the ladies, Zora Neale," Mr. Calhoun prompted and they took my hand one after the other and smiled. They asked if I loved school, and I lied that I did. There was *some* truth in it, because I liked geography and reading, and I liked to play at recess time. Who ever it was invented writing and arithmetic got no thanks from me. Neither did I like the arrangement where the teacher could sit up there with a palmetto stem and lick me whenever he saw fit. I hated things I couldn't do anything about. But I knew better than to bring that up right there, so I said yes, I *loved* school.

6. **pomegranate** (päm′ gran′ it) *n.* round, red-skinned fruit with many seeds.

8 **Critical Viewing**
How does the mood of this image compare or contrast with the mood of Hurston's writing? Explain. **[Compare and Contrast]**

Reading Strategy
Analyzing How a Writer Achieves Purpose Why do you think Hurston includes this description of her response to taunting classmates? How does it help you to understand young Zora's experience?

Vocabulary Builder
geography (jē äg′ rə fē) *n.* study of Earth's surface

11 
Reading Check
Why is Zora afraid to approach her teacher after reading so well?

8 Critical Viewing

Answer: The faces seem solemn and the face of the figure at far left seems almost desperate. Such joylessness is not characteristic of Hurston's ebullient personality or her writing. However, the bright colors of the image more closely echo Hurston's work.

9 Reading Strategy
Analyzing How a Writer Achieves Purpose

- Read aloud the bracketed passage to students.
- **Ask** the Reading Strategy question: Why do you think Hurston includes this description of her response to taunting classmates? How does it help you to understand young Zora's experience?
  Answer: Zora's reaction to her classmates shows her fearlessness and also her difference. She is taunted, at least in part, for being smart.

10 Vocabulary Builder
Greek Root *-graph-*

- Draw students' attention to Hurston's use of the word *geography,* and read its definition.
- Tell students that the word combines the prefix *geo-*, meaning "earth," with the root *-graph-*, meaning "to write."
- Write the following prefixes and their meanings on the board: *auto-* = "self"; *topo-* = "place," *biblio-* = "book," *bio-* = "life."
- Have students combine these prefixes with the root *-graph-* to create new words. **Ask** students to define each of the new words they create. **Answers:** An autograph is a signature. Topography is the contour of the land; the terrain. A bibliography is a list of books. A biography is a life story.

11 Reading Check

Answer: Zora looks dirty and untidy. She expects to be punished.

⓬ Reading Strategy
Analyzing How a Writer Achieves Purpose

- **Ask** students: Why does Hurston mention the "strange things" the ladies offer her to eat?
  Answer: She wants to stress how foreign and exotic the women seemed to her.
- Then, have students explain why Hurston describes the gift of the pennies in detail.
  Answer: She was overwhelmed by the gift and still remembers it years later. She wants readers to understand what a miracle it was for a black child in the Depression to have a hundred shiny pennies.
- Then, **ask** the Reading Strategy question: Why do you think Hurston includes this incident in which her mother prepares her for meeting the women at the hotel?
  Answer: Hurston wants to show how important this visit was to her family. She wants to emphasize that her invitation was a special, unusual event.

"I can tell you do," Brown Taffeta gleamed. She patted my head, and was lucky enough not to get sandspurs in her hand. Children who roll and tumble in the grass in Florida are apt to get sandspurs in their hair. They shook hands with me again and I went back to my seat.

When school let out at three o'clock, Mr. Calhoun told me to wait. When everybody had gone, he told me I was to go to the Park House, that was the hotel in Maitland,[7] the next afternoon to call upon Mrs. Johnstone and Miss Hurd. I must tell Mama to see that I was clean and brushed from head to feet, and I must wear shoes and stockings. The ladies liked me, he said, and I must be on my best behavior.

The next day I was let out of school an hour early, and went home to be stood up in a tub full of suds and be scrubbed and have my ears dug into. My sandy hair sported a red ribbon to match my red and white checked gingham dress, starched until it could stand alone. Mama saw to it that my shoes were on the right feet, since I was careless about left and right. Last thing, I was given a handkerchief to carry, warned again about my behavior, and sent off, with my big brother John to go as far as the hotel gate with me.

Reading Strategy
Analyzing How a Writer Achieves Purpose Why do you think Hurston includes this incident in which her mother prepares her for her meeting with the women at the hotel?

First thing, the ladies gave me strange things, like stuffed dates and preserved ginger, and encouraged me to eat all that I wanted. Then they showed me their Japanese dolls and just talked. I was then handed a copy of *Scribner's Magazine*,[8] and asked to read a place that was pointed out to me. After a paragraph or two, I was told with smiles, that that would do.

⓬

I was led out on the grounds and they took my picture under a palm tree. They handed me what was to me then a heavy cylinder done up in fancy paper, tied with a ribbon, and they told me goodbye, asking me not to open it until I got home.

My brother was waiting for me down by the lake, and we hurried home, eager to see what was in the thing. It was too heavy to be candy or anything like that. John insisted on toting it for me.

My mother made John give it back to me and let me open it. Perhaps, I shall never experience such joy again. The nearest thing to that moment was the telegram accepting my first book. One hundred goldy-new pennies rolled out of the cylinder. Their gleam lit up the world. It was not avarice that moved me. It was the beauty of the thing. I stood on the mountain. Mama let me play with my pennies for a while, then put them away for me to keep.

Vocabulary Builder
avarice (av′ ər is) *n.* extreme desire for wealth; greed

That was only the beginning. The next day I received an Episcopal hymn-book bound in white leather with a golden cross stamped into the front cover, a copy of *The Swiss Family Robinson*, and a book of fairy tales.

I set about to commit the song words to memory. There was no music written there, just the words. But there was to my consciousness music in between them just the same. "When I Survey the Wondrous Cross"

7. **Maitland** (māt′ lənd) city in Florida, close to Eatonville.
8. ***Scribner's Magazine*** literary magazine no longer published.

Enrichment

The Boxes of Books

Jonathan Swift's satire *Gulliver's Travels* (1727) recounts the amazing lands discovered by his fictional hero Lemuel Gulliver. The Lilliputians are miniature people, the Brobdingnagians are giants, and the Houyhnhnms are civilized horses whose servants are human savages.

Odin, Thor, and other Norse gods have counterparts in Greek and Roman mythology. Odin, like Zeus, is the unhappily-married chief of all the gods. Like Zeus' wife Hera, Odin's wife Fricka is the goddess of marriage and fidelity. Brunnhilde, Odin's favorite daughter, is a warrior maiden like Athena.

Robert Louis Stevenson is best known for his adventure stories—*Treasure Island, Kidnapped,* and *The Black Arrow.* Rudyard Kipling's *Just So Stories* is a collection of original Anglo-Indian legends explaining, among other things, how the camel got its hump and how the alphabet was invented.

seemed the most beautiful to me, so I committed that to memory first of all. Some of them seemed dull and without life, and I pretended they were not there. If white people liked trashy singing like that, there must be something funny about them that I had not noticed before. I stuck to the pretty ones where the words marched to a throb I could feel.

A month or so after the young ladies returned to Minnesota, they sent me a huge box packed with clothes and books. The red coat with a wide circular collar and the red tam[9] pleased me more than any of the other things. My chums pretended not to like anything that I had, but even then I knew that they were jealous. Old Smarty had gotten by them again. The clothes were not new, but they were very good. I shone like the morning sun.

But the books gave me more pleasure than the clothes. I had never been too keen on dressing up. It called for hard scrubbings with Octagon soap suds getting in my eyes, and none too gentle fingers scrubbing my neck and gouging in my ears.

In that box were *Gulliver's Travels, Grimm's Fairy Tales, Dick Whittington, Greek and Roman Myths,* and best of all, *Norse Tales.* Why did the Norse tales strike so deeply into my soul? I do not know, but they did. I seemed to remember seeing Thor swing his mighty short-handled hammer as he sped across the sky in rumbling thunder, lightning flashing from the tread of his steeds and the wheels of his chariot. The great and good Odin, who went down to the well of knowledge to drink, and was told that the price of a drink from that fountain was an eye. 14 Odin drank deeply, then plucked out one eye without a murmur and handed it to the grizzly keeper, and walked away. That held majesty for me.

Of the Greeks, Hercules moved me most. I followed him eagerly on his tasks. The story of the choice of Hercules as a boy when he met Pleasure and Duty, and put his hand in that of Duty and followed her steep way to the blue hills of fame and glory, which she pointed out at the end, moved me profoundly. I resolved to be like him. The tricks and turns of the other Gods and Goddesses left me cold. There were other thin books about this and that sweet and gentle little girl who gave up her heart to Christ and good works. Almost always they died from it, preaching as they passed. I was utterly indifferent to their deaths. In the first place I could not conceive of death, and in the next place they never had any funerals that amounted to a hill of beans, so I didn't care how soon they rolled up their big, soulful, blue eyes and kicked the bucket. They had no meat on their bones.

But I also met Hans Andersen and Robert Louis Stevenson. They seemed to know what I wanted to hear and said it in a way that tingled

9. **tam** (tam) *n.* cap with a wide, round, flat top and sometimes a center pompom.

13 ***Zora Neale Hurston Rediscovered***

Although she died in a welfare home in 1960 penniless and unknown, the rediscovery of Zora Neale Hurston in the 1970s is among the most dramatic events in American literary history. Hurston became a subject of author Alice Walker's 1983 essay, "In Search of Our Mother's Gardens." Ten years earlier, Walker's article "Looking for Zora" described her 1973 search to find and mark Hurston's unknown grave.

In both of her writings, Walker speaks of the importance of recovering and remembering Hurston as one of the greatest African American folklorists of all time and a major American writer. Walker championed the cause to resurrect Hurston's literary reputation and, once again, give her a prominent place in our literary heritage.

Connect to the Literature

Think about the incident that Hurston describes in this excerpt from her autobiography. Why do you think she became a writer?

15  **Reading Check**

Of all the gifts she receives, what gives Zora the most pleasure? Explain.

13 The American Experience

Zora Neale Hurston Rediscovered Writer Alice Walker, whose best-known work is *The Color Purple*, was determined to revive interest in Zora Neale Hurston. In August of 1973, Walker discovered and marked Hurston's grave in Fort Pierce, Florida. Walker described her search for Hurston's grave in her article "In Search of Zora Neale Hurston," published in *Ms.* magazine in March 1975.

Hurston's autobiographical work *Dust Tracks on a Road* recounts her growing interest in books and language.

Connect to the Literature Tell students to consider why Zora was chosen to meet Mrs. Johnstone and Miss Hurd at their hotel. Then have them think about the gifts Zora received and which ones she liked best.
Possible response: Zora loved reading stories, myths, and fairy tales. This intense interest coupled with a gift of new reading material most likely contributed to her desire to create stories.

14 Critical Thinking

Compare and Contrast

- Based on Hurston's descriptions of her favorite stories, **ask** students to compare and contrast Thor, Odin, and Hercules.
  Answer: Thor and Hercules are strong heroes. Odin and Hercules both make sacrifices for what they want (knowledge and glory).
- How is Zora like her heroes? How is she different?
  Answer: Like her heroes, Zora takes risks to get what she wants. She is brave. Her heroes have adventures and she, too, seeks adventure.
- Then, **ask** students to contrast Zora's personality with that of the "sweet and gentle little girl" she describes in the last paragraph on this page. Why do these stories bore her?
  Answer: Zora is the opposite of "sweet and gentle"; she is smart-alecky, disobedient, and high-spirited. She likes stories about bold spirits and is bored by tales of the lifeless and obedient.

15 Reading Check

Answer: Zora likes the books best because they tell exciting tales of bold characters whom she admires.

ASSESS

Answers

1. Students who like fantasy and adventure should share Zora's taste in stories.
2. (a) She calls to them and offers to accompany them up the road. (b) She is outgoing and assertive, likes talking to new people, and isn't afraid of strangers.
3. (a) Mrs. Johnstone and Miss Hurd are from Minnesota. Their interest in the school and their gifts to Zora suggest that they are involved in charity work. (b) Everything about them, from their hands to their clothing to the food they offer her, fascinates Zora. Their gift of the new roll of pennies resulted in one of the shining moments of Zora's life.
4. (a) Zora finds nearly everything about them fascinating, but is most taken with their hands. (b) She hasn't met many people outside her own community. Most of the people she knows are just like her and her family.
5. (a) She is happy with the clothes and thrilled by the pennies. It is the books that have the most enduring impact on her. (b) She loves to read, and likes things that appeal to her intelligence and imagination.
6. Students should say yes. People respond best to those who believe in and respect themselves.

Go Online Author Link For additional information about Zora Neale Hurston, have students type in the Web Code, then select *H* from the alphabet, and then select Zora Neale Hurston.

me. Just a little below these friends was Rudyard Kipling in his *Jungle Books*. I loved his talking snakes as much as I did the hero.

I came to start reading the Bible through my mother. She gave me a licking one afternoon for repeating something I had overheard a neighbor telling her. She locked me in her room after the whipping, and the Bible was the only thing in there for me to read. I happened to open to the place where David[10] was doing some mighty smiting, and I got interested. David went here and he went there, and no matter where he went, he smote 'em hip and thigh. Then he sung songs to his harp awhile, and went out and smote some more. Not one time did David stop and preach about sins and other things. All David wanted to know from God was who to kill and when. He took care of the other details himself. Never a quiet moment. I liked him a lot. So I read a great deal more in the Bible, hunting for some more active people like David. Except for the beautiful language of Luke and Paul,[11] the New Testament still plays a poor second to the Old Testament for me. The Jews had a God who laid about Him when they needed Him. I could see no use waiting until Judgment Day to see a man who was just crying for a good killing, to be told to go and roast. My idea was to give him a good killing first, and then if he got roasted later on, so much the better.

10. **David** in the Bible, the second king of Israel, the land of the Hebrews.
11. **Luke and Paul** two Christian Apostles who wrote parts of the New Testament.

Critical Reading

1. **Respond:** What do you think about young Zora's preferences in reading? Which of the stories would you like to read?
2. **(a) Recall:** What does Zora do when white travelers pass by her house? **(b) Infer:** What does this activity tell you about her?
3. **(a) Recall:** Who are the two white women Zora meets, and why are they at her school? **(b) Support:** How can you tell that these two women made an impression on Hurston?
4. **(a) Recall:** What does Zora find fascinating about the two visitors? **(b) Infer:** What does her fascination suggest about her life experiences so far?
5. **(a) Recall:** Describe Zora's response to the gifts she receives. **(b) Infer:** What does her preference reveal about her?
6. **Evaluate:** Do you think it is important to have self-confidence, as Zora did, in order to succeed in life? Why or why not?

For: More about Zora Neale Hurston
Visit: www.PHSchool.com
Web Code: ere-9523

Apply the Skills

from *Dust Tracks on a Road*

Literary Analysis

Social Context in Autobiography

1. **(a)** Why might Zora's grandmother be worried about her granddaughter's brazenness? **(b)** What can you infer about the **social context** and cultural attitudes, based on her grandmother's statements?
2. What do you learn about the social context through the following details of Hurston's **autobiography: (a)** the schoolroom being cleaned for visitors, **(b)** students reading mythology, and **(c)** Zora going to school barefoot?
3. Find three more details that reveal the attitudes of Hurston's culture. Record them in a chart like the one shown.

Connecting Literary Elements

4. What important information about Hurston is revealed in the opening **dialogue** she has with her grandmother?
5. Identify an example of dialogue that reveals a distinct trait of Hurston's personality. Explain how it does so.
6. What general impression do you get of the school and of education in the community based on the dialogue between Hurston, her teacher, and the two visitors?

Reading Strategy

Analyzing How a Writer Achieves Purpose

7. Why does Hurston include the actual words of her grandmother in dialect?
8. What small incidents and details does Hurston use to reveal her reputation as a smart-aleck in school?
9. For what purpose do you think Hurston included her meeting with the Minnesotans in her autobiography?

Extend Understanding

10. **Cultural Connection:** In what ways can relationships with mentors such as Hurston's improve a young person's life?

QuickReview

In **autobiography,** a writer tells his or her own life story.

Autobiographies often reveal **social context**—the attitudes or customs of a culture or specific time period.

The use of **dialogue,** or conversation between characters, makes a scene come alive and helps to define such things as the characters' personalities, social class, and education.

To **analyze how a writer achieves purpose,** consider the way details and events that are described work toward a specific goal.

Go Online Assessment
For: Self-test
Visit: www.PHSchool.com
Web Code: era-6515

Students may use the **Self-test** to prepare for **Selection Test A** or **Selection Test B.**

Answers

1. (a) She's afraid that Zora will get herself into trouble. (b) Experience tells the grandmother that many white people want black people to behave in a subservient manner, not to display the bold confidence that Zora shows.
2. (a) The teachers want to make a good impression on visitors; this suggests that they depend on the visitors in some way. (b) Students are exposed to classical literature. (c) The community is poor. The children's parents probably want to reserve shoes for special occasions.
3. **Possible answers:** Zora's classmates stumble through their reading; the culture is not highly literate. The ladies' gifts to Zora; some white people seek to redress the wrongs done to blacks. Zora's fascination with the ladies' slender white hands; she is used to seeing work-worn hands on women.

   Another sample answer can be found on **Literary Analysis Graphic Organizer B,** p. 204 in ***Graphic Organizer Transparencies.***
4. She risks punishment to do what she wants.
5. "Don't you want me to go a piece of the way with you?" shows that Hurston is gregarious and wants adventure.
6. The teachers seem to deal with the students as a group, not as individuals. They use force to discipline the children. An intelligent, curious child like Zora probably finds limited stimulation.
7. She wants to portray her grandmother realistically. She wants to remind readers of the heritage of slavery—fear and ignorance.
8. She reads aloud much better than the other students. Even when she thinks she is about to be punished, she makes a scornful gesture to the students who snicker at her.
9. Their gifts of books marked a turning point in her life. It gave her access in print to new places, stories, and people.
10. Mentors can share their life experiences, listen to confidences, give advice, and provide a model of success.

EXTEND/ASSESS

Answers

❶ Vocabulary Lesson

Word Analysis: Greek Root *-graph-*

1. to write one's signature
2. to send a message over wires
3. the story of someone's life
4. written or drawn

Spelling Strategy

1. judge
2. fudge
3. budge

Vocabulary Builder

1. foreknowledge
2. caper
3. brazenness
4. exalted
5. geography
6. avarice

❷ Grammar and Style Lesson

1. I kept right on gazing at them, and "going a piece of the way…"; conjunction: and
2. with the permission of my parents, nor with their foreknowledge; conjunction: nor
3. David sung songs and went out and smote; conjunction: and (twice)
4. I must tell Mama… and I must wear shoes and stockings; conjunction: and
5. I was given…, warned…, and sent off; conjunction: and

Writing Application

Have students exchange papers and check for the required grammatical elements. Students may review Writing and Grammar, Ruby Level, to settle any disagreements.

Build Language Skills

❶ Vocabulary Lesson

Word Analysis: Greek Root *-graph-*

The Greek root *-graph-* means "write." For example, *geography* means "the study of, or writing about, Earth." Define the following words, incorporating the meaning of *-graph-* into your definitions.

1. autograph
2. telegraph
3. biography
4. graphic

Spelling Strategy

In many words, the *j* sound is spelled *-dg-*, as in *knowledge* or *pudgy*. Complete each sentence with a word in which the *j* sound is spelled *-dg-*.

1. A __?__ rules in a court.
2. I ordered a hot __?__ sundae.
3. The heavy table would not __?__.

Vocabulary Builder: Analogies

Review the vocabulary list on page 913 and note how each word is used in the context of the selection. Then, select the correct word to complete each of the following analogies.

1. *Hindsight* is to *past* as __?__ is to *future.*
2. *Trick* is to *magician* as __?__ is to *prankster.*
3. *Indifference* is to *concern* as __?__ is to *shyness.*
4. *Dejected* is to *loser* as __?__ is to *winner.*
5. *Zoology* is to *animals* as __?__ is to *Earth's surface.*
6. *Cruelty* is to *kindness* as __?__ is to *selflessness.*

❷ Grammar and Style Lesson

Parallelism in Coordinate Elements

Parallel coordinate elements—those linked by coordinating conjunctions such as *and, but, or, nor,* or *so*—may be nouns, adjectives, adverbs, clauses, or phrases. To make elements that are linked with coordinating conjunctions parallel, put them in the same grammatical form.

Example: She *cut* her eyes and *gave* us a glare that meant trouble. (past tense verb)

Practice Copy the following sentences. Circle the coordinating conjunction(s) and underline the parallel coordinate elements.

1. Nevertheless, I kept right on gazing at them, and "going a piece of the way" . . .
2. I did not do this with the permission of my parents, nor with their foreknowledge.
3. Then [David] sung songs to his harp awhile, and went out and smote some more.
4. I must tell Mama to see that I was clean and brushed from head to feet, and I must wear shoes and stockings.
5. I was given a handkerchief to carry, warned again about my behavior, and sent off . . .

Writing Application Write a paragraph about the importance of self-confidence. Include at least two parallel coordinate elements linked by coordinating conjunctions.

WG *Prentice Hall Writing and Grammar Connection: Chapter 20, Section 6*

Assessment Practice

Sentence Completion **(For more practice, see *Standardized Test Preparation Workbook*, p. 55.)**

Many tests ask students to choose the best word to complete a sentence. Use the following sample test item to give students practice at this skill.

For African Americans, folklore and oral history served as an important means of preserving their cultural heritage. Thanks to anthropologists and writers such as Hurston, this folk tradition is now ___________ preserved in writing.

Which word best completes this passage?

A permanently
B temporarily
C emphatically
D tentatively

Students should know that short of deliberate destruction, written records last forever. The correct answer is *A*.

Writing Lesson

Personal Narrative

Hurston's encounter with the Minnesotans was a turning point in her life, leading to a greater love of reading and learning. Write a personal narrative about a moment in your life that inspired you to act or think differently.

Prewriting Jot down some of your interests, such as sports, hobbies, movies, or travel, and consider their origins. Think of incidents that were "moments of inspiration." Select one as the focus of your narrative, and explore its impact in a cause-and-effect diagram like the one shown.

Model: Analyzing Cause and Effect

Cause		Effects
My ninth-grade teacher introduced me to writing poetry in a creative way.	→	As a result, I feel confident in my ability and want to pursue a career as a poet.

Drafting Start your essay by showing the effects of your moment of inspiration and then flashing back to reconstruct the moment itself. Use the details in your cause-and-effect diagram to help you.

Revising Reread your narrative to make sure the connection between inspiration and reaction is clear. Make sure you have demonstrated, rather than explained, its impact on your life.

WG *Prentice Hall Writing and Grammar Connection: Chapter 4, Section 2*

Extend Your Learning

Listening and Speaking Develop and deliver a **campaign speech** in which young Zora hopes to persuade her classmates to elect her class president. Include details that reveal Zora's self-image and portray her character. The following tips will help you:

- Review the selection to identify Zora's qualities.
- Outline her accomplishments.
- Discuss goals that will benefit the class.

Practice the speech with a partner before presenting it to your class.

Research and Technology With a group, select three folk tales from Hurston's *Mules and Men* or from another book of folk tales collected in the United States. Compile them in a booklet, creating a **folk tale collection**. In the booklet, write an introduction, prepare a table of contents, choose art or illustrations and include brief reviews of each tale. **[Group Activity]**

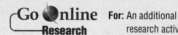

For: An additional research activity
Visit: www.PHSchool.com
Web Code: erd-7514

Assessment Resources

The following resources can be used to assess students' knowledge and skills.

Unit 5 Resources
Selection Test A, pp. 256–258
Selection Test B, pp. 259–261

General Resources
Rubrics for Narration: Autobiographical Narrative, pp. 43–44

Go Online Assessment — Students may use the **Self-test** to prepare for **Selection Test A** or **Selection Test B.**

❸ Writing Lesson

You may use this Writing Lesson as timed-writing practice, or you may allow students to develop the essay as a writing assignment over several days.

- To support students in preparing a personal narrative, give them the **Support for Writing Lesson** page (***Unit 5 Resources,*** p. 253).
- Students may find it helpful to begin by identifying a person who has strongly influenced their lives.
- Review the cause-and-effect chart. Explain to students that the impact of their chosen incident will be the effect.
- Tell students that the effect they define will be the main idea of their personal narratives. All the ideas and details they include in their narratives should contribute to this main idea.
- Use the Narration: Autobiographical Narrative rubrics in ***General Resources,*** pp. 43–44, to evaluate students' work.

❹ Research and Technology

- Encourage students to choose folk tales from a variety of cultures.
- Challenge students to write their own versions of old stories they heard while growing up.
- Students may want to collaborate on this project, with some students writing stories, others drawing illustrations, others working on the introductions, and others organizing the elements to create the actual books.
- The **Support for Extend Your Learning** page (***Unit 5 Resources,*** p. 254) provides guided note-taking opportunities to help students complete the Extend Your Learning activities.

Go Online Research — Have students type in the Web Code for another research activity.

Meeting Your Standards

Students will

1. **analyze and respond to literary elements.**
   - Literary Analysis: Speaker
2. **read, comprehend, analyze, and critique poetry.**
   - Reading Strategy: Drawing Inferences About the Speaker
   - Reading Check questions
   - Apply the Skills questions
   - Assessment Practice (ATE)
3. **develop vocabulary.**
   - Vocabulary Lesson: Latin Word Root: *-lib-*
4. **understand and apply written and oral language conventions.**
   - Spelling Strategy
   - Grammar and Style Lesson: Verb Tenses: Past and Present Perfect
5. **develop writing proficiency.**
   - Writing Lesson: Poetry Comparison
6. **develop appropriate research strategies.**
   - Extend Your Learning: Poster
7. **understand and apply listening and speaking strategies.**
   - Extend Your Learning: Presentation

Block Scheduling: Use one 90-minute class period to preteach the skills and have students read the selection. Use a second 90-minute class period to assess students' mastery of skills, extend their learning, and monitor their progress.

Homework Suggestions

Following are possibilities for homework assignments.

- Support pages from *Unit 5 Resources:*
  Literary Analysis
  Reading Strategy
  Vocabulary Builder
  Grammar and Style
- An Extend Your Learning project and the Writing Lesson for this selection group may be completed over several days.

Step-by-Step Teaching Guide	Pacing Guide
PRETEACH	
• Administer Vocabulary and Reading Warm-ups as necessary.	5 min.
• Engage students' interest with the motivation activity.	5 min.
• Read and discuss author and background features. **FT**	10 min.
• Introduce the Literary Analysis Skill: Speaker. **FT**	5 min.
• Introduce the Reading Strategy: Drawing Inferences About the Speaker. **FT**	10 min.
• Prepare students to read by teaching the selection vocabulary. **FT**	
TEACH	
• Informally monitor comprehension while students read independently or in groups. **FT**	30 min.
• Monitor students' comprehension with the Reading Check notes.	as students read
• Reinforce vocabulary with Vocabulary Builder notes.	as students read
• Develop students' understanding of speaker with the Literary Analysis annotations. **FT**	5 min.
• Develop students' ability to draw inferences about the speaker with the Reading Strategy annotations. **FT**	5 min.
ASSESS/EXTEND	
• Assess students' comprehension and mastery of the Literary Analysis and Reading Strategy by having them answer the Apply the Skills questions. **FT**	15 min.
• Have students complete the Vocabulary Lesson and the Grammar and Style Lesson. **FT**	15 min.
• Apply students' ability to use quotations to connect themes by using the Writing Lesson. **FT**	45 min. or homework
• Apply students' understanding by using one or more of the Extend Your Learning activities.	20–90 min. or homework
• Administer Selection Test A or Selection Test B. **FT**	15 min.

Resources

PRINT
Unit 5 Resources
Vocabulary Warm-up Word Lists **[L1, L2, EL]** .... p. 262
Vocabulary Warm-up Practice **[L1, L2, EL]** .... p. 263
Reading Warm-up A **[L1, L2, EL]** .... p. 264
Reading Warm-up B **[L1, L2, L3]** .... p. 265

TRANSPARENCY
Graphic Organizer Transparencies
Literary Analysis Graphic Organizer A **[L3]** .... p. 205
Literary Analysis Graphic Organizer B **[L1, L2, EL]** .... p. 206
Reading Strategy Graphic Organizer A **[L3]** .... p. 207
Reading Strategy Graphic Organizer B **[L1, L2, EL]** .... p. 208

PRINT
Reader's Notebook [L2]
Reader's Notebook: Adapted Version [L1]
Reader's Notebook: English Learner's Version [EL]
Unit 5 Resources
Literary Analysis **[L3]** .... p. 266
Reading Strategy **[L3]** .... p. 267
Vocabulary Builder **[L3]** .... p. 268

TECHNOLOGY
Listening to Literature Audio CDs [L2, EL]

PRINT
Unit 5 Resources
Grammar and Style **[L3]** .... p. 269
Support for Writing Lesson **[L3]** .... p. 270
Support for Extend Your Learning **[L3]** .... p. 271
Enrichment **[L4]** .... p. 272
Selection Test A **[L1, L2, EL]** .... pp. 273–275
Selection Test B **[L3, L4]** .... pp. 276–278
General Resources
Rubrics for Response to Literature **[L3]** .... pp. 65–66

TECHNOLOGY
Go Online: Research **[L3]**
Go Online: Self-test **[L3]**
***ExamView*® Test Bank [L3]**

Choosing Resources for Differentiated Instruction

[L1] Special Needs Students
[L2] Below-Level Students
[L3] All Students
[L4] Advanced Students
[EL] English Learners

For Vocabulary and Reading Warm-ups and for Selection Tests, **A** signifies "less challenging" and **B** "more challenging." For Graphic Organizer transparencies, **A** signifies "not filled in" and **B** "filled in."

FT Fast Track Instruction: To move the lesson more quickly, use the strategies and activities identified with **FT**.

Scaffolding for Less Proficient and Advanced Students

The leveled Critical Thinking questions after selections progress in the levels of thinking required to answer them. To address the needs of your different students, you may use the (a) level questions for your less proficient students and the (b) level questions with your on-level and advanced students. The occasional (c) level questions are appropriate for your advanced students.

PRENTICE HALL **TeacherEXPRESS**™ Plan · Teach · Assess — Use this complete suite of powerful teaching tools to make lesson planning and testing quicker and easier.

PRENTICE HALL **StudentEXPRESS**™ Learn · Study · Succeed — Use the interactive textbook (online and on CD-ROM) to make selections and activities come alive with audio and video support and interactive questions.

Go Online Professional Development
For: Information about Lexiles
Visit: www.PHSchool.com
Web Code: eue-1111

PRETEACH

Motivation

Play for the class the famous jazz song "Take the A Train" (composed by Billy Strayhorn, and arranged by Duke Ellington). Explain that during the 1920s, New York City's Harlem was a thriving center for literature, music, and the arts. This group of poems includes work by two important writers of the Harlem Renaissance: Langston Hughes and Claude McKay.

❶ Background

More About the Authors

In much of his work, which included lyrics, plays, and short stories as well as the poetry for which he is most famous, Langston Hughes sought to express the energy, immediacy, and improvisational feel of jazz and the blues. Although some critics took issue with these efforts, Hughes's insistence on the seriousness and integrity of these musical forms is one of his great artistic achievements. Hughes's interest in music was also evident in his work as a writer of librettos, including the one he wrote for the Kurt Weill/ Elmer Rice opera *Street Scene* (1947), that critics have praised as a groundbreaking work of the American musical theater.

For many critics, Claude McKay's poems of social protest, which he wrote fairly early in his career, remain his best and most influential work. Traditional in form but full of highly charged content, these poems influenced many of the younger writers of the Harlem Renaissance, including Langston Hughes. McKay wrote one of these poems of protest, the sonnet "If We Must Die," in response to a period of racial violence against blacks known as the Red Summer of 1919. The poem is an anthem of resistance to oppression and was later quoted by Winston Churchill during World War II.

❶ The Negro Speaks of Rivers • I, Too • Dream Variations • Refugee in America • The Tropics in New York

Langston Hughes (1902–1967)

Langston Hughes emerged from the Harlem Renaissance, a cultural movement of the 1920s, as the most prolific and successful African American writer in the country. In his poetry, he expressed pride in his heritage and voiced displeasure with the oppression he witnessed. Although Hughes is best known for his powerful poetry, he also wrote plays, fiction, autobiographical sketches, and screenplays.

Born in Missouri and raised in Kansas, Illinois, and Ohio, Hughes attended high school in Cleveland, where he contributed poetry to the school literary magazine. In 1921, he moved to New York City to attend Columbia University, but a year later he left school to travel to Europe and to Africa as a merchant seaman.

First Success On his return to New York, Hughes published his first volume of poetry, *The Weary Blues* (1926). The book attracted attention and earned him wide recognition. Hughes published several other volumes of poetry, including *The Dream Keeper* (1932), *Fields of Wonder* (1947), and *Montage of a Dream Deferred* (1951). He experimented with a variety of forms and techniques in his poetry and often tried to recreate the rhythms of contemporary jazz.

Like many of the Harlem Renaissance writers, Hughes was not born in Harlem and lived a large part of his life elsewhere. Nevertheless, he identified Harlem as a source of inspiration for black artists. Harlem was where he felt most welcome and nourished. Today, Hughes is recognized as one of the most popular and enduring African American writers of the twentieth century.

Claude McKay (1890–1948)

In much of his work, Claude McKay—poet, novelist, journalist, and activist—evokes the colors and rhythms of life on his native island of Jamaica. While McKay retained a lifelong attachment to Jamaica, he regarded Harlem as a spiritual home. Although he frequently lived elsewhere in the United States and overseas, including England, Russia, France, Germany, and Morocco, it was to Harlem that he would return in both his life and his work. Writing from abroad in 1930 to fellow Harlem Renaissance poet Langston Hughes, McKay said, "I write of America as home [although] I am really a poet without a country."

Jamaican Roots The son of farm workers, Festus Claudius McKay received his early education from his brother, who was a schoolteacher. When he was fourteen, McKay moved to Kingston, Jamaica's capital. There he met a British folklorist who encouraged him to write poetry that reflected Jamaica's culture. When his *Songs of Jamaica* (1912) won an award from the Institute of Arts and Letters, McKay was able to emigrate to the United States. He claimed he was coming to study agriculture, but he really came to advance his literary career.

After studying at Tuskegee Institute and Kansas State College, McKay moved to Harlem in 1914. There, he held various jobs and opened a restaurant with a friend. McKay's poem "The Tropics in New York" is marked by nostalgia for his homeland—a feeling echoed in the title of his autobiography, *A Long Way From Home* (1937).

Preview

Connecting to the Literature

Many factors shape our identities—the places we come from, the people who nurture us or cause us pain, and the experiences that touch our lives. In these poems, two eloquent writers examine the factors that helped to shape their identities.

2 Literary Analysis

Speaker

The **speaker** is the voice of a poem. Often, the speaker is the poet. However, a speaker may also be an imaginary person, a group of people, an animal, or an inanimate object. In "The Tropics in New York," Claude McKay's speaker is a homesick adult who is probably the poet himself:

A wave of longing through my body swept,
And, hungry for the old, familiar ways
I turned aside and bowed my head and wept.

As you read these poems, look for clues that reveal the identity of the speaker. Use a chart like the one shown to record your observations.

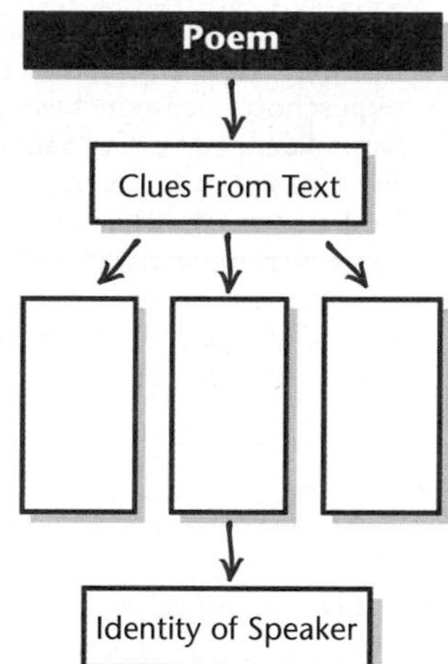

Comparing Literary Works

Through imagery and vivid memories, each of these poems expresses a sense of African American culture, identity, or homeland. For example, both "The Negro Speaks of Rivers" and "The Tropics in New York" describe homelands through references to ancient rivers, to the Mississippi, and to the tropics. As you read these poems, compare the images of African American culture and identity the poets describe.

3 Reading Strategy

Drawing Inferences About the Speaker

Most often, a poem's speaker is not revealed directly. Instead, the reader must **draw inferences,** or come to conclusions, based on the speaker's choice of words and the details included in the poem. Once you have determined the speaker's identity, you can draw inferences about the speaker's attitudes, feelings, and experiences.

As you read these poems, look for clues about the speakers, and draw inferences about both their personal qualities and the attitude toward life each expresses.

Vocabulary Builder

lulled (luld) *v.* calmed or soothed by a gentle sound or motion (p. 926)

dusky (dus′ kē) *adj.* dim; shadowy (p. 926)

liberty (lib′ ər tē) *n.* condition of being free from control by others (p. 931)

Differentiated Instruction

Solutions for All Learners

Support for Special Needs Students
Have students complete the **Preview** and **Build Skills** pages for these selections in the ***Reader's Notebook: Adapted Version.*** These pages provide a selection summary, an abbreviated presentation of the reading and literary skills, and the graphic organizer on the **Build Skills** page in the student book.

Support for Less Proficient Readers
Have students complete the **Preview** and **Build Skills** pages for these selections in the ***Reader's Notebook.*** These pages provide a selection summary, an abbreviated presentation of the reading and literary skills, and the graphic organizer on the **Build Skills** page in the student book.

Support for English Learners
Have students complete the **Preview** and **Build Skills** pages for these selections in the ***Reader's Notebook: English Learner's Version.*** These pages provide a selection summary, a presentation of the skills, contextual vocabulary, and the graphic organizer on the **Build Skills** page in the student book.

2 Literary Analysis

Speaker

- Explain that a speaker is to a poem what a narrator is to a work of prose. The poem presents the speaker's point of view, just as a story shares the narrator's point of view.
- List the following poems from previous units on the chalkboard and ask students to identify the speakers: "The Love Song of J. Alfred Prufrock" (a fictional character named Prufrock); excerpt from "Song of Myself" (Walt Whitman); "I heard a Fly buzz—when I died—" (speaker may or may not be the poet).
- Use this exercise to remind students that a speaker is simply a narrator, not necessarily the poet. In some cases, the speaker and the poet may be one and the same, but they are often completely different.
- Give students a copy of **Literary Analysis Graphic Organizer A,** p. 205 in ***Graphic Organizer Transparencies.*** Tell them to use this chart to list details that will help them identify the speaker of a poem.
- Challenge students to try to characterize the speaker of each poem in this grouping.

3 Reading Strategy

Drawing Inferences About the Speaker

- Critical Thinking annotations throughout this teacher's edition give students practice at drawing inferences. Briefly review this skill. An inference is a conclusion made from hints and implications in a text.
- Because the poems in this grouping are brief, students must infer almost all the information about the speakers—gender, appearance, age, and so on.
- Invite students to list the characteristics of each speaker and identify clues in the text that support each of their choices.

Vocabulary Builder

- Pronounce each vocabulary word for students and read the definitions as a class. Have students identify any words with which they are already familiar.

TEACH

Learning Modalities
Visual/Learners Invite students to choose any two poems and write brief essays comparing and contrasting the ways in which each poet uses words to create visual images. Do the poets create similar images? Do they use similar techniques to create vastly different images? How would students illustrate these poems if they had the opportunity?

❶ About the Selections

Four poems by Langston Hughes explore themes of ancestry, love, aspiration, and the longing for freedom and justice. Coming face to face with a window display of tropical fruit, the speaker of a Claude McKay poem is overcome with longing for home.

❷ Reading Strategy
Drawing Inferences About the Speaker

- **Ask** students what they can infer about the speaker of this poem. Have them explain their answers. **Answer:** The speaker describes memories of three African rivers, so he or she is probably of African descent. The speaker's reference to Lincoln and the Mississippi suggest that he or she has lived in the United States. The references to rivers suggest that they play an important role in the speaker's daily life.

➤ **Monitor Progress:** Have students use a graphic organizer like the one shown to determine who the speaker is in this poem. Help students to see that the final lines of the poem underscore the collective identity of the speaker.

dues
I've known rivers
I bathed in the Euphrates
I looked upon the Nile
. . .when Abe Lincoln . . .

↓

Inference

❶ The Negro Speaks of Rivers

Langston Hughes

Background "The Negro Speaks of Rivers" was Langston Hughes's first great poem. Hughes is said to have written it when he was a senior in high school, although it was published several years later. Hughes's poetry was influenced by Carl Sandburg and Walt Whitman, whom he considered the greatest American poets. Like Whitman's ~~poem~~ "Song of Myself," Hughes's poem "The Negro Speaks of Rivers" uses a first-person speaker to express the experience and identity of an entire community.

Hughes's poem "I, Too" is a direct response to Whitman's poem "I Hear America Singing" (page 448) and its opening line: "I hear America singing, the varied carols I hear."

I've known rivers:
I've known rivers ancient as the world and older than the flow
    of human blood in human veins.

My soul has grown deep like the rivers.

I bathed in the Euphrates when dawns were young.
I built my hut near the Congo and it lulled me to sleep.
❷ I looked upon the Nile and raised the pyramids above it.
I heard the singing of the Mississippi when Abe Lincoln went
    down to New Orleans, and I've seen its muddy bosom turn
    all golden in the sunset.

I've known rivers:
Ancient, dusky rivers.

My soul has grown deep like the rivers.

Vocabulary Builder
lulled (luld) *v.* calmed or soothed by a gentle sound or motion

Vocabulary Builder
dusky (dus′ kē) *adj.* dim; shadowy

Differentiated Instruction Solutions for All Learners

Accessibility at a Glance

	I, Too; Refugee	Negro Speaks; Dream; Tropics
Context	Harlem Renaissance; response to Whitman's poem	Harlem Renaissance
Language	Simple sentences and vocabulary	Simple sentences and vocabulary
Concept Level	Accessible (struggles; wanting freedom)	Challenging (meaning must be inferred from symbols and allusion)
Literary Merit	Cross-cultural experience	Cross-cultural experience
Lexile	NP	NP
Overall Rating	Average	More challenging

3

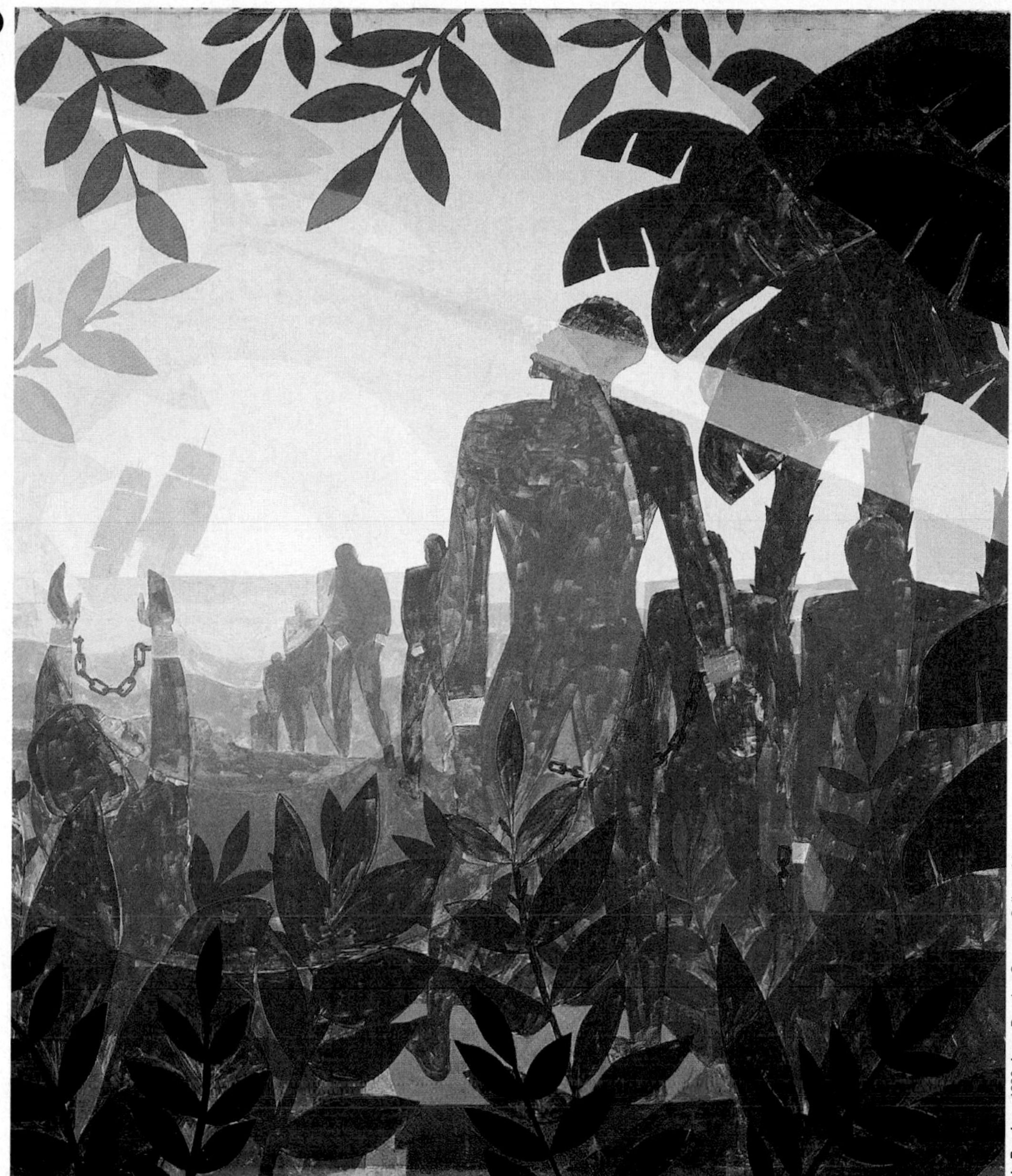

4 ▲ **Critical Viewing** What details in this painting, *Into Bondage*, by Harlem Renaissance painter Aaron Douglas, connect to Hughes's poem? **[Connect]**

Differentiated Instruction
Solutions for All Learners

Strategy for Special Needs Students
Remind students that the end of a line of poetry is often not the end of a sentence or complete thought. To aid their understanding, invite students to read the poem aloud, following the punctuation marks. As they read aloud, suggest that students also listen for the poem's sound elements, such as its use of repetition. Tell students that by reading in sentences, and listening for the poem's musical qualities, they will both understand and enjoy the poem more.

Strategy for Gifted/Talented Students
Hughes was famous for the musicality of his poems. He often built his poems using the rhythmic structure of the blues, or attempted to recreate the syncopations of jazz. Invite students to choose one of his poems and analyze it for its musical qualities. Suggest that students consider Hughes's uses of repetition, alliteration, assonance, rhyme, and rhythm. What songlike qualities does the poem demonstrate? If students were to set the poem to music, what kind of music would they choose?

3 Humanities
Into Bondage
by Aaron Douglas

Aaron Douglas (1898–1979) began his career as an art teacher in Kansas City. Then, under the advice from another artist, he sought inspiration from African art. Once Douglas incorporated African designs and subject matter, his work attracted attention. Eventually, he became a leader in the artistic movement during the "Harlem Renaissance." Douglas's work appeared in magazines, books, and even in a public library. This painting is part of a mural at the Harlem branch of the New York City Public Library. Douglas painted this as a commissioned artist under the "New Deal" program.

Use the following questions for discussion.

1. Who are the people in the painting, and where are they going?
   Possible answer: They are people from Africa, and they have been placed in chains so that they can come to America as slaves.
2. What do Hughes's poem and Douglas's painting reveal about each artist's self-identity?
   Possible answer: Hughes's poem makes a connection between the speaker and the ancient civilizations mentioned in the poem. The speaker is a descendant of these people. Douglas's painting of people being led into slavery is a connection to the artist's ancestry and the contribution to a continuing legacy.

4 Critical Viewing

Possible answer: The image shows a historical event in which people are being led in chains to slave ships. The speaker in the poem makes allusions to historical civilizations in Africa.

❺ Humanities

Nobody Around Here Calls Me Citizen,
by Robert Gwathmey

Robert Gwathmey (1903–1988) was an artist from Virginia. He attended art school in Pennsylvania and eventually became an art teacher in Philadelphia. Gwathmey's interest in racial issues shows in his artwork. He was troubled by the treatment African Americans received in the United States. He had hoped that his images would be enlightening and would advance positive race relations.

Use these questions for discussion.

1. **Ask** students what they think the number 2 in the painting symbolizes. Have them explain their answers.
   Possible answer: It may suggest that African Americans have two sides to them—the compliance that they show to be safe and the rebellion that they feel underneath. Others may say it suggests that African Americans are treated as second-class citizens.
2. Why did Gwathmey put the lion in the painting?
   Possible answer: He wanted to contrast the hopelessness in the man's face with the anger of the lion. The lion shows the anger that the man feels but does not show.

❻ Critical Viewing

Possible response: The figure of the man more closely resembles the image of the speaker in the reader's mind. However, like the voice in the poem, the lion is bold.

I, Too

Langston Hughes

Nobody Around Here Calls Me Citizen, 1943, Robert Gwathmey, Collection Frederick R. Weisman Art Museum at the University of Minnesota, Minneapolis,

❻ ▲ **Critical Viewing** Which image in this painting better illustrates the sentiments of this poem—the man or the lion? Explain. **[Make a Decision]**

Differentiated Instruction

Solutions for All Learners

Strategy for Less Proficient Readers
Have students create a word web for the poem "I, Too." In the center of the web, have students write the word *speaker.* Then, on the web's rays, invite them to list all the characteristics they have inferred about the speaker. They should also indicate the lines in the poem that support their inferences.

Strategy for English Learners
Have students clarify the language and meaning of the poem by reading it aloud with a partner. Remind students to read the poem as sentences, pausing where punctuation marks indicate. As they finish their oral readings, ask students to discuss their impressions of the speaker.

Enrichment for Advanced Readers
Invite students to reread the author biographies on page 924 and to conduct additional research into the life and work of Langston Hughes. After students read all of his poems in the grouping, ask them to discuss whether or not they think the speaker of each poem is Hughes.

I, too, sing America.

I am the darker brother.
They send me to eat in the kitchen
When company comes,
But I laugh,
And eat well,
And grow strong.

Tomorrow,
7 I'll be at the table
When company comes.
Nobody'll dare
Say to me,
"Eat in the kitchen,"
Then.

Besides,
They'll see how beautiful I am
And be ashamed—

I, too, am America.

Critical Reading

1. **(a) Respond:** What do you associate with the places Hughes describes in "The Negro Speaks of Rivers"? **(b) Respond:** What places do you associate with your culture or ancestry? Why?
2. **(a) Recall:** In "The Negro Speaks of Rivers," what has happened to the speaker's soul? **(b) Interpret:** Based on lines 3 and 10, what do you think is the theme of this poem?
3. **(a) Recall:** Which four rivers does the speaker mention? **(b) Interpret:** What does the age of these rivers imply about people of African ancestry?
4. **(a) Apply:** In what respects can the human race as a whole be compared with rivers? **(b) Speculate:** What other geological features or natural elements might a poet compare with the whole human race or a particular cultural group? Explain.
5. **(a) Interpret:** Why does the speaker in "I, Too" have to eat in the kitchen when company comes? **(b) Interpret:** What does eating in the kitchen represent? **(c) Interpret:** What is the significance of the fact that the speaker does not eat in the kitchen when company is not there?
6. **(a) Interpret:** What does the speaker mean when he says "I, too, am America"? **(b) Speculate:** Why do you think he refers so directly to Walt Whitman's poem?

For: More about Langston Hughes
Visit: www.PHSchool.com
Web Code: ere-9524

7 Reading Strategy
Drawing Inferences About the Speaker

- Have students reread Walt Whitman's poem "I Hear America Singing" on p. 448. Point out that Langston Hughes's opening line shows that his poem is a direct response to Whitman's poem. Have students discuss their reactions to Hughes's response.
  Possible answer: Students may note that many of the people Whitman describes could be African Americans. Nothing in Whitman's poem suggests that his American workers are all white. Suggest to students that Hughes's title asserts that he is also a singer of American songs—that his poetic voice is as valuable as Whitman's.
- After students have compared the two poems, **ask** them to draw an inference about the speaker's tone from "I, Too."
  Answer: The speaker is celebratory and defiant.

ASSESS

Answers

1. Students' responses will vary.
2. (a) It has "grown deep like the rivers." (b) The theme is the endurance of the African American people.
3. (a) The speaker names the Euphrates, Congo, Nile, and Mississippi rivers. (b) It implies that African Americans have roots that extend back to the earliest civilizations.
4. (a) **Possible answer:** Like rivers, the human race evolves and changes, shifting courses to adapt to those changes. (b) **Possible answer:** The human race can also be compared with the ocean's tides, which also evolve and change, constantly shifting.
5. (a) He does not have the same rights and status as "company," and he cannot sit with them. (b) **Possible answer:** The speaker is experiencing discrimination and is being segregated. (c) He is part of the family, but for the sake of appearances, he must be secluded in the kitchen when guests pay a visit.
6. (a) The speaker is saying that people like him are Americans and

Answers continued

should be viewed as having the same rights and freedoms as others. (b) **Possible answer:** Whitman's poem is well-known, and the speaker wants to tell another version.

For additional information about Langston Hughes, have students type in the Web Code, then select *H* from the alphabet, and then select Langston Hughes.

❽ Humanities

Girls Skipping,
by Hale Woodruff 1949

Hale Woodruff (1900–1980) was a painter, printmaker, muralist, and teacher. Born in Cairo, Illinois, he studied at the John Herron Art Institute and the Fogg Art Museum. He also studied with the great Mexican muralist Diego Rivera.

Use this question for discussion:

How does the artist create a sense of motion?
Answer: The swirls of color suggest motion. The girls' skirts and hair seem to blow in the breeze made by their movement. Looking from the bottom right corner, each figure leans or gestures toward the next, creating a circle of figures that ends at the top right.

❾ Critical Viewing

Answer: The poem is full of action verbs like *fling, whirl,* and *dance.* The figures enact these verbs.

❿ Reading Strategy

Drawing Inferences About the Speaker

- Explain to students that the poem describes experiences for which the speaker longs. What do students think the speaker's daily life is like?
  Answer: This poem works on at least two levels. On one level, the speaker dreams of playing in the sunshine and resting at night. The reader infers that he or she probably can't do these things. At the same time, the speaker is also expressing longing for a world in which darkness—like the skin of an African American person—is accepted. There is a strong suggestion that the speaker's daily life is full of struggle.
- **Ask** the Reading Strategy question: Based on lines 10–12, describe the speaker's personality.
  Answer: The speaker is burdened but hopeful and optimistic.

Dream Variations

LANGSTON HUGHES

❽

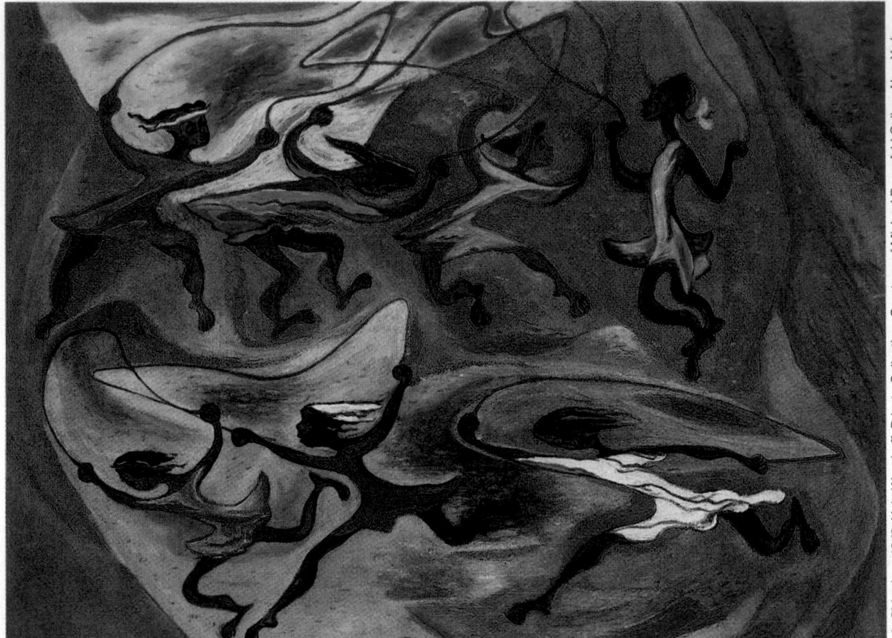

Girls Skipping, 1949, Hale Woodruff, Private Collection. Courtesy of Michael Rosenfeld Gallery, New York

To fling my arms wide
In some place of the sun,
To whirl and to dance
Till the white day is done.
Then rest at cool evening
Beneath a tall tree
While night comes on gently,
    Dark like me—
That is my dream!

❿
To fling my arms wide
In the face of the sun,
Dance! Whirl! Whirl!
Till the quick day is done.
Rest at pale evening . . .
A tall, slim tree . . .
Night coming tenderly
    Black like me.

❾ **▲ Critical Viewing**
How does the motion of the figures in this drawing reflect the mood of the poem? **[Connect]**

Reading Strategy
Drawing Inferences About the Speaker
Based on lines 10–12, decribe the speaker's personality.

Differentiated Instruction

Solutions for All Learners

Strategy for Advanced Readers

Invite students to analyze the form and style of the five poems in this grouping. Each is written in a different verse form; each uses rhyme differently; each has a different rhythm. Have students analyze the effect of each poem's form on its meaning and overall effect.

Students can consider how changes in form and style might have altered each poem's message. How do the poet's choices of form reveal their purposes in writing?

For example, "The Tropics in New York" echoes the sonnet form but is two lines short of a complete sonnet. Why might McKay have written only twelve lines instead of the usual fourteen? In traditional fourteen-line sonnets, what function does that final couplet often serve? By omitting it, in what ways does McKay reinforce the poem's meaning, and emphasize the speaker's feelings of loss and displacement?

Refugee in America

LANGSTON HUGHES

11 There are words like *Freedom*
Sweet and wonderful to say.
On my heart-strings freedom sings
All day everyday.

12 There are words like <u>*Liberty*</u>
That almost make me cry.
If you had known what I knew
You would know why.

Vocabulary Builder
liberty (lib′ ər tē) *n.* condition of being free from control by others

Critical Reading

1. **Respond:** What mood or emotions did you feel in reading "Dream Variations"? Explain.
2. **(a) Recall:** In "Dream Variations," what does the speaker want to do till the "white" day is done? **(b) Analyze:** What double meaning can you identify in the phrase "white day"?
3. **(a) Recall:** What words does the speaker use to describe color or images of darkness? **(b) Analyze:** In what ways are color and images of darkness used to express meaning?
4. **(a) Recall:** In "Refugee in America," what is the speaker's reaction to words like *freedom* and *liberty*? **(b) Interpret:** In what way does the title of the poem connect these words to the poem itself?
5. **(a) Recall:** What words of emotion are expressed in "Refugee in America"? **(b) Evaluate:** In what way do these emotions contribute to the mood conveyed by the poem? Explain.
6. **Apply:** What common goal do the speakers in these poems share? Explain.

For: More about Langston Hughes
Visit: www.PHSchool.com
Web Code: ere-9524

Go Online Author Link For additional information about Langston Hughes, have students type in the Web Code, then select *H* from the alphabet, and then select Langston Hughes.

11 Reading Strategy
Drawing Inferences About the Speaker

- **Ask** students to draw one inference about the speaker from each stanza of the poem.
  Answer: Stanza 1: The speaker is thrilled to be free. Stanza 2: The speaker values liberty because he or she has not always been free.
- Then, have students discuss what the title suggests about the speaker.
  Answer: He or she is a refugee. A refugee is a person who leaves his or her homeland in search of peace and freedom in another country.

12 Vocabulary Builder
Latin Root: *-lib-*

- Draw students' attention to Hughes's use of the word *liberty,* and read its definition.
- Write the following list of words that share the root *-lib-* on the chalkboard: *liberal, liberate, libertine.*
- Have students look up the definitions of the words on the list. Based on these definitions, **ask** students to infer what the Latin root *-lib-* means.
  Answer: The root *-lib-* derives from *liber,* the Latin word for "free."

ASSESS

Answers

1. **Possible answer:** I felt exhilarated by the vivid verbs.
2. (a) To whirl and dance in "some place of the sun." (b) The day is literally white with sunshine. The phrase also suggests that white people dominate, and define the entire world.
3. (a) Hughes uses the words *white, pale, dark,* and *black.* (b) The colors symbolize race as well as the difference between night and day.
4. (a) The speaker's reaction is strongly emotional. (b) The title suggests that the speaker is a refugee who came to the United States in search of freedom and liberty.
5. (a) Words of emotion include *sweet, wonderful, heart-strings,* and *cry.* (b) They show that the speaker's emotions are heightened and intensify the poem's power.
6. Both speakers long for freedom and an end to struggle.

ASSESS

Answers

1. Students' responses will vary.
2. (a) The fruits in the window include bananas, pears, tangerines, mangoes, and grapefruit. (b) They grow in tropical regions.
3. (a) The speaker recalls orchards of fruit trees, watching the dawn break, and looking at blue skies over the hills. (b) The speaker weeps with longing for the places he or she remembers.
4. (a) The title tells the reader that the speaker's experiences take place in New York, but are connected to the tropics. (b) The tropics can not exist in New York.
5. The speaker's homeland is beautiful, serene, and idyllic.
6. Students' responses will vary. Make sure they support their answers with details from their own experiences.

Go Online Author Link For additional information about Claude McKay, have students type in the Web Code, then select *M* from the alphabet, and then select Claude McKay.

The Tropics in New York

Claude McKay

Bananas ripe and green, and ginger-root,
    Cocoa in pods and alligator pears,
And tangerines and mangoes and grape fruit,
    Fit for the highest prize at parish fairs,

Set in the window, bringing memories
    Of fruit-trees laden by low-singing rills,
And dewy dawns, and mystical blue skies
    In benediction over nun-like hills.

My eyes grew dim, and I could no more gaze;
    A wave of longing through my body swept,
And, hungry for the old, familiar ways
    I turned aside and bowed my head and wept.

Critical Reading

1. **Respond:** The fruit in the window evokes memories of the speaker's birthplace. What objects could evoke memories of your own past?
2. **(a) Recall:** What fruits are set in the window? **(b) Assess:** In what regions are such fruits generally grown?
3. **(a) Recall:** What specific memories does the fruit stir in the speaker? **(b) Infer:** Why do you think the speaker weeps?
4. **(a) Interpret:** How does the title "The Tropics in New York" contribute to the poem's meaning? **(b) Interpret:** What is ironic about the title and the actual meaning of the poem?
5. **Analyze:** What impressions of his homeland does the speaker convey in this poem?
6. **Take a Position:** Do you think people can find happiness after they have made drastic changes? Why or why not?

For: More about Claude McKay
Visit: www.PHSchool.com
Web Code: ere-9525

Apply the Skills

The Negro Speaks of Rivers • I, Too • Dream Variations • Refugee in America • The Tropics in New York

Literary Analysis

Speaker

1. **(a)** Who is the **speaker** of "The Negro Speaks of Rivers"? **(b)** What effect does the title have on your ability to identify the speaker? Explain.
2. What can you infer about the identity and emotions of the speaker in "I, Too"?
3. Describe the speaker of "Refugee in America."
4. What might the effect of "Tropics in New York" be if it were delivered by an adolescent son or daughter of the speaker?

Comparing Literary Works

5. **(a)** Compare the references to homeland in "The Negro Speaks of Rivers" and "The Tropics in New York." **(b)** Which derive from personal experience? **(c)** Which are almost mythic? Explain.
6. Compare the messages about identity in "I, Too" and "Dream Variations," citing specific lines.
7. Explain the importance of place to the speakers in each poem.
8. What do these poems reveal about the shared experiences of African Americans with different backgrounds?

Reading Strategy

Drawing Inferences About the Speaker

9. In the third stanza of "The Negro Speaks of Rivers," what can you infer about the identity of a speaker who has raised the ancient pyramids and was also in New Orleans thousands of years later?
10. In each poem, find one line that reveals a characteristic of the speaker. Record your findings in a chart like the one shown.

Passage	What It Reveals About Speaker

Extend Understanding

11. **Cultural Connection:** What kinds of community and commercial services would you suggest to help immigrants stay in touch with their culture?

QuickReview

The **speaker** is the voice of a poem.

To **draw inferences about the speaker,** look closely at the speaker's choice of words and details included in a work.

For: Self-test
Visit: www.PHSchool.com
Web Code: era-6516

Students may use the **Self-test** to prepare for **Selection Test A** or **Selection Test B.**

Answers

1. (a) The speaker symbolizes all African Americans. (b)The title suggests that the speaker is not a single individual.
2. The speaker is an African American who is spirited and joyful because the future will be good.
3. The speaker is a refugee in the United States from another country. He seeks escape from oppression.
4. One would presume that an adolescent had not made the personal choice to live in the United States; therefore, the poem might have an additional poignancy.
5. (a) The speaker in "Rivers" does not seem to long for the past. The rivers and other references are symbolic. The speaker in "Tropics" longs for specific, tangible elements of home. (b) McKay's poem seems to be based on personal experience. (c) Hughes's poem presents a sweeping, almost mythic perspective that covers many centuries of history.
6. All lines in "I, Too," and all lines in "Dream Variations." Both speakers are African Americans who struggle to be accepted but seem confident about the future.
7. Their identities are shaped by the places in which they have lived.
8. The poems suggest that all African Americans have longed for, and sometimes found, freedom.
9. The speaker symbolizes a race of people whose history spans both places and times.
10. **Possible answers:** "Rivers" line 10: speaker is enduring. "I, Too" line 18: speaker asserts that he is also an American. "Variations" line 17: speaker is African American. "Refugee" lines 7–8: speaker has suffered oppression. "Tropics" line 12: speaker is homesick.

    Another sample answer can be found on **Reading Strategy Graphic Organizer B,** p. 208 in *Graphic Organizer Transparencies.*
11. Students may suggest programs offered by churches or community centers.

EXTEND/ASSESS

Answers

❶ Vocabulary Lesson

Word Analysis: Latin Root *-lib-*

1. b
2. c
3. a

Vocabulary Builder: Completing Sentences

1. dusky
2. lulled
3. liberty

Spelling Strategy

1. dull
2. steal
3. spell
4. extol

❷ Grammar and Style Lesson

1. has grown; present perfect
2. turned, bowed, wept; past
3. have known; present perfect
4. grew; past
5. bathed, were; past

Writing Application

Have students exchange papers with partners and check one another's work. Partners can review papers together and resolve any disagreements by referring to Writing and Grammar; Ruby Level.

WG Writing and Grammar, Ruby Level

Students will find further instruction and practice on verb tenses in Chapter 21, Section 2.

Build Language Skills

❶ Vocabulary Lesson

Word Analysis: Latin Root *-lib-*

The root *-lib-* derives from *liber,* the Latin word for "free." Match the following words with their definitions.

1. liberty	**a.** generous
2. liberate	**b.** freedom
3. liberal	**c.** release from slavery

Vocabulary Builder: Completing Sentences

Use words from the vocabulary list on page 925 to complete the following sentence.

The fading light, __?__ and soft, __?__ the prisoner to sleep, and soon he was dreaming again of his lost __?__ .

Spelling Strategy

One-syllable words, such as *lull* and *roll,* end in double *l* because the words have only one vowel. By contrast, one-syllable words such as *seal* and *peal* end with only one *l* because the words have two vowels. Considering this rule, choose a word that ends with a single or double *l* for each definition.

1. not shiny or bright (d ____)
2. to take something that does not belong to you (st ____)
3. to write the letters of a word correctly (sp ____)
4. to praise someone (ext ____)

❷ Grammar and Style Lesson

Verb Tenses: Past and Present Perfect

The tenses of verbs allow you to express time within one of three main categories; the present, the past, and the future. The **past tense** shows an action or condition that began and ended at a given time in the past. By contrast, the **present perfect tense** shows an action or condition that occurred at an indefinite time in the past—or one that begins in the past and continues into the present. This tense is formed with the helping verb *have* or *has* used before the past participle of the main verb.

Past: I *built* my hut near the Congo and it *lulled* me to sleep. (action ended)

Present Perfect: I'*ve known* rivers . . . (action continues into present)

Practice Copy these sentences in your notebook. Circle the verbs in each sentence, and label each verb as *past tense* or *present perfect tense.*

1. My soul has grown deep like the rivers.
2. I turned aside and bowed my head and wept.
3. I've known rivers ancient as the world and older than the flow of human blood in human veins.
4. My eyes grew dim . . .
5. I bathed in the Euphrates when dawns were young.

Writing Application Write a paragraph about a memory you have of your past. Include verbs in both the past tense and the present perfect tense.

WG Prentice Hall Writing and Grammar Connection: Chapter 21, Section 2

Assessment Practice

Sentence Completion **(For more practice, see *the Standardized Test Preparation Workbook*, p.56.)**

Many tests require students to choose the best word to complete a sentence. Use the following sample test item to give students practice at this skill.

In the 1920s, many writers identified Harlem as a source of ______ for African American artists, a supportive place where they felt a sense of ______.

Which pair of words best completes this sentence?

A embarrassment, loss
B inspiration, community
C comfort, bewilderment
D pride, abandonment

Only choices *A* and *B* contain pairs of words that work together. The word *supportive* in the sentence shows that Harlem was a good place for writers and artists. The correct answer is ***B***.

Writing Lesson

Timed Writing: Poetry Comparison

Langston Hughes committed himself to writing about the African American experience. His poetry focuses on themes of racial identity, pride, and perseverance. Write an essay addressing the themes you find in the Hughes poems you have read. ***(40 minutes)***

Prewriting ***(10 minutes)*** As you read the poems, list the images and messages you find in each one. Compare your notes and identify common themes that you can address.

Drafting ***(20 minutes)*** Begin your draft by introducing the common themes. In the body of your essay, include direct quotations to support your ideas. End with a conclusion that ties your ideas together.

Model: Using Quotations to Connect Themes

In "Refugee in America," Hughes refers to past suffering, saying, "If you had known what I knew." This message of perseverance parallels Hughes's message in "I, Too," in which he says, "But I laugh,/And eat well,/And grow strong."

Using quotations from the poems helps to make clear connections to the themes.

Revising ***(10 minutes)*** Reread your essay to make sure you have made strong connections between the poems. Review your introduction and conclusion to be sure they support your main points and provide insight to readers.

WG Prentice Hall Writing and Grammar Connection: Chapter 9, Section 2

Extend Your Learning

Listening and Speaking Working with a partner, research Jamaican life and culture. Consider the following in your research:

- What are the key aspects of Jamaican culture, including its music?
- Compare these ideas, beliefs, or customs with their parallels in American culture.

Give a **presentation** to classmates comparing American and Jamaican cultures. **[Group Activity]**

Research and Technology Using text and graphics, design a series of **posters** that depict the variety of cultural contributions made by African Americans during the 1920s. Include a range of mediums, such as literature, art, and drama. Display the work for your classmates.

For: An additional research activity
Visit: www.PHSchool.com
Web Code: erd-7515

Assessment Resources

The following resources can be used to assess students' knowledge and skills.

Unit 5 Resources
Selection Test A, pp. 273–275
Selection Test B, pp. 276–278

General Resources
Rubrics for Response to Literature, pp. 65–66

Go Online Assessment: Students may use the **Self-test** to prepare for **Selection Test A** or **Selection Test B.**

3 Writing Lesson

You may use this Writing Lesson as timed-writing practice, or you may allow students to develop it as a writing assignment over several days.

- To support students in preparing a comparison-and-contrast essay, give them the **Support for Writing Lesson** page (***Unit 5 Resources,*** p. 270).
- Students may want to read additional poems by Hughes and take them into account in their essays.
- Remind students that they should look for both similarities and differences among the poems.
- Use the Response to Literature Rubrics in ***General Resources,*** pp. 65–66 to assess students' essays.

4 Research and Technology

- The Harlem Renaissance influenced all areas of cultural activity, including literature, the visual arts, music, theater, philosophy, and social reform. Encourage students to focus their research on no more than three of these areas, but make sure that the full breadth of Renaissance activity is covered by the class as a whole.
- Encourage students to use a variety of research sources, including the Internet.
- Because students are creating posters, encourage them to find the most interesting images possible. Suggest a variety of ways in which to incorporate informational text, such as headlines, captions, quotes, and brief passages.
- Remind students that a poster should capture a central idea—theme or distinguishing trait—of its subject.
- Display students' finished posters in the classroom.
- The **Support for Extend Your Learning** page (***Unit 5 Resources,*** p. 271) provides guided note-taking opportunities to help students complete the Extend Your Learning activities.

Go Online Research: Have students type in the Web Code for another research activity.

Meeting Your Standards

Students will

1. **analyze and respond to literary elements.**
   - Literary Analysis: Metaphor
2. **read, comprehend, analyze, and critique poetry.**
   - Reading Strategy: Connecting to Historical Context
   - Reading Check questions
   - Apply the Skills questions
   - Assessment Practice (ATE)
3. **develop vocabulary.**
   - Vocabulary Lesson: Latin Word Root: *-cre-*
4. **understand and apply written and oral language conventions.**
   - Spelling Strategy
   - Grammar and Style Lesson: Placement of Adjectives
5. **develop writing proficiency.**
   - Writing Lesson: Comparison-and-Contrast Essay
6. **develop appropriate research strategies.**
   - Extend Your Learning: Research Report
7. **understand and apply listening and speaking strategies.**
   - Extend Your Learning: Dramatic Reading

Block Scheduling: Use one 90-minute class period to preteach the skills and have students read the selection. Use a second 90-minute class period to assess students' mastery of skills, extend their learning, and monitor their progress.

Homework Suggestions

Following are possibilities for homework assignments.

- Support pages from *Unit 5 Resources:*
  Literary Analysis
  Reading Strategy
  Vocabulary Builder
  Grammar and Style
- An Extend Your Learning project and the Writing Lesson for this selection group may be completed over several days.

Step-by-Step Teaching Guide	Pacing Guide
PRETEACH	
• Administer Vocabulary and Reading Warm-ups as necessary.	5 min.
• Engage students' interest with the motivation activity.	5 min.
• Read and discuss author and background features. **FT**	10 min.
• Introduce the Literary Analysis Skill: Metaphor **FT**	5 min.
• Introduce the Reading Strategy: Connecting to Historical Context **FT**	10 min.
• Prepare students to read by teaching the selection vocabulary. **FT**	
TEACH	
• Informally monitor comprehension while students read independently or in groups. **FT**	30 min.
• Monitor students' comprehension with the Reading Check notes.	as students read
• Reinforce vocabulary with Vocabulary Builder notes.	as students read
• Develop students' understanding of metaphor with the Literary Analysis annotations. **FT**	5 min.
• Develop students' ability to connect to historical context with the Reading Strategy annotations. **FT**	5 min.
ASSESS/EXTEND	
• Assess students' comprehension and mastery of the Literary Analysis and Reading Strategy by having them answer the Apply the Skills questions. **FT**	15 min.
• Have students complete the Vocabulary Lesson and the Grammar and Style Lesson. **FT**	15 min.
• Apply students' ability to identify points of comparison by using the Writing Lesson. **FT**	45 min. or homework
• Apply students' understanding by using one or more of the Extend Your Learning activities.	20–90 min. or homework
• Administer Selection Test A or Selection Test B. **FT**	15 min.

Resources

PRINT
Unit 5 Resources

TRANSPARENCY
Graphic Organizer Transparencies

PRINT
Reader's Notebook [L2]
Reader's Notebook: Adapted Version [L1]
Reader's Notebook: English Learner's Version [EL]
Unit 5 Resources

TECHNOLOGY
Listening to Literature Audio CDs [L2, EL]

PRINT
Unit 5 Resources

General Resources

TECHNOLOGY
Go Online: Research **[L3]**
Go Online: Self-test **[L3]**
***ExamView®* Test Bank [L3]**

Choosing Resources for Differentiated Instruction

[L1] Special Needs Students
[L2] Below-Level Students
[L3] All Students
[L4] Advanced Students
[EL] English Learners

For Vocabulary and Reading Warm-ups and for Selection Tests, **A** signifies "less challenging" and **B** "more challenging." For Graphic Organizer transparencies, **A** signifies "not filled in" and **B** "filled in."

FT Fast Track Instruction: To move the lesson more quickly, use the strategies and activities identified with **FT**.

Scaffolding for Less Proficient and Advanced Students

The leveled Critical Thinking questions after selections progress in the levels of thinking required to answer them. To address the needs of your different students, you may use the (a) level questions for your less proficient students and the (b) level questions with your on-level and advanced students. The occasional (c) level questions are appropriate for your advanced students.

PRENTICE HALL
TeacherEXPRESS™ Plan · Teach · Assess

Use this complete suite of powerful teaching tools to make lesson planning and testing quicker and easier.

PRENTICE HALL
StudentEXPRESS™ Learn · Study · Succeed

Use the interactive textbook (online and on CD-ROM) to make selections and activities come alive with audio and video support and interactive questions.

Go Online Professional Development

For: Information about Lexiles
Visit: www.PHSchool.com
Web Code: eue-1111

PRETEACH

Motivation

Obtain and display works by Harlem Renaissance artists such as Aaron Douglas, Hale Woodruff, or Palmer Hayden. Encourage volunteers to share their responses to the art. Tell students that both the art and the poems were created by some of the leading lights of the Harlem Renaissance. As they read, have students look for images or ideas in the poems that reflect those in the art.

1 Background

More About the Authors

God Sends Sunday, Arna Bontemps's first novel, tells the story of Little Augie, the most successful black jockey in St. Louis. In 1939, Bontemps and Countee Cullen collaborated on a musical play based on this novel. Titled *St. Louis Woman,* the play combined songs with folk beliefs to tell the story of Little Augie's romances as well as his life on the track. *St. Louis Woman* had a successful run on Broadway in 1946.

Build Skills *Poems*

1 From the Dark Tower • A Black Man Talks of Reaping • Storm Ending

Countee Cullen (1903–1946)

Unlike most other poets of his day, Countee Cullen used traditional forms and methods. Yet, no other poet expressed the sentiments of African Americans during the early 1900s more eloquently than did Cullen.

A Literary Life Cullen was born in Louisville, Kentucky, and raised by foster parents in New York. An outstanding student, Cullen worked on his high-school newspaper and literary magazine and began to write poetry seriously. He graduated from New York University and later earned a master's degree in English and French from Harvard University. His first collection of poetry, *Color,* was published in 1925. This was followed by *Copper Sun* (1927), *The Ballad of the Brown Girl* (1927), and *The Black Christ* (1929). In 1932, Cullen published *One Way to Heaven,* a satirical novel. In his later years, he published two children's books, *The Lost Zoo* (1940) and *My Lives and How I Lost Them* (1942).

Arna Bontemps (1902–1973)

Arna Bontemps was one of the most scholarly figures of the Harlem Renaissance. Throughout his career as an editor, a novelist, a dramatist, and a poet, his work for social justice made him "the conscience of an era."

Born in Louisiana and raised in California, Bontemps came to New York during the height of the Harlem Renaissance. After teaching at several religious academies, he wrote *Black Thunder* (1936), a highly acclaimed novel about a Virginia slave revolt. In subsequent years, he published poems, biographies, dramas, and books for young readers. He also ran the library at Fisk University in Nashville, making it a major center for African American studies. In 1967, after the death of his friend Langston Hughes, Bontemps compiled *Hold Fast to Dreams* (1969), a poetry anthology. The bulk of the extensive correspondence between Hughes and Bontemps was donated to Yale University, where scholars can study this vivid chronicle of African American literary life.

Jean Toomer (1894–1967)

Like other Harlem Renaissance writers, Jean Toomer was interested in the cultural roots of his people. In his work, he expressed the cultural belief that black heritage and pride were vital to the happiness and freedom of African Americans.

A Major Work Born in Washington, D.C., Nathan Pinchback Toomer attended New York University. He then taught for a few years in Georgia. In 1920, Toomer changed his first name to Jean, to honor the hero of a novel that inspired him. Following the appearance of *Cane* (1923), an unusual book of prose sketches, poems, stories, and a one-act play, Toomer was widely viewed as one of the most talented writers of the Harlem Renaissance. When Toomer's publishing output dwindled, *Cane* fell into obscurity. In recent years, however, *Cane* has been recognized and celebrated as a significant work of the Harlem Renaissance.

Preview

Connecting to the Literature

If you see trouble ahead, you might say that a storm is brewing. In the same way, these poems capture the experiences of the African American people through striking images of nature or familiar activities and events.

2 Literary Analysis

Metaphor

A **metaphor** is a comparison between two seemingly dissimilar things that does not use a connecting word such as *like* or *as.* A metaphor may be directly stated or implied. In these lines, Countee Cullen compares African American life to the toil of planting.

We shall not always plant while others reap
The golden increment of bursting fruit . . .

Although metaphors are usually brief, they may also be elaborate, lengthy comparisons. An **extended metaphor** is a comparison that is developed throughout several lines or an entire poem. As you read "Storm Ending," look for the extended metaphor Toomer develops.

Comparing Literary Works

Metaphors are often conveyed through the use of **imagery**—descriptive language that appeals to the senses. These three poets use imagery to express their feelings about the African American experience. Two of these poems offer images of planting, while the third presents images of a huge storm. Usually, readers associate agricultural imagery with growth, and storm imagery with destruction. However, these poems challenge readers' expectations. As you read, use a chart like the one shown to analyze each poem's imagery, and to assess the emotions and attitudes it conveys.

Metaphor
African Americans compared to farm workers

Image
silently working hard in fields of gold, weeping

Emotion / Ideas
sorrow, anger

3 Reading Strategy

Connecting to Historical Context

Many works of literature bear a direct relation to the time and place in which they were written. A reader must **connect** such works to their **historical contexts** in order to understand and appreciate them. To fully grasp the following poems—born in the cultural movement known as the Harlem Renaissance in the 1920s—review the information on pages 910–911.

Vocabulary Builder

increment (in′krə mənt) *n.* increase, as in a series (p. 938)

countenance (koun′ tə nəns) *v.* approve; tolerate (p. 938)

beguile (bē gīl′) *v.* charm or delight (p. 938)

stark (stärk) *adj.* severe (p. 939)

reaping (rēp′ iŋ) *v.* cutting or harvesting grain from a field (p. 939)

glean (glēn) *v.* collect the remaining grain after reaping (p. 939)

2 Literary Analysis

Metaphor

- Remind students of the difference between metaphor and simile. A simile is a comparison that states "A is like B." A metaphor is a more direct comparison stating that "A is B."
- List the following comparisons on the chalkboard and challenge students to identify similes and metaphors.

  "A poem should be palpable and mute/As a globed fruit." (simile) ("Ars Poetica" by Archibald MacLeish)

  "The actor is a metaphysician in the dark. . . ." (metaphor) ("Of Modern Poetry" by Wallace Stevens)

  "And indeed there will be time for the yellow smoke that slides along the street/Rubbing its back upon the window-panes. . . ." (metaphor) ("The Love Song of J. Alfred Prufrock" by T.S. Eliot)

3 Reading Strategy

Connecting to Historical Context

- Explain that all writers are products of the time and place in which they live. Readers can best appreciate literature if they have some understanding of the writer's social and historical circumstances.
- Have students read the author biographies on the previous page. In addition, you might encourage them to do a little further reading about these poets, or you may give the class a talk on both these poets and the Harlem Renaissance as a whole. Urge students to keep this information about the historical context in mind as they read.

Vocabulary Builder

- Pronounce each vocabulary word for students, and read the definitions as a class. Have students identify any words with which they are already familiar.

Differentiated Instruction

Solutions for All Learners

Support for Special Needs Students
Have students complete the **Preview** and **Build Skills** pages for these selections in the ***Reader's Notebook: Adapted Version.*** These pages provide a selection summary, an abbreviated presentation of the reading and literary skills, and the graphic organizer on the **Build Skills** page in the student book.

Support for Less Proficient Readers
Have students complete the **Preview** and **Build Skills** pages for these selections in the ***Reader's Notebook.*** These pages provide a selection summary, an abbreviated presentation of the reading and literary skills, and the graphic organizer on the **Build Skills** page in the student book.

Support for English Learners
Have students complete the **Preview** and **Build Skills** pages for these selections in the ***Reader's Notebook: English Learner's Version.*** These pages provide a selection summary, an abbreviated presentation of the skills, contextual vocabulary, and the graphic organizer on the **Build Skills** page in the student book.

TEACH

Learning Modalities
Visual Learners Have students consider the visual effects of each poem's language. Students can choose any two poems and write brief essays comparing and contrasting how each poet uses words to create visual images. Do the poets create similar images? Do they use similar techniques to create widely different images? How would students illustrate these poems if they had the opportunity?

❶ About the Selections

Three poems use extended metaphors—two of planting and one of a thunderstorm—to comment on social and historical issues.

❷ Vocabulary Builder

The Latin Root *-cre-*

- Call attention to the word *increment,* and have a volunteer read its definition.
- Tell students that increment shares the root *-cre-* with the words *create* and *increase.*
- **Ask:** Based on these words, what do you think the root *-cre-* means? **Answer:** The root *-cre-* means "to grow."

❸ Reading Strategy

Connecting to Historical Context

- Read the poem aloud and ask students to consider lines 4, 8, and 10.
- Then **ask** the Reading Strategy question: How does the historical context of this poem help you interpret the identity of "we?"
- **Answer:** The historical context of the poem tells us that the "we" of the poem are African American workers because the speaker tells us that they "always plant while others reap," and that "lesser men" who grow rich from their toil are holding them "cheap." Our knowledge of the unfair treatment of African Americans in America's past leads us to infer the identity of "we."

❶ From The Dark Tower

Countee Cullen (To Charles S. Johnson)

Background Countee Cullen dedicated this poem to Charles S. Johnson, an African American sociologist, editor, and author of a landmark study of race relations in the 1920s. Johnson was the editor of the publication *Opportunity: Journal of Negro Life* and helped to nurture the writers and artists of the Harlem Renaissance. Cullen served as assistant editor of the publication.

We shall not always plant while others reap
The golden increment of bursting fruit,
Not always countenance, abject and mute,
That lesser men should hold their brothers cheap;
Not everlastingly while others sleep
Shall we beguile their limbs with mellow flute,
Not always bend to some more subtle brute;
We were not made eternally to weep.

❸

The night whose sable breast relieves the stark,
White stars is no less lovely being dark,
And there are buds that cannot bloom at all
In light, but crumple, piteous, and fall;
So in the dark we hide the heart that bleeds,
And wait, and tend our agonizing seeds.

Vocabulary Builder

increment (inʹ krə mənt) *n.* increase, as in a series

countenance (kounʹ tə nəns) *v.* approve; tolerate

beguile (bē gīlʹ) *v.* charm or delight

Reading Strategy
Connecting to Historical Context How does the historical context of this poem help you interpret the identity of the "we"?

Critical Reading

1. **Respond:** Can you identify or empathize with the speaker of this poem? Why or why not?
2. **(a) Recall:** Which word is repeated five times in the first stanza? **(b) Analyze:** What is the effect of this repetition?
3. **(a) Recall:** What contrast or opposition does the speaker set up in lines 9–10? **(b) Interpret:** What does Cullen mean by "no less lovely being dark"?
4. **(a) Infer:** Who is the "we" in the poem? **(b) Interpret:** What distinction does the speaker draw between the circumstances of "we" and those of "others"?
5. **Evaluate:** Do you think that waiting is an appropriate response to the conflicts described in the poem? Explain.

Go Online
Author Link
For: More about Countee Cullen
Visit: www.PHSchool.com
Web Code: ere-9526

Differentiated Instruction Solutions for All Learners

Accessibility at a Glance

	Dark Tower; Storm Ending	Talks of Reaping
Context	Poems addressing social issues	Poem addressing social issues
Language	Simple sentences and repetitive phrases	Simple sentences and vocabulary
Concept Level	Accessible (struggles; desire for freedom)	Challenging (extended farming metaphor)
Literary Merit	Cross-cultural experience	Cross-cultural experience
Lexile	NP	NP
Overall Rating	Average	More challenging

Hoeing, 1943, Robert Gwathmey, Carnegie Institute Museum of Art, Pittsburgh, Pennsylvania, © Estate of Robert Gwathmey/Licensed by VAGA, New York, NY

◀ **Critical Viewing** 4
What emotion does this image convey? In what way does it compare with the mood of the poem? **[Compare and Contrast]**

5 A Black Man Talks of Reaping

Arna Bontemps

I have sown beside all waters in my day.
I planted deep, within my heart the fear
that wind or fowl would take the grain away.
I planted safe against this stark, lean year.

I scattered seed enough to plant the land
in rows from Canada to Mexico
but for my reaping only what the hand
can hold at once is all that I can show.

Yet what I sowed and what the orchard yields
my brother's sons are gathering stalk and root;
small wonder then my children glean in fields
they have not sown, and feed on bitter fruit.

Vocabulary Builder

stark (stärk) *adj.* severe

reaping (rēp′ iŋ) *v.* cutting or harvesting grain from a field

glean (glēn) *v.* collect the remaining grain after reaping

6  **Reading Check**
What does the speaker have to show for all his labor?

Differentiated Instruction
Solutions for All Learners

Strategy for Special Needs Students
Organize students into small groups to answer the Critical Reading questions on the previous and the following pages. Each group can then report on its answers to entire class. If there is significant disagreement, have students identify words, phrases, and lines from the poems that support their interpretations.

Enrichment for Gifted/Talented Students
Have each student choose one of the three poems and write a detailed analysis and interpretation of its meaning. Students can try paraphrasing lines and stanzas in their search for what the poems mean. Encourage them to do some background reading about Cullen, Bontemps, and Toomer, and to examine other works by the poets as they work on their interpretations.

ASSESS

Answers

1. Most students will empathize with the feeling of doing the work and watching others take the profits.
2. (a) "not" (b) The repetition gives the poem the quality of a protest.
3. (a) contrast between the dark night and the white stars
(b) Darkness is not inherently ugly.
4. (a) "We" can symbolize any oppressed people; Cullen probably had African Americans in mind. (b) "We" do the work while "others" take the profits.
5. **Possible Answer:** Waiting is appropriate because while the speakers wait, they build up strength.

4 Critical Viewing

Answer: The workers are all either toiling or pausing in exhaustion. The landscape is barren. Like the poem, the painting suggests that workers do not profit from their own labor.

5 Reading Strategy
Connecting to Historical Context

- **Ask** students to consider the poem's title. How does it affect their reading of the poem's meaning?
Answer: The title suggests that the poem is about race relations, not about sowing and reaping.

▶ **Monitor Progress:** Then, **ask** students to explain what Bontemps is saying about race relations.
Answer: Bontemps suggests that black people work and others reap the fruits of their labor.

6 Reading Check

The speaker gains only "what the hand can hold." The speaker does not profit from his work.

Answers

1. **Possible response:** I saw farmers toiling in fields, dark places with people hiding; I heard thunder and rain.
2. (a) The speaker is afraid that shallowly planted seeds would be stolen. (b) It might be a time in which people suffer from hunger or, symbolically, from a lack of freedom.
3. (a) He scatters an enormous amount of seed. (b) He can only harvest a handful. (c) His brother's sons reap what he has sown.
4. (a) a thunderstorm (b) The speaker is awed, impressed, and excited. (c) The words "gorgeously," "great," "full-lipped," and "golden" suggest the grandeur and beauty of the thunder.
5. (a) They have received only "the bitter fruit." (b) It suggests that this statement is not true in situations where people are denied their basic rights and freedoms.

Go Online **Author Link** For additional information about Countee Cullen, Arna Bontemps, and Jean Toomer, have students type in the Web Code, then select *C, B,* and *T* from the alphabet, and then select Countee Cullen, Arna Bontemps, and Jean Toomer.

Storm Ending

Jean Toomer

Thunder blossoms gorgeously above our heads,
Great, hollow, bell-like flowers,
Rumbling in the wind,
Stretching clappers to strike our ears . . .
Full-lipped flowers
Bitten by the sun
Bleeding rain
Dripping rain like golden honey—
And the sweet earth flying from the thunder.

Critical Reading

1. **Respond:** What did you see as you read these poems? What did you hear?
2. **(a) Recall:** In "A Black Man Talks of Reaping," why does the speaker plant "deep"? **(b) Draw Conclusions:** What do you think is meant by the "stark, lean year"?
3. **(a) Recall:** In "A Black Man Talks of Reaping," how much seed does the speaker scatter? **(b) Recall:** How much grain is he allowed to harvest? **(c) Infer:** Who reaps what the speaker has sown?
4. **(a) Recall:** In "Storm Ending," what natural event does the poem describe? **(b) Analyze:** What is the speaker's attitude toward the event described? **(c) Support:** Which words best convey this attitude?
5. **(a) Infer:** What does Bontemps suggest about what African Americans have received in exchange for their hard work? **(b) Apply:** In what way does Bontemps's poem comment on the idea that "Whatsoever a man soweth, that shall he also reap"?

For: More about Arna Bontemps and Jean Toomer
Visit: www.PHSchool.com
Web Code: ere-9527

Apply the Skills

From the Dark Tower • A Black Man Talks of Reaping • Storm Ending

Literary Analysis

Metaphor

1. **(a)** Identify the **metaphors** that Countee Cullen uses in "From the Dark Tower." **(b)** What details does he use to extend these metaphors?
2. **(a)** What metaphor appears in Bontemps's poem? **(b)** How does he express and develop the metaphor in each stanza?
3. **(a)** What two things are compared in the **extended metaphor** presented in "Storm Ending"? **(b)** Describe the way in which Toomer establishes this comparison in the first four lines. **(c)** Describe how he develops this metaphor in the lines that follow.

Comparing Literary Works

4. Using a chart like the one shown, identify and analyze the dominant **image** conveyed by each poem.

Poem	Image	Interpretation	Emotion

5. **(a)** What theme or central message do these poems share? **(b)** In what ways do their uses of imagery serve to convey those messages?
6. Rank the three poems from most optimistic to most pessimistic. Explain your assessments.

Reading Strategy

Connecting to Historical Context

7. How can you deepen your appreciation of "From the Dark Tower" by reflecting on the northern migration of nearly one million African Americans in the late 1800s and early 1900s?
8. Identify a fact of **historical context** that enriches your reading of "A Black Man Talks of Reaping." Explain.

Extend Understanding

9. **Historical Connection:** What historical factors may have contributed to the decline of the Harlem Renaissance around 1935?

QuickReview

A **metaphor** is a comparison between two seemingly dissimilar things that does not use *like* or *as*.

An **extended metaphor** is a metaphor that is developed over several lines or an entire poem.

Imagery is the descriptive language writers use to create word pictures or images for readers.

To **connect to historical context,** interpret a work by linking it with the time and place in which it was written.

For: Self-test
Visit: www.PHSchool.com
Web Code: era-6517

Go Online Assessment Students may use the **Self-test** to prepare for **Selection Test A** or **Selection Test B.**

Answers

1. (a) Cullen compares planting to labor and reaping to profiting from the labor of others.
   (b) Details include the mention of buds that will only bloom in the darkness.
2. (a) Bontemps compares sowing grain to struggling with oppression. (b) In stanza one, he describes sowing seed beside "all waters." In stanza two, he describes scattering seed across America, but reaping almost nothing. In stanza three, he describes others gathering the "stalk and root" while his own children are left with only "bitter fruit."
3. (a) The end of slavery is compared to a thunderstorm. (b) The clappers of thunder suggest bells ringing out freedom. (c) The "flowers" of thunder "bleed" the rain of freedom that is sweet "like golden honey."
4. **Possible answer:** Poem—"Tower"; Image—"buds that cannot bloom/In light"; Interpretation—some beautiful things require darkness to thrive; Emotion: sadness and controlled rage.

   Another sample answer can be found on **Literary Analysis Graphic Organizer B,** p. 212 in ***Graphic Organizer Transparencies.***
5. (a) All three deal with the oppression suffered by African Americans. (b) The images convey the idea of richness and plenty stolen from African Americans.
6. **Possible answer:** "Storm," "Tower," "Reaping." "Storm" has a positive message about achieving freedom. "Tower" suggests that freedom is possible. "Reaping" seems to have given up the fight.
7. African Americans migrated north in search of the opportunity to achieve equality but continued to find oppressive circumstances.
8. **Possible response:** The historical reality of slavery reminds the reader that the poem is no exaggeration.
9. The widespread poverty and unemployment brought by the Great Depression and the rise of fascism and Nazism in Europe caused the end of the Harlem Renaissance.

EXTEND/ASSESS

Answers

❶ Vocabulary Lesson

Word Analysis

1. A crescendo is a steady increase in sound.
2. A creation is something that is made.
3. An increment is a measure of growth.

Spelling Strategy

1. first g is hard, second g is soft
2. first g is hard, second g is soft
3. first g is soft, second g is hard

Vocabulary Builder

1. a 3. a 5. c
2. b 4. c 6. a

❷ Grammar and Style Lesson

1. The wind, cold and merciless, chilled us.
2. We saw the vast, cobalt ocean.
3. The refugees, penniless but determined, came to America to start anew.
4. The cold, hungry bird pecked the ground for worms.
5. We tired workers fell to exhaustion.

Writing Application

Have students exchange papers with partners and check one another's work. Partners can go over papers together and resolve any disagreements by referring to the Writing and Grammar book.

WG Writing and Grammar, Ruby Level

Students will find further instruction and practice on placement of adjectives in Chapter 27, Section 2.

Build Language Skills

❶ Vocabulary Lesson

Word Analysis: Latin Root *-cre-*

Like *increase,* and *create,* the word *increment* contains the Latin root *-cre-*, which means "to grow." Use your knowledge of the root *-cre-* to define these words:

1. crescendo
2. creation
3. increment

Spelling Strategy

The letter *g* usually makes a "hard" sound when it is followed by *a, h, o,* or *u,* as in *gather, ghost,* and *beguile.* For a "soft" sound, *g* is usually followed by *e, i,* or *y.* Indicate whether the *g* sounds in these words are hard or soft.

1. gorgeously **2.** garbage **3.** gyromagnetic

Vocabulary Builder: Synonyms

Review the vocabulary list on page 937. Then, write the letter of the best synonym for each numbered word.

1. reap: **(a)** harvest, **(b)** sow, **(c)** plow
2. countenance: **(a)** cheer, **(b)** tolerate, **(c)** disregard
3. increment: **(a)** increase, **(b)** stability, **(c)** decrease
4. stark: **(a)** gentle, **(b)** steep, **(c)** severe
5. glean: **(a)** distribute, **(b)** weigh, **(c)** collect
6. beguile: **(a)** amuse, **(b)** frighten, **(c)** behave

❷ Grammar and Style Lesson

Placement of Adjectives

An **adjective** is a word used to describe a noun or a pronoun. Adjectives can be placed *before* or *after* the nouns or pronouns they modify.

Before: this *stark, lean* year (modifies *year*)

After: I've scattered seed *enough* to plant the land (modifies *seed*)

When adjectives follow the noun they modify, they may have more emphasis in a sentence.

In poetry, a literary form characterized by precise word choice and deliberately sculpted lines and stanzas, adjectives can effectively add meaning and build imagery. While poets choose adjectives with care, they also select nouns and verbs to achieve poetic effects.

Practice Rewrite the following sentences, altering the position of the italicized adjectives. Be sure that the adjectives modify the same noun in your sentence as in the original. Make any necessary changes in wording and punctuation.

1. The *cold, merciless* wind chilled us.
2. We saw the ocean, *vast* and *cobalt.*
3. The *penniless* but *determined* refugees came to America to start anew.
4. The bird, *cold* and *hungry,* pecked the ground for worms.
5. *Tired,* we workers fell to exhaustion.

Writing Application Write a paragraph about a poem in this grouping. Include three adjectives and vary the placement of these modifiers.

WG *Prentice Hall Writing and Grammar Connection: Chapter 27, Section 2*

Assessment Practice

Sentence Completion **(For more practice, see *Standardized Test Preparation Workbook*, p. 57.)**

Many tests require students to choose the best word to complete a sentence. Use the following sample test item to give students practice at this skill.

Although the forms and techniques used by Harlem Renaissance writers varied widely, the poets and novelists had______purposes for creating their art.

Which word best completes this sentence?

A complex **C** similar
B unusual **D** different

The word *although* in the sentence suggests that the blank space must be filled by an antonym for *varied widely.* The correct answer is **C**.

3 Writing Lesson

Timed Writing: Comparison-and-Contrast Essay

Although Countee Cullen and Arna Bontemps were associated with the same literary movement, each had a distinct style. In an essay, compare and contrast "From the Dark Tower" and "A Black Man Talks of Reaping." ***(40 minutes)***

Prewriting *(10 minutes)* In a chart, identify the points of comparison between the two poets, such as their uses of metaphors and imagery. Then, consider each poem's message and its sound—the musical quality, which may be lilting and gentle or harsh and driving.

Model: Identifying Points of Comparison

Drafting *(20 minutes)* In your introduction, briefly describe the poems. Then, using your chart, draft a point-by-point comparison, addressing each element of comparison with examples from the poems.

Revising *(10 minutes)* Reread your essay to be sure you have addressed both similarities and differences between the two poems. Add vivid and descriptive language to strengthen comparisons, quoting sufficiently from the poems to support them.

WG *Prentice Hall Writing and Grammar Connection: Chapter 9, Section 2*

Extend Your Learning

Listening and Speaking Select and compare two other poems by Countee Cullen, and give a **dramatic reading** to the class. As you practice, consider these tips:

- Select the poems based on connections between theme and image.
- As you read, enhance meaning by emphasizing key words.

After reading the poems, invite questions and comments from the class.

Research and Technology With a group, choose an artist or musician from the Harlem Renaissance period and research his or her life and accomplishments. Present your findings to your class in an organized **research report. [Group Activity]**

For: An additional research activity
Visit: www.PHSchool.com
Web Code: erd-7516

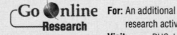

3 Writing Lesson

You may use this Writing Lesson as timed-writing practice, or you may allow students to develop it as a writing assignment over several days.

- Suggest that students try reading the poems aloud to compare their sound effects. Students may prefer to listen to the poems read on the CDs.
- In addition to the instruction and comparison chart in the Writing Lesson, give students the **Support for Writing Lesson** page (***Unit 5 Resources,*** p. 287).
- Have students consider form as well as content in their essays.
- Use the Exposition: Comparison-and-Contrast Essay rubrics in ***General Resources,*** pp. 69–70, to assess students' essays.

4 Research and Technology

- Have students clear their choices with you before they begin working. Students may want to work with partners or in small groups.
- This activity lends itself to a variety of class presentations. Encourage students to incorporate recordings, works of art, dramatic readings, or other elements into their presentations.
- To evaluate students' research presentations, use the Rubric for Speaking: Delivering a Research Presentation in ***General Resources,*** p. 92.
- The **Support for Extend Your Learning** page (***Unit 5 Resources,*** p. 288) provides guided note-taking opportunities to help students complete the Extend Your Learning activities.

Go Online Research Have students type in the Web Code for another research activity.

Assessment Resources

The following resources can be used to assess students' knowledge and skills.

Unit 5 Resources
- **Selection Test A,** pp. 290–292
- **Selection Test B,** pp. 293–295

General Resources
- **Rubrics for Exposition: Comparison-and-Contrast Essay,** pp. 69–70
- **Rubric for Speaking: Delivering a Research Presentation,** p. 92

Go Online Assessment Students may use the **Self-test** to prepare for **Selection Test A** or **Selection Test B.**

Meeting Your Standards

Students will

1. **understand and explain public relations documents.**
2. **read a public relations document.**

*See **Teacher Express™/Lesson View** for a detailed lesson plan for Reading Informational Materials.*

About Public Relations Documents

- Have students read "About Public Relations Documents."
- Point out to students that the purpose of a public relations document may be to sell a product or service, but it can also introduce the company, tell what it is doing and why, or explain a policy, a product, or an idea.
- Tell students that public relations documents they encounter may be sales brochures or advertisements in newspapers, in magazines, or on the Internet. They also might see public relations documents when they buy products such as computers or cellular phones. Invite students to give examples of public relations documents that they have received or seen.

Reading Strategy
Making Inferences

- Explain to students that an inference is based not just on what they read in a text, but on what they know from other sources, from experiences, and from observations.
- Tell students that making inferences is important when reading public relations documents because it allows them to check facts, assess bias, and decide what to believe and what to question.
- Review with students the graphic organizer for making and checking an inference, and invite them to talk about their experiences with fires. Ask them whether their experiences verify the inferences made.

Reading Informational Materials

Public Relations Documents

About Public Relations Documents

Businesses and organizations create many documents to convey messages to the public. These documents include brochures, advertisements, and flyers. They also include press releases and public service announcements. All of these documents are important; however, the heart of an organization lies in its mission, or purpose. For that reason, an organization's mission statement is one of its most important documents. Most mission statements contain three kinds of information:

- **Who We Are**—This is a set of basic facts about the business or organization that has issued the statement.
- **What We Do**—These details show what the business or organization offers.
- **Why We Do It**—This information expresses the philosophy and goals of the business or organization.

The mission statement on the next page outlines the *Who, What,* and *Why* for a museum in Boston, Massachusetts. As you read it, think about the information that it provides, why this information is offered, who is the intended audience, and why such a document would be useful.

Reading Strategy

Making Inferences

As you read, you gather information. Some information is stated in the text itself. Other information may take the form of assumptions that you make based on what you know or can figure out that is not directly stated in the text. Such assumptions and guesses, which combine a reading of the text with your own experience and prior knowledge, are called **inferences.**

Making an inference requires you to combine two kinds of knowledge and then to determine whether unstated information is likely to be supported by that knowledge.

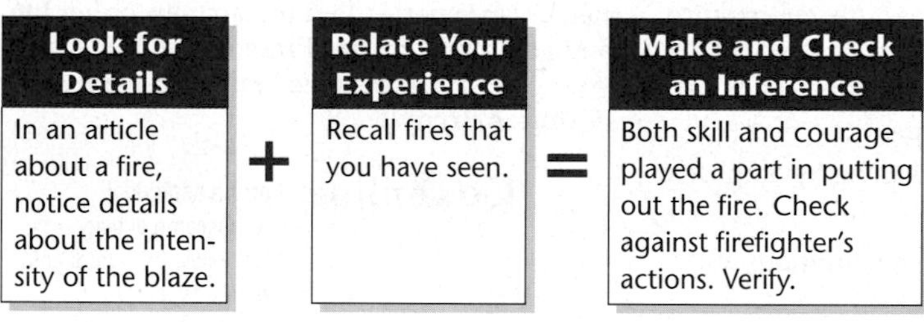

Look for Details
In an article about a fire, notice details about the intensity of the blaze.
+
Relate Your Experience
Recall fires that you have seen.
=
Make and Check an Inference
Both skill and courage played a part in putting out the fire. Check against firefighter's actions. Verify.

Differentiated Instruction Solutions for All Learners

Reading Support
Give students reading support with the appropriate version of the ***Reader's Notebooks:***

Reader's Notebook [L2, L3]

Reader's Notebook: Adapted Version [L1, L2]

Reader's Notebook: English Learner's Version [EL]

Mission Statement

Most businesses and organizations create informational documents that communicate to potential partners, customers, or contributors their overall purpose and the scope of their activities. The examples shown here include a mission statement on this page that briefly expresses the organization's purpose and a calendar of events on page 946 that shows how that purpose is carried out and invites people to come and participate.

Museum of Afro American History

Boston and Nantucket

MISSION STATEMENT

A Foundation for the Future

In one well-crafted sentence, the museum says, "This is *who we are.*" More details follow, but this is the single most important statement about the museum.

The mission of the Museum of Afro American History is to preserve, conserve and interpret the contributions of people of African descent and those who have found common cause with them in the struggle for liberty, dignity, and justice for all Americans. Therefore, we:

As part of a list of museum features, this explains *what we do* information. Similar information appears at the end of the statement, but its purpose is more general.

- collect and exhibit artifacts of distinction in this field and acquire and maintain physical structures and sites through the end of the 19th century;
- educate the public about the importance of the Afro American historical legacy in general, its Boston and New England heritages, in particular;
- celebrate the enduring vitality of African American culture;

Here is *why we do it* information—an expression of the museum's philosophy and goals.

- and advance on our own and in collaboration with others an appreciation of the past for the benefit of the custodians of the future.

Reading Public Relations Documents

- Tell students that they might encounter public relations documents packed in boxes with new purchases. They may see newspaper and magazine ads promoting new products and may read letters and brochures that come in the mail. They may also receive public relations documents when they visit public places, such as museums, zoos, festivals, and theme parks. Writers of these documents seek to explain the purpose and goals of the service or product and help orient readers to the kinds of services to expect.
- Have students read "Museum of Afro American History" and the side notes.
- **Ask** students to name the four basic tasks the museum has set for itself.
  Answer: The museum's tasks are to collect and exhibit artifacts, to educate the public, to celebrate African-American culture, and to promote an appreciation for the past.
- Point out that information is organized in bulleted segments that clearly distinguish the different tasks and make them easy to read.

Continued on page 946

Differentiated Instruction

Solutions for All Learners

Strategy for Special Needs Students

Help students clarify their understanding of a mission statement by working with them to create one for their school. Write the statement "Who we are" on the board and have students respond. Help them distill their ideas into a concise mission statement like that for the Museum of Afro American History. Then work with them to list two or three tasks that the school sponsors to fulfill the mission.

Support for English Learners

Provide background for students on the history underlying the Museum for Afro American History. Briefly review the history of African Americans in the United States, emphasizing that even though African Americans have enjoyed legal rights for more than a century, they have in fact been treated as second-class citizens for much of that time. The museum featured here and others around the country are helping to preserve African American history and to promote respect and pride in what African Americans have achieved.

Reading Public Relations Documents (cont.)

- Point out the Calendar of Events on this page. **Ask** students which events are free.
  Answer: The presentation on Madam C. J. Walker is free for everyone. The concert series is free for members, but non-members must pay ten dollars.
- Tell students to read the list of sponsoring organizations, and **ask** why this information is useful.
  Answer: When assessing whether to spend time and money at an event or place, some people want to know who sponsors the event and, therefore, who pays for it. Since different sponsors may have different standards, the list may offer clues about what to expect of the program.
- **Ask** students to whom this public relations document might be directed.
  Possible Response: It is directed to visitors, donors, and potential volunteers.
- **Ask** why visitors might want this information.
  Answer: Visitors also may want to know why the museum exists. This information helps them assess the exhibits and information there. Visitors might want information about program schedules, museum hours, and fees.
- **Ask** why donors and volunteers might want this information.
  Answer: Donors might want to know how their contributions are used so that they can decide whether to invest further in the project. Volunteers would like to know whether they are giving their time for a worthwhile purpose.

Reading Informational Materials

MUSEUM OF AFRO AMERICAN HISTORY BOSTON

CALENDAR OF EVENTS

Events take place at 8 Smith Court, Beacon Hill, unless otherwise noted.

A calendar of events provides basic information, such as where and when activities take place.

SATURDAY FEB. 3, 7:30 P.M.
READING AND BOOK SIGNING

On Her Own Ground: The Life and Times of Madam C.J. Walker

A'Lelia Bundles, former deputy bureau chief of ABC News in Washington and great-great granddaughter of Madam C.J. Walker, will discuss the writing of *On Her Own Ground*, the first historically accurate account of this legendary entrepreneur and social activist.

Information about sponsoring organizations is usually included.

Sponsored by the Collection of African American Literature, a partnership between the Museum of Afro American History, Suffolk University, and Boston African American Historic Site.

REFRESHMENTS AND BOOK SALES FOLLOWING. FREE

TUESDAYS, 10:30-11:30 A.M.

Stories from African American Literature and Lore

Vibrant stories and activities presenting history for preschool-aged children and parents. FREE

FRIDAY, FEB. 16, 6 P.M.-9 A.M.

Museum Overnight: Underground Railroad

Descriptions of events are brief but inviting.

Spend the night at the Museum exploring the Underground Railroad through the escape routes on Beacon Hill. Design and build your own safe house. Includes dinner, storytelling, activities, breakfast, and a special "bundle" to take home.

GRADE 5-6. $30 NON-MEMBER $25 MEMBER.

SUNDAY, MARCH 18, 3 P.M

Marian Anderson/Roland Hayes Concert Series: A New Beginning

Makanda Ken McIntyre Jazz Quartet. Original jazz selections and standard favorites from this world-class composer and improviser. McIntryre, a Boston native and NY resident, is a master of the alto sax, bass clarinet, oboe, flute, and bassoon. Reception immediately following.

Sponsored in part by the Office of Community Collaborations and Program Development at the New England Conservatory.

Any fees must be indicated.

$10 NON-MEMBER; FREE MEMBER; GROUP RATES AVAILABLE.

Monitor Your Progress

Assessment Practice

Reading: Making Inferences

Directions: *Choose the letter of the best answer to each question about the mission statement and the calendar of events.*

1. Which of the following is an inference that you can make from reading the mission statement and the calendar of events?
   - **A** The museum founders thought that African American history had been neglected.
   - **B** The museum founders knew that they would have a large audience.
   - **C** The museum founders wanted to create a museum just for serious scholars.
   - **D** The museum was created to celebrate the Harlem Renaissance.
2. Which of the following statements is an inference that you can make based on information in the calendar of events?
   - **A** The museum celebrates a variety of cultures.
   - **B** The museum places a special emphasis on the nineteenth century.
   - **C** The museum tries to educate the public.
   - **D** The museum believes that it should make history exciting for children.
3. Which of the following inferences is not supported by these documents?
   - **A** The museum supports the work of African American writers.
   - **B** The museum believes in collaborating with other organizations.
   - **C** The museum believes that it needs to attract more members.
   - **D** The museum wants children to learn about the Underground Railroad.
4. What can you infer about how the museum defines its audience?
   - **A** young children
   - **B** people of all ages
   - **C** African American scholars
   - **D** students of African American music

Reading: Comprehension and Interpretation

Directions: *Write your answers on a separate sheet of paper.*

5. State the museum's mission, and identify its main goal.
6. Explain how the museum works to achieve its mission and goals.
7. **(a)** Why do you think the program for preschool-aged children is free? **(b)** How might this admission policy advance the museum's mission?

Timed Writing: Exposition

Write a mission statement for an organization or publication that already exists or that you think should exist: for example, a specific type of museum, a charity or community service group, a school club, a magazine or a newspaper, or a Web site. In your mission statement, be sure to identify *who the group is, what it does,* and *why it does it.* **(25 minutes)**

ASSESS

Answers

Reading: Making Inferences

1. A
2. C
3. C
4. B

Reading: Comprehension and Interpretation

5. **Possible response:** The mission wants to preserve, conserve, and interpret the contributions of people of African descent and others who share an interest in liberty, dignity, and justice for all.
6. **Possible response:** The museum provides a program of stories and activities on African American literature and lore for children. It has an overnight visit to the museum that includes information about the Underground Railroad.
7. (a) The museum wants to encourage children to participate in programs and learn about African American history and culture. (b) By providing free information and knowledge to children, the museum educates the public about African American history and stimulates the interests of young people to help preserve this history and culture in years to come.

Timed Writing: Exposition

- Encourage students to choose an organization or subject about which they are familiar and in which they have a strong interest.
- Suggest that students plan how they will use their time, allotting about five minutes to planning, fifteen minutes to writing, and ten minutes for reviewing and revising.

Tips for Test Taking

Tell students that standardized tests that assess comprehension of an informational text often include multiple-choice questions.

They may find that the question limits in some way the scope of the answer required. The question may be more specific than they first thought, or it might ask what the text implies, not what it says explicitly.

Meeting Your Standards

Students will

1. understand the thematic connections between the pastoral poetry of Robert Frost and Dylan Thomas.
2. understand the characteristics of twentieth-century pastorals.

Connections

Literature Around the World

The American twentieth century was a time of fragmentation, uncertainty, and anxiety. For many, the peaceful and idyllic country life seemed the perfect remedy, and some poetry and prose addressed this theme. Although the pastoral is an ancient art that celebrates the simple life of the country, some writers, such as Robert Frost and Dylan Thomas, took it to a new level, using it to examine a wide range of human experiences. After students finish reading "Fern Hill," ask them to review the selections in Part 3 and to pay particular attention to the poems of Robert Frost.

The Modern Pastoral

- Point out that, until the modern era, the pastoral poem was highly conventionalized. It often involved a dialogue between shepherds (or a monologue) and frequently revolved around a shepherd's love for a maiden. Poets typically used courtly language even though the speaker was a shepherd far from the royal courts. In each case, the rural setting was idealized.
- In the late nineteenth and early twentieth centuries, the conventional formula broke down so that by the time of Frost and Dylan, the term *pastoral* referred to any poem that involved rural settings and rural people.
- By the twentieth century, poets used the pastoral form to introduce complex ideas. By contrasting the simplicity of the rural speaker and setting with the sophisticated concepts, the ideas gained power. The pastoral poetry of Frost and Dylan typifies this modern pastoral form.
- Ask students to look for the characteristics of the pastoral tradition in "Fern Hill" as well as in Frost's poetry and some of the other pieces in Part 3.

British Literature

Wales

The Modern Pastoral

The American poet Robert Frost (page 880) and the British poet Dylan Thomas are modern writers who used their experiences to write about country life. Their poems are part of a literary tradition known as the pastoral. A **pastoral** deals with rural life—usually its simple pleasures. Pastoral poetry originated in Greece and Rome, and the term comes from the Latin word for shepherd. Today, the term refers to any work that presents rural themes.

Twentieth-Century Pastoral While modern poets like Frost and Thomas work within the pastoral tradition, they also introduce complexities into their rural settings. As you read Thomas's "Fern Hill," consider how it connects to similar themes in Frost's poetry.

Fern Hill

Dylan Thomas

Now as I was young and easy under the apple boughs
About the lilting house and happy as the grass was green,
The night above the dingle starry,
Time let me hail and climb
Golden in the heydays of his eyes,
And honored among wagons I was prince of the apple towns
And once below a time I lordly had the trees and leaves
Trail with daisies and barley
Down the rivers of the windfall light.

And as I was green and carefree, famous among the barns
About the happy yard and singing as the farm was home,
In the sun that is young once only,
Time let me play and be
Golden in the mercy of his means,
And green and golden I was huntsman and herdsman, the calves
Sang to my horn, the foxes on the hills barked clear and cold,
And the sabbath rang slowly
In the pebbles of the holy streams.

All the sun long it was running, it was lovely, the hay
Fields high as the house, the tunes from the chimneys, it was air

Thematic Connections
What details in this stanza present a pastoral view?

And playing, lovely and watery
And fire green as grass.
And nightly under the simple stars
As I rode to sleep the owls were bearing the farm away,
All the moon long I heard, blessed among stables, the nightjars[1]
Flying with the ricks,[2] and the horses
Flashing into the dark.

And then to awake, and the farm, like a wanderer white
With the dew, come back, the cock on his shoulder; it was all
Shining, it was Adam and maiden,
The sky gathered again
And the sun grew round that very day.
So it must have been after the birth of the simple light
In the first, spinning place, the spellbound horses walking warm
Out of the whinnying green stable
On to the fields of praise.

And honored among foxes and pheasants by the gay house
Under the new made clouds and happy as the heart was long,
In the sun born over and over,
I ran my heedless ways,
My wishes raced through the house-high hay
And nothing I cared, at my sky blue trades, that time allows
In all his tuneful turning so few and such morning songs
Before the children green and golden
Follow him out of grace,

Nothing I cared, in the lamb white days, that time would take me
Up to the swallow thronged loft by the shadow of my hand,
In the moon that is always rising,
Nor that riding to sleep
I should hear him fly with the high fields
And wake to the farm forever fled from the childless land.
Oh as I was young and easy in the mercy of his means,
Time held me green and dying
Though I sang in my chains like the sea.

1. **nightjars** *n.* common nocturnal birds.
2. **ricks** *n.* haystacks.

Connecting British Literature

1. Compare and contrast the speakers' views of childhood in Thomas's "Fern Hill" and Frost's "Birches."
2. Which poem best represents the pastoral ideal, "Fern Hill" or "Out, Out—"? Explain.

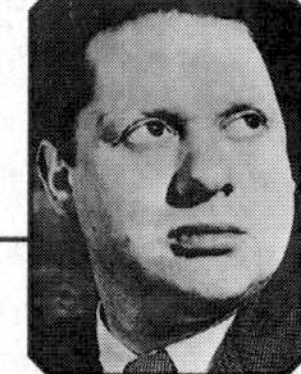

Dylan Thomas (1914–1953)

Born in the industrial city of Swansea, Wales, Dylan Thomas dropped out of school at the age of sixteen yet published his first book of poetry when he was only twenty. That same year, Thomas moved to London, where he worked in journalism, broadcasting, and filmmaking. In 1940, he published a collection of humorous stories about his childhood, *Portrait of the Artist as a Young Dog,* and in 1946, he published another poetry collection, *Deaths and Entrances.* Although acclaimed at an early age, Thomas struggled with poverty throughout his life, and he died at the age of thirty-nine.

Thematic Connections

Answer: Details include the hay fields, the references to grass and simple stars, owls that carry the farm away, stables, nightjars flying with the ricks, and the horses.

ASSESS

Answers

1. The speakers in both "Fern Hill" and "Birches" write from the perspective of adults looking back on childhood. They evoke the freedom and joy of childhood, and in the last lines, both speakers regret the passing of carefree childhood. Frost's speaker wants to return to childhood, swinging again in birches as a brief escape from daily life. In contrast, the speaker in "Fern Hill" does not look back on childhood as a time he would like to revisit; rather he sees himself in chains with childhood forever in the past and nothing but death ahead.
2. Students should recognize that "Fern Hill" most closely resembles the pastoral ideal. The speaker paints an idyllic and simple life in the country, only returning to a bleak reality in the final lines. "Out, Out" never presents a joyous or idyllic look at country life. The first lines describe a lovely setting, but even then the speaker sets a tone of dread that something dire will happen.

Differentiated Instruction

Solutions for All Learners

Strategy for English Learners
This poem may be quite difficult for English learners. To make it more accessible, read it aloud for them the first time, telling them to listen only to the sound of the lines. Then point out the poem's use of various sound devices, which create a rhythm that is obvious without knowing the meaning of the words. Then read the poem one or two lines at a time, and paraphrase the meaning, discussing the mood generated by the word choices.

Enrichment for Advanced Readers
Explain to students that Thomas finished "Fern Hill" in 1945, pointing out that this is the year World War II ended. The poem appeared in his poetry collection *Deaths and Entrances.* Ask students to look at a copy of the book, or at some of the poems from it, and identify the subjects, tone, and mood of the poems. Then have them compare these other poems from the book to "Fern Hill." Ask them how these poems reflect their composition during World War II and how "Fern Hill," one of the last composed, relates to the others.

Meeting Your Standards

Students will

1. write an analytical essay evaluating a literary trend.
2. understand and summarize criteria for a literary trend established in a literary essay.
3. evaluate poems by these established criteria.
4. use writing strategies to generate ideas, and to organize, evaluate, and revise writing.

Prewriting

- To give students guidance in developing this assignment, give them the **Writing About Literature** support pages in ***Unit 5 Resources.***
- Instruct students to reread Pound's essay A Fe w Don'ts." Ask students to carefully take notes identifying Pound's major ideas.
- Tell students to turn Pound's ideas into criteria for Imagist poetry by paraphrasing them, or rewriting the ideas in students' own words. As an example, **ask** them to paraphrase the following: "Use no superfluous word, no adjective, which does not reveal something." **Possible response:** An Imagist poem should have no purely descriptive adjectives.
- Students should select poems to evaluate from Unit 5. Encourage students to photocopy the poems they choose, enlarging them to make note taking easier.
- Call students' attention to the Analyzing According to Criteria model scorecard. Explain that by using a scorecard such as this, they can determine whether a poem meets or fails to meet the criteria. They can also identify why a poem succeeds or fails by these standards.

Tips for Test Taking

A writing prompt on the SAT or ACT test may assess students' ability to analyze literature. When writing under timed circumstances, they can use a Venn Diagram to help them organize the characteristics of each poem. This will help them decide which points to keep and which ones to eliminate.

Writing About Literature

Evaluate Literary Trends

The Imagist poets wrote with clear ideas about poetry and provided specific criteria with which to judge the success or failure of a poem. Ezra Pound expressed these ideas in his essay "A Few Don'ts." To a great extent, poems by such Imagists as Pound, William Carlos Williams, and H.D. can be measured according to the criteria Pound defined.

Using the assignment outlined in the yellow box, write an essay evaluating this literary trend.

Assignment: Following the Rules

Write an analytical essay that evaluates the success with which at least three Imagist poems fulfill the goals set out in Pound's essay "A Few Don'ts."

Criteria:

- Clearly restate Pound's main ideas.
- Evaluate the effectiveness of specific words, lines, and images in at least three poems according to Pound's ideas.
- Approximate length: 700 words.

Prewriting

Summarize Pound's main points. Reread Pound's essay, and take careful notes about each of his main points. Avoid using Pound's own language in your notes. Instead, paraphrase—or restate in your own words—his ideas. Translating his advice into your own words will allow you to be sure you understand his often complex concepts. It will also help you to determine which of his ideas will require additional explanation or definition for your readers.

Evaluate line by line. In all works of literature, every word plays an important part within the whole. In Imagist poetry, which, by its very nature, is compressed and focused, a single word carries even greater weight than in most other genres. Judge the success of each poem you have selected by weighing each word according to Pound's criteria. You may want to make a photocopy of the poems and write notes directly on the pages.

Create a scorecard. Use your notes to create an Imagist scorecard, like the one shown below. In the first column, list the criteria you will use to judge each poem. Across the top, list the titles of the poems you have chosen to analyze. In each box, place a *P* (for *Pass*) for each criterion that a given poem fulfills. Place an *F* (for *Fail*) for each criterion that a poem fails to meet.

Model: Analyzing According to Criteria

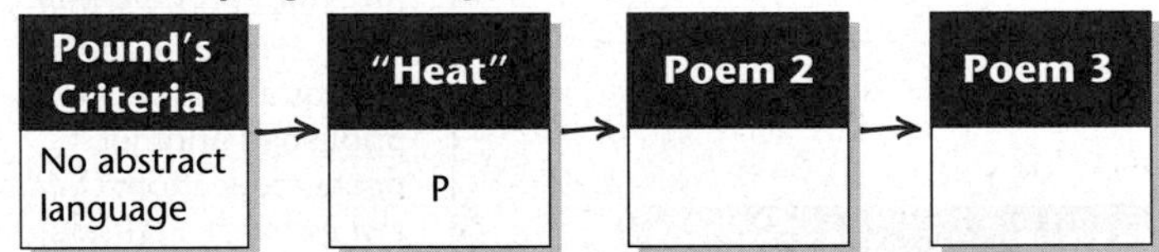

Pound's Criteria	"Heat"	Poem 2	Poem 3
No abstract language	P		

For each of the poems you are discussing, use the results of your scorecard to write a one-sentence statement about whether or not it fulfills Pound's criteria. These statements will serve as the foundation for the concepts you will develop more completely as you draft. Your statement should note the most prominent ways in which the poem succeeds or fails.

Read to Write

As you read each poem, ask yourself whether it meets Pound's criteria. The point is not whether or not you like the poem, but whether it fulfills specific artistic objectives.

Teaching Resources

The following resources can be used to extend or enrich the instruction for Writing About Literature.

Unit 5 Resources
Writing About Literature, pp. 296–297

General Resources
Rubrics for Response to Literature, pp. 65–66

Graphic Organizer Transparencies
Three-way Venn Diagram, p. 313

Drafting

Transform your notes into sentences. Notes written in preparation for writing an essay are abbreviated ideas—kernels of the points you will develop more completely in a draft. Using the notes you made as part of your prewriting activities, construct one or more complete sentences that fully express the idea each note represents.

Combine sentences into paragraphs. Write at least one paragraph on Pound's essay and at least one on each poem you have analyzed. In each paragraph about a poem, evaluate the author's success in meeting Pound's criteria. Refer to your scorecard for details. Make sure each sentence supports or explains your "grade."

Write to Learn

As you work on your essay, you may discover new ideas about the poems. Allow for this, and incorporate your discoveries into your work.

Revising and Editing

Review content: Check the soundness of your thinking. Check your evaluation of each poem to make sure it is based on the criteria you have compiled from Pound's essay. Remember: The point is not whether you personally like a poem but whether it fulfills the stated requirements.

Write to Explain

The foundation of your essay is your examination of Pound's essay. Make sure that your explanation of Pound's ideas is simple and clear.

Model: Revising to Focus On Criteria

"In a Station of the Metro" almost perfectly obeys Pound's dictate that a poem should "go in fear of abstractions." This brief description of faces in a crowd is intensely visual and concrete. ~~I love this poem because I know exactly what he means.~~ *One possible weakness is the word apparition. Because the word refers to something that is not really there, it can be interpreted as an abstraction.*

Review style: Vary sentence length and word choice. Poets select and arrange words not only for their meanings but also for their sounds and rhythms. Learn from their example. When revising your essay, work to avoid using the same words repeatedly, and make changes to avoid using sentences of the same length and structure.

Publishing and Presenting

Give an oral presentation. Share your ideas with the class. If possible, use an overhead projector or a slideshow program to project the poems you are discussing. Alternatively, you can simply copy the poems on the board. Then, as you read your essay aloud for the class, use a pointer to indicate words or phrases that are especially relevant to your discussion. Invite questions and comments from the class.

Prentice Hall Writing and Grammar Connection: Chapter 14

Differentiated Instruction

Solutions for All Learners

Support for Less Proficient Writers
These students may need help revising for variety. If they have drawn on their notes in drafting, their sentences and paragraphs may be highly repetitive. Have them vary their paragraphs by organizing their support for each evaluation differently.

Vocabulary for English Learners
These students may find revising for variety in word choice challenging. Encourage them to build vocabulary and vary word choice by using a thesaurus to find synonyms for repeated words. Then, have them look up the definitions of the new words in a dictionary. Be sure that they understand the difference between a synonym and a definition.

Strategy for Advanced Writers
As these students revise, encourage them to pay close attention to varying sentence structure. You might require students to incorporate two each of specific types of sentences—compound sentences, complex sentences, sentences using subordinate clauses, and so on—throughout their essays.

Drafting

- Suggest that students plan their essays with one paragraph to explain Pound's criteria and then one paragraph for each poem evaluated. Point out that this plan can easily be turned into an outline.
- Explain to students that their Analyze According to Criteria scorecards can provide the main points and evidence for each of their evaluation paragraphs.

Revising and Editing

- Be sure students understand that they are evaluating poems by *Pound's* standards—not by their own. Call their attention to the model on this page. Guide them to see the difference between the deleted passage and the revision.

Publishing and Presenting

- As students prepare their oral presentations, suggest that they include specific examples from the poems in their notes. Then, during presentations, students can point to specific words or phrases from the poems and explain why they meet or fail to meet Pound's criteria.

Writing and Grammar, Ruby Level

Students will find additional instruction on writing a literary evaluation in Chapter 14.

Writing and Grammar Interactive CD-ROM

Students can use the following tools as they complete their literary evaluations:

- Cluster Diagram
- Transition
- Sentence Length

Six Traits Focus

✔	Ideas		Word Choice
✔	Organization	✔	Sentence Fluency
	Voice	✔	Conventions

Assessing the Essay

To evaluate students' essays, use the Response to Literature rubrics, pp. 65–66 in ***General Resources.***

PRETEACH

Meeting Your Standards

Students will

1. **prepare, write, and deliver a multimedia presentation.**
2. **use writing strategies to generate ideas and to plan, organize, evaluate, and revise the presentation.**

From the Author's Desk

Tim O'Brien

Show students Segment 3 on Tim O'Brien on *From the Author's Desk DVD.* Discuss O'Brien's comments about his revision process.

Writing Genres

Using the Form Point out to students that multimedia presentations are often incorporated into many types of communications. Point out these examples:

- Family histories can include voice recordings and video clips, along with photographs and written accounts.
- Lectures often include slides and audio and video clips, along with charts, graphs, and other graphic organizers.
- Plays, concerts, and other live performances often use sound and visual effects.
- Business meetings frequently include slides, graphic organizers, and other media elements.

Writing Workshop

Research: Multimedia Presentation

The authors in this unit wrote poems, short stories, and nonfiction. The rise of technology has expanded the way we communicate. In the twenty-first century, media dominates the communications landscape. You may have encountered multimedia presentations on television, in art galleries, in documentaries, or on Web sites. The effect of these presentations on a viewer is quite different from the act of reading words on a page. Follow the steps outlined in this workshop to create your own multimedia presentation.

Assignment Create a multimedia presentation about a topic that interests you.

What to Include Your multimedia presentation should feature the following elements:

- integrated audio and visual components
- reinforcement of each element by the appropriate medium
- a scripted and logical organization that presents a focused message
- innovative use of media to convey concepts

To preview the criteria on which your multimedia presentation may be assessed, see the rubric on page 959.

Using the Form

You may use elements of a multimedia presentation in these situations:

- slide shows
- cable TV programs
- documentaries
- advertisements

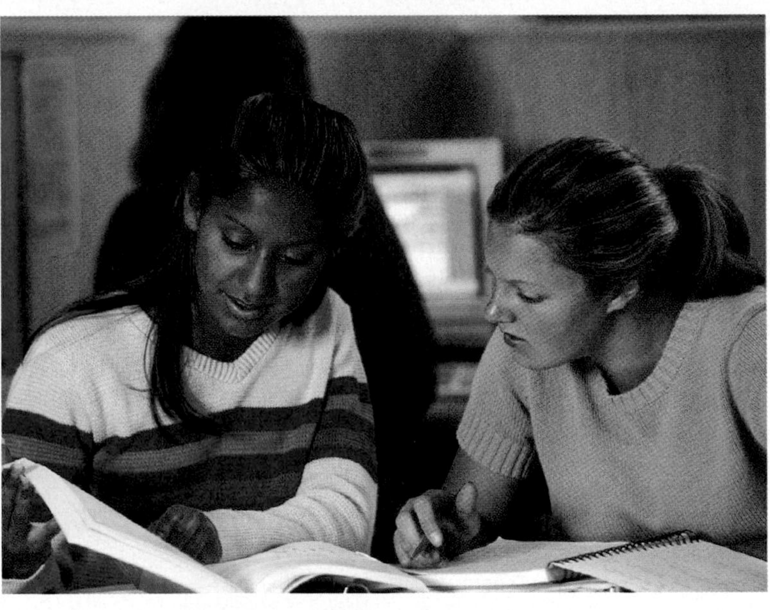

Teaching Resources

The following resources can be used to enrich or extend the instruction for the Writing Workshop.

Unit 5 Resources

Writing Workshop: Multimedia Presentation, pp. 298–299

General Resources

Rubrics for Multimedia Presentation, pp. 51–52

From the Author's Desk DVD

Tim O'Brien, Segments 3 and 4

Prewriting

Choosing Your Topic

To choose a subject for your multimedia presentation, use one of the following strategies:

- **List preferences.** Select a subject for which multimedia material will be readily available. Begin by listing musicians or artists whose work you enjoy, films you know well, or professional sports teams that you watch regularly. Make sure that you can imagine the audio or visual material that will support your ideas. Then choose a topic.
- **Create a media checklist.** In a chart like the one shown, list the various types of media that are available for several topics. Use the right-hand column of the chart to note specific media that would be most useful for your topic. Review your chart, and choose the topic that seems best suited to the assignment.

Media Checklist	Roller Coasters
☑ Music	*Mysterious music*
☑ Videos	*Historic roller coaster*
☑ Art	*Sketches of design*
☑ Photographs	*Dragon memorabilia*
☐ Computer Presentation	
☑ Interviews	*People waiting in line*

Narrowing Your Topic

Because images and sounds can be more difficult to locate than text, make sure that you can find enough media relevant to your topic. Continue your research, focusing on a topic narrow enough to be presented thoroughly. For example, the Civil War is too broad to address effectively, but you could research the role of women in the war or the effects of Sherman's march through Atlanta. As you narrow your topic, continue to check that you can find media that support your ideas.

Gathering Materials

Research your topic. As you gather materials, note creative ways to involve viewers. Consult your library for audio or video clips of interviews, documentaries, music, and art resources. Search the Internet for a wide range of media. You can use almost any medium, as long as it helps to explain your topic. Just make sure to credit all your media sources.

Identify a thesis. Review your notes and the materials you have gathered. Develop a thesis—one clear statement that will express the focus of your multimedia presentation. All aspects of your presentation, from the script to the visuals, audio, and charts, should support this main idea.

Tips for Using Rubrics

- Before students begin work on this assignment, have them preview the Rubric for Self-Assessment (p. 959) to know what is expected.
- Review the Assessment criteria in class. Before students use the Rubric for Self-Assessment, work with them to rate the student model by applying one or two criteria to it.
- If you wish to assess students' multimedia presentations with either a 4-point or a 5-point scoring rubric, see ***General Resources,*** pp. 51–52.

TEACH

Prewriting

- Have students choose topics by listing preferences or creating a media checklist.
- Use pp. 298–299 from ***Unit 5 Resources*** for support in creating a multimedia presentation.
- **Ask** students to evaluate the model checklist. Will this presentation be an interesting one? Explain.
  Possible response: The model checklist has five of the six media categories filled in. Therefore, the presentation will include a lot of variety, which should make it interesting.
- Give students the following broad topics, and have them **narrow** them into feasible subjects.
  1. Adolf Hitler; 2. The invention of the plane; 3. The Super Bowl.
  Possible responses: 1. Hitler's rise to power; 2. The design of the first effective airplane; 3. Memorable Super Bowl moments.
- Encourage students to consult with a librarian when visiting the library to gather materials.

Six Traits Focus

✔	Ideas		Word Choice
✔	Organization		Sentence Fluency
	Voice		Conventions

WG Writing and Grammar, Ruby Level

Students will find additional instruction on prewriting for a multimedia presentation in Chapter 28, Section 3.

Writing and Grammar Interactive CD-ROM

Students can use the following tools as they complete their multimedia presentations:

- Topic Bank
- Customizable Outliner
- Language Variety Revising Tool

Drafting

- Explain to students that adding sounds, images, and other media elements will not disguise a weak structure.
- Write the following thesis statement on the board: *Memorable Super Bowl moments stay with fans and compel them to watch the big game every year.* As a class, have students think of media that could be used to support this thesis. Have students decide how the media could be used together.
  Possible response: Video and audio clips of memorable Super Bowl moments could be played simultaneously. Video clips of the moments could be played with specially chosen music. Video clips of interviews with fans could be played with a background of specially chosen music.
- Explain to students that if they simultaneously played a video clip of a memorable Super Bowl moment, played music, and pointed to a chart detailing viewership of various Super Bowls, they would be overloading their audience. Emphasize to students the importance of focusing audience attention rather than dividing it.
- **Ask** students to explain how the changes have improved the excerpt from the student model.
  Answer: The change replaces a bland, general verb ("contains") with a more specific and active verb ("harnesses"), eliminates a vague and useless noun ("lots"), and describes the "power" ("of dragon lore").

Six Traits Focus

✔	Ideas	✔	Word Choice
✔	Organization		Sentence Fluency
	Voice		Conventions

Writing and Grammar, Ruby Level

Students will find additional instruction on drafting a multimedia presentation in Chapter 28, Section 3.

Writing Workshop

Drafting

Shaping Your Presentation

Sketch an outline. Your presentation needs the same solid structure as a persuasive essay or a research paper. Support your thesis with a unified approach and a script that details the sequence of your ideas. Your final script will orchestrate the complete presentation of multiple elements, but as you draft, a basic breakdown of your presentation's major components will keep you focused.

Plan your delivery. Start by jotting down the various media you will use in your multimedia presentation. Remember, your delivery will require a script and format that allow you to use two or more different media at the same time. Consider a two- or three-column chart to diagram what will occur at any given moment. Add stage directions to your diagram as you include text, audio, and video. Also note any props or equipment you will need as you present your work.

Too much at once

(cue audio, slide) Many of the more extreme sports **(point to chart)** have little to do with scoring or winning. **(cue interview film)**	**Audio:** *Tubular Bells* by Mike Oldfield **Slide:** Paragliding **Video:** Hot Air Balloons **Film:** Interview with Terry Edwards

Balanced

(cue audio) Many of the more extreme sports have little to do with scoring or winning. **(cue slide)**	**Audio:** *Tubular Bells* by Mike Oldfield **Slide:** Paragliding

Providing Elaboration

Strike a balance. Too many stimuli will overwhelm your viewer. Aim for a targeted interplay between two or three media at any one time. You want the viewer to be able to absorb primary materials along with any secondary elements, like music. Consult the sample notecards on this page for guidance.

Keep your narration lively. Your text anchors your presentation, but it also has to serve as part of the show. Avoid repeating in words what the other media are already communicating to the viewer. Your writing should sparkle and keep your audience's interest.

To read the complete student model, see page 958.

Student Model: Keep Narration Lively

^Today, Bombshell Roller Coasters ~~contain lots of~~ ^harnesses the power ^of dragon lore in a new roller coaster design **(pause for emphasis; cue video)**...the Dragon's Lair. **(Pause as video plays.)**

Livelier words heighten the effect of pauses.

From the Scholar's Desk
Tim O'Brien on Revision

Tim O'Brien

This is the opening to a novel called *The Things They Carried,* and it introduces the book's central motif: the physical and psychological burdens men carry through a war. I revised these sentences twenty or thirty times, sometimes deleting, sometimes adding bits of action to make the opening vivid and concret.

> *"I revised these sentences twenty or thirty times. . ."*
> — *Tim O'Brien*

Professional Model:

From *The Things They Carried*

First Lieutenant Jimmy Cross carried letters from a girl named Martha, a junior at Mount Sebastian College in New Jersey. They were not love letters, but Lieutenant Cross was hoping, so he kept them folded in plastic at the bottom of his rucksack. In the late afternoon, after a day's march, he would dig his foxhole, wash his hands under a canteen, unwrap the letters, hold them with the tips of his fingers, and spend the last hour of light pretending. He would imagine romantic camping trips into the White Mountains in New Hampshire. He would sometimes taste the envelope flaps, knowing her tongue had been there. More than anything, he wanted Martha to love him as he loved her, but the letters were mostly chatty, elusive on the matter of love. . . . She was an English major at Mount Sebastian, and she wrote beautifully about her professors and roommates and midterm exams, about her respect for Chaucer and her great affection for Virginia Woolf. She often quoted lines of poetry; she never mentioned the war, except to say, Jimmy, take care of yourself. The letters weighed ten ounces. They were signed Love, Martha, but Lieutenant Cross understood that Love was only a way of signing and did not mean what he sometimes pretended it meant.

Instead of writing abstractly about Jimmy's love for Martha, I inserted this line. These actions, I hope, convey a sense of how very precious the letters are to Jimmy Cross.

Although Martha isn't physically present in the scene, I wanted to hint at her character. I also wanted to suggest the vast emotional distance between college life and combat, how Jimmy and Martha are living in two different worlds.

By stating the precise weight of the letters, I hoped the reader might realize that some of the heaviest things we carry through life—letters, memories—can weigh almost nothing.

From the Author's Desk

- Show students Segment 3 on Tim O'Brien on **From the Author's Desk DVD.** Discuss why revision and rewriting are crucial to a final draft.
- **Ask** students if O'Brien was successful in making the opening vivid and concrete. Have students give examples to support their answers.
  Possible response: O'Brien made the opening vivid and concrete by using exact details, such as "folded in plastic at the bottom of his rucksack" and "taste the envelope flaps."
- Point out the first annotation to students. Tell students that O'Brien is showing, rather than telling, how much Jimmy loves Martha.
- Point out the third annotation to students. **Ask** students why the statement about the weight of the letters is so powerful.
  Possible response: This statement is powerful because O'Brien does not directly state this philosophical message; he gives readers this simple statement and allows them to make the inference.

Differentiated Instruction
Solutions for All Learners

Strategy for English Learners
Conducting media research may pose a special problem for these students, especially if they encounter audio and visual materials with unfamiliar vocabulary. Have these students research in small, mixed-skill level groups. Encourage group members to help one another determine the meanings of unfamiliar words and phrases.

Strategy for Advanced Readers
Encourage these students to find multimedia sources that express different positions on a topic. Using these sources, students should address a controversy within their topics as part of their presentations. Be sure students explain each position thoroughly and, then, take a clear position on this controversy and support it effectively.

Revising

- Emphasize to students that they should practice their presentations more than once. Once a partner has commented on a test run, the presenter should practice again, incorporating the partner's suggestions.
- Remind students to time their presentations accurately. They need to know how much time to allot to each phase of the presentation.
- Point out that presentations need to flow smoothly—and this flow can be interrupted when students stop to change media. Use the model as an example of revising to smooth transitions between different media.
- In addition to varying their media, encourage students to consider lengthening or shortening some of their media elements to improve the rhythm of their presentation. For the sake of variety and audience interest, they should avoid using media elements that are all approximately the same length.
- Call students' attention to the "Without Variety/With Variety" example. **Ask** students why the second version is likely to be more effective than the first.
  Answer: The first version uses only audio interviews. The second version uses video footage instead of an interview with the quarterback and enlivens a voiceover interview of the ballerina by using slides.

Six Traits Focus

	Ideas		Word Choice
✔	Organization		Sentence Fluency
	Voice		Conventions

Revising

Revising Your Overall Structure

Improve your sequence. A seamless delivery is the goal of any multimedia presentation. Because your presentation may involve apparatus that requires time for setup, practice in advance. Also make sure that the room you will be using is properly equipped for your presentation.

Peer Review: Hold a test-run with a partner.

- Run through your presentation, incorporating all audiovisual elements.
- Ask your partner to comment on parts that lacked clarity or seemed unpolished.

If necessary, revise the sequence to clarify connections between ideas or to smooth awkward transitions. Consider eliminating elements that are distracting or overly complicated.

Model: Revising to Smooth Transitions

(cue slide) ~~**(cue video)**~~ Our design represents the latest and best in roller coaster technology.	**Video:** computer ~~animation of Dragon's Lair~~
~~**(cue slide and audio)**~~ **(pointer to high lighter features)** The coaster will begin with a 95-meter peak, followed by a drop, followed by a 76-meter peak and drop. The rest of the ride includes banked turns, loops, and a smaller hill.	**Slide:** coaster route schematic design ~~**Audio:** People screaming~~

Afton deleted the video and audio elements of this section because the transitions were too complicated to handle smoothly.

Revising Your Selection of Media

Use a variety of effects. By using a variety of media to enhance your narration, you can spice up your presentation and hold your audience's interest. Review your script for overuse of one form of media. If you decide that your presention lacks variation, replace repetive elements with different media formats.

Without variety: Play audio interview of quarterback.
Play audio interview of ballerina.
Play recording of overture to the ballet.

With variety: Show video footage of quarterback.
Play voice-over interview of ballerina
Show slides of performance.

Tips for Using Technology in Writing

As students will probably know, there are many technology resources for preparing and delivering multimedia presentations. If you have access to audiocassette players, CD players, videocassette players, DVD players, and slide projectors for your class, encourage your students to make full use of them. A Power Point display can also be a very effective part of a multimedia presentation. If students are not familiar with this equipment, arrange for Audio/Visual staff members to give a tutorial.

Developing Your Style

Integrating Media

Choose different types of media. Your media must be appropriate to your intentions. For example, you would render a serious, thoughtful reflection less effective if you introduced silly cartoons and other lighter fare. Use the following chart as you integrate your media.

Media Checklist	Alternatives or Improvements
Is this image or sound appropriate for its use? Is it compelling and effective?	
Should it be moved to another position?	
Is there a smooth transition into the image or sound?	
Is there a smooth transition out of it?	
Does the image or sound help to unify the presentation?	

Find It in Your Reading Read or review the Student Model on page 958.

1. Locate elements of the presentation that have been properly integrated. Note the ways in which different media work together.
2. In particular, consider how the audio and video work together towards an appropriate effect.

Apply It to Your Writing Review the script for your multimedia presentation.

1. Evaluate the effect your media will have on the viewer. Consider each aspect individually, as well as its use with other media.
2. Circle each audio and video transition, as well as each stage direction, to make sure that all are working together. Look for ways to improve the transitions by making them more appropriate to your thesis or by blending components together more cleanly.
3. Experiment with different combinations of images and music. Varying the content or the order might produce unexpectedly effective results. Add transitions as you try several options to improve the flow of your work. Once you have developed your script, confirm your choices by previewing the presentation.

WG Prentice Hall Writing and Grammar Connection: Chapter 28, Section 3

Developing Your Style

- Remind students that media for media's sake will not enhance their presentations. They must use media selectively, choosing the most appropriate images and sounds to communicate and elaborate on their ideas.
- **Ask** students for examples of media choices that would not work well together.
  Possible answer: An image with a solemn tone would be undercut by upbeat music.
- Read the Student Model to the class, simulating the actual demonstration. Afterwards, have a class discussion about how Afton paced his presentation of the media. Point out how he integrated the media without overwhelming the audience.
- Explain to students that as they review their script they should be open to new organizational strategies. Tell students that if they become fixated with one structural idea they could close themselves off to another, more effective approach.

WG Writing and Grammar, Ruby Level

Students will find additional instruction on revising a multimedia presentation in Chapter 28, Section 3.

Tips for Test Taking

Although few tests will require students to make multimedia presentations, explain to students that the lessons they learn in preparing multimedia presentations will help them take tests more effectively. The clear focus required in multimedia presentations is useful in timed-writing situations. Also, the organization of their presentation into a series of steps can help students prepare for organizing their supporting evidence in a timed essay. Finally, students can apply their time-budgeting skills, honed in preparing and rehearsing a multimedia presentation, to test-taking situations.

Student Model

- Explain that the Student Model is a sample and that presentations may be longer.
- Call students' attention to Afton's subject—the power of dragons in the imagination. **Ask** students to evaluate this topic.
  Possible response: Students will likely agree that dragons are a stimulating subject, especially for a multimedia presentation that might have exciting visuals.
- After they have read the second note, make sure that students understand that multimedia material should not overwhelm the topic of a presentation. Therefore, the slide is more appropriate here than an exciting videotape.
- Remind students that a multimedia presentation must be organized as logically as an essay. **Ask** students to describe the organization used by Afton.
  Answer: The presentation moves from general to more specific information about the roller coaster.
- Call students' attention to the final note and encourage them to be innovative in their presentations, as well.

Writing Genres

Multimedia Presentations in the Workplace

Tell students that more and more jobs require skills in multimedia presentations—for selling goods and services, communicating goals and agendas, and informing audiences.

Fields such as teaching and law currently make extensive use of multimedia presentations. Share with students your own use of media in the classroom; encourage your colleagues in other departments to give you examples of their use of media. If possible, arrange for an attorney to visit the class and discuss the use of media presentations in the courtroom.

Student Model

Afton Kapala
Ventura, California

The Dragon's Lair

Text	Video and Audio
(cue video and audio) For thousands of years, dragons have played a major role in the human imagination. They represent the awesome power of nature and the extremes of human emotion.	**Video:** dragons from ancient China, Babylonia, Rome, to Wales, and Anglo-Saxon England, to today (film and TV shows) **Audio:** music from ancient past to today
Today, Bombshell Roller Coasters harnesses the power of dragon lore in our latest roller coaster design. **(pause for emphasis; cue video)** . . . the Dragon's Lair. **(pause as video plays)**	**Video:** computer animation of Dragon's Lair in motion with zooms in and out to show detail
(cue slide) Our design represents the latest and best in roller coaster technology. **(use pointer to highlight features)** The coaster will begin with a 95-meter peak, followed by a drop, followed by a 76-meter peak and drop. The rest of the ride includes banked turns, loops, and a smaller hill.	**Slide:** coaster route schematic design
(cue audio and first slide) After they buy tickets, customers will enter our air-conditioned concourse, **(cue second slide)** where they can buy snacks and dragon memorabilia. **(cue third slide)** Our Ground Dragons—customer service agents in costume—will provide customers with great photo opportunities.	**Slide:** dragon memorabilia (hats, flashlights, stuffed animals, etc.) **Slide:** costumed ground dragon
(cue slide) Why would Magic Mountain want to buy this ride? For nearly two centuries, roller coasters have been a huge public attraction. **(cue video)** All of those great roller coasters represent the past, but the Dragon's Lair is the future. It will keep crowds coming, generating great revenues for years to come.	**Slide:** question mark **Video with voiceover:** historic roller coasters—Russian Mountains (1800s), the Cyclone (1900s), the Fireball (1920s), and the Skyliner (1960s) **Video morphs to:** computer-animated image of the Dragon's Lair

Afton's subject is rich and well-suited to a multimedia format.

Afton does not attempt to be flashy if it is not appropriate. This slide of a schematic design is appropriate for the text.

The text, audio, and visual elements convey an increasing level of detail in a clear, logical way.

This use of video transforming into computer animation is an innovative and effective use of media.

Differentiated Instruction

Solutions for All Learners

Enrichment for Gifted/Talented Students

Many of these students are likely to have experience in multimedia work. Encourage them to challenge themselves and experiment with new media. Encourage them also to act as advisors to students who have less experience.

Enrichment for Advanced Students

Have students critique the multimedia elements used in a television news story or commercial. Challenge them to think of different ways to use the media in the story or commercial. Also, encourage students to think of new media that could be used in the story or commercial.

Editing and Proofreading

Review your script to eliminate errors in grammar, spelling, or punctuation.

Focus on Text: Review any writing in your presentation. Look for sentence fragments, and replace them with complete sentences. One way to revise a sentence fragment is to add the missing subject, verb, or both.

Fragment: A 95-meter peak, followed by a drop, followed by a 76-meter peak and drop.

Complete Sentence: The coaster will begin with a 95-meter peak, followed by a drop, followed by a 76-meter peak and drop.

Publishing and Presenting

Consider one of the following ways to share your multimedia presentation:

Stage a showing. Deliver your multimedia presentation to your class, followed by a question and discussion session.

Create a multimedia portfolio. Join with classmates to create a portfolio of multimedia presentations. Include a multimedia table of contents that uses catchy audio and visual components to summarize each presentation.

Reflecting on Your Writing

Writer's Journal Jot down your thoughts on the experience of creating a multimedia presentation. Begin by answering these questions:

- What did you learn about focusing your presentation?
- In what ways has creating a multimedia presentation changed the way you look at the different types of media you encounter daily?

Prentice Hall Writing and Grammar Connection: Chapter 28, Section 3

Rubric for Self-Assessment

Evaluate your multimedia presentation *using the following criteria and rating scale, or, with your classmates, determine your own reasonable evaluation criteria.*

Criteria	Rating Scale				
	not very				*very*
Focus: How clearly do you present your topic?	1	2	3	4	5
Organization: How logical is the organization?	1	2	3	4	5
Support/Elaboration: How well do you integrate audio and visual components to reinforce each element?	1	2	3	4	5
Style: How innovatively do you use media to convey concepts?	1	2	3	4	5
Conventions: How correct is the grammar, spelling, and punctuation in your presentation materials?	1	2	3	4	5

Editing and Proofreading

- Explain to students that text within their slides or printouts should be examined as thoroughly as text in a written report.
- Have students form pairs and, as a pair, examine the text of each other's slides and printouts.

Six Traits Focus

	Ideas		Word Choice
	Organization		Sentence Fluency
	Voice	✔	Conventions

ASSESS

Publishing and Presenting

- If students are unsure of delivering their oral presentation without a script, suggest that they use note cards to jot down notes for referral during their presentation.
- Tell students that in advertisements, information should not be overpowered by design and art. Tell students that an advertisement must catch a person's attention, but, most important, it must inform.

Reflecting on Your Writing

- Ask students what methods they found most effective to develop smooth transitions with their media. Was it difficult for them to coordinate operating the media with delivering a presentation?
- Ask students what they learned about the various media that they chose to work with. Would they feel at ease working with these types of media in the future?

Writing and Grammar, Ruby Level

Students will find additional guidance for editing and proofreading, publishing and presenting, and reflecting on a multimedia presentation in Chapter 28, Section 3.

Meeting Your Standards

Students will

1. **learn the terms *compare and contrast, conclude,* and *deduce.***
2. **apply knowledge of these terms in standardized-test situations.**

Know Your Terms: Recognizing Relationships

Explain that students will respond to the terms listed under Terms to Learn when asked to recall and use information from a reading passage in standardized-test situations.

Terms to Learn

- Review *compare and contrast.* Tell students that they may be asked to write responses that require them to explain how two or more literary works are alike and different. For example, students may compare the use of figurative language in two poems but contrast the type of figurative language each poem contains.
- Review *conclude.* If students are asked to conclude something about a theme, they are being asked to make a decision based on what they have read.
- Review *deduce.* Tell students that they can use their own knowledge to answer a question. If a test question asks them to *deduce,* they apply their own knowledge of what seems logical and reasonable to understand a situation.

ASSESS

Answers

1. Poetry should have rhythm, but it should not be descriptive.
2. **Possible answer:** He likes verse that is unburdened with descriptive language and uses precise wording to create rhythm.
3. **Possible answer:** He cares little for classical styles and he claims that most poetry labeled *classic* is b ad."

Vocabulary Workshop

High-Frequency Academic Words

High-frequency academic words are words that appear often in textbooks and on standardized tests. Though you may already know the meaning of many of these words, they usually have a more specific meaning when they are used in textbooks and on tests.

Know Your Terms: Recognizing Relationships

Each of the words listed is a verb that tells you to show that you can recognize logical relationships among different pieces of information.

Terms to Learn

Compare and Contrast Tell the important similarities and differences and explain why they are important.

Sample test item: ***Compare and contrast*** H. D.'s poems "Heat" and "Pear Tree."

Conclude Tell how you use reasoning to reach a decision or opinion based on the information provided.

Sample test item: What can you ***conclude*** about the theme of Cullen's poem?

Deduce Tell what you figure out by using logic to apply general information to a particular situation.

Sample test item: What do you ***deduce*** happens to the "fruits" of the narrator's labor?

Practice

Directions: *Read the following passage from Ezra Pound's essay "A Few Don'ts ." Then, answer questions 1–3.*

Don't be "viewy"—leave that to the writers of pretty little philosophic essays. Don't be descriptive; remember that a painter can describe a landscape much better than you can, and that he has to know a great deal more about it.

. . . Don't mess up the perception of one sense by trying to define it in terms of another. This is usually the result of being too lazy to find the exact word. To this clause there are possibly exceptions.

[These] simple proscriptions will throw out nine-tenths of all the bad poetry now accepted as standard and classic; and will prevent you from many a crime of production. . . .

1. *Compare and contrast* poetry, as Pound describes it, with painting.
2. What can you *conclude* about Pound's attitude toward "classic" poets?
3. What can you *deduce* from this passage about Pound's own poetic style?

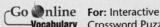

For: Interactive Crossword Puzzles
Visit: www.PHSchool.com
Web Code: erj-5101

Critical Reading: Sentence-Completion Questions

The reading sections of some tests require you to answer sentence-completion questions correctly. Use these strategies to help you understand and answer these types of questions.

- Use the context and your own knowledge to deduce which word would best complete the sentence.
- If the word you anticipated is not among the answers presented, look for a synonym of the word or other related words.
- Analyze the sentence meaning, and decide if it is positive or negative. Then, eliminate choices that have the opposite sense.

Practice

Directions: *Read the following sentences, and then select the answers that best complete their meanings.*

1. When Julia skipped three classes and two band practices after months of perfect attendance, her friends wondered about her __?__ behavior.

   A erratic **C** slow
   B reasonable **D** arrogant

2. Olivia's mastery of formal etiquette was just one example of her __?__ behavior.

   A crude **C** refined
   B suspicious **D** temporary

3. Those who believe it is barbaric and cruel to keep large animals in captivity think that to visit a zoo is __?__.

   A unfortunate **C** immoral
   B advisable **D** courageous

4. Surprisingly, Umberto loved peanuts but found peanut butter __?__.

   A creamy **C** old-fashioned
   B exquisite **D** repugnant

5. Although my friend had __?__ the movie, I was __?__ by the weak plot.

   A recommended; disappointed
   B enjoyed; impressed
   C criticized; convinced
   D proposed; frightened

Test-Taking Strategies

- Try each word choice in the sentence to see whether it makes sense. Often, you can eliminate some of the choices because they are illogical, the wrong part of speech, or inconsistent with the sentence's meaning.

Meeting Your Standards

Students will

1. **identify strategies for answering standardized-test questions.**
2. **apply sentence-completion strategies in a standardized-test situation.**

Critical Reading

- Review the word *deduce.* Explain to students that to answer sentence-completion questions, they must *deduce* their answers from the information they see on the test.
- Have students read the first practice item. Then **ask** them to visualize and describe the situation. **Possible response:** Julia's behavior seems alarming and unusual, especially because her friends "wondered" about it.
- Next, have students read the choice of answers. Guide them to recognize that only **A,** *erratic,* matches the situation they have visualized.
- In item 2, students should look for an answer choice that matches how someone with a mastery of etiquette would behave. A, B, and D are not behaviors that a person with a mastery of etiquette would show. Explain that only **C,** *refined,* matches the situation.
- For items 3 through 5, be sure that students read and match the behavior or sentiment in each situation with a logical answer choice.

Tips for Test Taking

Tell students that when they see sentence-completion questions on a standardized test, they need to carefully read the directions and especially each sentence in each item. Clues to the correct answer often may appear in a sentence. Students need to be sure that they completely understand the meaning of each sentence so that they can choose the most appropriate answer.

ASSESS

Answers

1. A
2. C
3. C
4. D
5. A

Meeting Your Standards

Students will

1. **critically evaluate the communication of messages in audiovisual media.**
2. **learn and apply strategies for evaluating the manner in which audiovisual media present information.**
3. **learn and apply strategies for evaluating the techniques audiovisual media use to present information.**

Evaluate Presentations

- Call students' attention to the chart. Explain that they will use this chart to evaluate audiovisual media communication methods.
- Tell students to begin their evaluations by determining the purpose of the media format. **Ask:** What do you think the purpose of a television newsmagazine program is? **Possible response:** Some students may say that their purpose is to inform; others will note that such programs also entertain.
- Explain to students that the structure of media communication—the length of news stories, for example, or the balance between audio and video—affects the way in which the message is conveyed.
- Be sure that students understand the difference between objective and subjective communication.

Evaluate Communication Techniques

- Encourage students to pay close attention to the music used with such audiovisual communication as a television news program.
- Instruct students to be on the lookout for sounds and images that appeal to the emotions without conveying relevant information.

Assess the Activity

To evaluate students' evaluations use the Listening: Evaluating Communication Methods rubric, p. 86 in *General Resources.*

Communications Workshop

Evaluating Communication Methods

Many of the communication methods we are most affected by, such as television broadcasts or films, appear in a visual medium. Listening and viewing skills can be useful in analyzing such materials and identifying the techniques used to present information and opinions. The strategies described below will help you interpret arguments and understand information presented through such media. Use the form on this page to record your responses.

Evaluate Presentations

Use the following strategies to evaluate presentations.

Recognize purpose. Distinct forms of media have specific goals. Some seek to entertain, some seek to persuade, and others seek to inform. Some seek to do all three.

Analyze structure. Note the ways in which each form of media structures information. For example, the evening news might build on short oral summaries supported by film footage. A TV ad might present a short persuasive message accompanied by a series of quick images.

Weigh objectivity and subjectivity. News reports are meant to present current events in a factual, objective manner, without bias or opinion. Often, such shows also include editorials that convey subjective opinions. Consider how the objectivity or subjectivity of a presentation affects your understanding of events. If a media report seems subjective, identify its perspective and evaluate its truthfulness. For some media messages, you may also need to identify the underlying moral or ethical values.

Feedback Form for Audiovisual Media

Presentation

Topic: entertainment _____ information _____

Structure: length _____

balance between visual and audio _____

Point of view: objective _____ subjective _____

Techniques

Note your responses to media makers' use of the techniques listed below. Use this ranking system:

+ = effective, ✓= acceptable, – = inappropriate.

Music/slogans: _____

Loaded sounds/images: _____

Your Evaluation:

Do you feel the events addressed by this medium were presented objectively and thoroughly?

How did the techniques you identified affect your response to the media? Explain.

Evaluate Communication Techniques

Media makers use various techniques to communicate information. Look for the following in evaluating audiovisual media:

- **Music or slogans:** Audiovisual media makers may use music to set a mood or emphasize visual imagery. Slogans, which you will often hear repeated, grab your attention and stick in your mind.
- **Charged images:** Powerful images, such as videos of gurgling babies or of starving children, evoke strong emotional reactions. Used responsibly, they give substance to reported facts. However, such nonverbal messages can sometimes be manipulative.

Activity ***Listen, View, and Evaluate*** Watch the television news, a film documentary, or a news magazine/interview program. Use the evaluation form shown here to analyze and evaluate media techniques.

Differentiated Instruction Solutions for All Learners

Support for Special Needs Students
Students may need to practice with videotapes of television news reports. Show students a news report, asking them to focus on and write down the facts of the story. Then, show the report again, this time having them evaluate presentation. Have them watch a third time for communication techniques.

Support for Less Proficient Readers
Students may find weighing objectivity and subjectivity challenging. Be sure that they understand that while a media format such as a news report may seem to be objective, it may have a subjective bias. Instruct them to search even seemingly objective media formats for signs of subjectivity.

Support for English Learners
These students may find the vocabulary of audiovisual media difficult, but they may be especially adept at recognizing the impact of music and charged sounds and images. Suggest that these students watch a news report, paying attention only to these techniques. What messages do they find?

Suggestions for Further Reading

Featured Titles:

The Great Gatsby
F. Scott Fitzgerald
Scribner, 1992

Novel Fitzgerald's celebrated novel incorporates all of the glamour and decadence that characterized America in the 1920s. This tragic tale of broken dreams and ruined lives explores self-made millionaire Jay Gatsby's quest to win the love of the wealthy, beautiful—and married—Daisy Buchanan. The narrator of the story is Nick Carraway, a young Midwesterner who becomes Gatsby's neighbor on Long Island one summer. Nick is caught up in the dazzling lives of Gatsby, Daisy, and their wealthy friends until tragic circumstances reveal the emptiness of their values. The mysterious Gatsby, an impure man with a pure dream, is the perfect symbol of America in the Jazz Age.

Winesburg, Ohio
Sherwood Anderson
Penguin Books, 1960

Fiction Inspired by Edgar Lee Masters's *Spoon River Anthology*, Sherwood Anderson wrote a group of related stories about small-town life. He based his fictional town of Winesburg on his own hometown of Clyde, Ohio. Central to the book is young George Willard, the sympathetic character to whom others try to explain themselves. The characters who open up to George are isolated people who usually have trouble communicating.

Black Voices: An Anthology of African-American Literature
Edited by Abraham Chapman
Signet Classic, 2001

Cultural Anthology This volume collects the best African American literature of the twentieth century in a variety of genres. The collection features works by Ralph Ellison, Frederick Douglass, James Baldwin, Malcolm X, Langston Hughes, Claude McKay, Countee Cullen, Robert Hayden, and Gwendolyn Brooks.

Work Presented in Unit Five:

If sampling a portion of the following texts has built your interest, treat yourself to the full works.

Poems by Robert Frost: A Boy's Will and North of Boston
Robert Frost
Signet Classic, 2001

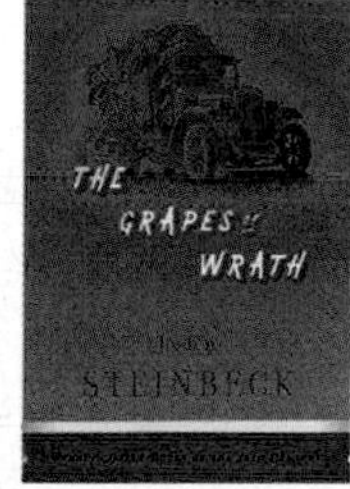

The Grapes of Wrath
John Steinbeck
Penguin Books, 1967

***Many of these titles are available in the* Prentice Hall/Penguin Literature Library.**
Consult your teacher before choosing one.

Planning Students' Further Reading

Discussions of literature can raise sensitive and often controversial issues. Before you recommend further reading to your students, consider the values and sensitivities of your community as well as the age, ability, and sophistication of your students. It is also good policy to preview literature before you recommend it to students. The notes below offer some guidance on specific titles.

The *Great Gatsby* by F. Scott Fitzgerald In writing about race and ethnicity, Fitzgerald occasionally used terms that are considered offensive today. Most of the characters in the book, excluding Gatsby, are heavy drinkers, and there are numerous scenes that describe alcohol consumption. The novel relates the effects of an extramarital affair, although there are no explicit sexual references. Students may be concerned about the hit-and-run accident that results in Myrtle's death or about Gatsby's murder and Wilson's suicide.

Lexile: 1070L

The *Grapes of Wrath* by John Steinbeck The novel depicts poverty, hardship, and social injustice in realistic detail. It contains drinking, smoking, sexual situations, coarse allusions, and derogatory language. It also contains details of religious hypocrisy and a character critical of religion who preaches a humanitarian philosophy that some may consider sacrilegious. It criticizes greed and commercialism and is unsympathetic to banks and other large business interests.

Lexile: 1230L

***Winesburg, Ohio* by Sherwood Anderson** Hands—Wing Biddlebaum's homosexuality; Paper Pills—pregnancy out of wedlock; Nobody Knows—George's sexual encounter; Goodliness--Louise's sexual promiscuity and alcoholism, as well as physical violence between David and his grandfather; Adventure—Alice's naked run in the rain; Respectability—Wash's naked wife; The Strength of God—Reverend Hartman's secretive watching of a naked woman in her bed; "Queer"—Elmer's physical violence with George; The Untold Lie—Nell's out-of-wedlock pregnancy; Drink—Tom's excessive drinking.

Lexile: 1050L

***Poems by Robert Frost: A Boy's Will* and *North of Boston* by Robert Frost** The following poems in *A Boy's Will* contain overtly religious references to God: "A Prayer in Spring" (p. 32), "Revelation" (p. 43), "The Trial by Existence" (p. 44), "In Equal Sacrifice" (p. 47). Several poems in *North of Boston* deal with death, including "The Death of the Hired Man (p. 69) and "Home Burial" (p. 86). "The Housekeeper" (p. 117) is about the problems of a man and a woman who have lived together for fifteen years but never married. "The Fear" (p. 125) is about the guilt a woman feels after she deserted her husband to be with another man.

Lexile: NP

***Black Voices: An Anthology of African-American Literature,* edited by Abraham Chapman** Students may expect to encounter a number of sensitive issues, including profanity, suicide, violence, sexual innuendo, graphic language, and the use of the words "nigger" and "nigra." Point out that many of the works in this collection were deliberately written with protest against discrimination and injustice as a major objective. Recommend that students always keep the social and cultural context in mind as they read.

Lexile: Appropriate for high school students

Meeting Your Standards

Students will

1. read selections from American literature written during the period of 1946 to the present.
2. apply a variety of reading strategies, particularly strategies for reading fiction, appropriate for reading these selections.
3. analyze literary elements.
4. use a variety of strategies to read unfamiliar words and to build vocabulary.
5. learn elements of grammar, usage, and style.
6. use recursive writing processes to write in a variety of forms.
7. develop listening and speaking skills.
8. express and support responses to various types of texts.
9. prepare, organize, and present literary interpretations.

Unit Instructional Resources

In **Unit 6 Resources,** you will find materials to support students in developing and mastering the unit skills and to help you assess their progress.

Vocabulary and Reading Additional vocabulary and reading support, based on Lexile scores of vocabulary words, is provided for each selection or grouping.

- **Word Lists A and B** and **Practices A and B** provide vocabulary-building activities for students reading two grades or one grade below level, respectively.
- **Reading Warm-ups A and B,** for students reading two grades or one grade below level, respectively, consist of short readings and activities that provide a context and practice for newly learned vocabulary.

Selection Support Practice and reinforcement pages support each selection:

- Reading Skills
- Literary Analysis
- Vocabulary
- Writing
- Extension
- Enrichment

PRENTICE HALL **TeacherEXPRESS™** Plan · Teach · Assess You may also access these resources on TeacherExpress.

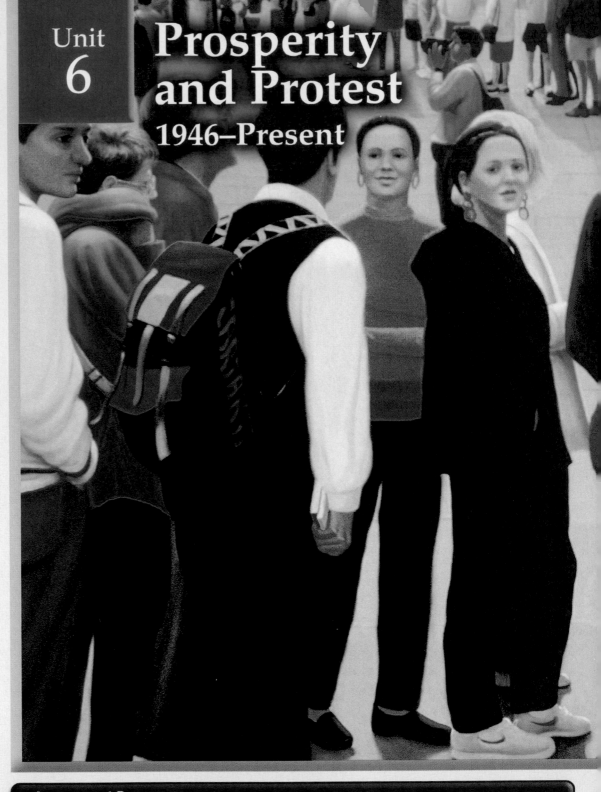

Unit 6 Prosperity and Protest

1946–Present

Assessment Resources

Listed below are the resources available to assess and measure students' progress in meeting the unit objectives and your state standards.

Skills Assessment

Unit 6 Resources
Selection Tests A and B

TeacherExpress™
ExamView® Test Bank Software

Adequate Yearly Progress Assessment

Unit 6 Resources
Diagnostic Tests 10, 11, and 12
Benchmark Tests 9, 10, 11, and 12

Standardized Assessment

Standardized Test Preparation Workbook

The Contemporary Period

"Sometimes I can see the future stretched out in front of me—just as plain as day. The future hanging over there at the edge of my days. Just waiting for me."

—Lorraine Hansberry

◀ This painting, *Blockbuster* by Dale Kennington, captures both the vibrancy and the anonymity of contemporary life.

Introduce Unit 6

- Direct students' attention to the title and time period of Unit 6. Have a student read the quotation. **Ask** them: What does the quotation suggest about Americans at this point in their history?
  Possible response: The quotation suggests that Americans are confident about the future.
- Have students look at the art. Read the Humanities note to them, and **ask** the discussion question.
- Then **ask:** What kinds of literature or themes in literature do you think might come out of this period in American history?
  Possible response: Students might suggest themes concerning anxiety, anticipation, and shared cultural experiences.

Humanities

Blockbuster, 1997 by Dale Kennington

Dale Kennington, a contemporary painter, was born in Savannah, Georgia. She completed her undergraduate education at the University of Alabama. At one time she was a faculty member at the School of Art and Architecture at Auburn. Kennington now spends eight to ten hours a day painting. Use the following question for discussion.

- How does the painting create a sense of community and isolation at the same time?
  Possible response: There are many people standing in line, but the faces looking toward the observer appear alone and disconnected from the crowd.

Unit Features

Arthur Miller

Each unit features commentary by a contemporary writer or scholar under the heading "From the Author's Desk." Playwright Arthur Miller introduces Unit 6 in Setting the Scene, in which he comments about the role of theater in contemporary experience and the unifying role of literature in the world. Later in the unit students can also read Miller's insights about writing on p. 1371 in the Writing Workshop.

Connections

Every unit contains a feature that connects the American literature of the period to World Literature. In this unit, students will connect English Romantic poet William Wordsworth's "I Wandered Lonely as a Cloud" with American writer Robert Penn Warren's "Gold Glade."

Use the information and questions on the Connections pages to help students enrich their understanding of the selections in this unit.

Reading Informational Materials

These selections will help students learn to analyze and evaluate informational texts, such as workplace documents, technical directions, and consumer materials. They will expose students to the organization and features unique to nonnarrative texts.

In this unit, students will read a critical review entitled "On Social Plays."

From the Author's Desk

Introduce Arthur Miller

- Arthur Miller introduces the unit and offers insights into contemporary literature and the American experience. His play *The Crucible,* and his commentary about it, appear later in the unit on pages 1252–1358.
- Have students read the introductory paragraph about Arthur Miller. Tell them that Miller wrote plays that addressed important social issues of the time. He often wrote about people who struggled against forces over which they had little or no control.
- Use the ***From the Author's Desk DVD*** to introduce Arthur Miller. Show Segment 1 to provide insight into his writing career. After students have watched the segment, **ask** what events in the United States inspired Miller to write *The Crucible*?
  Answer: Miller found a parallel between the Salem witch trials and the events orchestrated by Senator Joseph McCarthy.

The Purpose of Theater

- Have students read Miller's commentary on the purpose of theater.
- Miller explains that theater is more than entertainment. He asserts that theater has an important mission. **Ask:** According to Miller, what themes does theater need to confront?
  Possible answer: Theater needs to deal with the question of man's awareness of himself and his environment, his quest for justice, and the right to be human.
- Tell students that they will read *The Crucible* by Arthur Miller in Part 3 of this unit.

Critical Viewing

Possible response: Students may suggest that the audience is feeling anxiety or sadness.

Setting the Scene

Unit 6 features writing from a variety of writers who represent the contemporary American experience. The following remarks by playwright Arthur Miller introduce you to the role of theater in that experience as well as to the unifying role that literature plays in the world. As you read his commentary, the unit introduction, and the literature in Unit 6, challenge yourself to participate in the vivid cultural diversity of contemporary American literature.

From the Author's Desk
The Words of Arthur Miller on Literature

Arthur Miller

Introducing Arthur Miller (1915–2005) A legend of the contemporary American theater, Miller has chronicled the dilemmas of common people pitted against powerful social forces. His most famous plays are *Death of a Salesman,* for which he won a Pulitzer Prize, and *The Crucible.*

The Purpose of Theater

After a talk Arthur Miller gave at The University of Michigan, a member of the audience asked him: "What do you think the purpose, the ultimate purpose, of the theater is, really?" Miller responded: "I couldn't even speak in those terms because it's like asking, 'What is the ultimate purpose of the Universe?' To me the theater is not a disconnected entertainment, which it usually is to most people here. It's the sound and ring of the spirit of the people at any one time. It is where a collective mass of people, through the genius of some author, is able to project its terrors and its hopes and to symbolize them. Now how that's done—there are thousands of ways to do it of course. . . . I personally feel that the theater has to confront the basic themes always. And the faces change from generation to generation, but their roots are generally the same, and that is a question of man's increasing awareness of himself and

Teaching Resources

The following resources can be used to enrich or extend the instruction for the Unit 6 Introduction.

From the Author's Desk DVD
Arthur Miller, Segment 1

Unit 6 Resources
Names and Terms to Know, p. 2
Focus Questions, p. 3
Listening and Viewing, p. 338

his environment, his quest for justice and for the right to be human. That's a big order, but I don't know where else excepting a playhouse, where there's reasonable freedom, one should hope to see that."

Theater as a Bridge Between Cultures

Arthur Miller once wrote: "In a theater, people are themselves; they come of their own volition; they accept or reject, are moved or left cold not by virtue of reason alone or of emotion alone, but as whole human beings.

"A communion through art is therefore unusually complete; it can be a most reliable indication of a fundamental unity; and an inability to commune through art is, I think, a stern indication that cultures have not yet arrived at a genuine common ground. Had there been no Flaubert, no Zola, no Proust, de Maupassant, Stendhal, Balzac, Dumas;[1] had there been no Mark Twain, or Poe, Hawthorne, Emerson, Hemingway, Steinbeck, Faulkner,[2] or the numerous other American artists of the first rank, our conviction of essential union with France and of France with us would rest upon the assurances of the two Departments of State and the impression of tourists. I think that had there been no Tolstoy, no Gogol, no Turgenev, no Chekov or Dostoyevsky,[3] we should have no assurance at all nor any faint hope that the Russian heart was even ultimately comprehensible to us.

"Literature of the first rank is a kind of international signaling service, telling all who can read that wherever that distant blinker is shining live men of a common civilization."

1. **Flaubert . . . Dumas** influential French writers.
2. **Mark Twain . . . Faulkner** famous American writers.
3. **Tolstoy . . . Dostoyevsky** well-known Russian writers.

◀ Critical Viewing What emotions do you think this theater audience is feeling? **[Speculate]**

Go Online Author Link

For: An online video
Visit: www.PHSchool.com
Web Code: ere-8601

For: More about Arthur Miller
Visit: www.PHSchool.com
Web Code: ere-9635

Reading the Unit Introduction

Reading for Information and Insight Use the following terms and questions to guide your reading of the unit introduction on pages 970–977.

Names and Terms to Know
Silent Generation
Sputnik
Vietnam War
John F. Kennedy
Martin Luther King, Jr.
Modernism
Postmodernism

Focus Questions As you read this introduction, use what you learn to answer these questions:
- In what ways did World War II affect the position of the United States in the world?
- What was the impact of technology on daily life during this period?
- In what ways did American literature reflect the turbulence and confusion of this period?

Reading the Unit Introduction

Tell students that the terms and questions listed here are the key points in this introductory material. This information provides a context for the selections in the unit. Students should use the terms and questions as a guide to focus their reading of the unit introduction. When students have completed the unit introduction, they should be able to identify or explain each of these terms and answer or discuss the Focus Questions.

Concept Connector

After students have read the unit introduction, return to the Focus Questions to review the main points. For key points, see p. 977.

Go Online Author Link Typing in the Web Codes when prompted will bring students to a video clip and more information on Arthur Miller.

Using the Timeline

The Timeline can serve a number of instructional purposes, as follows:

Getting an Overview

Use the Timeline to help students get a quick overview of themes and events of the period. This approach will benefit all students but may be especially helpful for Visual/Spatial Learners, English Learners, and Less Proficient Readers. (For strategies in using the Timeline as an overview, see the bottom of this page.)

Thinking Critically

Questions are provided on the facing page. Use these questions to have students review the events, discuss their significance, and examine the *so what* behind the *what happened*.

Connecting to Selections

Have students refer to the Timeline when they begin to read individual selections. By consulting the Timeline regularly, they will gain a better sense of the period's chronology. In addition, they will appreciate what was occurring in the world that gave rise to these works of literature.

Projects

Students can use the Timeline as a launching pad for projects like these:

- **Timeline Follow-up** Have students bring the Timeline up-to-date by drawing an additional column in their notebooks and entering significant new American and world events. These can include new works of literature, scientific achievements, and political events.
- **Oral Reports** Have students choose an item on the Timeline and report to the class on some of its effects. For example, students might report on public reaction to the Vietnam Veterans Memorial, which was dedicated in 1982.

American and World Events

1945 1955 1965

AMERICAN EVENTS

- **1945** United States grants independence to the Philippines.
- **1949** *Death of a Salesman* by Arthur Miller is first produced.
- **1952** Ralph Ellison publishes *Invisible Man.* ▼
- **1954** Supreme Court rules public school segregation to be unconstitutional.

- **1955** Flannery O'Connor publishes *A Good Man Is Hard to Find.* ▼

- **1959** Alaska and Hawaii admitted to the Union as the 49th and 50th states.
- **1961** Joseph Heller publishes *Catch-22.*
- **1962** Environmental protection movement spurred by Rachel Carson's book *Silent Spring.*
- **1963** President John F. Kennedy assassinated in Dallas.
- **1966** *Ariel,* Sylvia Plath's last collection of poems, appears.
- **1968** Martin Luther King, Jr., civil rights leader, murdered in Memphis.
- **1969** Astronaut Neil Armstrong becomes the first person to set foot on the moon. ▲

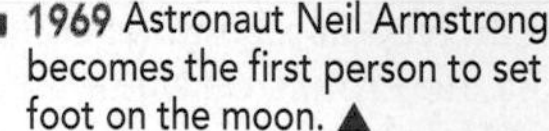

- **1972** Last U.S. combat troops leave Vietnam; peace pact signed in 1973. ▶

WORLD EVENTS

- **1947** India-Pakistan: India and Pakistan granted independence from Great Britain.
- **1948** Israel: United Nations establishes state of Israel.
- **1948** Germany: Soviet Union blockades Allied sectors of Berlin.
- **1950** England: Doris Lessing publishes *The Grass Is Singing.*
- **1954** England: *Lord of the Flies* by William Golding appears.
- **1956** Argentina: Jorge Luis Borges publishes *Extraordinary Tales.*
- **1957** Ghana: Ghana emerges as independent nation.
- **1957** USSR: *Doctor Zhivago* by Boris Pasternak appears.
- **1959** Germany: East Germany builds Berlin Wall.
- **1961** Cuba: Fidel Castro comes to power.
- **1962** USSR: *One Day in the Life of Ivan Denisovich* by Alexander Solzhenitsyn appears.
- **1967** Israel: Israel gains territory from Arab states in Six-Day War.
- **1969** Northern Ireland: Long period of violence begins between Catholics and Protestants.
- **1972** China: Nixon makes historic visit to China. ▼

Getting an Overview of the Period

Introduction To give students an overview of the period, have them indicate the span of dates in the title of the Timeline. Next, point out that the Timeline is divided into American Events (on the top) and World Events (on the bottom). Have them scan the Timeline, looking both at the American Events and the World Events. Finally, point out that the events in the Timeline often represent beginnings, turning points, and endings (for example, astronauts first landed on the moon in 1969).

Key Events Have students identify key events related to protest, one of the unit's themes.
Possible response: Supreme Court ruling against segregation (1954), assassination of Martin Luther King, Jr. (1968), end of the Vietnam War (1972–1973).

What events indicate progress or setbacks in technology?
Possible response: These include the first landing of humans on the moon (1969) and the nuclear disaster in Chernobyl (1986).

975 1985 1995

- **1980** Ronald Reagan elected president.
- **1982** Vietnam Veterans Memorial dedicated in Washington, D.C. ▼

- **1987** President Reagan and Soviet leader Mikhail Gorbachev sign the INF treaty, agreeing to ban short-range and medium-range nuclear missiles. ▲
- **1988** George Bush elected president.
- **1990** Congress passes the Americans With Disabilities Act, prohibiting discrimination against people with disabilities.
- **1992** Bill Clinton elected president.
- **1993** Toni Morrison wins Nobel Prize for Literature.
- **1995** Amy Tan publishes her third novel, *The Hundred Secret Senses.*
- **1996** Summer Olympic Games held in Atlanta, Georgia.
- **1997** Frank McCourt's autobiography *Angela's Ashes* wins Pulitzer Prize.
- **2000** George W. Bush defeats Al Gore in an extremely close and controversial presidential election.
- **2001** Novelist and short story writer Eudora Welty dies.
- **2001** Hijacked planes crash into the World Trade Center in New York, the Pentagon in Washington, D.C., and a field in Pennsylvania on the same day. Thousands of lives are lost.
- **2004** President George W. Bush is re-elected, defeating Senator John Kerry.

- 1979 India: Mother Teresa wins Nobel Prize for Peace.
- 1979 Vietnam: Hundreds of thousands of "boat people" flee Vietnam.
- 1979 Trinidad: V. S. Naipaul publishes *A Bend in the River.*
- 1979 England: Margaret Thatcher becomes British prime minister.
- 1981 Poland: Polish trade union movement, Solidarity, suppressed.
- 1986 USSR: Chernobyl nuclear disaster spreads radioactive cloud across Eastern Europe.
- 1989 Eastern Europe: Berlin Wall comes down.
- 1989 China: Pro-democracy demonstrations violently suppressed at Tiananmen Square.
- 1991 Middle East: Unified forces led by U.S. defeat Iraq in Persian Gulf War.
- 1994 South Africa: Nelson Mandela becomes the first democratically elected president.
- 1997 China: Hong Kong returns to Chinese rule, ending British rule. ▼

- 1999 Conflict between Albanians and Serbs in Kosovo leads to a war between Serbia and NATO forces. Then, a peace agreement is signed.
- 2001 Serbia: Serbian leader Slobodan Milosevic is arrested.

Analyzing the Timeline

1. (a) When did the Supreme Court rule that public school segregation is unconstitutional? (b) What is the relationship between that ruling and the civil rights movement of the 1950s and 1960s?
   Answer: (a) The Supreme Court ruling was in 1954. (b) Many students will realize that the Brown decision prompted further efforts to integrate schools.
2. (a) Name two important public figures who were assassinated during this period. (b) What do these events suggest about the decade in which they occurred?
   Answer: (a) John F. Kennedy was assassinated in 1963, and Martin Luther King, Jr. in 1968. (b) They suggest that the decade of the 1960s was turbulent.
3. (a) Identify two important political events occurring in Eastern Europe in the 1980s. (b) Taken together, what story do these events tell about Soviet control of Eastern Europe?
   Answer: (a) In 1981, the Polish trade union movement, Solidarity, was suppressed. In 1989, the Berlin Wall came down. (b) The first event suggests that the Soviet Union was having trouble with protest movements. The second suggests that the Soviet Union was coming apart.
4. (a) How long after the end of the Vietnam War was the Vietnam Veterans Memorial dedicated? (b) Do you think the dedication of the memorial meant that arguments over the war were finally coming to an end?
   Answer: (a) The Vietnam Veterans Memorial was dedicated in 1982, nine years after the peace pact was signed in 1973. (b) Some students may speculate that the dedication of a monument meant that some sense of conciliation had been reached. Others may point out that to this day, people disagree about the Vietnam War.
5. What other recent events from 2001 and after could be possible entries in a timeline like this one?
   Possible response: The events that students choose should be important turning points, firsts, or milestones in the fields of politics, literature, science, music, or art.

Critical Viewing

1. What is the mood of the image of the Vietnam Veterans Memorial (1982)? **[Interpret]**
   Possible response: Students may say that the names of the dead overpower the image of the soldier and that the image has a somber, sad mood.
2. (a) What is unusual about the flags in the 1987 photo featuring U.S. President Reagan and Soviet leader Gorbachev? **[Make Connections]** (b) How does this add to the moment as the men sign a treaty to ban certain nuclear missiles? **[Assess]**
   Possible response: (a) Each leader is sitting in front of the flag of the other's country. (b) It suggests that they are not enemies.

Literature of the Period

- In reading Flannery O'Connor's "The Life You Save May Be Your Own," students will experience a work that runs counter to the complacency of the 1950s. (The story first appeared in a full-length collection in 1955.)
- As students will read in this introductory essay, "The Contemporary Period," this era is one in which diverse groups have asserted their rights. Students have a chance to appreciate the diversity of contemporary literature by reading such selections as the excerpt from *The Names,* by N. Scott Momaday; "Mint Snowball," by Naomi Shihab Nye; "Suspended," by Joy Harjo; "Everyday Use," by Alice Walker; "Who Burns for the Perfection of Paper," by Martín Espada; and others.

Critical Viewing

Possible response: By demonstrating that African Americans could compete in professional baseball, Robinson prompted people to recognize that African Americans could succeed in other professional sports—and in all professions and trades.

The Contemporary Period

Looking to the future is a natural part of the human experience. Much of the technology that has become widespread since 1945—television and computers in particular—shows us a brighter future. The new technology often makes life easier. Paradoxically, it also introduces complexities that were unknown in earlier days.

The years from the end of World War II to the present day have been a time of change. Great strides have been made in civil rights and women's rights. Popular entertainment has changed dramatically, not just in presentation (for example, from radio to television, from phonograph records to CDs) but also in style (for example, from big bands to rock music and hip-hop). These changes and others have had an effect on American literature.

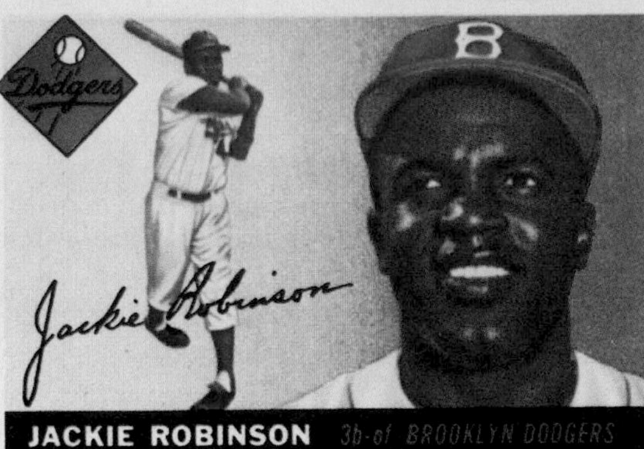

▲ **Critical Viewing** African Americans could not play baseball in the major leagues until Jackie Robinson broke the color barrier in 1947. What effects—both in sports and in society—did Robinson's breakthrough have? **[Analyze Cause and Effect]**

Historical Background

The United States emerged from World War II as the most powerful nation on Earth. Proud of their role in the Allied victory, Americans now wanted life to return to normal. Soldiers came home, the rationing of scarce goods ended, and the nation prospered. Despite postwar jubilation, however, the dawn of the nuclear age and the dominance of the Soviet Union throughout Eastern Europe meant that nothing would be the same again.

In 1945, the United Nations was created amid high hopes that it would prevent future wars. Nonetheless, the Cold War between the Soviet Union and the West began as soon as World War II ended. It was in Asia, however, that the first armed conflict came. In 1950, President Harry S. Truman sent American troops to help anticommunist South Korean forces turn back a North Korean invasion.

From Quiet Pride to Activism Americans of the 1950s are sometimes referred to as "the Silent Generation." Many of them had lived through both the Great Depression and World War II. When peace finally arrived, they were glad to adopt a quiet, somewhat complacent attitude. They greatly admired President Dwight D. Eisenhower, one of America's wartime heroes.

In October 1957, the Soviet Union launched *Sputnik,* the first artificial satellite to orbit Earth. This Soviet space triumph spurred many people to

Enrichment

Brown v. Board of Education

In 1951, Oliver Brown sued the Topeka, Kansas, Board of Education to allow his eight-year-old daughter Linda to attend a school that only white children had been allowed to attend. She had been going to a school farther away that was intended for African Americans only. When the case was argued before the Supreme Court, the African American lawyer Thurgood Marshall argued for Brown and against segregation in any of America's schools.

The court's ruling on May 17, 1954 was a historic one. It declared that "separate facilities are inherently unequal." President Eisenhower, who privately disagreed with the ruling, did not speak out for it publicly but said he would support "constitutional processes." Soon after, the court ruled that local schools should move to desegregate "with all deliberate speed."

Ask students why this ruling was so important. **Possible response:** Many will see that it challenged the decades-old doctrine of segregation.

call for changes in American science and education. President John F. Kennedy, elected in 1960, promised to "get the nation moving again." He had little time to do so, however, before his assassination in 1963.

After Kennedy's assassination came an escalating and increasingly unpopular war in Vietnam. A wave of protest followed. Gone were the calm of the Eisenhower years and the high hopes of Kennedy's brief administration. In their place came idealistic but strident demands for rapid change: greater "relevance" in education, more progress on civil rights, an immediate end to the Vietnam War. It was a time of crisis and confrontations, but it brought a great deal of genuine progress.

Real and lasting gains were made in civil rights after World War II. Segregation in the public schools was outlawed by the Supreme Court in 1954. Tragedy struck in 1968, however, when civil rights leader Martin Luther King, Jr., was assassinated in Memphis, Tennessee. Riots broke out in many cities across the nation.

Point/Counterpoint

The Dropping of the Atomic Bomb on Japan—Inevitable or Unjustifiable?

Was the dropping of the atomic bomb on Japan, an act that introduced the nuclear age, an inevitable event or an unjustifiable decision? Two equally distinguished historians disagree on this important question.

Inevitable Event

ìCo nceivably, as many would later argue, the Japanese might have surrendered before November and the scheduled invasion. Conceivably, they could have been strangled by naval blockade, forced to surrender by continued fire bombing, with its dreadful toll. . . . But no one close to Truman was telling him not to use the new weapon. General Marshall fully expected the Japanese to fight on even if the bomb were dropped. . . . That it might make the invasion unnecessary was too much to expect. . . . 'Truman made no decision because there was no decision to be made,' recalled George Elsey. . . . 'He could no more have stopped it than a train moving down a track. . . .'"

—*Truman*, David McCullough

Unjustifiable Decision

"The use of the atomic bomb was not really needed to produce this result [the surrender of Japan and the long-awaited end of the war]. With nine-tenths of Japan's shipping sunk or disabled, her air and sea forces crippled, her industries wrecked, and her people's food supplies shrinking fast, her collapse was already certain—as Churchill said.

"The U.S. Strategic Bombing Survey report emphasized this point, while adding: '. . . it seems clear that, even without the atomic bombing attacks, air supremacy could have exerted sufficient pressure to bring about unconditional surrender and obviate the need for invasion.'"

—*History of the Second World War*, B. H. Liddell Hart

The American Experience
Point/Counterpoint

Underscore that nuclear weapons—even the first atomic bombs, which were less powerful than today's weapons of mass destruction—proved to be a fearsome force in the modern world. The atomic bombing of Japan can now be seen as heralding in an age of unprecedented fear and anxiety. Then, ask the following questions.

1. What do the two viewpoints have in common? In what ways are they different?
   Possible response: Both viewpoints assume that Japan would ultimately have surrendered whether the bombs were dropped or not. They are different, however, because McCullough states that the surrender was not imminent, while Hart suggests that it was. Also, McCullough's focus is on President Truman, while Hart's is on Japan's condition.
2. Is it possible that both historians are correct? Explain.
   Possible response: Students should notice that Hart argues that Truman *should* have stopped the bombing, while McCullough argues that Truman *could not* have stopped it. Based on these excerpts, then, it is possible that both historians are correct.
3. Identify any effects of the bombing you see in today's world. How might the world be different if it had not happened?
   Possible response: Students may point to the ongoing issues of nuclear weapons and their proliferation as a long-term effect of the bombing—the fears and uncertainties that the bombings gave birth to still plague the world. Others may suggest, however, that the weapons would still exist and pose the same threat even if they had never been used in war.

Differentiated Instruction
Solutions for All Learners

Enrichment for Less Proficient Readers
Have students brainstorm to list issues and trends of contemporary life. After they have developed this framework of prior knowledge, have them look for evidence of these issues and trends in "Prosperity and Protest."

Enrichment for English Learners
Encourage students to consider key issues and trends of their first cultures in the present. Discuss how these issues and trends compare and contrast with those in contemporary America. Then, as they read "Prosperity and Protest," instruct them to find parallels between their own cultures and that of contemporary America.

Enrichment for Advanced Readers
Instruct students to create flowcharts that illustrate how American issues and trends evolved from 1946 until the present, becoming the issues and trends that dominate contemporary American society.

Historical Background

Comprehension Check

1. What international organization was created in 1945? Briefly describe this organization's chief goal.
   Answer: The United Nations was founded in 1945. Its goal was to prevent future wars.
2. Why are Americans of the 1950s sometimes referred to as "the Silent Generation"?
   Answer: Having lived through the Great Depression and World War II, they were glad to live quietly.
3. In what ways did the 1960s differ from the 1950s?
   Answer: The 1960s—which saw the assassinations of Kennedy and King and protests against the Vietnam War—were years of crisis and confrontation. The 1950s were characterized by a greater acceptance of things as they were.
4. In the years after World War II, what new medium changed the leisure habits of Americans?
   Answer: Television changed the leisure habits of Americans.
5. What type of regions grew most rapidly as a result of the automobile?
   Answer: The automobile made possible explosive suburban growth.

Critical Thinking

1. In what ways would America be different without cars and televisions? **[Speculate]**
   Possible response: Students may say that more people might travel by public transportation and that there might be more extensive rail lines connecting cities. Also, people might create more of their own entertainment.
2. Is it accurate to describe this era as one of protest? **[Evaluate]**
   Possible response: Students who agree will point out the civil rights movement, the women's movement, and the Vietnam War protests. Other students may distinguish among decades, pointing to the 1960s as a time of protest, with various movements continuing past that decade.

Literature of the Period

Variety and Promise The turbulence of contemporary times has contributed to the development of a looseknit variety of approaches known as Postmodernism. Listed here are some of the general ways in which Postmodernism tends to differ from its precursor, Modernism.

Modernism

- Viewed the massive casualties of World War I as undercutting pretensions to rationality and civilization
- Influenced by Freud's studies of the unconscious and a new interest in the art of primitive peoples
- Loss of trust in rationality, balanced by a newfound trust in the artist's ability to glean meaning from the irrational
- Confidence that the work of art is a unique and powerful creation with its own individual aura or atmosphere
- Tendency to view the work of art as a perfected product rather than as an incomplete and ongoing process
- Some confidence in the truth of the Renaissance notion that a great work of art is immortal and ensures immortality for its author
- Belief that "high" culture and "low" culture are separated by a meaningful dividing line and that a work of fine art is inherently superior to a cartoon

Postmodernism

- Viewed World War II, with the Holocaust and the dropping of the A-bomb, as undercutting assumptions of life's meaning
- Influenced by studies of media and language and by the explosive growth of information technology
- Some loss of trust in the artist's ability to access the irrational and return with a sense of renewal and greater meaning
- Less confidence that the work of art is unique, coupled with a sense that culture endlessly duplicates and copies itself
- Greater interest in the work of art as a process that reflects on its own making as it evolves
- Loss of confidence in the Renaissance notion that a great work of art is immortal and ensures immortality for its author
- Loss of belief in the meaningful dividing line between "high" culture and "low" culture, so that in Pop Art, the subject matter of fine art can be a cartoon

In the spirit of Postmodernism, some writers have explored new literary forms and techniques, composing works from dialogue alone, creating works that blend fiction and nonfiction, and experimenting with the physical appearance of their work. Still other writers, using more traditional forms, have focused on capturing the essence of contemporary life in the content of their works, addressing the impersonal and commercial nature of today's world.

Critical Thinking continued

3. What is the single most important development of this era? Explain. **[Support]**
   Possible response: Students should justify the importance of whatever issue or trend they choose to emphasize. For example, students might point to the civil rights movement as an attempt to fulfill the founders' promise of equality for all.

A Quest for Stability The upheavals of the 1960s brought a conservative reaction. Many Americans longed for a return to "the good old days." President Richard M. Nixon, elected in 1968, promised to end the Vietnam War and to restore order in the nation. Nixon's achievements were soon overshadowed by the Watergate affair—the burglarizing of Democratic Party headquarters under the direction of Nixon government officials. This scandal forced his resignation from the presidency in 1974.

Civil rights activism continued during the 1970s, and another movement attracted growing attention—the women's liberation movement. Although women had earned the right to vote in 1920, discrimination still existed. Betty Friedan's *The Feminine Mystique,* published in 1963, called for change. The women's movement grew steadily throughout the 1970s.

After Jimmy Carter's one-term presidency in the late 1970s, the nation sent Ronald Reagan to the White House. A former film star and governor of California, Reagan proved a popular and persuasive president. His re-election in 1984 was one of the biggest landslide victories in American history. In 1988, George Bush, Reagan's vice president, was elected to the presidency. Seeking reelection in 1992, Bush faced a tough fight against high unemployment, a recession, growing dissatisfaction with government, and his youthful opponent. Democrat Bill Clinton and his running mate, Al Gore—the youngest ticket in American history—won the election. Despite the 1994 elections that voted many Democratic Congress members out of office, Clinton won reelection in 1996. However, in 2000, Al Gore lost to George Bush's son, George W. Bush, in an election that was extremely controversial, and in 2004, Bush was re-elected, defeating Senator John Kerry.

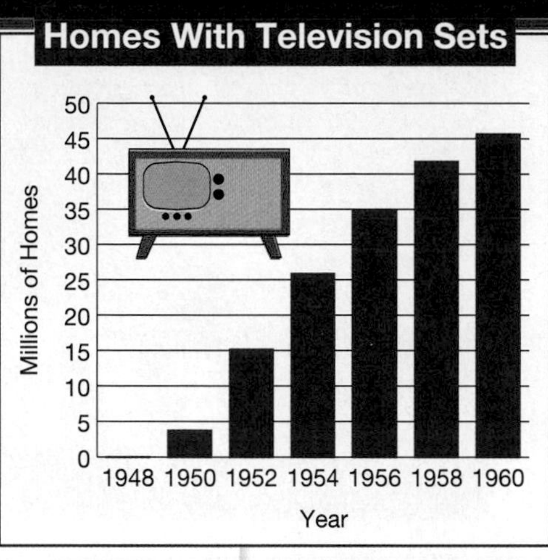

▲ **Critical Viewing** Before 1950, television was a novelty. By the end of the decade, however, television sets were a common feature in American homes. What factors might have influenced the steady rise in television ownership? **[Draw Conclusions]**

The Changing Scene Commercial television was still in its infancy at the end of World War II, but it was on the verge of spectacular growth. Over the next few years, television changed the leisure habits of Americans.

The postwar period was a time of explosive suburban growth, made possible by the automobile. At first, most suburban homeowners worked in a city and commuted to their jobs by train, bus, or car. Then, major corporations began establishing suburban headquarters, and workers could live nearby or commute short distances from one suburb to another. Even more recently, advanced technology has allowed people to "telecommute," or work in home offices and stay connected by Internet, phone, and fax.

The world has changed dramatically since 1945, and it is still changing. One of the most dramatic examples is the development of the Internet in a few short years from a military and scientific communication system to a global information network. The changes have had an impact on the literature of the time, although this impact has not always been obvious.

Background
Literature

Postmodernism involved a significant change of focus for American literature, away from the certainty of carefully crafted art and towards the process of creating. This shift is reflected in the literary scholarship of the time. Drawing on and responding to the ideas of such European critics as Jacques Derrida and Michel Foucault, such American *deconstructionists* as Paul de Man and J. Hillis Miller turned their attention to the uncertainties of language and literature. Some other critics examined historical contexts of literature; still others took literary criticism into political directions. Postmodernism in literary criticism may be as varied as in literature itself.

Background
Architecture

Postmodernism was not limited to literature. The movement flourished in other arts, including architecture. Modernist architecture had been simple, pure, and even utopian; postmodern architecture rebelled against this. Architectural postmodernism emerged in the United States, when modernist apartment buildings in St. Louis, Missouri, were demolished in 1972. The postmodern buildings drew on commercial architecture and art, as well as incorporating historical references. Robert Venturi was a major critic of modernist architecture, and he and his partner, John Rauch, were leading proponents of the new style, building houses in New York and Colorado.

Critical Viewing

Possible response: The steady rise in television ownership might have resulted from falling prices, improving technology, increased advertising, and appealing programs.

Enrichment

The Civil Rights Movement

After scoring major legal victories through the 1950s, including the famous decision in the *Brown v. Board of Education* case (see the note on p. 960), the civil rights movement gained support in the 1960s. African Americans and others attempted to end segregation and secure voting rights in the South. This battle was hard fought and sometimes violent, but it began to produce results by the mid-1960s. With desegregation progressing, the movement began to focus on economic injustice in cities.

Martin Luther King, Jr., was perhaps the most important leader in the civil rights movement. Both his father and grandfather were ministers, and he followed in their footsteps. He was also influenced by the teachings of the Indian leader Mohandas Gandhi, who believed that strong foes could be vanquished through nonviolence.

Ask students why King chose a nonviolent approach. **Possible response:** It is morally preferable to avoid violence. Also, when you are in the minority, it makes strategic sense to appeal to people's better instincts.

Critical Viewing

Answer: In 1950, the ratio of women's income to men's was about $800 to $1200, or 2/3. In 1975, the ratio was $4000 to $6500, which is less than 2/3. Although the ratios seem to remain relatively constant, the difference between men's and women's income in 1950 was $400, while the difference grew to $2500 in 1975.

Background
Literature

The South experienced a literary awakening between the world wars, in the heyday of Nobel Prize–winner William Faulkner. Writers emerging in the region after World War II inherited Faulkner's legacy. Flannery O'Connor was among the most prominent southern writers of the period. O'Connor captured southern social mores in richly detailed short stories. Students can find O'Connor's "The Life You Save May Be Your Own". Students may wish to compare her work with that of another southern writer, Eudora Welty. Welty's "A Worn Path" appears in Unit 5.

Background
Literature

A number of the new American writers who emerged after World War II brought absurdity, dark humor, and grim fantasy into their work. Such novelists as Joseph Heller and Kurt Vonnegut, Jr., portrayed the war in unrealistic terms, using absurdism to respond to its horrors. The atomic bomb and the rapidly escalating nuclear arms race that it heralded drove more American writers toward black humor and fantasy. These styles and concerns are reflected in the absurdist fables of Thomas Pynchon.

Median Incomes of Men and Women, 1950–1975

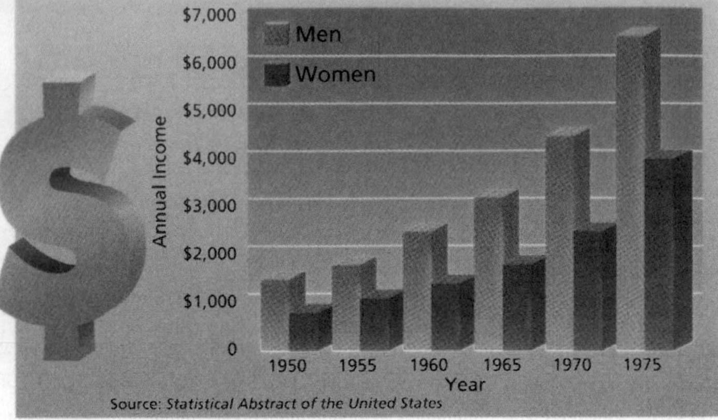

Source: *Statistical Abstract of the United States*

◀ **Critical Viewing** Between 1950 and 1975, women's incomes continued to lag behind men's earnings, partly because many low-paying fields such as nursing and teaching were traditionally considered "women's work." Did the income gap increase or decrease between 1950 and 1975? **[Analyze]**

Authors for a New Era Although contemporary writers have produced a wide variety of impressive works, it is all but impossible to predict which writers will achieve lasting fame and which will not. Time is needed to certify greatness. Modern readers and critics have their favorites, of course. Some of them will undoubtedly become part of America's enduring literary legacy.

Every writer owes a debt to those writers who have gone before. In that sense, literature is cumulative. The earliest American literature, except for that of the Native Americans, was based on European models. Writers in the United States today can look to a rich heritage of their own. Contemporary novelists are well aware of Nathaniel Hawthorne, Mark Twain, Ernest Hemingway, and William Faulkner. Short-story writers know Edgar Allan Poe, Willa Cather, and Eudora Welty. Poets study Emily Dickinson, Walt Whitman, and Langston Hughes. Playwrights are familiar with Eugene O'Neill and Thornton Wilder.

Renowned contemporary novelists include Carson McCullers, Norman Mailer, Bernard Malamud, John Updike, Flannery O'Connor, Joyce Carol Oates, Anne Tyler, and Alice Walker. Many of these novelists have written short stories as well. Flannery O'Connor and John Updike are modern masters of the short-story form. Other writers, such as Donald Barthelme and Ann Beattie, have written novels but are better known for their short stories. Isaac Bashevis Singer, a Polish-born New Yorker who wrote in Yiddish, was famous for both his novels and his short stories. He won the Nobel Prize for Literature in 1978. John Cheever, a respected novelist, won the Pulitzer Prize for Fiction in 1979 for his collected short stories, many of which concern suburban life.

Just as Realism and Romanticism have tended to merge in recent literature, so, curiously, have fiction and nonfiction. Truman Capote's *In Cold Blood,* published in 1966, was billed as a "nonfiction novel." Capote, primarily a novelist and short-story writer, used fictional techniques to

Enrichment

The Music of Aaron Copland

Tell students that Aaron Copland (1900–1990) is widely regarded as America's greatest composer. His works range from jazz- and blues-influenced compositions to orchestral pieces to ballets reflecting the influence of folk music.

Appalachian Spring, a ballet composed in 1944, is one of Copland's most popular works. It tells the story of a "pioneer celebration of Spring in a newly built farmhouse in Pennsylvania in the early 1800s." In one movement, Copland celebrates a young couple's new life together. Based on the Shaker hymn "Simple Gifts," the movement is a theme with variations, the theme being introduced by a solo clarinet and each variation becoming more elaborate.

If possible, find a recording of *Appalachian Spring* and play an excerpt for students—possibly the "Simple Gifts" movement described above. Have students discuss what is specifically American about this work. Guide them to recognize that the melodies come from old American songs.

analyze a real and seemingly senseless crime. Later authors, such as E. L. Doctorow in his novel *Ragtime,* combined historical figures with purely fictional characters. This technique has aroused some controversy.

Increasing attention has been paid recently to the place of nonfiction in the literary hierarchy. The essay has always been considered an important literary form, and some outstanding essays are published every year. James Baldwin and John McPhee are accomplished essayists. Among the many notable longer works of nonfiction are Paul Theroux's *The Great Railway Bazaar,* N. Scott Momaday's *The Names,* and Barry Lopez's *Arctic Dreams.*

Poetry Within the Tradition A number of the famed prewar poets continued to publish extensively after the war. Robert Frost, Marianne Moore, Wallace Stevens, E. E. Cummings, William Carlos Williams, and Ezra Pound all produced major collections of their works.

During the late 1940s and the 1950s, many poets starting out in the shadow of these great names were content to work within the technical boundaries established in the earlier part of the century. Nevertheless, poets like Theodore Roethke and Elizabeth Bishop created important and memorable work. Roethke, a master of poetic rhythm, was deeply influenced by his father, a strong-willed greenhouse owner in Saginaw, Michigan. The best of Roethke's poems recall his childhood life in and around the greenhouse. Bishop's poems are beautifully crafted, with precise and memorable descriptions that sometimes suggest realities beyond the physical.

Art in the Historical Context

California Artist Wayne Thiebaud

After World War II, Abstract Expressionists like Jackson Pollock inaugurated Postmodernist painting with works that seemed to be "about" their own making and whose swirls and shapes represented an inner rather than an outer reality. In California, however, a group of painters admired the energy of abstract work but wanted to use it in depicting what critic Donald Goddard called "California scenes filled with California light."

One of these artists was Wayne Thiebaud, a former cartoonist and designer. In his earlier work, Thiebaud demonstrated a fascination with such objects as shoes, ties, and ice cream cones. These paintings influenced the movement known as Pop Art. In later works, Thiebaud depicted landscapes. His San Francisco landscapes, like this one, render cityscapes in abstract terms but also capture "California light" and, in the roller-coaster swoop of a hill, convey a sense of surprise.

▶ **Critical Viewing** Which specific features in this painting suggest that Thiebaud was influenced by painters who use only abstract forms? Explain. **[Analyze]**

Corner Apartments (Down 18th Street). 1980, Wayne Thiebauc, at Hirshorn Museum, Smithsonian Institution

The American Experience
Art in the Historical Context

Corner Apartments (Down 18th Street), by Wayne Thiebaud

Thiebaud was born in Arizona in 1920. After working at a wide range of different jobs, including three years in the Air Force painting murals for the military, he began a career as an artist in 1947.

Thiebaud is best known in California, where he had his first solo exhibition in 1951. He has studied and taught at California universities. Although his most famous work captures such subjects as cakes and pastries in bright, striking colors, he has also painted a number of cityscapes such as this one.

Critical Viewing

Possible response: The tall geometric shapes of the buildings echo those of the roads and emphasize the formal, abstract qualities of these structures rather than their realistic details.

Enrichment

Rock and Roll

Tell students that after World War II, the United States entered a period of economic prosperity and rapid change. In what is popularly referred to as "The Baby Boom," the population expanded dramatically, altering the age balance of the American people. Making up an increasingly large percentage of the population, American teenagers became a major social and economic force.

The emerging economic importance of young Americans prompted major changes in popular entertainment. Among these was the development of rock-and-roll, a rebellious new type of music. "Rock Around the Clock," released in 1955 by Bill Haley and the Comets, was one of the earliest rock-and-roll hits.

If possible, find a recording of "Rock Around the Clock" and play it for students. Then, **ask** them how the song expresses the rebelliousness of early rock-and-roll.

Possible response: Its quick, insistent rhythms and lyrics advocating all-night dancing are rebellious.

Background
Poetry

Tell students that poetry experienced a renaissance in the 1990s, with many Americans becoming more aware of this art form. Signs of this renaissance include Bill Moyers's television show about poetry, *The Language of Life;* the increasing popularity of poetry readings, including contests known as poetry slams; and organizations like Poets House in New York, with its outreach program for libraries and high schools.

Tell students that poetry often appears in small literary magazines before it is published in books. Explain that thousands of these magazines are published throughout the country, including *Beloit Poetry Journal* (Maine), *Atlanta Review* (Georgia), *Threepenny Review* (California), and *Descant* (Texas). On the Internet, *Poetry Daily* features a new poem each day.

Humanities

Show students the Asian Women United Commemorative Quilt, on Transparency 11 in **Fine Art Transparencies, Volume 1.** Use the image to help students appreciate diversity and ethnic identity in the visual arts and in literature.

The American Experience
A Living Tradition

- Point out that the writing style of A.R. Ammons, a 20th-century poet, is inspired by William Carlos Williams. Mention that the loose form of the poem is appropriate, since it may give readers an impression of clutter.
- **Ask** students to identify which lines in the poem express the Emersonian theme of renewal. Where does the poem suggest that this renewal happens?
  Answer: The last two lines of the excerpt speak about beginnings and renewal. The place of renewal is a polluted stream.

A Living Tradition

A. R. Ammons, Emersonian Postmodernist

A. R. Ammons, a North Carolinian, brought the verve of Southern speech to poetry. In a long, outrageous poem humorously entitled *Garbage* (1993), Ammons takes trash—or the reprocessing of it—as a symbol of our times. Unlike Modernists who strove to create poems as perfect, well-constructed artifacts, Ammons, in good Postmodernist style, creates a talky, sprawling, shifting poem that is itself like a trash heap and that considers, among so many other things, its own making.

Emerson might have blinked and rubbed his eyes hard if he could have read this poem. However, he also might have recognized in it his own, distinctly American belief in renewal. He wrote in his essay "Compensation": "And such should be the outward biography of man in time, a putting off of dead circumstances day by day, as he renews his raiment day by day. . . ."

from *Garbage* by A. R. Ammons

garbage has to be the poem of our time because
garbage is spiritual, believable enough

to get our attention, getting in the way, piling
up, stinking, turning brooks brownish and

creamy white: what else deflects us from the
errors of our illusionary ways . . .

*　　*　　*

. . . here the driver knows,

where the consummations gather, where the disposal
flows out of form, where the last translations

cast away their immutable bits and scraps,
flits of steel, shivers of bottle and tumbler,

here is the gateway to beginning, here the portal
of renewing change . . .

New Directions in Poetry However, some poets challenged the boundaries of the art. Allen Ginsberg and A.R. Ammons, inspired by the work of William Carlos Williams, wrote bolder, more sprawling poems. In a Postmodernist spirit, Ginsberg's *Howl* and Ammons's *Tape for the Turn of the Year* and *Garbage* engaged powerfully with contemporary realities, dramatic and mundane alike. They dared to take in more confusion and chaos, even at the expense of their own apparent "perfection" as works of art.

The Literature of Personal and Group Identity Robert Lowell, a great-nephew of the poet James Russell Lowell, began his career in the postwar years as a creator of powerful, though traditional, poems. However, in the late 1950s, he began to reread William Carlos Williams. The result was *Life Studies,* a breakthrough book in which Lowell abandoned tight, traditional

Critical Thinking

1. What trends of this era explain the greater diversity among authors? **[Analyze Cause and Effect]**
   Possible response: This was an era of protest, in which various groups asserted their identities. The diversity among authors reflects these times.
2. Why do you think that this era caused no literary revolution of the kind that occurred in the 1920s? **[Speculate]**
   Possible response: Issues of identity took precedence over experimentation.
3. Do you think that computer technology will replace books? Will literature be written only for the screen? **[Analyze Cause and Effect]**
   Possible response: Some students may feel that the book will co-exist with computers. Other students may believe that the computer is bringing about revolution comparable to the invention of printed books. Students should support their answers.

forms and opened his work to the frustrations and confusions of his own personal and family history. Lowell was followed by others who revealed personal secrets, like Anne Sexton and Sylvia Plath. Rightly or wrongly, they were dubbed "confessional poets."

The tumultuous 1960s brought great changes in behavior and awareness—the civil rights movement, the protests against the Vietnam War, and the women's movement are three examples—that affected the subject matter of all literature. In poetry, as in fiction, these changes inspired a movement that encouraged the proud assertion and passionate exploration of personal, ethnic, and racial identity. It is important to realize, however, that this flowering of work that began in the 1960s, and still continues, had its roots in earlier decades. For example, African American poet Rita Dove, who won a Pulitzer Prize for *Thomas and Beulah* in 1986, could certainly acknowledge a debt to Robert Hayden and to Gwendolyn Brooks, who in 1950, became the first African American writer to win a Pulitzer Prize for her book *Annie Allen.*

Other writers in this rainbow movement are Native Americans N. Scott Momaday, also a Pulitzer Prize winner, and Joy Harjo; Asian Americans Maxine Hong Kingston, Amy Tan, and Garrett Hongo; and Latino and Latina writers Martín Espada, Sandra Cisneros, and Julia Alvarez. Adrienne Rich, strongly influenced by the women's movement, began changing her poetry in mid-career, loosening her formal structures and dealing with previously unexpressed conflicts and aspirations of women.

These and other writers are proving that, in literature as in society, America's strength lies in its diversity. Although it is too early to assess their achievements, it seems likely that some of the works they are producing today will become the classics of tomorrow.

Beyond the Horizon

One of the features of literary evolution is its unpredictability: No one knows in which direction it will develop next. Of this, however, we can be reasonably sure: The novel is not dead, as some were proclaiming in the 1950s and 1960s. Poetry is not dead, nor is the short story. Literature has great resilience. While it may be profoundly influenced by other media—radio, television, film—it has not been replaced by them. Indeed, for sheer technical virtuosity, there has probably never been a more impressive group of American writers at work than at the present time.

▼ Critical Viewing
In a few short years, the Internet has become an accepted part of American life. What benefits does it offer and what problems, if any, does it pose? **[Make a Judgment]**

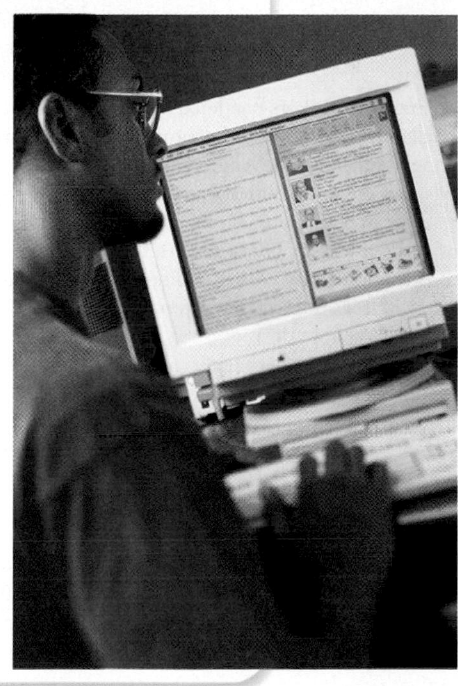

Critical Viewing

Possible response: Students will likely be familiar with many of the benefits of the Internet, such as easy long-distance communication and its value as a research tool and entertainment medium. Some students may say that people find the Internet a cause for concern because children can use it to access information that their parents might not want them to see. Others may point to issues such as problems in retaining control of intellectual property.

Literature of the Period
Comprehension Check

1. In what way does the literature of this era differ from that written in the earlier part of the twentieth century?
   Answer: Our time has not seen a literary revolution of the kind that occurred in the 1920s.
2. What new type of book did Truman Capote create?
   Answer: He created the nonfiction novel, which blends fiction and fact.
3. Name three important fiction writers from this era.
   Answer: Important fiction writers include Carson McCullers, Norman Mailer, Bernard Malamud, John Updike, Flannery O'Connor, Joyce Carol Oates, and Alice Walker, among others.
4. What important contemporary poet was a descendant of a well-known nineteenth-century poet?
   Answer: Robert Lowell was a great-nephew of James Russell Lowell.
5. What type of prose has received increased attention in recent years?
   Answer: Nonfiction and the essay have received increased attention.

Concept Connector

Have students return to the Focus Questions on p. 967. Ask them to use these questions to orally summarize the main points in the Unit Introduction. Students' summaries should include the following points:

Effect of World War II on the Position of the United States in the World

- The United States became a global political, economic, and millitary power.
- The United States became the leader in the battle to prevent the expansion of communism around the globe.
- The United States abandoned isolationism. It became a proponent of the United Nations and other international efforts to prevent war and promote stability.

The Impact of Technology on Post-War Daily Life

- Electric appliances and television changed the way Americans spent their time.
- Atomic weapons and the ensuing nuclear arms race led to persistent fear of nuclear war.
- The race with the Russians in the exploration of space spurred a new American commitment to excellence in science and mathematics, and to education generally.

How American Literature Reflected Post-War Turbulence

- The focus of American literature broadened, and literary approaches diversified.
- The increased emphasis on personal issues in literature reflected divergences in social identity.
- The lack of a dominant style reflected the ongoing American search for a common social identity.

Critical Thinking

1. At what time in American history have the most words been added to the language? Support your answer. **[Support]**
   Possible response: Students may respond that more words are added in the present than at any other time. The essay mentions that 5,000 words are added per year, and science and technology are advancing more dramatically now than ever.
2. What current developments in American society do you think will produce many new words in the future? Explain. **[Speculate]**
   Possible response: Students may point to any of a number of technological or medical developments in progress. Rapidly advancing communication technology is a likely response, as is the field of medications for mental health. Students should support their responses with examples.

Answers to the Activity

1. *Home page* is constructed from the English words *home,* from the Old English, and *page,* from the Latin. *Inkjet* is put together from *ink,* from the Medieval English, and *jet,* from the French word *jeter,* "to throw." *Laptop* is put together from *lap,* from the Old English word for a folding part of a garment, and *top,* from the Old English for a tuft of hair.
2. *Black hole* is formed from the English words *black,* from the Old English for "burn," and *hole,* from the Old English for "hollow." *Camcorder* is formed from camera, from the Latin word for "vault," and *recorder,* from the Latin word for "remember." *Supercluster* is formed from *super,* from the Latin for "above," and *cluster,* from Medieval English.

The Development of American English

Brave New Words

BY RICHARD LEDERER

The history of a living language like English is a history of constant change. Language is like a tree that sheds its leaves and grows new ones so that it may live on. New words, like new leaves, are essential to a living, healthy vocabulary.

A language draws its nutrients from the environment in which its speakers live. This growth is not new to English. Throughout history, as English speakers and writers have met with new objects, experiences, and ideas, they have needed new words to describe them. Nowadays, an average of 5,000 new words enter our language each year!

In almost every case, we cobble these new words from already existing word-making materials called *morphemes.* Morphemes are prefabricated bits of meaning from which words are made.

The Anglo-Saxons, who were the earliest speakers of our language, used a vivid term to describe the great wealth of English. They called it *word-hoard.* This stock of words grows considerably with each new development in science, medicine, and technology.

One of the major technologies of our lives is the computer. As the wonders of the computer have unfolded, we have acquired a new *user-friendly* (a compound composed of Latin and Anglo-Saxon word parts) vocabulary by piecing together morphemes from Latin, Greek, and early English.

We English speakers needed a name for the system of networks that connects computers around the world. So we combined the Latin prefix *inter,* "together," with the Anglo-Saxon word for a mesh fabric, and — presto! — we came up with the *Internet.* Then, we required a name for the complete set of documents on all Internet servers. So we mixed three Anglo-Saxon words into — ta da! — the *World Wide Web.*

The growing study of life on other worlds we have labeled *astrobiology* or *exobiology,* from the Greek word parts *astro* ("star") and *exo* ("outer") + *bio* ("life") + *logy* ("study of").

We have been aware of genes for more than a century, but only recently have scientists studied whole sets of genes and their interactions. The entire chomosomal makeup of an organism we now call the *genome*—a blend of two Greek words, *gen(e)* and *(chromos)ome.* The same blend names the field—*genomics.*

Over the past few decades, we have acquired countless new words for the brave new worlds of science, technology, and medicine. Scientific and medical breakthroughs seem to make the headlines almost every day, but our English "word-hoard" will never run out of prefixes, suffixes, and roots to identify these new concepts.

Activity

Identify the word parts and original languages for these words.

1. computer terms: *home page, inkjet,* and *laptop.*
2. scientific terms: *black hole, camcorder,* and *supercluster.*

Enrichment

The Globalization of English

The majority of the world's books, newspapers, and magazines are written in English. Most international telephone calls are made in English. Sixty percent of the world's radio programs are broadcast in English, and more than seventy percent of international mail is written and addressed in English. It is the language in which more than eighty percent of all stored computer texts and Web sites are written.

English is the first or official language of forty-five countries, including India, Pakistan, Malaysia, Switzerland, Holland, Denmark, and Sweden. One out of every seven people in the world understands and speaks the English language in some form. It is truly a global language.

It is no surprise, then, that English is a major source of new words for other languages. **Ask** students whether they can guess what the Japanese words *aisukurimo, chokoreto, banira,* and *sutorberi* mean.
Answer: The words are, respectively: ice cream, chocolate, vanilla, and strawberry.

Unit 6
Part
1

Literature Confronts the Everyday

Television Moon, 1978–79, Alfred Leslie, Wichita Art Museum, Wichita, Kansas

Differentiated Instruction
Solutions for All Learners

Accessibility at a Glance

More Accessible
from The Names
Mint Snowball
Suspended
Antojos
Who Burns for the Perfection of Paper

Average
The Life You Save May Be Your Own
The First Seven Years
Marigolds
Aliceville
Traveling Through the Dark
Average Waves in Unprotected Waters
Everyday Use
from The Woman Warrior
Most Satisfied by Snow
Hunger in New York City

More Challenging
Gold Glade
The Light Comes Brighter
What For

Selection Planning Guide

The writers whose work appears in this section reveal the variety of angles from which one can view everyday events. Both O'Connor's "The Life You Save May Be Your Own" and Malamud's "The First Seven Years" ask readers to consider the level of honesty between strangers, acquaintances, and co-workers. Walker's "Everyday Use" challenges students to decide the value of family heirlooms. Essays by Nye and Harjo reveal that ordinary happenings can be momentous. Finally, poetry by Espada, Ortiz, Chang, and Hongo suggests the filter that ethnicity and personal experience bring to the daily tasks of living.

Humanities

Television Moon, 1978–1979,
by Alfred Leslie

Like the writers of this period, Alfred Leslie has chosen an ordinary subject for this still life, adding significance to an otherwise mundane piece of furniture. Leslie converts the broad landscapes of earlier American artists into a limited, dim rendering shown on a television screen. Instead of facing the frontier through rugged exploration, citizens can now passively examine the landscape without leaving their armchairs. **Ask:**

- What might the artist be saying about America by focusing on the mundane items shown in this painting?
  Possible response: Americans are caught up in daily trivia and material goods, rather than focusing on more important issues.

Benchmark

After students have completed the essays by Momaday, Nye, and Harjo, administer **Benchmark Test 9.** If the Benchmark Test reveals that some students need further work, use the **Interpretation Guide** to determine the appropriate reteaching pages in the **Reading Kit** or on **Success Tracker.**

Monitoring Progress

Before students read "Everyday Use" by Alice Walker, administer **Diagnostic Test 10.** This test will determine students' level of readiness for the reading and vocabulary skills.

Meeting Your Standards

Students will

1. **analyze and respond to literary elements.**
   - Literary Analysis: Grotesque Characters
2. **read, comprehend, analyze, and critique a short story.**
   - Reading Strategy: Making Predictions
   - Reading Check questions
   - Apply the Skills questions
   - Assessment Practice (ATE)
3. **develop vocabulary.**
   - Vocabulary Lesson: Latin Root: *-sol-*
4. **understand and apply written and oral language conventions.**
   - Spelling Strategy
   - Grammar and Style Lesson: Subjunctive Mood
5. **develop writing proficiency.**
   - Writing Lesson: Deposition
6. **develop appropriate research strategies.**
   - Extend Your Learning: Body Language Presentation
7. **understand and apply listening and speaking strategies.**
   - Extend Your Learning: Readers Theatre

Block Scheduling: Use one 90-minute class period to preteach the skills and have students read the selection. Use a second 90-minute class period to assess students' mastery of skills, extend their learning, and monitor their progress.

Homework Suggestions

Following are possibilities for homework assignments.

- Support pages from ***Unit 6 Resources:***
  Literary Analysis
  Reading Strategy
  Vocabulary Builder
  Grammar and Style
- An Extend Your Learning project and the Writing Lesson for this selection may be completed over several days.

Step-by-Step Teaching Guide	Pacing Guide
PRETEACH	
• Administer Vocabulary and Reading Warm-ups as necessary.	5 min.
• Engage students' interest with the motivation activity.	5 min.
• Read and discuss author, and background features. **FT**	10 min.
• Introduce the Literary Analysis Skill: Grotesque Characters. **FT**	5 min.
• Introduce the Reading Strategy: Making Predictions. **FT**	10 min.
• Prepare students to read by teaching the selection vocabulary. **FT**	
TEACH	
• Informally monitor comprehension while students read independently or in groups. **FT**	30 min.
• Monitor students' comprehension with the Reading Check notes.	as students read
• Reinforce vocabulary with Vocabulary Builder notes.	as students read
• Develop students' understanding of grotesque characters with the Literary Analysis annotations. **FT**	5 min.
• Develop students' ability to make predictions with the Reading Strategy annotations. **FT**	5 min.
ASSESS/EXTEND	
• Assess students' comprehension and mastery of the Literary Analysis and Reading Strategy by having them answer the Apply the Skills questions. **FT**	15 min.
• Have students complete the Vocabulary Lesson and the Grammar and Style Lesson. **FT**	15 min.
• Apply students' ability to use transitions to show cause and effect by using the Writing Lesson. **FT**	45 min. or homework
• Apply students' understanding by using one or more of the Extend Your Learning activities.	20–90 min. or homework
• Administer Selection Test A or Selection Test B. **FT**	15 min.

Resources

PRINT

Unit 6 Resources

Vocabulary Warm-up Word Lists **[L1, L2, EL]** ....p. 4
Vocabulary Warm-up Practice **[L1, L2, EL]** ....p. 5
Reading Warm-up A **[L1, L2, EL]** ....p. 6
Reading Warm-up B **[L1, L2, L3]** ....p. 7

TRANSPARENCY

Graphic Organizer Transparencies

Literary Analysis Graphic Organizer A **[L3]** ....pp. 214, 216
Literary Analysis Graphic Organizer B **[L1, L2, EL]** ....pp. 215, 217

PRINT

Reader's Notebook [L2]
Reader's Notebook: Adapted Version [L1]
Reader's Notebook: English Learner's Version [EL]

Unit 6 Resources

Literary Analysis **[L3]** ....p. 8
Reading Strategy **[L3]** ....p. 9
Vocabulary Builder **[L3]** ....p. 10

TECHNOLOGY

Listening to Literature Audio CDs [L2, EL]

PRINT

Unit 6 Resources

Grammar and Style **[L3]** ....p. 11
Support for Writing Lesson **[L3]** ....p. 12
Support for Extend Your Learning **[L3]** ....p. 13
Enrichment **[L4]** ....p. 14
Selection Test A **[L1, L2, EL]** ....pp. 15–17
Selection Test B **[L3, L4]** ....pp. 18–20

General Resources

Rubrics for Response to Literature **[L3]** ....pp. 65–66
Rubric for Peer Assessment: Oral Interpretation **[L3]** ....p. 130

TECHNOLOGY

Go Online: Research **[L3]**
Go Online: Self-test **[L3]**
***ExamView*® Test Bank [L3]**

Choosing Resources for Differentiated Instruction

[L1] Special Needs Students
[L2] Below-Level Students
[L3] All Students
[L4] Advanced Students
[EL] English Learners

For Vocabulary and Reading Warm-ups and for Selection Tests, **A** signifies "less challenging" and **B** "more challenging." For Graphic Organizer transparencies, **A** signifies "not filled in" and **B** "filled in."

FT Fast Track Instruction: To move the lesson more quickly, use the strategies and activities identified with **FT**.

Scaffolding for Less Proficient and Advanced Students

The leveled Critical Thinking questions after selections progress in the levels of thinking required to answer them. To address the needs of your different students, you may use the (a) level questions for your less proficient students and the (b) level questions with your on-level and advanced students. The occasional (c) level questions are appropriate for your advanced students.

PRENTICE HALL **TeacherEXPRESS**™ Plan · Teach · Assess — Use this complete suite of powerful teaching tools to make lesson planning and testing quicker and easier.

PRENTICE HALL **StudentEXPRESS**™ Learn · Study · Succeed — Use the interactive textbook (online and on CD-ROM) to make selections and activities come alive with audio and video support and interactive questions.

Go Online Professional Development
For: Information about Lexiles
Visit: www.PHSchool.com
Web Code: eue-1111

PRETEACH

Motivation

The title of this story is a slogan that once commonly appeared on American highways. Such slogans—like this story—challenge readers' consciences and try to raise their moral standards. To spark students' interest in the story, post the title along with other common slogans, such as anti-drug or safety belt warnings. Discuss the motives to which these slogans appeal. Invite students to predict what this story may reveal about human nature.

❶ Background

More About the Author

In 1954,"The Life You Save May Be Your Own" won an O. Henry award for being one of the best short stories of the year. Flannery O'Connor was to win this award four more times—for "A Circle in the Fire," *Everything That Rises Must Converge,* "Greenleaf," and "Revelation." Like "The Life You Save," these stories share rural Southern settings, grotesque characters, moments of epiphany, religious symbols, and profound irony.

Build Skills *Short Story*

❶ The Life You Save May Be Your Own

Flannery O'Connor (1925–1964)

Flannery O'Connor's work reflects her intense commitment to her personal beliefs. In her exaggerated, tragic, and at times shockingly violent tales, she forces readers to confront such human faults as hypocrisy, insensitivity, self-centeredness, and prejudice. Many of her stories revolve around death and exhibit a dark sense of humor. Some critics have objected to the presence of such comic doom in her fiction, but O'Connor felt that she was portraying the world accurately. She once said, "People are always complaining that the modern novelist has no hope and that the picture he paints of the world is unbearable. The only answer to this is that people without hope do not write novels."

The Habit of Art Born in Savannah, Georgia, Flannery O'Connor was raised in the small Georgia town of Milledgeville. She earned her undergraduate degree from Georgia State College for Women and then left her home state to attend the celebrated University of Iowa Writers' Workshop. While still in graduate school, she published her first short story, "Geranium."

In 1950, O'Connor became ill with lupus, a serious disease that restricted her independence. She moved back to the family farm outside Milledgeville, where she lived with her mother. "I have never been anywhere but sick," she wrote. "In a sense, sickness is a place more instructive than a trip to Europe." Despite her illness, O' Connor committed herself not only to her writing but also to "the habit of art," an enlivened way of thinking and seeing. In 1952, at the age of twenty-seven, she published her first novel, *Wise Blood,* the story of a violent rivalry among members of a fictional religious sect in the South. In 1955, she published her first collection of stories, *A Good Man Is Hard to Find.* It was followed by a second novel, *The Violent Bear It Away* (1960), and *Everything That Rises Must Converge* (1965), another collection of short stories.

A Triumphant Spirit Throughout most of her adult life, O'Connor lived with physical pain and the awareness that she would probably die young. Despite her condition, she often seemed joyous, entertaining friends at home and painting watercolors of the peacocks that she and her mother raised on the farm. Still, her disease set her apart from other people, and O'Connor felt a deep sense of kinship with eccentrics and outsiders. In her fiction, she often portrays those who are outcast or suffering. Many of her characters are social misfits or people who are physically or mentally challenged. Although she paints these characters in an unsentimental way, O'Connor brings to their stories an underlying sense of sympathy, which reflects both her own physical problems and her strong Catholic faith.

Religious Faith Flannery O'Connor was raised as a devout Catholic in a region of the American South that was predominantly Protestant. She considered herself a religious writer in a world that had abandoned true religious values. In an effort to point out the spiritual failings of the modern world, O'Connor often highlights characters with powerfully stated convictions but dubious moral and intellectual capabilities. "The Life You Save May Be Your Own" is a typical O'Connor work. In its grim depiction of a group of outcasts with sharply exaggerated physical characteristics and personality traits, the story conveys shrewd insights, a powerful moral message, and an urgent sense of the tragic realities of life in the modern world.

Preview

Connecting to the Literature

In this story, a stranger appears at a remote farm where an elderly widow lives alone with her unmarried daughter. The woman must decide whether or not to trust the drifter. Similar decisions confront all of us as strangers enter our lives as potential friends or enemies.

Literary Analysis

Grotesque Characters

The word *grotesque* in literature does not mean "ugly" or "disgusting," as it sometimes does in popular speech. In literature, the **grotesque character** is one who has become bizarre or twisted, usually through some kind of obsession. Grotesque traits may be expressed in a character's physical appearance. Or, they may be hidden, visible only in a character's actions and emotions. In this story, all of the characters can be classified as grotesques. As you read, look for examples of absurd or extreme behavior, distortions, and striking incongruities that combine to create images of the grotesque.

Connecting Literary Elements

Writers create portraits of characters through **characterization**—the revelation of personality. There are two methods of characterization. With **direct characterization,** the writer simply tells the reader what a character is like. With **indirect characterization,** characters' traits are revealed

- through the character's words, thoughts, and actions.
- through descriptions of the character's appearance or background.
- through what other characters say about him or her.
- through the ways in which other characters react or respond.

Use a chart like the one shown to examine O'Connor's use of indirect characterization in portraying the cast of grotesque characters in this story.

Shiftlet

Physical Appearance One-armed
Words
Thoughts
Actions
How others react
What others say

Reading Strategy

Making Predictions

When you find yourself wondering how a series of events will unfold, pause and **predict** what will happen. Predict outcomes by looking back and weighing what you have read. Pay heed to hints the author has dropped, and measure these against your own understanding of human behavior.

Vocabulary Builder

desolate (des′ ə lit) *adj.* forlorn; wretched (p. 983)

listed (list′ id) *v.* tilted; inclined (p. 983)

ominous (äm′ ə nəs) *adj.* threatening; sinister (p. 985)

ravenous (rav′ ə nəs) *adj.* extremely eager (p. 987)

morose (mə rōs′) *adj.* gloomy; sullen (p. 990)

guffawing (gə fô′ iŋ) *adj.* laughing in a loud, coarse manner (p. 992)

Differentiated Instruction

Solutions for All Learners

Support for Special Needs Students
Have students complete the **Preview** and **Build Skills** pages for the selection in the ***Reader's Notebook: Adapted Version.*** These pages provide a selection summary, an abbreviated presentation of the reading and literary skills, and the graphic organizer on the **Build Skills** page in the student book.

Support for Less Proficient Readers
Have students complete the **Preview** and **Build Skills** pages for the selection in the ***Reader's Notebook.*** These pages provide a selection summary, an abbreviated presentation of the reading and literary skills, and the graphic organizer on the **Build Skills** page in the student book.

Support for English Learners
Have students complete the **Preview** and **Build Skills** pages for the selection in the ***Reader's Notebook: English Learner's Version.*** These pages provide a selection summary, an abbreviated presentation of the skills, and the graphic organizer on the **Build Skills** page in the student book.

❷ Literary Analysis

Grotesque Characters

- Go over the definition of grotesque characters with students.

  Remind them that in literature, *grotesque* has a meaning different from what it means in popular speech.
- Ask students to discuss the effects a writer might achieve with grotesque characters. Why might someone want to people a story with grotesque rather than more realistic characters? Have students share their ideas. Encourage them to cite examples from their reading.
- As students read, have them try to identify what makes each character in this story grotesque. Have them consider also whether the characters, in spite of being grotesque, are believable.
- Give students a copy of **Literary Analysis Graphic Organizer A,** p. 214 in ***Graphic Organizer Transparencies,*** to use as they read the story.

❸ Reading Strategy

Making Predictions

- Write the word *predict* on the chalkboard, drawing a vertical line between the prefix *pre-* and the root *dict.* Explain that *predict* comes from two Latin words and literally means "say before." When you predict, you state what will happen before it happens.
- Make sure students understand that a prediction is not a wild guess; it is based on details about the plot and characters. As students read, have them note details in the story that help them predict its outcome.
- Challenge students to pause at the end of every page or two of the story to predict what may come next. Remind them to identify details in the story that support these predictions.

Vocabulary Builder

- Pronounce each vocabulary word for students and read the definitions as a class. Have students identify any words with which they are already familiar.

TEACH

Learning Modalities
Visual/Spatial Learners
Encourage students to pay close attention to the details of the setting. Discuss how these details reflect the events in the story. For example, how do they suggest the decay in the characters' morality?

❶ About the Selection

This story of grotesque characters obsessed with outmaneuvering one another becomes a morality tale about the spiritual desert facing those who behave immorally. Mr. Shiftlet and Mrs. Lucynell Crater appear to be good people who denounce the moral deterioration of the world. They are motivated by goals that are not outwardly evil: Shiftlet wants a car, and Mrs. Crater wants a husband for her daughter, who is mentally retarded, deaf, and mute. As they plot to achieve their goals, they show that they are willing to sacrifice both human decency and the younger Lucynell's future. Their hypocrisy comes at a high price.

❷ Humanities

Deep Fork Overlook, by Joan Marron-LaRue

Joan Marron-La Rue grew up in rural Oklahoma. Interested in painting from early childhood, she worked in fashion design, for a time and later studied with various master painters. *Deep Fork Overlook* was a cover illustration for a poetry anthology written by students of Central State University. LaRue once lived down the road from the gas station and barn it depicts.

Use this question for discussion.

- What elements in this painting suggest the time period of the story?
  Answer: The old truck and barn, the antiquated gas pumps, and the wandering chickens suggest both the Depression time period and the rural setting.

2

Deep Fork Overlook, Joan Marron-LaRue

3 ▲ **Critical Viewing** Why might an automobile be so valuable in a rural area like the one in this story? **[Draw Conclusions]**

Differentiated Instruction Solutions for All Learners

Accessibility at a Glance

	The Life You Save May Be Your Own
Context	Southern Gothic
Language	Informal dialect
Concept Level	Accessible (clear, grotesque characterization, familiar setting)
Literary Merit	Noted author, widely anthologized
Lexile	1000L
Other	Contains irony
Overall Rating	Average

1 # The Life You Save May Be Your Own

Flannery O'Connor

Background Gothic literature, a genre of fiction that developed in Britain in the late 1700s, features horror and violence. Traditional gothic tales are often set against dramatic, gloomy backdrops—remote castles, deserted fortresses, and the like. Such literature acknowledges evil as a real force and ascribes to some characters a dark side that lures them to violent or wicked acts. Flannery O'Connor borrowed some devices from Gothic fiction, such as a foreboding atmosphere and grotesque characters, but she set her stories in an unremarkable American landscape. The story you are about to read is a perfect example of her exploration of the gothic under the familiar sunlight of the American South.

The old woman and her daughter were sitting on their porch when Mr. Shiftlet came up their road for the first time. The old woman slid to the edge of her chair and leaned forward, shading her eyes from the piercing sunset with her hand. The daughter could not see far in front of her and continued to play with her fingers. Although the old woman lived in this desolate spot with only her daughter and she had never seen Mr. Shiftlet before, she could tell, even from a distance, that he was a tramp and no one to be afraid of. His left coat sleeve was folded up to show there was only half an arm in it and his gaunt figure listed slightly to the side as if the breeze were pushing him. He had on a black town suit and a brown felt hat that was turned up in the front and down in the back and he carried a tin tool box by a handle. He came on, at an amble, up her road, his face turned toward the sun which appeared to be balancing itself on the peak of a small mountain.

The old woman didn't change her position until he was almost into her yard; then she rose with one hand fisted on her hip. The daughter, a large girl in a short blue organdy dress, saw him all at once and jumped up and began to stamp and point and make excited speechless sounds.

Mr. Shiftlet stopped just inside the yard and set his box on the ground and tipped his hat at her as if she were not in the least afflicted; then he turned toward the old woman and swung the hat all the way off. He had long black slick hair that hung flat from a part in the middle to beyond the tips of his ears on either side. His face descended in forehead for more than half its length and ended suddenly with his features just balanced over a jutting steel-trap jaw. He seemed to be

Vocabulary Builder
desolate (des′ ə lit) *adj.* forlorn; wretched

listed (list′ id) *v.* tilted; inclined

6 

Reading Check
In this opening scene, who does the old woman notice coming up her road?

3 Critical Viewing

Answer: There is probably no other means of transportation. A car is needed for emergencies and for hauling any heavy items like groceries from town.

4 Vocabulary Builder
The Latin Root *-sol-*

- Draw students' attention to the word *desolate* in the first paragraph.
- Explain that the root *-sol-* means "alone." Challenge students to use their knowledge of this root to define the word *desolate.*
  Answer: A *desolate* place is one that is abandoned, or left alone.

5 Literary Analysis
Grotesque Characters

- **Ask** students whether any aspects of Shiftlet seem grotesque. If so, what are they?
  Answer: He has only one whole arm and he doesn't stand up quite straight. His forehead is very long, and his features are all squashed together below it.
- Then, **ask:** Does the daughter seem grotesque in any way? If so, how?
  Answer: She apparently can't speak normally, and she is wearing a too-short dress. If the woman is old, the daughter must not be very young, but she is described as "a large girl"; it makes her seem like a parody of a child.

  As students continue reading, have them think about what words and actions make each character grotesque.

6 Reading Check

Answer: She sees a man—a tramp with one arm—whom she soon learns is named Shiftlet.

Differentiated Instruction Solutions for All Learners

Background for English Learners
The dialect in this story, with its double negatives, missing verbs, and slang idioms, may challenge some students' comprehension. Explain that it represents the everyday speech of uneducated Americans from the rural South. Have students choose partners with whom to read Mrs. Crater and Shiftlet's conversations aloud. Students can discuss any expressions they don't understand and try to work out their meaning. Tell them to use context clues and pay attention to the sense of the entire conversation. After partners work through the dialogue together, have the whole class gather to help one another resolve any questions that remain.

7 Literary Analysis
Grotesque Characters

- **Ask** students to give their reactions to the three characters at this point in the story.
  Possible answers: All three seem bizarre and unattractive. The old woman and the tramp seem suspicious of one another. The tramp doesn't seem as harmless as the old woman thinks he is.
- Then, **ask** the first Literary Analysis question: What exaggerated traits do you perceive in this description of the three characters?
  Answer: The old woman's smallness is exaggerated in the phrase "size of a cedar fence post." Mr. Shiftlet is again described as crooked. The colors associated with the daughter are overly bright.

8 Literary Analysis
Grotesque Characters

- Point out that Shiftlet does not answer any of Mrs. Crater's questions directly. **Ask** students what this suggests about his character.
  Answer: Mr. Shiftlet is being intentionally evasive, perhaps because he wishes to hide something unsavory in his past.
- **Ask** the second Literary Analysis question: What personality traits are suggested by this description of Mr. Shiftlet's "pale sharp glance"?
  Answer: The description suggests that Shiftlet's character is ultimately transparent and without substance, and that he is possibly dangerous.

a young man but he had a look of composed dissatisfaction as if he understood life thoroughly.

"Good evening," the old woman said. She was about the size of a cedar fence post and she had a man's gray hat pulled down low over her head.

7 The tramp stood looking at her and didn't answer. He turned his back and faced the sunset. He swung both his whole and his short arm up slowly so that they indicated an expanse of sky and his figure formed a crooked cross. The old woman watched him with her arms folded across her chest as if she were the owner of the sun, and the daughter watched, her head thrust forward and her fat helpless hands hanging at the wrists. She had long pink-gold hair and eyes as blue as a peacock's neck.

He held the pose for almost fifty seconds and then he picked up his box and came on to the porch and dropped down on the bottom step. "Lady," he said in a firm nasal voice, "I'd give a fortune to live where I could see me a sun do that every evening."

"Does it every evening," the old woman said and sat back down. The daughter sat down too and watched him with a cautious sly look as if he were a bird that had come up very close. He leaned to one side, rooting in his pants pocket, and in a second he brought out a package of chewing gum and offered her a piece. She took it and unpeeled it and began to chew without taking her eyes off him. He offered the old woman a piece but she only raised her upper lip to indicate she had no teeth.

8 Mr. Shiftlet's pale sharp glance had already passed over everything in the yard—the pump near the corner of the house and the big fig tree that three or four chickens were preparing to roost in—and had moved to a shed where he saw the square rusted back of an automobile. "You ladies drive?" he asked.

"That car ain't run in fifteen year," the old woman said. "The day my husband died, it quit running."

"Nothing is like it used to be, lady," he said. "The world is almost rotten."

"That's right," the old woman said. "You from around here?"

"Name Tom T. Shiftlet," he murmured, looking at the tires.

"I'm pleased to meet you," the old woman said. "Name Lucynell Crater and daughter Lucynell Crater. What you doing around here, Mr. Shiftlet?"

He judged the car to be about a 1928 or '29 Ford. "Lady," he said, and turned and gave her his full attention, "lemme tell you something. There's one of these doctors in Atlanta that's taken a knife and cut the human heart—the human heart," he repeated, leaning forward, "out of a man's chest and held it in his hand," and he held his hand out, palm up, as if it were slightly weighted with the human heart, "and studied it like it was a day-old chicken, and lady," he said, allowing a long significant pause in which his head slid forward and his clay-colored eyes brightened, "he don't know no more about it than you or me."

Literary Analysis
Grotesque Characters
What exaggerated traits do you perceive in this description of the three characters?

Literary Analysis
Grotesque Characters and Characterization
What personality traits are suggested by this description of Mr. Shiftlet's "pale sharp glance"?

"That's right," the old woman said.

"Why, if he was to take that knife and cut into every corner of it, he still wouldn't know no more than you or me. What you want to bet?"

"Nothing," the old woman said wisely. "Where you come from, Mr. Shiftlet?"

He didn't answer. He reached into his pocket and brought out a sack of tobacco and a package of cigarette papers and rolled himself a cigarette, expertly with one hand, and attached it in a hanging position to his upper lip. Then he took a box of wooden matches from his pocket and struck one on his shoe. He held the burning match as if he were studying the mystery of flame while it traveled dangerously toward his skin. The daughter began to make loud noises and to point to his hand and shake her finger at him, but when the flame was just before touching him, he leaned down with his hand cupped over it as if he were going to set fire to his nose and lit the cigarette.

He flipped away the dead match and blew a stream of gray into the evening. A sly look came over his face. "Lady," he said, "nowadays, people'll do anything anyways. I can tell you my name is Tom T. Shiftlet and I come from Tarwater, Tennessee, but you never have seen me before: how you know I ain't lying? How you know my name ain't Aaron Sparks, lady, and I come from Singleberry, Georgia, or how you know it's not George Speeds and I come from Lucy, Alabama, or how you know I ain't Thompson Bright from Toolafalls, Mississippi?"

"I don't know nothing about you," the old woman muttered, irked.

"Lady," he said, "people don't care how they lie. Maybe the best I can tell you is, I'm a man; but listen lady," he said and paused and made his tone more ominous still, "what is a man?"

The old woman began to gum a seed. "What you carry in that tin box, Mr. Shiftlet?" she asked.

"Tools," he said, put back. "I'm a carpenter."

"Well, if you come out here to work, I'll be able to feed you and give you a place to sleep but I can't pay. I'll tell you that before you begin," she said.

There was no answer at once and no particular expression on his face. He leaned back against the two-by-four that helped support the porch roof. "Lady," he said slowly, "there's some men that some things mean more to them than money." The old woman rocked without comment and the daughter watched the trigger that moved up and down in his neck. He told the old woman then that all most people were interested in was money, but he asked what a man was made for. He asked her if a man was made for money, or what. He asked her what she thought she was made for but she didn't answer, she only sat rocking and wondered if a one-armed man could put a new roof on her garden house. He asked a lot of questions that she didn't answer. He told her that he was twenty-eight years old and had lived a varied life. He had been a gospel singer, a foreman on the railroad, an assistant in an undertaking parlor, and he come over the radio for three months with Uncle Roy and his Red Creek Wranglers. He said he had fought

Reading Strategy
Making Predictions
In what ways might Mr. Shiftlet's speech about lying be a clue to later events?

Vocabulary Builder
ominous (äm′ ə nəs) *adj.* threatening; sinister

10  **Reading Check**
In what ways does young Lucynell try to communicate? Can she speak?

9 Reading Strategy
Making Predictions

- **Ask** students whether they think Shiftlet will accept the old woman's offer to work in exchange for room and board? Why do they think so?
  Answer: Hints on p. 984 suggest that he is interested in her car. He probably will take the job she offers.
- **Ask** the Reading Strategy question: In what way might Mr. Shiftlet's speech about lying be a clue to later events?
  Answer: Students might predict that Mr. Shiftlet will be dishonest, as a function of his duplicity thus far and the way he almost dares Lucynell to disbelieve him.

10 Reading Check

Answer: She communicates by gestures. She can "make loud noises" but does not speak in words.

Differentiated Instruction
Solutions for All Learners

Enrichment for Advanced Readers

Have students analyze the religious imagery and symbolism in this story. References include "his figure formed a crooked cross," "I'm a carpenter," "the monks of old slept in their coffins," and "She looks like an angel of Gawd." Have students work together to interpret these allusions and discuss their effect on the story's themes and its overall impact. Students can write essays based on their discussions and analysis.

11 Literary Analysis
Grotesque Characters and Characterization

- **Ask** students what the question "Are you married or are you single?" reveals about the old woman's plans.
  Answer: She may hope to marry him to Lucynell and get him to stay at the house permanently.
- Then, **ask** the Literary Analysis question: What does this dialogue about her daughter reveal about the old woman?
  Answer: The old woman seems to be focusing on and possibly exaggerating Lucynell's abilities in order to make her seem more attractive to Mr. Shiftlet.

12 Reading Strategy
Making Predictions

- After students read the bracketed passage, **ask** them why they think Shiftlet is working so hard and capably. What does he hope to gain?
  Answer: He wants the old woman to trust him enough to let him have the car.
- Then, **ask** the Reading Strategy question: What prediction can you make about Mr. Shiftlet based on his capable performance in his work?
  Possible answer: Mr. Shiftlet probably will not stay around long because he can take care of himself; he does not need the Craters' food or shelter. He might leave after getting what he wants.

and bled in the Arm Service of his country and visited every foreign land and that everywhere he had seen people that didn't care if they did a thing one way or another. He said he hadn't been raised thataway.

A fat yellow moon appeared in the branches of the fig tree as if it were going to roost there with the chickens. He said that a man had to escape to the country to see the world whole and that he wished he lived in a desolate place like this where he could see the sun go down every evening like God made it to do.

"Are you married or are you single?" the old woman asked.

There was a long silence. "Lady," he asked finally, "where would you find you an innocent woman today? I wouldn't have any of this trash I could just pick up."

The daughter was leaning very far down, hanging her head almost between her knees watching him through a triangular door she had made in her overturned hair; and she suddenly fell in a heap on the floor and began to whimper. Mr. Shiftlet straightened her out and helped her get back in the chair.

11 "Is she your baby girl?" he asked.

"My only," the old woman said "and she's the sweetest girl in the world. I would give her up for nothing on earth. She's smart too. She can sweep the floor, cook, wash, feed the chickens, and hoe. I wouldn't give her up for a casket of jewels."

"No," he said kindly, "don't ever let any man take her away from you."

"Any man come after her," the old woman said, "'ll have to stay around the place."

Literary Analysis
Grotesque Characters and Characterization
What does this dialogue about her daughter reveal about the old woman?

Mr. Shiftlet's eye in the darkness was focused on a part of the automobile bumper that glittered in the distance. "Lady," he said, jerking his short arm up as if he could point with it to her house and yard and pump, "there ain't a broken thing on this plantation that I couldn't fix for you, one-arm jackleg or not. I'm a man," he said with a sullen dignity, "even if I ain't a whole one. I got," he said, tapping his knuckles on the floor to emphasize the immensity of what he was going to say, "a moral intelligence!" and his face pierced out of the darkness into a shaft of doorlight and he stared at her as if he were astonished himself at this impossible truth.

The old woman was not impressed with the phrase. "I told you you could hang around and work for food," she said, "if you don't mind sleeping in that car yonder."

"Why listen, lady," he said with a grin of delight, "the monks of old slept in their coffins!"

"They wasn't as advanced as we are," the old woman said.

12 The next morning he began on the roof of the garden house while Lucynell, the daughter, sat on a rock and watched him work. He had not been around a week before the change he had made in the place was apparent. He had patched the front and back steps, built a new hog pen, restored a fence, and taught Lucynell, who was completely deaf and had

Reading Strategy
Making Predictions
What prediction can you make about Mr. Shiftlet based on his capable performance in his work?

Enrichment
The Great Depression

This story is set during the Great Depression of the 1930s. Jobs were so scarce that many men became drifters like Shiftlet. They wandered from place to place, often covering thousands of miles in their search for work. Drifters often hitched rides aboard slow-moving freight trains rather than walking from one city to another. Money was so hard to come by that many drifters would have welcomed Mrs. Crater's offer of room and board in exchange for work. When World War II began, many drifters and other unemployed men joined the armed services, with its steady paycheck. The war also created thousands of jobs for those who did not go overseas to fight.

Black Walnuts, 1945, Joseph Pollet, Oil on canvas, 30" × 40", Collection of Whitney Museum of American Art, Purchase, Gift of Gertrude Vanderbilt Whitney, by exchange

never said a word in her life, to say the word "bird." The big rosy-faced girl followed him everywhere, saying "Burrttddt ddbirrrttdt," and clapping her hands. The old woman watched from a distance, secretly pleased. She was ravenous for a son-in-law.

Mr. Shiftlet slept on the hard narrow back seat of the car with his feet out the side window. He had his razor and a can of water on a crate that served him as a bedside table and he put up a piece of mirror against the back glass and kept his coat neatly on a hanger that he hung over one of the windows.

In the evenings he sat on the steps and talked while the old woman and Lucynell rocked violently in their chairs on either side of him. The old woman's three mountains were black against the dark blue sky and were visited off and on by various planets and by the moon after it had left the chickens. Mr. Shiftlet pointed out that the reason he had improved this plantation was because he had taken a personal interest in it. He said he was even going to make the automobile run.

He had raised the hood and studied the mechanism and he said he could tell that the car had been built in the days when cars were really built. You take now, he said, one man puts in one bolt and another man puts in another bolt and another man puts in another bolt so that it's a man for a bolt. That's why you have to pay so much for a car: you're paying all those men. Now if you didn't have to pay but one man, you

14 ▲ Critical Viewing
Which aspects of the story are reflected in this painting? **[Connect]**

Vocabulary Builder
ravenous (rav′ ə nəs) *adj.* extremely eager

15 Reading Check
For what is the old woman "ravenous"?

13 Humanities

Black Walnuts by Joseph Pollet

Swiss-American painter Joseph Pollet studied at the Art Students' League in New York, under American realist painter John Sloan.

Black Walnuts shows both Sloan's influence—a highly realistic stop-action quality that conveys a great deal of emotion—and the general focus of painting during the Depression: capturing everyday American images for American viewers.

Use these questions for discussion:

1. How does the mood of this painting compare with that of the story?
Answer: The painting has a happier, brighter mood than the story does.
2. Do you think the story characters would fit in the painting's setting? Why or why not?
Answer: They would fit into the setting because it is rural; however, they would not belong in the sense that the scene is one of purity and goodness, while the characters—as students will see—are morally bankrupt.

14 Critical Viewing

Answer: Students should notice the rural setting and general air of dilapidation, the large tree, the shed, and the old car.

15 Reading Check

Answer: The old woman is ravenous for a son-in-law.

Differentiated Instruction

Solutions for All Learners

Background for Gifted/Talented Students

Tell students that Flannery O'Connor liked to employ her biting sense of irony in playing off of Southern manners. For instance, Tom Shiftlet mouths the platitudes of what she called elsewhere "good country people." We see this when he says to Lucynell Crater that "Nothing is like it used to be, lady . . . The world is almost rotten." The humor of his words comes from his timing—he offers this morally charged declaration after being told that the Craters' car stopped running years back. Encourage students to be aware of similar ironies in stereotypes and mannerisms.

16 Literary Analysis
Grotesque Characters

- **Ask** students what Shiftlet's reaction to Mrs. Crater suggests about his character.
  Answer: He knows what Mrs. Crater is up to. He turns his attention to the car immediately after she makes the suggestion, showing that he hopes to get the car running and leave the place as soon as possible.
- Finally, **ask** the first Literary Analysis question: In what way does Mrs. Crater's suggestion about teaching Lucynell reveal her obsession?
  Answer: She wants to force Shiftlet to speak endearingly to Lucynell.

17 Literary Analysis
Grotesque Characters

- Have a student read aloud the bracketed passage. Then, point out that Mr. Shiftlet's thoughts are on the car during his conversation about young Lucynell.
- **Ask** students the second Literary Analysis question: What does Mr. Shiftlet's remark about the car reveal about his obsession?
  Answer: It reveals that he cares more about the car than about the girl. He wants to repair it as much as possible while Mrs. Lucynell is footing the bill.

could get you a cheaper car and one that had had a personal interest taken in it, and it would be a better car. The old woman agreed with him that this was so.

Mr. Shiftlet said that the trouble with the world was that nobody cared, or stopped and took any trouble. He said he never would have been able to teach Lucynell to say a word if he hadn't cared and stopped long enough.

"Teach her to say something else," the old woman said.

"What you want her to say next?" Mr. Shiftlet asked.

The old woman's smile was broad and toothless and suggestive. "Teach her to say 'sugarpie,'" she said.

16 Mr. Shiftlet already knew what was on her mind.

The next day he began to tinker with the automobile and that evening he told her that if she would buy a fan belt, he would be able to make the car run.

Literary Analysis
Grotesque Characters
In what way does Mrs. Crater's suggestion about teaching Lucynell reveal her obsession?

The old woman said she would give him the money. "You see that girl yonder?" she asked, pointing to Lucynell who was sitting on the floor a foot away, watching him, her eyes blue even in the dark. "If it was ever a man wanted to take her away, I would say, 'No man on earth is going to take that sweet girl of mine away from me!' but if he was to say, 'Lady, I don't want to take her away, I want her right here,' I would say, 'Mister, I don't blame you none. I wouldn't pass up a chance to live in a permanent place and get the sweetest girl in the world myself. You ain't no fool,' I would say."

"How old is she?" Mr. Shiftlet asked casually.

"Fifteen, sixteen," the old woman said. The girl was nearly thirty but because of her innocence it was impossible to guess.

"It would be a good idea to paint it too," Mr. Shiftlet remarked. "You don't want it to rust out."

"We'll see about that later," the old woman said.

The next day he walked into town and returned with the parts he needed and a can of gasoline. Late in the afternoon, terrible noises issued from the shed and the old woman rushed out of the house, thinking
17 Lucynell was somewhere having a fit. Lucynell was sitting on a chicken crate, stamping her feet and screaming, "Burrddtt! bddurrddtttt!" but her fuss was drowned out by the car. With a volley of blasts it emerged from the shed, moving in a fierce and stately way. Mr. Shiftlet was in the driver's seat, sitting very erect. He had an expression of serious modesty on his face as if he had just raised the dead.

Literary Analysis
Grotesque Characters
What does Mr. Shiftlet's remark about the car reveal about his obsession?

That night, rocking on the porch, the old woman began her business, at once. "You want you an innocent woman, don't you?" she asked sympathetically. "You don't want none of this trash."

"No'm, I don't," Mr. Shiftlet said.

"One that can't talk," she continued, "can't sass you back or use foul language. That's the kind for you to have. Right there," and she pointed to Lucynell sitting crosslegged in her chair, holding both feet in her hands.

"That's right," he admitted. "She wouldn't give me any trouble."

"Saturday," the old woman said, "you and her and me can drive into town and get married."

Mr. Shiftlet eased his position on the steps.

"I can't get married right now," he said. "Everything you want to do takes money and I ain't got any."

"What you need with money?" she asked.

"It takes money," he said. "Some people'll do anything anyhow these days, but the way I think, I wouldn't marry no woman that I couldn't take on a trip like she was somebody. I mean take her to a hotel and treat her. I wouldn't marry the Duchesser Windsor," he said firmly, "unless I could take her to a hotel and giver something good to eat.

"I was raised thataway and there ain't a thing I can do about it. My old mother taught me how to do."

"Lucynell don't even know what a hotel is," the old woman muttered. "Listen here, Mr. Shiftlet," she said, sliding forward in her chair, "you'd be getting a permanent house and a deep well and the most innocent girl in the world. You don't need no money. Lemme tell you something: there ain't any place in the world for a poor disabled friendless drifting man."

The ugly words settled in Mr. Shiftlet's head like a group of buzzards in the top of a tree.

He didn't answer at once. He rolled himself a cigarette and lit it and then he said in an even voice, "Lady, a man is divided into two parts, body and spirit."

The old woman clamped her gums together.

"A body and a spirit," he repeated. "The body, lady, is like a house: it don't go anywhere; but the spirit, lady, is like a automobile: always on the move, always . . ."

"Listen, Mr. Shiftlet," she said, "my well never goes dry and my house is always warm in the winter and there's no mortgage on a thing about this place. You can go to the courthouse and see for yourself. And yonder under that shed is a fine automobile." She laid the bait carefully. "You can have it painted by Saturday. I'll pay for the paint."

In the darkness, Mr. Shiftlet's smile stretched like a weary snake waking up by a fire. After a second he recalled himself and said, "I'm only saying a man's spirit means more to him than anything else. I would have to take my wife off for the weekend without no regards at all for cost. I got to follow where my spirit says to go."

"I'll give you fifteen dollars for a weekend trip," the old woman said in a crabbed voice. "That's the best I can do."

"That wouldn't hardly pay for more than the gas and the hotel," he said. "It wouldn't feed her."

"Seventeen-fifty," the old woman said. "That's all I got so it isn't any use you trying to milk me. You can take a lunch." 20

Mr. Shiftlet was deeply hurt by the word "milk." He didn't doubt that she had more money sewed up in her mattress but he had already

Literary Analysis
Grotesque Characters and Characterization
What is revealed about Mr. Shiftlet and the old woman in this exchange about marriage and money?

Reading Strategy
Making Predictions
What predictions about Mr. Shiftlet can you make based on his discussion of body and spirit?

Reading Check
What does Mr. Shiftlet do with the old car?

18 Literary Analysis
Grotesque Characters and Characterization

- Read aloud the bracketed passage to students. Have students pay attention to the information they learn about Shiftlet and the old woman from their conversation.
- **Ask** the Literary Analysis question: What is revealed about Mr. Shiftlet and the old woman in this exchange about marriage and money?
  Answer: Each is trying to get what he or she wants from the other, while giving up as little as possible.
- Then, **ask** students to describe the part that Lucynell plays in this discussion. Have students consider what the others' attitude toward Lucynell in this passage reveals about them.
  Answer: Lucynell's future is decided for her without her input. The others regard her as property, or as a pawn in a chess game. She is simply a bargaining chip to both of them.

19 Reading Strategy
Making Predictions

- Have students read the bracketed passage to themselves. Then, have them explain in their own words what Shiftlet says in this passage.
- **Ask** the Reading Strategy question: What prediction about Mr. Shiftlet can you make based on his discussion of body and spirit?
  Answer: Like the spirit, he will soon be "on the move."

➤ **Monitor Progress: Ask** students what they think will happen to Lucynell once she is alone with Shiftlet.
Possible answers: He has been kind to her up to this point, so he probably won't hurt her. However, if he has the car, he will no longer have any motivation to impress Mrs. Crater by treating her daughter well.

20 Reading Check

Answer: Shiftlet repairs and paints it.

Differentiated Instruction
Solutions for All Learners

Enrichment for Gifted/Talented Students
The names Tom T. Shiftlet and Lucynell Crater are unusual and evocative, but what do they suggest to students? Have them free-associate phrases, adjectives, or images that these names bring to mind. What do they think were O'Connor's reasons for choosing each name?

Strategy for Advanced Readers
Have students analyze the figurative language in this story. Point out striking similes like "Shiftlet's smile stretched like a weary snake waking up by a fire" and "The ugly words settled in Mr. Shiftlet's head like a group of buzzards in the top of a tree." Have students find several such examples of figurative language and discuss how each one reveals information about a character's personality or motivations.

21 Reading Strategy
Making Predictions

- Have students read the bracketed passage. Remind them that they can use details from a story to make predictions about future events.
- Then, **ask** the Reading Strategy question: Based on this speech about his dissatisfaction, what do you predict will happen to the newlyweds?
  Possible answers: It is clear from his words that the ceremony was meaningless to Shiftlet. Based on this, we can predict that he does not feel bound to Lucynell and may harm or leave her.

➤ **Monitor Progress:** Challenge students to predict how the story will end. Have them give reasons for their predictions. At the end of the story, discuss whether anyone came close to predicting the story's actual end.

22 Literary Analysis
Grotesque Characters

- **Ask** the Literary Analysis question: Why is the old woman upset as she parts from her daughter?
  Possible answers: She has some genuine feelings for her daughter. She is suddenly afraid of what Shiftlet may do to Lucynell.
- Then, **ask** students whether the old woman really believes that Shiftlet "would do right" to her daughter. **Possible answer:** Students might say that the old woman is trying to convince herself that this is true.

told her he was not interested in her money. "I'll make that do," he said and rose and walked off without treating with her further.

On Saturday the three of them drove into town in the car that the paint had barely dried on and Mr. Shiftlet and Lucynell were married in the Ordinary's office while the old woman witnessed. As they came out of the courthouse, Mr. Shiftlet began twisting his neck in his collar. He looked morose and bitter as if he had been insulted while someone held him. 21 "That didn't satisfy me none," he said. "That was just something a woman in an office did, nothing but paper work and blood tests. What do they know about my blood? If they was to take my heart and cut it out," he said, "they wouldn't know a thing about me. It didn't satisfy me at all."

"It satisfied the law," the old woman said sharply.

"The law," Mr. Shiftlet said and spit. "It's the law that don't satisfy me."

He had painted the car dark green with a yellow band around it just under the windows. The three of them climbed in the front seat and the old woman said, "Don't Lucynell look pretty? Looks like a baby doll." Lucynell was dressed up in a white dress that her mother had uprooted from a trunk and there was a Panama hat on her head with a bunch of red wooden cherries on the brim. Every now and then her placid expression was changed by a sly isolated little thought like a shoot of green in the desert.

"You got a prize!" the old woman said.

Mr. Shiftlet didn't even look at her. They drove back to the house to let the old woman off and pick up the lunch. When they were ready to leave, she stood staring in the window of the car, with her fingers clenched around the glass. Tears began to seep sideways out of her eyes and run along the dirty creases in her face. "I ain't ever been parted with her for two days before," she said.

22 Mr. Shiftlet started the motor.

"And I wouldn't let no man have her but you because I seen you would do right. Goodbye, Sugarbaby," she said, clutching at the sleeve of the white dress. Lucynell looked straight at her and didn't seem to see her there at all. Mr. Shiftlet eased the car forward so that she had to move her hands.

The early afternoon was clear and open and surrounded by pale blue sky. Although the car would go only thirty miles an hour, Mr. Shiftlet imagined a terrific climb and dip and swerve that went entirely to his head so that he forgot his morning bitterness. He had always wanted an automobile but he had never been able to afford one before. He drove very fast because he wanted to make Mobile by nightfall.

Occasionally he stopped his thoughts long enough to look at Lucynell in the seat beside him. She had eaten the lunch as soon as they were out of the yard and now she was pulling the cherries off the hat one by one and throwing them out the window. He became depressed in spite of the car. He had driven about a hundred miles when he decided that she must be hungry again and at the next small town they came to, he stopped in front of an aluminum-painted eating

Vocabulary Builder
morose (mə rōs′) *adj.* gloomy; sullen

Reading Strategy
Making Predictions
Based on this speech about his dissatisfaction, what do you predict will happen to the newlyweds?

Literary Analysis
Grotesque Characters
Why is the old woman upset as she parts from her daughter?

place called The Hot Spot and took her in and ordered her a plate of ham and grits. The ride had made her sleepy and as soon as she got up on the stool, she rested her head on the counter and shut her eyes. There was no one in The Hot Spot but Mr. Shiftlet and the boy behind the counter, a pale youth with a greasy rag hung over his shoulder. Before he could dish up the food, she was snoring gently.

"Give it to her when she wakes up," Mr. Shiftlet said. "I'll pay for it now." The boy bent over her and stared at the long pink-gold hair and the half-shut sleeping eyes. Then he looked up and stared at Mr. Shiftlet. "She looks like an angel of Gawd," he murmured.

"Hitchhiker," Mr. Shiftlet explained. "I can't wait. I got to make Tuscaloosa."

The boy bent over again and very carefully touched his finger to a strand of the golden hair and Mr. Shiftlet left.

He was more depressed than ever as he drove on by himself. The late afternoon had grown hot and sultry and the country had flattened out. Deep in the sky a storm was preparing very slowly and without thunder as if it meant to drain every drop of air from the earth before it broke. There were times when Mr. Shiftlet preferred not to be alone. He felt too that a man with a car had a responsibility to others and he kept his eye out for a hitchhiker. Occasionally he saw a sign that warned: "Drive carefully. The life you save may be your own."

The narrow road dropped off on either side into dry fields and here and there a shack or a filling station stood in a clearing. The sun began to set directly in front of the automobile. It was a reddening ball that through his windshield was slightly flat on the bottom and top. He saw a boy in overalls and a gray hat standing on the edge of the road and he slowed the car down and stopped in front of him. The boy didn't have his hand raised to thumb the ride, he was only standing there, but he had a small cardboard suitcase and his hat was set on his head in a way to indicate that he had left somewhere for good. "Son," Mr. Shiftlet said, "I see you want a ride."

The boy didn't say he did or he didn't but he opened the door of the car and got in, and Mr. Shiftlet started driving again. The child held the suitcase on his lap and folded his arms on top of it. He turned his head and looked out the window away from Shiftlet. Mr. Shiftlet felt oppressed. "Son," he said after a minute, "I got the best old mother in the world so I reckon you only got the second best."

The boy gave him a quick dark glance and then turned his face back out the window.

"It's nothing so sweet," Mr. Shiftlet continued, "as a boy's mother. She taught him his first prayers at her knee, she give him love when no other would, she told him what was right and what wasn't, and she

23 

Southern Regionalism

While writers have the capacity to invent whole new worlds, they are human beings who are influenced by their environments. Regional writers are those who use specific geographical areas—usually their home turf—as settings. Yet regionalists do more than simply set their fiction in familiar locales; they incorporate the distinct culture of an area, including characteristic speech patterns, customs, beliefs, history, and folklore into the very fabric of their stories. This marriage of place, sensibility, and style goes beyond mere reporting to present a sophisticated treatment of the culture of a region. With the best regional writers, local detail helps to create stories of universal impact. You need not be from the American South to appreciate the work of such great Southern regional writers as Flannery O'Connor, Truman Capote, Carson McCullers, Tennessee Williams, William Faulkner, Eudora Welty, or Robert Penn Warren.

Connect to the Literature

What details in this story reflect a Southern sensibility? Could this story be set in a different region? Explain.

24 
Reading Check

What does Mr. Shiftlet do when Lucynell falls asleep at The Hot Spot?

23 The American Experience

Southern Regionalism Though accents vary throughout the American South, the region as a whole is known for its distinctive cadences and patterns of speech. These unique qualities were influenced by a number of circumstances. In the small towns of this agricultural region, people entertained themselves with storytelling and long chatting sessions. They heard only one another's voices; few outsiders came through.

The strong religious current in the southern states, sometimes referred to as the "Bible Belt," helped infuse the cadences of the King James Bible into Southern speech. In the years following the Civil War, Southerners struggled to retain a semblance of their pre-war lives. People preserved their speech patterns, which varied with social position, as a way of associating themselves with a particular social group.

Connect to the Literature Encourage students to provide at least two details from the text.

Possible response: The old woman's friendliness toward and lack of suspicion of Mr. Shiflet reflect Southern hospitality. The story could not be set in another region and still maintain the same characterization because people would not be as open as they are in the American South in the middle of the twentieth century.

24 Reading Check

Answer: He leaves money to pay for her meal and then abandons her.

Differentiated Instruction
Solutions for All Learners

Support for Special Needs Students

Discuss with students why Mr. Shiftlet leaves Lucynell in the diner. Help students determine that Shiftlet married her only in order to get the car and the honeymoon money; now that he has both, he no longer needs Lucynell.

Strategy for Advanced Readers

To encourage these students to respond thoughtfully to the story, initiate an analysis of Mr. Shiftlet's motivations throughout the story. Discuss whether he had always planned to abandon young Lucynell, or whether he was in fact willing to live with the Craters if only to gain access to the car.

ASSESS

Answers

1. Students will probably say that they are exaggerated and bizarre. They may recognize common character traits such as selfishness.
2. (a) She notices that he has only one arm and she thinks he is harmless. (b) He wants the car. (c) She doesn't seem aware that he is essentially untrustworthy.
3. (a) She points out that Lucynell is innocent and that she will never talk back or argue. (b) He wants the car and the money that Mrs. Crater agrees to give them for a honeymoon.
4. (a) He prays for the Lord to "break forth and wash this slime from the earth." (b) The rainstorm threatens to wash Shiftlet from the earth. (c) It suggests that people will ultimately pay for their hypocrisy.
5. Since Lucynell is disabled, she would be helpless if her mother died without making some arrangement for her future. Lucynell's limited reactions to Shiftlet are positive. The mother is justified on these grounds.

Go Online Author Link For additional information about Flannery O'Connor, have students type in the Web Code, then select *O* from the alphabet, and then Flannery O'Connor.

seen that he done the right thing. Son," he said, "I never rued a day in my life like the one I rued when I left that old mother of mine."

The boy shifted in his seat but he didn't look at Mr. Shiftlet. He unfolded his arms and put one hand on the door handle.

"My mother was a angel of Gawd," Mr. Shiftlet said in a very strained voice. "He took her from heaven and giver to me and I left her." His eyes were instantly clouded over with a mist of tears. The car was barely moving.

The boy turned angrily in the seat. "You go to the devil!" he cried. "My old woman is a flea bag and yours is a stinking pole cat!" and with that he flung the door open and jumped out with his suitcase into the ditch.

Mr. Shiftlet was so shocked that for about a hundred feet he drove along slowly with the door still open. A cloud, the exact color of the boy's hat and shaped like a turnip, had descended over the sun, and another, worse looking, crouched behind the car. Mr. Shiftlet felt that the rottenness of the world was about to engulf him. He raised his arm and let it fall again to his breast. "Oh Lord!" he prayed. "Break forth and wash the slime from this earth!"

The turnip continued slowly to descend. After a few minutes there was a guffawing peal of thunder from behind and fantastic raindrops, like tin-can tops, crashed over the rear of Mr. Shiftlet's car. Very quickly he stepped on the gas and with his stump sticking out the window he raced the galloping shower into Mobile.

Vocabulary Builder
guffawing (gə fô' iŋ) *adj.* laughing in a loud, coarse manner

Critical Reading

1. **Respond:** How did you react to the people in this story? In what way, if any, do they remind you of people you have met?
2. **(a) Recall:** What is Mrs. Crater's first reaction to Shiftlet when she sees him from a distance as the story begins? **(b) Infer:** What object on the Crater farm does Mr. Shiftlet want? **(c) Analyze:** What clues about Mr. Shiftlet's true character does Mrs. Crater seem to not notice?
3. **(a) Recall:** What arguments does Mrs. Crater use to persuade Shiftlet to marry Lucynell? **(b) Interpret:** What factors cause Shiftlet to agree to the marriage?
4. **(a) Recall:** What prayer does Shiftlet offer at the end of the story? **(b) Analyze:** What is ironic about the way in which his prayer is answered? **(c) Generalize:** What does this event suggest about those whose behavior contradicts their professed beliefs?
5. **Make a Judgment:** When Mrs. Crater decides to marry Lucynell to Shiftlet, the girl seems to have no control over her fate. Do Mrs. Crater's actions have any moral justification? Explain.

Go Online Author Link
For: More about Flannery O'Connor
Visit: www.PHSchool.com
Web Code: ere-9601

Apply the Skills

The Life You Save May Be Your Own

Literary Analysis

Grotesque Characters

1. Note two uses of physical description that create an exaggerated or **grotesque** effect for **(a)** Mrs. Crater, **(b)** Mr. Shiftlet, and **(c)** Lucynell.
2. Use a chart like the one shown to examine Mrs. Crater and Mr. Shiftlet. **(a)** What primary goal or obsession controls each character? **(b)** What actions does each undertake as a result of the obsession?

3. **(a)** In what ways are these characters exaggerated? **(b)** In what ways are they realistic?

Connecting Literary Elements

4. How does the narrator's observation that Mr. Shiftlet's figure "formed a crooked cross" contribute to his **characterization**?
5. What does Mr. Shiftlet's name suggest about his character?
6. **(a)** What is the cause of Lucynell's innocence? **(b)** What does the story suggest about the fate of such innocence?

Reading Strategy

Making Predictions

7. **(a)** What **predictions** did you make about Mr. Shiftlet's actions concerning Mrs. Crater and Lucynell when he first appeared? **(b)** What actually happened?
8. **(a)** What predictions did you make when Mr. Shiftlet departed with Lucynell after their wedding? **(b)** What actually happened?
9. In what ways do the story's actual events surprise the reader?

Extend Understanding

10. **Social Studies Connection:** In today's world, what educational opportunities or living situations might be available to a mentally challenged woman like Lucynell?

QuickReview

Grotesque characters become ludicrous or bizarre through their obsession with an idea, an assumption, or a value.

Characterization is the art of revealing character. With **direct characterization,** the writer simply states what a character is like. With **indirect characterization,** the writer reveals characters through their words, thoughts, actions, physical appearance, and by what other characters say and how they react.

To **make predictions,** use information from the text to anticipate how events will unfold later in the story.

Go Online Assessment

For: Self-test
Visit: www.PHSchool.com
Web Code: era-6601

Students may use the **Self-test** to prepare for **Selection Test A** or **Selection Test B.**

Answers

1. **Possible responses:** (a) The old woman is described as resembling "a cedar fence post" and having no teeth. (b) Shiftlet has lost part of one arm, and his figure is described as forming "a crooked cross." (c) Lucynell has "fat, helpless hands hanging at the wrists" and "long pink-gold hair."
2. Mrs. Crater: Goal: to marry Shiftlet to Lucynell. Actions undertaken: She tries to bribe him by allowing him to use the car. Shiftlet: Goal: to steal the car. Actions taken: He behaves well so that Mrs. Crater will trust him; he agrees to marry Lucynell and then promptly abandons her.

   Another sample answer can be found on **Literary Analysis Graphic Organizer B,** p. 217, in ***Graphic Organizer Transparencies.***
3. (a) Their physical characteristics are exaggerated. (b) Their personalities are realistic; the characters have problems and have been hurt by the world.
4. The cross suggests a religious symbol of love and sacrifice. The crookedness suggests that Shiftlet symbolizes the opposite: meanness and selfishness.
5. The name suggests the word *shiftless,* which means "lazy"; the word *makeshift,* which means "something that will do temporarily"; the word *shift,* which means "move," and the word *shifty,* which means "untrustworthy." All these words describe aspects of Shiftlet's character.
6. (a) She is deaf, mute, and mentally disabled. (b) The story suggests that innocent people will be manipulated and used.
7. (a) Students should have predicted that he intended to use them or harm them.
   (b) He used them for their money and their car.
8. (a) Students may have predicted that he would harm her.
   (b) He abandoned her far from home.
9. Students will probably say that the ending was a surprise. They may also have been surprised that Shiftlet went through with the marriage.
10. Students should note that many cities have schools for the deaf and the mentally challenged.

EXTEND/ASSESS

Answers

1 Vocabulary Lesson

Word Analysis

1. Solitaire is played by a single person.
2. A soliloquy involves one actor.
3. A pilot would not have a co-pilot on a solo flight.
4. Yes, a person who likes to be alone enjoys solitude.

Vocabulary Builder

1. With peeling paint and sagging window sashes, the cottage had a desolate appearance.
2. correct
3. correct
4. Having had no time to eat lunch, we were ravenous long before dinner.
5. Your morose reaction shows that your thoughts are gloomy.
6. correct

Spelling Strategy

1. shallower
2. glowing
3. withdrawal
4. hallowed

2 Grammar and Style Lesson

1. were
2. pay
3. rents
4. try
5. tastes

Writing Application

Have partners check one another's sentences to make sure they used the subjective verb form correctly.

WG Writing and Grammar, Ruby Level

Students will find further instruction and practice on subjunctive mood in Chapter 21, Section 3.

Build Language Skills

1 Vocabulary Lesson

Word Analysis: Latin Root *-sol-*

The Latin word root *-sol-*, meaning "alone," builds the meaning of these words:

a. *desolate:* isolated, uninhabited

b. *solitary:* alone, without company

c. *soloist:* one who performs by him- or herself

Use your knowledge of the Latin root *-sol-* to answer the following questions.

1. Is *solitaire* a game played by a single person or by a group of players?
2. In a *soliloquy,* do two actors have an exchange or does one actor address the audience?
3. Would a pilot have a co-pilot on a *solo* flight?
4. Would a person who usually loves to take long walks alone enjoy the state of *solitude*?

Vocabulary Builder: Context

For each sentence, indicate whether the word in italics is used correctly. If it is used incorrectly, write a new correct sentence.

1. With fresh paint and flower boxes, the cottage had a *desolate* appearance.
2. The rickety fence *listed* in the strong winds.
3. In an *ominous* voice, the jury foreperson read the guilty verdict.
4. After a huge dinner, we were *ravenous.*
5. Your *morose* reaction shows your happiness.
6. He was *guffawing* at the comic's antics.

Spelling Strategy

When you add a suffix to a word that ends in *w,* never double the *w.* For each word below, create a new word by adding the given suffix.

1. *-er* to shallow
2. *-ing* to glow
3. *-al* to withdraw
4. *-ed* to hallow

2 Grammar and Style Lesson

Subjunctive Mood

The **subjunctive mood** is any verb form indicating possibility, supposition, or desire.

- If a verb expresses a condition contrary to fact, use the past-tense form *were.*
- If a verb demands, recommends, or suggests, use the third-person singular verb form without the usual *-s, -es,* or *-ies* ending.

Look at these examples:

Contrary to fact: Mr. Shiftlet talked as if he *were* an ethical person.

Demands/suggests: Mrs. Crater suggested that Shiftlet *marry* her daughter.

Practice Determine whether the subjunctive mood is needed in each example. Then, write the correct form of the verb in parentheses to complete each sentence.

1. I wouldn't trust that broker, if I (be) you.
2. He requires that customers (pay) in cash.
3. Every summer, she (rent) a cottage.
4. He asks that each one (try) a sample.
5. The sample usually (taste) good.

Writing Application Write two different sentences using the subjunctive mood. For the first, express a condition contrary to fact. For the second, suggest a preferred course of action.

WG *Prentice Hall Writing and Grammar Connection: Chapter 21, Section 3*

Assessment Practice

Punctuation **(For more practice, see *Standardized Test Preparation Workbook*, p. 58.)**

Many tests require students to recognize errors in punctuation. Use the following sample test item to help students practice this skill.

"The Life You Save May Be Your Own" is the story of a drifter who meets a woman and her daughter. In the course of the story; the daughter is treated as if she were a piece of property.

Which punctuation mark above is incorrect?

A quotation marks around story title
B period after the word *daughter*
C semicolon after the word *story*
D period after the word *property*

The semicolon should be replaced by a comma. The correct answer is **C**.

Writing Lesson

Deposition

A deposition is a witness's formal, written testimony—a legal first-person recounting of events. Imagine that Mr. Shiftlet has been accused of stealing Mrs. Crater's car and of abandoning Lucynell. As a witness, write a deposition that may be used against him.

Prewriting List Mr. Shiftlet's statements and actions and the effects you know or imagine they had. Locate quotations from the story that support your testimony.

Drafting Begin by explaining, in objective detail, what Mr. Shiftlet did. Establish clear transitions that show cause and effect. Include relevant quotations to back up your statements. Finally, end by explaining why you believe that Mr. Shiftlet's actions were criminal.

Revising Be sure that you have described events in a clear and logical way. Add any transition words necessary to clarify causes and effects.

Model: Revising to Show Cause and Effect

At The Hot Spot, Mr. Shiftlet paid in advance for Lucynell's meal, ^so that^ he could leave her without arousing suspicion. He said that she was just a hitchhiker, ^thus^ justifying his leaving without her.

Transition words like *thus* and *so that* clarify cause and effect.

WG *Prentice Hall Writing and Grammar Connection: Chapter 10, Section 4*

Extend Your Learning

Listening and Speaking In a small group, conduct a **Readers Theatre** of the story.

- Name three students to be the narrator, Mrs. Crater, and Mr. Shiftlet.
- Have a fourth student act out Lucynell as the narrator describes her.

Follow your presentation with a discussion in which audience members comment on the author's use of stylistic devices to advance character and motive. **[Group Activity]**

Research and Technology People's posture or gestures may "speak" louder than their words. Conduct library and Internet research to prepare a **body language presentation.** Describe how body language reveals character. Link your findings to the selection and provide simple demonstrations to illustrate your main points.

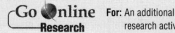

For: An additional research activity
Visit: www.PHSchool.com
Web Code: erd-7601

3 Writing Lesson

- Use the **Support for Writing Lesson** on p. 12 in ***Unit 6 Resources*** to help students as they write this deposition.
- Remind students that a deposition should give facts only, not opinions.
- Explain to students that depositions should describe only scenes and actions that the writer actually witnessed.
- Make sure students revise to show the causal relationships between events. Have students suggest other words and phrases that they can use to clarify these relationships.
- Use the Response to Literature rubrics, pp. 65–66 in ***General Resources*** to evaluate students' work.

4 Listening and Speaking

- Students might choose an excerpt from the story, rather than the whole text, so their presentations will be of manageable length.
- If necessary, a fifth student can take on the roles of the boy in the diner and the hitchhiker.
- Encourage students to adjust the tone, volume, and speed of their words to accurately reflect the character they are portraying.
- Give students a copy of the rubric for Peer Assessment: Oral Interpretation, p. 130 in ***General Resources,*** to use as they prepare their readings.
- The **Support for Extend Your Learning** page (***Unit 6 Resources,*** p. 13) provides guided note-taking opportunities to help students complete the Extend Your Learning activities.

Go Online Research Have students type in the Web Code for another research activity.

Assessment Resources

The following resources can be used to assess student's knowledge and skills.

Unit 6 Resources
- **Selection Test A,** pp. 15–17
- **Selection Test B,** pp. 18–20

General Resources
- **Rubrics for Response to Literature** pp. 65–66
- **Rubric for Peer Assessment: Oral Interpretation,** p. 130

Go Online Assessment Students may use the **Self-test** to prepare for **Selection Test A** or **Selection Test B.**

Meeting Your Standards

Students will

1. **analyze and respond to literary elements.**
   - Literary Analysis: Epiphany
2. **read, comprehend, analyze, and critique a short story.**
   - Reading Strategy: Identifying with Characters
   - Reading Check questions
   - Apply the Skills questions
   - Assessment Practice (ATE)
3. **develop vocabulary.**
   - Vocabulary Lesson: Latin Word Roots: *-litera-*
4. **understand and apply written and oral language conventions.**
   - Spelling Strategy
   - Grammar and Style Lesson: Usage: *who* and *whom*
5. **develop writing proficiency.**
   - Writing Lesson: Personality Profile
6. **develop appropriate research strategies.**
   - Extend Your Learning: Cultural Research
7. **understand and apply listening and speaking strategies.**
   - Extend Your Learning: Presentation

Block Scheduling: Use one 90-minute class period to preteach the skills and have students read the selection. Use a second 90-minute class period to assess students' mastery of skills, extend their learning, and monitor their progress.

Homework Suggestions

Following are possibilities for homework assignments.

- Support pages from ***Unit 6 Resources:***
  Literary Analysis
  Reading Strategy
  Vocabulary Builder
  Grammar and Style
- An Extend Your Learning project and the Writing Lesson for this selection may be completed over several days.

Step-by-Step Teaching Guide	Pacing Guide
PRETEACH	
• Administer Vocabulary and Reading Warm-ups as necessary.	5 min.
• Engage students' interest with the motivation activity.	5 min.
• Read and discuss author and background features. **FT**	10 min.
• Introduce the Literary Analysis Skill: Epiphany. **FT**	5 min.
• Introduce the Reading Strategy: Identifying with Characters. **FT**	10 min.
• Prepare students to read by teaching the selection vocabulary. **FT**	
TEACH	
• Informally monitor comprehension while students read independently or in groups. **FT**	30 min.
• Monitor students' comprehension with the Reading Check notes.	as students read
• Reinforce vocabulary with Vocabulary Builder notes.	as students read
• Develop students' understanding of epiphany with the Literary Analysis annotations. **FT**	5 min.
• Develop students' ability to identify with characters with the Reading Strategy annotations. **FT**	5 min.
ASSESS/EXTEND	
• Assess students' comprehension and mastery of the Literary Analysis and Reading Strategy by having them answer the Apply the Skills questions. **FT**	15 min.
• Have students complete the Vocabulary Lesson and the Grammar and Style Lesson. **FT**	15 min.
• Apply students' ability to generate details in their writing by using the Writing Lesson. **FT**	45 min. or homework
• Apply students' understanding by using one or more of the Extend Your Learning activities.	20–90 min. or homework
• Administer Selection Test A or Selection Test B. **FT**	15 min.

Resources

PRINT
Unit 6 Resources

Vocabulary Warm-up Word Lists **[L1, L2, EL]** ..... p. 21
Vocabulary Warm-up Practice **[L1, L2, EL]** ..... p. 22
Reading Warm-up A **[L1, L2, EL]** ..... p. 23
Reading Warm-up B **[L1, L2, L3]** ..... p. 24

TRANSPARENCY
Graphic Organizer Transparencies

Literary Analysis Graphic Organizer A **[L3]** ..... pp. 218, 220
Literary Analysis Graphic Organizer B **[L1, L2, EL]** ..... pp. 219, 221

PRINT
Reader's Notebook [L2]
Reader's Notebook: Adapted Version [L1]
Reader's Notebook: English Learner's Version [EL]
Unit 6 Resources

Literary Analysis **[L3]** ..... p. 25
Reading Strategy **[L3]** ..... p. 26
Vocabulary Builder **[L3]** ..... p. 27

TECHNOLOGY
Listening to Literature Audio CDs [L2, EL]
Reader's Notebook: Adapted Version Audio CD [L1, L2]

PRINT
Unit 6 Resources

Grammar and Style **[L3]** ..... p. 28
Support for Writing Lesson **[L3]** ..... p. 29
Support for Extend Your Learning **[L3]** ..... p. 30
Enrichment **[L4]** ..... p. 31
Selection Test A **[L1, L2, EL]** ..... pp. 32–34
Selection Test B **[L3, L4]** ..... pp. 35–37

General Resources

Rubrics for Descriptive Essay **[L3]** ..... pp. 63–64
Rubrics for Biographical Essay **[L3]** ..... pp. 76–77

TECHNOLOGY
Go Online: Research **[L3]**
Go Online: Self-test **[L3]**
***ExamView*® Test Bank [L3]**

Choosing Resources for Differentiated Instruction

[L1] Special Needs Students
[L2] Below-Level Students
[L3] All Students
[L4] Advanced Students
[EL] English Learners

For Vocabulary and Reading Warm-ups and for Selection Tests, **A** signifies "less challenging" and **B** "more challenging." For Graphic Organizer transparencies, **A** signifies "not filled in" and **B** "filled in."

FT Fast Track Instruction: To move the lesson more quickly, use the strategies and activities identified with **FT**.

Scaffolding for Less Proficient and Advanced Students

The leveled Critical Thinking questions after selections progress in the levels of thinking required to answer them. To address the needs of your different students, you may use the (a) level questions for your less proficient students and the (b) level questions with your on-level and advanced students. The occasional (c) level questions are appropriate for your advanced students.

PRENTICE HALL **TeacherEXPRESS™** Plan · Teach · Assess — Use this complete suite of powerful teaching tools to make lesson planning and testing quicker and easier.

PRENTICE HALL **StudentEXPRESS™** Learn · Study · Succeed — Use the interactive textbook (online and on CD-ROM) to make selections and activities come alive with audio and video support and interactive questions.

Go Online Professional Development — **For:** Information about Lexiles **Visit:** www.PHSchool.com **Web Code:** eue-1111

PRETEACH

Motivation

Write the following statements on the chalkboard:

I want you to have all the things I never had.

I want you to make something of yourself.

I only want what's best for you.

Ask students to respond to these statements. Do they sound familiar? Who might be the speaker? Who is the "you" being addressed? Explain that these are aspirations that parents commonly have for their children. Tell students that they are about to read a story of a father who has ambitious dreams for his daughter's future that, unfortunately for him, she does not share.

1 Background

More About the Author

Bernard Malamud began publishing fiction in the 1950s, one of a generation of gifted Jewish writers that included Saul Bellow, Norman Mailer, and Isaac Bashevis Singer. Among these, Malamud has been praised for the accessibility of his style and themes. The author himself, in speaking of the value of ordinary narrative forms, said, "The human race needs the novel. . . . Those who say the novel is dead can't write them."

Malamud's place among writers of his generation is further defined by his moral vision. The characters in his fiction often seem to struggle against base instincts in an attempt to lead better, more virtuous lives.

1 The First Seven Years

Bernard Malamud (1914–1986)

"I write . . . to explain life to myself and to keep me related to men," Bernard Malamud once commented when describing his life's work. He was a writer who possessed a strong social and political conscience, though he often insisted publicly that he was only interested in "the story." He explored the power of art to liberate people, always believing that "the purpose of freedom is to create it for others."

Childhood of Two Cultures Bernard Malamud was born in Brooklyn, New York, the son of Russian immigrants. His father was a grocer who, like so many immigrants, worked diligently to forge a better life for his family. According to his own account, Malamud's boyhood was "comparatively happy." He grew up hearing the constant mingling of Yiddish and English—an experience that contributed to his fine ear for the rhythms of spoken dialogue. Through his family's attention to Jewish culture, he developed a taste for Manhattan's Second Avenue Yiddish Theater, where two of his mother's relatives sometimes performed. A favored boyhood pastime was listening to his father recount tales of Jewish life in pre-Revolutionary Russia. Young Bernard began to display his father's gift for telling stories when, recovering from pneumonia at age nine, he spent hours in the back room of the family store writing down the stories he had composed to tell his friends.

A Literary Range Malamud attended City College of New York and Columbia University and began publishing stories in a number of well-known magazines. Despite his strong connection to Yiddish folk tales—many of Malamud's stories are drawn from this oral tradition—his work depicts a broad range of settings and characters. From the gifted baseball player in *The Natural* (1952), Malamud's first novel, to the handyman living in czarist Russia in the Pulitzer Prize-winning *The Fixer* (1966), all of his characters come across as real and accessible, with universal hopes and concerns.

Malamud's other novels include *The Assistant* (1957), *A New Life* (1961), *The Tenants* (1971), and *Dubin's Lives* (1979). He also wrote numerous short stories, many of which were published in *The Magic Barrel* (1958), which won the National Book Award.

Capturing Life's Lessons In much of his writing, Malamud uses Jewish characters to represent all of humanity, capturing their attempts to maintain a link to their cultural heritage while trying to cope with modern realities. While some of his characters achieve success, others experience disappointment. By portraying failure as well as triumph, Malamud reveals the essence of the human experience and creates a delicate balance between tragedy and comedy. Some of his stories amuse readers as the characters try to negotiate between fulfilling their ideals and meeting the practical demands of their lives.

A Touch of Magic Malamud often tells his stories in spare, compressed prose, sprinkled with flashes of highly charged metaphorical language. He allows magical events to happen in gloomy city neighborhoods, and gives his hard-working characters unexpected flashes of passion. Other Malamud stories move readers to sadness as characters struggle courageously within tragic circumstances. "The First Seven Years" depicts a Polish immigrant's desire to see his daughter achieve a better life. His notion of that life, however, is not the same as hers.

Preview

Connecting to the Literature

When parents or teachers push you to study hard, learn a skill, or practice an instrument, they hope to help you achieve a better life. Similarly, the father in this story pushes his daughter in a certain direction in the hope that she will find happiness. However, her idea of happiness does not match his.

2 Literary Analysis

Epiphany

In a traditional short story, the plot moves toward resolution, a point at which the conflict is untangled and the outcome of the action becomes clear. However, many twentieth-century writers turned away from such traditional plot structures. These writers constructed plots that move toward an **epiphany,** a moment when a character has a flash of insight that may alter the nature of the conflict without resolving it. In this story, the main character experiences an epiphany that requires him to reexamine long-held assumptions.

Connecting Literary Elements

Conflict, a struggle between opposing forces, is a key element of narrative literature because most plots develop from conflict. There are two main types of conflict:

- An **internal conflict** takes place within a character and involves a person's struggle with ideas, beliefs, or attitudes.
- An **external conflict** takes place between a character and an outside force, such as society, nature, or an enemy.

As you read this story, think about the conflicts each character experiences. Use a chart like the one shown to examine the conflicts, and categorize them as either internal or external.

External
1. with Sobel
2.

Feld's Conflicts

Internal
1.
2.

3 Reading Strategy

Identifying With Characters

When you **identify with characters,** you connect their thoughts, feelings, circumstances and actions to your own experience. Identifying with characters allows you to get more emotionally involved in your reading.

Vocabulary Builder

diligence (dil′ ə jəns) *n.* constant, careful effort; perseverance (p. 998)

connivance (kə nī′ vəns) *n.* secret cooperation (p. 999)

illiterate (i lit′ ər it) *adj.* unable to read or write (p. 999)

unscrupulous (un skrōō′ pyə ləs) *adj.* unethical; unprincipled (p. 1001)

repugnant (ri pug′ nənt) *adj.* offensive; disagreeable (p. 1001)

discern (di surn′) *v.* perceive or recognize; make out clearly (p. 1004)

Differentiated Instruction
Solutions for All Learners

Support for Special Needs Students
Have students read the adapted version of "The First Seven Years" in the ***Reader's Notebook: Adapted Version.*** This version provides basic-level instruction in an interactive format with questions and write-on lines. Completing these pages will prepare students to read the selection in the Student Edition.

Support for Less Proficient Readers
Have students read "The First Seven Years" in the ***Reader's Notebook.*** This version provides basic-level instruction in an interactive format with questions and write-on lines. After students finish the selection in the ***Reader's Notebook,*** have them complete the questions and activities in the Student Edition.

Support for English Learners
Have students read "The First Seven Years" in the ***Reader's Notebook: English Language Version.*** This version provides basic-level instruction in an interactive format with questions and write-on lines. Completing these pages will prepare students to read the selection in the Student Edition.

2 Literary Analysis
Epiphany

- Explain to students that an epiphany is literally a manifestation, or appearance, of divinity. In literary use, the term is broadened to mean an appearance of sudden understanding.
- Challenge students to recall epiphanies in other works they have read this year.
- Tell students to look for the epiphanies experienced by the characters in "The First Seven Years."
- Give students a copy of **Literary Analysis Graphic Organizer A,** p. 218 in ***Graphic Organizer Transparencies,*** to use as they read the story.

3 Reading Strategy
Identifying With Characters

- To identify with a character means to feel a sense of comradeship with him or her—to understand and sympathize with the character's feelings.
- Point out that it is often easiest to identify with the character from whose point of view the story is told, because this character shares his or her thoughts and feelings openly with the reader.
- As students read, have them try to put themselves in Feld's place. How would they feel if they wanted only the best for their daughter, only to have her refuse her opportunities?
- Encourage students to keep journals with them as they read. They can note a character's reactions to a given situation and compare these reactions to what they might think and do in the same circumstances.

Vocabulary Builder

- Pronounce each vocabulary word for students, and read the definitions as a class. Have students identify any words with which they are already familiar.

Learning Modalities
Musical/Rhythmic Learners
Explain that Feld's manner of speaking indicates a Yiddish accent characterized by a musical quality and an uprising tone at the end of each sentence. To help musical/rhythmic learners appreciate Feld's speech patterns, play the recording of this selection on the **Listening to Literature Audio CD.**

❶ About the Selection

This poignant story portrays the potentially tragic results that can occur as parents struggle to let go of their maturing children. The main character, the shoemaker Feld, loves his only child, Miriam, with a fierce and ambitious love. Wanting an easier life for her than the immigrant trials of his own young adulthood, Feld plots what he believes will be an advantageous relationship with a young accounting student, Max. When Sobel, Feld's assistant, hears Feld and Max talking about Miriam, he flees the store. After her second date with Max, Miriam reports that the aspiring CPA is a soulless bore. Circumstance forces Feld to swallow his pride and visit Sobel, who reveals that he has worked for the shoemaker for five years solely out of love for Miriam. Feld, devastated, relinquishes his plans for his daughter's brilliant future as he agrees to let the apprentice ask for Miriam's hand in marriage in two years. Feld discovers the hard way that emotions cannot be dictated and that children must choose their own path in life.

❷ Critical Viewing

Answer: Students should realize that the setting is a commercial section of a fairly large city, probably in the first half of the twentieth century. The prominent shoe repair sign suggests that the story involves a shoemaker.

❶ The First Seven Years

Bernard Malamud

Background This story takes place in the 1950s, a prosperous decade in the United States. Both the Great Depression and World War II had ended and the baby boom was in full swing. People were upwardly mobile; if they worked hard, they were virtually assured that their status in society would improve. Parents labored for wealth so that their children would have easier lives, yet some children took material comfort for granted. They became more interested in matters of the spirit. Malamud's story explores the gap in values that sometimes occurred between children of the 1950s and their parents.

Feld, the shoemaker, was annoyed that his helper, Sobel, was so insensitive to his reverie that he wouldn't for a minute cease his fanatic pounding at the other bench. He gave him a look, but Sobel's bald head was bent over the last[1] as he worked and he didn't notice. The shoemaker shrugged and continued to peer through the partly frosted window at the nearsighted haze of falling February snow. Neither the shifting white blur outside, nor the sudden deep remembrance of the snowy Polish village where he had wasted his youth could turn his thoughts from Max the college boy, (a constant visitor in the mind since early that morning when Feld saw him trudging through the snowdrifts on his way to school) whom he so much respected because of the sacrifices he had made throughout the years—in winter or direst heat—to further his education. An old wish returned to haunt the shoemaker: that he had had a son instead of a daughter, but this blew away in the snow for Feld, if anything, was a practical man. Yet he could not help but contrast the diligence of the boy, who was a peddler's son, with Miriam's unconcern for an education. True, she was always with a book in her hand, yet when the opportunity arose for a college education, she had said no she would rather find a job. He had begged her to go, pointing out how many fathers could not afford to send their children to college, but she said she wanted to be independent. As for education, what was it, she asked, but books, which Sobel, who diligently read the classics, would as usual advise her on. Her answer greatly grieved her father.

❷ ▲ **Critical Viewing**
What does this image reveal about the setting of the story? **[Predict]**

Vocabulary Builder
diligence (dil′ ə jəns) *n.* constant, careful effort; perseverance

1. **last** *n.* block shaped like a person's foot, on which shoes are made or repaired.

Differentiated Instruction Solutions for All Learners

Accessibility at a Glance

	The First Seven Years
Context	1950s urban; immigrant experience
Language	East European diction in dialogue
Concept Level	Accessible (parent/child relationships)
Literary Merit	Noted author
Lexile	1170L
Overall Rating	Average

A figure emerged from the snow and the door opened. At the counter the man withdrew from a wet paper bag a pair of battered shoes for repair. Who he was the shoemaker for a moment had no idea, then his heart trembled as he realized, before he had thoroughly discerned the face, that Max himself was standing there, embarrassedly explaining what he wanted done to his old shoes. Though Feld listened eagerly, he couldn't hear a word, for the opportunity that had burst upon him was deafening.

He couldn't exactly recall when the thought had occurred to him, because it was clear he had more than once considered suggesting to the boy that he go out with Miriam. But he had not dared speak, for if Max said no, how would he face him again? Or suppose Miriam, who harped so often on independence, blew up in anger and shouted at him for his meddling? Still, the chance was too good to let by: all it meant was an introduction. They might long ago have become friends had they happened to meet somewhere, therefore was it not his duty—an obligation—to bring them together, nothing more, a harmless connivance to replace an accidental encounter in the subway, let's say, or a mutual friend's introduction in the street? Just let him once see and talk to her and he would for sure be interested. As for Miriam, what possible harm for a working girl in an office, who met only loud-mouthed salesmen and illiterate shipping clerks, to make the acquaintance of a fine scholarly boy? Maybe he would awaken in her a desire to go to college; if not—the shoemaker's mind at last came to grips with the truth—let her marry an educated man and live a better life.

When Max finished describing what he wanted done to his shoes, Feld marked them, both with enormous holes in the soles which he pretended not to notice, with large white-chalk x's, and the rubber heels, thinned to the nails, he marked with o's, though it troubled him he might have mixed up the letters. Max inquired the price, and the shoemaker cleared his throat and asked the boy, above Sobel's insistent hammering, would he please step through the side door there into the hall. Though surprised, Max did as the shoemaker requested, and Feld went in after him. For a minute they were both silent, because Sobel had stopped banging, and it seemed they understood neither was to say anything until the noise began again. When it did, loudly, the shoemaker quickly told Max why he had asked to talk to him.

"Ever since you went to high school," he said, in the dimly-lit hallway, "I watched you in the morning go to the subway to school, and I said always to myself, this is a fine boy that he wants so much an education."

"Thanks," Max said, nervously alert. He was tall and grotesquely thin, with sharply cut features, particularly a beak-like nose. He was wearing a loose, long slushy overcoat that hung down to his ankles, looking like a rug draped over his bony shoulders, and a soggy, old brown hat, as battered as the shoes he had brought in.

Literary Analysis
Epiphany and Conflict Is Feld's conflict in speaking to Max primarily internal or external? Explain.

Vocabulary Builder
connivance (kə nī′ vəns) *n.* secret cooperation

illiterate (i lit′ ər it) *adj.* unable to read or write

5  **Reading Check**
What hope does Feld hold for his daughter Miriam and the college boy Max?

3 Literary Analysis
Epiphany and Conflict

- Have students make a two-column chart in their notebooks. In the left column, have them list, from Feld's point of view, the benefits of introducing Miriam to Max. In the right, have them list the potential drawbacks of doing so.
- **Ask** the Literary Analysis question: Is Feld's conflict in speaking to Max primarily internal or external? Explain.
  Answer: It is an internal conflict between his desire to play matchmaker and his fear of the consequences.

4 Vocabulary Builder
The Latin Root *-litera-*

- Draw students' attention to the word *illiterate* in the bracketed passage.
- **Ask** students to recall the word's meaning and to explain its basis in the Latin root *-litera-*.
  Answer: *Illiterate* means "unable to read letters" and derives from *littera,* which means "letter."

5 Reading Check

Answer: He wants Miriam and Max to marry.

Differentiated Instruction
Solutions for All Learners

Background for Less Proficient Readers
These students may have trouble understanding the concept of an epiphany. It may be helpful to relate it to a conventional conflict and resolution. Explain that many contemporary writers do not wish to resolve the conflict of a story entirely. Instead, an epiphany is used to focus attention on a particular insight or understanding.

Strategy for Advanced Readers
Prompt students to analyze how Malamud crafts a complex character portrait with relatively simple, almost spare language. Ask students to find examples of particularly vivid passages portraying Feld and to explain why these are so effective.

6 Reading Strategy
Identifying With Characters

- **Ask** students whom they identify with in this scene, Max or Feld. Have them explain their answers.
  Possible answers: Students might identify with Feld because they probably know how hard it can be to ask for something they truly want; other students may identify with Max because it can be embarrassing to have someone make such a request; also, it can be hard to say no.
- Have students **consider** what they would have charged Max for the repair job. Why?
  Possible answer: Students might say that they would have charged the regular price because this is the appropriate thing to do. Charging nothing would have seemed like a bribe.
- Then, **ask** the Reading Strategy question: How do you think Feld feels during this exchange with Max? Why?
  Answer: He is nervous and embarrassed because he wants so much to succeed in bringing the two young people together.

7 Literary Analysis
Epiphany and Conflict

- **Ask** students why Sobel reacts as he does. Have them look back in the story for a clue.
  Answer: Sobel lends Miriam books, which suggests that the two have a friendship. Sobel may be jealous; he may want to date Miriam himself.
- Then, **ask** the Literary Analysis question: What do Sobel's actions and Feld's reactions suggest about a conflict between the two men?
  Answer: Sobel is upset that Feld has not considered him as a potential husband for Miriam.

"I am a business man," the shoemaker abruptly said to conceal his embarrassment, "so I will explain you right away why I talk to you. I have a girl, my daughter Miriam—she is nineteen—a very nice girl and also so pretty that everybody looks on her when she passes by in the street. She is smart, always with a book, and I thought to myself that a boy like you, an educated boy—I thought maybe you will be interested sometime to meet a girl like this." He laughed a bit when he had finished and was tempted to say more but had the good sense not to.

Max stared down like a hawk. For an uncomfortable second he was silent, then he asked, "Did you say nineteen?"

"Yes."

"Would it be all right to inquire if you have a picture of her?"

"Just a minute." The shoemaker went into the store and hastily returned with a snapshot that Max held up to the light.

"She's all right," he said.

6 Feld waited.

"And is she sensible—not the flighty kind?"

"She is very sensible."

After another short pause, Max said it was okay with him if he met her.

"Here is my telephone," said the shoemaker, hurriedly handing him a slip of paper. "Call her up. She comes home from work six o'clock."

Max folded the paper and tucked it away into his worn leather wallet.

"About the shoes," he said. "How much did you say they will cost me?"

"Don't worry about the price."

"I just like to have an idea."

"A dollar—dollar fifty. A dollar fifty," the shoemaker said.

At once he felt bad, for he usually charged two twenty-five for this kind of job. Either he should have asked the regular price or done the work for nothing.

Later, as he entered the store, he was startled by a violent clanging and looked up to see Sobel pounding with all his might upon the
7 naked last. It broke, the iron striking the floor and jumping with a thump against the wall, but before the enraged shoemaker could cry out, the assistant had torn his hat and coat from the hook and rushed out into the snow.

So Feld, who had looked forward to anticipating how it would go with his daughter and Max, instead had a great worry on his mind. Without his temperamental helper he was a lost man, especially since it was years now that he had carried the store alone. The shoemaker had for an age suffered from a heart condition that threatened collapse if he dared exert himself. Five years ago, after an attack, it had appeared as though he would have either to sacrifice his business upon the auction block and live on a pittance thereafter, or put himself at the mercy of

Reading Strategy
Identifying With Characters How do you think Feld feels during this exchange with Max? Why?

Literary Analysis
Epiphany and Conflict
What do Sobel's actions and Feld's reactions suggest about a conflict between the two men?

Enrichment

America's Immigrants

This story is about Polish immigrants to the United States. The Poles are just one of many groups whose members left their homelands to seek better lives in America. For example, a huge immigration surge occurred in the mid-1800s as Irish, Chinese, and Germans—along with many others—fled economic or political difficulties. Additional immigration waves have swelled America's population since that time, whether comprising Russian Jews escaping mob attacks in the late 1870s or Vietnamese seeking freedom from a changing government in the late 1980s.

Immigrants often settle first in coastal cities, straining the urban infrastructure. During the nineteenth and early twentieth centuries, large numbers of newcomers were forced to live in dark and dreary tenement house apartments, which often lacked windows, indoor plumbing, and fire escapes. Many new Americans arrived with limited financial resources, and even more limited English.

some unscrupulous employee who would in the end probably ruin him. But just at the moment of his darkest despair, this Polish refugee, Sobel, appeared one night from the street and begged for work. He was a stocky man, poorly dressed, with a bald head that had once been blond, a severely plain face and soft blue eyes prone to tears over the sad books he read, a young man but old—no one would have guessed thirty. Though he confessed he knew nothing of shoemaking, he said he was apt and would work for a very little if Feld taught him the trade. Thinking that with, after all, a landsman,[2] he would have less to fear than from a complete stranger, Feld took him on and within six weeks the refugee rebuilt as good a shoe as he, and not long thereafter expertly ran the business for the thoroughly relieved shoemaker.

Feld could trust him with anything and did, frequently going home after an hour or two at the store, leaving all the money in the till, knowing Sobel would guard every cent of it. The amazing thing was that he demanded so little. His wants were few; in money he wasn't interested—in nothing but books, it seemed—which he one by one lent to Miriam, together with his profuse, queer written comments, manufactured during his lonely rooming house evenings, thick pads of commentary which the shoemaker peered at and twitched his shoulders over as his daughter, from her fourteenth year, read page by sanctified page, as if the word of God were inscribed on them. To protect Sobel, Feld himself had to see that he received more than he asked for. Yet his conscience bothered him for not insisting that the assistant accept a better wage than he was getting, though Feld had honestly told him he could earn a handsome salary if he worked elsewhere, or maybe opened a place of his own. But the assistant answered, somewhat ungraciously, that he was not interested in going elsewhere, and though Feld frequently asked himself what keeps him here? why does he stay? he finally answered it that the man, no doubt because of his terrible experiences as a refugee, was afraid of the world.

After the incident with the broken last, angered by Sobel's behavior, the shoemaker decided to let him stew for a week in the rooming house, although his own strength was taxed dangerously and the business suffered. However, after several sharp nagging warnings from both his wife and daughter, he went finally in search of Sobel, as he had once before, quite recently, when over some fancied slight—Feld had merely asked him not to give Miriam so many books to read because her eyes were strained and red—the assistant had left the place in a huff, an incident which, as usual, came to nothing for he had returned after the shoemaker had talked to him, and taken his seat at the bench. But this time, after Feld had plodded through the snow to Sobel's house—he had thought of sending Miriam but the idea became repugnant to him—the burly landlady at the door informed him in a nasal voice that Sobel was not at home, and though **9** Feld knew this was a nasty lie, for where had the refugee to go? still

2. **landsman** *n.* fellow countryman.

Vocabulary Builder
unscrupulous (un skrōōp′ yə ləs) *adj.* unethical; unprincipled

Literary Analysis
Epiphany and Conflict
What are some of the conflicts Feld experiences in regard to Sobel?

Vocabulary Builder
repugnant (ri pug′ nənt) *adj.* offensive; disagreeable

Reading Check
Under what circumstances did Sobel begin working for Feld?

8 Literary Analysis
Epiphany and Conflict

- Read aloud the bracketed passage to students. Have them look for signs of conflict between Feld and Sobel.
- **Ask** the Literary Analysis question: What are some of the conflicts Feld experiences in regard to Sobel?
  Answer: Feld feels guilty for paying Sobel less than he could earn elsewhere. He is thankful that Sobel stays with him, but he is puzzled by his reasons.
- Challenge students to guess why Sobel stays with Feld. **Ask** them to think about whether Feld senses why Sobel stays and refuses to acknowledge it, even to himself.
  Answer: Sobel stays so that he can see Miriam every day. Since Feld wants Miriam to marry an educated man, he doesn't want to see that Sobel cares for her.

9 Reading Check

Answer: When Feld needed to find an assistant because of his weak heart, Sobel appeared and asked for a job.

⑩ Reading Strategy
Identifying With Characters

- Have students read the bracketed passage, and discuss with them Feld's hopes for the date between Miriam and Max.
- To help them identify with the characters, **ask** students to consider experiences they have had with dates arranged by others. How do they think Max and Miriam's date is likely to turn out? **Possible answers:** Students may mention disastrous arranged dates or their surprise at successful arrangements. They will likely speculate that the date between Max and Miriam will not go well.

⑪ The American Experience
The Rooming House

Rooming houses are far less common today. In the early twentieth century, social conditions created a need for a safe, respectable, and inexpensive place to live for immigrants who came to this country alone or for individuals who came from rural areas to the city to work. Rooming houses filled this need.

Connect to the Literature Ask students to elaborate on the reasons Sobel lived in a rooming house. Then ask the Connect to the Literature question.

Possible response: Students may feel sorry that Sobel is poor and lonely. His living in a rooming house emphasizes that he has no family and lives a circumscribed life in a foreign place. He lives in the rooming house because he cannot afford an apartment of his own and has no family with whom to live. If he did have means and family, readers might sympathize less with his situation and his love for Miriam.

for some reason he was not completely sure of—it may have been the cold and his fatigue—he decided not to insist on seeing him. Instead he went home and hired a new helper.

Having settled the matter, though not entirely to his satisfaction, for he had much more to do than before, and so, for example, could no longer lie late in bed mornings because he had to get up to open the store for the new assistant, a speechless, dark man with an irritating rasp as he worked, whom he would not trust with the key as he had Sobel. Furthermore, this one, though able to do a fair repair job, knew nothing of grades of leather or prices, so Feld had to make his own purchases: and every night at closing time it was necessary to count the money in the till and lock up. However, he was not dissatisfied, for he lived much in his thoughts of Max and Miriam. The college boy had called her, and they had arranged a meeting for this coming Friday night. The shoemaker would
⑩ personally have preferred Saturday, which he felt would make it a date of the first magnitude, but he learned Friday was Miriam's choice, so he said nothing. The day of the week did not matter. What mattered was the aftermath. Would they like each other and want to be friends? He sighed at all the time that would have to go by before he knew for sure. Often he was tempted to talk to Miriam about the boy, to ask whether she thought she would like his type—he had told her only that he considered Max a nice boy and had suggested he call her—but the one time he tried she snapped at him—justly—how should she know?

At last Friday came. Feld was not feeling particularly well so he stayed in bed, and Mrs. Feld thought it better to remain in the bedroom with him when Max called. Miriam received the boy, and her parents could hear their voices, his throaty one, as they talked. Just before leaving, Miriam brought Max to the bedroom door and he stood there a minute, a tall, slightly hunched figure wearing a thick, droopy suit, and apparently at ease as he greeted the shoemaker and his wife, which was surely a good sign. And Miriam, although she had worked all day, looked fresh and pretty. She was a large-framed girl with a well-shaped body, and she had a fine open face and soft hair. They made, Feld thought, a first-class couple.

Miriam returned after 11:30. Her mother was already asleep, but the shoemaker got out of bed and after locating his bathrobe went into the kitchen, where Miriam, to his surprise, sat at the table, reading.

"So where did you go?" Feld asked pleasantly.

"For a walk," she said, not looking up.

"I advised him," Feld said, clearing his throat, "he shouldn't spend so much money."

"I didn't care."

⑪ *The Rooming House*

In this story, Sobel lives in a rooming house. Though rooming houses still exist today, up until the mid-twentieth century, they were a far more common form of shelter. Sometimes called boarding houses, rooming houses were inexpensive places to live. The roomer—or boarder—paid the owner a weekly fee for a bedroom, with access to a shared bathroom. The fee also covered meals, typically served family style. This setting was well suited to those with small incomes, new immigrants, and single people. Because they brought together strangers from all walks of life, rooming houses provided a rich setting for writers. They figure in some famous works of literature, including the short story "Tea-Time for Stout-Hearted Ladies" by Jean Stafford and, more recently, Frank McCourt's memoir *'Tis*.

Connect to the Literature

Would your reaction to Sobel be different if he lived in his own apartment or with his family, instead of in a rooming house? Explain.

Enrichment
Local Business

The main drama of this story takes place in a shoe repair shop, where people like Feld and Max have become acquainted while transacting routine business. Have students analyze the kinds of interactions they have had with businesses in your community. Have they worked in local businesses? Are they acquainted with any proprietors or workers? Then, discuss how local business owners participate in the community. Do they live locally? What, if any, role do they play in community decisions?

The shoemaker boiled up some water for tea and sat down at the table with a cupful and a thick slice of lemon.

"So how," he sighed after a sip, "did you enjoy?"

"It was all right."

He was silent. She must have sensed his disappointment, for she added, "You can't really tell much the first time."

"You will see him again?"

Turning a page, she said that Max had asked for another date.

"For when?"

"Saturday."

"So what did you say?"

"What did I say?" she asked, delaying for a moment—"I said yes."

Afterwards she inquired about Sobel, and Feld, without exactly knowing why, said the assistant had got another job. Miriam said nothing more and began to read. The shoemaker's conscience did not trouble him; he was satisfied with the Saturday date.

During the week, by placing here and there a deft question, he managed to get from Miriam some information about Max. It surprised him to learn that the boy was not studying to be either a doctor or lawyer but was taking a business course leading to a degree in accountancy. Feld was a little disappointed because he thought of accountants as bookkeepers and would have preferred "a higher profession." However, it was not long before he had investigated the subject and discovered that Certified Public Accountants were highly respected people, so he was thoroughly content as Saturday approached. But because Saturday was a busy day, he was much in the store and therefore did not see Max when he came to call for Miriam. From his wife he learned there had been nothing especially revealing about their meeting. Max had rung the bell and Miriam had got her coat and left with him—nothing more. Feld did not probe, for his wife was not particularly observant. Instead, he waited up for Miriam with a newspaper on his lap, which he scarcely looked at so lost was he in thinking of the future. He awoke to find her in the room with him, tiredly removing her hat. Greeting her, he was suddenly inexplicably afraid to ask anything about the evening. But since she volunteered nothing he was at last forced to inquire how she had enjoyed herself. Miriam began something noncommittal but apparently changed her mind, for she said after a minute, "I was bored."

When Feld had sufficiently recovered from his anguished disappointment to ask why, she answered without hesitation, "Because he's nothing more than a materialist."

"What means this word?"

"He has no soul. He's only interested in things."

He considered her statement for a long time but then asked, "Will you see him again?"

"He didn't ask."

"Suppose he will ask you?"

"I won't see him."

Literary Analysis
Epiphany and Conflict
What does this conversation suggest are some of Miriam's conflicts with her father?

Literary Analysis
Epiphany and Conflict
Why do you think Feld was "suddenly inexplicably afraid to ask anything about the evening"?

14 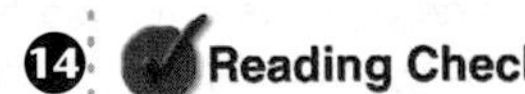

Reading Check
What is Miriam's reaction to her first date with Max?

12 Literary Analysis
Epiphany and Conflict

- **Ask** the first Literary Analysis question: What does this conversation suggest are some of Miriam's conflicts with her father?
  Answer: Miriam seems more interested in Sobel than in Max. In addition, Miriam's answers are curt, which suggests that she does not want her father interfering in her personal life.
- **Ask:** Why do you think Miriam says nothing further about Sobel?
  Possible answers: She may be hurt by Sobel's having left without saying goodbye. She may sense that her father would not react well to her interest in Sobel.

13 Literary Analysis
Epiphany and Conflict

- After students have read the bracketed passage, ask them to restate the action in their own words.
- **Ask** the second Literary Analysis question: Why do you think Feld was "suddenly inexplicably afraid to ask anything about the evening"?
  Answer: Feld knows instinctively that the evening did not go well. He is afraid that if he asks questions, Miriam will confirm his fear.
- **Ask** students why Miriam decides to be honest about her reaction to Max.
  Answer: She knows that this will save her from having to see him again. She hopes that honesty now will prevent arguments in the future.
- Finally, **ask:** What does Miriam's reaction to Max suggest about a conflict between her values and Feld's?
  Answer: Feld wants Miriam to have material comforts; Miriam does not care as much about such things.

14 Reading Check

Answer: Miriam is unenthusiastic, but she agrees to see him again.

Differentiated Instruction
Solutions for All Learners

Strategy for Special Needs Students

Read aloud the descriptions of Max and Miriam. Ask students to compare and contrast the two characters' appearances—allow them to draw pictures, if necessary. What impression of each character Is suggested by the comparison? Why is Feld's description of the couple ironic?

Students should see that Max appears physically unattractive—"droopy"—while Miriam is "fresh and pretty." Ironically, though Feld describes the two as a "first-class couple," readers can see that they are obviously ill suited to each other.

Encourage students to be aware of characters' physical descriptions when they read. These details often provide insights into the characters and the plot.

15 Literary Analysis
Epiphany and Conflict

- As students read this passage, have them identify the conflicts that Feld experiences.
- Then, **ask** the Literary Analysis question: What many conflicts does Feld experience in this passage? Which are internal and which are external?
  Answer: Internal conflicts include Feld's illness, his pride versus his need to apologize to Sobel and ask him to return, and his inability to understand Sobel. External conflicts include Feld's disagreement with Miriam about going for Sobel and his struggle to climb the stairs.

➤ **Monitor Progress: Ask** students what conflicts they think Sobel feels at seeing Feld again and hearing his request.
Answer: Sobel probably resents Feld's failure to value and respect him. He does not want to return to the store, but he does want to see Miriam again.

16 Critical Viewing

Answer: The last, shaped like a foot, is mentioned in the story.

He did not argue: however, as the days went by he hoped increasingly she would change her mind. He wished the boy would telephone, because he was sure there was more to him than Miriam, with her inexperienced eye, could discern. But Max didn't call. As a matter of fact he took a different route to school, no longer passing the shoemaker's store, and Feld was deeply hurt.

Then one afternoon Max came in and asked for his shoes. The shoemaker took them down from the shelf where he had placed them, apart from the other pairs. He had done the work himself and the soles and heels were well built and firm. The shoes had been highly polished and somehow looked better than new. Max's Adam's apple went up once when he saw them, and his eyes had little lights in them.

"How much?" he asked, without directly looking at the shoemaker.

"Like I told you before," Feld answered sadly. "One dollar fifty cents."

Max handed him two crumpled bills and received in return a newly-minted silver half dollar.

He left. Miriam had not been mentioned. That night the shoemaker discovered that his new assistant had been all the while stealing from him, and he suffered a heart attack.

Vocabulary Builder
discern (di surn′) *v.* perceive or recognize; make out clearly

15 Though the attack was very mild, he lay in bed for three weeks. Miriam spoke of going for Sobel, but sick as he was Feld rose in wrath against the idea. Yet in his heart he knew there was no other way, and the first weary day back in the shop thoroughly convinced him, so that night after supper he dragged himself to Sobel's rooming house.

He toiled up the stairs, though he knew it was bad for him, and at the top knocked at the door. Sobel opened it and the shoemaker entered. The room was a small, poor one, with a single window facing the street. It contained a narrow cot, a low table and several stacks of books piled haphazardly around on the floor along the wall, which made him think how queer Sobel was, to be uneducated and read so much. He had once asked him, Sobel, why you read so much? and the assistant could not answer him. Did you ever study in a college someplace? he had asked but Sobel shook his head. He read, he said, to know. But to know what, the shoemaker demanded, and to know, why? Sobel never explained, which proved he read much because he was queer.

Feld sat down to recover his breath. The assistant was resting on his bed with his heavy back to the wall. His shirt and trousers were clean, and his stubby fingers, away from the shoemaker's bench, were strangely pallid. His face was thin and pale, as if he had been shut in this room since the day he had bolted from the store.

"So when you will come back to work?" Feld asked him.

To his surprise, Sobel burst out, "Never."

Literary Analysis
Epiphany and Conflict
What conflicts does Feld experience in this passage? Which are internal, and which external?

16 ▼**Critical Viewing**
Which item mentioned in the story is shown in this photograph? **[Connect]**

Enrichment

Jacob and Rachel
"The First Seven Years" echoes the Biblical story of Jacob, Leah, and Rachel (Genesis 29–31). Like Sobel, Jacob falls in love with a young girl (Rachel) and agrees to work for her father Laban for seven years if, at the end of that time, Laban will allow them to marry. Laban agrees, but the morning after the wedding, Jacob discovers that Leah, Rachel's older sister, has taken Rachel's place. Laban explains that it would not be proper for the younger sister to be married before the older. Jacob agrees to serve Laban for another seven years if he can take Rachel as his second wife. Rachel eventually bears Joseph, Jacob's favorite son.

Jumping up, he strode over to the window that looked out upon the miserable street. "Why should I come back?" he cried.

"I will raise your wages."

"Who cares for your wages!"

The shoemaker, knowing he didn't care, was at a loss what else to say.

"What do you want from me, Sobel?"

"Nothing."

"I always treated you like you was my son."

Sobel vehemently denied it. "So why you look for strange boys in the street they should go out with Miriam? Why you don't think of me?"

The shoemaker's hands and feet turned freezing cold. His voice became so hoarse he couldn't speak. At last he cleared his throat and croaked, "So what has my daughter got to do with a shoemaker thirty-five years old who works for me?"

"Why do you think I worked so long for you?" Sobel cried out. "For the stingy wages I sacrificed five years of my life so you could have to eat and drink and where to sleep?"

"Then for what?" shouted the shoemaker.

"For Miriam," he blurted—"for her."

The shoemaker, after a time, managed to say, "I pay wages in cash, Sobel," and lapsed into silence. Though he was seething with excitement, his mind was coldly clear, and he had to admit to himself he had sensed all along that Sobel felt this way. He had never so much as thought it consciously, but he had felt it and was afraid.

"Miriam knows?" he muttered hoarsely.

"She knows."

"You told her?"

"No."

"Then how does she know?"

"How does she know?" Sobel said, "because she knows. She knows who I am and what is in my heart."

Feld had a sudden insight. In some devious way, with his books and commentary, Sobel had given Miriam to understand that he loved her. The shoemaker felt a terrible anger at him for his deceit.

"Sobel, you are crazy," he said bitterly. "She will never marry a man so old and ugly like you."

Sobel turned black with rage. He cursed the shoemaker, but then, though he trembled to hold it in, his eyes filled with tears and he broke into deep sobs. With his back to Feld, he stood at the window, fists clenched, and his shoulders shook with his choked sobbing.

Watching him, the shoemaker's anger diminished. His teeth were on edge with pity for the man, and his eyes grew moist. How strange and sad that a refugee, a grown man, bald and old with his miseries, who had by the skin of his teeth escaped Hitler's incinerators,[3] should fall in 19

Reading Strategy
Identifying With Characters Put yourself in Sobel's position. Why is he so angry with Feld?

Literary Analysis
Epiphany How can you tell that Feld is having an epiphany?

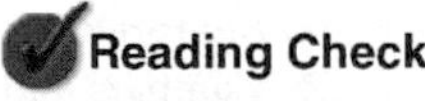
Reading Check
How does Sobel feel about Miriam? In what way has he expressed his feelings?

3. **Hitler's incinerators** During World War II, millions of Jews were murdered by the Nazis under the direction of German dictator Adolf Hitler (1889–1945).

17 Reading Strategy
Identifying With Characters

- **Ask** students with whom they identify in this exchange and why.
  Answer: Students will probably identify with Sobel because he has done his best to achieve what he truly wants.
- **Ask** the Reading Strategy question: Put yourself in Sobel's position. Why is he so angry with Feld?
  Answer: He resents Feld's failure to consider him as a possible son-in-law.

18 Literary Analysis
Epiphany

- Remind students that an epiphany is a moment of insight or understanding. Have them read the passage and look for details of an epiphany.
- **Ask** the Literary Analysis question: How can you tell that Feld is having an epiphany?
  Answer: The sentence "Feld had a sudden insight" shows that he is having an epiphany.
- **Ask** students to explain Feld's epiphany. Why is he angry at Sobel?
  Answer: Feld believes that Sobel has been dishonest about his motives. He also feels that Sobel has ruined Feld's plan to marry Miriam to a wealthy man.

19 Reading Check

Answer: Sobel is deeply in love with Miriam. He has continued to work where he can see her even though he could make more money elsewhere.

Differentiated Instruction
Solutions for All Learners

Strategy for English Learners
Discuss with these students the difficulty in reading the unpunctuated dialogue in the paragraph beginning "He toiled up the stairs" on p. 1004. Encourage students to rewrite the paragraph, adding quotation marks to indicate dialogue.

Strategy for Advanced Readers
Challenge students to speculate about whether Feld will tell Miriam about his discussion with Sobel. Students may say that Feld won't tell Miriam because he wants to discourage the relationship. On the other hand, he might tell her in the hope that she will respond negatively and end Sobel's hopes herself.

⑳ Literary Analysis
Epiphany and Conflict

- After students read the bracketed passage, **ask** them what Feld means when he says that Miriam's life will be "ugly" if she marries Sobel.
  Answer: Feld means that Miriam will have no hope of attaining the material comforts that he wished for her.
- Then, **ask** the Literary Analysis question: What realization brings Feld such a strong feeling of sorrow?
  Answer: Feld realizes that if his daughter marries Sobel, her future will be bleak. His dreams for his daughter have been crushed.

ASSESS
Answers

1. Students may admire Feld for seeking a better life for his daughter, while others may sympathize with Miriam.
2. (a) He sees Max trudging through the snow to school. (b) Feld admires Max's college education and the comfortable future he thinks it will bring him.
3. (a) Max represents the possibility of a better, more comfortable life. (b) Miriam says that Max cares only for material things; Max seems to want these things for himself, while Feld wants them for his daughter.
4. (a) She is disappointed and shows no interest in future dates. (b) Miriam likes and respects Sobel, and she finds Max materialistic and dull.
5. (a) He is a refugee from Poland. (b) Sobel has known hardship and sorrow. To Feld, he represents a lifetime of hardship, which he has hoped his daughter could avoid.
6. (a) Education represents the opportunity for a better life than their own. (b) Sobel views education as an opportunity to expand his knowledge and understanding of the world. Feld and Max look on education as a means of making money.
7. Some students will say that Feld had the right to interfere as Miriam's parent; others will say he should have stayed out of her love life.

love, when he had got to America, with a girl less than half his age. Day after day, for five years he had sat at his bench, cutting and hammering away, waiting for the girl to become a woman, unable to ease his heart with speech, knowing no protest but desperation.

"Ugly I didn't mean," he said half aloud.

Then he realized that what he had called ugly was not Sobel but Miriam's life if she married him. He felt for his daughter a strange and gripping sorrow, as if she were already Sobel's bride, the wife, after all, of a shoemaker, and had in her life no more than her mother had had. And all his dreams for her—why he had slaved and destroyed his heart with anxiety and labor—all these dreams of a better life were dead.

Literary Analysis
Epiphany and Conflict What realization brings Feld such a strong feeling of sorrow?

The room was quiet. Sobel was standing by the window reading, and it was curious that when he read he looked young.

"She is only nineteen," Feld said brokenly. "This is too young yet to get married. Don't ask her for two years more, till she is twenty-one, then you can talk to her."

Sobel didn't answer. Feld rose and left. He went slowly down the stairs but once outside, though it was an icy night and the crisp falling snow whitened the street, he walked with a stronger stride.

But the next morning, when the shoemaker arrived, heavy-hearted, to open the store, he saw he needn't have come, for his assistant was already seated at the last, pounding leather for his love.

Critical Reading

1. **Respond:** Which ambitions for Miriam's future seem more worthy to you—Feld's or Miriam's? Explain.
2. **(a) Recall:** Under what circumstances does Feld first notice Max? **(b) Interpret:** Why is Max so appealing to Feld?
3. **(a) Recall:** To Feld, what values does Max seem to embody? **(b) Interpret:** Does Max really share Feld's values? Explain.
4. **(a) Recall:** How does Miriam react to her second date with Max? **(b) Compare and Contrast:** Explain the differences between Miriam's feelings for Max and her feelings for Sobel.
5. **(a) Recall:** What is Sobel's background? **(b) Speculate:** In what ways do the events of history that Sobel experienced add to his characterization?
6. **(a) Interpret:** What does education represent to Feld and Max? **(b) Compare and Contrast:** How does Sobel's love of reading compare with both Feld's and Max's feelings about education?
7. **Make a Judgment:** Do you think Feld was right to interfere in Miriam's life? Explain.

Author Link
For: More about Bernard Malamud
Visit: www.PHSchool.com
Web Code: ere-9602

Go Online Author Link For additional information about Bernard Malamud, have students type in the Web Code, and then select Bernard Malamud.

Apply the Skills

The First Seven Years

Literary Analysis

Epiphany

1. Use a chart like the one shown to examine the **epiphanies** the characters experience in this story.

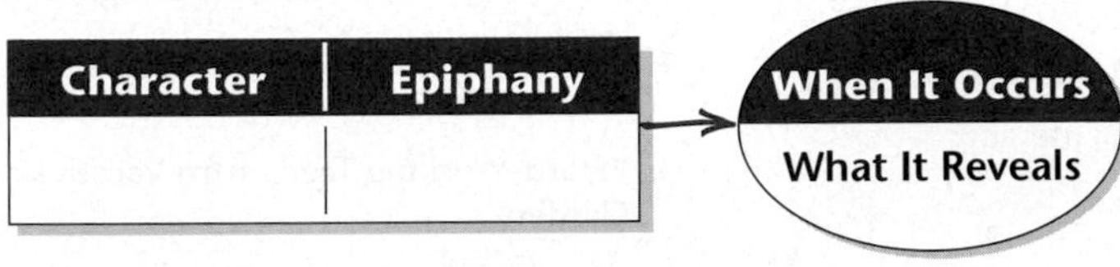

2. What new ideas does Feld's epiphany introduce that challenge the values he has always held?
3. In what ways might Feld's epiphany **(a)** change his thinking in the future? **(b)** affect his attitude toward Miriam? **(c)** affect his attitude toward Sobel?

Connecting Literary Elements

4. **(a)** With what external **conflicts** does Feld struggle? **(b)** What internal conflicts trouble him? **(c)** Which conflicts affect Feld the most?
5. **(a)** What external conflicts does Sobel face? **(b)** What internal conflicts trouble him?
6. **(a)** What image of Sobel begins the story? **(b)** What image of Sobel ends it? **(c)** What meaning do you find in the relationship of the beginning of the story to its ending?
7. **(a)** At the end of this story, have the characters' situations changed? **(b)** If so, in what ways? If not, how might they change in the future?

Reading Strategy

Identifying With Characters

8. **(a)** Choose a character from "The First Seven Years" and list as many connections as possible to your own experience. **(b)** Imagine yourself in the character's situation. How would you feel? What actions might you take?

Extend Understanding

9. **Social Studies Connection:** For generations, many skilled trades in the United States, such as shoemaking, baking, stone cutting, or woodworking, have attracted immigrant workers. Why do you think this has so often been the case?

QuickReview

An **epiphany** is a sudden revelation or flash of insight.

A **conflict** is a struggle between opposing forces. **Internal conflict** takes place within a character who is struggling with ideas and emotions. **External conflict** takes place between a character and an outside force, such as society, nature, or an enemy.

To **identify with characters,** connect their thoughts, feelings, circumstances, and actions to your own experience.

For: Self-test
Visit: www.PHSchool.com
Web Code: era-6602

Answers

1. **Possible answers:** Feld realizes that Sobel truly loves Miriam. He realizes what the past five years must have been like for Sobel.
2. Feld realizes that people may have other things to offer than material success.
3. (a) He may try harder to see situations from other people's points of view. (b) He may have learned that she has to make her own decisions. (c) He may treat Sobel with greater respect and understanding.
4. (a) He struggles to succeed in his business and provide for his family. (b) His pride and his need for help come into conflict after his heart attack. He struggles with the differences between his goals and Miriam's. (c) The greatest conflict is the one between his desires for Miriam's future, and Miriam's own desires for her life.
5. (a) He earns little money. (b) He loves Miriam but fears that his age and his low salary will prevent him from being with her.
6. (a) Sobel is pounding on the last in the shoe shop. (b) The same image ends the story. (c) It echoes the constancy of Sobel's love and his determination to wait.
7. (a) All the characters' situations have changed. (b) Feld has abandoned his dreams for his daughter; Sobel will wait two years but has permission to ask for Miriam's hand in marriage; Miriam will be able to pursue her love for Sobel.
8. (a) Answers will vary depending on students' experiences. (b) **Possible answer:** A student in Miriam's situation might act as she does: be polite to the interfering parent, but stick to his or her own goals and plans.
9. Some immigrant workers may have continued trades in the U.S. that they practiced in their countries of origin. However, for many immigrants, the trades were attractive because they did not usually require formal schooling or fluency in English and they provided reasonable pay.

Go Online Assessment Students may use the **Self-test** to prepare for **Selection Test A** or **Selection Test B.**

EXTEND/ASSESS

Answers

❶ Vocabulary Lesson

Word Analysis

1. having to do with letters
2. exactly as the letters say
3. the repetition of sounds from a letter or letters, used to create a particular effect in writing
4. the ability to read

Spelling Strategy

1. intelligent
2. originality
3. injustice
4. adjudicate

Vocabulary Builder

1. illiterate
2. repugnant
3. diligence
4. unscrupulous
5. discern
6. connivance

❷ Grammar and Style Lesson

1. who (subject)
2. who (subject)
3. who (subject)
4. whom (direct object)
5. who (subject)

Writing Application

Have partners check each other's sentences to make sure they have used *who* and *whom* correctly.

WG Writing and Grammar, Ruby Level

Students will find further instruction and practice on the use of *who* and *whom* in Chapter 22, Section 2.

Build Language Skills

Vocabulary Lesson

Word Analysis: Latin Root *-litera-*

The root *-litera-* comes from the Latin word *littera,* which means "letter." Write a definition for each of the following words containing the root *-litera-*. Then, check your definitions against those in a dictionary.

1. literary
2. literal
3. alliteration
4. literacy

Spelling Strategy

When you hear the *j* sound in the middle of a word, that sound is often produced by the letter *g,* as in *diligence.* In your notebook, spell each word below by adding the letter that forms the *j* sound.

1. intelli__ent
2. ori__inality
3. in__ustice
4. ad__udicate

Vocabulary Builder: Context

Review the vocabulary list on p. 997. Then, select the word you might find in each of these newspaper articles.

1. "Reading Rate Declines Among Adults"
2. "Residents Complain of Dump's Disagreeable Smell"
3. "Hard-Working Teens Turn Vacant Lot Into Garden"
4. "Dishonorable Band of Thieves Gets Nabbed"
5. "Girl of Ten Recognizes Error in Mayor's Speech"
6. "Five Executives Caught Plotting a Takeover"

Grammar and Style Lesson

Usage: *who* and *whom*

The correct use of *who* and *whom* helps an author clarify which character is being described. **Who,** like *he* or *she,* is used as a subject or subject complement. **Whom,** like *him* or *her,* is used as a direct object or object of the preposition. Study these examples:

Subject: The diligence of the boy, *who* was a poor man's son, was inspiring. (*Who* serves as the subject of the adjective clause *who was . . . son.*)

Object: Max, the college boy, *whom* he so much respected, was not a deep thinker. (*Whom* serves as the direct object of *respected.*)

Practice Identify which word—*who* or *whom*—correctly completes each sentence. Then, identify the word's function in the sentence.

1. She knows __?__ I am . . .
2. Feld, __?__ had looked forward to hearing about Max, was too nervous to ask.
3. There was little hope for a girl __?__ met only loud-mouthed salesmen.
4. He had to open the store for the assistant, __?__ he would not trust with the key.
5. He called Sobel, __?__ he expected would be eagerly waiting.

Writing Application Write two sentences using *who* and *whom* correctly. In the first sentence, use the word that functions as a subject. In the second, use the word that functions as an object.

WG Prentice Hall Writing and Grammar Connection: Chapter 22, Section 2

Assessment Practice

Punctuation (For more practice, see *Standardized Test Preparation Workbook*, p. 59.)

Many tests require students to recognize errors in punctuation. Use the following sample test item to help students practice this skill.

Feld is a shoemaker. Who emigrated from Poland to America.

Which choice below corrects the error in the underlined phrase?

A shoemaker who emigrated
B shoemaker—who emigrated
C shoemaker; who emigrated
D correct as is

No punctuation is necessary between *shoemaker* and *who.* The correct answer is *A.*

Writing Lesson

Personality Profile

Malamud creates a believable and engaging character in Feld, the shoemaker. Suppose you are developing a television show based on "The First Seven Years." Write a personality profile of Feld to be used by your producers.

Prewriting Before Feld's television character can be fully crafted, actors and producers need to know what he looks like and how he behaves. Use a cluster diagram like the one shown to jot down physical characteristics and personal qualities you observe in Feld.

Model: Clustering to Generate Details

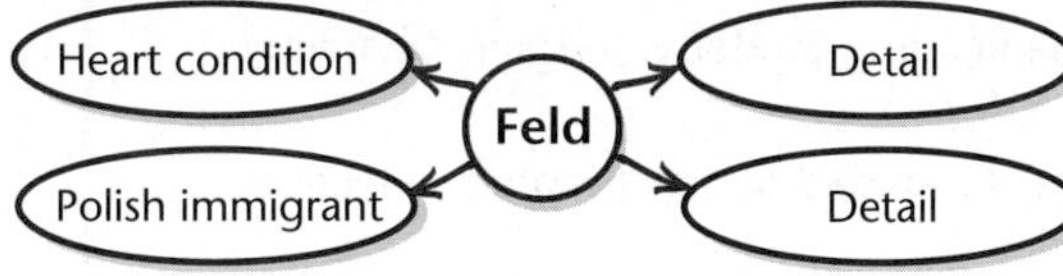

Drafting Begin with an informative detail or image of Feld. Expand your profile in layers, referring to your cluster diagram as needed.

Revising Have a classmate create a new cluster diagram based on your profile. Compare it to your prewriting diagram to discover key information you may have omitted.

WG Prentice Hall Writing and Grammar Connection: Chapter 6, Section 2

Extend Your Learning

Listening and Speaking Review the story to find details about Sobel's past, and create a **presentation** explaining how his past has affected his personality, values, and decisions. Use these tips to prepare:

- Estimate Sobel's date of birth and possible birthplace.
- Conduct historical research to identify events Sobel may have experienced.

Following your presentation, lead a class discussion about the issues raised by Sobel's life. **[Group Activity]**

Research and Technology Using a variety of sources including the Internet, conduct **cultural research** on a present-day society that adheres to the tradition of arranged marriages. Prepare a multimedia report, including text, quotations, images, and sound. In your report, balance the positive and negative aspects of such a tradition.

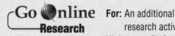

For: An additional research activity
Visit: www.PHSchool.com
Web Code: erd-7602

3 Writing Lesson

- Use the **Support for Writing Lesson** on p. 29 in ***Unit 6 Resources*** to help students as they write this personality profile.
- Remind students that since the story is written from Feld's point of view, they have a good idea of what he thinks and feels. The profiles they write should reflect this.
- Remind students to consider the way other characters react to Feld. What would Miriam say about him? How does Sobel feel about him?
- Use the Descriptive Essay rubrics, pp. 63–64 in ***General Resources,*** to evaluate students' work.

4 Listening and Speaking

- Students should start by summarizing what they know of Sobel's history, characteristics, and values.
- Remind students that Sobel fled Poland because of Nazi persecution. They might focus their research on the German occupation of Poland during World War II.
- Students may want to work with partners on this activity.
- Use the rubrics for Biographical Essay, pp. 76–77 in ***General Resources,*** to evaluate students' presentations.
- The **Support for Extend Your Learning** page (***Unit 6 Resources,*** p. 30) provides guided note-taking opportunities to help students complete the Extend Your Learning activities.

Go Online Research — Have students type in the Web Code for another research activity.

Assessment Resources

The following resources can be used to assess students' knowledge and skills.

Unit 6 Resources
- **Selection Test A,** pp. 32–34
- **Selection Test B,** pp. 35–37

General Resources
- **Rubrics for Descriptive Essay,** pp. 63–64
- **Rubrics for Biographical Essay,** pp. 76–77

Go Online Assessment — Students may use the **Self-test** to prepare for **Selection Test A** or **Selection Test B.**

Meeting Your Standards

Students will

1. **analyze and respond to literary elements.**
   - Literary Analysis: Static and Dynamic Characters
2. **read, comprehend, analyze, and critique a short story.**
   - Reading Strategy: Judging Characters' Actions
   - Reading Check questions
   - Apply the Skills questions
   - Assessment Practice (ATE)
3. **develop vocabulary.**
   - Vocabulary Lesson: Greek Root: *-morph-*
4. **understand and apply written and oral language conventions.**
   - Spelling Strategy
   - Grammar and Style Lesson: Commonly Confused Words: *then* and *than*
5. **develop writing proficiency.**
   - Writing Lesson: Advice Column
6. **develop appropriate research strategies.**
   - Extend Your Learning: Graph of the Great Migration
7. **understand and apply listening and speaking strategies.**
   - Extend Your Learning: Eulogy

Block Scheduling: Use one 90-minute class period to preteach the skills and have students read the selection. Use a second 90-minute class period to assess students' mastery of skills, extend their learning, and monitor their progress.

Homework Suggestions

Following are possibilities for homework assignments.

- Support pages from ***Unit 6 Resources:***
  Literary Analysis
  Reading Strategy
  Vocabulary Builder
  Grammar and Style
- An Extend Your Learning project and the Writing Lesson for this selection group may be completed over several days.

Step-by-Step Teaching Guide	Pacing Guide
PRETEACH	
• Administer Vocabulary and Reading Warm-ups as necessary.	5 min.
• Engage students' interest with the motivation activity.	5 min.
• Read and discuss author and background features. **FT**	10 min.
• Introduce the Literary Analysis skill: Static and Dynamic Characters. **FT**	5 min.
• Introduce the Reading Strategy: Judging Characters' Actions. **FT**	10 min.
• Prepare students to read by teaching the selection vocabulary. **FT**	
TEACH	
• Informally monitor comprehension while students read independently or in groups. **FT**	30 min.
• Monitor students' comprehension with the Reading Check notes.	as students read
• Reinforce vocabulary with Vocabulary Builder notes.	as students read
• Develop students' understanding of static and dynamic characters with the Literary Analysis annotations. **FT**	5 min.
• Develop students' ability to judge characters' actions with the Reading Strategy annotations. **FT**	5 min.
ASSESS/EXTEND	
• Assess students' comprehension and mastery of the Literary Analysis and Reading Strategy by having them answer the Apply the Skills questions. **FT**	15 min.
• Have students complete the Vocabulary Lesson and the Grammar and Style Lesson. **FT**	15 min.
• Apply students' ability to elaborate to support an argument by using the Writing Lesson. **FT**	45 min. or homework
• Apply students' understanding by using one or both of the Extend Your Learning activities.	20–90 min. or homework
• Administer Selection Test A or Selection Test B. **FT**	15 min.

Resources

PRINT

Unit 6 Resources

Vocabulary Warm-up Word Lists **[L1, L2, EL]** .... p. 38
Vocabulary Warm-up Practice **[L1, L2, EL]** .... p. 39
Reading Warm-up A **[L1, L2, EL]** .... p. 40
Reading Warm-up B **[L1, L2, L3]** .... p. 41

TRANSPARENCY

Graphic Organizer Transparencies

Literary Analysis Graphic Organizer A **[L3]** .... p. 222
Literary Analysis Graphic Organizer B **[L1, L2, EL]** .... p. 223
Reading Strategy Graphic Organizer A **[L3]** .... p. 224
Reading Strategy Graphic Organizer B **[L1, L2, EL]** .... p. 225

PRINT

Reader's Notebook [L2]
Reader's Notebook: Adapted Version [L1]
Reader's Notebook: English Learner's Version [EL]

Unit 6 Resources

Literary Analysis **[L3]** .... p. 42
Reading Strategy **[L3]** .... p. 43
Vocabulary Builder **[L3]** .... p. 44

PRINT

Unit 6 Resources

Grammar and Style .... p. 45
Support for Writing Lesson **[L3]** .... p. 46
Support for Extend Your Learning **[L3]** .... p. 47
Enrichment **[L4]** .... p. 48
Selection Test A **[L1, L2, EL]** .... pp. 49–51
Selection Test B **[L3, L4]** .... pp. 52–54

General Resources

Rubrics for Exposition: Problem-Solution Essay **[L3]** .... p. 59–60
Rubric for Speaking: Delivering a Speech **[L3]** .... p. 89

TECHNOLOGY

Go Online: Research **[L3]**
Go Online: Self-test **[L3]**
***ExamView®* Test Bank [L3]**

Choosing Resources for Differentiated Instruction

[L1] Special Needs Students
[L2] Below-Level Students
[L3] All Students
[L4] Advanced Students
[EL] English Learners

For Vocabulary and Reading Warm-ups and for Selection Tests, **A** signifies "less challenging" and **B** "more challenging." For Graphic Organizer transparencies, **A** signifies "not filled in" and **B** "filled in."

FT Fast Track Instruction: To move the lesson more quickly, use the strategies and activities identified with **FT**.

Scaffolding for Less Proficient and Advanced Students

The leveled Critical Thinking questions after selections progress in the levels of thinking required to answer them. To address the needs of your different students, you may use the (a) level questions for your less proficient students and the (b) level questions with your on-level and advanced students. The occasional (c) level questions are appropriate for your advanced students.

PRENTICE HALL **TeacherEXPRESS™** Plan · Teach · Assess — Use this complete suite of powerful teaching tools to make lesson planning and testing quicker and easier.

PRENTICE HALL **StudentEXPRESS™** Learn · Study · Succeed — Use the interactive textbook (online and on CD-ROM) to make selections and activities come alive with audio and video support and interactive questions.

Go Online Professional Development — **For:** Information about Lexiles **Visit:** www.PHSchool.com **Web Code:** eue-1111

PREACH

Motivation

Ask students the following question: Can something positive come out of something you regret? Lead students in a discussion of the question, pointing out that this is actually a common situation found in novels and stories: An action, a word, or even a thought leads to regret, a series of unwanted consequences, the achievement of self-knowledge, and an eventual positive resolution. Point out that "Marigolds" begins in rage, leads to regret, and ends in a kind of wisdom.

❶ Background

More About the Author

The power of a person's emotional life is one of Eugenia Collier's prominent themes. Like "Marigolds," several of her stories focus on the interplay between a difficult, even brutal, reality and the dynamic inner life of a person. For example, "A Present for Sarah" tells the tale of a grandmother who buys a dollhouse for her granddaughter for Christmas. Because of tension in the family, the girl's mother refuses to let the girl visit her grandmother on Christmas. Disappointed and depressed, the grandmother keeps the dollhouse and creates a doll family that reflects family life the way she wishes it to be.

❶ Marigolds

Eugenia W. Collier (b. 1928)

Her love of African American literature, drama, and culture inspires the writing of Eugenia W. Collier. A writer of fiction, poetry, personal essays, and numerous critical articles on the work of African American writers, she has also co-edited an anthology, *Afro-American Writing: An Anthology of Prose and Poetry* (1972), with fellow professor Richard A. Long. Collier's own writing has deep roots in her African American experience. As she herself explains, "The rich African American culture that nurtured me, the people I knew along the way, and our endless, complex struggle—these are the forces that informed my writing."

Early Years Collier was the second of two children born to a young physician and a teacher. She spent her early childhood in a racially segregated neighborhood of Baltimore, Maryland, where she and her family lived in her grandmother's large row house. When she was eight years old, her family moved into their own home.

As a child, Collier was educated in public schools in Baltimore. After high school, she attended Howard University, a prominent and historically black university in Washington, D.C., where she majored in English. After graduating in 1948, she went on to Columbia University in New York City, where she earned a Master of Arts degree. She later earned her doctorate in American Studies at the University of Maryland.

Work and Family Collier married in 1948 and is the mother of three sons. In her first career, she worked as a case worker at the Baltimore Department of Public Welfare and at Crownsville State Hospital, a facility for the mentally ill. Collier left that job to begin a teaching career at Morgan State College in 1955. Since then, Collier has taught at a number of colleges and universities, including Community College of Baltimore, the University of Maryland, and her alma mater, Howard University. She served as the head of the department of Languages, Literature, and Journalism at Coppin State College in Baltimore, and in 1992 she returned to Morgan State College as a professor of English. She retired in 1996 and has spent the years since then in what she calls "joyful idleness."

The Craft of Writing Eugenia Collier wanted to be a writer all her life. "My love of reading," she says, "instilled in me by my father, taught me to appreciate literature, and teaching students to write taught me the craft of writing." The day-to-day struggle with life—the practical, personal, and often internal struggles of average people—is a frequent theme in Collier's writing. The short story "Marigolds" was her first published story and as such, it has special meaning for her. "Marigolds" won the prestigious Gwendolyn Brooks Award for Fiction in 1969 and is featured in a collection of short stories by Collier entitled *Breeder and Other Stories* (1993). Collier identifies the publication of this collection as "a highlight of my life."

Collier's work has appeared in many anthologies, magazines, and literary collections. In addition to *Breeder and Other Stories,* works by Collier include "The Caregiver" (2002), a short story that appeared in *African American Review.* She is currently working on a series of autobiographical sketches.

A Writer's Task Collier believes that "a writer must speak to the generations. A writer must have a vision of a world beyond the physical; he/she must have a sense of the timelessness of human experience and the limitless potential of the human self." For Collier, "writers, like all serious artists, have a special task: to tell the truth as they see the truth, to strive to perfect their craft, to be mercilessly honest, and ultimately to change the world."

Preview

Connecting to the Literature

Most people can remember doing or saying something hurtful to another person and then wishing they could take it back. In this story, the main character learns a key lesson from her shame.

Literary Analysis

Static and Dynamic Characters

Collier uses static and dynamic characters to create a heightened sense of contrast in her story.

- A **static character** is one whose attitudes and behavior remain essentially stable throughout a literary work.
- A **dynamic character** experiences a change in attitude or behavior during the course of a work.

As you read "Marigolds," organize a character list like the one shown, identifying each of the characters as either static or dynamic. Consider how the contrasts between these character types add to the story's impact.

Character → Condition at Beginning of Story → Condition at End of Story → Dynamic or Static?

Connecting Literary Elements

Characters arise in part from their **cultural context,** the economic and social environment that they inhabit. In this story, that context is a dusty, impoverished town in rural Maryland during the 1930s. The characters are residents of an African American community that has never known prosperity. They live in an old broken-down shack, have very little food to eat, and wear nothing but tattered clothes. As you read, notice how the cultural context influences the characters' goals, aspirations, and values. Consider the impact that the struggles of the parents have on the lives of their children.

Reading Strategy

The characters in this story live under difficult conditions. When you **judge the characters' actions,** you evaluate their behavior against ethical or other criteria. While reading the story, consider the actions of each character. Think about how you would behave if faced with similar circumstances. Then, decide whether or not you find each character ethical or unethical.

Vocabulary Builder

nostalgia (nä stal′ jə) *n.* a feeling of longing for home, for something far away or long ago, or for happier circumstances (p. 1013)

amorphous (ə môr′ fəs) *adj.* shapeless, without a well-defined form (p. 1013)

retribution (re′ trə byo͞o shən) *n.* payback for evil done, especially punishment (p. 1016)

squalor (skwäl′ ər) *n.* extremely dirty, unsafe, and unhealthy conditions (p. 1023)

poignancy (poi′ nyən sē) *n.* a state of deeply felt distress or sorrow (p. 1024)

❷ Literary Analysis

Static and Dynamic Characters

- Tell students that, as they read "Marigolds," they will focus on static (unchanging) and dynamic (evolving) characters. Read the instruction about static and dynamic characters aloud. Discuss examples of each character type from stories students have recently read.
- Use the Connecting Literary Elements instruction to point out that understanding cultural context will help students recognize the forces that shape the actions of the characters in "Marigolds" and that both prevent and propel change.
- Note the graphic organizer and model its use. Give students a copy of **Literary Analysis Graphic Organizer A,** p. 222 in ***Graphic Organizer Transparencies,*** to use as they read the story.

❸ Reading Strategy

Judging Characters' Actions

- Remind students that judging characters' actions requires readers to enter the story situation and thus engage in active reading.
- To judge characters' actions, readers must develop a set of standards. They should, however, judge in light of the circumstances of the story.
- Urge students to use their knowledge of human behavior in judging characters' actions.

Vocabulary

- Pronounce each vocabulary word for students and read the definitions as a class. Have students identify any words with which they are already familiar.

Differentiated Instruction

Solutions for All Learners

Support for Special Needs Students

Give students an alternative method for grasping the cultural context of "Marigolds." Show students photographs or a video about the hard times that many Americans faced during the Depression. Be sure students understand that the 1930s occurred before World War II, before television, and before the Civil Rights movement. Challenge them to identify details of the daily lives of people affected by poverty, unemployment, and racism.

Strategy for Less Proficient Readers

Help students understand the concept of dynamic characters by giving them examples of the kinds of changes that a character can experience. A character may begin a story as lonely and loveless, and end a story happily and deeply in love—or vice versa. A character may begin a story as an immature and irresponsible person, and end as a mature and responsible one. Have students come up with additional examples of their own.

TEACH

Learning Modalities
Intrapersonal Learners

Have students reflect on the narrator's perceptions, motives, and actions. Encourage them to write a journal entry in which they both speculate about why Lizabeth acts as she does and assess the ethics of her actions.

1 About the Selection

In "Marigolds, " an African American woman tells the story of a life-changing experience she had when she was fourteen years old. In a small town in rural Maryland during the 1930s, the narrator Lizabeth, her brother Joey, and some of the local children take malicious pleasure in tormenting an old woman, Miss Lottie, who lives in a shack with her mentally troubled son John Burke. In this time and place of great poverty, Miss Lottie's only solace is a garden of marigolds on which she lavishes tender care and attention. One day, the children throw stones at the flowers and are chased away. However, that night, after overhearing her father cry in desperation over his joblessness, Lizabeth sneaks back to Miss Lottie's and, in a furious rage that she does not understand, utterly destroys the marigolds. Arriving too late, Miss Lottie stands silently over her. At that moment Lizabeth feels the depths of both humiliation and compassion, and she realizes her childhood is over.

1

Marigolds

EUGENIA W. COLLIER

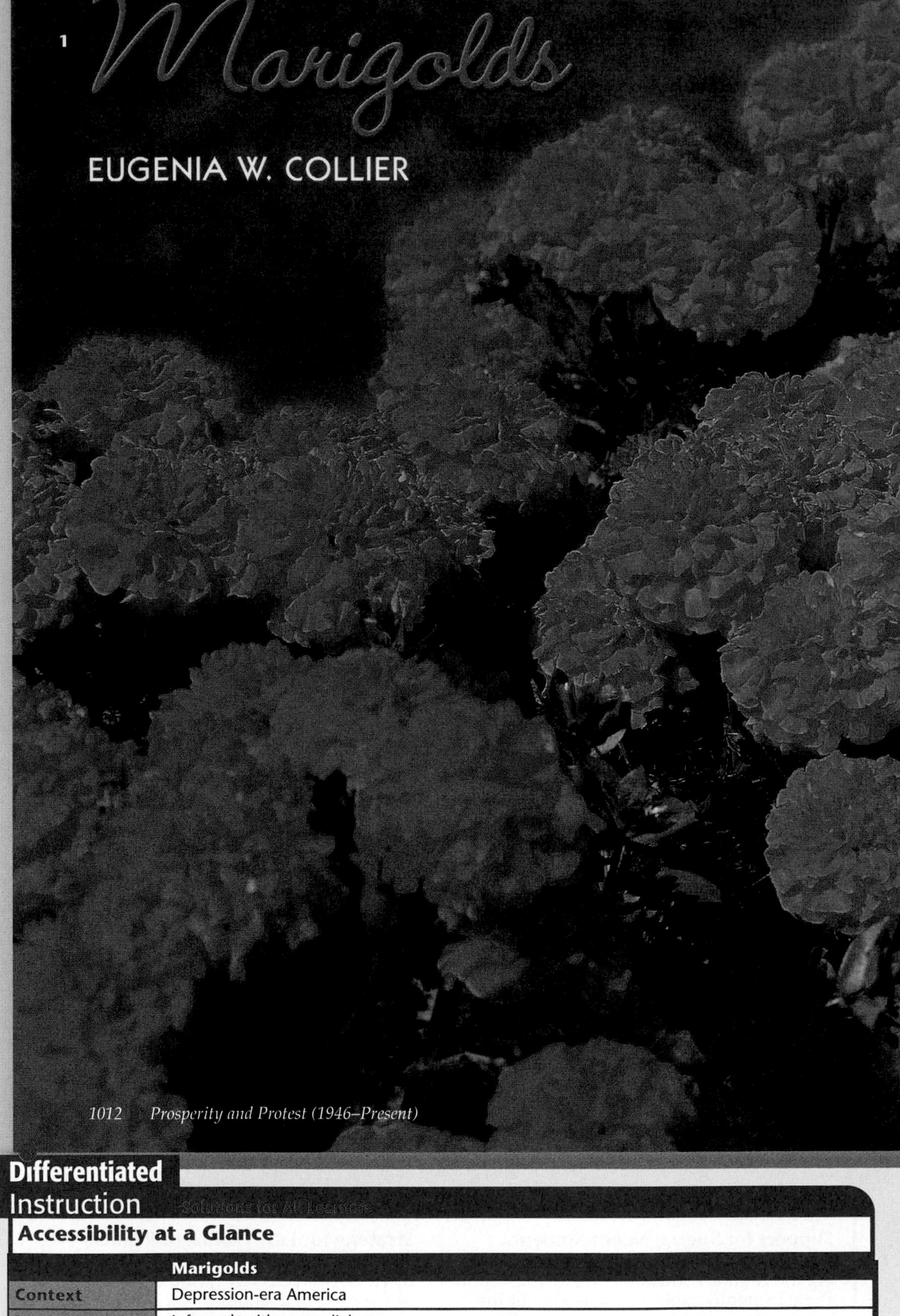

Differentiated Instruction Solutions for All Learners

Accessibility at a Glance

	Marigolds
Context	Depression-era America
Language	Informal, with some dialect
Concept Level	Accessible (self-discovery)
Literary Merit	Noted author
Lexile	1190L
Overall Rating	Average

Background This story is set in rural Maryland during the 1930s. At this time in the United States, poverty, discrimination, and natural agricultural disasters had driven thousands of African Americans out of their rural southern communities. Like several of the narrator's siblings, they migrated to northern cities in search of better economic, social, and political opportunities. By the 1960s, more than six million African Americans had relocated to the North. This population shift became known as "The Great Migration."

When I think of the home town of my youth, all that I seem to remember is dust—the brown, crumbly dust of late summer—arid, sterile dust that gets into the eyes and makes them water, gets into the throat and between the toes of bare brown feet. I don't know why I should remember only the dust. Surely there must have been lush
2 green lawns and paved streets under leafy shade trees somewhere in town; but memory is an abstract painting—it does not present things as they are, but rather as they *feel.* And so, when I think of that time and that place, I remember only the dry September of the dirt roads and grassless yards of the shanty-town where I lived. And one other thing I remember, another incongruency[1] of memory—a brilliant splash of sunny yellow against the dust—Miss Lottie's marigolds.

Whenever the memory of those marigolds flashes across my mind, a strange nostalgia comes with it and remains long after the picture has faded. I feel again the chaotic emotions of adolescence, illusive as smoke, yet as real as the potted geranium before me now. Joy and rage and wild animal gladness and shame become tangled together in the multicolored skein[2] of 14-going-on-15 as I recall that devastating moment when I was suddenly more woman than child, years ago in Miss Lottie's yard. I think of those marigolds at the strangest times; I remember them vividly now as I desperately pass away the time waiting for you, who will not come.

I suppose that futile waiting was the sorrowful background music of our impoverished little community when I was young. The Depression that gripped the nation was no new thing to us, for the black workers of rural Maryland had always been depressed. I don't know what it was that we were waiting for; certainly not for the prosperity that was "just around the corner," for those were white folks' words, which we never believed. Nor did we wait for hard work and thrift to pay off in shining success as the American Dream promised, for we knew better than that, too. Perhaps we waited for a miracle, amorphous in concept but necessary if one were to have the grit to rise before dawn each day and labor in the white man's vineyard until

Literary Analysis
Static and Dynamic Characters and Cultural Context What does this passage reveal about the cultural context of the narrator's youth?

Vocabulary Builder
nostalgia (nä stal´ jə) *n.* a feeling of longing for home, for something far away or long ago, or for happier circumstances

Vocabulary Builder
amorphous (ə môr´ fəs) *adj.* shapeless, without a well-defined form

3  **Reading Check**
What "gripped the nation" when the narrator was young?

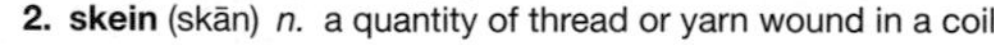

1. **incongruency** (in´ käŋ´ grōō ən sē) *n.* the condition of being irrational or meaningless.
2. **skein** (skān) *n.* a quantity of thread or yarn wound in a coil.

4 ◀ **Critical Viewing** What kind of person might grow flowers like these? Explain. **[Speculate]**

2 Literary Analysis
Static and Dynamic Characters and Cultural Context

- **Ask** students to identify the specific details of time and place that the narrator remembers in the opening paragraph.
  Answer: The narrator remembers a dusty town, a dry September, dirt roads, grassless yards, a shanty-town, and the marigolds. She recalls that there must have been green lawns and paved streets somewhere else in the town.
- **Ask** students the Literary Analysis question.
  Answer: The passage reveals that the cultural context is the shanty-town section of an American town at a time of great poverty. The division of the town into a grassy and paved section and a shanty-town section suggests a time and place in which race divided America.

3 Reading Check

The Depression gripped the nation when the narrator was young.

4 Critical Viewing

Possible responses: Anyone who loves flowers might grow marigolds. Anyone who loves nature, who craves color, or who simply wants to create a place of beauty might grow them.

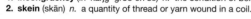

Differentiated Instruction
Solutions for All Learners

Strategy for Special Needs Students
Students may need help recognizing that the narrator is now a grown woman looking back on a life-changing incident of her youth. Have students list the clue words on this page that show that the story that is about to be told is a memory. Students might list *remember, memory, that time, that place, where I lived, nostalgia, years ago, when I was young.*

Vocabulary for English Learners
The narrator describes her neighborhood as a shanty-town. Explain to students that a shanty is a shabby, rundown, or poorly-built dwelling, and a shanty-town is a section of a town or city that consists of many of these types of dwellings. The narrator describes the grassless yards, dirt roads, and ramshackle homes that characterize the shanty-town where she lives. Have students keep in mind this setting and its effect on the events of the story.

5 Critical Thinking
Making Inferences About a Character

- Have students read the sentence beginning "But God was chary. . . ." **Ask** them to paraphrase the sentence.
  Possible response: Escaping poverty in those days seemed to demand an act of divine intervention, and those acts were few and far between, so we endured and kept hoping for something to happen.
- **Ask** students what they can infer about the narrator's character and beliefs from the information in this sentence.
  Possible responses: The narrator believes in God but does not experience any supernatural rescue from poverty. The narrator and her family have the strength and willpower that enables them to continue to endure hardship.

6 Critical Viewing

Possible responses: The image compares with Lizabeth because the figure is a young African American girl with a serious expression in a log house with newspapers over the windows. The image contrasts with Lizabeth because the figure does not look like someone who would maliciously torment an old woman.

after dark, or to wander about in the September dust offering one's sweat in return for some meager share of bread. But God was chary[3] with miracles in those days, and so we waited—and waited.

We children, of course, were only vaguely aware of the extent of our poverty. Having no radios, few newspapers, and no magazines, we were somewhat unaware of the world outside our community. Nowadays we would be called "culturally deprived" and people would write books and hold conferences about us. In those days everybody we knew was just as hungry and ill-clad as we were. Poverty was the cage in which we all were trapped, and our hatred of it was still the vague, undirected restlessness of the zoo-bred flamingo who knows that nature created him to fly free.

As I think of those days I feel most poignantly the tag-end of summer, the bright dry times when we began to have a sense of shortening days and the imminence of the cold.

6 ▲ **Critical Viewing** In what ways does this image compare or contrast with your impression of Lizabeth? **[Compare and Contrast]**

3. **chary** (cher´ ē) *adj.* not giving freely; sparing.

Enrichment

Music of the Great Depression

The narrator of "Marigolds" says that her family and the people in her community had "no radios," so their access to the music of the time was limited. However, the 1930s witnessed the flourishing of blues, jazz, folk, and popular music that reflected the hard lives of struggling Americans. Blues singers Robert Johnson and Big Bill Broonzy made classic recordings during the 1930s, and T-Bone Walker began experimenting with a prototype of the electric guitar. Folk singer Woody Guthrie composed the "Dust Bowl Blues," summarizing the Depression with the image of dust that "turned my farm into a pile of sand." Yip Harburg's "Brother, Can You Spare a Dime?" (1931) echoed an all-too-common question, while some folks tried to forget their anxiety briefly by singing "Life Is Just a Bowl of Cherries" (1931). Encourage students to find other songs of the Depression era.

By the time I was 14 my brother Joey and I were the only children left in our house, the older ones having left home for early marriage or the lure of the city, and the two babies having been sent to relatives who might care for them better than we. Joey was three years younger than I, and a boy, and therefore vastly inferior. Each morning our mother and father trudged wearily down the dirt road and around the bend, she to her domestic job, he to his daily unsuccessful quest for work. After our few chores around the tumble-down shanty, Joey and I were free to run wild in the sun with other children similarly situated.

For the most part, those days are ill-defined in my memory, running together and combining like a fresh water-color painting left out in the rain. I remember squatting in the road drawing a picture in the dust, a picture which Joey gleefully erased with one sweep of his dirty foot. I remember fishing for minnows in a muddy creek and watching sadly as they eluded my cupped hands, while Joey laughed uproariously. And I remember, that year, a strange restlessness of body and of spirit, a feeling that something old and familiar was ending, and something unknown and therefore terrifying was beginning.

One day returns to me with special clarity for some reason, perhaps because it was the beginning of the experience that in some inexplicable way marked the end of innocence. I was loafing under the great oak tree in our yard, deep in some reverie[4] which I have now forgotten except that it involved some secret, secret thoughts of one of the Harris boys across the yard. Joey and a bunch of kids were bored now with the old tire suspended from an oak limb which had kept them entertained for awhile.

"Hey, Lizabeth," Joey yelled. He never talked when he could yell. "Hey, Lizabeth, let's go somewhere."

I came reluctantly from my private world. "Where do you want to go? What you want to do?"

The truth was that we were becoming tired of the formlessness of our summer days. The idleness whose prospect had seemed so beautiful during the busy days of spring now had degenerated to an almost desperate effort to fill up the empty midday hours.

"Let's go see can we find some locusts[5] on the hill," someone suggested.

Joey was scornful. "Ain't no more locusts there. Y'all got 'em all while they was still green."

The argument that followed was brief and not really worth the effort. Hunting locust trees wasn't fun any more by now.

"Tell you what," said Joey finally, his eyes sparkling. "Let's go over to Miss Lottie's."

The idea caught on at once, for annoying Miss Lottie was always

4. **reverie** (rev′ ə rē) *n.* daydreaming; dreamy thinking or imagining.
5. **locust** (lō′ kəst) *n.* a spiny tree of the pea family that reproduces by dropping long seed pods.

Literary Analysis
Static and Dynamic Characters and Cultural Context What additional information does this passage reveal about the cultural context of the story?

Reading Strategy
Judging the Characters' Actions Which of Joey's actions are thoughtless or unkind?

9 

Reading Check
Where have all the other children of the narrator's family gone?

7 Static and Dynamic Characters and Cultural Context

- **Ask** students to identify details of the family's everyday life revealed in this paragraph. **Answer:** The older children have left home for marriage or the city, the babies were sent to relatives, the mother works as a domestic, and the father looks unsuccessfully every day for a job.
- **Ask** students the Literary Analysis question.
  Answer: These details of cultural context reveal that poverty has separated the family and that drudgery and joblessness are facts of Depression-era life. As a result, the children are left unsupervised.

8 Reading Strategy
Judging Characters' Actions

- **Ask** students to identify Joey's actions in this passage.
  Answer: Joey erases Lizabeth's picture and laughs at Lizabeth's inability to catch minnows.
- **Ask** students the Reading Strategy question.
  Answer: Both of Joey's actions seem thoughtless and unkind; they seem to be performed out of mean-spiritedness and mockery.

9 Reading Check

Answer: The older children have gotten married or gone to the city, and the babies have been sent to live with relatives.

Differentiated Instruction
Solutions for All Learners

Strategy for Less Proficient Readers

To help students recognize how the cultural context directly affects the daily lives of the characters in "Marigolds," have students make a cause-and-effect chain (a string of ovals or squares), or give them a copy of a the Cause-and-Effect Flowchart, p. 305 in ***Graphic Organizer Transparencies.*** State that the Stock Market Crash of 1929 and the Great Depression of the 1930s are the cause. Then lead students to follow the string of effects from "Depression" which causes "unemployment" which causes "poverty" which causes "family separation" which causes the children to "run wild."

Support for English Learners

Point out to students that the characters in "Marigolds," especially Joey, speak in a **dialect**—a way of using words that is particular to a time, place, and cultural context. Have students list some of Joey's expressions: *ain't no more, y'all got 'em all, look at 'er, go 'way.* Point out that the apostrophes represent missing letters—*o, ou, th, h,* and *a*. Have students write out Joey's words in standard English.

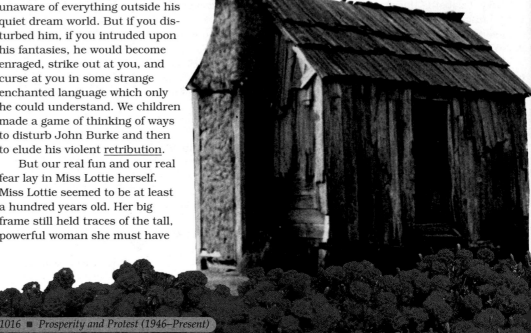

⑩ Critical Thinking
Making Inferences About a Character

- Point out to students that cultural context includes the houses in which characters live. Writers often use houses to reveal aspects of the lives or personalities of characters.
- **Ask** students what they can infer about the character of Miss Lottie from the description of her house.
  Possible responses: Miss Lottie is extremely poor and unable to fix up her house or build a new one. Like her house, Miss Lottie barely survives.

⑪ Critical Viewing

Answer: Details that connect to Miss Lottie's house include "ramshackle," "rickety frame," "boards . . . leaning together," "gray rotting thing with no porch, no shutters, no steps, set on a cramped lot with no grass," "a monument to decay."

fun. I was still child enough to scamper along with the group over rickety fences and through bushes that tore our already raggedy clothes, back to where Miss Lottie lived. I think now that we must have made a tragicomic spectacle, five or six kids of different ages, each of us clad in only one garment—the girls in faded dresses that were too long or too short, the boys in patchy pants, their sweaty brown chests gleaming in the hot sun. A little cloud of dust followed our thin legs and bare feet as we tramped over the barren land.

⑩ When Miss Lottie's house came into view we stopped, ostensibly to plan our strategy, but actually to reinforce our courage. Miss Lottie's house was the most ramshackle of all our ramshackle homes. The sun and rain had long since faded its rickety frame siding from white to a sullen gray. The boards themselves seemed to remain upright not from being nailed together but rather from leaning together like a house that a child might have constructed from cards. A brisk wind might have blown it down, and the fact that it was still standing implied a kind of enchantment that was stronger than the elements. There it stood, and as far as I know is standing yet—a gray rotting thing with no porch, no shutters, no steps, set on a cramped lot with no grass, not even any weeds—a monument to decay.

In front of the house in a squeaky rocking chair sat Miss Lottie's son, John Burke, completing the impression of decay. John Burke was what was known as "queer-headed." Black and ageless, he sat, rocking day in and day out in a mindless stupor, lulled by the monotonous squeak-squawk of the chair. A battered hat atop his shaggy head shaded him from the sun. Usually John Burke was totally unaware of everything outside his quiet dream world. But if you disturbed him, if you intruded upon his fantasies, he would become enraged, strike out at you, and curse at you in some strange enchanted language which only he could understand. We children made a game of thinking of ways to disturb John Burke and then to elude his violent retribution.

But our real fun and our real fear lay in Miss Lottie herself. Miss Lottie seemed to be at least a hundred years old. Her big frame still held traces of the tall, powerful woman she must have

Vocabulary Builder
retribution (re′ trə byo͞o shən) *n.* payback for evil done, especially punishment

⑪ **▼ Critical Viewing**
What details connect this photograph to the description of Miss Lottie's house? **[Connect]**

Enrichment

Horticulture: Symbolism of Marigolds
Marigolds, originally native to Mexico, are one of the most common flowers in many sections of the United States and throughout the world. Their popularity rests on being deeply colorful, easy to cultivate, and able to last throughout the warm months. Marigolds do have a strong smell, however, not the usual pleasant smell that most people associate with flowers.

Like many flowers, marigolds have acquired symbolic meanings throughout the ages. What is unusual about the meanings attached to marigolds is that they are contradictory. Marigolds are said to stand not only for affection but also for cruelty, jealousy, and grief. Discuss with students how all four of these emotions play a role in the changes of Lizabeth's dynamic character in "Marigolds."

been in youth, although it was now bent and drawn. Her smooth skin was a dark reddish-brown, and her face had Indian-like features and the stern stoicism[6] that one associates with Indian faces. Miss Lottie didn't like intruders either, especially children. She never left her yard, and nobody ever visited her. We never knew how she managed those necessities which depend on human interaction—how she ate, for example, or even whether she ate. When we were tiny children, we thought Miss Lottie was a witch and we made up tales, that we half believed ourselves, about her exploits. We were far too sophisticated now, of course, to believe the witch-nonsense. But old fears have a way of clinging like cobwebs, and so when we sighted the tumble-down shack, we had to stop to reinforce our nerves.

"Look, there she is," I whispered, forgetting that Miss Lottie could not possibly have heard me from that distance. "She's fooling with them crazy flowers."

"Yeh, look at 'er."

Miss Lottie's marigolds were perhaps the strangest part of the picture. Certainly they did not fit in with the crumbling decay of the rest of her yard. Beyond the dusty brown yard, in front of the sorry gray house, rose suddenly and shockingly a dazzling strip of bright blossoms, clumped together in enormous mounds, warm and passionate and sun-golden. The old black witch-woman worked on them all summer, every summer, down on her creaky knees, weeding and cultivating and arranging, while the house crumbled and John Burke rocked. For some perverse reason, we children hated those marigolds. They interfered with the perfect ugliness of the place; they were too beautiful; they said too much that we could not understand; they did not make sense. There was something in the vigor with which the old woman destroyed the weeds that intimidated us. It should have been a comical sight—the old woman with the man's hat on her cropped white head, leaning over the bright mounds, her big backside in the air—but it wasn't comical, it was something we could not name. We had to annoy her by whizzing a pebble into her flowers or by yelling a dirty word, then dancing away from her rage, revelling in our youth and mocking her age. Actually, I think it was the flowers we wanted to destroy, but nobody had the nerve to try it, not even Joey, who was usually fool enough to try anything.

"Y'all git some stones," commanded Joey now, and was met with instant giggling obedience as everyone except me began to gather

6. **stoicism** (stō′ i siz′ əm) *n.* indifference to pleasure or pain; impassivity.

Literary Analysis
Static and Dynamic Characters and Cultural Context What differences and similarities does this passage reveal between Miss Lottie's life and the children's experiences?

Reading Strategy
Judging the Characters' Actions What details in this passage tell you why the children dislike Miss Lottie?

14 

Reading Check
What do the children want to destroy?

12 Literary Analysis
Static and Dynamic Characters and Cultural Context

- **Ask** students the Literary Analysis question.
  Answer: Both the children and Miss Lottie are poor, although Miss Lottie is worse off than anyone else. She lives a solitary life, apparently cut off from interaction with the community. Her isolation probably contributed to being labeled a witch by the children.
- Point out to students that the cultural context allows the children to imagine that Miss Lottie is a witch. In a different cultural context—say, that of ancient China—a very old person would be given great honor and respect.

13 Reading Strategy
Judging the Characters' Actions

- **Ask** students the Reading Strategy question.
  Answer: The children dislike Miss Lottie because she is a solitary and isolated "witch-woman," and because she tends obsessively to the shockingly beautiful flowers in a place of "perfect ugliness."
- **Ask** students how people often judge the actions of others that "do not make sense."
  Possible responses: People often fear, mock, or reject actions they do not understand.

14 Reading Check

Answer: The children want to destroy the marigolds.

Differentiated Instruction
Solutions for All Learners

Strategy for Less Proficient Readers
Point out the words that describe the physical placement of elements in the scene: *beyond, in front of, together, over, through, bordered.* Help students visualize the scene by identifying the elements and sketching them: "*beyond* the dusty brown yard," "*in front of* the sorry gray house," the "dazzling strip" of marigolds "clumped *together* in enormous mounds," the old woman "leaning *over,*" the children "peering *through* the bushes," "the bushes that *bordered* the narrow road *in front of* Miss Lottie's place."

Support for English Learners
Point out to students that Collier uses several hyphenated adjectives in "Marigolds." Explain that these compound adjectives are made of two words joined by a hyphen, and that one of the words is often a verb form. Have students list and identify these adjectives: *ill-clad, ill-defined, tumble-down, queer-headed, dew-soaked, age-distorted.* Then help them define these words.

15 Literature in Context

The Great Depression One of President Roosevelt's programs for combating the Depression was the Works Progress Administration, a system of work-relief that gave jobs to many Americans and enabled them to survive. WPA workers built new public buildings and bridges, created parks, and repaired roads. In addition, the WPA had a direct effect on American literature and culture by employing thousands of writers and artists.

Through the WPA, the federal government commissioned writers to create literary works—fiction, nonfiction, and drama—that brought good writing to many people whose hard lives deprived them of fulfilling imaginative experiences. Writers also wrote useful state guidebooks that described in detail the features of each state—from the geographical and political, to the cultural and culinary. The WPA commissioned thousands of artists to paint murals and create sculptures, many of which can still be seen, especially in the nation's public buildings. Eventually the programs of the WPA would evolve into the National Foundation for the Arts and the National Endowment for the Humanities.

Connect to the Literature As students examine the photos, have them think about the details of Lizabeth's life.

Possible responses: Both photographs reflect the poverty and desperation that is also a part of Lizabeth's life, and the bottom picture shows a shanty-town perhaps similar to Lizabeth's. The top picture, however, shows an urban setting with unemployed white men, different from Lizabeth's small-town, African American experience.

Literature in Context

15 History Connection

The Great Depression

The Great Depression was the most severe economic crisis in U.S. history. It started with the U.S. stock market crash in 1929, but the country did not fully recover until the early 1940s. At the depression's worst point, there were sixteen million people unemployed—about one third of the country's work force. Inflation was so high that necessities such as bread were too expensive for most people to buy. The first photograph shown, for example, shows unemployed people lined up to receive free coffee.

The impact of the depression was not limited to the poor, however. Many wealthy members of society who had investments in the stock market lost all their money, completing a total collapse of the prosperity the country had enjoyed throughout the 1920s. Hundreds of thousands of people lost their homes and were forced to live in makeshift shantytowns like the one shown in the second photograph. These settlements were called "Hoovervilles," named after the president, President Herbert Hoover. Hoover was blamed for the problems that led to the Great Depression and for failling to enact measures to save the country from the crisis. In 1932, Franklin Delano Roosevelt was elected, and his "New Deal" policies are credited with ending the crisis and bringing new hope to the nation.

Connect to the Literature

In what ways do you think Lizabeth's poor rural life is similar to what these photographs reveal? In what ways do you think life in her community is different?

pebbles from the dusty ground.

"Come on, Lizabeth."

I just stood there peering through the bushes, torn between wanting to join the fun and feeling that it was all a bit silly.

"You scared, Lizabeth?"

I cursed and spat on the ground—my favorite gesture of phony bravado.[7]

"Y'all children get the stones, I'll show you how to use 'em."

I said before that we children were not consciously aware of how thick were the bars of our cage. I wonder now, though, whether we

7. **bravado** (brə vä′ dō) *n.* pretended courage or defiant courage when one is really afraid.

Enrichment

Hollywood and the Great Depression

When they could afford it, Americans did go to the movies during the Great Depression. In fact, scholars estimate that 60 to 80 million Americans went to the movies each week during the Depression. Along with baseball, movies played a huge role in keeping up American morale.

Many movies addressed the gritty social realities of the time, such as *I Am a Fugitive from a Chain Gang* (1932). However, escapism in the form of zany comedies (The Marx Brothers' *Duck Soup,* 1933), amazing fantasies (*King Kong,* 1933), and "all-singing, all dancing!" musicals (*Forty-Second Street,* 1933) gave people a chance to forget their woes, at least for a little while.

were not more aware of it than I thought. Perhaps we had some dim notion of what we were, and how little chance we had of being anything else. Otherwise, why would we have been so preoccupied with destruction? Anyway, the pebbles were collected quickly, and everybody looked at me to begin the fun.

"Come on, y'all."

We crept to the edge of the bushes that bordered the narrow road in front of Miss Lottie's place. She was working placidly, kneeling over the flowers, her dark hand plunged into the golden mound. Suddenly "zing"—an expertly-aimed stone cut the head off one of the blossoms.

"Who out there?" Miss Lottie's backside came down and her head came up as her sharp eyes searched the bushes. "You better git!"

We had crouched down out of sight in the bushes, where we stifled the giggles that insisted on coming. Miss Lottie gazed warily across the road for a moment, then cautiously returned to her weeding. "Zing"—Joey sent a pebble into the blooms, and another marigold was beheaded.

Miss Lottie was enraged now. She began struggling to her feet, leaning on a rickety cane and shouting, "Y'all git! Go on home!" Then the rest of the kids let loose with their pebbles, storming the flowers and laughing wildly and senselessly at Miss Lottie's impotent rage. She shook her stick at us and started shakily toward the road crying, "Git 'long! John Burke! John Burke, come help!"

Then I lost my head entirely, mad with the power of inciting such rage, and ran out of the bushes in the storm of pebbles, straight toward Miss Lottie chanting madly, "Old witch, fell in a ditch, picked up a penny and thought she was rich!" The children screamed with delight, dropped their pebbles and joined the crazy dance, swarming around Miss Lottie like bees and chanting, "Old lady witch!", while she screamed curses at us. The madness lasted only a moment, for John Burke, startled at last, lurched out of his chair, and we dashed for the bushes just as Miss Lottie's cane went whizzing at my head.

I did not join the merriment when the kids gathered again under the oak in our bare yard. Suddenly I was ashamed, and I did not like being ashamed. The child in me sulked and said it was all in fun, but the woman in me flinched at the thought of the malicious attack that I had led. The mood lasted all afternoon. When we ate the beans and rice that was supper that night, I did not notice my father's silence, for he was always silent these days, nor did I notice my mother's absence, for she always worked well into evening. Joey and I had a particularly bitter argument after supper; his exuberance got on my nerves. Finally I stretched out upon the pallet[8] in the room we shared and fell into a fitful doze.

When I awoke, somewhere in the middle of the night, my mother had returned, and I vaguely listened to the conversation that was **17**

8. **pallet** (pal′ it) *n.* a small bed or a pad filled as with straw and used directly on the floor.

Reading Strategy
Judging the Characters' Actions Do you think Lizabeth and the other children realize that what they are doing is wrong? Explain your answer.

Reading Check
What was Miss Lottie doing when the children arrived at her house?

16 Reading Strategy
Judging the Characters' Actions

- **Ask** students what it is that Lizabeth thinks the children were "more aware of" than she thought.
  Answer: They may have been more aware of the depth and power of the poverty that imprisoned them and that constituted the major part of their cultural context.
- **Ask** students the Reading Strategy question.
  Possible response: Lizabeth and the other children may very well have some sense that what they are doing to Miss Lottie is cruel and wrong. The same "dim notion" they have of the cruelty and wrongness of their poverty may have given them a "dim notion" of the destructive malice of their own actions.

17 Reading Check

Answer: Miss Lottie was "working placidly, kneeling over the flowers."

Differentiated Instruction Solutions for All Learners

Strategy for Less Proficient Readers
Students who have trouble seeing the difference between static and dynamic characters may be helped by a visual demonstration. Draw the visual shown here on the board. **Ask** students which pair of figures represents Joey and which pair represents Lizabeth. Students should realize that Joey is static and Lizabeth is dynamic.

malicious	malicious
Static	
malicious	regretful
Dynamic	

⓲ Literary Analysis
Static and Dynamic Characters

- Remind students that a static character in literature may be multidimensional and even somewhat complex. However, a character that does not significantly *change* is still static.
- **Ask** students the Literary Analysis question.
  Answer: Based on this passage, Lizabeth's mother is a static character—unchangingly persevering and supportive of her husband.

⓳ Reading Strategy
Judging the Characters' Actions

- **Ask** students what they can infer about the father's character from this passage.
  Possible response: Lizabeth's father is a proud and independent man who does not want charity; he wants a job. He had always been strong, but poverty has finally driven him to despair. He cries only after a long and fruitless struggle to provide for himself and his family.
- **Ask** students the Reading Strategy question.
  Possible response: Students are likely to sympathize with Lizabeth's father because, although his intentions are good, he is the victim of social and economic circumstances beyond his control.

audible through the thin walls that separated our rooms. At first I heard no words, only voices. My mother's voice was like a cool, dark room in summer—peaceful, soothing, quiet. I loved to listen to it; it made things seem all right somehow. But my father's voice cut through hers, shattering the peace.

"Twenty-two years, Maybelle, 22 years," he was saying, "and I got nothing for you, nothing, nothing."

"It's all right, honey, you'll get something. Everybody's out of work now, you know that."

"It ain't right. Ain't no man ought to eat his woman's food year in and year out, and see his children running wild. Ain't nothing right about that."

"Honey, you took good care of us when you had it. Ain't nobody got nothing nowadays."

"I ain't talking about nobody else, I'm talking about *me.* God knows
18 I try." My mother said something I could not hear, and my father cried out louder, "What must a man do, tell me that?"

"Look, we ain't starving. I git paid every week, and Mrs. Ellis is real nice about giving me things. She's gonna let me have Mr. Ellis's old coat for you this winter—"

"Forget Mr. Ellis's coat! And forget his money! You think I want white folks' leavings? Oh, Maybelle"—and suddenly he sobbed, loudly and painfully, and cried helplessly and hopelessly in the dark night. I had never heard a man cry before. I did not know men ever cried. I covered my ears with my hands but could not cut off the sound of my father's harsh, painful, despairing sobs. My father was a strong man
19 who could whisk a child upon his shoulders and go singing through the house. My father whittled toys for us and laughed so loud that the great oak seemed to laugh with him, and taught us how to fish and hunt rabbits. How could it be that my father was crying? But the sobs went on, unstifled, finally quieting until I could hear my mother's voice, deep and rich, humming softly as she used to hum to a frightened child.

The world had lost its boundary lines. My mother, who was small and soft, was now the strength of the family; my father, who was the rock on which the family had been built, was sobbing like the tiniest child. Everything was suddenly out of tune, like a broken accordion. Where did I fit into this crazy picture? I do not now remember my thoughts, only a feeling of great bewilderment and fear.

Long after the sobbing and the humming had stopped, I lay on the pallet, still as stone with my hands over my ears, wishing that I too could cry and be comforted. The night was silent now except for the sound of the crickets and of Joey's soft breathing. But the room was too crowded with fear to allow me to sleep, and finally, feeling the terrible aloneness of 4 A.M., I decided to awaken Joey.

"Ouch! What's the matter with you? What you want?" he demanded disagreeably when I had pinched and slapped him awake.

Reading Strategy
Judging the Characters' Actions Do you sympathize with Lizabeth's father in this passage? Explain.

Literary Analysis
Static and Dynamic Characters Based on this passage, would you say that Lizabeth's mother is a static or dynamic character? Why?

Enrichment

Oral Histories of the Depression

Oral histories are audio recordings of personal recollection—memoirs of experiences great and small, momentous and trivial—that convey a vivid sense of the past. Most oral histories exist only on audio recordings, but some of the finest oral histories of the Great Depression were collected and transcribed by Studs Terkel for his book *Hard Times: An Oral History of the Great Depression* (re-released in paperback by W. W. Norton in 2000). As Terkel says, his "memory book" is an attempt to "get the story" directly from the mouths of the era's survivors.

Encourage students to explore the collections of oral histories at The Smithsonian Institution and the Library of Congress, as well as printed collections. The Library of Congress also houses a unique group of written documents called "American Life Histories, Manuscripts from the Federal Writers' Project, 1936-1940." More than 300 writers, as part of a WPA project, produced narratives of the lives of families, historical documentaries that detail the daily lives of American families from education and occupations to views on politics, religion, diet, and a wide variety of miscellaneous observations.

"Come on, wake up."

"What for? Go 'way."

I was lost for a reasonable reply. I could not say, "I'm scared and I don't want to be alone," so I merely said, "I'm going out. If you want to come, come on."

The promise of adventure awoke him. "Going out now? Where to, Lizabeth? What you going to do?"

I was pulling my dress over my head. Until now I had not thought of going out.

"Just come on," I replied tersely.

I was out the window and halfway down the road before Joey caught up with me.

"Wait, Lizabeth, where you going?"

I was running as if the furies[9] were after me, as perhaps they were—running silently and furiously until I came to where I had half-known I was headed: to Miss Lottie's yard.

9. **furies** (fyoor′ ēz) *n.* the three terrible female spirits of Greek and Roman myth with snaky hair who punish the doers of unavenged crimes.

21 **Critical Viewing** In what ways does this photo compare with your impression of Lizabeth's father? **[Compare and Contrast]**

22  **Reading Check** What upsets Lizabeth's father?

20 Humanities

Lunch Hour, 1942, by Joseph Hirsch

Many artists of the 1930s and 1940s felt a close connection to the working class American. The style adopted by these artists is a straightforward realism that enabled them not only to represent working class life with unadorned authenticity but also to reach the general public with works of art that were considered accessible. Although *Lunch Hour* presents a man who might have almost any occupation, it was Joseph Hirsch's father, a well-known surgeon, who posed for the picture.

Ask students: What do you think this lithograph conveys about the man in it?

Possible response: He appears to be very tired, but he may also be depressed or feeling despair.

21 Critical Viewing

Possible responses: The picture shows a resting, perhaps exhausted, man. The image might suggest the despair of Lizabeth's father, although the title of the lithograph suggests that this man has a job and is resting on his lunch hour.

22 Reading Check

Answer: Lizabeth's father is upset because he cannot find a job and provide for his family. He erupts at the thought of accepting someone else's old clothes.

Differentiated Instruction
Solutions for All Learners

Strategy for Advanced Readers

Lizabeth says that she runs "as if the Furies were after me, as perhaps they were." Have students further research the Furies and report on why the classical reference is especially appropriate in this story. (The Furies not only punish crimes; they are especially devoted to family wrongs and blood-guilt. They carry out the curses of a father or a mother. After Lizabeth witnesses her father "curse" his poverty, she rushes out into the night.)

Strategy for Gifted/Talented Students

To help the class feel the emotionally wrenching scene on page 1020 that Lizabeth overhears, have students read the scene aloud as if it were a radio play. Begin the scene with the line "At first I heard no words," and end with the line "great bewilderment and fear." Assign the parts of Lizabeth, her father, and her mother. Identify key words that each character should emphasize in order to convey the ideas and emotions of the scene—for example, *shattering, nothing, right, leavings, helplessly, crying, humming.* Have students rehearse their parts and present the scene to the class.

23 Critical Viewing

Answer: The sky in the picture is not completely dark, but cloudy and dramatic. It suggests the "grotesque" and "haunted" atmosphere described by Lizabeth.

24 Critical Thinking

Recognizing Causes and Effects

- Point out that Lizabeth lists the multiple causes of her present state of mind. **Ask** students to identify them. **Answer:** Lizabeth cites a need for mother, hopelessness of poverty, bewilderment of being both child and woman, and fear at her father's breakdown.
- Point out that Lizabeth says the effect of all these causes was an "impulse toward destruction." **Ask** students to speculate about other possible effects of these causes. **Possible answers:** Other possible effects might be depression, withdrawal into herself, retreat into fantasy, anger at her parents, desire to run away, and a resolve to help her family.

25 Reading Strategy

Judging the Characters' Actions

- Have a student summarize Lizabeth's actions. **Answer:** She jumps on the marigolds and tears them out of the ground.
- **Ask** the Reading Strategy question. **Possible response:** Her malicious, destructive behavior is wrong. She knows it is wrong, but she is unable to control herself.

The half-dawn light was more eerie than complete darkness, and in it the old house was like the ruin that my world had become—foul and crumbling, a grotesque caricature. It looked haunted, but I was not afraid because I was haunted too.

"Lizabeth, you lost your mind?" panted Joey.

24 I had indeed lost my mind, for all the smoldering emotions of that summer swelled in me and burst—the great need for my mother who was never there, the hopelessness of our poverty and degradation, the bewilderment of being neither child nor woman and yet both at once, the fear unleashed by my father's tears. And these feelings combined in one great impulse toward destruction.

"Lizabeth!"

25 I leaped furiously into the mounds of marigolds and pulled madly, trampling and pulling and destroying the perfect yellow blooms. The fresh smell of early morning and of dew-soaked marigolds spurred me on as I went tearing and mangling and sobbing while Joey tugged my dress or my waist crying, "Lizabeth, stop, please stop!"

And then I was sitting in the ruined little garden among the uprooted and ruined flowers, crying and crying, and it was too late to undo what I had done. Joey was sitting beside me, silent and frightened, not knowing what to say. Then, "Lizabeth, look."

I opened my swollen eyes and saw in front of me a pair of large calloused feet; my gaze lifted to the swollen legs, the age-distorted body clad in a tight cotton night

23 ◀ **Critical Viewing** In what ways does this image of the sky compare or contrast with the eerie, half-dawn light that Lizabeth describes? **[Compare and Contrast]**

Reading Strategy
Judging the Characters' Actions Evaluate Lizabeth's behavior in this passage. **[Evaluate]**

dress, and then the shadowed Indian face surrounded by stubby white hair. And there was no rage in the face now, now that the garden was destroyed and there was nothing any longer to be protected.

"M-miss Lottie!" I scrambled to my feet and just stood there and stared at her, and that was the moment when childhood faded and womanhood began. That violent, crazy act was the last act of childhood. For as I gazed at the immobile face with the sad, weary eyes, I gazed upon a kind of reality which is hidden to childhood. The witch was no longer a witch but only a broken old woman who had dared to create beauty in the midst of ugliness and sterility. She had been born in squalor and lived in it all her life. Now at the end of that life she had nothing except a falling-down hut, a wrecked body, and John Burke, the mindless son of her passion. Whatever verve[10] there was left in her, whatever was of love and beauty and joy that had not been squeezed out by life, had been there in the marigolds she had so tenderly cared for.

Of course I could not express the things that I knew about Miss Lottie as I stood there awkward and ashamed. The years have put words to the things I knew in that moment, and as I look back upon it, I know that that moment marked the end of innocence. People

10. **verve** (vurv) *n.* vigor and energy; exuberant enthusiasm, spirit.

27 **▲ Critical Viewing**
Which elements of this painting represent the emotional tone of Lizabeth's memories? **[Connect]**

Vocabulary Builder
squalor (skwäl′ ər) *n.* extremely dirty, unsafe, and unhealthy conditions

28 **Reading Check**
What does Lizabeth say was her "last act of childhood"?

26 Humanities

Moonflowers, 1997, Karl J. Kuerner III

Karl Kuerner (born 1957) seemed destined to be an artist. He grew up surrounded by artists on his family's farm, the site of many of the landscapes painted by the renowned artist Andrew Wyeth. Wyeth became Kuerner's friend and teacher, and later said that the young man's painting "exhibits a strong honest quality that comes from deep within and touches the ordinary in a profound way." Kuerner's paintings are straightforward and yet intimate, realistic and yet primarily composed of strong abstract shapes. **Ask** students the following questions:

1. What is the mood of this painting?
   Possible response: The mood is quiet, serene, reflective.
2. How does the mood of this painting compare with that of the story?
   Possible response: The mood of the narrator is reflective as she remembers the events years later. However, the mood of the specific night of her memory is disturbed, angry, violent, and very sad, whereas the mood of the painting is quiet and content.

27 Critical Viewing

Possible response: Lizabeth's emotional tone may be reflected in the painting's dream-like landscape, the cloudy night sky, and the solitary human figure, apparently alone with nature and her thoughts.

28 Reading Check

Answer: Lizabeth says her "last act of childhood" was the "violent, crazy act" of destroying the marigolds.

Differentiated Instruction
Solutions for All Learners

Support for Special Needs Students
Students may need help in understanding the emotional growth that Lizabeth describes. Point out that many people do things that they do not fully understand at the time. Later, as they grow up and gain experience of themselves and the world, they are able to look back, gain perspective, and understand why they did certain things. This *progress toward self-knowledge* is what "Marigolds" is about. Remind students that, when they judge a character's actions, they need to take into account the age and experience of the character.

Strategy for Advanced Readers
Point out to students that Collier does not tell readers how the nighttime scene in front of Miss Lottie's house ends. What exactly does Miss Lottie do? What does she feel? What exactly does Lizabeth say? (Note that on the next page she refers to "wild contrition.") What does Joey do? **Ask** students to write a more detailed ending. Encourage them to show how and why Lizabeth and Miss Lottie express themselves in the following moments.

29 Literary Analysis
Static and Dynamic Characters

Ask students the Literary Analysis question.

Possible responses: Lizabeth has grown emotionally and become a compassionate woman. She is now able to look back with understanding on her own childhood. Because she has "planted marigolds," she has recognized how much she has in common with Miss Lottie.

30 Critical Viewing

Possible responses: The road is an accurate symbol for Lizabeth's life because she has "traveled" emotionally and made "progress" on the path to maturity. The road is not an accurate symbol because it erroneously suggests that gaining maturity and understanding is a straight line with inevitable "progress" as one gets older.

think of the loss of innocence as meaning the loss of virginity, but this is far from true. Innocence involves an unseeing acceptance of things at face value, an ignorance of the area below the surface. In that humiliating moment I looked beyond myself and into the depths of another person. This was the beginning of compassion, and one cannot have both compassion and innocence. 29

The years have taken me worlds away from that time and that place, from the dust and squalor of our lives and from the bright thing that I destroyed in a blind childish striking out at God-knows-what. Miss Lottie died long ago and many years have passed since I last saw her hut, completely barren at last, for despite my wild contrition she never planted marigolds again. Yet, there are times when the image of those passionate yellow mounds returns with a painful poignancy. For one does not have to be ignorant and poor to find that his life is barren as the dusty yards of our town. And I too have planted marigolds.

Literary Analysis
Static and Dynamic Characters In what ways has Lizabeth changed since the beginning of the story?

30 **◄ Critical Viewing**
Do you think the road is an accurate symbol for Lizabeth's life? Why or why not? **[Interpret]**

Vocabulary Builder
poignancy (poiˊ nyən sē) *n.* a state of deeply felt distress or sorrow

Critical Reading

1. **Respond:** What did you find admirable or disappointing about the narrator?
2. **(a) Recall:** When does the narrator remember marigolds? **(b) Compare and Contrast:** In what ways do the marigolds differ from the other things she recalls? **(c) Infer:** What do these differences suggest about the narrator's childhood?
3. **(a) Recall:** To what does the narrator compare poverty? **(b) Interpret:** What does this comparison suggest about the narrator's view of her poverty?
4. **(a) Recall:** Why do the children hate the marigolds? **(b) Compare and Contrast:** In what ways do Lizabeth's feelings after the attack on Miss Lottie differ from Joey's feelings? **(c) Infer:** Why do you think their feelings differ?
5. **(a) Recall:** What event upsets Lizabeth in the middle of the night? **(b) Analyze Cause and Effect:** How does this event lead to the destruction of the marigolds?
6. **(a) Analyze:** What does the narrator mean when she says that one "does not have to be ignorant and poor to realize one's life is barren as the dusty yards of our town"? **(b) Interpret:** What do you think the narrator means when she says "I, too, have planted marigolds?"

Go Online Author Link
For: More about Eugenia W. Collier
Visit: www.PHSchool.com
Web Code: ere-9603

ASSESS
Answers

1. Sample answers may include Lizabeth's ability to admit when she is wrong and her patience with her younger brother, both of which are admirable. Her insensitivity towards Miss Lottie and John Burke, as well as her destructive tantrum, are disappointing.
2. (a) She remembers the marigolds whenever she thinks of her hometown. (b) The marigolds are brilliantly colored, alive, and beautiful. Everything else—dust, shanties, dirt roads—is colorless and ugly. (c) The differences suggest that her childhood is poor, with little beauty or liveliness.
3. (a) She compares poverty to a cage. (b) It suggests she views poverty as a prison she was unable to escape, an environment that affected her behavior.
4. (a) The children hate the marigolds because they "interfere with the perfect ugliness" of the place. (b) Joey feels happy and exuberant, but Lizabeth is ashamed. (c) Joey is still a child and has not developed compassion or understanding, but Lizabeth is becoming an adult and feels ashamed of her childish malice.
5. (a) She hears her father sobbing because he cannot find a job, and she hears her mother comforting him as if he were a child. (b) The event makes her feel afraid and so angry about her family's hopelessness and helplessness that she throws a tantrum. The object of her rage is the one thing she is able to destroy—the marigolds.
6. (a) **Possible response:** A person's life can lack beauty or friendship or compassion even if the person is not poor or ignorant. (b) **Possible response:** She has made efforts to create beauty in some way in her own life.

Go Online Author Link For additional information about Eugenia Collier, have students type in the Web Code and then select Eugenia Collier.

Apply the Skills

Marigolds

Literary Analysis

Static and Dynamic Characters

1. **(a)** Is Lizabeth a **static** or a **dynamic character**? **(b)** Cite two examples from the story to support your answer.
2. Is Lizabeth's brother Joey a static or a dynamic character? Explain.
3. Classify Miss Lottie as either a static or dynamic character. Support your answer.

Connecting Literary Elements

4. Use the **cultural context** of Lizabeth's family to explain the motives or reasons behind her destructive act.
5. What cultural meaning does the dust have for Lizabeth?
6. **(a)** Explain the role that hope plays in Lizabeth's life. **(b)** In what ways does it affect her behavior?

Reading Strategy

Judging the Character's Actions

7. **(a)** What do you think of Joey's actions throughout the story? **(b)** In what ways do you think he influenced Lizabeth's actions? **(c)** In what ways did Lizabeth influence Joey's behavior?
8. At the end of the story, Lizabeth explains that she saw Miss Lottie first from a child's perspective and then from an adult's perspective. Use the chart shown to record the differences between these two perspectives.

Miss Lottie

Lizabeth as a child:	
Lizabeth as an adult:	

9. **(a)** Review Lizabeth's actions throughout the story. Identify at least two actions that you judge to be right and two that you judge to be wrong. **(b)** How would you have behaved if you faced similar circumstances? Explain your answer.

Extend Understanding

Cultural Connection

10. In the story, Lizabeth compares poverty to a "trap" and a "cage." **(a)** In what ways do you see poverty as a "trap" today? **(b)** In what ways can our society and our government help those trapped in poverty?

QuickReview

A **static character** is one whose attitudes and behavior remain essentially stable throughout a literary work.

A **dynamic character** experiences a shift or change in attitude or behavior during the course of a work.

Cultural context is the social and economic environment that the characters inhabit.

To **judge the characters' actions,** evaluate their behaviors and actions according to your standards of right and wrong.

For: Self-Test
Visit: www.PHSchool.com
Web Code: era-6603

Answers

1. (a) Lizabeth is a dynamic character: she changes in attitude and behavior through the course of the story. (b) She feels ashamed of throwing stones and screaming rude things at Miss Lottie; she regrets her destructive, childish behavior and recognizes that she is becoming an adult.
2. Lizabeth's brother is a static character: he does not change through the course of the story.
3. She is dynamic: she changes—at least in Lizabeth's mind—from an angry "witch" to a broken old woman. She is static: the author does not show us any changes in her character.
4. Lizabeth's family is very poor, without enough money to keep the family together. They are without hope in an ugly, barren neighborhood. The marigolds enrage Lizabeth because Miss Lottie dares to try to make her ugly yard beautiful despite overwhelming poverty.
5. **Possible responses:** The dust means barrenness and poverty. The people of Lizabeth's community are too poor to have green lawns.
6. **Possible responses:** The absence of hope is common in Lizabeth's community. Hopelessness is the core of the scene with Lizabeth's father and mother. (b) The hopelessness makes her angry and motivates her destruction of the marigolds, which she sees as a hopeless attempt at beauty amidst poverty.
7. (a) **Possible responses:** Joey's actions are mean, such as his destruction of Lizabeth's picture and his attack on the flowers. (b) It is Joey who suggests that they go to Miss Lottie's home, and Joey eggs Lizabeth on the first time they attack the marigolds. (c) As Joey's older sister, Lizabeth has influence over him. When she begins to taunt Miss Lottie, he joins her. He follows her on the night she destroys the marigolds.
8. **Possible responses:** As a child: "witch"; mean; scary. As an adult: old broken woman, trying to have a little joy and beauty; sad, defeated, vulnerable.

Another sample answer can be found on Reading Strategy Graphic Organizer B, p. 225 in ***Graphic Organizer Transparencies.***

9. (a) **Possible responses:** Actions judged to be right may include contrition over destructive behavior, shame about the first attack on Miss Lottie, concern for her father. Actions judged to be wrong may include the two attacks on Miss Lottie's flowers, fighting with her brother, thinking her brother is "vastly inferior" to her, the fact that she led the other children in the first attack. (b) Students' answers should include their reasons and should take age, economic situation, and emotional states into account.
10. **Possible responses:** (a) Inflation, unemployment, low salaries, lack of education, and housing issues can "trap" people in poverty because these things prevent them from getting ahead. (b) The government can raise the minimum wage, create better schools, and fund more charities.

Go Online Assessment Students may use the **Self-test** to prepare for **Selection Test A** or **Selection Test B.**

EXTEND/ASSESS

Answers

1 Vocabulary Lesson

Word Analysis

1. Branch of biology that deals with form and structure of animals and plants
2. Special-effects process in film or video production in which persons or objects change form or shape
3. Transformation; change in form, shape, structure, or substance
4. Substance that can crystallize in different forms

Spelling Strategy

1. pallor
2. collar
3. polar
4. bother

Vocabulary Builder

1. retribution
2. poignancy
3. nostalgia
4. squalor
5. amorphous

2 Grammar and Style Lesson

1. than
2. then
3. then
4. than
5. then

Writing Application

Paragraphs should be consistent with the characters and events of the story. Check to see that students have used both *then* and *than* correctly at least once.

WG Writing and Grammar, Ruby Level

Students will find further instruction and practice on the use of *then* and *than* in Chapter 25, Section 2.

Build Language Skills

1 Vocabulary Lesson

Word Analysis: Greek Root *-morph-*

The Greek root *-morph-* means "form." *Amorphous* means "without form." With this knowledge, define the following words. Use a dictionary to check your definitions.

1. morphology
2. morphing
3. metamorphosis
4. polymorph

Spelling Strategy

The "er" sound can be spelled with *er, ar,* or *or.* For example, in *squalor, or* spells the "er" sound. When you are uncertain about the spelling of a word with the "er" sound, consult a dictionary. Complete the spelling of each word.

1. pall__r
2. coll__r
3. pol__r
4. both__r

Vocabulary Builder: Sentence Completion

Consult the vocabulary list on page 1011 and review the way each word is used in the context of the story. Then, select the vocabulary word that fits best in each of the following sentences.

1. The family demanded _____ for the wrongs committed against it.
2. The _____ of the eulogy given by the fallen hero's grandson was overwhelming.
3. A visit to the old baseball field evoked a sense of _____ in the retired player.
4. The apartment was so filthy that it was clear that the previous tenants had lived in _____.
5. Jeanne's _____ ideas for a story began to take shape with the help of her classmates.

2 Grammar and Style Lesson

Commonly Confused Words: *then* and *than*

Then and *than* are two examples of commonly confused words that look or sound alike but have different meanings. *Then* is an adverb that means "at that time, next in order, next in time," or "in that case; therefore." *Than* is a conjunction that is often used to introduce the second element of a comparison. It is also used to express an exception.

Correct use of *then*: We children made a game of thinking of ways to disturb John Burke and ***then*** elude his violent retribution. (Here, *then* means "next in time.")

Correct use of *than*: ...the two babies having been sent to live with relatives who might care for them better ***than*** we. (Here, *than* introduces the second element of a comparison, *we,* which is being compared to *relatives.*)

Practice Complete each sentence correctly, using either *then* or *than.*

1. Lizabeth is older _____ Joey.
2. The kids collected rocks and _____ threw them at Miss Lottie's flowers.
3. Back _____, candy bars and gum only cost a nickel.
4. Miss Lottie knew that the guilty party was none other _____ Lizabeth.
5. If you didn't hear me last time, _____ you'd better listen now!

Writing Application Write a paragraph about one of the characters in this story. In the paragraph, use the words *then* and *than* correctly at least once.

WG *Prentice Hall Writing and Grammar Connection: Chapter 25, Section 2*

Assessment Practice

Grammar and Usage **(For more practice, see *Standardized Test Preparation Workbook*, p. 74.)**

Many tests require students to recognize and correct errors in grammar and usage. Use the following sample item to help students practice this skill.

Eugenia Collier's collection called *Breeder and Other Stories* were published in 1994.

Choose the best way to rewrite the underlined section of the passage. If the underlined section needs no change, choose "Correct as is."

A was published
B had been published
C could have been published
D Correct as is.

The best way to rewrite the underlined section is to rewrite it for correct verb usage. The correct answer is *A*.

Writing Lesson

Advice Column

Collier's story presents Lizabeth's guilt over her actions. Write an advice column in response to a brief letter from Lizabeth in which she asks what she should do to make up for her destruction of Miss Lottie's marigold bed. As a columnist, propose specific actions and support your advice with solid reasoning and evidence.

Prewriting: First, list the elements and results of Lizabeth's offense. Then, identify ways she could make retribution to Miss Lottie. Keep in mind Lizabeth's financial limitations. Next, decide on the best advice. Then, provide several reasons to persuade Lizabeth to follow your advice.

Draft: Begin your response by expressing support and praise for Lizabeth's desire to make up for her behavior. Then, summarize your proposed action. Elaborate each point with logical arguments, reasons, or facts.

Model: Elaborate to Support an Argument

First, apologize to Miss Lottie because it is the mature thing to do. According to psychologists, apologizing allows both people to heal and reduces stress.

Coherent reasons and expert evidence help support an argument.

Revising: Reread your column to be sure that Lizabeth's problem and your response are clearly stated. Consider additional reasons and support you might add to make your advice more persuasive.

Prentice Hall Writing and Grammar Connection: Chapter 11, Connected Assignment

Extend Your Learning

Research and Technology During the time period of this story, many poor African Americans, lured by the opportunities offered by the cities, left their rural hometowns in what became known as the "Great Migration." With a partner, conduct library and Internet research to learn more about the Great Migration of African Americans. Create a **bar graph** that depicts the number of people that migrated to northern cities between 1910 and 1930, and a series of **pie charts** that depict population percentages of African Americans in rural versus urban settings before and after the Great Migration. Present your work to your classmates. **[Group Activity]**

Listening and Speaking As Lizabeth, write a **eulogy** for Miss Lottie's memorial service. Use the following tips as a guide:

- Mention two or three special qualities that Miss Lottie may have possessed, based on the information you have of her.
- Explain how she enhanced your life.

After you have rehearsed enough to feel comfortable speaking aloud, present the eulogy to your class.

For: An additional research activity
Visit: www.PHSchool.com
Web Code: erd-7603

3 Writing Lesson

- Use the **Support for Writing Lesson,** p. 46 in ***Unit 6 Resources,*** to help students in writing this advice column.
- Review the story's central event with students. Then, read through the Writing Lesson and help students address the prompt in the Prewriting section.
- Urge students to focus first on identifying their central piece of advice. They can then develop supporting arguments.
- Use the Problem-Solution Essay rubrics, pp. 59–60 in ***General Resources*** to evaluate students' work.

4 Listening and Speaking

- Review the definition of a eulogy with students, and invite any volunteers who have delivered or heard eulogies to share their knowledge.
- Encourage students to scan the selection for details about Miss Lottie.
- Remind students to use formal speaking guidelines in delivering their eulogies: Speak clearly and slowly, make eye contact, and confine movement to appropriate gestures.
- Give students a copy of the rubric for Speaking: Delivering a Speech, p. 89 in ***General Resources,*** to help them as they prepare their eulogies.
- The **Support for Extend Your Learning** page (***Unit 6 Resources,*** p. 47) provides guided note-taking opportunities to help students complete the Extend Your Learning activities.

Go Online Research: Have students type in the Web Code for another research activity.

Assessment Resources

The following resources can be used to assess students' knowledge and skills.

Unit 6 Resources
- **Selection Test A,** pp. 49–51
- **Selection Test B,** pp. 52–54

General Resources
- **Rubric for Exposition: Problem-Solution Essay,** pp. 59–60
- **Rubric for Speaking: Delivering a Speech,** p. 89

Go Online Assessment: Students may use the **Self-test** to prepare for **Selection Test A** or **Selection Test B.**

Meeting Your Standards

Students will

1. **analyze and respond to literary elements.**
   - Literary Analysis: Tone
2. **read, comprehend, analyze, and critique a short story.**
   - Reading Strategy: Visualizing
   - Reading Check questions
   - Apply the Skills questions
3. **develop vocabulary.**
   - Vocabulary Lesson: Word Analysis: The meanings of *dis-*
4. **understand and apply written and oral language conventions.**
   - Spelling Strategy
   - Grammar and Style Lesson: Using *Like, As,* and *As If*
5. **develop writing proficiency.**
   - Writing Lesson: Critical Response
6. **develop appropriate research strategies.**
   - Extend Your Learning: Debate
7. **understand and apply listening and speaking strategies.**
   - Extend Your Learning: Monologue

Block Scheduling: Use one 90-minute class period to preteach the skills and have students read the selection. Use a second 90-minute class period to assess students' mastery of skills, extend their learning, and monitor their progress.

Homework Suggestions

Following are possibilities for homework assignments.

- Support pages from ***Unit 6 Resources:***
  Literary Analysis
  Reading Strategy
  Vocabulary Builder
  Grammar and Style
- An Extend Your Learning project and the Writing Lesson for this selection group may be completed over several days.

Step-by-Step Teaching Guide	Pacing Guide
PRETEACH	
• Administer Vocabulary and Reading Warm-ups as necessary.	5 min.
• Engage students' interest with the motivation activity.	5 min.
• Read and discuss author and background features. **FT**	10 min.
• Introduce the Literary Analysis Skill: Tone. **FT**	5 min.
• Introduce the Reading Strategy: Visualizing. **FT**	10 min.
• Prepare students to read by teaching the selection vocabulary. **FT**	
TEACH	
• Informally monitor comprehension while students read independently or in groups. **FT**	30 min.
• Monitor students' comprehension with the Reading Check notes.	as students read
• Reinforce vocabulary with Vocabulary Builder notes.	as students read
• Develop students' understanding of tone with the Literary Analysis annotations. **FT**	5 min.
• Develop students' ability to visualize with the Reading Strategy annotations. **FT**	5 min.
ASSESS/EXTEND	
• Assess students' comprehension and mastery of the Literary Analysis and Reading Strategy by having them answer the Apply the Skills questions. **FT**	15 min.
• Have students complete the Vocabulary Lesson and the Grammar and Style Lesson. **FT**	15 min.
• Apply students' ability to use literary evidence by using the Writing Lesson. **FT**	45 min. or homework
• Apply students' understanding by using one or more of the Extend Your Learning activities.	20–90 min. or homework
• Administer Selection Test A or Selection Test B. **FT**	15 min.

Resources

PRINT
Unit 6 Resources
Vocabulary Warm-up Word Lists **[L1, L2, EL]** ....p. 55
Vocabulary Warm-up Practice **[L1, L2, EL]** ....p. 56
Reading Warm-up A **[L1, L2, EL]** ....p. 57
Reading Warm-up B **[L1, L2, L3]** ....p. 58

TRANSPARENCY
Graphic Organizer Transparencies
Literary Analysis Graphic Organizer A **[L3]** ....p. 228
Literary Analysis Graphic Organizer B **[L1, L2, EL]** ....p. 229
Reading Strategy Graphic Organizer A **[L3]** ....p. 226
Reading Strategy Graphic Organizer B **[L1, L2, EL]** ....p. 227

PRINT
Reader's Notebook [L2]
Reader's Notebook: Adapted Version [L1]
Reader's Notebook: English Learner's Version [EL]
Unit 6 Resources
Literary Analysis **[L3]** ....p. 59
Reading Strategy **[L3]** ....p. 60
Vocabulary Builder **[L3]** ....p. 61

TECHNOLOGY
Listening to Literature Audio CDs [L2, EL]

PRINT
Unit 6 Resources
Grammar and Style **[L3]** ....p. 62
Support for Writing Lesson **[L3]** ....p. 63
Support for Extend Your Learning **[L3]** ....p. 64
Enrichment **[L4]** ....p. 65
Selection Test A **[L1, L2, EL]** ....pp. 66–68
Selection Test B **[L3, L4]** ....pp. 69–71
General Resources
Rubrics for Response to Literature **[L3]** ....pp. 65–66

TECHNOLOGY
Go Online: Research **[L3]**
Go Online: Self-test **[L3]**
***ExamView®* Test Bank [L3]**

Choosing Resources for Differentiated Instruction

[L1] Special Needs Students
[L2] Below-Level Students
[L3] All Students
[L4] Advanced Students
[EL] English Learners

For Vocabulary and Reading Warm-ups and for Selection Tests, **A** signifies "less challenging" and **B** "more challenging." For Graphic Organizer transparencies, **A** signifies "not filled in" and **B** "filled in."

FT Fast Track Instruction: To move the lesson more quickly, use the strategies and activities identified with **FT**.

Scaffolding for Less Proficient and Advanced Students

The leveled Critical Thinking questions after selections progress in the levels of thinking required to answer them. To address the needs of your different students, you may use the (a) level questions for your less proficient students and the (b) level questions with your on-level and advanced students. The occasional (c) level questions are appropriate for your advanced students.

PRENTICE HALL **TeacherEXPRESS™** Plan · Teach · Assess
Use this complete suite of powerful teaching tools to make lesson planning and testing quicker and easier.

PRENTICE HALL **StudentEXPRESS™** Learn · Study · Succeed
Use the interactive textbook (online and on CD-ROM) to make selections and activities come alive with audio and video support and interactive questions.

Go Online Professional Development
For: Information about Lexiles
Visit: www.PHSchool.com
Web Code: eue-1111

PREteach

Motivation

Sometimes moments that seem inconsequential from the outside are actually important turning points in people's lives. Ask students to think about times when something very ordinary—for example, completing an everyday task, facing a small disappointment, or having a minor disagreement with someone—has had an outsized effect on how they see the world. Instruct students to write journal entries describing the experience and how it affected them. Journal entries should attempt to explain how something so ordinary could actually be so significant. If their topics are not too personal, encourage volunteers to read their journal entries to the class.

1 Background

More About the Author

Writing *Jim the Boy* proved to be a monumental struggle for Tony Earley. As the deadline for his first novel approached, Earley found himself trapped by the pressure to achieve brilliance. He composed some 150 pages of one story before deciding it was a false start and abandoning it. Periodically plagued by depression throughout his life, he now sank into it deeply.

Earley found the solution to his personal and artistic crisis in E.B. White's *Charlotte's Web.* The book inspired him primarily in terms of its style. In its seemingly simple prose and story, Earley saw depth. He decided to write the story of Jim Glass's youth, using straightforward language that would enable him to capture emotional truths that a flashier novel might miss. Published in 2000, the finished novel was praised by *The New York Times, Time Magazine, Newsweek, The Chicago Tribune,* and countless authors.

1 Aliceville

Tony Earley (b. 1961)

Tony Earley decided to become a writer at the ripe old age of seven. "My second-grade teacher made us write a story every Monday about what we did over the weekend. And one Monday morning she read mine and said, 'This is very good. You should be a writer.' I thought, 'OK, I'll be a writer,' and I never really got over that." After his second-grade teacher set him on the path to becoming a writer, Earley says he found himself narrating his daily experiences in his head, almost as if they were short stories.

Earley was born in San Antonio, Texas, but his parents, who originally hailed from North Carolina, moved the family back to that state before he was two. His upbringing in North Carolina is reflected in the settings and characters of his fiction and essays. Earley spent his boyhood in Rutherford County, a place much like the fictional Aliceville of the story he later wrote. Many of his characters are farmers or live in farming communities like the ones where his parents and grandparents grew up.

Family Tragedy The death of his sister, while Earley was attending Warren Wilson College in North Carolina, affected him deeply, darkening his view of life. After graduating, he worked for four years as a newspaper writer. However, he felt that newspaper work did not satisfy his need to write about life more deeply, so he attended graduate school at the University of Alabama. Soon he began publishing stories in increasingly prominent journals, like *The New Yorker* and *Harper's.* In 1996, Tony Earley was hailed as one of the best young writers in the country by the influential journal *Granta.*

The Character of Jim Glass Earley's novel *Jim the Boy* (2001) focuses on the character of Jim Glass, who is the narrator of "Aliceville." Earley wrote three stories about Jim and then decided to write a novel with him at its heart. The novel, which became a national bestseller, was also inspired by the children's classic *Charlotte's Web,* by E. B. White, a book Earley first discovered as an adult when his wife read it to him. He decided that he wanted to write a contemporary adult novel that used the conventions of the children's book. Earley says that he is "a long way from finished" with the character of Jim Glass and may write several sequels to *Jim the Boy.*

Earley currently teaches creative writing at Vanderbilt University in Nashville, Tennessee. His other books are *Here We Are in Paradise* (1994), a collection of short stories, and *Somehow Form a Family* (2001), a collection of essays. Earley has said of his work, which mixes fiction and autobiographical elements:

> Memory and imagination seem to me the same human property, known by different names. Clark Kent and Superman are, after all, the same muscular guy; the only difference between them lies in how they are packaged and perceived. While it is necessary for our sanity to keep the line between fiction and nonfiction clearly drawn, that particular boundary, as with the boundaries between nations, is more arbitrary than we might care to think. Good novels and short stories are most often praised as "true" by critics, while successful memoirs are invariably compared to novels. The personal essayist recounting a conversation he participated in twenty-five years ago . . . and the short story writer making up a conversation between fictional characters are basically engaged in the same exercise. Both are taking subjective human experience and converting it into narrative.

Preview

Connecting to the Literature

Sometimes one incident provides a clear dividing line between childhood and adulthood. "Aliceville" focuses on such a moment, an experience that leaves the main character feeling older and wiser—and sadder.

2 Literary Analysis

Tone

The **tone** of a literary work is the writer's attitude toward his or her subject and audience. The tone may be serious or playful, analytical or emotional, sarcastic or sympathetic. Tone comes chiefly from a writer's word choice—through the emotional associations and images that the words create. Notice the simple but vivid words that set the scene and the tone for "Aliceville":

> This was in December, on one of those still evenings in the new part of winter when you cannot decide whether it is a good thing to inhale deeply, the air is so clear and sharp.

As you read "Aliceville," listen for the tone that Earley's narrator uses as he takes you further into his confidence.

Connecting Literary Elements

Imagery refers to language that appeals to the senses of sight, hearing, touch, taste, and smell. Images can draw readers into a literary work by creating the sensory feel of actual experience. Imagery also influences tone. As you step into the world of "Aliceville," enjoy the way the sights, sounds, and other sensations make this imaginary place so real.

3 Reading Strategy

Visualizing

When you **visualize** a written text, you form a mental image of what you are reading—the scenes and actions described by the writer's words. Visualizing helps you enter the world of the story and follow the action. The narrator of "Aliceville" uses visual details to paint memorable word pictures of his family members, of the town, of nature, and of the story's central experience. Look at this description of a flock of geese:

> The geese flew across the field and turned in a climbing curve against the wooded ridge on the other side of the creek, back the way they had come, toward Uncle Zeno and me.

You might be able to visualize this scene by imagining the "climbing curve" of the geese flying out one way and then turning back. As you read, record other especially vivid details in a chart like the one shown.

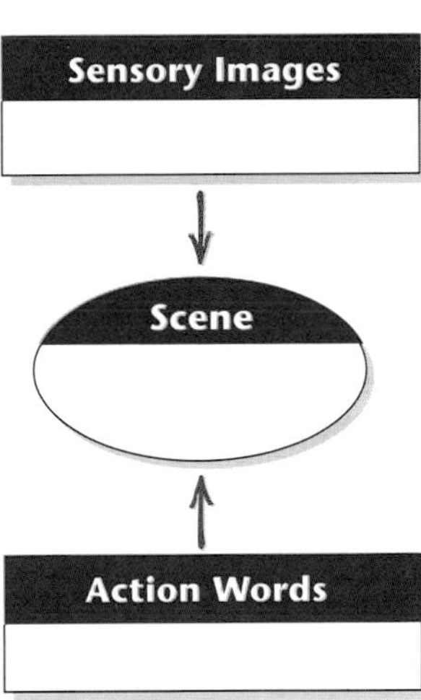

Vocabulary Builder

revelation (rev´ ə lā´ shən) *n.* discovery (p. 1031)

excluded (eks klo͞od´ id) *v.* kept out (p. 1035)

allegiances (ə lē´ jəns əz) *n.* loyalties (p. 1035)

disdain (dis dān´) *n.* scorn (p. 1036)

stealthy (stel´ thē) *adj.* avoiding detection (p. 1041)

gingerly (jin´ jər lē) *adv.* very carefully, cautiously (p. 1042)

Differentiated Instruction

Solutions for All Learners

Support for Special Needs Students

Have students complete the **Preview** and **Build Skills** pages for "Aliceville" in the ***Reader's Notebook: Adapted Version.*** These pages provide a selection summary, an abbreviated presentation of the reading and literary skills, and the graphic organizer on the **Build Skills** page in the student book.

Support for Less Proficient Readers

Have students complete the **Preview** and **Build Skills** pages for "Aliceville" in the ***Reader's Notebook***. These pages provide a selection summary, an abbreviated presentation of the reading and literary skills, and the graphic organizer on the **Build Skills** page in the student book.

Support for English Learners

Have students complete the **Preview** and **Build Skills** pages for "Aliceville" in the ***Reader's Notebook: English Learner's Version.*** These pages provide a selection summary, an abbreviated presentation of the skills, additional contextual vocabulary, and the graphic organizer on the **Build Skills** page in the student book.

2 Literary Analysis

Tone

- Explain to students that the *tone* of a literary work is the writer's attitude towards his or her subject. For example, a writer might have a warm, affectionate tone describing his or her hometown or a cold and angry tone when describing someone who has mistreated him or her.
- Point out to students that the main tool writers use to create tone is word choice. The words that writers use have an emotional content that reveals the writer's feelings about his or her subject—and helps shape readers' feelings about that subject.
- Read the passage from "Aliceville" with the class. Discuss its tone with students, guiding them to recognize that the simple but vivid language reveals the importance Earley sees in the seemingly ordinary. Encourage students to continue looking for tone as they read "Aliceville."

3 Reading Strategy

Visualizing

- Explain to students that when they visualize, they are forming mental images of what they read. Students can use this strategy to enter the worlds writers create. Point out that visualizing is especially useful when reading texts as rich in imagery as "Aliceville."
- Give students a copy of **Reading Strategy Graphic Organizer A,** (*Graphic Organizer Transparencies,* p. 226). Then, read the passage from "Aliceville" to the class. Lead the class to identify the *sensory image* (a flock of geese flying), the *scene* (a wooded ridge near a creek), and *action words* from the passage (*flew, climbing curve*).
- Discuss the passage with the class. Ask students to describe how they visualize the scene. Encourage them to use this chart as they read "Aliceville."

Vocabulary Builder

- Pronounce each vocabulary word for students, and read the definitions as a class. Have students identify any words with which they are already familiar.

5 Literary Analysis
Tone

- Remind students that tone is the writer's attitude toward his or her subject. In literary works with first-person narrators, such as "Aliceville," tone can describe the narrator's attitude toward the people, places, and events he or she describes for readers. Remind students that writers create tone through their word choice.
- Have students read the bracketed passage. Ask students to **identify** words and phrases that help create the tone. You may want to write the words and phrases on the board.
  Possible response: Words and phrases include *climbing curve, great wings, as if they had been ghosts, listened to our blood,* and *the winter silence.*
- Have students consider the words and phrases on the board. Then **ask** them to identify the narrator's tone, or attitude, as he describes what he and Uncle Zeno saw.
  Possible response: Jim's tone is one of wonder at the sight of the geese. His description makes the geese seem more beautiful and mysterious than they might otherwise appear to be.
- You may wish to discuss the effect of this passage's tone with students. Suggest to the class that readers can feel the narrator's sense of wonder at the geese and share his attitude towards this moment. Have students consider how their perceptions might change along with the narrator's tone.

3 so close and flying so fast that they seemed in danger of crashing into the truck. Their rising shouts and the rushing sound of their wings, coming on us so suddenly, were as loud and frightening as unexpected gunshots, and as strange to our ears as ancient tongues. Uncle Zeno slammed on the brakes so hard that the truck fishtailed[1] in the gravel and left us crosswise in the road, facing the bottom.

5 The geese flew across the field and turned in a climbing curve against the wooded ridge on the other side of the creek, back the way they had come, toward Uncle Zeno and me. They spread out their great wings, beating straight downward in short strokes, catching themselves in the air, and settled into the short corn stubble, probably a half mile from the road. And they disappeared then, in the middle of the field as we watched, through the distance and the dim winter light, as completely as if they had been ghosts. Uncle Zeno turned off the headlights, and then the engine, and we leaned forward and stared out into the growing darkness, until the ridge was black against the sky. Canadian geese just did not on an ordinary day fly over the small place in which we lived our lives. We did not speak at first, and listened to our blood, and the winter silence around us, and wondered at the thing we had seen.

We decided on the way home, the sounds of flight still wild in our ears, that the geese bedded down in the

1. **fishtailed** *v.* swung from side to side in the back.

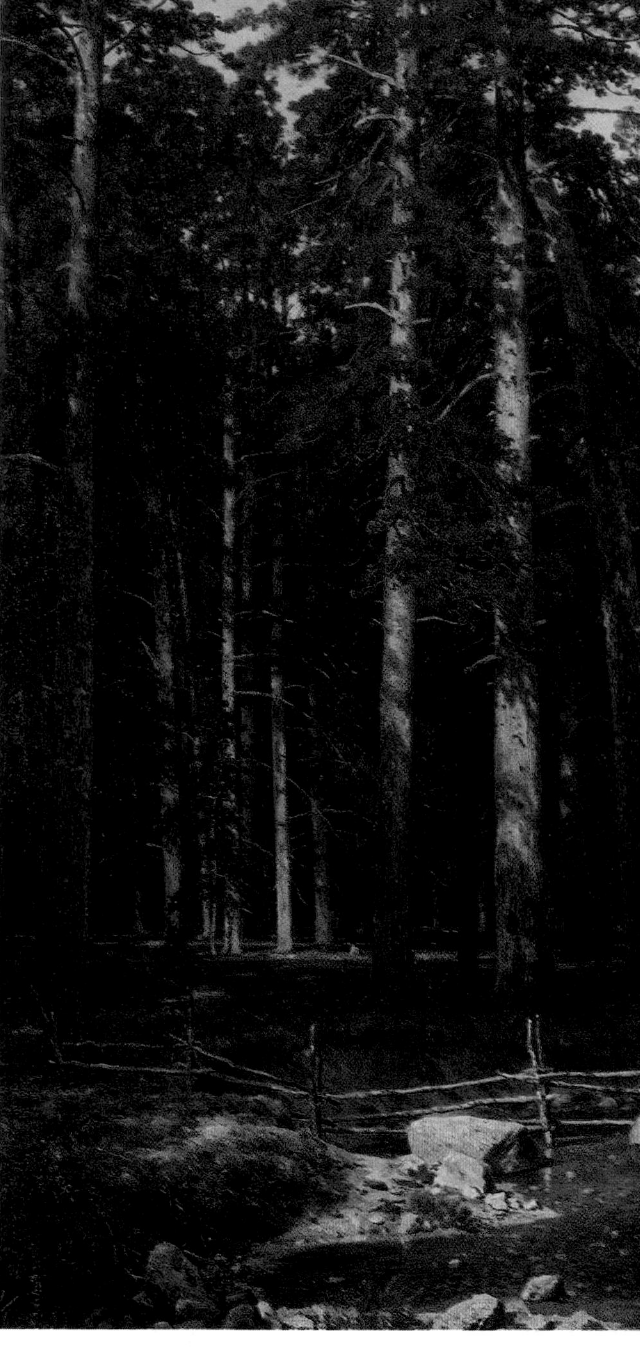

6 ▶ **Critical Viewing** What elements in this landscape remind you of the landscape described in the story? **[Connect]**

Enrichment

Canada Geese

The words *goose* and *geese* are applied to a range of different birds. Actual geese, however, are water birds closely related to ducks and swans. The geese that Jim and Uncle Zeno see in "Aliceville" are Canada geese, *Branta canadensis,* the most common species of goose in North America. These birds have black feathers on their heads, tails, and necks, and brown-feathered bodies. They can be as large as 45 inches from beak to tail.

Canada geese are migratory birds. Each year, they move among nesting grounds that stretch from the arctic reaches of Alaska and Canada to the American prairie states. Geese migrate to find warmer nesting grounds in winter and cooler ones in summer, but other factors, such as the availability of food and water, play a role as well. Flocks of geese fly in a formation that resembles a letter V. In the spring or fall, you may see flocks of these birds forming giant, moving Vs in the sky.

❻ Critical Viewing

Possible Response: The creek and the woods could be a part of the land described in this scene. The landscape in the picture does not, however, include a ridge or the stubble of cornfields in winter. Still, the picture evokes emotions similar to the story's tone: a sense of wonder at the beauty of the natural world.

Differentiated Instruction

Solutions for All Learners

Support for Less Proficient Readers

Students may benefit from extra support in understanding the Literary Analysis skill, tone. Present students with the **Literary Analysis Graphic Organizer A** (*Graphic Organizer Transparencies,* p. 228) and explain that they can use the chart to help determine the tone of a passage. Instruct students to identify the scene of a passage and write words and details they find on their charts. Then, have students complete the charts by describing what emotions those details convey, and even how they feel when they read these details.

Enrichment for Advanced Readers

In this passage, the narrator tells readers "Canadian geese just did not on an ordinary day fly over the small place in which we lived our lives." Encourage these students to investigate this statement. Students should research the migratory routes of Canadian geese and determine whether they might fly over parts of North Carolina. If Jim's statement is not literally true, what do students think it means? You may have students present their findings to the class.

7 Critical Viewing

Possible response: The photograph will match the way many students imagine Jim's mother and the scene he describes at mealtime. The story describes a family structure in which Jim's mother does all of the cooking and the family eats all meals together.

8 Critical Thinking

Infer

- Have students read the bracketed passage. **Ask** them to summarize the information it presents.
  Answer: Of the adults in the family, Jim's mother is the youngest, his Uncles Al and Coran are in the middle, and Uncle Zeno is the oldest. The men live in three houses, one next to the other, and Jim and his mother live in Zeno's house. Jim's mother does all of the cooking.
- **Ask** students what important information this passage leaves out.
  Answer: The passage offers no information about Jim's father.
- **Ask** students what they can infer about Jim's family from this passage.
  Possible response: Jim's father does not live with the family or has died. Jim's mother relies on her family—her brothers—for her and Jim's well being. Al, Coran, and Zeno are bachelors and are happy to have their family together. It is an old-fashioned household, one in which Jim's mother does all of the cooking, and possibly all of the housework, too.
- Encourage students to consider how this family structure might affect Jim and shape his attitudes towards the events in the story.

7

Enrichment

The Depression in the South

"Aliceville" takes place around 1934 at the peak of the Great Depression. This socioeconomic calamity struck the United States hard—and it hit the American South very hard. Southern states, including Jim Glass's North Carolina, were in a precarious economic condition before the stock market collapsed in 1929. In the 1930s, the south became the poorest region of the nation.

In "Aliceville," Jim and his family, who own farms and multiple houses and eat three meals a day, seem to have escaped the worst of the Depression. Many others were not so lucky. Countless southerners had no choice but to live in houses that were poorly constructed and unsanitary. Unemployment and low wages were problems before the stock market crash, and the Depression only made them worse. Many people were wracked with hunger and disease. By 1938, more than half of southern farmers did not own their own land.

bottom would be our secret, one that we would not share with Uncle Coran and Uncle Al, who were Uncle Zeno's brothers. My uncles were close, but they were competitive in the way that brothers often are—they could not fish or hunt without keeping score—and Uncle Zeno said that we could get a good one over on Uncle Coran and Uncle Al, who were twins, if we walked in at breakfast the next morning carrying a brace of Canadian geese. He hoped that we could sneak up on the flock just before dawn, while they were still bedded and cold, and thought that he could drop two, maybe three if he could reload fast enough, before they managed to get into the air and climb away from the bottom. He was as excited on the way home as I had ever seen him.

My mother was also to be excluded from our plans, because Uncle Zeno said that if she even looked at Uncle Coran and Uncle Al, they would know something was up, and would gang up on her until she told them our secret. My mother was fourteen years younger than Uncle Al and Uncle Coran, and twenty-one years younger than Uncle Zeno. They called her Sissy, and knew—even after she was a grandmother, and they were men of ancient and remarkable age—exactly what to say to make her mad enough to fight. It was impossible for her to lie to them about anything. We lived with Uncle Zeno on Depot Street, and Uncle Coran and Uncle Al lived on either side of us, in houses of their own. The five of us together ate as a family three times a day, at the long table in Uncle Zeno's dining room, meals that my mother cooked.

I managed to keep quiet about the geese during supper, although Uncle Coran and Uncle Al more than once commented on the possum-like[2] nature of my grin. Uncle Zeno twice nudged me under the table with his foot, and narrowed his eyes in warning. The whole family knew something was up, and that Uncle Zeno was behind it. I enjoyed every minute of letting them know that I knew what it was. It was a position I was not often in. My mother slipped into my room that night after I went to bed, bearing in her apron a rare stick of peppermint. She broke it in two and presented me with half, which I accepted. We sucked on our candy in silence, staring at each other, until she asked, misjudging my allegiances, just what exactly Uncle Zeno and I were up to. I told her that we were going to see a man about a dog, which is what Uncle Zeno would have said in reply to such a transparent attempt at bribery. My mother smiled—she always considered it a good sign to see parts of her brothers, particularly parts of Uncle Zeno, coming out in me—and told me to make sure that the dog would bark at a stranger, which was one of the many appropriate responses. After she kissed me and left the room, I heard Uncle Zeno in the kitchen loudly proclaiming that he didn't know what in the world they were talking about, that we weren't up to anything at all.

2. **possum-like** *adj.* pretending to be asleep, dead, or unaware, as in "playing possum."

◄ Critical Viewing
How effectively does this photograph match the way you visualize the mother and the setting in the story? **[Evaluate]**

Vocabulary Builder
excluded (eks klo͞od´ id) *v.* kept out

Literary Analysis
Tone Identify the narrator's tone, or attitude, as he describes his mother and uncles.

Reading Strategy
Visualizing Describe the scene that the narrator creates at the dinner table.

Vocabulary Builder
allegiances (ə lē´ jəns əz) *n.* loyalties

Reading Check
11 What secret do the narrator and Uncle Zeno keep from the rest of the family?

9 Literary Analysis
Tone

Ask the Literary Analysis question: Identify the narrator's tone, or attitude, as he describes his mother and uncles.
Answer: Jim is very matter-of-fact in his description of his family, but the description of the uncles and the mother fighting as if they are still children gives the passage a playful tone.

10 Reading Strategy
Visualizing

- Have students read the bracketed passage. Suggest that this scene, the dinner at which Jim and his Uncle Zeno are clearly keeping a secret from the rest of the family, would be an excellent one to visualize.
- Encourage students to complete Visualizing charts for the dinner scene. **Ask** students to identify sensory images and action words they included on their charts.
  Possible response: Sensory images include *the long table, the possum-like nature of my grin,* and *Uncle Zeno twice nudged me under the table with his foot.* Action words include *nudged* and *narrowed.*
- **Ask** students to respond to the Reading Strategy prompt: Describe the scene the narrator creates at the dinner table.
  Possible response: The family is sitting together at a big table, eating a rich, hearty meal. Jim is the only child there, and his uncles Coran and Al think they can get the secret out of him. He is clearly enjoying the attention. His mother wants to know what Jim and Uncle Zeno are up to, but she is also proud of her son.
- Encourage students to continue creating Visualizing charts as they read.

11 Reading Check

Answer: Jim and Uncle Zeno keep the geese—and their plan to sneak back and hunt them—secret.

Differentiated Instruction
Solutions for All Learners

Strategy for Special Needs Students
Students may need extra support visualizing. Before discussing with students the Reading Strategy item on this page, be sure students understand that *sensory images* are details that appeal to one or more of the five senses—sight, hearing, smell, taste, and touch. Have students assign details from the bracketed passage to these five headings before moving on to the Reading Strategy item.

Vocabulary for English Learners
Although much of "Aliceville" is written in simple, if vivid, language, the dinner scene uses vocabulary that may be new and challenging for these students. Two Vocabulary Builder words appear on this page (*excluded* and *allegiances*), as well as several other high-level and idiomatic words and phrases: *Sissy, possum-like nature of my grin, misjudging, transparent, bribery,* and *proclaiming.* Write these words and phrases on the board, and ask students for any additional words they find challenging. Then, teach the meanings of these terms.

⓬ Vocabulary Builder
The Meanings of *dis-*

- Read the bracketed passage aloud and **ask** students to identify the word that contains the Latin prefix *dis-*.
  Answer: The word *disdain* contains the prefix *dis-*.
- Tell students that the Latin prefix *dis-* can have several meanings, including "apart" or "away" and "not."
- Call students' attention to the definition of the word *disdain*. Explain that the root of *disdain* is the Latin *dignus,* which means "worthy."
- Then, **ask** students to explain which meaning the prefix dis- has in the word disdain.
  Answer: In *disdain,* the prefix *dis-* means "not." To treat something with *disdain* is to treat it as if it is "not worthy."

⓭ Literary Analysis
Tone

- Be sure students understand that tone is created primarily by the writer's word choice. The words in Jim's narration, for example, create images and emotional associations that reveal his attitudes.
- Have students read the bracketed passage. Then, **ask** them to describe the narrator's tone.
  Possible response: His tone is one of excitement, strong enough to banish thoughts of sleep.
- **Ask** students the Literary Analysis question: Which words here reveal the narrator's tone as he describes setting out for the hunt?
  Possible response: Words that describe Jim's excitement include *what seemed like only minutes, the dreams I had traveled through, geese exploding into the air,* and *secret adventure.*
- Encourage students to discuss how the emotional content of these words reflects the narrator's excitement.

That night on their way back to their houses, Uncle Coran and Uncle Al stopped outside my window, pressed their faces against the glass, and growled like bears. I treated their performance with the disdain it deserved. I could not know then what the next day would bring, what Uncle Zeno and I would discover on our hunt. Most of the things that make you see the world and yourself in it differently, you do not imagine beforehand, and I suppose that is the best way. It enables us to live moment to moment in the things we hope to be true. I went to sleep that night possessor, along with my uncle, of what we thought to be a magnificent secret: in the morning a flock of Canadian geese would rise up before us into the air. They would be waiting, there in the frozen field, when we sneaked up on them in the new light.

In what seemed like only minutes, Uncle Zeno pulled my toe and held a finger to his lips. It was dark outside, for all I knew the deepest part of the night. I thought briefly about going back to sleep, into the dreams I had traveled through, and whose thresholds were still close by, but the thought of the geese exploding into the air, the secret adventure that I would share with Uncle Zeno, brought me fully awake. I kicked back the covers and gathered up my clothes and shoes and ran into the kitchen to dress beside the fire. Uncle Zeno was already wearing his hunting coat, and the legs of his overalls were stuffed down into the tall, black rubber boots he wore when he fed the stock. He was grinning. "Get a move on, Doc," he whispered, blowing on a cup of coffee. "Tonight me and you'll be eating a big old goose for dinner. You think we should let anybody else have any?" His shotgun was broken open and lying on the table. Neither his stock boots nor the gun, by my mother's decree, were supposed to be in the kitchen. I shook my head no. Let the rest of the world find their own geese.

When I was dressed, still shivering from my dash between sleep and the fire, Uncle Zeno and I started down the hall toward the darkness outside, and the things that waited for us in it, most of which we did not know. As we tiptoed past my mother's open door, she coughed, which stopped Uncle Zeno in his tracks. He shifted his gun to the other hand and dragged me by the collar back into the kitchen. From out of the straw basket that sat on the second shelf of the cupboard, he removed a piece of corn bread left over from supper the night before. "Here, Doc," he said, "you better eat this." He also poured me a glass of buttermilk. I gulped it all down. When we passed my mother's room a second time, we didn't hear a thing.

Once we made it out of the house, Uncle Zeno and I left in a hurry, pausing only long enough to scrape the ice off the windshield. If Uncle Al and Uncle Coran heard the sound of the truck starting in the yard, they did not dash barefoot out of their houses to see where we were going. And if our flight woke any of the hounds and pointers and assorted feists[3] that divided their time and allegiances between our

3. **feists** (fīsts) *n.* small, snappish dogs.

Vocabulary Builder
disdain (dis dān′) *n.* scorn

Literary Analysis
Tone Which words here reveal the narrator's tone as he describes setting out for the hunt?

◀ Critical Viewing ⓯
What inferences can you make about this boy, based on the photograph? [Infer]

⓮ Reading Strategy
Visualizing

- Remind students that details in a story are what help them visualize what they are reading.
- Have students read the bracketed passage. **Ask** them to identify strong visual details that might help them visualize the scene.
  Possible response: Visual details include *the legs of his overalls were stuffed down into the tall, black rubber boots; he was grinning; blowing on a cup of coffee;* and *his shotgun was broken open and lying on the table.*
- **Ask** students to describe the scene as they visualize it.
  Possible response: The only light in the house comes from the kitchen fire. Uncle Zeno is wearing hunting clothes and drinking coffee. Jim dresses fast, excited about the big, secret adventure he and his uncle are about to have.
- Encourage students to use these details to fill in their Visualizing charts.

⓯ Critical Viewing

Possible Response: The boy's clothing suggests that he lived a long time ago, possibly during the Great Depression of the 1930s. His overalls and bare feet suggest that he lives in a rural area. From his bare feet, viewers can also infer that he is from a less than wealthy family.

Differentiated Instruction
Solutions for All Learners

Enrichment for Gifted/Talented Students
After answering the Reading Strategy question on page 1035, these students may want to create artworks illustrating the scene they have visualized. First, point out to students that this is a high point in the narrator's secret adventure and a moment during which he and Uncle Zeno are forming a strong bond. Encourage students to capture this emotional content as well as the visual details in their illustrations. Students may use any medium they wish. Have students present their work to the class. They should be prepared to answer questions about how their work reflects the emotions of the scene.

Strategy for Advanced Readers
Call these students' attention to the striking example of foreshadowing in the first paragraph on p. 1036. Encourage students to make predictions about what will happen. Will the outcome of the hunt be tragic, or will it seem insignificant outside of Jim's mind? Lead students in a discussion of Jim's musings on "things that make you see the world and yourself in it differently." Students should consider whether these things need to be dramatic events—or if the mundane can change us, as well.

⑯ Critical Viewing

Possible response: The photograph shows a town that could be as small as, or even smaller than, Aliceville. The houses are small, there are few trees and no sidewalk, and the road is not paved. There are no cars visible and virtually no activity; the only person in the photograph is a woman walking along the road. The town does seem all but entirely forgotten. If the people who presumably lived there were to move away, it would entirely cease to exist.

Enrichment

How a Town Is Planned

Jim tells readers that Aliceville is a circle, one mile across. Although few towns are planned this simply, Americans have a long history of planning the layouts of their towns and cities, dating back to the colonial period. Towns in colonial New England, for example, were carefully planned as a means of populating the wilderness. The early and mid-nineteenth century was a time of rapid growth in America. New towns and cities were established across the nation, most of them following a grid.

Aliceville, of course, is not a city; it is a town "like a small idea in danger of being forgotten." The town's residents live within a half-mile of the stake under the depot, most likely left there by a land surveyor hired to draw the town's boundaries. The fields farmed by families like Jim's lie outside the circle, surrounding the town.

Critical Viewing 16 In what ways does this photograph capture the narrator's description of Aliceville as "a small idea in danger of being forgotten" (page 1041)? **[Connect]**

three houses, they did not crawl from out of their beds beneath the porches to investigate. We escaped cleanly, down the single block of Depot Street to the state highway.

Aliceville was still asleep as far as I could tell, the houses dark, and before Uncle Zeno even finished shifting into high gear we were out of town completely and into the open country. There is a surveyor's iron stake driven into the ground underneath the depot that marks the exact center of Aliceville — I suppose that small boys still play games whose rules involve crawling through the spiderwebs and imagined snakes beneath the building to touch the stake, there at the center of things — and from that point the imaginary line marking

Reading Check 18

Why do the narrator and Uncle Zeno try not to make any noise as they leave the house?

17 Literary Analysis

Tone

- Explain to students that tone often plays a major role in shaping readers' perceptions of the people, places, and events in a story.
- **Ask** students to describe the tone of Jim's narration up to this point of "Aliceville."
  Possible response: When Jim describes the geese, his tone is one of wonder. He is thrilled about sharing a secret with Uncle Zeno and excited about the hunting adventure they have planned.
- Point out to students that although the story is named for the town where Jim lives, he has said very little about Aliceville. His tone towards the town is not yet clear.

18 Reading Check

Answer: Jim and Uncle Zeno try to be so quiet because they do not want any of their relatives to wake up and discover their secret.

⑲ Reading Strategy
Visualizing

- Discuss the visualizing strategy with the class. Encourage students to explain how visualizing has helped them enter the imaginary world of "Aliceville." Students may wish to share their successes in "seeing" the flock of geese and Jim's family.
- Then, have students read the bracketed passage. Instruct them to pay close attention to the visual details and record them in a Visualization chart.
- **Ask** students to respond to the Reading Strategy prompt on the next page: Describe Aliceville as the narrator portrays it here. **Possible response:** Aliceville seems to be a small, quiet town where children grow up playing together. It is a town that, late at night, can seem entirely asleep.
- Discuss with students what growing up in the town that they have visualized might be like. Encourage them to consider how the human landscape of Aliceville might have shaped Jim Glass, the narrator.

⑳ Critical Viewing

Possible response: Most students will say the painting presents a positive attitude towards hunting. The image shows a hunter who appears to be responsible in the woods on a beautiful day with a loyal hunting dog. It is the peaceful, bucolic image many hunters have of their sport. Some students will find any image of hunting negative, because hunting necessarily involves shooting wild animals.

the city limits is only a half mile away in any direction. Aliceville is a small but perfect circle on a map,
19 and it sits in the middle of the fields that surround it like a small idea in danger of being forgotten. We lived our lives inside that circle, and made it a town by saying that it was.

The stars were still bright and close above us, but strange somehow, stopped at some private point in their spinning that I had never seen. The state highway was white in the beams of our headlights, and black beyond, and the expansion strips in the concrete bumped under our tires in the countable
21 rhythm of distance passing. There was no sign yet of the coming day, although in the east, down close to the tops of the trees beyond the fields, there was a faint purple tint that disappeared if you stared at it very long and tried, in your wishing for light and warmth, to turn it into dawn. The fields beside the highway were white with a hard frost.

Two miles outside town, Uncle Zeno turned off the state highway onto the dirt road that ran past the bottom where the geese waited for us in the dark. He cut the headlights and slowed the truck to a stealthy crawl, the engine barely above idle. We crept along the road in the starlight until he stopped the truck and turned off the engine a mile or more away from the bottom, at the place where the creek that ran on the other side of it forded the road. "Don't slam the door, Doc," Uncle Zeno whispered. "From here on out, if we poot, they'll hear it. If we make 22
a sound, we'll never see them."

Uncle Zeno loaded his double barrel with two shells out of the

Reading Strategy
Visualizing Describe Aliceville as the narrator portrays it here.

20 **◄ Critical Viewing**
Do you think this painting presents a positive or a negative attitude toward hunting? Explain. **[Assess]**

Vocabulary Builder
stealthy (stelʹ thē) *adj.* avoiding detection

Reading Check
Why does Uncle Zeno stop the truck and turn off the engine?

21 Literary Analysis
Tone

- Point out to students that imagery—language that appeals to the senses of sight, hearing, touch, taste, and smell—can play an important part in creating tone.
- Have students read the bracketed passage. **Ask** them to identify examples of imagery in this passage and the senses to which they appeal.
- **Possible response:** Imagery that appeals to sight includes *[t]he stars were still bright and close. [T]he expansion strips in the concrete bumped under our tires* appeals to both touch and hearing. *The fields beside the highway were white with a hard frost* appeals to sight.
- **Ask** students to describe the tone the imagery in this passage creates. **Possible response:** The tone is full of anticipation of the adventure Jim expects to have. The strangeness of the stars and the disappearing of the purple light hint that Jim is worried that the hunting trip will not go as he hopes.

22 Reading Check

Answer: Uncle Zeno stops and turns off the truck's engine because he does not want to startle the sleeping geese.

Differentiated Instruction
Solutions for All Learners

Strategy for Special Needs Students
Students may need extra help understanding tone, the Literary Analysis skill for this selection. Explain that Jim's description of the countryside and night sky helps set the tone for this section of the story and that these details tend to make readers feel the same way the writer feels. Have students list details from the page that describe how Jim feels about the hunting trip. Then, have students describe how each detail makes them feel. Explain to students that these emotions are the tone of the piece.

Support for Less Proficient Readers
Students may need extra help understanding Jim's feelings in this section of the story. Ask students to write a few sentences describing how they felt when going on a special trip or doing a special activity, such as playing a sport or going shopping, with a parent or other relative. Ask students: Did you like having the special attention from your parent or relative? Why? Did going on the trip or doing this activity make you feel more grown up and part of the family? Why or why not? Make sure students use words that describe sensory details in their sentences.

23 Reading Strategy
Visualizing

- Discuss the visualizing strategy with students. Encourage them to describe the success they have had forming mental pictures of the scenes Jim describes in "Aliceville." Guide students to recognize that visualizing has helped them enter the world of the story.
- Have students pause before reading the bracketed passage. Point out that at the top of the page, Jim is doing something similar to visualizing: he is creating a mental picture of the goose hunt he and Uncle Zeno anticipate. **Ask** students why they think Jim does this.
  Possible response: Jim is trying to imagine already experiencing the hunt. He is trying to enter the world of the future he is so eagerly anticipating.
- Then, have students read the bracketed passage. Tell them to pay close attention to the sensory images and action words they find. **Ask** students to describe the scene in the bracketed passage, as they have visualized it.
  Possible response: It is still dark, although the stars are beginning to fade. Uncle Zeno is a huge man, and Jim is riding on his shoulders as he strides through the creek. Despite his size, Zeno walks quietly, even gracefully. He never drops his nephew, and he manages to keep from colliding with the vines and tree branches that hang in their path.

24 Critical Viewing

Possible response: The painting presents geese very differently from the narrator's description. In the painting, the geese are active but seem essentially at peace. They appear to be landing, as if to rest along a shallow stream. In contrast, the narrator never even sees the geese; they fly away in the dark before he and Uncle Zeno can get anywhere near them. The sounds they make are "exotic" and "urgent," full of mystery and even fear.

pocket of his hunting coat, and gingerly clicked it shut. We were going to sneak up on the flock by walking in the creek, which had high banks and was hidden from view on both sides by thick underbrush. When we got close enough, we would run up out of the brush like Indians, and into the middle of the sleeping geese. They would explode into the frozen air around us for Uncle Zeno to shoot. I did not have any rubber boots, so I climbed onto Uncle Zeno's back—my uncles were tall, strong men who ran their last footrace down Depot Street on Uncle Zeno's sixtieth birthday—and I looped my arms around his neck and my legs around his waist. He shrugged once to get me higher on his back, and stepped over the thick mush ice that grew up out of the bank, and into
23 the cold creek.

Uncle Zeno carried his gun in his right hand, and I felt its stock against my hip. We moved slowly downstream, and in a few steps the brush and trees that grew on the sides of the creek closed above our heads and hid us from whatever might have been watching. Uncle Zeno slid each foot in and out of the creek so quietly that I could not distinguish his steps from the noise made by the water.

We ducked beneath low-hanging vines and limbs and the trunks of trees that had fallen across the creek. I looked up through the thick branches and vines that were tangled above our heads, and could only occasionally see a star. They were dimmer, though it was still night, than when we had left home. I rested my chin on Uncle Zeno's shoulder and closed my eyes and listened to the sound of the creek moving by us in the dark. I might've even dozed off. When I opened my eyes I could sense the bottom on my left, its openness beneath the sky, but I could not see it yet through the laurel and briars. We were still a long way from the geese. Uncle Zeno tilted his head back until the stubble of his beard brushed my cheek, and he said "Shh" so softly that I almost couldn't hear it.

To this day, I do not know what sound we made that caused the geese to fly—how they knew we were there. We never saw them. We were still four or five hundred yards away when they took off, but I knew when it happened it was because of something we had done. We had been silly to think we could get close. When they rose from the bottom their wings pushing against the air sounded like a hard rain, one that might wake you up in the middle of the night. Their shouted
25 cries were as exotic and urgent as they had been the night before, and I heard inside those cries frozen places we would never see. Uncle Zeno and I didn't move when they went up — we were so far away that it didn't startle us, but seemed inevitable somehow — and we stood still in the creek, with our heads cocked upward, listening. We could hear them a long time after they took off, spiraling upward in the sky, calling out, until they were high above us, almost out of earshot, and leaving our part of the world for good.

We listened to those last fading calls until even the possibility of hearing them again was gone, until not even our wishing could keep

Vocabulary Builder
gingerly (jin′ jər lē) *adv.* very carefully, cautiously

24 ▶Critical Viewing Compare and contrast this painting with the narrator's description of the geese and the setting on this page. **[Compare and Contrast]**

Literary Analysis
Tone Which words reveal the narrator's tone as he and his uncle surprise the geese?

Enrichment

Hunting

Although some students may find aspects of hunting objectionable, the sport has an extremely long tradition. Indeed, in prehistoric times, hunting was not a sport; it was an essential activity that provided people with food and pelts to use as clothing. Hunting remained a central part of life for societies with limited agriculture and industry. As human societies evolved, however, hunting became less of a necessity, but it remained a popular and well-regarded sport. Ancient Egyptians, Greeks, and Romans hunted, as did Europeans in the Middle Ages. The introduction of firearms in the fourteenth and fifteenth centuries changed the sport significantly.

Laws and other rules regulate hunting. Since 1871, Congress (as well as state and local governments) has passed laws that affect how people may and may not hunt.

the familiar sounds we tried not to hear from returning into our lives. The creek moved around us as if we weren't there, along the edge of the bottom toward the river. A truck bound for New Carpenter on the state highway downshifted in the distance. A dog barked. I hid my face against Uncle Zeno's neck, suddenly ashamed of what we had wanted to do, of the dark thing we had held in our hearts. At that moment I would have said a prayer to bring the geese back, to hide them again in the field, had I thought it would work. But I knew there was nothing I could do, no desperate bargain I could make, that it was over, just over. The simple presence of the geese had made our

Reading Check

What prevents Jim and Uncle Zeno from shooting the geese?

25 Literary Analysis
Tone

- Explain to students that a story's tone can shift. Point out that in the beginning of "Aliceville," the tone reflects Jim's wonder at the sight of the Canada geese and his excited pleasure at sharing a secret adventure with Uncle Zeno.
- Have students read the bracketed passage on the previous page. Then, **ask** them the Literary Analysis question: Which words reveal the narrator's tone as he and his uncle surprise the geese?
Possible response: Words that reveal tone include *silly, exotic, urgent, frozen places we would never see, inevitable, spiraling upward,* and *leaving our part of the world for good.*
- **Ask** students to describe the narrator's tone in this passage.
Possible response: The tone is sad but resigned, Jim seeing as inevitable that something as wondrous as a flock of Canada geese would not stay long in Aliceville.

➤ **Monitor Progress:** Have students write a paragraph explaining how the tone of "Aliceville" evolves from the beginning of the story to this point.

➤ **Reteach:** If students do not recognize the change in tone, have them reread the story to this point, listing details from the beginning and the end that describe Jim's attitude and emotions about the hunting trip and his town. When students have finished, have them compare those details and explain how Jim's attitude has changed. Emphasize that emotions or attitudes convey tone.

26 Reading Check

Answer: The geese become aware of Jim and Uncle Zeno's approach, and fly away long before they are in range.

Differentiated Instruction
Solutions for All Learners

Support for English Learners

These students may find language in the climax of "Aliceville" challenging. Have students return to the **Preview** and **Build Skills** pages for "Aliceville" in the ***Reader's Notebook: English Learner's Version***. After they review this material, read the climax with the students. Be sure they recognize that the climax is internal: a shift in Jim's feelings that may seem disproportionate to what happens in the plot.

Enrichment for Gifted/Talented Students

A hunting scene at the climax of a story is often filled with dramatic action. In "Aliceville," however, the drama of the hunt is internal. These students may wish to dramatize Jim's experience in a monologue. Students should write monologues from Jim's perspective, using and expanding on his narration in the story. They may wish to write from the point of view of an older Jim. Encourage students to explore how the disappointment changes his life and how he sees it. Encourage students to perform their monologues for the class.

ASSESS

Answers

1. **Possible answer:** Some students may find Jim's discovery surprising, considering that he is just going on a simple goose hunt. Others will respond that Jim's narration foreshadows a disappointing end.
2. (a) They plan to keep the secret from the rest of their family and sneak back before dawn to hunt the geese.
   (b) He is excited by the chance to catch geese, but he is even more excited by the chance to best his brothers at hunting.
3. (a) They remain silent at dinner, and Jim lies to his mother. (b) Jim is thrilled to be at the center of a secret plan, to be the object of attention, and to share a secret with Uncle Zeno. He is also excited by the prospect of the hunt.
4. (a) Jim and Uncle Zeno wake before dawn, sneak out of their houses, and head to the creek bottom. However, the geese sense their presence and fly away. (b) Zeno is open to the wonder the geese inspire in Jim, and he is as excited about the hunt as his nephew is. Despite his age, he also seems saddened when the geese leave.
5. (a) **Possible answer:** Jim means that the sense of possibility, wonder, and magic the geese represent has left his world and quite possibly his life. (b) Jim has learned that life is not filled with the wondrous possibilities.

Go Online Author Link For additional information about Tony Earley, have students type in the Web Code, then select *E* from the alphabet, and then select Tony Earley.

world seem less small, and we were smaller than we had been, once they were gone.

When Uncle Zeno finally moved, I was surprised to see that it was daylight. The trunks of the trees around us had changed from black to gray, as if the day had been waiting only for the geese to climb back into the sky. I could make out the faint red of the sand on the bottom of the creek, the dark green of the laurel on its banks. It was like waking up. Uncle Zeno let out a long breath and turned toward the bottom and waded out of the creek. I slid down onto the ground. "Well, Doc," he said, "I guess me and you might as well go on home." Through the undergrowth I saw the gray sky curving down toward the field. Somewhere a crow called out a warning. There was nothing remarkable about any of it, not that I could tell, not anymore.

Critical Reading

1. **Respond:** Were you surprised by the discovery that Jim makes near the end of the story? Why or why not?
2. **(a) Recall:** At the beginning of the story, what do Jim and Uncle Zeno plan to do about the geese they see? **(b) Infer:** Why would Uncle Zeno be excited about such an opportunity?
3. **(a) Recall:** Describe the efforts Jim and Zeno use to keep their plans secret. **(b) Draw Conclusions:** How do you think Jim feels about Uncle Zeno and the expedition?
4. **(a) Recall:** Describe the hunting expedition and its outcome. **(b) Generalize:** What does Zeno's behavior during the expedition reveal about him as a person?
5. **(a) Interpret:** As they head home, what does the narrator mean when he says: "There was nothing remarkable about any of it, not that I could tell, not anymore"? **(b) Speculate:** What has the experience taught Jim about life?

For: More about Tony Earley
Visit: www.PHSchool.com
Web Code: ere-9604

Apply the Skills

Aliceville

Literary Analysis

Tone

1. Choose two or three adjectives (such as *personal, pompous, indifferent*) to describe the **tone** in this story. Support each adjective with an example from the text.
2. Select two passages from the story in which the tone clearly sounds like that of an adult, and identify language that creates this impression.
3. **(a)** Choose two passages from the beginning and the end of the story, and complete a chart like the one shown to analyze the tone of each. **(b)** How has the narrator's attitude changed by the story's end?

Summary	Words/Details Creating Tone	→	Tone

Connecting Literary Elements

4. Choose three sound **images** in "Aliceville." For each, explain what the image contributes to the tone of the narrative, and why. Be as specific as possible.
5. Find a passage that draws on at least two senses. Identify the senses and describe the tone of the passage.

Reading Strategy

Visualizing

6. Identify an action, a description, or a scene in the story that you can **visualize.** What makes the passage especially vivid to you?
7. Reread and visualize the passage that describes how Zeno carries Jim downstream toward the geese. Then, describe it in your own words.

Extend Understanding

8. **Science Connection:** What does "Aliceville" tell you about the behavior of geese that a zoology textbook would not?

QuickReview

Tone is a writer's attitude toward his or her subject and audience.

Imagery is language that appeals to one or more of the five senses.

When you **visualize,** you create a mental picture of the people, events, or descriptions in the text.

For: Self-test
Visit: www.PHSchool.com
Web Code: era-6624

Answers

1. **Possible answer:** The tone can be described as wondrous ("the geese came down on us like a revelation") and saddened and resigned ("We listened to those last fading calls until even the possibility of hearing them again was gone").
2. **Possible answer:** "Most of the things that make you see the world and yourself in it differently, you do not imagine beforehand." The phrase *you do not imagine beforehand* suggests Jim is looking back on the experience from the future. "I suppose that small boys still play games whose rules involve crawling through the spider webs and imagined snakes." The phrases *small boys, still play,* and *imagined snakes* suggest Jim is looking back from adulthood.
3. (a) **Possible answer:** **Summary:** "Their rising shouts and the rushing sound of their wings, coming on us so suddenly, were as loud and frightening as unexpected gunshots, and as strange to our ears as ancient tongues." The sound of the geese startles Jim and Uncle Zeno. **Words/details creating tone:** *rising shouts, rushing sound, unexpected gunshots, ancient tongues.*

   Tone: Strange, wondrous, unsettling.
3. (b) By the story's end, the narrator seems more grown up and less innocent and wide-eyed.
4. **Possible answer:** "[T]he air around us exploded with honking geese"; the image adds to the narrator's amazement at the geese. "We did not speak at first, and listened to our blood, and the winter silence around us, and wondered at the thing we had seen"; the image emphasizes how extraordinary this event is for the narrator. "A truck bound for New Carpenter on the state highway downshifted in the distance"; the image adds to the ordinariness of the scene.
5. **Possible answer:** "We sucked our candy in silence, staring at each other, until she asked, misjudging my allegiances, just what exactly Uncle Zeno and I were up to." This passage appeals to taste, hearing, and sight. The tone is one of delight.

Continued from right column

6. **Possible answer:** The scene in which Jim dresses by firelight and sneaks out of the house with Uncle Zeno is full of motion and vivid details such as the gun on the table, and Zeno dragging Jim back into the kitchen for breakfast.
7. Jim rides on Uncle Zeno's back. Zeno strides slowly through the creek. It's still dark out, and the darkness gets even deeper as the vegetation above gets thicker.
8. **Possible answer:** The story tells readers that Canada geese rarely fly over this part of North Carolina and that they are so sensitive that there is no real chance of sneaking up on them.

Go Online Assessment — Students may use the **Self-test** to prepare for **Selection Test A** or **Selection Test B.**

EXTEND/ASSESS

Answers

❶ Vocabulary Lesson

Word Analysis

1. put or force something out of its place; *dis-* means "not"
2. shame, loss of honor or respect; *dis-* means "not"
3. purify a liquid by heating it, drawing away its vapors, and condensing them; *dis-* means "away"
4. deprive of a natural or established privilege; *dis-* means "not"
5. recognize as different, pick out; *dis-* means "away"
6. look on someone with scorn; *dis-* means "not"

Spelling Strategy

1. gorgeous
2. manageable
3. advantageous

Vocabulary Builder

1. a	4. c
2. c	5. c
3. b	6. a

❷ Grammar and Style Lesson

1. as if	4. as
2. like	5. as if
3. like	

Writing Application

Students' paragraphs should reflect the correct use of *like, as,* and *as if.*

WG Writing and Grammar, Ruby Level

Students will find further instruction and practice on using *like, as,* and *as if* in Chapter 25, Section 2.

Build Language Skills

❶ Vocabulary Lesson

Word Analysis: The Meanings of *dis-*

The Latin prefix *dis-* can have several meanings. In some words it means "apart" or "away" (as in *disseminate* or *distribute*), while in other words it means "not" (as in *dishonest* or *disbelief*).

Use a dictionary to check the meanings of the following words, noting whether the prefix *dis-* means "away" or "not" in each.

1. dislocate	**4.** disinherit
2. disgrace	**5.** distinguish
3. distill	**6.** disdain

Spelling Strategy: *g* + *i*

The pronunciation of the letter *g* can be either hard, as in *ground,* or soft, as in *giant.* In a word containing a soft *g,* the *g* must always be followed by *i* or *e.* Correct the spelling of the following words.

1. gorgous **2.** managable **3.** advantagous

Vocabulary Builder: Antonyms

Antonyms are words that are opposite or nearly opposite in meaning. For each item, choose the letter of the antonym of the numbered word.

1. stealthy: **(a)** open **(b)** successful **(c)** covert
2. allegiances: **(a)** alliances **(b)** pledges **(c)** betrayals
3. revelation: **(a)** boredom **(b)** mystery **(c)** fact
4. gingerly: **(a)** timidly **(b)** sadly **(c)** carelessly
5. disdain: **(a)** ridicule **(b)** hope **(c)** admiration
6. excluded: **(a)** welcomed **(b)** disbarred **(c)** voted

❷ Grammar and Style Lesson

Using *Like, As,* and *As If*

The words ***like, as,*** and ***as if*** help create comparisons. Be careful to use these words correctly.

- ***Like*** is a preposition and should never be used to introduce a subordinate clause.
- Use the words ***as*** or ***as if*** to introduce subordinate clauses.
- ***As*** can also be used as a preposition, substituting for ***like.***

Prepositional phrase: "growled like bears"
Subordinate clause: "moved around us as if we weren't there"

Practice Copy the following sentences, filling in *like, as,* or *as if* in each blank space.

1. Zeno sees hunting the geese _____ it is a chance to get an edge over his brothers.
2. Jim's grin about their secret is _____ that of a possum.
3. Winter days _____ the one the narrator describes are beautiful in a very spare, cold way.
4. Their expedition turns out not to be triumphant, _____ Jim and Zeno thought it would be.
5. By the end, Jim feels _____ he is doing something shameful.

Writing Application Write a paragraph that includes two or three comparisons. Use the correct word or words (*like, as,* or *as if*) to create these comparisons.

WG *Prentice Hall Writing and Grammar Connection: Chapter 25, Section 2*

Writing Lesson

Critical Response

Write a **critical response** to the following statement by literary critic Michael Pearson: ". . . Earley has a talent that seems lost to so many contemporary writers: the ability to speak straightforwardly, expressing an honest, deep-felt emotion, without ever lapsing into sentimentality." Do you agree with this assessment? Use specific evidence from "Aliceville" to support your opinion.

Prewriting Reread the story and think about whether you agree or disagree with Pearson's comment. As you formulate your opinion, note events and passages from the story that you could use to support it.

Drafting Start your response by quoting Pearson's comment and indicating whether you agree or disagree with it. Then, elaborate by providing details and by quoting passages from the story to prove your point.

Revising Reread your critical response to confirm that you have provided solid literary evidence to support your ideas. Consider adding images, statements by the narrator, and other specific story details.

Model: Revising to Add Literary Evidence

Earley uses simple yet powerful language to evoke the feelings of both a young boy setting out on an adventure and the mature narrator looking back on it with rueful wisdom. For example, he creates a sense of mature hindsight: "Most of the things that make you see the world and yourself in it differently, you do not imagine beforehand, and I suppose that is the best way."

This quotation from the text builds the writer's argument about the narrator's age and experience.

Prentice Hall Writing and Grammar Connection: Chapter 14, Section 3

Extend Your Learning

Research and Technology With a classmate, stage a **debate** about the pros and cons of hunting. Argue from the viewpoint of farmers, animal-rights supporters, hunters, and others.

- Take notes during your opponent's argument so that you can respond effectively.
- Paraphrase or summarize your opponent's points before offering your rebuttal.
- Show respect for and sensitivity to your opponent's viewpoint at all times.

At the end of your debate, ask the class for feedback on the effectiveness of presenting multiple perspectives. **[Group Activity]**

Listening and Speaking Prepare and present a **monologue** based on "Aliceville." As the character of the narrator, tell a new story or anecdote about one or several of his uncles. Think about the mood, or overall feeling, that you want to convey. Use humor, slang, dialect, and idioms, if appropriate, to express the personality of the uncle(s).

For: An additional research activity
Visit: www.PHSchool.com
Web Code: erd-7620

3 Writing Lesson

You may use this Writing Lesson as timed-writing practice, or you may allow students to develop the essay as a writing assignment over several days.

- To give students guidance for writing this critical response essay, give them the **Support for Writing Lesson,** p. 63 in ***Unit 6 Resources.***
- Students' critical response essays should address Pearson's assessment of Earley as a writer who expresses emotion honestly without sentimentality. They should state whether they agree with Pearson and use examples from "Aliceville" to support their positions.
- Students will benefit from rereading "Aliceville" carefully, making note of passages with clear emotional content. Have students evaluate these passages. Are they straightforward and honest, or do they tend towards the sentimental?
- Use the Response to Literature rubrics in ***General Resources,*** pp. 65–66, to evaluate students' Critical Response essays.

4 Research and Technology

- Ask students to approach the topic with an open mind. No matter what their personal feelings about hunting are, students should assess the views of different groups as objectively as possible.
- Most students will wish to use the Internet to research this topic. Provide supervision and guidance throughout the research process.
- The **Support for Extend Your Learning** page (***Unit 6 Resources,*** p. 64) provides guided note-taking opportunities to help students complete the Extend Your Learning activities.

Go Online Research — Have students type in the Web Code for another research activity.

Assessment Resources

The following resources can be used to assess students' knowledge and skills.

Unit 6 Resources
- **Selection Test A,** pp. 66–68
- **Selection Test B,** pp. 69–71

General Resources
- **Rubrics for Response to Literature,** pp. 65–66

Go Online Assessment — Students may use the **Self-test** to prepare for **Selection Test A** or **Selection Test B.**

Meeting Your Standards

Students will

1. **analyze and respond to literary elements.**
   - Literary Analysis: Style and Diction
2. **read, comprehend, analyze, and critique poetry.**
   - Reading Strategy: Paraphrasing
   - Reading Check questions
   - Apply the Skills questions
   - Assessment Practice (ATE)
3. **develop vocabulary.**
   - Vocabulary Lesson: Related Words: *exhaust*
4. **understand and apply written and oral language conventions.**
   - Spelling Strategy
   - Grammar and Style Lesson: Subject and Verb Agreement
5. **develop writing proficiency.**
   - Writing Lesson: Critical Response
6. **develop appropriate research strategies.**
   - Extend Your Learning: Oral Presentation
7. **understand and apply listening and speaking strategies.**
   - Extend Your Learning: Evaluation

Block Scheduling: Use one 90-minute class period to preteach the skills and have students read the selection. Use a second 90-minute class period to assess students' mastery of skills, extend their learning, and monitor their progress.

Homework Suggestions

Following are possibilities for homework assignments.

- Support pages from ***Unit 6 Resources:***
  Literary Analysis
  Reading Strategy
  Vocabulary Builder
  Grammar and Style
- An Extend Your Learning project and the Writing Lesson for this selection group may be completed over several days.

Step-by-Step Teaching Guide	Pacing Guide
PRETEACH	
• Administer Vocabulary and Reading Warm-ups as necessary.	5 min.
• Engage students' interest with the motivation activity.	5 min.
• Read and discuss author and background features. **FT**	10 min.
• Introduce the Literary Analysis Skill: Style and Diction. **FT**	5 min.
• Introduce the Reading Strategy: Paraphrasing. **FT**	10 min.
• Prepare students to read by teaching the selection vocabulary. **FT**	
TEACH	
• Informally monitor comprehension while students read independently or in groups. **FT**	30 min.
• Monitor students' comprehension with the Reading Check notes.	as students read
• Reinforce vocabulary with Vocabulary Builder notes.	as students read
• Develop students' understanding of style and diction with the Literary Analysis annotations. **FT**	5 min.
• Develop students' ability to paraphrase with the Reading Strategy annotations. **FT**	5 min.
ASSESS/EXTEND	
• Assess students' comprehension and mastery of the Literary Analysis and Reading Strategy by having them answer the Apply the Skills questions. **FT**	15 min.
• Have students complete the Vocabulary Lesson and the Grammar and Style Lesson. **FT**	15 min.
• Apply students' ability to use suitable criteria to judge literary works by using the Writing Lesson. **FT**	45 min. or homework
• Apply students' understanding by using one or more of the Extend Your Learning activities.	20–90 min. or homework
• Administer Selection Test A or Selection Test B. **FT**	15 min.

Resources

PRINT
Unit 6 Resources

TRANSPARENCY
Graphic Organizer Transparencies

PRINT
Reader's Notebook [L2]
Reader's Notebook: Adapted Version [L1]
Reader's Notebook: English Learner's Version [EL]
Unit 6 Resources

TECHNOLOGY
Listening to Literature Audio CDs [L2, EL]

PRINT
Unit 6 Resources

General Resources

TECHNOLOGY
Go Online: Research **[L3]**
Go Online: Self-test **[L3]**
ExamView® **Test Bank [L3]**

Choosing Resources for Differentiated Instruction

[L1] Special Needs Students
[L2] Below-Level Students
[L3] All Students
[L4] Advanced Students
[EL] English Learners

For Vocabulary and Reading Warm-ups and for Selection Tests, **A** signifies "less challenging" and **B** "more challenging." For Graphic Organizer transparencies, **A** signifies "not filled in" and **B** "filled in."

FT Fast Track Instruction: To move the lesson more quickly, use the strategies and activities identified with **FT**.

Scaffolding for Less Proficient and Advanced Students

The leveled Critical Thinking questions after selections progress in the levels of thinking required to answer them. To address the needs of your different students, you may use the (a) level questions for your less proficient students and the (b) level questions with your on-level and advanced students. The occasional (c) level questions are appropriate for your advanced students.

PRENTICE HALL **TeacherEXPRESS™** Plan · Teach · Assess Use this complete suite of powerful teaching tools to make lesson planning and testing quicker and easier.

PRENTICE HALL **StudentEXPRESS™** Learn · Study · Succeed Use the interactive textbook (online and on CD-ROM) to make selections and activities come alive with audio and video support and interactive questions.

Go Online Professional Development **For:** Information about Lexiles
Visit: www.PHSchool.com
Web Code: eue-1111

PREPEACH

Motivation

Introduce students to the poetry by asking what inspires strong emotions or awe in them. You might show students some photographs of natural and man-made wonders as a stimulus. Ask how the emotions awakened by these images might take root in poetic form. Urge students to read on for the answer three poets give.

❶ Background
More About the Authors

Aside from winning three Pulitzer Prizes, Robert Penn Warren was appointed the first poet laureate of the United States in 1985.

Theodore Roethke was an acclaimed teacher of poetry. His pupils included James Wright, David Wagoner, and Richard Hugo. He advised his beginning students to "write like someone else": many critics believe that he followed his own advice too faithfully.

William Stafford's writings have won numerous awards, and he served as the Consultant in Poetry for the Library of Congress.

Build Skills *Poems*

❶ Gold Glade • The Light Comes Brighter • Traveling Through the Dark

Robert Penn Warren (1905–1989)

Born in Guthrie, Kentucky, Robert Penn Warren went to college at Vanderbilt University. There, he became the youngest member of the Fugitives, a group of poets who promoted Southern rural life and its traditions. Among the most versatile, prolific, and distinguished writers of our time, Warren won the first of his three Pulitzer Prizes for *All the King's Men* (1946), a fictional study of a Southern politician (based on Louisiana Governor Huey Long). Warren went on to become the only writer who has ever won a Pulitzer Prize for both fiction and poetry. He was also an important literary critic—one of the leading theorists of an influential school of literary criticism called the New Criticism. Warren's poetry collections include *Promises* (1957) and *Now and Then: Poems* (1978). Although Warren consistently used Southern settings and characters in his writing, he treated universal themes, such as the love of the land that fills the poem "Gold Glade."

Theodore Roethke (1908–1963)

Theodore Roethke (ret′ kē) was born in Saginaw, Michigan, where his family owned several large commercial greenhouses. As a boy, Roethke was a passionate observer of the plants that grew in the greenhouses. These observations later provided him with ideas for many of his poems. In 1923, Roethke's father lost his battle with cancer, an event that heavily influenced Roethke's poetry.

Throughout his life, Roethke found it difficult to relate to other people. He found a refuge, though, in nature and poetry. At age thirty-three, Roethke published his first volume of poetry, launching a career as one of the most acclaimed poets of his day. He won the Pulitzer Prize for *The Waking* (1953) and the National Book Award for *The Far Field* (1964). From short, witty poems to complex, philosophical free verse, Roethke's poetry reflects a wide range of feelings and poetic styles.

William Stafford (1914–1993)

William Stafford spent key parts of his life in Kansas, Iowa, and Oregon. These regions influenced his poetry, both in its content and in its serene, unadorned language. A believer in the sanctity of life, Stafford served in World War II as a conscientious objector. Focusing on such subjects as the threat of nuclear war and the beauty of nature, Stafford wrote of his fear that modern technology would someday destroy the wilderness. He did not publish his first volume of verse, *West of Your City* (1960), until he was forty-six, after years of working in the U.S. Forest Service. Stafford's other poetry collections include *The Rescued Year* (1966) and *Stories That Could Be True: New and Collected Poems* (1977). In 1970, Stafford was appointed Consultant of Poetry to the Library of Congress, a position now known as Poet Laureate of the United States.

Preview

Connecting to the Literature

Sometimes, when you least expect it, you make the most surprising discoveries about yourself and the world around you. In a similar way, the speakers in the three poems that follow make discoveries in unexpected places.

Literary Analysis

Style and Diction

A writer's **style** is the manner in which he or she puts ideas into words. Style generally concerns *form* rather than *content*. In poetry, style is determined by a poet's use of these elements:

- Tone
- Sound devices
- Symbolism
- Rhythm
- The length and arrangement of lines
- Figurative language
- Punctuation and capitalization

Another important aspect of style is **diction,** or word choice. As you read these poems, note the ways in which each poet's style and diction not only reflect varying degrees of formality but also help establish a unique voice—a distinctive or characteristic sound or way of "speaking" on the page.

Comparing Literary Works

Poets often search for important ideas through the lens of ordinary life. This approach helps readers see everyday experiences in new ways. For example, in Robert Penn Warren's poem "Gold Glade," the speaker makes an important discovery during an ordinary walk through the woods. As you read these poems, try to identify the abstract idea—the larger truth or insight—that each poet is really addressing through his exploration of the ordinary.

Reading Strategy

Paraphrasing

Some poems contain passages that are especially difficult to understand because of unusual vocabulary, complex sentences, or the ambiguities of poetic language. To improve your comprehension, **paraphrase,** or restate in your own words, any difficult passages you encounter. As you read these poems, use a chart like the one shown to aid your understanding.

Roethke's Words
Soon field and wood will wear an April look.
Paraphrase
Soon it will be spring.

Vocabulary Builder

declivity (dē kliv′ ə tē) *n.* downward slope (p. 1050)

domain (dō mān′) *n.* territory; sphere of knowledge, activity, or influence (p. 1051)

vestiges (ves′ tij iz) *n.* traces (p. 1052)

exhaust (eg zôst′) *n.* discharge of used steam or gas from an engine (p. 1054)

Differentiated Instruction

Solutions for All Learners

Support for Special Needs Students
Have students complete the **Preview** and **Build Skills** pages for these selections in the ***Reader's Notebook: Adapted Version.*** These pages provide a selection summary, an abbreviated presentation of the reading and literary skills, and the graphic organizer on the **Build Skills** page in the student book.

Support for Less Proficient Readers
Have students complete the **Preview** and **Build Skills** pages for these selections in the ***Reader's Notebook.*** These pages provide a selection summary, an abbreviated presentation of the reading and literary skills, and the graphic organizer on the **Build Skills** page in the student book.

Support for English Learners
Have students complete the **Preview** and **Build Skills** pages for these selections in the ***Reader's Notebook: English Learner's Version.*** These pages provide a selection summary, an abbreviated presentation of the skills, and the graphic organizer on the **Build Skills** page in the student book.

2 Literary Analysis

Style and Diction

- Point out that both style and diction have to do with the choices a writer makes. Write the following sentences on the board, pointing out that each gives the same information. Students can compare and contrast the styles and diction of the two sentences. *The right fielder hit a home run. Flexing mighty arms, the batter swung powerfully and smashed the ball over the fences.*
- Have students try to **characterize** the style and diction of some of the poets they have read earlier this year. **Possible answers:** T.S. Eliot: elevated style, sophisticated and formal diction. Carl Sandburg: plain style, colloquial and informal diction.
- As students read the poems in this group, have them try to characterize the style and diction of each poet.

3 Reading Strategy

Paraphrasing

- A good first step in paraphrasing poetry is to write out complete sentences, ignoring line breaks and the capital letters at the start of lines. Students will have an easier time paraphrasing when they can see where the sentences end.
- Remind students that paraphrasing and summarizing are not the same. A paraphrase should restate the original idea without leaving out any details.
- Give students a copy of **Reading Strategy Graphic Organizer A,** p. 230 in ***Graphic Organizer Transparencies,*** to use as they read the poems.

Vocabulary Builder

- Pronounce each vocabulary word for students, and read the definitions as a class. Have students identify any words with which they are already familiar.

TEACH

❶ About the Selections

These three poems describe different aspects of America: forest glade in autumn, an unexpected highway encounter with a dead doe, and the breaking of dawn at a lake in winter.

❷ Literary Analysis
Style and Diction

- Have a volunteer read aloud the first ten lines of the poem. Ask students to describe the poet's diction.
- **Ask** the Literary Analysis question: In the very first stanza, what do you notice about the poet's innovative diction?
  Answer: The whole first stanza is only part of the poem's first sentence. The word order is unusual. Articles and other words one would expect to see are missing.
- **Ask** students what they think the speaker means by "boy-blankness of mood"? Which words and phrases in lines 1–10 support their answers?
  Answer: The speaker's mood is carefree. He is wandering for the sheer pleasure of it. Supporting words: wandering, aimless.

❸ Reading Check

Answer: The speaker is wandering through the woods in autumn.

1

Gold Glade

Robert Penn Warren

Background Following an English tradition dating back to 1616, the Library of Congress named Robert Penn Warren as the first Poet Laureate of the United States in 1985. Since then, some of America's best and brightest literary talents have held the title of Poet Laureate. Unlike their British counterparts, American poets laureate are under no obligation to write poems to commemorate special occasions. Though they receive a sizable stipend and an office in the Library of Congress for the duration of the one-year term, poets laureate are free to continue writing (or not writing) as they choose.

2

Wandering, in autumn, the woods of boyhood,
Where cedar, black, thick, rode the ridge,
Heart aimless as rifle, boy-blankness of mood,
I came where ridge broke, and the great ledge,
Limestone, set the toe high as treetop by dark edge

Of a gorge, and water hid, grudging and grumbling,
And I saw, in mind's eye, foam white on
Wet stone, stone wet-black, white water tumbling,
And so went down, and with some fright on
Slick boulders, crossed over. The gorge-depth drew night on,

But high over high rock and leaf-lacing, sky
Showed yet bright, and declivity wooed
My foot by the quietening stream, and so I
Went on, in quiet, through the beech wood:
There, in gold light, where the glade gave, it stood.

Literary Analysis
Style and Diction In the very first stanza, what do you notice about the poet's innovative diction?

Vocabulary Builder
declivity (dē kliv′ ə tē) *n.* downward slope

3 
Reading Check
Where is the speaker wandering?

Differentiated Instruction Solutions for All Learners

Accessibility at a Glance

	Gold Glade	The Light Comes Brighter	Traveling Through the Dark
Language	Accessible diction; complex sentence structure	Uncomplicated sentence structure	Conversational
Concept Level	Accessible (descriptions of nature)	Accessible (descriptions of nature)	Accessible (familiar setting and situation)
Literary Merit	Classic	Notable Author	Poignant anecdote
Lexile	NP	NP	NP
Overall Rating	More challenging	More accessible	Average

The glade was geometric, circular, gold,
No brush or weed breaking that bright gold of leaf-fall.
4 In the center it stood, absolute and bold
Beyond any heart-hurt, or eye's grief-fall.
Gold-massy in air, it stood in gold light-fall,

No breathing of air, no leaf now gold-falling,
No tooth-stitch of squirrel, or any far fox bark,
5 No woodpecker coding, or late jay calling.
Silence: gray-shagged, the great shagbark[1]
Gave forth gold light. There could be no dark.

But of course dark came, and I can't recall
What county it was, for the life of me.
Montgomery, Todd, Christian—I know them all.
Was it even Kentucky or Tennessee?
Perhaps just an image that keeps haunting me.

No, no! in no mansion under earth,
Nor imagination's domain of bright air,
But solid in soil that gave it its birth,
It stands, wherever it is, but somewhere.
I shall set my foot, and go there.

1. **shagbark** hickory tree.

Literary Analysis
Style and Diction Which words in this stanza are repeated? What is the effect?

Reading Strategy
Paraphrasing How might you paraphrase lines 21–25?

Vocabulary Builder
domain (dō mān′) *n.* territory; sphere of knowledge, activity, or influence

Critical Reading

1. **Respond:** What are some of your memories of autumn? In what ways do they compare to the speaker's memories?
2. **(a) Recall:** What majestic thing does the speaker find in the center of the glade? **(b) Define:** What are "heart-hurt" and "grief-fall"? **(c) Analyze:** Why is the glade "beyond" those things?
3. **(a) Recall:** Where does the action of the poem shift from past to present? **(b) Interpret:** Describe the change in tone that occurs at that point.
4. **(a) Interpret:** In lines 21–25, what are the dominant sensory impressions? **(b) Deduce:** What emotions does the speaker seem to feel in that stanza? **(c) Analyze:** What does the speaker mean by saying, "There could be no dark"?
5. **(a) Interpret:** What does the gold glade represent to the speaker? **(b) Speculate:** Is the glade a real place to which the speaker could actually return? Explain. **(c) Evaluate:** Is this poem an accurate portrayal of memory? Explain.

For: More about Robert Penn Warren
Visit: www.PHSchool.com
Web Code: ere-9605

4 Literary Analysis
Style and Diction

- Point out that the poem has a regular rhyme scheme. **Ask** students to identify the rhyme scheme and describe its effect on the poem.
  Answer: The rhyme scheme is *ababb.* It is the only fixed element in the poem; the lines are all of different lengths and the rhythm is irregular. Students may say that the rhyme scheme gives the poem a stately, rhythmic sound that matches the poet's reverent tone.
- Then, **ask** the Literary Analysis question: Which words in this stanza (lines 16–20) are repeated? What is the effect?
  Possible answers: The word *gold* is used four times; *fall* is used three times. Effect: readers can visualize the gold leaves falling from the trees.

5 Reading Strategy
Paraphrasing

- Remind students that paraphrasing means restating the text in the reader's own words.
- Ask a volunteer to read aloud the stanza.
- Then, **ask** the Reading Strategy question: How might you paraphrase lines 21–25?
- **Possible answer:** It was silent in the glade near the hickory tree, and it was so bright near the tree that it seemed it would always be so.

ASSESS
Answers

1. Make sure students offer similarities and differences as they compare their memories with those of the speaker.
2. (a) a great shagbark (hickory tree) (b) human suffering and grief (c) The glade's beauty made it seem eternal, untouched by time or human suffering.
3. (a) line 26 (b) The tone becomes prosaic, everyday—the reader becomes aware that the glade and great tree are only an uncertain memory.
4. (a) The images appeal to sight and hearing. (b) He feels awe and reverence for the hickory tree's beauty. (c) He means that the gold and light seem to be eternal, even sacred.

Answers continued

5. (a) It represents beauty and eternity. (b) The glade seems real; it is described in detail and realistically but the speaker is ambivalent about whether it is only a haunting image or a real place. (c) Students should say yes; the speaker remembers the beauty of the place and the feelings it evoked, but finds that the specifics connected with the memory fade and waver, as often happens with memories.

Go Online Author Link For additional information about Robert Penn Warren, have students type in the Web Code, then select *W* from the alphabet, and then select Robert Penn Warren.

❻ Literary Analysis
Style and Diction

- Review with students the elements writers use to construct their writing style: tone, sound devices, symbolism, rhythm, line length and arrangement, figurative language, and punctuation and capitalization.
- **Ask** students the Literary Analysis question: What do you notice about the rhythm, length, and arrangement of lines in this poem?
  Answer: Students should be able to recognize that Roethke uses iambic pentameter with a rhyme scheme of *abab* in this poem.

❼ Reading Strategy
Paraphrasing

- **Ask** students to paraphrase this line to denote what natural activity line 4 describes.
  Possible answer: Students should paraphrase to indicate that the walker hears ice cracking as the river thaws.
- **Ask** students what effect the poet has on the reader by using words that suggest action, even violence, such as "cannon crack," cuts," and "buckled."
  Answer: Students should note that the poet creates an image of spring as being a powerful force—Roethke even says it "breaks" like a storm.

❽ Reading Check

Answer: The poem describes the coming of spring.

The Light Comes Brighter

Theodore Roethke

The light comes brighter from the east; the caw
Of restive crows is sharper on the ear.
A walker at the river's edge may hear
A cannon crack announce an early thaw.

The sun cuts deep into the heavy drift,
Though still the guarded snow is winter-sealed,
At bridgeheads buckled ice begins to shift,
The river overflows the level field.

Once more the trees assume familiar shapes,
As branches loose last vestiges of snow.
The water stored in narrow pools escapes
In rivulets; the cold roots stir below.

Soon field and wood will wear an April look,
The frost be gone, for green is breaking now;
The ovenbird[1] will match the vocal brook,
The young fruit swell upon the pear-tree bough.

And soon a branch, part of a hidden scene,
The leafy mind, that long was tightly furled,
Will turn its private substance into green,
And young shoots spread upon our inner world.

Literary Analysis
Style and Diction What do you notice about the rhythm, length, and arrangements of lines in this poem?

Vocabulary Builder
vestiges (vesˊ tij iz) *n.* traces

❽

Reading Check
What seasonal process does this poem describe?

1. **ovenbird** common name for any of the many birds that build a domelike nest on the ground.

Differentiated Instruction
Solutions for All Learners

Enrichment for Gifted/Talented Students
Challenge students to write poems of their own, based on something that inspires them in one of these five poems. Remind students that they are free to write free verse or to use whatever poetic form best expresses their ideas. Have students give brief explanations of their sources of inspiration before reading the poems aloud in class.

Enrichment for Advanced Readers
Have students do further reading about one of the poets represented in this group. Students can give a class presentation on the poet's life, read more of his poems and discuss them in an essay, or design some other kind of project based on their research.

Traveling Through the Dark

William Stafford

9 Traveling through the dark I found a deer
dead on the edge of the Wilson River road.
It is usually best to roll them into the canyon:
that road is narrow; to swerve might make more dead.

9 Literary Analysis
Style and Diction

- Draw students' attention to the bracketed passage. **Ask** how they would characterize William Stafford's diction in this poem.
  Possible answer: Students may observe that Stafford's diction is like ordinary speech.
- **Ask** students to identify the stylistic techniques that Stafford uses to craft poetry in this piece.
  Answer: Students should note that Stafford uses highly original line arrangement and sentence rhythms, punctuation, and capitalization to create the poem, rather than the more traditional techniques of rhyme and meter.

Differentiated Instruction
Solutions for All Learners

Strategy for Special Needs Students
Have students work together to answer the questions on pages 1051 and 1054. They can meet in a small group afterwards to compare answers. If there is significant disagreement, have students identify words, phrases, and lines from the poems that support their interpretations.

Strategy for Advanced Readers
Point out to students the moral and medical dilemma facing the speaker when he realizes the fawn is still alive. Have students speculate about the speaker's chain of thought as he knelt beside the dead deer—why do they think the speaker acted in this way? Challenge students to develop alternative courses of action the speaker might have considered to try to save the fawn. How practical and successful might these be?

⑩ Critical Thinking

Analyze and Connect

- **Ask** students how they feel the mood of the poem is affected by the time of day in which it is set.
  Possible answer: Students may observe that nighttime and the resulting lighting from the car's lights creates a mood of loneliness, isolation, and danger.
- Draw students' attention to the image of the warm, still-living fawn within the belly of the dead deer. **Ask** students to look for a parallel image in the poem.
  Answer: Students should link the image with that of the warm engine purring beneath the hood of the car.

⑪ Vocabulary Builder

Related Words: *exhaust*

- Point out that the word *exhaust* in this line is a noun meaning "fumes from an engine." **Ask** students to define the verb *exhaust* in a different way.
  Answer: to tire out
- **Ask** what effect this second meaning of *exhaust* has on this line of poetry.
  Answer: The word *exhaust* might suggest the speaker's fatigue, or how the doe must have felt as her life ebbed away. It adds emotion to the scene.

ASSESS

Answers

1. **Possible response:** "Light" makes the stronger impression because it describes a familiar phenomenon; "Traveling" because of its vivid imagery and use of sensory details.
2. (a) The poem describes the change from winter into spring. (b) The "cannon crack" of the early thaw and the sun "cutting deep" into the snow drifts describe action.
3. (a) The poet uses *inner.* (b) The inner creative process is fuled by the creativity of the external world in the form of nature.
4. (a) The doe is carrying a fawn. (b) His impulse is to try to save the fawn.

By glow of the tail-light I stumbled back of the car
and stood by the heap, a doe, a recent killing;
she had stiffened already, almost cold.
I dragged her off; she was large in the belly.

⑩
My fingers touching her side brought me the reason—
her side was warm; her fawn lay there waiting,
alive, still, never to be born.
Beside that mountain road I hesitated.

The car aimed ahead its lowered parking lights;
under the hood purred the steady engine.
⑪ I stood in the glare of the warm exhaust turning red;
around our group I could hear the wilderness listen.

I thought hard for us all—my only swerving—,
then pushed her over the edge into the river.

Vocabulary Builder
exhaust (eg zôst′) *n.* discharge of used steam or gas from an engine

Critical Reading

1. **Respond:** Which of these poems made a stronger impression on you? Why?
2. **(a) Recall:** In "The Light Comes Brighter," what change of seasons is described? **(b) Distinguish:** Identify two images that suggest that change involves action and even violence.
3. **(a) Recall:** In the final line, what adjective does the poet use to describe the "world"? **(b) Analyze:** What do you think the poet is saying about the creative process?
4. **(a) Recall:** In "Traveling Through the Dark," what discovery does the speaker make when he examines the deer? **(b) Infer:** Why does the speaker hesitate upon making this discovery?
5. **(a) Interpret:** In the fourth stanza, what details make the car seem alive? **(b) Connect:** In what ways does this description echo the speaker's discovery about the deer?
6. **(a) Deduce:** What factors does the speaker weigh in his decision about what to do with the deer? **(b) Analyze:** How does the title reflect the speaker's moral dilemma?
7. **Generalize:** What does this poem reveal about the relationship between humanity and nature in the modern world?

For: More about Theodore Roethke and William Stafford
Visit: www.PHSchool.com
Web Code: ere-9606

Answers continued

5. (a) The words "aimed" and "purred" suggest that the car is alive. (b) The car is cold on the outside, like the dead doe, but has a warm, purring engine.
6. (a) The speaker weighs motorists' safety against the life of the fawn. (b) The speaker can't clearly see what he should do and is thus literally and metaphorically "travelling in the dark."
7. Human beings are taking up more space than ever, and animals like deer are threatened.

Go Online Author Link For additional information about Theodore Roethke and William Stafford, have students type in the Web Code, then select *R* or *S* from the alphabet, and then select Theodore Roethke or William Stafford.

Apply the Skills

Gold Glade* • *The Light Comes Brighter* • *Traveling Through the Dark

Literary Analysis

Style and Diction

1. **(a)** In "Gold Glade," which letter sounds does Warren use most to create alliteration—the repetition of initial consonants? **(b)** What is the effect?
2. **(a)** What formal structure does Roethke use in his poem "The Light Comes Brighter"? **(b)** Why would such an orderly structure make sense for this poem?
3. In "Traveling Through the Dark," how does Stafford's use of a conversational rhythm reinforce the meaning of the poem?
4. **(a)** Use a chart like the one shown to analyze each poet's **diction.** **(b)** How does diction help to create a distinct voice in each poem?

Poet	Formal or Informal	Plain or Ornate	Abstract or Concrete	Effect
Stafford	informal	plain	concrete	casual, familiar

Comparing Literary Works

5. **(a)** Which of these poems describe everyday life? Explain. **(b)** What important ideas, if any, do the poets discover through the lens of ordinary experience?
6. **(a)** Which poem attempts to define an abstract idea? Explain. **(b)** What details do the poets use to give form to their ideas?
7. Compare and contrast two of these poems and how they use an experience from ordinary life to reflect on an abstract idea or truth.

Reading Strategy

Paraphrasing

8. Paraphrase each of the following passages: **(a)** "Gold Glade," lines 16–20; **(b)** "The Light Comes Brighter," lines 1–4.
9. For each, explain whether the paraphrase helped you to see something that was previously unclear.

Extend Understanding

10. **Science Connection:** Society sometimes tries to accommodate the needs of wildlife by making creative modifications to modern technology. Discuss some examples.

QuickReview

Style is the manner in which a writer puts ideas into words. **Diction** is a writer's word choice.

To clarify the meaning of a difficult passage, **paraphrase** it—restate it in your own words.

For: Self-test
Visit: www.PHSchool.com
Web Code: era-6605

Go Online Assessment Students may use the **Self-test** to prepare for **Selection Test A** or **Selection Test B.**

Answers

1. (a) "g" (b) The stress on this sound emphasizes and reiterates both the sounds of *gold* and *glade.* "G" is a hard sound.
2. (a) "Light" is written in quatrains of iambic pentameter. Stanza 1 is *abba;* the other stanzas are *abab.* (b) The fixed structure is appropriate for a poem that describes the eternal *cycle* of the change in seasons.
3. The conversational rhythm and ordinary diction offset the significance of the life and death decision the speaker must make.
4. (a) Students should say that all the poems use a mix of formal and informal diction; in "Gold Glade," for instance, many of the words are quite simple and everyday but the combinations are ornate and poetic.
   (b) Each poem contains a mixture of concrete and abstract.
   Another sample answer can be found on **Literary Analysis Graphic Organizer B,** p. 233 in ***Graphic Organizer Transparencies.***
5. (a) A return to a leafy glade, the change from winter to spring, and an encounter with a dead deer describe everyday life.
   (b) Roethke compares the change from winter to spring to the awakening of the creative process.
6. (a) "Light" comments on truth and the creative process.
   (b) It compares everyday sights to abstract concepts.
7. Students should consider how the poems use concrete details to reveal larger, abstract meanings.
8. (a) The glade is perfectly round. Its floor is covered with a carpet of gold leaves. A majestic object stands in the center of the glade in the gold light. (b) Spring's arrival is intense, not gentle.
9. Students may find that paraphrasing clarifies ideas.
10. Students may discuss cars that have features that repel wildlife.

EXTEND/ASSESS

Answers

1 Vocabulary Lesson

Related Words

1. exhaustion
2. exhausted
3. inexhaustible

Vocabulary Builder

1. c
2. d
3. a
4. b

Spelling Strategy

1. meditate
2. sustain
3. demonstrate
4. explain
5. refrain
6. manipulate

2 Grammar and Style Lesson

1. water escapes
2. walkers hear
3. shoots spread
4. fingers reveal
5. mind turns

Writing Application

1. A walker at the river's edge pauses to watch.
2. Once more the trees sway with the wind.
3. My fingers touching her side feel the steady beat of her heart.
4. The water stored in narrow pools shimmers in the moonlight.

WG Writing and Grammar, Ruby Level

Students will find further instruction and practice on subject and verb agreement in Chapter 23, Section 1.

Build Language Skills

1 Vocabulary Lesson

Related Words: *exhaust*

As a noun, the word *exhaust* means "the discharge of used steam or gas from an engine." *Exhaust* may also function as a verb meaning "to empty completely" or "to tire out." Other words related to *exhaust* include the following:

inexhaustible exhausted exhaustion

Complete each of the following sentences with one of the related words listed above.

1. The __?__ I felt was due to lack of sleep.
2. The marathon runner had become completely __?__.
3. A fit athlete, her energy level was usually __?__.

Vocabulary Builder: Synonyms

Select the word in the second column that is the best synonym for each word in the first column.

1. declivity	a. traces
2. domain	b. fumes
3. vestiges	c. slope
4. exhaust	d. territory

Spelling Strategy

The long *a* sound can be spelled *a*-consonant-*e*, as in *glade,* or it can be spelled *ai,* as in *domain*. In your notebook, complete the spelling of these words. If you are unsure of a word's spelling, check a dictionary.

1. medit __?__
2. sust __?__
3. demonstr __?__
4. expl __?__
5. refr __?__
6. manipul __?__

2 Grammar and Style Lesson

Subject and Verb Agreement

Subjects and verbs must agree in number, even if the verb is separated from its subject by intervening words. Study this example from "The Light Comes Brighter:"

Example: . . . the caw (S) / Of restive crows is (V) sharper on the ear.

The singular verb *is* agrees with the singular subject *caw,* not with the plural noun *crows,* which is not the subject of its clause.

Practice Identify the subject in each of the following sentences. Then, choose the correct form of the verb in parentheses.

1. The water (escapes, escape) in rivulets.
2. Walkers at the river's edge (hears, hear) a cannon crack.
3. And young shoots (spreads, spread) upon our inner world.
4. My fingers touching her side (reveals, reveal) the reason.
5. The leafy mind, that was tightly furled, (turns, turn) its private substance into green.

Writing Application For each of the following fragments, add a verb that agrees in number with the subject, and complete the sentence.

1. A walker at the river's edge . . .
2. Once more the trees . . .
3. My fingers touching her side . . .
4. The water stored in narrow pools . . .

WG Prentice Hall Writing and Grammar Connection: Chapter 23, Section 1

Assessment Practice

Grammar and Usage

Many tests require students to complete sentences with the correct form of a verb. Use the following sample test item to give students practice at this skill.

In 1946, Robert Penn Warren published *All the King's Men* and __________ the Pulitzer Prize.

Choose the correct form of the verb.

A wins
B had won
C won
D has won

(For more practice, see the Standardized *Test Preparation Workbook*, p. 61.)

Since *published* is in the past tense and both events happened during the same year, the other verb in the sentence must also be past tense. The correct answer is ***C***.

Writing Lesson

Timed Writing: Critical Response

The twentieth century American poet Robert Lowell once said, "In life we speak with many false voices; occasionally, if we are lucky, we find a true one in our poems." Choose one of these poems and write an essay in which you discuss whether or not it achieves a "true" voice. ***(40 minutes)***

Prewriting *(10 minutes)* Select the poem that you like the most. Reread it, taking notes about its message, imagery, and style. Assess why the poem speaks to you. Based on your assessment, create a list of criteria for a poem that has a "true" voice.

Model: Identifying Criteria

Judging from my reading of "Traveling Through the Dark," a true voice

- uses plain words, but in a beautiful way
- deals with a moral question
- makes me think or see in a new way

A list of criteria lays the foundation for the development of ideas in an essay.

Drafting *(20 minutes)* Begin by identifying the poem you have selected, and briefly describe its subject. Then, introduce your criteria. Use body paragraphs to explain how each of your criteria applies to the poem.

Revising *(10 minutes)* Review your essay, and make sure that each body paragraph clearly speaks to one item on your list of criteria.

Prentice Hall Writing and Grammar Connection: Chapter 14, Section 3

Extend Your Learning

Listening and Speaking Watch the film based on Robert Penn Warren's novel "All the King's Men." Take notes, and then prepare an **evaluation** of the film. To prepare, keep these tips in mind:

- Offer a brief summary of the story.
- Evaluate how effectively the film expresses ideas visually.

As you work, pay close attention to strategies the filmmakers use to shape viewers' perceptions of events and characters. **[Group Activity]**

Research and Technology Conduct library and Internet research to learn more about Robert Penn Warren, Theodore Roethke, or William Stafford. Prepare and give an **oral presentation** in which you share your findings on this poet and his work. Recite two or three of the poems you like best.

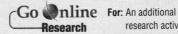

For: An additional research activity
Visit: www.PHSchool.com
Web Code: erd-7605

❸ Writing Lesson

You may use this Writing Lesson as timed-writing practice, or you may allow students to develop it as a writing assignment over several days.

- Give students the **Support for Writing Lesson,** p. 80 in ***Unit 6 Resources,*** to use as they write their critical responses.
- Encourage students to read their chosen poems several times. Repeated reading often leads to greater understanding of a literary work.
- Encourage students to paraphrase their chosen poems. This will help clarify any ideas that seem difficult or obscure.
- Use the **Response to Literature** rubric in ***General Resources*** pp. 65–66, to assess students' critical responses.

❹ Listening and Speaking

- Students may want to view the film as a group and discuss it afterwards.
- As an extension, interested students may want to try reading the novel on which the film was based.
- Use the rubrics for Critique, pp. 75–76 in ***General Resources.***
- The **Support for Extend Your Learning** page (***Unit 6 Resources,*** p. 81) provides guided note-taking opportunities to help students complete the Extend Your Learning activities.

Go Online Research — Have students type in the Web Code for another research activity.

Assessment Resources

The following resources can be used to assess students' knowledge and skills.

Unit 6 Resources
Selection Test A, pp. 83–85
Selection Test B, pp. 86–88

General Resources
Rubrics for Response to Literature, pp. 65–66
Rubrics for Critique, pp. 75–76

Go Online Assessment — Students may use the **Self-test** to prepare for **Selection Test A** or **Selection Test B.**

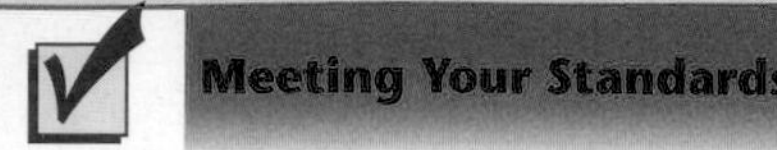

Meeting Your Standards

Students will

1. understand the connections between poems that describe chance encounters with nature.
2. understand the main idea of a poem.

Connections

Literature Around the World

Have students reread Robert Penn Warren's "Gold Glade." Like "I Wandered Lonely as a Cloud," Warren's poem describes a chance discovery about nature. Have students identify similarities between the poems' main ideas.

Moments of Discovery

- Have students discuss the seemingly random occurrences in both poems. **Ask** why such images in nature would be meaningful to poets and readers across several centuries.
  Answer: Such images in nature would be meaningful to poets and readers across several centuries because nature's beauty evokes the same emotional responses in people, no matter what century they're living in. Nature's beauty has a soothing effect on the human soul, yet its unpredictability and its power are awe-inspiring.
- Encourage students to **visualize** the images in both poems. Which poem gives the clearer image? Why?
  Possible response: Wordsworth's poem gives the clearer image because his sentence structure is much more simple and he does not use as many compound and hyphenated words as Warren.
- Point out that both revelations of nature are spontaneous. **Discuss** how the unplanned discovery affects the poets.
  Possible response: Each poet finds himself filled with awe by his spontaneous discovery in nature. The fact that each discovery was unplanned made them all the more breathtaking and memorable.

British Literature

England

Moments of Discovery

Taking a walk with no particular place to go or just wandering aimlessly through the woods can be a surprising opportunity for discovery. You might spot a deer standing still as stone among the trees or stumble upon a field of flowers shimmering in the morning light.

Wandering Into Nature Although the modern American poet Robert Penn Warren was born 135 years after the English Romantic poet William Wordsworth, both writers have explored what it means to encounter nature in just such an unexpected moment of discovery. Both Warren's "Gold Glade" (page 1050) and Wordsworth's "I Wandered Lonely as a Cloud," presented here, show a speaker's chance discovery of natural beauty while taking an aimless, ambling walk—"wandering" without any formal destination in mind. Both speakers are transformed by what they see: a startling image that haunts their mind's eye forever. As you read Wordsworth's famous poem, think about why the sight of the daffodils affects the speaker the way it does. Then, consider the ways in which his experience connects to the speaker's encounter with nature in "Gold Glade."

I Wandered Lonely as a Cloud

William Wordsworth

I wandered lonely as a cloud
That floats on high o'er vales[1] and hills,
When all at once I saw a crowd,
A host, of golden daffodils;
Beside the lake, beneath the trees,
Fluttering and dancing in the breeze.

Continuous as the stars that shine
And twinkle on the milky way,
They stretched in never-ending line
Along the margin of a bay:
Ten thousand saw I at a glance,
Tossing their heads in sprightly dance.

The waves beside them danced; but they
Outdid the sparkling waves in glee;
A poet could not but be gay,
In such a jocund[2] company;
I gazed—and gazed—but little thought
What wealth the show to me had brought:

For oft, when on my couch I lie
In vacant or in pensive mood,
They flash upon that inward eye
Which is the bliss of solitude;
And then my heart with pleasure fills,
And dances with the daffodils.

1. **o'er vales** over valleys.
2. **jocund** (jak′ ənd) *adj.* cheerful.

CONNECTIONS

Vocabulary Builder

host (hōst) *n.* great number

pensive (pen′ siv) *adj.* thinking deeply

William Wordsworth (1770–1850)

William Wordsworth was born in England's rural Lake District. As a young man, he spent time in France and became a supporter of the French Revolution's ideals of equality, social justice, and individual rights. Although Wordsworth became disillusioned with the Revolution as it turned bloody, he transferred his ideals to the realm of literature. In 1798, Wordsworth and fellow poet Samuel Taylor Coleridge published a poetry collection called *Lyrical Ballads.* Unlike the formal, elaborate verse that was popular at the time, the poems in this book used simple language to exalt remarkable moments in everyday life—and to express a deep connection between nature and the human mind.

Connecting British Literature

1. **(a)** In Wordsworth's "I Wandered Lonely as a Cloud" and Warren's "Gold Glade," what color does each speaker use to describe what he discovers on his walk? **(b)** What larger meaning might this color suggest? Explain your answer.
2. **(a)** Compare and contrast each speaker's description of his encounter with nature. **(b)** Compare and contrast the ways in which each speaker's memory of that encounter affects his experience with nature.
3. **(a)** What is the "inward eye" (line 21) that the speaker mentions in "I Wandered Lonely as a Cloud"? **(b)** What is the "mind's eye" (line 7) that the speaker mentions in "Gold Glade"? **(c)** Do you think that the two speakers are referring to the same thing? Explain your answer.

ASSESS

Answers

1. (a) Both speakers mention gold. (b) It could suggest joy, happiness, or hope because this color is considered bright and cheerful. Gold is also a metal of enduring value and could indicate permanence.
2. (a) Wordsworth's description is more cheerful; he describes flowers and uses words such as "floats," "twinkle," and "dance." Warren's description is more melancholy. He uses words that evoke sorrow, such as "heart-hurt" and "grief-fall," and he describes trees rather than flowers. Both speakers look back on the discovery after many years. (b) Wordsworth's speaker's encounter with nature brings joy; Warren's speaker seems puzzled about whether the image is real, although, like Wordsworth's speaker, Warren's cherishes the memory and wishes to return, whether in reality or in the mind's eye.
3. (a) The "inward eye" refers to memory and reflection. (b) The "mind's eye" sees an image of the hidden water. (c) They are not referring to the same thing. Wordsworth uses the term as his speaker recalls concrete images from the past; Warren's speaker's "mind's eye" is imagining what remains unseen but has become part of memory.

Differentiated Instruction

Solutions for All Learners

Vocabulary for English Learners
Students may feel some confusion about the poetic diction in Wordsworth's poem. Point out these words that are used in an uncommon way: c rowd, "dancing," and "wealth." Help them discover the sense that Wordsworth meant for the words by looking at the alternate definitions. For example, "wealth" in line 18 does not refer to money, which is the first definition in many dictionaries. Have students determine the intended meanings of words that puzzle them.

Enrichment for Gifted/Talented Students
Students may be struck by the imagery or rhythm of the Wordsworth poem. Invite artistically talented students to transform Wordsworth's verbal description into a sketch or painting of the field of daffodils. Challenge them to make their portrayal as colorful and memorable as the original. Musically talented students may wish to compose a piece that duplicates the rhythm of the original poem or to find a recording of a classical work that would be appropriate background music for reading the poem.

Meeting Your Standards

Students will

1. **analyze and respond to literary elements.**
   - Literary Analysis: Foreshadowing
2. **read, comprehend, analyze, and critique a short story.**
   - Reading Strategy: Putting Events in Order
   - Reading Check questions
   - Apply the Skills questions
   - Assessment Practice (ATE)
3. **develop vocabulary.**
   - Vocabulary Lesson: Latin Prefix: *trans-*
4. **understand and apply written and oral language conventions.**
   - Spelling Strategy
   - Grammar and Style Lesson: Correct Use of Adjectives and Adverbs
5. **develop writing proficiency.**
   - Writing Lesson: Social Worker's Report
6. **develop appropriate research strategies.**
   - Extend Your Learning: Research Report
7. **understand and apply listening and speaking strategies.**
   - Extend Your Learning: Political Speech

Block Scheduling: Use one 90-minute class period to preteach the skills and have students read the selection. Use a second 90-minute class period to assess students' mastery of skills, extend their learning, and monitor their progress.

Homework Suggestions

Following are possibilities for homework assignments.

- Support pages from ***Unit 6 Resources:***
  - **Literary Analysis**
  - **Reading Strategy**
  - **Vocabulary Builder**
  - **Grammar and Style**
- An Extend Your Learning project and the Writing Lesson for this selection may be completed over several days.

Step-by-Step Teaching Guide	Pacing Guide
PRETEACH	
• Administer Vocabulary and Reading Warm-ups as necessary.	5 min.
• Engage students' interest with the motivation activity.	5 min.
• Read and discuss author and background features. **FT**	10 min.
• Introduce the Literary Analysis Skill: Foreshadowing. **FT**	5 min.
• Introduce the Reading Strategy: Putting Events in Order. **FT**	10 min.
• Prepare students to read by teaching the selection vocabulary. **FT**	
TEACH	
• Informally monitor comprehension while students read independently or in groups. **FT**	30 min.
• Monitor students' comprehension with the Reading Check notes.	as students read
• Reinforce vocabulary with Vocabulary Builder notes.	as students read
• Develop students' understanding of foreshadowing with the Literary Analysis annotations. **FT**	5 min.
• Develop students' ability to put events in order with the Reading Strategy annotations. **FT**	5 min.
ASSESS/EXTEND	
• Assess students' comprehension and mastery of the Literary Analysis and Reading Strategy by having them answer the Apply the Skills questions. **FT**	15 min.
• Have students complete the Vocabulary Lesson and the Grammar and Style Lesson. **FT**	15 min.
• Apply students' ability to use transitions to show cause and effect by using the Writing Lesson. **FT**	45 min. or homework
• Apply students' understanding by using one or more of the Extend Your Learning activities.	20–90 min. or homework
• Administer Selection Test A or Selection Test B. **FT**	15 min.

Resources

PRINT

Unit 6 Resources

TRANSPARENCY

Graphic Organizer Transparencies

PRINT

Reader's Notebook [L2]
Reader's Notebook: Adapted Version [L1]
Reader's Notebook: English Learner's Version [EL]

Unit 6 Resources

TECHNOLOGY

Listening to Literature Audio CDs [L2, EL]

PRINT

Unit 6 Resources

TRANSPARENCY

Graphic Organizer Transparencies

General Resources

TECHNOLOGY

Go Online: Research **[L3]**
Go Online: Self-test **[L3]**
***ExamView®* Test Bank [L3]**

Choosing Resources for Differentiated Instruction

[L1] Special Needs Students
[L2] Below-Level Students
[L3] All Students
[L4] Advanced Students
[EL] English Learners

For Vocabulary and Reading Warm-ups and for Selection Tests, **A** signifies "less challenging" and **B** "more challenging." For Graphic Organizer transparencies, **A** signifies "not filled in" and **B** "filled in."

FT Fast Track Instruction: To move the lesson more quickly, use the strategies and activities identified with **FT**.

Scaffolding for Less Proficient and Advanced Students

The leveled Critical Thinking questions after selections progress in the levels of thinking required to answer them. To address the needs of your different students, you may use the (a) level questions for your less proficient students and the (b) level questions with your on-level and advanced students. The occasional (c) level questions are appropriate for your advanced students.

PRENTICE HALL **TeacherEXPRESS™** Plan · Teach · Assess Use this complete suite of powerful teaching tools to make lesson planning and testing quicker and easier.

PRENTICE HALL **StudentEXPRESS™** Learn · Study · Succeed Use the interactive textbook (online and on CD-ROM) to make selections and activities come alive with audio and video support and interactive questions.

Go Online Professional Development **For:** Information about Lexiles **Visit:** www.PHSchool.com **Web Code:** eue-1111

Motivation

Students may find this story of ambivalence in the face of seemingly unavoidable change both touching and depressing. Involve them in considering the range of human reactions to change by presenting the following dramatization. Ask the school principal to announce to your class an impending major change—for example, relocating the school, the retirement of a popular teacher, or cancellation of the athletic program. Ask students to identify both positive and negative reactions to the proposed change. Lead from this discussion of change to the story, in which the main character experiences emotional extremes when facing an important life change.

❶ Background

More About the Author

Author Anne Tyler is celebrated for her sensitive ear for dialogue and her lifelike contemporary characters with whom readers can relate. Tyler's themes are human experiences—relationships between husbands and wives, parents and children, siblings; the meaning of love; the nature of identity; impermanence and change.

Tyler, who strives to make each novel an "extremely believable lie," hopes to be known as a writer of serious, not necessarily important, books, ones that have "layers and layers and layers, like life does."

Build Skills *Short Story*

❶Average Waves in Unprotected Waters

Anne Tyler (b. 1941)

As the wife of a child psychiatrist and the mother of two daughters, Anne Tyler has for years successfully juggled the demands of family life while maintaining her commitment to writing. She works at home in her starkly plain study, seated on a daybed. She pens her fiction in longhand so that, as she explains it, she can hear her characters speak. During occasional bouts of insomnia, she records her ideas in boxes of index cards.

Everyday People Tyler, who has remained a private person despite her fame, lives in Baltimore, Maryland, a city that provides a strong setting for her work. Many of her stories focus on the loneliness and isolation of ordinary middle-class people.

Young Talent Born in Minneapolis, Tyler spent most of her early childhood in Quaker communes in the Midwest and South. This experience, she recalls, was helpful to her as a writer because it enabled her to look "at the normal world with a certain amount of distance and surprise." After attending high school in Raleigh, North Carolina, she enrolled at Duke University to study Russian when she was sixteen. After graduating from college, she worked as a bibliographer at Duke and then moved to Montreal, Canada, where she held a job as a librarian at McGill University.

Tyler began her writing career with a series of short stories, few of which were published. Then, at age twenty-four, she published her first work, the novel *If Morning Ever Comes.* The book depicts a young man who returns home and attempts to find his identity amid overpowering family expectations. Since then Tyler has produced a string of novels to ever-increasing acclaim. Among them are *Dinner at the Homesick Restaurant* (1982); *The Accidental Tourist* (1985), which was made into a film in 1988; *Breathing Lessons* (1988), winner of the 1989 Pulitzer Prize for Fiction; *Back When We Were Grown Ups* (2000); and *The Amateur Marriage* (2004). Tyler has also published numerous short stories in literary magazines like *The New Yorker.*

Serious Fiction When Tyler works on a novel, she follows a pattern. First, she writes out a draft in longhand. She then reads the draft to "find out what it means." She revises the draft to enhance "the subconscious intentions" she has discovered in the work. Tyler keeps the goal of writing "serious fiction" firmly in sight. Her characters are not fictionalized versions of people from her own life; instead, they are products of a fertile imagination that are drawn with her gift for fine, realistic detail.

Eccentrics Tyler has a flair for creating eccentric people in improbable yet touching plots. Her compassion, wit, and use of the precise details of domestic life flavor her tales of relationships and family dynamics. Her overall theme may be seen as the persistent endurance of the human spirit in the face of the inevitable struggles and strains of daily life.

"Average Waves in Unprotected Waters," which was first published in *The New Yorker* in 1977, displays Tyler's ability to create well-developed, realistic characters and to evoke an emotional response through an unsentimental portrayal of the characters' tragic lives.

Preview

Connecting to the Literature

A family move, a transfer to a new school—these events can present both problems and challenges. In this story, the main character faces the reality that a painful change in her life just may be for the better.

2 Literary Analysis

Foreshadowing

Foreshadowing is the use of details or clues that hint at what will occur later in a plot or suggest a certain outcome. Foreshadowing builds suspense because it makes the reader wonder what will happen next or how the story will end, as this passage demonstrates:

> Maybe she felt to blame that he was going. But she'd done the best she could: babysat him all these years and only given up when he'd grown too strong and wild to manage.

As you read, notice how Tyler's use of foreshadowing keeps you guessing about the story's outcome.

Connecting Literary Elements

An effective use of foreshadowing can heighten the suspense for readers and pique their interest to read further. **Suspense** is a feeling of growing uncertainty about the outcome of events in a literary work. Writers create suspense by raising questions in readers' minds. Because most people are curious or concerned, they keep reading to find out what will happen next. As you read, notice how the suspense makes you anxious to learn the outcome.

3 Reading Strategy

Putting Events in Order

Most stories are written in chronological order—the order in which events happen in real time. Sometimes, however, the writer interrupts the sequence to present a flashback—a scene or an event from an earlier time. As you read Tyler's story, **put the events in order** by noting the sequence in which they actually occurred. Create a chain-of-events diagram like the one shown to record the events in order, from the earliest to the latest.

Order of Events

Vocabulary Builder

orthopedic (ôr′ thō pē′ dik) *adj.* correcting posture or other disorders of the skeletal system (p. 1064)

transparent (trans per′ ənt) *adj.* capable of being seen through (p. 1065)

stocky (stäk′ ē) *adj.* solidly built; sturdy (p. 1065)

staunch (stônch) *adj.* strong; unyielding (p. 1066)

viper (vī′ pər) *n.* type of snake; a malicious person (p. 1066)

2 Literary Analysis

Foreshadowing

- Explain to students that they will focus on foreshadowing, clues to events that will occur later in the story, as they read "Average Waves in Unprotected Waters."
- Draw students' attention to the example of foreshadowing. Have them consider how foreshadowing builds suspense.

3 Reading Strategy

Putting Events in Order

- Reiterate to students that most stories are written in chronological order. Tell students that strict chronological order in a story may be interrupted by a flashback or flash forward, a memory of an action that has already taken place or one that is yet to come.
- On the board, draw a chart like the one on p. 1061 and have volunteers tell a few events from a common fairy tale in the order that they occurred.
- Give students a copy of **Reading Strategy Graphic Organizer A,** p. 234 in ***Graphic Organizer Transparencies,*** to record the main events in "Average Waves in Unprotected Waters" in chronological order. Caution them to watch out for flashbacks.

Vocabulary Builder

- Pronounce each vocabulary word for students, and read the definitions as a class. Have students identify any words with which they are already familiar.

Differentiated Instruction
Solutions for All Learners

Support for Special Needs Students
Have students complete the **Preview** and **Build Skills** pages for the selection in the ***Reader's Notebook: Adapted Version.*** These pages provide a selection summary, an abbreviated presentation of the reading and literary skills, and the graphic organizer on the **Build Skills** page in the student book.

Support for Less Proficient Readers
Have students complete the **Preview** and **Build Skills** pages for the selection in the ***Reader's Notebook***. These pages provide a selection summary, an abbreviated presentation of the reading and literary skills, and the graphic organizer on the **Build Skills** page in the student book.

Support for English Learners
Have students complete the **Preview** and **Build Skills** pages for the selection in the ***Reader's Notebook: English Learner's Version.*** These pages provide a selection summary, an abbreviated presentation of the skills, and the graphic organizer on the **Build Skills** page in the student book.

Learning Modalities
Musical/Rhythmic Learners Point out the care with which Bet modulates her tone of voice, sure that it will reveal too much of her feelings to Arnold. As Bet, have students read portions of the text aloud, listening for the intonations that might signal to Arnold that something is amiss.

❶ About the Selection

In this story, readers meet Bet, a woman torn apart emotionally by the difficult decision she has made about the care of her mentally challenged son, Arnold. As Bet accompanies Arnold to his new home, guiding him and helping him negotiate the obstacles of travel, she recalls the events that have brought her to this point. Readers learn of the gritty perseverance that has enabled her to endure the catastrophic events of her life, which have washed over her like "average waves in unprotected waters." As Bet leaves her son behind in a mental hospital, she is torn with ambivalent feelings of guilt and relief as she realizes that she will no longer participate in the daily agonies of caring for Arnold.

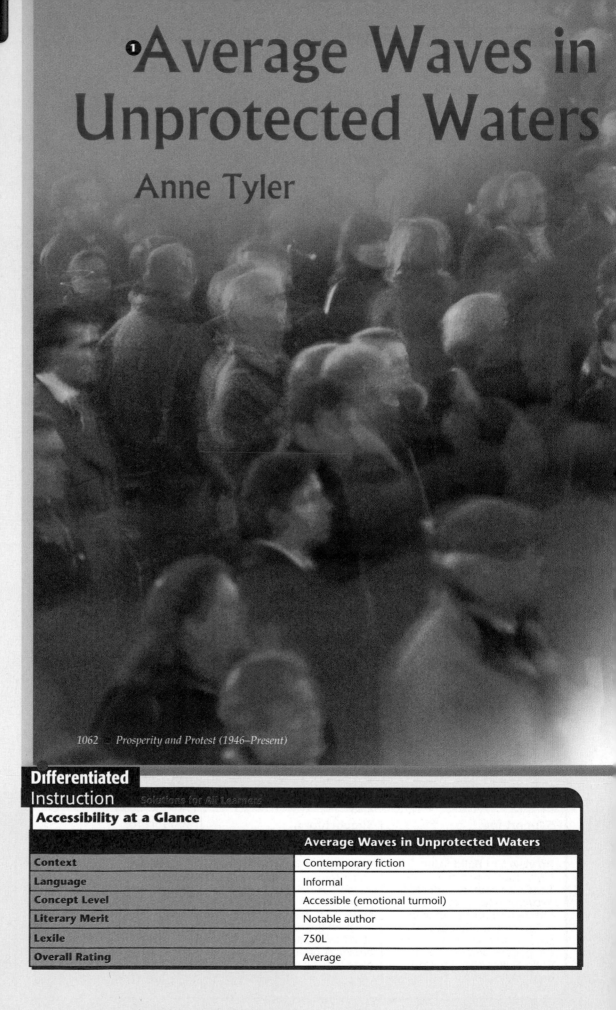

❶ Average Waves in Unprotected Waters

Anne Tyler

Differentiated Instruction Solutions for All Learners

Accessibility at a Glance

	Average Waves in Unprotected Waters
Context	Contemporary fiction
Language	Informal
Concept Level	Accessible (emotional turmoil)
Literary Merit	Notable author
Lexile	750L
Overall Rating	Average

Background

The decision to institutionalize a child is an extremely difficult one. In this story, Anne Tyler explores a single mother's attempts to care for a severely mentally challenged child. When this story was written in the mid-1970s, a single parent may have felt she had few other options available to her. Then, as now, the cost of private care was so high that many patients were placed in state-run or charitable hospitals where lack of funding sometimes resulted in grim conditions, outdated equipment, and an inadequate staff. Fortunately, an array of educational, medical, and counseling programs for children with special needs today makes it possible for many of them who might once have been institutionalized to remain at home.

As soon as it got light, Bet woke him and dressed him, and then she walked him over to the table and tried to make him eat a little cereal. He wouldn't, though. He could tell something was up. She pressed the edge of the spoon against his lips till she heard it click on his teeth, but he just looked off at a corner of the ceiling—a knobby child with great glassy eyes and her own fair hair. Like any other nine-year-old, he wore a striped shirt and jeans, but the shirt was too neat and the jeans too blue, unpatched and unfaded, and would stay that way till he outgrew them. And his face was elderly—pinched, strained, tired—though it should have looked as unused as his jeans. He hardly ever changed his expression.

She left him in his chair and went to make the beds. Then she raised the yellowed shade, rinsed a few spoons in the bathroom sink, picked up some bits of magazines he'd torn the night before. This was a rented room in an ancient, crumbling house, and nothing you could do to it would lighten its cluttered look. There was always that feeling of too many lives layered over other lives, like the layers of brownish wallpaper her child had peeled away in the corner by his bed.

She slipped her feet into flat-heeled loafers and absently patted the front of her dress, a worn beige knit she usually saved for Sundays. Maybe she should take it in a little; it hung from her shoulders like a sack. She felt too slight and frail, too wispy for all she had to do today. But she reached for her coat anyhow, and put it on and tied a blue kerchief under her chin. Then she went over to the table and slowly spun, modeling the coat. "See, Arnold?" she said. "We're going out."

Arnold went on looking at the ceiling, but his gaze turned wild and she knew he'd heard.

Literary Analysis
Foreshadowing What details in this paragraph hint that something unusual, or even unpleasant, may lie ahead?

Reading Check 4

What is Arnold's reaction as his mother busily prepares to leave the house?

◀ **Critical Viewing** How might this busy scene at a train station represent the isolation or alienation Bet feels in this story? **[Connect]**

Differentiated Instruction
Solutions for All Learners

Strategy for Special Needs Students
To help students gain some insight into the two characters, ask them to list adjectives to describe Arnold and Bet. Then, have small groups of students discuss these questions: What are Bet's feelings toward Arnold? How does her son feel about her?

Enrichment for Gifted/Talented Students
Ask students to think of songs and poems that capture the feeling they get from reading this page. Ask students to gather in small groups to share their songs and poems. Then, have them discuss the emotions this page arouses and the devices the author uses to evoke these emotions.

Enrichment for Advanced Readers
Ask students to gather in small groups to discuss the beginning of the story. What mood or tone does the author establish in the first paragraph? How does she accomplish this task? In what ways do the figurative language and the point of view contribute to the emotional content of this page?

2 Literary Analysis
Foreshadowing

- Point out that the bracketed passage is an example of foreshadowing.
- **Ask** whether the event coming up is likely to be pleasant or unpleasant.
  Answer: Most students will believe that the event will be unpleasant because the boy seems upset.
- **Ask** the Literary Analysis question: What details in this paragraph hint that something unusual, or even unpleasant, may lie ahead?
  Answer: Details include the following: The boy and his mother are up before daylight. The boy won't eat. He seems upset.

3 Literary Analysis
Foreshadowing

- **Ask** students to identify the foreshadowing in the passage.
  Answer: Bet wears a dress she usually wears only on Sunday, and she feels too frail for all she has to do this day.
- Point out to students that the foreshadowing indicates the importance of an upcoming journey.

▶ **Monitor Progress:** Have students who can't identify the foreshadowing or speculate about its possible implications consider why the author included the information. Remind them that authors have a purpose for all the details they include. Good readers will wonder why the author decided to have Bet wear her Sunday dress on a weekday. They will realize that the Sunday dress suggests that Bet faces a day of great importance.

4 Reading Check
Answer: Arnold is upset. He refuses to eat and gazes about wildly.

5 Critical Viewing
Possible response: It is said that people feel most alone in a crowd. No matter how many people Bet is surrounded by, she will always be lonely for her son.

❻ Literary Analysis
Foreshadowing

- Remind students that foreshadowing builds suspense by hinting at what might happen next.
- Read the bracketed passage aloud, and **ask** students to describe Mrs. Puckett's behavior.
Answer: Mrs. Puckett waits outside her door with tear-filled eyes and quavering voice, and makes Arnold peanut butter cookies.
- Then, **ask** the Literary Analysis question: What does Mrs. Puckett's behavior hint about the events to come?
Answer: Mrs. Puckett is distressed; her behavior indicates she is worried about what will happen to Arnold.

❼ Reading Strategy
Putting Events in Order

- **Ask** students to identify when in the chronology of the story the bracketed passage occurs.
Answer: Mrs. Puckett had cared for Arnold from early childhood until recently.
- **Ask:** How does inserting this information about past events help clarify the current situation?
Answer: The reference to the change in Arnold's behavior explains why his mother feels she must make new arrangements for his care.

❽ Critical Thinking
Predict

- Have students **predict** where Bet and Arnold are going.
- Have students give reasons for their predictions. Remind them that they should base their ideas on details about the characters and the plot.
Answer: Many students will predict that Arnold is going to some sort of institution because his mother can no longer care for him.

She fetched his jacket from the closet—brown corduroy, with a hood. It had set her back half a week's salary. But Arnold didn't like it; he always wanted his old one, a little red duffel coat he'd long ago outgrown. When she came toward him, he started moaning and rocking and shaking his head. She had to struggle to stuff his arms in the sleeves. Small though he was, he was strong, wiry; he was getting to be too much for her. He shook free of her hands and ran over to his bed. The jacket was on, though. It wasn't buttoned, the collar was askew, but never mind; that just made him look more real. She always felt bad at how he stood inside his clothes, separate from them, passive, unaware of all the buttons and snaps she'd fastened as carefully as she would a doll's.

She gave a last look around the room, checked to make sure the hot plate was off, and then picked up her purse and Arnold's suitcase. "Come along, Arnold," she said.

He came, dragging out every step. He looked at the suitcase suspiciously, but only because it was new. It didn't have any meaning for him. "See?" she said. "It's yours. It's Arnold's. It's going on the train with us."

But her voice was all wrong. He would pick it up, for sure. She paused in the middle of locking the door and glanced over at him fearfully. Anything could set him off nowadays. He hadn't noticed, though. He was too busy staring around the hallway, goggling at a freckled, walnut-framed mirror as if he'd never seen it before. She touched his shoulder. "Come, Arnold," she said.

❻ They went down the stairs slowly, both of them clinging to the sticky mahogany railing. The suitcase banged against her shins. In the entrance hall, old Mrs. Puckett stood waiting outside her door—a huge, soft lady in a black crepe dress and orthopedic shoes. She was holding a plastic bag of peanutbutter cookies, Arnold's favorites. ❼ There were tears in her eyes. "Here, Arnold," she said, quavering. Maybe she felt to blame that he was going. But she'd done the best she could: babysat him all these years and only given up when he'd grown too strong and wild to manage. Bet wished Arnold would give the old lady some sign—hug her, make his little crowing noise, just take the cookies, even. But he was too excited. He raced on out the front door, and it was Bet who had to take them. "Well, thank you, Mrs. Puckett," she said. "I know he'll enjoy them later."

"Oh, no . . ." said Mrs. Puckett, and she flapped her large hands and gave up, sobbing.

They were lucky and caught a bus first thing. Arnold sat by the window. He must have thought he was going to work with her; when they passed the red-and-gold Kresge's sign, he jabbered and tried to stand up. "No, honey," she said, and took hold of his arm. He settled down then and let his hand stay curled in hers awhile. He had very small, cool fingers, and nails as smooth as thumbtack heads.

❽ At the train station, she bought the tickets and then a pack of Wrigley's spearmint gum. Arnold stood gaping at the vaulted ceiling,

Vocabulary Builder
orthopedic (ôr′ thō pē′ dik) *adj.* correcting posture or other disorders of the skeletal system

Literary Analysis
Foreshadowing What does Mrs. Puckett's behavior hint about the events to come?

Differentiated Instruction
Solutions for All Learners

Enrichment for Gifted/Talented Students
Have students do some research to find out what resources are available in their community to help support parents, especially single parents, who are caretakers of children with mental disabilities similar to Arnold's. Then, have them write a dialogue between Bet and a social worker who has been assigned to help her find the best ways to take care of her son and make the most of his potential for learning. Have students perform their dialogues for the rest of the class.

Enrichment for Advanced Readers
Have students research the mainstreaming of mentally and physically disabled students into general classrooms. Have them consider such questions as when and why mainstreaming began and what the goal of mainstreaming is. Have students write about or discuss the benefits and liabilities of mainstreaming. Urge students to suggest ways that mainstreaming could be modified to work even better than it now does.

with his head flopped back and his arms hanging limp at his sides. People stared at him. She would have liked to push their faces in. "Over here, honey," she said, and she nudged him toward the gate, straightening his collar as they walked.

He hadn't been on a train before and acted a little nervous, bouncing up and down in his seat and flipping the lid of his ashtray and craning forward to see the man ahead of them. When the train started moving, he crowed and pulled at her sleeve. "That's right, Arnold. Train. We're taking a trip," Bet said. She unwrapped a stick of chewing gum and gave it to him. He loved gum. If she didn't watch him closely, he sometimes swallowed it—which worried her a little because she'd heard it clogged your kidneys; but at least it would keep him busy. She looked down at the top of his head. Through the blond prickles of his hair, cut short for practical reasons, she could see his skull bones moving as he chewed. He was so thin-skinned, almost transparent; sometimes she imagined she could see the blood traveling in his veins.

When the train reached a steady speed, he grew calmer, and after a while he nodded over against her and let his hands sag on his knees. She watched his eyelashes slowly drooping—two colorless, fringed crescents, heavier and heavier, every now and then flying up as he tried to fight off sleep. He had never slept well, not ever, not even as a baby. Even before they'd noticed anything wrong, they'd wondered at his jittery, jerky catnaps, his tiny hands clutching tight and springing open, his strange single wail sailing out while he went right on sleeping. Avery said it gave him the chills. And after the doctor talked to them Avery wouldn't have anything to do with Arnold anymore—just walked in wide circles around the crib, looking stunned and sick. A few weeks later, he left. She wasn't surprised. She even knew how he felt, more or less. Halfway, he blamed her; halfway, he blamed himself. You can't believe a thing like this will just fall on you out of nowhere.

She'd had moments herself of picturing some kind of evil gene in her husband's ordinary, stocky body—a dark little egg like a black jelly bean, she imagined it. All his fault. But other times she was sure the gene was hers. It seemed so natural; she never could do anything as well as most people. And then other times she blamed their marriage. They'd married too young, against her parents' wishes. All she'd wanted was to get away from home. Now she couldn't remember why. What was wrong with home? She thought of her parents' humped green trailer, perched on cinder blocks near a forest of masts in Salt Spray, Maryland. At this distance (parents dead, trailer rusted to bits, even Salt Spray changed past recognition), it seemed to her that her old life had been beautifully free and spacious. She closed her eyes and saw wide gray skies. Everything had been ruled by the sea. Her father (who'd run a fishing boat for tourists) couldn't arrange his day till he'd heard the marine forecast—the wind, the tides, the small-craft warnings, the height of average waves in unprotected waters. He loved to fish, offshore and on, and he swam every chance he could get. He'd tried to teach her to bodysurf, but it hadn't worked out.

Vocabulary Builder
transparent (trans per′ ənt) *adj.* capable of being seen through

Vocabulary Builder
stocky (stäk′ ē) *adj.* solidly built; sturdy

Reading Strategy
Putting Events in Order
What clues tell you that Bet is recalling the past?

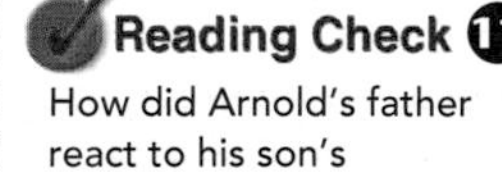
Reading Check 11
How did Arnold's father react to his son's condition?

9 Vocabulary Builder
Latin Prefix *trans-*

- Call students' attention to the word *transparent.* Tell them that the prefix *trans-* means "across," "over," or "through." *Transparent* means "able to be seen through."
- Have volunteers **suggest** other words with the prefix *trans-* and explain what each word means. Write the words on the board.
  Answer: Words with the prefix *trans-* include, among many others, *transfix, transcend, transcribe, transfer, translate, transportation,* and *transit.*

10 Reading Strategy
Putting Events in Order

- Have a volunteer read the bracketed passage aloud. Then, **ask** the Reading Strategy question: What clues tell you that Bet is recalling the past?
  Answer: Clues include Arnold's sleep habits, which remind Bet of how Arnold slept as a baby. Moreover, Bet is described as "picturing" events from the past. Bet lets memories of those times propel her further into her own childhood.
- Make sure that students realize that the flashback begins with Arnold's childhood, then moves to Bet's childhood, and finally explores her marriage to Avery.

➤ **Monitor Progress: Ask** students to suggest some reasons why Bet might recall events out of chronological order.
Answer: Students may point out that thinking of Arnold's childhood naturally leads Bet to contrast it with her own childhood. The memory of her father then leads to memories of Arnold's father.

11 Reading Check

Answer: Avery left his baby and wife a few weeks after they learned that the baby had a mental disability.

12 Critical Thinking
Connect

- **Ask** students whether they think Bet's habit of enduring is a good and useful one.
  Possible answers: Some students will believe that Bet's stoicism is useful since she can't change Arnold's condition; many students will believe Bet could do more for Arnold and herself if she were more assertive.
- Have students **identify** an episode from Bet's childhood that demonstrates this character trait.
  Answer: Bet demonstrates her stoic endurance when she lets the waves slam into her rather than attempting to bodysurf.

13 Literary Analysis
Foreshadowing and Suspense

- **Ask** students what details and phrases clue them in to the threatening tone of the bracketed passage.
  Possible response: The conductor "lurched down the aisle, plucking pink tickets"; the lady's coat has a "fox fur piece biting its own tail," her muscles twitch; she waves a "spidery hand."
- Then, **ask** the Literary Analysis question: In what ways does this scene raise questions in your mind and create suspense?
  Answer: The scene is suspenseful because the reader has no idea whether the woman is going to pay for her ticket or be put off the train.

There was something about the breakers: she just gritted her teeth and stood staunch and let them slam into her. As if standing staunch were a virtue, really. She couldn't explain it. Her father thought she was scared, but it wasn't that at all.

She'd married Avery against their wishes and been sorry ever since—sorry to move so far from home, sorrier when her parents died within a year of each other, sorriest of all when the marriage turned grim and cranky. But she never would have thought of leaving him. It was Avery who left; she would have stayed forever. In fact, she did stay on in their apartment for months after he'd gone, though the rent
12 was far too high. It wasn't that she expected him back. She just took some comfort from enduring.

Arnold's head snapped up. He looked around him and made a gurgling sound. His chewing gum fell onto the front of his jacket. "Here, honey," she told him. She put the gum in her ashtray. "Look out the window. See the cows?"

He wouldn't look. He began bouncing in his seat, rubbing his hands together rapidly.

"Arnold? Want a cookie?"

If only she'd brought a picture book. She'd meant to and then forgot. She wondered if the train people sold magazines. If she let him get too bored, he'd go into one of his tantrums, and then she wouldn't be able to handle him. The doctor had given her pills just in case, but she was always afraid that while he was screaming he would choke on them. She looked around the car. "Arnold," she said, "see the . . . see the hat with feathers on? Isn't it pretty? See the red suitcase? See the, um . . ."

The car door opened with a rush of clattering wheels and the conductor burst in, singing "Girl of my dreams, I love you." He lurched down the aisle, plucking pink tickets from the back of each seat. Just across from Bet and Arnold, he stopped. He was looking down at a tiny black lady in a purple coat, with a fox fur piece biting its own tail around her neck. "You!" he said.

The lady stared straight ahead.

"You, I saw you. You're the one in the washroom."

13 A little muscle twitched in her cheek.

"You got on this train in Beulah, didn't you. Snuck in the washroom. Darted back like you thought you could put something over on me. I saw that bit of purple! Where's your ticket gone to?"

She started fumbling in a blue cloth purse. The fumbling went on and on. The conductor shifted his weight.

"Why!" she said finally. "I must've left it back in my other seat."

"What other seat?"

"Oh, the one back . . ." She waved a spidery hand.

The conductor sighed. "Lady," he said, "you owe me money."

"I do no such thing!" she said. "Viper! Monger! Hitler!"[1] Her voice screeched up all at once; she sounded like a parrot. Bet winced and felt

Vocabulary Builder
staunch (stônch) *adj.* strong; unyielding

Literary Analysis
Foreshadowing and Suspense In what ways does this scene raise questions in your mind and create suspense?

Vocabulary Builder
viper (vī′ pər) *n.* type of snake; a malicious person

1. **Hitler** German dictator Adolf Hitler (1889–1945).

Enrichment

Specialized Skills
Several characters in the story—the narrator, Mrs. Puckett, and the nurse—must care for a young, mentally challenged boy. Challenge students to brainstorm for a list of skills a caregiver would need to care for the mentally challenged properly and kindly. Discuss how interested students might acquire these skills. Does your community offer training classes, or does a local hospital offer internships? Then, discuss whether these skills might be useful in other workplace or family situations.

herself flushing, as if *she* were the one. But then at her shoulder she heard a sudden, rusty clang, and she turned and saw that Arnold was laughing. He had his mouth wide open and his tongue curled, the way he did when he watched "Sesame Street." Even after the scene had worn itself out, and the lady had paid and the conductor had moved on, Arnold went on chortling and la-la-ing, and Bet looked gratefully at the little black lady, who was settling her fur piece fussily and muttering under her breath.

From the Parkinsville Railroad Station, which they seemed to be tearing down or else remodeling—she couldn't tell which—they took a taxicab to Parkins State Hospital. "Oh, I been out there many and many a time," said the driver. "Went out there just the other—"

But she couldn't stop herself; she had to tell him before she forgot. "Listen," she said, "I want you to wait for me right in the driveway. I don't want you to go on away."

"Well, fine," he said.

"Can you do that? I want you to be sitting right by the porch or the steps or whatever, right where I come out of, ready to take me back to the station. Don't just go off, and—"

"I *got* you, I got you," he said.

She sank back. She hoped he understood.

Arnold wanted a peanut-butter cookie. He was reaching and whimpering. She didn't know what to do. She wanted to give him anything he asked for, anything; but he'd get it all over his face and arrive not looking his best. She couldn't stand it if they thought he was just ordinary and unattractive. She wanted them to see how small and neat he was, how somebody cherished him. But it would be awful if he went into one of his rages. She broke off a little piece of cookie from the bag. "Here," she told him. "Don't mess, now."

He flung himself back in the corner and ate it, keeping one hand flattened across his mouth while he chewed.

The hospital looked like someone's great, pillared mansion, with square brick buildings all around it. "Here we are," the driver said.

"Thank you," she said. "Now you wait here, please. Just wait till I get—"

"*Lady,*" he said. "I'll wait."

She opened the door and nudged Arnold out ahead of her. Lugging the suitcase, she started toward the steps. "Come on, Arnold," she said.

He hung back.

"Arnold?"

Maybe he wouldn't allow it, and they would go on home and never think of this again.

But he came, finally, climbing the steps in his little hobbled way. His face was clean, but there were a few cookie crumbs on his jacket. She set down the suitcase to brush them off. Then she buttoned all his buttons and smoothed his shirt collar over his jacket collar before she pushed open the door.

Literary Analysis
Foreshadowing and Suspense What questions does Bet's request raise in your mind?

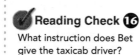

Reading Check 16
What instruction does Bet give the taxicab driver?

14 Literary Analysis
Foreshadowing and Suspense

- Ask a volunteer to read the bracketed passage aloud.
- **Ask** students what words they might use to characterize Bet in this passage.
  Possible responses: Students might say that Bet is nervous, unsure, paranoid or panic-stricken.
- Then, **ask** the Literary Analysis question: What questions does Bet's request raise in your mind?
  Answer: The urgency of Bet's request makes the reader wonder what might happen at the hospital that would make her want to leave in a hurry. It also makes the reader ask what would happen if the taxi driver were to leave before Bet was through with her business at the hospital.

15 Critical Thinking
Draw Conclusions

- **Discuss** with students Bet's state of mind at this point in the story. What conclusions can they draw from her thought that Arnold might refuse to get out of the taxicab and go into the hospital?
  Answer: Students may conclude that Bet is conflicted about taking Arnold to the hospital. If he refuses to cooperate, she will be relieved of responsibility for making this difficult decision.
- **Ask** students how much control Bet feels she has over her life. Have them support their responses with examples from the story.
  Answer: Students should recognize a pattern of passive endurance in Bet dating from the incident with the waves and including her response to Avery's departure.

16 Reading Check

Answer: Bet tells the taxi driver to wait for her in the driveway of the hospital.

Differentiated Instruction
Solutions for All Learners

Support for Less Proficient Readers
Discuss this part of the story in detail to make sure students understand Bet's conflicting feelings of relief, guilt, and love. What are students' feelings about Bet? Is she trying to shirk her responsibility, or is she doing a difficult but necessary thing? Have students give examples from the story to support their opinions.

Background for English Learners
English learners who come from cultures in which members of the extended family provide childcare may find it difficult to understand Bet's decision. Discuss Bet's isolation and her lack of support by social service agencies or her family so that students understand how limited her choices are.

Enrichment for Gifted/Talented Students
Have students discuss Bet's range of feelings about Arnold, and then express her feelings in an original performance piece. They may want to write and recite a poem, write and perform a monologue that reveals Bet's thoughts, or create a movement piece that shows without words her emotional state.

17 Literary Analysis
Foreshadowing and Suspense

- Have students read the bracketed passage.
- **Ask** students to answer the Literary Analysis question: Why does the mundane smell of disinfectant create suspense?
  Answer: Since smells sometimes cause Arnold to have a temper tantrum, the reader wonders whether the smell of disinfectant will have this effect on the boy and whether he will realize that he is in a mental health facility.

18 Critical Thinking
Evaluate

- **Ask** students why the hospital might want visitors to wait six months before visiting new patients.
  Answer: The hospital believes new patients will accept their new home more easily if they are not reminded of their former lives.
- **Ask** students whether they agree or disagree with the hospital's policy.
  Possible answers: Some students will agree for the reason cited above; other students will think that this policy is cruel and will make patients believe that their families no longer care about them.

19 Critical Thinking
Analyze

- Have students **describe** the nurse's attitude toward Bet and Arnold.
  Answer: Students may say that the nurse seems emotionally uninvolved.
- **Ask** students to explain why the nurse might have this attitude.
  Answer: The nurse has seen relatives say good-bye and leave their loved ones in the hospital many times before. She would be too upset to do her work well if she got involved emotionally with every patient.

In the admitting office, a lady behind a wooden counter showed her what papers to sign. Secretaries were clacketing typewriters all around. Bet thought Arnold might like that, but instead he got lost in the lights—chilly, hanging ice-cube-tray lights with a little flicker to them. He gazed upward, looking astonished. Finally a flat-fronted nurse came in and touched his elbow. "Come along, Arnold. Come, Mommy. We'll show you where Arnold is staying," she said.

17 They walked back across the entrance hall, then up wide marble steps with hollows worn in them. Arnold clung to the banister. There was a smell Bet hated, pine-oil disinfectant, but Arnold didn't seem to notice. You never knew; sometimes smells could just put him in a state.

Literary Analysis Foreshadowing and Suspense Why does the mundane smell of disinfectant create suspense?

The nurse unlocked a double door that had chicken-wired windows. They walked through a corridor, passing several fat, ugly women in shapeless gray dresses and ankle socks. "Ha!" one of the women said, and fell giggling into the arms of a friend. The nurse said, "*Here* we are." She led them into an enormous hallway lined with little white cots. Nobody else was in it; there wasn't a sign that children lived here except for a tiny cardboard clown picture hanging on one vacant wall. "This one is your bed, Arnold," said the nurse. Bet laid the suitcase on it. It was made up so neatly, the sheets might have been painted on. A steely-gray blanket was folded across the foot. She looked over at Arnold, but he was pivoting back and forth to hear how his new sneakers squeaked on the linoleum.

18 "Usually," said the nurse, "we like to give new residents six months before the family visits. That way they settle in quicker, don't you see." She turned away and adjusted the clown picture, though as far as Bet could tell it was fine the way it was. Over her shoulder, the nurse said, "You can tell him goodbye now, if you like."

19 "Oh," Bet said. "All right." She set her hands on Arnold's shoulders. Then she laid her face against his hair, which felt warm and fuzzy. "Honey," she said. But he went on pivoting. She straightened and told the nurse, "I brought his special blanket."

"Oh, fine," said the nurse, turning toward her again. "We'll see that he gets it."

"He always likes to sleep with it; he has ever since he was little."

"All right."

"Don't wash it. He hates if you wash it."

"Yes. Say goodbye to Mommy now, Arnold."

"A lot of times he'll surprise you. I mean there's a whole lot to him. He's not just—"

"We'll take very good care of him, Mrs. Blevins, don't worry."

"Well," she said. " 'Bye, Arnold."

She left the ward with the nurse and went down the corridor. As

20 the nurse was unlocking the doors for her, she heard a single, terrible scream, but the nurse only patted her shoulder and pushed her gently on through.

In the taxi, Bet said, "Now, I've just got fifteen minutes to get to the station. I wonder if you could hurry?"

Literary Analysis Foreshadowing and Suspense What actions do you anticipate after Arnold's scream?

Differentiated Instruction
Solutions for All Learners

Strategy for Gifted/Talented Students
Invite these students to role-play the scene between Bet and the nurse. Ask students playing Bet how the nurse's behavior makes them feel. Discuss with those playing the nurse the conflicting emotions they may feel about taking on the care of another child with severe problems.

Enrichment for Advanced Readers
Have students research the changes in treatment for people with schizophrenia, bipolar disorder, and other mental illnesses that have taken place in the last forty or fifty years. Encourage students to conduct direct research by interviewing health care providers. Ask students to consider whether the enormous changes in the approach to treatment have been helpful for most mentally ill people.

Girl Looking at Landscape, 1957, Richard Diebenkorn, oil on canvas, 59 × 60 3/8 inches, (149.9 × 153.4 cm), Gift of Mr. and Mrs. Alan H. Temple, 61.49, Collection of Whitney Museum of American Art, photograph by Geoffrey Clements, N.Y., Photograph copyright © 1997: Whitney Museum of American Art

▲ **Critical Viewing** Bet probably experienced a range of emotions after leaving the hospital. Which of her possible emotions are reflected in this painting? **[Interpret]**

"Sure thing," the driver said.

She folded her hands and looked straight ahead. Tears seemed to be coming down her face in sheets.

Once she'd reached the station, she went to the ticket window. "Am I in time for the twelve-thirty-two?" she asked.

"Easily," said the man. "It's twenty minutes late."

"What?"

"Got held up in Norton somehow."

"But you can't!" she said. The man looked startled. She must be a sight, all swollen-eyed and wet-cheeked. "Look," she said, in a lower voice. "I figured this on purpose. I chose the one train from Beulah that would let me catch another one back without waiting. I do not want to sit and wait in this station."

  **Reading Check**

What is the physical appearance of Arnold's hospital room?

⑳ Literary Analysis
Foreshadowing and Suspense

- Have a volunteer read the bracketed passage aloud.
- **Ask** students what words Tyler uses to heighten the suspense.
  Answer: The use of the adjectives *single* and *terrifying* to characterize the scream heightens the suspense.
- **Ask** students the second Literary Analysis question on the previous page: What action do you anticipate after Arnold's scream?
  Answer: Most students will believe that Arnold will have a severe temper tantrum after he screams and may hurt himself and/or others.

㉑ Critical Viewing

Answer: Many students will suggest that this painting reflects Bet's sadness over leaving her son. This emotion is conveyed by the posture of the slumped, still figure of the woman.

㉒ Reading Check

Answer: Arnold's bed is in a long hallway with many small cots in it. The cot to which Arnold is assigned is made up neatly and has a gray blanket folded at the foot. The only indication that children live there is a picture of a clown.

Enrichment

Girl Looking at Landscape, 1957, by Richard Diebenkorn

Richard Diebenkorn (1922–1993) was educated in California and New Mexico and migrated to New York in the 1940s, the heyday of abstract expressionism. Throughout his career, Diebenkorn switched from abstract to figurative works, such as *Girl Looking at Landscape,* and back again. Known for luscious color and underlying geometric rigor, Diebenkorn was influenced by many, including painters Edward Hopper, Paul Cezanne, and Henri Matisse.

Ask students how the painting symbolizes Bet's relationship to the world.
Answer: Like Bet, the girl in the painting is an observer of, rather than a participant in, the world around her.

ASSESS

Answers

1. **Possible answer:** Most students will disapprove of Bet's new outlook on life because it indicates she has given up. Students may say that it is unlikely that Bet will maintain this attitude.
2. (a) Bet is taking Arnold to the Parkins State Hospital, a mental hospital. (b) Bet can no longer care for Arnold adequately at home. (c) Arnold seems to suspect something is amiss. He is upset and uneasy, constantly on the verge of a temper tantrum.
3. (a) She grew up in a trailer and married at a young age to get away from home. Her husband left her when Arnold was still an infant. (b) Bet takes pride in enduring. She does little to change the flow of events.
4. (a) Bet wants to escape from the hospital as soon as possible because she feels guilty about leaving Arnold there. (b) Students may say that Bet is not sure she is doing the right thing and wants to get away before she can change her mind.
5. (a) Bet will no longer participate in the daily care for Arnold that had been the center of her life. (b) The title refers to those events in life that can catch a person off guard, such as Bet's son's condition and her husband's leaving the family.
6. **Possible answer:** Many students will feel that Bet did the only thing she could do under the circumstances. Students should realize that there were not as many options for high-quality care available at that time, particularly for those who, like Bet, lacked financial resources.

Go Online Author Link For additional information about Anne Tyler, have students type in the Web Code, then select *T* from the alphabet, and then select Anne Tyler.

"Twenty *minutes*, lady. That's all it is."

"What am I going to do?" she asked him.

He turned back to his ledgers.

She went over to a bench and sat down. Ladders and scaffolding towered above her, and only ten or twelve passengers were dotted through the rest of the station. The place looked bombed out—nothing but a shell. "Twenty minutes!" she said aloud. "What am I going to do?"

Through the double glass doors at the far end of the station, a procession of gray-suited men arrived with briefcases. More men came behind them, dressed in work clothes, carrying folding chairs, black trunklike boxes with silver hinges, microphones, a wooden lectern, and an armload of bunting. They set the lectern down in the center of the floor, not six feet from Bet. They draped the bunting across it—an arc of red, white, and blue. Wires were connected, floodlights were lit. A microphone screeched. One of the workmen said, "Try her, Mayor." He held the microphone out to a fat man in a suit, who cleared his throat and said, "Ladies and gentlemen, on the occasion of the expansion of this fine old railway station—"

"Sure do get an echo here," the workman said. "Keep on going."

The Mayor cleared his throat again. "If I may," he said, "I'd like to take about twenty minutes of your time, friends."

He straightened his tie. Bet blew her nose, and then she wiped her eyes and smiled. They had come just for her sake, you might think. They were putting on a sort of private play. From now on, all the world was going to be like that—just something on a stage, for her to sit back and watch.

Critical Reading

1. **Respond:** What do you think of Bet's new outlook? Explain.
2. **(a) Recall:** Where is Bet taking Arnold? **(b) Recall:** Why is she taking him there? **(c) Interpret:** Does Arnold seem to suspect anything different? Support your answer.
3. **(a) Summarize:** Summarize what you learn about Bet's childhood and marriage. **(b) Connect:** How does Bet's behavior while her father teaches her to bodysurf relate to her behavior later in life?
4. **(a) Infer:** Why does Bet insist that the cab driver wait for her outside the hospital? **(b) Draw Conclusions:** What does this action reveal about Bet's needs and fears?
5. **(a) Analyze:** What is the meaning of the story's final sentence? **(b) Connect:** How does the story's title relate to its meaning?
6. **Take a Position:** Do you think that most people today would act as Bet did if they were in her place? Why or why not?

Go Online Author Link

For: More about Anne Tyler
Visit: www.PHSchool.com
Web Code: ere-9608

Apply the Skills

Average Waves in Unprotected Waters

Literary Analysis

Foreshadowing

1. How does Arnold's reluctance to cooperate with his mother at the beginning of the story **foreshadow** the story's main event?
2. Using a chart like the one shown, find three other examples of foreshadowing from the story, and analyze their effect on the reader.

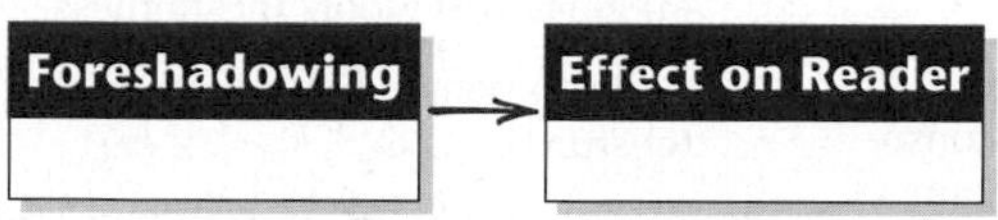

3. Would the story be less effective if Tyler did not use foreshadowing? Explain.

Connecting Literary Elements

4. How does Tyler's use of foreshadowing help to build **suspense**?
5. In what ways does Bet's concern that the cab driver may not wait for her create suspense?
6. **(a)** What is suspenseful about the train being delayed twenty minutes? **(b)** Did you anticipate a different ending? Explain.
7. **(a)** Note three points in the story where you felt the greatest suspense. **(b)** List the questions each of these moments raised in your mind. **(c)** In what ways were those questions answered?
8. At what point in the story does the suspense end? Why?

Reading Strategy

Putting Events in Order

9. State the main events and details of the story in chronological order.
10. **(a)** What flashback does Bet have? **(b)** What prompts this flashback, and what causes it to end?
11. **(a)** What does this flashback add to your understanding of the story? **(b)** Do you think the story would suffer without it? Why or why not?

Extend Understanding

12. **Career Connection:** Bet entrusts the life of her son to others. What qualities would you look for in a caregiver for children like Arnold who are mentally challenged?

QuickReview

Foreshadowing is the placement of hints or clues in a narrative to suggest later events.

Suspense is a feeling of growing uncertainty about the outcome of events in a literary work.

A **flashback** is a scene or an event from an earlier time that interrupts the chronological presentation of events.

To **put events in order,** note the sequence in which they occur in real time.

For: Self-test
Visit: www.PHSchool.com
Web Code: era-6606

Answers

1. Arnold senses that something unsettling is going to happen.
2. **Foreshadowing:** Descriptions of Arnold in the opening paragraph **Effect on Reader:** The reader becomes concerned about Arnold. **Foreshadowing:** Arnold eyes the suitcase suspiciously. **Effect on Reader:** The reader wonders where Arnold is going. **Foreshadowing:** Bet's nervousness **Effect on Reader:** The reader suspects that the change will be bad.
3. The foreshadowing gives the reader a sense of suspenseful anticipation; without it, the flashbacks would have less significance and the story might have less appeal.
4. It increases the reader's interest in learning the trip's purpose.
5. The reader becomes concerned about the effect on Bet if the cab driver does not wait.
6. (a) The reader is not sure whether Bet can gain some equanimity about her decision. (b) The ending is fitting because Bet's behavior follows established patterns in her life.
7. (a), (b), and (c) Students' answers should be supported by references to the story.
8. The suspense ends in the last paragraph when the reader realizes that Bet will not change her mind about Arnold.
9. Bet's father tried unsuccessfully to teach her to bodysurf. She married Avery against her parents' wishes. Her parents died. She and Avery had Arnold and learned about his condition. Avery deserted the family. Bet took Arnold to a state hospital where he would remain. While she waited for the train, the mayor came to give a speech, and she watched.
10. (a) She flashes back to Arnold as a baby, her husband's desertion, and the history of her childhood and marriage. (b) The flashback is prompted by remembering, as Arnold falls asleep, that he has never slept well; it ends when Arnold's head snaps up.

Answers continued

11. (a) The flashback sheds new light on Bet's personality and circumstances. (b) Without it, the story would lack the insight the flashback provides.
12. Students may mention patience and knowledge about patients' conditions.

Go Online Assessment Students may use the **Self-test** to prepare for **Selection Test A** or **Selection Test B.**

EXTEND/ASSESS

Answers

1 Vocabulary Lesson

Word Analysis

1. *Transcribe* means to make a copy, or write something over.
2. *Transcontinental* means across a continent.
3. *Transportation* is the act of carrying something across or over.
4. *Transplant* is to replant or plant something over.

Spelling Strategy

1. childhood
2. kindness
3. resistance

Vocabulary Builder

1. a
2. c
3. b
4. b
5. a

2 Grammar and Style Lesson

1. suspiciously (modifies *stared*)
2. pathetic (modifies *Arnold*)
3. well (modifies *behaved*)
4. carefully (modifies *chewed*)
5. awful (modifies *hospital*)
6. bad (modifies *she*)

Writing Application

Remind students to use adverbs to modify action verbs, and to use adjectives after linking verbs if the modifier describes the subject.

WG Writing and Grammar, Ruby Level

Students will find further instruction and practice on the correct use of adjectives and adverbs in Chapter 17, Section 3.

Build Language Skills

1 Vocabulary Lesson

Word Analysis: Latin Prefix *trans-*

The Latin prefix *trans-* means "across," "over," or "through." Something *transparent* is clear enough to be seen through. Explain how the meaning of the prefix relates to the meaning of each word.

1. transcribe
2. transcontinental
3. transportation
4. transplant

Spelling Strategy

To add a suffix to a word ending in two consonants, retain both consonants. For example, *bunt* + *ing* = *bunting* and *thank* + *ful* = *thankful*. Using this rule, add a suffix to each word.

1. Bet thought back on her child_____.
2. Treat everyone with kind_____.
3. Arnold offered resist _____ to his mother.

Vocabulary Builder: Sentence Completion

Review the words in the vocabulary list on page 1061. Then, choose the letter of the word or phrase that best completes each of the following statements.

1. Something *transparent* might be made of **(a)** glass, **(b)** wool, **(c)** stainless steel.
2. A *stocky* person looks **(a)** bored, **(b)** rich, **(c)** sturdy.
3. A *staunch* ally **(a)** betrays you, **(b)** always stands by you, **(c)** abandons you.
4. *Orthopedic* shoes **(a)** make you look taller, **(b)** correct your posture, **(c)** cost less than most other shoes.
5. A *viper* might **(a)** bite you, **(b)** sing to you, **(c)** shake your hand.

2 Grammar and Style Lesson

Correct Use of Adjectives and Adverbs

Adjectives modify nouns or pronouns; **adverbs** modify verbs, adjectives, or other adverbs. Always use an adjective, not an adverb, after linking verbs such as *am, is, are, feel, smell,* or *seem* if the modifier describes the subject. Always use an adverb, not an adjective, to modify an action verb.

In the following examples, the verbs are underlined and the modifiers are in italics.

Adverb: She never could do anything as *well* as most people. (modifies the verb *could do*)

Adjective: The collar was *askew.* (modifies the noun *collar*)

Practice For each item, choose the correct modifier and identify the word it modifies.

1. Arnold stared (suspicious, suspiciously).
2. Sometimes Arnold looked (pathetic, pathetically) in his neatly buttoned clothes.
3. Arnold usually behaved (good, well).
4. Arnold chewed his gum (careful, carefully).
5. The hospital smelled (awful, awfully).
6. After Bet left, she felt very (bad, badly).

Writing Application Write two sentences for each modifier given. Construct one sentence so that the modifier serves as an adjective, and the other so that the modifier serves as an adverb.

1. early
2. much

WG *Prentice Hall Writing and Grammar Connection: Chapter 17, Section 3*

Assessment Practice

Grammar and Usage

(For more practice, see *Standardized Test Preparation Workbook*, p. 62.)

The writing sections of tests often require students to choose the correct word or group of words to complete a sentence. Use the following sample item to show students how to recognize correct and incorrect grammar and choose the correct word to complete a sentence.

A writer who wishes to create serious fiction should be willing to revise ____ work as many times as necessary.

Choose the word or group of words that belong in the blank.

A their
B they're
C him or her
D his or her

A is plural, whereas the antecedent is singular. *B* is not a possessive pronoun, but a contraction meaning "they are." *C* is not possessive. *D* is both singular and possessive, and is therefore the correct answer.

Writing Lesson

Social Worker's Report

Imagine that you are the social worker assigned to Bet and Arnold's case. Write a report explaining Arnold's condition and summarizing the events that led to Bet's decision to have her son institutionalized.

Prewriting Scan the story for details that indicate that Bet can no longer care for Arnold. Categorize the information into causes and effects to show how each detail contributes to Bet's decision.

Model: Listing Causes and Effects

Causes		Effects
1. Arnold cannot dress or feed himself.	→	1. He requires a lot of care.
2. He is getting bigger and stronger.		2. "He was getting to be too much for her."

Drafting Build your report on the information you gathered. Use clear transitions to show cause-and-effect and other relationships. Work to maintain the objective tone of an effective social worker.

Revising Read your report as though you were a supervisor reviewing the case for the first time. Make sure the draft includes sufficient details to support the conclusion. Check that your facts are accurate, your word choice is precise, and that you establish clear cause-and-effect relationships.

Prentice Hall Writing and Grammar Connection: Chapter 10, Section 4

Extend Your Learning

Listening and Speaking Imagine that the subject of the mayor's speech was the need for more funding and improved care at state-run institutions. Prepare and present a **political speech** he might give using Arnold's case to support his points. Consider these ideas in your speech:

- The benefits for the needy children
- The expertise of health care professionals
- The humanitarian effort

Present the speech to the class.

Research and Technology With a group, research autism, Down's syndrome, or another childhood condition that causes severe mental or emotional challenges. Check the Internet or the library for information. Present your findings in a medical **research report. [Group Activity]**

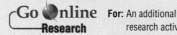

For: An additional research activity
Visit: www.PHSchool.com
Web Code: erd-7604

Assessment Resources

The following resources can be used to assess students' knowledge and skills.

Unit 6 Resources
Selection Test A, pp. 100–102
Selection Test B, pp. 103–105

General Resources
Rubrics for Cause-and-Effect Essay, pp. 55–56
Rubrics for Research: Research Report, pp. 49–50

Go Online Assessment — Students may use the **Self-test** to prepare for **Selection Test A** or **Selection Test B.**

3 Writing Lesson

- Give students the **Support for Writing Lesson,** p. 97 in ***Unit 6 Resources,*** to use as they write their reports.
- Review the model on p. 1073. Have students add other effects caused by Arnold's behavior. Ask students to make a similar chart to list all the causes and effects having to do with Arnold's condition. Students may wish to record their notes in the Cause-and-Effect Flowchart on page 305 in ***Graphic Organizer Transparencies.***
- Discuss the form a social worker's report on Bet and Arnold's case would take. Remind students first to describe Arnold's condition and then to summarize the events that led to Bet's decision.
- Use the Writing Lesson to guide students in writing their reports.
- Use the Cause-and-Effect Essay rubrics in ***General Resources*** pp. 55–56, to evaluate students' reports.

4 Research and Technology

- Suggest that students try to interview an expert on the condition they have chosen as the subject of their paper. Students should do as much research as possible before the interview, so their questions can be focused and on target. If possible, they should tape the interview.
- Urge students to make formal or informal outlines to organize the information they have gathered.
- Encourage students to include charts, graphs, and diagrams to make the information in their report clear.
- Use the rubrics for Research: Research Report, pp. 49–50 in ***General Resources,*** to evaluate students' reports.
- The **Support for Extend Your Learning** page (***Unit 6 Resources,*** p. 98) provides guided note-taking opportunities to help students complete the Extend Your Learning activities.

Go Online Research — Have students type in the Web Code for another research activity.

Meeting Your Standards

Students will

1. **analyze and respond to literary elements.**
   - Literary Analysis: Anecdote
2. **read, comprehend, analyze, and critique nonfiction.**
   - Reading Strategy: Relating to Your Own Experiences
   - Reading Check questions
   - Apply the Skills questions
   - Assessment Practice (ATE)
3. **develop vocabulary.**
   - Vocabulary Lesson: Latin Prefix: *con-*
4. **understand and apply written and oral language conventions.**
   - Spelling Strategy
   - Grammar and Style Lesson: Elliptical Clauses
5. **develop writing proficiency.**
   - Writing Lesson: Reflective Essay
6. **develop appropriate research strategies.**
   - Extend Your Learning: Class Anthology
7. **understand and apply listening and speaking strategies.**
   - Extend Your Learning: Musical Analysis

Block Scheduling: Use one 90-minute class period to preteach the skills and have students read the selection. Use a second 90-minute class period to assess students' mastery of skills, extend their learning, and monitor their progress.

Homework Suggestions

Following are possibilities for homework assignments.

- Support pages from ***Unit 6 Resources:***
  Literary Analysis
  Reading Strategy
  Vocabulary Builder
  Grammar and Style
- An Extend Your Learning project and the Writing Lesson for this selection group may be completed over several days.

Step-by-Step Teaching Guide	Pacing Guide
PRETEACH	
• Administer Vocabulary and Reading Warm-ups as necessary.	5 min.
• Engage students' interest with the motivation activity.	5 min.
• Read and discuss author and background features. **FT**	10 min.
• Introduce the Literary Analysis Skill: Anecdote. **FT**	5 min.
• Introduce the Reading Strategy: Relating to Your Own Experiences. **FT**	10 min.
• Prepare students to read by teaching the selection vocabulary. **FT**	
TEACH	
• Informally monitor comprehension while students read independently or in groups. **FT**	30 min.
• Monitor students' comprehension with the Reading Check notes.	as students read
• Reinforce vocabulary with Vocabulary Builder notes.	as students read
• Develop students' understanding of anecdote with the Literary Analysis annotations. **FT**	5 min.
• Develop students' ability to relate to their own experiences with the Reading Strategy annotations. **FT**	5 min.
ASSESS/EXTEND	
• Assess students' comprehension and mastery of the Literary Analysis and Reading Strategy by having them answer the Apply the Skills questions. **FT**	15 min.
• Have students complete the Vocabulary Lesson and the Grammar and Style Lesson. **FT**	15 min.
• Apply students' ability to add emotional depth to their writing through elaboration by using the Writing Lesson. **FT**	45 min. or homework
• Apply students' understanding by using one or more of the Extend Your Learning activities.	20–90 min. or homework
• Administer Selection Test A or Selection Test B. **FT**	15 min.

Resources

PRINT
Unit 6 Resources
Vocabulary Warm-up Word Lists **[L1, L2, EL]** . . . . . p. 106
Vocabulary Warm-up Practice **[L1, L2, EL]** . . . . . p. 107
Reading Warm-up A **[L1, L2, EL]** . . . . . p. 108
Reading Warm-up B **[L1, L2, L3]** . . . . . p. 109

TRANSPARENCY
Graphic Organizer Transparencies
Literary Analysis Graphic Organizer A **[L3]** . . . . . p. 238
Literary Analysis Graphic Organizer B **[L1, L2, EL]** . . . . . p. 239
Reading Strategy Graphic Organizer A **[L3]** . . . . . p. 240
Reading Strategy Graphic Organizer B **[L1, L2, EL]** . . . . . p. 241

PRINT
Reader's Notebook [L2]
Reader's Notebook: Adapted Version [L1]
Reader's Notebook: English Learner's Version [EL]
Unit 6 Resources
Literary Analysis **[L3]** . . . . . p. 110
Reading Strategy **[L3]** . . . . . p. 111
Vocabulary Builder **[L3]** . . . . . p. 112

TECHNOLOGY
Listening to Literature Audio CDs [L2, EL]

PRINT
Unit 6 Resources
Grammar and Style **[L3]** . . . . . p. 113
Support for Writing Lesson **[L3]** . . . . . p. 114
Support for Extend Your Learning **[L3]** . . . . . p. 115
Enrichment **[L4]** . . . . . p. 116
Selection Test A **[L1, L2, EL]** . . . . . pp. 117–119
Selection Test B **[L3, L4]** . . . . . pp. 120–122
General Resources
Rubrics for Reflective Essay **[L3]** . . . . . pp. 47–48

TECHNOLOGY
Go Online: Research **[L3]**
Go Online: Self-test **[L3]**
***ExamView*® Test Bank [L3]**

Choosing Resources for Differentiated Instruction

[L1] Special Needs Students
[L2] Below-Level Students
[L3] All Students
[L4] Advanced Students
[EL] English Learners

For Vocabulary and Reading Warm-ups and for Selection Tests, **A** signifies "less challenging" and **B** "more challenging." For Graphic Organizer transparencies, **A** signifies "not filled in" and **B** "filled in."

FT Fast Track Instruction: To move the lesson more quickly, use the strategies and activities identified with **FT**.

Scaffolding for Less Proficient and Advanced Students

The leveled Critical Thinking questions after selections progress in the levels of thinking required to answer them. To address the needs of your different students, you may use the (a) level questions for your less proficient students and the (b) level questions with your on-level and advanced students. The occasional (c) level questions are appropriate for your advanced students.

PRENTICE HALL **TeacherEXPRESS™** Plan · Teach · Assess Use this complete suite of powerful teaching tools to make lesson planning and testing quicker and easier.

PRENTICE HALL **StudentEXPRESS™** Learn · Study · Succeed Use the interactive textbook (online and on CD-ROM) to make selections and activities come alive with audio and video support and interactive questions.

Benchmark

After students have completed these essays, administer **Benchmark Test 9** *(Unit 6 Resources,* p. 123). If the Benchmark Test reveals that some students need further work, use the **Interpretation Guide** to determine the appropriate reteaching pages in the **Reading Kit** or on **Success Tracker.**

Go Online Professional Development **For:** Information about Lexiles **Visit:** www.PHSchool.com **Web Code:** eue-1111

PRETEACH

Motivation

In preparation for reading these essays, ask students to find a piece of music that is especially meaningful to them. Invite students to bring recordings to class and, in small groups, share the feelings or memories that the music evokes. Alternatively, you might play segments of music and ask the class to respond. Consider using music that will evoke childhood memories: the sound of the ice cream truck, music from "A Charlie Brown Christmas," or a lullaby.

❶ Background

More About N. Scott Momaday

N. Scott Momaday has spent a good part of his life trying to safeguard the oral tradition and other aspects of Indian culture. He is the chairman and founder of the Buffalo Trust, a nonprofit organization founded to preserve and return their heritage to Native Americans. Momaday, a professor of English at the University of Arizona at Tucson and a consultant for the National Endowment for the Humanities and the National Endowment for the Arts since 1970, has this to say about his interest in preserving the oral tradition:

> My father was a great storyteller and he knew many stories from the Kiowa oral tradition…But it was only after I became an adult that I understood how fragile they are, because they exist only by word of mouth, always just one generation away from extinction. That's when I began writing down the tales my father and others had told me.

Build Skills | *Memoir • Essays*

❶ *from* The Names • Mint Snowball • Suspended

N. Scott Momaday (b. 1934)

A member of the Kiowa nation, N. Scott Momaday was born in Lawton, Oklahoma. As a child, he often visited his grandparents, whose home was a meeting place for elderly Kiowas. Momaday describes these people as being "made of lean leather."

Inspired by his boyhood experiences, Momaday devoted himself to preserving his Kiowa heritage. His first book, *House Made of Dawn* (1969), is a novel about a young Native American torn between his roots and white society. The book earned Momaday a Pulitzer Prize. In the mid-1960s, the author made a pilgrimage to his grandmother's grave in western Oklahoma. He wrote about that experience in his best-known work, *The Way to Rainy Mountain* (1969), a collection of personal anecdotes and retellings of Kiowa myths and legends.

Momaday has since published poetry, essays, and a memoir, *The Names* (1996). His work provides the reader with a deeper understanding of Native American culture, both past and present. Momaday earned a doctoral degree from Stanford University, and now teaches at the University of Arizona.

Naomi Shihab Nye (b. 1952)

Arab American poet Naomi Shihab Nye spent her teenage years in Jerusalem, far from the cities of St. Louis, Missouri, and San Antonio, Texas, where she had been a child. Her father had emigrated from Palestine and settled in St. Louis, Missouri, where he and his wife operated stores specializing in imported goods. When Naomi was fourteen, the family moved back to Jerusalem to be near her father's Arab relatives. Nye says the family's years in Jerusalem enabled her to discover her heritage.

In addition to publishing award-winning volumes of poetry, Nye has also created picture books for children. This versatile writer, whose work is built on the sturdy foundation of everyday experiences, believes that "the primary source of poetry has always been local life, random characters met on the streets, our own ancestry sifting down to us through small essential daily tasks."

Joy Harjo (b. 1951)

The influence of Joy Harjo's Native American Creek (or Muscogee) and Cherokee heritage is evident in many aspects of her life, including her writing. Born in Tulsa, Oklahoma, Harjo became interested in dance and joined a troupe of Native American dancers when she was a teenager. Her essay "Suspended" demonstrates music's ability to become a transport, a vehicle through which Harjo can connect her cultural heritage to her creative and everyday world.

Harjo attended the Institute of American Indian Arts, the University of New Mexico, and the Writers' Workshop of the University of Iowa. In addition to publishing books of poetry and prose, Harjo has also written film scripts and taught at the state universities of California, New Mexico, and Montana.

Preview

Connecting to the Literature

Watching home videos or flipping through family photos may bring back special memories of a treasured toy, a long-forgotten friend, or a special occasion. As you read these selections, think about childhood experiences that helped form your sense of self.

2 Literary Analysis

Anecdote

An **anecdote** is a short account of an amusing or interesting event. People tell anecdotes all the time, mostly for entertainment. Essayists recount anecdotes to make a point, make generalizations, or illustrate conclusions, as in this example from "Mint Snowball":

> Perhaps the clue to my entire personality connects to the lost Mint Snowball. I have always felt out-of-step with my environment, disjointed in the modern world.

Identify the anecdotes in these essays and the generalizations or conclusions they inspire. Use a chart like the one shown to help you.

Anecdote → Generalization

Comparing Literary Works

These writers describe **rites of passage**—events that mark personal transitions that have cultural significance. Momaday and Harjo write about unique experiences, while Nye describes a lost recipe that was a link to her cultural heritage. As you read, compare how the experiences of the writers created in them a new awareness of self and the world around them.

3 Reading Strategy

Relating to Your Own Experiences

Many common experiences know no cultural boundaries. If you have ever taken a journey, yearned for the past, or experienced an inner awakening, you can find a connection between your experiences and the ones expressed in these selections. **Relating to your own experiences** will increase your understanding and enjoyment of the essays.

Vocabulary Builder

supple (sup′ əl) *adj.* able to bend and move easily and nimbly (p. 1077)

concocted (kən käkt′ əd) *v.* made by combining various ingredients (p. 1081)

flamboyant (flam boi′ ənt) *adj.* too extravagant (p. 1081)

elixir (i liks′ ər) *n.* supposed remedy for all ailments (p. 1081)

permeated (pur′ mē āt′ id) *adj.* penetrated and spread through (p. 1081)

replicate (rep′ li kāt′) *v.* to duplicate (p. 1082)

revelatory (rev′ ə lə tôr′ ē) *adj.* revealing; disclosing (p. 1083)

confluence (kän′ floo əns) *n.* a flowing together (p. 1084)

2 Literary Analysis

Anecdote

- Ask students to pay particular attention to the anecdotes, short accounts of amusing or interesting events, as they read these three essays. Ask them to think about the purposes the anecdotes serve.
- Have a volunteer read the generalization Naomi Shihab Nye drew from the anecdote she shares in her essay, "Mint Snowball."
- Give students a copy of **Literary Analysis Graphic Organizer A,** p. 238 in ***Graphic Organizer Transparencies,*** to record the anecdotes they relate in their essays and the generalizations they drew from these anecdotes.
- Tell students that the authors may state the generalizations they drew from the experiences they describe, as did Naomi Shihab Nye, or students may have to infer generalizations.

3 Reading Strategy

Relating to Your Own Experiences

- Discuss with students the essential similarities among human experiences despite cultural differences.
- Urge students to compare their own experiences with the authors' as they read these essays. Remind them that such comparisons will increase their understanding and enjoyment of the essays.

Vocabulary Builder

- Pronounce each vocabulary word for students, and read the definitions as a class. Have students identify any words with which they are already familiar.

Differentiated Instruction

Solutions for All Learners

Support for Special Needs Students
Have students complete the **Preview** and **Build Skills** pages for the selections in the **Reader's Notebook: Adapted Version.** These pages provide a selection summary, an abbreviated presentation of the reading and literary skills, and the graphic organizer on the **Build Skills** page in the student book.

Support for Less Proficient Readers
Have students complete the **Preview** and **Build Skills** pages for the selections in the **Reader's Notebook.** These pages provide a selection summary, an abbreviated presentation of the reading and literary skills, and the graphic organizer on the **Build Skills** page in the student book.

Support for English Learners
Have students complete the **Preview** and **Build Skills** pages for the selections in the **Reader's Notebook: English Learner's Version.** These pages provide a selection summary, an abbreviated presentation of the skills, and the graphic organizer on the **Build Skills** page in the student book.

❽ Reading Strategy
Relating to Your Own Experiences

- Have students **discuss** the reasons Momaday was ashamed to admit that he had made a bad bargain in exchanging horses.
  Possible response: People often don't like to admit that they have made a mistake.
- Then, have students think about decisions they made that they later regretted. Encourage volunteers to give examples.
- Ask students whether they were ashamed to admit their mistakes and to give reasons for their reactions.

▶ **Monitor Progress:** Have students compare their experiences and reactions to Momaday's.

❾ Literary Analysis
Anecdote

- Have students **discuss** the attraction that Pasqual's horse might have had for the boy.
  Possible responses: The boy was curious about the horse. The horse was half wild and would be a challenge to ride.

▶ **Monitor Progress: Ask** what Pasqual's goal was when he began praising the horse.
Answer: Pasqual was probably hoping that the boy would want to trade horses, possibly to show up his friend as unable to ride the stallion.

- **Ask** students why they think the narrator fell for Pasqual's smooth talk.
  Possible response: He felt challenged to prove something; he was intrigued by the wildness of the stallion.
- **Ask** the Literary Analysis question: What do you think Momaday means by "wiser and better mounted?"
  Answer: The boy has come to appreciate the virtues of his horse, which is much more comfortable to ride than Pasqual's horse is.

I overtook my friend Pasqual Fragua. He was riding a rangy, stiff-legged black and white stallion, half wild, which horse he was breaking for the rancher Cass Goodner. The horse skittered and blew as I drew up beside him. Pecos began to prance, as he did always in the company of another horse. "Where are you going?" I asked in the Jemez language. And he replied, "I am going down the road." The stallion was hard to manage, and Pasqual had to keep his mind upon it; I saw that I had taken him by surprise. "You know," he said after a moment, "when you rode up just now I did not know who you were." We rode on for a time in silence, and our horses got used to each other, but still they
❽ wanted their heads.[4] The longer I looked at the stallion the more I admired it, and I suppose that Pasqual knew this, for he began to say good things about it: that it was a thing of good blood, that it was very strong and fast, that it felt very good to ride it. The thing was this: that the stallion was half wild, and I came to wonder about the wild half of it; I wanted to know what its wildness was worth in the riding. "Let us trade horses for a while," I said, and, well, all right, he agreed. At first it was exciting to ride the stallion, for every once in a while it pitched and bucked and wanted to run. But it was heavy and raw-boned and full of resistance, and every step was a jolt that I could feel deep down in my bones. I saw soon enough that I had made a bad bargain, and I wanted my horse back, but I was ashamed to admit it. There came a time in the late afternoon, in the vast plain far south of San Ysidro, after thirty miles, perhaps, when I no longer knew whether it was I who was riding the stallion or the stallion who was riding me. "Well, let us go back now," said Pasqual at last. "No. I am going on; and I will have my horse back, please," I said, and he was surprised and sorry to hear it, and we said goodbye. "If you are going south or east," he said, "look out for the sun, and keep your face in the shadow of your hat. *Vaya con Dios*."[5]
❾ And I went on my way alone then, wiser and better mounted, and thereafter I held on to my horse. I saw no one for a long time, but I saw four falling stars and any number of jackrabbits, roadrunners, and coyotes, and once, across a distance, I saw a bear, small and black, lumbering in the ravine. The mountains drew close and withdrew and drew close again, and after several days I swung east.

Now and then I came upon settlements. For the most part they were dry, burnt places with Spanish names: Arroyo Seco, Las Piedras, Tres Casas. In one of these I found myself in a narrow street between high adobe walls. Just ahead, on my left, was a door in the wall. As I approached the door was flung open, and a small boy came running out, rolling a hoop. This happened so suddenly that Pecos shied very sharply, and I fell to the ground, jamming the thumb of my left hand. The little boy looked very worried and said that he was sorry to have caused such an accident. I waved the matter off, as if it were nothing;

Literary Analysis
Anecdote What do you think Momaday means by the phrase "wiser and better mounted"?

4. **. . . they wanted their heads** The horses wanted to be free of the control of the reins.
5. **Vaya con Dios** (vī yə kən dē′ ōs) "Go with God" (Spanish).

Enrichment

The Kiowa

The Kiowa are a Native American people of the southern Great Plains. A fierce tribe of expert horsemen, the Kiowa were one of the last Plains Indian tribes to capitulate to the U.S. government.

The Kiowa were in many ways typical of nomadic Plains tribes. They hunted buffalo on horseback, did no farming, and lived in skin tepees supported by three poles. The Kiowa society had a warrior tradition; exploits in war enabled members to rise in rank.

The Kiowa believed that dreams and visions gave them supernatural powers. They came close to a written language in their twice yearly recording of events using pictographs on animal skins.

At the time of the 1990 census, there were 9,421 Kiowa. Most of them live in Southwestern Oklahoma, where their people have shared a reservation with the Comanche since 1868.

but as a matter of fact my hand hurt so much that tears welled up in my eyes. And the pain lasted for many days. I have fallen many times from a horse, both before and after that, and a few times I fell from a running horse on dangerous ground, but that was the most painful of them all.

In another settlement there were some boys who were interested in racing. They had good horses, some of them, but their horses were not so good as mine, and I won easily. 11 After that, I began to think of ways in which I might even the odds a little, might give some advantage to my competitors. Once or twice I gave them a head start, a reasonable head start of, say, five or ten yards to the hundred, but that was too simple, and I won anyway. Then it came to me that I might try this: we should all line up in the usual way, side by side, but my competitors should be mounted and I should not. When the signal was given I should then have to get up on my horse while the others were breaking away; I should have to mount my horse during the race. This idea appealed to me greatly, for it was both imaginative and difficult, not to mention dangerous; Pecos and I should have to work very closely together. The first few times we tried this I had little success, and over a course of a hundred yards I lost four races out of five. The principal problem was that Pecos simply could not hold still among the other horses. Even before they broke away he was hard to manage, and when they were set running nothing could hold him back, even for an instant. I could not get my foot in the stirrup, but I had to throw myself up across the saddle on my stomach, hold on as best I could, and twist myself into position, and all this while racing at full speed. I could ride well enough to accomplish this feat, but it was a very awkward and inefficient business. I had to find some way to use the whole energy of my horse, to get it all into the race. Thus far I had managed only to break his motion, to divert him from his purpose and mine. To correct this I took Pecos away and worked with him through the better part of a long afternoon on a broad reach of level ground beside an irrigation ditch. And it was hot, hard work. I began by teaching him to run straight away while I ran beside him a few steps, holding on to the saddle horn, with no pressure on the reins. Then, when we had mastered this trick, we proceeded to the next one, which was this: I placed my weight on my arms, hanging from the saddle horn, threw my feet out in front of me, struck them to the ground, and sprang up against the saddle. This I did again and again, until Pecos came to expect it and did not flinch or lose his stride. I sprang a little higher each time. It was in all a slow process of trial and error, and after two or three hours both Pecos and I

Literature in Context

10 Mythology Connection

The Centaur

In his first paragraph, N. Scott Momaday refers to the Plains Indian culture as "the centaur culture." In alluding to that mythical creature with the upper body of a man and the lower body of a horse, Momaday indirectly places his discussion within the larger context of cultural history. According to Greek myth, centaurs like the one shown here were a race of wild, inhospitable beings who dwelled in the mountains of northern Greece. However, one centaur, Chiron, taught many Greek heroes and was well known for his wisdom and knowledge of medicine.

Connect to the Literature

Why do you think Momaday calls the Plains Indian culture a "centaur culture" rather than a "horse culture"?

12 Reading Check

Why were Momaday and Pecos training together?

10 Literature in Context

Mythology Connection One Greek legend describes Chiron as the first centaur. According to the myth, Chiron was originally a Titan—the son of Chronos and the sea nymph Philyra—and he received the half-man/half-horse form as punishment from Apollo (Greek god of light and reason) because Chiron was bold enough to declare war on the young Olympians.

Chiron was said to have been educated by the gods, and in his wilderness surroundings he instructed mythical heroes such as Achilles, Jason, and Acteon.

Connect to the Literature Before asking the Connect to the Literature question, ask students to summarize what they have read so far about the author and his horse.

Possible response: Referring to the Plains Indian culture as a "centaur culture" suggests that the people and animals serve as a unit. The horse is considered an extension of the body.

11 Reading Strategy

Relating to Your Own Experiences

- Have students **discuss** Momaday's motivation for wanting to give an advantage to his competitors in horse races.
  Possible response: Momaday was winning all the time and grew bored.
- **Ask** students whether they would feel the same way Momaday did.
  Answer: Many students will agree that winning constantly would eventually become dull.
- Have volunteers discuss situations in their lives in which they either sought out or avoided competition, and ask them to explain their reasons.

12 Reading Check

Answer: Momaday and Pecos were training together so that the horse would get used to being mounted while a race was in progress.

Differentiated Instruction

Solutions for All Learners

Background for Less Proficient Readers
Help students understand the process through which Momaday trained Pecos not to break stride as the author ran alongside him and leaped into the saddle. Discuss the training process with students. Write each step on the board. You may have students sketch the actions as you describe them.

Strategy for Gifted/Talented Students
Have students write a journal entry in which they describe a time when they successfully mastered a goal. What lessons did they learn from working hard to meet a challenge? When they finish, have students discuss their answers.

Enrichment for Advanced Readers
Have students research horse-training techniques. After they learn about some of the latest and most effective training techniques, ask them to evaluate the methods Momaday used to train Pecos.

ASSESS

Answers

1. Most students will choose animals with which they have had contact or wild animals such as the bald eagle or lion that hold symbolic significance.
2. (a) After he was given a horse at age thirteen, the feeling of exhilaration on horseback was so strong that he felt compelled to make a journey. (b) The journey was a rite of passage for him, and completing it successfully made him feel accomplished and close to nature and his Kiowa heritage.
3. (a) He trades his horse for Pasqual's. (b) He is motivated by curiosity and admiration for the half wild horse.
4. (a) He meets a friend and trades horses; he hurts his hand; he travels through many settlements and experiences the beauty of nature; he becomes involved in horse racing. (b) Since horses are an important element of Kiowa culture, this journey on horseback connects him with his heritage.
5. (a) **Possible response:** Pecos allows himself to be trained. (b) Pecos worked hard but was treated fairly and with appreciation. (c) Momaday probably became involved in activities for which he could not use a horse, or lived in places where he could not have a horse.
6. Possible responses include compassion, patience, perseverance, courage, and the value of friendship.

Go Online Author Link For additional information about N. Scott Momaday, have students type in the Web Code, then select *M* from the alphabet, and then select N. Scott Momaday.

were covered with bruises and soaked through with perspiration. But we had much to show for our efforts, and at last the moment came when we must put the whole performance together. I had not yet leaped into the saddle, but I was quite confident that I could now do so; only I must be sure to get high enough. We began this dress rehearsal then from a standing position. At my signal Pecos lurched and was running at once, straight away and smoothly. And at the same time I sprinted forward two steps and gathered myself up, placing my weight precisely at my wrists, throwing my feet out and together, perfectly. I brought my feet down sharply to the ground and sprang up hard, as hard as I could, bringing my legs astraddle of my horse—and everything was just right, except that I sprang too high. I vaulted all the way over my horse, clearing the saddle by a considerable margin, and came down into the irrigation ditch. It was a good trick, but it was not the one I had in mind, and I wonder what Pecos thought of it after all. Anyway, after a while I could mount my horse in this way and so well that there was no challenge in it, and I went on winning race after race.

I went on, farther and farther into the wide world. Many things happened. And in all this I knew one thing: I knew where the journey was begun, that it was itself a learning of the beginning, that the beginning was infinitely worth the learning. The journey was well undertaken, and somewhere in it I sold my horse to an old Spanish man of Vallecitos. I do not know how long Pecos lived. I had used him hard and well, and it may be that in his last days an image of me like thought shimmered in his brain.

Critical Reading

1. **Respond:** What kind of animal seems "sacred" or special in some way to you? Why?
2. **(a) Recall:** What inspires Momaday's decision to take a journey? **(b) Draw Conclusions:** What do you think such a journey meant to him, and how did it make him feel?
3. **(a) Recall:** What does Momaday trade with Pasqual? **(b) Analyze:** What motivates him to make this trade?
4. **(a) Recall:** What does Momaday see and do on his journey? **(b) Draw Conclusions:** Why is it significant that his first long journey was on horseback?
5. **(a) Support:** Provide one detail that shows that Pecos was an extremely good horse. **(b) Infer:** What does the writer mean when he says that he "had used him hard and well"? **(c) Draw Conclusions:** Why do you suppose Momaday sold the horse?
6. **Apply:** What life lesson have you learned that was "infinitely worth the learning"?

Go Online Author Link
For: More about N. Scott Momaday
Visit: www.PHSchool.com
Web Code: ere-9609

Enrichment

Horses and Plains Indians

Plains Indians have not always had horses. There were no horses in North America until some were left behind in the 1540s by the expeditions of Spanish explorers Coronado and DeSoto. But Indians didn't ride or use horses until much later.

In the 1600s, Pueblo and Navaho Indians learned to train and ride horses at Spanish missions in New Mexico, but were not allowed to own the animals. In 1680, Pueblo Indians revolted against the Spanish and drove them back to Old Mexico, where they stayed for over a decade. The Spanish left behind many horses, which the Indians used. Soon the Pueblo Indians began selling and trading horses to other Indians such as the Kiowa and Comanche. Soon after, horses spread across the Southern Plains very quickly.

Mint Snowball

Naomi Shihab Nye

My great-grandfather on my mother's side ran a drugstore in a small town in central Illinois. He sold pills and rubbing alcohol from behind the big cash register and creamy ice cream from the soda fountain. My mother remembers the counter's long polished sweep, its shining face. She twirled on the stools. Dreamy fans. Wide summer afternoons. Clink of nickels in anybody's hand. He sold milkshakes, cherry cokes, old fashioned sandwiches. What did an old fashioned sandwich look like? Dark wooden shelves. Silver spigots on chocolate dispensers.

My great-grandfather had one specialty: a Mint Snowball which he invented. Some people drove all the way in from Decatur just to taste it. First he stirred fresh mint leaves with sugar and secret ingredients in a small pot on the stove for a very long time. He concocted a flamboyant elixir of mint. Its scent clung to his fingers even after he washed his hands. Then he shaved ice into tiny particles and served it mounted in a glass dish. Permeated with mint syrup. Scoops of rich vanilla ice cream to each side. My mother took a bite of minty ice and ice cream mixed together. The Mint Snowball tasted like winter. She closed her eyes to see the Swiss village my great-grandfather's parents came from. Snow frosting the roofs. Glistening, dangling spokes of ice.

Before my great-grandfather died, he sold the recipe for the mint syrup to someone in town for one hundred dollars. This hurt my

Vocabulary Builder

concocted (kən käkt′ əd) *v.* made by combining various ingredients

flamboyant (flam boi′ ənt) *adj.* too extravagant

elixir (i liks′ ər) *n.* supposed remedy for all ailments

permeated (pur′ mē āt′ id) *adj.* penetrated and spread through

16 

Reading Check

Describe Nye's great-grandfather's specialty.

Differentiated Instruction Solutions for All Learners

Background for Less Proficient Readers
Explain that the text break in this essay indicates a shift in focus. Prior to the break, the essay describes an earlier time. After the break, Nye jumps forward in time to focus on her own personal experiences.

Background for English Learners
Students may be unfamiliar with the soda fountains once found in old-fashioned drugstores. Explain the words and phrases the author uses to describe her great-grandfather's store, such as milkshakes, cherry cokes, and silver spigots.

Enrichment for Advanced Readers
Have students discuss the effect of memories and family stories on children's personalities. Ask students to talk about experiences they had early in their lives, as well as stories they heard from relatives, that affected them.

13 About the Selection

This brief essay vividly captures a flash of memory that illuminates the present with the power of the past. The speaker recalls the atmosphere of *her* great-grandfather's soda shop as her mother had described. In this magical place, Nye's great-grandfather had concocted a wondrous dessert called a Mint Snowball. Since the recipe was lost to the family, Naomi and her mother feel a palpable loss, a break in the chain of memories leading to heritage and identity.

14 Reading Strategy
Relating to Your Own Experiences

- Discuss the description of the author's great-grandfather's drugstore. Have students ever seen a drugstore like this? Have they ever heard a parent or grandparent mention a drugstore or soda fountain similar to this one?
- **Ask** students to think of universal qualities in the description in the paragraph.
  Answer: Students may note the slow pace of summer, the magical perspective of childhood, and perhaps the love of sweets.

15 Vocabulary Builder
Latin Prefix *con-*

- Invite a volunteer to read aloud the definition of *concocted.*
- Then, have students **link** their knowledge of the Latin prefix *con-* to the definition.
  Answer: Concocted means "made by combining various ingredients." The prefix *con-,* which means "with" or "together," is combined with the root *coquere,* which means "to cook."

16 Reading Check

Answer: A Mint Snowball is shaved ice covered with a special syrup— a cooked concoction of mint leaves mixed with sugar and secret ingredients—and surrounded by scoops of vanilla ice cream.

ASSESS

Answers

1. **Possible response:** Students may feel out of step with some aspects of the modern world, such as the pace of life, the many choices, and the emphasis on physical appearance.
2. (a) Nye's mother describes the drugstore and the Mint Snowball. (b) The cold, minty taste reminds Nye's mother of Switzerland.
3. (a) Nye's great-grandfather sold the recipe. (b) Nye's mother came close to duplicating the recipe. (c) It was impossible to replicate the recipe because it contained ingredients that had never been identified.
4. (a) The author longs for old-fashioned things that have been lost, such as the recipe for the Mint Snowball. (b) The author feels that many of the possible futures that she and members of her family might have had have been lost.
5. (a) A wistful longing is expressed in the last paragraph. (b) Details include images of her great-grandfather and her mother in the drugstore and descriptions of mint and ice.
6. Most students will believe that the image of the dessert captures a past time successfully because it is described in such loving detail and has had such a great effect on the author.

Go Online Author Link For additional information about Naomi Shihab Nye, have students type in the Web Code, then select *N* from the alphabet, and then select Naomi Shihab Nye.

grandfather's feelings. My grandfather thought he should have inherited it to carry on the tradition. As far as the family knew, the person who bought the recipe never used it. At least not in public. My mother had watched my grandfather make the syrup so often she thought she could replicate it. But what did he have in those little unmarked bottles? She experimented. Once she came close. She wrote down what she did. Now she has lost the paper.

Vocabulary Builder
replicate (rep´ li kāt) *v.* duplicate

Perhaps the clue to my entire personality connects to the lost Mint Snowball. I have always felt out-of-step with my environment, disjointed in the modern world. The crisp flush of cities makes me weep. Strip centers, Poodle grooming and Take-out Thai. I am angry over lost department stores, wistful for something I have never tasted or seen.

Although I know how to do everything one needs to know—change airplanes, find my exit off the interstate, charge gas, send a fax—there is something missing. Perhaps the stoop of my great-grandfather over the pan, the slow patient swish of his spoon. The spin of my mother on the high stool with her whole life in front of her, something fine and fragrant still to happen. When I breathe a handful of mint, even pathetic sprigs from my sunbaked Texas earth, I close my eyes. Little chips of ice on the tongue, their cool slide down. Can we follow the long river of the word "refreshment" back to its spring? Is there another land for me? Can I find any lasting solace in the color green?

Critical Reading

1. **Respond:** Do you feel out of step with the modern world or in tune with it? Explain your feelings.
2. **(a) Recall:** Whose memory provides the description of the drugstore and of the Mint Snowball? **(b) Connect:** Why does this memory evoke the country from which her ancestors came?
3. **(a) Recall:** What happened to the original Mint Snowball recipe? **(b) Recall:** Which family member comes close to duplicating the recipe? **(c) Infer:** Why do you think it was impossible to replicate?
4. **(a) Interpret:** What connection is made between the Mint Snowball and the author's life? **(b) Infer:** What does Nye consider lost as a result of the vanished recipe?
5. **(a) Analyze:** What is the mood of the final paragraph of the essay? **(b) Analyze:** Which details create that mood?
6. **Evaluate:** Does the image of this family dessert successfully capture a time long passed? Explain.

For: More about Naomi Shihab Nye
Visit: www.PHSchool.com
Web Code: ere-9610

Differentiated Instruction
Solutions for All Learners

Enrichment for Gifted/Talented Students
Have students make a mural showing the soda fountain the author's great-grandfather owned. First, students should reread the first two paragraphs of the essay and list every detail that describes the soda fountain. Then, they should gather visual resources, illustrations, and photographs of old-time soda fountains. They will then be ready to draw some preliminary sketches of the soda fountain based on their notes, photos, and illustrations, striving to make their sketches as accurate as possible. After they choose sketches they like, students can refer to them as they make a mural of a life-size soda fountain, on large sheets of paper.

17 # SUSPENDED

Joy Harjo

18 

Getting Down, Joseph Holston

19 ◀ **Critical Viewing** Does this illustration of a jazz musician effectively convey Harjo's belief that jazz is "a way to speak beyond the confines of ordinary language"? Explain. **[Evaluate]**

Once I was so small that I could barely peer over the top of the backseat of the black Cadillac my father polished and tuned daily; I wanted to see everything. It was around the time I acquired language, or even before that time, when something happened that changed my relationship to the spin of the world. My concept of language, of what was possible with music was changed by this revelatory moment. It changed even the way I looked at the sun. This suspended integer of time probably escaped ordinary notice in my parents' universe, which informed most of my vision in the ordinary world. They were still omnipresent gods. We were driving somewhere in Tulsa, the northern border of the Creek Nation.[1] I don't know where we were going or

Vocabulary Builder
revelatory (rev′ ə lə tôr′ ē) *adj.* revealing; disclosing

20 

Reading Check
At what stage of Harjo's life does this narrative take place?

1. **Creek Nation** nation of Native American peoples, mainly Muscogean, formerly of Georgia and Alabama. Most now live in Oklahoma and Florida.

17 About the Selection

This essay illustrates how a single sensory experience can radically change a person's life. The speaker recalls a critical moment in which the glory of jazz reached her pre-verbal childhood mind. Blended with the heat of the day and the scent of her father's aftershave, the music became a catalyst, a medium through which the author could suddenly connect her creative dream world to everyday existence.

18 Humanities

Getting Down, by Joseph Holston

This painting—gouache on paper—illustrates an African American jazz musician, like Miles Davis, whom the speaker in the story hears on the radio.

Joseph Holston was born in Washington, D.C. Self-taught during a career in advertising art, he also studied with Marcus Blahove and Richard Goetz. Encouraged by Harlem Renaissance artists Lois Mailou Jones and James Wells, Holston developed a cubist abstractionist style in both his paintings and prints. *Getting Down,* with its fragmented forms and emphasis on line, tone, and shadow, illustrates that style.

Use this question for discussion:

- How might the speaker respond to this painting?
  Possible response: She would likely enjoy it as a bridge between reality—the musician and his instrument—and visual art—the play of shadow and form.

19 Critical Viewing

Answer: Students may say that the painting conveys emotions such as excitement, moodiness, and pleasure without words in a fashion similar to the way jazz communicates these emotions without words.

20 Reading Check

Answer: Harjo writes about an incident that happened when she was very young, at about the time she learned to speak.

Differentiated Instruction

Solutions for All Learners

Support for Special Needs Students
This short essay can be challenging because of its complex syntax and vocabulary. Have students listen to the essay on the **Listening to Literature Audio CD.** Then, have them discuss the essay and use the Got It! Assessment Videotape to test their comprehension.

Support for Less Proficient Readers
Ask students to listen to the essay on the **Listening to Literature Audio CD** before they read it on their own. Ask students to form pairs to read and discuss the essay together paragraph by paragraph.

Support for English Learners
Guide students through the essay and have them listen to it on the **Listening to Literature Audio CD** before they attempt to read it on their own. You may want to pair English learners with students whose first language is English and have pairs read and discuss the essay together.

ASSESS

Answers

1. Students may recall experiences from their early childhood. Encourage them to think about why words cannot always sufficiently communicate a past event.
2. (a) Harjo's experience took place in the summer. (b) She describes the boiling hot sun and her attempts to get a breeze.
3. (a) Harjo describes her father as a "handsome god" who dresses impeccably and smells like aftershave. (b) These details reveal her affection and respect for her father.
4. (a) She hears a trumpet playing jazz on the car radio. (b) It teaches her that music can speak in ways that reach beyond words.
5. Growing up means losing childhood innocence and becoming aware of people's failings and the finite nature of life.
6. The essay suggests that everyone's inner world is unique and that different experiences are important to people in indescribable ways.

Go Online Author Link For additional information about Joy Harjo, have students type in the Web Code, then select *H* from the alphabet, and then select Joy Harjo.

where we had been, but I know the sun was boiling the asphalt, the car windows open for any breeze as I stood on tiptoes on the floorboard behind my father, a handsome god who smelled of Old Spice, whose slick black hair was always impeccably groomed, his clothes perfectly creased and ironed. The radio was on. I loved the radio, jukeboxes or any magic thing containing music even then.

I wonder now what signaled this moment, a loop of time that on first glance could be any place in time. I became acutely aware of the line the jazz trumpeter was playing (a sound I later associated with Miles Davis). I didn't know the word jazz or trumpet, or the concepts. I don't know how to say it, with what sounds or words, but in that confluence of hot southern afternoon, in the breeze of aftershave and humidity, I followed that sound to the beginning, to the place of the birth of sound. I was suspended in whirling stars, a moon to which I'd traveled often by then. I grieved my parents' failings, my own life which I saw stretched the length of that rhapsody.

My rite of passage into the world of humanity occurred then, via jazz. The music made a startling bridge between familiar and strange lands, an appropriate vehicle, for though the music is predominantly west African in concept, with European associations, jazz was influenced by the Creek (or Muscogee) people, for we were there when jazz was born. I recognized it, that humid afternoon in my formative years, as a way to speak beyond the confines of ordinary language. I still hear it.

Vocabulary Builder
confluence (kän′ flo͞o əns) *n.* a flowing together

Critical Reading

1. **Respond:** Can you recall a personal experience that was important in your life but is difficult for you to analyze or describe?
2. **(a) Recall:** During what season did Harjo's experience take place? **(b) Support:** How do you know?
3. **(a) Recall:** Describe the appearance of Harjo's father. **(b) Analyze:** Which details of her description reveal the way she feels about her father?
4. **(a) Recall:** What kind of music was playing on the car radio? **(b) Draw Conclusions:** What did the music teach Harjo about communication?
5. **Deduce:** How does Harjo suggest that growing up involves sadness and disillusion?
6. **Apply:** What does this essay suggest about the mysterious workings of every person's inner world?

For: More about Joy Harjo
Visit: www.PHSchool.com
Web Code: ere-9611

Apply the Skills

from *The Names* • *Mint Snowball* • *Suspended*

Literary Analysis

Anecdote

1. **(a)** Identify two **anecdotes** in Momaday's piece. **(b)** What connects these anecdotes to the theme introduced in the opening paragraph?
2. In what ways is the lost recipe significant in Nye's life and in the development of her personality?
3. **(a)** Describe the way in which Harjo's experience of jazz affected her in a single moment. **(b)** How did the experience change her life?

Comparing Literary Works

4. What **rite of passage** did Momaday experience through his journey and the later selling of his horse?
5. Explain the significance of Harjo's statement, "My rite of passage into the world of humanity occurred then . . ."
6. Nye feels a great loss over her inability to recreate the Mint Snowball. If she still had the recipe, how might it have served as a rite of passage for her?
7. When a person experiences a rite of passage, he or she learns an adult truth about life and leaves childhood behind. What truths about life do each of these authors learn? Support your answer.

Reading Strategy

Relating to Your Own Experiences

8. Use a chart like the one shown to note the relationships you can find between these selections and your own experiences.

Writer's Experience	My Experience	How They Relate

9. Which writer's experiences or reflections were most accessible to you? Why?

Extend Understanding

10. **Literature Connection:** Relate "The Mint Snowball" to another literary work that expresses the theme of yearning for a way of life that is long gone. How are they similar? How do they differ?

QuickReview

An **anecdote** is a short account of an amusing or interesting event or experience.

A **rite of passage** is a significant event in a person's life that marks a transition.

To **relate to your own experiences**, connect your personal situations, emotions, attitudes, and behaviors with those of the writers.

For: Self-test
Visit: www.PHSchool.com
Web Code: era-6607

Answers

1. (a) **Possible response:** Two anecdotes include Momaday's trading horses with Pasqual and training his horse Pecos. (b) Both anecdotes demonstrate the importance of horses to people of Kiowa descent.
2. The lost recipe contributes to Nye's wistfulness and longing for things that have been lost in modern society.
3. (a) Harjo was fascinated and transported, and she experienced a "rite of passage."
(b) The experience made her realize that there are worlds beyond what she knew and that connected her with all of humankind.
4. Momaday tested himself physically and tested his courage on his journey. His courage was again tested as he moved out into the world after selling his horse.
5. Harjo understands that feelings beyond words connect her with the rest of humanity.
6. The recipe might have connected Nye to her great-grandfather and, through him, to other relatives whom she never knew.
7. **Possible response:** Momaday's rite of passage is most traditional because he tests his physical strength and courage. Nye's rite of passage is the most subtle, because for most people losing a recipe is an insignificant event. Harjo's rite of passage may be the most powerful, because she was so dramatically changed from it and because she still experiences the feelings she had during the experience.
8. Many students will relate physical challenges and experiences with music and art.

   Another sample answer can be found on **Reading Strategy Graphic Organizer B**, p. 241, in ***Graphic Organizer Transparencies.***
9. Many students will find Harjo's experience with music most accessible because of the accessibility of various kinds of music.

Answers continued

10. Students might connect "Mint Snowball" to accounts of Native American or pioneer life in America.

Go Online Assessment Students may use the **Self-test** to prepare for **Selection Test A** or **Selection Test B.**

EXTEND/ASSESS

Answers

❶ Vocabulary Lesson

Word Analysis

1. conference: conferring with
2. congregated: got together with
3. concocted: made by putting ingredients together
4. conform: go along with

Spelling Strategy

1. reluctant
2. deference
3. descendant

Vocabulary Builder

1. a
2. a
3. a
4. a
5. b
6. b
7. b
8. a

❷ Grammar and Style Lesson

1. Pecos ran faster than the other horses [ran].
2. Momaday thought the stallion was better than his own horse [was].
3. Nye's great-grandfather sold the recipe [that] he had invented.
4. Harjo recalls hearing the music in the car more vividly than [she recalls] any other early experience.
5. She noticed more than she had [noticed] before.

Writing Application

The sentences must contain elliptical clauses. Make sure students understand that elliptical clauses are clauses in which one or more words are omitted because they are understood.

Writing and Grammar, Ruby Level

Students will find further instruction and practice on elliptical clauses in Chapter 22, Section 2.

Build Language Skills

❶ Vocabulary Lesson

Word Analysis: Latin Prefix *con-*

The Latin prefix *con-* means "with" or "together." Combined with *fluence,* it produces *confluence,* meaning "flowing together." Define each of the following words, using "with" or "together."

1. conference
2. congregated
3. concocted
4. conform

Spelling Strategy

Many words end in *-ent* or *-ence,* such as *dependent* and *dependence.* However, there are exceptions, such as *flamboyant* and *flamboyance,* which end in *-ant* or *-ance.* In your notebook, complete the spelling of words in each sentence.

1. He was reluct____ to ride on the horse.
2. She showed defer____ to her grandfather.
3. She was a descend____ of the pilgrims.

Vocabulary Builder: Analogies

Select the word that best completes the analogy.

1. comfortable : chair :: supple : __?__
   (a) dancer **(b)** flexible
2. stitched : clothing :: concocted : __?__
   (a) potion **(b)** scientist
3. shy : timid :: flamboyant : __?__
   (a) showy **(b)** nervous
4. treatment : disease :: elixir : __?__
   (a) ailment **(b)** doctor
5. spread : rumor :: permeated : __?__
   (a) filled **(b)** odor
6. design : create :: replicate : __?__
   (a) count **(b)** copy
7. illuminating : lamp :: revelatory : __?__
   (a) celebration **(b)** news
8. join : split :: confluence : __?__
   (a) divergence **(b)** river

❷ Grammar and Style Lesson

Elliptical Clauses

The term *elliptical* comes from the word *ellipsis,* meaning "omission." In an **elliptical clause,** one or more words are omitted because they are understood. An elliptical clause is only understood if the context makes clear what the missing elements are—for example, in many cases, the word *that* is omitted.

Examples: Her mother enjoyed the dessert *more than* [. . .] *any other.* (*she enjoyed* is understood)

I hoped [. . .] *she would like it.* (*that* is understood)

Practice Copy each sentence, underline the elliptical clause, and write the understood word(s).

1. Pecos ran faster than the other horses.
2. Momaday thought the stallion was better than his own horse.
3. Nye's great-grandfather sold the recipe he had invented.
4. Harjo recalls hearing the music in the car more vividly than any other early experience.
5. She noticed more than she had before.

Writing Application Write two sentences containing elliptical clauses.

Prentice Hall Writing and Grammar Connection: Chapter 22, Section 2

Assessment Practice

Sentence Structure

(For more practice, see the Standardized *Test Preparation Workbook*, p. 63.)

Standardized tests often require students to choose the best way to correct the structure of a sentence. Use the sample test item below to demonstrate.

If you don't know much about horses, riding one can be quite dangerous. A horse can easily throw an inexperienced rider, this can cause serious injury.

Choose the best way to write the underlined section of the passage.

A A horse can easily throw an inexperienced rider, can cause serious injury.

B A horse can easily throw an inexperienced rider, causing serious injury.

C A horse, easily throwing an inexperienced rider, causing serious injury.

D Correct as is.

B is the best answer; it is the only complete sentence that is correctly structured and punctuated.

Writing Lesson

Reflective Essay

Each of these writers shares a moment from the past and reflects on its importance. Choose a significant event and write a reflective essay exploring its meaning.

Prewriting Brainstorm for a list of events that affected you earlier. For each, write two or three reasons why the event was significant. Decide which one you will write about.

Drafting After describing the event or experience, provide the insight to explain its effect on you. Include details that build the emotional impact of your insight.

Model: Elaborating to Add Emotional Depth

It was during my aunt's visit in the summer of 1996 that I discovered my pride in my Native American heritage. Through her stories about my grandparents and their struggles, I finally learned to celebrate what makes my life different instead of trying to hide it.

Words like *proud, finally,* and *celebrate* relate the symbolic meaning of the event.

Revising Ask a classmate to read your draft to see if he or she can identify with your experience. Then, revise your draft, adding elaboration to ensure that readers will understand the importance of the event and the feelings it inspired in you.

Prentice Hall Writing and Grammar Connection: Chapter 4, Section 3

Extend Your Learning

Listening and Speaking A line of jazz gave Joy Harjo a new vision of the world. Listen to a piece of music that does the same for you. Then, using these tips, conduct a **musical analysis,** explaining the music's effect on you:

- Describe the images that are evoked by the melody.
- If there are any lyrics, connect them with your own experiences.

Play the music for your class and discuss your feelings about it.

Research and Technology Like music, photography also has the power to evoke memory. With a group, create a **class anthology** of photographs and written memories. Include personal photographs with anecdotal notes. Provide an introduction and illustrations or art to enhance your anthology. **[Group Activity]**

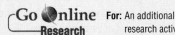

For: An additional research activity
Visit: www.PHSchool.com
Web Code: erd-7607

❸ Writing Lesson

You may use this Writing Lesson as timed-writing practice, or you may allow students to develop it as a writing assignment over several days.

- Give students the **Support for Writing Lesson** page in ***Unit 6 Resources,*** p. 114, to use as they write their reflective essays.
- Review the prewriting, drafting, and revising steps that students will undertake as they write their reflective essays. Remind students that they will want to give at least two reasons why the event they chose is significant.
- Use the Reflective Essay rubrics in ***General Resources,*** pp. 47–48, to evaluate students' essays.

❹ Research and Technology

- Suggest that students work in groups of at least five to produce their class anthologies.
- Each student in the group should take on a task: choosing and assembling the photographs, writing the introduction, editing copy, illustrating, and assembling the anthology.
- When the students are done with their booklets, have them present their work to the rest of the class. You may wish to display the booklets so students can view them on their own time.
- The **Support for Extend Your Learning** page (***Unit 6 Resources,*** p. 115) provides guided note-taking opportunities to help students complete the Extend Your Learning activities.

Go Online Research — Have students type in the Web Code for another research activity.

Assessment Resources

The following resources can be used to assess students' knowledge and skills.

Unit 6 Resources
- **Selection Test A,** pp. 117–119
- **Selection Test B,** pp. 120–122
- **Benchmark Test 9,** pp. 123–128

General Resources
- **Rubrics for Reflective Essay,** pp. 47–48

Go Online Assessment — Students may use the **Self-test** to prepare for **Selection Test A** or **Selection Test B.**

Benchmark

Administer **Benchmark Test 9.** If the Benchmark Test reveals that some students need further work, use the **Interpretation Guide** to determine the appropriate reteaching pages in the **Reading Kit** or on **Success Tracker.**

Meeting Your Standards

Students will

1. **analyze and respond to literary elements.**
   - Literary Analysis: Character's Motivation
2. **read, comprehend, analyze, and critique a short story.**
   - Reading Strategy: Contrasting Characters
   - Reading Check questions
   - Apply the Skills questions
   - Assessment Practice (ATE)
3. **develop vocabulary.**
   - Vocabulary Lesson: Latin Root: *-doc-, -doct-*
4. **understand and apply written and oral language conventions.**
   - Spelling Strategy
   - Grammar and Style Lesson: Sentence Fragments
5. **develop writing proficiency.**
   - Writing Lesson: Critical Review
6. **develop appropriate research strategies.**
   - Extend Your Learning: African Languages Presentation
7. **understand and apply listening and speaking strategies.**
   - Extend Your Learning: Television Talk Show

Block Scheduling: Use one 90-minute class period to preteach the skills and have students read the selection. Use a second 90-minute class period to assess students' mastery of skills, extend their learning, and monitor their progress.

Homework Suggestions

Following are possibilities for homework assignments:

- Support pages from ***Unit 6 Resources:***
  Literary Analysis
  Reading Strategy
  Vocabulary Builder
  Grammar and Style
- An Extend Your Learning project and the Writing Lesson for this selection may be completed over several days.

Step-by-Step Teaching Guide	Pacing Guide
PRETEACH	
• Administer Vocabulary and Reading Warm-ups as necessary.	5 min.
• Engage students' interest with the motivation activity.	5 min.
• Read and discuss author and background features. **FT**	10 min.
• Introduce the Literary Analysis skill: Motivation. **FT**	5 min.
• Introduce the Reading Strategy: Contrasting Characters. **FT**	10 min.
• Prepare students to read by teaching the selection vocabulary. **FT**	
TEACH	
• Informally monitor comprehension while students read independently or in groups. **FT**	30 min.
• Monitor students' comprehension with the Reading Check notes.	as students read
• Reinforce vocabulary with Vocabulary Builder notes.	as students read
• Develop students' understanding of the character's motivation with the Literary Analysis annotations. **FT**	5 minutes
• Develop students' ability to contrast characters with the Reading Strategy annotations. **FT**	5 minutes
ASSESS/EXTEND	
• Assess students' comprehension and mastery of the Literary Analysis and Reading Strategy by having them answer the Apply the Skills questions. **FT**	15 min.
• Have students complete the Vocabulary Lesson and the Grammar and Style Lesson. **FT**	15 min.
• Apply students' ability to use precise details by using the Writing Lesson. **FT**	45 min. or homework
• Apply students' understanding using one or more of the Extend Your Learning activities.	20–90 min. or homework
• Administer Selection Test A or Selection Test B. **FT**	15 min.

Resources

PRINT
Unit 6 Resources
Vocabulary Warm-up Word Lists **[L1, L2, EL]** .... p. 132
Vocabulary Warm-up Practice **[L1, L2, EL]** .... p. 133
Reading Warm-up A **[L1, L2, EL]** .... p. 134
Reading Warm-up B **[L1, L2, L3]** .... p. 135

TRANSPARENCY
Graphic Organizer Transparencies
Literary Analysis Graphic Organizer A **[L3]** .... p. 244
Literary Analysis Graphic Organizer B **[L1, L2, EL]** .... p. 245
Reading Strategy Graphic Organizer A **[L3]** .... p. 242
Reading Strategy Graphic Organizer B **[L1, L2, EL]** .... p. 243

PRINT
Reader's Notebook [L2]
Reader's Notebook: Adapted Version [L1]
Reader's Notebook: English Learner's Version [EL]
Unit 6 Resources
Literary Analysis **[L3]** .... p. 136
Reading Strategy **[L3]** .... p. 137
Vocabulary Builder **[L3]** .... p. 138

TECHNOLOGY
Listening to Literature Audio CDs [L2, EL]
Reader's Notebook: Adapted Version Audio CD [L1, L2]

PRINT
Unit 6 Resources
Grammar and Style **[L3]** .... p. 139
Support for Writing Lesson **[L3]** .... p. 140
Support for Extend Your Learning **[L3]** .... p. 141
Enrichment **[L4]** .... p. 142
Selection Test A **[L1, L2, EL]** .... pp. 143–145
Selection Test B **[L3, L4]** .... pp. 146–148
General Resources
Rubrics for Critique **[L3]** .... pp. 75–76
Rubric for Speaking: Delivering a Research Presentation **[L3]** .... p. 92

TECHNOLOGY
Go Online: Research **[L3]**
Go Online: Self-test **[L3]**
***ExamView*® Test Bank [L3]**

Choosing Resources for Differentiated Instruction

[L1] Special Needs Students
[L2] Below-Level Students
[L3] All Students
[L4] Advanced Students
[EL] English Learners

For Vocabulary and Reading Warm-ups and for Selection Tests, **A** signifies "less challenging" and **B** "more challenging." For Graphic Organizer transparencies, **A** signifies "not filled in" and **B** "filled in."

FT Fast Track Instruction: To move the lesson more quickly, use the strategies and activities identified with **FT**.

Scaffolding for Less Proficient and Advanced Students

The leveled Critical Thinking questions after selections progress in the levels of thinking required to answer them. To address the needs of your different students, you may use the (a) level questions for your less proficient students and the (b) level questions with your on-level and advanced students. The occasional (c) level questions are appropriate for your advanced students.

PRENTICE HALL **TeacherEXPRESS**™ Plan · Teach · Assess Use this complete suite of powerful teaching tools to make lesson planning and testing quicker and easier.

PRENTICE HALL **StudentEXPRESS**™ Learn · Study · Succeed Use the interactive textbook (online and on CD-ROM) to make selections and activities come alive with audio and video support and interactive questions.

Monitoring Progress

Before students read "Everyday Use," administer **Diagnostic Test 10** ***(Unit 6 Resources*,** p. 129). This test will determine students' level of readiness for the reading and vocabulary skills.

Go Online Professional Development **For:** Information about Lexiles
Visit: www.PHSchool.com
Web Code: eue-1111

PREТEACH

Motivation

Ask students to bring to class, or be prepared to discuss, mementos that represent their heritage. These items might be anything from a treasured photograph or great-grandfather's watch to a china teapot that has been in the family for generations. Ask students how their families use or display these items: Are they tucked away in storage or display cabinets, or do their families use them regularly? Is the risk of damaging the objects outweighed by the pleasure of seeing and using them regularly? Tell students that the story they are about to read poses the question of whether such family heirlooms belong in "everyday use."

❶ Background

More About the Author

Alice Malsenior Walker was the eighth and youngest child of poor sharecroppers, Minnie Tallulah Grant Walker and Willie Lee Walker. Her family was rich in spirit, love, and family pride. Walker often heard stories about her father's great-great-great grandmother, Mary Poole—who was a slave forced to walk from Virginia to Georgia carrying two babies—and her mother's grandmother Tallulah, who was mostly Cherokee Indian.

Walker remembered her heritage throughout her years of education at Spelman College and Sarah Lawrence College, her participation in the civil rights movement, and her career as a novelist and poet. Strong women and love of the earth are recurring themes in Walker's work.

Build Skills *Short Story*

❶ Everyday Use

Alice Walker (b. 1944)

Born in Eatonton, Georgia, Alice Walker was the eighth and youngest child in a family of sharecroppers. Of her childhood, Walker writes, "It was great fun being cute. But then, one day, it ended."

The self-confidence of her childhood was challenged by an accident with a BB gun that scarred and nearly blinded her. Eight years old when the accident happened, Walker reports that she did not lift her head for six years. It was during this time of self-imposed isolation that she indulged her passion for reading. It was not until the family could afford surgery that Walker finally had the scar tissue on her eye removed. With that surgery, her self-confidence returned.

Civil Rights Walker became one of the most popular students in her high school and graduated as both class valedictorian and prom queen. She attended Spelman College, an elite college for African American women in Atlanta. While at Spelman, Walker became deeply involved in the civil rights movement. In August 1963, she traveled to Washington, D.C., to take part in the March on Washington for Jobs and Freedom. The guest speaker that day was Dr. Martin Luther King. Unable to see him through the crowd, Walker perched in a tree to get a better view. From there, she heard Dr. King deliver his famous "I Have a Dream" address.

After two years at Spelman, Walker learned that she had won a scholarship for full tuition to Sarah Lawrence College in Bronxville, New York. Although she was reluctant to leave Spelman and her civil rights activities, Walker's teachers persuaded her to accept the offer.

From Prom Queen to Poet At Sarah Lawrence, Walker studied under famed poets Muriel Rukeyser and Jane Cooper, who nurtured her talent. Walker's first collection of poetry, *Once* (1968), was written while she was a student at Sarah Lawrence.

After graduating from Sarah Lawrence, Walker moved to Mississippi to continue her work in the civil rights movement. During this period, she also taught African American studies at Jackson State University, where she was a writer-in-residence.

Cultural Pride Much of Alice Walker's fiction—novels including *The Third Life of Grange Copeland* (1970) and story collections including *In Love and Trouble* (1973) and *You Can't Keep a Good Woman Down* (1981)—delves into the lives of African American women and their experiences throughout history and in the modern world. Her most recent novel is *Now Is the Time to Open Your Heart* (2004).

Walker's fiction and essays reflect a pride in her personal heritage and the culture of her people. She draws inspiration from the creative efforts of countless African American artists who, long ago, survived the oppression of slavery. In looking at today's world, Walker explores the connections between sexism and racism and the effects of both on individuals and their relationships.

The Color Purple With the publication of *The Color Purple* in 1982, Walker shot to international fame. The novel portrays women who are oppressed by the abusive men in their lives, but go on to find inner strength and personal dignity. Awarded both a Pulitzer Prize and a National Book Award, the book was later adapted into a successful film.

"Everyday Use" explores Walker's maternal heritage, describing the creative legacy of "ordinary" black southern women. The title essay of Walker's *In Search of Our Mothers' Gardens* can be considered the nonfiction counterpart of "Everyday Use."

Preview

Connecting to the Literature

Time and new experiences can create divisions between people—even close relatives. In this story, distance and the passage of time lead a mother and her daughter to two very different views of the world.

2 Literary Analysis

Motivation

To truly know a character, you have to understand that character's **motivation,** the reasons behind his or her thoughts, actions, and speech. Characters may be motivated by their values, experiences, needs, or dreams. These lines of "Everyday Use" are clues to the narrator's motivation.

> Maggie will be nervous until her sister goes . . . She thinks her sister has held life always in the palm of one hand, that "no" is a word the world never learned to say to her.

This quotation suggests that the narrator is motivated, at least in part, by feelings of love and protectiveness for Maggie. As you read, ask yourself these questions:

- Why is this character doing or saying this?
- What need or goal does she hope to satisfy?

Connecting Literary Elements

"Everyday Use" is written in the **first-person point of view,** featuring a narrator who is a character in the story and who uses the first-person pronoun *I*. When a story is told from the first-person point of view, the narrator's motivations may be easily understood. As you read, examine the thoughts and feelings of the narrator to understand her actions in the story.

3 Reading Strategy

Contrasting Characters

As this story opens, you learn that two sisters and their life experiences are quite different. By **contrasting characters,** or identifying the ways in which they differ, you can uncover the major conflict in the story. Use a Venn diagram like the one shown to note the character traits, such as details in behavior and speech, that separate Dee from Maggie. Consider the ways their experiences have shaped their differences.

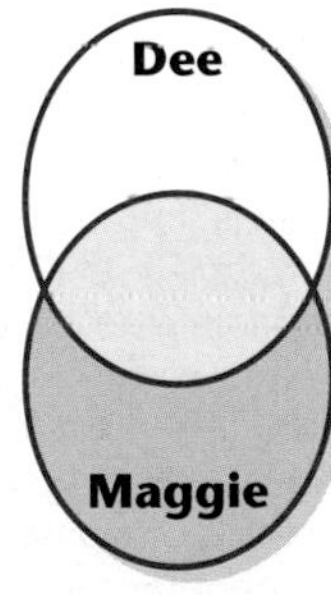

Vocabulary Builder

furtive (fur′ tiv) *adj.* sneaky (p. 1093)

lye (lī) *n.* strong alkaline solution used in cleaning and making soap (p. 1093)

oppress (ə pres′) *v.* keep down by cruel or unjust use of power or authority (p. 1094)

doctrines (däk′ trinz) *n.* religious beliefs or principles (p. 1095)

Differentiated Instruction

Solutions for All Learners

Support for Special Needs Students
Have students read the adapted version of "Everyday Use" in the ***Reader's Notebook: Adapted Version.*** This version provides basic-level instruction in an interactive format with questions and write-on lines. Completing these pages will prepare students to read the selection in the Student Edition.

Support for Less Proficient Readers
Have students read "Everyday Use" in the ***Reader's Notebook.*** This version provides basic-level instruction in an interactive format with questions and write-on lines. After students finish the selection in the ***Reader's Notebook,*** have them complete the questions and activities in the Student Edition.

Support for English Learners
Have students read "Everyday Use" in the ***Reader's Notebook: English Language Version.*** This version provides basic-level instruction in an interactive format with questions and write-on lines. Completing these pages will prepare students to read the selection in the Student Edition.

2 Literary Analysis

Motivation

- Reiterate to students that to understand fictional characters, readers must notice clues to their motivation, the causes that underlie the characters' behavior.
- Have a volunteer read the quotation from "Everyday Use" on p. 1089. Discuss with students what these few words reveal about the narrator's values and beliefs.
- Explain that because the story is written from the first-person point of view, readers learn a great deal about the motivation of the narrator, the mother of the two other main characters, Maggie and Dee.
- Remind students that all the details that Walker provides about her characters are important to fully understanding them. Urge students to keep questions such as the following in mind as they read: Why do characters behave as they do? What is important to them? What are their values, beliefs, fears, and joys?

3 Reading Strategy

Contrasting Characters

- Refer students to the Venn diagram on this page.
- Remind students that the overlapping portion of the Venn diagram indicates those traits that are shared by both characters. The parts of the circles that don't overlap indicate contrasting traits.
- Ask students to use a copy of **Reading Strategy Graphic Organizer A,** p. 242 in ***Graphic Organizer Transparencies,*** to track the similarities and differences between Maggie and Dee as they read "Everyday Use."

Vocabulary Builder

- Pronounce each vocabulary word for students, and read the definitions as a class. Have students identify any words with which they are already familiar.

TEACH

Learning Modalities
Visual/Spatial Learners Have students search in books, magazines, or web sites for examples of slave-era and contemporary African American quilts or other folk arts. Students can use the examples they locate to help them visualize the items that are so pivotal to the story.

1 About the Selection

In this short story, a mother and daughter struggle to make themselves known to each other across the considerable chasm that time and change have created between them. Educated and self-assured, Dee, who now uses the African name Wangero, visits her rural Georgia childhood home. She has returned after a long absence, ostensibly to reintroduce herself to her cultural heritage, but also to display her spiritual growth to the mother and sister she has left behind. As Dee tries to extract some material trappings of her African American heritage from the house, her mother and sister discover their own personal brand of cultural pride.

2 Critical Viewing

Answer: The pieces stitched together to make the quilts are remnants of the family's clothing. The quilt patterns may be traditional and handed down from generation to generation.

1 Everyday Use

Alice Walker

Background In this story, the character Dee, the narrator's daughter, is interested in a butter churn and a quilt—two homely artifacts that reveal her family's history. Today, such home-crafted pieces are celebrated for their beauty, but most folk art was originally created for utilitarian purposes. People took pride in creating items that were attractive as well as useful. The quilt in this story is an especially important symbol. Like most folk art, quilts served many purposes: keeping people warm, recycling worn-out clothing, providing a focal point for social gatherings of women, and preserving precious bits of family history for future generations. The differing ways in which each character regards the quilt become a critical point of division in this story.

▲ Critical Viewing 2
In what ways can quilts like these and the ones described in "Everyday Use" represent people's lives? **[Connect]**

Differentiated Instruction
Solutions for All Learners

Accessibility at a Glance

	Everyday Use
Context	Contemporary fiction
Language	Informal, conversational
Concept Level	Accessible (family dynamics)
Literary Merit	Cross generational, character driven
Lexile	820L
Overall Rating	Average

I will wait for her in the yard that Maggie and I made so clean and wavy yesterday afternoon. A yard like this is more comfortable than most people know. It is not just a yard. It is like an extended living room. When the hard clay is swept clean as a floor and the fine sand around the edges lined with tiny, irregular grooves, anyone can come and sit and look up into the elm tree and wait for the breezes that never come inside the house.

Maggie will be nervous until after her sister goes: she will stand hopelessly in corners, homely and ashamed of the burn scars down her arms and legs, eyeing her sister with a mixture of envy and awe. She thinks her sister has held life always in the palm of one hand, that "no" is a word the world never learned to say to her.

Reading Strategy
Contrasting Characters What contrasts do you learn about Maggie and her sister from the narrator's comments in this passage?

You've no doubt seen those TV shows where the child who has "made it" is confronted, as a surprise, by her own mother and father, tottering in weakly from backstage. (A pleasant surprise, of course: What would they do if parent and child came on the show only to curse out and insult each other?) On TV mother and child embrace and smile into each other's faces. Sometimes the mother and father weep, the child wraps them in her arms and leans across the table to tell how she would not have made it without their help. I have seen these programs.

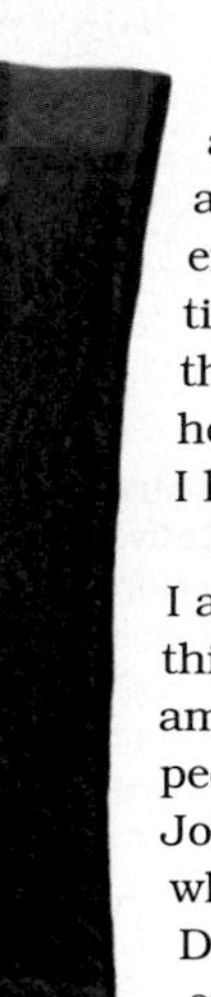

Sometimes I dream a dream in which Dee and I are suddenly brought together on a TV program of this sort. Out of a dark and soft-seated limousine I am ushered into a bright room filled with many people. There I meet a smiling, gray, sporty man like Johnny Carson who shakes my hand and tells me what a fine girl I have. Then we are on the stage and Dee is embracing me with tears in her eyes. She pins on my dress a large orchid, even though she has told me once that she thinks orchids are tacky flowers.

In real life I am a large, big-boned woman with rough, man-working hands. In the winter I wear flannel nightgowns to bed and overalls during the day. I can kill and clean a hog as mercilessly as a man. My fat keeps me hot in zero weather. I can work outside all day, breaking ice to get water for washing; I can eat pork liver cooked over the open fire minutes after it comes steaming from the hog. One winter I knocked a bull calf straight in the brain between the eyes with a sledge hammer and had the meat hung up to chill before nightfall. But of course all of this does not show on television. I am the way my daughter would want me to be: a hundred pounds lighter, my skin like an uncooked barley pancake. My hair glistens in the hot bright lights. Johnny Carson has much to do to keep up with my quick and witty tongue.

4

Literary Analysis
Motivation What do you think motivates the narrator to feel this way about herself in her dream?

Reading Check 5
Who are Maggie and her mother waiting to welcome?

3 Reading Strategy
Contrasting Characters

- Have a volunteer read the second paragraph of the story.
- If Maggie is *homely,* **ask** students what word would best describe Dee.
  Possible response: Attractive, pretty or sophisticated
- **Ask** the Reading Strategy question: What contrasts do you learn about Maggie and her sister from the narrator's comments in this passage?
  Answer: Dee is beautiful, self-assured, and lucky; Maggie has been unlucky; she is physically and, consequently, emotionally scarred and lacking in self-confidence.

4 Literary Analysis
Motivation

- **Ask** students to describe the narrator, both physically and psychologically.
  Possible response: She is a big, strong woman who can handle difficult farm tasks, like slaughtering a hog or cow—jobs usually reserved for men. She can take care of herself and her family, and seems confident in her abilities.
- **Ask** students the Literary Analysis question: What do you think motivates the character to feel this way about herself in her dream?
  Answer: The narrator's motivation probably comes from her desire to please her daughter Dee.

5 Reading Check

Answer: Maggie and her mother are waiting for Maggie's older sister Dee.

Differentiated Instruction
Solutions for All Learners

Background for Special Needs Students
Help students build some of the background they will need to understand the narrator's dream. Explain that the television show to which she refers is *This Is Your Life,* which aired during the 1950s. The program reunited celebrities with surprise visitors from their past.

Background for Gifted/Talented Students
Explain that the television show described in the narrator's dream is *This Is Your Life,* which aired during the 1950s. Ask students to act out the narrator's dream scene from the television show.

Background for Advanced Readers
Explain that the television show described in this part of the story is *This Is Your Life,* which aired during the 1950s. Have students research the show and write about its importance to popular culture at the time.

❻ Literary Analysis
Motivation and First-Person Point of View

- Have a volunteer read the bracketed passage aloud.
- Remind students that descriptions told from the first-person point of view can be very powerful because they serve as eyewitness accounts, both observed and experienced.
- **Ask** students why the narrator is moved to remember details of the night the fire burned down her house and injured Maggie.
  Possible response: The narrator is thinking about the differences between Maggie and Dee, and Dee's light beautiful skin emphasizes Maggie's suffering.
- **Ask** the Literary Analysis question: What does the narrator's memory of the fire reveal about her point of view toward her two daughters?
  Answer: The narrator feels pity for Maggie and anger toward Dee.

❼ Reading Strategy
Contrasting Characters

- Have students reread the bracketed passage.
- **Ask** the Reading Strategy question: What contrasts between herself and Dee does the narrator describe?
  Answer: The narrator is large, uninterested in fashion, strong in both mind and body, and compassionate. She sees Dee as stylish, pretty, determined, and strong-minded but also self-centered.

But that is a mistake. I know even before I wake up. Who ever knew a Johnson with a quick tongue? Who can even imagine me looking a strange white man in the eye? It seems to me I have talked to them always with one foot raised in flight, with my head turned in whichever way is farthest from them. Dee, though. She would always look anyone in the eye. Hesitation was no part of her nature.

"How do I look, Mama?" Maggie says, showing just enough of her thin body enveloped in pink skirt and red blouse for me to know she's there, almost hidden by the door.

"Come out into the yard," I say.

Have you ever seen a lame animal, perhaps a dog run over by some careless person rich enough to own a car, sidle up to someone who is ignorant enough to be kind to him? That is the way my Maggie walks. She has been like this, chin on chest, eyes on ground, feet in shuffle, ever since the fire that burned the other house to the ground.

Dee is lighter than Maggie, with nicer hair and a fuller figure. ❻ She's a woman now, though sometimes I forget. How long ago was it that the other house burned? Ten, twelve years? Sometimes I can still hear the flames and feel Maggie's arms sticking to me, her hair smoking and her dress falling off her in little black papery flakes. Her eyes seemed stretched open, blazed open by the flames reflected in them. And Dee. I see her standing off under the sweet gum tree she used to dig gum out of; a look of concentration on her face as she watched the last dingy gray board of the house fall in toward the red-hot brick chimney. Why don't you do a dance around the ashes? I'd want to ask her. She had hated the house that much.

I used to think she hated Maggie, too. But that was before we raised the money, the church and me, to send her to Augusta to school. She used to read to us without pity; forcing words, lies, other folks' habits, whole lives upon us two, sitting trapped and ignorant underneath her voice. She washed us in a river of make-believe, burned us with a lot of knowledge we didn't necessarily need to know. Pressed us to her with the serious way she read, to shove us away at just the moment, like dimwits, we seemed about to understand.

❼ Dee wanted nice things. A yellow organdy dress to wear to her graduation from high school; black pumps to match a green suit she'd made from an old suit somebody gave me. She was determined to stare down any disaster in her efforts. Her eyelids would not flicker for minutes at a time. Often I fought off the temptation to shake her. At sixteen she had a style of her own, and knew what style was.

I never had an education myself. After second grade the school was closed down. Don't ask me why: in 1927 colored asked fewer questions than they do now. Sometimes Maggie reads to me. She stumbles along good-naturedly but can't see well. She knows she is not bright. Like good looks and money, quickness passed her by. She will marry John

Literary Analysis
Motivation and First-Person Point of View
What does the narrator's memory of the fire reveal about her point of view toward her two daughters?

Reading Strategy
Contrasting Characters
What contrasts between herself and Dee does the narrator describe?

Enrichment

TV Shows

The story's narrator alludes to several popular television shows that were a well-established feature of American popular culture in the mid-to-late-twentieth century. The television show *This Is Your Life* ran from 1952 to 1961. Hosted by Ralph Edwards, the show staged reunions between celebrities and influential people from various phases of their lives. The narrator also mentions Johnny Carson, who hosted late-night television's *Tonight Show* from 1962 until 1992. With wry humor, Carson interviewed celebrities from various walks of life, with the emphasis on comedy and show business.

Thomas (who has mossy teeth in an earnest face) and then I'll be free to sit here and I guess just sing church songs to myself. Although I never was a good singer. Never could carry a tune. I was always better at a man's job. I used to love to milk till I was hooved in the side in '49. Cows are soothing and slow and don't bother you, unless you try to milk them the wrong way.

I have deliberately turned my back on the house. It is three rooms, just like the one that burned, except the roof is tin; they don't make shingle roofs any more. There are no real windows, just some holes cut in the sides, like the portholes in a ship, but not round and not square, with rawhide holding the shutters up on the outside. This house is in a pasture, too, like the other one. No doubt when Dee sees it she will want to tear it down. She wrote me once that no matter where we "choose" to live, she will manage to come see us. But she will never bring her friends. Maggie and I thought about this and Maggie asked me, "Mama, when did Dee ever *have* any friends?"

She had a few. Furtive boys in pink shirts hanging about on washday after school. Nervous girls who never laughed. Impressed with her they worshiped the well-turned phrase, the cute shape, the scalding humor that erupted like bubbles in lye. She read to them.

When she was courting Jimmy T she didn't have much time to pay to us, but turned all her faultfinding power on him. He *flew* to marry a cheap city girl from a family of ignorant flashy people. She hardly had time to recompose herself.

When she comes I will meet—but there they are!

Maggie attempts to make a dash for the house, in her shuffling way, but I stay her with my hand. "Come back here," I say. And she stops and tries to dig a well in the sand with her toe.

It is hard to see them clearly through the strong sun. But even the first glimpse of leg out of the car tells me it is Dee. Her feet were always neat-looking, as if God himself had shaped them with a certain style. From the other side of the car comes a short, stocky man. Hair is all over his head a foot long and hanging from his chin like a kinky mule tail. I hear Maggie suck in her breath. "Uhnnnh," is what it sounds like. Like when you see the wriggling end of a snake just in front of your foot on the road. "Uhnnnh."

Dee next. A dress down to the ground, in this hot weather. A dress so loud it hurts my eyes. There are yellows and oranges enough to throw back the light of the sun. I feel my whole face warming from the heat waves it throws out. Earrings gold, too, and hanging down to her shoulders. Bracelets dangling and making noises when she moves her arm up to shake the folds of the dress out of her armpits. The dress is loose and flows, and as she walks closer, I like it. I hear Maggie go "Uhnnnh" again. It is her sister's hair. It stands straight up like the wool on a sheep. It is black as night and around the edges are two long pigtails that rope about like small lizards disappearing behind her ears.

Vocabulary Builder

furtive (fur′ tiv) *adj.* sneaky

lye (lī) *n.* strong alkaline solution used in cleaning and making soap

Literary Analysis
Motivation What motivates Maggie to try to run for the house?

Reading Check 11
What traumatic event occurred in the lives of the mother and her daughters?

8 Critical Thinking
Infer

- Have students **describe** what Dee's friends thought of her.
  Answer: They looked up to her.
- **Ask:** What did their behavior indicate about their feelings toward Dee?
  Answer: They seemed to be intimidated by Dee.
- Then, **ask** what Dee's friends reveal to the reader about Dee.
  Answer: She likes to be surrounded by those who do not challenge her.

9 Literary Analysis
Motivation

- **Ask** students who Jimmy T was and how Dee treated him.
  Answer: Jimmy T was Dee's boyfriend, and he was the constant target of her criticism.
- Have students **explain** why Dee's behavior motivated Jimmy T to break up with her and marry another woman.
  Answer: Most students will agree that no one likes to be the target of someone's incessant criticism. Dee made Jimmy T feel inferior, so he found a woman who didn't make him feel this way.

10 Literary Analysis
Motivation

- Read the bracketed passage aloud to the class.
- **Ask** the Literary Analysis question: What motivates Maggie to try to run for the house?
  Answer: Maggie tries to run into the house because she is shy, self-conscious, and afraid to face her sister or meet her sister's companion.
- Then, **ask** students how Maggie reacts to Dee's companion.
  Answer: Maggie sucks in her breath as if she had seen a snake.
- Have students **explain** what this reaction indicates about Maggie's feelings toward the man.
  Answer: Maggie finds the man scary and repellent.

11 Reading Check

Answer: Their house burned down and Maggie was badly injured.

Differentiated Instruction
Solutions for All Learners

Support for Less Proficient Readers
Help students note the narrator's negative feelings toward Dee. Explain that the reason the word *choose* in the first complete paragraph on p. 1093 is in quotation marks is because it is ironic. The narrator and Maggie cannot choose where they want to live. Help students notice how even her compliments are bitter.

Strategy for Gifted/Talented Students
Encourage students to discuss how the narrator feels about Dee based on what they read on this page. Have them select paragraphs to memorize and then recite for an audience, using a tone of voice that expresses the narrator's feelings toward her oldest daughter.

Enrichment for Advanced Readers
Invite students to analyze the text carefully for evidence about the narrator's feelings about her daughter Dee. Have them describe the tone of the narrator's thoughts and explain the complexity of the narrator's feelings. Ask students to back up their opinions with evidence from this page.

12 Literary Analysis
Motivation

- Have a volunteer read the bracketed passage aloud.
- Then, **ask** the Literary Analysis question: Why does Dee take so many photographs?
  Possible response: Dee takes numerous photographs of the house, its surroundings, and her relatives as a reminder of her "heritage." In doing so, she diminishes her family by portraying them and their home as quaint. She may be gathering pictures to show her friends because she does not plan to return again soon.

13 Literary Analysis
Motivation

- Discuss with students the reasons behind Dee's decision to change her name. What do they think of this decision?
  Possible answer: Students may say that Dee's name change reinforces her African heritage but distances her from her immediate family.
- Then, discuss the narrator's reaction to the name change.
  Ask: Does the narrator understand Dee's perspective? Does she approve?
  Answer: Most students will believe that her mother does understand but that she does not approve.

▶ **Monitor Progress: Ask** students what feelings and thoughts may motivate the narrator's behavior in this discussion with her daughter.
Answer: Most students will believe that the narrator is deliberately "playing dumb" by pretending not to understand that the family name ultimately derives from the days of slavery. She does this to irritate her daughter and to make the point that wherever the name came from, it has become their own, and she is proud of it.

"Wa-su-zo-Tean-o!"[1] she says, coming on in that gliding way the dress makes her move. The short stocky fellow with the hair to his navel is all grinning and he follows up with "Asalamalakim,[2] my mother and sister!" He moves to hug Maggie but she falls back, right up against the back of my chair. I feel her trembling there and when I look up I see the perspiration falling off her chin.

"Don't get up," says Dee. Since I am stout it takes something of a push. You can see me trying to move a second or two before I make it. She turns, showing white heels through her sandals, and goes back to the car. Out she peeks next with a Polaroid. She stoops down quickly and lines up picture after picture of me sitting there in front of
12 the house with Maggie cowering behind me. She never takes a shot without making sure the house is included. When a cow comes nibbling around the edge of the yard she snaps it and me and Maggie and the house. Then she puts the Polaroid in the back seat of the car, and comes up and kisses me on the forehead.

Meanwhile Asalamalakim is going through motions with Maggie's hand. Maggie's hand is as limp as a fish, and probably as cold, despite the sweat, and she keeps trying to pull it back. It looks like Asalamalakim wants to shake hands but wants to do it fancy. Or maybe he don't know how people shake hands. Anyhow, he soon gives up on Maggie.

"Well," I say. "Dee."

"No, Mama," she says. "Not 'Dee,' Wangero Leewanika Kemanjo!"

"What happened to 'Dee'?" I wanted to know.

"She's dead," Wangero said. "I couldn't bear it any longer, being named after the people who oppress me."

"You know as well as me you was named after your aunt Dicie," I said. Dicie is my sister. She named Dee. We called her "Big Dee" after
13 Dee was born.

"But who was *she* named after?" asked Wangero.

"I guess after Grandma Dee," I said.

"And who was she named after?" asked Wangero.

"Her mother," I said, and saw Wangero was getting tired. "That's about as far back as I can trace it," I said. Though, in fact, I probably could have carried it back beyond the Civil War through the branches.

"Well," said Asalamalakim, "there you are."

"Uhnnnh," I heard Maggie say.

"There I was not," I said, "before 'Dicie' cropped up in our family, so why should I try to trace it that far back?"

He just stood there grinning, looking down on me like somebody inspecting a Model A car. Every once in a while he and Wangero sent eye signals over my head.

"How do you pronounce this name?" I asked.

Literary Analysis
Motivation Why does Dee take so many photographs?

Vocabulary Builder
oppress (ə pres′) *v.* keep down by cruel or unjust use of power or authority

1. **Wa-su-zo-Tean-o** (wä so͞o zō tēn′ ō) African greeting.
2. **Asalamalakim** *Salaam aleikhim* (sə läm′ ä lī′ kēm′) Islamic greeting meaning "Peace be with you."

Enrichment

African American Identity and Islam

In the 1960s and early 1970s, as part of their quest for an African American identity, some African Americans began to emphasize their links to their African ancestry. They celebrated their cultural heritage, dressed in African clothing, and wore their hair in the natural "afro" style. Some took African or Arabic names, rejecting the names acquired through their American slave ancestry, and some became Muslims.

African Americans who converted to Islam followed the teachings of Mohammed established in the seventh century and expressed in the Koran, the Muslim holy book. The Koran forbids usury, games of chance, and the consumption of pork and alcohol. Practicing Muslims believe in a single God, pray five times a day facing Mecca, donate to charity, fast during Ramadan, and make a pilgrimage to Mecca once in their lifetime.

"You don't have to call me by it if you don't want to," said Wangero.

"Why shouldn't I?" I asked. "If that's what you want us to call you, we'll call you."

"I know it might sound awkward at first," said Wangero.

"I'll get used to it," I said. "Ream it out again."

Well, soon we got the name out of the way. Asalamalakim had a name twice as long and three times as hard. After I tripped over it two or three times he told me to just call him Hakim-a-barber. I wanted to ask him was he a barber, but I didn't really think he was, so I didn't ask.

"You must belong to those beef-cattle people down the road," I said. They said "Asalamalakim" when they met you, too, but they didn't shake hands. Always too busy: feeding the cattle, fixing the
4 fences, putting up salt-lick shelters, throwing down hay. When the white folks poisoned some of the herd the men stayed up all night with rifles in their hands. I walked a mile and a half just to see the sight.

5 Hakim-a-barber said, "I accept some of their doctrines, but farming and raising cattle is not my style." (They didn't tell me, and I didn't ask, whether Wangero (Dee) had really gone and married him.)

We sat down to eat and right away he said he didn't eat collards[3] and pork was unclean. Wangero, though, went on through the chitlins[4] and corn bread, the greens and everything else. She talked a blue streak over the sweet potatoes. Everything delighted her. Even the fact that we still used the benches her daddy made for the table when we couldn't afford to buy chairs.

"Oh, Mama!" she cried. Then turned to Hakim-a-barber. "I never knew how lovely these benches are. You can feel the rump prints," she said, running her hands underneath her and along the bench. Then she gave a sigh and her hand closed over Grandma Dee's butter dish. "That's it!" she said. "I knew there was something I wanted to ask you if I could have." She jumped up from the table and went over in the corner where the churn stood, the milk in it clabber by now. She looked at the churn and looked at it.

"This churn top is what I need," she said. "Didn't Uncle Buddy whittle it out of a tree you all used to have?"

"Yes," I said.

"Uh huh," she said happily. "And I want the dasher, too."

"Uncle Buddy whittle that, too?" asked the barber.

---

3. **collards** (käl′ ərdz) *n.* leaves of the collard plant, often referred to as "collard greens."
4. **chitlins** (chit′ lənz) *n.* chitterlings, a pork dish popular among southern African Americans.

Vocabulary Builder
doctrines (däk′ trinz) *n.* religious beliefs or principles

Reading Check 16
Why has Dee changed her name?

14 Critical Thinking
Infer

- Invite a volunteer to read the bracketed passage aloud.
- **Ask** students what the narrator thinks of her Muslim neighbors down the road. Why does she call them "beef-cattle people"?
  Answer: She thinks they are enterprising but not neighborly. Thus, they are "beef-cattle people," who would rather spend time with their herd than say hello. However, she admires their ability to defend themselves against white people who threaten them.

15 Vocabulary Builder
The Latin Root *-doc-* / *-doct-*

- Draw students' attention to the word *doctrines* and read its definition.
- Explain that the Latin root *-doc-* or *-doct-* means "teach."
- Give an example of a word with this Latin root, and **ask** students to think of some others.
- **Possible answers:** *doctrinaire, doctor, doctorate, document, docudrama,* and *indoctrinate*
- Finally, have students choose three words from the list and construct sentences with them.

16 Reading Check

Answer: Dee says she has changed her name because she no longer wanted to use a name given to her by the oppressor. The reader may suspect that she has also changed her name because it was a fashionable thing to do among a select group of African Americans at the time.

Differentiated Instruction
Solutions for All Learners

Strategy for English Learners
Students who are learning English may have had the experience of being treated as though they were stupid because their grasp of English was limited. Have students discuss this problem and compare their feelings with the feelings of the mother and Maggie. What advice would students give Hakim-a-barber to help him get along better with the narrator and Maggie? Note students' suggestions on the chalkboard and have them use your notes to write a letter of advice to Hakim-a-barber.

Strategy for Gifted/Talented Students
Have students gather in small groups to describe the behavior of Hakim-a-barber toward Maggie and her mother. Ask the groups to discuss the reasons why Maggie and her mother don't like him very much. Urge students to compare his behavior with that of people they have known. Then, ask students to work together to write Hakim-a-barber a letter of advice about getting along with people who are different from him.

⓱ Critical Viewing

Answer: Students are likely to say that the young girl's shy glance and poor clothing are similar to their mental image of Maggie. Some students may believe that the girl's glance and posture are more self-confident than Maggie's would be.

⓲ Reading Strategy
Contrasting Characters

- **Ask** students to describe what the two sisters do after dinner.
  Answer: Dee goes through her mother's trunk. Maggie starts washing the dinner dishes.
- Invite students to **explain** what this difference in behavior reveals about the sisters' personalities.
  Answer: Dee immediately thinks about getting what she wants. Maggie thinks first about helping out. Maggie "hanging back" in the kitchen also demonstrates her shyness.

⓳ Critical Thinking
Analyze

- **Ask** students what event is described in this sentence.
  Answer: Maggie drops something in the kitchen and slams the door.
- Invite students to **explain** why Maggie did this.
  Answer: Maggie was upset at the prospect of Dee getting the quilts.
- **Ask** students to explain what this behavior reveals about Maggie.
  Answer: Maggie cannot express her feelings directly, but she is angry.

Dee (Wangero) looked up at me.

"Aunt Dee's first husband whittled the dash," said Maggie so low you almost couldn't hear her. "His name was Henry, but they called him Stash."

"Maggie's brain is like an elephant's," Wangero said, laughing. "I can use the churn top as a centerpiece for the alcove table," she said, sliding a plate over the churn, "and I'll think of something artistic to do with the dasher."

When she finished wrapping the dasher the handle stuck out. I took it for a moment in my hands. You didn't even have to look close to see where hands pushing the dasher up and down to make butter had left a kind of sink in the wood. In fact, there were a lot of small sinks; you could see where thumbs and fingers had sunk into the wood. It was beautiful light yellow wood, from a tree that grew in the yard where Big Dee and Stash had lived.

⓲ After dinner Dee (Wangero) went to the trunk at the foot of my bed and started rifling through it. Maggie hung back in the kitchen over the dishpan. Out came Wangero with two quilts. They had been pieced by Grandma Dee and then Big Dee and me had hung them on the quilt frames on the front porch and quilted them. One was in the Lone Star pattern. The other was Walk Around the Mountain. In both of them were scraps of dresses Grandma Dee had worn fifty and more years ago. Bits and pieces of Grandpa Jarrell's Paisley shirts. And one teeny faded blue piece, about the size of a penny matchbox, that was from Great Grandpa Ezra's uniform that he wore in the Civil War.

"Mama," Wangero said sweet as a bird. "Can I have these old quilts?"

⓳ I heard something fall in the kitchen, and a minute later the kitchen door slammed.

"Why don't you take one or two of the others?" I asked. "These old things was just done by me and Big Dee from some tops your grandma pieced before she died."

▼ Critical Viewing ⓱ Look at the expression on this young girl's face and the clothing she is wearing. Compare and contrast them with your perception of Maggie. **[Compare and Contrast]**

Enrichment

African American Quilts

Enslaved African American women became expert quilters during slavery times, using their master's fabrics and patterns to make quilts for their master's use.

After the Civil War, black women continued to create quilts, but now did so for their own families. They used scraps of clothing and feed sacks—whatever fabric was available. Few examples of these quilts remain because the quilts were used until they wore out. Many everyday quilts were made of fabric strips, the "string" technique, a quick and efficient quilting method.

African American women also made story quilts that used appliqué over fabric to create pictures that tell stories. No one knows how common these quilts were, but story quilt techniques have been handed down through the generations. Today, many African American women still make story quilts.

"No," said Wangero. "I don't want those. They are stitched around the borders by machine."

"That'll make them last better," I said.

"That's not the point," said Wangero. "These are all pieces of dresses Grandma used to wear. She did all this stitching by hand. Imagine!" She held the quilts securely in her arms, stroking them.

"Some of the pieces, like those lavender ones, come from old clothes her mother handed down to her," I said, moving up to touch the quilts. Dee (Wangero) moved back just enough so that I couldn't reach the quilts. They already belonged to her.

"Imagine!" she breathed again, clutching them closely to her bosom.

"The truth is," I said, "I promised to give them quilts to Maggie, for when she marries John Thomas."

She gasped like a bee had stung her.

"Maggie can't appreciate these quilts!" she said. "She'd probably be backward enough to put them to everyday use."

"I reckon she would," I said. "God knows I been saving 'em for long enough with nobody using 'em. I hope she will!" I didn't want to bring up how I had offered Dee (Wangero) a quilt when she went away to college. Then she had told me they were old-fashioned, out of style.

"But they're *priceless*!" she was saying now, furiously; for she has a temper. "Maggie would put them on the bed and in five years they'd be in rags. Less than that!"

"She can always make some more," I said. "Maggie knows how to quilt."

Dee (Wangero) looked at me with hatred. "You just will not understand. The point is these quilts, *these quilts*!"

"Well," I said, stumped. "What would *you* do with them?"

"Hang them," she said. As if that was the only thing you *could* do with quilts.

Maggie by now was standing in the door. I could almost hear the sound her feet made as they scraped over each other.

"She can have them, Mama," she said, like somebody used to never winning anything, or having anything reserved for her.

"I can 'member Grandma Dee without the quilts."

I looked at her hard. She had filled her bottom lip with checker-berry snuff and it gave her face a kind of dopey, hangdog look. It was Grandma Dee and Big Dee who taught her how to quilt herself. She stood there with her scarred hands hidden in the folds of her skirt.

Reading Strategy
Contrasting Characters
In what way does the dispute over the quilts reveal differences between the two sisters?

 **Reading Check** 21
Why does Dee think Maggie should not have the quilts?

20 Reading Strategy
Contrasting Characters

- **Ask** students to discuss Dee's behavior after she retrieves the quilts from the trunk. Why does she act as though the quilts already belong to her?
  Answer: Dee is very self-confident and self-centered. She is accustomed to getting what she wants.
- Then, **ask** the Reading Strategy question: In what way does the dispute over the quilts reveal differences between the two sisters?
  Answer: The dispute reveals Maggie's practical unassuming nature and Dee's quest for the latest in fashion. Dee will fight as hard as she can to acquire the quilts; Maggie is willing to give them up without a battle because she doesn't expect to get things she wants.

21 Reading Check

Answer: Dee thinks Maggie should not have the quilts because Maggie does not appreciate their artistic and historical value. Dee believes that Maggie will use the quilts every day and quickly wear them out.

Differentiated Instruction
Solutions for All Learners

Enrichment for Gifted/Talented Students
Invite students to work together to make a story quilt. Each student should design a quilt square that represents him or herself. Students should then choose a design that says something about them: what they like, what is important to them, how they see themselves, and so on. Each student should appliqué the design on a quilt square. After all the squares are complete, an adult volunteer can stitch the squares together and add stuffing and a backing.

Enrichment for Advanced Readers
Have students research quilting techniques and designs. Suggest that they focus particularly on quilts made by African American women. Ask students to make presentations to the rest of the class in which they display photographs or actual examples of the various techniques and designs. If possible, encourage students to invite a quilt maker to class for a lecture demonstration.

ASSESS

Answers

1. Many students will feel upset that Dee treated her mother and sister in such a thoughtless, high-handed, and condescending fashion.
2. (a) Maggie was burned in a fire. (b) Maggie was upset at losing her home; Dee seemed glad to see it go.
3. (a) Dee asks for a churn top, dasher, and two quilts. (b) She intends to display them as art objects. (c) She hated both these items and her heritage when she lived with them.
4. (a) The quilts symbolize the experiences and shared heritage of the women's family. (b) For Dee, the quilts are a quaint reminder of a heritage she has left behind; for Maggie, the quilts are part of a living heritage to be used and enjoyed in her daily life.
5. Dee's main purpose in visiting her childhood home seems to have been to show it to her friend and to gather keepsakes to take away.
6. Many students will believe that Dee's behavior was so offensive that her mother should not have given her anything. Other students will say that Dee's mother should have given her some family heirlooms, but not the ones she had already promised to Maggie.

Go Online **Author Link** For additional information about Alice Walker, have students type in the Web Code, then select *W* from the alphabet, and then select Alice Walker.

She looked at her sister with something like fear but she wasn't mad at her. This was Maggie's portion. This was the way she knew God to work.

When I looked at her like that something hit me in the top of my head and ran down to the soles of my feet. Just like when I'm in church and the spirit of God touches me and I get happy and shout. I did something I never had done before: hugged Maggie to me, then dragged her on into the room, snatched the quilts out of Miss Wangero's hands and dumped them into Maggie's lap. Maggie just sat there on my bed with her mouth open.

"Take one or two of the others," I said to Dee.

But she turned without a word and went out to Hakim-a-barber.

"You just don't understand," she said, as Maggie and I came out to the car.

"What don't I understand?" I wanted to know.

"Your heritage," she said. And then she turned to Maggie, kissed her, and said, "You ought to try to make something of yourself, too, Maggie. It's really a new day for us. But from the way you and Mama still live you'd never know it."

She put on some sunglasses that hid everything above the tip of her nose and her chin.

Maggie smiled; maybe at the sunglasses. But a real smile, not scared. After we watched the car dust settle I asked Maggie to bring me a dip of snuff. And then the two of us sat there just enjoying, until it was time to go in the house and go to bed.

Critical Reading

1. **Respond:** How did you feel about Dee's behavior on her visit home? Explain.
2. **(a) Recall:** How was Maggie injured? **(b) Compare and Contrast:** How did Maggie and Dee each react to that dramatic experience?
3. **(a) Recall:** What objects does Dee ask to have?
   (b) Recall: What does Dee intend to do with the items she requests?
   (c) Interpret: What is ironic about her request for these objects and her professed interest in her heritage?
4. **(a) Interpret:** What do the quilts symbolize?
   (b) Compare and Contrast: In what ways do the quilts hold different meanings for Dee and for Maggie?
5. **Infer:** What seems to have been Dee's main purpose in visiting her home?
6. **Take a Position:** Should Dee's mother have given some of the family heirlooms to Dee? Why or why not?

Go Online **Author Link**
For: More about Alice Walker
Visit: www.PHSchool.com
Web Code: ere-9612

Apply the Skills

Everyday Use

Literary Analysis

Motivation

1. What appears to **motivate** Dee's interest in her heritage?
2. **(a)** List three personality traits that enable Dee to return home after a long absence and assume she may take things from the house. **(b)** Give three examples that reveal Maggie's character.
3. What does the narrator's act of snatching the quilts from Dee reveal about her personal values?
4. Explain Dee's complex motivations when she uses the word "heritage" and describes Maggie as "backward."

Connecting Literary Elements

5. Using a chart like the one shown, analyze the narrator's feelings toward Dee and Maggie.

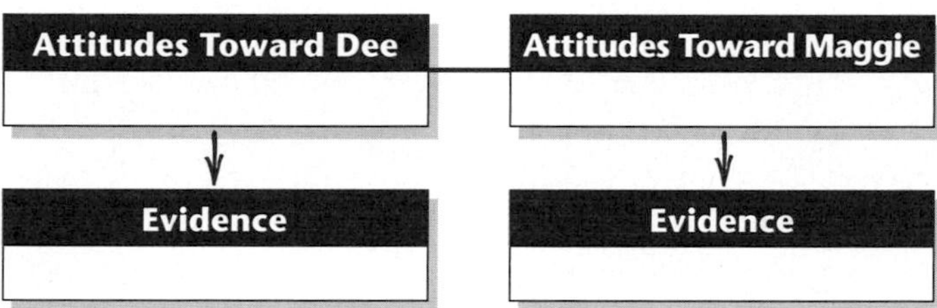

6. **(a)** What is your attitude toward each sister? **(b)** How does Walker's choice of narrator influence your response?
7. In what ways might the story change if it were told by Dee? Explain.

Reading Strategy

Contrasting Characters

8. How do Maggie and Dee differ **(a)** physically, **(b)** intellectually, and **(c)** emotionally?
9. **(a)** What does each sister know about her heritage? **(b)** To what extent does each sister think it is important to incorporate knowledge of her African heritage into her daily life?

Extend Understanding

10. **Cultural Connection:** What message does the story convey about family relationships and the meaning of heritage?

QuickReview

A character's **motivations** are the reasons for his or her thoughts, feelings, actions, and speech.

A story using the **first-person point of view** is told by a narrator who is a character in the story and who uses the first-person pronoun *I*.

To **contrast characters,** identify the ways in which they differ.

For: Self-test
Visit: www.PHSchool.com
Web Code: era-6608

Go Online Assessment Students may use the **Self-test** to prepare for **Selection Test A** or **Selection Test B**.

Answers

1. **Possible response:** A desire to keep up with the fashionable trend of connecting with one's African American heritage seems to motivate Dee's interest.
2. (a) Personality traits include self-confidence, lack of sensitivity to others, and selfishness. (b) Maggie's hanging back to avoid meeting the visitors; Maggie's cleaning up after dinner; Maggie's willingness to give up the quilts.
3. The narrator can be pushed only so far. When Maggie is being hurt once again, she defends her.
4. Dee has turned her back on her family but pretends to value her heritage.
5. Attitudes Toward Dee: Dislike; Evidence: Dee's happiness at seeing their house burn, treating her mother and sister as if they were stupid. Attitudes Toward Maggie: Pity; Evidence: Descriptions of Maggie's burns and her cringing posture.

   Another sample answer can be found on **Literary Analysis Graphic Organizer B,** p. 245 in ***Graphic Organizer Transparencies.***
6. (a) Most students will dislike Dee and feel sorry for Maggie. (b) The mother has ambivalent feelings about Dee but she loves Maggie. These feelings influence the reader's perceptions of the characters.
7. Dee might be a far more sympathetic character and might present details of her experiences growing up that alter readers' perceptions of her and her family.
8. (a) Dee is prettier and more stylish than Maggie. (b) Dee has had a much better formal education than Maggie has had and is much more quick-witted than her sister. (c) Dee is more self-confident and less sensitive than Maggie is.
9. (a) Dee has learned about her heritage from books; Maggie from everyday life. (b) To Dee, her heritage is something to be studied; for Maggie, it is something to be lived.
10. Many students will comment on the importance of maintaining close family relationships and appreciating everyday aspects of one's heritage.

Build Language Skills

❶ Vocabulary Lesson

Word Analysis: Latin Root *-doc-* / *-doct-*

The word *doctrines,* meaning "teachings, ideas, or beliefs," includes the Latin root *-doc-* / *-doct-*, meaning "teach." By combining this information with context clues, choose the best word to complete each sentence.

documents indoctrinate docile documentary

1. We watched a __?__ on the history of quilt-making in America.
2. A __?__ learner is one who accepts without question anything he or she is taught.
3. The political leader worked to __?__ his followers by repeating his ideology every day.
4. Immigrants were asked to show __?__ to prove their citizenship in their original country.

Vocabulary Builder: Analogies

Complete each analogy using a word from the vocabulary list on page 1089.

1. *Flour* is to *pie crust* as __?__ is to *soap.*
2. *Encourage* is to *coach* as __?__ is to *dictator.*
3. *Competitive* is to *athlete* as __?__ is to *prowler.*
4. *Moral* is to *lesson* as __?__ is to *belief.*

Spelling Strategy

To add a suffix to a word ending in two consonants, retain both consonants and add the suffix: *oppress + -ive = oppressive.* Add a suffix to each of the words below and write a sentence for each.

1. distress 2. will 3. obsess

❷ Grammar and Style Lesson

Sentence Fragments

A sentence expresses a complete thought with a subject and a verb. **Sentence fragments** are parts of sentences incorrectly punctuated as though they were complete. The fragment in this example lacks a subject:

Example: Never could carry a tune. (missing a subject: *Who?*)

Although it was a quilt made by my mother. (does not express a complete thought)

While fragments are not acceptable in formal writing, writers do use them to imitate the way people speak.

Practice Explain why each example is a sentence fragment, and identify the missing sentence part. Rewrite each fragment as a complete sentence.

1. Furtive boys in pink shirts hanging about on washday after school.
2. Nervous girls who never laughed.
3. Earrings gold, too, and hanging down to her shoulder.
4. Always too busy: feeding the cattle, fixing the fences, putting up salt-lick shelters.
5. Your heritage.

Writing Application Write a dialogue between characters from "Everyday Use." Incorporate fragments to capture speech patterns.

WG Prentice Hall Writing and Grammar Connection: Chapter 20, Section 4

EXTEND/ASSESS

Answers

❶ Vocabulary Lesson

Word Analysis

1. documentary
2. docile
3. indoctrinate
4. documents

Vocabulary Builder

1. lye
2. oppress
3. furtive
4. doctrines

Spelling Strategy

1. distressing
2. willing
3. obsessive

❷ Grammar and Style Lesson

1–3. Students may say that these fragments are missing a verb, or both a subject and verb. Either answer is acceptable.

In fragment 4, there is no subject or verb. In fragment 5, there is no verb.

1. Her friends were furtive boys in pink shirts hanging about on washday after school.
2. Her friends were nervous girls who never laughed.
3. Her earrings were gold, too, and hanging down to her shoulder.
4. They were always too busy: feeding the cattle, fixing the fences, putting up salt-lick shelters.
5. Your heritage is important to you.

Writing Application

The dialogue must be among characters from "Everyday Use" and include sentence fragments.

WG Writing and Grammar, Ruby Level

Students will find further instruction and practice on sentence fragments in Chapter 20, Section 4.

Assessment Practice

Grammar and Usage (For more practice, see *Standardized Test Preparation Workbook*, p. 64.)

The writing sections of some tests often require students to choose the correct word or group of words to complete a sentence. Use the following sample item to demonstrate.

The pieces of the unfinished quilt _____ scattered on the floor.

Choose the word that belongs in the blank.

A lay
B lied
C laid
D lain

B is the past tense of the word *lie,* meaning "to tell an untruth"; *C* is the past tense of the transitive verb *lay; D* is the past participle of *lie; A* is the simple past tense of *lie,* meaning "to rest or recline," and is therefore the correct answer.

❸ Writing Lesson

Timed Writing: Critical Review

Write a critical review of "Everyday Use," explaining whether you think the story is effective. Note your reactions to the story and explain whether the characters are believable and interesting. Consider the story's message, and express your opinion about its importance. ***(40 minutes)***

Prewriting *(10 minutes)* Review the story and list your responses, both positive and negative. Beside each item, note the page numbers of appropriate examples. Review your chart, and summarize your opinion in a sentence or two.

Drafting *(20 minutes)* Begin by stating your overall opinion of the story. Then, present a series of paragraphs in which you support your ideas with details.

Revising *(10 minutes)* Evaluate your draft to replace weak modifiers with precise adjectives and adverbs that capture your reactions. Be sure your writing is accurate by checking that you have copied all quotations exactly.

Model: Revising to Add Precise Details

Dee, as Wangero, appears ~~nice,~~ genuine but she is ~~really quite~~ insincere. She is not at all interested in ~~the things,~~ her heritage but rather in appearances.

Replacing weak modifiers with specific words makes writing more precise and interesting. Words like *really* do not add meaning to the work.

WG *Prentice Hall Writing and Grammar Connection: Chapter 14, Section 3*

❹ Extend Your Learning

Listening and Speaking With a partner, dramatize the narrator's dream of a **television talk show** reunion with Dee. Consider these techniques:

- Use appropriate dialogue for the scene.
- Create skillful and artistic staging.
- Make your characters interesting and believable.

After rehearsing to achieve command of your text, present the dramatization to your class. **[Group Activity]**

Research and Technology The names *Wangero* and *Hakim-a-barber* come from one of the more than 800 languages spoken in Africa today. Conduct research on one of the four major language families. Create an **African languages presentation** for your class, including audio and videotapes and maps of the region.

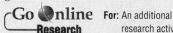

For: An additional research activity
Visit: www.PHSchool.com
Web Code: erd-7608

❸ Writing Lesson

You may use this Writing Lesson as timed-writing practice, or you may allow students to develop the review as a writing assignment over several days.

- Give students the **Support for Writing Lesson**, p. 140 in ***Unit 6 Resources,*** to use as they write their critical reviews.
- Read a brief book review to students and discuss it with the class. What evidence did the writer of the review provide to back up his or her opinions of the book?
- Explain that regardless of their opinion of the story, their reviews of "Everyday Use" must offer well-supported reasons and examples from the story.
- Use the Critique rubrics in ***General Resources,*** pp. 75–76, to evaluate students' reviews.

❹ Research and Technology

- Suggest that students work in small groups to research an African language and present their findings.
- Each group member should check at least one source for information.
- If possible, encourage students to tape native speakers of the language they are researching. If this is not possible, they may be able to locate sound clips on the Internet to share during their presentations.
- Use the Speaking: Delivering a Research Presentation rubric in ***General Resources,*** p. 92, to assess students' presentations.
- The **Support for Extend Your Learning** page (***Unit 6 Resources,*** p. 141) provides guided note-taking opportunities to help students complete the Extend Your Learning activities.

Go Online Research — Have students type in the Web Code for another research activity.

Assessment Resources

The following resources can be used to assess students' knowledge and skills.

Unit 6 Resources
- **Selection Test A,** pp. 143–145
- **Selection Test B,** pp. 146–148

General Resources
- **Rubrics for Critique,** pp. 75–76
- **Rubric for Speaking: Delivering a Research Presentation,** p. 92

Go Online Assessment — Students may use the **Self-test** to prepare for **Selection Test A** or **Selection Test B.**

Meeting Your Standards

Students will

1. **analyze and respond to literary elements.**
   - Literary Analysis: Memoirs
2. **read, comprehend, analyze, and critique a short story.**
   - Reading Strategy: Applying Background Information
   - Reading Check questions
   - Apply the Skills questions
   - Assessment Practice (ATE)
3. **develop vocabulary.**
   - Vocabulary Lesson: Latin Root: *-aud-*
4. **understand and apply written and oral language conventions.**
   - Spelling Strategy
   - Grammar and Style Lesson: Punctuating a Quotation Within a Quotation
5. **develop writing proficiency.**
   - Writing Lesson: Character Analysis
6. **develop appropriate research strategies.**
   - Extend Your Learning: Immigration Report
7. **understand and apply listening and speaking strategies.**
   - Extend Your Learning: Panel Discussion

Block Scheduling: Use one 90-minute class period to preteach the skills and have students read the selection. Use a second 90-minute class period to assess students' mastery of skills, extend their learning, and monitor their progress.

Homework Suggestions

Following are possibilities for homework assignments:

- Support pages from ***Unit 6 Resources:***
  Literary Analysis
  Reading Strategy
  Vocabulary Builder
  Grammar and Style
- An Extend Your Learning project and the Writing Lesson for this selection may be completed over several days.

Step-by-Step Teaching Guide	Pacing Guide
PRETEACH	
• Administer Vocabulary and Reading Warm-ups as necessary.	5 min.
• Engage students' interest with the motivation activity.	5 min.
• Read and discuss author and background features. **FT**	10 min.
• Introduce the Literary Analysis Skill: Memoirs **FT**	5 min.
• Introduce the Reading Strategy: Applying Background Information **FT**	10 min.
• Prepare students to read by teaching the selection vocabulary. **FT**	
TEACH	
• Informally monitor comprehension while students read independently or in groups. **FT**	30 min.
• Monitor students' comprehension with the Reading Check notes.	as students read
• Reinforce vocabulary with Vocabulary Builder notes.	as students read
• Develop students' understanding of memoirs with the Literary Analysis annotations. **FT**	5 minutes
• Develop students' ability to apply background information with the Reading Strategy annotations. **FT**	5 minutes
ASSESS/EXTEND	
• Assess students' comprehension and mastery of the Literary Analysis and Reading Strategy by having them answer the Apply the Skills questions. **FT**	15 min.
• Have students complete the Vocabulary Lesson and the Grammar and Style Lesson. **FT**	15 min.
• Apply students' ability to revise to provide support by using the Writing Lesson. **FT**	45 min. or homework
• Apply students' understanding using one or more of the Extend Your Learning activities.	20–90 min. or homework
• Administer Selection Test A or Selection Test B. **FT**	15 min.

Resources

PRINT
Unit 6 Resources
- Vocabulary Warm-up Word Lists **[L1, L2, EL]** ....p. 149
- Vocabulary Warm-up Practice **[L1, L2, EL]** ....p. 150
- Reading Warm-up A **[L1, L2, EL]** ....p. 151
- Reading Warm-up B **[L1, L2, L3]** ....p. 152

TRANSPARENCY
Graphic Organizer Transparencies
- Literary Analysis Graphic Organizer A **[L3]** ....p. 248
- Literary Analysis Graphic Organizer B **[L1, L2, EL]** ....p. 249
- Reading Strategy Graphic Organizer A **[L3]** ....p. 246
- Reading Strategy Graphic Organizer B **[L1, L2, EL]** ....p. 247

PRINT
Reader's Notebook [L2]
Reader's Notebook: Adapted Version [L1]
Reader's Notebook: English Learner's Version [EL]
Unit 6 Resources
- Literary Analysis **[L3]** ....p. 153
- Reading Strategy **[L3]** ....p. 154
- Vocabulary Builder **[L3]** ....p. 155

TECHNOLOGY
Listening to Literature Audio CDs [L2, EL]

PRINT
Unit 6 Resources
- Grammar and Style **[L3]** ....p. 156
- Support for Writing Lesson **[L3]** ....p. 157
- Support for Extend Your Learning **[L3]** ....p. 158
- Enrichment **[L4]** ....p. 159
- Selection Test A **[L1, L2, EL]** ....pp. 160–162
- Selection Test B **[L3, L4]** ....pp. 163–165

TRANSPARENCY
Graphic Organizer Transparencies
- Character Wheel ....p. 306

General Resources
- Rubrics for Response to Literature **[L3]** ....pp. 65–66
- Rubric for Speaking: Delivering a Research Presentation **[L3]** ....p. 92

TECHNOLOGY
Go Online: Research **[L3]**
Go Online: Self-test **[L3]**
***ExamView*® Test Bank [L3]**

Choosing Resources for Differentiated Instruction

[L1] Special Needs Students
[L2] Below-Level Students
[L3] All Students
[L4] Advanced Students
[EL] English Learners

For Vocabulary and Reading Warm-ups and for Selection Tests, **A** signifies "less challenging" and **B** "more challenging." For Graphic Organizer transparencies, **A** signifies "not filled in" and **B** "filled in."

FT Fast Track Instruction: To move the lesson more quickly, use the strategies and activities identified with **FT**.

Scaffolding for Less Proficient and Advanced Students

The leveled Critical Thinking questions after selections progress in the levels of thinking required to answer them. To address the needs of your different students, you may use the (a) level questions for your less proficient students and the (b) level questions with your on-level and advanced students. The occasional (c) level questions are appropriate for your advanced students.

PRENTICE HALL
TeacherEXPRESS™ Plan · Teach · Assess
Use this complete suite of powerful teaching tools to make lesson planning and testing quicker and easier.

PRENTICE HALL
StudentEXPRESS™ Learn · Study · Succeed
Use the interactive textbook (online and on CD-ROM) to make selections and activities come alive with audio and video support and interactive questions.

Go Online Professional Development
For: Information about Lexiles
Visit: www.PHSchool.com
Web Code: eue-1111

PRETEACH

Motivation

In reading this memoir, students will experience the excitement, impatience, and surprise of a long-awaited family reunion. Engage student interest with the following activity. Provide childhood pictures of yourself and other teachers, or ask students to contribute their own baby photos. Challenge the class to match up the photos with the correct people. How difficult might it be to recognize someone who has changed this much? What feelings might such a reunion produce in both parties?

❶ Background

More About the Author

Writing has long been central to Maxine Hong Kingston's life. She explains, "My writing is an ongoing function, like breathing or eating. . . . I have the habit of writing things down. Anything. And then some of it falls into place. . . ."

In 1976, while Kingston was teaching creative writing at the Mid-Pacific Institute, she published *The Woman Warrior.* In this book, her first, she weaves folklore and autobiography to give the popular topic of mother-daughter relationships an exotic setting and a unique voice. By the end of the memoir, the shy Kingston has broken her silence to carry on the Chinese oral tradition through her writing.

Build Skills *Memoir*

❶ *from* The Woman Warrior

Maxine Hong Kingston (b. 1940)

"I was born to be a writer," Maxine Hong Kingston once told an interviewer. "In the midst of any adventure, a born writer has a desire to hurry home and put it into words."

Crossing Cultures Although Kingston was born in America, she did not begin describing her adventures in English until she was nearly ten because the language spoken at home was Say Yup, a Chinese dialect spoken around Canton, now known as Guangzhou, China. Kingston's parents came from a village near Canton. Her father left first for "the Golden Mountain" of America and settled in New York City. His training as a poet and calligrapher was unmarketable in the United States, so he earned a living working in the laundry business. Kingston's mother, who was trained as a midwife, used the money her husband sent home to run a clinic in their native village. She did so until 1939, when she escaped war-torn China and joined her husband. Not long afterward, the couple resettled in Stockton, California, where Maxine Hong was born.

Building a Love for Story Young Maxine, whose Chinese name is Ting Ting, was a shy and quiet girl who repeated kindergarten because she spoke very little English. While at home, however, she listened intently to the stories told by family members and friends; this love of storytelling later influenced her writing style as Kingston developed her "talk stories." By the time she was nine years old, she mastered English and began writing poetry. Soon, she began to earn straight A's in school.

Kingston won a scholarship to the University of California at Berkeley, which she attended in the 1960s during its heyday as a center of intellectual activity and political activism. There, she met Earll Kingston and married him in 1962. After graduation, the Kingstons supported themselves as teachers while pursuing success in their chosen fields—Earll in acting, Maxine in writing. They lived in Hawaii for many years but returned to the mainland with their son, settling in Oakland, California.

A Bestseller Kingston shot to success with her first and best-known book, *The Woman Warrior: Memoirs of a Girlhood Among Ghosts.* The subtitle refers to the pale "ghosts" of white America as well as the "ghosts" of the narrator's ancestors in China. *The Woman Warrior,* a unique blend of folklore, myth, feminism, and autobiography, won the National Book Critics' Circle Award in 1976. The major focus of the book is on Brave Orchid—Kingston's mother. Brave Orchid tells her daughter about China and the female members of their family through her talk stories—a blend of truth and fiction, tales of ancient heroes, family secrets, and important cultural traditions and values that have been passed down from generation to generation.

Kingston earned the National Book Critics' Circle Award a second time in 1980 for *China Men,* which chronicles the lives of three generations of Chinese men in America. In 1989, she published the novel *Tripmaster Monkey.* A slow, methodical writer, Kingston labors over numerous revisions to her books. Her latest book, *The Fifth Book of Peace* (2003), tells the true story of the fire that destroyed her novel-in-progress, titled *The Fourth Book of Peace.*

Preview

Connecting to the Literature

At some point in your life, you have probably felt that your older relatives view the world quite differently than you do. In families whose adults and children were born in different countries, these differences can be especially pronounced, as they are in this selection.

2 Literary Analysis

Memoirs

Most **memoirs** are first-person nonfiction narratives that recount historically or personally significant events in which the writer was a participant or an eyewitness. The following excerpt from Kingston's memoir blends the historical and the personal:

> To while away time, she and her niece talked about the Chinese passengers. These new immigrants had it easy. On Ellis Island the people were thin after forty days at sea and had no fancy luggage.

Kingston skillfully incorporates details of culture and time period into an account of a memorable day in her life.

Connecting Literary Elements

Memoirs are, by definition, acts of memory—accounts of individual experience told in the first person point of view. In most memoirs, the writer uses *I* to narrate events. Kingston, however, defies convention by using the **limited third-person point of view**—the story is related by a narrator who uses the pronoun *she* to describe herself. This unusual use of point of view helps to blur the line between fact and fiction. As you read, think about why Kingston made this choice.

3 Reading Strategy

Applying Background Information

Background information given in a book jacket, an introduction, or footnote can help you fully appreciate a literary work. In this textbook, you can gain such information from the author biography, the Build Skills pages, and the Background. As you read, record the information you learn from these features in a chart like the one shown.

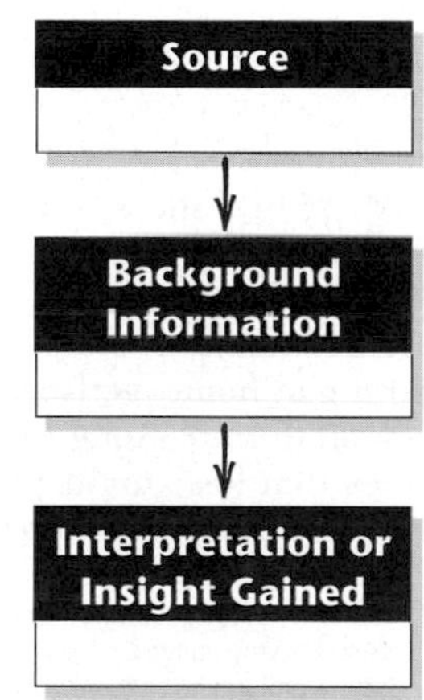

Vocabulary Builder

hysterically (hi ster′ i klē) *adv.* in a highly emotional manner (p. 1105)

encampment (en kamp′ mənt) *n.* place where a person has set up camp (p. 1106)

inaudibly (in ôd′ ə blē) *adv.* in a manner that cannot be heard (p. 1108)

gravity (grav′ i tē) *n.* seriousness (p. 1109)

oblivious (ə bliv′ ē əs) *adj.* lacking all awareness (p. 1109)

2 Literary Analysis

Memoirs

- Remind students that traditional memoirs are accounts of people's personal experiences and observations. Kingston incorporates folklore and history into her memoir, *The Woman Warrior.*
- Discuss the information under Connecting Literary Elements with students. Make sure they understand that though memoirs are usually told from the first-person point of view, *The Woman Warrior* uses the limited third-person point of view. Readers gain access to the thoughts and feelings of Brave Orchid; to learn about the other characters, readers must observe their words and actions.

3 Reading Strategy

Applying Background Information

- Encourage students to activate relevant background information as they read the excerpt from *The Woman Warrior,* including the information in their textbook about Maxine Hong Kingston.
- Give students a copy of **Reading Strategy Graphic Organizer A,** p. 246 in ***Graphic Organizer Transparencies,*** to track some of the sources of the background information they used to gain greater insight into the selection.

Vocabulary Builder

- Pronounce each vocabulary word for students, and read the definitions as a class. Have students identify any words with which they are already familiar.

Differentiated Instruction

Solutions for All Learners

Support for Special Needs Students
Have students complete the **Preview** and **Build Skills** pages for the selection in the ***Reader's Notebook: Adapted Version.*** These pages provide a selection summary, an abbreviated presentation of the reading and literary skills, and the graphic organizer on the **Build Skills** page in the student book.

Support for Less Proficient Readers
Have students complete the **Preview** and **Build Skills** pages for the selection in the ***Reader's Notebook.*** These pages provide a selection summary, an abbreviated presentation of the reading and literary skills, and the graphic organizer on the **Build Skills** page in the student book.

Support for English Learners
Have students complete the **Preview** and **Build Skills** pages for the selection in the ***Reader's Notebook: English Learner's Version.*** These pages provide a selection summary, an abbreviated presentation of the skills, and the graphic organizer on the **Build Skills** page in the student book.

Learning Modalities
Verbal/Linguistic Learners To understand and appreciate Brave Orchid's personality and behavior, students will benefit from hearing her words and thoughts read aloud. Have students take turns reading the selection aloud, or have them listen to it on the **Listening to Literature Audio CD** before they read it on their own.

❶ About the Selection

This memoir captures the strange distortion that passing time can create. When the main character, Brave Orchid, arrives at the airport to meet the sister she has not seen for thirty years, she brings along the unique perspective of her memories—sure that she and Moon Orchid remain unchanged by time. Determined as well to resist the effects of the alien American culture in which she now lives, Brave Orchid evokes the universal struggle between tradition and change.

❷ Critical Viewing

Answer: The China that Brave Orchid remembers probably had few automobiles, and the inhabitants probably wore more traditional clothing.

❸ Reading Strategy
Applying Background Information

- **Ask** students why authors and editors use footnotes.
  Possible answer: Footnotes are used to clarify phrases and words, and to cite sources. They enrich the reader's enjoyment of a story by providing helpful background information.
- **Ask** students: What does the footnoted information suggest about Moon Orchid's life since she and Brave Orchid last saw each other?
  Answer: Moon Orchid has probably had a difficult life and has had to adapt to many changes. She may have immigrated to Hong Kong before traveling to the United States.

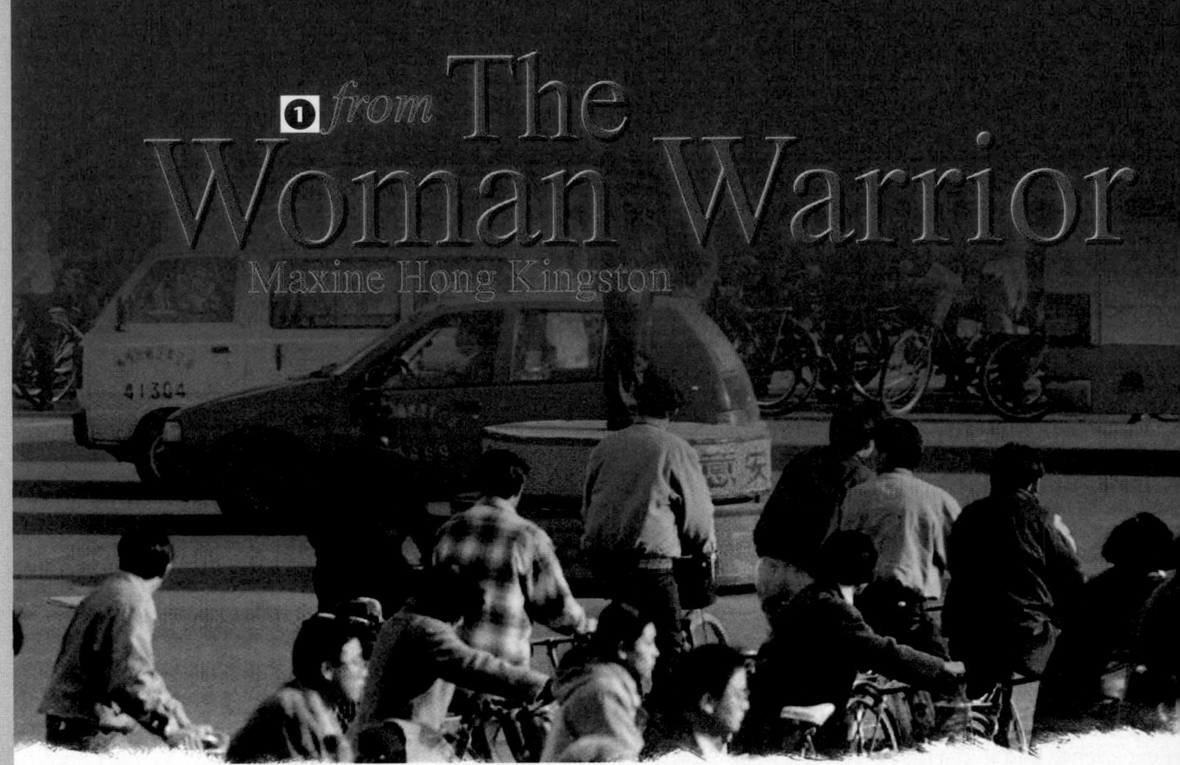

❶ *from* The Woman Warrior

Maxine Hong Kingston

Background The *Woman Warrior* is an innovative memoir that attempts to capture the experience of growing up in a bicultural world—part Chinese, part American. To accomplish her purpose, Kingston mingles the narrative with "talk stories," tales full of magical events that she heard as a girl from her mother, Brave Orchid. The subtitle of the book, *Memoir of a Girlhood Among Ghosts*, refers both to white America, whose pale inhabitants remind Brave Orchid of ghosts, and to the family's ancestors in China. In this excerpt, Brave Orchid reunites with her sister, one of the ghosts of her past.

▲ **Critical Viewing** ❷ Do you think this scene at a chaotic Beijing intersection might represent the China Brave Orchid remembers? Why or why not? **[Compare]**

When she was about sixty-eight years old, Brave Orchid took a day off to wait at San Francisco International Airport for the plane that was bringing her sister to the United States. She had not seen Moon Orchid for thirty years. She had begun this waiting at home, getting up a half-hour before Moon Orchid's plane took off in Hong Kong.[1] Brave Orchid would add her will power to the forces that keep an airplane up. Her head hurt with the concentration. The plane had to be light, so no matter how tired she felt, she

❸ 1. **took off in Hong Kong** After mainland China fell to the Communists in the late 1940's, many native Chinese fled first to Hong Kong (a British colony until 1997) before emigrating to the United States.

Differentiated Instruction Solutions for All Learners

Accessibility at a Glance

	from The Woman Warrior
Context	Contemporary memoir
Language	Informal
Concept Level	Accessible (tradition versus change)
Literary Merit	Cross-cultural; cross-generational
Lexile	800L
Overall Rating	Average

dared not rest her spirit on a wing but continuously and gently pushed up on the plane's belly. She had already been waiting at the airport for nine hours. She was wakeful.

Next to Brave Orchid sat Moon Orchid's only daughter, who was helping her aunt wait. Brave Orchid had made two of her own children come too because they could drive, but they had been lured away by the magazine racks and the gift shops and coffee shops. Her American children could not sit for very long. They did not understand sitting; they had wandering feet. She hoped they would get back from the pay TV's or the pay toilets or wherever they were spending their money before the plane arrived. If they did not come back soon, she would go look for them. If her son thought he could hide in the men's room, he was wrong.

"Are you all right, Aunt?" asked her niece.

"No, this chair hurts me. Help me pull some chairs together so I can put my feet up."

She unbundled a blanket and spread it out to make a bed for herself. On the floor she had two shopping bags full of canned peaches, real peaches, beans wrapped in taro leaves,[2] cookies, Thermos bottles,[3] enough food for everybody, though only her niece would eat with her. Her bad boy and bad girl were probably sneaking hamburgers, wasting their money. She would scold them.

Many soldiers and sailors sat about, oddly calm, like little boys in cowboy uniforms. (She thought "cowboy" was what you would call a Boy Scout.) They should have been crying hysterically on their way to Vietnam.[4] "If I see one that looks Chinese," she thought, "I'll go over and give him some advice." She sat up suddenly; she had forgotten about her own son, who was even now in Vietnam. Carefully she split her attention, beaming half of it to the ocean, into the water to keep him afloat. He was on a ship. He was in Vietnamese waters. She was sure of it. He and the other children were lying to her. They had said he was in Japan, and then they said he was in the Philippines. But when she sent him her help, she could feel that he was on a ship in Da Nang.[5] Also she had seen the children hide the envelopes that his letters came in.

"Do you think my son is in Vietnam?" she asked her niece, who was dutifully eating.

"No. Didn't your children say he was in the Philippines?"

"Have you ever seen any of his letters with Philippine stamps on them?"

"Oh, yes. Your children showed me one."

---

2. **taro** (te´ rō) **leaves** leaves of an edible tuberous plant widely eaten in Asia.
3. **Thermos** (thʉr´ məs) **bottles** insulated containers for holding liquids and keeping them warm or cold.
4. **Vietnam** southeast Asian nation where, in the late 1960s when this selection takes place, the U.S. had joined the conflict known as the Vietnam War (1954–1975).
5. **Da Nang** (da naŋ) city in central Vietnam that was the site of an important U.S. military base during the Vietnam War; also spelled Danang.

Literary Analysis
Memoirs Whose impressions are described in this passage about "her American children"?

Vocabulary Builder
hysterically (hi ster´ i klē) *adv.* in a highly emotional manner

Reading Strategy
Applying Background Information How do footnotes 4 and 5 help to clarify this passage?

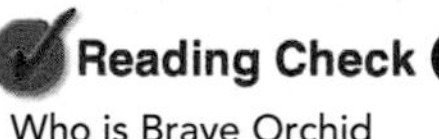

Reading Check 6
Who is Brave Orchid waiting to meet?

4 Literary Analysis
Memoirs

- Have a volunteer read the bracketed passage aloud.
- **Ask** the Literary Analysis question: Whose impressions are described in this passage about "her American children"?
  Answer: Brave Orchid's impressions are described in this passage.

➤ **Monitor Progress: Ask** students what Brave Orchid's musings reveal about her impression of American values.
Answer: Brave Orchid seems to believe that American children are restless, impatient, and wasteful.

5 Reading Strategy
Applying Background Information

- After students read the bracketed passage, **ask** them to write down questions about it.
  Possible answers: Why were the soldiers being shipped to Vietnam? Where is Da Nang? Why does Brave Orchid believe that her son is in Da Nang?
- **Ask** students the Reading Strategy question: How do footnotes 4 and 5 help to clarify this passage?
  Answer: The footnotes explain why the boys "should have been crying": They were on their way to the Vietnam War. The footnotes also provide information about Da Nang, which is where Brave Orchid believes her son has been stationed.

6 Reading Check

Answer: Brave Orchid is waiting to meet her sister, Moon Orchid, whom she has not seen for thirty years.

7 Reading Strategy
Applying Background Information

- **Ask** students the Reading Strategy question: What information in footnote 8 helps to clarify this passage?
  Answer: To understand Brave Orchid's comparison of "old immigrants" and "new immigrants," readers need to know that Ellis Island is where many "old immigrants" arrived in the United States.
- Then, **ask** students to apply background knowledge to explain why Brave Orchid, who lives in California, would be familiar with Ellis Island.
  Answer: Students should recall from the author information on p. 1102 that the author's mother, upon whom Brave Orchid is based, was an immigrant who arrived in New York City. She would therefore have passed through Ellis Island.

"I wouldn't put it past them to send the letters to some Filipino they know. He puts Manila[6] postmarks on them to fool me."

"Yes, I can imagine them doing that. But don't worry. Your son can take care of himself. All your children can take care of themselves."

"Not him. He's not like other people. Not normal at all. He sticks erasers in his ears, and the erasers are still attached to the pencil stubs. The captain will say, 'Abandon ship,' or 'Watch out for bombs,' and he won't hear. He doesn't listen to orders. I told him to flee to Canada,[7] but he wouldn't go."

She closed her eyes. After a short while, plane and ship under control, she looked again at the children in uniforms. Some of the blond ones looked like baby chicks, their crew cuts like the downy yellow on baby chicks. You had to feel sorry for them even though they were Army and Navy Ghosts.

Suddenly her son and daughter came running. "Come, Mother. The plane's landed early. She's here already." They hurried, folding up their mother's encampment. She was glad her children were not useless. They must have known what this trip to San Francisco was about then. "It's a good thing I made you come early," she said.

Vocabulary Builder
encampment (en kamp′ mənt) *n.* place where a person has set up camp

Brave Orchid pushed to the front of the crowd. She had to be in front. The passengers were separated from the people waiting for them by glass doors and walls. Immigration Ghosts were stamping papers. The travellers crowded along some conveyor belts to have their luggage searched. Brave Orchid did not see her sister anywhere. She stood watching for four hours. Her children left and came back. "Why don't you sit down?" they asked.

"The chairs are too far away," she said.

"Why don't you sit on the floor then?"

No, she would stand, as her sister was probably standing in a line she could not see from here. Her American children had no feelings and no memory.

7 To while away time, she and her niece talked about the Chinese passengers. These new immigrants had it easy. On Ellis Island[8] the people were thin after forty days at sea and had no fancy luggage.

Reading Strategy
Applying Background Information What information in footnote 8 helps to clarify this passage?

"That one looks like her," Brave Orchid would say.

"No, that's not her."

Ellis Island had been made out of wood and iron. Here everything was new plastic, a ghost trick to lure immigrants into feeling safe and spilling their secrets. Then the Alien Office could send them right back. Otherwise, why did they lock her out, not letting her help her sister answer questions and spell her name? At Ellis Island when the ghost asked Brave Orchid what year her husband had cut off his

6. **Manila** (mə nil′ ə) capital of the Philippines.
7. **flee to Canada** During the Vietnam War era, thousands of Americans fled to Canada to escape the military draft, even though such draft dodgers were subject to prosecution upon returning to the U.S.
8. **Ellis Island** island in the harbor off New York City that was the chief U.S. immigration station from 1892 to 1943.

Enrichment

Literary Criticism
The critic *Sharon Wong* reviewed Kingston's work: "In this beautifully written collection of interrelated reminiscences, Kingston tells the story of a Chinese American woman searching for her past to explain her present…Kingston grows painfully aware that she cannot accept the old values, yet she is somehow saddened by her loss."

Use this question to discuss Wong's review.

How does Kingston use the characters to reveal the conflict within her?

Answer: The two sisters have changed and seem to disapprove of each other; they might be compared as the products of two cultures.

pigtail, a Chinese who was crouching on the floor motioned her not to talk. "I don't know," she had said. If it weren't for that Chinese man, she might not be here today, or her husband either. She hoped some Chinese, a janitor or a clerk, would look out for Moon Orchid. Luggage conveyors fooled immigrants into thinking the Gold Mountain was going to be easy.

Brave Orchid felt her heart jump—Moon Orchid. "There she is," she shouted. But her niece saw it was not her mother at all. And it shocked her to discover the woman her aunt was pointing out. This was a young woman, younger than herself, no older than Moon Orchid the day the sisters parted. "Moon Orchid will have changed a little, of course," Brave Orchid was saying. "She will have learned to wear western clothes." The woman wore a navy blue suit with a bunch of dark cherries at the shoulder.

"No, Aunt," said the niece. "That's not my mother."

"Perhaps not. It's been so many years.

Yes, it is your mother. It must be. Let her come closer, and we can tell. Do you think she's too far away for me to tell, or is it my eyes getting bad?"

"It's too many years gone by," said the niece.

Brave Orchid turned suddenly—another Moon Orchid, this one a neat little woman with a bun. She was laughing at something the person ahead of her in line said. Moon Orchid was just like that, laughing at nothing. "I would be able to tell the difference if one of them would only come closer," Brave Orchid said with tears, which she did not wipe. Two children met the woman with the cherries, and she shook their hands. The other woman was met by a young man. They looked at each other gladly, then walked away side by side.

Up close neither one of those women looked like Moon Orchid at all. "Don't worry, Aunt," said the niece. "I'll know her."

"I'll know her too. I knew her before you did."

The niece said nothing, although she had seen her mother only five years ago. Her aunt liked having the last word.

Finally Brave Orchid's children quit wandering and drooped on a railing. Who knew what they were thinking? At last the niece called out, "I see her! I see her! Mother! Mother!" Whenever the doors parted, she shouted, probably embarrassing the American cousins, but she didn't care. She called out, "Mama! Mama!" until the crack in the sliding doors became too small to let in her voice. "Mama!" What a strange word in an adult voice. Many people turned to see what adult was calling, "Mama!" like a child. Brave Orchid saw an old, old woman jerk her head up, her little eyes blinking confusedly, a woman whose nerves leapt toward the sound anytime she heard "Mama!" Then she relaxed to her own business again. She was a tiny, tiny lady, very thin, with little fluttering hands, and her hair was in a

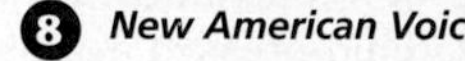

8 ***New American Voices***

During the 1970s, two vigorous social movements—feminism and multiculturalism—had a major impact on American literature. For the first time, the writings of minority women began to appear in the mainstream press. In 1970, African American author Toni Cade Bambara published an influential anthology of fiction, nonfiction, and poetry entitled *The Black Woman*. That same year, Toni Morrison, who would later win the 1993 Nobel Prize for Literature, published her first novel, *The Bluest Eye*. When Maxine Hong Kingston's memoir *The Woman Warrior* appeared in 1976, it represented yet another utterly new voice. In the decades to follow, these writings influenced the work of younger minority women, including Julia Alvarez, Sandra Cisneros, Amy Tan, and Gish Jen. A new subgenre emerged, giving voice to women of all backgrounds and enriching the landscape of American literature.

Connect to the Literature

In what ways does Kingston's voice as a woman minority writer emerge in this excerpt from her memoir?

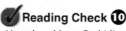

Reading Check 10

How does Moon Orchid's physical appearence compare with those of the women Brave Orchid mistakes for her sister?

Differentiated Instruction
Solutions for All Learners

Strategy for Less Proficient Readers
Have students make a chart on which to record the feelings of the characters as they wait for Moon Orchid to arrive. How are the niece's feelings different from those of her cousins? What conflicting feelings might Brave Orchid have?

Strategy for Gifted/Talented Students
Have students perform a Readers Theater presentation of pp. 1106–1107. Volunteers should take the parts of the narrator, the niece, and Brave Orchid. Urge students to consider the characters' feelings as they decide how to interpret their parts.

Strategy for Advanced Readers
Have students analyze in detail Brave Orchid's feelings at this point in the story. What might be some of her hopes and fears about her sister? Why does she seem unable to realize that Moon Orchid is quite old? Ask students to discuss their ideas with classmates and then record them in writing.

8 The American Experience

New American Voices Like Maxine Hong Kingston, Amy Tan is a Chinese American and a Californian. Writing in the wake of Kingston's success, Tan has published numerous short stories, essays, and novels. Her first novel, *The Joy Luck Club* (1989), received critical acclaim and was made into a film in 1993.

In her work, Tan, like Kingston, explores the cultural implications of being a Chinese American. Her characters often struggle to understand and reconcile threads of the two disparate cultures.

Connect to the Literature Have students review what Kingston has mentioned about herself and her relationship with her mother.
Possible response: The details about Kingston's Chinese heritage and her relationship with her mother reveal both her minority status and issues of gender.

9 Critical Thinking
Interpret

- Have a volunteer **recall** what the phrase "Gold Mountain" means.
Answer: "Gold Mountain" is a term the Chinese immigrants used for the United States.
- **Ask** students to explain what this term implies about the immigrants' view of the United States.
Answer: The term implies that the immigrants expected to find great wealth in their new home.
- **Ask** why Brave Orchid thinks that luggage conveyors fooled immigrants into thinking that life in America was going to be easy.
Answer: Because the conveyors transported her luggage without her having to expend any energy, Brave Orchid was fooled into thinking all the other difficult parts of her new life would be taken care of as easily.

10 Reading Check

Answer: Moon Orchid is small, thin, and much older than the women whom Brave Orchid mistakes for her.

⓫ Vocabulary Builder

Latin Root *–aud-*

- Write *inaudibly* on the board and circle the root *-aud-*. Tell students that *-aud-* is a Latin root that means "hearing" or "sound."
- Have students give other examples of words with this root. Write their suggestions on the board and circle the root *-aud-*. Some words with *-aud-* include the following: *auditory, audience, audition, audiotape,* and *auditorium.*
- Finally, have students explain how the root *-aud-* helps them understand the meaning of three words on the list.

⓬ Critical Viewing

Answer: In Hong Kong, nearly 98 percent of the population is ethnic Han Chinese; in 1990, about 30 percent of San Francisco's population was of Asian descent. In San Francisco, Moon Orchid will probably experience a wider variety of cultures and values than she did in Hong Kong.

gray knot. She was dressed in a gray wool suit; she wore pearls around her neck and in her earlobes. Moon Orchid *would* travel with her jewels showing. Brave Orchid momentarily saw, like a larger, younger outline around this old woman, the sister she had been waiting for. The familiar dim halo faded, leaving the woman so old, so gray. So old. Brave Orchid pressed against the glass. *That* old lady? Yes, that old lady facing the ghost who stamped her papers without questioning her was her sister. Then, without noticing her family, Moon Orchid walked smiling over to the Suitcase Inspector Ghost, who took her boxes apart, pulling out puffs of tissue. From where she was, Brave Orchid could not see what her sister had chosen to carry across the ocean. She wished her sister would look her way. Brave Orchid thought that if she were entering a new country, she would be at the windows. Instead Moon Orchid hovered over the unwrapping, surprised at each reappearance as if she were opening presents after a birthday party.

"Mama!" Moon Orchid's daughter kept calling. Brave Orchid said to her children, "Why don't you call your aunt too? Maybe she'll hear us if all of you call out together." But her children slunk away. Maybe that shame-face they so often wore was American politeness.

"Mama!" Moon Orchid's daughter called again, and this time her mother looked right at her. She left her bundles in a heap and came ⓫ running. "Hey!" the Customs Ghost yelled at her. She went back to clear up her mess, talking inaudibly to her daughter all the while. Her daughter pointed toward Brave Orchid. And at last Moon Orchid looked at her—two old women with faces like mirrors.

Vocabulary Builder
inaudibly (in ôd′ə blē) *adv.* in a manner that cannot be heard

▼ Critical Viewing ⓬
How might life in the city of San Francisco, shown in this image, compare or contrast with life in Hong Kong from where Moon Orchid has just arrived? **[Compare and Contrast]**

Enrichment

Hong Kong

Hong Kong has been an administrative region of China since 1997, when it passed to Chinese sovereignty from Britain. The British control of Hong Kong began in 1842, when China was forced to cede it after the First Opium War.

The government of Hong Kong is headed by a chief executive who is selected by a committee appointed by China. Members of a Legislative Council, whose members assist the chief executive in making policy decisions, are elected by the people of Hong Kong.

Hong Kong consists of a mainland portion, which is located on the southeastern coast of China, and about 235 islands. The total area is only 422 square miles. The city of Hong Kong, also known as Victoria, is located on Hong Kong Island and is home to both the government offices and the central business district.

Their hands reached out as if to touch the other's face, then returned to their own, the fingers checking the grooves in the forehead and along the sides of the mouth. Moon Orchid, who never understood the gravity of things, started smiling and laughing, pointing at Brave Orchid. Finally Moon Orchid gathered up her stuff, strings hanging and papers loose, and met her sister at the door, where they shook hands, oblivious to blocking the way.

"You're an old woman," said Brave Orchid.

"Aiaa. *You're* an old woman."

"But *you* are really old. Surely, you can't say that about me. I'm not old the way you're old."

"But you really are old. You're one year older than I am."

"Your hair is white and your face all wrinkled."

"You're so skinny."

"You're so fat."

"Fat women are more beautiful than skinny women."

The children pulled them out of the door-way. One of Brave Orchid's children brought the car from the parking lot, and

Vocabulary Builder

gravity (grav′ i tē) *n.* seriousness

oblivious (ə bliv′ ē əs) *adj.* lacking all awareness

14

Reading Check

Why is the reunion between Brave Orchid and her sister delayed?

13 Critical Thinking

Infer

- Have two volunteers read the dialogue between Brave Orchid and Moon Orchid.
- **Ask** students what they can infer about Brave Orchid and Moon Orchid's relationship from the dialogue on this page.
  Answer: Brave Orchid and Moon Orchid do not openly demonstrate their affection for one another, as shown by their formal handshake. However, they do talk to each other in a blunt and open manner.

14 Reading Check

Answer: The reunion is delayed as Moon Orchid waits to enter the terminal, passes through customs, and has her luggage examined.

Differentiated Instruction

Solutions for All Learners

Vocabulary for English Learners
Point out that the three main characters in the memoir are all women. In describing them, Kingston frequently uses the pronouns *her* and *she.* To avoid confusion, suggest that students replace pronouns with proper nouns to clarify which character is being described.

Enrichment for Gifted/Talented Students
Have students invent and perform a dialogue between Brave Orchid and Moon Orchid in which the two women say what's really on their minds, without the constraints of custom and habit. Have the audience determine whether the dialogue is convincing, and why.

Enrichment for Advanced Readers
Challenge students to create, from their own knowledge or research, additional footnotes to explain Brave Orchid's references to American culture and to the events of the memoir's historical setting (the late 1960s).

ASSESS

Answers

1. Students should be prepared to explain their responses.
2. (a) Family members include Brave Orchid, who is anxiously awaiting her sister's arrival; Brave Orchid's niece, who is attentive to her aunt and keeps her company; and Brave Orchid's children, who restlessly roam the airport. (b) Brave Orchid has not embraced American culture the way her children have.
3. (a) Brave Orchid attempts to keep her sister's plane in the air and her son's ship afloat. (b) She seems to be a reserved, dignified woman who clings to traditional Chinese values and customs.
4. (a) Brave Orchid cannot believe how old her sister has grown. (b) **Possible response:** They fall back into old habits, bickering with one another as they did in their youth.
5. (a) Brave Orchid seems to feel that they are inferior to China and its culture. (b) It suggests that immigrants struggle to hold on to their cultural heritage while making their way in a new culture. Their children are often caught between the old and new cultures, and may feel that they do not fully belong in either.
6. Students may suggest that Kingston succeeds in showing how Brave Orchid is still staunchly Chinese in her attitudes and behavior. They may cite Brave Orchid's supply of Chinese foods, her insistence on standing for hours as her sister goes through customs, and the way she formally shakes her sister's hand when they finally meet.

Go Online Author Link For additional information about Maxine Hong Kingston, have students type in the Web Code, then select *K* from the alphabet, and then select Maxine Hong Kingston.

the other heaved the luggage into the trunk. They put the two old ladies and the niece in the back seat. All the way home—across the Bay Bridge,[9] over the Diablo hills,[10] across the San Joaquin River[11] to the valley, the valley moon so white at dusk—all the way home, the two sisters exclaimed every time they turned to look at each other, "Aiaa! How old!"

Brave Orchid forgot that she got sick in cars, that all vehicles but palanquins[12] made her dizzy. "You're so old," she kept saying. "How did you get so old?"

Brave Orchid had tears in her eyes. But Moon Orchid said, "You look older than I. You *are* older than I," and again she'd laugh. "You're wearing an old mask to tease me." It surprised Brave Orchid that after thirty years she could still get annoyed at her sister's silliness.

---

9. **Bay Bridge** one of the bridges across San Francisco Bay.
10. **Diablo** (dē äb´ lō) **hills** hills outside San Francisco.
11. **San Joaquin** (wô kēn´) **River** river of central California; its valley is one of the state's richest agricultural areas.
12. **palanquins** (pal´ ən kēnz´) hand-carried covered litters once widely used to transport people in China and elsewhere in eastern Asia.

Critical Reading

1. **Respond:** With which character do you identify the most? Why?
2. **(a) Recall:** Identify the family members waiting for Moon Orchid at the airport, and briefly describe each one's behavior. **(b) Interpret:** What do Brave Orchid's thoughts about her children's behavior reveal about her?
3. **(a) Recall:** What two things does Brave Orchid try to keep safe by applying her willpower? **(b) Connect:** What does this behavior reveal about Brave Orchid's worldview?
4. **(a) Interpret:** What is Brave Orchid's main impression when she finally sees Moon Orchid? **(b) Draw Conclusions:** When the two sisters finally meet, why do they speak to each other as they do?
5. **(a) Infer:** What seems to be Brave Orchid's attitude toward America and American culture? **(b) Apply:** What does this selection suggest about the conflicts that face immigrants and the children of immigrants in America?
6. **Evaluate:** Do you think Kingston succeeds in evoking the lives of people from very different cultures? Explain your answer.

For: More about Maxine Hong Kingston
Visit: www.PHSchool.com
Web Code: ere-9613

Apply the Skills

from *The Woman Warrior*

Literary Analysis

Memoirs

1. Using a chart like the one shown, list details to show how this **memoir** incorporates historical details with personal ones.

Historical Details	Personal Details

2. **(a)** Cite two memories Brave Orchid has while waiting at the airport. **(b)** Are these memories typical features of a memoir? Why or why not?
3. Explain how a memoir such as Kingston's could be meaningful to many women growing up in a bicultural world.

Connecting Literary Elements

4. Whose impressions provide the **limited third-person point of view** of this excerpt?
5. Brave Orchid is Kingston's mother. **(a)** What role does Kingston herself play in this excerpt? **(b)** What techniques more commonly found in fiction does Kingston use to create her mother as a literary character?
6. How might Brave Orchid's story have been different if the narrative had been written with her voice, using *I* instead of *she*? Explain.

Reading Strategy

Applying Background Information

7. **(a)** From what province in China might Moon Orchid be coming? **(b)** What evidence did you use to draw your conclusion?
8. What does the narrator mean by **(a)** Army and Navy Ghosts? **(b)** Customs Ghosts?
9. **(a)** Where might the family be headed in the last paragraphs? **(b)** How do you know?

Extend Understanding

10. **Social Studies Connection:** Immigration brings with it the timeless struggle between tradition and change. Choose a culture—your own or another—and discuss the conflicts that people of this culture are likely to face when they come to live in America.

QuickReview

Memoirs are usually first-person nonfiction narratives that recount historically or personally significant events in which the writer was a participant or an eyewitness.

A narrative that uses the **limited third-person point of view** relates the inner thoughts and feelings of only one character but is told by a narrator who speaks in the third person.

When you **apply background information,** you read information in book jackets, forewords, introductions, and footnotes to gain better understanding of the text.

For: Self-test
Visit: www.PHSchool.com
Web Code: era-6609

Go Online Assessment Students may use the **Self-test** to prepare for **Selection Test A** or **Selection Test B.**

Answers

1. Historical detail: Vietnam War Personal detail: Brave Orchid's son is in the Navy. Historical detail: Ellis Island was the chief immigration station of the U.S. Personal detail: Brave Orchid came through Ellis Island. Historical detail: Chinese men wore pigtails. Personal detail: Brave Orchid is asked when her husband cut off his pigtail.

   Another sample answer can be found on **Literary Analysis Graphic Organizer B,** p. 249, in ***Graphic Organizer Transparencies.***
2. (a) She remembers entering the U.S. through Ellis Island. She remembers telling her son to go to Canada rather than be drafted. (b) The memories are not typical in that they recall events in which the writer was not directly involved. The memories are, on the other hand, personally significant to the subject of the memoir, Brave Orchid—a typical feature of the events recounted in memoirs.
3. The struggle to hold onto one culture while embracing another is probably typical of many women growing up in a bicultural world.
4. The narrator's impressions provide the limited third-person point of view for the selection.
5. (a) Kingston plays the role of the narrator. (b) Kingston imagines not only Brave Orchid's actions, but her thoughts and emotions, as if she were a literary character that Kingston had created.
6. The reader would have known more about the reasons Brave Orchid acted as she did, but would not have been sure whether she was relating events accurately.
7. (a) Moon Orchid is probably coming from Canton. (b) The author's biography reveals that her family came from this region.
8. (a) The narrator means white soldiers and sailors. (b) The narrator means white customs officers.
9. (a) They are probably heading to Stockton, California. (b) The author's biography reveals that her family relocated to this area.
10. Many students will comment on differences in values between American culture and the culture they choose.

EXTEND/ASSESS

Answers

❶ Vocabulary Lesson

Word Analysis

1. Sound is recorded and played back on an audiocassette.
2. *Auditory* describes something that relates to hearing.
3. An auditorium is where one hears musical or theatrical performances.
4. An audition is a chance to be heard.

Spelling Strategy

1. suddenly
2. hysterically

Vocabulary Builder

1. encampment
2. Oblivious
3. inaudibly
4. hysterically
5. gravity

❷ Grammar and Style Lesson

"My sister wrote, 'I am coming to America,'" Brave Orchid told her family. "She asked, 'Will you be able to pick me up?' I told her, 'Yes, I will leave my house before your plane takes off from Hong Kong.' Do you think she knows I am excited?"

Writing Application

The paragraph must include properly punctuated quotations within quotations.

WG Writing and Grammar, Ruby Level

Students will find further instruction and practice on punctuating a quotation within a quotation in Chapter 27, Section 4.

Build Language Skills

❶ Vocabulary Lesson

Word Analysis: Latin Root *-aud-*

The Latin word root *-aud-* indicates "hearing" or "sound." The adverb *inaudibly* means "in a tone too low to be heard." Explain how the meaning of the root is connected to each of these words.

1. audiocassette
2. auditory
3. auditorium
4. audition

Spelling Strategy

When adding the suffix *-ly* or *-less* to a word ending in *l*, or when adding *-ness* to a word ending in *n*, keep all the letters of the base word. For example, *tail* becomes *tailless*.

Add *-ly, -less*, or *-ness* to each word in italics to create a new word that fits the clue.

1. happening all of a *sudden*
2. with *hysterical* feelings

Vocabulary Builder: Sentence Completion

Review the vocabulary list on page 1103. Then, copy each sentence, replacing the blank with the appropriate word.

1. We left our homey __?__ and hiked up the mountain.
2. __?__ to the clock, she worked on into the night.
3. When she replied __?__, I asked her to speak up.
4. The boy yelled __?__ when he thought he was lost.
5. The __?__ of the situation silenced all bickering.

❷ Grammar Lesson

Punctuating a Quotation Within a Quotation

For clarity, use single quotation marks to enclose a quotation within a quotation.

Example: "The captain will say, 'Abandon ship,' or 'Watch out for bombs,' and he won't hear."

Also remember to place commas and periods inside closing quotation marks, but keep colons, and semicolons outside. Question marks and exclamation points can be placed either inside or outside the quotation marks, depending on the words to which they apply.

Practice Copy this paragraph about the characters in *The Woman Warrior*, adding all the missing single quotation marks.

"My sister wrote, I am coming to America," Brave Orchid told her family. "She asked, Will you be able to pick me up? I told her, Yes, I will leave my house before your plane takes off from Hong Kong. Do you think she knows I am excited?"

Writing Application Write a second paragraph in which Brave Orchid quotes her sister. Use single quotation marks to indicate quotations within quotations. Punctuate according to the rules that apply.

WG Prentice Hall Writing and Grammar Connection: Chapter 27, Section 4

Assessment Practice

Punctuation **(For more practice, see *Standardized Test Preparation Workbook*, p.65.)**

Many tests require students to identify the type of error in a sentence. Use the following sample test item to demonstrate.

Immigrants who arrived at Ellis Island had often spent months at sea; and were thin and weak by the time they landed.

Read the passage and decide which type of error, if any, appears in the underlined section.

A Spelling error
B Capitalization error
C Punctuation error
D No error

C is the correct answer. The underlined section contains a semicolon separating two parts of a compound predicate. Remind students that semicolons are used to separate independent clauses.

Writing Lesson

Timed Writing: Character Analysis

In an essay, analyze Brave Orchid's character. Identify three or four of her personality traits, and connect them to her background and behavior. Cite appropriate supporting examples from the selection. *(40 minutes)*

Prewriting *(10 minutes)* List Brave Orchid's character traits, using such words as *bossy* or *nervous*. Next to each trait, note the background, attitudes, and behaviors connected with them. Then, select the traits you will write about.

Drafting *(20 minutes)* In the first paragraph of your essay, introduce Brave Orchid and *The Woman Warrior*. Include information about where she was born, her culture, her emigration to America, and her character. In the body paragraphs of your essay, address each one of those elements.

Revising *(10 minutes)* Highlight Brave Orchid's character traits and be sure you have connected them with her behaviors. To do so, cite examples from the selection.

Model: Revising to Provide Support

Because of her hard life, Brave Orchid is skeptical about American conveniences. For example, she feels that the luggage conveyors at American airports fooled immigrants into thinking life would be much easier here.

Added information from the selection supports a specific idea.

WG Prentice Hall Writing and Grammar Connection: Chapter 28, Section 3

Extend Your Learning

Listening and Speaking When *The Woman Warrior* won a 1976 award for nonfiction, many debated whether or not it fit that category. Hold a **panel discussion** to address the issue. Use the following tips:

- Identify criteria to determine whether the work fits the definition of nonfiction.
- Quote Kingston's own comments on the topic.

Present the discussion, inviting questions from classmates. **[Group Activity]**

Research and Technology Conduct research to prepare a written **immigration report** about the arrival of Chinese immigrants to the United States. Find at least two historical records to analyze. Supplement your report with a chart of statistical information. Present your findings to your class.

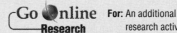

For: An additional research activity
Visit: www.PHSchool.com
Web Code: erd-7609

Assessment Resources

The following resources can be used to assess students' knowledge and skills.

Unit 6 Resources
- **Selection Test A,** pp. 160–162
- **Selection Test B,** pp. 163–165

General Resources
- **Rubrics for Response to Literature,** pp. 65–66
- **Rubric for Speaking: Delivering a Research Presentation,** p. 92

Go Online Assessment — Students may use the **Self-test** to prepare for **Selection Test A** or **Selection Test B.**

❸ Writing Lesson

You may use this Writing Lesson as timed-writing practice, or you may allow students to develop it as a writing assignment over several days.

- Give students the **Support for Writing Lesson,** p. 157 in ***Unit 6 Resources*** to use as they write their character analyses.
- Briefly discuss a favorite character from literature with students. What were the character's outstanding traits? How did the character demonstrate these traits?
- Lead students into a discussion of Brave Orchid. Remind students to support their descriptions of Brave Orchid with specific examples from the selection.
- Use the Writing Lesson to guide students in writing their character analyses.
- You may want to give students the Character Wheel graphic organizer, p. 306 in ***Graphic Organizer Transparencies,*** to use for this lesson.
- To evaluate students' character analyses, use the rubrics for Response to Literature, pp. 65–66 in ***General Resources.***

❹ Research and Technology

- Suggest that students work in small groups to complete their projects.
- Encourage students to use the Internet as a source of up-to-date information. However, stress to students that they must evaluate Internet sources carefully. Information from the official Ellis Island Web site, for example, may be presumed to be reliable. Information from an individual's Web site, on the other hand, should be corroborated. Urge students to corroborate statistics from at least three sources before considering them reliable.
- Use the rubric for Speaking: Delivering a Research Presentation, p. 92 in ***General Resources,*** to evaluate students' presentations.
- The **Support for Extend Your Learning** page (***Unit 6 Resources,*** p. 158) provides guided note-taking opportunities to help students complete the Extend Your Learning activities.

Go Online Research — Have students type in the Web Code for another research activity.

Meeting Your Standards

Students will

1. **analyze and respond to literary elements.**
   - Literary Analysis: Plot
2. **read, comprehend, analyze, and critique a short story.**
   - Reading Strategy: Identifying With a Character
   - Reading Check questions
   - Apply the Skills questions
   - Assessment Practice (ATE)
3. **develop vocabulary.**
   - Vocabulary Lesson: Words From Spanish
4. **understand and apply written and oral language conventions.**
   - Spelling Strategy
   - Grammar and Style Lesson: Absolute Phrases
5. **develop writing proficiency.**
   - Writing Lesson: New Version of the Story
6. **develop appropriate research strategies.**
   - Extend Your Learning: Multimedia Report
7. **understand and apply listening and speaking strategies.**
   - Extend Your Learning: Cause-and-Effect Flowchart

Block Scheduling: Use one 90-minute class period to preteach the skills and have students read the selection. Use a second 90-minute class period to assess students' mastery of skills, extend their learning, and monitor their progress.

Homework Suggestions

Following are possibilities for homework assignments.

- Support pages from *Unit 6 Resources:*
  Literary Analysis
  Reading Strategy
  Vocabulary Builder
  Grammar and Style
- An Extend Your Learning project and the Writing Lesson for this selection group may be completed over several days.

Step-by-Step Teaching Guide	Pacing Guide
PRETEACH	
• Administer Vocabulary and Reading Warm-ups as necessary.	5 min.
• Engage students' interest with the motivation activity.	5 min.
• Read and discuss author and background features. **FT**	10 min.
• Introduce the Literary Analysis Skill: Plot. **FT**	5 min.
• Introduce the Reading Strategy: Identifying With a Character. **FT**	10 min.
• Prepare students to read by teaching the selection vocabulary. **FT**	
TEACH	
• Informally monitor comprehension while students read independently or in groups. **FT**	30 min.
• Monitor students' comprehension with the Reading Check notes.	as students read
• Reinforce vocabulary with Vocabulary Builder notes.	as students read
• Develop students' understanding of plot with the Literary Analysis annotations. **FT**	5 min.
• Develop students' ability to identify with a character with the Reading Strategy annotations. **FT**	5 min.
ASSESS/EXTEND	
• Assess students' comprehension and mastery of the Literary Analysis and Reading Strategy by having them answer the Apply the Skills questions. **FT**	15 min.
• Have students complete the Vocabulary Lesson and the Grammar and Style Lesson. **FT**	15 min.
• Apply students' ability to use details to create a vivid portrayal by using the Writing Lesson. **FT**	45 min. or homework
• Apply students' understanding by using one or more of the Extend Your Learning activities.	20–90 min. or homework
• Administer Selection Test A or Selection Test B. **FT**	15 min.

Resources

PRINT
Unit 6 Resources
Vocabulary Warm-up Word Lists **[L1, L2, EL]** .... p. 166
Vocabulary Warm-up Practice **[L1, L2, EL]** .... p. 167
Reading Warm-up A **[L1, L2, EL]** .... p. 168
Reading Warm-up B **[L1, L2, L3]** .... p. 169

TRANSPARENCY
Graphic Organizer Transparencies
Literary Analysis Graphic Organizer A **[L3]** .... p. 252
Literary Analysis Graphic Organizer B **[L1, L2, EL]** .... p. 253
Reading Strategy Graphic Organizer A **[L3]** .... p. 250
Reading Strategy Graphic Organizer B **[L1, L2, EL]** .... p. 251

PRINT
Reader's Notebook [L2]
Reader's Notebook: Adapted Version [L1]
Reader's Notebook: English Learner's Version [EL]
Unit 6 Resources
Literary Analysis **[L3]** .... p. 170
Reading Strategy **[L3]** .... p. 171
Vocabulary Builder **[L3]** .... p. 172

TECHNOLOGY
Listening to Literature Audio CDs [L2, EL]

PRINT
Unit 6 Resources
Grammar and Style **[L3]** .... p. 173
Support for Writing Lesson **[L3]** .... p. 174
Support for Extend Your Learning **[L3]** .... p. 175
Enrichment **[L4]** .... p. 176
Selection Test A **[L1, L2, EL]** .... pp. 177–179
Selection Test B **[L3, L4]** .... pp. 180–182

TRANSPARENCY
Graphic Organizer Transparencies
Plot Diagram .... p. 310
General Resources
Rubrics for Narration: Short Story **[L3]** .... pp. 57–58
Rubrics for Multimedia Presentation **[L3]** .... pp. 51–52

TECHNOLOGY
Go Online: Research **[L3]**
Go Online: Self-test **[L3]**
ExamView® **Test Bank [L3]**

Choosing Resources for Differentiated Instruction

[L1] Special Needs Students
[L2] Below-Level Students
[L3] All Students
[L4] Advanced Students
[EL] English Learners

For Vocabulary and Reading Warm-ups and for Selection Tests, **A** signifies "less challenging" and **B** "more challenging." For Graphic Organizer transparencies, **A** signifies "not filled in" and **B** "filled in."

FT Fast Track Instruction: To move the lesson more quickly, use the strategies and activities identified with **FT**.

Scaffolding for Less Proficient and Advanced Students

The leveled Critical Thinking questions after selections progress in the levels of thinking required to answer them. To address the needs of your different students, you may use the (a) level questions for your less proficient students and the (b) level questions with your on-level and advanced students. The occasional (c) level questions are appropriate for your advanced students.

PRENTICE HALL **TeacherEXPRESS**™ Plan · Teach · Assess — Use this complete suite of powerful teaching tools to make lesson planning and testing quicker and easier.

PRENTICE HALL **StudentEXPRESS**™ Learn · Study · Succeed — Use the Interactive textbook (online and on CD-ROM) to make selections and activities come alive with audio and video support and interactive questions.

Go Online Professional Development
For: Information about Lexiles
Visit: www.PHSchool.com
Web Code: eue-1111

PRETEACH

Motivation

Like a travel diary, this story of a young woman's journey to her homeland is immediate and engaging. To entice travelers to visit particular places, travel agents often show photographs and excerpt travel diaries. Invite your students into the world of the Dominican Republic by displaying some photos of the region and travel advertisements. Write these passages on the board:

"She hadn't had her favorite *antojo, guavas,* since her last trip seven years ago."

"She ate right on the spot, relishing the slightly bumpy feel of the skin in her hand, devouring the crunchy, sweet, white meat."

Ask students to describe journeys they have taken and identify moments they found enjoyable.

❶ Background
More About the Author

Reared in a Spanish-speaking home, as a girl Julia Alvarez failed English classes again and again. How ironic that she is now a fluent and successful writer of novels and poetry in English!

Alvarez's work draws heavily on her own experiences and those of her family as she explores themes of family expectations conflicting with personal ambitions and the difficulties of living in two cultures. When interviewer Marny Requa asked her whether it was inspiring to have a foot in both Anglo and Latino cultures, Alvarez replied," . . . It was a burden because I felt torn—I wanted to be part of the other . . . Now I see the richness. Part of what I want to show with my work is that complexity, that richness. I don't want it to be simplistic and either/or."

Build Skills *Short Story*

❶ Antojos

Julia Alvarez
(b. 1950)

Julia Alvarez was born in New York City but raised in the Dominican Republic. When her father's involvement in a plot to overthrow that country's dictator, Rafael Trujillo, was uncovered, the family was forced to flee to the United States. It was 1960. When Alvarez arrived in the United States, she spoke only Spanish and had few friends. "I came into English as a ten-year-old from the Dominican Republic, and I consider this radical uprooting from my culture, my native language, my country, the reason I began writing," Alvarez once explained.

Writing to Ease the Pain

While moving to a new country changed her life forever, Alvarez quickly found her voice as a writer. She said, "I landed, not in the United States, but in the English language. That became my new home . . . which you never had to lose, because it was a portable homeland." As a young adult, Alvarez found that writing helped her deal with the pain of adjustment to a new culture and language. "In high school, I fell in love with how words can make you feel complete in a way that I hadn't felt complete since leaving the island," she said. Alvarez found herself turning more and more to writing "as the one place where I felt I belonged and could make sense of myself, my life, all that was happening to me."

After graduating from college, where she was awarded several poetry prizes, Alvarez earned a masters degree in creative writing at Syracuse University. She went on to join the Kentucky Arts Commission's poetry-in-the-schools program. For two years, she traveled around Kentucky teaching poetry. She then held a variety of teaching jobs before settling in Vermont as a Professor of English at Middlebury College.

Writing to Understand For Alvarez, writing "is happening all the time. When you go outside and you see the way a blade of grass bends in the breeze—when you're a writer, you're thinking about how that's happening." She also says that writing "is a way to understand yourself. You learn how you feel about things, but you're also making your little statement about things, and that makes you feel a little bit more powerful."

Alvarez's poetry often focuses on her personal experiences as well as her Caribbean heritage. She has published three volumes of poetry: *Homecoming* (1984), *The Other Side* (1995), and *The Woman I Kept to Myself* (2004).

A Storytelling Tradition After *Homecoming* was published, Alvarez began to focus on a new area of writing: fiction. "My own island background was steeped in a tradition of storytelling that I wanted to explore in prose," Alvarez explained. The move to prose proved fruitful, for Alvarez has won fame for four novels rooted in Hispanic American tradition: *How the García Girls Lost Their Accents* (1991), *In the Time of the Butterflies* (1994), *¡Yo!* (1997) and *In the Name of Salomé* (2000). Her fiction, like her poetry, deals with both the immigrant experience and her own bicultural identity.

"Antojos," which became the first chapter of *How the García Girls Lost Their Accents*, relates the story of a Dominican woman who has settled in the United States. The story captures what happens when she revisits her homeland and confronts the culture she had left behind.

Preview

Connecting to the Literature

If you have ever felt vulnerable in the presence of strangers whose motives might be questionable, you will understand how the main character in this story feels. Read to discover if her fears are justified.

Literary Analysis

Plot

Plot is the sequence of events in a literary work. In most narrative literature, the plot involves characters and a central conflict. Most plots follow a specific sequence, often referred to as the dramatic arc:

- **Exposition:** The basic situation is introduced.
- **Inciting incident:** The central conflict or struggle is revealed.
- **Development:** The conflict increases in intensity.
- **Climax:** The conflict reaches its most intense point.
- **Resolution,** or **Denouement:** The conflict is resolved, and some insight or change in the main character is revealed.

Plot events that lead up to the climax comprise the **rising action.** The events that follow the climax comprise the **falling action.**

Connecting Literary Elements

A **flashback** is an interruption in the chronological presentation of events in a story. Writers use flashbacks to highlight a scene or event from an earlier time, thus providing valuable information about the characters' backgrounds, personalities, and motives. When you come to a flashback in "Antojos," consider what it reveals about the character and her situation.

Reading Strategy

Identifying With a Character

You can often understand literature better if you **identify with a character** who appears in the work. Think about what you and the character have in common. For example, as you read "Antojos," note qualities you share with the main character, Yolanda. List similarities in a chart like the one shown.

	Yolanda	Me
Background		
Personality		
Attitudes		
Motives		
Behavior		

Vocabulary Builder

dissuade (di swād′) *v.* convince someone not to do something (p. 1118)

loath (lōth) *adj.* reluctant (p. 1120)

appease (ə pēz′) *v.* satisfy (p. 1121)

machetes (mə shet′ ēz) *n.* large heavy knives with broad blades (p. 1122)

collusion (kə lo͞o′ zhən) *n.* secret agreement; conspiracy (p. 1123)

docile (däs′ əl) *adj.* easy to direct or manage; obedient (p. 1123)

enunciated (ē nun′ sē āt′ əd) *v.* pronounced; stated precisely (p. 1125)

❷ Literary Analysis

Plot

- Tell students to focus on the dramatic arc of the plot, the rising action before the climax and the falling action after it, as they read "Antojos." They should decide whether the story includes all the classic stages and follows the plot order of exposition, inciting incident, development, climax, denouement and resolution.
- Go over each stage in the plot sequence from exposition to resolution. Have a volunteer define the term for each stage of the plot and give an example from his or her reading, preferably from a work that the class has read together.
- Mention that "Antojos" includes several flashbacks, interruptions in the chronological order of events. Ask students to note at which junctures in the story the flashbacks occur.

❸ Reading Strategy

Identifying With a Character

- Explain that the main character, Yolanda, is a young woman who has returned to the Dominican Republic for a visit after living in the United States for many years. Might she be similar in any way to themselves?
- Draw students' attention to the chart on p. 1115. Give students a copy of **Reading Strategy Graphic Organizer A,** p. 250 in **Graphic Organizer Transparencies,** to record any similarities they discover between Yolanda and themselves as they read the story.

Vocabulary Builder

- Pronounce each vocabulary word for students, and read the definitions as a class. Have students identify any words with which they are already familiar.

Differentiated Instruction

Solutions for All Learners

Support for Special Needs Students
Have students complete the **Preview** and **Build Skills** pages for "Antojos" in the **Reader's Notebook: Adapted Version.** These pages provide a selection summary, an abbreviated presentation of the reading and literary skills, and the graphic organizer on the **Build Skills** page in the student book.

Support for Less Proficient Readers
Have students complete the **Preview** and **Build Skills** pages for "Antojos" in the **Reader's Notebook.** These pages provide a selection summary, an abbreviated presentation of the reading and literary skills, and the graphic organizer on the **Build Skills** page in the student book.

Support for English Learners
Have students complete the **Preview** and **Build Skills** pages for "Antojos" in the **Reader's Notebook: English Learner's Version.** These pages provide a selection summary, an abbreviated presentation of the skills, and the graphic organizer on the **Build Skills** page in the student book.

Learning Modalities
Visual/Spatial Learners
Have students make maps of Yolanda's journey. The purpose of the maps is not to record Yolanda's exact route, but to visualize the various settings through which she passes.

❶ About the Selection

If students have ever taken a journey of any significant length alone, they will recognize the mix of confidence, anticipation, and fear that the main character, Yolanda, experiences in this story. Yolanda has returned to her Caribbean island homeland intent on demonstrating her adult independence from the family. As she travels through the countryside, aware of the region's unpredictable political climate, Yolanda must decide whom to trust and whom to fear. By facing some risks and making choices, she begins to consider how high a price she is willing to pay for her independence.

❷ Critical Viewing

Answer: The painting shows an abundant and beautiful arrangement of fruit: colorful, ripe, and inviting. In a similar way, Yolanda thinks of guavas as inviting, craving them all the more since it has been so long since she has eaten them in her homeland.

❶ 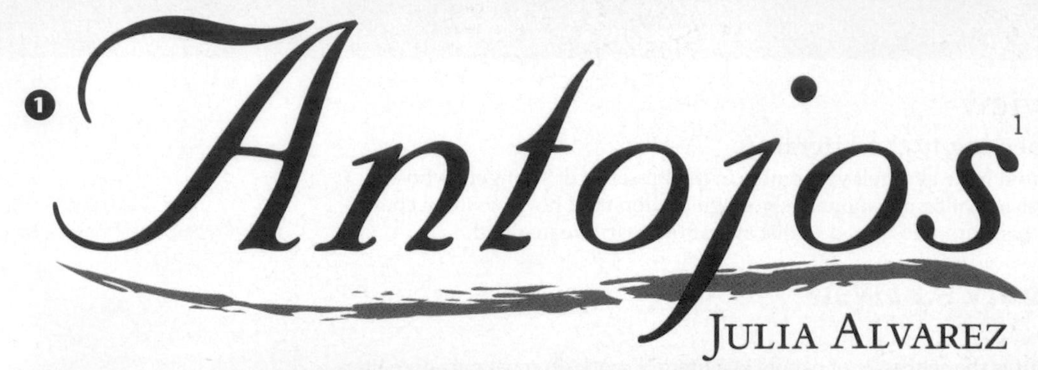

Antojos[1]

JULIA ALVAREZ

❸ 

Fruit Vendor, 1951, Olga Costa, Museo de Arte Moderno, Mexico

❷ ▲ **Critical Viewing** What elements of this artist's portrayal of fruit mirror Yolanda's feelings about guavas? **[Compare]**

1. **Antojos** (än tō′ hōs) Spanish for "cravings." The story explores the additional connotations of the word.

Differentiated Instruction Solutions for All Learners

Accessibility at a Glance

	Antojos
Context	Contemporary
Language	Informal, conversational, foreign words defined in footnotes
Concept Level	Accessible (homecoming)
Literary Merit	Cross-cultural experience
Lexile	980L
Overall Rating	More accessible

Background

Alvarez's homeland, the Dominican Republic, won independence in 1844 after a successful rebellion against Haitian rule. Since then, however, the country has suffered through several dictatorships and frequent foreign domination. One of the most ruthless dictators was Rafael Trujillo, who ruled the country from 1930 until he was assassinated in 1961. Julia Alvarez's father was part of the underground movement against Trujillo, and it was this involvement that forced the Alvarez family to flee the country. Three months after the family left, three of her father's co-conspirators were killed. Alvarez's emigration experience and her feelings of displacement and exile have influenced much of her writing, including the story that appears here.

4 For the first time since Yolanda had reached the hills, there was a shoulder on the left side of the narrow road. She pulled the car over out of a sense of homecoming: every other visit she had stayed with her family in the capital.

Once her own engine was off, she heard the sound of another motor, approaching, a pained roar as if the engine were falling apart. She made out an undertow of men's voices. Quickly, she got back into the car, locked the door, and pulled off the shoulder, hugging her right side of the road.

—Just in time too. A bus came lurching around the curve, obscuring her view with a belching of exhaust, the driver saluting or warning with a series of blasts on his horn. It was an old army bus, the official name brushed over with paint that didn't quite match the regulation gray. The passengers saw her only at the last moment, and all up and down her side of the bus, men poked out of the windows, hooting and yelling, waving purple party flags, holding out bottles and beckoning to her. She speeded up and left them behind, the small compact climbing easily up the snakey highway, its well-oiled hum a gratifying sound after the hullabaloo of the bus.

She tried the radio again, but all she could tune to was static even here on the summit hills. She would have to wait until she got to the coast to hear news of the hunger march in the capital. Her family had been worried that trouble would break out, for the march had been scheduled on the anniversary of the failed revolution nineteen years ago today. A huge turnout was expected. She bet that bus she had just passed had been delayed by breakdowns on its way to the capital. In fact, earlier on the road when she had first set out, Yolanda had passed buses and truckloads of men, drinking and shouting slogans. It crossed her mind that her family had finally agreed to loan her a car because they knew she'd be far safer on the north coast than in the capital city where revolutions always broke out.

The hills began to plane out into a high plateau, the road widening. Left and right, roadside stands began appearing. Yolanda slowed

Literary Analysis
Plot In this opening paragraph, what do you learn about the story's basic situation, including the character and setting?

5 
Reading Check
What political event is occurring in the city as Yolanda drives into the hills?

3 Humanities

Fruit Vendor, by Olga Costa

This painting vividly illustrates a fruit stand similar to those Yolanda passes in the story.

The artist, Olga Costa, was born in Leipzig, Germany, but has been a resident of Mexico since 1945. Largely self-taught, Costa's realistic style has been exhibited countless times during her years in Mexico and was ultimately honored by Mexico's National Art Prize in 1990.

Use this question for discussion:

- What elements of the painting capture the sensory images of the story setting?
  Possible response: The bright colors, bountiful quantities, and tropical nature of the fruits all reflect the vivid sensory images of the story setting.

4 Literary Analysis
Plot

- Read the opening paragraph aloud.
- **Ask** students the Literary Analysis question: In this opening paragraph, what do you learn about the story's basic situation, including the character and setting?
  Answer: Yolanda is an adult woman who is on a visit but is not staying with her family in the capital city, as she usually does. She has been driving a car on a narrow road in the hills, and her feelings have caused her to pull the car over to the side of the road.

5 Reading Check

Answer: People are going on a hunger march in the capital city as Yolanda is driving through the hills.

Differentiated Instruction
Solutions for All Learners

Enrichment for Advanced Readers

Suggest that students read additional works by Julia Alvarez. You may wish to use **Authors in Depth,** *The American Experience,* which contains the following selections:

Snow, *from* How the García Girls Lost Their Accents, (fiction, p. 179)
Papi Working (poem, p. 180)
Storm Windows (poem, p. 181)
Writing Matters (nonfiction, p. 182)

After students have read these or other works by Alvarez, have them form discussion groups in which they compare and contrast the selections they have read. Suggest criteria for comparison, such as setting, theme, and characters. To extend the activity, have volunteers present to the class brief oral reports on their favorite Alvarez selections.

❻ Literary Analysis
Plot and Flashback

- Have a volunteer read the passage aloud.
- Remind students that a flashback is a break in the chronological presentation of events in a story. Then, **ask** them why writers use flashbacks.
  Answer: Writers use flashbacks to provide important background information about characters.
- **Ask** Literary Analysis question: What information about Yolanda and her family is conveyed in this flashback?
  Answer: Yolanda and her aunts are quite wealthy. They don't see each other very often.

➤**Monitor Progress** **Ask** students to discuss the relationship between Yolanda and her aunts revealed in this passage. How does Yolanda feel about her aunts? How do they feel about her?
Answer: The relationship is cordial on both sides, but the aunts think that Yolanda is too "American," and Yolanda is slightly exasperated by her aunts, who in her opinion lead overly sheltered lives.

❼ Reading Strategy
Identifying With a Character

- **Ask** students why Yolanda wants to head off by herself.
  Possible response: Yolanda wants to be an independent adult.

➤**Monitor Progress** **Ask** students whether they think Yolanda's behavior is universal. How often and under what circumstances have they felt the way Yolanda feels?
Answer: Most students will feel that Yolanda's behavior is typical of young adults and will be able to provide plenty of similar examples from their own lives.

down and kept an eye out for guavas, supposedly in season this far north. Piled high on wooden stands were fruits she hadn't seen in so many years: pinkish-yellow mangoes, and tamarind pods oozing their rich sap, and small cashew fruits strung on a rope to keep them from bruising each other. There were little brown packets of roasted cashews and bars of milk fudge wrapped in waxed paper and tied with a string, the color of which told what filling was inside the bar. Strips of meat, buzzing with flies, hung from the windows of butcher stalls. An occasional display of straw hats and baskets and hammocks told that tourists sometimes did pass by here. Looking at the stores spread before her, it was hard to believe the poverty the organizers of the march kept discussing on the radio. There seemed to be plenty here to eat—except for guavas.

In the capital, her aunts had plied her with what she most craved after so many years away. "Any little *antojo*, you must tell us!" They wanted to spoil her, so she'd stay on in her nativeland before she forgot where she had come from. "What exactly does it mean, *antojo?*" Yolanda asked. Her aunts were proven right: After so many years away, their niece was losing her Spanish.

"An *antojo*—" The aunts exchanged quizzical looks. "How to put it? An *antojo* is like a craving for something you have to eat."

A cousin blew out her cheeks. "Calories."

An *antojo*, one of the older aunts continued, was a very old Spanish word from before "your United States was thought of," she added tartly. In the countryside some *campesinos*[2] still used the word to mean possession by an island spirit demanding its due.

❻ Her island spirit certainly was a patient soul, Yolanda joked. She hadn't had her favorite *antojo*, guavas, since her last trip seven years ago. Well, on this trip, her aunts promised, Yoyo could eat guavas to her heart's content. But when the gardener was summoned, he wasn't so sure. Guavas were no longer in season, at least not in the hotter lowlands of the south. Maybe up north, the chauffeur could pick her up some on his way back from some errand. Yolanda took this opportunity to inform her aunts of her plans: she could pick the guavas herself when she went up north in a few days.

❼ —She was going up north? By herself? A woman alone on the road! "This is not the States." Her old aunts had tried to dissuade her. "Anything can happen." When Yolanda challenged them, "What?" they came up with boogeymen stories that made her feel as if she were talking to china dolls.[3] Haitian hougans[4] and Communist kidnappers. "And Martians?" Yolanda wanted to tease them. They had led such sheltered lives, riding from one safe place to another in their air-conditioned cars.

Literary Analysis
Plot and Flashback What information about Yolanda and her family is conveyed in this flashback?

Vocabulary Builder
dissuade (di swād′) *v.* convince someone not to do something

2. ***campesinos*** (käm′ pe sē′ nōs) "poor farmers; simple rural dwellers" (Spanish).
3. **china dolls** old-fashioned, delicate dolls made of fragile high-quality porcelain or ceramic ware.
4. **Haitian hougans** (o͞o gänz′) voodoo priests or cult leaders.

Enrichment

The Guava

The guava is a tropical fruit native to Central and South America that grows on trees and shrubs. It belongs to the genus Psidium. There are several species of guava: the common guava, the cattley, the cás, the guisaro, and the Brazilian guava. The fruit referred to as the pineapple guava is actually a feijoa.

The guava that Yolanda craves is the common guava. The tree of the common guava has four-petal white flowers. The three-inch-long yellow-skinned guava fruit is round to pear shaped. The flesh can be pink, white, or yellow. Some people don't care for the strong smell of guava pulp or the multitude of small, hard seeds.

Guavas are very healthful fruit loaded with vitamins A, B, and C. People eat guavas right off the tree or sliced with sugar and cream. These fruits are also made into jams, jellies, and preserves.

She had left the fruit stands behind her and was approaching a compound very much like her family's in the capital. The underbrush stopped abruptly at a high concrete wall, topped with broken bottle glass. Parked at the door was a chocolate brown Mercedes. Perhaps the owners had come up to their country home for the weekend to avoid the troubles in the capital?

Just beyond the estate, Yolanda came upon a small village—ALTAMIRA in rippling letters on the corrugated tin roof of the first little house. It was a little cluster of houses on either side of the road, a good place to stretch her legs before what she'd heard was a steep and slightly (her aunts had warned "very") dangerous descent to the coast. Yolanda pulled up at a cantina, the thatched roof held up by several posts. Instead of a menu, there was a yellowing, grimy poster for Palmolive soap tacked on one of the posts with a picture of a blonde woman under a spraying shower, her head thrown back in seeming ecstasy, her mouth opened in a wordless cry. ("Palmolive"? Yolanda wondered.) She felt even thirstier and grimier looking at this lathered beauty after her hot day on the road.

An old woman emerged at last from a shack behind the cabana, buttoning up a torn housedress, and followed closely by a little boy, who kept ducking behind her whenever Yolanda smiled at him. Asking him his name just drove him further into the folds of the old woman's skirt.

"You must excuse him, Doña,"[5] she apologized. "He's not used to being among people." But Yolanda knew the old woman meant, not the people in the village, but the people with money who drove through Altamira to the beaches on the coast. "Your name," the old woman repeated, as if Yolanda hadn't asked him in Spanish. The little boy mumbled at the ground. "Speak up!" the old woman scolded, but her voice betrayed pride when she spoke up for him. "This little know-nothing is Jose Duarte Sanchez y Mella García."

Yolanda laughed. Not only were those a lot of names for such a little boy, but they certainly were momentous: the surnames of the three liberators of the country!

"Can I serve the Doña in any way?" the woman asked. Yolanda gave the tree line beyond the woman's shack a glance. "You think you might have some guavas around?"

The old woman's face scrunched up. "Guavas?" she murmured and thought to herself a second. "Why, they're all around, Doña. But I can't say as I've seen any."

5. **Doña** (dō̃ nyä) "Madam" (Spanish).

Literature in Context

8 Geography Connection

The Dominican Republic

Located in the West Indies, the Dominican Republic takes up the eastern two thirds of the island of Hispaniola. The country is bounded on the north by the Atlantic Ocean; on the east by the Mona Passage, which separates it from Puerto Rico; on the south by the Caribbean Sea; and on the west by Haiti.

In Alvarez's story, Yolanda begins her journey in Santo Domingo, the capital city, which is located on the country's southern coast. Yolanda's journey takes her into the Cordillera Central Range, which includes Pico Duarte, the highest mountain in the Caribbean. The slopes of many of these mountains are covered with dense semi-tropical forests, like those in which Yolanda searches for guavas.

Connect to the Literature

In what ways does the story's setting—both geographical and cultural—contribute to Yolanda's conflict?

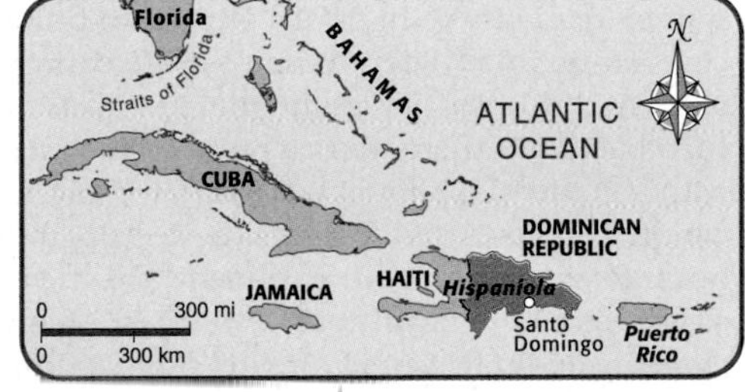

10 Reading Check

Who does Yolanda meet at the roadside cantina?

8 Literature in Context

Geography Connection The Dominican Republic is a country of the West Indies that occupies the eastern two-thirds of the Island of Hispaniola.

The capital of the Dominican Republic, Santo Domingo, is on the southern coast of the country. To reach the northern part of the Dominican Republic from the capital city, Yolanda would have had to drive across the Cordillera Central, a highland area containing the West Indies's highest mountain, the Pico Duarte, which is 10,417 ft. (3,175 m) high.

Though the transportation system in the Dominican Republic is generally considered adequate, the mountainous center of the country is challenging to motorists. Traveling through the mountains is slow, though scenic. In fact, the name of the village where Yolanda stops—Altamira—can be translated as "View from Above."

Connect to the Literature Ask students to describe the landscape and the people presented in the story. Then ask the Connect to the Literature question.

Possible response: The Dominican Republic's unstable environment mirrors Yolanda's unstable emotional state.

9 Critical Thinking

Infer

- **Ask** students what evidence indicates that the owners of the compound are of the same social class as Yolanda's family.
  Answer: They have a compound similar to her family's compound in the capital city.
- Have students **speculate** about why rich families lived in compounds surrounded by high walls topped by broken glass.
  Answer: Rich families wanted to protect themselves against political unrest and thievery.

10 Reading Check

Answer: Yolanda meets an old woman and a little boy.

Differentiated Instruction *Solutions for All Learners*

Support for Less Proficient Readers
Help students clarify the settings and characters introduced on this page by listing where Yolanda is, what she sees, and whom she sees. Write the headings *Where, What,* and *Whom* on the board and have volunteers fill in the information, or ask them to do this independently using their notebooks.

Strategy for Gifted/Talented Students
Have students discuss where Yolanda is at this point in the story and what and whom she sees there. Then, have students draw illustrations of the cantina and the people Yolanda meets there. Urge students to refer to the text in order to include as many accurate details as possible in their illustrations.

Strategy for Advanced Readers
Have students analyze the settings and characters introduced on this page. For each concrete detail the author provides, have students speculate about why the author included that detail and what conclusions readers can draw from it.

⓫ Reading Strategy
Identifying With a Character

- **Ask** a volunteer to explain why Yolanda becomes irritated when the woman tries to discourage her from going with the boys to pick guavas.
  Answer: Yolanda feels overprotected by the old woman. She feels that the old woman, much like Yolanda's family, is keeping her from exploring her country.
- Then, **ask** the Reading Strategy question: Can you identify with Yolanda's feelings as she responds to the old woman? Why or why not?
  Answer: Most students will identify with Yolanda's feelings. Teenagers often experience constraints imposed by their families on their growing independence.

⓬ Critical Thinking
Analyze/Predict

- **Ask** students to explain why the boys are so excited about going for a ride in Yolanda's car.
  Answer: The boys probably have few chances to ride in cars. It is unlikely that their families own cars.
- Have students **speculate** about what might happen as Yolanda and the boys ride off together in her car to look for guavas.
  Possible response: Students may predict that they will have some kind of problem to provide an inciting incident in the plot.

⓭ Critical Viewing

Answer: Since the people shown in the photograph are peasants, they have more in common with the people Yolanda meets in the mountains than with her wealthy family back in the capital city.

"With your permission—" Jose Duarte had joined a group of little boys who had come out of nowhere and were milling around the car, boasting how many automobiles they had ridden in. At Yolanda's mention of guavas, he sprung forward, pointing across the road towards the summit of the western hills. "I know where there's a whole grove of them." Behind him, his little companions nodded.

"Go on, then!" His grandmother stamped her foot as if she were scatting a little animal. "Get the Doña some."

A few boys dashed across the road and disappeared up a steep path on the hillside, but before Jose could follow, Yolanda called him back. She wanted to go along too. The little boy looked towards his grandmother, unsure of what to think. The old woman shook her head. The Doña would get hot, her nice clothes would get all dirty. Jose would get
⓫ the Doña as many guavas as she was wanting.

"But they taste so much better when you've picked them yourself," Yolanda's voice had an edge, for suddenly, it was as if the woman had turned into the long arm of her family, keeping her away from seeing her country on her own.

The few boys who had stayed behind with Jose had congregated around the car. Each one claimed to be guarding it for the Doña. It occurred to Yolanda that there was a way to make this a treat all the way around. "What do you say we take the car?"

⓬ "*Sí, Sí, Sí*,"[6] the boys screamed in a riot of excitement.

The old woman hushed them but agreed that was not a bad idea if the Doña insisted on going. There was a dirt road up ahead she could follow a ways and then cross over onto the road that was paved all the way to the coffee barns. The woman pointed south in the direction of the big house. Many workers took that short cut to work.

They piled into the car, half a dozen boys in the back, and Jose as co-pilot in the passenger seat beside Yolanda. They turned onto a bumpy road off the highway, which got bumpier and bumpier, and climbed up into wilder, more desolate country. Branches scraped the sides and pebbles pelted the underside of the car. Yolanda wanted to turn back, but there was no room to maneuver the car around. Finally, with a great snapping of twigs and thrashing of branches across the windshield, as if the countryside were loath to release them, the car burst forth onto smooth pavement and the light of day. On either side of the road were groves of guava trees. Among them, the boys who had gone ahead on foot were already pulling down branches and shaking loose a rain of guavas. The fruit was definitely in season.

For the next hour or so, Yolanda and her crew scavenged the grove, the best of the pick going into the beach basket Yolanda had gotten out of the trunk, with the exception of the ones she ate right on the spot, relishing the slightly bumpy feel of the skin in her hand, devouring the crunchy, sweet, white meat. The boys watched her, surprised by her odd hunger.

6. ***Sí, Sí, Sí*** (sē) "Yes, Yes, Yes" (Spanish).

Reading Strategy
Identifying With a Character Can you identify with Yolanda's feelings as she responds to the old woman? Why or why not?

Vocabulary Builder
loath (lōth) *adj.* reluctant

⓭ **► Critical Viewing**
Do you think the people in this picture have more in common with Yolanda and her family or with the people she meets in the mountains? Explain. **[Analyze]**

Yolanda and Jose, partners, wandered far from the path that cut through the grove. Soon they were bent double to avoid getting entangled in the thick canopy of branches overhead. Each addition to the basket caused a spill from the stash already piled high above the brim. Finally, it was a case of abandoning the treasure in order to cart some of it home. With Jose hugging the basket to himself and Yolanda parting the wayward branches in front of them, they headed back toward the car.

When they finally cleared the thicket of guava branches, the sun was low on the western horizon. There was no sign of the other boys. "They must have gone to round up the goats," Jose observed.

Yolanda glanced at her watch: it was past six o'clock. She'd never make the north coast by nightfall, but at least she could get off the dangerous mountain roads while it was still light. She hurried Jose back to the car, where they found a heap of guavas the other boys had left behind on the shoulder of the road. Enough guavas to appease even the greediest island spirit for life!

15 They packed the guavas in the trunk quickly and climbed in, but the car had not gone a foot before it lurched forward with a horrible hobble. Yolanda closed her eyes and laid her head down on the wheel, then glanced over at Jose. The way his eyes were searching

Vocabulary Builder
appease (ə pēz′) *v.* satisfy

Reading Check
What do Jose and his friends help Yolanda to gather?

14 Critical Thinking
Infer

- **Ask** students to name the likeliest reason for Yolanda's car lurching "with a horrible hobble."
  Answer: Yolanda's car probably has a flat tire.
- **Ask** what motivates Yolanda to close her eyes and rest her head on the wheel.
  Answer: Yolanda is upset and discouraged.
- Discuss with students what they would do if they found themselves in a similar situation. What would they advise Yolanda to do?
  Answer: Suggestions may include changing the tire with Jose's help, waiting in the car for help, and hiking out with Jose to look for help.

15 Reading Check
Answer: Jose and his friends help Yolanda gather guavas.

Differentiated Instruction
Solutions for All Learners

Strategy for Gifted/Talented Students
Have students choose a food they love to eat that holds special meaning for them as guavas do for Yolanda. Ask them to make a word web that includes all the reasons the food is significant to them. They should then refer to this web to write a poem about the food. If they like, they can use the letters of the food to begin each line of the poem.

Enrichment for Advanced Readers
Have students choose a food that holds special significance for them as guavas do for Yolanda in "Antojos." Ask students to do some research to find out all they can about the food they choose. Students should blend some of the interesting information they learned while doing research with their personal feelings to write a short personal essay in which they explain why they chose the food as their favorite.

⓰ Literary Analysis
Plot

- **Ask** students the Literary Analysis question: What elements of the setting serve to intensify Yolanda's conflict?
  Answer: The bad road and the rapidly setting sun intensify Yolanda's conflict.
- **Ask** students to discuss the relationship between setting and plot.
  Answer: Students should understand that the setting and plot are interwoven. If the setting in this story had not turned threatening, for example, there would have been less difficulty for the main character to face.

⓱ Reading Strategy
Identifying With a Character

- Have a volunteer read the bracketed passage aloud.
- Then, **ask** the Reading Strategy question: What is Yolanda feeling as she waits for Jose? Do you think you would react with similar emotions if you were in her situation? Explain.
  Answer: Yolanda is enjoying the beauty and sense of connectedness she feels in the countryside, a feeling she has missed while living in the United States. Most students will say that they would not feel as Yolanda does; they would be too worried about being in a potentially dangerous situation.

⓲ Vocabulary Builder
Words From Spanish

- Have a volunteer read aloud the definition of *machete* in the margin. Point out that *machete* comes from the Spanish word for *sledgehammer.*
- Remind students that we use many words that come from Spanish, such as *hammock,* as well as words that are Spanish, such as *Latino.*
- Encourage students to note other Spanish words and words that came from Spanish as they read. Explain that English has borrowed more words from other languages—French, German, Yiddish, Italian, and many others—than has any other language.

the inside of the car for a clue as to what could have happened, she could tell he didn't know how to change a flat tire either.

⓰ It was no use regretting having brought the car up that bad stretch of road. The thing to do now was to act quickly. Soon the sun would set and night would fall swiftly, no lingering dusk as in the States. She explained to Jose that they had a flat tire and had to hike back to town and send for help down the road to the big house. Whoever tended to the brown Mercedes would know how to change the tire on her car.

"With your permission," Jose offered meekly. He pointed down the paved road. "This goes directly to the big house." The Doña could just wait in the car and he would be back in no time with someone from the Miranda place.

She did not like the idea of staying behind in the car, but Jose could probably go and come back much quicker without her. "All right," she said to the boy. "I'll tell you what." She pointed to her watch. It was almost six thirty. "If you're back by the time this hand is over here, I'll give you"—she held up one finger "a dollar." The boy's mouth fell open. In no time, he had shot out of his side of the car and was headed at a run toward the Miranda place. Yolanda climbed out as well and walked down a pace, until the boy had disappeared in one of the turnings of the road.

⓱ Suddenly, the countryside was so very quiet. She looked up at the purple sky. A breeze was blowing through the grove, rustling the leaves, so they whispered like voices, something indistinct. Here and there a light flickered on the hills, a *campesino* living out his solitary life. This was what she had been missing without really knowing that she was missing it all these years. She had never felt at home in the States, never, though she knew she was lucky to have a job, so she could afford her own life and not be run by her family. But independence didn't have to be exile. She could come home, home to places like these very hills, and live here on her own terms.

Heading back to the car, Yolanda stopped. She had heard footsteps in the grove. Could Jose be back already? Branches were being thrust aside, twigs snapped. Suddenly, a short, dark man, and then a slender, light-skin man emerged from a footpath on the opposite side of the grove from the one she and Jose had scavenged. They wore ragged work clothes stained with patches of sweat; their faces were drawn and
⓲ tired. Yolanda's glance fell on the <u>machetes</u> that hung from their belts.

The men's faces snapped awake from their stupor at the sight of her. They looked beyond her at the car. "Yours?" the darker man spoke first. It struck her, even then, as an absurd question. Who else's would it be here in the middle of nowhere?

"Is there some problem?" the darker man spoke up again. The taller one was looking her up and down with interest. They were now both in front of her on the road, blocking her escape. Both—she had looked them up and down as well—were strong and quite capable of catching her if she made a run for the Miranda's. Not that she could have moved, for her legs seemed suddenly to have been hammered

Literary Analysis
Plot What elements of the setting serve to intensify Yolanda's conflict?

Reading Strategy
Identifying With a Character What is Yolanda feeling as she waits for Jose? Do you think you would react with similar emotions if you were in her situation? Explain.

Vocabulary Builder
machetes (mə shet′ ēz) *n.* large heavy knives with broad blades

Enrichment

eople o the ominican epu lic

The people of the Dominican Republic are mostly mulatto (of mixed European and African descent). The original Indian inhabitants of the island of Hispaniola, of which the Dominican Republic occupies the eastern part, were long ago decimated by disease, warfare, and the ravages of slavery. Spanish is the dominant language of the Dominican Republic, and most of the inhabitants are Roman Catholic. The original Spanish colonizers of the Dominican Republic were joined in the 1800s and 1900s by East Asians and immigrants from France, England, and Germany. Small numbers of Jews, Middle Easterners, and Japanese also emigrated to the Dominican Republic during this time.

into the ground beneath her. She thought of explaining that she was just out for a drive before dinner at the big house, so that these men would think someone knew where she was, someone would come looking for her if they tried to carry her off. But she found she could not speak. Her tongue felt as if it'd been stuffed in her mouth like a rag to keep her quiet.

The men exchanged a look—it seemed to Yolanda of collusion. Then the shorter, darker one spoke up again, "Señorita,[7] are you all right?" He peered at her. The darkness of his complexion in the growing darkness of the evening made it difficult to distinguish an expression. He was no taller than Yolanda, but he gave the impression of being quite large, for he was broad and solid, like something not yet completely carved out of a piece of wood. His companion was tall and of a rich honey-brown color that matched his honey-brown eyes. Anywhere else, Yolanda would have found him extremely attractive, but here on a lonely road, with the sky growing darker by seconds, his good looks seemed dangerous, a lure to catch her off her guard.

"Can we help you?" the shorter man repeated.

The handsome one smiled knowingly. Two long, deep dimples appeared like gashes on either side of his mouth. "*Americana*," he said to the other in Spanish, pointing to the car. "She doesn't understand."

The darker man narrowed his eyes and studied Yolanda a moment. "*Americana?*" he asked her as if not quite sure what to make of her.

She had been too frightened to carry out any strategy, but now a road was opening before her. She laid her hand on her chest—she could feel her pounding heart—and nodded. Then, as if the admission itself loosened her tongue, she explained in English how it came that she was on a back road by herself, her craving for guavas, her never having learned to change a flat. The two men stared at her, uncomprehendingly, rendered docile by her gibberish. Strangely enough, it soothed her to hear herself speaking something they could not understand. She thought of something her teacher used to say to her when as a young immigrant girl she was learning English, "Language is power." It was her only defense now.

Yolanda made the motions of pumping. The darker man looked at the other, who had shown better luck at understanding the foreign lady. But his companion shrugged, baffled as well. "I'll show you," Yolanda waved for them to follow her. And suddenly, as if after pulling and pulling at roots, she had finally managed to yank them free of the soil they had clung to, she found she could move her own feet forward to the car.

The small group stood staring at the sagging tire a moment, the two men kicking at it as if punishing it for having failed the Señorita. They squatted by the passenger's side, conversing in low tones. Yolanda led them to the rear of the car, where the men lifted the spare out of its sunken nest—then set to work, fitting the interlocking pieces of the

7. **Señorita** (se´ nyō rē´ tä) "Miss" (Spanish).

Vocabulary Builder
collusion (kə lo͞o´ zhən) *n.* secret agreement; conspiracy

Literary Analysis
Plot In what ways is Yolanda's conflict growing more intense and complex?

Vocabulary Builder
docile (däs´ əl) *adj.* easy to direct or manage; obedient

21

Reading Check
What does Yolanda pretend when she is approached by the two men?

19 Literary Analysis
Plot

- Have students **identify** Yolanda's predominant emotion in the bracketed passage.
  Answer: Yolanda's predominant emotion is fear.
- Then, **ask** the Literary Analysis question: In what ways is Yolanda's conflict growing more intense and complex?
  Answer: Her conflict is more intense because she is unable to follow her normal instincts. Her feelings are complicated by finding the man attractive yet fearing him.

20 Reading Strategy
Identifying With a Character

- Have students **discuss** the phrase "language is power." What does it mean? Do they agree?
  Possible response: The person whose language dominates defines the terms of debate. Language can be used to wound and manipulate, and in many ways language may be a more powerful tool than a weapon.
- Have students **give** examples of the power of language.
  Possible response: Students may mention instances in which someone's words made them feel either awful or great.

21 Reading Check

Answer: Yolanda pretends she is an American who doesn't speak Spanish.

Differentiated Instruction
Solutions for All Learners

Strategy for Special Needs Students
Students may understand the story better by discussing the swings of emotions Yolanda displays on pp. 1122 and 1123. Ask students how Yolanda feels in the fourth full paragraph on p. 1122. What happens shortly after that to change her mood?

Strategy for Less Proficient Readers
Have students chart the trajectory of Yolanda's emotions that the author describes on pp. 1122 and 1123. If necessary, prompt students with questions such as the following: How does Yolanda feel as she walks outside the car? How do her feelings change when she sees the men? Why is Yolanda afraid of the men? Are her fears rational?

Strategy for Advanced Readers
Have students trace the arc of Yolanda's emotions as they are revealed on pp. 1122 and 1123. Then, ask students to imagine the point of view of the men she encounters on the path. How did they feel when they saw Yolanda and listened to her speak in English? What is the meaning of the looks they shoot at each other?

22 Critical Viewing

Answer: The boys seem slightly awe-stricken and overwhelmed, yet interested in the photographer, which is similar to Jose's reaction to Yolanda in the story.

23 Reading Strategy
Identifying With a Character

- Have students **speculate** about how Yolanda is feeling now that the men are fixing her tire and one of them has injured his hand. Which sentence gives a clue about her feeling?
  Answer: Yolanda is probably feeling guilty about her suspicions about the men. The sentence that gives readers a clue about her feelings is the following: "She had been sure that if any blood were going to be spilled tonight, it would be hers."
- Ask students to think of similar situations in their lives in which they made an assumption about someone that turned out to be faulty. How did they feel when that happened? What did they learn from the incident?

jack, unpacking the tools from the deeper hollows of the trunk. They laid their machetes down on the side of the road, out of the way. Yolanda turned on the headlights to help them see in the growing darkness. Above the small group, the sky was purple with twilight.

There was a problem with the jack. It squeaked and labored, but the car would not rise. The shorter man squirmed his way underneath and placed the mechanism deeper under the bowels of the car. There, he pumped vigorously, his friend bracing him by holding him down by the ankles. Slowly, the car rose until the wheel hung suspended. When the man came out from under the car, his hand was bloody where his knuckles had scraped against the pavement.

23 Yolanda pointed to the man's hand. She had been sure that if any blood were going to be spilled tonight, it would be hers. She offered him the towel she kept draped on her car seat to absorb her perspiration. But he waved it away and sucked his knuckles to make the bleeding stop.

Once the flat had been replaced with the spare, the two men lifted the deflated tire into the trunk and put away the tools. They handed Yolanda her keys. There was still no sign of Jose and the Miranda's.

22 ▲ Critical Viewing In what ways might these boys' reactions to the photographer taking their picture be similar to Jose's reaction to Yolanda in the story? **[Connect]**

Enrichment

Raising Mangoes

The tropical climate of the Dominican Republic is well suited to growing fruits such as guavas, mangoes, tamarind pods, and cashew nuts. In fact, mangoes are one of the nation's major agricultural products. Like many tropical fruits, mangoes are evergreen while also sensitive to cold temperatures. Grown widely in India and other parts of Asia, as well as tropical parts of Central and South America, mangoes range from plum-size to almost five pounds. A reddish-yellow to green skin covers orange-yellow flesh and a single large stone. Mangoes contain vitamins A, C, and D. Unfortunately, they are highly perishable and therefore difficult and expensive to transport.

If possible, offer students the opportunity to taste a mango. Otherwise, display pictures of the fruit and some foods prepared with it. Discuss how its succulence suggests the tropical setting of the story.

Yolanda was relieved. As she had waited, watching the two men hard at work, she had begun to dread the boy's return with help. The two men would realize she spoke Spanish. It was too late to admit that she had tricked them, to explain she had done so only because she thought her survival was on the line. The least she could do now was to try and repay them, handsomely, for their trouble.

"I'd like to give you something," she began reaching for the purse she'd retrieved from the trunk. The English words sounded hollow on her tongue. She rolled up a couple of American bills and offered them to the men. The shorter man held up his hand. Yolanda could see where the blood had dried dark streaks on his palm. "No, no, Señorita. *Nuestro placer.*"[8] Our pleasure.

Yolanda turned to the other man, who had struck her as more pliant than his sterner companion. "Please," she urged the bills on him. But he too looked down at the ground with the bashfulness she had observed in Jose of country people not wanting to offend. She felt the poverty of her response and stuffed the bills quickly into his pocket.

The two men picked up their machetes and raised them to their shoulders like soldiers their guns. The tall man motioned towards the big house. "*Directo, directo,*"[9] he enunciated the words carefully. Yolanda looked in the direction of his hand. In the faint light of what was left of day, she could barely make out the road ahead. It was as if the guava grove had overgrown into the road and woven its mat of branches so securely and tightly in all directions, she would not be able to escape.

But finally, she was off! While the two men waited a moment on the shoulder to see if the tire would hold, Yolanda drove a few yards, poking her head out the window before speeding up. "*Gracias!*"[10] she called, and they waved, appreciatively, at the foreign lady making an effort in their native tongue. When she looked for them in her rear-view mirror, they had disappeared into the darkness of the guava grove.

Just ahead, her lights described the figure of a small boy: Jose was walking alone, listlessly, as if he did not particularly want to get to where he was going.

Yolanda leaned over and opened the door for him. The small overhead light came on; she saw that the boy's face was streaked with tears.

"Why, what's wrong, Jose?"

The boy swallowed hard. "They would not come. They didn't believe me." He took little breaths between words to keep his tears at bay. He had lost his chance at a whole dollar. "And the guard, he said if I didn't stop telling stories, he was going to whip me."

"What did you tell him, Jose?"

"I told him you had broken your car and you needed help fixing it."

8. ***Nuestro placer*** (no͞o es´ trō plä ser´) "Our pleasure" (Spanish).
9. ***Directo, directo*** (dē rek´ tō) "Straight, straight" (Spanish).
10. ***Gracias*** (grä´ sē äs) "Thank you" (Spanish).

Literary Analysis
Plot Is Yolanda's problem fully addressed now that the men have fixed her tire? What is still unresolved?

Vocabulary Builder
enunciated (ē nun´ sē āt´ əd) *v.* pronounced; stated precisely

26 **Reading Check**
What do the two men do to help Yolanda?

24 Literary Analysis
Plot

- Read the bracketed passage aloud, and have students **identify** Yolanda's primary emotion.
  Answer: Though all her problems aren't solved, Yolanda is overwhelmingly relieved that the men haven't harmed her and have fixed the flat tire on her car.

▶ **Monitor Progress: Ask** the Literary Analysis question: Is Yolanda's problem fully addressed now that the men have fixed her tire? What is unresolved?
Answer: Students should understand that Yolanda has sent Jose to get help from the Mirandas. If he returns before the men leave, they will know that she speaks Spanish. If he doesn't return, Yolanda will have to worry about what happened to him.

25 Reading Strategy
Identifying With a Character

- **Ask** students to explain why such poor men have turned down an offer of money for changing the tire.
  Answer: The men don't think it's proper to take money for performing a good deed.
- **Ask:** Why is Yolanda embarrassed?
  Answer: She realizes that offering money for the men's politeness could be considered insulting to them.
- **Ask** students whether they have made a similar *faux pas,* perhaps with people they didn't know well or in an unfamiliar situation. How did they feel? What did they learn?
  Answer: Many students will be able to relate to Yolanda's social gaffe and her feelings of embarrassment.

26 Reading Check

Answer: The men change the tire on Yolanda's car.

Differentiated Instruction
Solutions for All Learners

Strategy for Special Needs Students
To help students understand the characters' motivations, have them analyze the characters' behavior on pp. 1124 and 1125. Have students make a chart with the headings *Yolanda, The Campesinos,* and *Jose.* Along the side of the chart, ask them to write What the Character(s) Do(es) and Why the Character(s) Do(es) It. As they read these pages, students can fill in the chart. After completing their charts, students should discuss them. You may want to draw a similar chart on the board and fill in an item or two to provide a model.

Strategy for Gifted/Talented Readers
Have students discuss the characters' various motivations and behavior in this part of the story. Then, have each student take the part of Yolanda, Jose, or one of the two campesinos. Have them get together in groups for a heart-to-heart chat. The characters should tell each other what lies behind their behavior—what they truly think and why they are behaving as they are.

ASSESS

Answers

1. Some students might be surprised that the campesinos didn't harm Yolanda, given her aunt's worries. Other students may be surprised by Yolanda's shame at her behavior and Jose's distress at not being believed.
2. (a) Her aunts tell Yolanda anything could happen, such as attacks by Haitian hougans and kidnappings by Communists. (b) Yolanda does encounter campesinos in a remote area, though no harm comes to her.
3. (a) Her aunts are concerned and upset. (b) Yolanda has led a less sheltered life than her aunts; she is more adventurous and is not concerned about traveling on her own. (c) Yolanda is from a different generation than her aunts and has lived on her own in the United States.
4. (a) *Antojos* are cravings for certain foods. (b) The title emphasizes the theme of longing for connection with one's heritage.
5. (a) Jose is delighted with the promise of a dollar. (b) A segment of the population in the Dominican Republic is not making a living wage. (c) The issue of social and economic inequity is central to the story, defining the characters' behavior and underlying the assumptions they make about one another.
6. (a) Yolanda is afraid of the men, though she acknowledges that under different circumstances, she would find one of the men attractive. (b) Yolanda thinks she will be safer if she pretends to be an American who does not speak Spanish.
7. (a) Yolanda learns that the campesinos are more complex and sensitive than her simplistic view of them had led her to believe. (b) Many students will believe that Yolanda might make light of her experiences to her family because she would not want her family to believe that their fears had been justified.

She should have gone along with Jose to the Miranda's. Given all the trouble in the country, they would be suspicious of a boy coming to their door at nightfall with some story about a lady on a back road with a broken car. "Don't you worry, Jose," Yolanda patted the boy. She could feel the bony shoulder through the thin fabric of his worn shirt. "You can still have your dollar. You did your part."

But the shame of being suspected of lying seemed to have obscured any immediate pleasure he might feel in her offer. Yolanda tried to distract him by asking what he would buy with his money, what he most craved, thinking that on a subsequent trip, she might bring him his little *antojo*. But Jose Duarte Sanchez y Mella said nothing, except a bashful thank you when she left him off at the cantina with his promised dollar. In the glow of the headlights, Yolanda made out the figure of the old woman in the black square of her doorway, waving good-bye. Above the picnic table on a near post, the Palmolive woman's skin shone; her head was thrown back, her mouth opened as if she were calling someone over a great distance.

Critical Reading

1. **Respond:** Did this story surprise you in any way? Explain.
2. **(a) Recall:** What warnings do her aunts give Yolanda before she starts on her journey? **(b) Interpret:** How do these warnings anticipate, or foreshadow, Yolanda's experiences on her trip?
3. **(a) Recall:** With what emotions do her aunts react to Yolanda's announcement that she plans to drive north on her own? **(b) Compare and Contrast:** In what ways is Yolanda different from her aunts? **(c) Speculate:** What factors might account for the differences between Yolanda and her aunts?
4. **(a) Recall:** What are *antojos*? **(b) Connect:** What theme does the title of the story stress?
5. **(a) Recall:** How does the boy Jose react to Yolanda's promise of a dollar? **(b) Infer:** What is suggested about the country's political situation by the idea of a "hunger march" taking place in the capital? **(c) Analyze:** What role do issues of money and social inequity play in this story?
6. **(a) Interpret:** When Yolanda first sees the two men what emotions does she experience? **(b) Analyze:** Why does Yolanda pretend not to speak Spanish?
7. **(a) Evaluate:** Does Yolanda learn or grow in the story? Explain. **(b) Speculate:** How might Yolanda describe her experiences to her family when she returns from her trip?

Go Online
Author Link
For: More about Julia Alvarez
Visit: www.PHSchool.com
Web Code: ere-9614

Go Online Author Link For additional information about Julia Alvarez, have students type in the Web Code, then select *A* from the alphabet, and then select Julia Alvarez.

Apply the Skills

Antojos

Literary Analysis

Plot

1. Use a chart like the one shown to analyze the **plot** and answer the following questions: **(a)** What events in the story form the **rising action**? **(b)** What events form the **falling action**? **(c)** What is the story's main **conflict**? **(d)** How does it resolve?

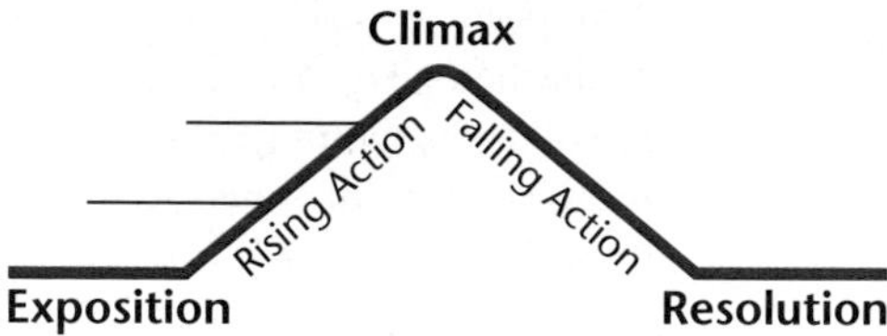

2. In what ways does the story's central conflict mirror other, deeper conflicts that may not be so easily resolved?

Connecting Literary Elements

3. **(a)** What does the **flashback** to Yolanda's visit with her aunts reveal about her family's social and economic circumstances? **(b)** What does the flashback reveal about Yolanda's reasons for traveling north?
4. **(a)** How else might Alvarez have conveyed the information given in the flashback? **(b)** Is her use of flashback more or less effective than another technique might be? Explain.

Reading Strategy

Identifying With a Character

5. **(a)** Examine Yolanda's attitudes and behavior toward her aunts, Jose, and the two men who approach her. **(b)** Do you **identify** with Yolanda in her dealings with these people? Explain.
6. **(a)** What information about the country's political turmoil adds to the weight of Yolanda's feelings about the two men? **(b)** How might her aunts' feelings about solo travel have affected Yolanda?

Extend Understanding

7. **Cultural Connection:** How might it feel to return to one's country of origin after a long absence? Respond from your own experience, or interview a family member, friend, or neighbor to find out.

QuickReview

Plot is the sequence of events in narrative writing. The sequence of a plot follows these stages: the **exposition,** when the basic situation is introduced; the **inciting incident,** when the conflict is revealed; the **development,** when the conflict intensifies; the **climax,** when the conflict reaches its most intense point; and the **resolution,** or **denouement,** when the conflict is resolved and changes or insights are conveyed.

A **flashback** is an interruption in the chronological narrative that is used to present a scene or an event from an earlier time.

To **identify with a character,** think about character traits and experiences you share.

Go Online Assessment

For: Self-test
Visit: www.PHSchool.com
Web Code: era-6610

Students may use the **Self-test** to prepare for **Selection Test A** or **Selection Test B.**

Answers

1. (a) Yolanda's visiting with the aunts, setting out on her trip north, meeting with the peasant woman and Jose, and gathering guavas are events that form the rising action. (b) Picking up Jose crying on the road, dropping him off at home, and waving good-bye to the woman and boy form the falling action. (c) The story's conflict is between Yolanda's desire for a closer connection with her homeland and her alienation from her country. (d) Though Yolanda isn't aware of it, she has chosen through her behavior American values over the values of the campesinos of the countryside.

   Another sample answer can be found on **Literary Analysis Graphic Organizer B**, p. 253, in ***Graphic Organizer Transparencies.***
2. The upper and lower classes of the Dominican Republic may not be able to resolve their differences easily.
3. (a) The family is wealthy and upper class. (b) Yolanda wants to be independent of her family and come to terms with her country on her own.
4. (a) She might have described the scene in chronological order. (b) Many students will believe the use of flashback is effective because it conveys information from Yolanda's point of view vividly and economically.
5. (a) Yolanda is affectionate toward her aunts but slightly exasperated with their fears and protectiveness. Yolanda is friendly toward Jose. Yolanda is afraid of the men at first but ends up impressed by their simple dignity. (b) Some students will identify with Yolanda's habit of making assumptions about people she doesn't really know.
6. (a) Knowing that the country is experiencing a hunger strike and that a threat of revolution exists causes Yolanda to fear that the men will identify her with the upper class and resent her. (b) Though she scoffed at her aunts' fears, their nervousness may have added to her own unease.
7. Most students will understand that one's memories of one's homeland may not conform to reality.

EXTEND/ASSESS

Answers

1 Vocabulary Lesson

Words From Spanish

1. guava
2. canteen
3. In the story, people live in a village comprised of *cabanas,* or small shacks.

Vocabulary Builder

1. synonyms
2. antonyms
3. antonyms
4. synonyms
5. synonyms
6. antonyms
7. antonyms

Spelling Strategy

1. skated
2. defining
3. captured

2 Grammar and Style Lesson

1. It was an old army bus, the official name brushed over with paint.
2. She speeded up and left them behind, the small compact climbing easily.
3. Yolanda pulled at a cantina, the thatched roof held up by several posts.
4. Yolanda and her crew scavenged the grove, the best of the pick going into the basket.
5. The small group stared at the sagging tire, the two men kicking it.

Writing Application

Students must include three or more absolute phrases in their descriptions of childhood memories.

WG Writing and Grammar, Ruby Level

Students will find further instruction and practice on absolute phrases in Chapter 19, Section 2.

Build Language Skills

1 Vocabulary Lesson

Concept Development: Words From Spanish

Many words, such as *machete, tortilla,* and *sombrero,* come to English directly from Spanish. Use the story context to help you answer these questions about three other Spanish words.

1. Which English word used in the story probably comes from *guayaba,* the Spanish name for the same tropical fruit?
2. *Cantina,* from the Spanish for "bar" or "tavern," is related to an Italian word for "wine cellar." Which English word probably has a similar origin?
3. In English, a *cabana* or *cabaña* is usually a small building at a swimming pool or beach. Is that the word's meaning on page 1119 in the story? Explain.

Vocabulary Builder: Synonyms or Antonyms

Classify each of the following pairs of words as either synonyms or antonyms.

1. dissuade, discourage
2. loath, eager
3. appease, arouse
4. machetes, knives
5. collusion, plotting
6. docile, cantankerous
7. enunciated, slurred

Spelling Strategy

For words ending in silent *e,* drop the *e* before adding a suffix beginning with a vowel (*enunciate +-ed = enunciated*). Correctly add the indicated suffix to each word listed.

1. skate (*-ed*) 2. define (*-ing*) 3. capture (*-ed*)

2 Grammar and Style Lesson

Absolute Phrases

An **absolute phrase** consists of a noun or noun phrase modified by a participle or participial phrase. Though it modifies the clause to which it is attached, it is not part of the subject or predicate and is set off from the rest of the sentence by commas.

Example: A bus came lurching around the curve, *the driver saluting.*

Practice Identify the absolute phrases in the following sentences.

1. It was an old army bus, the official name brushed over with paint.
2. She speeded up and left them behind, the small compact climbing easily.
3. Yolanda pulled up at a cantina, the thatched roof held up by several posts.
4. Yolanda and her crew scavenged the grove, the best of the pick going into the basket.
5. The small group stared at the sagging tire, the two men kicking it.

Writing Application Write a one-paragraph description of an important childhood memory. Include at least three absolute phrases in your account to add descriptive detail.

WG Prentice Hall Writing and Grammar Connection: Chapter 19, Section 2

Assessment Practice

Grammar and Usage (For more practice, see *Standardized Test Preparation Workbook*, p. 66.)

The writing sections of many tests require students to recognize and correct errors in grammar. Use the following sample test item to give students practice in this skill.

The latest sales reports indicate that the popularity of guavas are growing in the United States.

Choose the best way to rewrite the underlined section of the passage. If the underlined section needs no change, choose "Correct as is."

A of guavas were growing
B of guavas is growing
C of guavas was growing
A Correct as is

A and *C* are in the past tense, while the passage refers to the present. The plural verb *are* does not agree with the singular subject *popularity,* so *D* is incorrect. The correct choice is *B.*

3 Writing Lesson

New Version of the Story

In both literature and life, stories are shaped by the points of view of those who tell them. For example, in this story you see events and people through Yolanda's eyes. You can only speculate about the thoughts of the people she encounters. Write a new version of the story from the point of view of one of the men who changes Yolanda's tire.

Prewriting Choose the character whose point of view you will use and reread the story considering that perspective. Note details to incorporate and develop. Then, write a brief outline of your new version.

Drafting Write the story from the new point of view you have selected. Use sensory details, flashbacks, and dialogue to provide background and flesh out the character's world.

Model: Using Details to Create a Vivid Portrayal

Paulo saw a small white car stuck in the foliage. The tire was busted, and a lady stood there. Her eyes were nervous and black. She reminded Paulo of a cornered chihuahua, and he thought she might bite. He laughed at the thought. ìHo w can we help you, Doña?" he asked.

The inclusion of dialogue and a character's inner thoughts add to the vividness of a narrative.

Revising Reread your story, and look for points where you may have strayed from the perspective you have chosen. Delete details the character might not know, and add information to strengthen your use of point of view.

WG *Prentice Hall Writing and Grammar Connection: Chapter 5, Section 4*

Extend Your Learning

Listening and Speaking Create a **cause-and-effect flowchart** that examines the series of decisions each character makes. Use the flowchart as the basis for a class presentation. Use these tips to prepare:

- Diagram the characters' choices in each situation.
- Note how the decisions made by Yolanda and other characters affect the plot.

After your presentation, lead a discussion about the conflicts and decisions portrayed in this story.

Research and Technology Work with several classmates to prepare a **multimedia report** about the Dominican Republic. Choose one area to research—for example, geography, or economics. Add music and images, and report your findings in a presentation. **[Group Activity]**

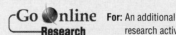

For: An additional research activity
Visit: www.PHSchool.com
Web Code: erd-7610

Assessment Practice

The following resources can be used to assess students' knowledge and skills.

Unit 6 Resources
- **Selection Test A**, pp. 177–179
- **Selection Test B**, pp. 180–182

General Resources
- **Rubrics for Narration: Short Story**, pp. 57–58
- **Rubrics for Multimedia Presentation**, pp. 51–52

Go Online Assessment — Students may use the **Self-test** to prepare for **Selection Test A** or **Selection Test B.**

3 Writing Lesson

- Give students the **Support for Writing Lesson,** p. 174 in ***General Resources,*** to use as they write a new version of "Antojos." You may also wish to supply students with the Plot Diagram, p. 310 in ***Graphic Organizer Transparencies.***
- To prepare them to write a new version of "Antojos," have students reread the part of the story in which the campesinos appear. Remind students to jot down relevant details.
- Use the Writing Lesson to guide students in preparing to write and draft their versions of the stories. Remind them to use sensory details, flashbacks, and dialogue.
- Use the drafting model to provide an example for students. Urge students to revise their stories to add details or dialogue to make the character come alive.
- Use the Narration: Short Story rubric in **General Resources,** pp. 57–58, to evaluate students' stories.

4 Research and Technology

- Suggest that students work in small groups to research the Dominican Republic.
- Have group members choose a topic for their group, such as geography, demographics, or the economy.
- Make sure that each student in the group contributes to the presentation, either by doing research, writing, or preparing one of the elements of the presentation.
- Use the rubrics for Multimedia Presentation, pp. 51–52 in ***General Resources,*** to evaluate students' work.
- The **Support for Extend Your Learning** page (***Unit 6 Resources,*** p. 175) provides guided note-taking opportunities to help students complete the Extend Your Learning activities.

Go Online Research — Have students type in the Web Code for another research activity.

Meeting Your Standards

Students will

1. **analyze and respond to literary elements.**
   - Literary Analysis: Voice
2. **read, comprehend, analyze, and critique poetry.**
   - Reading Strategy: Summarizing
   - Reading Check questions
   - Apply the Skills questions
   - Assessment Practice (ATE)
3. **develop vocabulary.**
   - Vocabulary Lesson: Greek Prefix: *auto-*
4. **understand and apply written and oral language conventions.**
   - Spelling Strategy
   - Grammar and Style Lesson: Participial Phrases
5. **develop writing proficiency.**
   - Writing Lesson: Comparison-and-Contrast Essay
6. **develop appropriate research strategies.**
   - Extend Your Learning: Anthology
7. **understand and apply listening and speaking strategies.**
   - Extend Your Learning: Interview

Block Scheduling: Use one 90-minute class period to preteach the skills and have students read the selection. Use a second 90-minute class period to assess students' mastery of skills, extend their learning, and monitor their progress.

Homework Suggestions

Following are possibilities for homework assignments:

- Support pages from ***Unit 6 Resources:***
  Literary Analysis
  Reading Strategy
  Vocabulary Builder
  Grammar and Style
- An Extend Your Learning project and the Writing Lesson for this selection group may be completed over several days.

Step-by-Step Teaching Guide	Pacing Guide
PRETEACH	
• Administer Vocabulary and Reading Warm-ups as necessary.	5 min.
• Engage students' interest with the motivation activity.	5 min.
• Read and discuss author, and background features. **FT**	10 min.
• Introduce the Literary Analysis Skill: Voice **FT**	5 min.
• Introduce the Reading Strategy: Summarizing **FT**	10 min.
• Prepare students to read by teaching the selection vocabulary. **FT**	
TEACH	
• Informally monitor comprehension while students read independently or in groups. **FT**	30 min.
• Monitor students' comprehension with the Reading Check notes.	as students read
• Reinforce vocabulary with Vocabulary Builder notes.	as students read
• Develop students' understanding of voice with the Literary Analysis annotations. **FT**	5 minutes
• Develop students' ability to summarize with the Reading Strategy annotations. **FT**	5 minutes
ASSESS/EXTEND	
• Assess students' comprehension and mastery of the Literary Analysis and Reading Strategy by having them answer the Apply the Skills questions. **FT**	15 min.
• Have students complete the Vocabulary Lesson and the Grammar and Style Lesson. **FT**	15 min.
• Apply students' ability to elaborate for a stronger statement by using the Writing Lesson. **FT**	45 min. or homework
• Apply students' understanding using one or more of the Extend Your Learning activities.	20–90 min. or homework
• Administer Selection Test A or Selection Test B. **FT**	15 min.

Resources

PRINT

Unit 6 Resources

Vocabulary Warm-up Word Lists **[L1, L2, EL]** .... p. 183
Vocabulary Warm-up Practice **[L1, L2, EL]** .... p. 184
Reading Warm-up A **[L1, L2, EL]** .... p. 185
Reading Warm-up B **[L1, L2, L3]** .... p. 186

TRANSPARENCY

Graphic Organizer Transparencies

Literary Analysis Graphic Organizer A **[L3]** .... p. 256
Literary Analysis Graphic Organizer B **[L1, L2, EL]** .... p. 257
Reading Strategy Graphic Organizer A **[L3]** .... p. 254
Reading Strategy Graphic Organizer B **[L1, L2, EL]** .... p. 255

PRINT

Reader's Notebook [L2]
Reader's Notebook: Adapted Version [L1]
Reader's Notebook: English Learner's Version [EL]

Unit 6 Resources

Literary Analysis **[L3]** .... p. 187
Reading Strategy **[L3]** .... p. 188
Vocabulary Builder **[L3]** .... p. 189

TECHNOLOGY

Listening to Literature Audio CDs [L2, EL]

PRINT

Unit 6 Resources

Grammar and Style **[L3]** .... p. 190
Support for Writing Lesson **[L3]** .... p. 191
Support for Extend Your Learning **[L3]** .... p. 192
Enrichment **[L4]** .... p. 193
Selection Test A **[L1, L2, EL]** .... pp. 194–196
Selection Test B **[L3, L4]** .... pp. 197–199

TRANSPARENCY

Graphic Organizer Transparencies

Venn Diagram .... p. 316

General Resources

Rubrics for Comparison-and-Contrast Essay **[L3]** .... pp. 69–70

TECHNOLOGY

Go Online: Research **[L3]**
Go Online: Self-test **[L3]**
***ExamView*® Test Bank [L3]**

Choosing Resources for Differentiated Instruction

[L1] Special Needs Students
[L2] Below-Level Students
[L3] All Students
[L4] Advanced Students
[EL] English Learners

For Vocabulary and Reading Warm-ups and for Selection Tests, **A** signifies "less challenging" and **B** "more challenging." For Graphic Organizer transparencies, **A** signifies "not filled in" and **B** "filled in."

FT Fast Track Instruction: To move the lesson more quickly, use the strategies and activities identified with **FT**.

Scaffolding for Less Proficient and Advanced Students

The leveled Critical Thinking questions after selections progress in the levels of thinking required to answer them. To address the needs of your different students, you may use the (a) level questions for your less proficient students and the (b) level questions with your on-level and advanced students. The occasional (c) level questions are appropriate for your advanced students.

PRENTICE HALL **TeacherEXPRESS**™ Plan · Teach · Assess — Use this complete suite of powerful teaching tools to make lesson planning and testing quicker and easier.

PRENTICE HALL **StudentEXPRESS**™ Learn · Study · Succeed — Use the interactive textbook (online and on CD-ROM) to make selections and activities come alive with audio and video support and interactive questions.

Go Online Professional Development
For: Information about Lexiles
Visit: www.PHSchool.com
Web Code: eue-1111

PRETEACH

Motivation

As students question and define their own identities in relation to their cultural heritages, they will find these poems—statements of cultural pride and definition—intensely relevant. Begin a discussion of this topic by displaying a selection of advertisements featuring people of various ethnicities and cultures. Ask students to discuss why the advertisers chose to use these models. Discuss as a class the growing role of cultural identity in America's multicultural society.

❶ Background

More About the Authors

Martín Espada's work has appeared in the *New York Times Book Review, Harper's, The Nation,* and *The Best American Poetry.* He has received the Pen/Revson Award, Paterson Poetry Prize, two NEA fellowships, and the National Book Award.

Diana Chang received a John Hay Whitney Foundation Fellowship in order to complete her first novel, *The Frontiers of Love* (1956). She is a charter life member of the International Society of Poets and The Library of Congress.

Simon Ortiz's books of poetry include *Going for Rain* (1976), *Woven Stone* (1992), and *After and Before the Lightning* (1994).

Garrett Hongo's *The River of Heaven* was the Lamont Poetry Selection of the Academy of American Poets and a finalist for the Pulitzer Prize in 1988. He has also received fellowships from the National Endowment for the Arts and the Rockefeller Foundation.

Build Skills Poems

❶ Who Burns for the Perfection of Paper • Most Satisfied by Snow • Hunger in New York City • What For

Martín Espada (b. 1957)

Not many lawyers pursue simultaneous careers as poets, but, until 1993, Martín Espada was an exception. Espada's creativity was inspired by his father, a photographer based in Brooklyn, New York. Father and son worked together on a 1981 photo documentary called *The Puerto Rican Diaspora Documentary Project.* A year later, Espada published his first volume of poetry, *The Immigrant Iceboy's Bolero.* His other collections include *The City of Coughing and Dead Radiators* (1993), *A Mayan Astronomer in Hell's Kitchen* (2000), and *Alabanza: New and Selected Poems: 1982–2002* (2004). Called "the Latino poet of his generation," Espada draws on both his Puerto Rican heritage and his work as a legal-aid lawyer. He now teaches poetry at the University of Massachusetts at Amherst.

Diana Chang (b. 1934)

Born in New York City, Diana Chang spent most of her childhood in China. She returned to the United States after World War II and attended Barnard College. After college, Chang worked as an editor. In addition to writing poetry, she has written several novels, including *The Frontiers of Love* (1956), *Eye to Eye* (1974), and *A Perfect Love* (1978). Chang's spare, introspective poetry, collected in volumes such as *What Matisse Is After* (1984) and *Earth, Water, Light* (1991), shows the influence of traditional Asian verse forms. She has also translated Asian writings into English. Perhaps due to the many views and voices in her experience, Chang's work "moves beyond ethnicity" to examine "identity and self."

Simon J. Ortiz (b. 1941)

Born in Albuquerque, New Mexco, Simon J. Ortiz grew up steeped in the oral tradition of his Native American people—the Acoma Pueblo of New Mexico. Writing came naturally to him, and in 1981 he was honored at a White House "Salute to Poetry and American Poets." Ortiz has published more than a dozen books of poetry and prose, including *After and Before the Lightning* (1994), *Men on the Moon: Collected Short Stories* (1999), *From Sand Creek* (2000), and *Somewhere Out There* (2002). He has also edited several anthologies, including *Earth Power Coming: Short Fiction in Native American Literature* (1988). Ortiz currently teaches at the University of Toronto.

Garrett Hongo (b. 1951)

One of the stars among contemporary Asian American poets, Garrett Hongo is a fourth-generation Japanese American who spent his early childhood in Hawaii. His father, an electrical technician, figures prominently in Hongo's poems and is profiled in his book *Volcano: A Memoir of Hawaii* (1995). Hongo's poetry gives the reader a vivid look into the lives of Japanese Americans, including the racial discrimination and alienation they have suffered. Hongo has won numerous awards, including fellowships from the Thomas Watson and Guggenheim foundations. Among Hongo's other works are the poetry collections *Yellow Light* (1982) and *The River of Heaven* (1988). He is also the editor of *Under Western Eyes* (1995), an anthology of personal essays about growing up Asian American.

Preview

Connecting to the Literature

The poets whose work appears here represent some of the many distinct cultural groups that make up the American fabric. As you read, think about the role that family and cultural heritage play in your life.

2 Literary Analysis

Voice

Just as each person has a distinctive way of speaking, every poet has a unique **voice,** or literary personality. A poet's voice is based on word choice, tone, sound devices, rhyme (or its absence), pace, attitude, and even the patterns of vowels and consonants. Consider these examples:

- *Espada:* No gloves: fingertips required / for the perfection of paper . . .
- *Chang:* Against my windows, / fog knows / what to do, too

As you read these poems, note the distinctive voice each one reveals.

Comparing Literary Works

Issues of cultural and personal **alienation** are a common theme in American poetry of the late twentieth century. Alienation is the feeling of being separate, or detached from a group. Feelings of alienation arise from internal sources, such as questions of personal identity, or from external sources, such as clashes between cultures. As you read these poems, think about the poet's relationship to his or her subject, and whether or not it expresses acceptance or the more difficult feelings of alienation.

3 Reading Strategy

Summarizing

Sometimes, you can understand a poem better if you briefly restate the main points in a **summary.** A summary should match these criteria:

- It includes content from the beginning, middle, and end.
- It is concise—no longer than a single sentence.
- It is precise, clearly conveying the poem's essence.

Use a chart like the one shown to create summaries of each poem.

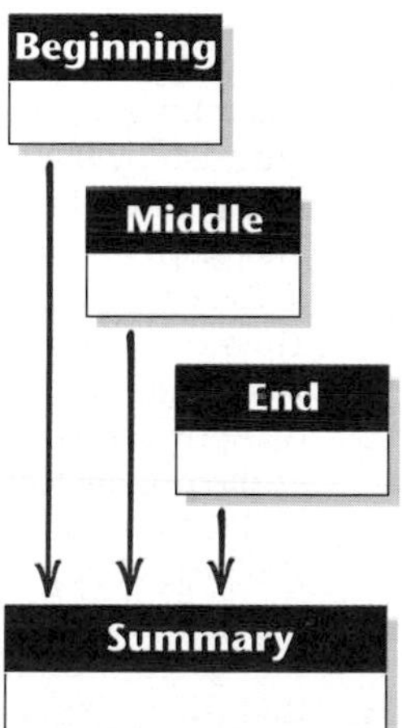

Vocabulary Builder

crevices (krev′ is iz) *n.* narrow cracks or splits (p. 1132)

pervade (pər vād′) *v.* spread throughout (p. 1133)

automation (ôt′ ə mā′ shən) *n.* manufacturing conducted with partly or fully self-operating machinery (p. 1134)

liturgy (lit′ ər jē) *n.* public religious ceremonies; religious ritual (p. 1135)

conjure (kän′ jər) *v.* summon by magic or as if by magic; call forth (p. 1135)

calligraphy (kə lig′ rə fē) *n.* artistic handwriting (p. 1136)

trough (trôf) *n.* a low point of a wave (p. 1136)

2 Literary Analysis

Voice

- As they read these four poems, students will think about how each poet's culture and heritage are reflected in his or her work. Are the poets integrated into their culture, or do they seem alienated?
- Encourage students to read the poems carefully and repeatedly, considering as they read each one how they would describe the poet's voice, or literary personality.
- Discuss the elements that make up a poet's voice, and have volunteers compare the voices reflected in the two examples on this page.

3 Reading Strategy

Summarizing

- Remind students that summaries are concise statements that contain the essential ideas of a selection. Mention that attempting to write a summary can help students realize whether or not they understood what they read.
- Have students write a one-sentence summary of each of the four poems.
- Give students a copy of **Reading Strategy Graphic Organizer A,** p. 254 in ***Graphic Organizer Transparencies,*** to help them write the summaries. They should use it to make sure they include information from the beginning, middle, and end of each poem.

Vocabulary Builder

- Pronounce each vocabulary word for students, and read the definitions as a class. Have students identify any words with which they are already familiar.

Differentiated Instruction

Solutions for All Learners

Support for Special Needs Students

Have students complete the **Preview** and **Build Skills** pages for the selections in the ***Reader's Notebook: Adapted Version.*** These pages provide a selection summary, an abbreviated presentation of the reading and literary skills, and the graphic organizer on the **Build Skills** page in the student book.

Support for Less Proficient Readers

Have students complete the **Preview** and **Build Skills** pages for the selections in the ***Reader's Notebook.*** These pages provide a selection summary, an abbreviated presentation of the reading and literary skills, and the graphic organizer on the **Build Skills** page in the student book.

Support for English Learners

Have students complete the **Preview** and **Build Skills** pages for the selections in the ***Reader's Notebook: English Learner's Version.*** These pages provide a selection summary, an abbreviated presentation of the reading and literary skills, and the graphic organizer on the **Build Skills** page in the student book.

TEACH

Learning Modalities
Visual/Spatial Learners
Encourage these students to respond freely to the illustrations that accompany the poems. Challenge them to make predictions about the content and mood of the poems based on the illustrations.

❶ About the Selections

The speaker in "Who Burns for the Perfection of Paper" recalls the harsh physical labor that was part of a job he held at age 16 to remind readers that behind his outward accomplishments are the painful memories of hard work and sacrifice—and more generally that anonymous workers have performed demanding physical labor to produce the products we enjoy.

In "Most Satisfied by Snow," the speaker contrasts the empty spaces of fog with the substance of snow, characterizing nature as a teacher urging awareness of both physical and spiritual components.

❷ Reading Strategy
Summarizing

- Have a volunteer read aloud the first stanza of the poem. Ask students to identify the main idea of the stanza.
- Then, **ask** students to summarize the first stanza of the poem. **Answer:** At 16, the speaker cut his hands working at a plant that made legal pads.

❶ Who Burns for the Perfection of Paper

Martín Espada

Background The poems you are about to read reflect the cultural roots of their authors. Espada recalls the harsh labor of an after-school job. Chang offers a poem whose subject and style are reminiscent of Asian verse. Ortiz describes how life in New York City prompts a hunger for his southwestern home. Chinese American writer Hongo draws on his heritage as Hawaiian of Japanese descent.

At sixteen, I worked after high school hours
at a printing plant
that manufactured legal pads:
Yellow paper
stacked seven feet high
and leaning
as I slipped cardboard
between the pages,
then brushed red glue
up and down the stack.
❷ No gloves: fingertips required
for the perfection of paper,
smoothing the exact rectangle.
Sluggish by 9 PM, the hands
would slide along suddenly sharp paper,
and gather slits thinner than the crevices
of the skin, hidden.
Then the glue would sting,
hands oozing
till both palms burned
at the punchclock.

Ten years later, in law school,
I knew that every legal pad
was glued with the sting of hidden cuts,
that every open lawbook
was a pair of hands
upturned and burning.

Vocabulary Builder
crevices (krev′ is iz) *n.* narrow cracks or splits

Differentiated Instruction Solutions for All Learners

Accessibility at a Glance

	Who Burns for the Perfection of Paper	Most Satisfied by Snow	Hunger in New York City	What For
Language	Informal diction, uncomplicated syntax	Informal diction	Long and short sentence structures	Formal, vocabulary covered in footnotes
Concept Level	Accessible (details of physical labor)	Challenging (Nature as teacher)	Challenging (longing for connection to nature)	Challenging (using words to alleviate pain)
Literary Merit	Factual account	Inspirational	Notable Author	Award-winning Author
Lexile	NP	NP	NP	NP
Overall Rating	Accessible	Average	Average	More challenging

MOST SATISFIED BY SNOW

Diana Chang

Against my windows,
fog knows
what to do, too

Spaces pervade
us, as well

But occupied by snow,
I see

Matter
matters

I, too,
flowering

3 ▲ **Critical Viewing**
In what ways does this image of trees relate to the last two lines of the poem? **[Connect]**

Vocabulary Builder
pervade (pər vād′) *v.* spread throughout

Critical Reading

1. **Respond:** In what ways were you surprised by these poems?
2. **(a) Recall:** In "Who Burns for the Perfection of Paper," what was the speaker's first experience with legal pads? **(b) Recall:** What were the speaker's later job with legal pads? **(c) Interpret:** What did the speaker learn from the first job?
3. **(a) Recall:** What word does the speaker use twice to describe cuts on the hands? **(b) Interpret:** What role does the idea of anonymity play in this poem?
4. **(a) Classify:** In "Most Satisfied by Snow," the speaker observes two kinds of weather. What are they? **(b) Compare and Contrast:** What differences between these two types of weather does the poem highlight?
5. **(a) Interpret:** What might the speaker mean by the comment that "spaces pervade us"? **(b) Interpret:** What is the relationship of "matter" to these "spaces"?

For: More about Martín Espada and Diana Chang
Visit: www.PHSchool.com
Web Code: ere-9615

3 Critical Viewing

Answer: The trees appear to be flowering as the poem's speaker is, though they are actually covered with snow or, like the speaker, occupied by snow.

ASSESS

Answers

1. Some students were probably surprised that nothing was being burned by fire in the first poem and that the subject of the second poem is not snow but matter.
2. (a) The speaker worked in a plant that manufactured legal pads. (b) The speaker used legal pads in law school. (c) The speaker learned that behind every manufactured item lies an untold story of effort and pain.
3. (a) The speaker uses the word *sting*. (b) The stories of the people who labor to produce items we use remain anonymous.
4. (a) The speaker observes foggy and snowy weather. (b) The fog represents space; the snow stands for substance.
5. (a) The speaker may mean that we are made of matter, but matter includes space. (b) Matter occupies space and space occupies matter. We often refer to people's spirit (space) and flesh (matter).

Go Online Author Link For additional information about Martín Espada or Diana Chang, have students type in the Web Code, then select *E* or *C* from the alphabet, and then select Martín Espada or Diana Chang.

Differentiated Instruction Solutions for All Learners

Background for Less Proficient Readers
Help students relate to "Who Burns for the Perfection of Paper" by discussing jobs they have held. What were the most difficult parts of those jobs?

Background for Gifted/Talented Students
Help students relate to "Who Burns for the Perfection of Paper" by discussing jobs they have held. What were the most difficult parts of those jobs? Have students pantomime doing various jobs and ask classmates to guess which jobs they are acting out and how they feel about doing the work.

Background for Advanced Readers
Help students relate to "Who Burns for the Perfection of Paper" by discussing jobs they have held. What were the most difficult parts of those jobs? Ask students to research child labor practices in the United States and list some suggestions for improving the lives of children who work.

4 About the Selection

The speaker in "Hunger in New York City" acknowledges a longing for his home, where nature is more accessible, and draws on memories of a closer connection to the earth to satisfy his longing.

5 Critical Viewing

Answer: The poem and photograph both convey sadness and longing.

6 Vocabulary Builder

Greek Prefix *auto*–

- Draw students' attention to the definition of the word *automation* in the margin. Have a volunteer read the definition.
- Tell students that the prefix *auto*– means "self." Have them **explain** how the prefix relates to the meaning of *automation*.
  Answer: Automation is self-operated machinery.

7 Reading Strategy

Summarizing

- Have a volunteer read aloud the last stanza of the poem. Ask students to identify the main idea of this stanza.
- Then, **ask** students the Reading Strategy question: Summarize the final stanza to determine what it reveals about the speaker's struggle.
  Answer: The speaker nurtures and heals himself by communing with nature.

4 Hunger in New York City

Simon J. Ortiz

Hunger crawls into you
from somewhere out of your muscles
or the concrete or the land
or the wind pushing you.

It comes to you, asking
for food, words, wisdom, young memories
of places you ate at, drank cold spring water,
or held somebody's hand,
or home of the gentle, slow dances,
the songs, the strong gods, the world
you know.

That is, hunger searches you out.
It always asks you,
How are you, son? Where are you?
Have you eaten well?
Have you done what you as a person
of our people is supposed to do?

And the concrete of this city,
the oily wind, the blazing windows,
6 the shrieks of automation cannot,
truly cannot, answer for that hunger
although I have hungered,
truthfully and honestly, for them
to feed myself with.

So I sang to myself quietly:
I am feeding myself
with the humble presence
of all around me;
7 I am feeding myself
with your soul, my mother earth;
make me cool and humble.
Bless me.

5 ▲ Critical Viewing What words would you use to describe the emotions conveyed by both the poem and this photograph? **[Interpret]**

Vocabulary Builder

automation (ôt′ ə mā′ shən) *n.* manufacturing conducted with partly or fully self-operating machinery

Reading Strategy

Summarizing Summarize the final stanza to determine what it reveals about the speaker's struggle.

Enrichment

New York City

New York City covers 309 square miles at the mouth of the Hudson River in southeast New York State. The city includes Manhattan and Staten Islands, parts of Long Island, and the mainland north of Manhattan. New York consists of five sections called boroughs: Manhattan, the Bronx, Brooklyn, Queens, and Staten Island.

New York has the largest population of any city in the United States, nearly 7,500,000 people. Its population is the most varied and international of any U.S. city.

New York is nothing like it was years ago when Native Americans hunted and fished there. Today, New York's most common animal inhabitants are the cockroach and the Norway rat. But 80 species of fish and dozens of species of birds still live in New York, and mammals that live in New York include raccoons and opossums and even the occasional coyote.

8

What For

GARRETT HONGO

At six I lived for spells:
how a few Hawaiian words could call
up the rain, could hymn like the sea
in the long swirl of chambers
10 curling in the nautilus of a shell,[1]
how Amida's[2] ballads of the Buddhaland
in the drone of the priest's <u>liturgy</u>
could <u>conjure</u> money from the poor
and give them nothing but mantras,[3]
the strange syllables that healed desire.

1. **nautilus** (nôt′ əl əs) **of a shell** spiral of a seashell such as the chambered nautilus or paper nautilus.
2. **Amida's** (ä mēd ä) referring to Amida, the great savior worshiped by members of the Pure Land sect of Buddhism popular in eastern Asia.
3. **mantras** (män′ trəz) sacred words repeated in prayers, hymns, or chants.

9 ▲**Critical Viewing** In the poem's final stanza, what does the fragrant plumeria flower represent to the speaker? **[Analyze]**

Vocabulary Builder

liturgy (lit′ ər jē) *n.* public religious ceremonies; religious ritual

conjure (kän′ jər) *v.* summon by magic or as if by magic; call forth

8 About the Selection

In this poem, the speaker recalls childhood moments of waiting patiently for his father to come home from a physically demanding job and the fervent wish to use the power of his Japanese and Hawaiian heritage to ease his father's pain.

9 Critical Viewing

Answer: The plumeria flower is particularly fragrant, and the speaker equates the sweet smell of the flower with sweet words that he wishes could cure his father's aches and pains.

10 Critical Thinking

Infer

- Read aloud the bracketed stanza to students. Have them clarify what the speaker means by "spells." Have them point out other words in the stanza that support their responses, such as *liturgy, conjure,* and *mantras.*
- Then, **ask** students to decide what makes spells so powerful to the speaker.
  Answer: The speaker seems most impressed by the way words are used in spells to affect natural forces and people.

Differentiated Instruction

Solutions for All Learners

Background for English Learners
Ask students who are familiar with any of the items mentioned in the poem, such as the chambered nautilus, *hana* cards, volcanic soil, *pikake* flowers, and plumeria to describe these items to their classmates. Encourage students who are familiar with Buddhism to explain aspects of the religion that are mentioned in the poem.

Enrichment for Gifted/Talented Students
Have students learn the names of several plants and animals in Hawaiian and find out what they look like. Ask students to draw on their research to write, illustrate, and produce an illustrated glossary of Hawaiian flora and fauna.

Enrichment for Advanced Readers
Have students learn some Hawaiian words, for example the names of fruits and flowers. Encourage students to research the origins of the words. Then, have students teach their classmates several Hawaiian words.

11 Reading Strategy
Summarizing

- Have students read lines 24–40 to themselves. As they read, instruct them to record all the details that relate to the father's daily experience.
- Then, **ask** them the Reading Strategy question: Summarize the father's daily experience.
  Answer: The father works hard at a physically demanding job that is destroying his health and leaves him too tired at the end of a day to play with his child.

▶**Monitor Progress:** **Ask** students how they decided what information to include in the summary.
Answer: Students should understand that the important points in a passage should be included in a summary: in this case, the physical demands of the father's job and the effect his job has on him.

12 Literary Analysis
Voice

- Read aloud the bracketed stanza to students. Have students close their eyes as you read, and ask them to think about the effects of the speaker's words on them.
- Then, **ask** them the Literary Analysis question: In what way would you describe the speaker's voice in lines 41–46?
  Answer: The speaker's voice is straightforward and clear, as would be typical of a child. The speaker's longing is expressed in the first two words in the stanza: "I wanted." The poet uses two figures of speech in this stanza, a metaphor comparing hearing to crystal chimes and a simile comparing crystal chimes to "fins of glass."

13 Literary Analysis
Voice and Alienation

- Ask students to restate the meaning of the last stanza in their own words.
- Then, **ask** the Literary Analysis question: What is the speaker's desire in the last stanza of this poem?
  Answer: The speaker wants to be able to cure his father through the power of words.

I lived for stories about the war
my grandfather told over *hana* cards,[4]
slapping them down on the mats
with a sharp Japanese *kiai*.[5]

I lived for songs my grandmother sang
stirring curry into a thick stew,
weaving a calligraphy of Kannon's[6] love
into grass mats and straw sandals.

I lived for the red volcano dirt
staining my toes, the salt residue
of surf and sea wind in my hair,
the arc of a flat stone skipping
in the hollow trough of a wave.

I lived a child's world, waited
for my father to drag himself home,
dusted with blasts of sand, powdered rock,
and the strange ash of raw cement,
his deafness made worse by the clang
of pneumatic drills,[7] sore in his bones
11 from the buckings of a jackhammer.

He'd hand me a scarred lunchpail,
let me unlace the hightop G.I. boots,[8]
call him the new name I'd invented
that day in school, write it for him
on his newspaper. He'd rub my face
with hands that felt like gravel roads,
tell me to move, go play, and then he'd
walk to the laundry sink to scrub,
rinse the dirt of his long day
from a face brown and grained as koa wood.[9]

I wanted to take away the pain
in his legs, the swelling in his joints,
12 give him back his hearing,
clear and rare as crystal chimes,
the fins of glass that wrinkled
and sparked the air with their sound.

Vocabulary Builder
calligraphy (kə lig′ rə fē) *n.* artistic handwriting

Vocabulary Builder
trough (trôf) *n.* a low point of a wave

Reading Strategy
Summarizing Summarize the father's daily experience.

Literary Analysis
Voice In what way would you describe the speaker's voice in lines 41–46?

4. ***hana*** (hä′ nä) **cards** cards with flower patterns that players try to pair up in a popular Japanese card game. *Hana* is Japanese for "flower."
5. ***kiai*** (kē ī′) Japanese word for the sound made by slapping down *hana* cards.
6. **Kannon's** (kä′ nənz) referring to an enlightened savior of Japanese Buddhism who, out of infinite compassion and mercy, forgoes the heavenly state of nirvana in order to save others.
7. **pneumatic** (no͞o mat′ ik) **drills** air drills used in construction.
8. **hightop G.I. boots** army boots.
9. **koa** (kō′ ə) **wood** grainy wood of the Hawaiian acacia tree.

Enrichment

Noise Pollution
Noise pollution has been an unwanted side effect of the growth and development of cities and transportation systems.

The intensity of sound is commonly measured in logarithmic units called decibels. A change from a level of 10 decibels to 20 decibels represents a 100% increase in sound. Steady noise at 80 decibels is annoying, but steady exposure to 90 decibels or more—which is what the speaker's father experienced using a pneumatic drill—is dangerous. Besides causing hearing loss, such loud noises may have other bad effects on health and productivity at work.

Many large cities have tried to limit noise pollution—especially at airports—with limited success.

I wanted to heal the sores that work
and war had sent to him,
let him play catch in the backyard
with me, tossing a tennis ball
past papaya trees without the shoulders
of pain shrugging back his arms.

I wanted to become a doctor of pure magic,
to string a necklace of sweet words
fragrant as pine needles and plumeria,[10]
fragrant as the bread my mother baked,
place it like a lei of cowrie shells[11]
and *pikake*[12] flowers around my father's neck,
and chant him a blessing, a sutra.[13]

Literary Analysis
Voice and Alienation
What is the speaker's desire in the last stanza of this poem?

10. **plumeria** (plo͞o mer′ ē ə) tropical tree bearing flowers known for their fragrance.
11. **lei** (lā) **of cowrie** (kou′ rē) **shells** garland made of brightly colored seashells found in the South Pacific.
12. ***pikake*** (pē kä′ kā) Hawaiian word for jasmine, a fragrant flowering shrub.
13. **sutra** (so͞o′ trə) one of the sacred texts or scriptures of Buddhism.

Critical Reading

1. **Respond:** Do you think the speaker of "What For" had a happy childhood? Why or why not?
2. **(a) Recall:** In "Hunger in New York City," what four questions does hunger ask? **(b) Analyze:** What kind of hunger does the speaker mean?
3. **(a) Interpret:** What key words does the speaker use to paint a harsh portrait of New York City? **(b) Compare and Contrast:** In what ways is the city unlike the world the speaker has known—the world of his home?
4. **(a) Recall:** In the first four stanzas of "What For," what forms of communication did the speaker live for? **(b) Infer:** What do these forms of communication suggest about the child's relationship to adults?
5. **(a) Deduce:** From where did the father "drag himself home" each day? **(b) Analyze:** What values are expressed in the father's behavior?
6. **(a) Classify:** In what ways does the landscape of the poem change in the fifth stanza? **(b) Interpret:** Is this shift connected to the child's wish for the father in the final stanza? Explain.
7. **Evaluate:** Evaluate the title's relationship to the content of the poem. Is the title an effective one? Explain.

For: More about Simon J. Ortiz and Garrett Hongo
Visit: www.PHSchool.com
Web Code: ere-9616

ASSESS

Answers

1. Many students will feel that the speaker had a fairly happy childhood, but that he was sad about his father's aches and pains and his inability to spend much time with the speaker.
2. (a) Hunger asks these questions: How are you? Where are you? Have you eaten well? Have you done what you are supposed to do? (b) The hunger is for a connection to a person's cultural heritage and to nature.
3. (a) The poet uses the words "Concrete," "oily wind," "blazing windows," and "shrieks of automation" to describe New York City. (b) New York City is unlike the speaker's home because it holds no memories of the speaker's cultural heritage and connectedness with nature.
4. (a) The speaker lived for spells, stories, songs, and volcanic dirt. (b) Significant adults were very important to the child.
5. (a) He dragged himself home from work. (b) The behavior of the speaker's father expresses the values of working hard and not complaining or discussing difficulties.
6. (a) The landscape shifts from the speaker's world to his father's. (b) Yes, this shift permits readers to appreciate how hard the father works and how exhausted he is so that the speaker's wish in the last stanza makes sense.
7. The title asks a question that the poem answers by listing the things for which the speaker lived as a boy and describing how the father works to support the family. Most students will think that the title is effective because it addresses the central concerns of the poem.

Go Online Author Link For additional information about Simon Ortíz or Garrett Hongo, have students type in the Web Code, then select *O* or *H* from the alphabet, and then select Simon Ortíz or Garrett Hongo.

Answers

1. (a) Possible response for "Most Satisfied": Adjective: meditative; Evidence: the speaker is considering nature. (b) Another adjective would be *reverent*.

   Another sample answer can be found on **Literary Analysis Graphic Organizer B,** p. 257 in ***Graphic Organizer Transparencies.***
2. (a) The poet's descriptions of customs and use of his first language reflect his cultural background. (b) The poets' descriptions of physical labor reflect their working class backgrounds. Ortiz's longing for a connection with nature reflects the importance of nature to his heritage. The form of Chang's poem as well as her contemplation of nature may reflect her heritage.
3. (a) Ortiz expresses alienation. (b) Ortiz is alienated from the earth.
4. (a) These settings are all products of an industrial society. (b) The plant lets Espada earn money. It deprives him of the time to do other things. The city deprives Ortiz of his connection to nature. It presumably supplies him with a job and housing. The construction site deprives the speaker's father of his health. It permits him to earn a living.
5. Espada has not forgotten his background as he strives to get ahead. Hongo appreciates the sacrifices his family has made for him.
6. (a) The speaker relies on memories of a closer connection to nature for comfort. The speaker appreciates the labor of ordinary workers because he remembers his own efforts. (b) Rhyme, meter, and figurative language are lost.
7. (a) The speaker remembers the stories and songs that he heard, as well as his interaction with nature. (b)The speaker remembers the toll hard work took on his father and how he wished he could heal him. (c) The summaries reveal that the poem is divided roughly in half.
8. Students may mention various holiday celebrations, foods, dress, and other customs.

Apply the Skills

Who Burns for the Perfection of Paper • Most Satisfied by Snow • Hunger in New York City • What For

Literary Analysis

Voice

1. **(a)** Use a chart like the one shown to select the adjective that best describes each poet's **voice. (b)** Then, choose another adjective that additionally characterizes each poet's voice.

Adjectives: angry, meditative, remorseful, yearning, reverent

Poet	Voice	Evidence

→

Additional Adjectives

2. **(a)** What aspects of Hongo's voice reflect his culture? **(b)** In what ways do the voices of the other poets reflect their cultural backgrounds?

Comparing Literary Works

3. **(a)** Which of these poets express **alienation**? **(b)** In each case, what is the cause of that alienation?
4. **(a)** What traits do the printing plant, the urban setting, and the construction site share? **(b)** What do these settings bring to the speakers in these poems? What does each take away?
5. Simon Ortiz notes that the "hunger" asks "Have you done what you as a person / of our people is supposed to do?" How does this question apply to the poems by Espada and Hongo?

Reading Strategy

Summarizing

6. **(a)** Write a **summary** of "Hunger in New York City" and "Who Burns for the Perfection of Paper." **(b)** What poetic effects and meanings are lost in the summaries?
7. **(a)** Write a summary of stanzas 1–4 of "What For." **(b)** Write a summary of stanzas 5–8. **(c)** What do these summaries reveal to you about the poem's structure?

Extend Understanding

8. **Cultural Connection:** What aspects of American popular culture reflect the country's growing diversity?

QuickReview

Voice is a poet's distinctive literary personality, created by word choice, tone, sound devices, rhyme, pace, and attitude.

Alienation, a sense of detachment or separation from a group, is a common theme in American literature of the twentieth century.

To **summarize,** briefly restate the main points of a poem in a concise way.

For: Self-test
Visit: www.PHSchool.com
Web Code: era-6611

Go Online Assessment Students may use the **Self-test** to prepare for **Selection Test A** or **Selection Test B.**

Build Language Skills

Vocabulary Lesson

Word Analysis: Greek Prefix *auto-*

Explain how the meaning of *auto-*, defined as "self," is expressed in each of the following words:

1. automobile
2. autopilot
3. autograph
4. autobiography
5. automatic
6. autocratic

Spelling Strategy

The *shun* sound in a suffix is usually formed by the letters *sion* or *tion*, as in percus*sion* or automa*tion*. Add the suffix *-sion* or *-tion* to change each of the following verbs into a noun.

1. fascinate
2. extend
3. intervene
4. devote

Vocabulary Builder: Definitions

Choose the definition that best matches each numbered word.

1. trough **(a)** high point of a wave, **(b)** low point of a wave, **(c)** surf
2. conjure **(a)** quickly follow, **(b)** harshly criticize, **(c)** magically summon
3. calligraphy **(a)** bright tapestry, **(b)** intricate hairdo, **(c)** artistic handwriting
4. liturgy **(a)** a religious ritual, **(b)** dinner menu, **(c)** architectural blueprint
5. automation **(a)** electrification, **(b)** mechanization, **(c)** termination
6. crevices **(a)** gorges, **(b)** rivers, **(c)** narrow cracks
7. pervade **(a)** spread, **(b)** withdraw, **(c)** request

Grammar and Style Lesson

Participial Phrases

A **participial phrase** is a participle—a verb form that can be used as an adjective—and the words that modify or complete it. The entire phrase works as an adjective to modify a noun or a pronoun.

Present participle: My hands, *smoothing the exact rectangle*, would slide along the paper. (modifies *hands*)

Past participle: *Reminded of the experience*, he winced. (modifies *he*)

Practice Identify the participial phrase in each sentence. Determine the noun or pronoun it modifies.

1. Seeking an after-school job, I found one at a printing plant.
2. I worked hard, slipping cardboard between the papers.
3. Cut by sharp edges, my hands were often stinging.
4. The glue, oozing over them, made the stinging worse.
5. I can still visualize my hands, upturned in pain.

Writing Application Write a paragraph about a place you know or can picture, using the following participial phrases:

1. nestled among climbing roses
2. sitting beside the freeway
3. abandoned in the open lots

WG *Prentice Hall Writing and Grammar Connection: Chapter 19, Section 2*

Assessment Practice

Sentence Structure (For more practice, see *Standardized Test Preparation Workbook*, p. 68.)

Many tests require students to identify correctly written sentences that should be combined. Use the following sample item to demonstrate.

<u>Poets often do other work. They work to support themselves.</u> Among the members of most professions, you can find a poet or two.

Choose the best way to write the underlined section. If the underlined section needs no change, choose "Correct as is."

A Poets often do other work to support themselves.
B Poets often do other work, or they work to support themselves.
C Among the members of most professions, poets work to support themselves.
D Correct as is.

Students should recognize that choice *A* combines two choppy sentences, but maintains the sense of both.

Answers

1 Vocabulary Builder

Word Analysis

1. An automobile is a vehicle that is self-powered.
2. Autopilot is a system that lets a vehicle navigate itself.
3. An autograph is a signature that someone writes.
4. An autobiography is the story of a person's life told by him- or herself.
5. Something that is automatic works by itself.
6. Someone who is autocratic is self-ruled.

Spelling Strategy

1. fascination
2. extension
3. intervention
4. devotion

Vocabulary Builder

1. b
2. c
3. c
4. a
5. b
6. c
7. a

2 Grammar and Style Lesson

1. Seeking an after-school job; *I*
2. slipping cardboard between the papers; *I*
3. Cut by sharp edges; *hands*
4. oozing over them; *glue*
5. upturned in pain; *hands*

Writing Application

Students' paragraphs must include the three participial phrases.

WG **Writing and Grammar, Ruby Level**

Students will find further instruction and practice on participial phrases in Chapter 19, Section 2.

❸ Writing Lesson

You may use this Writing Lesson as timed-writing practice, or you may allow students to develop it as a writing assignment over several days.

- Give students the **Support for Writing Lesson**, p. 191 in ***Unit 6 Resources***, to use as they write their comparison-and-contrast essays.
- Suggest that students use the Venn Diagram organizer, p. 316 in ***Graphic Organizer Transparencies.***
- Discuss with students the views of childhood portrayed in "Who Burns" and "What For."
- Explain that students will write comparisons of the messages about childhood and adolescence in these poems and the means the poets use to relay their messages.
- Remind students that they are to take notes on the language, meaning, and structure of both poems and then compare the two poems.
- Go over the model with students so that they understand how to revise their own work to make the modifiers as precise as possible.
- Use the Comparison-and-Contrast Essay rubrics on pp. 69–70 of **General Resources** to evaluate students' work.

❹ Listening and Speaking

- Suggest that students work in small groups to interview someone about his or her heritage.
- Have students find out as much as they can beforehand about the person's background so that their interviews can be as focused as possible. Remind students to let the interviewee talk—silence while the person considers a question is fine.
- The **Support for Extend Your Learning** page (***Unit 6 Resources,*** p. 192) provides guided note-taking opportunities to help students complete the Extend Your Learning activities.

Go Online Research — Have students type in the Web Code for another research activity.

❸ Writing Lesson

Timed Writing: Comparison-and-Contrast Essay

The poems by Hongo and Espada present childhood and adolescence in distinctly different ways. In a comparison-and-contrast essay, evaluate the sensory images each poem uses to convey the speaker's memories. Compare and contrast the nature of the wisdom each speaker gains in adulthood. ***(40 minutes)***

Prewriting *(10 minutes)* Reread each poem, and take notes about its language, images, meaning, and structure. Then compare how each poem portrays its speaker's memories.

Drafting *(20 minutes)* Introduce the poets and summarize the poems. Then, state your main ideas about the way each poem portrays childhood or adolescence. As you draft, include precise modifiers—adjectives and adverbs—that clearly express praise or criticism.

Revising *(10 minutes)* Review your essay to make sure you have expressed your points about each poem with clarity and conviction. Identify any weak or unclear modifiers and replace them with stronger choices.

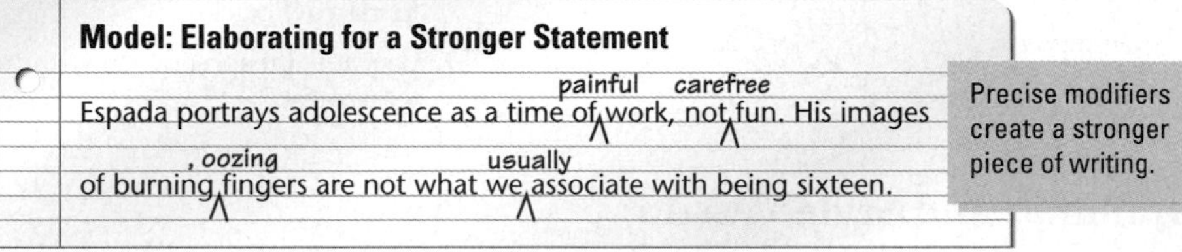

Model: Elaborating for a Stronger Statement
painful carefree
Espada portrays adolescence as a time of work, not fun. His images
, oozing usually
of burning fingers are not what we associate with being sixteen.
Precise modifiers create a stronger piece of writing.

Prentice Hall Writing and Grammar Connection: Chapter 14, Section 4

❹ Extend Your Learning

Listening and Speaking You probably know someone whose life centers around his or her cultural heritage. With a classmate, conduct an **interview** with such a person. To prepare, use the following tips:

- Develop questions to establish the subject's background and personal history.
- Create a list of suitable follow-up questions.

Videotape or record the interview to share with classmates. **[Group Activity]**

Research and Technology Locate and gather Asian poetry in English translation, using library or Internet resources. Create an **anthology** of these poems. In a brief introduction to your anthology, explain how Diana Chang's "Most Satisfied by Snow" demonstrates the influence of Asian verse.

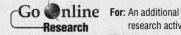

For: An additional research activity
Visit: www.PHSchool.com
Web Code: erd-7611

Assessment Resources

The following resources can be used to assess students' knowledge and skills.

Unit 6 Resources
Selection Test A, pp. 194–196
Selection Test B, pp. 197–199

General Resources
Rubrics for Comparison-and-Contrast Essay, pp. 69–70

Go Online Assessment — Students may use the **Self-test** to prepare for **Selection Test A** or **Selection Test B.**

Unit 6 Part 2

Focus on Literary Forms: Essays

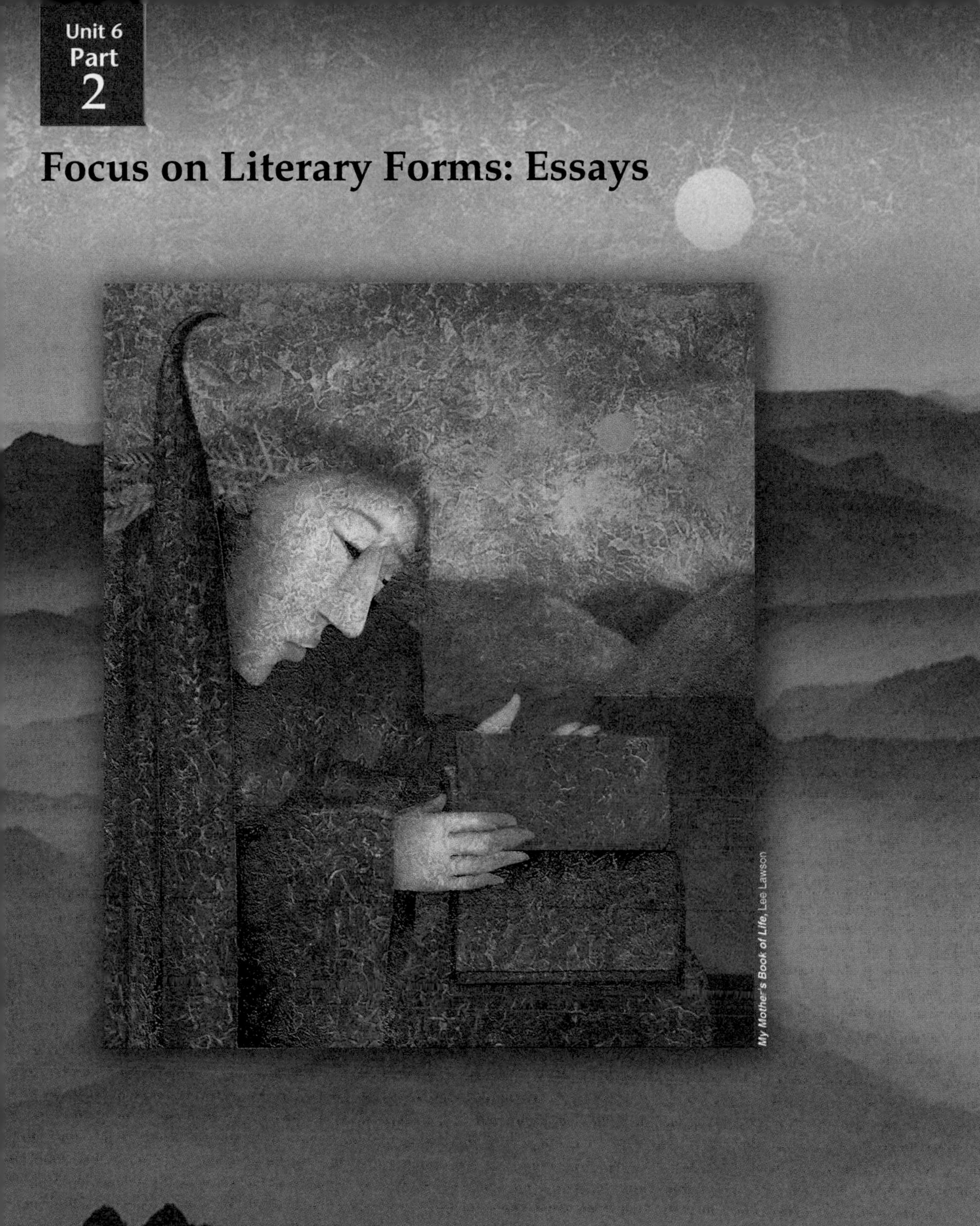

Differentiated Instruction

Solutions for All Learners

Accessibility at a Glance

More Accessible	Average	More Challenging
Onomatopoeia	Coyote v. Acme	Loneliness . . . An American Malady
For the Love of Books	Straw Into Gold	
	Mother Tongue	
	One Day, Broken in Two	

Selection Planning Guide

The selections in this section offer students a sampling of a wide range of styles and subjects. Carson McCullers's "Loneliness . . . An American Malady" addresses the issue of loneliness. Safire's expository essay "Onomatopoeia" presents an interesting segment of language. Frazier's satirical "Coyote v. Acme" takes a humorous look at the court system. Reflective essays by Cisneros, Dove, and Tan address each author's thoughts about life.

Humanities

My Mother's Book of Life, 1987, by Lee Lawson

Encourage students to contrast this painting with *Television Moon* (p. 979), which introduced Part 1. Help them to see not only the difference in subject matter—a real moon, as opposed to a televised one, along with a human being reading—but also the differences in style. This painting has visible texture, which softens the edges of the images, as opposed to the hard, almost photographic quality of *Television Moon.*

Use these questions for discussion:

1. What mood would you say this painting creates, and how?
   Possible answer: The painting creates a quiet, reflective, tender mood through the use of soft colors and interesting textures and through its title.
2. An essay is a highly personal form of literature, directly expressing the author's thoughts, feelings, and opinions. What do you feel this painting reveals about its creator?
   Possible answer: The artist expresses love for a mother who cherished books and natural beauty.

Benchmark

After students have completed the grouping of essays by Sandra Cisneros, Rita Dove, and Amy Tan, administer **Benchmark Test 10.** If the Benchmark Test reveals that some students need further work, use the **Interpretation Guide** to determine the appropriate reteaching pages in the **Reading Kit** or on **Success Tracker.**

Meeting Your Standards

Students will

1. **recognize and appreciate the types and elements of essays.**
2. **apply strategies for reading essays.**

❶ Classifying Essays by Tone

- Tell students that in Part 2 they will focus on essays. **Ask:** What makes essays different from other types of nonfiction writing?
- **Possible answer:** Essays explore a small aspect of a subject rather than treat it extensively. Although they are not fiction, they often contain anecdotes as well as the author's thoughts, feelings, or opinions.
- Introduce students to the two main categories in which they can classify essays. Clarify the distinctions between formal and informal essays. Tell students that essays can cover a wide range of topics, tone, and appeal; essays can be political, personal, humorous, or serious. They can be persuasive, informative, critical, or narrative.
- Suggest that students refer to these pages as they read the essays in Part 2.

❷ Classifying Essays by Purpose

- Review and clarify with students the different purposes for writing essays. Review and discuss the examples shown.
- Reinforce the idea that a writer may have more than one purpose for writing an essay or may use multiple essay styles to achieve one purpose. In such cases, a writer may combine elements from more than one category to make a point.

Focus on Literary Forms

Defining Essays

An **essay** is a brief nonfiction work about a specific subject. The term was first used in 1580 by the French philosopher Michel de Montaigne, who published a collection of short prose pieces entitled *Essais.* The French word means "attempts" or "tries," and Montaigne used the title to suggest that his discussions were casual explorations of a subject, rather than thorough interpretations. That quality of inquisitive exploration remains a defining feature of the essay form.

THE ESSAY IS A LITERARY DEVICE FOR SAYING ALMOST EVERYTHING ABOUT ALMOST ANYTHING. —*Aldous Huxley*

Classifying Essays by Tone

Essays are often divided into two main categories, according to the writer's general **tone,** or attitude toward the subject matter or reader:

- **Formal essays** use a serious tone and often analyze public issues or philosophical topics. "The Crisis, Number 1" by Thomas Paine, page 174, and "Self-Reliance" by Ralph Waldo Emerson, page 393, are examples of formal essays.
- **Informal essays,** also called **personal essays,** use a casual tone and explore everyday topics in a conversational style. They may use a loose structure, circling around a topic and developing ideas in an indirect way. "Here Is New York" by E. B. White, page 903, and "Mother Tongue" by Amy Tan, page 1172, are examples of informal essays.

Classifying Essays by Purpose

Within these two broad categories, essays can be further classified according to the writer's **purpose:** for example, to inform, to persuade, to tell a story, to convey a sense of place, or to analyze an idea.

- A **persuasive essay** (sometimes called an **argumentative essay**) tries to get readers to accept the writer's opinion about an issue or to take a course of action. **Example:** "Civil Disobedience" by Henry David Thoreau, page 416.
- A **descriptive essay** uses sensory details to present a portrait of a person, a place, or an object. **Example:** "Nature" by Ralph Waldo Emerson, page 390.

Extend the Lesson

Activity

- Read aloud the fourth paragraph of "Mother Tongue" on p. 1173, beginning with "Just last week . . ."
- **Ask** students the following questions:
  1. What is the tone of the essay?
     Answer: The tone is conversational and casual.
  2. What is the purpose of the essay?
     Answer: The essay probably was written to show the kinds of language the writer uses with her family.
  3. Predict the content of the essay.
     Answer: The essay will probably have examples of how people use language.

- A **narrative essay** tells a true story about real people. **Example:** Introduction to *Frankenstein* by Mary Shelley, page 379.

This way of classifying essays is loose at best, since essayists often combine different types of writing to achieve their overall purpose. For example, a descriptive essay might also be making a persuasive argument, while a persuasive essay might contain narrative anecdotes to drive home its arguments.

3 Classifying Essays by Content

Essays are also frequently classified according to their topic or the writer's approach to that topic. The chart on this page shows some categories.

Once again, these essay categories frequently overlap—both with one another and with the other classification labels for essays. For example, an autobiographical essay is a type of narrative essay, and it may also be humorous. A persuasive essay may also be considered a satirical essay if it uses satire in its attempt to persuade.

Type of Essay	Example
An **autobiographical essay** tells about the writer's own life.	"Straw Into Gold" by Sandra Cisneros, p. 1164
An **analytical essay** explores a topic by breaking it down into parts.	"Loneliness . . . An American Malady" by Carson McCullers, p. 1153
A **reflective essay** shares the writer's personal thoughts and feelings about a topic.	"One Day, Now Broken in Two" by Anna Quindlen, p. 1156
A **humorous essay** presents a topic in an amusing way.	"The Night the Ghost Got In" by James Thurber, p. 898
A **satirical essay** uses irony, ridicule, sarcasm, or parody to comment on a topic.	"Coyote v. Acme" by Ian Frazier, p. 1148

4 Strategies for Reading Essays

Use these strategies as you read essays.

Identify the Author's Purpose As you read an essay, think about the writer's purpose, or reason for writing. Understanding what the writer is trying to accomplish will help you interpret the essay and evaluate its effectiveness.

Identify the Author's Thesis As you read, look for the author's **main idea,** or **thesis**—the essential point of the essay. Then, notice the ways in which the writer develops and supports this central idea.

Analyze the Writer's Tone Listen to the writer's tone. Consider whether the writer is being serious or playful, gentle or bitter, sympathetic or hostile. Often, "hearing" the tone of an essay is the key to understanding its meaning.

3 Classifying Essays by Content

- Refer to the chart to discuss information about classifying essays according to their topics.
- Point out that students have already encountered some of these types of essays, such as autobiography and satire.
  Ask students why it may be beneficial to classify essays by content.
  Answer: Two or more essays may have the same purpose and tone yet discuss different topics. Classifying by content provides another trait with which to identify and analyze an essay.

4 Strategies for Reading Essays

- Tell students that they will need to analyze an essay in order to fully understand its meaning.
- Suggest that students consider the authors purpose as they read an essay.
- Remind students that a thesis may not be stated outright; it may be implied by the writer.
- A writer's tone may be determined by reading aloud parts of an essay. Demonstrate this by reading the first paragraph of "Onomatopoeia" on page 1146.

Meeting Your Standards

Students will

1. **analyze and respond to literary elements.**
   - Literary Analysis: Essay
2. **read, comprehend, analyze, and critique nonfiction.**
   - Reading Strategy: Identifying a Line of Reasoning
   - Reading Check questions
   - Apply the Skills questions
   - Assessment Practice (ATE)
3. **develop vocabulary.**
   - Vocabulary Lesson: Latin Root: *-ten-*
4. **understand and apply written and oral language conventions.**
   - Spelling Strategy
   - Grammar and Style Lesson: Pronouns with Appositives
5. **develop writing proficiency.**
   - Writing Lesson: Parody
6. **develop appropriate research strategies.**
   - Extend Your Learning: Essay
7. **understand and apply listening and speaking strategies.**
   - Extend Your Learning: Opening Statement

Block Scheduling: Use one 90-minute class period to preteach the skills and have students read the selections. Use a second 90-minute class period to assess students' mastery of skills, extend their learning, and monitor their progress.

Homework Suggestions

Following are possibilities for homework assignments:

- Support pages from *Unit 6 Resources:*
  Literary Analysis
  Reading Strategy
  Vocabulary Builder
  Grammar and Style
- An Extend Your Learning project and the Writing Lesson for this selection group may be completed over several days.

Step-by-Step Teaching Guide	Pacing Guide
PRETEACH	
• Administer Vocabulary and Reading Warm-ups as necessary.	5 min.
• Engage students' interest with the motivation activity.	5 min.
• Read and discuss author and background features. **FT**	10 min.
• Introduce the Literary Analysis skill: Essay **FT**	5 min.
• Introduce the Reading Strategy: Identifying Line of Reasoning **FT**	10 min.
• Prepare students to read by teaching the selection vocabulary. **FT**	
TEACH	
• Informally monitor comprehension while students read independently or in groups. **FT**	30 min.
• Monitor students' comprehension with the Reading Check notes.	as students read
• Reinforce vocabulary with Vocabulary Builder notes.	as students read
• Develop students' understanding of the essay with the Literary Analysis annotations. **FT**	5 minutes
• Develop students' ability to identify line of reasoning with the Reading Strategy annotations. **FT**	5 minutes
ASSESS/EXTEND	
• Assess students' comprehension and mastery of the Literary Analysis and Reading Strategy by having them answer the Apply the Skills questions. **FT**	15 min.
• Have students complete the Vocabulary Lesson and the Grammar and Style Lesson. **FT**	15 min.
• Apply students' ability to write a parody by using the Writing Lesson. **FT**	45 min. or homework
• Apply students' understanding using one or more of the Extend Your Learning activities.	20–90 min. or homework
• Administer Selection Test A or Selection Test B. **FT**	15 min.

Resources

PRINT
Unit 6 Resources

TRANSPARENCY
Graphic Organizer Transparencies

PRINT
Reader's Notebook [L2]
Reader's Notebook: Adapted Version [L1]
Reader's Notebook: English Learner's Version [EL]
Unit 6 Resources

TECHNOLOGY
Listening to Literature Audio CDs [L2, EL]

PRINT
Unit 6 Resources

General Resources

TECHNOLOGY
Go Online: Research **[L3]**
Go Online: Self-test **[L3]**
***ExamView*® Test Bank [L3]**

Choosing Resources for Differentiated Instruction

[L1] Special Needs Students
[L2] Below-Level Students
[L3] All Students
[L4] Advanced Students
[EL] English Learners

For Vocabulary and Reading Warm-ups and for Selection Tests, **A** signifies "less challenging" and **B** "more challenging." For Graphic Organizer transparencies, **A** signifies "not filled in" and **B** "filled in."

FT Fast Track Instruction: To move the lesson more quickly, use the strategies and activities identified with **FT**.

Scaffolding for Less Proficient and Advanced Students

The leveled Critical Thinking questions after selections progress in the levels of thinking required to answer them. To address the needs of your different students, you may use the (a) level questions for your less proficient students and the (b) level questions with your on-level and advanced students. The occasional (c) level questions are appropriate for your advanced students.

PRENTICE HALL **TeacherEXPRESS**™ Plan Teach Assess — Use this complete suite of powerful teaching tools to make lesson planning and testing quicker and easier.

PRENTICE HALL **StudentEXPRESS**™ Learn Study Succeed — Use the interactive textbook (online and on CD-ROM) to make selections and activities come alive with audio and video support and interactive questions.

Go Online Professional Development — **For:** Information about Lexiles **Visit:** www.PHSchool.com **Web Code:** eue-1111

PREPARE

Motivation

As you show a Roadrunner cartoon to the class, ask students to count the times Coyote meets with disaster. Ask students to draw a few conclusions about Coyote as a predator. (Students will probably decide he is incompetent.) Then, ask for student reaction to the cartoon. Point out that essays—like cartoons, movies, or advertisements—generate a variety of responses. Invite students to be open to the range of expression this genre, and this grouping, offers.

❶ Background
More About the Authors

In addition to his "On Language" column, William Safire has published a number of books. His 1975 book, *Before the Fall,* describes the pre-Watergate White House. His *New Language of Politics* is considered the definitive study on the language of politics.

Ian Frazier has a great love for the American West. In an interview, he said of the West, "I'm afraid of people thinking, 'There's nothing out there anyway, so let's ruin it.' There's an idea of the Plains as the middle of nowhere, something to be contemptuous of. But it's really a heroic place."

Best-selling author Anna Quindlen has written two children's books. *Happily Ever After* tells the tale of a young girl's foray into fairy tale life. *The Tree That Came to Stay* is a whimsical look at one family's attempt to capture the spirit of Christmas.

In all McCullers's works, which fit in the category of Southern gothic, characters suffer from physical and psychological problems, perhaps reflecting the author's own difficulties.

Build Skills *Essays*

❶ Onomatopoeia • Coyote v. Acme • Loneliness . . . An American Malady • One Day, Now Broken in Two

William Safire (b. 1929)

When it comes to questions about the use—and misuse—of the English language, few people have more answers or observations than William Safire. A political columnist for the *New York Times* until his retirement in 2005, Safire continues to write the *Times* magazine's "On Language" column and is one of the world's most widely read writers on language. The 1978 Pulitzer Prize winner for Distinguished Commentary, Safire was once a speech writer for the Nixon White House. He has written many books on language, including his most recent collection of "On Language" columns, *The Right Word in the Right Place at the Right Time* (2004).

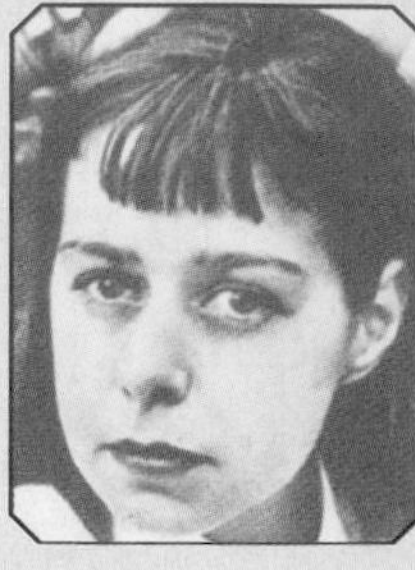

Carson McCullers (1917–1967)

Carson McCullers, whose writing has been praised as a brilliant fusion of the compassionate and the grotesque, led a troubled life marked by serious health problems. She was raised in Columbus, Georgia, a town that later formed the backdrop for all her fiction. At the age of seventeen, McCullers moved to New York, and while still in her twenties, she suffered a series of strokes. In later years, partial paralysis confined her to a wheelchair, yet she still managed to type new manuscripts. Her loneliness and suffering are reflected in her novels, which include *The Heart Is a Lonely Hunter* (1940) and *The Member of the Wedding* (1946), which was made into a movie.

Ian Frazier (b. 1951)

Ian Frazier was born in Cleveland, Ohio, and now lives in New York City, where he works as a staff writer for *The New Yorker* magazine. Known for both humorous essays and affectionate descriptions of rural and urban America, Frazier brings "an antic sense of fun" to much of his work. His books include *Dating Your Mom* (1986), *Nobody Better, Better Than Nobody* (1987), *Family* (1994), *Coyote v. Acme* (1996), and *On the Rez* (2000). "Coyote v. Acme" is typical of his work: a ludicrous premise packaged in serious style.

Anna Quindlen (b. 1953)

Anna Quindlen was a *New York Times* reporter when the paper asked her to write a weekly column in 1986. "Life in the '30s" was a popular feature for more than two years. Her next *Times* column, "Public and Private," won the Pulitzer Prize for Commentary in 1992. Quindlen's nonfiction books include *Living Out Loud* (1988) and *Loud and Clear* (2004), and her novels include *One True Thing* (1994), which was made into a movie, and *Blessings* (2002). She currently writes a column for *Newsweek* magazine called "The Last Word."

Preview

Connecting to the Literature

Perhaps you explore subjects that matter to you, such as friendship or creativity, in a journal. Some writers use a more public form of writing—the essay—to discuss ideas they find important.

❷ Literary Analysis

Essay

An **essay** is a short piece of nonfiction in which a writer expresses a personal view on a topic. The many types of essays include

- the **analytical essay,** which breaks down and interprets various elements of a topic.
- the **expository essay,** which explains a topic.
- the **satirical essay,** which uses irony, ridicule, parody, or sarcasm to comment on a topic.
- the **reflective essay,** which explores the meaning of a personal experience or pivotal event.

Look for the elements in these essays that will help you decide how to classify each one.

Comparing Literary Works

These different types of essays illustrate the flexibility of the essay form. Yet their greatest difference lies in their **tone,** the author's attitude toward the subject or audience. You can hear that tone—humorous, critical, or serious—in each writer's choice of words and details. As you read, note how each essay's tone contributes to its structure and meaning.

❸ Reading Strategy

Identifying a Line of Reasoning

When presenting an argument, an essayist offers a **line of reasoning** to convince readers of the soundness of his or her ideas. As you read these essays, identify the key points and note the reasons, facts, and examples that support them. Record each line of reasoning, and its evidence, in a chart like the one shown.

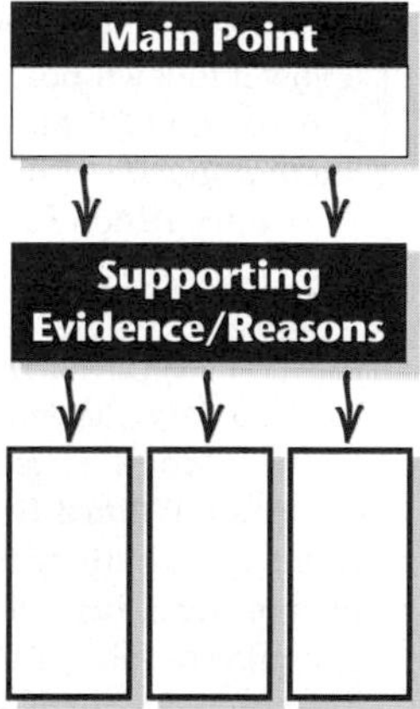

Vocabulary Builder

contiguous (kən tig′ yo͞o əs) *adj.* bordering; adjacent (p. 1148)

precipitate (prē sip′ ə tit) *adj.* very sudden (p. 1149)

caveat (kā′ vē at′) *n.* formal notice; warning (p. 1149)

tensile (ten′ sil) *adj.* stretchable (p. 1151)

pristine (pris′ tēn) *adj.* pure; uncorrupted (p. 1154)

corollary (kôr′ ə ler′ ē) *n.* easily drawn conclusion (p. 1154)

aesthetic (es thet′ ik) *adj.* pertaining to the study or theory of beauty (p. 1154)

maverick (mav′ ər ik) *n.* nonconformist (p. 1154)

❷ Literary Analysis

Essay

- Tell students that they should label each essay one of the following: an analytical essay, an expository essay, a satirical essay, or a reflective essay. As they read, they should compare the tone of the essays, and the author's attitude toward the subject, characters, and audience.
- Discuss the instruction under Literary Analysis on this page. If possible, select a model of each type of essay and read aloud several paragraphs from each one. Then, decide as a class how to classify each excerpt.

❸ Reading Strategy

Identifying a Line of Reasoning

- Explain to students that they should use a chart similar to the one on this page to record the main points that the essayists make, as well as the evidence and the arguments they provide that support those points.
- Remind students that evidence can include reasons, facts, examples, and relationships of cause and effect.
- Give students a copy of **Reading Strategy Graphic Organizer A,** p. 258, in ***Graphic Organizer Transparencies*** to use as they read the essays.

Vocabulary Builder

- Pronounce each vocabulary word for students, and read the definitions as a class. Have students identify any words with which they are already familiar.

Differentiated Instruction

Solutions for All Learners

Support for Special Needs Students
Have students complete the **Preview** and **Build Skills** pages for these selections in the ***Reader's Notebook: Adapted Version.*** These pages provide a selection summary, an abbreviated presentation of the reading and literary skills, and the graphic organizer on the **Build Skills** page in the student book.

Support for Less Proficient Readers
Have students complete the **Preview** and **Build Skills** pages for the selections in the ***Reader's Notebook.*** These pages provide a selection summary, an abbreviated presentation of the reading and literary skills, and the graphic organizer on the **Build Skills** page in the student book.

Support for English Learners
Have students complete the **Preview** and **Build Skills** pages for the selections in the ***Reader's Notebook: English Learner's Version.*** These pages provide a selection summary, an abbreviated presentation of the skills, and the graphic organizer on the **Build Skills** page in the student book.

Learning Modalities Musical/Rhythmic Learners
Remind students that loneliness is a prime topic for songwriters. Many songs, in styles as varied as rock, jazz, and country and western, focus on the speaker's isolation. Invite students to share favorites, prompting them with classics such as The Beatles' "Eleanor Rigby."

❶ About the Selection

This expository essay explains the origin and meaning of *onomatopoeia.* As a linguistic tool, onomatopoeia—"words that are made by people making sounds like the action to be described"—has proved appealing to writers, both serious and commercial, as well as to readers and consumers, for centuries. In recounting some history and applications of onomatopoeia, Safire humorously confirms the extraordinary power of words and sounds to engage the human mind.

❷ Humanities

Blam, 1962, by Roy Lichtenstein
This illustration depicts a cartoon character ejecting from an exploding airplane and features an onomatopoetic word—*BLAM.*

The artist, Roy Lichtenstein, was born and raised in New York City, where in his boyhood he was a fan of science and science fiction. He studied at the Art Students League and later with Hoyt Sherman at Ohio State University.

Use these questions for discussion:

1. How is the word *BLAM* an example of the onomatopoetic effects explained in this essay?
Answer: It imitates the sound of the explosion as it might be heard in the viewer's ears.
2. According to the essay, why are words and images like those in the painting so enduring?
Answer: They engage the human imagination through multiple senses.

❸ Critical Viewing

Answer: *Blam* conveys the sound of the exploding plane.

❶ ONOMATOPOEIA

William Safire

Background The vocabulary of English is the largest of any language in the world. English readily incorporates new words from a wide variety of sources, including borrowing them from other languages. William Safire, a former presidential speechwriter, describes another way in which English evolves. According to Safire, when we consider onomatopoeia—the figure of speech in which a word sounds like what it means—we discover that new words are not just based on what we experience, but on what we merely imagine.

❷

Blam, 1962, Roy Lichtenstein

❹ The word *onomatopoeia* was used above, and it had better be spelled right or one usage dictator and six copy editors will get zapped. That word is based on the Greek for "word making"—the *poe* is the same as in *poetry,* "something made"—and is synonymous with *imitative* and *echoic,* denoting words that are made by people making sounds like the action to be described. (The *poe* in *onomatopoeia* has its own rule for pronunciation. Whenever a vowel follows *poe,* the *oe* combination is pronounced as a long *e: onomato-PEE-ia.* Whenever a consonant follows, as in *poetry* and *onomatopoetic,* pronounce the long *o* of Edgar Allan's name.)

Henry Peacham, in his 1577 book on grammar and rhetoric called *The Garden of Eloquence,* first used *onomatopoeia* and defined it as "when we invent, devise, fayne, and make a name intimating the sound of that it signifieth, as *hurlyburly,* for an uprore and tumultuous stirre." He also gave *flibergib* to "a gossip," from which we derive *flibbertigibbet,* and the long-lost *clapperclaw* and *kickle-kackle.*

Since Willard Espy borrowed the title of Peacham's work for his rhetorical bestiary in 1983, the author went beyond the usual examples of *buzz, hiss, bobwhite* and *babble.* He pointed out that one speculation about the origin of language was the *bow-wow theory,* holding that words originated in imitation of natural sounds of animals and thunder. (Proponents of the *pooh-pooh theory* argued that

❸ ▲ **Critical Viewing**
What meaning does the onomatopoeia *Blam* convey in this image? **[Analyze]**

Differentiated Instruction Solutions for All Learners

Accessibility at a Glance

	Onomatopoeia	Coyote v. Acme	Loneliness . . . An American Malady	One Day, Now Broken in Two
Language	Accessible	Subject-specific (legal terminology)	Formal	Vocabulary covered in footnotes
Concept Level	Accessible (examination of language)	Challenging (satire)	Challenging (examination of emotion)	Accessible (impact of 9–11)
Literary Merit	High-interest	High-interest	Noted author	High-interest
Lexile	1320L	1520L	1320L	1060L
Overall Rating	Accessible	Average	Challenging	Average

interjections like *ow!* and *oof!* started us all yakking toward language. Other theories—arrgh!—abound.)

Reaching for an alliterative onomatope, the poet Milton chose "melodious *murmurs*;" Edgar Allan Poe one-upped him with "the *tintinnabulation* of the bells." When carried too far, an obsession with words is called *onomatomania;* in the crunch (a word imitating the sound of an icebreaker breaking through ice) Gertrude Stein turned into an *onomatomaniac.*

What makes a word like *zap* of particular interest is that it imitates an imaginary noise—the sound of a paralyzing ray gun. Thus we can see another way that the human mind creates new words: imitating what can be heard only in the mind's ear. The coinage filled a need for an unheard sound and—*pow!*—slammed the vocabulary right in the kisser. Steadily, surely, under the watchful eye of great lexicographers and with the encouragement of columnists and writers who ache for color in verbs, the creation of Buck Rogers's creator has blasted its way into the dictionaries. The verb will live long after superpowers agree to ban ray guns; no sound thunders or crackles like an imaginary sound turned into a new word.

Took me a while to get to the point today, but that is because I did not know what the point was when I started.

"I now zap all the commercials," says the merry Ellen Goodman. "I zap to the memory of white tornadoes past. I zap headaches, arthritis, bad breath and laundry detergent. I zap diet-drink maidens and hand-lotion mavens . . . Wiping out commercials could entirely and joyfully upend the TV industry. Take the word of The Boston Zapper."

Literary Analysis
Essay What kind of essay do you think Safire is writing? Explain.

Critical Reading

1. **Respond:** Had you ever noticed the connection between the onomatopoetic words Safire discusses and the sounds they describe?
2. **(a) Recall:** What is onomatopoeia? **(b) Classify:** What is the origin of this word?
3. **(a) Recall:** What is the *bow-wow theory* concerning the origin of language? **(b) Compare and Contrast:** Compare and contrast it with the *pooh-pooh theory* of language. **(c) Make a Judgment:** Do you think either of these terms is actually used by linguists? Explain.
4. **(a) Recall:** What does Safire find so interesting about the word *zap*? **(b) Analyze:** Why does he believe that this word will "live long after superpowers agree to ban ray guns"?
5. **(a) Infer:** Based on Safire's comment, what would you expect to find in Gertrude Stein's writing? **(b) Infer:** How do you think Safire views the use of onomatopoeia by writers?
6. **Evaluate:** Do you think Safire's humorous style is more or less effective than a factual explanation? Explain.

For: More about William Safire
Visit: www.PHSchool.com
Web Code: ere-9621

4 Literary Analysis
Essay

- Read the bracketed passage aloud, and **ask** the Literary Analysis question: What kind of essay do you think Safire is writing? Explain.
  Answer: Safire is writing an expository essay because the essay explains the origin of the word *onomatopoeia.*

ASSESS

Answers

1. Many students will have learned about onomatopoetic words in earlier grades and will have explored the connections between onomatopoetic words and the sounds they describe.
2. (a) Onomatopoeia is the use of words whose sounds suggest their meaning. (b) The word comes from the Greek for "word making."
3. (a) The "bow-wow theory" posits that words began as people imitated natural sounds.
   (b) The "pooh-pooh theory" holds that interjections started people on the path toward language. (c) Most students will say that these theories probably have more official or scholarly names that linguists use.
4. (a) Safire thinks zap is particularly interesting because the word imitates an imaginary noise.
   (b) He thinks that the word has enough power that it will live on.
5. (a) Based on Safire's comment, one would expect to find many onomatopoetic words in Stein's writing. (b) Safire seems to enjoy the use of onomatopoeia by writers.
6. Many students will find Safire's humorous style an appropriate and enjoyable way to learn about a topic such as onomatopoeia. Students may point out that the amusing examples Safire uses will help them remember the information he presents.

Go Online Author Link For additional information about William Safire, have students type in the Web Code, then select *S* from the alphabet, and then William Safire.

Enrichment

Buck Rogers

Buck Rogers made his first appearance in a comic strip in *Amazing Stories* in the late 1920s. In 1934, the first Buck Rogers movie appeared—*Buck Rogers in the 25th Century.* In this 10-minute-long film, Buck and Wilma Deering battle the Tiger Men of Mars. The movie, with its cliffhanger ending that clearly indicated that the short film was the first in a series, was a great hit at the 1935 World's Fair in Chicago.

During the latter part of the 1930s, Buster Crabbe starred in twelve Buck Rogers serials. As in the comic book, Buck awakens in the 25th century and battles various villains, including the terrifying Killer Kane.

❺ About the Selection

Most students will find this satirical take on a legal brief amusing and enjoyable. The fictional defendant, Wile E. Coyote of cartoon fame, becomes an outraged victim whose terrible injuries are listed in great detail. This "brief's" lambaste of the Acme Company for its supposed negligence presents a scathing—but hilarious—commentary on the litigious relationship that exists between consumers and business.

❻ Critical Thinking

Interpret/Assess

- Have a volunteer explain why the beginning of the essay takes the form it does. What are a plaintiff and a defendant? What does *v.* mean?
  Answer: Students should understand that the essay takes the form of a legal brief, and begins as an actual legal brief would by listing the court, case number, and judge, as well as the plaintiff (the party who has initiated the lawsuit) and the defendant (the party against which the action has been brought). The *v.* stands for *versus,* which means "against."
- **Ask** students to discuss the effect this opening has on the reader.
  Answer: The legal heading establishes the tone and purpose of the rest of the piece.

❼ Reading Strategy

Identifying Line of Reasoning

- Have a volunteer read this page.
- **Ask** students what line of reasoning the brief will employ to make its case for an award of damages to the plaintiff, Wile E. Coyote.
  Answer: The brief will provide details that support the claim that negligence by the Acme Company caused injuries and loss of income to the plaintiff.

❺

COYOTE V. ACME

Ian Frazier

Background This essay is the fictional opening statement of a lawsuit by Mr. Wile E. Coyote, charging the Acme Company with the sale of defective merchandise. If these names sound familiar, you may have a childhood memory of watching Wile E. Coyote chase the Road Runner around the desert. The Warner Brothers cartoon "Road Runner and Coyote" made its debut in 1949; more than half a century later, both the coyote and the elusive bird are still going strong. Perhaps fifty years from now your grandchildren will be watching Coyote's ill-fated attempts—many involving Acme products—to capture the fleet-footed bird. As you read the essay, consider what Frazier is really satirizing—the cartoon character who is his subject or the legal profession.

❻

In the United States District Court,
Southwestern District,
Tempe, Arizona
Case No. B19294,
Judge Joan Kujava, Presiding

WILE E. COYOTE, Plaintiff
—v.—
ACME COMPANY, Defendant

❼

Opening Statement of Mr. Harold Schoff, attorney for Mr. Coyote: My client, Mr. Wile E. Coyote, a resident of Arizona and contiguous states, does hereby bring suit for damages against the Acme Company, manufacturer and retail distributor of assorted merchandise, incorporated in Delaware and doing business in every state, district, and territory. Mr. Coyote seeks compensation for personal injuries, loss of business income, and mental suffering caused as a direct result of the actions and/or gross negligence of said company, under Title 15 of the United States Code, Chapter 47, section 2072, subsection (a), relating to product liability.

Mr. Coyote states that on eighty-five separate occasions he has purchased of the Acme Company (hereinafter, "Defendant"), through

Vocabulary Builder
contiguous (kən tigʹ yo͞o əs) *adj.* bordering; adjacent

Enrichment

Animation

The animation techniques used to create cartoon figures such as Wile E. Coyote date back to 1908 when Frenchman Émile Cohl drew white matchstick figures on a black background. Later methods, such as those used by Walt Disney, were based on drawings either inked or painted onto clear plastic sheets. Repeated or unmoving elements could be reproduced on many sheets, while moving elements had to be redrawn in their new position for each image. When the many images were photographed and linked together, the elements appeared to be animated, or moving. Today's animation is often computer generated, saving a great deal of time and enhancing the range of possible effects.

Have students discuss why an animated character is so suited for the satirical essay Ian Frazier chose to write. How does the animation process lend itself to portraying exaggeration and irony?

that company's mail-order department, certain products which did cause him bodily injury due to defects in manufacture or improper cautionary labeling. Sales slips made out to Mr. Coyote as proof of purchase are at present in the possession of the Court, marked Exhibit A. Such injuries sustained by Mr. Coyote have temporarily restricted his ability to make a living in his profession of predator. Mr. Coyote is self-employed and thus not eligible for Workmen's Compensation.[1]

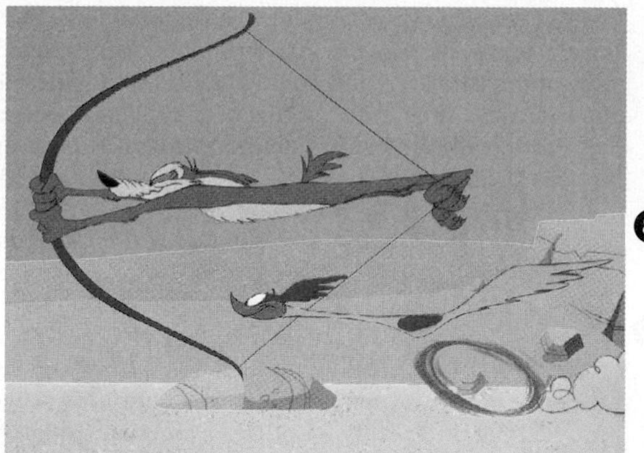
8

Mr. Coyote states that on December 13th he received of Defendant via parcel post one Acme Rocket Sled. The intention of Mr. Coyote was to use the Rocket Sled to aid him in pursuit of his prey. Upon receipt of the Rocket Sled Mr. Coyote removed it from its wooden shipping crate and, sighting his prey in the distance, activated the ignition. As Mr. Coyote gripped the handlebars, the Rocket Sled accelerated with such sudden and precipitate force as to stretch Mr. Coyote's forelimbs to a length of fifty feet. Subsequently, the rest of Mr. Coyote's body shot forward with a violent jolt, causing severe strain to his back and neck
10 and placing him unexpectedly astride the Rocket Sled. Disappearing over the horizon at such speed as to leave a diminishing jet trail along its path, the Rocket Sled soon brought Mr. Coyote abreast of his prey. At that moment the animal he was pursuing veered sharply to the right. Mr. Coyote vigorously attempted to follow this maneuver but was unable to, due to poorly designed steering on the Rocket Sled and a faulty or nonexistent braking system. Shortly thereafter, the unchecked progress of the Rocket Sled brought it and Mr. Coyote into collision with the side of a mesa.[2]

Paragraph One of the Report of Attending Physician (Exhibit B), prepared by Dr. Ernest Grosscup, M.D., D.O., details the multiple fractures, contusions, and tissue damage suffered by Mr. Coyote as a result of this collision. Repair of the injuries required a full bandage around the head (excluding the ears), a neck brace, and full or partial casts on all four legs.

Hampered by these injuries, Mr. Coyote was nevertheless obliged to support himself. With this in mind, he purchased of Defendant as an aid to mobility one pair of Acme Rocket Skates. When he attempted to use this product, however, he became involved in an accident remarkably similar to that which occurred with the Rocket Sled. Again, Defendant sold over the counter, without caveat, a product which attached powerful jet engines (in this case, two) to inadequate vehicles,

1. **Workmen's Compensation** form of disability insurance that provides income to workers who are unable to work due to injuries sustained on the job.
2. **mesa** (mā′ sə) *n.* small, high plateau with steep sides.

▲ Critical Viewing 9
Which word from the vocabulary list on page 1145 might be used to describe Coyote's bow? Explain. **[Connect]**

Vocabulary Builder
precipitate (prē sip′ ə tit) *adj.* very sudden

Vocabulary Builder
caveat (kā′ vē at′) *n.* formal notice; warning

Reading Check 11
For what three reasons does Mr. Coyote seek compensation from The Acme Company?

8 Humanities

Road Runner and Wile E. Coyote, by Chuck Jones, still-photo from animated film

This illustration shows the cartoon figure of Wile E. Coyote chasing his prey, the Road Runner, in a situation similar to the one in the essay.

Chuck Jones created the hilarious Road Runner cartoons, in which the obsessive and indefatigable Wile E. Coyote is forever chasing his nemesis, the Road Runner, with a notable lack of success. The duo first appeared in 1949 in "Fast and Furry-ous."

Jones, who has worked in animation for more than 60 years as a director, producer, and animator, studied at the Chouinard Art Institute in Los Angeles and eventually joined the animation team at Warner Bros. Jones stayed with the innovative animation company until it closed in the early 1960s. With colleagues, he came up with such cartoon favorites as Bugs Bunny, Tweety Pie, Sylvester, Daffy Duck, Elmer Fudd, Porky Pig, and Pepe Le Pew. In the 1960s, Jones founded his own animation company to create cartoons for television, the best-known being an adaptation of a Dr. Seuss classic, "How the Grinch Stole Christmas."

9 Critical Viewing

Answer: The vocabulary word *tensile* might be used to describe Coyote's bow.

10 Reading Strategy
Identifying Line of Reasoning

- **Ask** students to speculate about what purpose is served by the detailed description of exactly how the Rocket Sled did—or rather didn't—function.
  Answer: This level of detail is needed to explain exactly how the Rocket Sled was supposed to work in order to support the claim of negligence.

▶ **Monitor Progress: Ask** students how this evidence supports the accusation in the legal brief.
Answer: The Rocket Sled did not operate as it was supposed to.

11 Reading Check

Answer: Mr. Coyote seeks compensation from the Acme Company for injuries, loss of income, and mental suffering.

Differentiated Instruction
Solutions for All Learners

Strategy for Special Needs Students
To help students appreciate the humor in the essay, show them a selection of Road Runner cartoons. Make available three or four of these cartoons, and provide time for students to enjoy them. Then, read aloud part or all of the legal brief and help students understand the absurdity of the essay.

Support for English Learners
Appreciating the satire in this essay requires a grasp of "legalese," which may be beyond the knowledge of English learners. Pair English learners with students whose first language is English. If English learners get bogged down in the legal language of the brief, they can call on their partners to translate them into plain English.

Enrichment for Advanced Readers
Have students represent the defendant, the Acme Company. They should write a brief in the same style as the essay on these pages in which they defend the Acme Company from the spurious suit brought by the attorneys for Mr. Coyote.

12 Literary Analysis
Essay and Tone

- Read the bracketed passage aloud, and remind students that tone refers to the writer's attitude towards his or her subject, characters, and audience.
- Then, **ask** the Literary Analysis question: How would you describe the tone created by the use of legal language to describe the exaggerated events of the cartoon?
Answer: The author creates a tone of hilarious absurdity through the use of dry legal language to describe the exaggerated, nonsensical events that take place in a cartoon.

13 Critical Thinking
Infer

- **Ask** students why preparers of legal briefs might use language that is hard to understand rather than simple, straightforward English.
Answer: Students may think that using language that is difficult for laypeople to understand makes the legal claims seem more impressive. Legal language can distract people who are not used to reading it from the lack of evidence or the weakness of arguments.
- Have students **explain** how the word choices in this passage heighten the hilarity.
Answer: The more elevated the language is, the further it is from matching the tone of the events in the cartoons.

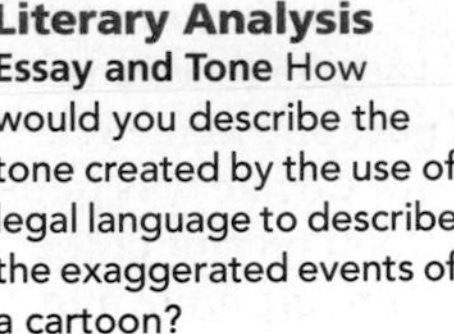

with little or no provision for passenger safety. Encumbered by his heavy casts, Mr. Coyote lost control of the Rocket Skates soon after strapping them on, and collided with a roadside billboard so violently as to leave a hole in the shape of his full silhouette.

Mr. Coyote states that on occasions too numerous to list in this document he has suffered mishaps with explosives purchased of Defendant: the Acme "Little Giant" Firecracker, the Acme Self-Guided Aerial Bomb, etc. (For a full listing, see the Acme Mail Order Explosives Catalogue and attached deposition,[3] entered in evidence as Exhibit C.) Indeed, it is safe to say that not
12 once has an explosive purchased of Defendant by Mr. Coyote performed in an expected manner. To cite just one example: At the expense of much time and personal effort, Mr. Coyote constructed around the outer rim of a butte[4] a wooden trough beginning at the top
13 of the butte and spiraling downward around it to some few feet above a black X painted on the desert floor. The trough was designed in such a way that a spherical explosive of the type sold by Defendant would roll easily and swiftly down to the point of detonation indicated by the X. Mr. Coyote placed a generous pile of birdseed directly on the X, and then, carrying the spherical Acme Bomb (Catalogue #78–832), climbed to the top of the butte. Mr. Coyote's prey, seeing the birdseed, approached, and Mr. Coyote proceeded to light the fuse. In an instant, the fuse burned down to the stem, causing the bomb to detonate.

In addition to reducing all Mr. Coyote's careful preparations to naught, the premature detonation of Defendant's product resulted in the following disfigurements to Mr. Coyote:

1. Severe singeing of the hair on the head, neck, and muzzle.
2. Sooty discoloration.
3. Fracture of the left ear at the stem, causing the ear to dangle in the aftershock with a creaking noise.
4. Full or partial combustion of whiskers producing kinking, frazzling, and ashy disintegration.
5. Radical widening of the eyes, due to brow and lid charring.

Literary Analysis
Essay and Tone How would you describe the tone created by the use of legal language to describe the exaggerated events of a cartoon?

3. **deposition** (dep´ ə zish´ ən) *n.* legal term for the written testimony of a witness.
4. **butte** (byo͞ot) *n.* steep hill standing alone in a plain.

We come now to the Acme Spring-Powered Shoes. The remains of a pair of these purchased by Mr. Coyote on June 23rd are Plaintiff's Exhibit D. Selected fragments have been shipped to the metallurgical laboratories of the University of California at Santa Barbara for analysis, but to date no explanation has been found for this product's sudden and extreme malfunction. As advertised by Defendant, this product is simplicity itself: two wood-and-metal sandals, each attached
14 to milled-steel springs of high tensile strength and compressed in a tightly coiled position by a cocking device with a lanyard release. Mr. Coyote believed that this product would enable him to pounce upon his prey in the initial moments of the chase, when swift reflexes are at a premium.

To increase the shoes' thrusting still further, Mr. Coyote affixed them by their bottoms to the side of a large boulder. Adjacent to the boulder was a path which Mr. Coyote's prey was known to frequent. Mr. Coyote put his hind feet in the wood-and-metal sandals and crouched in readiness, his right forepaw holding firmly to the lanyard release. Within a short time Mr. Coyote's prey did indeed appear on the path coming toward him. Unsuspecting, the prey stopped near Mr. Coyote, well within range of the springs at full extension. Mr. Coyote gauged the distance with care and proceeded to pull the lanyard release.

At this point, Defendant's product should have thrust Mr. Coyote forward and away from the boulder. Instead, for reasons yet unknown, the Acme Spring-Powered Shoes thrust the boulder away from Mr. Coyote. As the intended prey looked on unharmed, Mr. Coyote hung suspended in air. Then the twin springs recoiled, bringing Mr. Coyote to a violent feet-first collision with the boulder, the full weight of his head and forequarters falling upon his lower extremities.

The force of this impact then caused the springs to rebound, whereupon Mr. Coyote was thrust skyward. A second recoil and collision followed. The boulder, meanwhile, which was roughly ovoid in shape, had begun to bounce down a hillside, the coiling and recoiling of the springs adding to its velocity. At each bounce, Mr. Coyote came into contact with the boulder, or the boulder came into contact with Mr. Coyote, or both came into contact with the ground. As the grade was a long one, this process continued for some time.

The sequence of collisions resulted in systemic physical damage to Mr. Coyote, viz., flattening of the cranium, sideways displacement of the tongue, reduction of length of legs and upper body, and compression of vertebrae from base of tail to head. Repetition of blows along a vertical axis produced a series of regular horizontal folds in Mr. Coyote's body tissues—a rare and painful condition which caused Mr. Coyote to expand upward and contract downward alternately as he walked, and to emit an off-key accordion-like wheezing with every step. The

Literature in Context

15 Literature Connection

Parody

Satirists use many tools to ridicule a topic. One of the methods Frazier uses in this satiric essay is parody. A **parody** is a humorous piece of writing that mocks the characteristics of a literary form, a specific work, or the style of a certain writer. By exaggerating typical themes, characters, language, or plot devices, a parody calls attention to ridiculous elements of the original, particularly those that have become clichés.

There are many famous parodies in American literature. Mark Twain's novel *A Connecticut Yankee in King Arthur's Court* parodies the chivalric romance. Stephen Crane's story "The Bride Comes to Yellow Sky" parodies the western. Popular culture is full of parodies, such as Elvis Presley impersonators, the movies of Mel Brooks, and the songs of Weird Al Yankovic.

Connect to the Literature

What do you think Frazier is parodying in this essay?

Vocabulary Builder

tensile (ten′ sil) *adj.* stretchable

Reading Check 16

Have Acme products performed well for Mr. Coyote? Explain.

14 Vocabulary Builder

Latin Root *-ten-*

- Have a volunteer read the sentence in which the word *tensile* appears.
- Draw students' attention to the definition of *tensile* that appears in the margin.
- Point out that *tensile* begins with the Latin root *ten-*, which means "stretch tightly."
- **Challenge** students to think of other words with this root.
  Answer: Some examples include *tendon, tender, attenuate, extenuate, extend,* and *portend.*

15 Literature in Context

Parody

Although this parody is used in a satirical piece, parody did not originate in satire. The ancient Greeks and Romans wrote parodies in which one poem imitated the style of another poem for humorous ends. Imitating the art of the Classical world, French writers began to write parodies as well. It was not until Ben Johnson wrote his first original play, "Every Man in His Humour," that an English writer used the word *parody* to describe a form of literature. Jonathan Swift, however, was the first English writer to refer to his piece of narrative prose as *parody.* Furthermore, Swift's work was intended not only to be humorous but to demean and ridicule the original author's work as well; thus, the nature of *parody* has evolved into a much more biting form of humor than that which entertained the Greeks and the Romans.

Connect to the Literature

Have students reread the essay before answering the Connect to the Literature question. Students should support their answers with examples from the text.
Answer: Frazier is parodying legal language and our litigious society.

16 Reading Check

Answer: Acme products have not performed well for Mr. Coyote. He has injured himself every time he has used an Acme product. In addition, Acme products have not helped him catch his prey, the Road Runner.

Differentiated Instruction

Solutions for All Learners

Strategy for Less Proficient Readers

To help students picture the sequence of events, encourage them to draw simple thumbnail sketches of what happened, step by step, to Mr. Coyote when he tried to use the Acme Spring-Powered Shoes.

Strategy for English Learners

To help students picture the sequence of events, help them "translate" the legal language into ordinary words and simplify the complex sentences. Then, have students make thumbnail sketches of the sequence of events when Mr. Coyote tried to use the Acme Spring-Powered Shoes.

Enrichment for Gifted/Talented Students

Have students make a catalogue of Acme Company products. Ask students to list the products and to explain how each one functions.

17 Literary Analysis

Essay

- Read the bracketed passage aloud.
- **Ask** the Literary Analysis question: What aspects of the legal and business professions does the line about "our trading partners" satirize?
  Answer: The line about "our trading partners" satirizes the United States' sensitivity to international opinion.

ASSESS

Answers

1. Most students will feel sorry for Wile E. Coyote, though they will laugh at his exploits. Some students will be unsympathetic because they will believe Wile E. Coyote deserved his fate.
2. (a) His forelimbs stretched 50 feet. (b) Things happen to Wile E. Coyote, such as his legs stretching 50 feet, that could never happen in real life.
3. (a) Wile E. Coyote buys Acme products frequently. The essay states that he has bought them 85 times. (b) The essay states that Wile E. Coyote has no other source of the goods he needs for his "work" trying to catch the Road Runner.
4. (a) Wile E. Coyote is trying to collect $38,750,000 in damages. (b) Many students will believe that Wile E. Coyote has misused Acme products and thus is not eligible for damages.
5. Most students will understand that Frazier is not only trying to be funny but is also satirizing the legal profession and frivolous product liability claims.

Go Online Author Link For additional information about Ian Frazier, have students type in the Web Code, then select *F* from the alphabet, and then Ian Frazier.

distracting and embarrassing nature of this symptom has been a major impediment to Mr. Coyote's pursuit of a normal social life.

As the Court is no doubt aware, Defendant has a virtual monopoly of manufacture and sale of goods required by Mr. Coyote's work. It is our contention that Defendant has used its market advantage to the detriment of the consumer of such specialized products as itching powder, giant kites, Burmese tiger traps, anvils, and two-hundred-foot-long rubber bands. Much as he has come to mistrust Defendant's products, Mr. Coyote has no other domestic source of supply to which to turn. 17 [One can only wonder what our trading partners in Western Europe and Japan would make of such a situation, where a giant company is allowed to victimize the consumer in the most reckless and wrongful manner over and over again.]

Mr. Coyote respectfully requests that the Court regard these larger economic implications and assess punitive damages in the amount of seventeen million dollars. In addition, Mr. Coyote seeks actual damages (missed meals, medical expenses, days lost from professional occupation) of one million dollars; general damages (mental suffering, injury to reputation) of twenty million dollars; and attorney's fees of seven hundred and fifty thousand dollars. Total damages: thirty-eight million seven hundred and fifty thousand dollars. By awarding Mr. Coyote the full amount, this Court will censure Defendant, its directors, officers, shareholders, successors, and assigns, in the only language they understand, and reaffirm the right of the individual predator to equal protection under the law.

Literary Analysis
Essay What aspects of the legal and business professions does the line about "our trading partners" satirize?

Critical Reading

1. **Respond:** As you read the attorney's statement, did you sympathize with Wile E. Coyote? Why or why not?
2. **(a) Recall:** What happens to Wile E. Coyote's forelimbs when he uses the Rocket Sled? **(b) Support:** What details in this essay suggest that Wile E. Coyote is a cartoon character?
3. **(a) Recall:** How often does Wile E. Coyote buy products from the Acme Company? **(b) Support:** Find evidence to explain why he maintains this relationship with Acme, despite the outcomes he has faced with their products.
4. **(a) Recall:** What action is Wile E. Coyote seeking from the court? **(b) Make a Judgment:** If you were a member of the jury in this case, what would your verdict be? Explain.
5. **Evaluate:** What do you believe was Frazier's purpose in writing this essay? Was he simply trying to be funny or was he making a point? Explain.

For: More about Ian Frazier
Visit: www.PHSchool.com
Web Code: ere-9618

Loneliness...
18 An American Malady

Carson McCullers

This city, New York—consider the people in it, the eight million of us. An English friend of mine, when asked why he lived in New York City, said that he liked it here because he could be so alone. While it was my friend's desire to be alone, the aloneness of many Americans who live in cities is an involuntary and fearful thing. It has been said that loneliness is the great American malady. What is
19 the nature of this loneliness? It would seem essentially to be a quest for identity.

To the spectator, the amateur philosopher, no motive among the complex ricochets of our desires and rejections seems stronger or more
20 enduring than the will of the individual to claim his identity and belong. From infancy to death, the human being is obsessed by these dual motives. During our first weeks of life, the question of identity shares urgency with the need for milk. The baby reaches for his toes,

Literary Analysis
Essay In what ways does the question about the nature of loneliness signal to readers that this is an analytical essay?

18 About the Selection

As young adults working to define their own place in the world, students will find "Loneliness . . . An American Malady" both poignant and highly relevant. McCullers begins with the challenge of understanding American loneliness. She follows the path of human growth to track the development of Americans' sense of isolation and offers examples of real-life responses to loneliness. By analyzing this apparently ingrained element of the human experience and urging self-examination as a method for relief, McCullers offers hope to any reader who has ever felt like an outsider.

19 Literary Analysis
Essay

- Remind students that an analytical essay attempts to explain a topic by breaking it down into parts.
- Read the bracketed section aloud, and **ask** students the Literary Analysis question: In what ways does the question about the nature of loneliness signal to the readers that this is an analytical essay?
  Answer: The question deals with what *constitutes* a particular kind of loneliness: American loneliness. The question signals that McCullers is going to break down this notion and assess it from different angles.

20 Reading Strategy
Identifying a Line of Reasoning

- **Ask** students to explain "this primitive grasp of identity."
Answer: It is self-consciousness.
- Then, **ask** the Reading Strategy question: What evidence does McCullers offer to support the connections between her ideas about identity and loneliness?
Answer: McCullers offers the example of a baby establishing his or her sense of self, and the separation that is implicit in self-awareness. McCullers explains that throughout their lives, humans are concerned with the desire to establish an individual identity and forge connections with others.

21 Reading Strategy
Identifying a Line of Reasoning

- Draw students' attention to this paragraph, in which McCullers introduces an element in her argument.
- **Ask** students to paraphrase the text and restate McCullers's position.
Possible response: Love helps people reduce their loneliness by offering a bridge to others, by creating a positive lens through which to view the world, and by casting out fear.

then explores the bars of his crib; again and again he compares the difference between his own body and the objects around him, and in the wavering, infant eyes there comes a pristine wonder.

20 Consciousness of self is the first abstract problem that the human being solves. Indeed, it is this self-consciousness that removes us from lower animals. This primitive grasp of identity develops with constantly shifting emphasis through all our years. Perhaps maturity is simply the history of those mutations that reveal to the individual the relation between himself and the world in which he finds himself.

After the first establishment of identity there comes the imperative need to lose this new-found sense of separateness and to belong to something larger and more powerful than the weak, lonely self. The sense of moral isolation is intolerable to us.

In *The Member of the Wedding*[1] the lonely twelve-year-old girl, Frankie Addams, articulates this universal need: "The trouble with me is that for a long time I have just been an *I* person. All people belong to a *We* except me. Not to belong to a *We* makes you too lonesome."

21 Love is the bridge that leads from the *I* sense to the *We*, and there is a paradox about personal love. Love of another individual opens a new relation between the personality and the world. The lover responds in a new way to nature and may even write poetry. Love is affirmation; it motivates the *yes* responses and the sense of wider communication. Love casts out fear, and in the security of this togetherness we find contentment, courage. We no longer fear the age-old haunting questions: "Who am I?" "Why am I?" "Where am I going?"—and having cast out fear, we can be honest and charitable.

For fear is a primary source of evil. And when the question "Who am I?" recurs and is unanswered, then fear and frustration project a negative attitude. The bewildered soul can answer only: "Since I do not understand 'Who I am,' I only know what I am *not*." The corollary of this emotional incertitude is snobbism, intolerance and racial hate. The xenophobic[2] individual can only reject and destroy, as the xenophobic nation inevitably makes war.

The loneliness of Americans does not have its source in xenophobia; as a nation we are an outgoing people, reaching always for immediate contacts, further experience. But we tend to seek out things as individuals, alone. The European, secure in his family ties and rigid class loyalties, knows little of the moral loneliness that is native to us Americans. While the European artists tend to form groups or aesthetic schools, the American artist is the eternal maverick—not only from society in the way of all creative minds, but within the orbit of his own art.

Thoreau took to the woods to seek the ultimate meaning of his life. His creed was simplicity and his *modus vivendi*[3] the deliberate stripping of

1. ***The Member of the Wedding*** novel and play by Carson McCullers.
2. **xenophobic** (zen′ ə fō′ bik) *adj.* afraid of strangers or foreigners.
3. ***modus vivendi*** (mō′ dəs vi ven′ dī) "manner of living" (Latin).

Vocabulary Builder
pristine (pris′ tēn) *adj.* pure; uncorrupted

Reading Strategy
Identifying a Line of Reasoning What evidence does McCullers offer to support the connections between her ideas about identity and loneliness?

Vocabulary Builder
corollary (kôr′ ə ler′ ē) *n.* easily drawn conclusion

Vocabulary Builder
aesthetic (es thet′ ik) *adj.* pertaining to the study or theory of beauty

maverick (mav′ ər ik) *n.* nonconformist

Differentiated Instruction
Solutions for All Learners

Support for Special Needs Students
Students may have difficulty identifying McCullers's arguments in this essay. Model this process with the help of the **Reading Strategy Graphic Organizer A,** p. 258 in ***Graphic Organizer Transparencies.***

Support for Less Proficient Readers
Discuss with students the sorts of evidence and reasoning authors use to support their main points, such as definitions, examples, and logical arguments. Which of these kinds of evidence can students find on the first two pages of McCullers's essay?

Strategy for Advanced Readers
Have students summarize McCullers's main points and list the evidence and reasons she uses to support them. Then, have students take a position: Do they agree or disagree with McCullers? Ask students to give logical reasons for their opinions and support their opinions with facts and examples.

external life to the Spartan[4] necessities in order that his inward life could freely flourish. His objective, as he put it, was to back the world into a corner. And in that way did he discover "What a man thinks of himself, that it is which determines, or rather indicates, his fate."

On the other hand, Thomas Wolfe turned to the city, and in his wanderings around New York he continued his frenetic and lifelong search for the lost brother, the magic door. He too backed the world into a corner, and as he passed among the city's millions, returning their stares, he experienced "That silent meeting [that] is the summary of all the meetings of men's lives."

Whether in the pastoral joys of country life or in the labyrinthine city, we Americans are always seeking. We wander, question. But the answer waits in each separate heart—the answer of our own identity and the way by which we can master loneliness and feel that at last we belong.

4. **Spartan** (spär′ tən) *adj.* characteristic of the people of ancient Sparta: hardy, stoical, severe, frugal.

Critical Reading

1. **Respond:** If you could meet Carson McCullers, which of the observations in this essay would you most like to discuss with her? Explain your reasons for choosing this observation.
2. **(a) Recall:** Why does McCullers's English friend like living in New York City? **(b) Interpret:** In what way is his explanation seemingly contradictory or paradoxical?
3. **(a) Recall:** According to McCullers, what is "the great American malady"? **(b) Analyze:** When McCullers describes this American malady, she speaks of *moral* isolation and *moral* loneliness. What does she mean by these terms?
4. **(a) Recall:** What is a primary source of evil? **(b) Analyze Cause and Effect:** What are the consequences of evil? **(c) Speculate:** According to McCullers, how might the personal experience of love change society?
5. **(a) Distinguish:** What does McCullers say is the main difference between Europeans and Americans? **(b) Interpret:** In what ways does she believe this difference is expressed?
6. **(a) Define:** What is the *I* sense? **(b) Define:** What is the *We* sense? **(c) Interpret:** According to McCullers, how does love lead from one to the other?
7. **(a) Evaluate:** In what ways does McCullers think American individualism hurts people? **(b) Take a Position:** Do you see any positive effects of our emphasis on individualism? Explain.

For: More about Carson McCullers
Visit: www.PHSchool.com
Web Code: ere-9619

ASSESS

Answers

1. **Possible responses:** Many students would like to talk to McCullers about her idea that love helps people move from concentrating on establishing their individual identify to forging connections with others.
2. (a) McCullers's friend likes New York because he can be alone. (b) New York is a huge, crowded city, so it seems paradoxical that people feel alone there.
3. (a) "The great American malady" is loneliness. (b) She uses "moral" to imply conformity to accepted ideas of right and wrong. A child loses moral isolation by learning the standards of family and society. Without strict class structure of Europeans, Americans experience the "moral isolation" of deciding correct behavior.
4. (a) McCullers believes that fear is the main cause of evil. (b) "Emotional incertitude," which begets xenophobia, is a consequence of evil. (c) McCullers believes that experiencing love leads from a concentration on the individual to thinking of oneself as part of a group, and thus being concerned with society.
5. (a) Americans seek out things as individuals, whereas Europeans are secure in groups, such as families and classes. (b) An example of this difference is that European artists form schools, while the American artist is the "eternal maverick."
6. (a) The *I* sense is the sense of the individual. (b) The *We* sense is identifying with another person or people. (c) Love expands the sense of self from the individual to include the beloved.
7. (a) McCullers thinks that American individualism makes people lonely. (b) Students may state that positive aspects of it include self-reliance and creative problem solving.

Go Online Author Link For additional information about Carson McCullers, have students type in the Web Code, then select *M* from the alphabet, and then Carson McCullers.

Enrichment

Thomas Wolfe

Thomas Wolfe (1900–1938) is best known for his classic American novel, *Look Homeward, Angel.* Wolfe grew up in Asheville, North Carolina, the setting of several of his plays and novels, and left for New York City as a young man.

Look Homeward, Angel was published in 1929. The novel, which has become an American classic, tells of the coming of age of Eugene Gant in the mountain town of Altamont. The thinly disguised autobiographical novel was an immediate success but caused quite a scandal in Wolfe's hometown of Asheville.

㉒ About the Selection

In this essay, Anna Quindlen examines the impact of the events of 9-11 and the way in which those events separated American life into "the mundane and the monstrous."

㉓ Reading Strategy

Identifying a Line of Reasoning

- Have students reread Paragraph 4 and summarize the meaning of each sentence.
- Then **ask** students the Reading Strategy question: What is Quindlen's main point in this paragraph?
  Answer: Quindlen's main point in this paragraph states that Americans don't all agree on how 9-11 shaped our identity and our self-perception; however, she does agree with the realists, who believe that 9-11 displayed both the best and the worst in human beings.

㉒

One Day, Now Broken in Two

Anna Quindlen

Background Anna Quindlen writes a weekly column for *Newsweek* magazine called "The Last Word." "One Day, Now Broken in Two" was published one year after the September 11, 2001, terrorist attacks on the World Trade Center in New York City and the Pentagon building in Washington, D. C. Her column was part of a commemorative edition of *Newsweek* entitled *America: A Year After.*

September 11 is my eldest child's birthday. When he drove cross-country this spring and got pulled over for pushing the pedal on a couple of stretches of monotonous highway, two cops in two different states said more or less the same thing as they looked down at his license: aw, man, you were really born on 9-11? Maybe it was coincidence, but in both cases he got a warning instead of a ticket.

Who are we now? A people who manage to get by with the help of the everyday, the ordinary, the mundane, the old familiar life muting the terror of the new reality. The day approaching will always be bifurcated[1] for me: part September 11, the anniversary of one of the happiest days of my life, and part 9-11, the day America's mind reeled, its spine stiffened, and its heart broke.

That is how the country is now, split in two. The American people used their own simple routines to muffle the horror they felt looking at that indelible[2] loop of tape—the plane, the flames, the plane, the fire, the falling bodies, the falling buildings. Amid the fear and the shock there were babies to be fed, dogs to be walked, jobs to be done. After the first months almost no one bought gas masks anymore; fewer people than expected in New York City asked for the counseling that had been provided as part of the official response. Slowly the planes filled up again. A kind of self-hypnosis prevailed, and these were the words used to induce the happy trance: life goes on.

㉓ Who are we now? We are better people than we were before. That's what the optimists say, soothed by the vision of those standing in line to give blood and money and time at the outset, vowing to stop and smell the flowers as the weeks ticked by. We are people living in a world of unimaginable cruelty and savagery. So say the pessimists. The realists insist that both are right, and, as always, they are correct.

Reading Strategy
Identifying a Line of Reasoning What is Quindlen's main point in this paragraph?

1. **bifurcated** (bī´ fər kā təd) *adj.* divided into two parts.
2. **indelible** (in del´ ə bəl) *adj.* permanent; that cannot be erased.

24 Critical Viewing

Answer: Students may respond to images of 9-11 memorials with a mixture of sorrow and anger. Seeing the faces of the victims of the terrorist attacks, and acknowledging that they've left behind grieving loved one's, somehow makes the tragedy more personal.

25 Reading Check

Answer: Some Americans are outraged at the question that many people have asked after 9-11: "Why do they hate us?"

We are people whose powers of imagination have been challenged by the revelations of the careful planning, the hidden leaders, the machinations[3] from within a country of rubble and caves and desperate want, the willingness to slam headlong into one great technological achievement while piloting another as a way of despising modernity. Why do they hate us, some asked afterward, and many Americans were outraged at the question, confusing the search for motivation with mitigation.[4] But quietly, as routine returned, a new routine based on a new bedrock of loss of innocence and loss of life, a new question crept almost undetected into the national psyche: did we like ourselves? Had we become a people who confused prosperity with probity,[5] whose culture had become personified by oversize sneakers and KFC? Our own individual transformations made each of us wonder what our legacy would be if we left the world on a sunny September day with a "to do" list floating down eighty stories to the street below.

So we looked at our lives a little harder, called our friends a little more often, hugged our kids a little tighter. And then we complained about the long lines at the airport and obsessed about the stock market in lieu of soul-searching. Time passed. The blade dulled. The edges softened. Except, of course, for those who lived through birthdays, anniversaries, holidays, without someone lost in the cloud of silvery dust, those families the living embodiment of what the whole nation had first felt and then learned not to feel.

We are people of two minds now, the one that looks forward and the one that unwillingly and unexpectedly flashes back. Flying over lower Manhattan, the passengers reflexively lean toward the skyline below,

▲ Critical Viewing 24 How do you respond when you see photographs of spontaneous 9-11 memorials like this one? **[Respond]**

Reading Check 25 What question outrages some Americans, according to Quindlen?

3. **machinations** (mak´ ə nā´ shənz) *n.* secret schemes.
4. **mitigation** (mit´ ə gā´ shən) *n.* relief; moderation; lessening of severity.
5. **probity** (prō´ bə tē) *n.* integrity; moral uprightness.

Differentiated Instruction
Solutions for All Learners

Strategy for Less Proficient Readers
If students have difficulty identifying Quindlen's main idea, have them revisit the Reading Strategy graphic organizer. Work with them to record reasons, facts, and examples in the "Supporting Evidence/Reasons" boxes before completing the "Main Point" box. Alternatively, students may be given a copy of the **Reading Strategy Graphic Organizer B**, p. 259 in ***Graphic Organizer Transparencies,*** to model how to identify a main idea.

Vocabulary for English Learners
This essay contains challenging vocabulary such as *monotonous, mundane, induce,* and *monstrous.* To help English learners, encourage them to read the selection with a dictionary at hand. Each time students cannot figure out the meaning of a word from context, they should pause to look up the word's definition.

Enrichment for Advanced Readers
Have students gather in groups to discuss their memories of the events of September 11, 2001. Then, encourage them to consider whether their lives were "broken in two." Do they agree with Quindlen's assertion? Why or why not?

㉖ Literary Analysis

Essay and Tone

- Read aloud the bracketed paragraph. Have students pay special attention to the different events she mentions to have taken place on September 10.
- **Ask** students the Literary Analysis question: How would you describe Quindlen's tone in this paragraph?
- **Answer:** Quindlen's tone is stressful and unpleasant. She is recalling a serious of very intense and emotional events, and as September 10 drew to a close, she did not believe she could experience a day worse than that.

ASSESS

Answers

1. Students' responses will vary.
2. (a) He was given a warning instead of a ticket. (b) The officers probably felt sorry for Quindlen's son because his birthday falls on the date of such a horrific event.
3. (a) Optimists feel that Americans are better people than they were before 9-11. (b) Pessimists feel that the events of 9-11 have made Americans aware of the world's cruelty and savagery. (c) Quindlen understands that both viewpoints are correct. Americans have become better people as a result of having to face such cruelty.
4. (a) Americans have asked themselves "Why do they hate us?" and "Do we like ourselves?" (b) It is a mistake to be outraged because people ask the first question in order to make sense of what happened, not to find an excuse. (c) Quindlen's response to the second question is that most of us do not like ourselves.
5. (a) We are a people who have been forever changed by the events of 9-11 and who will forever live with the duality of "the mundane and the monstrous." (b) One must live a bifurcated life.
6. Students should support their responses with examples.

looking for ghost buildings. "Is everything back to normal?" someone asked me in another country not long ago, and I said yes. And no. The closest I could come to describing what I felt was to describe a bowl I had broken in two and beautifully mended. It holds everything it once did; the crack is scarcely visible. But I always know it's there. My eye worries it without even meaning to.

㉖ On September 10 of last year my daughter and I went to the funeral of a neighbor we both loved greatly. We rushed home so I could go to the hospital, where my closest friend had just had serious surgery. Someone else took the cat to the vet after we discovered that he was poisoned and was near death. That night, as my daughter got ready for bed, I said to her, without the slightest hint of hyperbole,[6] "Don't worry, honey. We'll never again have a day as bad as this one."

Literary Analysis
Essay and Tone How would you describe Quindlen's tone in this paragraph?

Who are we now? We are people who know that we never understood what "bad day" meant until that morning that cracked our world cleanly in two, that day that made two days, September 11 and 9-11. The mundane and the monstrous. "Tell me how do you live brokenhearted?" Bruce Springsteen sings on his new album about the aftermath. September 11 is my boy's birthday; 9-11 is something else. That is the way we have to live, or we cannot really go on living at all.

---

6. **hyperbole** (hī pur′ bə lē) *n.* exaggeration.

Critical Reading

1. **Respond:** What were your reactions as you read this essay?
2. **(a) Recall:** What happened to Quindlen's son when he was stopped for speeding? **(b) Infer:** Why do you think the police officers responded the way they did?
3. **(a) Recall:** According to Quindlen, what is the optimists' view of who Americans have become as a result of 9-11? **(b) Compare and Contrast:** What is the pessimists' answer to the same question, and why? **(c) Analyze:** In Quindlen's opinion, which viewpoint is correct? Explain.
4. **(a) Recall:** According to Quindlen, what two questions have Americans asked themselves as a result of 9-11? **(b) Interpret:** Why does she believe that it is a mistake to be outraged by the first question? **(c) Infer:** What is Quindlen's answer to the second question?
5. **(a) Analyze:** What is Quindlen's answer to the question "Who are we now?" **(b) Infer:** What is her answer to the question that she quotes from Bruce Springsteen's song?
6. **Take a Position:** Do you think it is possible to divide life into "the mundane and the monstrous," as Quindlen suggests we must do? Explain your opinion.

For: More about Anna Quindlen
Visit: www.PHSchool.com
Web Code: ere-9620

Go Online Author Link For additional information about Anna Quindlen, have students type in the Web Code, then select *Q* from the alphabet, and then Anna Quindlen.

Apply the Skills

Onomatopoeia* • *Coyote v. Acme* • *Loneliness . . . An American Malady* • *One Day, Now Broken in Two

Literary Analysis

Essay

1. **(a)** What type of **essay** is "Onomatopoeia"? **(b)** Give an example of an idea that Safire explains.
2. **(a)** In "Coyote v. Acme," in what ways does the use of humor convey a serious idea? **(b)** What is the main point of the essay?
3. **(a)** What type of essay is "Loneliness . . . An American Malady"? **(b)** What aspects of loneliness does McCullers explore? **(c)** What is her main point?
4. **(a)** What type of essay is "One Day, Now Broken in Two"? **(b)** What is Quindlen's main point?

Comparing Literary Works

5. **(a)** Use a chart like the one shown to analyze the first paragraph of each essay and determine the author's **tone.** **(b)** What attitude toward his or her subject is revealed in each author's tone?

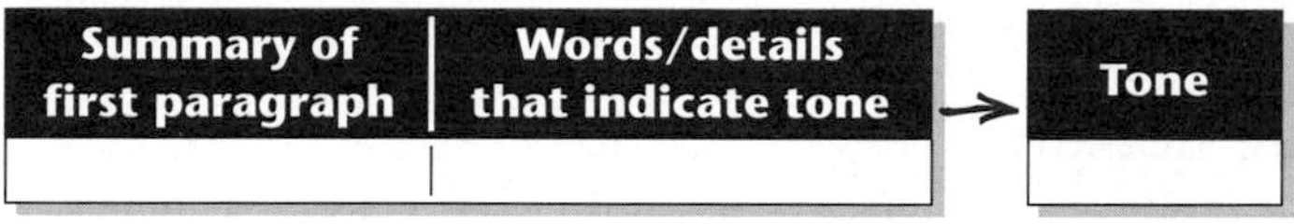

6. Both Safire's and Frazier's essays rely on humor, but of different kinds. In your own words, describe the kind of humor used in each essay.
7. What role does tone play in the overall effect of each essay?

Reading Strategy

Identifying a Line of Reasoning

8. **(a)** Summarize the attorney's case for Mr. Coyote in "Coyote v. Acme." **(b)** What is the connection between Exhibits A–D and the main points of the attorney's arguments?
9. What supporting information does McCullers use to convince the reader that **(a)** loneliness stems from the quest for identity and **(b)** love is the means of overcoming loneliness?

Extend Understanding

10. **Social Studies Connection:** Do you think Americans today are likely to be more or less lonely than the early settlers? Explain the societal changes that prompted your answer.

QuickReview

In an **analytical essay,** the writer explores and clarifies a topic. In an **expository essay,** the writer explains or provides information about a topic. In a **satirical essay,** the writer uses irony, ridicule, parody, or sarcasm to comment on a topic. In a **reflective essay,** the writer explores the meaning of a personal experience or pivotal event.

A writer's **tone** reflects his or her attitude toward the subject or audience.

To **identify a line of reasoning,** note the author's main points and the evidence that supports them.

For: Self-test
Visit: www.PHSchool.com
Web Code: era-6612

Answers

1. (a) "Onomatopoeia" is an expository essay (b) Safire explains the "bow-wow theory," which posits that words began in imitation of natural sounds.
2. (a) "Coyote v. Acme" satirizes a product liability lawsuit. (b) The main point is that some product liability suits are frivolous.
3. (a) "Loneliness" is an analytical essay. (b) McCullers explores the development of a social consciousness from birth and American tendencies toward loneliness. (c) Everyone experiences the conflicting pulls of establishing self-identity and needing connection with others.
4. (a) It is a reflective essay. (b) Quindlen's main point is that 9-11 created a duality of "the mundane and the monstrous."
5. (a) McCullers uses a philosophical question about loneliness to convey a serious tone. Safire uses casual language to convey a lighthearted tone. Frazier uses legal jargon to convey a satirical tone. (b) McCullers takes her subject very seriously. Safire provides information in a lighthearted way, and Frazier satirizes his subject.
6. Safire jokes openly in his essay. Frazier pretends to be serious, but his basic premise is absurd, resulting in a satire.
7. McCullers's serious tone encourages the reader to take her points seriously. Safire teaches through humor. Frazier makes his point through exaggeration.
8. (a) Acme's products have malfunctioned, causing bodily harm and loss of employment to Mr. Coyote. (b) The exhibits are various kinds of documentation that support the attorney's contention.
9. (a) She describes a baby's growing self-identity. (b) She describes how loves change from identifying with the *I* to identifying with the *we.* (c) Most students will find her evidence convincing.
10. Some students may argue that Americans today are more likely to be lonely than early settlers because extended family may live far apart. Others may argue that Americans are less lonely because travel is easier and modes of communication quicker and more reliable.

Go Online Assessment Students may use the **Self-test** to prepare for **Selection Test A** or **Selection Test B.**

EXTEND/ASSESS

Answers

1 Vocabulary Lesson

Word Analysis: Latin Root –*ten*–

Paragraphs about disastrous camping trips must include four of the following six words: *tension, tense, tent, extent, tendon, intensify.*

Spelling Strategy

1. athletic
2. basic
3. fantastic

Vocabulary Builder

1. c	5. d
2. f	6. g
3. a	7. b
4. h	8. e

2 Grammar and Style Lesson

1. Loneliness is common among us Americans.
2. Love can help you and me.
3. Two students, she and Carlos, were tied for the best grades.
4. We cartoon lovers all know Wile E. Coyote.
5. He would like to gain sympathy amongst us predators.

Writing Application

Paragraphs must include at least three appositives.

WG **Writing and Grammar, Ruby Level**

Students will find further instruction and practice on pronouns with appositives in Chapter 19, Section 1.

Build Language Skills

1 Vocabulary Lesson

Word Analysis: Latin Root *-ten-*

The word *tensile* contains the Latin root *-ten-*, meaning "to stretch tightly." Tensile springs would be "stretchable." The words below take their meaning from the root *-ten-*. Use at least four of the words to write a paragraph about a disastrous camping trip.

tension	tense	tent
extent	tendon	intensify

Spelling Strategy

When you add the suffix *-ic* to nouns ending in *e* or *y*, drop the final *e*, as in *aesthete* + *-ic* = *aesthetic*. Notice that the new word is an adjective. Add the suffix *-ic* to create the adjective form for each of the following words.

1. athlete **2.** base **3.** fantasy

Vocabulary Builder: Definitions

Review the vocabulary list on page 1145. Then, choose the definition from the right column that best fits the word in the left column.

1. precipitate	**a.** share a common border
2. tensile	**b.** conclusion
3. contiguous	**c.** sudden, abrupt
4. pristine	**d.** formal warning
5. caveat	**e.** nonconformist
6. aesthetic	**f.** stretchable quality
7. corollary	**g.** sense of beauty
8. maverick	**h.** completely untouched

2 Grammar and Style Lesson

Pronouns With Appositives

McCullers observes that ". . . we Americans are always seeking." Notice that the pronoun *we* is followed by the noun *Americans* and acts as the subject of the clause. When a **pronoun** is followed by an **appositive**—a noun that renames the pronoun—choose the correct pronoun by mentally dropping the appositive.

Subject: We players had to win. (We had to win.)

Object: It was up to us players. (It was up to us.)

Use *I, he, she, we,* or *they* to rename subjects and *me, him, her, us,* or *them* to rename objects.

Practice For each of the sentences below, choose the correct form of the pronoun in parentheses. Then, rewrite the complete sentence correctly.

1. Loneliness is common among (we, us) Americans.

2. Love can help (us, you) and (I, me).

3. Two students, (she, her) and Carlos, were tied for the best grades.

4. (We, Us) cartoon lovers all know Wile E. Coyote.

5. He would like to gain sympathy amongst (us, we) predators.

Writing Application Write a paragraph in which you describe a sporting event. Use the correct form of pronouns with appositives at least three times.

WG *Prentice Hall Writing and Grammar Connection: Chapter 19, Section 1*

Assessment Practice

Punctuation **(For more practice, see *Standardized Test Preparation Workbook*, p. 68.)**

The writing sections of many tests require students to identify and correct punctuation errors. Use the following sample test item to give students practice in this skill.

A coyote could not possibly use the following items! a rocket sled, rocket skates, a bomb, and spring-powered shoes.

What is the BEST way to rewrite the underlined section of the passage.

A NO CHANGE **C** items a rocket

B items: a rocket **D** items. A rocket

An exclamation mark is not appropriate preceding a list, so *A* is incorrect. *C* does not provide the necessary punctuation between the clause and the list. *D* creates a sentence fragment. *B* is the correct answer because it uses a colon to introduce the list.

Writing Lesson

Parody

In his satiric essay "Coyote v. Acme," Frazier parodies aspects of the legal profession. Write a parody of your favorite—or least favorite—writer, genre, or writing style. For example, you could parody a love poem, a heroic epic, or a scary Gothic poem such as Edgar Allen Poe's "The Raven."

Prewriting Choose the writing style, genre, or writer that you want to parody. Use a cluster diagram to organize your thoughts about the characteristics of the piece you are imitating and to set a goal for your parody.

Model: Using a Cluster Diagram to Write a Parody

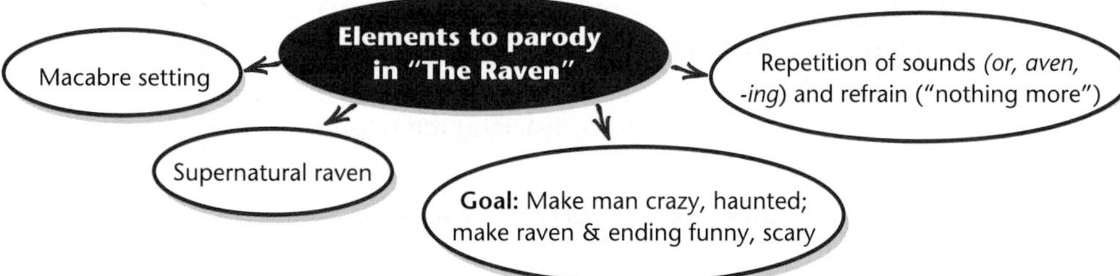

Drafting Begin by imitating the original in a straightforward way. Then, use your cluster diagram to add humor or irony to poke fun at the piece.

Revising Reread your parody to make sure that you have addressed all the elements you wanted to imitate to reach your goal.

WG *Prentice Hall Writing and Grammar Connection: Chapter 3, Section 2*

Extend Your Learning

Listening and Speaking Working in groups as teams of attorneys defending the Acme Company, develop a response to the arguments presented in "Coyote v. Acme." Present your **opening statement** for the defense to the class. Use these tips to prepare:

- Respond to each of the main arguments presented in the essay.
- Appeal both to logic and to the emotions.

Present your opening statements using appropriate body language. **[Group Activity]**

Research and Technology View episodes of the Roadrunner cartoon. As you watch, evaluate the various ways the cartoon makers present events and communicate characters' motivations. Then, write a short **essay** analyzing the cartoon and discussing the expository methods you identified. Exchange your essay with classmates and discuss points of agreement and disagreement.

For: An additional research activity
Visit: www.PHSchool.com
Web Code: erd-7612

Assessment Resources

The following resources can be used to assess students' knowledge and skills.

Unit 6 Resources
Selection Test A, pp. 211–213
Selection Test B, pp. 214–216

General Resources
Rubrics for Response to Literature, pp. 65–66
Rubric for Listening: Analyzing Persuasive Techniques, p. 83

Go Online Assessment Students may use the **Self-test** to prepare for **Selection Test A** or **Selection Test B**.

3 Writing Lesson

You may use this Writing Lesson as timed-writing practice, or you may allow students to develop the essay as a writing assignment over several days.

- Review the characteristics that make Frazier's essay a parody.
- Give students the **Support for Writing Lesson**, p. 208 in ***Unit 6 Resources***, to use as they write their parodies.
- Use the Writing Lesson to guide students in planning and drafting their own parodies.
- Remind students that they should include these features in their parody: humor, exaggerations, clichés, and a mocking tone.
- Use the rubrics for Response to Literature, pp. 65–66 in ***General Resources***, to evaluate students' parodies.

4 Listening and Speaking

- Suggest that each group of students work its way through the plaintiff's brief, brainstorming for arguments to refute each point.
- Students should decide as a group which arguments are most convincing and use those in their opening statement.
- After preparing a draft of the statement, a group member should read it aloud to the rest of their group and have them critique it before it is revised.
- Encourage presenters to practice reading the opening statement several times so that they can maintain eye contact with the audience when they present it.
- Use the rubric for Analyzing Persuasive Techniques in ***General Resources***, p. 83, to evaluate students' work.
- The **Support for Extend Your Learning** page (***Unit 6 Resources***, p. 209) provides guided note-taking opportunities to help students complete the Extend Your Learning activities.

Go Online Research Have students type in the Web Code for another research activity.

Meeting Your Standards

Students will

1. **analyze and respond to literary elements.**
   - Literary Analysis: Reflective Essay
2. **read, comprehend, analyze, and critique nonfiction.**
   - Reading Strategy: Evaluating a Writer's Message
   - Reading Check questions
   - Apply the Skills questions
   - Assessment Practice (ATE)
3. **develop vocabulary.**
   - Vocabulary Lesson: Latin Root: *-scrib-, -script-*
4. **understand and apply written and oral language conventions.**
   - Spelling Strategy
   - Grammar and Style Lesson: Varying Sentences Structure
5. **develop writing proficiency.**
   - Writing Lesson: Letter to the Author
6. **develop appropriate research strategies.**
   - Extend Your Learning: Team Report
7. **understand and apply listening and speaking strategies.**
   - Extend Your Learning: Speech

Block Scheduling: Use one 90-minute class period to preteach the skills and have students read the selection. Use a second 90-minute class period to assess students' mastery of skills, extend their learning, and monitor their progress.

Homework Suggestions

Following are possibilities for homework assignments:

- Support pages from ***Unit 6 Resources:***
  Literary Analysis
  Reading Strategy
  Vocabulary Builder
  Grammar and Style
- An Extend Your Learning project and the Writing Lesson for this selection group may be completed over several days.

Step-by-Step Teaching Guide	Pacing Guide
PRETEACH	
• Administer Vocabulary and Reading Warm-ups as necessary.	5 min.
• Engage students' interest with the motivation activity.	5 min.
• Read and discuss author and background features. **FT**	10 min.
• Introduce the Literary Analysis Skill: Reflective Essay **FT**	5 min.
• Introduce the Reading Strategy: Evaluating a Writer's Message **FT**	10 min.
• Prepare students to read by teaching the selection vocabulary. **FT**	
TEACH	
• Informally monitor comprehension while students read independently or in groups. **FT**	30 min.
• Monitor students' comprehension with the Reading Check notes.	as students read
• Reinforce vocabulary with Vocabulary Builder notes.	as students read
• Develop students' understanding of the reflective essay with the Literary Analysis annotations. **FT**	5 minutes
• Develop students' ability to evaluate a writer's message with the Reading Strategy annotations. **FT**	5 minutes
ASSESS/EXTEND	
• Assess students' comprehension and mastery of the Literary Analysis and Reading Strategy by having them answer the Apply the Skills questions. **FT**	15 min.
• Have students complete the Vocabulary Lesson and the Grammar and Style Lesson. **FT**	15 min.
• Apply students' ability to revise to include precise language in their writing by using the Writing Lesson. **FT**	45 min. or homework
• Apply students' understanding using one or more of the Extend Your Learning activities.	20–90 min. or homework
• Administer Selection Test A or Selection Test B. **FT**	15 min.

Resources

PRINT

Unit 6 Resources

Vocabulary Warm-up Word Lists **[L1, L2, EL]** .... p. 217
Vocabulary Warm-up Practice **[L1, L2, EL]** .... p. 218
Reading Warm-up A **[L1, L2, EL]** .... p. 219
Reading Warm-up B **[L1, L2, L3]** .... p. 220

TRANSPARENCY

Graphic Organizer Transparencies

Literary Analysis Graphic Organizer A **[L3]** .... p. 262
Literary Analysis Graphic Organizer B **[L1, L2, EL]** .... p. 263
Reading Strategy Graphic Organizer A **[L3]** .... p. 264
Reading Strategy Graphic Organizer B **[L1, L2, EL]** .... p. 265

PRINT

Reader's Notebook [L2]
Reader's Notebook: Adapted Version [L1]
Reader's Notebook: English Learner's Version [EL]

Unit 6 Resources

Literary Analysis **[L3]** .... p. 221
Reading Strategy **[L3]** .... p. 222
Vocabulary Builder **[L3]** .... p. 223

TECHNOLOGY

Listening to Literature Audio CDs [L2, EL]
Reader's Notebook: Adapted Version Audio CD [L1, L2]

PRINT

Unit 6 Resources

Grammar and Style **[L3]** .... p. 224
Support for Writing Lesson **[L3]** .... p. 225
Support for Extend Your Learning **[L3]** .... p. 226
Enrichment **[L4]** .... p. 227
Selection Test A **[L1, L2, EL]** .... pp. 228–230
Selection Test B **[L3, L4]** .... pp. 231–233

General Resources

Rubrics for Critique **[L3]** .... pp. 75–76
Rubric for Peer Assessment: Speech **[L3]** .... p. 129

TECHNOLOGY

Go Online: Research **[L3]**
Go Online: Self-test **[L3]**
***ExamView®* Test Bank [L3]**

Choosing Resources for Differentiated Instruction

[L1] Special Needs Students
[L2] Below-Level Students
[L3] All Students
[L4] Advanced Students
[EL] English Learners

For Vocabulary and Reading Warm-ups and for Selection Tests, **A** signifies "less challenging" and **B** "more challenging." For Graphic Organizer transparencies, **A** signifies "not filled in" and **B** "filled in."

FT Fast Track Instruction: To move the lesson more quickly, use the strategies and activities identified with **FT**.

Scaffolding for Less Proficient and Advanced Students

The leveled Critical Thinking questions after selections progress in the levels of thinking required to answer them. To address the needs of your different students, you may use the (a) level questions for your less proficient students and the (b) level questions with your on-level and advanced students. The occasional (c) level questions are appropriate for your advanced students.

PRENTICE HALL **TeacherEXPRESS™** Plan · Teach · Assess

Use this complete suite of powerful teaching tools to make lesson planning and testing quicker and easier.

PRENTICE HALL **StudentEXPRESS™** Learn · Study · Succeed

Use the interactive textbook (online and on CD-ROM) to make selections and activities come alive with audio and video support and interactive questions.

Benchmark

After students have completed these essays, administer **Benchmark Test 10** (*Unit 6 Resources*, pp. 234–239). If the Benchmark Test reveals that some students need further work, use the **Interpretation Guide** to determine the appropriate reteaching pages in the **Reading Kit** or on **Success Tracker.**

Go Online **Professional Development**
For: Information about Lexiles
Visit: www.PHSchool.com
Web Code: eue-1111

PRETEACH

Motivation

These essays offer a convincing mosaic of the many reasons people write and the myriad experiences that fan writers' imaginations. To interest students in the essays, ask students to bring or suggest a favorite title for a classroom library from each student's most recently enjoyed reading material. Urge students to be candid; all reading is worthwhile. Discuss what inspired these many writers to share their experiences, topics, and issues: what makes an idea worth writing about.

❶ Background

More About the Authors

As a young girl in a large Mexican American family, Sandra Cisneros mourned her lack of a "normal" childhood, like the ones she saw on *Leave It to Beaver* and *Father Knows Best.* The Cisneros family moved frequently between Mexico City and Chicago. She had, as she says, "seven fathers," or six brothers and a father, and was lonely for a sister and female friends.

Her loneliness drove Cisneros into the library and motivated her to write. She began writing poetry in high school, but she didn't really take writing seriously until she took her first creative writing class in college. In college, she searched for her unique voice and developed a writing style that was deliberately different from that of her classmates.

In "Ghosts and Voices: Writing from Obsession," Cisneros writes, "If I were asked what it is I write about, I would have to say I write about those ghosts that haunt me, that will not let me sleep, of that which even memory does not like to mention."

In addition to her poetry, Dove has also created texts for musical stage productions and symphonies. Her work with music was actually inspired by an incident in which a lightning bolt set her house on fire, destroying the manuscripts she had been working on. In an attempt to help Dove and her husband recover from the devastating loss, their neighbors gave them tickets to a benefit dinner dance. Dove says that the healing night of music and dancing led to her new passion for dance, which has greatly influenced her writing ever since.

Amy Tan's second novel, *The Kitchen God's Wife,* was inspired by her mother's harrowing early life in China. Her mother was forced to leave three daughters behind in China during her escape on the last boat out of Shanghai during the Communist takeover in 1949. In 1987, Tan brought her mother back to China in an attempt to find the missing daughters. The trip kindled a new connection between Tan and her mother and her Chinese heritage, which in turn influenced her writing.

Build Skills *Essays*

❶ Straw Into Gold • For the Love of Books • Mother Tongue

Sandra Cisneros (b. 1954)

Sandra Cisneros was born in Chicago into a large Mexican American family. Because her family was poor, Cisneros moved frequently and lived for the most part in small, cramped apartments. To cope with these conditions, she retreated into herself and spent much of her time reading fairy tales and classic literature. She attended Loyola University in Chicago and the Writer's Workshop at the University of Iowa. During her college years, Cisneros met writers from many other backgrounds. At first uncomfortable about her family's struggles, she soon realized that her heritage provided her with something unique. Cisneros began writing about her childhood in a book of connected short stories. *The House on Mango Street* (1984) was a modest success. However, her next book, *Woman Hollering Creek* (1991), earned Cisneros widespread recognition, and her most recent novel, *Caramelo* (2002) was selected for the Today Show Book Club. Of her desire to write about her family and community, Cisneros has said, "I'm trying to write stories that haven't been written. I feel like a cartographer; I'm determined to fill a literary void."

Rita Dove (b. 1952)

Now a famous poet, Rita Dove's first writing efforts—at the age of nine or ten—were comic books with female superheroes. Dove was born in Akron, Ohio, to highly educated parents. Dove attended Miami University in Oxford, Ohio, and the University of Iowa. She has published many volumes of poetry, including the Pulitzer Prize–winning *Thomas and Beulah* (1986), *On the Bus with Rosa Parks* (1999), and *American Smooth* (2004). Dove has also written a play, a novel, and a collection of short stories. In 1993, she was appointed Poet Laureate of the United States, becoming the first African American and the youngest person ever to hold that position. "Every time I write a poem," Dove has said, "I try to imagine the reader—the reader that I was—curled up on the couch, at the moment of opening a book and absolutely having my world fall away and entering into another one."

Amy Tan (b. 1952)

As a child, Amy Tan—the daughter of Chinese immigrants—would answer her mother's Chinese questions in English. Growing up in Oakland, California, Tan continued to embrace typical American values, which she assumed defined her identity. These assumptions were upended when the thirty-five-year old Tan visited China with her mother. There she came to appreciate her Chinese roots. At the time, she was leaving a successful career as a business writer to become a fiction writer. When she returned to the United States, she began *The Joy Luck Club* (1989), a novel about four Chinese American women and their mothers. The book made Tan a celebrity. Although she struggled with writer's block, Tan triumphed with her second novel, *The Kitchen God's Wife* (1991). Her other books include *The Hundred Secret Senses* (1995); *The Bonesetter's Daughter* (2001); and *The Opposite of Fate* (2003), a collection of essays.

Preview

Connecting to the Literature

Perhaps, like the writers of these essays when they were girls, you are not as confident as you would like to be. These writers discovered the world of books, and their love of reading led them to write. In writing, each found her own voice.

2 Literary Analysis

Reflective Essay

An essay is a short piece of nonfiction in which a writer expresses a personal view of a topic. In a **reflective essay,** the writer uses an informal tone to explore the meaning of a personal experience or pivotal event. In her essay Rita Dove focuses on her love of books:

> . . . always, I have been passionate about books. . . . I loved to feel their heft in my hand . . .

An essay writer often explores an experience in order to arrive at a deeper understanding of its significance. To help you track each writer's reflections, use a chart like the one shown.

Experiences → Feelings / Significance → Understanding

Comparing Literary Works

Each of these three writers discusses her struggle to create her own true sense of **identity.** As you read, examine how each writer describes the role played by other people in her creation of a genuine sense of self. Determine if a true sense of identity is to be discovered among our companions, in the recesses of our own privacy, or in some combination of the two.

3 Reading Strategy

Evaluating a Writer's Message

As a reader, your job is not only to get a writer's point, but also to decide what you think about it. When you **evaluate a writer's message,** you assess the validity of the writer's ideas and decide whether you agree or disagree with them. As you read these essays, identify and then evaluate the message of each writer.

Vocabulary Builder

nomadic (nō mad′ ik) *adj.* wandering; leading the life of a nomad (p. 1166)

transcribed (tran skrībd′) *v.* wrote or typed a copy (p. 1173)

empirical (em pir′ i kəl) *adj.* derived from observation or experiment (p. 1174)

benign (bi nīn′) *adj.* not injurious or malignant; not cancerous (p. 1175)

semantic (sə man′ tik) *adj.* pertaining to meaning in language (p. 1176)

quandary (kwän′ də rē; kwän′ drē) *n.* state of uncertainty; dilemma (p. 1177)

nascent (nas′ ənt; nā′ sənt) *adj.* coming into existence; emerging (p. 1177)

2 Literary Analysis

Reflective Essay

- Tell students that as they read the three essays, they will become familiar with the essay form called the reflective essay, in which a writer reflects on important life experiences.
- As they read, students should compare the writers' struggles to forge their own identity to their own. How closely can students relate to the writers' experiences and feelings and the conclusions they drew in their essays?
- Draw a chart on the board similar to the one on this page of the student book. Read the example from Rita Dove's essay and use it to fill in the chart as a model for the chart students will fill in as they read the essays. Under the heading Experiences, write "Loved to handle books." Under Feelings, write "Passion," and under Significance, write "Importance of books." Have the class decide as a group what to write under Understanding. (Answers should reflect the enormous influence her experiences with books have had on Rita Dove's life and career.)
- Give students a copy of **Literary Analysis Graphic Organizer A,** p. 262 in ***Graphic Organizer Transparencies,*** to use as they read the selections.

3 Reading Strategy

Evaluating a Writer's Message

- Urge students to make sure that they have read the essays carefully and feel confident that they have understood each writer's message before they attempt to evaluate it.
- Ask students to evaluate the message each of the three writers transmits in her essay. Remind students to support their opinions with reasoned arguments and examples from the text.

Vocabulary Builder

- Pronounce each vocabulary word for students and read the definitions as a class. Have students identify any words with which they are already familiar.

Differentiated Instruction

Solutions for All Learners

Support for Special Needs Students
Have students read the adapted version of "Mother Tongue" in the ***Reader's Notebook: Adapted Version.*** This version provides basic-level instruction in an interactive format with questions and write-on lines. Completing these pages will prepare students to read the selection in the Student Edition.

Support for Less Proficient Readers
Have students read "Mother Tongue" in the ***Reader's Notebook.*** This version provides basic-level instruction in an interactive format with questions and write-on lines. After students finish the selection in the ***Reader's Notebook,*** have them complete the questions and activities in the Student Edition.

Support for English Learners
Have students read "Mother Tongue" in the ***Reader's Notebook: English Language Version.*** This version provides basic-level instruction in an interactive format with questions and write-on lines. Completing these pages will prepare students to read the selection in the Student Edition.

Learning Modalities
Bodily/Kinesthetic Learners
Invite students to demonstrate for the class a physical skill—analogous to the tortilla making in the story—they have recently mastered. As all students attempt the task, urge them to share their feelings about facing and managing challenges.

❶ About the Selection

This essay connects life experiences and a writer's imaginative powers. The essayist, Sandra Cisneros shares anecdotes about her childhood in a Mexican American family and her travels through Europe as a fledgling writer. In recounting some unexpected turns in her life, Cisneros highlights the contrast between her inner experience and the world's view of her and emphasizes strengths she had been surprised to discover in herself.

❷ Literary Analysis
Reflective Essay

- **Ask** a volunteer to read the bracketed passage aloud.
- Then, **ask** the Literary Analysis question: What aspects of the author's tone and word choice let you know right away that this is an informal, personal piece of writing?
Answer: The informal tone is established by the use of sentence fragments and informal sentence openers, such as the word *so*.
- Remind students that reflective essays often describe seemingly insignificant events and draw universal conclusions from them.
- **Ask:** What event does the essayist mention? What problem crops up as a result?
Answer: Cisneros mentions being invited to share a home-cooked dinner of Mexican food. Cisneros has been asked to make tortillas, but she doesn't know how.

➤ **Monitor Progress:** Have students **suggest** a larger lesson that readers could learn from this incident.
Answer: Students are likely to suggest the following: People should not make assumptions based on others' cultural background.

❶ Straw Into Gold: The Metamorphosis of the Everyday

Sandra Cisneros

Background The term "essay" from the French *essai,* meaning "try," historically described an exploratory piece of writing that lacked finish. In 1597, Francis Bacon called his own *Essays* "grains of salt which will rather give an appetite than offend with satiety." Eventually, the essay lost its original "unfinished" sense and writers began to think of it as an elegant, logically reasoned, polished piece of writing. Today, the essay has become one of the most popular literary forms among writers and readers.

❷ When I was living in an artists' colony in the south of France, some fellow Latin-Americans who taught at the university in Aix-en-Provence[1] invited me to share a home-cooked meal with them. I had been living abroad almost a year then on an NEA[2] grant, subsisting mainly on French bread and lentils while in France so that my money could last longer. So when the invitation to dinner arrived, I accepted without hesitation. Especially since they had promised Mexican food.

What I didn't realize when they made this invitation was that I was supposed to be involved in preparing this meal. I guess they assumed I knew how to cook Mexican food because I was Mexican. They wanted specifically tortillas, though I'd never made a tortilla in my life.

It's true I had witnessed my mother rolling the little armies of dough into perfect circles, but my mother's family is from Guanajuato,[3] *provinciales,*[4] country folk. They only know how to make flour tortillas. My father's family, on the other hand, is chilango,[5] from Mexico City.

Literary Analysis
Reflective Essay What aspects of the author's tone and word choice let you know right away that this is an informal, personal piece of writing?

1. **Aix-en-Provence** (eks än prō väns′) city in southeastern France.
2. **NEA** National Endowment for the Arts.
3. **Guanajuato** (gwä′ nä hwä′ tō) state in central Mexico.
4. **provinciales** (prō bēn sē ä′ lās) "country folk" (Spanish).
5. **chilango** (chē län′ gō) "city folk" (Spanish).

Differentiated Instruction Solutions for All Learners

Accessibility at a Glance

	Straw Into Gold	For the Love of Books	Mother Tongue
Language	Informal diction	Informal diction	Informal diction
Concept Level	Accessible (consideration of identity)	Accessible (consideration of identity)	Accessible (consideration of identity)
Literary Merit	Noted author	Award-winning author	Cross-cultural experience
Lexile	930L	1080L	1120L
Overall Rating	Average	Easy	Average

Biography, 1988, Marina Gutierrez, Courtesy of the artist ❸

We ate corn tortillas but we didn't make them. Someone was sent to the corner tortilleria to buy some. I'd never seen anybody make corn tortillas. Ever.

Well, somehow my Latino hosts had gotten a hold of a packet of corn flour, and this is what they tossed my way with orders to produce tortillas. *Asi como sea.* Any ol' way, they said and went back to their cooking.

❺ Why did I feel like the woman in the fairy tale who was locked in a room and ordered to spin straw into gold? I had the same sick feeling when I was required to write my critical essay for my MFA[6] exam—the only piece of noncreative writing necessary in order to get my graduate degree. How was I to start? There were rules involved here, unlike writing a poem or story, which I did intuitively. There was a step-by-step process needed and I had better know it. I felt as if making tortillas, or writing a critical paper for that matter, were tasks so impossible I wanted to break down into tears.

Somehow though, I managed to make those tortillas—crooked and burnt, but edible nonetheless. My hosts were absolutely ignorant when it came to Mexican food; they thought my tortillas were delicious. (I'm glad my mama wasn't there.) Thinking back and

6. **MFA** Master of Fine Arts.

▲ Critical Viewing ❹
This painting, titled *Biography,* challenges the viewer to piece together the experiences of a lifetime from a variety of small objects. What parallels can you draw between the picture and this essay? **[Connect]**

Reading Check ❻
What Mexican dish was Cisneros asked to prepare?

❸ Humanities

Biography, 1988, by Marina Gutierrez

The creator of the painting is Marina Gutierrez, a contemporary Latin American artist (b.1954). In titling this painting *Biography,* Gutierrez offers viewers a guiding hand through the painting's complexity, just as Sandra Cisneros points the way for readers of her "biography," each recognizing that a life and a personality are often more complex than they initially appear to be.

Use these questions for discussion:

1. Which objects in the painting suggest experiences mentioned in the essay?
   Possible response: The apartment building, red house, table with food, and open book all suggest aspects of Cisneros's life experiences.
2. How might each of the young women depicted in the painting represent aspects of Sandra Cisneros?
   Possible response: One might be her eleven-year-old self, one her intellectual/writer self, and one her proud Mexican American self.

❹ Critical Viewing

Answer: Students should note that Cisneros also pieces together a picture of her life experiences from a collection of anecdotes and incidents.

❺ Critical Thinking

Interpret

- Read the bracketed passage aloud.
- **Ask** students to suggest reasons why Cisneros does not tell her hosts that she does not know how to make tortillas.
  Answer: Students' responses should focus on Cisneros's personality. Cisneros is clearly a proud person who rises to a challenge. She had wanted to break down in tears and give up as she had wanted to when she had to write a critical essay for her MFA, but she didn't in either case.

❻ Reading Check

Answer: Cisneros was asked to prepare corn tortillas.

Differentiated Instruction

Solutions for All Learners

Background for Special Needs Students
Read aloud a version of the fairy tale *Rumplestiltskin* to refresh students' memory of the tale and make sure they understand the title and references to *Rumplestiltskin* in the body of the essay. Discuss why Cisneros felt like the miller's daughter in the tale when she was asked to make tortillas.

Background for English Learners
Students learning English may not be familiar with the fairy tale *Rumplestiltskin* and will be puzzled by the title and references to the fairy tale in the text of the essay. Read *Rumplestiltskin* aloud to students or have them listen to the story on CD. Then point out and discuss the references to the fairy tale in the essay.

Strategy for Advanced Readers
Have a volunteer summarize the fairy tale *Rumplestiltskin* and suggest reasons Cisneros drew on this tale in her essay. Then ask students to make a chart that compares Cisneros with the miller's daughter in the fairy tale.

7 Literary Analysis
Reflective Essay

- Have a volunteer read the bracketed passage aloud.
- Remind students that in a reflective essay, the writer uses a personal tone.
- **Ask** the Literary Analysis question: What words or phrases in this paragraph signal the fact that this is a reflective essay on a personal topic?
  Answer: Cisneros reflects on her heritage by describing herself as a Latina and an only daughter in a family of six brothers. She explains that in her culture women don't leave home until they get married. Words and phrases that suggest the reflective nature of the essay include *because I am a woman, an only daughter,* and *I crossed my father's threshold.*

8 Reading Strategy
Evaluating a Writer's Message

- Ask students to consider in what ways their heritage or culture defines the roles of men and women. How does their cultural heritage compare to Cisneros's?
- What aspects of Cisneros' background shaped her as a writer?
  Answer: Her family, her ethnicity, and her poverty all influenced Cisneros.
- Point out that many people have backgrounds in some ways similar to Cisneros's, yet they don't become writers. Have students **discuss** what is unique about Cisneros.
  Answer: Students should understand that each person is influenced by his or her background in a unique way.

looking at that photograph documenting the three of us consuming those lopsided circles I am amazed. Just as I am amazed I could finish my MFA exam (lopsided and crooked, but finished all the same). Didn't think I could do it. But I did.

I've managed to do a lot of things in my life I didn't think I was capable of and which many others didn't think me capable of either.

7 Especially because I am a woman, a Latina, an only daughter in a family of six men. My father would've liked to have seen me married long ago. In our culture, men and women don't leave their father's house except by way of marriage. I crossed my father's threshold with nothing carrying me but my own two feet. A woman whom no one came for and no one chased away.

Literary Analysis
Reflective Essay What words or phrases in this paragraph signal that this is a reflective essay on a personal topic?

To make matters worse, I had left before any of my six brothers had ventured away from home. I had broken a terrible taboo. Somehow, looking back at photos of myself as a child, I wonder if I was aware of having begun already my own quiet war.

8 I like to think that somehow my family, my Mexicanness, my poverty all had something to do with shaping me into a writer. I like to think my parents were preparing me all along for my life as an artist even though they didn't know it. From my father I inherited a love of wandering. He was born in Mexico City but as a young man he traveled into the U.S. vagabonding. He eventually was drafted and thus became a citizen. Some of the stories he has told about his first months in the U.S. with little or no English surface in my stories in *The House on Mango Street* as well as others I have in mind to write in the future. From him I inherited a sappy heart. (He still cries when he watches the Mexican soaps—especially if they deal with children who have forsaken their parents.)

My mother was born like me—in Chicago but of Mexican descent. It would be her tough, streetwise voice that would haunt all my stories and poems. An amazing woman who loves to draw and read books and can sing an opera. A smart cookie.

When I was a little girl we traveled to Mexico City so much I thought my grandparents' house on La Fortuna, Number 12, was home. It was the only constant in our nomadic ramblings from one Chicago flat to another. The house on Destiny Street, Number 12, in the colonia Tepeyac,[7] would be perhaps the only home I knew, and that nostalgia for a home would be a theme that would obsess me.

Vocabulary Builder
nomadic (nō madʹ ik) *adj.* wandering; leading the life of a nomad

My brothers also figured greatly in my art. Especially the oldest two; I grew up in their shadows. Henry, the second oldest and my favorite, appears often in poems I have written and in stories which at times only borrow his nickname, Kiki. He played a major role in my childhood. We were bunkbed mates. We were co-conspirators. We were pals. Until my oldest brother came back from studying in Mexico and left me odd-woman-out for always.

What would my teachers say if they knew I was a writer? Who would've guessed it? I wasn't a very bright student. I didn't much like

7. **colonia Tepeyac** (cô lōʹ nēä tā päʹ yäc) district of Mexico City.

Enrichment

Mexico City

Mexico City, the capital of Mexico, is located in the central plateau of Mexico in the Valley of Mexico, which is ringed by mountains. The city was founded by Aztec Indians in the 1300s and called Tenochtitlan. It quickly became the center of the powerful Aztec empire.

Modern Mexico City is the center of Mexico's cultural, economic, and political life. Though overcrowded and plagued by water and air pollution as well as social unrest, Mexico City has beautiful parks and neighborhoods, important museums, and significant architecture.

Mexico City is one of the fastest growing areas in the world. About 17 million people live in the metropolitan area (nearly 10 million people live in Mexico City proper). Most of the people who live in Mexico City are mestizos, people of mixed Spanish and Indian heritage, and the vast majority of people who live in Mexico City (as in the rest of Mexico) are Roman Catholics.

school because we moved so much and I was always new and funny-looking. In my fifth-grade report card, I have nothing but an avalanche of C's and D's, but I don't remember being that stupid. I was good at art and I read plenty of library books and Kiki laughed at all my jokes. At home I was fine, but at school I never opened my mouth except when the teacher called on me, the first time I'd speak all day.

9 When I think how I see myself, it would have to be at age eleven. I know I'm thirty-two on the outside, but inside I'm eleven. I'm the girl in the picture with skinny arms and a crumpled shirt and crooked hair. I didn't like school because all they saw was the outside me. School was lots of rules and sitting with your hands folded and being very afraid all the time. I liked looking out the window and thinking. I liked staring at the girl across the way writing her name over and over again in red ink. I wondered why the boy with the dirty collar in front of me didn't have a mama who took better care of him.

I think my mama and papa did the best they could to keep us warm and clean and never hungry. We had birthday and graduation parties
10 and things like that, but there was another hunger that had to be fed. There was a hunger I didn't even have a name for. Was this when I began writing?

In 1966 we moved into a house, a real one, our first real home. This meant we didn't have to change schools and be the new kids on the block every couple of years. We could make friends and not be afraid we'd have to say goodbye to them and start all over. My brothers and the flock of boys they brought home would become important characters eventually for my stories—Louie and his cousins, Meme Ortiz and his dog with two names, one in English and one in Spanish.

My mother flourished in her own home. She took books out of the library and taught herself to garden, producing flowers so envied we had to put a lock on the gate to keep out the midnight flower thieves. My mother is still gardening to this day.

This was the period in my life, that slippery age when you are both child and woman and neither, I was to record in *The House on Mango Street*. I was still shy. I was a girl who couldn't come out of her shell.

How was I to know I would be recording and documenting the women who sat their sadness on an elbow and stared out a window? It would be the city streets of Chicago I would later record, but from a child's eyes.

I've done all kinds of things I didn't think I could do since then. I've gone to a prestigious university, studied with famous writers, and taken away an MFA degree. I've taught poetry in the schools in Illinois and Texas. I've gotten an NEA grant and run away with it as far as my courage would take me. I've seen the bleached and bitter mountains of the Peloponnesus.[8] I've lived on a Greek island. I've been to Venice[9]

---

8. **Peloponnesus** (pel´ ə pə nē´ səs) peninsula forming the southeastern part of the Greek mainland.
9. **Venice** (ven´ is) seaport in northern Italy.

Literary Analysis
Reflective Essay and Identity When she was a child, in what ways did Cisneros's inner life not communicate itself to those around her?

Reading Strategy
Evaluating a Writer's Message Why do you think Cisneros does not go into greater detail about the nature of her "hunger"?

Reading Check 11
In Cisneros's culture, under what circumstances do women usually leave home?

9 Literary Analysis
Reflective Essay

- Read the bracketed passage aloud.
- **Ask** the Literary Analysis question: When she was a child, in what ways did Cisneros's inner life not communicate itself to those around her?
  Answer: Cisneros did not speak in school unless the teacher called on her. Her alertness, love of reading, talent for art, and sense of humor were not apparent to teachers and students at school. At home, Cisneros had longings she couldn't put a name to, so these feelings probably went unnoticed by her family.

10 Reading Strategy
Evaluating a Writer's Message

- Read the bracketed passage aloud, and **ask** students what kinds of hunger Cisneros is discussing.
  Answer: literal and figurative hunger
- **Ask** students the Reading Strategy question: Why do you think Cisneros does not go into greater detail about the nature of her "hunger"?
  Answer: Cisneros probably cannot go into greater detail because as a child she could not name or understand this figurative or abstract "hunger."

11 Reading Check
Answer: In Cisneros's culture, women normally leave home only when they marry.

Differentiated Instruction
Solutions for All Learners

Enrichment for Gifted/Talented Students
Do students think that their interior selves remain hidden, or do their friends, family, and acquaintances have a pretty good idea of what they are really like? Invite students to describe and express their essential selves through a medium of their choice. They might create a work of art, such as a painting or piece of sculpture, do a dance or recite a monologue, or write a song, poem, or personal essay. Regardless of the medium they choose, students should keep in mind their goal of giving voice to the person that they are on the inside.

Enrichment for Advanced Readers
Do students believe that their own inner and outer selves are in sync? Invite students to assemble an anthology of poems or excerpts from memoirs, short stories, and other works of literature that discuss the writers' sense of self. If they like, students can invite contributions from their classmates and write selections themselves. Urge students to include an introduction to the anthology that describes the theme that unites the anthology and explains how it was put together.

⓯ Reading Strategy
Evaluating a Writer's Message

- Have a volunteer read the bracketed passage aloud.
- Then, **ask** students to recall the first time they read Shakespeare, and ask them if they enjoyed the experience? What was the most difficult aspect of reading Shakespeare?
  Possible response: Most students will say that they had a difficult time with Shakespeare's diction.
- **Ask** the Reading Strategy question: What point is Dove making about the value of reading when she notes that she did not understand every word she read?
  Answer: Readers can be thrilled by the language they read even though they may not understand every word. Imperfect understanding does not preclude enjoyment.

⓰ Literary Analysis
Reflective Essay

- Read the bracketed passage aloud.
- **Ask** the students the Literary Analysis Question: What sense of herself as a child does Dove's description of the boy in the story convey?
  Answer: Dove identifies with the "dreamy, mild, scatter-brained" boy in the story because she was shy and people who observed her had no idea of what she was really like.

the shelf and discovered a cornucopia of emotional and linguistic delights, from "The Ballad of Barbara Fritchie," which I adored for its sheer length and rather numbing rhymes, to Langston Hughes's dazzlingly syncopated "Dream Boogie." Then there was Shakespeare—daunting for many years because it was his entire oeuvre,[1] in matching wine-red volumes that were so thick they looked more like over-sized bouillon cubes than books, and yet it was that ponderous title—*The Complete Works of William Shakespeare*—that enticed me, because here was a lifetime's work—a lifetime!—in two compact, dense packages. I
⓯ began with the long poem "The Rape of Lucrece" . . . I sampled a few sonnets, which I found beautiful but rather adult; and finally wandered into the plays—first *Romeo and Juliet*, then *Macbeth, Julius Caesar, A Midsummer Night's Dream, Twelfth Night*—enthralled by the language, by the fact that poetry was spinning the story. Of course I did not understand every single word, but I was too young to know that this was supposed to be difficult; besides, no one was waiting to test me on anything, so, free from pressure, I dove in.

At the same time, my brother, two years my senior, had become a science fiction buff, so I'd read his *Analog* and *Fantasy* and Science Fiction magazines after he was finished with them. One story particularly fascinated me: A retarded boy in a small town begins building a sculpture in his backyard, using old and discarded materials—coke bottles, scrap iron, string, and bottle caps. Everyone laughs at him, but he continues building. Then one day he disappears. And when the neighbors investigate, they discover that the sculpture has been dragged onto the back porch and that the screen door is open. Somehow the narrator of the story figures out how to switch on the sculpture: The back door frame begins to glow, and when he steps through it, he's in an alternate universe, a town the mirror image of his own—even down to the colors, with green roses and an orange sky. And he walks through this town until he comes to the main square, where there is a statue erected to—who else?—the village idiot.

I loved this story, the idea that the dreamy, mild, scatter-brained boy
⓰ of one world could be the hero of another. And in a way, I identified with that village idiot because in real life I was painfully shy and awkward; the place where I felt most alive was between the pages of a book.

Although I loved books, for a long time I had no aspirations to be a writer. The possibility was beyond my imagination. I liked to write, however—and on long summer days when I ran out of reading material or my legs had fallen asleep because I had been curled up on the couch for hours on end, I made up my own stories. Most were abandoned midway. Those that I did bring to a conclusion I neither showed to others nor considered saving.

My first piece of writing I thought enough of to keep was a novel called *Chaos*, which was about robots taking over the earth. I had just

Reading Strategy
Evaluating a Writer's Message What point is Dove making about the value of reading when she notes that she did not understand every word she read?

Literary Analysis
Reflective Essay and Identity What sense of herself as a child does Dove's description of the boy in the story convey?

1. **oeuvre** (ë´ vrə) *n.* all the works, usually of a lifetime, of a particular writer, artist, or composer.

Enrichment

Bookbinding

The art of bookbinding, which so enchanted young Rita Dove, began with the production of beautifully illuminated, or decorated, bibles and other religious books used in worship services in churches. These magnificently adorned volumes sometimes included ivory carvings, jewels, gold leaf, or embroidery. Later, decorated leather bindings became the norm. These books were hand-bound with carefully tooled leather.

Today's books are usually machine bound, though they can be quite beautiful. Some books have lettering or illustrations impressed into the fabric covering. Paper jackets, often incorporating paintings, illustrations, or stylized text, are contemporary examples of the bookbinder's art.

entered third or fourth grade; the novel had forty-three chapters, and each chapter was twenty lines or less because I used each week's spelling list as the basis for each chapter, and there were twenty words per list. In the course of the year I wrote one installment per week, and I never knew what was going to happen next—the words led me, not the other way around.

At that time I didn't think of writing as an activity people admited doing. I had no living role models—a "real" writer was a long-dead white male, usually with a white beard to match. Much later, when I was in eleventh grade, my English teacher, Miss Oechsner, took me to a book-signing in a downtown hotel. She didn't ask me if I'd like to go—she asked my parents instead, signed me and a classmate (who is now a professor of literature) out of school one day, and took us to meet a writer. The writer was John Ciardi, a poet who also had translated Dante's *Divine Comedy*, which I had heard of, vaguely. At that moment I realized that writers were real people and how it was possible to write down a poem or story in the intimate sphere of one's own room and then share it with the world.

Critical Reading

1. **Respond:** Would you have been friends with Rita Dove if you had known her as a child? Why or why not?
2. **(a) Recall:** Which emotion did Dove feel in the presence of an unopened book? **(b) Interpret:** For Dove, what traits did an unopened book and a genie's lamp share? **(c) Analyze:** What attitude toward the imagination is suggested by this simile?
3. **(a) Recall:** What books does Dove note most delighted her as a child? **(b) Interpret:** What point is Dove making about the imaginative life of a child through this catalog of her favorite literature?
4. **(a) Recall:** What happens in the science fiction story that Dove enjoys so much? **(b) Connect:** Why is the story especially meaningful to Dove?
5. **(a) Recall:** Which experience made Dove realize that she could be a "real" writer? **(b) Speculate:** Do you think Dove would have gone on to become a writer if she had not had that experience? Why or why not?
6. **Take a Position:** When Dove started reading Shakespeare, she did not know that it "was supposed to be difficult" and so she loved it. What does this statement suggest about our expectations when approaching challenges?

For: More about Rita Dove
Visit: www.PHSchool.com
Web Code: ere-9622

ASSESS

Answers

1. Some students will respond that they would have been friends with Rita Dove because they were shy or shared her passion for books. Other students, who were more active and had other interests, will feel it unlikely that they would have been friends with Dove.
2. (a) Dove felt excitement and anticipation. (b) They were both entrees into magical worlds with endless possibilities. (c) The importance of the imagination is suggested by this simile.
3. (a) Books that delighted Dove included *A Thousand and One Nights, Treasury of Best Loved Poems,* and *The Complete Works of William Shakespeare.* (b) Dove is making the point that children's imaginative lives are unlimited.
4. (a) A retarded boy is appreciated for his creativity in an alternate universe. (b) Dove had an active and imaginative interior life that was not apparent to others.
5. (a) She met the poet John Ciardi. (b) Some students will believe that Dove would never have gone on to become a writer without a role model. Others will believe that she was so imaginative, she would somehow have found her way to writing.
6. The statement suggests that we can succeed at many challenging activities if we have self-confidence, and if we do not know that the challenges we face are considered difficult.

Go Online — Author Link For additional information about Rita Dove, have students type in the Web Code, then select *D* from the alphabet, and then Rita Dove.

Differentiated Instruction

Solutions for All Learners

Background for Special Needs Students
Special needs students may find it very difficult to relate to someone such as Rita Dove who is so enamored of books and reading. Share some of your favorite childhood books with these students and talk about why the books are important to you. Encourage students to discuss their favorite books.

Background for Less Proficient Readers
Share some favorite childhood books with students and have students recall some of their own favorites. Discuss together what qualities make some books so important to children. How unusual do students think Rita Dove's attitude toward books and reading was?

Background for Advanced Readers
Ask advanced readers to gather in small groups to recall their favorite childhood books and discuss the reasons they loved them. Have students poll their classmates to find out their favorite books. Ask students to make a graph or chart that displays the results of the poll.

⓱ About the Selection

This essay demonstrates how much people miss when they make snap judgments or apply stereotypes. Amy Tan paints a portrait of her mother as an intelligent and perceptive woman who encounters difficulties because of her non-standard English. Tan contrasts the valuable lessons she has learned from her mother with the English-speaking world's view of her mother. This essay celebrates the many ways people can communicate and identifies Tan's central goal as a writer: to be readable.

⓲ Critical Viewing

Answer: Judging from the photograph, Tan and her mother have a close and cordial relationship.

⓳ Literary Analysis
Reflective Essay

- Read the bracketed passage aloud.
- Have students **explain** which characteristics comprise a reflective essay.
  Answer: A reflective essay is a short piece of nonfiction in which the author uses informal language and draws conclusions from personal experiences.

➤ **Monitor Progress: Ask** the Literary Analysis question: Which ideas in these opening paragraphs signal that this will be a reflective essay?
Answer: Tan establishes an informal tone immediately. She uses the personal experience of giving a talk on *The Joy Luck Club* to talk about the "different Englishes" she uses as a Chinese American writer.

⓱ Mother Tongue

Amy Tan

⓳ I am not a scholar of English or literature. I cannot give you much more than personal opinions on the English language and its variations in this country or others.

I am a writer. And by that definition, I am someone who has always loved language. I am fascinated by language in daily life. I spend a great deal of my time thinking about the power of language—the way it can evoke an emotion, a visual image, a complex idea, or a simple truth. Language is the tool of my trade. And I use them all—all the Englishes I grew up with.

Recently, I was made keenly aware of the different Englishes I do use. I was giving a talk to a large group of people, the same talk I had already given to half a dozen other groups. The nature of the talk was about my writing, my life, and my book, *The Joy Luck Club.* The talk was ⓴ going along well enough, until I remembered one major difference that made the whole talk sound wrong. My mother was in the room. And it was perhaps the first time she had heard me give a lengthy speech, using the kind of English I have never used with her. I was saying things like,

⓲ ▲ **Critical Viewing** Based on this photograph of Amy Tan and her mother, what kind of a relationship do you think they share? Explain. **[Infer]**

Literary Analysis
Reflective Essay Which ideas in these opening paragraphs signal that this will be a reflective essay?

Enrichment

The English Language

English is the primary language spoken in the United States, United Kingdom, Ireland, Canada, Australia, New Zealand, and many islands in the Caribbean and Pacific. English is the official language of India, the Philippines, and many African countries.

English belongs to one of the three main language branches, West Germanic, and thus is closely related to German and Dutch. English is even more closely related to Frisian, a language spoken by the people of the Dutch province of Friesland. (Old English is most closely related to Icelandic.) As part of the Indo-European language family, English is also related to most of the languages of Europe and Western Asia.

20 "The intersection of memory upon imagination" and "There is an aspect of my fiction that relates to thus-and-thus"—a speech filled with carefully wrought grammatical phrases, burdened, it suddenly seemed to me, with nominalized forms, past perfect tenses, conditional phrases, all the forms of standard English that I had learned in school and through books, the forms of English I did not use at home with my mother.

Just last week, I was walking down the street with my mother, and I again found myself conscious of the English I was using, the English I do use with her. We were talking about the price of new and used furniture and I heard myself saying this: "Not waste money that way." My husband was with us as well, and he didn't notice any switch in my English. And then I realized why. It's because over the twenty years we've been together I've often used the same kind of English with him, and sometimes he even uses it with me. It has become our language of intimacy, a different sort of English that relates to family talk, the language I grew up with.

21 So you'll have some idea of what this family talk I heard sounds like, I'll quote what my mother said during a recent conversation which I videotaped and then transcribed.

During this conversation, my mother was talking about a political gangster in Shanghai[1] who had the same last name as her family's, Du, and how the gangster in his early years wanted to be adopted by her family, which was rich by comparison. Later, the gangster became more powerful, far richer than my mother's family, and one day showed up at my mother's wedding to pay his respects. Here's what she said in part:

"Du Yusong having business like fruit stand. Like off the street kind. He is Du like Du Zong—but not Tsung-ming Island people. The local people call putong, the river east side, he belong to that side local people. That man want to ask Du Zong father take him in like become own family. Du Zong father wasn't look down on him, but didn't take seriously, until that man big like become a mafia. Now important person, very hard to inviting him. Chinese way, come only to show respect, don't stay for dinner. Respect for making big celebration, he shows up. Mean gives lots of respect. Chinese custom. Chinese social life that way. If too important won't have to stay too long. He come to my wedding. I didn't see, I heard it. I gone to boy's side, they have YMCA[2] dinner. Chinese age I was nineteen."

You should know that my mother's expressive command of English belies how much she actually understands. She reads the Forbes[3] report, listens to *Wall Street Week*,[4] converses daily with her stockbroker, reads all of Shirley MacLaine's[5] books with ease—all kinds of things I

1. **Shanghai** (shaŋ′ hī′) seaport city in eastern China.
2. **YMCA** Young Men's Christian Association.
3. ***Forbes*** magazine of business and finance.
4. ***Wall Street Week*** weekly television program that reports business and investment news.
5. **Shirley MacLaine's** (mək lānz′) Shirley MacLaine is an American actress who has written several books.

Literary Analysis
Reflective Essay and Identity What division in her sense of identity does Tan experience while giving her lecture?

Vocabulary Builder
transcribed (tran skrībd′) *v.* wrote or typed a copy

22  **Reading Check**
How does Tan's language change when she gives her speech?

Differentiated Instruction
Solutions for All Learners

Support for Special Needs Students
Before students read the selection, work with them to preview the footnoted terms. Make sure students understand each term's meaning, and answer any questions they may have.

Support for Less Proficient Readers
Before students read the selection, ask them to work with partners and list the footnoted terms. For terms that both partners do not know, ask them to check print or online dictionaries to find the meaning of each.

Vocabulary for English Learners
Students may have difficulty understanding the acronyms YMCA, CAT, and SAT. Explain that an acronym is an abbreviation formed from the first letters or syllables in a group of words. For example, YMCA is formed from the first letters of Young Men's Christian Association.

20 Literary Analysis
Reflective Essay

- Have a student volunteer read the bracketed passage aloud.
- **Ask** students the Literary Analysis question: What division in her sense of identity does Tan experience while giving her lecture?
Answer: Tan experiences a conflict between the formally educated aspect of herself that she developed in school and her at-home self, which she experiences with her mother.
- **Ask** students how the languages they speak at home are similar to or different from the one they speak at school.
Possible response: Most students will acknowledge a difference between private, family language and public, or formal language. These languages may be entirely different or simply subtle variations of English.

21 Vocabulary Builder
The Latin Word Root *-scrib-*, *-script-*

- Read the sentence in which the word *transcribed* appears and have students define *transcribed*. Make sure that students understand that *transcribing* means "copying out in full."
- Point out the root *-scrib-* appears in the word *transcribed* and that *-scrib-* and *-script-* are Latin word roots that mean "write."
- **Invite** students to think of other common words with this root.
Answer: Some examples include *script, scripture, scribe,* and *scribble.*

22 Reading Check

Answer: Tan's language in her speech changes from informal to formal or standard English "with carefully wrought grammatical forms, past perfect tenses, conditional phrases, all the forms of standard English."

㉓ Literary Analysis
Reflective Essay

- Read the bracketed passage aloud.
- Have students **state** some of the "I" phrases that Tan uses in this passage.
  Answer: "I've been giving more thought . . . "; "I have described it . . . ""I wince when I say . . . "
- Then, **ask** the Literary Analysis question: What language in this paragraph reinforces the idea that the essay is reflective?
  Answer: The idea that the essay is reflective is reinforced by the personal language and Tan's reference to her mother's English to illustrate that language is often a reflection of identity. Tan explicitly states that she has been "giving more thought" to the English her mother speaks.

㉔ Reading Strategy
Evaluating a Writer's Message

- Have a volunteer read the bracketed passage aloud.
- **Ask** the Reading Strategy question: What point does Tan make through this anecdote about speaking for her mother? Do you find her point valid? Explain.
  Answer: The author is making the point that people don't take those who speak fractured, or imperfect, English seriously. Tan herself was guilty of thinking that her mother's non-standard English reflected the quality of her mother's thinking.
- Have students **speculate** about how important the author's mother feels her lack of proper English is and explain why they hold that opinion.
  Answer: Many students will remark that the author's mother believes that her lack of formal English has been a hindrance because she calls on her daughter to help her in difficult situations. Still, the author's mother hasn't let her limited English stand in her way too much, as demonstrated by her meeting with her stockbroker.

can't begin to understand. Yet some of my friends tell me they understand 50 percent of what my mother says. Some say they understand 80 to 90 percent. Some say they understand none of it, as if she were speaking pure Chinese. But to me, my mother's English is perfectly clear, perfectly natural. It's my mother tongue. Her language, as I hear it, is vivid, direct, full of observation and imagery. That was the language that helped shape the way I saw things, expressed things, made sense of the world.

㉓ Lately, I've been giving more thought to the kind of English my mother speaks. Like others, I have described it to people as "broken," or "fractured" English. But I wince when I say that. It has always bothered me that I can think of no way to describe it other than "broken," as if it were damaged and needed to be fixed, as if it lacked a certain wholeness and soundness. I've heard other terms used, "limited English," for example. But they seem just as bad, as if everything is limited, including people's perceptions of the limited English speaker.

Literary Analysis
Reflective Essay What language in this paragraph reinforces the idea that the essay is reflective?

I know this for a fact, because when I was growing up, my mother's "limited" English limited my perception of her. I was ashamed of her English. I believed that her English reflected the quality of what she had to say. That is, because she expressed them imperfectly her thoughts were imperfect. And I had plenty of empirical evidence to support me: the fact that people in department stores, at banks, and at restaurants did not take her seriously, did not give her good service, pretended not to understand her, or even acted as if they did not hear her.

Vocabulary Builder
empirical (em pir′ i kəl) *adj.* derived from observation or experiment

My mother has long realized the limitations of her English as well. When I was fifteen, she used to have me call people on the phone to pretend I was she. In this guise, I was forced to ask for information or even to complain and yell at people who had been rude to her. One time it was a call to her stockbroker in New York. She had cashed out her small portfolio and it just so happened we were going to go to New York the next week, our very first trip outside California. I had to get on the phone and say in an adolescent voice that was not very convincing, "This is Mrs. Tan."

And my mother was standing in the back whispering loudly, "Why he don't send me check, already two weeks late. So mad he lie to me, losing me money."

㉔ And then I said in perfect English, "Yes, I'm getting rather concerned. You had agreed to send the check two weeks ago, but it hasn't arrived."

Then she began to talk more loudly. "What he want, I come to New York tell him front of his boss, you cheating me?" And I was trying to calm her down, make her be quiet, while telling the stockbroker, "I can't tolerate any more excuses. If I don't receive the check immediately, I am going to have to speak to your manager when I'm in New York next week." And sure enough, the following week there we were in front of this astonished stockbroker, and I was sitting there red-faced and quiet, and my mother, the real Mrs. Tan, was shouting at his boss in her impeccable broken English.

Reading Strategy
Evaluating a Writer's Message What point does Tan make through this anecdote about speaking for her mother? Do you find her point valid? Explain.

Enrichment

Attitudes Toward Chinese Americans

The Anti-Defamation League and the Committee of 100 (an organization of prominent Chinese Americans) released a poll in the spring of 2001 that examined Americans' attitudes toward Chinese Americans, though the poll found that most Americans do not distinguish between Chinese Americans and other Asian Americans.

According to the poll, 32% of Americans believe Chinese Americans are more loyal to China than to America. Thirty-four percent said that Chinese Americans have too much control over the high-tech industry. Twenty-four percent of Americans do not approve of intermarriage between Chinese Americans and Americans of other backgrounds, and 23% said they would not vote for a Chinese American for president.

The ADL believes that Chinese Americans face a combination of racial and political prejudice, one that discussion and education can help overcome.

We used a similar routine just five days ago, for a situation that was far less humorous. My mother had gone to the hospital for an appointment, to find out about a benign brain tumor a CAT scan[6] had revealed a month ago. She said she had spoken very good English, her best English, no mistakes. Still, she said, the hospital did not apologize when they said they had lost the CAT scan and she had come for nothing. She said they did not seem to have any sympathy when she told them she was anxious to know the exact diagnosis, since her husband and son had both died of brain tumors. She said they would not give her any more information until the next time and she would have to make another appointment for that. So she said she would not leave until the doctor called her daughter. She wouldn't budge. And when the doctor finally called her daughter, me, who spoke in perfect English—lo and behold—we had assurances the CAT scan would be found, promises that a conference call on Monday would be held, and apologies for any suffering my mother had gone through for a most regrettable mistake.

Vocabulary Builder
benign (bi nīn′) *adj.* not injurious or malignant; not cancerous

I think my mother's English almost had an effect on limiting my possibilities in life as well. Sociologists and linguists probably will tell you that a person's developing language skills are more influenced by peers. But I do think that the language spoken in the family, especially in immigrant families which are more insular, plays a large role in shaping the language of the child. And I believe that it affected my results on
25 achievement tests, IQ tests, and the SAT.[7] While my English skills were never judged as poor, compared to math, English could not be considered my strong suit. In grade school I did moderately well, getting perhaps B's, sometimes B-pluses, in English and scoring perhaps in the sixtieth or seventieth percentile on achievement tests. But those scores were not good enough to override the opinion that my true abilities lay in math and science, because in those areas I achieved A's and scored in the ninetieth percentile or higher.

This was understandable. Math is precise; there is only one correct answer. Whereas, for me at least, the answers on English tests were always a judgment call, a matter of opinion and personal experience. Those tests were constructed around items like fill-in-the-blank sentence completion, such as, "Even though

6. **CAT scan** method used by doctors to diagnose brain disorders.
7. **SAT** Scholastic Aptitude Test; national college entrance exam.

26 ▶ **Critical Viewing** Is the language on these signs in San Francisco's Chinatown district the "mother tongue" to which Tan refers? Explain. **[Distinguish]**

25 Reading Strategy
Evaluating a Writer's Message

- Read the bracketed passage aloud.
- Remind students of how Tan's mother felt about her limited English. Then, **ask** students to describe the effect Tan believes her mother's English has had on her own life.
  Answer: Tan feels that her mother's lack of English has lowered her own results on tests of language skills and caused people to assume that Tan's true abilities are in mathematics.

26 Critical Viewing

Answer: Students should recall that Tan describes her mother's "broken English," not Chinese, as her mother tongue.

Differentiated Instruction
Solutions for All Learners

For Special Needs Students
Discuss how the author's mother was treated by the stockbroker and the hospital staff. Use a graphic organizer such as a Problem/Solution organizer to help students identify the mother's problem, the reasons for it, and possible solutions.

For Less Proficient Readers
Ask students to use a Problem/Solution graphic organizer to help them analyze the causes of the mother's problem and possible solutions for it. Ask students to use the information on the organizer to write a note of advice to the mother.

For Advanced Readers
Ask students to use a Problem/Solution graphic organizer to analyze why the broken English of the author's mother causes people to treat her so shabbily. Ask students to use their data on the graphic organizer to write a brief essay on this topic.

27 Literary Analysis
Reflective Essay and Identity

- Read the bracketed passage aloud.
- Then, **ask** the Literary Analysis question: What conflict between her personal sensibilities and the values of society does Tan highlight in this discussion of her struggles in English classes?
  Answer: Tan's imagination felt limited by the choices she had to make on multiple-choice tests she took in English class because her model, her mother's English, was so imaginative and fluid and admitted so many possibilities.

28 Reading Strategy
Evaluating a Writer's Message

- Have a volunteer read the bracketed passage.
- **Ask** the Reading Strategy question: What point about defying expectations is Tan making? Do you agree with her?
  Possible response: Because she is Chinese American, people expected Tan to go into a field that relies on logic and mathematics. Tan defied expectations by majoring in English, and she began to write after a boss told her that writing was her weakest skill.
- **Ask** students how Tan's behavior—defying expectations— relates to her mother's English.
  Possible response: Much like Tan's behavior in the face of doubt and adversity, Tan's mother's limited English defied expectations by reinforcing imagination and engendering possibility for Tan.

Tom was _______, Mary thought he was ______." And the correct answer always seemed to be the most bland combinations of thoughts, for example, "Even though Tom was shy, Mary thought he was charming," with the grammatical structure "even though" limiting the correct answer to some sort of semantic opposites, so you wouldn't get answers like, "Even though Tom was foolish, Mary thought he was ridiculous." Well, according to my mother, there were very few limitations as to what Tom could have been and what Mary might have thought of him. So I never did well on tests like that.

27 The same was true with word analogies, pairs of words in which you were supposed to find some sort of logical, semantic relationship — for example, "*Sunset* is to *nightfall* as _______ is to _______." And here you would be presented with a list of four possible pairs, one of which showed the same kind of relationship: *red* is to *stoplight, bus* is to *arrival, chills* is to *fever, yawn* is to *boring*. Well, I could never think that way. I knew what the tests were asking, but I could not block out of my mind the images already created by the first pair, "*sunset* is to *nightfall*"—and I would see a burst of colors against a darkening sky, the moon rising, the lowering of a curtain of stars. And all the other pairs of words—red, bus, stoplight, boring—just threw up a mass of confusing images, making it impossible for me to sort out something as logical as saying: "A sunset precedes nightfall" is the same as "a chill precedes a fever." The only way I would have gotten that answer right would have been to imagine an associative situation, for example, my being disobedient and staying out past sunset, catching a chill at night, which turns into feverish pneumonia as punishment, which indeed did happen to me.

I have been thinking about all this lately, about my mother's English, about achievement tests. Because lately I've been asked, as a writer, why there are not more Asian Americans represented in American literature. Why are there few Asian Americans enrolled in creative writing programs? Why do so many Chinese students go into engineering? Well, these are broad sociological questions I can't begin to answer. But I have noticed in surveys—in fact, just last week—that Asian students, as a whole, always do significantly better on math achievement tests than in English. And this makes me think that there are other Asian-American students whose English spoken in the home might also be described as "broken" or "limited." And perhaps they also have teachers who are steering them away from writing and into math and science, which is what happened to me.

28 Fortunately, I happen to be rebellious in nature and enjoy the challenge of disproving assumptions made about me. I became an English major my first year in college, after being enrolled as pre-med. I started writing nonfiction as a freelancer the week after I was told by my former boss that writing was my worst skill and I should hone my talents toward account management.

But it wasn't until 1985 that I finally began to write fiction. And at first I wrote using what I thought to be wittily crafted sentences,

Vocabulary Builder
semantic (sə man′ tik) *adj.* pertaining to meaning in language

Literary Analysis
Reflective Essay and Identity What conflict between her personal sensibilities and the values of society does Tan highlight in this discussion of her struggles in English classes?

Reading Strategy
Evaluating a Writer's Message What point about defying expectations is Tan making? Do you agree with her?

Enrichment

Standardized Achievement Tests

In this essay Amy Tan describes difficulties she had with standardized tests. What are standardized tests and what do they measure? Some tests are criteria-based—that is, they measure a body of knowledge. Others are norm-referenced. Norm-referenced tests compare a test-taker's score against the scores of people who have already taken the test.

Common norm-referenced tests include the California Achievement Test, Comprehensive Test of Basic Skills, Iowa Test of Basic Skills, Metropolitan Achievement Test, and Stanford Achievement Test. Scores on norm-referenced tests are reported in percentile ranks. For example, if a student scored in the 75th percentile, the student had a higher score than 75% of the other students who took the test.

Should schools use tests that rank and sort students, rather than determine whether they have learned the material they have been taught? Norm-referenced tests are a continuing topic of debate in schools.

sentences that would finally prove I had mastery over the English language. Here's an example from the first draft of a story that later made its way into *The Joy Luck Club,* but without this line: "That was my mental quandary in its nascent state." A terrible line, which I can barely pronounce.

Fortunately, for reasons I won't get into today, I later decided I should envision a reader for the stories I would write. And the reader I decided upon was my mother, because these were stories about mothers. So with this reader in mind—and in fact she did read my early drafts—I began to write stories using all the Englishes I grew up with: the English I spoke to my mother, which for lack of a better term might be described as "simple"; the English she used with me, which for lack of a better term might be described as "broken"; my translation of her Chinese, which could certainly be described as "watered down"; and what I imagined to be her translation of her Chinese if she could speak in perfect English, her internal language, and for that I sought to preserve the essence, but neither an English nor a Chinese structure. I wanted to capture what language ability tests can never reveal: her intent, her passion, her imagery, the rhythms of her speech and the nature of her thoughts.

Apart from what any critic had to say about my writing, I knew I had succeeded where it counted when my mother finished reading my book and gave me her verdict: "So easy to read."

Vocabulary Builder

quandary (kwän′ dä rē) *n.* state of uncertainty; dilemma

nascent (nas′ ənt, nā′ sənt) *adj.* coming into existence; emerging

Critical Reading

1. **Respond:** Having read this essay, what are your feelings about Tan and her mother? Explain.
2. **(a) Recall:** What does Tan realize while speaking to an audience that includes her mother? **(b) Infer:** What circumstances account for Tan's having developed more than one "English"?
3. **(a) Recall:** According to Tan, in what ways do math skills differ from language skills? **(b) Interpret:** In what ways did Tan's sense of different "Englishes" prevent her from answering correctly on grammar tests?
4. **(a) Summarize:** Summarize one experience Tan had involving her mother's difficulty with Standard English.
   (b) Compare and Contrast: In what ways does Tan's sense of her mother's English differ from the perceptions of strangers?
   (c) Analyze: What influence has Tan's mother had on her daughter's writing? Support your answer.
5. **Speculate:** What would it be like to live in a place where a language barrier made it difficult for you to communicate with others? What actions might you take to overcome the barrier?

For: More about Amy Tan
Visit: www.PHSchool.com
Web Code: ere-9623

ASSESS

Answers

1. Many students will admire both Tan and her mother because the mother fought prejudice against her poor English by continuing to demand what she wanted and needed and because Tan overcame her embarrassment at her mother's non-standard English and went on to achieve in an area in which people assumed she could not do well.
2. (a) Tan realizes she is using a kind of complex standard English that she would never use at home with her mother. (b) Tan had to use English her mother would understand at home and more formal English to succeed in school and in her profession.
3. (a) In math, there is one precise correct answer to a problem; language skills cannot be evaluated as precisely. (b) Tan sees too many possible answers and cannot figure out which of the many possibilities is considered "correct."
4. (a) The author's mother often asked that Tan pretend to be her own mother on the phone, because she spoke standard English. (b) Tan knows that her mother is bright and capable despite her fractured English. Strangers assume Tan's mother is stupid because of her limited English. (c) Tan's mother has provided an example of some of the many creative ways English may be used through her imaginative "broken" English.
5. Most students will state that they would dislike living in a place where a language barrier prevented them from communicating with other people. They would likely try to keep a sense of humor as they learned the native language as quickly and thoroughly as possible.

Go Online Author Link For additional information about Amy Tan, have students type in the Web Code, then select *T* from the alphabet, and then Amy Tan.

Answers

1. (a) Cisneros believes that people can transform their lives; she thinks that education, travel, and writing about a variety of experiences are very important. (b) The last paragraph confirms this idea as it describes the places her writing has taken her.
2. (a) Dove was a shy and awkward child. (b) Dove is grateful for the worlds she discovered in books.
3. Tan is no longer embarrassed by her mother's non-standard English, which doesn't indicate her mother's intelligence.
4. A reflective essay may provide the opportunity for a more logical, extended analysis of a personal experience.
5. (a) Both Dove and Cisneros were awkward youngsters who discovered books and writing. Cisneros became a writer almost as a reaction to people's expectations; Dove became a writer as a result of meeting a writer. (b) Both authors drew on childhood experiences in their essays.
6. All three authors had to fight against prejudice and feeling like outsiders. Through their reading and writing, they gained and strengthened their unique identities.
7. (a) Students should support their answers. (b) Writing has helped all three authors bridge the gap between their inner lives and their outward circumstances.
8. (a) **Author's Message:** Books are magical and transformative. **Evidence For:** Dove describes several books and stories and her reactions to them. **Your Response:** Most students will believe that books transformed Dove's life. (b) **Author's Message:** Language abilities indicate nothing about intelligence. **Evidence For:** Tan's mother is intelligent and her English is expressive, though non-standard. **Your Response:** Most students will agree based on what they have learned about Tan's mother. (c) Students should explain their answers.
9. A community can provide various social services and English language instruction.

Go Online Assessment Students may use the **Self-test** to prepare for **Selection Test A** or **Selection Test B**.

Apply the Skills

Straw Into Gold • For the Love of Books • Mother Tongue

Literary Analysis

Reflective Essay

1. **(a)** What does Cisneros's list of accomplishments reveal about her values? **(b)** Does the last paragraph confirm or contradict that idea? Explain.
2. **(a)** What kind of child does Dove say she was? **(b)** How do you think Dove feels about her childhood?
3. In what ways has Tan's attitude toward her mother changed as she has grown older? Explain.
4. Based on these examples, why might an author use a **reflective essay** instead of fiction or poetry to explore a specific subject?

QuickReview

A **reflective essay** explores the meaning of a writer's personal experiences or observations.

Comparing Literary Works

5. **(a)** Compare and contrast Dove's and Cisneros's childhoods and the paths each took to become a writer. **(b)** In what ways do you think their backgrounds might be expressed in their work?
6. What evidence do you find in these essays that each writer struggled or sacrificed to create a true sense of **identity**?
7. **(a)** In what ways do these author's inner lives contrast—or conflict—with the outside world? **(b)** What role does writing play in the relationship between each writer's inner and outer life?

The struggle for a true sense of **identity,** which reflects a person's values, experiences, heritage, and interests, is often a shaping force in a writer's life and work.

Reading Strategy

Evaluating a Writer's Message

8. Use a chart like the one shown to answer the following questions: **(a)** What does Dove believe about the power of books? **(b)** What does Tan's essay reveal about how language differences can lead to misconceptions or stereotypes? **(c)** For each essay, explain whether you do or do not agree with the author's message.

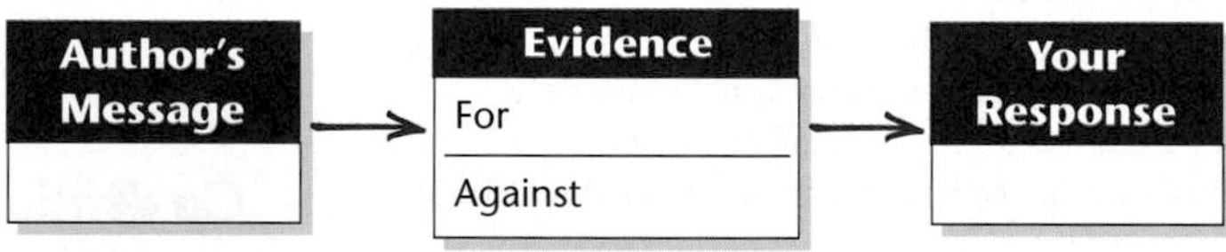

To **evaluate a writer's message,** judge it critically and decide whether you do or do not agree with it.

Extend Understanding

9. **Community Connection:** Amy Tan's mother struggled to communicate effectively in the United States. What services can a community provide to people with limited abilities in English?

For: Self-test
Visit: www.PHSchool.com
Web Code: era-6613

Build Language Skills

❶ Vocabulary Lesson

Word Analysis: Latin Root *-scrib-*, *-script-*

The word *transcribe,* which means "write out or type out in full," is formed from the Latin root *-scrib-*, which means "write." Using each pair of words below, write a sentence that demonstrates the meaning of this root.

1. scribble, child
2. prescription, doctor
3. inscription, trophy
4. author, manuscript

Spelling Strategy

When adding a suffix beginning with a vowel to words of more than one syllable ending with a single consonant, do not double the final consonant: *nomad* + *-ic* = *nomadic.* Often, however, when a word's final syllable has the accent, the final consonant is doubled: *regrettable.* Correctly add the indicated suffix to each word below.

1. benefit + *-ed* **2.** refer + *-ing* **3.** travel + *-er*

Vocabulary Builder: Sentence Completions

Complete each sentence by filling in each blank with a vocabulary word from the list on page 1163.

1. The wandering tribe led a __?__ life in the desert.
2. A person who loves language might pursue __?__ studies.
3. The kindly old woman had a __?__ influence on her children.
4. Her __?__ social extroversion revealed itself before she could talk.
5. The archaeologist __?__ the message that was carved on the wall of the tomb.
6. Having accepted two invitations, he found himself in a social __?__.
7. Scientists use __?__ evidence to prove or disprove a hypothesis.

❷ Grammar and Style Lesson

Varying Sentence Structure

Simple sentences—those consisting of one independent clause—convey ideas concisely and directly. **Compound sentences** contain two or more independent clauses. **Complex sentences** contain an independent clause and one or more subordinate clauses. In this example, Sandra Cisneros follows a complex sentence with a simple one:

Example: To make matters worse, I had left before any of my six brothers had ventured away from home. I had broken a terrible taboo.

Looking at Style Compare Amy Tan's first two paragraphs with the rest of her essay.

1. What do you notice about the sentence structure?
2. What affect does her choice of sentence structure have on the rhythm of her writing?
3. How does Tan's style relate to her message?

Writing Application Using a variety of sentence structures, write a paragraph in which you discuss the essay you enjoyed most. In your writing, explain your choice.

 *Prentice Hall Writing and Grammar Connection: Chapter 20, Section 3*

Assessment Practice

Identifying Errors (For more practice, see *Standardized Test Preparation Workbook*, p. 69.)

The writing sections of many tests require students to identify the type of error, if any, present in a sentence or phrase. Use the following sample item to show students how to determine the type of error a passage contains.

Many people have too different selves: the one they show to the outside world and the one they keep hidden.

Which type of error, if any, appears in the underlined section of the passage?

A Spelling error **C** Punctuation error
B Capitalization error **D** No error

There are no capitalization errors or punctuation errors, but *too* should be spelled "two." The correct answer is *A*.

Answers

❶ Vocabulary Lesson

Word Analysis

Sentences should include word pairs in a way that shows understanding of the root *-scrib-* or *-script-*.

Spelling Strategy

1. benefited
2. referring
3. traveler

Vocabulary Builder

1. nomadic
2. semantic
3. benign
4. nascent
5. transcribed
6. quandary
7. empirical

❷ Grammar and Style Lesson

Looking at Style

1. The first two paragraphs are written in short, simple sentences.
2. The first two paragraphs present information bluntly and forcefully. The following paragraphs are more flowing.
3. The first two paragraphs may represent the simpler writing of a mother tongue. The next paragraphs are more fluent. Tan's message is about fluency and the ability to communicate with ease using different styles.

Writing Application

Students must use a variety of sentence structures in their paragraphs about the essay they enjoyed most.

Writing and Grammar, Ruby Level

Students will find further instruction and practice on varying sentence structure in Chapter 20, Section 3.

❸ Writing Lesson

- Give students **Support for the Writing Lesson**, p. 225 in ***Unit 6 Resources***, to use as they write their letters to the author.
- To prepare students to write their letters to authors, choose one of the three essays and discuss what students liked and didn't like about it, as well as aspects of the essay that puzzled them. Summarize the students' comments in a list that you write on the board.
- Review the Writing Lesson with students to help them take notes for, draft, and revise their letters.
- Go over the writing model so that students gain practice in substituting stronger modifiers for weaker ones. Urge them to revise their own drafts to make their writing more vivid and precise.
- Use the rubrics for Critique, pp. 75–76 in ***General Resources***, to evaluate students' letters.

❹ Listening and Speaking

- Urge students to reread the essay by the author they have chosen. As they reread it, they should note the main points that they plan to include in their speech.
- Have students look over their notes and summarize the most important points on the index cards. Encourage them to write words and phrases rather than complete sentences so they are not tempted to read from the cards when they give the speech rather than referring to them from time to time.
- Ask students to practice their speeches for a classmate or two before they present them to the entire class.
- Use the rubric for Peer Assessment: Speech, p. 129 in ***General Resources***, to evaluate students' work.
- The **Support for Extend Your Learning** page (***Unit 6 Resources***, p. 226) provides guided note-taking opportunities to help students complete the Extend Your Learning Activities.

Go Online Research Have students type in the Web Code for another research activity.

❸ Writing Lesson

Letter to the Author

Because they seem so personal and are written in a conversational style, these reflective essays invite response. Write a letter to the author of the essay you found most interesting. Explain what you liked, what you did not like, and ask any questions you might have.

Prewriting Choose the essay you wish to discuss and reread it. Take notes about the author's message and style. List statements and images that you like, or that disturb you in some way.

Drafting In your opening paragraph, state how much you enjoyed the essay and why. In the body paragraphs, go into greater detail, and ask any relevant questions. Consider drawing parallels to your own life.

Revising Review your letter, and determine whether or not you have used the best language to communicate your thoughts. Highlight and replace any vague words with more specific ones.

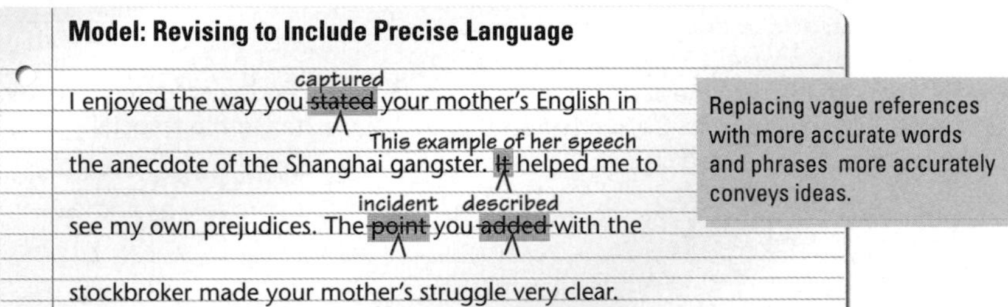

Model: Revising to Include Precise Language
I enjoyed the way you ~~stated~~ captured your mother's English in
the anecdote of the Shanghai gangster. ~~It~~ This example of her speech helped me to
see my own prejudices. The ~~point~~ incident you ~~added~~ described with the
stockbroker made your mother's struggle very clear.
Replacing vague references with more accurate words and phrases more accurately conveys ideas.

WG *Prentice Hall Writing and Grammar Connection: Chapter 14, Section 4*

Extend Your Learning

❹ **Listening and Speaking** Write and deliver a **speech** that Cisneros, Dove, or Tan might present to aspiring young authors. Keep the following tips in mind as you prepare:

- List each main point on an index card.
- Practice until you refer only occasionally to your index cards.

As you deliver your speech, speak slowly and clearly, using appropriate tone, pitch, and pacing. Be sure to maintain eye contact with the audience.

Research and Technology Both Tan and Cisneros grew up with more than one language. In a group, research the ways in which multilingual environments affect the development of language skills. Then, deliver a **team report** on the advantages of language studies for young children. **[Group Activity]**

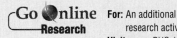

For: An additional research activity
Visit: www.PHSchool.com
Web Code: erd-7613

Assessment Resources

The following resources can be used to assess students' knowledge and skills.

Unit 6 Resources
Selection Test A, pp. 228–230
Selection Test B, pp. 231–233
Benchmark Test 10, pp. 234–239

General Resources
Rubrics for Critique, pp. 75–76
Rubric for Peer Assessment: Speech, p. 129

Go Online Assessment Students may use the **Self-test** to prepare for **Selection Test A** or **Selection Test B.**

Benchmark
Administer **Benchmark Test 10.** If the Benchmark Test reveals that some students need further work, use the **Interpretation Guide** to determine the appropriate reteaching pages in the **Reading Kit** or on **Success Tracker.**

Unit 6
Part
3

Social Protest

Choke, 1964, Robert Rauschenberg oil and screenprint on canvas, 60" × 48", Washington University Gallery of Art, St. Louis.

Differentiated Instruction

Solutions for All Learners

Accessibility at a Glance

More Accessible	Average	More Challenging
Losses	The Rockpile	*from* Hiroshima
The Death of the Ball Turret Gunner	Mirror	In a Classroom
Frederick Douglass	Inaugural Address	The Explorer
Runagate Runagate	*from* Letter from Birmingham City Jail	Camouflaging the Chimera
	For My Children	
	Bidwell Ghost	
	The Crucible	

Selection Planning Guide

From Hersey's account of the bombing of Hiroshima to the dark themes of *The Crucible,* the selections in this section capture the mood of the second half of the twentieth century. Social protest threads through poems such as "Mirror," which questions society's emphasis on youth, and "Frederick Douglass," which assesses the progress African Americans have made toward equality. A poem by Yusef Komunyakaa brings home the lessons of the Vietnam War.

Humanities

Choke, 1964, by Robert Rauschenberg

Born in Texas in 1925, Robert Rauschenberg has been one of the leading experimental American artists of the late twentieth century. The work shown here uses a technique he developed in the early 1960s: combining images from media and other artifacts of everyday life in silk-screen prints. Encourage students to identify specific images in this work. For example, guide students to see the upside-down Public Shelter sign, the One Way sign, the grainy Army helicopter, and the Statue of Liberty. **Ask:**

- There are references to the military and bomb shelters in this work. Given that Rauschenberg created this image a few years after the Cuban Missile Crisis, what aspect of American life might he be protesting?
  Possible answer: He might be protesting the possibility of nuclear war or the power of the military.

Monitoring Progress

Before students read "The Rockpile," administer **Diagnostic Test 11.** Before students read *The Crucible,* administer **Diagnostic Test 12.** These tests will determine students' level of readiness for the reading and vocabulary skills.

Benchmark

After students have completed the poems by Colleen McElroy, Louise Erdrich, and Yusef Komunyakaa, administer **Benchmark Test 11.** After students have completed *The Crucible,* administer **Benchmark Test 12.**

If the Benchmark Tests reveal that some students need further work, use the **Interpretation Guide** to determine the appropriate reteaching pages in the **Reading Kit** or on **Success Tracker.**

Meeting Your Standards

Students will

1. **analyze and respond to literary elements.**
   - Literary Analysis: Setting
2. **read, comprehend, analyze, and critique a short story.**
   - Reading Strategy: Identifying Cause and Effect
   - Reading Check questions
   - Apply the Skills questions
   - Assessment Practice (ATE)
3. **develop vocabulary.**
   - Vocabulary Lesson: Latin Prefix: *mal-*
4. **understand and apply written and oral language conventions.**
   - Spelling Strategy
   - Grammar and Style Lesson: Restrictive and Nonrestrictive Adjective Clauses
5. **develop writing proficiency.**
   - Writing Lesson: Roy's Journal
6. **develop appropriate research strategies.**
   - Extend Your Learning: Illustrated Report
7. **understand and apply listening and speaking strategies.**
   - Extend Your Learning: Radio Play

Block Scheduling: Use one 90-minute class period to preteach the skills and have students read the selection. Use a second 90-minute class period to assess students' mastery of skills, extend their learning, and monitor their progress.

Homework Suggestions

Following are possibilities for homework assignments.

- Support pages from *Unit 6 Resources:*
  Literary Analysis
  Reading Strategy
  Vocabulary Builder
  Grammar and Style
- An Extend Your Learning project and the Writing Lesson for this selection may be completed over several days.

Step-by-Step Teaching Guide	Pacing Guide
PRETEACH	
• Administer Vocabulary and Reading Warm-ups as necessary.	5 min.
• Engage students' interest with the motivation activity.	5 min.
• Read and discuss author and background features. **FT**	10 min.
• Introduce the Literary Analysis Skill: Setting. **FT**	5 min.
• Introduce the Reading Strategy: Identifying Cause and Effect. **FT**	10 min.
• Prepare students to read by teaching the selection vocabulary. **FT**	
TEACH	
• Informally monitor comprehension while students read independently or in groups. **FT**	30 min.
• Monitor students' comprehension with the Reading Check notes.	as students read
• Reinforce vocabulary with Vocabulary Builder notes.	as students read
• Develop students' understanding of setting with the Literary Analysis annotations. **FT**	5 min.
• Develop students' ability to identify cause and effect with the Reading Strategy annotations. **FT**	5 min.
ASSESS/EXTEND	
• Assess students' comprehension and mastery of the Literary Analysis and Reading Strategy by having them answer the Apply the Skills questions. **FT**	15 min.
• Have students complete the Vocabulary Lesson and the Grammar and Style Lesson. **FT**	15 min.
• Apply students' ability to develop a personal tone in their writing by using the Writing Lesson. **FT**	45 min. or homework
• Apply students' understanding by using one or more of the Extend Your Learning activities.	20–90 min. or homework
• Administer Selection Test A or Selection Test B. **FT**	15 min.

Resources

PRINT

Unit 6 Resources

Vocabulary Warm-up Word Lists **[L1, L2, EL]** .... p. 243
Vocabulary Warm-up Practice **[L1, L2, EL]** .... p. 244
Reading Warm-up A **[L1, L2, EL]** .... p. 245
Reading Warm-up B **[L1, L2, L3]** .... p. 246

TRANSPARENCY

Graphic Organizer Transparencies

Literary Analysis Graphic Organizer A **[L3]** .... p. 268
Literary Analysis Graphic Organizer B **[L1, L2, EL]** .... p. 269
Reading Strategy Graphic Organizer A **[L3]** .... p. 266
Reading Strategy Graphic Organizer B **[L1, L2, EL]** .... p. 267

PRINT

Reader's Notebook [L2]
Reader's Notebook: Adapted Version [L1]
Reader's Notebook: English Learner's Version [EL]

Unit 6 Resources

Literary Analysis **[L3]** .... p. 247
Reading Strategy **[L3]** .... p. 248
Vocabulary Builder **[L3]** .... p. 249

TECHNOLOGY

Listening to Literature Audio CDs [L2, EL]

PRINT

Unit 6 Resources

Grammar and Style **[L3]** .... p. 250
Support for Writing Lesson **[L3]** .... p. 251
Support for Extend Your Learning **[L3]** .... p. 252
Enrichment **[L4]** .... p. 253
Selection Test A **[L1, L2, EL]** .... pp. 254–256
Selection Test B **[L3, L4]** .... pp. 257–259

TRANSPARENCY

Graphic Organizer Transparencies

Timeline **[L3]** .... p. 314

General Resources

Rubrics for Response to Literature **[L3]** .... pp. 65–66
Rubrics for Research: Research Report **[L3]** .... pp. 49–50

TECHNOLOGY

Go Online: Research **[L3]**
Go Online: Self-test **[L3]**
***ExamView®* Test Bank [L3]**

Choosing Resources for Differentiated Instruction

[L1] Special Needs Students
[L2] Below-Level Students
[L3] All Students
[L4] Advanced Students
[EL] English Learners

For Vocabulary and Reading Warm-ups and for Selection Tests, **A** signifies "less challenging" and **B** "more challenging." For Graphic Organizer transparencies, **A** signifies "not filled in" and **B** "filled in."

FT Fast Track Instruction: To move the lesson more quickly, use the strategies and activities identified with **FT**.

Scaffolding for Less Proficient and Advanced Students

The leveled Critical Thinking questions after selections progress in the levels of thinking required to answer them. To address the needs of your different students, you may use the (a) level questions for your less proficient students and the (b) level questions with your on-level and advanced students. The occasional (c) level questions are appropriate for your advanced students.

PRENTICE HALL **TeacherEXPRESS™** Plan · Teach · Assess — Use this complete suite of powerful teaching tools to make lesson planning and testing quicker and easier.

PRENTICE HALL **StudentEXPRESS™** Learn · Study · Succeed — Use the interactive textbook (online and on CD-ROM) to make selections and activities come alive with audio and video support and interactive questions.

Monitoring Progress

Before students read "The Rockpile," administer **Diagnostic Test 11** (*Unit 6 Resources,* pp. 240–242). This test will determine students' level of readiness for the reading and vocabulary skills.

Go Online Professional Development — **For:** Information about Lexiles **Visit:** www.PHSchool.com **Web Code:** eue-1111

PREACHING

Motivation

Write the following statement on the board: "I am not my brother's keeper." Discuss its meaning with students. You might use some of the following questions to shape the discussion:

- To whom does the word *brother* refer?
- What does the word *keeper* mean in this context?
- When would someone be apt to make such a statement?
- Do you agree with the sentiments expressed by this statement? Why or why not?

Encourage students to keep this statement in mind as they read "The Rockpile" and to note which characters might agree with its meaning.

❶ Background

More About the Author

Much of James Baldwin's work reflects his experience growing up in Harlem. This New York City neighborhood has been a vital center of African American life and culture since southern blacks began migrating there in the 1910s. In the 1920s, it was the hub of the Harlem Renaissance, an African American literary and artistic movement. One of the leading writers of that movement was Baldwin's teacher, Countee Cullen.

When the Depression hit in the 1930s, the largely poor population of Harlem plunged even deeper into poverty. This was the Harlem in which Baldwin grew up. Despite economic hardship, however, Harlem's culture—its theaters, music and dance centers, and the churches where the young Baldwin preached—remained strong.

Build Skills | Short Story

❶ The Rockpile

James Baldwin (1924–1987)

James Baldwin once told an interviewer that he "never had a childhood." Because his stepfather worked long hours as both a preacher and a factory hand, Baldwin was given much of the responsibility for raising his eight half brothers and half sisters. The only leisure activity he was able to pursue was reading. He explained, "As [my half brothers and half sisters] were born, I took them over with one hand and held a book with the other. . . . In this way I read *Uncle Tom's Cabin* and *A Tale of Two Cities* over and over again; in this way, in fact, I read just about everything I could get my hands on." Baldwin's early love for reading deepened his imagination, planting the seeds of inspiration for his later success as a writer.

A Harlem Childhood Baldwin was born in Harlem, the New York community that served as a cultural center for African Americans during the 1920s and 30s. Even as a young boy, it was clear that he had a gift for words. He published his first short story in a church newspaper when he was twelve years old. Despite his obvious gift, Baldwin's deeply religious parents disapproved of his interest in literature. At age fourteen, Baldwin followed their wishes and became a preacher, earning a degree of fame in churches around Harlem, but he continued to pursue his literary ambitions.

Baldwin was encouraged by African American poet Countee Cullen, who taught in his junior high school. With Cullen's support, he wrote poetry and worked on his school's literary magazine. Inspired by the success of Richard Wright's novel *Native Son,* which proved to him that an African American could have success as a writer, Baldwin eventually decided to abandon preaching and devote his life to writing.

The Road to "Writer" For several years, Baldwin worked at odd jobs while writing and reading in his spare time. He wrote book reviews and essays, which were published in several New York journals. Some of these articles were later collected in *Notes of a Native Son* (1955). When he was twenty-four, Baldwin won a fellowship that enabled him to travel to Europe and write. He lived in Paris for the next four years, where he completed his first novel, *Go Tell It on the Mountain* (1953). The novel marked the beginning of a distinguished literary career that included the novels *Giovanni's Room* (1956), *Another Country* (1962), *The Fire Next Time* (1963), and *Tell Me How Long the Train's Been Gone* (1968); a play set in the American South called *Blues for Mr. Charlie* (1964); a collection of short stories titled *Going to Meet the Man* (1965); and several successful collections of essays.

A Powerful Witness Baldwin once said, "One writes out of one thing only—one's own experience. Everything depends on how relentlessly one forces from this experience the last drop, sweet or bitter, it can possibly give." Baldwin's work bears powerful witness to his own experience as an African American. In his writing, he expresses the need for social justice as well as the universal desire for love. Because his books dig deeply into contemporary life, they are sometimes painful to read, but the pain is always tempered by hope, and by Baldwin's magnificent language. Of Baldwin's essays, the poet Langston Hughes once wrote, "He uses words like the sea uses waves, to flow and beat, advance and retreat, rise and take a bow in disappearing." In interviews throughout his life, Baldwin often repeated one phrase: "People can be better than they are." This simple idea is woven into everything he wrote.

Preview

Connecting to the Literature

This story centers on a family living in a poor neighborhood where the setting itself presents a conflict. The children of the family are caught between two sources of danger—the street life they are forbidden to join and the tensions between their parents.

❷ Literary Analysis

Setting

The **setting** of a story is the time and place in which it occurs, and may include details about the weather, physical features of the landscape, and other elements of an environment. "The Rockpile" is set in Harlem during the 1930s. Life in that place and time was influenced by the difficult economic and social realities that people faced. As you read, think about how the setting helps to shape the characters' personalities and actions.

Connecting Literary Elements

A **symbol** is a person, place, or object that has a meaning in itself but also suggests a larger meaning. For example, in this story, the rockpile represents both failure in the community and conflict within the family.

> They fought on the rockpile. Sure footed, dangerous, and reckless, they rushed each other and grappled on the heights . . .

As you read, note the ways in which the rockpile is described, the characters associated with it, and the events that take place there. These details will help reveal the symbolic meaning of the rockpile.

❸ Reading Strategy

Identifying Cause and Effect

In this story, a child's disobedience reveals a complicated family dynamic. You will understand the characters in the story better if you **identify cause-and-effect** relationships among them. Use a chart like the one shown to determine the motives for characters' actions and their effects on others.

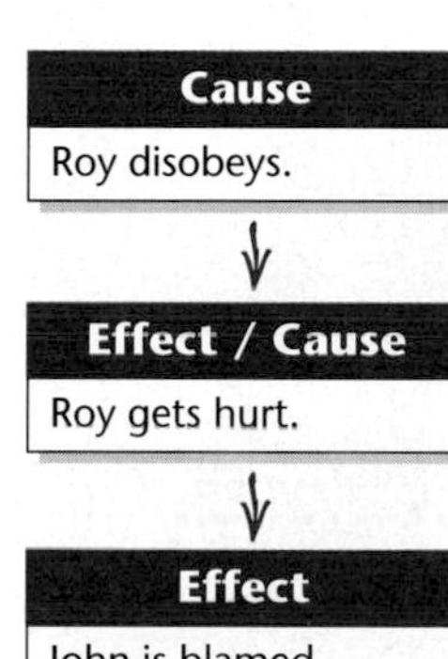

Cause
Roy disobeys.
Effect / Cause
Roy gets hurt.
Effect
John is blamed.

Vocabulary Builder

intriguing (in trē′ giŋ) *adj.* interesting or curious (p. 1185)

benevolent (bə nev′ ə lənt) *adj.* kindly; charitable (p. 1186)

decorously (dek′ ə rəs lē) *adv.* characterized by or showing decorum and good taste (p. 1186)

latent (lāt′ 'nt) *adj.* present but invisible or inactive (p. 1186)

engrossed (en grōst′) *adj.* occupied wholly; absorbed (p. 1187)

jubilant (jo͞o′ bə lənt) *adj.* joyful and triumphant (p. 1187)

arrested (ə res′ tid) *adj.* stopped (p. 1188)

malevolence (mə lev′ ə ləns) *n.* malice; spitefulness (p. 1192)

perdition (pər dish′ ən) *n.* complete and irreparable loss; ruin (p. 1192)

❷ Literary Analysis
Setting

- Explain to students that setting—the time and place in which a story occurs—can shape the characters of a literary work.
- Ask students to consider how a setting like the one described in the story might shape a young boy's personality.
- Instruct students as they read to take notes on the influence the setting has on the characters in "The Rockpile."

❸ Reading Strategy
Identifying Cause and Effect

- Be sure students understand that "cause and effect" refers to the causes of a character's actions, and the effects those actions have on others.
- As an example, suggest that if a student's younger sibling disobeys rules, he or she might get hurt. Write on the chalkboard: **Cause:** *Sibling disobeys;* **Effect:** *Sibling gets hurt.*
- Then, suggest that if the younger sibling gets hurt, parents might blame the student. Write on the chalkboard: **Cause:** *Sibling gets hurt;* **Effect:** *Student is blamed.*
- Point out that the chart on this page illustrates such a chain of cause and effects in "The Rockpile."
- Give students a copy of **Reading Strategy Graphic Organizer A,** p. 266 in ***Graphic Organizer Transparencies,*** to use as they read the story.

Vocabulary Builder

- Pronounce each vocabulary word for students, and read the definitions as a class. Have students identify any words with which they are already familiar.

Differentiated Instruction
Solutions for All Learners

Support for Special Needs Students
Have students complete the **Preview** and **Build Skills** pages for "The Rockpile" in the ***Reader's Notebook: Adapted Version.*** These pages provide a selection summary, an abbreviated presentation of the reading and literary skills, and the graphic organizer on the **Build Skills** page in the student book.

Support for Less Proficient Readers
Have students complete the **Preview** and **Build Skills** pages for "The Rockpile" in the ***Reader's Notebook.*** These pages provide a selection summary, an abbreviated presentation of the reading and literary skills, and the graphic organizer on the **Build Skills** page in the student book.

Support for English Learners
Have students complete the **Preview** and **Build Skills** pages for "The Rockpile" in the ***Reader's Notebook: English Learner's Version.*** These pages provide a selection summary, an abbreviated presentation of the reading and literary skills, and the graphic organizer on the **Build Skills** page in the student book.

Learning Modalities
Verbal/Linguistic Learners

Baldwin's use of language reveals the influence of the evangelical church, where both he and his father preached. Encourage students to find and listen to recordings of evangelical preachers, and identify resonances in Baldwin's prose. Students can make a presentation based on their findings.

❶ About the Selection

Family relationships are complicated, and family conflicts are studies in cause and effect. As students read this story about one family's response to a child's seemingly ordinary act of disobedience, they will see that the characters' actions have both obvious and underlying causes and both immediate and far-reaching effects. Tracing these strands will help students understand the forces of love, need, resentment, and fear that bind and divide Baldwin's fictional family.

❷ Literary Analysis
Setting

- Remind students that a story's setting—the time and place in which it occurs—can shape the characters in important ways.
- Have students read the bracketed passage. Then, **ask** the Literary Analysis question: What unique features of the rockpile are described in the opening paragraph?
  Answer: It is "a mass of natural rock jutting out of the ground" in the middle of a city block.
- Ask students to keep these physical details about the rockpile in mind as they read.

Differentiated Instruction
Solutions for All Learners

Accessibility at a Glance

	The Rockpile
Context	Modern literature, urban experience
Language	Informal, vernacular
Concept Level	Accessible (clear characterization, familiar setting)
Literary Merit	Noted author, cross-generational
Lexile	850L
Overall Rating	Average

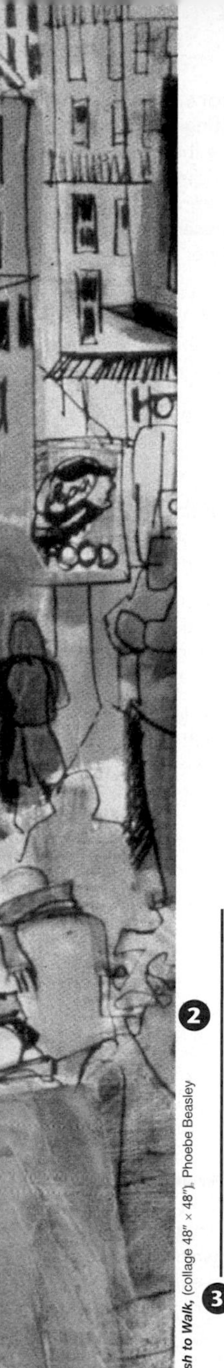

Push to Walk, (collage 48" × 48"), Phoebe Beasley

❶

The Rockpile

James Baldwin

Background Even though he spent most of his adult life in Europe, James Baldwin's impassioned voice is full of the rhythms and details of life in Harlem, the New York City neighborhood where he grew up. This story, about a struggling Harlem family, is a strong example of Baldwin's connection to the place that shaped him both as a writer and as a person.

❷ Across the street from their house, in an empty lot between two houses, stood the rockpile. It was a strange place to find a mass of natural rock jutting out of the ground; and someone, probably Aunt Florence, had once told them that the rock was there and could not be taken away because without it the subway cars underground would fly apart, killing all the people. This, touching on some natural mystery concerning the surface and the center of the earth, was far too intriguing an explanation to be challenged, and it invested the rockpile, moreover, with such mysterious importance that Roy felt it to be his right, not to say his duty, to play there.

❸ Other boys were to be seen there each afternoon after school and all day Saturday and Sunday. They fought on the rockpile. Sure footed, dangerous, and reckless, they rushed each other and grappled on the

❹ ◀ **Critical Viewing** What details shown in this painting connect to Baldwin's story? **[Connect]**

Literary Analysis
Setting and Symbol
Which unique features of the rockpile are described in the opening paragraph?

Vocabulary Builder
intriguing (in trē´ giŋ) *adj.* interesting or curious

❺ **Reading Check**
Where is the rockpile located?

❸ Humanities

Push to Walk, by Phoebe Beasley

This urban image captures the busy setting that Baldwin's story describes. An African American born in Ohio, Phoebe Beasley studied at the Cleveland Art Institute and received her BFA from Ohio University. She became a high school art teacher and eventually moved to Los Angeles to pursue her art full-time. Beasley has created work to celebrate presidential inaugurations and the official artwork for the 1987 Los Angeles Marathon. She has won many awards, including the Presidential Seal.

Use these questions for discussion:

1. Draw students' attention to the artist's vibrant use of color. What is the effect of this feature?
   Possible response: Students may say that it makes the scene seem vividly real and alive.
2. In "The Rockpile," Baldwin offers a glimpse into the lives and relationships of one family living in Harlem in the 1930s. How does Beasley suggest that there are many "stories" waiting to be told on the block that she depicts?
   Possible response: Students may point out the numerous and intriguing figures on the street.

❹ Critical Viewing

Possible response: Both painting and story include urban details—such as tenement buildings, a wide range of people, and much activity—that suggest the crowded and energetic nature of life on city streets.

❺ Reading Check

Answer: It is located in a vacant lot across the street from the main characters' apartment building.

Differentiated Instruction
Solutions for All Learners

Strategy for Less Proficient Readers
To help students better understand the story, point out that the first two and a half pages convey setting and background information, and that the main incident is recounted immediately afterward. Encourage students to make a timeline of the series of events that unfold on the rockpile.

Strategy for Advanced Readers
Encourage students to consider the significance of the description of the rockpile on this page. Remind them that the story's title is "The Rockpile," indicating that the rock formation itself will be important to the plot. Based on its physical description alone, can students predict what conflicts might develop for parents who are trying to keep their children safe, and for children who wish to explore their world?

6 Literary Analysis
Setting and Symbol

- Remind students that some elements of setting—such as the rockpile—can be symbols, a person, place, or object that has a meaning in itself but suggests a larger meaning.
- After students have read the first two paragraphs, be sure that they understand that the rockpile is a rock formation where children play—and where Roy and John are forbidden to go.
- **Ask** students the first part of the first Literary Analysis question: What does the rockpile represent to the neighborhood children?
  Possible response: The rockpile represents a mysterious, exciting, and dangerous place beyond the strict control of their parents.
- Then, **ask** the second part of the question: What does it represent to Roy's mother?
  Possible response: It represents the dangers from which she must protect her children.

Monitor Progress: Encourage students to discuss how the rockpile is likely to shape the events of the story. Have them write down their ideas and review them after completing the story.

7 Literary Analysis
Setting and Symbol

- Point out to students that actions and events, as well as places and objects, can be symbols with larger meanings.
- Have students read the bracketed passage. Then, **ask** them what the drowning reveals about the setting.
  Answer: There are many dangers for children in this neighborhood.
- Then, **ask** students the second Literary Analysis question: Can the tragedy of the boy's drowning in the river be seen as a symbol? If so, of what?
  Possible response: Students may respond that it can be, because for Roy and John's mother it represents the dangers of the world outside their home.

6 heights, sometimes disappearing down the other side in a confusion of dust and screams and upended, flying feet. "It's a wonder they don't kill themselves," their mother said, watching sometimes from the fire escape. "You children stay away from there, you hear me?" Though she said "children" she was looking at Roy, where he sat beside John on the fire escape. "The good Lord knows," she continued, "I don't want you to come home bleeding like a hog every day the Lord sends." Roy shifted impatiently, and continued to stare at the street, as though in this gazing he might somehow acquire wings. John said nothing. He had not really been spoken to: he was afraid of the rockpile and of the boys who played there.

Each Saturday morning John and Roy sat on the fire escape and watched the forbidden street below. Sometimes their mother sat in the room behind them, sewing, or dressing their younger sister, or nursing the baby, Paul. The sun fell across them and across the fire escape with a high, benevolent indifference; below them, men and women, and boys and girls, sinners all, loitered; sometimes one of the church-members passed and saw them and waved. Then, for the moment that they waved decorously back, they were intimidated. They watched the saint, man or woman, until he or she had disappeared from sight. The passage of one of the redeemed made them consider, however vacantly, the wickedness of the street, their own latent wickedness in sitting where they sat; and made them think of their father, who came home early on Saturdays and who would soon be turning this corner and entering the dark hall below them.

But until he came to end their freedom, they sat, watching and longing above the street. At the end of the street nearest their house was the bridge which spanned the Harlem River[1] and led to a city called the Bronx; which was where Aunt Florence lived. Nevertheless, when they saw her coming, she did not come from the bridge, but from the opposite end of the street. This, weakly, to their minds, she explained by saying that she had taken the subway, not wishing to walk, and that, besides, she did not live in that section of the Bronx. Knowing that the Bronx was across the river, they did not believe this story ever, but, adopting toward her their father's attitude, assumed that she had just left some sinful place which she dared not name, as, for example, a movie palace.

7 In the summertime boys swam in the river, diving off the wooden dock, or wading in from the garbage-heavy bank. Once a boy, whose name was Richard, drowned in the river. His mother had not known where he was; she had even come to their house, to ask if he was there. Then, in the evening, at six o'clock, they had heard from the street a woman screaming and wailing; and they ran to the windows and looked out. Down the street came the woman, Richard's mother, screaming, her face raised to the sky and tears running down her face. A woman walked beside her, trying to make her quiet and trying

Literary Analysis
Setting and Symbol What does the rockpile represent to the neighborhood children? What does it represent to Roy's mother?

Vocabulary Builder

benevolent (bə nevˊ ə lənt) *adj.* kindly; charitable

decorously (dekˊ ər əs lē) *adv.* characterized by or showing decorum and good taste

latent (lātˊ ənt) *adj.* present but invisible or inactive

Literary Analysis
Setting and Symbol Can the tragedy of the boy's drowning in the river be seen as a symbol? If so, of what?

1. **Harlem River** river that separates Manhattan Island from the Bronx in New York City.

Enrichment

Countee Cullen

Countee Cullen, who taught and encouraged James Baldwin, was a leading writer of the Harlem Renaissance. Cullen grew up in Kentucky and moved to Harlem when he was fifteen. He received several important poetry awards while he was a college student at New York University and published *Color,* his first book of poetry, shortly before his graduation.

Cullen went on to earn a Masters degree at Harvard; to teach French and English in New York City's public schools; and to publish several more volumes of poetry, a novel, two collections of children's stories, and several plays. He is best known for his poems, which he often wrote in sonnet form, and in which he explored such themes as race, creativity, and spirituality.

Refer students to Cullen's poem "From the Dark Tower." After they read the poem, ask students how Countee Cullen and other Harlem Renaissance writers and artists might have influenced James Baldwin.

to hold her up. Behind them walked a man, Richard's father, with Richard's body in his arms. There were two white policemen walking in the gutter, who did not seem to know what should be done. Richard's father and Richard were wet, and Richard's body lay across his father's arms like a cotton baby. The woman's screaming filled all the street; cars slowed down and the people in the cars stared; people opened their windows and looked out and came rushing out of doors to stand in the gutter, watching. Then the small procession disappeared within the house which stood beside the rockpile. Then, *"Lord, Lord, Lord!"* cried Elizabeth, their mother, and slammed the window down.

One Saturday, an hour before his father would be coming home, Roy was wounded on the rockpile and brought screaming upstairs. He and John had been sitting on the fire escape and their mother had gone into the kitchen to sip tea with Sister McCandless. By and by Roy became bored and sat beside John in restless silence; and John began drawing into his schoolbook a newspaper advertisement which featured a new electric locomotive. Some friends of Roy passed beneath the fire escape and called him. Roy began to fidget, yelling down to them through the bars. Then a silence fell. John looked up. Roy stood looking at him.

"I'm going downstairs," he said.

"You better stay where you is, boy. You know Mama don't want you going downstairs."

"I be right *back*. She won't even know I'm gone, less you run and tell her."

"I ain't *got* to tell her. What's going to stop her from coming in here and looking out the window?"

"She's talking," Roy said. He started into the house.

"But Daddy's going to be home soon!"

"I be back before *that*. What you all the time got to be so *scared* for?" He was already in the house and he now turned, leaning on the windowsill, to swear impatiently, "I be back in *five* minutes."

John watched him sourly as he carefully unlocked the door and disappeared. In a moment he saw him on the sidewalk with his friends. He did not dare to go and tell his mother that Roy had left the fire escape because he had practically promised not to.

He started to shout, *Remember, you said five minutes!* but one of Roy's friends was looking up at the fire escape. John looked down at his schoolbook: he became engrossed again in the problem of the locomotive.

When he looked up again he did not know how much time had passed, but now there was a gang fight on the rockpile. Dozens of boys fought each other in the harsh sun: clambering up the rocks and battling hand to hand, scuffed shoes sliding on the slippery rock; filling the bright air with curses and jubilant cries. They filled the air, too, with flying weapons: stones, sticks, tin cans, garbage, whatever could be picked up and thrown. John watched in a kind of absent amazement—until he remembered that Roy was still downstairs, and that he was one of the

Reading Strategy
Identifying Cause and Effect What causes Roy to go down to the street?

Vocabulary Builder
engrossed (en grōst′) *adj.* occupied wholly; absorbed

jubilant (jo͞o′ bə lənt) *adj.* joyful and triumphant

10 **Reading Check**
Does Roy obey the instructions his mother gives him regarding the rockpile?

8 Reading Strategy
Identifying Cause and Effect

- Draw a chart on the board that consists of two boxes linked by an arrow, one labeled "Cause" and the other "Effect." Instruct students to copy it into their notebooks.
- Have students read the bracketed passage. Then, **ask** them the Reading Strategy question: What causes Roy to go down to the street?
- Ask students to write their answers on their cause-and-effect charts.
  Possible response: Cause: Roy's friends call him from the street. Effect: Roy goes to the rockpile.

9 Critical Thinking
Infer

- Have students read the bracketed passage. Be sure they understand that Roy runs downstairs to see his friends although John urges him not to go.
- **Ask** students what inferences they can make about John's character, based on the argument he has with his brother Roy.
  Possible response: Students should recognize that John is the older brother, and is supposed to watch out for Roy. However, he is also less bold, and afraid that something bad will happen.

10 Reading Check

Answer: Roy does not obey his mother; instead, he goes to play on the rockpile.

Differentiated Instruction
Solutions for All Learners

Enrichment for Gifted/Talented Students
Aunt Florence had offered one explanation of why the rockpile cannot be moved. Ask students to consider what other adults in Roy and John's neighborhood might have told the children about the rockpile. Challenge students to invent a series of alternative explanations to account for the rockpile's presence. They can present these explanations in a dramatic reading representing how the neighborhood children might perceive the rockpile.

Strategy for Advanced Readers
Encourage students to begin to analyze the differences between Roy and John. Students should notice that Roy "tunes out" their mother's scolding and is rebellious and disobedient. John appears to be the opposite—he is afraid to misbehave. Students can use a Cause-and-Effect chart to examine these characteristics as causes of events and effects in a chain of circumstances.

⓫ Literary Analysis
Setting

- Remind students of the importance of setting—that it can have a direct impact on the lives of characters.
- Have students read the bracketed passage. Then, **ask** them to explain what happened to Roy on the rockpile.
  Answer: Roy joined in a rough game; he tore his shirt; he stood on top of the rockpile; a can hit him in the head, cutting him; he fell to the ground.
- **Ask** students the Literary Analysis question: What details of Roy's accident reflect the difficulties of life in this place?
  Possible response: The rowdiness, the presence of jagged tin cans, the lack of a safe place for children to play, and the danger of the rockpile all reflect the difficulties of life in this setting.

▶ **Monitor Progress:** Encourage students to discuss how these details of the setting have shaped Roy's and John's personalities.

⓬ Reading Strategy
Identifying Cause and Effect

- Have students read the bracketed passage. Then, **ask** them the Reading strategy question: What causes Elizabeth to look "with apprehension" toward the clock?
  Possible response: Students should understand that both John and Elizabeth are frightened of the father who is expected home momentarily.

boys on the rockpile. Then he was afraid; he could not see his brother among the figures in the sun; and he stood up, leaning over the fire-escape railing. Then Roy appeared from the other side of the rocks; John saw that his shirt was torn; he was laughing. He moved until he stood at the very top of the rockpile. Then, something, an empty tin can, flew out of the air and hit him on the forehead, just above the eye. Immediately, one side of Roy's face ran with blood, he fell and rolled on ⓫ his face down the rocks. Then for a moment there was no movement at all, no sound, the sun, arrested, lay on the street and the sidewalk and the arrested boys. Then someone screamed or shouted; boys began to run away, down the street, toward the bridge. The figure on the ground, having caught its breath and felt its own blood, began to shout. John cried, "Mama! Mama!" and ran inside.

"Don't fret, don't fret," panted Sister McCandless as they rushed down the dark, narrow, swaying stairs, "don't fret. Ain't a boy been born don't get his knocks every now and again. *Lord!*" they hurried into the sun. A man had picked Roy up and now walked slowly toward them. One or two boys sat silent on their stoops; at either end of the street there was a group of boys watching. "He ain't hurt bad," the man said, "wouldn't be making this kind of noise if he was hurt real bad."

Elizabeth, trembling, reached out to take Roy, but Sister McCandless, bigger, calmer, took him from the man and threw him over her shoulder as she once might have handled a sack of cotton. "God bless you," she said to the man, "God bless you, son." Roy was still screaming. Elizabeth stood behind Sister McCandless to stare at his bloody face.

"It's just a flesh wound," the man kept saying, "just broke the skin, that's all." They were moving across the sidewalk, toward the house. John, not now afraid of the staring boys, looked toward the corner to see if his father was yet in sight.

Upstairs, they hushed Roy's crying. They bathed the blood away, to find, just above the left eyebrow, the jagged, superficial scar. "Lord, ⓬ have mercy," murmured Elizabeth, "another inch and it would've been his eye." And she looked with apprehension toward the clock. "Ain't it the truth," said Sister McCandless, busy with bandages and iodine.

"When did he go downstairs?" his mother asked at last.

Sister McCandless now sat fanning herself in the easy chair, at the head of the sofa where Roy lay, bound and silent. She paused for a moment to look sharply at John. John stood near the window, holding the newspaper advertisement and the drawing he had done.

"We was sitting on the fire escape," he said. "Some boys he knew called him."

"When?"

"He said he'd be back in five minutes."

"Why didn't you tell me he was downstairs?"

He looked at his hands, clasping his notebook, and did not answer.

"Boy," said Sister McCandless, "you hear your mother a-talking to you?"

Literary Analysis
Setting Which details of Roy's accident reflect the difficulties of life in this place?

Vocabulary Builder
arrested (ə res′ tid) *adj.* stopped

Reading Strategy
Identifying Cause and Effect What causes Elizabeth to look "with apprehension" toward the clock?

Enrichment

Communities and Families

One of the problems that contributes to the conflict in this story is that John and Roy did not have a place outside the home where they could safely play. Many communities, however, provide programs and facilities for both children and teenagers, making such places as the rockpile less attractive. Local newspapers and community bulletins often offer information about such community resources. Interested students can explore the youth facilities and programs in their own community.

The other major source of conflict in the story lies within the family. Writers like James Baldwin delve into family problems and family dynamics as part of their creative work. Social workers—professionals trained to provide support and counseling to individuals and families who need help—deal with these issues on a practical, real-life level. Students can research the various types of services that social workers provide, and then consider how a social worker could be of assistance to the family Baldwin describes.

He looked at his mother. He repeated:

"He said he'd be back in five minutes."

13 "He said he'd be back in five minutes," said Sister McCandless with scorn, "don't look to me like that's no right answer. You's the man of the house, you supposed to look after your baby brothers and sisters—you ain't supposed to let them run off and get half-killed. But I expect," she added, rising from the chair, dropping the cardboard fan, "your Daddy'll make you tell the truth. Your Ma's way too soft with you."

He did not look at her, but at the fan where it lay in the dark red, depressed seat where she had been. The fan advertised a pomade[2] for the hair and showed a brown woman and her baby, both with glistening hair, smiling happily at each other.

"Honey," said Sister McCandless, "I got to be moving along. Maybe I drop in later tonight. I don't reckon you going to be at Tarry Service tonight?"

Tarry Service was the prayer meeting held every Saturday night at church to strengthen believers and prepare the church for the coming of the Holy Ghost on Sunday.

"I don't reckon," said Elizabeth. She stood up; she and Sister McCandless kissed each other on the cheek. "But you be sure to remember me in your prayers."

"I surely will do that." She paused, with her hand on the door knob, and looked down at Roy and laughed. "Poor little man," she said, "reckon he'll be content to sit on the fire escape *now*."

Elizabeth laughed with her. "It sure ought to be a lesson to him. You don't reckon," she asked nervously, still smiling, "he going to keep that scar, do you?"

14 "Lord, no," said Sister McCandless, "ain't nothing but a scratch. I declare, Sister Grimes, you worse than a child. Another couple of weeks and you won't be able to *see* no scar. No, you go on about your housework, honey, and thank the Lord it weren't no worse." She opened the door; they heard the sound of feet on the stairs. "I expect that's the Reverend," said Sister McCandless, placidly, "I *bet* he going to raise cain."[3]

"Maybe it's Florence," Elizabeth said. "Sometimes she get here about this time." They stood in the doorway, staring, while the steps reached the landing below and began again climbing to their floor. "No," said Elizabeth then, "that ain't her walk. That's Gabriel."

"Well, I'll just go on," said Sister McCandless, "and kind of prepare his mind." She pressed Elizabeth's hand as she spoke and started into the hall, leaving the door behind her slightly ajar. Elizabeth turned slowly back into the room. Roy did not open his eyes, or move; but she knew that he was not sleeping; he wished to delay until the last possible moment any contact with his father. John put

2. **pomade** (päm ād′) *n.* perfumed ointment.
3. **raise cain** slang for "cause trouble."

15 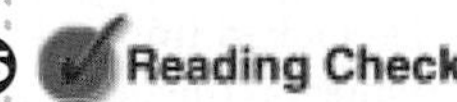

Reading Check

What happens to Roy on the rockpile?

13 Critical Thinking

Making a Judgment

- Ask students to consider the character of Sister McCandless. Be sure they understand that she is Elizabeth's friend and that she seems to take control of the situation when Roy is hurt.
- Have students read the bracketed passage. Then, **ask** them whether they think that Sister McCandless's scolding of John is justified or not.
  Possible response: Some students may feel that it is justified—John should have stopped Roy from going downstairs. Others may say it is not justified because John did try to stop Roy, and he is only a child himself, not a responsible adult.
- Encourage students to keep their judgment in mind as more is revealed about Sister McCandless's character.

14 Critical Thinking

Analyze

- Have students read the bracketed passage. Ask them to keep in mind their thoughts about Sister McCandless.
- **Ask** students: What do Sister McCandless's words reveal about her relationship with Elizabeth? Explain.
  Possible response: Students may say that Sister McCandless dominates Elizabeth, treating her as she would a child. They should note that she says Elizabeth is "worse than a child," and that she seems to usurp Elizabeth's responsibilities.

15 Reading Check

Answer: First, Roy's shirt is torn. Then, he is hit in the head and cut by a thrown tin can.

Differentiated Instruction

Solutions for All Learners

Support for Special Needs Students
Students may need to pause and review the events of the story's plot. Be sure that students understand that Roy has gone to the rockpile against his parents' wishes; he has been hurt; and Elizabeth, John, and Sister McCandless are awaiting Roy's father.

Support for Less Proficient Readers
Students may find the Reading Strategy exercise challenging. Guide them to recognize that Elizabeth's glance at the clock is caused by her fear of Gabriel's imminent return.

Support for English Learners
Students might have difficulty with the dialogue between John, Elizabeth, and Sister McCandless. Encourage them to reread the dialogue, perhaps as they listen to the story read aloud on **Listening to Literature Audio CD**.

16 Literature in Context

James Baldwin and the Church

Evangelism refers to winning converts to Christianity. The evangelical church focuses on conversion, strict reliance on biblical scripture, and on preaching. Baldwin's childhood in the church is likely a major source of inspiration for "The Rockpile." The author's experiences as a preacher can be seen most clearly in *The Fire Next Time,* a long essay in which Baldwin directly addresses racism, its effects on society, and what must be done to combat it.

Connect to the Literature Have students follow along as you select two strong readers to read the next two pages aloud, paying close attention to phrases and internal punctuation. Then ask the Connect to the Literature question.

Possible response: Two examples are the sentence beginning with "He turned back to Roy," p. 1191, and "She looked back at Gabriel," p. 1192.

17 Reading Strategy
Identifying Cause and Effect

- Remind students that they have already learned a great deal about this family by examining cause and effect.
- Have students read the bracketed passage. Be sure they understand that Roy begins to cry when his father asks him what happened.
- **Ask** students the Reading Strategy question: How does Gabriel react to Roy's tears?
  Answer: He comforts Roy and reassures him, implying that he will not punish Roy no matter what happened.
- Encourage students to consider what the effect of Roy's tears on Gabriel suggests about the family dynamic.

his newspaper and his notebook on the table and stood, leaning on the table, staring at her.

"It wasn't my fault," he said. "I couldn't stop him from going downstairs." 16

"No," she said, "you ain't got nothing to worry about. You just tell your Daddy the truth."

He looked directly at her, and she turned to the window, staring into the street. What was Sister McCandless saying? Then from her bedroom she heard Delilah's thin wail and she turned, frowning, looking toward the bedroom and toward the still open door. She knew that John was watching her. Delilah continued to wail, she thought, angrily, *Now that girl's getting too big for that,* but she feared that Delilah would awaken Paul and she hurried into the bedroom. She tried to soothe Delilah back to sleep. Then she heard the front door open and close—too loud, Delilah raised her voice, with an exasperated sigh Elizabeth picked the child up. Her child and Gabriel's, her children and Gabriel's: Roy, Delilah, Paul. Only John was nameless and a stranger, living, unalterable testimony to his mother's days in sin.

"What happened?" Gabriel demanded. He stood, enormous, in the center of the room, his black lunchbox dangling from his hand, staring at the sofa where Roy lay. John stood just before him, it seemed to her astonished vision just below him, beneath his fist, his heavy shoe.

The child stared at the man in fascination and terror—when a girl down home she had seen rabbits stand so paralyzed before the barking dog. She hurried past Gabriel to the sofa, feeling the weight of Delilah in her arms like the weight of a shield, and stood over Roy, saying:

"Now, ain't a thing to get upset about, Gabriel. This boy sneaked downstairs while I had my back turned and got hisself hurt a little. He's alright now."

Roy, as though in confirmation, now opened his eyes and looked gravely at his father. Gabriel dropped his lunchbox with a clatter and knelt by the sofa.

"How you feel, son? Tell your Daddy what happened?"

Roy opened his mouth to speak and then, relapsing into panic, began to cry. His father held him by the shoulder.

"You don't want to cry. You's Daddy's little man. Tell your Daddy what happened."

17 "He went downstairs," said Elizabeth, "where he didn't have no business to be, and got to fighting with them bad boys playing on the rockpile. That's what happened and it's a mercy it weren't nothing worse."

He looked up at her. "Can't you let this boy answer me for hisself?"

Ignoring this, she went on, more gently: "He got cut on the forehead, but it ain't nothing to worry about."

Literature in Context

Cultural Connection

James Baldwin and the Church

Baldwin's choice of words, and often the subject matter of his stories, was influenced by the evangelical church, of which his father was a minister. In this story, many details reflect this influence:

- references to "the good Lord" and "saints"
- reference to the father as "the Reverend"
- mention of prayer services
- the fact that the mother and her friend call each other "Sister"
- conflicts between the family's strict religious values and the temptations of the neighborhood

As a teenager, Baldwin earned renown for his gifts as a preacher. He brought those same gifts, including the use of impassioned, rhythmic language, to his writing, creating prose of great beauty and power.

Connect to the Literature

List two or three examples of Baldwin's rhythmic language in this story.

Reading Strategy
Identifying Cause and Effect How does Gabriel react to Roy's tears?

"You call a doctor? How you know it ain't nothing to worry about?"

"Is you got money to be throwing away on doctors? No, I ain't called no doctor. Ain't nothing wrong with my eyes that I can't tell whether he's hurt bad or not. He got a fright more'n anything else, and you ought to pray God it teaches him a lesson."

"You got a lot to say now," he said, "but I'll have *me* something to say in a minute. I'll be wanting to know when all this happened, what you was doing with your eyes *then*." He turned back to Roy, who had lain quietly sobbing eyes wide open and body held rigid: and who now, at his father's touch, remembered the height, the sharp, sliding rock beneath his feet, the sun, the explosion of the sun, his plunge into darkness and his salty blood; and recoiled, beginning to scream, as his father touched his forehead. "Hold still, hold still," crooned his father, shaking, "hold still. Don't cry. Daddy ain't going to hurt you, he just wants to see this bandage, see what they've done to his little man." But Roy continued to scream and would not be still and Gabriel dared not lift the bandage for fear of hurting him more. And he looked at Elizabeth in fury: "Can't you put that child down and help me with this boy? John, take your baby sister from your mother—don't look like neither of you got good sense."

John took Delilah and sat down with her in the easy chair. His mother bent over Roy, and held him still, while his father, carefully—but still Roy screamed—lifted the bandage and stared at the wound. Roy's sobs began to lessen. Gabriel readjusted the bandage. "You see," said Elizabeth, finally, "he ain't nowhere near dead."

"It sure ain't your fault that he ain't dead." He and Elizabeth considered each other for a moment in silence. "He came mightly close to losing an eye. Course, his eyes ain't as big as your'n, so I reckon you don't think it matters so much." At this her face hardened; he smiled. "Lord, have mercy," he said, "you think you ever going to learn to do right? Where was you when all this happened? Who let him go downstairs?"

"Ain't nobody let him go downstairs, he just went. He got a head just like his father, it got to be broken before it'll bow. I was in the kitchen."

"Where was Johnnie?"

"He was in here."

"Where?"

"He was on the fire escape."

"Didn't he know Roy was downstairs?"

"I reckon."

"What you mean, you reckon? He ain't got your big eyes for nothing, does he?" He looked over at John. "Boy, you see your brother go downstairs?"

"Gabriel, ain't no sense in trying to blame Johnnie. You know right well if you have trouble making Roy behave, he ain't going to listen to his brother. He don't hardly listen to me." 19

"How come you didn't tell your mother Roy was downstairs?"

John said nothing, staring at the blanket which covered Delilah.

Reading Strategy
Identifying Cause and Effect What is Gabriel's reaction to Elizabeth's efforts to downplay the incident?

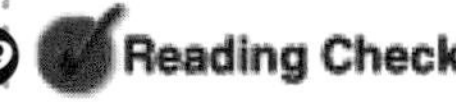

On whom does Gabriel attempt to pin the blame for Roy's accident?

18 Reading Strategy
Identifying Cause and Effect

- Briefly review student responses to the Reading Strategy question. Ask students to keep in mind what has been revealed about the family.
- Have students read the bracketed passage. Then, **ask** the Reading Strategy question: What is Gabriel's reaction to Elizabeth's efforts to downplay the incident?
  Answer: Gabriel responds angrily to his wife, threatening to punish her for Roy's accident, then shouting at her.

  Monitor Progress: Ask students what Gabriel's words and actions following his return home reveal about the family dynamic.
  Possible response: Gabriel views himself as the head of his household; he is an authority figure and scolds his wife as if she were a naughty child. Roy appears to be his favorite child; Gabriel is overly protective of Roy and spoils him.

19 Reading Check

Answer: Gabriel attempts to blame John for Roy's accident.

Differentiated Instruction
Solutions for All Learners

Support for Less Proficient Readers
The family discussion that begins with Gabriel's entrance would be a good point to play the **Listening to Literature Audio CD.** Students can read along with the text and draw conclusions about the relationships within the family.

Enrichment for Gifted/Talented Students
Call students' attention to the complicated relationships within this family. Some students may have direct personal experience with the complicated emotions that can develop between a step-child and step-parent. Instruct students to create collages that capture the emotions of this family, using whatever materials they prefer.

Enrichment for Advanced Readers
Ask students to consider this question: Is Gabriel a completely bad person? Students are likely to find both good—his tenderness for his family—and bad—his dominance and quick temper—in Gabriel. Instruct students to write brief but well-reasoned statements evaluating Gabriel's character.

20 Vocabulary Builder
The Latin Prefix *mal-*

- Call students' attention to the word *malevolence* and its definition. Tell students that the Latin prefix *mal-* means "bad," "wrong," or "ill."
- Have students **suggest** words and phrases that contain this prefix, and list them on the chalkboard. **Possibilities include:** malfunction, maladjusted, malodorous, and malnutrition.
- Next, have students create their own definitions for these words, and check their answers in a dictionary.

ASSESS
Answers

1. **Possible response:** Students may recall a time when they or a younger sibling disobeyed.
2. (a) They sit on the fire escape and watch the street. (b) **Possible response:** The street is forbidden because their parents see it as dangerous and filled with sinners.
3. (a) Gabriel is John's stepfather. (b) **Possible response:** Gabriel sees John as evidence of his wife's sinful past.
4. (a) Richard drowns in the river. (b) **Possible response:** Baldwin shows that the family is separate from and somewhat frightened by the community.
5. (a) He blames first Elizabeth and then John for Roy's injury. (b) **Possible response:** They have a strained relationship in which Gabriel is harsh and domineating. (c) **Possible response:** He remembers that she is his partner and the mother of his children.
6. **Possible response:** Students may wish to blame Roy himself for his injury. Students should support their opinions.

Go Online Author Link For additional information about James Baldwin, have students type in the Web Code, then select *B* from the alphabet, and then James Baldwin.

"Boy, you hear me? You want me to take a strap to you?"

"No, you ain't," she said. "You ain't going to taken no strap to this boy, not today you ain't. Ain't a soul to blame for Roy's lying up there now but you—you because you done spoiled him so that he thinks he can do just anything and get away with it. I'm here to tell you that ain't no way to raise no child. You don't pray to the Lord to help you do better than you been doing, you going to live to shed bitter tears that the Lord didn't take his soul today." And she was trembling. She moved, unseeing, toward John and took Delilah from his arms. She looked back at Gabriel, who had risen, who stood near the sofa, staring at her. And she found in his face not fury alone, which would not have surprised her; but hatred so deep as to become insupportable in its lack of personality. His eyes were struck alive, unmoving, blind
20 with malevolence—she felt, like the pull of the earth at her feet, his longing to witness her perdition. Again, as though it might be propitiation, she moved the child in her arms. And at this his eyes changed, he looked at Elizabeth, the mother of his children, the helpmeet given by the Lord. Then her eyes clouded; she moved to leave the room; her foot struck the lunchbox lying on the floor.

"John," she said, "pick up your father's lunchbox like a good boy."

She heard, behind her, his scrambling movement as he left the easy chair, the scrape and jangle of the lunchbox as he picked it up, bending his dark head near the toe of his father's heavy shoe.

Vocabulary Builder

malevolence (mə lev′ ə ləns) *n.* malice; spitefulness

perdition (pər dish′ ən) *n.* complete and irreparable loss; ruin

Critical Reading

1. **Respond:** Does this story call to mind any of your own childhood experiences? Explain.
2. **(a) Recall:** What do John and Roy do each Saturday morning? **(b) Deduce:** Why is the street "forbidden"?
3. **(a) Recall:** How is John related to Gabriel? **(b) Support:** What evidence is there that Gabriel's relationship with John is different from his relationship with the other children?
4. **(a) Recall:** What happens to the boy, Richard, at the river? **(b) Analyze:** Through this anecdote, what is Baldwin saying about this family's relationship to their community?
5. **(a) Recall:** Whom does Gabriel blame for Roy's injury? **(b) Draw Conclusions:** What conclusions can you draw about Gabriel's relationship with Elizabeth? Explain. **(c) Speculate:** Why do Gabriel's feelings toward Elizabeth soften at the end of the story?
6. **Make a Judgment:** Who do you think is responsible for Roy's injury?

For: More about James Baldwin
Visit: www.PHSchool.com
Web Code: ere-9624

Apply the Skills

The Rockpile

Literary Analysis

Setting

1. Find three details that describe the psychological environment of the story's **setting**—the mood and atmosphere of the neighborhood.
2. Find three details that describe the physical environment—the landmarks of the neighborhood.
3. What are some of the potential dangers the setting presents?
4. In what ways do you think the setting has influenced Gabriel's and Elizabeth's decisions about how to raise their children?

Connecting Literary Elements

5. **(a)** Use a chart like the one shown to analyze the rockpile, the main **symbol** in this story. **(b)** What does the rockpile represent?

The Rockpile				What It Means
What people say about it	Events linked with it	Details used to describe it	→	

6. **(a)** What does "the toe of his father's heavy shoe," mentioned at the end of the story, symbolize? **(b)** In what way does this image capture John's relationship to Gabriel? **(c)** How would you define their relationship?

Reading Strategy

Identifying Cause and Effect

7. **(a)** What **causes** John to avoid telling his mother that Roy went to the rockpile? **(b)** What is the **effect** of his delay?
8. **(a)** What are the causes of Elizabeth's protectiveness toward John? **(b)** What is the effect on Gabriel of this protectiveness?

Extend Understanding

9. **Psychology Connection:** In this story, John is given a heavy responsibility: monitoring his brother's behavior. What problems might such responsibility create for a young boy like John?

QuickReview

The **setting** of a story is the time and place in which it occurs.

A **symbol** is a person, place, or object that has a meaning in itself but suggests other meanings as well.

To **identify cause-and-effect** relationships, note the circumstances that cause characters' actions and the effects their actions have on others.

For: Self-test
Visit: www.PHSchool.com
Web Code: era-6614

Answers

1. Details include the reckless games the children play on the rockpile, the "sinners" loitering in the street, the anxiety of John and Roy's parents.
2. Details include the rockpile, the crowds in the street, the river, the garbage strewn about the lot, and the fire escape from which John and Roy watch the neighborhood.
3. **Possible response:** There is the danger of succumbing to violence, of killing or being killed in the fight for survival.
4. **Possible response:** Because they feel the neighborhood is not safe, the parents impose strict rules on their children.
5. (a. and b.) **Possible responses:** What people say about it: It cannot be removed; it is intriguing; it is a dangerous place; Events Linked With It: Children play recklessly; children fall and get hurt; Details: "mass of natural rock jutting out of the ground"; "slippery rock"; What it Means: It represents the dangers of the world outside from which Gabriel and Elizabeth want to shield their children.

   Another sample answer can be found on **Literary Analysis Graphic Organizer B**, p. 269 in ***Graphic Organizer Transparencies.***
6. **Possible responses:** (a) It symbolizes Gabriel's power over John. (b) It shows that Gabriel's authority in the family is crushing to John. (c) Their relationship is strained because John is not Gabriel's son.
7. **Possible responses:** (a) John does not tell his mother because he had "practically promised not to." (b) Roy gets hurt, and then everyone looks to John for an explanation.
8. **Possible responses:**(a) Elizabeth may be trying to compensate for the fact that Gabriel doesn't treat John with kindness. (b) It makes Gabriel angry.
9. **Possible response:** Students may say that John could become excessively anxious. John could feel he missed his childhood, as Baldwin did.

Go Online Assessment Students may use the **Self-test** to prepare for **Selection Test A** or **Selection Test B**.

EXTEND/ASSESS

Answers

❶ Vocabulary Lesson

Word Analysis

1. to work improperly
2. producing an unpleasant scent
3. poorly adjusted to the conditions of life
4. a disease resulting from a poor diet

Spelling Strategy

1. recklessly
2. dressing
3. passed

Vocabulary Builder

1. antonyms
2. synonyms
3. synonyms
4. antonyms
5. antonyms
6. antonyms
7. synonyms
8. antonyms
9. antonyms

❷ Grammar and Style Lesson

1. "who seemed at a loss"; *policemen;* nonrestrictive
2. "which spanned the river"; *bridge;* restrictive
3. "who came home early on Saturdays"; *father;* nonrestrictive
4. "which stood beside the rockpile"; *house;* restrictive
5. "where it lay"; *fan;* restrictive; "where she had been"; *seat;* restrictive

Writing Application

Students should include a restrictive adjective clause and a nonrestrictive adjective clause.

WG Writing and Grammar, Ruby Level

Students will find further instruction and practice on restrictive and nonrestrictive adjective clauses in Chapter 19, Section 3.

Build Language Skills

❶ Vocabulary Lesson

Word Analysis: Latin Prefix *mal-*

The Latin prefix *mal-* means "bad," "wrong," or "ill." Combined with the root *-vol-*, meaning "wish," *malevolence* means "ill will." Use this root to determine the meaning of each of these words.

1. malfunction
2. malodorous
3. maladjusted
4. malnutrition

Spelling Strategy

If a word ends in a double consonant, do not make a change when you add a suffix. For example, *engross* + *-ed* = *engrossed.* Correctly add the indicated suffix to the following words.

1. reckless + *-ly* **2.** dress + *-ing* **3.** pass + *-ed*

Vocabulary Builder: Synonyms or Antonyms

Identify each of the following pairs of words as either synonyms or antonyms.

1. intriguing, boring
2. benevolent, charitable
3. decorously, tastefully
4. latent, obvious
5. engrossed, detached
6. jubilant, despondent
7. arrested, halted
8. malevolence, kindness
9. perdition, salvation

❷ Grammar and Style Lesson

Restrictive and Nonrestrictive Adjective Clauses

Containing both a subject and a verb, **adjective clauses** add information about nouns in the main part of a sentence.

A **restrictive adjective clause** is necessary to complete the meaning of the noun or pronoun it modifies.

Restrictive: He was afraid of the rockpile and the boys *who played there.* (essential; tells which *boys*)

A **nonrestrictive adjective clause** provides additional but inessential information and must be set off by commas.

Nonrestrictive: Once a boy, whose name was Richard, drowned in the river. (nonessential; modifies *boy*)

Practice Identify the adjective clause(s), and indicate the word it modifies. Then, state whether it is restrictive or nonrestrictive.

1. There were two white policemen, who seemed at a loss, walking in the street.
2. At the end of the street nearest the house was the bridge which spanned the river . . .
3. . . . made them think of their father, who came home early on Saturdays . . .
4. Then the small procession disappeared into the house which stood beside the rockpile.
5. He did not look at her, but at the fan where it lay in the seat where she had been.

Writing Application Write two sentences. In the first, use a restrictive adjective clause. In the second, use a nonrestrictive adjective clause.

WG Prentice Hall Writing and Grammar Connection: Chapter 19, Section 3

Assessment Practice

Punctuation **(For more practice, see *Standardized Test Preparation Workbook*, p. 70.)**

Some tests require students to identify the best way to correct an error in punctuation. Use the following sample test item to demonstrate.

Because he had much of the responsibility of raising his eight siblings—James Baldwin claimed that he "never had a childhood."

Which is the best way to correct this passage?

A Because he had much of the responsibility of raising his eight siblings; James Baldwin claimed that he "never had a childhood."

B Because he had much of the responsibility of raising his eight siblings: James Baldwin claimed that he "never had a childhood."

C Because he had much of the responsibility of raising his eight siblings, James Baldwin claimed that he "never had a childhood."

D Correct as is

C correctly places a comma after an adverb clause preceding an independent clause.

3 Writing Lesson

Roy's Journal

In "The Rockpile," Roy's actions spark a family crisis in which much is revealed about the family as a whole, but very little about Roy himself. Write a journal entry for Roy in which he discusses his inner thoughts and conflicts. Use appropriate language to express the genuine thoughts and feelings of a young boy.

Prewriting Reread the story to create a timeline of events. Then, for each point on the line, jot down ideas about Roy's thoughts and feelings.

Drafting As you draft Roy's journal, refer to your notes for detail. Keep the language personal and informal.

Revising Look for opportunities to make the tone of the journal more personal. Replace words that may be too formal with more appropriate choices. Determine whether or not your writing provides new insight into Roy's behavior.

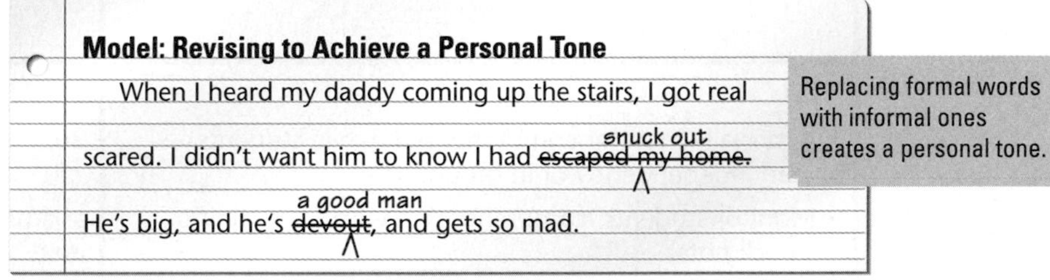

Model: Revising to Achieve a Personal Tone
When I heard my daddy coming up the stairs, I got real
scared. I didn't want him to know I had escaped my home.
snuck out
He's big, and he's devout, and gets so mad.
a good man
Replacing formal words with informal ones creates a personal tone.

Prentice Hall Writing and Grammar Connection: Chapter 14, Section 3

Extend Your Learning

Listening and Speaking In a group, adapt "The Rockpile" as a **radio play.** Divide the story into scenes and develop a script. Keep the following tips in mind as you write and rehearse:

- Assign one person to be the narrator.
- Choose appropriate sound effects and music that evokes the time and place of the story.

Rehearse the play until you are satisfied that you are presenting it as effectively as possible. Then, perform it for the class. **[Group Activity]**

Research and Technology Using a wide range of sources, including the Internet, prepare an **illustrated report** comparing Harlem today with Harlem in the 1930s. Explain the reasons for any similarities and differences between Harlem past and Harlem present. Share your report with the class.

For: An additional research activity
Visit: www.PHSchool.com
Web Code: erd-7614

3 Writing Lesson

- Instruct students to consider what they already know about Roy and his relationships with family members before they reread and create timelines.
- As they begin drafting, remind students that their primary goal is to convey Roy's feelings and conflicts in a believable way.
- Use the writing model to guide students in achieving a personal tone. Give students the **Support for Writing Lesson,** p. 251 in ***Unit 6 Resources,*** to help students as they write their journal entries. Suggest also that students use the Timeline, p. 314 in ***Graphic Organizer Transparencies,*** to complete the assignment.
- Use the rubrics for Response to Literature, pp. 65–66 in ***General Resources*** to assess students' work.

4 Research and Technology

- Be sure that students understand that their reports should compare information about Harlem in the 1930s and today.
- Encourage students to work in small research groups, assigning research and presentation tasks.
- Remind students to look for images that they can use to illustrate their reports.
- Adapt the Research: Research Report rubrics in ***General Resources,*** pp. 49–50, to assess students' reports.
- The **Support for Extend Your Learning** page (***Unit 6 Resources,*** p. 252) provides guided note taking opportunities to help students complete the Extend Your Learning activities.

Go Online Research — Have students type in the Web Code for another research activity.

Assessment Resources

The following resources can be used to assess students' knowledge and skills.

Unit 6 Resources
- **Selection Test A,** pp. 254–256
- **Selection Test B,** pp. 257–259

General Resources
- **Rubrics for Response to Literature,** pp. 65–66
- **Rubrics for Research: Research Report,** pp. 49–50

Go Online Assessment — Students may use the **Self-test** to prepare for **Selection Test A** or **Selection Test B.**

Meeting Your Standards

Students will

1. **analyze and respond to literary elements.**
   - Literary Analysis: Implied Theme
2. **read, comprehend, analyze, and critique nonfiction and poetry.**
   - Reading Strategy: Drawing Inferences About Theme
   - Reading Check questions
   - Apply the Skills questions
   - Assessment Practice (ATE)
3. **develop vocabulary.**
   - Vocabulary Lesson: Latin Root: *-vol-*
4. **understand and apply written and oral language conventions.**
   - Spelling Strategy
   - Grammar and Style Lesson: Transitions and Transitional Phrases
5. **develop writing proficiency.**
   - Writing Lesson: Book Review
6. **develop appropriate research strategies.**
   - Extend Your Learning: Written Report
7. **understand and apply listening and speaking strategies.**
   - Extend Your Learning: Dramatic Reading

Block Scheduling: Use one 90-minute class period to preteach the skills and have students read the selection. Use a second 90-minute class period to assess students' mastery of skills, extend their learning, and monitor their progress.

Homework Suggestions

Following are possibilities for homework assignments.

- Support pages from *Unit 6 Resources:*
  Literary Analysis
  Reading Strategy
  Vocabulary Builder
  Grammar and Style
- An Extend Your Learning project and the Writing Lesson for this selection group may be completed over several days.

Step-by-Step Teaching Guide	Pacing Guide
PRETEACH	
• Administer Vocabulary and Reading Warm-ups as necessary.	5 min.
• Engage students' interest with the motivation activity.	5 min.
• Read and discuss author and background features. **FT**	10 min.
• Introduce the Literary Analysis Skill: Implied Theme. **FT**	5 min.
• Introduce the Reading Strategy: Drawing Inferences About Theme. **FT**	10 min.
• Prepare students to read by teaching the selection vocabulary. **FT**	
TEACH	
• Informally monitor comprehension while students read independently or in groups. **FT**	30 min.
• Monitor students' comprehension with the Reading Check notes.	as students read
• Reinforce vocabulary with Vocabulary Builder notes.	as students read
• Develop students' understanding of implied theme with the Literary Analysis annotations. **FT**	5 min.
• Develop students' ability to draw inferences about theme with the Reading Strategy annotations. **FT**	5 min.
ASSESS/EXTEND	
• Assess students' comprehension and mastery of the Literary Analysis and Reading Strategy by having them answer the Apply the Skills questions. **FT**	15 min.
• Have students complete the Vocabulary Lesson and the Grammar and Style Lesson. **FT**	15 min.
• Apply students' ability to write to the knowledge level of readers by using the Writing Lesson. **FT**	45 min. or homework
• Apply students' understanding by using one or more of the Extend Your Learning activities.	20–90 min. or homework
• Administer Selection Test A or Selection Test B. **FT**	15 min.

Resources

PRINT

Unit 6 Resources

Vocabulary Warm-up Word Lists **[L1, L2, EL]** . . . . p. 260
Vocabulary Warm-up Practice **[L1, L2, EL]** . . . . p. 261
Reading Warm-up A **[L1, L2, EL]** . . . . p. 262
Reading Warm-up B **[L1, L2, L3]** . . . . p. 263

TRANSPARENCY

Graphic Organizer Transparencies

Literary Analysis Graphic Organizer A **[L3]** . . . . p. 272
Literary Analysis Graphic Organizer B **[L1, L2, EL]** . . . . p. 273
Reading Strategy Graphic Organizer A **[L3]** . . . . p. 270
Reading Strategy Graphic Organizer B **[L1, L2, EL]** . . . . p. 271

PRINT

Reader's Notebook [L2]
Reader's Notebook: Adapted Version [L1]
Reader's Notebook: English Learner's Version [EL]

Unit 6 Resources

Literary Analysis **[L3]** . . . . p. 264
Reading Strategy **[L3]** . . . . p. 265
Vocabulary Builder **[L3]** . . . . p. 266

TECHNOLOGY

Listening to Literature Audio CDs [L2, EL]

PRINT

Unit 6 Resources

Grammar and Style **[L3]** . . . . p. 267
Support for Writing Lesson **[L3]** . . . . p. 268
Support for Extend Your Learning **[L3]** . . . . p. 269
Enrichment **[L4]** . . . . p. 270
Selection Test A **[L1, L2, EL]** . . . . pp. 271–273
Selection Test B **[L3, L4]** . . . . pp. 274–276

General Resources

Rubrics for Critique **[L3]** . . . . pp. 75–76
Rubric for Peer Assessment: Oral Interpretation **[L3]** . . . . p. 130

TECHNOLOGY

Go Online: Research **[L3]**
Go Online: Self-test **[L3]**
***ExamView®* Test Bank [L3]**

Choosing Resources for Differentiated Instruction

[L1] Special Needs Students
[L2] Below-Level Students
[L3] All Students
[L4] Advanced Students
[EL] English Learners

For Vocabulary and Reading Warm-ups and for Selection Tests, **A** signifies "less challenging" and **B** "more challenging." For Graphic Organizer transparencies, **A** signifies "not filled in" and **B** "filled in."

FT Fast Track Instruction: To move the lesson more quickly, use the strategies and activities identified with **FT**.

Scaffolding for Less Proficient and Advanced Students

The leveled Critical Thinking questions after selections progress in the levels of thinking required to answer them. To address the needs of your different students, you may use the (a) level questions for your less proficient students and the (b) level questions with your on-level and advanced students. The occasional (c) level questions are appropriate for your advanced students.

PRENTICE HALL **TeacherEXPRESS™** Plan · Teach · Assess — Use this complete suite of powerful teaching tools to make lesson planning and testing quicker and easier.

PRENTICE HALL **StudentEXPRESS™** Learn · Study · Succeed — Use the interactive textbook (online and on CD-ROM) to make selections and activities come alive with audio and video support and interactive questions.

Go Online Professional Development — **For:** Information about Lexiles **Visit:** www.PHSchool.com **Web Code:** eue-1111

PREteach

Motivation

What do today's young people fear most? Conduct a brief discussion in which students offer their responses to this question. Follow the discussion by explaining that about a half century ago, young people lived with the very real fear of atomic war and its massive destructive force. In elementary schools of the post-World War II age, students were taught to duck beneath their desks and cover their heads to protect themselves from bombs (a response that, from John Hersey's description, we know would have been futile in a real atomic bomb attack). Tell students that the selections they are about to read will give them a glimpse of the horrors of modern warfare and help them understand people's anxieties and fears in the aftermath of World War II.

❶ Background

More About the Authors

Hiroshima, the book by John Hersey excerpted here, grew from the idea that a first-person account of the bombing and its aftermath would be especially moving. The book begins a few hours before the explosion and follows the city until one year later. Hersey focuses on six survivors, including the four described here. These people— including two doctors and two members of the Christian clergy—are not representative of the population of Hiroshima; rather, they are meant to be recognizable for American readers, who may have known of the bombing only from such unpeopled photographs as those that illustrate this excerpt.

Many of Randall Jarrell's southern contemporaries—including his Vanderbilt University connections Tate, Warren, and Ransom—were members of a writers' group called the Fugitives. This group advocated the rural Southern agrarian tradition, Southern political and cultural ideals, and traditional poetic form, but Jarrell was not interested in these issues. Instead, his writing was apocalyptic and surreal. His main influences were W.H. Auden and Robert Frost.

Build Skills *Nonfiction • Poems*

❶ *from* Hiroshima • Losses • The Death of the Ball Turret Gunner

John Hersey (1914–1993)

Born in China to American parents and raised there until age ten, John Hersey returned repeatedly to East Asia during his long career as a war correspondent, novelist, and essayist.

In his twenty-five books and countless articles, Hersey combined a profound moral sensibility with the highest artistry. His novels and essays not only examine the moral implications of the major political and historical events of his day, they do so with high literary grace. In 1945, Hersey won a Pulitzer Prize for his novel *A Bell for Adano,* in which an American major discovers the human dignity of the Italian villagers who were his enemies in World War II.

The Atomic Bomb During the 1940s, Hersey traveled to China and Japan as a correspondent for *The New Yorker* and *Time* magazines. He also used these visits to gather material for his most famous and acclaimed book, *Hiroshima* (1946), a shocking, graphic depiction of the devastation caused by the atomic bomb that was dropped on the Japanese city of Hiroshima at the end of World War II. This remarkable report first appeared in *The New Yorker* on August 31, 1946. Wallace Shawn, then editor of *The New Yorker,* made the unprecedented decision to bump all of the magazine's other editorial content in order to publish Hersey's four-part article.

Stories of Inhumanity and Courage In 1950, Hersey published the novel *The Wall,* which tells of the extinction of the Warsaw ghetto by the Germans during World War II. Hersey's later works include *A Single Pebble* (1956), *The War Lover* (1959), *The Child Buyer* (1960), *The Algiers Motel Incident* (1968), *The Writer's Craft* (1974), *Blues* (1987), and *Fling and Other Stories* (1990).

Randall Jarrell (1914–1965)

Randall Jarrell was a talented poet, literary critic, and teacher whose work was praised by both writers and critics. His literary essays, many of which appear in his book *Poetry and the Age* (1953), have been credited with changing the critical tastes and trends of his time.

Literary Ambitions Born in Nashville, Tennessee, Jarrell graduated from Vanderbilt University, where he studied under writers Robert Penn Warren, Allen Tate, and John Crowe Ransom. All of these men would prove helpful in promoting Jarrell's career. Warren and Tate published Jarrell's early poetry and criticism, and Tate helped land Jarrell his first teaching job at Kenyon College.

During World War II, Jarrell enlisted in the U.S. Air Force. He served only briefly as a pilot, and spent the remaining war years as an aviation instructor, training pilots to fly the famed B-29 bombers that helped secure victory. Jarrell's war experiences provided him with the material for the poems in his books *Little Friend, Little Friend* (1945) and *Losses* (1948). These books rank among the finest literature to emerge from the war.

American Language Jarrell was a great admirer of the poetry of Robert Frost, and, like Frost, he wrote poems based on the sounds and rhythms of American speech. Jarrell's collections *The Seven-League Crutches* (1951) and *The Lost World* (1965) focus on childhood and innocence. *The Woman at the Washington Zoo* (1960) deals with the theme of aging and loneliness. "The Death of the Ball Turret Gunner"—a brief poem told in the first person of a soldier experiencing his last moments in a World War II bomber plane—is one of Jarrell's most famous works.

Preview

Connecting to the Literature

You may have seen movies about World War II. You may even have a relative who experienced the war firsthand. Yet, it is probably still difficult for you to imagine what it was like to live through a conflict of such immensity. These selections will give you a better sense of the war and provide a picture of events that changed the world forever.

❷ Literary Analysis

Implied Theme

The **theme** is the central idea that a writer conveys in a work of literature. Most often a theme is **implied,** or revealed indirectly, through the writer's choice of details, portrayal of characters and events, and use of literary devices. These selections all present implied themes about war.

Comparing Literary Works

Usually, we expect works of journalism to be objective, while we expect poems to be subjective. These selections, however, challenge our expectations.

- An **objective account** of a story is one in which the narrator is an outside observer who reports events without emotion or bias.
  Hersey: A hundred thousand people were killed by the atomic bomb . . .
- A **subjective account** is one in which the narrator reveals his or her feelings about the events described.
  Jarrell: I woke to black flak and the nightmare fighters.

As you read these powerful pieces, compare how the authors mix objectivity and subjectivity in surprising and effective ways.

❸ Reading Strategy

Drawing Inferences About Theme

When the theme of a literary work is conveyed indirectly, it is up to the reader to **draw inferences,** or conclusions, by looking closely at the writer's choice of details, events, and characters. As you read, use a chart like the one shown to note important details that point to an implied theme.

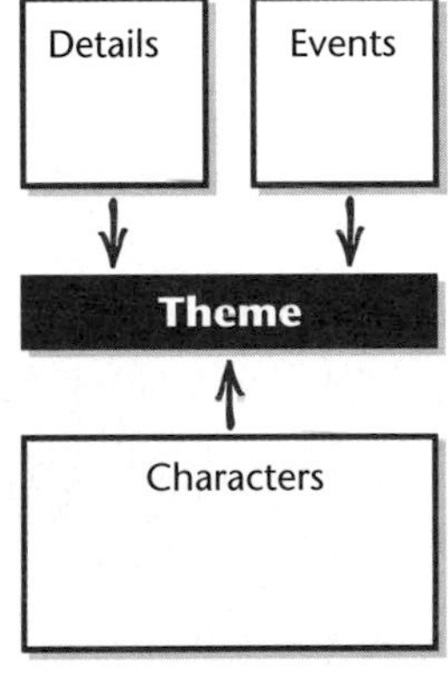

Vocabulary Builder

evacuated (ē vak′ yo͞o āt′ id) *v.* to have made empty; withdrawn (p. 1199)

volition (vō lish′ ən) *n.* act of using the will (p. 1199)

rendezvous (rän′ dā vo͞o′) *n.* meeting place (p. 1200)

philanthropies (fə lan′ thrə pēz) *n.* charitable acts or gifts (p. 1201)

incessant (in ses′ ənt) *adj.* constant; continuing or repeating in a way that seems endless (p. 1206)

convivial (kən viv′ ē əl) *adj.* fond of good company; sociable (p. 1207)

❷ Literary Analysis

Implied Theme

- Remind students that the *theme* is the central idea conveyed in a literary work. Explain that an *implied theme* is revealed indirectly, rather than stated explicitly.
- Explain to students that they can identify the implied theme of a literary work by examining the characters, details, and literary devices the author employs.

❸ Reading Strategy

Drawing Inferences About Theme

- Be sure students understand that if a work's theme is implied, a reader must draw inferences about it, based on the details the author includes.
- Present students with this line from Randall Jarrell's "Losses": . . . we burned/The cities we had learned about in school—
- Guide students to recognize the contrast between education and destruction. What inference about the poem's theme can they draw? **Possible response:** The poem's theme is the apparent senselessness of war.
- Give students a copy of **Reading Strategy Graphic Organizer A,** p. 270 in ***Graphic Organizer Transparencies,*** to use as they read.

Vocabulary Builder

- Pronounce each vocabulary word for students, and read the definitions as a class. Have students identify any words with which they are already familiar.

Differentiated Instruction

Solutions for All Learners

Support for Special Needs Students
Have students complete the **Preview** and **Build Skills** pages for these selections in the ***Reader's Notebook: Adapted Version.*** These pages provide a selection summary, an abbreviated presentation of the reading and literary skills, and the graphic organizer on the **Build Skills** page in the student book.

Support for Less Proficient Readers
Have students complete the **Preview** and **Build Skills** pages for these selections in the ***Reader's Notebook.*** These pages provide a selection summary, an abbreviated presentation of the reading and literary skills, and the graphic organizer on the **Build Skills** page in the student book.

Support for English Learners
Have students complete the **Preview** and **Build Skills** pages for these selections in the ***Reader's Notebook: English Learner's Version.*** These pages provide a selection summary, an abbreviated presentation of the reading and literary skills, and the graphic organizer on the **Build Skills** page in the student book.

TEACH

Learning Modalities
Intrapersonal Learners
Before they read, ask students to think about and record in writing their personal feelings about war. As they read, have them note particular phrases or descriptions that they find especially moving or disturbing. After they read, discuss how the three works affected their original feelings.

❶ About the Selection

World War II was a so-called "popular" war in which the issues that spurred the conflict were clearly defined. With the future of many of the nations of the world in grave danger, the majority of Americans believed that fighting the enemy was both just and necessary for survival. Nevertheless, technological advances in weaponry; the sheer magnitude of the global conflict; and the ability to report on the progress of the war from virtually any location around the world via print, radio, and film media, brought home the horrors of war in a new way. Although the antiwar movement did not become a political force until the 1960s, these works by Hersey and Jarrell take their place in the ranks of early antiwar literature.

❶ FROM HIROSHIMA

John Hersey

Differentiated Instruction Solutions for All Learners

Accessibility at a Glance

	from Hiroshima	Losses	The Death of the Ball Turret Gunner
Context	World War II, Hiroshima bombing	World War II	World War II
Language	Straightforward, reportorial	Conversational	Specialized terminology
Concept Level	Challenging (effect of war)	Challenging (nature of war)	Challenging (nature of war)
Literary Merit	High-interest, anti-war	Government indifference to loss of life	Striking imagery
Lexile	1230L	NP	NP
Overall Rating	More challenging	More accessible	More accessible

Background In August 1945, American President Harry Truman was faced with a terrible decision. The world had been at war for six years. Germany had surrendered in May, but Japan refused to give up. The United States had just finished developing an atomic bomb. President Truman had to decide whether or not to use this new technology to bring an end to the war. On August 6, Truman ordered that the atomic bomb be dropped on the Japanese city of Hiroshima. Three days later, another bomb was dropped on Nagasaki. These two bombs killed more than 200,000 people and forced the Japanese surrender. Like so many events of World War II, the atomic bomb gave the world a new horror, as John Hersey so carefully documents in this selection.

At exactly fifteen minutes past eight in the morning, on August 6, 1945, Japanese time, at the moment when the atomic bomb flashed above Hiroshima, Miss Toshiko Sasaki, a clerk in the personnel department of the East Asia Tin Works, had just sat down at her place in the plant office and was turning her head to speak to the girl at the next desk. At that same moment, Dr. Masakazu Fujii was settling down cross-legged to read the Osaka *Asahi* on the porch of his private hospital, overhanging one of the seven deltaic rivers which divide Hiroshima; Mrs. Hatsuyo Nakamura, a tailor's widow, stood by the window of her kitchen, watching a neighbor tearing down his house because it lay in the path of an air-raid-defense fire lane . . . and the Reverend Mr. Kiyoshi Tanimoto, pastor of the Hiroshima Methodist Church, paused at the door of a rich man's house in Koi, the city's western suburb, and prepared to unload a handcart full of things he had evacuated from town in fear of the massive B-29 raid which everyone expected Hiroshima to suffer. A hundred thousand people were killed by the atomic bomb, and these [four] were among the survivors. They still wonder why they lived when so many others died. Each of them counts many small items of chance or volition—a step taken in time, a decision to go indoors, catching one streetcar instead of the next—that spared him. And now each knows that in the act of survival he lived a dozen lives and saw more death than he ever thought he would see. At the time, none of them knew anything.

The Reverend Mr. Tanimoto got up at five o'clock that morning. He was alone in the parsonage, because for some time his wife had been commuting with their year-old baby to spend nights with a friend in Ushida, a suburb to the north. Of all the important cities of Japan, only two, Kyoto and Hiroshima, had not been visited in strength by *B-san*, or Mr. B, as the Japanese, with a mixture of respect

3 ◄ **Critical Viewing** How effectively do these remains of the sacred tree of a Hiroshima temple convey the physical and emotional devastation of the blast? Explain. **[Evaluate]**

Vocabulary Builder

evacuated (ē vak´ yo͞o āt´ id) *v.* to have made empty; withdrawn

volition (vō lish´ ən) *n.* act of using the will

4 

Reading Check

What happened at exactly 8:15 in the morning on August 6, 1945?

2 Vocabulary Builder

The Latin Root *-vol-*

- Call students' attention to the word *volition* and its definition. Tell students that the Latin word root *-vol-* means "to will" or "to wish."
- Have students **suggest** words and phrases that contain this root, and list them on the chalkboard. **Possible answers:** volunteer, malevolence, benevolence, and involuntary.
- Next, have students look up the meanings of these words in a dictionary.
- Have students write sentences in which they use these words correctly. Call on volunteers to read their sentences aloud—and to define the word "volunteer"!

3 Critical Viewing

Possible response: The remains of the sacred tree convey the physical and emotional devastation of the blast quite effectively. First of all, the gnarled remnants of the tree and the bricks and debris scattered about illustrate the magnitude of physical damage. Perhaps more importantly, the fact that the decimated tree is a sacred one helps to underscore the emotional pain that the people of Hiroshima must have felt.

4 Reading Check

Answer: At 8:15 that morning, the atomic bomb was dropped on the Japanese city of Hiroshima.

Differentiated Instruction
Solutions for All Learners

Strategy for Less Proficient Readers
Help students keep track of the characters in the excerpt from *Hiroshima* by making a chart with the following headings and filling it in as they read:

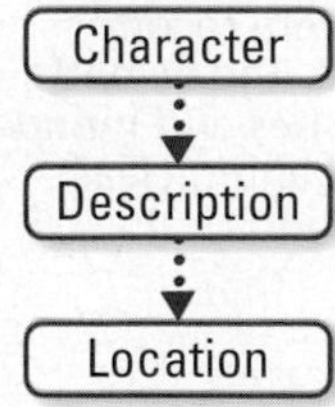

Strategy for English Learners
Movement back and forth in time in *Hiroshima* may confuse some English language learners. As students read, ask them to determine whether each paragraph deals with a time well before the bomb drops, early on the day of the bombing, or immediately after the bomb explodes.

5 Reading Strategy
Drawing Inferences About Theme

- Remind students that when the theme of a literary work is implied, rather than stated explicitly, readers must draw inferences about the theme based on details, events, and characters.
- Call students' attention to the chart modeled with the Reading Strategy instruction. Have them prepare such a chart as they read.
- Have students read the bracketed passage. Ask them to use their charts to note the details, events, and characters it describes.
- **Ask** students what inferences they can draw about Hersey's theme based on these details, events, and characters.
  Possible response: Students may infer that Hersey implies that in a war, "the enemy" is actually made up of ordinary people no different from ourselves.

6 Literature in Context
B-29 Bombers

The Allied bombing campaign against Japan carried out by the United States Army Air Force relied on the B-29. Coming at the very end of the war, the atomic bombing of Hiroshima and Nagasaki made it clear that long-range bombers which, like the B-29, could deliver nuclear weapons would be crucial in military strategy for the post-war world. After the war, the U.S. Air Force was established as a part of the Department of Defense, and the Strategic Air Command was put in charge of nuclear-armed bombers.

Connect to the Literature Ask students whether they would be more comfortable knowing or *not* knowing about danger. Then, **ask** the Connect to the Literature question.
Possible response: Knowing the extent of the B-29's destructive capabilities would increase Mr. Tanimoto's anxiety.

and unhappy familiarity, called the B-29♦; and Mr. Tanimoto, like all his neighbors and friends, was almost sick with anxiety. He had heard uncomfortably detailed accounts of mass raids on Kure, Iwakuni, Tokuyama, and other nearby towns; he was sure Hiroshima's turn would come soon. He had slept badly the night before, because there had been several air-raid warnings. Hiroshima had been getting such warnings almost every night for weeks, for at that time the B-29s were using Lake Biwa, northeast of Hiroshima, as a rendezvous point, and no matter what city the Americans planned to hit, the Super-fortresses streamed in over the coast near Hiroshima. The frequency of the warning and the continued abstinence of Mr. B with respect to Hiroshima had made its citizens jittery; a rumor was going around that the Americans were saving something special for the city.

Vocabulary Builder
rendezvous (rän′dā vo͞o′) *n.* meeting place

5 Mr. Tanimoto was a small man, quick to talk, laugh, and cry. He wore his black hair parted in the middle and rather long; the prominence of the frontal bones just above his eyebrows and the smallness of his mustache, mouth, and chin gave him a strange old-young look, boyish and yet wise, weak and yet fiery. He moved nervously and fast, but with a restraint which suggested that he is a cautious, thoughtful man. He showed, indeed, just those qualities in the uneasy days before the bomb fell. Mr. Tanimoto had been carrying all the portable things from his church, in the close-packed residential district called Nagaragawa, to a house that belonged to a rayon manufacturer in Koi, two miles from the center of town. The rayon man, a Mr. Matsui, had opened his then unoccupied estate to a large number of his friends and acquaintances, so that they might evacuate whatever they wished to a safe distance from the probable target area. Mr. Tanimoto had had no difficulty in moving chairs, hymnals, Bibles, altar gear, and church records by pushcart himself, but the organ console and an upright piano required some aid. A friend of his named Matsuo had, the day before, helped him get the piano out to Koi; in return, he had promised this day to assist Mr. Matsuo in hauling out a daughter's belongings. That is why he had risen so early.

Mr. Tanimoto cooked his own breakfast. He felt awfully tired. The effort of moving the piano the day before, a sleepless night, weeks of worry and unbalanced diet, the cares of his parish—all combined to make him feel hardly adequate to the new day's work. There was another thing, too: Mr. Tanimoto had studied theology at Emory College, in Atlanta, Georgia; he had graduated in 1940; he spoke excellent English; he dressed in American clothes; he had corresponded with many American friends right up to the time the war began; and among a people obsessed with a fear of being spied upon—perhaps almost obsessed himself—he found himself growing increasingly uneasy. The police had questioned

Literature in Context

6 **History Connection**

♦ ***B-29 Bombers***
The Second World War saw major advances in the technology of mechanized warfare—warfare that relied heavily on machines. The B-29 Superfortress bomber that Hersey mentions was an aircraft capable of long-range, heavy bombing runs. It was used frequently against Japan during 1944 and 1945. Firebomb B-29 raids against industrial cities in Japan totaled nearly 7,000 flights and dropped 41,600 tons of bombs.

Connect to the Literature
In what way would having more information about the B-29 bomber increase Mr. Tanimoto's anxiety level?

Enrichment

Hiroshima and Nagasaki

Share with the class the following information about Japan and the cities of Hiroshima and Nagasaki. Have one or more volunteers point out the places you cite on a wall map.

Japan is a chain of islands—which means that it can be attacked only by air or by sea. The four main islands of Japan are Hokkaido, Honshu, Shikoku, and Kyushu. Its western neighbors are North and South Korea, Russia, and China.

Hiroshima is a port city on the southwest coast of Honshu. Nagasaki is a port city on the west coast of Kyushu. Both had a certain amount of industry and military installations in 1945, but neither was as major a target as the capital, Tokyo, was. The cities were in large part destroyed by the bombs but were reconstructed throughout the 1950s. Today, both cities house important tourist sites and monuments that attract antiwar and antinuclear supporters from around the world.

him several times, and just a few days before, he had heard that an influential acquaintance, a Mr. Tanaka, a retired officer of the Toyo Kisen Kaisha steamship line, an anti-Christian, a man famous in Hiroshima for his showy philanthropies and notorious for his personal tyrannies, had been telling people that Tanimoto should not be trusted. In compensation, to show himself publicly a good Japanese, Mr. Tanimoto had taken on the chairmanship of his local *tonarigumi*, or Neighborhood Association, and to his other duties and concerns this position had added the business of organizing air-raid defense for about twenty families.

Before six o'clock that morning, Mr. Tanimoto started for Mr. Matsuo's house. There he found that their burden was to be a *tansu*, a large Japanese cabinet, full of clothing and household goods. The two men set out. The morning was perfectly clear and so warm that the day promised to be uncomfortable. A few minutes after they started, the air-raid siren went off—a minute-long blast that warned of approaching planes but indicated to the people of Hiroshima only a slight degree of danger, since it sounded every morning at this time, when an American weather plane came over. The two men pulled and pushed the handcart through the city streets. Hiroshima was a fan-shaped city, lying mostly on the six islands formed by the seven estuarial rivers that branch out from the Ota River; its main commercial and residential districts, covering about four square miles in the center of the city, contained three-quarters of its population, which had been reduced by several evacuation programs from a wartime peak of 380,000 to about 245,000. Factories and other residential districts, or suburbs, lay compactly around the edges of the city. To the south were the docks, an airport, and the island-studded Inland Sea. A rim of mountains runs around the other three sides of the delta. Mr. Tanimoto and Mr. Matsuo took their way through the shopping center, already full of people, and across two of the rivers to the sloping streets of Koi, and up them to the outskirts and foothills. As they started up a valley away from the tight-ranked houses, the all-clear sounded. (The Japanese radar operators, detecting only three planes, supposed that they comprised a reconnaissance.) Pushing the handcart up to the rayon man's house was tiring, and the men, after they had maneuvered their load into the driveway and to the front steps, paused to rest awhile. They stood with a wing of the house between them and the city. Like most homes in this part of Japan, the house consisted of a wooden frame and wooden walls supporting a heavy tile roof. Its front hall, packed with rolls of bedding and clothing, looked like a cool cave full of fat cushions. Opposite the house, to the right of the front door, there was a large, finicky rock garden. There was no sound of planes. The morning was still; the place was cool and pleasant.

Then a tremendous flash of light cut across the sky. Mr. Tanimoto has a distinct recollection that it travelled from east to west, from the city toward the hills. It seemed a sheet of sun. Both he and Mr. Matsuo reacted in terror—and both had time to react (for they were 3,500 yards, or two miles, from the center of the explosion). Mr. Matsuo dashed up

Vocabulary Builder
philanthropies (fə lan′ thrə pēz) *n.* charitable acts or gifts

Literary Analysis
Implied Theme In light of the bombing, what is ironic about an air-raid siren indicating only a "slight degree of danger"?

9 
Reading Check
Why does Mr. Tanimoto move all the portable things in his church to a home farther from the town center?

Differentiated Instruction
Solutions for All Learners

Strategy for Special Needs Students
This long selection provides a good opportunity for students to develop their ability to read independently for a sustained period of time. Suggest to students that, while reading independently, they use sticky notes to mark any passages that present them with confusing ideas or vocabulary and continue reading. During class discussion, have students ask questions about passages they have marked.

Support for Advanced Readers
Encourage students to discuss Hersey's development of the passage of time. Call students' attention to the author's use of transitions on this page. Guide them to recognize that before the bomb strikes, Hersey advances time by describing the sequence of Mr. Tanimoto's actions. When the bomb strikes, the author uses the very simple transition "Then," echoing the terrifying suddenness of the devastation that seems to end normal time.

7 Literary Analysis
Implied Theme

- Remind students that in many works of literature, the *theme* is not stated explicitly. Instead, it is *implied* through the characters, details, and literary devices.
- Have students read the bracketed passage. Be sure they are aware that the passage relates details of Mr. Tanimoto's actions just before the atomic bomb hit Hiroshima.
- **Ask** students the Literary Analysis question: In light of the bombing, what is ironic about an air-raid siren indicating only a "slight degree of danger"?
  Answer: This is an example of dramatic irony, because readers know what the characters do not: that the city is about to be destroyed by an atomic bomb.

➤ **Monitor Progress:** Encourage students to discuss how this and other details might express the implied theme.

8 Critical Thinking
Analyze

- Have students read the bracketed passage. Instruct them to **visualize** the scene Hersey describes here. How would they characterize it?
  Possible response: Students will likely respond that the scene is peaceful, even serene.
- **Ask** students: Considering what is about to happen—the atomic blast—why do you think Hersey includes this peaceful moment here?
  Possible response: This scene sharply contrasts with the chaos and devastation that is about to erupt, showing the suddenness and brutality of the atomic bomb attack.

9 Reading Check

Answer: He moves the things in his church because the Japanese believed that Hiroshima would be bombed, perhaps very heavily.

⑩ Critical Viewing

Possible response: Students may say that they relate the devastation more to real people's lives now that they have read about some real people affected by the bombing.

⑪ Reading Strategy
Drawing Inferences About Theme

- Remind students that readers often must infer the theme of a literary work based on the details the author chooses to include.
- Have students read the bracketed passage. Then, **ask** them the Reading strategy question: What does the detail about the bleeding, dazed soldiers imply about the catastrophe that has just taken place?
  Possible response: Whatever has happened was worse than anything the soldiers had anticipated; the attack was so unpredictable and immense a suitable defense was impossible.

➤ **Monitor Progress:** **Ask** students, based on their responses, what this detail implies about Hersey's theme.
Possible response: Hersey conveys the idea that the atomic bomb is a weapon of tremendous, almost unthinkable power.

the front steps into the house and dived among the bedrolls and buried himself there. Mr. Tanimoto took four or five steps and threw himself between two big rocks in the garden. He bellied up very hard against one of them. As his face was against the stone, he did not see what happened. He felt a sudden pressure, and then splinters and pieces of board and fragments of tile fell on him. He heard no roar. (Almost no one in Hiroshima recalls hearing any noise of the bomb. But a fisherman in his sampan on the Inland Sea near Tsuzu, the man with whom Mr. Tanimoto's mother-in-law and sister-in-law were living, saw the flash and heard a tremendous explosion; he was nearly twenty miles from Hiroshima, but the thunder was greater than when the B-29s hit Iwakuni, only five miles away.)

⑩ ▲ **Critical Viewing** You may have seen photographs like this one of the aftermath of the Hiroshima bombing. Does Hersey's account change the way you view such pictures? Explain. **[Relate]**

When he dared, Mr. Tanimoto raised his head and saw that the rayon man's house had collapsed. He thought a bomb had fallen directly on it. Such clouds of dust had risen that there was a sort of twilight around. In panic, not thinking for the moment of Mr. Matsuo under the ruins, he dashed out into the street. He noticed as he ran that the concrete wall of the estate had fallen over—toward the house rather than away from it. In the street, the first thing he saw was a squad of soldiers who had been

⑪  burrowing into the hillside opposite, making one of the thousands of

Enrichment

Radio Broadcasting

The Second World War occurred at a time when there was as yet only limited television broadcasting. Therefore, the most important source of up-to-the-minute news about the war was radio. This was true for Americans and their allies as well as for Japanese citizens such as Mrs. Nakamura. Radio broadcasting is still a vital link to the news of the day for thousands of people, many of whom keep the radio on as they go about their business at work.

The importance of radio news today may seem to be eclipsed by that of television, but radio is still a vital news source. Just as in the golden age of radio (from 1925 until the early 1950s), today's on-air news reporters interview subjects and distill key ideas from masses of information. Encourage students to discuss how they get information about what is happening in your area, in the country, and in the world. Invite students to explore radio as a news source and consider what it was like to rely on radio as do Hersey's subjects.

dugouts in which the Japanese apparently intended to resist invasion, hill by hill, life for life; the soldiers were coming out of the hole, where they should have been safe, and blood was running from their heads, chests, and backs. They were silent and dazed.

Under what seemed to be a local dust cloud, the day grew darker and darker.

At nearly midnight, the night before the bomb was dropped, an announcer on the city's radio station said that about two hundred B-29s were approaching southern Honshu and advised the population of Hiroshima to evacuate to their designated "safe areas." Mrs. Hatsuyo Nakamura, the tailor's widow, who lived in the section called Nobori-cho and who had long had a habit of doing as she was told, got her three children—a ten-year-old boy, Toshio, an eight-year-old girl, Yaeko, and a five-year-old girl, Myeko—out of bed and dressed them and walked with them to the military area known as the East Parade Ground, on the northeast edge of the city. There she unrolled some mats and the children lay down on them. They slept until about two, when they were awakened by the roar of the planes going over Hiroshima.

As soon as the planes had passed, Mrs. Nakamura started back with her children. They reached home a little after two-thirty and she immediately turned on the radio, which, to her distress, was just then broadcasting a fresh warning. When she looked at the children and saw how tired they were, and when she thought of the number of trips they had made in past weeks, all to no purpose, to the East Parade Ground, she decided that in spite of the instructions on the radio, she simply could not face starting out all over again. She put the children in their bedrolls on the floor, lay down herself at three o'clock, and fell asleep at once, so soundly that when planes passed over later, she did not waken to their sound.

The siren jarred her awake at about seven. She arose, dressed quickly, and hurried to the house of Mr. Nakamoto, the head of her Neighborhood Association, and asked him what she should do. He said that she should remain at home unless an urgent warning—a series of intermittent blasts of the siren—was sounded. She returned home, lit the stove in the kitchen, set some rice to cook, and sat down to read that mornings Hiroshima *Chugoku*. To her relief, the all-clear sounded at eight o'clock. She heard the children stirring, so she went and gave each of them a handful of peanuts and told them to stay in their bedrolls, because they were tired from the night's walk. She had hoped that they would go back to sleep, but the man in the house directly to the south began to make a terrible hullabaloo of hammering, wedging, ripping, and splitting. The prefectural government,[1] convinced, as everyone in Hiroshima was, that the city would be attacked soon, had begun to press with threats and warnings for the completion of wide

1. **prefectural government** regional districts of Japan which are administered by a governor.

Reading Strategy
Drawing Inferences About Theme What does the detail about the bleeding, dazed soldiers imply about the catastrophe that has just taken place?

Literary Analysis
Implied Theme and Objective/Subjective Accounts What do the details about Mrs. Nakamura's tired children suggest about the author's objectivity?

13 
Reading Check
Why are Mrs. Nakamura's children so tired?

12 Literary Analysis
Implied Theme and Objective/Subjective Accounts

- Remind students that a literary work can present either an objective or a subjective account of the events it describes, depending upon the emotions the author reveals toward his subject.
- Have students read the bracketed passage. Be sure that they understand that Mrs. Nakamura's children are so tired she cannot bring herself to take them back to the "safe area" again.
- **Ask** students the Literary Analysis question: What do the details about Mrs. Nakamura's tired children suggest about the author's objectivity?
  Possible response: These details suggest that Hersey sympathizes strongly with Mrs. Nakamura and other ordinary people; his is a subjective account.
- Encourage students to consider what Hersey's feelings—and the details through which he reveals them—imply about his theme.

13 Reading Check

Answer: The children are so tired because Mrs. Nakamura brought them to the "safe area" at midnight, and they did not get home until two-thirty in the morning.

Differentiated Instruction
Solutions for All Learners

Support for Less Proficient Readers
Students might be confused by the transition from the moments following the explosion back to the moments preceding it. Guide them to understand that Hersey will show them the atomic blast from the perspectives of four different individuals.

Support for English Learners
Students may find Hersey's highly detailed descriptions of his subjects and their activities challenging. Allow them to first read the selection along with **Listening to Literature Audio CD**. Then, have them reread the descriptions carefully, pausing to look up any unfamiliar words.

Enrichment for Gifted/Talented Students
Ask students to discuss Hersey's description of the atomic bomb's impact. Is this the first such description that they have read? If so, encourage them to look for photographs and videotaped images of nuclear explosions and their aftermath. Students can assemble a visual presentation for the class to complement Hersey's writing.

⓮ Literary Analysis
Implied Theme

- Be sure students recognize that the theme of Hersey's text is not stated explicitly—instead, Hersey implies his theme through the details he describes.
- Have students read the bracketed passage. Instruct them to pay close attention to the details about daily life in Hiroshima before the bomb.
- **Ask** students the Literary Analysis question: Why do you think the author included information about the citizens' attempts to defend their city and its population?
  Possible response: The information is ironic because readers know that the defensive measures are futile; one cannot prepare for nuclear warfare.

➤ **Monitor Progress: Ask** students to look at the picture on this spread and explain how it illustrates the irony of the passage.
Possible response: The neighbor is knocking down his house to make way for a fire lane; however, the house will soon be hit by a bomb more devastating than any incendiary device ever seen.

⓯ Literary Analysis
Implied Theme

- Have students read the bracketed passage. Then, **ask** them to discuss Hersey's characterization of Mrs. Nakamura. How would they describe her experience of the war?
  Possible response: Mrs. Nakamura has already suffered so much that it seems impossible she will have to endure more, but the reader knows that she will.
- **Ask** students what the description suggests about Hersey's implied themes.
  Possible response: It implies a theme of the strength of the human spirit. Mrs. Nakamura embodies the resilience and strength of the human spirit.

fire lanes, which, it was hoped, might act in conjunction with the rivers to localize any fires started by an incendiary[2] raid; and the neighbor was reluctantly sacrificing his home to the city's safety. Just the day before, the prefecture had ordered all able-bodied girls from the secondary schools to spend a few days helping to clear these lanes, and they started work soon after the all-clear sounded.

⓮ Mrs. Nakamura went back to the kitchen, looked at the rice, and began watching the man next door. At first, she was annoyed with him for making so much noise, but then she was moved almost to tears by pity. Her emotion was specifically directed toward her neighbor, tearing down his home, board by board, at a time when there was so much unavoidable destruction, but undoubtedly she also felt a generalized, community pity, to say nothing of self-pity. She had not had an easy time. Her husband, Isawa, had gone into the Army just after Myeko was born, and she had heard nothing from or of him for a long time, until, ⓯ on March 5, 1942, she received a seven-word telegram: "Isawa died an honorable death at Singapore." She learned later that he had died on February 15th, the day Singapore fell, and that he had been a

Literary Analysis
Implied Theme Why do you think the author included information about the citizens' attempts to defend their city and its population?

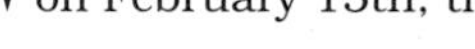

2. **incendiary** (in sen′ dē er′ ē) *adj.* designed to cause fires.

16 ◄ Critical Viewing
There are no people shown in this photograph—nor in many others—depicting the devastation wrought by the Hiroshima bomb. Does the lack of humanity lessen or intensify the power of the image? Explain. **[Assess]**

corporal. Isawa had been a not particularly prosperous tailor, and his only capital was a Sankoku sewing machine. After his death, when
5 his allotments stopped coming, Mrs. Nakamura got out the machine and began to take in piecework herself, and since then had supported the children, but poorly, by sewing.

As Mrs. Nakamura stood watching her neighbor, everything flashed whiter than any white she had ever seen. She did not notice what happened to the man next door; the reflex of a mother set her in
7 motion toward her children. She had taken a single step (the house was 1,350 yards, or three-quarters of a mile, from the center of the explosion) when something picked her up and she seemed to fly into the next room over the raised sleeping platform, pursued by parts of her house.

Timbers fell around her as she landed, and a shower of tiles pommelled her; everything became dark, for she was buried. The debris did not cover her deeply. She rose up and freed herself. She heard a child cry, "Mother, help me!" and saw her youngest—Myeko, the five-year-old—buried up to her breast and unable to move. As Mrs. Nakamura started frantically to claw her way toward the baby, she could see or hear nothing of her other children.

18 Reading Check
What happens as Mrs. Nakamura stands watching her neighbor?

16 Critical Viewing

Possible response: Students may say that the impact of the image is greater without people because the bomb appears to have erased all signs of life.

17 Critical Thinking

Analyze

- Have students read the bracketed passage. Then, **ask** them to describe their responses to this description of the blast.
  Possible response: Students may respond that this description is especially moving because of Mrs. Nakamura's impulse to protect her children.
- **Ask** students to explain why using a mother of three as one of his subjects would be an effective way for Hersey to make his points about war.
  Possible response: A mother's desire to protect her children is something every reader understands. The fate of a mother and her children will touch readers in a way that other subjects might not. The passage emphasizes the extreme vulnerability of the bomb's victims.

18 Reading Check

Answer: The bomb exploded over Hiroshima, destroying her home as "everything flashed whiter than any white she had ever seen."

Differentiated Instruction
Solutions for All Learners

Strategy for Special Needs Students
Students might have difficulty following Hersey's shifts through time. Encourage them to create a chart using the following headings:

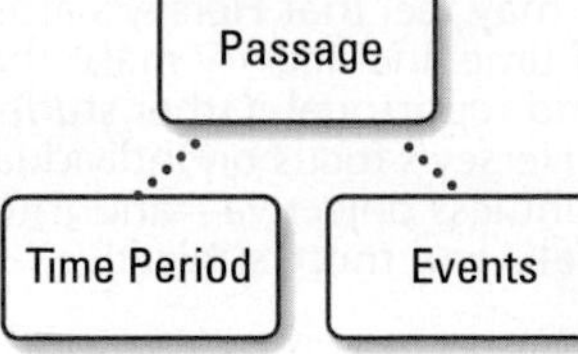

After completing their charts, suggest that students create brief summaries of each character's experience.

⑲ The American Experience

World War II Although World War II was a "popular" war with clearly defined issues involving crucial American and global interests, it was a conflict that included abhorrent actions on both sides. Hersey writes that the Japanese had "a fear of being spied upon," but they were not the only people who held such fears. After the attack on Pearl Harbor, the United States government rounded up Japanese American families living in the West and locked them up in detention camps for the duration of the war. While this action cannot be compared to the atrocities visited by Nazi Germany on the Jews of Europe, it nonetheless illustrates that thinking in terms of enemies versus allies can bring out irrational fears.

Connect to the Literature Ask students to share their views on how they react to news of tragic occurrences. Focus on whether people feel stronger about anonymous victims or victims whom they know or with whom they can identify. Then, **ask** the Connect to the Literature question.

Possible response: The information about the individuals involved humanizes the losses. They become more than "soft targets."

⑳ Reading Strategy

Drawing Inferences About Theme

- Remind students that when they read a literary work with an implied theme they must draw inferences about the theme from details in the text.
- Have students read the bracketed passage. Be sure they understand that a portion of Dr. Fujii's house hangs over the river and has stood fast against a number of floods.
- **Ask** students: Considering what is about to happen, what is Hersey saying about nuclear warfare with this description?

  Possible response: Hersey compares the devastation of which nature is capable to the devastation caused by the bomb and finds the latter much more powerful.

In the days right before the bombing, Dr. Masakazu Fujii, being prosperous, hedonistic,[3] and at the time not too busy, had been allowing himself the luxury of sleeping until nine or nine-thirty, but fortunately he had to get up early the morning the bomb was dropped to see a house guest off on a train. ⑲ He rose at six, and half an hour later walked with his friend to the station, not far away, across two of the rivers. He was back home by seven, just as the siren sounded its sustained warning. He ate breakfast and then, because the morning was already hot, undressed down to his underwear and went out on the porch to read the paper. This porch—in fact, the whole building—was curiously constructed. Dr. Fujii was the proprietor of a peculiarly Japanese institution; a private, single-doctor hospital. This building, perched beside and over the water of the Kyo River, and next to the bridge of the same name, contained thirty rooms for thirty patients and their kinfolk—for, according to Japanese custom, when a person falls sick and goes to a hospital, one or more members of his family go and live there with him, to cook for him, bathe, massage, and read to him, and to offer incessant familial sympathy, without which a Japanese patient would be miserable indeed. Dr. Fujii had no beds—only straw mats—for his patients. He did, however, have all sorts of modern equipment: an X-ray machine, diathermy[4] apparatus, and a fine tiled laboratory. The structure rested two-thirds on the land, one-third on piles over the tidal waters of the Kyo. This overhang, the part of the building where Dr. Fujii lived, was queer-looking, but it was cool in summer and from the porch, which faced away from the center of the city, the prospect of the river, with pleasure boats ⑳ drifting up and down it, was always refreshing. Dr. Fujii had occasionally had anxious moments when the Ota and its mouth branches rose to flood, but the piling was apparently firm enough and the house had always held.

Dr. Fujii had been relatively idle for about a month because in July, as the number of untouched cities in Japan dwindled and as Hiroshima seemed more and more inevitably a target, he began turning patients away, on the ground that in case of a fire raid he would not be able to evacuate them. Now he had only two patients left—a woman from Yano, injured in the shoulder, and a young man of twenty-five recovering from burns he had suffered when the steel factory near Hiroshima in which he worked had been hit. Dr. Fujii had six nurses to tend his patients. His wife and children were safe; his wife and one son were living outside Osaka, and another son and two daughters were in the country on Kyushu. A niece was living

World War II

World War II began in September 1939 when German forces, following the orders of the dictator Adolf Hitler, invaded Poland. In response to this unprovoked invasion, France and Great Britain declared war on Germany. Just over two years later, the United States entered the war when Japan, a German ally, launched a surprise attack on an American naval base at Pearl Harbor in Hawaii. The war continued to escalate during the early 1940s. More than two dozen nations were eventually drawn into the conflict, and tens of millions of soldiers were killed. By 1945, the tide had turned strongly in favor of the United States and its allies. In early May 1945, the German forces surrendered. Fighting continued in the Pacific however, as the Japanese refused to give up. The war finally ended in 1945 when the United States dropped two atomic bombs on the Japanese cities of Hiroshima and Nagasaki. The bombs killed more than 200,000 people and forced Japan's surrender.

Connect to the Literature

In what way does getting to know Dr. Fujii and the others affect your feelings about the dropping of the atomic bombs?

Vocabulary Builder

incessant (in ses′ ənt) *adj.* constant; continuing or repeating in a way that seems endless

3. **hedonistic** (he de nis′ tik) *adj.* indulgently seeking out pleasure.
4. **diathermy** (dī′ ə thur′ mē) *n.* medical treatment in which heat is produced beneath the skin to warm or destroy tissue.

Enrichment

More About the Author

Commenting on John Hersey's *Hiroshima,* one reviewer wrote: "This is not a treatise. It is a factual account, in straightforward reportorial style, of what happened in Hiroshima on the morning of August 6, 1945, and in the sad days that followed. It is John Hersey at his best." Share this comment with students. Then, encourage them to discuss the reviewer's reactions.

Guide discussion by asking students if they agree that Hersey's book is "a factual account" written "in straightforward reportorial style." Students may feel that Hersey's attention to details of time and activity make the narrative factual and reportorial. Other students may feel that Hersey's focus on individuals makes his account less objective—and thus less reportorial—and more subjective.

with him, and a maid and a manservant. He had little to do and did not mind, for he had saved some money. At fifty, he was healthy, convivial, and calm, and he was pleased to pass the evenings drinking whiskey with friends, always sensibly and for the sake of conversation. Before the war, he had affected brands imported from Scotland and America; now he was perfectly satisfied with the best Japanese brand, Suntory.

Dr. Fujii sat down cross-legged in his underwear on the spotless matting of the porch, put on his glasses, and started reading the Osaka *Asahi.* He liked to read the Osaka news because his wife was there. He saw the flash. To him—faced away from the center and looking at his paper—it seemed a brilliant yellow. Startled, he began to rise to his feet. In that moment (he was 1,550 yards from the center), the hospital leaned behind his rising and, with a terrible ripping noise, toppled into the river. The Doctor, still in the act of getting to his feet, was thrown forward and around and over; he was buffeted and gripped; he lost track of everything, because things were so speeded up; he felt the water.

Dr. Fujii hardly had time to think that he was dying before he realized that he was alive, squeezed tightly by two long timbers in a V across his chest, like a morsel suspended between two huge chopsticks—held upright, so that he could not move, with his head miraculously above water and his torso and legs in it. The remains of his hospital were all around him in a mad assortment of splintered lumber and materials for the relief of pain. His left shoulder hurt terribly. His glasses were gone. . . .

Miss Toshiko Sasaki, the East Asia Tin Works clerk, . . . got up at three o'clock in the morning on the day the bomb fell. There was extra housework to do. Her eleven-month-old brother, Akio, had come down the day before with a serious stomach upset; her mother had taken him to the Tamura Pediatric Hospital and was staying there with him. Miss Sasaki, who was about twenty, had to cook breakfast for her father, a brother, a sister, and herself, and—since the hospital, because of the war, was unable to provide food—to prepare a whole day's meals for her mother and the baby, in time for her father, who worked in a factory making rubber earplugs for artillery crews, to take the food by on his way to the plant. When she had finished and had cleaned and put away the cooking things, it was nearly seven. The family lived in Koi, and she had a forty-five-minute trip to the tin works, in the section of town called Kannonmachi. She was in charge of the personnel records in the factory. She left Koi at seven, and as soon as she reached the plant, she went with some of the other girls from the personnel department to the factory auditorium. A prominent local Navy man, a former employee, had committed suicide the day before by throwing himself under a train—a death considered honorable enough to warrant a memorial service, which was to be held at the tin works at ten o'clock 23 that morning. In the large hall, Miss Sasaki and the others made suitable preparations for the meeting. This work took about twenty minutes.

Vocabulary Builder
convivial (kən viv′ ē əl) *adj.* fond of good company; sociable

Literary Analysis
Implied Theme and Objective/Subjective Accounts Is Hersey's description of Dr. Fujii objective or subjective? Explain.

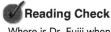

Reading Check
Where is Dr. Fujii when the bomb hits?

Differentiated Instruction
Solutions for All Learners

Vocabulary for English Learners
Call students' attention to the use of the word *affected* at the top of this page: "Before the war, he had affected brands imported from Scotland and America." Explain that *affected* here means "showed a liking for," with a connotation of trying to make an impression by putting on airs.

Strategy for Advanced Readers
Students should recognize that Dr. Fujii is a less sympathetic character than Mr. Tanimoto, Mrs. Nakamura, or Miss Sasaki. He is "prosperous, hedonistic," and somewhat idle. Ask them to consider why Hersey might have included Dr. Fujii as a subject, despite his self-centered, pleasure-seeking lifestyle. Does this section of the text effectively advance Hersey's themes?

21 Literary Analysis
Implied Theme and Objective/Subjective Accounts

- Encourage students to recall Hersey's descriptions of Mr. Tanimoto and Mrs. Nakamura. Remind them that details in each description suggest that Hersey's has been a subjective account.
- Have students read the bracketed passage. Instruct them to consider carefully the details in Hersey's description of Dr. Fujii.
- **Ask** students the Literary Analysis question: Is Hersey's description of Dr. Fujii objective or subjective? Explain.
  Possible response: Hersey's description of Dr. Fujii appears to be objective, because there are no strongly emotional details. Some students may suggest that the magnitude of the destruction makes all of Hersey's descriptions subjective.
- **Monitor Progress:** Encourage students to discuss how the description of Dr. Fujii develops Hersey's theme.

22 Critical Thinking
Analyze

- Have students read the bracketed passage. Point out that Hersey includes a number of mundane details about Miss Sasaki's morning. **Ask** students to list some of these details.
  Answer: Details include Akio's stomach upset, Miss Sasaki's making breakfast for her family and food for the hospital, and her long walk to work.
- **Ask** students: Knowing that the bomb is about to fall, how do these details affect your response to the text?
  Possible response: The details help you to relate to Miss Sasaki as a fellow human being, making the coming disaster seem more tragic and painful.

23 Reading Check
Answer: Dr. Fujii was on his porch overlooking the Kyo River.

ASSESS

Answers

1. **Possible response:** Responses will probably focus upon the terrible destructive power of an atomic bomb.
2. (a) The bomb was dropped at eight-fifteen on the morning of August 6, 1945. (b) **Possible response:** Hersey's precision emphasizes the immensity of the attack; this one horrific event destroyed hundreds of thousands of lives in an instant.
3. (a) He repeatedly refers to the moment when the bomb exploded. (b) **Possible response:** By returning to the moment of the explosion, Hersey forces the reader to witness the bomb's destructive power again and again.
4. **Possible responses:** (a) Residents of the city expected to be bombed with conventional weapons; evacuation orders were given frequently; an air-raid siren sounded early every morning. (b) By describing the city before the blast, he shows readers Hiroshima as a living community before it is destroyed.
5. (a) She is crushed by books. (b) **Possible response:** The effect is sadly ironic. Miss Sasaki is crushed by the weight of "knowledge" and "learning"; the explosion that caused the books to fall, of course, was the fruit of many expert scientists' labors.
6. (a) They are merely ordinary citizens. (b) **Possible response:** By telling the story through the eyes of ordinary citizens, Hersey implies that the atomic bomb devastated everyone in the same way—regardless of background, class, or vocation.
7. **Possible response:** After reading this selection, students may feel that Truman's decision was wrong because the devastation visited upon ordinary citizens was so great. Other students may agree with Truman's decision because conventional warfare may have been equally deadly.

Go Online **Author Link** For additional information about John Hersey, have students type in the Web Code, then select *H* from the alphabet, and then John Hersey.

Miss Sasaki went back to her office and sat down at her desk. She was quite far from the windows, which were off to her left, and behind her were a couple of tall bookcases containing all the books of the factory library, which the personnel department had organized. She settled herself at her desk, put some things in a drawer, and shifted papers. She thought that before she began to make entries in her lists of new employees, discharges, and departures for the Army, she would chat for a moment with the girl at her right. Just as she turned her head away from the windows, the room was filled with a blinding light. She was paralyzed by fear, fixed still in her chair for a long moment (the plant was 1,600 yards from the center).

Everything fell, and Miss Sasaki lost consciousness. The ceiling dropped suddenly and the wooden floor above collapsed in splinters and the people up there came down and the roof above them gave way; but principally and first of all, the bookcases right behind her swooped forward and the contents threw her down, with her left leg horribly twisted and breaking underneath her. There, in the tin factory, in the first moment of the atomic age, a human being was crushed by books.

Critical Reading

1. **Respond:** What thoughts remain with you after reading this account of the bombing of Hiroshima?
2. **(a) Recall:** At what time and on what day was the bomb dropped on Hiroshima? **(b) Draw Conclusions:** Why do you think Hersey is so precise in noting the exact date and time?
3. **(a) Recall:** In describing each individual's experience, which moment does Hersey refer to again and again? **(b) Interpret:** What is the effect of Hersey's returning to this moment repeatedly?
4. **(a) Recall:** Note three details describing the city of Hiroshima in the hours preceding the bomb. **(b) Analyze:** Why does Hersey spend so much time describing the city before the blast?
5. **(a) Recall:** By what is Miss Sasaki crushed? **(b) Infer:** What effect do you think Hersey intended when he described Miss Sasaki's experience?
6. **(a) Classify:** Are the people Hersey portrays important decision makers or merely ordinary citizens? **(b) Draw Conclusions:** What is Hersey implying about the fates of individuals in the midst of war?
7. **Take a Position:** President Truman's hope that the atomic bomb would end the war proved true but at a huge cost. Do you think he made the right decision? Why or why not?

Go Online **Author Link**
For: More about John Hersey
Visit: www.PHSchool.com
Web Code: ere-9625

24 # Losses

Randall Jarrell

25 It was not dying: everybody died.
It was not dying: we had died before
In the routine crashes—and our fields
Called up the papers, wrote home to our folks,
And the rates rose, all because of us.
We died on the wrong page of the almanac,
Scattered on mountains fifty miles away;
Diving on haystacks, fighting with a friend,
We blazed up on the lines we never saw.
We died like aunts or pets or foreigners.
(When we left high school nothing else had died
For us to figure we had died like.)

In our new planes, with our new crews, we bombed
The ranges by the desert or the shore,
Fired at towed targets, waited for our scores—
And turned into replacements and woke up
One morning, over England, operational.
It wasn't different: but if we died
It was not an accident but a mistake
(But an easy one for anyone to make).
We read our mail and counted up our missions—
In bombers named for girls, we burned
The cities we had learned about in school—
Till our lives wore out; our bodies lay among
The people we had killed and never seen.
When we lasted long enough they gave us medals;
When we died they said, "Our casualties were low."

They said, "Here are the maps"; we burned the cities.

It was not dying—no, not ever dying;
But the night I died I dreamed that I was dead,
And the cities said to me: "Why are you dying?
We are satisfied, if you are; but why did I die?"

Reading Strategy
Drawing Inferences About Theme In lines 1–2, what surprising comments does the poet make about death?

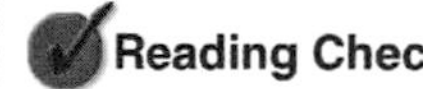
Reading Check
Who is speaking? Who are "we"?

24 About the Selections

The indifference with which governments sacrifice human lives during wartime is the implied theme of "Losses." According to the speaker, this indifference extends to both the young World War II fliers like himself—men whose deaths were regarded as either "accidents" or "mistakes"—and to the enemy they fired at—"the people we had killed and never seen." In "The Death of the Ball Turret Gunner," Jarrell juxtaposes images of sleeping, waking, birth, and death to expose the deadly and all-powerful nature of war.

25 Reading Strategy
Drawing Inferences About Theme

- Point out to students that poems often do not state their themes explicitly. A reader often must draw inferences about the theme of a poem.
- Have students read the bracketed lines. Then, **ask** the Reading Strategy question: In lines 1–2, what surprising comments does the poet make about death?
  Answer: The poet says that death was not real to the fliers, nor was it dramatic. It was just part of the job.

➤ **Monitor Progress: Ask** students what inferences about the poem's theme they can draw from these comments.
Possible response: The poet implies that soldiers and fliers are often removed from the reality of war, and from the likelihoods of their own, very real deaths.

26 Reading Check

Answer: The speaker is an Allied flier during World War II; "we" are all of the fliers with whom the speaker is massed together.

Differentiated Instruction
Solutions for All Learners

Support for Less Proficient Readers
Check students' comprehension by asking them what Jarrell means in lines 11–12 of "Losses." Be sure they understand he means that the fliers— "we"—were so young and untouched by death that they had no frame of reference other than the deaths of relatives, pets, and distant strangers to which to compare their own.

Strategy for Gifted/Talented Students
Encourage students to discuss their emotional responses to the images in Jarrell's very short poem, "The Death of the Ball Turret Gunner." Instruct students to capture those emotions in a visual representation of the poem's speaker before his death.

Strategy for Advanced Readers
After they have completed the excerpt from *Hiroshima,* encourage students to consider whether or not Truman's decision to use the atomic bomb was justified. Encourage them to form teams and stage a debate for the class.

ASSESS

Answers

1. **Possible response:** While students may not have considered war from this perspective before reading the poem, they may agree with Jarrell's attitude. Student responses should be supported by citations from the poem.
2. (a) They die in "routine crashes," "Scattered on mountains," "Diving on haystacks," and "fighting with a friend." In all cases, they die like "aunts or pets or foreigners." (b) **Possible response:** They place little value on individual lives, even their own.
3. (a) They do not see the people they kill. (b) **Possible response:** It demonstrates that part of the horror of modern warfare is its impersonal nature.
4. (a) He refers to it as a "dream of life." (b) **Possible response:** He might view life on earth as a dream because he is completely removed from it while experiencing the "nightmare" of the turret.
5. **Possible response:** (a) "State" seems to refer to both the government and the fighter plane that is flown to support its war efforts. (b) He suggests that the state takes children from their mothers and drops them into war to fight and to die.
6. **Possible response:** Students may concede that some wars, such as World War II, are more justified than others, but may still feel that "good" is not an appropriate adjective for any war.

Go Online Author Link For additional information about Randall Jarrell, have students type in the Web Code, then select *J* from the alphabet, and then Randall Jarrell.

24

The Death of the Ball Turret Gunner

Randall Jarrell

A ball turret was a plexiglass sphere, or circular capsule, in the underside of certain World War II bombers; it held a small man and two machine guns. When the bomber was attacked by a plane below, the gunner, hunched in his little sphere, would revolve with the turret to fire his guns from an upside-down position.

From my mother's sleep I fell into the State,
And I hunched in its belly till my wet fur froze.
Six miles from earth, loosed from its dream of life,
I woke to black flak[1] and the nightmare fighters.
When I died they washed me out of the turret with a hose.

1. **flak** *n.* anti-aircraft fire.

Critical Reading

1. **Respond:** Do you share the poet's attitude toward war as he expresses it in "Losses"? Why or why not?
2. **(a) Recall:** In the first stanza of "Losses," in what variety of ways do the pilots die? **(b) Interpret:** What do these descriptions suggest about the pilots' attitude toward death?
3. **(a) Recall:** Do the pilots see the people they kill? **(b) Analyze:** What is the poet suggesting about the horror of modern warfare?
4. **(a) Recall:** In "The Death of the Ball Turret Gunner," which words does the gunner use to describe his view of life on Earth?
(b) Analyze: In what way is this view of life related to the "nightmare" in the turret?
5. **(a) Interpret:** To what does the word "State" refer?
(b) Draw Conclusions: What is the poet suggesting about the relationship between a soldier in a war and the government?
6. **Take a Position:** Jarrell based his poems on observations of World War II, a war that has been called "the good war." Is there such a thing as a "good war"? Explain.

For: More about Randall Jarrell
Visit: www.PHSchool.com
Web Code: ere-9626

Apply the Skills

from *Hiroshima* • *Losses* • *The Death of the Ball Turret Gunner*

Literary Analysis

Implied Theme

1. **(a)** Which details in *Hiroshima* give clues to the **implied theme**? **(b)** What is that theme?
2. **(a)** In "Losses," what does line 26 imply about the value of the medals? **(b)** What is the poet saying about honor and valor in war?
3. In "The Death of the Ball Turret Gunner," what is the poet saying about the value of human life during war?
4. **(a)** Use a chart like the one shown to explore similarities and differences in Hersey's and Jarrell's portrayals of victims in war. **(b)** Do the three pieces share a common theme? Explain.

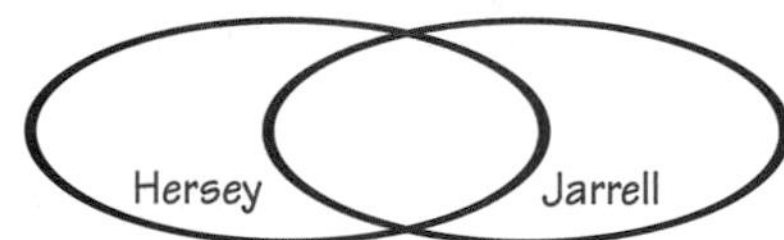

Comparing Literary Works

5. **(a)** In *Hiroshima,* which descriptions evoke the strongest emotions in you? **(b)** Is Hersey writing an **objective account** as a reporter or a **subjective account** as a commentator? Explain.
6. **(a)** Which lines in Jarrell's poems are stated as pure fact, seemingly without emotional bias? **(b)** What is the effect?

Reading Strategy

Drawing Inferences About Theme

7. **(a)** Explain the underlying meaning of this line from *Hiroshima*:

   > . . . the night before the bomb was dropped, an announcer . . . advised the population . . . to evacuate to their designated 'safe areas.'

   (b) In what ways does that line help to communicate the theme?
8. In "Losses," the speaker notes, "We died like aunts or pets or foreigners." What does this line suggest about the poem's theme?

Extend Understanding

9. **Science Connection:** When the atom bomb was dropped on Hiroshima, no one knew about fallout, radiation sickness, or long-term contamination of the land. How might such knowledge have changed the decision to drop the bomb?

QuickReview

An **implied theme** is the message the author suggests through details, characterization, and events but does not directly state.

In an **objective account,** the narrator is an outside observer who comments on the events without emotion. In a **subjective account,** the narrator reveals his or her feelings about the events described.

To **draw inferences about theme,** examine clues from the work for their underlying meanings.

For: Self-test
Visit: www.PHSchool.com
Web Code: era-6615

Go Online Assessment Students may use the **Self-test** to prepare for **Selection Test A** or **Selection Test B.**

Answers

1. **Possible responses:** (a) The details of the ordinary activities of Japanese citizens and the details of the physical impact of the bomb give clues about the theme. (b) The implied theme is the great destructive power of the bomb.
2. **Possible responses:** (a) The medals have little value, only signifying that someone has "lasted long enough." (b) Honor and valor have no real meaning in modern war.
3. **Possible responses:** Individual lives have no value in war.
4. **Possible responses:** (a) Hersey: Our "enemies" are ordinary people like ourselves; Jarrell: Our soldiers are not heroes but victims; Overlap: Victims of war are destroyed, regardless of the nature of their involvement with the conflict. (b) Students may respond that all three pieces imply that modern war is a purely destructive evil.

   Another sample answer can be found on **Literary Analysis Graphic Organizer B,** p. 273, in ***Graphic Organizer Transparencies.***
5. **Possible responses:** (a) Students may say that Mrs. Nakamura evoked the strongest emotions because of her young children. (b) Some students may feel Hersey's account is objective because of its reportorial style; others will say it is subjective because of its strong emotions.
6. (a) The first stanza of "Losses" and the last line of "The Death of the Ball Turret Gunner" seem to be pure fact. (b) The "facts" stated in these lines are of extreme horror, so the objective style heightens their effect.
7. **Possible responses:** (a) This line suggests that there are no "safe areas." (b) It communicates the theme by emphasizing the immensity of the bomb's destructive power.
8. **Possible responses:** These words show that the deaths of the pilots are not important.
9. **Possible responses:** Some students may feel that the United States would not have used the bomb had such effects been known. Others will feel that the desire to end the war would have outweighed even this knowledge.

EXTEND/ASSESS

Answers

❶ Vocabulary Lesson
Word Analysis
1. *volunteer:* a person who offers to do something
2. *malevolence:* the quality or state of wishing evil or harm to others
3. *benevolence:* an inclination or wish to do good; kindness
4. *involuntary:* a reaction over which one has no conscious control

Spelling Strategy
1. losses
2. parishes
3. crashes
4. reflexes
5. churches
6. glasses

Vocabulary Builder
1. evacuated
2. volition
3. rendezvous
4. philanthropies
5. incessant
6. convivial

❷ Grammar and Style Lesson

Possible response: After Mr. Tanimoto cooked his own breakfast, he started for Mr. Matsuo's house. Later, as the two men set out, an air-raid siren went off. Then, the all-clear sounded. Suddenly, although there was no sound of planes, a tremendous flash of light cut across the sky. Both Mr. Tanimoto and Mr. Matsuo reacted in terror.

Writing Application
Students' paragraphs should present a chronological sequence of events. Details within paragraphs should be logically linked by transitions.

WG Writing and Grammar, Ruby Level

Students will find further instruction and practice on the use of transitions and transitional phrases in Chapter 3, Section 2.

Build Language Skills

❶ Vocabulary Lesson

Word Analysis: Latin Root *-vol-*
The meaning of the word *volition,* "the act of using the will," is derived from the Latin root *-vol-,* meaning "to will" or "to wish." Using your knowledge of the roots, define each of the following words. Then, check your answers in a dictionary.

1. volunteer
2. malevolence
3. benevolence
4. involuntary

Spelling Strategy
The plural of words ending in *z, x, sh, ch,* or *s* is usually formed by adding *-es* to the base word. For example, *porch* + *-es* = *porches.* Write the plural of each of the following words.

1. loss
2. parish
3. crash
4. reflex
5. church
6. glass

Vocabulary Builder: Sentence Completion
Select the word from the vocabulary list on p. 1197 that best completes each of these sentences.

1. The birds __?__ their nest and never returned to it.
2. She did extra homework of her own __?__.
3. Let's establish a __?__ point, so we don't miss each other.
4. Among the financier's __?__ was a fund to send young musicians to music camp.
5. The child's __?__ whining bothered fellow train passengers.
6. The __?__ friends attend parties together often.

❷ Grammar and Style Lesson

Transitions and Transitional Phrases
Transitions are words that show chronological, spatial, comparison and contrast, cause and effect, and order of importance relationships among ideas. Groups of words that function in the same way are called **transitional phrases.**

Transition: *Then,* a tremendous flash of light cut across the sky.

Transitional phrase: *At the time,* none of them knew anything.

Common transitions like *because, as a result, if, therefore, in addition, although, next, in contrast, similarly, despite,* and *recently* can clarify the connections between ideas.

Practice Add transitions or transitional phrases to the following paragraph.

Mr. Tanimoto cooked his own breakfast. He started for Mr. Matsuo's house. The two men set out. An air-raid siren went off. The all-clear sounded. There was no sound of planes. A tremendous flash of light cut across the sky. Both Mr. Tanimoto and Mr. Matsuo reacted in terror.

Writing Application Write a series of sentences summarizing your activities during a typical day. Use transitions and transitional phrases to link ideas.

WG *Prentice Hall Writing and Grammar Connection: Chapter 3, Section 2*

Assessment Practice

Grammar and Usage **(For more practice, see *Standardized Test Preparation Workbook*, p. 71.)**

The writing sections of many tests require students to choose the correct word to complete a sentence. Use the following sample item to show students how to recognize correct and incorrect grammar and choose the correct word to complete each sentence.

If you ever see photographs of the devastation of Hiroshima, _____ senses will be overwhelmed.

Choose the word or group of words that belongs in the blank.

A yourself
B your
C you're
D you

A, C, and *D* are not possessive forms. *B* is the correct possessive form.

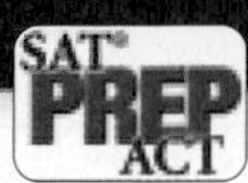

Writing Lesson

Timed Writing: Book Review

John Hersey's book *Hiroshima* was published in 1946. Imagine that, more than fifty years later, you have been asked to write a review of the book celebrating its anniversary. In your review, discuss the book as both a work of literature and an important historical document. ***(40 minutes)***

Prewriting *(10 minutes)* Reread the excerpt from *Hiroshima.* Speculate about the effect the book had on its first readers who were just learning about the power of nuclear weapons. Take notes about Hersey's use of description, and identify his attitude toward his subject.

Drafting *(20 minutes)* Begin with a vivid opening sentence. Then, describe the book and state why it is both a moving and an important piece of writing. Present point-by-point detail in your body paragraphs, and write a conclusion that reinforces Hersey's insights for modern readers.

Revising *(10 minutes)* Read your review to make sure you have conveyed a clear sense of the book. Determine whether you have appropriately targeted the knowledge level of your expected audience.

Model: Revising for Knowledge Level of Readers

When the United States bombed ^the Japanese city of^ Hiroshima ^on August 6, 1945^, a catastrophic power was unleashed. This event contributed to a fear of nuclear war that would last for decades.

An audience unfamiliar with an event requires the basic information added in revision.

Prentice Hall Writing and Grammar Connection: Chapter 13, Section 2

Extend Your Learning

Listening and Speaking Present a **dramatic reading** of one of Randall Jarrell's poems. To prepare, try the following tips:

- Supplement the reading with evocative music and appropriate sound effects.
- Vary your pitch, pacing, and tone of voice to draw out shades of meaning.
- Include visual aids, such as a photograph of a World War II bomber, to accompany your reading.

Research and Technology Working with a partner, use library and Internet sources to conduct research on the city of Hiroshima. Focus your investigation on the state of the city just before and after August 1945, when the bomb was dropped. Gather your findings in a **written report. [Group Activity]**

For: An additional research activity
Visit: www.PHSchool.com
Web Code: erd-7615

Assessment Resources

The following resources can be used to assess students' knowledge and skills.

Unit 6 Resources
- **Selection Test A,** pp. 271–273
- **Selection Test B,** pp. 274–276

General Resources
- **Rubric for Critique,** pp. 75–76
- **Rubric for Peer Assessment: Oral Interpretation,** p. 130

Go Online Assessment Students may use the **Self-test** to prepare for **Selection Test A** or **Selection Test B.**

❸ Writing Lesson

You may use this Writing Lesson as timed-writing practice, or you may allow students to develop the review as a writing assignment over several days.

- Give students **Support for Writing Lesson,** p. 268 in ***Unit 6 Resources,*** to use as they write their book reviews.
- Explain that students' book reviews should present assessments of *Hiroshima,* both as a literary work and as an historical document.
- After students reread and take notes on the selection, instruct them to write one-sentence assessments of the work. Students may construct outlines focusing on their assessments.
- As students revise, be sure that they include basic information appropriate for their audience.
- Use the Rubrics for Critique, pp. 75–76 in ***General Resources,*** to evaluate students' book reviews.

❹ Listening and Speaking

- Explain that a dramatic reading is similar to a reading of a play. The reader uses vocal expression to show emotion and may incorporate visual elements, music, and sound effects.
- Have each participant choose one of the Jarrell poems. Provide time for students to locate and record music and other sounds. Students may also gather visual materials, such as photographs.
- Have students take turns performing for the class. Provide necessary audio/video equipment.
- Use the Peer Assessment: Oral Interpretation rubric in ***General Resources,*** p. 130, to assess students' dramatic readings.
- The **Support for Extend Your Learning** page (***Unit 6 Resources,*** p. 269) provides guided note-taking opportunities to help students complete the Extend Your Learning activities.

Go Online Research Have students type in the Web Code for another research activity.

Meeting Your Standards

Students will

1. **analyze and respond to literary elements.**
   - Literary Analysis: Theme
2. **read, comprehend, analyze, and critique poetry.**
   - Reading Strategy: Interpreting
   - Reading Check questions
   - Apply the Skills questions
   - Assessment Practice (ATE)
3. **develop vocabulary.**
   - Vocabulary Lesson: Latin Root: *-cep-/-cept-*
4. **understand and apply written and oral language conventions.**
   - Spelling Strategy
   - Grammar and Style Lesson: Parallel Structure
5. **develop writing proficiency.**
   - Writing Lesson: Literary Analysis
6. **develop appropriate research strategies.**
   - Extend Your Learning: Multimedia Presentation
7. **understand and apply listening and speaking strategies.**
   - Extend Your Learning: Debate

Block Scheduling: Use one 90-minute class period to preteach the skills and have students read the selection. Use a second 90-minute class period to assess students' mastery of skills, extend their learning, and monitor their progress.

Homework Suggestions

Following are possibilities for homework assignments:

- Support pages from ***Unit 6 Resources:***
  Literary Analysis
  Reading Strategy
  Vocabulary Builder
  Grammar and Style
- An Extend Your Learning project and the Writing Lesson for this selection group may be completed over several days.

Step-by-Step Teaching Guide	Pacing Guide
PRETEACH	
• Administer Vocabulary and Reading Warm-ups as necessary.	5 min.
• Engage students' interest with the motivation activity.	5 min.
• Read and discuss author and background features. **FT**	10 min.
• Introduce the Literary Analysis Skill: Theme. **FT**	5 min.
• Introduce the Reading Strategy: Interpreting. **FT**	10 min.
• Prepare students to read by teaching the selection vocabulary. **FT**	
TEACH	
• Informally monitor comprehension while students read independently or in groups. **FT**	30 min.
• Monitor students' comprehension with the Reading Check notes.	as students read
• Reinforce vocabulary with Vocabulary Builder notes.	as students read
• Develop students' understanding of theme with the Literary Analysis annotations. **FT**	5 min.
• Develop students' ability to interpret with the Reading Strategy annotations. **FT**	5 min.
ASSESS/EXTEND	
• Assess students' comprehension and mastery of the Literary Analysis and Reading Strategy by having them answer the Apply the Skills questions. **FT**	15 min.
• Have students complete the Vocabulary Lesson and the Grammar and Style Lesson. **FT**	15 min.
• Apply students' ability to use quotations by using the Writing Lesson. **FT**	45 min. or homework
• Apply students' understanding by using one or more of the Extend Your Learning activities.	20–90 min. or homework
• Administer Selection Test A or Selection Test B. **FT**	15 min.

Resources

PRINT

Unit 6 Resources

TRANSPARENCY

Graphic Organizer Transparencies

PRINT

Reader's Notebook [L2]

Reader's Notebook: Adapted Version [L1]

Reader's Notebook: English Learner's Version [EL]

Unit 6 Resources

TECHNOLOGY

Listening to Literature Audio CDs [L2, EL]

PRINT

Unit 6 Resources

General Resources

TECHNOLOGY

Go Online: Research **[L3]**
Go Online: Self-test **[L3]**
***ExamView*® Test Bank [L3]**

Choosing Resources for Differentiated Instruction

[L1] Special Needs Students
[L2] Below-Level Students
[L3] All Students
[L4] Advanced Students
[EL] English Learners

For Vocabulary and Reading Warm-ups and for Selection Tests, **A** signifies "less challenging" and **B** "more challenging." For Graphic Organizer transparencies, **A** signifies "not filled in" and **B** "filled in."

FT Fast Track Instruction: To move the lesson more quickly, use the strategies and activities identified with **FT**.

Scaffolding for Less Proficient and Advanced Students

The leveled Critical Thinking questions after selections progress in the levels of thinking required to answer them. To address the needs of your different students, you may use the (a) level questions for your less proficient students and the (b) level questions with your on-level and advanced students. The occasional (c) level questions are appropriate for your advanced students.

PRENTICE HALL **TeacherEXPRESS**™ Plan · Teach · Assess Use this complete suite of powerful teaching tools to make lesson planning and testing quicker and easier.

PRENTICE HALL **StudentEXPRESS**™ Learn · Study · Succeed Use the interactive textbook (online and on CD-ROM) to make selections and activities come alive with audio and video support and interactive questions.

Go Online Professional Development **For:** Information about Lexiles
Visit: www.PHSchool.com
Web Code: eue-1111

PRETEACH

Motivation

Ask students to suggest ways that they might cope with injustice and lack of opportunity. Would they give up? Protest actively? Express their anger in writing? Why or why not? Remind them that the writers of these poems protest through poetry.

❶ Background

More About the Authors

Sylvia Plath's father died during her childhood, leaving her mother to struggle financially. Plath's anger and sense of loss over this stayed with her, and is revealed in poems such as "Daddy" and "Medusa."

A staunch feminist, Adrienne Rich devoted much of her poetry to protesting male and female roles in American society. Rich carried her protests into real life as well. For example, she refused a National Medal of Honor in 1997 in protest of some of the policies of President Bill Clinton.

Gwendolyn Brooks's poetry became more political as her career progressed. She increasingly focused her work on building an African American protest community. In later years, Brooks was the poet laureate of Illinois.

In addition to his focus on social protest and interest in racial themes, Robert Hayden worked hard to perfect poetic techniques. From 1976–78, Hayden consulted about poetry at the Library of Congress.

❶ Mirror • In a Classroom • The Explorer • Frederick Douglass • Runagate Runagate

Sylvia Plath (1932–1963)

Despite her success as a writer, Sylvia Plath lived a short, unhappy life. In many of her poems, she expresses intense feelings of despair and deep inner pain. Born in Boston, Plath wrote poetry and received scholastic and literary awards as a youth. Although she suffered a nervous breakdown in her junior year, she graduated with highest honors from Smith College. She also studied at Cambridge University in England, where she met and married poet Ted Hughes in 1956. Her first book of verse, *The Colossus and Other Poems* (1960), was the only one published during her lifetime. Four more books of poetry and a novel, *The Bell Jar* (1963), were published posthumously.

Adrienne Rich (b. 1929)

Adrienne Rich's most recent books of poetry are *The School Among the Ruins: Poems 2000-2004* and *Fox: Poems 1998-2000* (Norton). A selection of her essays, *Arts of the Possible: Essays and Conversations,* was published in 2001. A new edition of *What Is Found There: Notebooks on Poetry and Politics* appeared in 2003. She is the recipient of the Lannan Foundation Lifetime Achievement Award, the Lambda Book Award, the Lenore Marshall/*Nation* Prize, the Wallace Stevens Award, and the Bollingen Prize in Poetry, among other honors. She lives in California.

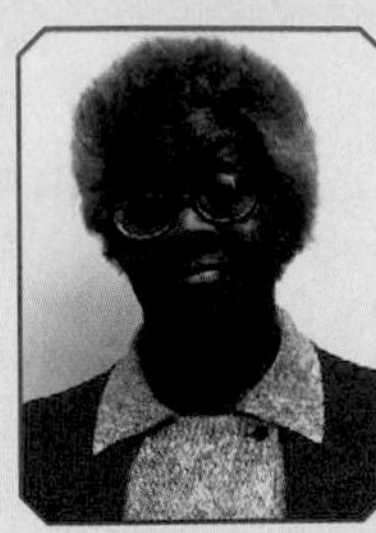

Gwendolyn Brooks (1917–2000)

Gwendolyn Brooks was raised in a Chicago neighborhood known as "Bronzeville"—the setting for her first book, *A Street in Bronzeville* (1945). Although her early poems focus on suffering urban blacks who feel uprooted and are unable to make a living, Brooks's own youth was quite different. Her home was warm and her family loving, supportive, and confident that Brooks would find success as a writer. Brooks began writing poetry at the age of seven. In 1950, she became the first African American writer to win a Pulitzer Prize. After that, her reputation grew steadily, and she became one of the most highly regarded poets of our time.

Robert Hayden (1913–1980)

Born in Detroit, Robert Hayden was a young, politically active writer in the 1930s who protested not only the social and economic conditions of African Americans but also what he saw as the nation's inadequate care of the poor. Hayden was an extremely versatile writer who used a variety of poetic forms and techniques. He published several collections of poetry, including *Heart-Shape in the Dust* (1940), *The Lion and the Archer* (1948), and *The Night-Blooming Cereus* (1972). His collection *A Ballad of Remembrance* received the Grand Prize for Poetry at the First World Festival for Negro Arts in 1966.

Preview

Connecting to the Literature

It is human nature to find fault with the situations, policies, and attitudes we experience in everyday life. While you may discuss your social concerns with your family and friends, some poets use their writing as a means of expressing their views.

2 Literary Analysis

Theme

A poem's **theme** is the central idea it conveys. Poets suggest themes through the **connotations,** or emotional overtones, of the words and images they choose. For example, in these lines about aging by Sylvia Plath, the words *drowned* and *terrible* have negative associations; thus, you can infer that the theme has something to do with the fear of growing old:

In me she has drowned a young girl, and in me an old woman
Rises toward her day after day, like a terrible fish.

As you read these poems, find clues to the themes in words and images that evoke either negative or positive responses.

Comparing Literary Works

Poetry has long been a vehicle for **social criticism.** In some poems, the social critique addresses topics we usually categorize as personal. In the poet's message, however, the personal takes on larger meaning. Other poems address large social themes and show the ways in which broad social problems affect the lives of individuals. All the poems you are about to read carry messages of social critique. As you read, examine the ways in which each one explores the intersection between the individual and the society of which he or she is part.

3 Reading Strategy

Interpreting

In most poems, the central message is not directly stated. It is up to you to **interpret** it by looking for an underlying meaning in the words and images. Consider the connotations of the words and the associations they call to mind, and then try to determine what common thread ties them together. Use an organizer like the one shown to record words and images that will help you interpret the theme.

Words and Images	Potential Meaning

Vocabulary Builder

preconceptions (prē´ kən sep´ shənz) *n.* ideas formed beforehand (p. 1216)

meditate (med´ ə tāt´) *v.* think deeply; ponder (p. 1216)

din (din) *n.* loud, continuous noise; uproar or clamor (p. 1218)

wily (wī´ lē) *adj.* sly; cunning (p. 1218)

2 Literary Analysis

Theme

- Tell students that as they read, they will focus on theme, the central idea that a poem conveys.
- After discussing the Literary Analysis instruction, have a volunteer read aloud the excerpt from "Mirror." Discuss how Plath's words and images yield a predominantly negative effect.
- Urge students as they read to monitor their emotional reactions as a way to recognize themes.
- Discuss the instruction under Comparing Literary Works. Point out that identifying a poem's historical context can help the reader recognize the target of its social critique.

3 Reading Strategy

Interpreting

- Explain to students that interpreting—building meaning from poetic language—is critical to understanding and enjoying poetry.
- Review the organizer on this page with students. Choose a sample sentence from one of the poems, and use it to model the organizer's use.
- Give students a copy of **Reading Strategy Graphic Organizer A,** p. 274, in ***Graphic Organizer Transparencies,*** to use as they read the poems.
- Remind students that connotations are the associations a word evokes.

Vocabulary Builder

- Pronounce each vocabulary word for students, and read the definitions as a class. Have students identify any words with which they are already familiar.

Differentiated Instruction

Solutions for All Learners

Support for Special Needs Students
Have students complete the **Preview** and **Build Skills** pages for these selections in the ***Reader's Notebook: Adapted Version.*** These pages provide a selection summary, an abbreviated presentation of the reading and literary skills, and the graphic organizer on the **Build Skills** page in the student book.

Support for Less Proficient Readers
Have students complete the **Preview** and **Build Skills** pages for these selections in the ***Reader's Notebook.*** These pages provide a selection summary, an abbreviated presentation of the reading and literary skills, and the graphic organizer on the **Build Skills** page in the student book.

Support for English Learners
Have students complete the **Preview** and **Build Skills** pages for these selections in the ***Reader's Notebook: English Learner's Version.*** These pages provide a selection summary, an abbreviated presentation of the skills, and the graphic organizer on the **Build Skills** page in the student book.

Learning Modalities
Interpersonal Learners
Through literature, the poets in this group protest attitudes and circumstances. Ask students to identify and describe values or attitudes that they might find difficult to accept. If they were poets living in each place, what might they feel compelled to challenge through their art?

❶ About the Selection

The speaker of this poem, a mirror, describes a woman's reaction to viewing her image day after day. The woman, aware that she is growing older, responds "with tears and agitation of hands."

❷ Humanities

Mirror II by George Tooker

Born in 1920, George Tooker is an American painter whose style is known as "Magic Realism." Magic Realism is realistic art that uses everyday images symbolically, as Tooker uses the mirror in this painting. As in most of Tooker's paintings, the setting, lighting, and mood of *Mirror II* are clean, cold, and barren.

Use this question for discussion:

- In what way does the woman in the painting resemble the woman in the poem?
  Answer: Each woman searches "for what she really is"; each senses an older woman "rising toward her."

❸ Critical Viewing

Answer: Both suggest that aging is an inevitable part of the human condition.

❶ Mirror

Sylvia Plath

❷

Mirror II, George Tooker, © Addison Gallery of American Art, Phillips Academy, Andover, Massachusetts

❸ **◄ Critical Viewing**
The artist titled this painting *Mirror II.* What ideas are common to both the painting and poem? **[Connect]**

I am silver and exact. I have no preconceptions.
Whatever I see I swallow immediately
Just as it is, unmisted by love or dislike.
I am not cruel, only truthful—
The eye of a little god, four-cornered.
Most of the time I meditate on the opposite wall.
It is pink, with speckles. I have looked at it so long
I think it is a part of my heart. But it flickers.
Faces and darkness separate us over and over.
Now I am a lake. A woman bends over me,
Searching my reaches for what she really is.
Then she turns to those liars, the candles or the moon.
I see her back, and reflect it faithfully.
She rewards me with tears and an agitation of hands.
I am important to her. She comes and goes.
Each morning it is her face that replaces the darkness.
In me she has drowned a young girl, and in me an old woman
Rises toward her day after day, like a terrible fish.

❹ **Vocabulary Builder**

preconceptions (prē´ kən sep´ shənz) *n.* ideas formed beforehand

meditate (med´ ə tāt´) *v.* think deeply; ponder

Differentiated Instruction Solutions for All Learners

Accessibility at a Glance

	Mirror	In a Classroom	The Explorer	Frederick Douglass	Runagate Runagate
Language	Use of metaphor and simile	Use of simile	Complicated diction and syntax	Use of metaphor and simile	Complicated syntax
Concept Level	Accessible (the toll of time)	Accessible (classroom atmosphere)	Challenging (search for peace)	Accessible (struggle for freedom)	Accessible (Underground Railroad)
Literary Merit	Noted author	Noted author	Noted author	Inspirational	Suspenseful
Lexile	NP	NP	NP	NP	NP
Overall Rating	Average	More challenging	More challenging	More accessible	More accessible

In a Classroom

Adrienne Rich

Talking of poetry, hauling the books
arm-full to the table where the heads
bend or gaze upward, listening, reading aloud,
talking of consonants, elision,[1]
caught in the how, oblivious of why:
I look in your face, Jude,
neither frowning nor nodding,
opaque in the slant of dust-motes over the table:
a presence like a stone, if a stone were thinking
What I cannot say, is me. For that I came.

1. **elision** (ē lizh′ ən) *n.* omission or slurring over of a vowel or syllable; often used in poetry to preserve meter.

Critical Reading

1. **Respond:** The speaker of "Mirror" maintains, "I am not cruel, only truthful—." If the truth hurts, do you think being truthful is cruel? Explain.
2. **(a) Recall:** What two reflecting surfaces does the speaker name? **(b) Infer:** Who is the speaker?
3. **(a) Recall:** In what way does the woman "reward" the speaker? **(b) Interpret:** Explain why she reacts this way.
4. **(a) Recall:** To whom does the woman turn? **(b) Interpret:** Why are they called liars?
5. **(a) Infer:** Who is the "old woman"? **(b) Draw Conclusions:** What are the woman's feelings about aging?
6. **Extend:** The woman searches the mirror for "what she really is." Can one's true self be seen in a mirror? Explain.

For: More about Sylvia Plath and Adrienne Rich
Visit: www.PHSchool.com
Web Code: ere-9627

❹ Vocabulary Builder

Latin Root *-cep-/-cept-*

- Point out the word *preconceptions* in line 1 of "Mirror" and have a volunteer read the line aloud.
- Direct students' attention to the definition of *preconceptions,* and explain that the Latin word root *-cep-/-cept-* means "to take, hold, or seize."
- If time allows, refer students to the Vocabulary Lesson on the Build Language Skills page. Have them look up the listed words in the dictionary.

ASSESS

Answers

1. Accept reasonable responses.
2. (a) The speaker mentions a "four-cornered mirror" and a lake. (b) The mirror is the speaker in the poem.
3. (a) She rewards the speaker with tears and an agitation of hands. (b) She reacts that way because she is upset to see herself aging.
4. (a) She turns to "those liars, the candles or the moon." (b) They create deceptively complimentary images of the speaker.
5. (a) The old woman is the person the woman is becoming. (b) She is unhappy about aging and has difficulty accepting it.
6. **Possible response:** Students may say that a mirror can reveal physical traits but shows little of a person's feelings or thoughts.

Go Online Author Link For additional information about Sylvia Plath or Adrienne Rich, have students type in the Web Code, then select *P* or *R* from the alphabet, and then Sylvia Plath or Adrienne Rich.

Differentiated Instruction
Solutions for All Learners

Background for Special Needs Students
Explain that the opening lines of "Mirror" establish the identity of the speaker. Help students search the poem for words that describe the speaker's qualities or traits. With this information, have students draw their image of the speaker. Guide students to see that the speaker is a mirror. It is accurate, truthful, and objective.

Strategy for English Learners
Tell students that sentence inversion can make it difficult for readers to interpret meaning. Point out the inversion in line 17 of "Mirror." Encourage students to reorder the words by placing "in me" after "young girl." Then, help them interpret the line's meaning as "She has lost her youthfulness over time."

Background for Advanced Readers
Challenge students to interpret line 10 of "Mirror." Share the myth of Narcissus, the beautiful youth who fell in love with his own image in a pool, whereupon he turned into a flower. Ask students: What is meant when we say someone is narcissistic? How is Narcissus similar to the woman in the poem?

❺ About the Selection

A person, identified only as "he," explores an apartment building, searching for "a still spot in the noise." His search for peace—for inner peace—is unsuccessful, however, as all he finds are noises connected with human activities and the frightening prospect of "choices, that cried to be taken."

ASSESS

Answers

1. Students should support their responses.
2. (a) The "inner want" is peace of mind. (b) The title suggests that the speaker will explore in order to fulfill that inner want.
3. (a) He is searching in an apartment building. (b) No, he doesn't find it.
4. **Possible responses:** (a) The apartment building may represent the speaker's life, and the rooms represent his choices in life. (b) His actions and feelings might symbolize his inability to find solace and the limitations of the choices with which he is presented.
5. **Possible response:** People are afraid they will not be happy with the results of their decision.

❻ About the Selection

In this poem, the speaker describes the way Frederick Douglass will be remembered when freedom "is finally ours": not through statues, legends, poems, or wreaths, but through the lives that will realize the visionary's dream.

Go Online Author Link For additional information about Gwendolyn Brooks, have students type in the Web Code, then select *B* from the alphabet, and then Gwendolyn Brooks.

❺

The Explorer

Gwendolyn Brooks

Somehow to find a still spot in the noise
Was the frayed inner want, the winding, the frayed hope
Whose tatters he kept hunting through the din.
A satin peace somewhere.
A room of wily hush somewhere within.

So tipping down the scrambled halls he set
Vague hands on throbbing knobs. There were behind
Only spiraling, high human voices,
The scream of nervous affairs,
Wee griefs,
Grand griefs. And choices.

He feared most of all the choices, that cried to be taken.

There were no bourns.[1]
There were no quiet rooms.

1. **bourns** (bōrnz) *n.* limits; boundaries

Vocabulary Builder

din (din) *n.* loud, continuous noise; uproar or clamor

wily (wī′ lē) *adj.* sly; cunning

Critical Reading

1. **Respond:** What did you see and hear as you read this poem?
2. **(a) Recall:** What is the "inner want" the poem's speaker expresses? **(b) Interpret:** In what way does the title of the poem relate to the "inner want"?
3. **(a) Recall:** Where is the explorer searching for the "inner want"? **(b) Assess:** Does he find it?
4. **(a) Interpret:** What might the explorer's apartment building symbolize? **(b) Interpret:** What might the explorer's actions and feelings symbolize?
5. **Apply:** Why do you think people often fear having to make choices?

For: More about Gwendolyn Brooks
Visit: www.PHSchool.com
Web Code: ere-9628

Frederick Douglass[1]

Robert Hayden

When it is finally ours, this freedom, this liberty,
 this beautiful
and terrible thing, needful to man as air,
usable as earth; when it belongs at last to all,
when it is truly instinct, brain matter, diastole, systole,[2]
reflex action; when it is finally won; when it is more
than the gaudy mumbo jumbo of politicians:
this man, this Douglass, this former slave, this Negro
beaten to his knees, exiled, visioning a world
where none is lonely, none hunted, alien,
this man, superb in love and logic, this man
shall be remembered. Oh, not with statues' rhetoric,
not with legends and poems and wreaths of bronze alone,
but with the lives grown out of his life, the lives
fleshing his dream of the beautiful, needful thing.

Part II, The Free Man, No. 30, The Frederick Douglass Series, Jacob Lawrence, Hampton University Museum, Hampton, Virginia

▲ Critical Viewing What impression of Douglass does this painting convey? **[Analyze]**

---

1. **Frederick Douglass** American abolitionist (1817?–1895).
2. **diastole** (dī as′ tə lē′), **systole** (sis′ tə lē′) Diastole is the normal rhythmic dilation, or opening, of the heart. Systole is the normal rhythmic closing of the heart.

Critical Reading

1. **Respond:** What impression do you have of Frederick Douglass after reading this poem? What kind of person was he?
2. **(a) Recall:** What is the "beautiful and terrible" thing? **(b) Infer:** To whom does it not yet belong?
3. **(a) Recall:** In what ways does the speaker say that Douglass will not be remembered? **(b) Infer:** What does the speaker think are the limitations of statues and memorials?
4. **(a) Interpret:** In what way does the speaker say Douglass truly will be remembered? **(b) Analyze:** What does the speaker mean by "the lives fleshing his dream of the beautiful, needful thing"?
5. **Apply:** How do you think Frederick Douglass would respond to this poem? Explain.

For: More about Robert Hayden
Visit: www.PHSchool.com
Web Code: ere-9629

Differentiated Instruction

Solutions for All Learners

Vocabulary for English Learners

Point out the words *diastole* and *systole* in line 4 of "Frederick Douglass." Have a volunteer read aloud the numbered footnote definitions. Explain to students that these words, which refer to the steady beating of the heart, suggest that for Douglass freedom is as necessary as breathing.

Background for Less Proficient Readers

Direct students' attention to lines 2–3 of "Frederick Douglass." Help students understand the figurative ways in which Hayden describes freedom. Point out, for example, that the phrase *usable as earth* can be interpreted to mean "Freedom is as necessary to people as earth is."

Enrichment for Gifted/Talented Students

Challenge students to interpret the meaning of "Frederick Douglass." Then, ask them to write an essay in which they compare and contrast Hayden's meaning with that of Paul Laurence Dunbar's poem about Frederick Douglass.

7 Humanities

Part II, The Free Man, No. 30, The Frederick Douglass Series by Jacob Lawrence

African American artist Jacob Lawrence utilizes bold geometric shapes and bright colors to depict the daily lives of ordinary black Americans as well as the lives of distinguished blacks. This painting is of the latter variety, part of a series completed during 1938 and 1939 on the life of Frederick Douglass. Use this question for discussion:

- Does the painting correspond with the image of Douglass presented in the poem? **Possible response:** Yes, because the poem alludes to a highly intelligent man "superb in love and logic," who would therefore probably be fond of reading.

8 Critical Viewing

Answer: The impression is one of a thoughtful, scholarly Douglass.

ASSESS

Answers

1. **Possible response:** Douglass had a difficult life but kept alive the dream of freedom.
2. (a) **Possible response:** Freedom is beautiful because it is dignifying and precious, especially after a long, hard struggle; it can also be terrible if it comes at a price. (b) Freedom does not yet belong to anyone because it is not yet instinctual.
3. (a) He won't be remembered by statue inscriptions, legends, poems, or memorials. (b) **Possible response:** Statues and memorials are not vital as tools for remembering.
4. (a) He will be remembered in the lives of those living out his dreams. (b) **Possible response:** He is referring to the lives of those who make Douglass's dream a reality by achieving the freedom for which he fought.
5. **Possible response:** He would be proud to think that his work is continuing.

Go Online Author Link For additional information about Robert Hayden, have students type in the Web Code, then select *H* from the alphabet, and then Robert Hayden.

❾ About the Selection

A chorus of voices conveys the risks, the rewards, and the emotions that accompany a journey on the Underground Railroad.

❿ Reading Strategy
Interpreting

- Have students read the bracketed text several times. Then, call on a volunteer to read it aloud.
- Discuss with students how the poetry invites a rapid and escalating pace and tone of voice.

▶ **Monitor Progress: Ask** students the Reading Strategy question: How do the words in lines 1–7 capture the feeling of running?
Answer: The use of repetition, the lack of punctuation, and the non-stop litany of actions and imagery convey a sense of movement and of breathlessness.

❾ Runagate Runagate

Robert Hayden

Background Although Robert Hayden's poetry spans the range of human experience, much of it reflects his passionate, lifelong interest in African American history. His first job after graduating from Detroit City College was to research local African American history with Detroit's Federal Writer's Project. Throughout his career as a professor of literature, Hayden continued to research and write about his heritage. In "Frederick Douglass," he pays tribute to the famous African American abolitionist. "Runagate Runagate" brings the experiences of the Underground Railroad vividly to life.

I

❿
Runs falls rises stumbles on from darkness into darkness
and the darkness thicketed with shapes of terror
and the hunters pursuing and the hounds pursuing
and the night cold and the night long and the river
to cross and the jack-muh-lanterns beckoning beckoning
and blackness ahead and when shall I reach that somewhere
morning and keep on going and never turn back and keep on going

Runagate[1]
Runagate
Runagate

Many thousands rise and go
many thousands crossing over

O mythic North
O star-shaped yonder Bible city[2]

Some go weeping and some rejoicing
some in coffins and some in carriages
some in silks and some in shackles

Rise and go or fare you well

No more auction block for me
no more driver's lash for me

Reading Strategy
Interpreting How do the words in lines 1–7 capture the feeling of running?

1. **Runagate** (run′ ə gāt) runaway; fugitive.
2. **star-shaped yonder Bible city** Bethlehem, a town in the free state of Pennsylvania.

If you see my Pompey, 30 yrs of age,
new breeches, plain stockings, negro shoes;
if you see my Anna, likely young mulatto
branded E on the right cheek, R on the left,
catch them if you can and notify subscriber.[3]
Catch them if you can, but it won't be easy.
They'll dart underground when you try to catch them,
plunge into quicksand, whirlpools, mazes,
turn into scorpions when you try to catch them.

And before I'll be a slave
I'll be buried in my grave

North star and bonanza gold
I'm bound for the freedom, freedom-bound
and oh Susyanna don't you cry for me.

Runagate

Runagate

II

Rises from their anguish and their power,

Harriet Tubman,[4]

woman of earth, whipscarred,
a summoning, a shining

Mean to be free

And this was the way of it, brethren brethren,
way we journeyed from Can't to Can.
Moon so bright and no place to hide,
the cry up and the patterollers[5] riding,
hound dogs belling in bladed air.
And fear starts a-murbling, Never make it,
we'll never make it. *Hush that now,*
and she's turned upon us, leveled pistol
glinting in the moonlight:
Dead folks can't jaybird-talk, she says;
you keep on going now or die, she says.

Wanted Harriet Tubman alias The General
alias Moses Stealer of Slaves
In league with Garrison Alcott Emerson
Garrett Douglass Thoreau John Brown[6]

3. **subscriber** slave holder from whom the slaves are fleeing.
4. **Harriet Tubman** (c. 1820–1913) African American slave who escaped and led other slaves to safety in the North.
5. **patterollers** patrollers, hunting the escaped slaves.
6. **Garrison . . . John Brown** prominent abolitionists.

12 **Critical Viewing**
What inspiration might the moon have offered runaways? **[Hypothesize]**

13 **Reading Check**
To where is the speaker journeying? Why?

11 Literary Analysis
Theme

- Point out that Robert Hayden fills his poem with allusions to African American spirituals and folk songs.
- **Ask** students: How does this line from a spiritual illuminate the poem's theme?
  Answer: The theme relates to the risks people take to be free, and this line expresses that even death is better than slavery.

12 Critical Viewing

Answer: By lighting their way during nighttime travel, the moon might have made the travelers' journey a bit easier.

13 Reading Check

Answer: The speaker is journeying north in the hope of finding freedom.

Differentiated Instruction
Solutions for All Learners

Strategy for Less Proficient Readers

Suggest that students visualize a thread of meaning linking the poem's words and images together, and point out that their interpretive challenge is to state what that thread of meaning may be. On the board, draw the following graphic organizer, depicting a thread linking images from "Runagate, Runagate." Have students reproduce the graphic, adding more images from the poem. Finally, ask them to write one sentence on a line labeled "Interpretation," stating the underlying idea that links the images together.

Stumbles on from darkness into darkness

North Star and bonanza gold

No more auction block for me

Armed and known to be Dangerous

Wanted Reward Dead or Alive

Tell me, Ezekiel, oh tell me do you see
mailed Jehovah[7] coming to deliver me?

Hoot-owl calling in the ghosted air,
five times calling to the hants[8] in the air.
Shadow of a face in the scary leaves,
shadow of a voice in the talking leaves:

Come ride-a my train

Oh that train, ghost-story train
through swamp and savanna movering movering,
over trestles of dew, through caves of the wish,
Midnight Special on a sabre track movering movering,
first stop Mercy and the last Hallelujah.

Come ride-a my train

Mean mean mean to be free.

7. **Ezekiel** (ē zē′ kē əl) . . . **Jehovah** (ji hō′ və) Ezekiel was a sixth-century B.C. Hebrew prophet; Jehovah is an Old Testament name for the Judeo-Christian God.
8. **hants** haunts; ghosts.

Critical Reading

1. **Respond:** How did your response change as the poem moved from stanza to stanza?
2. **(a) Recall:** What is being described in this poem? **(b) Interpret:** What feeling do the words "Runagate, Runagate, Runagate" convey? Explain.
3. **(a) Recall:** Who "rises from their anguish and their power"? **(b) Interpret:** In what ways does this person prevent the frightened fugitives from giving themselves up?
4. **(a) Draw Conclusions:** Whom do you think is wanted dead or alive? **(b) Draw Conclusions:** Who will pay the reward?
5. **(a) Interpret:** Do you think this poem reflects the experiences of a single speaker, or does it reflect a chorus of voices? Explain. **(b) Interpret:** If there is more than one voice, whose voices are they? Support your answers with examples from the poem.
6. **(a) Apply:** What do you think were some of the risks involved in the struggle for freedom? **(b) Take a Position:** If you had been in the situation of a "runagate," would you have put yourself at such risk? Explain.

For: More about Robert Hayden
Visit: www.PHSchool.com
Web Code: ere-9629

ASSESS

Answers

1. Accept reasonable responses grounded in the poem.
2. (a) The poem describes a trip on the Underground Railroad. (b) They convey the feeling of hurrying in fear through sound and repetition.
3. (a) Harriet Tubman rises from their anguish and power. (b) She threatens to kill them if they try to give themselves up.
4. (a) Harriet Tubman is wanted dead or alive. (b) Slave owners will pay the reward.
5. (a) The poem's shifts in viewpoint from stanza to stanza reflect a chorus of voices. (b) The first seven lines voice the words of a slave on the run; the references to obstacles and the determination to "keep on going" are supporting examples. Lines 19–27 give the voice of a slave owner asking people to catch runaway slaves. Evidence of this are the descriptions of the slaves and the pleas to "catch them if you can." Lines 30–32 again represent the voice of a runaway slave. Lines 34–39 give the voice of a runaway slave describing Harriet Tubman. Lines 50–55 present the voice of a slave owner wanting Harriet Tubman captured or killed. The remaining lines of the poem present the voice of a runaway slave's impressions of the Underground Railroad.
6. (a) The risks involve being captured or killed. (b) Students should support their responses.

Go Online — Author Link For additional information about Robert Hayden, have students type in the Web Code, then select *H* from the alphabet, and then Robert Hayden.

Apply the Skills

Mirror • In a Classroom • The Explorer • Frederick Douglass • Runagate Runagate

Literary Analysis

Theme

1. **(a)** Using a chart like the one shown, list the sensory images used in "Runagate Runagate." **(b)** Explain how the words you have listed express the **theme** that a journey on the Underground Railroad was full of risk, danger, reward, and emotion.

Sight	Hearing	Smell	Touch	Taste

2. List three images in "The Explorer" that help to identify the theme.
3. **(a)** In "Frederick Douglass," what words does Hayden use to describe Douglass and his work? **(b)** Based on the **connotations** of these words, what would you say is the theme of the poem?
4. In "Mirror," what does the line "I am important to her" suggest about the theme of the poem?

Comparing Literary Works

5. **(a)** In what ways do both "The Explorer" and "Frederick Douglass" express the longing for an end to struggle? **(b)** What are the struggles each poem addresses?
6. **(a)** In what way can "Mirror" be read as a poem of social critique? **(b)** What social change, if any, does the poem advocate?
7. **(a)** How does "Runagate Runagate" demonstrate the suffering of individuals caused by a social injustice? **(b)** Does the poem propose a specific social change, or not? Explain.

Reading Strategy

Interpreting

8. **(a)** In "Mirror," what is the significance of the word *swallow*? **(b)** How does this word contribute to the message of the poem?
9. What is the significance of the medical terms Hayden uses to describe a time when freedom is "diastole, systole, reflex action"?

Extend Understanding

10. **Cultural Connection:** Do you think most people share the attitude toward aging that the woman in "Mirror" has? Why or why not?

QuickReview

The **theme** is the central message of a work of literature.

The **connotations** of a word are the emotions it suggests.

Literature of **social criticism** expresses the effects of social ills on individuals and often advocates change.

To **interpret** a work of literature is to determine its meaning by looking for messages in the words and images.

For: Self-test
Visit: www.PHSchool.com
Web Code: era-6616

Go Online Assessment — Students may use the **Self-test** to prepare for **Selection Test A** or **Selection Test B.**

Answers

1. (a) **Sight:** Stumbles on from darkness into darkness; shapes of terror; blackness ahead; moon so bright; glinting in the moonlight; shadow of a face; **Hearing:** weeping; dogs belling; jaybird talk; hoot-owl calling; shadow of a voice; **Touch:** Night cold; silks and some in shackles; driver's lash; whip-scarred (b) These images suggest people's willingness to make sacrifices and take risks for freedom.

   Another sample answer can be found on **Literary Analysis Graphic Organizer B,** p. 277 in ***Graphic Organizer Transparencies.***
2. Images might include "a still spot in the noise," "hunting through the din," and "no quiet rooms."
3. (a) He uses the words "visioning a world where none is lonely, none hunted." (b) The poem's theme is that Douglass's hard work has not yet been realized.
4. The poet thinks people care a lot about their looks.
5. (a) Both poems seek an end to a problem. (b) "Explorer" describes an internal struggle for peace of mind; "Frederick Douglass" describes the struggle for freedom.
6. (a) "Mirror" can be said to critique society's obsession with youth and good looks. (b) It might advocate more respect for the elderly or an end to judging people on appearance.
7. (a) The poem describes how it feels to be pursued in the night by slave catchers. (b) The poem describes a problem; it aims to inspire the reader to find a solution.
8. (a) The word *swallow* personifies the mirror and indicates that the mirror takes in anything it sees without question. (b) *Swallow* implies that the mirror reflects the stark reality it takes in.
9. The medical terms describe phenomena that occur naturally the way Hayden hopes freedom will occur for everyone.
10. Many older people do share the woman's attitude toward aging because of society's preoccupation with good looks and youthfulness.

EXTEND/ASSESS

Answers

❶ Vocabulary Lesson
Word Analysis

Students' poems should reflect knowledge of the precise meanings of the given words.

Spelling Strategy

1. discover
2. preschool
3. redress
4. misconstrue

Vocabulary Builder

1. meditate
2. preconceptions
3. din
4. wily

❷ Grammar and Style Lesson

1. The woman rewards the mirror's faithful accuracy with tears, tantrums, and depression.
2. High human voices are heard in one room, and the scream of nervous affairs is heard from another room.
3. There is no quiet or peace for the explorer.
4. The runagates escaped from slavery, some in coffins, some in carriages, some in silks, and some in shackles.
5. They saw the shadow of a face in the scary leaves and heard the shadow of a voice in the talking leaves.

Writing Application

Check to see that students have used parallel structure correctly.

WG Writing and Grammar, Ruby Level

Students will find further instruction and practice on the use of parallel structure in Chapter 8, Section 4.

Build Language Skills

❶ Vocabulary Lesson

Word Analysis: Latin Root *-cep-/-cept-*

The word *preconception,* like other English words such as *deception, inception, conception, concept, reception,* and *intercept,* derives from the Latin root *-cep-/-cept-,* meaning "to take, hold, or seize." Using these words, write a reflective poem about an experience you have had.

Spelling Strategy

A prefix added to a word does not affect the spelling of the original word. For example, when you add the prefix *pre-* to the word *conceptions,* you create *preconceptions.* Use the prefixes given with a word root you know to make new words.

1. *dis-*
2. *pre-*
3. *re-*
4. *mis-*

Vocabulary Builder: Sentence Completion

Review the list of vocabulary words on page 1215. Then, select the word that best completes each sentence below.

1. The guru will __?__ on the question I posed.
2. To keep the trial fair, the jurors had no __?__ about the case.
3. The __?__ of the machines was ear-splitting.
4. The raccoon is one of the most __?__ of animals.

❷ Grammar and Style Lesson

Parallel Structure

Parallel structure is the expression of similar ideas in similar grammatical forms. Parallelism is especially helpful in poetry where it can add to the rhythm and sound of a poem. When writing, be careful to avoid faulty parallelism—the use of dissimilar grammatical structures to express similar ideas.

> **Example:** *when it is* truly instinct . . . / *when it is* finally won; *when it is* more / than the gaudy mumbo jumbo . . .

Practice Rewrite the following sentences using correct parallel structure.

1. The woman rewards the mirror's faithful accuracy with tears, tantrums, and getting depressed.
2. High human voices are heard in one room, and from another room comes the scream of nervous affairs.
3. There is no quiet place for the explorer and he's not finding any peace.
4. The runagates escaped from slavery, some in coffins, some in carriages, some in silks, and some were wearing shackles.
5. They saw the shadow of a face in the scary leaves and heard the shadow of a voice in the leaves that were talking.

Writing Application Write three sentences about a hero whose actions or attitudes you admire. In each sentence, use parallel structure to express your ideas eloquently.

WG Prentice Hall Writing and Grammar Connection: Chapter 8, Section 4

Assessment Practice

Sentence Structure **(For more practice, see *Standardized Test Preparation Workbook*, p. 72.)**

Many tests require students to choose the best way to correct the structure of a sentence.

Robert Hayden wrote about folklore, mythology, spiritual matters, and he also wrote about historical events.

Choose the best way to write the passage.

A Robert Hayden wrote about folklore, mythology, and spiritual matters, he also wrote about historical events.

B Robert Hayden wrote about folklore, mythology, spiritual matters, historical events.

C Robert Hayden wrote about folklore, mythology, and spiritual matters, about historical events.

D Robert Hayden wrote about folkore, mythology, spiritual matters, and historical events.

D is correct. It is a complete sentence with parallel structure

3 Writing Lesson

Timed Writing: Literary Analysis

The purpose of a literary analysis is to show how various elements of a work of literature combine to convey an overall meaning or effect. Write a literary analysis of one of the poems you have just read. *(40 minutes)*

Prewriting *(10 minutes)* Select a poem and read it several times, taking notes on how you will describe its overall effect or meaning. Gather examples of the poet's use of various elements such as imagery, personification, or metaphor to achieve this effect.

Drafting *(20 minutes)* Begin your analysis with a general statement about the poem and the points you will cover. Then, in a separate paragraph, support each point with examples and quotations from the poem. Conclude a well-phrased summary of your analysis.

Revising *(10 minutes)* Identify places in your draft at which you make important general statements about the poem. Strengthen your analysis by adding accurate quotations from the poem to support your interpretation.

Model: Using Quotations to Support Interpretation

Plath personifies the inanimate objects and contrasts them, giving them positive and negative human traits: The mirror says, "I am not cruel, only truthful," but Plath adds, "Then she turns to those liars, the candles or the moon."

Using direct quotations supports the interpretation of the poem.

Prentice Hall Writing and Grammar Connection: Chapter 14, Section 4

Extend Your Learning

Listening and Speaking With a group of classmates, stage a **debate** that answers these questions: What does freedom mean to you? Do you believe that everyone in present-day America is free? Be sure to follow these rules:

- With your own team, negotiate to reach a consensus about the argument you will present.
- Allow each side to speak without interruption, observing time limits.

After both sides speak, give each one a chance for rebuttal. **[Group Activity]**

Research and Technology In "Mirror," a woman is preoccupied with her appearance and upset at the signs of aging. With a partner, use magazine ads, song tracks, and oral commentary to create a **multimedia presentation** exploring our culture's emphasis on youth.

For: An additional research activity
Visit: www.PHSchool.com
Web Code: erd-7616

3 Writing Lesson

You may use this Writing Lesson as timed-writing practice, or you may allow students to develop the review as a writing assignment over several days.

- Give students the **Support for Writing Lesson,** p. 285 in ***Unit 6 Resources,*** to use as they write their literary analyses.
- Review poetic elements such as imagery, personification, and metaphor with students to confirm understanding.
- Discuss the Writing Lesson to guide students in developing their analyses.
- Use the Response to Literature rubrics on pp. 65–66 of ***General Resources*** to assess students' work.

4 Listening and Speaking

- Make sure all students understand the structure and rules of the debate. Encourage each group to assign specific tasks, such as argument or rebuttal, to each student.
- Suggest that groups prioritize their arguments from most effective to least—or the other way around.
- Encourage students to anticipate the other side's arguments and to identify weaknesses in them.
- Use the rubric for Speaking: Delivering a Speech, p. 89 in ***General Resources,*** to evaluate students' debates.
- The **Support for Extend Your Learning** page (***Unit 6 Resources,*** p. 286) provides guided note-taking opportunities to help students complete the Extend Your Learning activities.

Go Online Research — Have students type in the Web Code for another research activity.

Assessment Resources

The following resources can be used to assess students' knowledge and skills.

Unit 6 Resources
- **Selection Test A,** pp. 288–290
- **Selection Test B,** pp. 291–293

General Resources
- **Rubrics for Response to Literature,** pp. 65–66
- **Rubric for Speaking: Delivering a Speech,** p. 89

Go Online Assessment — Students may use the **Self-test** to prepare for **Selection Test A** or **Selection Test B.**

Meeting Your Standards

Students will

1. **analyze and respond to literary elements.**
   - Literary Analysis: Parallelism
2. **read, comprehend, analyze, and critique a speech and a letter.**
   - Reading Strategy: Identifying the Main Idea and Supporting Details
   - Reading Check questions
   - Apply the Skills questions
3. **develop vocabulary.**
   - Vocabulary Lesson: Word Analysis: Latin Root: *-vert-* or *–vers-*
4. **understand and apply written and oral language conventions.**
   - Spelling Strategy
   - Grammar and Style Lesson: Parallel Structure
5. **develop writing proficiency.**
   - Writing Lesson: Public Letter
6. **develop appropriate research strategies.**
   - Extend Your Learning: Multimedia Presentation
7. **understand and apply listening and speaking strategies.**
   - Extend Your Learning: Speech

Block Scheduling: Use one 90-minute class period to preteach the skills and have students read the selection. Use a second 90-minute class period to assess students' mastery of skills, extend their learning, and monitor their progress.

Homework Suggestions

Following are possibilities for homework assignments.

- Support pages from *Unit 6 Resources:*
  Literary Analysis
  Reading Strategy
  Vocabulary Builder
  Grammar and Style
- An Extend Your Learning project and the Writing Lesson for this selection group may be completed over several days.

Step-by-Step Teaching Guide	Pacing Guide
PRETEACH	
• Administer Vocabulary and Reading Warm-ups as necessary.	5 min.
• Engage students' interest with the motivation activity.	5 min.
• Read and discuss author and background features. **FT**	10 min.
• Introduce the Literary Analysis Skill: Parallelism. **FT**	5 min.
• Introduce the Reading Strategy: Identifying the Main Idea and Supporting Details. **FT**	10 min.
• Prepare students to read by teaching the selection vocabulary. **FT**	
TEACH	
• Informally monitor comprehension while students read independently or in groups. **FT**	30 min.
• Monitor students' comprehension with the Reading Check notes.	as students read
• Reinforce vocabulary with Vocabulary Builder notes.	as students read
• Develop students' understanding of parellelism with the Literary Analysis annotations. **FT**	5 min.
• Develop students' ability to identify the main idea and supporting details with the Reading Strategy annotations. **FT**	5 min.
ASSESS/EXTEND	
• Assess students' comprehension and mastery of the Literary Analysis and Reading Strategy by having them answer the Apply the Skills questions. **FT**	15 min.
• Have students complete the Vocabulary Lesson and the Grammar and Style Lesson. **FT**	15 min.
• Apply students' ability to use language persuasively by using the Writing Lesson. **FT**	45 min. or homework
• Apply students' understanding using one or more of the Extend Your Learning activities.	20–90 min. or homework
• Administer Selection Test A or Selection Test B. **FT**	15 min.

Resources

PRINT

Unit 6 Resources

TRANSPARENCY

Graphic Organizer Transparencies

PRINT

Reader's Notebook [L2]

Reader's Notebook: Adapted Version [L1]

Reader's Notebook: English Learner's Version [EL]

Unit 6 Resources

TECHNOLOGY

Listening to Literature Audio CDs [L2, EL]

PRINT

Unit 6 Resources

General Resources

TECHNOLOGY

Go Online: Research **[L3]**

Go Online: Self-test **[L3]**

ExamView® **Test Bank [L3]**

Choosing Resources for Differentiated Instruction

[L1] Special Needs Students

[L2] Below-Level Students

[L3] All Students

[L4] Advanced Students

[EL] English Learners

For Vocabulary and Reading Warm-ups and for Selection Tests, **A** signifies "less challenging" and **B** "more challenging." For Graphic Organizer transparencies, **A** signifies "not filled in" and **B** "filled in."

FT Fast Track Instruction: To move the lesson more quickly, use the strategies and activities identified with **FT**.

Scaffolding for Less Proficient and Advanced Students

The leveled Critical Thinking questions after selections progress in the levels of thinking required to answer them. To address the needs of your different students, you may use the (a) level questions for your less proficient students and the (b) level questions with your on-level and advanced students. The occasional (c) level questions are appropriate for your advanced students.

PRENTICE HALL **TeacherEXPRESS™** Plan · Teach · Assess — Use this complete suite of powerful teaching tools to make lesson planning and testing quicker and easier.

PRENTICE HALL **StudentEXPRESS™** Learn · Study · Succeed — Use the interactive textbook (online and on CD-ROM) to make selections and activities come alive with audio and video support and interactive questions.

Go Online **Professional Development** **For:** Information about Lexiles **Visit:** www.PHSchool.com **Web Code:** eue-1111

PRETEACH

Motivation

Tell students that among the most memorable words John F. Kennedy spoke in his Inaugural Address are these: "Ask not what your country can do for you—ask what you can do for your country." Ask students what they think he meant. Then have them name people who answered the call of their country. Students might suggest Martin Luther King, Jr., Rosa Parks, and Rachel Carson. Ask students how they can meet this challenge.

❶ Background

More About the Authors

John F. Kennedy became president during a difficult period in American history. The United States and the Soviet Union were engaged in the Cold War and were armed with huge nuclear arsenals. John F. Kennedy stepped to center stage in this conflict. He confronted the Soviet Union in Cuba and in West Berlin. Kennedy recognized the immense danger of nuclear weapons and began an effort that led to the 1963 test ban treaty.

President Kennedy set a tone of hope and idealism. In addition to working for civil rights legislation, he started the Peace Corps to help developing countries and to spread the American ideal of freedom.

Martin Luther King, Jr., was born in Atlanta, Georgia, and grew up in a South torn apart by racism. He attended Morehouse College, studied theology at Crozer Theological Seminary, and earned a Ph.D. at Boston University in 1953.

In 1955, King led the Montgomery, Alabama, bus boycott. It lasted 382 days. King suffered personal abuse. He was arrested, and his house was bombed. After the boycott succeeded, King became one of America's great civil rights leaders. In the years that followed, he traveled over six million miles and gave more than twenty-five hundred speeches. In 1964, he was awarded the Nobel Peace Prize.

❶ Inaugural Address • *from* Letter from Birmingham City Jail

John F. Kennedy (1917–1963)

A Tradition of Service John Fitzgerald Kennedy was born into a family with a tradition of public service. His father Joseph served as U.S. Ambassador to Great Britain, and his maternal grandfather was elected mayor of Boston. After graduation from Harvard University, Kennedy served with distinction in the U.S. Navy during World War II. Having barely escaped death in battle, Kennedy returned home as a war hero, and in 1946 he easily won election to the House of Representatives. Kennedy served three terms in the House before he was elected senator from Massachusetts in 1952.

Thirty-Fifth President Eight years later, in 1960, Kennedy won a hard-fought contest for the presidency. At the age of forty-three, he became the youngest person ever to be elected to that office. While he was president, he witnessed events as diverse as the launch of the first communications satellite, *Telstar,* and the signing of the first nuclear nonproliferation treaty with the Soviet Union. The United States teetered on the brink of nuclear war during the Cuban missile crisis and put its first astronaut into orbit around the Earth.

Fallen Leader Tragically, Kennedy was assassinated on November 22, 1963, in Dallas, Texas. Two days after the president's murder, Lee Harvey Oswald, who had been arrested for the crime, was himself assassinated. In 1964, the Warren Commission, charged with investigating the circumstances of Kennedy's murder, ruled that Oswald had acted alone. Nevertheless, conspiracy theories have continued to swirl about the assassination.

Martin Luther King, Jr. (1929–1968)

Martin Luther King, Jr., was born into a family of ministers: both his father and maternal grandfather were Baptist preachers. At Morehouse College in Atlanta, Georgia, King originally planned to study both medicine and law. However, under the influence of his mentor, the college president and eloquent orator Benjamin Mays, King committed himself to the ministry and to the struggle for racial equality.

Formative Years King prepared for the ministry at Crozer Theological Seminary in Chester, Pennsylvania. Here, the nonviolent philosophy of the Indian leader Mohandas K. ("Mahatma") Gandhi made a critical impression on him. At Boston University a few years later, King earned a doctorate in theology.

Civil Rights Leader Convinced that political and social freedoms were attainable through nonviolence, King first gained prominence as the leader of the Montgomery Bus Boycott of 1955–1956. Thereafter, he led boycotts, marches, and sit-ins to protest segregation, injustice, and the economic oppression of African Americans. A charismatic orator, King soon became known as the most eloquent and influential leader of the civil rights movement. In April 1963, he crystallized the movement's aims and methods in "Letter from Birmingham City Jail." Four months later, he helped organize the March on Washington, where he delivered his memorable speech "I Have a Dream." Although King stressed nonviolence, he became a martyr for freedom when he was assassinated in Memphis, Tennessee, on April 4, 1968. His widow, Coretta Scott King, works to keep King's message and achievements alive.

Preview

Connecting to the Literature

The words *American, patriot,* and *democracy* suggest a range of responses. As you read, think about what the words mean to you and what each writer tells you about the privileges and obligations of freedom.

❷ Literary Analysis

Parallelism

Parallelism is the repetition of words, phrases, clauses, or sentences that have the same grammatical structure or the same meaning. Also known as **parallel structure,** it is a rhetorical device used in poetry, speeches, and other types of writing to balance related ideas, to stress contrasting ones, or to create a memorable rhythm.

> . . . the torch has been passed to a new generation of Americans— born in this century, tempered by war, disciplined by a hard and bitter peace, proud of our ancient heritage . . .

Comparing Literary Works

Persuasion is writing or speech meant to get a reader or listener to think or act in a particular way. Writers use a variety of persuasive techniques:

- *logical appeals,* or reasoned arguments based on evidence
- *emotional appeals,* or efforts to engage the feelings of the audience
- *ethical appeals,* or references to the writer's own sensitivity and fairness

Identify each author's political beliefs and his outlook on major public issues, and consider how effectively the authors speak to their respective audiences.

❸ Reading Strategy

Identifying the Main Idea and Supporting Details

The **main ideas** in a selection are the key points that the writer wants to convey. The **supporting details** consist of the facts, examples, or reasons that explain or justify these ideas. Use a chart like the one shown to identify main ideas and supporting details as you read these selections.

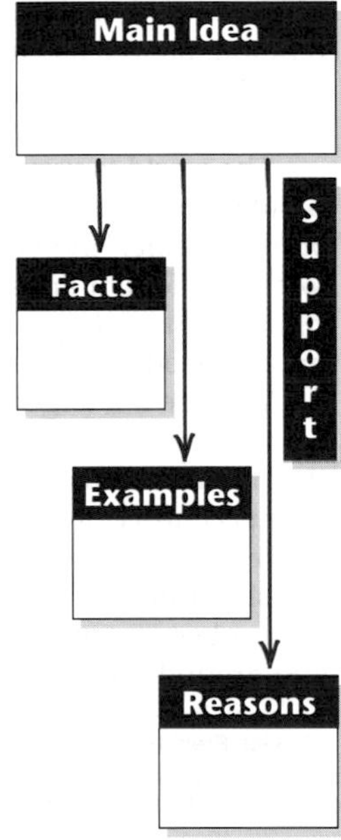

Vocabulary Builder

heirs (erz) *n.* people who carry on the tradition of predecessors (p. 1228)

tyranny (tir′ ə nē) *n.* oppressive and unjust government (p. 1229)

alliance (ə lī′ əns) *n.* union of nations for a specific purpose (p. 1229)

invective (in vek′ tiv) *n.* verbal attack; strong criticism (p. 1229)

adversary (ad′ vər ser′ ē) *n.* opponent; enemy (p. 1229)

eradicate (ē rad′ i kāt′) *v.* wipe out; destroy (p. 1230)

impelled (im peld′) *v.* moved; forced (p. 1232)

flagrant (flā′ grənt) *adj.* glaring; outrageous (p. 1233)

profundity (prō fun′ də tē) *n.* intellectual depth (p. 1233)

monotony (mə nät′ ən ē) *n.* unchanging sameness; lack of variety (p. 1234)

❷ Literary Analysis

Parallelism

- Point out that parallelism helps make the meaning of complex topics clearer and easier to understand. By putting similar or contrasting ideas in a parallel structure, writers and speakers highlight similarities and differences.
- Explain that parallelism not only creates a memorable rhythm, but it also creates a sentence structure that enables sound devices to stand out and work together.
- Have students look at the underlined examples in their texts. Point out that the underlined words all begin adjective phrases modifying *Americans.* The phrases in this series are all in the same, or parallel, grammatical structure.

❸ Reading Strategy

Identifying the Main Idea and Supporting Details

- Give students a copy of **Reading Strategy Graphic Organizer A** from ***Graphic Organizer Transparencies,*** p. 278, to use as they read these selections.
- Tell students that speakers sometimes do not state main ideas. Readers must go through the passage and infer the big ideas from the details the writer provides. This technique occurs most often when the main idea is controversial or when writers want subtlety.
- Point out that supporting ideas are especially important in persuasive writing. These details may be facts, examples, statistics, or other concrete information. They may also be reasons that support the main ideas with logic and common sense.

Vocabulary Builder

- Pronounce each vocabulary word for students, and read the definitions as a class. Have students identify any words with which they are already familiar.

Differentiated Instruction

Solutions for All Learners

Support for Special Needs Students
Have students complete the **Preview** and **Build Skills** pages for these selections in the ***Reader's Notebook: Adapted Version.*** Completing these pages will prepare students to read the selection in the Student Edition.

Support for Less Proficient Readers
Have students complete the **Preview** and **Build Skills** pages for these selections in the ***Reader's Notebook.*** Completing these pages will prepare students to read the selection in the Student Edition.

Support for English Learners
Have students complete the **Preview** and **Build Skills** pages for these selections in the ***Reader's Notebook: English Learner's Version.*** Completing these pages will prepare students to read the selection in the Student Edition.

❻ Humanities

Retroactive I, 1964, by Robert Rauschenberg

Born in Texas in 1925, Rauschenberg experimented with different combinations of materials and techniques. In the early 1960s, he began to combine media images with printmaking techniques to create striking works like the one shown here.

Use this question for discussion:

- Does the work capture the mood and content of the Inaugural Address? Explain.
  Answer: The speech refers to the world's ills and causes of fear. However, the speech is confident and strong. In the same way, the chaotic images of the painting are dominated by the confident image of Kennedy.

❼ Literary Analysis
Parallelism

- **Ask** students: What elements of parallel structure in this passage develop balance and contrast?
  Answer: Kennedy contrasts "let us never negotiate out of fear" with "let us never fear to negotiate."

➤ **Monitor Progress:** Ask students to comment on the rhythm of the speech. Then **ask** how parallelism helps make the meaning clear and easy to follow.
Answer: The parallelism shows a clear relationship between ideas by demonstrating that they are opposites.

❽ Literary Analysis
Parallelism

- Point out the use of parallelism to connect ideas from paragraph to paragraph. For example, each paragraph begins with "Let both sides."
- **Ask** students the Literary Analysis question: What parallel elements does Kennedy use to make both logical and emotional appeals?
  Answer: Logical structures include the repetition of the phrase "let both sides," which recurs through the paragraphs. Emotional appeals include the repetition of "absolute" in "absolute power to destroy" and "absolute control"; and the parallel series referring to stars, deserts, disease, ocean depths, arts, and commerce.

deadly atom, yet both racing to alter that uncertain balance of terror that stays the hand of mankind's final war.

7 So let us begin anew—remembering on both sides that civility is not a sign of weakness, and sincerity is always subject to proof. Let us never negotiate out of fear. But let us never fear to negotiate.

Let both sides explore what problems unite us instead of belaboring those problems which divide us.

Let both sides, for the first time, formulate serious and precise proposals for the inspection and control of arms—and bring the absolute power to destroy other nations under the absolute control of all nations.

8 Let both sides seek to invoke the wonders of science instead of its terrors. Together let us explore the stars, conquer the deserts, eradicate disease, tap the ocean depths, and encourage the arts and commerce.

Let both sides unite to heed in all corners of the earth the command of Isaiah—to "undo the heavy burdens . . . and let the oppressed go free."[4]

❻

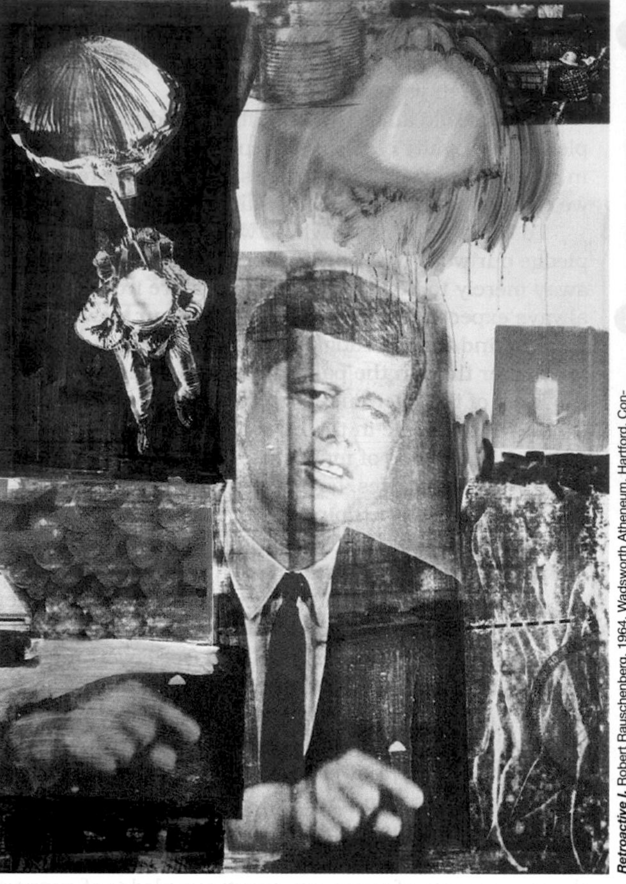

Retroactive I, Robert Rauschenberg, 1964, Wadsworth Atheneum, Hartford, Con-

And if a beachhead of cooperation may push back the jungle of suspicion, let both sides join in creating a new endeavor, not a new balance of power, but a new world of law, where the strong are just and the weak secure and the peace preserved.

All this will not be finished in the first 100 days. Nor will it be finished in the first 1,000 days, nor in the life of this Administration, nor even perhaps in our lifetime on this planet. But let us begin.

In your hands, my fellow citizens, more than in mine, will rest the final success or failure of our course. Since this country was founded, each generation of Americans has been summoned to give testimony to its national loyalty. The graves of young Americans who answered the call to service surround the globe.

9 Now the trumpet summons us again—not as a call to bear arms, though arms we need; not as a call to battle, though embattled we are—but a call to bear the burden of a long twilight struggle, year in

4. **Isaiah . . . free** the quotation refers to the passage in Isaiah 58:6.

Vocabulary Builder
eradicate (e rad′ i kāt′) *v.* wipe out; destroy

Literary Analysis
Parallelism and Persuasion What parallel elements does Kennedy use to make both logical and emotional appeals?

and year out, "rejoicing in hope, patient in tribulation"[5]—a struggle against the common enemies of man: tyranny, poverty, disease, and war itself.

Can we forge against these enemies a grand and global alliance, North and South, East and West, that can assure a more fruitful life for all mankind? Will you join in that historic effort?

In the long history of the world, only a few generations have been granted the role of defending freedom in its hour of maximum danger. I do not shrink from this responsibility—I welcome it. I do not believe that any of us would exchange places with any other people or any other generation. The energy, the faith, the devotion which we bring to this endeavor will light our country and all who serve it—and the glow from that fire can truly light the world.

And so, my fellow Americans: ask not what your country can do for you—ask what you can do for your country.

My fellow citizens of the world: ask not what America will do for you, but what together we can do for the freedom of man.

Finally, whether you are citizens of America or citizens of the world, ask of us here the same high standards of strength and sacrifice which we ask of you. With a good conscience our only sure reward, with history the final judge of our deeds, let us go forth to lead the land we love, asking His blessing and His help, but knowing that here on earth God's work must truly be our own.

5. **"rejoicing . . . tribulation"** from Romans 12:12. In Paul's letter to the Romans, he enjoins people to work together in love and mutual respect.

Reading Strategy
Identifying the Main Idea and Supporting Details
What key idea does Kennedy stress in this paragraph?

◀ Critical Viewing
What do the images in this montage—and the unfinished quality of the upper right corner—suggest about Kennedy? **[Infer]**

Critical Reading

1. **Respond:** If you had been among those to hear Kennedy's inaugural address, what ideas might have sparked the strongest response in you? Explain.
2. **(a) Recall:** What difference does Kennedy stress between the world now and the world of the Revolutionary War? **(b) Interpret:** How does Kennedy want his audience to respond to this difference?
3. **(a) Recall:** In paragraphs 6–11, which groups does Kennedy specifically address? **(b) Generalize:** What common message does he have for each of these groups?
4. **(a) Recall:** What project does Kennedy urge both sides of the Cold War to begin? **(b) Infer:** Why would this project be important, even though it may not be completed in our lives?
5. **Evaluate:** How effective is the challenge that Kennedy offers in the final paragraphs of the speech? Explain your answer.

For: More about John F. Kennedy
Visit: www.PHSchool.com
Web Code: ere-9630

❾ Reading Strategy
Identifying the Main Idea and Supporting Details

- **Ask** students the Reading Strategy question: What key idea does Kennedy stress in this paragraph?
  Answer: Americans are called to help fight tyranny, poverty, disease, and war.
- Discuss how the main idea of this paragraph reflects the main idea of the speech by pointing out that Kennedy began by talking about the responsibilities of Americans as the "heirs of that first revolution."

❿ Critical Viewing

Answer: The images suggest that Kennedy controlled a variety of issues. The unfinished corner may allude to his unfinished term of office.

ASSESS
Answers

1. Students may state that Kennedy's challenge sparked a strong response because he calls listeners personally contribute to the country.
2. (a) People now have the power to end poverty and the power to destroy human life. (b) He wants members of his audience to work for peace and freedom.
3. (a) He urges the two powers to cooperate on issues on which they agree. (b) It will create a better world for future generations.
4. It is a powerful challenge because he has already spelled out the responsibilities of Americans, the problems to be solved, and the solution. Now he asks people to do their part and start working.

Go Online Author Link For additional information about John F. Kennedy, have students type in the Web Code, then select *K* from the alphabet, and then select Kennedy.

Differentiated Instruction
Solutions for All Learners

Strategy for Advanced Readers
Share the following reactions to Kennedy's speech:

". . . his "Inaugural Address" really inspired people; it was a feeling of renewal."

". . . that business of bearing any burden and taking on any foe was great at the time, but looking back on it, I think it was really quite arrogant."

Challenge students to write essays supporting one of these two reactions. Remind them to use specific evidence from the speech and from their knowledge of history to support their arguments. If students disagree with both views, have them articulate and support their own reactions.

13 Literary Analysis
Parallelism

- Read the paragraph aloud to students. Then **ask** the Literary Analysis question: What parallel structures does King use in these sentences?
  Answer: In the first lines, King says "I have no despair" and "I have no fear." Next he uses the parallel of "the goal of freedom" and "the goal of America." Then he states "before the Pilgrims" and "before the pen," and then "they made" and "they built."
- **Ask** students what effect these parallel structures have.
  Answer: The parallelism links and balances ideas and it creates a rhythm that makes the writing enjoyable and memorable.

from Letter from Birmingham City Jail

Martin Luther King, Jr.

Background By the late 1950s, Martin Luther King, Jr., had emerged as a key figure of the civil rights movement—the struggle by African Americans to gain full equality, justice, and economic opportunity. During the Kennedy administration, King was arrested in April, 1963, for protesting racial segregation in Birmingham, Alabama. As he sat in jail, he read a newspaper article in which eight white clergymen criticized him for "unwise and untimely" demonstrations. Without proper writing paper, King drafted a response—the "Letter from Birmingham City Jail"—in the cramped margins of that newspaper. A few months later, King led the March on Washington. On that occasion, more than 200,000 Americans of all races gathered around the Lincoln Memorial and heard his voice ring out again for the causes of racial justice and freedom.

13 I hope the church as a whole will meet the challenge of this decisive hour. But even if the church does not come to the aid of justice, I have no despair about the future. I have no fear about the outcome of our struggle in Birmingham, even if our motives are presently misunderstood. We will reach the goal of freedom in Birmingham and all over the nation, because the goal of America is freedom. Abused and scorned though we may be, our destiny is tied up with the destiny of America. Before the Pilgrims landed at Plymouth we were here. Before the pen of Jefferson etched across the pages of history the majestic words of the Declaration of Independence, we were here. For more than two centuries our fore-parents labored in this country without wages; they made cotton king; and they built the homes of their masters in the midst of brutal injustice and shameful humiliation—and yet out of a bottomless vitality they continued to thrive and develop. If the inexpressible cruelties of slavery could not stop us, the opposition we now face will surely fail. We will win our freedom because the sacred heritage of our nation and the eternal will of God are embodied in our echoing demands.

14 I must close now. But before closing I am impelled to mention one other point in your statement that troubled me profoundly. You warmly commended the Birmingham police force for keeping "order" and "preventing violence." I don't believe you would have so warmly commended the police force if you had seen its angry violent dogs literally biting six unarmed, nonviolent Negroes. I don't believe you would so quickly

Literary Analysis
Parallelism What parallel structures does King use in these sentences?

Vocabulary Builder
impelled (im peld′) *v.* moved; forced

Reading Strategy
Identifying the Main Idea and Supporting Details Identify two details King uses in this paragraph to support his main idea.

Enrichment

The Montgomery Bus Boycott
Martin Luther King, Jr. was thrust into the leadership of the Montgomery [Alabama] Improvement Association (MIA) in 1955 when Rosa Parks refused to relinquish her seat on a Montgomery bus to a white passenger. The MIA was a group composed mostly of black citizens of Montgomery who sponsored a boycott of city buses. Their goal was to win fair treatment for blacks, who made up 75 percent of the city's bus passengers. Despite their dependence on public transportation, African Americans held to the boycott with remarkable solidarity. MIA leaders arranged car pools, and black taxi drivers charged only the ten-cent bus fare to transport black passengers. The boycott lasted for a little over a year; finally the bus company and the city agreed to desegregate the buses. By this time, Dr. King had become a front-page name and was viewed as the spokesperson of the Civil Rights Movement.

commend the policemen if you would observe their ugly and inhuman treatment of Negroes here in the city jail; if you would watch them push and curse old Negro women and young Negro girls; if you would see
4 them slap and kick old Negro men and young Negro boys; if you will observe them, as they did on two occasions, refuse to give us food because we wanted to sing our grace together. I'm sorry that I can't join you in your praise for the police department.

It is true that they have been rather disciplined in their public handling of the demonstrators. In this sense they have been rather publicly "nonviolent." But for what purpose? To preserve the evil system of segregation. Over the last few years I have consistently preached that nonviolence demands that the means we use must be as pure as the ends we seek. So I have tried to make it clear that it is wrong to use immoral means to attain moral ends. But now I must affirm that it is just as wrong, or even more so, to use moral means to preserve immoral ends. Maybe Mr. Connor and his policemen have been rather publicly nonviolent, as Chief Pritchett was in Albany, Georgia, but they have used the moral means of nonviolence to maintain the immoral end of flagrant racial injustice. T. S. Eliot has said that there is no greater treason than to do the right deed for the wrong reason.

I wish you had commended the Negro sit-inners and demonstrators of Birmingham for their sublime courage, their willingness to suffer and their amazing discipline in the midst of the most inhuman provocation. One day the South will recognize its real heroes. They will be the James Merediths, courageously and with a majestic sense of purpose facing jeering and hostile mobs and the agonizing loneliness that characterizes the life of the pioneer. They will be old, oppressed, battered Negro women, symbolized in a seventy-two-year-old woman of Montgomery, Alabama, who rose up with a sense of dignity and with her people decided not to ride the segregated buses, and responded to one who inquired about her tiredness with ungrammatical profundity: "My feet is tired, but my soul is rested." They will be the young high school and college students, young ministers of the gospel and a host of their elders courageously and nonviolently sitting-in at lunch counters and willingly going to jail for conscience's sake. One day the South will know that when these disinherited children of God sat down at lunch counters they were in reality standing up for the best in the American dream and the most sacred values in our Judeo-Christian heritage, and thusly, carrying our whole nation back

Vocabulary Builder

flagrant (flā′ grənt) *adj.* glaring, outrageous

profundity (prō fun′ də tē) *n.* intellectual depth

15 ▼ **Critical Viewing** To prevent others from joining this African American sitting at a "whites only" lunch counter, the other seats were piled with linen supplies. Based on their posture and activity, what might the customer and the waitress be feeling? **[Hypothesize]**

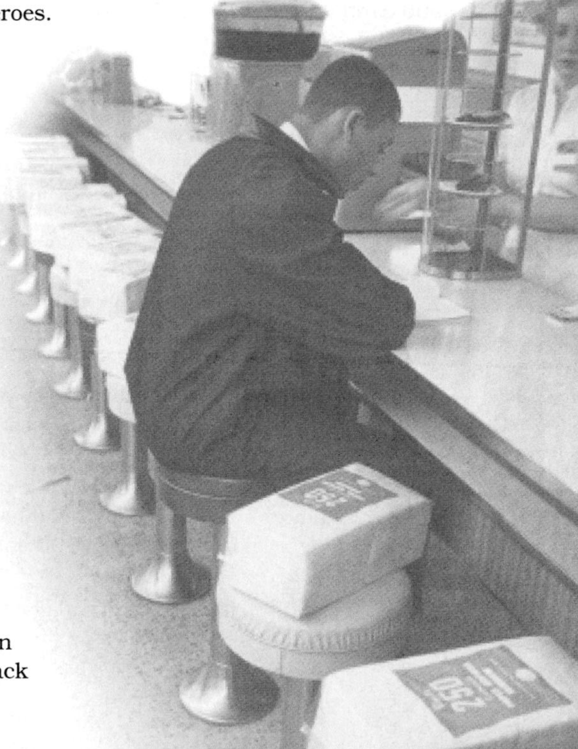

14 Reading Strategy
Identifying the Main Idea and Supporting Details

- Have a volunteer read aloud the bracketed paragraph. **Ask** students to identify the main idea.
  Answer: The main idea is that the police department treated the black demonstrators badly.

Monitor Progress: Now **ask** students to respond to the Reading Strategy prompt: Identify two details King uses in this paragraph to support his main idea.
Answer: Details include the police allowing their dogs to bite demonstrators; pushing, cursing, and kicking people; and withholding food.

15 Critical Viewing

Answer: The man seems engaged in his book. He may feel vulnerable, but he seems relaxed. The waitress is busy with her chores; perhaps she feels awkward and prefers to focus on her work.

Differentiated Instruction
Solutions for All Learners

Support for Less Proficient Readers
Make sure students understand the situation and purpose that prompted King to write this letter. Create a K-W-L chart on the board before students begin reading. Tell them to read the title of the speech and to look at the pictures. Then ask them what they know and what they want to know. Enter the information in the chart. Then, pause occasionally as students read to add to the chart. At the end of the class discussion, check back with students and guide them in completing the Learn column.

Vocabulary for English Learners
Students may be unfamiliar with abstract civil rights words in this letter. Ask students to identify any unfamiliar words. Make a chart on the board with two columns, one for negative words such as *segregation* and *injustice* and the other for positive words such as *rights* and *nonviolence*. Suggest that students copy the chart for later reference. Discuss with students the meanings of these words.

16 Reading Strategy
Identifying the Main Idea and Supporting Details

- Read the final paragraph aloud. Ask a volunteer to paraphrase what King has said.
- **Ask** students the Reading Strategy question: What is King's key idea in the final paragraph?
  Answer: King hopes that peace and brotherhood will replace fear and misunderstanding.

ASSESS

Answers

1. Students may point to the description of the "real heroes" because they exhibited courage while demonstrating for their rights.
2. (a) King says that he is confident because the goal of America is freedom and because African Americans have struggled without giving up. (b) **Possible response:** King wants to demonstrate his conviction that what is happening is right. He also may want to show that he will never give in.
3. (a) King shows that the police were cruel and violent. (b) He says that it is wrong to use immoral means to achieve moral ends and that it is equally wrong to use moral means to gain immoral ends.
4. (a) King believes they are worthy of praise because such demonstrations are courageous and moral acts. (b) King's allusions show that the demonstrators are doing God's will, not fighting for something new but for the rights Americans have already earned.
5. **Possible response:** It is effective because it urges communication and cooperation.

Go Online Author Link For additional information about Martin Luther King, Jr., have students type in the Web Code, then select *K* from the alphabet, and then select King.

to those great wells of democracy which were dug deep by the Founding Fathers in the formulation of the Constitution and the Declaration of Independence.

Never before have I written a letter this long (or should I say a book?). I'm afraid that it is much too long to take your precious time. I can assure you that it would have been much shorter if I had been writing from a comfortable desk, but what else is there to do when you are alone for days in the dull monotony of a narrow jail cell other than write long letters, think strange thoughts, and pray long prayers?

Vocabulary Builder
monotony (mə nät′ ən ē) *n.* tiresome unchanging sameness; lack of variety

If I have said anything in this letter that is an overstatement of the truth and is indicative of an unreasonable impatience, I beg you to forgive me. If I have said anything in this letter that is an understatement of the truth and is indicative of my having a patience that makes me patient with anything less than brotherhood, I beg God to forgive me.

14 I hope this letter finds you strong in the faith. I also hope that circumstances will soon make it possible for me to meet each of you, not as an integrationist or a civil rights leader, but as a fellow clergyman and a Christian brother. Let us all hope that the dark clouds of racial prejudice will soon pass away and the deep fog of misunderstanding will be lifted from our fear-drenched communities and in some not too distant tomorrow the radiant stars of love and brotherhood will shine over our great nation with all of their scintillating beauty.

Reading Strategy
Identifying the Main Idea and Supporting Details
What is King's key idea in the final paragraph?

Yours for the cause of Peace
and Brotherhood,
Martin Luther King, Jr.

Critical Reading

1. **Respond:** What do you think is the most persuasive part of this letter? Why?
2. **(a) Recall:** In the first paragraph, what reasons does King give for his confidence in the outcome of the struggle? **(b) Infer:** Why do you think he stresses his attitude about the outcome?
3. **(a) Recall:** How does King refute the clergymen's warm praise of the Birmingham police force? **(b) Distinguish:** What two points does King make about means and ends in this passage of the letter?
4. **(a) Recall:** Why does King feel that those who participate in sit-ins and demonstrations are worthy of praise? **(b) Analyze:** How do King's allusions to religion and to history bolster his persuasive appeal in this passage?
5. **Evaluate:** Do you think the final paragraph of the letter is an effective conclusion? Why or why not?

For: More about Martin Luther King, Jr.
Visit: www.PHSchool.com
Web Code: ere-9631

Apply the Skills

Inaugural Address • from *Letter from Birmingham City Jail*

Literary Analysis

Parallelism

1. Identify examples of **parallelism** in the sixth paragraph of Kennedy's inaugural address, beginning "To those old allies . . . ."
2. **(a)** Reread the nineteenth paragraph in Kennedy's inaugural that begins "And if a beachhead of cooperation . . . ." Using a chart like the one shown, identify the parallel words and phrases.

Parallel Words	Parallel Phrases

   (b) Choose the strongest example in your chart and explain your choice.
3. How does the passage that begins "Ask not what your country can do for you . . ." combine parallelism with *antithesis,* or a striking, balanced contrast?
4. **(a)** In "Letter from Birmingham City Jail," identify parallelism in the paragraph beginning "If I have said anything in this letter that is an overstatement . . . ." **(b)** What is the effect of this rhetorical device?

Comparing Literary Works

Persuasion

5. When Kennedy addresses "both sides" of the Cold War in his inaugural, is his **persuasive** appeal primarily logical, emotional, or a mixture of both? Explain.
6. **(a)** What emotionally charged words and phrases can you identify in the twenty-second paragraph of Kennedy's inaugural? **(b)** In what way does the choice of words contribute to Kennedy's persuasive goal in this part of the speech?
7. **(a)** What double audience does King address in his letter? **(b)** What details in the final paragraph show an awareness of both audiences? Explain.

Reading Strategy

Identifying the Main Idea and Supporting Details

8. What details support Kennedy's **main idea** that the task of defending freedom should be welcomed?
9. According to King, who will eventually be recognized as the "real heroes" of the South?

Extend Understanding

10. **Social Studies Connection:** Is eloquence a necessary or important requirement for effective leadership? Explain.

QuickReview

Parallelism is the repetition of words, phrases, clauses, or sentences that have the same grammatical structure.

Persuasion is writing or speech meant to convince a reader or listener to think or act in a particular way.

When you **identify the main idea and supporting details,** you distinguish a writer's key points from the facts, examples, or reasons that justify or support them.

For: Self-test
Visit: www.PHSchool.com
Web Code: era-6617

Answers

1. Examples include the parallel structure of the sentences that begin "United" and "Divided." Kennedy repeats the phrase ". . . there is little . . ." This paragraph is also the first of several that begin with the phrase "To those . . ."
2. (a) Parallel words include "new"; parallel phrases include "a new endeavor," "a new balance," and "a new world" and "the strong are just," and "the weak secure." (b) **Possible response:** The strongest example includes the parallel phrases "the strong are just," "the weak secure," and "the peace preserved," because it includes an emotional appeal and ends the paragraph.
3. The lines combine a parallel sentence structure that contrasts two related but opposite ideas.
4. (a) King uses two parallel structures. First, he begins each of the first two sentences with the clause "If I have said anything in this letter." Then he contrasts the words "indicative of an unreasonable impatience" with "indicative of my having a patience." (b) The effect shows a balance between the ideas.
5. The effect is both logical and emotional because he first links examples and facts; then, he adds emotional appeal by referring to the "uncertain balance of terror."
6. (a) Words include "trumpet summons us again," "burden," "twilight struggle," "rejoicing in hope, patient in tribulation," and "tyranny, poverty, disease, and war itself." (b) It shows both hope that something can be done and horror if nothing is done.
7. (a) King addresses the clergymen and the public. (b) He refers to himself as a "fellow clergyman and a Christian brother" and to the "fear-drenched communities."
8. Details include his reference to the opportunity that "few generations have been granted the role of defending freedom in its hour of maximum danger" and his statement that "I do not believe that any of us would exchange places with any other people or any other generation."
9. The people of the South will be recognized.

Answers continued

10. **Possible response:** It is not necessary but it is important because it enables a leader to inspire followers and give them courage.

Go Online Assessment Students may use the **Self-test** to prepare for **Selection Test A** or **Selection Test B.**

EXTEND/ASSESS

Answers

1 Vocabulary Lesson

Word Analysis

1. to change from one thing into another; *-vert-*
2. to turn aside; *-vert-*
3. person who tends to turn one's thoughts upon oneself; *-vert-*
4. able to do many things, to turn easily from one thing to another; *-vers-*
5. to turn upside down; *-vert-*
6. an arguing of an important question on which differences of opinion exist—that is, on which the arguers are turned in opposite directions; *-vers-*

Spelling Strategy

1. compelled
2. referred
3. combated
4. offered
5. waxed
6. permitted

Vocabulary Builder

1. b
2. c
3. a
4. a
5. c
6. b
7. b
8. a
9. c
10. a

2 Grammar and Style Lesson

1. In his inaugural, Kennedy reassured our allies, addressed our adversaries, and reaffirmed our commitment to liberty.
2. Kennedy reminded his audience that civility was not a sign of weakness and that sincerity was always subject to proof.
3. Kennedy's words, sentences, and inspired paragraphs thrilled listeners at the time.
4. King compares and contrasts the use of immoral means to attain moral ends with the use of moral means to preserve immoral ends.
5. King employs a variety of rhetorical devices, including parallelism, repetition, antithesis, and questions.

Writing Application

Students' descriptions should mention in parallel structure a series of related points.

Build Language Skills

1 Vocabulary Lesson

Word Analysis: Latin Root *-vert-* or *-vers-*

The Latin root *-vert-* or *-vers-* means "to turn." Write the definition of each word shown below. Then, find the root of the word in a dictionary.

1. convert
2. divert
3. introvert
4. versatile
5. invert
6. controversy

Spelling Strategy

To add a suffix beginning with a vowel to a word ending in a vowel plus a consonant in a stressed syllable, double the final consonant: *impel* becomes *impelled*. There are two exceptions: words ending in *-x* or *-w*, and words in which the stress changes after the suffix is added.

Using a dictionary, if necessary, complete each word below, using the suffix *-ed*.

1. compel_____
2. refer_____
3. combat_____
4. offer_____
5. wax_____
6. permit_____

Vocabulary Builder: Synonyms

For each item, choose the letter of the word or phrase that is closest in meaning.

1. flagrant: **(a)** tasty **(b)** obvious **(c)** contorted
2. monotony: **(a)** difference **(b)** excitement **(c)** uniformity
3. tyranny: **(a)** harshness **(b)** monarchy **(c)** rebellion
4. heirs: **(a)** descendents **(b)** critics **(c)** listeners
5. impelled: **(a)** erased **(b)** weakened **(c)** urged
6. alliance: **(a)** contact **(b)** association **(c)** program
7. profundity: **(a)** exploration **(b)** intense thought **(c)** ambiguity
8. invective: **(a)** insult **(b)** apology **(c)** rhetorical device
9. eradicate: **(a)** analyze **(b)** redefine **(c)** erase
10. adversary: **(a)** antagonist **(b)** friend **(c)** minister

2 Grammar and Style Lesson

Parallel Structure

In your writing, be careful to avoid **faulty parallelism**—the use of dissimilar grammatical structures to express similar ideas.

Faulty: The goals of the civil rights movement included *full equality, racial justice,* and *to have economic opportunity.*

Parallel: The goals of the civil rights movement included *full equality, racial justice,* and *economic opportunity.*

Practice Rewrite the following sentences, using correct parallel structure.

1. In his inaugural, Kennedy reassured our allies, addressed our adversaries, and reaffirming our commitment to liberty.
2. Kennedy reminded his audience that civility was not a sign of weakness and that sincerity to be always subject to proof.
3. Kennedy's words, sentences, and the way he spoke in inspiring paragraphs thrilled listeners at the time.
4. King compares and contrasts using immoral means to attain moral ends with the use of moral means for immoral ends.
5. King employs a variety of rhetorical devices, including parallelism, repetition, antithesis, and questions that are rhetorical.

Writing Application Write a description of a political event, like an inauguration. Use parallel structure to call attention to the key details.

WG Prentice Hall Writing and Grammar Connection: Chapter 20, Section 6

Writing Lesson

Timed Writing: Public Letter

Write a **public letter** or **letter to the editor** commenting on an issue that you feel strongly about. In your letter, keep in mind the needs, views, and prior knowledge of the particular audience you are addressing. ***(40 minutes)***

Prewriting ***(10 minutes)*** Briefly freewrite to generate ideas for your letter. Use a chart like the one shown to list your ideas.

Issue: ____________________

Opinion Statement: ____________________

Persuasive Support:

Logical	Emotional	Ethical
______	______	______
______	______	______

Drafting ***(20 minutes)*** Present your main idea or viewpoint about the issue in an opinion statement. As you draft, support your main idea with a variety of details, using logical, emotional, and ethical appeals. In addition, use parallel structure as a rhetorical device.

Revising ***(10 minutes)*** Review your paper to be sure that you have used language persuasively and that you have supported your opinion statement adequately. Then, revise for coherence, making sure you link ideas smoothly and logically.

WG *Prentice Hall Writing and Grammar Connection: Chapter 7, Section 4*

Extend Your Learning

Listening and Speaking Develop a **speech** that presents a vision for the future. Use rhetorical devices to persuade your audience to accept your vision. Challenge yourself to develop at least one memorable line (such as Kennedy's "Ask not . . ."). Record the draft to evaluate your own speaking skills. Use these tips:

- Choose words that suit your audience.
- Work to convey poise and confidence and to control any public-speaking anxiety.
- Avoid distracting behaviors such as fidgeting or unintended pausing.

Research and Technology With a partner or a group, use library resources and the Internet to research the April 1963 protests held in Birmingham, Alabama, that led to the arrest of Martin Luther King, Jr. Locate newspaper and magazine articles, photographs, cartoons, television news reports, and protest songs. Present your findings in a **multimedia presentation. [Group Activity]**

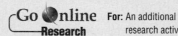

For: An additional research activity
Visit: www.PHSchool.com
Web Code: erd-7617

❸ Writing Lesson

You may use this Writing Lesson as timed-writing practice, or you may allow students to develop the letter as a writing assignment over several days.

- Give students the **Support for Writing Lesson,** p. 302 in ***Unit 6 Resources,*** to use as they write their letters.
- Read through the Writing Lesson steps with students and clarify any confusion.
- Suggest to students that they list ideas for their letters. Tell them to jot down controversial topics that interest them. After they have built a list, tell them to go back and choose one entry as a topic for their letters.
- Use the Persuasion: Persuasive Essay rubrics in ***General Resources,*** pp. 45–46, to evaluate students' letters.

❹ Listening and Speaking

- Suggest that students work in pairs to practice their speeches and to give each other feedback. Alternatively, suggest that students record their practice sessions so they can critique themselves.
- Encourage students to consider how gestures and facial expressions can enhance their presentation. Tell them to also think about how they can use changes in tone, pacing, and loudness to convey important ideas.
- Use the Peer Assessment: Speech rubric in ***General Resources,*** p. 129, to evaluate students' letters.
- The **Support for Extend Your Learning,** p. 303, in ***Unit 6 Resources*** provides guided note-taking opportunities to help students complete the Extend Your Learning activities.

Go Online Research Have students type in the Web Code for another research activity.

Assessment Resources

The following resources can be used to assess students' knowledge and skills.

Unit 6 Resources
Selection Test A, pp. 305–307
Selection Test B, pp. 308–310

General Resources
Rubrics for Persuasion: Persuasive Essay, pp. 45–46
Rubric for Peer Assessment: Speech, p. 129

Go Online Assessment Students may use the **Self-test** to prepare for **Selection Test A** or **Selection Test B.**

Meeting Your Standards

Students will

1. **analyze and respond to literary elements.**
   - Literary Analysis: Lyric Poetry
2. **read, comprehend, analyze, and critique poetry.**
   - Reading Strategy: Reading in Sentences
   - Reading Check questions
   - Apply the Skills questions
   - Assessment Practice (ATE)
3. **develop vocabulary.**
   - Vocabulary Lesson: Related Words: *Heritage*
4. **understand and apply written and oral language conventions.**
   - Spelling Strategy
   - Grammar and Style Lesson: Sequence of Tenses
5. **develop writing proficiency.**
   - Writing Lesson: Ghost Story
6. **develop appropriate research strategies.**
   - Extend Your Learning: Multimedia Cultural Presentation
7. **understand and apply listening and speaking strategies.**
   - Extend Your Learning: Interview

Block Scheduling: Use one 90-minute class period to preteach the skills and have students read the selection. Use a second 90-minute class period to assess students' mastery of skills, extend their learning, and monitor their progress.

Homework Suggestions

Following are possibilities for homework assignments.

- Support pages from *Unit 6 Resources:*
  Literary Analysis
  Reading Strategy
  Vocabulary Builder
  Grammar and Style
- An Extend Your Learning project and the Writing Lesson
  for this selection group may be completed over several days.

Step-by-Step Teaching Guide	Pacing Guide
PRETEACH	
• Administer Vocabulary and Reading Warm-ups as necessary.	5 min.
• Engage students' interest with the motivation activity.	5 min.
• Read and discuss author and background features. **FT**	10 min.
• Introduce the Literary Analysis Skill: Lyric Poetry. **FT**	5 min.
• Introduce the Reading Strategy: Reading in Sentences. **FT**	10 min.
• Prepare students to read by teaching the selection vocabulary. **FT**	
TEACH	
• Informally monitor comprehension while students read independently or in groups. **FT**	30 min.
• Monitor students' comprehension with the Reading Check notes.	as students read
• Reinforce vocabulary with Vocabulary Builder notes.	as students read
• Develop students' understanding of lyric poetry with the Literary Analysis annotations. **FT**	5 min.
• Develop students' ability to read in sentences with the Reading Strategy annotations. **FT**	5 min.
ASSESS/EXTEND	
• Assess students' comprehension and mastery of the Literary Analysis and Reading Strategy by having them answer the Apply the Skills questions. **FT**	15 min.
• Have students complete the Vocabulary Lesson and the Grammar and Style Lesson. **FT**	15 min.
• Apply students' ability to use sensory details by using the Writing Lesson. **FT**	45 min. or homework
• Apply students' understanding by using one or more of the Extend Your Learning activities.	20–90 min. or homework
• Administer Selection Test A or Selection Test B. **FT**	15 min.

Resources

PRINT

Unit 6 Resources

Vocabulary Warm-up Word Lists **[L1, L2, EL]** .... p. 311
Vocabulary Warm-up Practice **[L1, L2, EL]** .... p. 312
Reading Warm-up A **[L1, L2, EL]** .... p. 313
Reading Warm-up B **[L1, L2, L3]** .... p. 314

TRANSPARENCY

Graphic Organizer Transparencies

Literary Analysis Graphic Organizer A **[L3]** .... p. 282
Literary Analysis Graphic Organizer B **[L1, L2, EL]** .... p. 283
Reading Strategy Graphic Organizer A **[L3]** .... p. 284
Reading Strategy Graphic Organizer B **[L1, L2, EL]** .... p. 285

PRINT

Reader's Notebook [L2]
Reader's Notebook: Adapted Version [L1]
Reader's Notebook: English Learner's Version [EL]

Unit 6 Resources

Literary Analysis **[L3]** .... p. 315
Reading Strategy **[L3]** .... p. 316
Vocabulary Builder **[L3]** .... p. 317

TECHNOLOGY

Listening to Literature Audio CDs [L2, EL]

PRINT

Unit 6 Resources

Grammar and Style **[L3]** .... p. 318
Support for Writing Lesson **[L3]** .... p. 319
Support for Extend Your Learning **[L3]** .... p. 320
Enrichment **[L4]** .... p. 321
Selection Test A **[L1, L2, EL]** .... pp. 322–324
Selection Test B **[L3, L4]** .... pp. 325–327

General Resources

Rubrics for Narration: Short Story **[L3]** .... pp. 57–58
Rubric for Speaking: Delivering a Research Presentation **[L3]** .... p. 92

TECHNOLOGY

Go Online: Research **[L3]**
Go Online: Self-test **[L3]**
ExamView® **Test Bank [L3]**

Choosing Resources for Differentiated Instruction

[L1] Special Needs Students
[L2] Below-Level Students
[L3] All Students
[L4] Advanced Students
[EL] English Learners

For Vocabulary and Reading Warm-ups and for Selection Tests, **A** signifies "less challenging" and **B** "more challenging." For Graphic Organizer transparencies, **A** signifies "not filled in" and **B** "filled in."

FT Fast Track Instruction: To move the lesson more quickly, use the strategies and activities identified with **FT**.

Scaffolding for Less Proficient and Advanced Students

The leveled Critical Thinking questions after selections progress in the levels of thinking required to answer them. To address the needs of your different students, you may use the (a) level questions for your less proficient students and the (b) level questions with your on-level and advanced students. The occasional (c) level questions are appropriate for your advanced students.

PRENTICE HALL **TeacherEXPRESS™** Plan · Teach · Assess Use this complete suite of powerful teaching tools to make lesson planning and testing quicker and easier.

PRENTICE HALL **StudentEXPRESS™** Learn · Study · Succeed Use the interactive textbook (online and on CD-ROM) to make selections and activities come alive with audio and video support and interactive questions.

Benchmark

After students have completed these poems, administer **Benchmark Test 11.** If the Benchmark Test reveals that some students need further work, use the **Interpretation Guide** to determine the appropriate reteaching pages in the **Reading Kit** or on **Success Tracker.**

Go Online Professional Development **For:** Information about Lexiles
Visit: www.PHSchool.com
Web Code: eue-1111

PRETEACH

Motivation

How important is it that children learn about history and experiences of previous generations? In what ways can one generation help educate another when the world changes so drastically every year? Ask students to consider these questions and the ideas they would stress if they were to write a letter to the children of the future. What important lessons about life or what lessons from history would they want to convey? You might pair students to write the letters and then have the class compare their ideas with those expressed in McElroy's poem.

❶ Background

More About the Authors

Colleen McElroy discovered her interest in the past and in stories as a young girl captivated by her grandmother's boudoir mirror and wind-up Victrola. Travel soon added a dimension to this "romance with language." It began during her childhood when she moved frequently with her mother and army sergeant stepfather, and continues to this day. Says McElroy about traveling and writing: "Each piece of writing is a new port of call, full of surprises and disappointments, pleasures and intrigue."

Louise Erdrich's experiences raising her five children have changed the way she writes. She says that being a mother sometimes makes it hard to face the world's cruelties. A mother instinctively "protects the imagination against . . . [negative] intrusion."

Yusef Komunyakaa was born on April 29, 1947, in Bogalusa, Louisiana. He is the eldest of five children. Komunyakaa uses his childhood experiences to inform many of his works: His familial relationships, his maturation in a rural Southern community, and the musical environment afforded by the close proximity of the jazz and blues center of New Orleans provide fundamental themes for several of his volumes.

❶ For My Children • Bidwell Ghost • Camouflaging the Chimera

Colleen McElroy (b. 1935)

Like a modern-day explorer, Colleen McElroy enjoys experiencing new places and has traveled widely throughout the United States and abroad. Her many adventures have included island hopping in Fiji, exploring Malaysia, climbing Machu Picchu, and riding a motorcycle at age 58 across the Australian desert. In her poetry, McElroy often delves into her rich African American and Pacific Islander heritage to find connections between experiences of the past, realities of the present, and hopes for the future.

After growing up in St. Louis, Missouri, McElroy graduated from Kansas State University and earned a doctorate from the University of Washington, where she is now a professor of English. A prolific writer, her books include the poetry collection *What Madness Brought Me Here* (1990) and the travel memoir entitled *A Long Way from St. Louie* (1997).

Louise Erdrich (b. 1954)

Louise Erdrich was born in Little Falls, Minnesota. Her mother was of Chippewa and French descent, and her father was German American. Both of her parents were teachers at the Bureau of Indian Affairs school in Wahpeton, North Dakota.

After graduating from Dartmouth College, Erdrich taught poetry and writing to young people and then earned a master's degree in creative writing from Johns Hopkins University.

Erdrich settled in New Hampshire and published her first volume of poems, *Jacklight* (1984). Her debut novel, *Love Medicine* (1984), is the story of three Chippewa families living on a North Dakota reservation in the early part of the twentieth century. Erdrich's reputation grew with the publication of three sequels to the book, *The Beet Queen* (1986), *Tracks* (1988), and *The Bingo Palace* (1994). Her most recent novel is *Four Souls* (2004).

Yusef Komunyakaa (b. 1947)

"It took me fourteen years to write poems about Vietnam," said Yusef Komunyakaa (yo͞o′ sef kō mun yä′ kä) in 1994, shortly after winning the Pulitzer Prize for *Neon Vernacular.* "I had never thought about writing about it, and in a way I had been systematically writing around it."

Komunyakaa was born in Bogalusa, Louisiana. He joined the army and went to Vietnam in 1965. Serving as an "information specialist," he reported from the front lines, edited a military newspaper called *The Southern Cross*, and earned a Bronze Star. After the war, he pursued his education, earning a B.A. at the University of Colorado, an M.A. at Colorado State University, and an M.F.A. at the University of California, Irvine. In 1977, he published his first collection of poetry, and he has been publishing poetry ever since, including *Dien Cai Dau* (1988) and *Taboo* (2004). Komunyakaa teaches at Princeton University and is Chancellor of the Academy of American Poets.

Preview

Connecting to the Literature

The stories we hear from relatives, family friends, and neighbors help shape our awareness of our heritage and our history. In different ways, all of these poems explore the mythic power of stories and memories.

Literary Analysis

Lyric Poetry

Lyric poetry is melodic poetry that expresses the observations and feelings of a single speaker. Lyric poems were originally sung to the accompaniment of a stringed instrument called a lyre. Though rarely set to music today, lyric poems are still brief and melodic. Unlike narrative poems that tell stories, lyric poems focus on producing a single effect. In these lines from "Bidwell Ghost," for example, the speaker recalls vivid impressions of a fiery tragedy.

It has been twenty years
since her house surged and burst in the dark trees

As you read each poem, use a chart like the one shown to record the words and phrases that contribute to a single unifying effect.

Detail

Detail | Detail | Detail

Single Effect

Comparing Literary Works

All of these poems speak about memories of the past. In "For My Children," the past is presented in a positive light, as a pleasant place that holds a family's history. In "Bidwell Ghost," the past is seen in a terrifying light, as a dangerous place, where a great tragedy occurred. In "Camouflaging the Chimera," the past is a place of terror and moral ambiguity. As you read, think about how each speaker presents and responds to the memory that is the focus of the poem.

Reading Strategy

Reading in Sentences

Like prose, many poems are written in sentences. They are also written in lines, but poets do not always complete sentences at the end of a line. Instead, a sentence may extend for several lines and then end in the middle of a line so that the poet can keep to a chosen rhythm and rhyme scheme. To understand the meaning of a poem, **read in sentences**. Notice the punctuation. Do not make a full stop at the end of a line unless there is a period, colon, semicolon, or dash.

Vocabulary Builder

shackles (shakʹ əlz) *n.* restraints on freedom of expression or action (p. 1241)

heritage (herʹ i tij) *n.* something handed down from one's ancestors or from the past (p. 1241)

effigies (efʹ i jēz) *n.* likenesses; figures, such as dolls or statues (p. 1241)

refuge (refʹ yo͞oj) *n.* shelter or protection from danger (p. 1246)

2 Literary Analysis
Lyric Poetry

- Tell students that as they read, they will focus on lyric poetry, in which words and phrases create a single unifying effect.
- After discussing the Literary Analysis instruction, have two volunteers read the poems aloud. Discuss each poet's use of vivid verbs such as *surged* and *burst* to create strong images.
- Model the use of the chart on the student page and direct students to complete **Literary Analysis Graphic Organizer A,** p. 282, in ***Graphic Organizer Transparencies*** as they read the poems.
- Discuss the instruction under Comparing Literary Works. Guide students to understand how flashback provides information that contributes to the meaning of a lyric poem.

3 Reading Strategy
Reading in Sentences

- Explain to students that reading in sentences helps readers better understand the meaning of a poem.
- Review with students the stops indicated by various types of punctuation. For example, a period indicates a longer pause than does a comma.

Vocabulary Builder

- Pronounce each vocabulary word for students, and read the definitions as a class. Have students identify any words with which they are already familiar.

Differentiated Instruction
Solutions for All Learners

Support for Special Needs Students

Have students complete the **Preview** and **Build Skills** pages for these selections in the ***Reader's Notebook: Adapted Version.*** These pages provide a selection summary, an abbreviated presentation of the reading and literary skills, and the graphic organizer on the **Build Skills** page in the student book.

Support for Less Proficient Readers

Have students complete the **Preview** and **Build Skills** pages for these selections in the ***Reader's Notebook.*** These pages provide a selection summary, an abbreviated presentation of the reading and literary skills, and the graphic organizer on the **Build Skills** page in the student book.

Support for English Learners

Have students complete the **Preview** and **Build Skills** pages for these selections in the ***Reader's Notebook: English Learner's Version.*** These pages provide a selection summary, an abbreviated presentation of the skills, and the graphic organizer on the **Build Skills** page in the student book.

TEACH

Learning Modalities
Interpersonal Learners Encourage students to respond to the poems by writing journal entries. Suggest that the entries take the form of poems based on their own cultural heritage or on stories that have been passed down to them.

❶ About the Selection

The speaker of "For My Children" searches for a heritage to share with her children, an African American heritage that extends "beyond St. Louis" all the way back "to Ashanti mysteries and rituals." As she delves into her store of tales, thoughts, and memories, she invokes many rich possibilities. She also discovers that the present and past are not as separate and discontinuous as they may seem—they mingle joyously in the children she observes.

❷ Humanities

The Madonna and Child by Momodou Ceesay

In this watercolor, contemporary artist Momodou Ceesay combines traditional elements of both African and European art. The effect is simultaneously tender and vibrant. The painting—filled with strong angles, vivid colors, and intense pattern repetition—pulses with life and contrast.

Use these questions for discussion:

1. How does the subject of the painting reflect the theme of the poem?
   Answer: The mother in the painting looks closely at the child, just as the speaker in the poem looks closely at her children to find links between the past and present.
2. How does the artist's use of color correspond to the images in the poem?
   Answer: The painting's vibrant colors appeal to the sense of sight; sensory images in the poem appeal to the sense of sight as well as hearing and touch.

❶

Colleen McElroy

❷

❸ ▲ **Critical Viewing** In what ways does this painting reflect the heritage that the speaker seeks to hand on to her children? Explain. **[Analyze]**

Differentiated Instruction Solutions for All Learners

Accessibility at a Glance

	For My Children	Bidwell Ghost	Camouflaging the Chimera
Context	African American heritge	Native American heritage	Vietnam War
Language	Conversational	Uncomplicated diction and syntax	Informal
Concept Level	Accessible (examination of heritage)	Accessible (legend)	Challenging (experience of war)
Literary Merit	Cross-cultural experience	Cross-cultural	Suspenseful
Lexile	NP	NP	NP
Overall Rating	Average	Average	More challenging

Background

In recent years, many Americans have become fascinated by oral history—the information gathered through interviews with individuals who can recall events and people of years past. Oral histories of families and communities are especially popular.

In societies without a written language, oral information that was passed down from one generation to the next took the place of written historical accounts. The speaker of "For My Children" is a collector of the oral history of her people. In telling this poem, she sifts through many facts and images of the past and passes on to the reader those she finds most striking.

I have stored up tales for you, my children
My favorite children, my only children;
Of <u>shackles</u> and slaves and a bill of rights.
But skin of honey and beauty of ebony begins
In the land called Bilad as-Sudan,[1]
❹ So I search for a <u>heritage</u> beyond St. Louis.

❺ My memory floats down a long narrow hall,
A calabash[2] of history.
Grandpa stood high in Watusi[3] shadows
In this land of yearly rituals for alabaster beauty;
Where <u>effigies</u> of my ancestors are captured
In Beatle tunes,
And crowns never touch Bantu[4] heads.

My past is a slender dancer reflected briefly
Like a leopard in fingers of fire.
The future of Dahomey[5] is a house of 16 doors,
The totem of the Burundi[6] counts 17 warriors—
In reverse generations.
While I cling to one stray Seminole.[7]

1. **Bilad as-Sudan** (bē lād′ äs so͞o dan′) "land of the blacks," an Arabic expression by which Arab geographers referred to the settled African countries north of the southern edge of the Sahara.
2. **calabash** (kal′ ə bash′) *n.* dried, hollow shell of a gourd, used as a bowl or a cup.
3. **Watusi** (wä to͞o′ sē) people of east-central Africa.
4. **Bantu** (ban′ to͞o) Bantu-speaking peoples of southern Africa.
5. **Dahomey** (də hō′ mē) old name for Benin, in west-central Africa.
6. **Burundi** (boo roon′ dē) country in east-central Africa.
7. **Seminole** (sem′ ə nōl′) Native American people from Florida.

Vocabulary Builder

shackles (shak′ əlz) *n.* restraints on freedom of expression or action

heritage (her′ i tij′) *n.* something handed down from one's ancestors or from the past

effigies (ef′ i jēz) *n.* likenesses; figures, such as dolls or statues

❻  **Reading Check**

What has the speaker stored up for her children?

Differentiated Instruction Solutions for All Learners

Strategy for Special Needs Students
Students may find the figurative language of the poems confusing, particularly the metaphors in "For My Children." Encourage students to identify difficult images as they read. Guide them in questioning and determining the meaning of each image.

Strategy for English Learners
To help students understand the cultural references in "For My Children," encourage them to make a chart listing unfamiliar names of places, objects, and people. Then, have them jot down a brief explanation of each reference, using information from the numbered side notes.

Strategy for Advanced Readers
Advanced readers can be challenged to analyze some of the more difficult figurative language in the poem. Encourage them to explain the meaning of phrases such as "yearly rituals for alabaster beauty," "The wrought-iron rail of first stairs," and "her house surged and burst."

❸ Critical Viewing

Answer: The mother's traditional African clothing and the painting's stylized African landscape reflect the ancient African heritage McElroy describes.

❹ Vocabulary Builder
Related Words: *heritage*

- Call students' attention to the word *heritage* and its definition. Tell students that there are several words related to *heritage.*
- List the words presented in the Vocabulary Lesson: *heredity, inherit,* and *inheritance.* Have students suggest meanings for these words, using a dictionary if necessary.
- Invite students to write sentences using these words and the context of the two poems presented here.

❺ Literary Analysis
Lyric Poetry

- **Ask** students to note details or allusions that they recognize in the bracketed stanza. List these on the chalk board.
  Possible responses: Students will likely recognize allusions to the Beatles and the Bantu and Watusi peoples.
- Lead students to see how the progression of images in the stanza contributes to a single effect, which illuminates the speaker's sense of her own history.
- Let students know that in Africa, the calabash gourd was dried and used as a container. The speaker compares her memory to such an ancestral gourd.
- Help students to interpret the remaining images and references, and summarize the stanza's effect. Students should note that the figure of the speaker's grandfather is pictured in a country celebrating "yearly rituals for alabaster beauty" —perhaps beauty pageants—and in which rock-and-roll tunes founded on black musical traditions make millions for white artists. The stanza closes with an image of purloined African royal crowns. The effect of the stanza is to evoke long years of exile and discrimination.

❻ Reading Check

Answer: She has stored up tales of their shared heritage.

ASSESS

Answers

1. Urge students to generalize beyond the specific cultures mentioned in the poem.
2. (a) She addresses her children. (b) She wants to share stories of their heritage with them.
3. (a) She names the Watusi, Bantu, Seminole, Ashanti, and Ibo cultures. (b) The images suggest a grand and noble family, full of regal power. (c) Images include a house of 16 doors and a 17-warrior totem.
4. (a) She mentions the Mississippi and Congo rivers. (b) The Congo reflects the deep past and their African ancestry, while the Mississippi ties them to present-day America.
5. (a) The ancestral heritage of African Americans, with all its depth and grandeur, continues in current and future generations. (b) The speaker sees reflections of Africa—its physical landscape, art, and the beauty of its people—in the young children around her.
6. **Possible responses:** Children who are aware of their heritage can appreciate not only their own ancestral culture, but may also be more respectful of cultural diversity in general; they may be able to share their heritage with others; and they may develop more self-confidence.

Go Online Author Link For additional information about Colleen McElroy, have students type in the Web Code, then select *M* from the alphabet, and then Colleen McElroy.

My thoughts grow thin in the urge to travel
Beyond Grandma's tale
Of why cat fur is for kitten britches;
Past the wrought-iron rail of first stairs
In baby white shoes,
To Ashanti[8] mysteries and rituals.

Back in the narrow hallway of my childhood.
I cradled my knees
In limbs as smooth and long as the neck of a bud vase,
I began this ancestral search that you children yield now
In profile and bust
By common invention, in being and belonging.

The line of your cheeks recalls Ibo[9] melodies
As surely as oboe and flute.
The sun dances a honey and cocoa duet on your faces.
I see smiles that mirror schoolboy smiles
In the land called Bilad as-Sudan;
I see the link between the Mississippi and the Congo.

8. **Ashanti** (ə shän′ tə) people of western Africa.
9. **Ibo** (ē′ bō′) African people of southeastern Nigeria.

Critical Reading

1. **Respond:** Does this poem stir up thoughts about your own ancestors and cultural traditions? Why or why not?
2. **(a) Recall:** To whom does the speaker address this poem?
   (b) Infer: What is the speaker's reason for addressing the poem to them?
3. **(a) Recall:** Identify the cultures in which the speaker searches for evidence of her heritage. **(b) Analyze:** In the second and third stanzas, what impressions of her ancestors does the speaker convey? **(c) Analyze:** What images shape these impressions?
4. **(a) Recall:** Which two rivers does the speaker mention in the last stanza? **(b) Interpret:** Why might these two rivers be important to the speaker and to her children?
5. **(a) Interpret:** What is the poem's theme, or central message?
   (b) Support: What details or ideas in the poem support your interpretation?
6. **Apply:** In what specific ways might educating children about their heritage affect the choices they make in life?

For: More about Colleen McElroy
Visit: www.PHSchool.com
Web Code: ere-9632

Enrichment

Oral History

Oral history is as old as the study of history itself. As early as the fifth century B.C., the Greek historians Herodotus and Thucydides relied upon the oral accounts of survivors of wars to provide a basis for their written histories.

Among Native American cultures, such as the Chippewa from whom Louise Erdrich gains much of her identity, oral literature was the primary means of communicating the history and values of a people. Oral literature includes oral histories, ritual drama, chanting, ceremonies, and songs, speeches, and narratives.

Today, interest in oral history has been advanced by the commitment of anthropologists, sociologists, historians, and artists who regard the oral tradition as a serious and vital part of all cultures.

7

Bidwell Ghost

Louise Erdrich

Winter, Ozz Franca

8

9 ◄ **Critical Viewing**

What features of this painting are reminiscent of phrases from the poem? Explain. **[Connect]**

Each night she waits by the road
in a thin white dress
embroidered with fire.

It has been twenty years
since her house surged and burst in the dark trees.
Still nobody goes there.

The heat charred the branches
of the apple trees,
but nothing can kill that wood.

10 

Reading Check

What is remarkable about the apple trees?

7 About the Selection

Like "For My Children," "Bidwell Ghost" is a multi-layered lyric poem that explores the effect of the past on the present. On one level, the poem presents a legend passed on to the poet and storyteller, who in turn passes it on to the reader. On another level, it probes the fate of a figure who is haunted and tormented by a tragic past.

8 Humanities

Winter by Ozz Franca

Like the Bidwell ghost, the figure in *Winter* emanates mystery and seems immersed in her own thoughts. The shadowy features give the figure an air of mystery. The red area adds warmth that could symbolize fire or blood.

Use these questions for discussion:

1. In what ways is the mood of this illustration similar to the mood of the poem?
   Answer: Both have dramatic, mysterious, and somber moods.
2. Does the illustration reflect the mental image you have of the Bidwell ghost? Explain.
   Possible response: The illustration mostly matches the image I formed while reading, however, the ghost in the poem wears a "thin white dress" while the figure in the illustration seems to be wrapped in a warm cloak.

9 Critical Viewing

Answer: The woman in the painting appears to have a "blackened nest of hair," and the images of cold in the poem are reflected in her posture. Like the ghost, the woman in the painting stands alone, dressed in a white garment edged in flame-like color that suggests it has been "embroidered with fire."

10 Reading Check

Answer: They were charred by heat, but not killed.

Differentiated Instruction

Solutions for All Learners

Support for Less Proficient Readers
Share the information given under the heading **Support for English Learners** with less proficient readers. Tell them to assume that the word *bidwell* means "bids well." Then, help them confirm the sense of this definition by searching for a synonym. Invite students to present their alternative title ideas to the class.

Support for English Learners
Read the title aloud to students. Tell them that the word *bidwell* is not in a dictionary. Explain that it may be a surname, the name of a place, or an invented word made by combining the verb *bid* and the adverb *well.* After students read the poem, invite their opinion as to which explanation makes the most sense.

Enrichment for Gifted/Talented Students
Discuss the title with students, asking them to share any knowledge they may have of literature about ghosts. Challenge students to complete the Writing Lesson, and then to share their ghost stories orally with the class.

⓫ Reading Strategy
Reading in Sentences

- Draw students' attention to the bracketed stanza. **Ask** students how many sentences appear in these four lines.
  Answer: There are two sentences.
- **Ask** students to read the stanza as sentences, and note how Erdrich breaks the sentences into lines. What effect does this have on the reader?
  Answer: Students should note that Erdrich's line breaks work to divide the sentences into smaller units of meaning. This forces the reader to slow down and appreciate the solemnity of the account of the ghost.

  Then **ask** students the Reading Strategy question: In the last stanza, where should you pause in the middle of a line?
  Answer: You should pause at the end of the first sentence.

ASSESS
Answers

1. Students may have questions about the identity or history of the woman the poem describes.
2. (a) A house burned down. (b) A young woman was affected.
3. (a) She waits by the road for a ride to her old house. (b) Her behavior is strange, antisocial, and full of pain. (c) She might behave this way because she has been hurt by the loss of her home.
4. (a) They blossom. (b) It suggests that new life emerges despite crippling losses.
5. (a) The child is the ghost. (b) Erdrich uses this word to suggest that the ghost is vulnerable to pain and dependent on others.
6. **Possible response:** Ghosts are one way in which people deal with the mystery of death.
7. (a) She suggests that tragedy has an open-ended, permanent effect on people. (b) Students should be able to support their responses.

Go Online **Author Link** For additional information about Louise Erdrich, have students type in the Web Code, then select *E* from the alphabet, and then Louise Erdrich.

She will climb into your car
but not say where she is going
and you shouldn't ask.

Nor should you try to comb the blackened nest of hair
or press the agates of tears
back into her eyes.

First the orchard bowed low and complained
of the unpicked fruit,
then the branches cracked apart and fell.

The windfalls sweetened to wine
beneath the ruined arms and snow.
Each spring now, in the grass, buds form on the tattered wood.

⓫
The child, the child, why is she so persistent
in her need? Is it so terrible
to be alone when the cold white blossoms
come to life and burn?

Reading Strategy
Reading in Sentences
In the last stanza, where should you pause in the middle of a line?

Critical Reading

1. **Respond:** What questions arose in your mind as you read this poem? Were they all answered? Explain.
2. **(a) Recall:** What occurred twenty years ago?
   (b) Draw Conclusions: Who or what was affected by that event?
3. **(a) Recall:** What does the Bidwell ghost do each night?
   (b) Interpret: How would you describe the Bidwell ghost's attitude or behavior? **(c) Speculate:** Why might the ghost feel or behave this way?
4. **(a) Recall:** What happens to the apple trees each spring?
   (b) Analyze: What does this image suggest about nature's resilience?
5. **(a) Analyze:** Who is "the child" in the final stanza? **(b) Speculate:** Why do you think the speaker uses this term?
6. **Speculate:** Why do you think people from so many cultures are fascinated with ghosts?
7. **(a) Interpret:** What does the poet suggest about the lasting impact of tragedy? **(b) Take a Position:** Do you agree with this idea? Explain.

Author Link
For: More about Louise Erdrich
Visit: www.PHSchool.com
Web Code: ere-9633

Camouflaging the Chimera[1]

Yusef Komunyakaa

Background American involvement in the Vietnam War lasted from 1961 to 1973. The war presented American military forces with the frustrating and terrifying problem of how to fight in dense jungle against the Viet Cong (or VC), an enemy capable of magically "merging" with the landscape. As this poem demonstrates, part of the answer to this problem involved sending small groups of American soldiers into the jungle to wait in ambush for the elusive enemy.

We tied branches to our helmets.
We painted our faces & rifles
with mud from a riverbank,

blades of grass hung from the pockets
of our tiger suits. We wove
13 ourselves into the terrain,
content to be a hummingbird's target.

We hugged bamboo & leaned
against a breeze off the river,
slow-dragging with ghosts

from Saigon to Bangkok,
with women left in doorways

1. **Chimera** (kī′ mir′ ə) from Greek mythology, a firebreathing monster with a lion's head, a goat's body, and a serpent's tail.

12 About the Selection

"Camouflaging the Chimera" is a suspenseful, first-person description of how it feels to lie in ambush for hours, waiting for the approach of enemy soldiers.

Differentiated Instruction

Solutions for All Learners

Support for Less Proficient Readers
These students may be unfamiliar with the cities of Saigon and Bangkok. Use a map or globe to show students the location of the cities.

Enrichment for English Learners
Your class may include Vietnamese or Hmong immigrants whose relatives fought in the Vietnam War, or whose families were relocated to the United States as a result of the war. Speak to these students privately before beginning these selections and ask whether there are any family stories about the war they would be willing to share with the class.

Strategy for Advanced Readers
Encourage these students to compare the two works. What similar ideas and images, if any, do they convey about the Vietnam War? How do the different forms—poetry and fictional memoir—affect these ideas and images? Which piece did students prefer, and why?

⓭ Reading Strategy
Reading in Sentences

- Remind students that reading in sentences can help a reader understand a poem's meaning.
- Then, **ask** the Reading Strategy question: Which stanzas contain sentences that continue into the next stanza?
  Answer: The first, third, fifth, sixth, seventh, and eighth stanzas all continue into the next stanza.

ASSESS

Answers

1. Possible responses include fear, anticipation, anxiety, and excitement. Students should support their responses with details.
2. (a) It is set in the jungles of Vietnam. (b) **Possible response:** The speaker faces the danger of being seen and the burden of remaining silent and motionless despite the growing tension.
3. (a) The river runs through their bones. (b) Possible images include "blades of grass" hanging from pockets, soldiers weaving "into the terrain," and the speaker "hugg[ing] bamboo."
   (c) **Possible response:** The soldiers have blended into the jungle, disappearing as individuals.
4. **Possible responses:** (a) In the end, the speaker has no feelings toward the VC or anything else.
   (b) Students may respond that the poem takes no political position but portrays the soldiers' interaction with nature.
5. (a) A *chimera* is a mythical creature that breathes fire.
   (b) **Possible response:** The title suggests that the soldiers have become a single, deadly monster.
6. **Possible response:** The poet successfully uses details of the jungle to convey abstract feelings of anticipation.

Go Online Author Link For additional information about Yusef Komunyakaa, have students type in the Web Code, then select *K* from the alphabet, and then Yusef Komunyakaa.

reaching in from America.
We aimed at dark-hearted songbirds.

In our way station of shadows
rock apes tried to blow our cover,
throwing stones at the sunset. Chameleons

crawled our spines, changing from day
to night: green to gold,
gold to black. But we waited
till the moon touched metal,

⓭ till something almost broke
inside us. VC struggled
with the hillside, like black silk

wrestling iron through grass.
We weren't there. The river ran
through our bones. Small animals took refuge
against our bodies; we held our breath,

ready to spring the L-shaped
ambush, as a world revolved
under each man's eyelid.

Reading Strategy
Reading in Sentences Which stanzas contain sentences that continue into the next stanza?

Vocabulary Builder
refuge (ref′ yo͞oj) *n.* shelter or protection from danger

Critical Reading

1. **Respond:** What emotions did this poem evoke in you? Explain.
2. **(a) Recall:** Where does this poem take place? **(b) Analyze:** What obstacles and burdens does the speaker face?
3. **(a) Recall:** What runs through the soldiers' bones? **(b) Support:** What other images suggest that the speaker is merging with his surroundings? **(c) Interpret:** What does the speaker mean by his observation that "We weren't there"?
4. **(a) Interpret:** How would you describe the speaker's feelings toward the VC? Support your answer. **(b) Analyze:** Do the images in this poem suggest that the speaker is opposed to the war? Explain.
5. **(a) Define:** What is a chimera? **(b) Interpret:** What effect does the title have on your interpretation of the poem? Explain.
6. **Evaluate:** Komunyakaa has said, "I like connecting the abstract to the concrete." Has he succeeded in this poem? Explain.

For: More about Yusef Komunyakaa
Visit: www.PHSchool.com
Web Code: ere-9634

Apply the Skills

For My Children • Bidwell Ghost • Camouflaging the Chimera

Literary Analysis

Lyric Poetry

1. Describe, in your own words, the thoughts that the speaker expresses in the opening stanza of "For My Children."
2. In what way would you describe the "observations and feelings" the speaker expresses in "Bidwell Ghost"?
3. What is the single effect in **(a)** "For My Children," **(b)** "Bidwell Ghost," and **(c)** "Camouflaging the Chimera"?

Comparing Literary Works

4. Explain where the speaker's thoughts are "traveling" in the fourth stanza of "For My Children."
5. **(a)** In "Bidwell Ghost," analyze the effect that the past has on the present. **(b)** What connection can you find between the ghost and the people who see her?
6. **(a)** How do you think the speaker in "Camouflaging the Chimera" feels about his war memories? **(b)** In what way are the ghosts in Komunyakaa's poem different from the ghost in Erdrich's poem? **(c)** Are there any ghosts in "For My Children"? Explain.

Reading Strategy

Reading in Sentences

7. **(a)** By focusing on Erdrich's use of punctuation, what do you notice about every stanza? **(b)** Why do you think she chose to punctuate this poem as she did?
8. **(a)** Using a chart like the one shown, identify the figurative language in the last stanza of "For My Children." **(b)** Did reading the poem in sentences help you to understand these figures of speech? Explain.

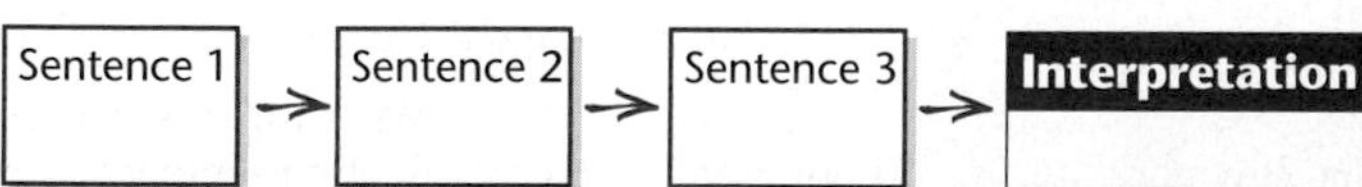

Extend Understanding

9. **Cultural Connection:** Could each of these poems be understood as a form of social protest? Explain.

QuickReview

Lyric poetry is melodic poetry that expresses the observations and feelings of a single speaker.

To understand a poem's meaning, **read it in sentences,** pausing according to the punctuation rather than stopping automatically at the end of every line.

For: Self-test
Visit: www.PHSchool.com
Web Code: era-6618

Go Online Assessment Students may use the **Self-test** to prepare for **Selection Test A** or **Selection Test B.**

Answers

1. The speaker would like to convey a heritage beyond that of slavery to her African American children.
2. The feelings reflect sadness, a sense of mystery, and helplessness.
3. (a) The single effect is inspirational. (b) The single effect is anguished. (c) The single effect is haunting.
4. They are traveling to her Ashanti heritage.
5. (a) The past disturbs the present. (b) The people who see the ghost recognize her pain but cannot help her.
6. (a) **Possible response:** The poet seems to have little emotion about his war memories. He seems neither angry nor afraid, and when he tells what happened, it is as if he was not a part of it. (b) The ghosts in Komunyakaa's poem are the nameless victims of the war that the soldiers bring with them, while the ghost in Erdrich's poem is a child who insists on attention from the living. (c) **Possible response:** The ancestors named in "For My Children" can be considered to be ghosts of a sort; they are the family ghosts of the past that live on in the descendants of the present and future.
7. (a) Most stanzas are complete sentences. (b) **Possible response:** The punctuation clarifies the separate images and gives the poem's mysterious events a sense of order.
8. (a) **Sentence 1:** The line of your cheek recalls Ibo melodies . . . ; **Sentence 2:** The sun dances . . . ; **Sentence 3:** Smiles that mirror schoolboy smiles in the land called Bilad as-Sudan; **Interpretation:** A face is likened to music; the sun is personified; the children's smiles are likened to smiles of faraway children. (b) Reading in sentences makes it easier to isolate and understand the figures of speech.

   Another sample answer can be found on **Reading Strategy Graphic Organizer B,** p. 285, in ***Graphic Organizer Transparencies.***
9. **Possible response:** "For My Children" could be read as a poem of social protest if the speaker feels that the country she lives in fails to acknowledge the power and dignity of her heritage.

EXTEND/ASSESS

Answers

1 Vocabulary Lesson

Related Words

1. heredity
2. inheritance
3. heritage
4. inherit

Vocabulary Builder

1. a
2. c
3. b
4. b

Spelling

1. memories
2. melodies
3. mysteries

2 Grammar and Style Lesson

1. *waits:* present. The waiting takes place in the present.
2. *charred:* past. The charring was completed in the past.
3. *form:* present. The action of the buds' forming occurs in the present.
4. *has wondered:* present-perfect. The action of this sentence started in the past and continues to the present.
5. *tied:* past. The tying was completed in the past.

Writing Application

Check to see that students have used the correct verb tense in the specified location.

WG Writing and Grammar, Ruby Level

Students will find further instruction and practice on sequence of tenses in Chapter 21, Section 2.

Build Language Skills

1 Vocabulary Lesson

Related Words: *heritage*

The word *heritage* means "something handed down from ancestors." It derives from the Latin word *heres,* meaning "heir," and usually refers more to cultural ideas, values, and tales than to objects or artifacts. Several English words, such as *heredity, inherit,* and *inheritance,* are related to this word. Use these four related words to complete the sentences below.

1. His slender physique is a result of __?__.
2. The siblings' __?__ included their uncle's prized collection of hand tools.
3. My twin cousins are very proud of their Scandinavian __?__.
4. Children __?__ physical characteristics from both parents.

Vocabulary Builder: Synonyms

A synonym is a word that has a meaning similar to that of another word. Choose the best synonym for each of the first words.

1. effigies: **(a)** representations, **(b)** toys, **(c)** machines
2. shackles: **(a)** anger, **(b)** worries, **(c)** chains
3. heritage: **(a)** folk art, **(b)** traditions, **(c)** society
4. refuge: **(a)** garbage, **(b)** shelter, **(c)** denial

Spelling Strategy

When forming the plural of a word that ends in a consonant plus *y*, change the *y* to *i* and add *es*. *Effigy* thus becomes *effigies.* Write the plural form of these words.

1. memory **2.** melody **3.** mystery

2 Grammar and Style Lesson

Sequence of Tenses

Using the correct **sequence of verb tenses** allows you to show the relationship of events in time. The *present tense* shows action that exists in the present. *The present-perfect tense* indicates something that began in the past and continues to the present. The *past tense* shows action that began and ended at a given time in the past.

Present: So I **search** for a heritage beyond St. Louis . . .

Present-Perfect: I **have stored** up tales for you . . .

Past: First the orchard **bowed** low and **complained** . . .

Practice Identify the tense of the italicized verbs in the following sentences, and then explain the relationship of events in time that the verbs express.

1. Each night she *waits* by the road.
2. The heat *charred* the branches of the trees.
3. Each spring now, in the grass, buds *form* on the tattered wood.
4. She *has wondered* about this all her life.
5. We *tied* branches to our helmets.

Writing Application Write three sentences about your own heritage. In the first sentence, use a verb in the present tense. In the second, use a verb in the present-perfect tense. In the third, use a verb in the past tense.

WG *Prentice Hall Writing and Grammar Connection: Chapter 21, Section 2*

Assessment Practice

Identify Errors **(For more practice, see *Standardized Test Preparation Workbook*, p. 73.)**

Many tests require students to identify the type of error in a written passage. Use the following sample test item to give students practice in this skill.

Poets often use details of culture to add depth to their poems. The poem's details communicate its theme.

Read the passage and decide which type of error, if any, appears in the underlined section.

A Spelling error
B Capitalization error
C Punctuation error
D No error

Some students may choose *C*, thinking that *its* should have an apostrophe. Have a volunteer explain why this is not an error. Use this example to show students that some test items will contain no errors. *D* is the correct choice here.

Writing Lesson

Ghost Story

Ghost stories are common in Gothic fiction, folk literature, legends, and oral histories. Almost all ghost stories contain an element of mystery and eeriness; some also feature a noticeable air of humor or melancholy. Write a ghost story based on "The Bidwell Ghost."

Prewriting Reread the poem and take notes about the characteristics of the Bidwell ghost. Use a chart like the one shown to organize the poem's sensory details into categories. Then, decide which elements will best convey an aura of mystery.

Model: Categorizing Sensory Details

Sight	Hearing	Touch	Taste	Smell

Drafting Grab your audience's interest from the start with a vivid description of the setting or a description of an eerie event. As you develop your story, focus on building suspense by including descriptions, events, or hints that raise questions for readers. Be sure to answer most questions by the story's end.

Revising Read your story several times, both silently and aloud. Revise it to make it more suspenseful, adding or deleting as needed.

WG *Prentice Hall Writing and Grammar Connection: Chapter 5, Section 3*

Extend Your Learning

Listening and Speaking Conduct an **interview** with a Vietnam War veteran about his or her experiences during the war. Use these tips to prepare:

- Choose a focus for your interview based on your prior knowledge of the war.
- Ask questions requiring in-depth, not "yes" or "no," responses.
- Ask questions about lessons that he or she feels can be learned from the war.

Record the interview on audio- or videotape, and share highlights with the class.

Research and Technology In a small group, research and deliver a short **multimedia cultural presentation** about one of the African cultures mentioned in "For My Children"—Watusi, Bantu, Dahomey, Burundi, Ashanti, or Ibo. Describe the culture, and include posters, photographs, art, and music to present the culture in an interesting way. **[Group Activity]**

For: An additional research activity
Visit: www.PHSchool.com
Web Code: erd-7618

❸ Writing Lesson

- Give students **Support for Writing Lesson,** p. 319 in ***Unit 6 Resources,*** to use as they write their ghost stories.
- Have students explore their associations with *ghosts* by creating a cluster diagram with the word *ghost* in the center.
- Encourage students to use a story map organizer to help them plan their stories.
- Review the Writing Lesson to guide students in developing their story.
- Use the Narration: Short Story rubrics in ***General Resources,*** pp. 57–58, to evaluate students' stories.

❹ Research and Technology

- Make sure that all the listed cultures are assigned to at least one group of students. For groups focusing on the same culture, suggest divergent focal points for research.
- Discuss potential research sources, such as web sites for universities with African Studies programs.
- Invite students to present their reports as part of a cultural heritage festival.
- Use the Speaking: Delivering a Research Presentation rubric in ***General Resources,*** p. 92, to assess student presentations.
- The **Support for Extend Your Learning** page (***Unit 6 Resources,*** p. 320) provides guided note-taking opportunities to help students complete the Extend Your Learning activities.

Go Online Research — Have students type in the Web Code for another research activity.

Assessment Resources

The following resources can be used to assess students' knowledge and skills.

Unit 6 Resources
- **Selection Test A,** pp. 322–324
- **Selection Test B,** pp. 325–327
- **Benchmark Test 11,** pp. 240–242

General Resources
- **Rubrics for Narration: Short Story,** pp. 57–58
- **Rubric for Speaking: Delivering a Research Presentation,** p. 92

Go Online Assessment — Students may use the **Self-test** to prepare for **Selection Test A** or **Selection Test B.**

Benchmark
Administer **Benchmark Test 11.** If the Benchmark Test reveals that some students need further work, use the **Interpretation Guide** to determine the appropriate reteaching pages in the **Reading Kit** or on **Success Tracker.**

Meeting Your Standards

Students will

1. understand changes in American theater during the twentieth century.
2. participate in a discussion about contemporary theater.

Background
Drama/Literature

A Streetcar Named Desire is the story of two sisters, Stella and Blanche, who are from a genteel Southern family. Stella has married Stanley Kowalski, a working-class man with no pretension to intellect or manners. When Blanche comes for a long visit, she reacts to Stanley with fear and loathing. In his turn, he realizes her contempt and resents it, believing she will try to turn Stella against him. In an act of brutal violence, Stanley eventually triumphs over the weaker Blanche. The film of Williams's play won Academy Awards for both Leigh and Brando; it is perhaps the role with which he is most widely identified.

Critical Viewing

Answer: Students may mention the expressions on the actors' faces or the fact that they are standing so close together. The position of their hands and Brando's hold on Leigh's arm add to the emotional impact.

A Closer Look

Twentieth Century Drama: America on Stage

It is opening night at the theater. As the curtain rises, you are filled with anticipation of an exciting new play. No, it is not a big-budget musical with elaborate sets and costumes. It is a night of talk—sometimes loud and angry, sometimes hushed and mournful, but always riveting.

> "*For much of the twentieth century, the theater was the center of American intellectual life.*"

For much of the twentieth century, the theater was the center of American intellectual life. Great plays offered thrilling stories, crackling dialogue, and philosophical truth. The best American playwrights of the twentieth century chronicled different aspects of the American experience.

- **Thornton Wilder** (1897–1975), best known for *Our Town* (1938), revealed the secrets of small-town America.
- **Arthur Miller** (1915–2005) combined politics and realism to give America some of its most moving plays, including *Death of a Salesman* (1949) and *The Crucible* (1953) (see page 1257).
- **Lorraine Hansberry** (1930–1965) dramatized the lives of African Americans. Her play *A Raisin in the Sun* (1959) was the first drama by a black woman to be produced on Broadway.
- **Edward Albee** (b. 1928) shocked audiences with his psychological dramas, including the harsh and powerful *Who's Afraid of Virginia Woolf* (1962).

▼ **Critical Viewing** This photograph shows a scene from Tennessee Williams's *A Streetcar named Desire*. In what ways does this scene depict the "raw power of human emotion"? **[Interpret]**

The American theater had not always been so powerful. Before the 1920s, the American stage was known for light, escapist fare. It was Eugene O'Neill who ushered in a century of great drama.

America's First Great Playwright "I want to be an artist or nothing," O'Neill said at the age of twenty-five. When he died forty years later, he had written more than fifty plays and won the Nobel Prize and four Pulitzer Prizes.

O'Neill's work reflects his troubled childhood and rough-and-tumble youth. He was born in New York City in 1888. In his mid-twenties, hard living landed O'Neill in the hospital, where he pondered his life for the first time: "It was in this enforced period of reflection that the urge to write first came to me," he said.

Enrichment

Song and Dance

Remind students that musicals contain elements of serious drama. With the premiere of *Showboat,* the Broadway musical took its rightful place in American theater history. This show by Oscar Hammerstein III and Jerome Kern adapted a novel by Edna Ferber. In song, dance, and dialogue, it took on the difficult subject of miscegenation (mixing of races) as well as the more popular, general theme of romance. This straightforward willingness to deal with serious issues in American society—in this case racial prejudice, in other shows gang warfare *(West Side Story),* urban loneliness *(Company),* spousal abuse *(Carousel)*—give the Broadway musical a depth and passion that makes it a serious genre of our theater.

O'Neill experimented with different styles—realistic, symbolic, and political. *Beyond the Horizon* (1920), his first Broadway play, was a smash hit. *The Iceman Cometh* (1946) tells the stories of dreamers and losers who frequent a waterfront bar. *A Long Day's Journey Into Night* (1956), O'Neill's masterpiece, recounts his troubled childhood.

A Woman's Voice Born in 1905 in New Orleans, Lillian Hellman became the most influential female playwright of the twentieth century. Her first play, *The Children's Hour* (1934), is the tale of two teachers whose lives are ruined by malicious accusations. Her best-known work, *The Little Foxes* (1939), takes a harsh look at a rich and powerful southern family. Her political drama *Watch on the Rhine* (1941) warned the world of the dangers of Nazism. By the time of her death in 1984, Hellman had helped shape a golden age in American theater and paved the way for women playwrights to exert influence and express powerful views.

The Raw Power of Human Emotion Born in 1911 in rural Mississippi, Tennessee Williams decided to become a writer while he was still a teenager. His first major play, *The Glass Menagerie* (1945), moved audiences with its compassion for a mother and sister who cling to their ever-fading dreams. In 1947, Williams shocked audiences with *A Streetcar Named Desire*, a hard-hitting story filled with both cruelty and beauty. Its effect on audiences was so great that it inspired dozens of imitations. By the time Williams died in 1983, he had written more than 60 plays and become one of the most important dramatists of all time.

Activity

American Theater Today

In midcentury America, Broadway in New York City was the center of the theater world. Broadway is still the heart of New York's theater district, but theater as an artistic institution has changed. With a group, discuss your thoughts about theater today. Use these questions to guide your discussion:

- What kinds of theatrical plays are presented where you live, both in your community and at your school? Are these performances well attended?
- In what ways is the experience of seeing live theater different from watching a movie or television show?
- Do you think that theater continues to be an important cultural force today, or has it been overshadowed by other forms of expression? Explain.

Choose a point person to share your thoughts with the class.

Critical Thinking

1. What may have prompted the rise of intellectual dramas in the twentieth century?
   Answer: Perhaps events, such as World War I, prompted Americans to consider issues that had not been widely scrutinized before. When a few playwrights became successful by writing plays that featured intellectual issues, others began to imitate them.
2. Why do you think interest in theater took so long to find a popular market in American society while in England, theater had been popular since the 1500s?
   Answer: Puritans did not approve of theater, and this disapproval permeated society throughout many years time.

Activity

Organize students in groups. Suggest that they list the theatrical venues available within their community. As the groups progress to the second and third question, encourage them to share personal observations about the effect of theater. Allow time for the point person from each group to report back to the class.

Meeting Your Standards

Students will

1. **analyze and respond to literary elements.**
   - Literary Analysis: Dialogue and Stage Directions
2. **read, comprehend, analyze, and critique a drama.**
   - Reading Strategy: Questioning the Characters' Motives
   - Reading Check questions
   - Apply the Skills questions
   - Assessment Practice (ATE)
3. **develop vocabulary.**
   - Vocabulary Lesson: Latin Root: *-grat-*
4. **understand and apply written and oral language conventions.**
   - Spelling Strategy
   - Grammar and Style Lesson: Pronoun Case in Incomplete Construction
5. **develop writing proficiency.**
   - Writing Lesson: Defense of a Character's Actions (After Act IV)
6. **develop writing strategies.**
   - Extend Your Learning: News Account
7. **understand and apply listening and speaking strategies.**
   - Extend Your Learning: Oral Report

Block Scheduling: Use one 90-minute class period to preteach the skills and have students read the selection. Use a second 90-minute class period to assess students' mastery of skills, extend their learning, and monitor their progress.

Homework Suggestions

Following are possibilities for homework assignments.

- Support pages from *Unit 6 Resources:*
  Literary Analysis
  Reading Strategy
  Vocabulary Builder
  Grammar and Style
- An Extend Your Learning project and the Writing Lesson for this selection may be completed over several days.

Step-by-Step Teaching Guide	Pacing Guide
PRETEACH	
• Administer Vocabulary and Reading Warm-ups as necessary.	5 min.
• Engage students' interest with the motivation activity.	5 min.
• Read and discuss author, background, and From the Author's Desk features. **FT**	10 min.
• Introduce the Literary Analysis Skill: Dialogue and Stage Directions. **FT**	5 min.
• Introduce the Reading Strategy: Questioning the Characters' Motives. **FT**	10 min.
• Prepare students to read by teaching the selection vocabulary. **FT**	
TEACH	
• Informally monitor comprehension while students read independently or in groups. **FT**	30 min.
• Monitor students' comprehension with the Reading Check notes.	as students read
• Reinforce vocabulary with Vocabulary Builder notes.	as students read
• Develop students' understanding of dialogue and stage directions with the Literary Analysis annotations. **FT**	5 min.
• Develop students' ability to question the characters' motives with the Reading Strategy annotations. **FT**	5 min.
ASSESS/EXTEND	
• Assess students' comprehension and mastery of the Literary Analysis and Reading Strategy by having them answer the Apply the Skills questions. **FT**	15 min.
• Have students complete the Vocabulary Lesson and the Grammar and Style Lesson. **FT**	15 min.
• Apply students' understanding by using one or more of the Extend Your Learning activities.	20–90 min. or homework
• Administer Selection Test A or Selection Test B. **FT**	15 min.

Resources

PRINT

Unit 6 Resources

From the Author's Desk ....p. 337
Listening and Viewing ....p. 338
Vocabulary Warm-up Word Lists **[L1, L2, EL]** ....p. 339
Vocabulary Warm-up Practice **[L1, L2, EL]** ....p. 340
Reading Warm-up A **[L1, L2, EL]** ....p. 341
Reading Warm-up B **[L1, L2, L3]** ....p. 342

TRANSPARENCY

Graphic Organizer Transparencies

Literary Analysis Graphic Organizer A **[L3]** ....p. 288
Literary Analysis Graphic Organizer B **[L1, L2, EL]** ....p. 289
Reading Strategy Graphic Organizer A **[L3]** ....p. 286
Reading Strategy Graphic Organizer B **[L1, L2, EL]** ....p. 287

TECHNOLOGY

From the Author's Desk DVD .... Arthur Miller, Segment 2

PRINT

Reader's Notebook [L2]
Reader's Notebook: Adapted Version [L1]
Reader's Notebook: English Learner's Version [EL]

Unit 6 Resources

Literary Analysis **[L3]** ....p. 343
Reading Strategy **[L3]** ....p. 344
Vocabulary Builder **[L3]** ....p. 345

PRINT

Unit 6 Resources

Grammar and Style **[L3]** ....p. 346
Support for Extend Your Learning **[L3]** ....p. 347
Enrichment **[L4]** ....p. 348
Selection Test A **[L1, L2, EL]** ....pp. 349–351
Selection Test B **[L3, L4]** ....pp. 352–354

TECHNOLOGY

Go Online: Research **[L3]**
Go Online: Self-test **[L3]**
***ExamView®* Test Bank [L3]**

Choosing Resources for Differentiated Instruction

[L1] Special Needs Students
[L2] Below-Level Students
[L3] All Students
[L4] Advanced Students
[EL] English Learners

For Vocabulary and Reading Warm-ups and for Selection Tests, **A** signifies "less challenging" and **B** "more challenging." For Graphic Organizer transparencies, **A** signifies "not filled in" and **B** "filled in."

FT Fast Track Instruction: To move the lesson more quickly, use the strategies and activities identified with **FT**.

Scaffolding for Less Proficient and Advanced Students

The leveled Critical Thinking questions after selections progress in the levels of thinking required to answer them. To address the needs of your different students, you may use the (a) level questions for your less proficient students and the (b) level questions with your on-level and advanced students. The occasional (c) level questions are appropriate for your advanced students.

PRENTICE HALL **TeacherEXPRESS™** Plan · Teach · Assess
Use this complete suite of powerful teaching tools to make lesson planning and testing quicker and easier.

PRENTICE HALL **StudentEXPRESS™** Learn · Study · Succeed
Use the interactive textbook (online and on CD-ROM) to make selections and activities come alive with audio and video support and interactive questions.

Monitoring Progress

Before students read the *The Crucible,* administer **Diagnostic Test 12** (***Unit 6 Resources,*** p. 334). This test will determine students' level of readiness for the reading and vocabulary skills.

Go Online Professional Development
For: Information about Lexiles
Visit: www.PHSchool.com
Web Code: eue-1111

From the Author's Desk

Introduce Arthur Miller

- Tell students that Arthur Miller was examining events in his own time that seemed to have many parallels with events from another period in United States history—the witch trials in Salem, Massachusetts.
- Show Segment 2 on Miller on the *From the Author's Desk DVD* to provide insight into how *The Crucible* came to be. Discuss why Arthur Miller saw similarities between the witch trials in Salem, Massachusetts, and the McCarthy Senate hearings.

The Writing of *The Crucible*

- Have students read about Arthur Miller's inspiration for *The Crucible.* **Ask:** Why do you think Miller chose to set his play in seventeenth-century Massachusetts and not during the time of the Senate hearings?
  Possible answer: It was a creative way to juxtapose two separate time periods, connecting them by a common set of issues. Miller also may have feared retribution from the House Un-American Activities Committee.

From the Author's Desk

The Words of ARTHUR MILLER *on* The Crucible

Arthur Miller's *The Crucible* failed at the box office in its initial production in 1953, but it has since become one of the most popular American plays of the twentieth century.

The Historical Background of *The Crucible*

In *Echoes Down the Corridor,* published in 2000, Arthur Miller writes: "It would probably never have occurred to me to write a play about the Salem witch trials of 1692 had I not seen some astonishing correspondences with that calamity in the America of the late forties and early fifties. . . . my basic need was to respond to a phenomenon which, with only small exaggeration, one could say was paralyzing a whole generation and in an amazingly short time was drying up the habits of trust and toleration in public discourse.

"I refer, of course, to the anticommunist rage that threatened to reach hysterical proportions and sometimes did. I can't remember anyone calling it an ideological war, but I think now that that is what it amounted to. Looking back at the period, I suppose we very rapidly passed over anything like a discussion or debate and into something quite different, a hunt not alone for subversive people but ideas and even a suspect language."

The Writing of *The Crucible*

Miller explains where his ideas for *The Crucible* came from, saying, "On a lucky afternoon I happened upon a book, *The Devil in Massachusetts,* by Marion Starkey, a narrative of the Salem witch-hunt of 1692. I knew this story from my college reading more than a decade earlier, but now in this changed and darkened America it turned a wholly new aspect toward me, namely, the poetry of the hunt. Poetry may seem an odd word for a witch-hunt, but I saw now that there was something of the marvelous in the spectacle of the whole village, if not an entire province, whose imagination was literally captured by a vision of something that wasn't there. . . .

"As I stood in the stillness of the Salem courthouse, surrounded by the miasmic swirl of the images of the 1950s but with my head in 1692, what the two eras had in common was gradually gaining definition. In both was the menace of concealed plots, but most startling were the similarities in the rituals of defense and the investigative routines. Three hundred years apart, both prosecutions were alleging membership in a secret, disloyal group; should the accused confess, his honesty could be proved only in precisely the

Teaching Resources

The following resources can be used to enrich or extend the instruction for From the Author's Desk.

Unit 6 Resources
From the Author's Desk, p. 337
Listening and Viewing, p. 338

From the Author's Desk DVD
Arthur Miller, Segment 2

same way—by naming former confederates, nothing less. Thus the informer became the very proof of the plot and the investigator's necessity."

How the Play Has Lasted Musing on the eventual popularity of *The Crucible,* Miller says, "*The Crucible* is my most-produced play, here and abroad. . . . And it is part of the play's history, I think, that to people in so many parts of the world its story seems so like their own. . . . In fact, I used to think, half seriously—although it was not far from the truth—that you could tell when a dictator was about to take power in a Latin American country or when one had just been overthrown, by whether *The Crucible* was suddenly being produced there."

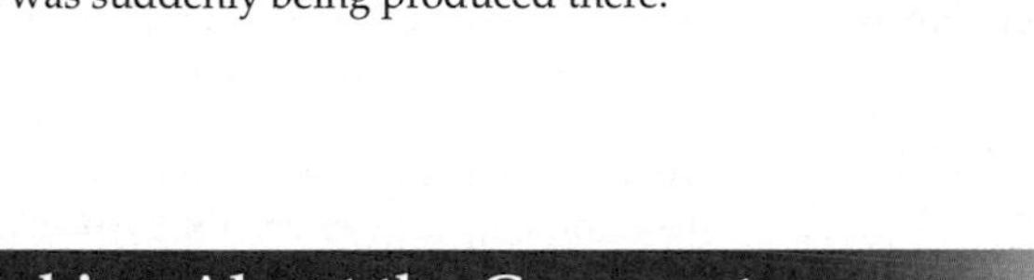

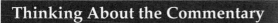

▲ **Critical Viewing** This photograph shows a scene from a contemporary production of *The Crucible*. What can you infer about the relationship between these two characters, based on this photograph? **[Infer]**

Thinking About the Commentary

1. **(a) Recall:** What experience gave Miller the original idea for *The Crucible*? **(b) Infer:** What aspects of this experience helped Miller connect the Salem of 1692 with the United States of the late 1940s and 1950s?
2. **(a) Recall:** What specific similarities does Miller see between the Salem witch trials of 1692 and the anticommunist hearings of the 1950s? **(b) Speculate:** In what ways do you think these similarities have contributed to the fact that *The Crucible* is Miller's most-produced play?

As You Read *The Crucible* . . .

3. Notice how the conflict in the play can represent a universal conflict.
4. Consider ways in which reading this commentary enhances your experience of the play.

Critical Viewing

Possible responses: They may be a married couple at their dining table. Judging from their looks and their body language, there may be some tension between them.

ASSESS

Answers

1. (a) Miller gathers inspiration from the anti-communist rage of the early 1950s. (b) Miller notes that the prosecution approached the case in much the same manner as did the prosecution in Salem, Massachusetts.
2. (a) The prosecution in both cases accused people of belonging to a secretive, disloyal group. In both cases, the accused were required to name people who were part of this group. (b) Possible answer: The story rests on a common theme about a powerful group who abuses the rights of others. Both time periods also reveal how people invent or distort other people's actions to create sensationalism and scandal for public consumption.

PREPARE

Motivation

Have students think about situations in which they have been subjected to pressure from their peers or their families. Explain that they are about to read a play in which the population of an entire town splits into two factions—the accusers and the accused. Into this town come judges who try to force the accused to confess to the crimes of which they are accused. Those who refuse to confess will be sentenced to death.

❶ Background

Literature

In an essay titled *"The Crucible* in History," Arthur Miller discussed his reasons for writing the play:

"In 1948, '49, '50, '51, I had the sensation of being trapped inside a perverse work of art, one of those Escher constructs in which it is impossible to know whether a stairway is going up or down. Practically everyone I knew, all survivors of the Great Depression of course as well as World War II, was somewhere within the conventions of the political left of center, one or two were Communist Party members, some were sort of fellow travelers, as I suppose I was. . . . I have never been able to believe in the reality of these people being actual or putative traitors any more than I could be, yet others like them were being fired from teaching or other jobs in government or large corporations. The unreality of it all never left me. . . . *The Crucible* was an attempt to make life real again, palpable and structured—a work of art created in order to interpret an anterior work of art that was called reality but was not."

Build Skills *Drama*

❶ The Crucible

Arthur Miller (1915–2005)

A legend of the modern American theater, Arthur Miller has chronicled the dilemmas of common people pitted against powerful and unyielding social forces. A native New Yorker, Miller has known bad times as well as good. During the Depression, his family lost its money and was forced to move from Manhattan to more modest living quarters in Brooklyn. Although Miller graduated from Abraham Lincoln High School in 1932, he was forced to delay his enrollment at the University of Michigan for more than two years in order to raise money for tuition. He did so by working at a variety of jobs, including singing for a local radio station, driving a truck, and working as a stock clerk in an automobile parts warehouse.

Promising Playwright Miller first began writing drama while still in college. In 1947, his play *All My Sons* opened on Broadway to immediate acclaim, establishing Miller as a bright new talent. Two years later, he won international fame and a Pulitzer Prize for *Death of a Salesman* (1949), which critics hailed as a modern American tragedy.

His next play, *The Crucible* (1953), was less warmly received, because it uses the Salem witchcraft trials of 1692 as a means of attacking the anti-communist "witch hunts" in Congress in the 1950s. Miller believed that the hysteria surrounding the witchcraft trials in Puritan New England paralleled the contemporary climate of McCarthyism—Senator Joseph McCarthy's obsessive quest to uncover Communist party infiltration of American institutions.

In the introduction to his *Collected Plays* (1957), Miller described his perceptions of the atmosphere during the McCarthy era and the way in which those perceptions influenced the writing of *The Crucible*. He said, "It was as though the whole country had been born anew, without a memory even of certain elemental decencies which a year or two earlier no one would have imagined could be altered, let alone forgotten. Astounded, I watched men pass me by without a nod whom I had known rather well for years; and again, the astonishment was produced by my knowledge, which I could not give up, that the terror in these people was being knowingly planned and consciously engineered, and yet that all they knew was terror. That so interior and subjective an emotion could have been so manifestly created from without was a marvel to me. It underlies every word in *The Crucible*."

In the Shadows of McCarthyism During the two years following the publication and production of *The Crucible,* Miller was investigated for possible associations with the Communist party. In 1956, he was called to testify before the House Committee on Un-American Activities. Although he never became a member of the Communist party, Miller, like so many of his contemporaries, had advocated principles of social justice and equality among the classes. He had become disillusioned, however, by the reality of communism as practiced in the Soviet Union. At the hearings, he testified about his own experiences, but he refused to discuss his colleagues and associates. He was found guilty of contempt of Congress for his refusal, but the sentence was later overturned.

Hollywood Glamour In 1956, the spotlight was focused on Miller's personal life when he married glamorous film star Marilyn Monroe. Although he did little writing during their five-year marriage, he did pen the screenplay for a film, *The Misfits* (1961), in which Monroe starred. After their divorce, Miller wrote other noteworthy plays, including *The Price* (1968) and *The Last Yankee* (1993).

Background

In 1692, the British colony of Massachusetts was swept by a witchcraft hysteria that resulted in the execution of twenty people and the jailing of at least 150 others. The incident was not isolated. It is estimated that between 1 million and 9 million Europeans were accused of being witches and then executed in the sixteenth and seventeenth centuries. Many of these people were merely practicing folk customs that had survived in Europe since pre-Christian times. In addition, in an era when religion and politics were closely allied, witch hunts were often politically motivated. England's James I, for example, wrote a treatise on witchcraft and sometimes accused his enemies of practicing the black arts. It was a cry that resonated well among a superstitious populace.

For the New England colonies, however, the witchcraft episode was unusual, though perhaps inevitable. The colonists endured harsh conditions and punishing hardship in their lives. Finding themselves at the mercy of forces beyond their control—bitter weather, sickness and death, devastating fires, drought, and insect infestations that killed their crops—many colonists attributed their misfortunes to the Devil. They were fearful (some would say paranoid) people, and their Puritan faith stressed the biblical teaching that witches were real and dangerous.

In the small parish of Salem Village, many were quick to blame witchcraft when the minister's daughter and several other girls were afflicted by seizures and lapses into unconsciousness, especially after it was learned that the girls had been dabbling in fortunetelling with the minister's slave, Tituba. (They were not dancing in the woods, as portrayed in the play.) At first, only Tituba and two elderly women were called witches, but then the hunt spread until some of the colony's most prominent citizens stood accused. Many historians have

seen a pattern of social and economic animosity behind the accusations, but most feel that mass hysteria was also a strong contributing factor.

When *The Crucible* was first published, Arthur Miller added a note about the play's historical accuracy: "This play is not history in the sense in which the word is used by the academic historian. Dramatic purposes have sometimes required many characters to be fused into one; the number of girls involved in the 'crying-out' has been reduced; Abigail's age has been raised; while there were several judges of almost equal authority, I have symbolized them in Hathorne and Danforth. However, I believe that the reader will discover here the essential nature of one of the strangest and most awful chapters in human history. The fate of each character is exactly that of his historical model, and there is no one in the drama who did not play a similar—and in some cases exactly the same—role in history."

❷ Background
History

In 1643, the four colonies of New England—Plymouth, Massachusetts, Connecticut, and Rhode Island—formed a confederation called the United Colonies of New England. Each was the stronghold of a different religious body. The Plymouth Puritans were separatists who wanted a break from the Church of England. The Massachusetts Puritans were not separatist, but were still extremely conservative. Connecticut was governed by a Presbyterian system, while Rhode Island was home to Quakers, Anabaptists, and other free thinkers.

In 1660, Puritan Oliver Cromwell's reign over England came to an end with the restoration of the monarchy and the coronation of the Roman Catholic Charles II. Charles revoked the charters that guaranteed the American colonies self-government. This alarmed the Puritans on both economic and religious grounds; they wanted no interference with their profitable trade or with their systems of religion. This halt in colonial self-government would eventually lead to the American Revolution of the late 1700s. This resentment of authority was mirrored in the gradual changes to the Puritan system that finally erupted in the witchcraft trials.

Between 1662 and 1676, conflicts between the Indians and the Europeans escalated. In 1676, the all-out war known as King Philip's War ("King Philip" was a Wampanoag chief whose Indian name was Metacomet) broke out between them. Many on both sides were killed.

The Salem witchcraft trials grew out of this climate of unrest and fear of enemies attacking from all sides—the English king eroding colonial rights, Native Americans trying to repossess their land, and liberal factions within the church seeking to ease standards for membership.

❸ Literary Analysis
Dialogue and Stage Directions

- Point out the designation "An Overture" at the start of the stage directions. Tell students that in modern theater, an overture is a short piece of music that is played before the curtain goes up on Act I of an opera or a musical play. Overtures often consist of melodies and motifs that will be heard later in the show. **Ask** what Miller's calling this an overture suggests to them about this act. **Answer:** Act I may introduce themes and motifs that will be explored more fully in the later acts. It may be entirely expository in nature, like a musical overture. Its purpose may be simply to set a mood.
- **Ask** students the Literary Analysis question: What important information is revealed in the third paragraph of the stage direction? **Answer:** This paragraph identifies the two people on stage and their relationship to each other.

▶ **Monitor Progress:** Have students find the place where they would first find out this information if they were attending a performance rather than reading the script. **Answer:** Some students may know that the cast is listed in order of appearance, so they might infer that the characters on stage are Reverend Parris and Betty Parris, and are related in some way. Other students will say they would not know until p. 1261 when Parris refers to Betty as his child.

CHARACTERS

REVEREND PARRIS
BETTY PARRIS
TITUBA
ABIGAIL WILLIAMS
SUSANNA WALCOTT
MRS. ANN PUTNAM
THOMAS PUTNAM
MERCY LEWIS
MARY WARREN
JOHN PROCTOR
REBECCA NURSE
GILES COREY
MARTHA COREY
REVEREND JOHN HALE
ELIZABETH PROCTOR
FRANCIS NURSE
EZEKIEL CHEEVER
MARSHAL HERRICK
JUDGE HATHORNE
DEPUTY GOVERNOR DANFORTH
SARAH GOOD
HOPKINS

(An Overture)

A small upper bedroom in the home of REVEREND SAMUEL PARRIS, *Salem, Massachusetts, in the spring of the year 1692.*

There is a narrow window at the left. Through its leaded panes the morning sunlight streams. A candle still burns near the bed, which is at the right. A chest, a chair, and a small table are the other furnishings. At the back a door opens on the landing of the stairway to the ground floor. The room gives off an air of clean spareness. The roof rafters are exposed, and the wood colors are raw and unmellowed.

❸ *As the curtain rises,* REVEREND PARRIS *is discovered kneeling beside the bed, evidently in prayer. His daughter,* BETTY PARRIS, *aged ten, is lying on the bed, inert.*

At the time of these events Parris was in his middle forties. In history he cut a villainous path, and there is very little good to be said for him. He believed he was being persecuted wherever he went, despite his best efforts to win people and God to his side. In meeting, he felt insulted if someone rose to shut the door without first asking his permission. He was a widower with no interest in children, or talent with them. He regarded them as young adults, and until this strange crisis he, like the rest of Salem, never conceived that the children were anything but thankful for being permitted to walk straight, eyes slightly lowered, arms at the sides, and mouths shut until bidden to speak.

His house stood in the "town"—but we today would hardly call it a village. The meeting house was nearby, and from this point outward—toward the bay or inland—there were a few small-windowed, dark houses snuggling against the raw Massachusetts winter. Salem had been established hardly forty years before. To the European world the whole province was a barbaric frontier inhabited by a sect of fanatics who, nevertheless, were shipping out products of slowly increasing quantity and value.

Literary Analysis
Dialogue and Stage Directions What important information is revealed in the third paragraph of the stage direction?

Arthur Miller
Author's Insight
Miller once speculated that *The Crucible*, with its large cast, would not be accepted by today's "commercialized" Broadway and was too large for off-Broadway theaters: ". . . what would one do with *The Crucible* on a shoebox stage [off-Broadway] with its twenty-one characters and several sets?"

Differentiated Instruction
Solutions for All Learners

Enrichment for Gifted/Talented Students
Have students research childhood in early America. In the commentary above, Miller says that children were expected to "walk straight, eyes slightly lowered, arms at the sides, and mouths shut." Have students find out what Puritan children wore, how they were educated, what games they played, at what age they began working, and what the differences were between a boy's upbringing and a girl's. Ask students to research particularly Miller's observation that children were regarded simply as small adults. Can students find any evidence to the contrary? Have students share the results of their research with their classmates so that everyone has the background information to understand the context in which the girls of Salem began accusing adults of witchcraft.

No one can really know what their lives were like. They had no novelists—and would not have permitted anyone to read a novel if one were handy. Their creed forbade anything resembling a theater or "vain enjoyment." They did not celebrate Christmas, and a holiday from work meant only that they must concentrate even more upon prayer.

Which is not to say that nothing broke into this strict and somber way of life. When a new farmhouse was built, friends assembled to "raise the roof," and there would be special foods cooked and probably some potent cider passed around. There was a good supply of ne'er-do-wells in Salem, who dallied at the shovelboard[2] in Bridget Bishop's tavern. Probably more than the creed, hard work kept the morals of the place from spoiling, for the people were forced to fight the land like heroes for every grain of corn, and no man had very much time for fooling around.

That there were some jokers, however, is indicated by the practice of appointing a two-man patrol whose duty was to "walk forth in the time of God's worship to take notice of such as either lye about the meeting house, without attending to the word and ordinances, or that lye at home or in the fields without giving good account thereof, and to take the names of such persons, and to present them to the magistrates, whereby they may be accordingly proceeded against." This predilection for minding other people's business was time-honored among the people of Salem, and it undoubtedly created many of the suspicions which were to feed the coming madness. It was also, in my opinion, one of the things that a John Proctor would rebel against, for the time of the armed camp had almost passed, and since the country was reasonably—although not wholly—safe, the old disciplines were beginning to rankle. But, as in all such matters, the issue was not clear-cut, for danger was still a possibility, and in unity still lay the best promise of safety.

The edge of the wilderness was close by. The American continent stretched endlessly west, and it was full of mystery for them. It stood, dark and threatening, over their shoulders night and day, for out of it Indian tribes marauded from time to time, and Reverend Parris had parishioners who had lost relatives to these heathen.

The parochial snobbery of these people was partly responsible for their failure to convert the Indians. Probably they also preferred to take land from heathens rather than from fellow Christians. At any rate, very few Indians were converted, and the Salem folk believed that the virgin forest was the Devil's last preserve, his home base and the citadel of his final stand. To the best of their knowledge the American forest was the last place on earth that was not paying homage to God.

For these reasons, among others, they carried about an air of innate resistance, even of persecution. Their fathers had, of course, been persecuted in England. So now they and their church found it necessary to deny any other sect its freedom, lest their New Jerusalem[3] be defiled and corrupted by wrong ways and deceitful ideas.

2. **shovelboard** game in which a coin or other disk is driven with the hand along a highly polished board, floor, or table marked with transverse lines.
3. **New Jerusalem** in the Bible, the holy city of heaven.

Literary Analysis
Dialogue, Stage Directions, and Dramatic Exposition In what way does the information Miller provides in these essay-like passages differ from the typical stage direction or dialogue?

Vocabulary Builder
predilection (pred′ ə lek′ shən) *n.* preexisting preference

Literary Analysis
Dialogue, Stage Directions, and Dramatic Exposition Why is this background information about Salem important to your understanding of the play?

5  **Reading Check**
What is a time-honored activity among the people of Salem?

4 Literary Analysis
Dialogue, Stage Directions, and Dramatic Exposition

- What does the opening paragraph of the commentary tell the reader about Parris? Why would Miller do this?
  Answer: The commentary prejudices readers against him by saying that he is a villain. Miller wants readers to know right away that Parris's motives are base.
- **Ask** students the first Literary Analysis question: In what way does the information Miller provides in these essay-like passages differ from the typical stage direction or dialogue?
  Answer: In this commentary, Miller speaks directly to the reader. He provides information about the historical figures and events on which his play is based.
- **Ask** students the second Literary Analysis question: Why is this background information about Salem important to your understanding of the play?
  Answer: Readers may not know much about the long-ago time and the place in which the play is set. This information fills in this background for readers.

▶ **Monitor Progress:** What does the presence of this commentary suggest about Miller's intentions?
Answer: Miller wanted his play to be read as well as performed. This commentary will not appear in a performance, so it is clearly written especially for the reader.

5 Reading Check

Answer: Minding one another's business is a time-honored activity among the people of Salem.

Differentiated Instruction
Solutions for All Learners

Strategy for Advanced Readers

Explain that the passage of lengthy prose commentary that appears here is one of several that appear throughout Act I. Tell students that these commentaries are included only for readers of the play—they are not part of its theatrical performance. Have students write brief critical essays discussing the reasons they think Miller included these commentaries and evaluating what they contribute to the play. Given that the theater audience does not read them or hear them, are they in any sense necessary? If not, why did Miller include them? What do they add to a reader's understanding and appreciation of the play? Might Miller have communicated the same information in dialogue, in a narration, or in other ways?

❻ Reading Strategy
Questioning the Characters' Motives

- Have students **paraphrase** the motives Miller ascribes for the Puritan way of life in New England.
Answer: The Puritans banded together to protect and perpetuate their religious beliefs.
- **Ask** students what they think might happen to any Puritans whose behavior did not conform to the community's beliefs.
Answer: Such people would most likely be targeted by their watchful neighbors and turned over to authorities, since any sign of disunity would have been perceived as a threat to the ordered life of the community.

▶ **Monitor Progress:** Have students keep this motivation for unity in mind as they continue reading Act I. Have them look for characters whose ideas seem to be different from those of their neighbors. What may happen to these characters later in the play?

❼ Critical Viewing

Answer: He is looking toward the sky, which suggests an attitude of prayer.

They believed, in short, that they held in their steady hands the candle that would light the world. We have inherited this belief, and it has helped and hurt us. It helped them with the discipline it gave them. They were a dedicated folk, by and large, and they had to be to survive the life they had chosen or been born into in this country.

The proof of their belief's value to them may be taken from the opposite character of the first Jamestown settlement, farther south, in Virginia. The Englishmen who landed there were motivated mainly by a hunt for profit. They had thought to pick off the wealth of the new country and then return rich to England. They were a band of individualists, and a much more ingratiating group than the Massachusetts men. But Virginia destroyed them. Massachusetts tried to kill off the Puritans, but they combined; they set up a communal society which, in the beginning, was little more than an armed camp with an autocratic and very devoted leadership. It was, however, an autocracy by consent, for they were united from top to bottom by a commonly held ideology whose perpetuation was the reason and justification for all their sufferings. So their self-denial, their purposefulness, their suspicion of all vain pursuits, their hard-handed justice, were altogether perfect instruments for the conquest of this space so antagonistic to man.

Vocabulary Builder
ingratiating (in grā´ shē āt´ iŋ) *adj.* charming or flattering

❻ But the people of Salem in 1692 were not quite the dedicated folk that arrived on the *Mayflower.* A vast differentiation had taken place, and in their own time a revolution had unseated the royal government and substituted a junta[4] which was at this moment in power. The times, to their eyes, must have been out of joint, and to the common folk must have seemed as insoluble and complicated as do ours today. It is not hard to see how easily many could have been led to believe that the time of confusion had been brought upon them by deep and darkling forces. No hint of such speculation appears on the court record, but social disorder in any age breeds such mystical suspicions, and when, as in Salem, wonders are brought forth from below the social surface, it is too much to expect people to hold back very long from laying on the victims with all the force of their frustrations.

❼ **▲ Critical Viewing** This nineteenth-century engraving shows the hanging of the Reverend Stephen Burroughs during the Salem witchcraft trials. What does this image suggest about the condemned man's state of mind? **[Infer]**

The Salem tragedy, which is about to begin in these pages, developed from a paradox. It is a paradox in whose grip we still live, and there is no prospect yet that we will discover its resolution. Simply, it was this: for good purposes, even high purposes, the people of Salem developed a theocracy, a combine of state and religious power whose function was to keep the community together, and to prevent any kind of disunity that might open it to destruction by material or ideological enemies. It was forged for a necessary purpose and accomplished that purpose. But all organization is and must

4. **junta** (hoon´ tə) *n.* assembly or council.

be grounded on the idea of exclusion and prohibition, just as two objects cannot occupy the same space. Evidently the time came in New England when the repressions of order were heavier than seemed warranted by the dangers against which the order was organized. The witch-hunt was a perverse manifestation of the panic which set in among all classes when the balance began to turn toward greater individual freedom.

When one rises above the individual villainy displayed, one can only pity them all, just as we shall be pitied someday. It is still impossible for man to organize his social life without repressions, and the balance has yet to be struck between order and freedom.

The witch-hunt was not, however, a mere repression. It was also, and as importantly, a long overdue opportunity for everyone so inclined to express publicly his guilt and sins, under the cover of accusations against the victims. It suddenly became possible—and patriotic and holy—for a man to say that Martha Corey had come into his bedroom at night, and that, while his wife was sleeping at his side, Martha laid herself down on his chest and "nearly suffocated him." Of course it was her spirit only, but his satisfaction at confessing himself was no lighter than if it had been Martha herself. One could not ordinarily speak such things in public.

Long-held hatreds of neighbors could now be openly expressed, and vengeance taken, despite the Bible's charitable injunctions. Land-lust which had been expressed before by constant bickering over boundaries and deeds, could now be elevated to the arena of morality; one
8 could cry witch against one's neighbor and feel perfectly justified in the bargain. Old scores could be settled on a plane of heavenly combat between Lucifer[5] and the Lord; suspicions and the envy of the miserable toward the happy could and did burst out in the general revenge.

REVEREND PARRIS *is praying now, and, though we cannot hear his words, a sense of his confusion hangs about him. He mumbles, then seems about to weep; then he weeps, then prays again; but his daughter does not stir on the bed.*

The door opens, and his Negro slave enters. TITUBA *is in her forties.* PARRIS *brought her with him from Barbados, where he spent some years as a merchant before entering the ministry. She enters as one does who can no longer bear to be barred from the sight of her beloved, but she is also very frightened because her slave sense has warned her that, as always, trouble in this house eventually lands on her back.*

TITUBA, *already taking a step backward:* My Betty be hearty soon?

PARRIS: Out of here!

TITUBA, *backing to the door:* My Betty not goin' die . . .

PARRIS, *scrambling to his feet in a fury:* Out of my sight! *She is gone.* Out of my—*He is overcome with sobs. He clamps his teeth against them and closes the door and leans against it, exhausted.* Oh, my God! God help me! *Quaking with fear, mumbling to himself through his sobs, he goes to the bed and gently takes* BETTY'S *hand.* Betty. Child. Dear child. 9
Will you wake, will you open up your eyes! Betty, little one . . .

5. **Lucifer** (lo͞o′ sə fər) the Devil.

Reading Strategy
Questioning the Characters' Motives
What do you learn here about Tituba's motives?

Reading Check
What accusation surfaces among the residents of Salem?

8 Reading Strategy
Questioning the Characters' Motives

- Miller's commentary suggests various motives for the accusations of witchcraft. Have students **discuss** these motives. Do they seem reasonable? Remind students that the penalty for witchcraft was death.
Answer: Miller suggests that petty quarrels over property and other disagreements of long-standing caused people to accuse one another. Students may think that these are insufficient motives for what amounts to murder.
- **Ask** students the Reading Strategy question: What do you learn here about Tituba's motives?
Answer: Tituba is afraid of Parris.

9 Reading Check

Answer: Some residents of Salem accuse others of witchcraft.

Differentiated Instruction
Solutions for All Learners

Support for Special Needs Students
Assign peer tutors for students. Have each pair work through the play a few pages at a time, reading the dialogue aloud. At natural breaks in the action, the tutor should make sure that his or her partner can identify the characters and summarize the action up to this point. Since most scenes in the play involve several characters, a few tutors and their partners may want to work together in a group.

Strategy for Gifted/Talented Students
Miller's richly metaphorical language was meant to be heard rather than read silently. Have students form a group in which to read the play aloud together. Readers can maintain the same roles or alternate so that everyone has a chance to read both major and minor characters. Have students discuss how hearing the language enriches their experience of the play.

⑩ Reading Strategy
Questioning the Characters' Motives

- Draw students' attention to the vocabulary word, *dissembling.* If necessary, discuss what kind of person has a capacity for dissembling.
- **Ask** students the first Reading Strategy question: Based on what stage directions have revealed about Abigail's personality, what can you conclude about her "worry" and "apprehension"?
Answer: She isn't really worried or apprehensive.

⑪ Reading Strategy
Questioning the Characters' Motives

- **Ask** students the second Reading Strategy question: Why is Parris so quick to dismiss the possibility that Betty's ailment is the result of "unnatural causes"?
Answer: He knows that if people believe this rumor he will be in serious trouble.
- Why is Parris unwilling to tell the congregation that he discovered the girls dancing in the forest?
Answer: They will blame him for being an irresponsible guardian.

He is bending to kneel again when his niece, ABIGAIL WILLIAMS, *seventeen, enters—a strikingly beautiful girl, an orphan, with an endless capacity for dissembling. Now she is all worry and apprehension and propriety.*

ABIGAIL: Uncle? *He looks to her.* Susanna Walcott's here from Doctor Griggs.

PARRIS: Oh? Let her come, let her come.

ABIGAIL, *leaning out the door to call to Susanna, who is down the hall a few steps:* Come in, Susanna.

SUSANNA WALCOTT, *a little younger than Abigail, a nervous, hurried girl, enters.*

PARRIS, *eagerly:* What does the doctor say, child?

SUSANNA, *craning around* PARRIS *to get a look at* BETTY: He bid me come and tell you, reverend sir, that he cannot discover no medicine for it in his books.

PARRIS: Then he must search on.

⑩ **SUSANNA:** Aye, sir, he have been searchin' his books since he left you, sir. But he bid me tell you, that you might look to unnatural things for the cause of it.

PARRIS, *his eyes going wide:* No—no. There be no unnatural cause here. Tell him I have sent for Reverend Hale of Beverly, and Mr. Hale will surely confirm that. Let him look to medicine and put out all thought of unnatural causes here. There be none.

SUSANNA: Aye, sir. He bid me tell you. *She turns to go.*

ABIGAIL: Speak nothin' of it in the village, Susanna.

PARRIS: Go directly home and speak nothing of unnatural causes.

SUSANNA: Aye, sir. I pray for her. *She goes out.*

ABIGAIL: Uncle, the rumor of witchcraft is all about; I think you'd best go down and deny it yourself. The parlor's packed with people, sir. I'll sit with her.

PARRIS, *pressed, turns on her:* And what shall I say to them? That my daughter and my niece I discovered dancing like heathen in the forest?

ABIGAIL: Uncle, we did dance; let you tell them I confessed it—and I'll be whipped if I must be. But they're speakin' of witchcraft. Betty's not witched.

PARRIS: Abigail, I cannot go before the congregation when I know you have not opened with me. What did you do with her in the forest?

ABIGAIL: We did dance, uncle, and when you leaped out of the bush so suddenly, Betty was frightened and then she fainted. And there's the whole of it.

PARRIS: Child. Sit you down.

ABIGAIL, *quavering, as she sits:* I would never hurt Betty. I love her dearly.

PARRIS: Now look you, child, your punishment will come in its time. But if you trafficked with spirits in the forest I must know it now, for surely my enemies will, and they will ruin me with it.

ABIGAIL: But we never conjured spirits.

Vocabulary Builder
dissembling (di sem′ bliŋ) *n.* disguising one's real nature or motives

Reading Strategy
Questioning the Characters' Motives
Based on what stage directions have revealed about Abigail's personality, what can you conclude about her "worry" and "apprehension"?

Reading Strategy
Questioning the Characters' Motives
Why is Parris so quick to dismiss the possibility that Betty's ailment is the result of "unnatural causes"?

PARRIS: Then why can she not move herself since midnight? This child is desperate! *Abigail lowers her eyes.* It must come out—my enemies will bring it out. Let me know what you done there. Abigail, do you understand that I have many enemies?

ABIGAIL: I have heard of it, uncle.

PARRIS: There is a faction that is sworn to drive me from my pulpit. Do you understand that?

ABIGAIL: I think so, sir.

PARRIS: Now then, in the midst of such disruption, my own household is discovered to be the very center of some obscene practice. Abominations are done in the forest—

ABIGAIL: It were sport, uncle!

PARRIS, *pointing at* BETTY: You call this sport? *She lowers her eyes. He pleads:* Abigail, if you know something that may help the doctor, for God's sake tell it to me. *She is silent.* I saw Tituba waving her arms over the fire when I came on you. Why was she doing that? And I heard a screeching and gibberish coming from her mouth. She were swaying like a dumb beast over that fire!

ABIGAIL: She always sings her Barbados songs, and we dance.

PARRIS: I cannot blink what I saw, Abigail, for my enemies will not blink it. I saw a dress lying on the grass.

ABIGAIL, *innocently:* A dress?

PARRIS—*it is very hard to say:* Aye, a dress. And I thought I saw—someone naked running through the trees!

ABIGAIL, *in terror:* No one was naked! You mistake yourself, uncle!

PARRIS, *with anger:* I saw it! *He moves from her. Then, resolved:* Now tell me true, Abigail. And I pray you feel the weight of truth upon you, for now my ministry's at stake, my ministry and perhaps your cousin's life. Whatever abomination you have done, give me all of it now, for I dare not be taken unaware when I go before them down there.

ABIGAIL: There is nothin' more. I swear it, uncle.

PARRIS, *studies her, then nods, half convinced:* Abigail, I have fought here three long years to bend these stiff-necked people to me, and now, just now when some good respect is rising for me in the parish, you compromise my very character. I have given you a home, child, I have put clothes upon your back—now give me upright answer. Your name in the town—it is entirely white, is it not?

ABIGAIL, *with an edge of resentment:* Why, I am sure it is, sir. There be no blush about my name.

PARRIS, *to the point:* Abigail, is there any other cause than you have told me, for your being discharged from Goody[6] Proctor's service? I have heard it said, and I tell you as I heard it, that she comes so rarely to the church this year for she will not sit so close to something soiled. 13 What signified that remark?

6. **Goody** title used for a married woman; short for Goodwife.

Literary Analysis
Dialogue What do his references to his "enemies" reveal about Parris's personality?

Reading Check
What did Abigail and Betty do in the forest with Tituba?

12 Literary Analysis
Dialogue and Stage Directions

- **Ask** students the Literary Analysis question: What do his references to his "enemies" reveal about Parris's personality?
  Answer: His statements suggest that he is a hostile, and even paranoid, man.
- **Ask** students why they think the girls danced naked in the woods when they knew they would be punished if they were caught.
  Answer: Abigail's statement, "It were sport," together with her feigned innocence and unwillingness to tell the truth suggest that Referend Parris's repressive ways prompted the girls to rebel.

13 Reading Check
Answer: They danced.

Differentiated Instruction
Solutions for All Learners

Background for English Learners
Students may be puzzled by the unconventional English the play's characters speak. Write some examples from these two pages on the chalkboard:

- . . . he cannot discover no medicine for it . . .
- . . . he have been searchin' his books since he left you . . .
- It were sport, uncle!
- What signified that remark?

Explain that Miller wrote in a style that suggests the speech of early America. Grammar and spelling were not standardized at the time; rules of speech were much more lax than today. Help students "translate" the above examples into modern English. As students read the play, have them use context clues to figure out what the characters are saying.

17 Reading Strategy
Questioning the Characters' Motives

- Why does Abigail accuse Tituba and Ruth of "conjuring spirits"?
  Answer: Since Mrs. Putnam has already admitted that she asked Ruth to ask Tituba to communicate with the dead, Abigail makes a safe accusation. She won't be blamed for the accusation, nor will she be punished for her behavior in the woods.
- What does this passage reveal about the Putnams' motives for blaming Ruth's illness on witchcraft?
  Answer: They don't want to take any blame for having sent Ruth on a dangerous errand or making Ruth participate in the sin of "conjuring up the dead." Therefore, they look for a witch as a scapegoat.

18 Critical Viewing

Answer: Tituba is frightened of the consequences of this accusation. She doesn't expect her denials to be believed.

your part in all contention here, and I would continue; but I cannot if you hold back in this. There are hurtful, vengeful spirits layin' hands on these children.

PARRIS: But, Thomas, you cannot—

PUTNAM: Ann! Tell Mr. Parris what you have done.

MRS. PUTNAM: Reverend Parris, I have laid seven babies unbaptized in the earth. Believe me, sir, you never saw more hearty babies born. And yet, each would wither in my arms the very night of their birth. I have spoke nothin', but my heart has clamored intimations. And now, this year, my Ruth, my only—I see her turning strange. A secret child she has become this year, and shrivels like a sucking mouth were pullin' on her life too. And so I thought to send her to your Tituba—

PARRIS: To Tituba! What may Tituba—?

MRS. PUTNAM: Tituba knows how to speak to the dead, Mr. Parris.

PARRIS: Goody Ann, it is a formidable sin to conjure up the dead!

MRS. PUTNAM: I take it on my soul, but who else may surely tell us what person murdered my babies?

PARRIS, *horrified:* Woman!

17 **MRS. PUTNAM:** They were murdered, Mr. Parris! And mark this proof! Mark it! Last night my Ruth were ever so close to their little spirits; I know it, sir. For how else is she struck dumb now except some power of darkness would stop her mouth? It is a marvelous sign, Mr. Parris!

PUTNAM: Don't you understand it, sir? There is a murdering witch among us, bound to keep herself in the dark. PARRIS *turns to* BETTY, *a frantic terror rising in him.* Let your enemies make of it what they will, you cannot blink it more.

PARRIS, *to* ABIGAIL: Then you were conjuring spirits last night.

ABIGAIL, *whispering:* Not I, sir—Tituba and Ruth.

PARRIS *turns now, with new fear, and goes to* BETTY, *looks down at her, and then, gazing off:* Oh, Abigail, what proper payment for my charity! Now I am undone.

PUTNAM: You are not undone! Let you take hold here. Wait for no one to charge you—declare it yourself. You have discovered witchcraft—

PARRIS: In my house? In my house, Thomas? They will topple me with this! They will make of it a—

Enter MERCY LEWIS, *the Putnams' servant, a fat, sly, merciless girl of eighteen.*

MERCY: Your pardons. I only thought to see how Betty is.

PUTNAM: Why aren't you home? Who's with Ruth?

MERCY: Her grandma come. She's improved a little, I think—she give a powerful sneeze before.

MRS. PUTNAM: Ah, there's a sign of life!

18 ▼ **Critical Viewing** Abigail Williams has accused Tituba of conjuring up spirits. What can you infer about Tituba's reaction from her expression here? **[Infer]**

Enrichment

African Religion

The Puritans consider Tituba's ability to speak to the dead shocking and scandalous, but communication with the dead is a basic part of many African religions. In many religions derived from African cultures, the dead are honored and considered to be able to provide wisdom and advice to the living.

Vodoun, or voodoo, is a folk religion from the West Indies, which developed from Roman Catholic beliefs mixed with African religious practices.

In a voodoo ritual service, the priestess leads a gathering of people in song, drumming, dance, prayer, cooking, or animal sacrifice. As students read on, they will see that most of these details apply to the descriptions of what Tituba and the girls were doing in the woods. Ironically, a voodoo priestess is said to have the power to protect her followers from witchcraft.

MERCY: I'd fear no more, Goody Putnam. It were a grand sneeze; another like it will shake her wits together, I'm sure. *She goes to the bed to look.*

PARRIS: Will you leave me now, Thomas? I would pray a while alone.

ABIGAIL: Uncle, you've prayed since midnight. Why do you not go down and—

PARRIS: No—no. *To* PUTNAM: I have no answer for that crowd. I'll wait till Mr. Hale arrives. *To get* MRS. PUTNAM *to leave:* If you will, Goody Ann . . .

PUTNAM: Now look you, sir. Let you strike out against the Devil, and the village will bless you for it! Come down, speak to them—pray with them. They're thirsting for your word, Mister! Surely you'll pray with them.

PARRIS, *swayed:* I'll lead them in a psalm, but let you say nothing of witchcraft yet. I will not discuss it. The cause is yet unknown. I have had enough contention since I came; I want no more.

MRS. PUTNAM: Mercy, you go home to Ruth, d'y'hear?

MERCY: Aye, mum.

MRS. PUTNAM *goes out.*

PARRIS, *to* ABIGAIL: If she starts for the window, cry for me at once.

ABIGAIL: I will, uncle.

PARRIS, *to* PUTNAM: There is a terrible power in her arms today. *He goes out with* PUTNAM.

ABIGAIL, *with hushed trepidation:* How is Ruth sick?

MERCY: It's weirdish, I know not—she seems to walk like a dead one since last night.

ABIGAIL, *turns at once and goes to* BETTY, *and now, with fear in her voice:* Betty? BETTY *doesn't move. She shakes her.* Now stop this! Betty! Sit up now!

19 BETTY *doesn't stir.* MERCY *comes over.*

MERCY: Have you tried beatin' her? I gave Ruth a good one and it waked her for a minute. Here, let me have her.

ABIGAIL, *holding* MERCY *back:* No, he'll be comin' up. Listen, now; if they be questioning us, tell them we danced—I told him as much already.

MERCY: Aye. And what more?

ABIGAIL: He knows Tituba conjured Ruth's sisters to come out of the grave.

MERCY: And what more?

ABIGAIL: He saw you naked.

20 **MERCY:** *clapping her hands together with a frightened laugh:* Oh, Jesus!

Enter MARY WARREN, *breathless. She is seventeen, a subservient, naive, lonely girl.*

MARY WARREN: What'll we do? The village is out! I just come from the farm; the whole country's talkin' witchcraft! They'll be callin' us witches, Abby!

MERCY, *pointing and looking at* MARY WARREN: She means to tell, I know it.

***Arthur Miller* Author's Insight**
In *The Crucible*, Miller uses dialogue that sounds like the speech of New England Puritans. Commenting on the language of his plays, Miller wrote: "My own tendency has been to shift styles according to the nature of my subject. . . . I have done this in order to find speech that springs naturally out of the characters and their backgrounds. . . . "

Literary Analysis
Dialogue and Stage Directions What does this conversation reveal about the two young women?

Literary Analysis
Dialogue and Stage Directions What are the contrasting character traits of Mary Warren and of Mercy Lewis?

21 
Reading Check
Why do the Putnams believe there is witchcraft in Salem Village?

19 Literary Analysis
Dialogue and Stage Directions

- Draw students' attention to the stage direction preceding Abigail's line, "How is Ruth sick?" If necessary, define the word *trepidation,* and **ask** students what the phrase "hushed trepidation" indicates about Abigail's state of mind.
  Answer: Abigail is frightened, and wishes not to be overheard.
- **Ask** students the first Literary Analysis question: What does this conversation reveal about the two young women?
  Answer: They don't think Ruth and Betty are bewitched. They know they have done something wrong and they may get into trouble. Abigail wants to be sure that they all tell the same story.

20 Literary Analysis
Dialoque and Stage Directions

- **Ask** students the second Literary Analysis question: What are the contrasting character traits of Mary Warren and of Mercy Lewis?
  Answer: Mary feels guilty about her behavior in the woods. Mercy treats it as a joke.
- Have students compare and contrast Abigail with the other two girls.
  Answer: Abigail seems to be the leader of the group. She takes charge of the most practical aspect of the situation by deciding exactly what the girls should admit to.

21 Reading Check

Answer: They blame Ruth's illness on witchcraft.

22 Critical Thinking
Assess

- **Ask** students to assess Abigail's character.
  Answer: She is mean to the other girls. She is a leader who rules the group by inspiring fear. She is strong. She hates Goody Proctor.
- **Ask** students whether the other girls are likely to give Abigail away.
  Answer: Betty and Mary seem too frightened of her to give her away, but Mary also seems frightened of the consequences of lying.

23 Critical Viewing

Answer: Betty exhibits pain and fear.

MARY WARREN: Abby, we've got to tell. Witchery's a hangin' error, a hangin' like they done in Boston two year ago! We must tell the truth, Abby! You'll only be whipped for dancin', and the other things!

ABIGAIL: Oh, *we'll* be whipped!

MARY WARREN: I never done none of it, Abby. I only looked!

MERCY, *moving menacingly toward* MARY: Oh, you're a great one for lookin', aren't you, Mary Warren? What a grand peeping courage you have!

BETTY, *on the bed, whimpers.* ABIGAIL *turns to her at once.*

ABIGAIL: Betty? *She goes to* BETTY. Now, Betty, dear, wake up now. It's Abigail. *She sits* BETTY *up and furiously shakes her.* I'll beat you, Betty! BETTY *whimpers.* My, you seem improving. I talked to your papa and I told him everything. So there's nothing to—

BETTY, *darts off the bed, frightened of* ABIGAIL, *and flattens herself against the wall:* I want my mama!

23 ▲ **Critical Viewing** What emotion is conveyed in this image of Betty Parris's attempt to fly? Explain. **[Interpret]**

ABIGAIL, *with alarm, as she cautiously approaches* BETTY: What ails you, Betty? Your mama's dead and buried.

BETTY: I'll fly to Mama. Let me fly! *She raises her arms as though to fly, and streaks for the window, gets one leg out.*

ABIGAIL, *pulling her away from the window:* I told him everything; he knows now, he knows everything we—

BETTY: You drank blood, Abby! You didn't tell him that!

ABIGAIL: Betty, you never say that again! You will never—

BETTY: You did, you did! You drank a charm to kill John Proctor's wife! You drank a charm to kill Goody Proctor!

22 **ABIGAIL,** *smashes her across the face:* Shut it! Now shut it!

BETTY: *collapsing on the bed:* Mama, Mama! *She dissolves into sobs.*

ABIGAIL: Now look you. All of you. We danced. And Tituba conjured Ruth Putnam's dead sisters. And that is all. And mark this. Let either of you breathe a word, or the edge of a word, about the other things, and I will come to you in the black of some terrible night and I will bring a pointy reckoning that will shudder you. And you know I can do it; I saw Indians smash my dear parents' heads on the pillow next to mine, and I have seen some reddish work done at night, and I can make you wish you had never seen the sun go down! *She goes to* BETTY *and roughly sits her up.* Now, you—sit up and stop this!

But BETTY *collapses in her hands and lies inert on the bed.*

Enrichment

Indians Versus Settlers

Abigail remembers seeing "Indians smash my dear parents' heads on the pillows next to mine." As the immigrant population rose, settlers took over more and more of what had been Native American territory. Native Americans retaliated by attacking the settlements.

At dawn on February 10, 1676, the Narragansett people attacked the tiny village of Lancaster, Massachusetts. They set fire to every building and killed most of the settlers, except for a few whom they carried away and held for ransom. Ironically, the Narragansett were armed with guns for which they had once traded with the Europeans. Mary Rowlandson, freed after a £20 ransom was paid, published an account of the raid and her captivity. "Captivity narratives" such as hers were best-sellers in Puritan New England—they were among the very few books whose publication the Puritans allowed.

MARY WARREN, *with hysterical fright:* What's got her? ABIGAIL *stares in fright at* BETTY. Abby, she's going to die! It's a sin to conjure, and we—

ABIGAIL, *starting for* MARY: I say shut it, Mary Warren!

Enter JOHN PROCTOR. *On seeing him.* MARY WARREN *leaps in fright.*

Proctor was a farmer in his middle thirties. He need not have been a partisan of any faction in the town, but there is evidence to suggest that he had a sharp and biting way with hypocrites. He was the kind of man—powerful of body, even-tempered, and not easily led—who cannot refuse support to partisans without drawing their deepest resentment. In Proctor's presence a fool felt his foolishness instantly—and a Proctor is always marked for calumny therefore.

But as we shall see, the steady manner he displays does not spring from an untroubled soul. He is a sinner, a sinner not only against the moral fashion of the time, but against his own vision of decent conduct. These people had no ritual for the washing away of sins. It is another trait we inherited from them, and it has helped to discipline us as well as to breed hypocrisy among us. Proctor, respected and even feared in Salem, has come to regard himself as a kind of fraud. But no hint of this has yet appeared on the surface, and as he enters from the crowded parlor below it is a man in his prime we see, with a quiet confidence and an unexpressed, hidden force. Mary Warren, his servant, can barely speak for embarrassment and fear.

MARY WARREN: Oh! I'm just going home, Mr. Proctor.

PROCTOR: Be you foolish, Mary Warren? Be you deaf? I forbid you leave the house, did I not? Why shall I pay you? I am looking for you more often than my cows!

MARY WARREN: I only come to see the great doings in the world.

PROCTOR: I'll show you a great doin' on your arse one of these days. Now get you home; my wife is waitin' with your work! *Trying to retain a shred of dignity, she goes slowly out.*

MERCY LEWIS, *both afraid of him and strangely titillated:* I'd best be off. I have my Ruth to watch. Good morning, Mr. Proctor.

MERCY *sidles out. Since* PROCTOR'S *entrance,* ABIGAIL *has stood as though on tiptoe, absorbing his presence, wide-eyed. He glances at her then goes to* BETTY *on the bed.*

ABIGAIL: Gad. I'd almost forgot how strong you are, John Proctor!

PROCTOR, *looking at* ABIGAIL *now, the faintest suggestion of a knowing smile on his face:* What's this mischief here?

ABIGAIL, *with a nervous laugh:* Oh, she's only gone silly somehow.

PROCTOR: The road past my house is a pilgrimage to Salem all morning. The town's mumbling witchcraft.

ABIGAIL: Oh, posh! *Winningly she comes a little closer, with a confidential, wicked air.* We were dancin' in the woods last night, and my uncle leaped in on us. She took fright, is all. ㉕

PROCTOR, *his smile widening:* Ah, you're wicked yet, aren't y'! *A trill of expectant laughter escapes her, and she dares come closer, feverishly*

Literary Analysis
Dialogue, Stage Directions, and Dramatic Exposition What does Miller reveal about Proctor through this dramatic exposition?

Vocabulary Builder
calumny (kal' əm nē) *n.* false accusation; slander

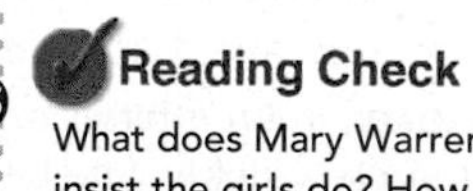

Reading Check
What does Mary Warren insist the girls do? How does Abigail react?

㉔ Literary Analysis
Dialogue, Stage Directions, and Dramatic Exposition

- **Ask** students the Literary Analysis question: What does Miller reveal about Proctor through this dramatic exposition?
  Answer: Proctor is a loner who relies on his own judgment. He is not necessarily popular. He doesn't like hypocrites.
- Have students **speculate** about the sins Proctor may have committed. Point out the stage direction describing Abigail "absorbing his presence, wide-eyed" and remind them of her desire to kill Proctor's wife.
  Answer: Proctor and Abigail may have been lovers; Abigail is clearly attracted to him and hates his wife. Dialogue earlier in the play states that Goody Proctor avoids church because she doesn't want to "sit so close to something soiled," and that she threw Abigail out of her house.

㉕ Reading Check

Answer: Mary insists that they tell the truth. Abigail threatens violence if anyone talks.

26 Literary Analysis
Dialogue and Stage Directions

- **Ask** students the Literary Analysis question: What important information about Abigail's behavior and emotions is conveyed through these stage directions?
  Answer: The stage directions mention her "concentrated desire" and "grasping his hand." She wants Proctor.
- **Ask** students what Proctor's dialogue suggests about his intentions toward Abigail.
  Answer: He has made up his mind that the affair is over. He does not love her or want her to take his wife's place.

▶ **Monitor Progress:** Given Abigail's character, how is she likely to react to this rejection?
Answer: She may threaten Proctor. She has already "drunk a charm to kill Goody Proctor"; she may try something like that again.

27 Reading Strategy
Questioning the Characters' Motives

- **Ask** students the Reading Strategy question: What does this paragraph reveal about Abigail's motivations?
  Answer: She drank blood to kill Goody Proctor because she wants to take her place.
- **Ask** students to deduce Proctor's motivation for taking Abigail as a lover.
  Possible answers: He was captivated by her beauty. He responded to her feelings for him. He is not in love with his wife. His wife is, as Abigail says, a cold woman.
- Why is Proctor angry with himself? What does this suggest about him?
  Answer: His anger at himself after Abigail's remark about his wife suggests that he also has resented Elizabeth, and used this resentment as an excuse for his affair.

looking into his eyes. You'll be clapped in the stocks before you're twenty. *He takes a step to go, and she springs into his path.*

ABIGAIL: Give me a word, John. A soft word. *Her concentrated desire destroys his smile.*

PROCTOR: No, no, Abby. That's done with.

ABIGAIL, *tauntingly:* You come five mile to see a silly girl fly? I know you better.

26 **PROCTOR,** *setting her firmly out of his path:* I come to see what mischief your uncle's brewin' now. *With final emphasis:* Put it out of mind, Abby.

ABIGAIL, *grasping his hand before he can release her:* John—I am waitin' for you every night.

PROCTOR: Abby, I never give you hope to wait for me.

ABIGAIL, *now beginning to anger—she can't believe it:* I have something better than hope, I think!

PROCTOR: Abby, you'll put it out of mind. I'll not be comin' for you more.

ABIGAIL: You're surely sportin' with me.

PROCTOR: You know me better.

ABIGAIL: I know how you clutched my back behind your house and sweated like a stallion whenever I come near! Or did I dream that? It's she put me out, you cannot pretend it were you. I saw your face when she put me out, and you loved me then and you do now!

PROCTOR: Abby, that's a wild thing to say—

ABIGAIL: A wild thing may say wild things. But not so wild, I think. I have seen you since she put me out; I have seen you nights.

PROCTOR: I have hardly stepped off my farm this seven-month.

ABIGAIL: I have a sense for heat, John, and yours has drawn me to my window, and I have seen you looking up, burning in your loneliness. Do you tell me you've never looked up at my window?

PROCTOR: I may have looked up.

27 **ABIGAIL,** *now softening:* And you must. You are no wintry man. I know you, John. I *know* you. *She is weeping.* I cannot sleep for dreamin'; I cannot dream but I wake and walk about the house as though I'd find you comin' through some door. *She clutches him desperately.*

PROCTOR, *gently pressing her from him, with great sympathy but firmly:* Child—

ABIGAIL, *with a flash of anger:* How do you call me child!

PROCTOR: Abby, I may think of you softly from time to time. But I will cut off my hand before I'll ever reach for you again. Wipe it out of mind. We never touched, Abby.

ABIGAIL: Aye, but we did.

PROCTOR: Aye, but we did not.

ABIGAIL, *with a bitter anger:* Oh, I marvel how such a strong man may let such a sickly wife be—

PROCTOR, *angered—at himself as well:* You'll speak nothin' of Elizabeth!

Literary Analysis
Dialogue and Stage Directions What important information about Abigail's behavior and emotions is conveyed through these stage directions?

Reading Strategy
Questioning the Characters' Motives What does this paragraph reveal about Abigail's motivations?

ABIGAIL: She is blackening my name in the village! She is telling lies about me! She is a cold, sniveling woman, and you bend to her! Let her turn you like a—

PROCTOR, *shaking her:* Do you look for whippin'?

A psalm is heard being sung below.

ABIGAIL, *in tears:* I look for John Proctor that took me from my sleep and put knowledge in my heart! I never knew what pretense Salem was, I never knew the lying lessons I was taught by all these Christian women and their covenanted men! And now you bid me tear the light out of my eyes? I will not, I cannot! You loved me, John Proctor, and whatever sin it is, you love me yet! *He turns abruptly to go out. She rushes to him.* John, pity me, pity me!

The words "going up to Jesus" are heard in the psalm, and BETTY *claps her ears suddenly and whines loudly.*

ABIGAIL: Betty? *She hurries to* BETTY, *who is now sitting up and screaming.* PROCTOR *goes to* BETTY *as* ABIGAIL *is trying to pull her hands down, calling "Betty!"*

PROCTOR, *growing unnerved:* What's she doing? Girl, what ails you? Stop that wailing!

The singing has stopped in the midst of this, and now PARRIS *rushes in.*

PARRIS: What happened? What are you doing to her? Betty! *He rushes to the bed, crying,* "Betty, Betty!" MRS. PUTNAM *enters, feverish with curiosity, and with her* PUTNAM *and* MERCY LEWIS. PARRIS, *at the bed, keeps lightly slapping* BETTY'S *face, while she moans and tries to get up.*

ABIGAIL: She heard you singin' and suddenly she's up and screamin'.

MRS. PUTNAM: The psalm! The psalm! She cannot bear to hear the Lord's name!

PARRIS: No, God forbid. Mercy, run to the doctor! Tell him what's happened here! MERCY LEWIS *rushes out.*

MRS. PUTNAM: Mark it for a sign, mark it!

REBECCA NURSE, *seventy-two, enters. She is white-haired, leaning upon her walking-stick.*

PUTNAM, *pointing at the whimpering* BETTY: That is a notorious sign of witchcraft afoot, Goody Nurse, a prodigious sign!

MRS. PUTNAM: My mother told me that! When they cannot bear to hear the name of—

PARRIS, *trembling:* Rebecca, Rebecca, go to her, we're lost. She suddenly cannot bear to hear the Lord's—

GILES COREY, *eighty-three, enters. He is knotted with muscle, canny, inquisitive, and still powerful.*

REBECCA: There is hard sickness here, Giles Corey, so please to keep the quiet.

GILES: I've not said a word. No one here can testify I've said a word. Is she going to fly again? I hear she flies.

PUTNAM: Man, be quiet now!

Literary Analysis
Dialogue and Stage Directions What do these lines reveal about Mrs. Putnam's eagerness to see signs of witchcraft?

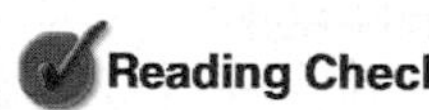

Reading Check
What effect does the psalm have on Betty? Why?

28 Literary Analysis
Dialogue and Stage Directions

- **Ask** students what effect the sound of the psalm has in this scene.
  Answer: It frightens Betty. It is ironic because it accompanies Abigail's speech condemning virtue and praising sin.
- **Ask** students to analyze Abigail's speech beginning "I look for John Proctor." What does this speech tell them about Abigail? Does it alter their opinions of her? Does it make her more or less sympathetic?
  Answers: The speech suggests that the passion Abigail shared with John has made her question the values of Salem—purity, chastity, and virtue. She judges the people of Salem as hypocrites, because they share passion but preach against it. Students should sympathize with Abigail's suffering, and they may agree with her view of her neighbors.

29 Literary Analysis
Dialogue and Stage Directions

- **Ask** students the Literary Analysis question: What do these lines reveal about Mrs. Putnam's eagerness to see signs of witchcraft?
  Answer: She jumps to the conclusion that Betty's reaction to the psalm means that she is bewitched.
- How does Proctor react to Betty's screams?
  Answer: He asks why she screams instead of making an assumption.

▶ **Monitor Progress:** Have students discuss what the characters' reactions suggest about them.

30 Reading Check

Answer: It seems to give her pain.

Differentiated Instruction
Solutions for All Learners

Support for English Learners
Have a student read aloud John's speech beginning "Abby, I may think of you". Make sure students understand that when he says, "We never touched, Abby," he does not mean this literally—he is urging her to think and behave as if it had never happened and trying to tell her that on the deepest level, they never touched.

Strategy for Advanced Readers
Ask students to analyze Abigail's motivation. They can begin with her actions in this conversation with Proctor and continue weighing her motives as they read further. Have students think about whether they sympathize at all with Abigail, or whether they condemn her entirely as they watch her begin to accuse people of witchcraft.

❸❶ Critical Thinking

Analyze

- **Ask** students what reputation Francis and Rebecca Nurse had had in the community until now. **Answer:** They had been greatly respected, and perhaps envied.
- Go over the information in the last two paragraphs of this passage with students. Clarify for them that bad feeling has arisen between the Putnam and Nurse clans over land.
- Draw students' attention to the last sentence in the passage, and define the word *iniquity*—"wickedness" or "unrighteousness."
- **Ask** students to summarize what Miller is suggesting when he says ironically that Mrs. Putnam's charge that Rebecca Nurse had "tempted her to iniquity" was more true than Mrs. Putnam realized. **Answer:** Students should recognize that the competitive envy between the two groups is prompting the Putnams' persecution of Rebecca Nurse. Miller is suggesting that although she may be unconscious of the fact, Mrs. Putnam's own resentment caused her to yield to the temptation of charging an innocent woman with a crime punishable by death—which is indeed iniquitous.

❸❷ Critical Viewing

Answer: Students may say that the rolled-up sleeves, open collar, and hoe suggest hard physical labor, and that the actor's expression is solemn and stern.

Everything is quiet. REBECCA *walks across the room to the bed. Gentleness exudes from her.* BETTY *is quietly whimpering, eyes shut.* REBECCA *simply stands over the child, who gradually quiets.*

And while they are so absorbed, we may put a word in for Rebecca. Rebecca was the wife of Francis Nurse, who, from all accounts, was one of those men for whom both sides of the argument had to have respect. He was called upon to arbitrate disputes as though he were an unofficial judge, and Rebecca also enjoyed the high opinion most people had for him. By the time of the delusion, they had three hundred acres, and their children were settled in separate homesteads within the same estate. However, Francis had originally rented the land, and one theory has it that, as he gradually paid for it and raised his social status, there were those who resented his rise.

Another suggestion to explain the systematic campaign against Rebecca, and inferentially against Francis, is the land war he fought with his neighbors, one of whom was a Putnam. This squabble grew to the proportions of a battle in the woods between partisans of both sides, and it is said to have lasted for two days. As for Rebecca herself, the general opinion of her character was so high that to explain how anyone dared cry her out for a witch—and more, how adults could bring themselves to lay hands on her—we must look to the fields and boundaries of that time.

❸❶ As we have seen, Thomas Putnam's man for the Salem ministry was Bayley. The Nurse clan had been in the faction that prevented Bayley's taking office. In addition, certain families allied to the Nurses by blood or friendship, and whose farms were contiguous with the Nurse farm or close to it, combined to break away from the Salem town authority and set up Topsfield, a new and independent entity whose existence was resented by old Salemites.

That the guiding hand behind the outcry was Putnam's is indicated by the fact that, as soon as it began, this Topsfield-Nurse faction absented themselves from church in protest and disbelief. It was Edward and Jonathan Putnam who signed the first complaint against Rebecca; and Thomas Putnam's little daughter was the one who fell into a fit at the hearing and pointed to Rebecca as her attacker. To top it all, Mrs. Putnam—who is now staring at the bewitched child on the bed—soon accused Rebecca's spirit of "tempting her to iniquity," a charge that had more truth in it than Mrs. Putnam could know.

MRS. PUTNAM, *astonished:* What have you done?

REBECCA, *in thought, now leaves the bedside and sits.*

PARRIS, *wondrous and relieved:* What do you make of it, Rebecca?

PUTNAM, *eagerly:* Goody Nurse, will you go to my Ruth and see if you can wake her?

REBECCA, *sitting:* I think she'll wake in time. Pray calm yourselves. I have eleven children, and I am twenty-six

❸❷ ▼ **Critical Viewing** How would you characterize John Proctor, based on this photograph? After you have finished reading the play, see if your prediction was accurate. **[Predict]**

Enrichment

Church Membership

Church membership among the Puritans was the result of religious conversion. Everyone in the community was expected to attend services, but only those who had been converted ("born again," in present-day terminology) were entitled to membership in the congregation and the power and privileges that went with membership (Proctor refers to the ability to vote). Before 1662, only the children of church members were baptized and admitted to the church. However, as church membership fell, Boston Puritans began to adopt the Halfway Covenant, which opened baptism and church membership to children of those who were virtuous Christians but not church members. Conservative congregations were violently opposed to this relaxation of standards, and some churches adopted the Halfway Covenant only after the Salem trials.

times a grandma, and I have seen them all through their silly seasons, and when it come on them they will run the Devil bowlegged keeping up with their mischief. I think she'll wake when she tires of it. A child's spirit is like a child, you can never catch it by running after it; you must stand still, and, for love, it will soon itself come back.

PROCTOR: Aye, that's the truth of it, Rebecca.

MRS. PUTNAM: This is no silly season, Rebecca. My Ruth is bewildered, Rebecca; she cannot eat.

REBECCA: Perhaps she is not hungered yet. *To* PARRIS: I hope you are not decided to go in search of loose spirits, Mr. Parris. I've heard promise of that outside.

PARRIS: A wide opinion's running in the parish that the Devil may be among us, and I would satisfy them that they are wrong.

PROCTOR: Then let you come out and call them wrong. Did you consult the wardens before you called this minister to look for devils?

PARRIS: He is not coming to look for devils!

PROCTOR: Then what's he coming for?

PUTNAM: There be children dyin' in the village, Mister!

PROCTOR: I seen none dyin'. This society will not be a bag to swing around your head, Mr. Putnam. *To Parris:* Did you call a meeting before you—?

PUTNAM: I am sick of meetings; cannot the man turn his head without he have a meeting?

PROCTOR: He may turn his head, but not to Hell!

REBECCA: Pray, John, be calm. *Pause. He defers to her.* Mr. Parris, I think you'd best send Reverend Hale back as soon as he come. This will set us all to arguin' again in the society, and we thought to have peace this year. I think we ought rely on the doctor now, and good prayer.

MRS. PUTNAM: Rebecca, the doctor's baffled!

REBECCA: If so he is, then let us go to God for the cause of it. There is prodigious danger in the seeking of loose spirits. I fear it, I fear it. Let us rather blame ourselves and—

PUTNAM: How may we blame ourselves? I am one of nine sons; the Putnam seed have peopled this province. And yet I have but one child left of eight—and now she shrivels!

REBECCA: I cannot fathom that.

MRS. PUTNAM, *with a growing edge of sarcasm:* But I must! You think it God's work you should never lose a child, nor grandchild either, and I bury all but one? There are wheels within wheels in this village, and fires within fires!

PUTNAM, *to* PARRIS: When Reverend Hale comes, you will proceed to look for signs of witchcraft here.

PROCTOR, *to* PUTNAM: You cannot command Mr. Parris. We vote by name in this society, not by acreage.

Reading Strategy
Questioning the Characters' Motives
What do the Putnams suggest by their remarks?

34 
Reading Check
What is Rebecca Nurse's effect on Betty? Why?

33 Reading Strategy
Questioning the Characters' Motives

- **Ask** students the Reading Strategy question: What do the Putnams suggest by their remarks?
  Answer: They suggest that other people are to blame for their misfortunes.
- **Ask** students to summarize Rebecca's motives for her actions and comments in this sequence.
  Answer: Rebecca wants peace in the community. She doesn't want Hale coming among them because she doesn't welcome the strife that rumors of witchcraft will cause between neighbors. She is tolerant and calm and tries to make everyone else see reason and get along better.
- What was Parris's motive for calling Hale without consulting the congregation?
  Answer: He knows he is not popular in the parish. He doesn't want to call attention to his lack of control over his daughter and niece.

34 Reading Check

Answer: Rebecca Nurse's presence, which is filled with her calm strength, seems to quiet and soothe Betty.

Differentiated Instruction
Solutions for All Learners

Strategy for Gifted/Talented Students

Have students work as a group to make a large chart or diagram assessing the responsibility of each character for the trials that begin in Act II. Each student can choose one or two characters and carefully read through Act I, looking for speeches and actions in which this character sets something in motion that helps bring the town to the point of the trials. The diagram should clearly show what each character says and does that brings about this outcome. Students can create a bulletin-board display showing the results of their search for responsibility. The entire class can use the display as a springboard for a discussion of the issue of guilt in Salem. Remind students to consider the idea that apparently innocent characters like John Proctor may also bear some responsibility.

35 Reading Strategy
Questioning the Characters' Motives

- **Ask** students the Reading Strategy question: Of what charge does Parris accuse members of his congregation? What does this accusation reveal about him?
  Answer: Parris accuses the congregation of persecuting him, and suggests that this may be the work of the devil.
- Why does Parris preach "hellfire and damnation" when he knows this drives away the parishioners?
  Answer: He doesn't understand their needs. He is frightened and paranoid, and he reveals these emotions in his sermons.

36 Literary Analysis
Dialogue and Stage Directions

- **Ask** students the Literary Analysis question: How does the playwright indicate that Parris interrupts Proctor?
  Answer: The dash after the word *house* shows that Parris has cut Proctor off in midsentence.
- Have students **identify** the sources of the conflict between Parris and Proctor.
  Answer: Proctor thinks Parris is unfit to preach; he also thinks he is too much concerned with the material advantages of being a minister. Parris resents Proctor's contempt; he believes that the congregation should show their respect for the church by showing respect for his wishes.
- Why is everyone shocked when Proctor says he wants to join the faction against Parris?
  Answer: They live in a society where everyone agrees to accept the authority of the minister and the church.

▶ **Monitor Progress:** Have students discuss who is right in this argument—Parris, Proctor, both to some degree, or neither? Have students give reasons for their opinions. Remind them to evaluate the men's opinions in the context of the time and place in which the play is set.

PUTNAM: I never heard you worried so on this society, Mr. Proctor. I do not think I saw you at Sabbath meeting since snow flew.

PROCTOR: I have trouble enough without I come five mile to hear him preach only hellfire and bloody damnation. Take it to heart, Mr. Parris. There are many others who stay away from church these days because you hardly ever mention God any more.

35 **PARRIS,** *now aroused:* Why, that's a drastic charge!

REBECCA: It's somewhat true; there are many that quail to bring their children—

PARRIS: I do not preach for children, Rebecca. It is not the children who are unmindful of their obligations toward this ministry.

REBECCA: Are there really those unmindful?

PARRIS: I should say the better half of Salem village—

PUTNAM: And more than that!

PARRIS: Where is my wood? My contract provides I be supplied with all my firewood. I am waiting since November for a stick, and even in November I had to show my frostbitten hands like some London beggar!

GILES: You are allowed six pound a year to buy your wood, Mr. Parris.

PARRIS: I regard that six pound as part of my salary. I am paid little enough without I spend six pound on firewood.

PROCTOR: Sixty, plus six for firewood—

PARRIS: The salary is sixty-six pound, Mr. Proctor! I am not some preaching farmer with a book under my arm; I am a graduate of Harvard College.

GILES: Aye, and well instructed in arithmetic!

PARRIS: Mr. Corey, you will look far for a man of my kind at sixty pound a year! I am not used to this poverty; I left a thrifty business in the Barbados to serve the Lord. I do not fathom it, why am I persecuted here? I cannot offer one proposition but there be a howling riot of argument. I have often wondered if the Devil be in it somewhere; I cannot understand you people otherwise.

PROCTOR: Mr. Parris, you are the first minister ever did demand the deed to this house—

PARRIS: Man! Don't a minister deserve a house to live in?

36 **PROCTOR:** To live in, yes. But to ask ownership is like you shall own the meeting house itself; the last meeting I were at you spoke so long on deeds and mortgages I thought it were an auction.

PARRIS: I want a mark of confidence, is all! I am your third preacher in seven years. I do not wish to be put out like the cat whenever some majority feels the whim. You people seem not to comprehend that a minister is the Lord's man in the parish; a minister is not to be so lightly crossed and contradicted—

PUTNAM: Aye!

PARRIS: There is either obedience or the church will burn like Hell is burning!

Reading Strategy
Questioning the Characters' Motives Of what charge does Parris accuse members of his congregation? What does this accusation reveal about him?

Literary Analysis
Dialogue and Stage Direction How does the playwright indicate that Parris interrupts Proctor?

PROCTOR: Can you speak one minute without we land in Hell again? I am sick of Hell!

PARRIS: It is not for you to say what is good for you to hear!

PROCTOR: I may speak my heart, I think!

PARRIS, *in a fury:* What, are we Quakers?[8] We are not Quakers here yet,
36 Mr. Proctor. And you may tell that to your followers!

PROCTOR: My followers!

PARRIS—*now he's out with it:* There is a party in this church. I am not blind; there is a faction and a party.

PROCTOR: Against you?

PUTNAM: Against him and all authority!

PROCTOR: Why, then I must find it and join it.

There is shock among the others.

REBECCA: He does not mean that.

PUTNAM: He confessed it now!

PROCTOR: I mean it solemnly, Rebecca; I like not the smell of this "authority."

REBECCA: No, you cannot break charity with your minister. You are another kind, John. Clasp his hand, make your peace.

PROCTOR: I have a crop to sow and lumber to drag home. *He goes angrily to the door and turns to* COREY *with a smile.* What say you, Giles, let's find the party. He says there's a party.

GILES: I've changed my opinion of this man, John. Mr. Parris, I beg your pardon. I never thought you had so much iron in you.

PARRIS, *surprised:* Why, thank you, Giles!

GILES: It suggests to the mind what the trouble be among us all these years. *To all:* Think on it. Wherefore is everybody suing everybody else? Think on it now, it's a deep thing, and dark as a pit. I have been six time in court this year—

PROCTOR, *familiarly, with warmth, although he knows he is approaching the edge of Giles' tolerance with this:* Is it the Devil's fault that a man cannot say you good morning without you clap him for defamation? You're old, Giles, and you're not hearin' so well as you did.

37 **GILES**—*he cannot be crossed:* John Proctor, I have only last month collected four pound damages for you publicly sayin' I burned the roof off your house, and I—

PROCTOR, *laughing:* I never said no such thing, but I've paid you for it, so I hope I can call you deaf without charge. Now come along, Giles, and help me drag my lumber home.

PUTNAM: A moment, Mr. Proctor. What lumber is that you're draggin', if I may ask you?

8. **Quakers** members of the Society of Friends, a Christian religious sect that was founded in the mid-17th century and has no formal creed, rites, or priesthood. Unlike the Quakers, the Puritans had a rigid code of conduct and were expected to heed the words of their ministers.

Literary Analysis
Dialogue and Stage Directions What does this dialogue between Proctor and Giles reveal about the mood and atmosphere in Salem?

38 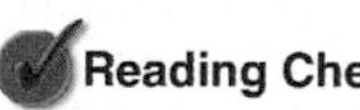

Reading Check
How do Proctor's and Parris's beliefs about authority differ?

37 Literary Analysis
Dialogue and Stage Directions

- **Ask** students the Literary Analysis question: What does this dialogue between Proctor and Giles reveal about the mood and atmosphere in Salem?
  Answer: Giles's dialogue suggests that, in general, the people of Salem don't get along well. They easily lose patience with one another, and instead of settling their quarrels among themselves they take one another to court.
- How does Proctor's manner with Giles contrast with the general mood in Salem?
  Answer: Proctor is patient and good-humored with Giles. He has even paid him damages for something he never said, rather than risk his friendship.

▶ **Monitor Progress:** What does Proctor's manner toward Giles suggest about Proctor's character?
Answer: He doesn't look for trouble. He is easygoing and tolerant as a rule.

38 Reading Check
Answer: Proctor believes that the minister should use his authority as minister to help and guide his people, whereas Parris believes his authority inheres in his ability to exact obedience from the congregation.

Differentiated Instruction
Solutions for All Learners

Strategy for Advanced Readers
Proctor and Rebecca both express some distaste for Parris's preaching "hellfire and bloody damnation." Earlier this year, students read a prime example of this style of sermon, Jonathan Edwards's "Sinners in the Hands of an Angry God" (Unit 1). Have students reread Edwards's sermon in light of *The Crucible.* Have them put themselves in the place of the congregation and imagine how they would have felt at hearing such sermons week in and week out. How might Parris's style of preaching have alienated "the better half of Salem village"? What evidence can students find that Parris's harshness has itself created an atmosphere in which paranoia can flourish?

39 Reading Strategy
Questioning the Characters' Motives

- **Ask** students the Reading Strategy question: Why does Giles feel a "sudden will to work"?
  Answer: Giles has had enough of Putnam's company. He much prefers Proctor to Putnam and is glad to help Proctor do something that will annoy Putnam.
- Why does Putnam threaten Proctor and Corey?
  Answer: Putnam is greedy and belligerent. He will do whatever he must to hang on to property, even if it means making enemies of his neighbors.

40 Literary Analysis
Dialogue, Stage Directions, and Dramatic Exposition

- **Ask** students to characterize Mr. Hale. What is his area of expertise in the church?
  Answer: Mr. Hale is a learned man and an expert in demonology.
- **Ask** students the Literary Analysis question: What important information does Miller provide about his view of the world?
  Possible Answer: Miller introduces the idea that we, like the Puritans, are still gripped by the assumption that the world is neatly divided into clearly identifiable good and evil—the realms of God and the Devil.

PROCTOR: My lumber. From out my forest by the riverside.

PUTNAM: Why, we are surely gone wild this year. What anarchy is this? That tract is in my bounds, it's in my bounds, Mr. Proctor.

PROCTOR: In your bounds! *Indicating* REBECCA: I bought that tract from Goody Nurse's husband five months ago.

39 PUTNAM: He had no right to sell it. It stands clear in my grandfather's will that all the land between the river and—

PROCTOR: Your grandfather had a habit of willing land that never belonged to him, if I may say it plain.

GILES: That's God's truth; he nearly willed away my north pasture but he knew I'd break his fingers before he'd set his name to it. Let's get your lumber home, John. I feel a sudden will to work coming on.

PUTNAM: You load one oak of mine and you'll fight to drag it home!

GILES: Aye, and we'll win too, Putnam—this fool and I. Come on! *He turns to* PROCTOR *and starts out.*

PUTNAM: I'll have my men on you, Corey! I'll clap a writ on you!

Enter REVEREND JOHN HALE *of Beverly.*

Mr. Hale is nearing forty, a tight-skinned, eager-eyed intellectual. This is a beloved errand for him; on being called here to ascertain witchcraft he felt the pride of the specialist whose unique knowledge has at last been publicly called for. Like almost all men of learning, he spent a good deal of time pondering the invisible world, especially since he had himself encountered a witch in his parish not long before. That woman, however, turned into a mere pest under his searching scrutiny, and the child she had allegedly been afflicting recovered her normal behavior after Hale had given her his kindness and a few days of rest in his own house. However, that experience never raised a doubt in his mind as to the reality of the underworld or the existence of Lucifer's
40 many-faced lieutenants. And his belief is not to his discredit. Better minds than Hale's were—and still are—convinced that there is a society of spirits beyond our ken. One cannot help noting that one of his lines has never yet raised a laugh in any audience that has seen this play; it is his assurance that "We cannot look to superstition in this. The Devil is precise." Evidently we are not quite certain even now whether diabolism is holy and not to be scoffed at. And it is no accident that we should be so bemused.

Like Reverend Hale and the others on this stage, we conceive the Devil as a necessary part of a respectable view of cosmology. Ours is a divided empire in which certain ideas and emotions and actions are of God, and their opposites are of Lucifer. It is as impossible for most men to conceive of a morality without sin as of an earth without "sky." Since 1692 a great but superficial change has wiped out God's beard and the Devil's horns, but the world is still gripped between two diametrically opposed absolutes. The concept of unity, in which positive and negative are attributes of the same force, in which good and evil are relative, ever-changing, and always joined to the same phenomenon—such a concept

Reading Strategy
Questioning the Characters' Motives Why does Giles feel a "sudden will to work"?

Literary Analysis
Dialogue, Stage Directions, and Dramatic Exposition What important information does Miller provide about his view of the world?

Enrichment

Voltaire on the Inquisition

François-Marie Arouet, better known as Voltaire (1694–1778), is probably the best-known thinker of the French Enlightenment. The Spanish Inquisition was in power throughout Voltaire's lifetime, and it was the epitome of everything he despised about organized religion and Christianity in particular. Here is the opening of Voltaire's entry "On the Inquisition" from his *Philosophical Dictionary* (1764):

> "The Inquisition is well known to be an admirable and truly Christian invention for increasing the power of the pope and monks, and rendering the population of a whole kingdom hypocrites."

is still reserved to the physical sciences and to the few who have grasped the history of ideas. When it is recalled that until the Christian era the underworld was never regarded as a hostile area, that all gods were useful and essentially friendly to man despite occasional lapses; when we see the steady and methodical inculcation into humanity of the idea of man's worthlessness—until redeemed—the necessity of the Devil may become evident as a weapon, a weapon designed and used time and time again in every age to whip men into a surrender to a particular church or church-state.

Our difficulty in believing the—for want of a better word—political inspiration of the Devil is due in great part to the fact that he is called up and damned not only by our social antagonists but by our own side, whatever it may be. The Catholic Church, through its Inquisition, is famous for cultivating Lucifer as the arch-fiend, but the Church's enemies relied no less upon the Old Boy to keep the human mind enthralled. Luther[9] was himself accused of alliance with Hell, and he in turn accused his enemies. To complicate matters further, he believed that he had had contact with the Devil and had argued theology with him. I am not surprised at this, for at my own university a professor of history—a Lutheran,[10] by the way—used to assemble his graduate students, draw the shades, and commune in the classroom with Erasmus.[11] He was never, to my knowledge, officially scoffed at for this, the reason being that the university officials, like most of us, are the children of a history which still sucks at the Devil's teats. At this writing, only England has held back before the temptations of contemporary diabolism. In the countries of the Communist ideology, all resistance of any import is linked to the totally malign capitalist succubi,[12] and in America any man who is not reactionary in his views is open to the charge of alliance with the Red hell. Political opposition, thereby, is given an inhumane overlay which then justifies the abrogation[13] of all normally applied customs of civilized intercourse. A political policy is equated with moral right, and opposition to it with diabolical malevolence. Once such an equation is effectively made, society becomes a congerie[14] of plots and counterplots, and the main role of government changes from that of the arbiter to that of the scourge of God.

9. **Luther** Martin Luther (1483–1546), German theologian who led the Protestant Reformation.
10. **Lutheran** member of the Protestant denomination founded by Martin Luther.
11. **Erasmus** Erasmus Desiderius (1466?–1536), Dutch humanist, scholar, and theologian.
12. **succubi** (suk′ yoo bī) female demons thought to lie on sleeping men.
13. **abrogation** (ab′ rō gā′ shən) abolishment.
14. **congerie** (kän′ jə rē′) heap; pile.

Literature in Context

41 History Connection

♦ *The Inquisition*

Miller alludes to the Inquisition, a "court of justice" established by the Catholic Church in the thirteenth century, but he does not describe it. It bears a close resemblance to the Salem witch hunts of the 1690s and to the Red Scare during the 1950s. In each case, a panel of judges decided allegations of heresy or treason. The Salem judges sentenced some to death, as had the Catholic judges of the Middle Ages. No one died in the 1950s as a result of Senator McCarthy's accusations, but many suffered damage to their personal and professional reputations.

Connect to the Literature

What else might the Salem trials have in common with the Inquisition?

Vocabulary Builder

inculcation (in′ kul kā′ shən) *n.* teaching by repetition and urging

42  **Reading Check**

What is Reverend Hale's experience with witchcraft?

41 Literature in Context

The Inquisition

The first Roman Catholic Inquisition was called in 1231. Anyone accused of heresy, witchcraft, or sorcery was brought before the inquisitor and offered the opportunity to confess. Anyone who did not confess was tried and interrogated. Beginning in 1252, torture was commonly used to extract confessions. A secular branch of the Inquisition sentenced condemned heretics to death. The Inquisition was at its most powerful in northern Italy and southern France until 1478, when Pope Sixtus IV created the Spanish Inquisition, headed by the infamous Torquemada, who probably condemned about 2,000 people to death at the stake. The Spanish Inquisition continued to wield power off and on until 1834, when it was permanently suppressed.

Connect to the Literature Have students read the Literature in Context note and summarize what they have read so far. Then, **ask** the Literature in Context question.

Answer: Both the Inquisition and the Salem trials sought to impose religious doctrine upon those who did not conform to established religions. Both used techniques of humiliation and fear to destroy the lives of those who did not follow the doctrines of the tribunals. In both, with the confession of a subject's sins, the subject would be released from imprisonment or tortured and reaccepted into the community. Without confession, the subject might be condemned to death. Both the Inquisition and the Salem trials encouraged subjects to name or testify against their friends and family members.

42 Reading Check

Answer: Hale has examined and acquitted one accused witch and her child. Most of his experience with witchcraft comes from books.

Differentiated Instruction

Solutions for All Learners

Strategy for Less Proficient Readers

The commentary that begins on the left-hand page is dense and complex, both in its language and its arguments. Have students break it down into paragraphs, find the main idea and key supporting details in each paragraph, and use these notes to summarize Miller's arguments. Students can then gather for a discussion of their reactions to what Miller says.

Vocabulary for English Learners

This commentary is filled with sophisticated and unfamiliar vocabulary. Assign peer tutors to help students read the commentary. Students learning English should try as much as possible to use context clues or cognates to define unfamiliar words before checking a dictionary.

43 Critical Thinking
Evaluate

- **Ask** students to summarize Miller's arguments about the devil in society and human beliefs about the devil.
  Answer: Miller asserts that in the same way that the Puritans ascribed negative events to the influence of the devil on witches, modern people attributed the ills of the world to communism and communists.
- **Ask** students whether they accept Miller's argument. Does he support his contention? What evidence does he use? Is his evidence convincing?

The results of this process are no different now from what they ever were, except sometimes in the degree of cruelty inflicted, and not always even in that department. Normally, the actions and deeds of a man were all that society felt comfortable in judging. The secret intent of an action was left to the ministers, priests, and rabbis to deal with. When diabolism rises, however, actions are the least important manifests of the true nature of a man. The Devil, as Reverend Hale said, is a wily one, and until an hour before he fell, even God thought him beautiful in Heaven.

The analogy, however, seems to falter when one considers that, while there were no witches then, there are Communists and capitalists now, and in each camp there is certain proof that spies of each side are at work undermining the other. But this is a snobbish objection and not at all warranted by the facts. I have no doubt that people *were* communing with, and even worshiping, the Devil in Salem, and if the whole truth could be known in this case, as it is in others, we should discover a regular and conventionalized propitiation of the dark spirit. One certain evidence of this is the confession of Tituba, the slave of Reverend Parris, and another is the behavior of the children who were known to have indulged in sorceries with her.

Vocabulary Builder
propitiation (prə pish′ ē ā′ shən) *n.* action designed to soothe or satisfy a person, a cause, etc.

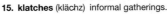

There are accounts of similar *klatches*[15] in Europe, where the daughters of the towns would assemble at night and, sometimes with fetishes,[16] sometimes with a selected young man, give themselves to love, with some bastardly results. The Church, sharp-eyed as it must be when gods long dead are brought to life, condemned these orgies as
43 witchcraft and interpreted them, rightly, as a resurgence of the Dionysiac[17] forces it had crushed long before. Sex, sin, and the Devil were early linked, and so they continued to be in Salem, and are today. From all accounts there are no more puritanical mores in the world than those enforced by the Communists in Russia, where women's fashions, for instance, are as prudent and all-covering as any American Baptist would desire. The divorce laws lay a tremendous responsibility on the father for the care of his children. Even the laxity of divorce regulations in the early years of the revolution was undoubtedly a revulsion from the nineteenth-century Victorian[18] immobility of marriage and the

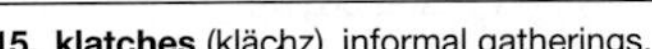

15. **klatches** (klächz) informal gatherings.
16. **fetishes** (fet′ ish iz) objects believed to have magical power.
17. **Dionysiac** (dī′ ə nis′ ē ak′) characteristic of Dionysus, Greek god of wine and revelry; thus, wild, frenzied, sensuous.
18. **Victorian** characteristic of the time when Victoria was queen of England (1837–1901), an era associated with respectability, prudery, and hypocrisy.

consequent hypocrisy that developed from it. If for no other reasons, a state so powerful, so jealous of the uniformity of its citizens, cannot long tolerate the atomization of the family. And yet, in American eyes at least, there remains the conviction that the Russian attitude toward women is lascivious. It is the Devil working again, just as he is working within the Slav who is shocked at the very idea of a woman's disrobing herself in a burlesque show. Our opposites are always robed in sexual sin, and it is from this unconscious conviction that demonology gains both its attractive sensuality and its capacity to infuriate and frighten.

Coming into Salem now, Reverend Hale conceives of himself much as a young doctor on his first call. His painfully acquired armory of symptoms, catchwords, and diagnostic procedures are now to be put to use at last. The road from Beverly is unusually busy this morning, and he has passed a hundred rumors that make him smile at the ignorance of the yeomanry in this most precise science. He feels himself allied with the best minds of Europe—kings, philosophers, scientists, and ecclesiasts of all churches. His goal is light, goodness and its preservation, and he knows the exaltation of the blessed whose intelligence, sharpened by minute examinations of enormous tracts, is finally called upon to face what may be a bloody fight with the Fiend himself.

He appears loaded down with half a dozen heavy books.

44 **HALE:** Pray you, someone take these!

PARRIS, *delighted:* Mr. Hale! Oh! it's good to see you again! *Taking some books:* My, they're heavy!

HALE, *setting down his books:* They must be; they are weighted with authority.

PARRIS, *a little scared:* Well, you do come prepared!

HALE: We shall need hard study if it comes to tracking down the Old Boy. *Noticing* REBECCA: You cannot be Rebecca Nurse?

REBECCA: I am, sir. Do you know me?

HALE: It's strange how I knew you, but I suppose you look as such a good soul should. We have all heard of your great charities in Beverly.

PARRIS: Do you know this gentleman? Mr. Thomas Putnam. And his good wife Ann.

HALE: Putnam! I had not expected such distinguished company, sir.

PUTNAM, *pleased:* It does not seem to help us today, Mr. Hale. We look to you to come to our house and save our child.

HALE: Your child ails too?

MRS. PUTNAM: Her soul, her soul seems flown away. She sleeps and yet she walks . . .

PUTNAM: She cannot eat.

HALE: Cannot eat! *Thinks on it. Then, to* PROCTOR *and* GILES COREY: Do you men have afflicted children?

PARRIS: No, no, these are farmers. John Proctor—

GILES COREY: He don't believe in witches.

Reading Strategy
Questioning the Characters' Motives
According to this passage, what motivates Reverend Hale to study and expose witchcraft?

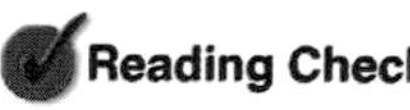

Reading Check
What is the "armory" Hale brings with him to Salem?

44 Reading Strategy
Questioning the Characters' Motives

- **Ask** students the Reading Strategy question: According to this passage, what motivates Reverend Hale to study and expose witchcraft?
  Answer: Hale wants to cure people. He wants to best the devil in combat for human souls.
- How do students evaluate Hale's fitness for his task, based on the information in the commentary?
  Answer: The case of the woman acquitted of witchcraft shows that Hale doesn't rush to judgment. However, he seems to rely too much on books and not on his own observations of people.
- What does Hale's recognition of Rebecca suggest about both characters?
  Answer: Rebecca's goodness is visible in her expression; Hale is observant enough to sense it.

45 Reading Check

Answer: It is an armory of "symptoms, catchwords, and diagnostic procedures."

50 Literary Analysis
Dialogue and Stage Directions

- **Ask** students the Literary Analysis question: In what ways do Hale's questions to Betty suggest the answers he wants to hear?
  Answer: He asks her instead of just waiting to see if she has anything to say.
- **Ask** students where they have seen this method of questioning before.
  Answer: In the play's opening passages, Parris suggests to Abigail that she and the others were conjuring spirits, rather than just asking her what they were doing.

▶ **Monitor Progress:** Point out that Hale repeats this method when he questions Abby about the soup. **Ask** students what they think of this method of questioning.
Answers: Students may object because it puts ideas into people's heads. When people are questioned about any serious crime, they can be so frightened that they may say anything; leading them is not the best way to find out the truth.

51 Critical Viewing

Answer: The photograph suggests that the girls are romping, dancing, literally "letting their hair down" and having fun.

knew it to be the Devil in an animal's shape. "What frighted you?" he was asked. He forgot everything but the word "frighted," and instantly replied, "I do not know that I ever spoke that word in my life."

HALE: Ah! The stoppage of prayer—that is strange. I'll speak further on that with you.

GILES: I'm not sayin' she's touched the Devil, now, but I'd admire to know what books she reads and why she hides them. She'll not answer me, y' see.

HALE: Aye, we'll discuss it. To all: Now mark me, if the Devil is in her you will witness some frightful wonders in this room, so please to keep your wits about you. Mr. Putnam, stand close in case she flies. Now, Betty, dear, will you sit up? PUTNAM *comes in closer, ready-handed.* HALE *sits* BETTY *up, but she hangs limp in his hands.* Hmmm. *He observes her carefully. The others watch breathlessly.* Can you hear me? I am John Hale, minister of Beverly. I have come to help you, dear. Do you remember my two little girls in Beverly? *She does not stir in his hands.*

PARRIS, *in fright:* How can it be the Devil? Why would he choose my house to strike? We have all manner of licentious people in the village!

HALE: What victory would the Devil have to win a soul already bad? It is the best the Devil wants, and who is better than the minister?

GILES: That's deep, Mr. Parris, deep, deep!

PARRIS, *with resolution now:* Betty! Answer Mr. Hale! Betty!

HALE: Does someone afflict you, child? It need not be a woman, mind you, or a man. Perhaps some bird invisible to others comes to you—perhaps a pig, a mouse, or any beast at all. Is there some figure bids you fly? *The child remains limp in his hands. In silence he lays her back on the pillow. Now, holding out his hands toward her, he intones:* In nomine Domini Sabaoth sui filiique ite ad infernos.[20] *She does not stir. He turns to* ABIGAIL, *his eyes narrowing.* Abigail, what sort of dancing were you doing with her in the forest?

50 **ABIGAIL:** Why—common dancing is all.

PARRIS: I think I ought to say that I—I saw a kettle in the grass where they were dancing.

ABIGAIL: That were only soup.

HALE: What sort of soup were in this kettle, Abigail?

ABIGAIL: Why, it were beans—and lentils, I think, and—

HALE: Mr. Parris, you did not notice, did you, any living thing in the kettle? A mouse, perhaps, a spider, a frog—?

PARRIS, *fearfully:* I—do believe there were some movement—in the soup.

ABIGAIL: That jumped in, we never put it in!

HALE, *quickly:* What jumped in?

---

20. **In nomine Domini Sabaoth sui filiique ite ad infernos** (in nō´ mē nā dō´ mē nē sab´ ā āth sōō´ ē fē´ lēē kwā ē´ tā äd in fur´ nōs) "In the name of the lord of hosts and his son, get thee to the lower world" (Latin).

Vocabulary Builder
licentious (lī sen´ shəs) *adj.* lacking moral restraint

Literary Analysis
Dialogue and Stage Directions In what way do Hale's questions to Betty suggest the answers he wants to hear?

51 ▶ **Critical Viewing**
Based on this photograph of Abigail and Tituba surrounded by other girls of Salem, how would you describe what actually happened in the woods? **[Interpret]**

ABIGAIL: Why, a very little frog jumped—

PARRIS: A frog, Abby!

HALE, *grasping* ABIGAIL: Abigail, it may be your cousin is dying. Did you call the Devil last night?

ABIGAIL: I never called him! Tituba, Tituba . . .

PARRIS, *blanched:* She called the Devil?

HALE: I should like to speak with Tituba.

PARRIS: Goody Ann, will you bring her up? MRS. PUTNAM *exits.*

HALE: How did she call him?

ABIGAIL: I know not—she spoke Barbados.

HALE: Did you feel any strangeness when she called him? A sudden cold wind, perhaps? A trembling below the ground?

ABIGAIL: I didn't see no Devil! *Shaking* BETTY: Betty, wake up. Betty! Betty!

HALE: You cannot evade me, Abigail. Did your cousin drink any of the brew in that kettle?

ABIGAIL: She never drank it!

HALE: Did you drink it?

ABIGAIL: No, sir!

HALE: Did Tituba ask you to drink it?

ABIGAIL: She tried, but I refused.

HALE: Why are you concealing? Have you sold yourself to Lucifer?

Reading Strategy
Questioning the Characters' Motives Why does Hale want to speak with Tituba?

53 **Reading Check**
What important details does Parris add to Abigail's story? How does she explain them?

52 Reading Strategy
Questioning the Characters' Motives

- **Ask** students the Reading Strategy question: Why does Hale want to speak with Tituba?
  Answer: Hale wishes to gain more information about Tituba's actions in the forest.
- Have students **predict** what is likely to happen when Tituba comes into the room. Have them base their predictions on what has happened since Hale's entrance.
  Answer: Hale is likely to question Tituba on the assumption that she is guilty of witchcraft.
- Point out that Hale also questions Abigail, assuming that she too is guilty of witchcraft. Have students note Abigail's response to these questions. What does her response suggest about her character?
  Answer: To divert attention from herself, she accuses Tituba. She points to Tituba as soon as Tituba enters the room. She is willing to sacrifice others to save herself.

53 Reading Check

Answer: Parris reveals that he saw a kettle being used to cook something, and that he saw something moving in it. Abigail claims it was only soup, and that a frog accidentally jumped in.

Differentiated Instruction
Solutions for All Learners

Strategy for Less Proficient Readers
Have students work together on cause-and-effect chains that trace the development of Act I from Parris's first questions to Abigail through the accusations of witchcraft that end the act. Students may want to consider causes that were in place before the play begins, such as Puritan disapproval of children having fun. They should also try predicting what will come of the accusations made at the end of the act.

Strategy for English Learners
To help students understand the complex set of motives and causes that drive the plot of the play, have them work together in groups with more proficient English speakers. Have students use a list of characters to brainstorm for dialogue and expository passages that reveal each character's motivations, and list these on the chalkboard. Then help students to create a timeline for the events in Act I, annotated with the characters' motivations for each action.

54 Reading Strategy
Questioning the Characters' Motives

- **Ask** students the first Reading Strategy question: What do you think Abigail is trying to do in accusing Tituba of making her "laugh at prayer"?
  Possible answers: Abigail is trying to divert attention from herself and her own guilt in trying to practice witchcraft against John Proctor's wife. On the previous page, Hale was beginning to accuse her of witchcraft.
- Why does Abigail attack Tituba rather than one of the other girls?
  Answer: Because Tituba is a slave and from a foreign culture, she is in a weak position. Abigail knows that her word will likely be taken against Tituba's.

55 Reading Strategy
Questioning the Characters' Motives

- **Ask** students the second Reading Strategy question: What does this dialogue reveal about the motives for Tituba's sudden confusion?
  Answer: Tituba confesses because Parris and Putnam tell her that the alternative is death.
- Why does Tituba not argue more strongly with Abigail?
  Possible answers: She is bewildered. She is shocked that Abigail has turned on her. She knows that no one will believe the word of a slave against that of the minister's niece. She doesn't want Abigail hanged.

ABIGAIL: I never sold myself! I'm a good girl! I'm a proper girl!

MRS. PUTNAM *enters with* TITUBA, *and instantly* ABIGAIL *points at* TITUBA.

ABIGAIL: She made me do it! She made Betty do it!

TITUBA, *shocked and angry:* Abby!

ABIGAIL: She makes me drink blood!

PARRIS: Blood!!

MRS. PUTNAM: My baby's blood?

TITUBA: No, no, chicken blood. I give she chicken blood!

HALE: Woman, have you enlisted these children for the Devil?

TITUBA: No, no, sir, I don't truck with no Devil!

HALE: Why can she not wake? Are you silencing this child?

TITUBA: I love me Betty!

54 **HALE:** You have sent your spirit out upon this child, have you not? Are you gathering souls for the Devil?

ABIGAIL: She sends her spirit on me in church; she makes me laugh at prayer!

PARRIS: She have often laughed at prayer!

ABIGAIL: She comes to me every night to go and drink blood!

TITUBA: You beg *me* to conjure! She beg *me* make charm—

ABIGAIL: Don't lie! *To* HALE: She comes to me while I sleep; she's always making me dream corruptions!

TITUBA: Why you say that, Abby?

ABIGAIL: Sometimes I wake and find myself standing in the open doorway and not a stitch on my body! I always hear her laughing in my sleep. I hear her singing her Barbados songs and tempting me with—

TITUBA: Mister Reverend, I never—

HALE, *resolved now:* Tituba, I want you to wake this child.

TITUBA: I have no power on this child, sir.

HALE: You most certainly do, and you will free her from it now! When did you compact with the Devil?

TITUBA: I don't compact with no Devil!

PARRIS: You will confess yourself or I will take you out and whip you to your death, Tituba!

55 **PUTNAM:** This woman must be hanged! She must be taken and hanged!

TITUBA, *terrified, falls to her knees:* No, no, don't hang Tituba! I tell him I don't desire to work for him, sir.

PARRIS: The Devil?

HALE: Then you saw him! TITUBA *weeps.* Now Tituba, I know that when we bind ourselves to Hell it is very hard to break with it. We are going to help you tear yourself free—

TITUBA, *frightened by the coming process:* Mister Reverend, I do believe somebody else be witchin' these children.

HALE: Who?

Reading Strategy
Questioning the Characters' Motives
What do you think Abigail is trying to do in accusing Tituba of making her "laugh at prayer"?

Reading Strategy
Questioning the Characters' Motives
What does this dialogue reveal about the motives for Tituba's sudden confusion?

TITUBA: I don't know, sir, but the Devil got him numerous witches.

HALE: Does he! *It is a clue.* Tituba, look into my eyes. Come, look into me. *She raises her eyes to his fearfully.* You would be a good Christian woman, would you not, Tituba?

TITUBA: Aye, sir, a good Christian woman.

HALE: And you love these little children?

TITUBA: Oh, yes, sir, I don't desire to hurt little children.

HALE: And you love God, Tituba?

TITUBA: I love God with all my bein'.

HALE: Now, in God's holy name—

TITUBA: Bless Him. Bless Him. *She is rocking on her knees, sobbing in terror.*

HALE: And to His glory—

TITUBA: Eternal glory. Bless Him—bless God . . .

HALE: Open yourself, Tituba—open yourself and let God's holy light shine on you.

TITUBA: Oh, bless the Lord.

HALE: When the Devil come to you does he ever come—with another person? *She stares up into his face.* Perhaps another person in the village? Someone you know.

PARRIS: Who came with him?

PUTNAM: Sarah Good? Did you ever see Sarah Good with him? Or Osburn?

PARRIS: Was it man or woman came with him?

56 **TITUBA:** Man or woman. Was—was woman.

PARRIS: What woman? A woman, you said. What woman?

TITUBA: It was black dark, and I—

PARRIS: You could see him, why could you not see her?

TITUBA: Well, they was always talking; they was always runnin' round and carryin' on—

PARRIS: You mean out of Salem? Salem witches?

TITUBA: I believe so, yes, sir.

Now HALE *takes her hand. She is surprised.*

HALE: Tituba. You must have no fear to tell us who they are, do you understand? We will protect you. The Devil can never overcome a
57 minister. You know that, do you not?

TITUBA, *kisses* HALE'S *hand:* Aye, sir, oh, I do.

HALE: You have confessed yourself to witchcraft, and that speaks a wish to come to Heaven's side. And we will bless you, Tituba.

TITUBA, *deeply relieved:* Oh, God bless you, Mr. Hale!

HALE, *with rising exaltation:* You are God's instrument put in our hands 58
to discover the Devil's agent among us. You are selected, Tituba, you are chosen to help us cleanse our village. So speak utterly, Tituba,

Literary Analysis
Dialogue and Stage Directions What techniques does Miller use to indicate that Tituba is making things up?

Literary Analysis
Dialogue and Stage Directions To what does Tituba confess in this dialogue?

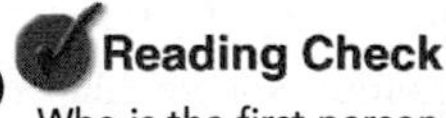
Reading Check
Who is the first person to name specific individuals?

56 Literary Analysis
Dialogue and Stage Directions

- **Ask** students whether they think Tituba believes her own statements.
  Answer: Students should recognize that Tituba, in fear for her life, is saying anything she can think of that Parris wants to hear.
- **Ask** students the first Literary Analysis question: What techniques does Miller use to indicate that Tituba is making things up?
  Answer: Miller has Tituba repeat the questions she is asked, to gain time for thought, and then hesitate before she answers. Her hesitations are indicated with a dash.

57 Literary Analysis
Dialogue and Stage Directions

- **Ask** students the second Literary Analysis question: To what does Tituba confess in this dialogue?
  Answer: She confesses to witchcraft and to having seen an unidentified woman with the Devil.
- Point out that Tituba's "confession" is entirely the result of suggestions that Hale and Parris make to her. They prompt her, telling her what they want to hear, and she tries to satisfy them without actually accusing any innocent people.

58 Reading Check
Answer: Putnam, who asks about Sarah Good and Goody Osburn, is the first to name specific people.

Differentiated Instruction
Solutions for All Learners

Strategy for Special Needs Students
Have students work together to answer the Review and Assess questions at the end of Act I. You might make this a homework assignment. The next day in class, students can gather in a group to discuss their answers. Have them go back to the text of the play to resolve any disagreements.

Strategy for Gifted/Talented Students
Through acting, students can better grasp the emotional upheaval of the events that end Act I. Encourage volunteers to play the roles of Hale, Parris, Abigail, Tituba, and Putnam through to the end of Act I, beginning from Parris's line, "How can it be the Devil?" Have students run through, rehearse, and then perform their roles for the class. Ask students what emotions best describe the characters' motivations in this scene (fear, hysteria, hate, excitement, ambition, helplessness).

59 Reading Strategy
Questioning the Characters' Motives

- **Ask** students the Reading Strategy question: What do you think motivates Hale to speak "kindly" to Tituba?
  Answer: He believes that she is trying her best to fight off the influence of the Devil. He is a compassionate man who truly wants to help.
- What motivates Tituba to name Goody Good and Goody Osburn?
  Answer: She responds to Hale's kindness. Putnam has just put these two names into her head, so she knows these are the names her questioners want to hear.
- What motivates Abigail to make this false confession?
  Answer: Abigail's motives are complex. She sees that a confession makes Tituba the center of attention and that Tituba's importance in the community has risen. Abigail wants to be important. Parris had already told her that her reputation was not good, and she wants to change that. She also wants to make sure that she is safe from any accusation about using witchcraft to kill Goody Proctor. She has also seen that a confession will guarantee safety from hanging.

turn your back on him and face God—face God, Tituba, and God will protect you.

TITUBA, *joining with him:* Oh, God, protect Tituba!

HALE, *kindly:* Who came to you with the Devil? Two? Three? Four? How many?

Tituba pants, and begins rocking back and forth again, staring ahead.

TITUBA: There was four. There was four.

PARRIS, *pressing in on her:* Who? Who? Their names, their names!

TITUBA, *suddenly bursting out:* Oh, how many times he bid me kill you, Mr. Parris!

PARRIS: Kill me!

TITUBA, *in a fury:* He say Mr. Parris must be kill! Mr. Parris no goodly man, Mr. Parris mean man and no gentle man, and he bid me rise out of my bed and cut your throat! *They gasp.* But I tell him "No! I don't hate that man. I don't want kill that man." But he say, "You work for me, Tituba, and I make you free! I give you pretty dress to wear, and put you way high up in the air, and you gone fly back to Barbados!" And I say, "You lie, Devil, you lie!" And then he come one stormy night to me, and he say, "Look! I have *white* people belong to me." And I look—and there was Goody Good.

PARRIS: Sarah Good!

TITUBA, *rocking and weeping:* Aye, sir, and Goody Osburn.

MRS. PUTNAM: I knew it! Goody Osburn were midwife to me three times. I begged you, Thomas, did I not? I begged him not to call Osburn because I feared her. My babies always shriveled in her hands!

HALE: Take courage, you must give us all their names. How can you bear to see this child suffering? Look at her, Tituba. *He is indicating* BETTY *on the bed.* Look at her God-given innocence; her soul is so tender; we must protect her, Tituba; the Devil is out and preying on her like a beast upon the flesh of the pure lamb. God will bless you for your help.

ABIGAIL *rises, staring as though inspired, and cries out.*

ABIGAIL: I want to open myself! *They turn to her, startled. She is enraptured, as though in a pearly light.* I want the light of God, I want the sweet love of Jesus! I danced for the Devil; I saw him; I wrote in his book; I go back to Jesus; I kiss His hand. I saw Sarah Good with the Devil! I saw Goody Osburn with the Devil! I saw Bridget Bishop with the Devil!

As she is speaking, BETTY *is rising from the bed, a fever in her eyes, and picks up the chant.*

BETTY, *staring too:* I saw George Jacobs with the Devil! I saw Goody Howe with the Devil!

PARRIS: She speaks! *He rushes to embrace* BETTY. She speaks!

HALE: Glory to God! It is broken, they are free!

Reading Strategy
Questioning the Characters' Motives
What do you think motivates Hale to speak "kindly" to Tituba?

BETTY, *calling out hysterically and with great relief:* I saw Martha Bellows with the Devil!

ABIGAIL: I saw Goody Sibber with the Devil! *It is rising to a great glee.*

PUTNAM: The marshal, I'll call the marshal!

PARRIS *is shouting a prayer of thanksgiving.*

BETTY: I saw Alice Barrow with the Devil!

The curtain begins to fall.

HALE, *as* PUTNAM *goes out:* Let the marshal bring irons!

ABIGAIL: I saw Goody Hawkins with the Devil!

BETTY: I saw Goody Bibber with the Devil!

ABIGAIL: I saw Goody Booth with the Devil!

On their ecstatic cries—

THE CURTAIN FALLS

Critical Reading

1. **Respond:** Were you surprised when the accusations against specific individuals multiplied? Explain.
2. **(a) Recall:** What is Betty's condition when the play opens? **(b) Recall:** What does Abigail say that she and Betty were doing in the forest? **(c) Infer:** What seems to be the main motivation for Reverend Parris's concern about the girls' behavior in the forest?
3. **(a) Recall:** What do Abigail, Betty, Mercy, and Mary discuss after Reverend Parris leaves his daughter's room? **(b) Interpret:** What events does this scene suggest may occur later in the play?
4. **(a) Recall:** Who is Reverend Hale? **(b) Recall:** Why is he contacted? **(c) Evaluate:** Do you think he is being fair and impartial so far? Why or why not?
5. **(a) Summarize:** Summarize Abigail's prior relationship with the Proctors. **(b) Interpret:** What does Betty's revelation about Abigail's actions in the forest suggest about Abigail's feelings for Goody Proctor?
6. **(a) Support:** What evidence suggests that sharp divisions exist among the people of Salem Village? **(b) Apply:** Name two others who may be accused. Explain your choices.
7. **Evaluate:** Which situations, if any, in contemporary life might cause an American town to be afflicted with a general hysteria? Explain.

For: More about Arthur Miller
Visit: www.PHSchool.com
Web Code: ere-9635

ASSESS

Answers

1. Students were probably surprised. One accusation would have been enough for the girls to escape punishment for their games in the woods.
2. (a) She is in a heavy sleep. (b) She says they were dancing. (c) He is afraid of how it may affect his position in the community if his enemies find out.
3. (a) They try to agree on what story they will tell; Abigail threatens the others with vengeance if they say that she tried to kill Goody Proctor. (b) It suggests that the girls will be asked what happened in the woods and that they will lie.
4. (a) He is a pastor from Beverly. (b) He is reputed to be an expert on demonic possession. (c) He does not rush to judgment, but he presumes guilt instead of innocence.
5. (a) Abigail was their servant and, briefly, John's lover. (b) Abigail is clearly filled with jealous hatred of her.
6. (a) Parris mentions having enemies who want to drive him from the pulpit. Rebecca mentions strife in the town. Proctor and Corey suggest that the Putnam family cheats and angers everyone. (b) **Possible answer:** Proctor and Rebecca may be accused because others resent them.
7. Students might refer to such actual events as unfounded accusations of child abuse at daycare centers, or some people's preparations for the end of the world at New Year, 2000.

Go Online Author Link For additional information about Arthur Miller, have students type in the Web Code, then select *M* from the alphabet, and then select Arthur Miller.

Answers

1. Both stage directions and dialogue reveal that Abigail is a liar. Dialogue reveals that she hates Goody Proctor: "It's a bitter woman, a lying, cold, sniveling woman" and "You drank a charm to kill Goody Proctor!" Dialogue and stage directions show that she loves John: "I walk and walk about the house as though I'd find you comin' through some door." *She clutches him desperately.*

   Another sample answer can be found on **Literary Analysis Graphic Organizer B**, p. 289, in ***Graphic Organizer Transparencies.***
2. Stage directions mention her "concentrated desire" for him and indicate that she tries to touch him and make him touch her. They also mention her anger and resentment at his rejection.
3. (a) He wants the readers to understand the attitudes and beliefs in the time and place in which his play is set. (b) The comments are addressed to the reader; they will not be read or spoken in a staged performance.
4. The stage directions identify the time and place, describe the room, and identify the two characters currently on stage.
5. Their recent behavior is revealed in dialogue.
6. He compares the Inquisition and the Red Scare to the threat of witchcraft in Salem.
7. His main concern is to protect himself from those in the parish who would like to see him leave his position as minister.
8. Abigail wants John. Her threats make it clear that she doesn't want this becoming public knowledge.
9. He has a grudge against them and wants them accused without having to do so openly.
10. He criticizes greed and irresponsibility. Putnam is greedy for property; Parris is jealous of his salary and privileges. Both seek to blame others for their own misfortunes.

Go Online Assessment Students may use the **Self-test** to prepare for **Selection Test A** or **Selection Test B**.

Apply the Skills

The Crucible, Act I

Literary Analysis

Dialogue and Stage Directions

1. Use a chart like the one shown to analyze the character of Abigail Williams. To respond, combine details from her **dialogue** with Miller's descriptions of her in the **stage directions.**

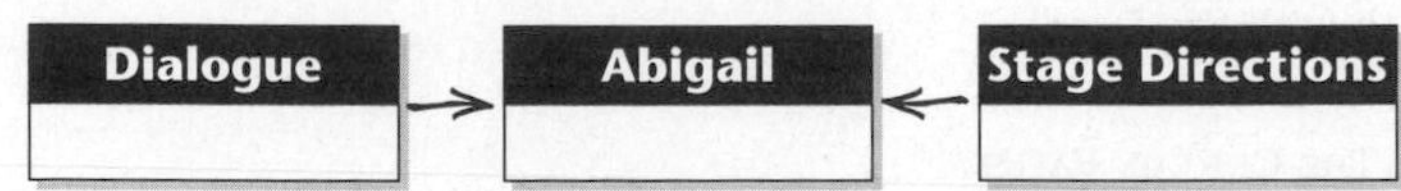

2. In the scene between Abigail and John Proctor, in what ways do the stage directions add to your understanding of their relationship?

Connecting Literary Elements

3. **(a)** Why does Miller include such extensive background information about seventeenth-century Salem and its inhabitants? **(b)** To whom is this information addressed? Explain.
4. What information is conveyed about the play's basic situation in the first three paragraphs of stage directions?
5. What technique does Miller use to provide important information about the recent activities of several village girls? Explain.
6. When Reverend Hale enters the scene, what two historic events does Miller compare in his **dramatic exposition**?

Reading Strategy

Questioning the Characters' Motives

7. What do Reverend Parris's comments and actions reveal about his **motivations**?
8. What do Abigail's actions in the forest and her threat to the girls reveal about her motives?
9. What is Putnam's motive for asking Tituba whether she saw Sarah Good or Goody Osburn in the woods?

Extend Understanding

10. **Cultural Connection:** Which elements of society does Miller seem to be criticizing through the characters of Reverend Parris and the Putnams? Explain.

QuickReview

Dialogue refers to the words characters speak; it reveals characters' personalities and backgrounds.

Stage directions are the instructions the playwright provides for the director, actors, and technicians involved in putting on the play.

Dramatic exposition conveys important background information about the setting and characters.

To better understand a plot, **question characters' motives** by identifying the reasons behind their actions.

For: Self-test
Visit: www.PHSchool.com
Web Code: era-6620

Build Language Skills

1 Vocabulary Lesson

Word Analysis: Latin Root *-grat-*

From *gratus,* Latin for "pleasing," comes the root *-grat-*, which means "pleasing" or "agreeable." An *ingratiating* attitude, for example, is one designed to please others. Explain how *-grat-* relates to the meaning of these words.

1. gratify **2.** grateful **3.** congratulate

Spelling Strategy

When adding a suffix that begins with a vowel to a word that ends in a silent *e,* drop the *e* and then add the suffix: *ingratiate* becomes *ingratiating.* For each word below, add the suffix given to form a new word.

1. ignite (*-ion*) **2.** observe (*-ance*)

Vocabulary Builder: Context

Complete each of the following sentences with the appropriate vocabulary word from page 1256.

1. __?__ can destroy a person's reputation.
2. Months of __?__ helped me to learn.
3. He hid his true nature by __?__.
4. His __?__ behavior was scandalous.
5. To soothe their gods, they made sacrifices as an act of __?__.
6. Her __?__ manner pleased the customers.
7. With my __?__ for history I knew I would enjoy *The Crucible.*

2 Grammar and Style Lesson

Pronoun Case in Incomplete Constructions

In an **incomplete construction,** you may be uncertain about which form of pronoun to use. To decide, mentally complete the construction by inserting the missing words.

Example: They want slaves, not such as *I.* (complete construction: *as I am.*)

Practice Choose the pronoun that best completes each sentence.

1. Proctor is not more sinful than (he, him).
2. Proctor has some affection for Abigail but cares more for his wife than (she, her).
3. Betty lies, but Abigail is craftier than (she, her).
4. "Blame her more than (I, me)," she says.
5. Abigail is manipulative, but Mercy Lewis is more cruel than (she, her).

Writing Application Write three sentences in which you compare two people. Use both proper nouns and correct pronouns in your sentences.

WG *Prentice Hall Writing and Grammar Connection: Chapter 22, Section 2*

Extend Your Learning

Writing Write a series of **news accounts** of the events in Salem as they might be described in a Boston newspaper of the day.

Listening and Speaking Working in a group, research and then report on the belief in witches in seventeenth-century Europe. Present your findings in an **oral report. [Group Activity]**

EXTEND/ASSESS

1 Vocabulary Lesson

Word Analysis

1. To gratify means to please.
2. Someone who is grateful is pleased and thankful.
3. To congratulate means to express pleasure at someone's good fortune.

Spelling

1. ignition 2. observance

Vocabulary Builder

1. Calumny
2. inculcation
3. dissembling
4. licentious
5. propitiation
6. ingratiating
7. predilection

2 Grammar and Style Lesson

1. he 2. her 3. she 4. me 5. she

Writing Application

Have students check one another's sentences and use **Writing and Grammar,** Ruby Level, to resolve disagreements.

3 Extension Activities

Writing Lesson

Students might write using seventeenth-century diction.

Listening and Speaking

- Students' social studies teachers may be able to suggest sources of information for the report.
- The **Support for Extend Your Learning** page (*Unit 6 Resources,* p. 347) provides guided note-taking opportunities to help students complete Extend Your Learning activities.

Go Online Research Have students type in the Web Code for another research activity.

Assessment Practice

Grammar and Usage **(For more practice, use *Standardized Test Preparation Workbook,* p. 76)**

Many tests require students to choose the best word to complete a sentence. Use this sample test item.

Among the plays written by Arthur Miller ___ The Crucible, Death of a Salesman, and *A View from the Bridge.*

Which word correctly completes this sentence:

A is
B are
C was
D remains

Since the subject ("the plays") is plural, the verb must be plural. Choice *B* is correct.

Meeting Your Standards

Students will

1. **analyze and respond to literary elements.**
   - Literary Analysis: Allusion
2. **read, comprehend, analyze, and critique a drama.**
   - Reading Strategy: Reading Drama
   - Reading Check questions
   - Apply the Skills questions
   - Assessment Practice (ATE)
3. **develop vocabulary.**
   - Vocabulary Lesson: Greek Suffix: *-logy*
4. **understand and apply written and oral language conventions.**
   - Spelling Strategy
   - Grammar and Style Lesson: Commas After Introductory Words
5. **develop writing proficiency.**
   - Writing Lesson: Defense of a Character's Actions (After Act IV)
6. **develop writing strategies.**
   - Extend Your Learning: Wanted Poster
7. **understand and apply listening and speaking strategies.**
   - Extend Your Learning: Scene

Block Scheduling: Use one 90-minute class period to preteach the skills and have students read the selection. Use a second 90-minute class period to assess students' mastery of skills, extend their learning, and monitor their progress.

Homework Suggestions

Following are possibilities for homework assignments.

- Support pages from ***Unit 6 Resources:***
  Literary Analysis
  Reading Strategy
  Vocabulary Builder
  Grammar and Style
- An Extend Your Learning project and the Writing Lesson for this selection may be completed over several days.

Step-by-Step Teaching Guide	Pacing Guide
PRETEACH	
• Administer Vocabulary and Reading Warm-ups as necessary.	5 min.
• Engage students' interest with the motivation activity.	5 min.
• Read and discuss author and background features. **FT**	10 min.
• Introduce the Literary Analysis skill: Allusion. **FT**	5 min.
• Introduce the Reading Strategy: Reading Drama. **FT**	10 min.
• Prepare students to read by teaching the selection vocabulary. **FT**	
TEACH	
• Informally monitor comprehension while students read independently or in groups. **FT**	30 min.
• Monitor students' comprehension with the Reading Check notes.	as students read
• Reinforce vocabulary with Vocabulary Builder notes.	as students read
• Develop students' understanding of allusion with the Literary Analysis annotations. **FT**	5 min.
• Develop students' ability to read drama with the Reading Strategy annotations. **FT**	5 min.
ASSESS/EXTEND	
• Assess students' comprehension and mastery of the Literary Analysis and Reading Strategy by having them answer the Apply the Skills questions. **FT**	15 min.
• Have students complete the Vocabulary Lesson and the Grammar and Style Lesson. **FT**	15 min.
• Apply students' understanding by using one or more of the Extend Your Learning activities.	20–90 min. or homework
• Administer Selection Test A or Selection Test B. **FT**	15 min.

Resources

PRINT

Unit 6 Resources

Vocabulary Warm-up Word Lists **[L1, L2, EL]** .... p. 355
Vocabulary Warm-up Practice **[L1, L2, EL]** .... p. 356
Reading Warm-up A **[L1, L2, EL]** .... p. 357
Reading Warm-up B **[L1, L2, L3]** .... p. 358

TRANSPARENCY

Graphic Organizer Transparencies

Literary Analysis Graphic Organizer A **[L3]** .... p. 290
Literary Analysis Graphic Organizer B **[L1, L2, EL]** .... p. 291
Reading Strategy Graphic Organizer A **[L3]** .... p. 292
Reading Strategy Graphic Organizer B **[L1, L2, EL]** .... p. 293

PRINT

Reader's Notebook [L2]
Reader's Notebook: Adapted Version [L1]
Reader's Notebook: English Learner's Version [EL]

Unit 6 Resources

Literary Analysis **[L3]** .... p. 359
Reading Strategy **[L3]** .... p. 360
Vocabulary Builder **[L3]** .... p. 361

PRINT

Unit 6 Resources

Grammar and Style **[L3]** .... p. 362
Support for Extend Your Learning **[L3]** .... p. 363
Enrichment **[L4]** .... p. 364
Selection Test A **[L1, L2, EL]** .... pp. 365–367
Selection Test B **[L3, L4]** .... pp. 368–370

TECHNOLOGY

Go Online: Research **[L3]**
Go Online: Self-test **[L3]**
ExamView® **Test Bank [L3]**

Choosing Resources for Differentiated Instruction

[L1] Special Needs Students
[L2] Below-Level Students
[L3] All Students
[L4] Advanced Students
[EL] English Learners

For Vocabulary and Reading Warm-ups and for Selection Tests, **A** signifies "less challenging" and **B** "more challenging." For Graphic Organizer transparencies, **A** signifies "not filled in" and **B** "filled in."

FT Fast Track Instruction: To move the lesson more quickly, use the strategies and activities identified with **FT**.

Scaffolding for Less Proficient and Advanced Students

The leveled Critical Thinking questions after selections progress in the levels of thinking required to answer them. To address the needs of your different students, you may use the (a) level questions for your less proficient students and the (b) level questions with your on-level and advanced students. The occasional (c) level questions are appropriate for your advanced students.

PRENTICE HALL **TeacherEXPRESS™** Plan · Teach · Assess — Use this complete suite of powerful teaching tools to make lesson planning and testing quicker and easier.

PRENTICE HALL **StudentEXPRESS™** Learn · Study · Succeed — Use the interactive textbook (online and on CD-ROM) to make selections and activities come alive with audio and video support and interactive questions.

Go Online Professional Development — **For:** Information about Lexiles **Visit:** www.PHSchool.com **Web Code:** eue-1111

❹ Reading Strategy
Reading Drama

- **Ask** students the first Reading Strategy question: What do you learn about Elizabeth's feelings toward her husband from these stage directions?
  Answer: She finds it hard to show her feelings for him.
- Ask students to characterize the Proctors' relationship. **Ask** what their behavior suggests about their feelings for each other.
  Answer: There is tension between them. Each is careful to please the other. The effort they both make suggests that they care about their marriage and want to work through the tension.

❺ Reading Strategy
Reading Drama

- **Ask** students the second Reading Strategy question: How do these stage directions help prepare you for Proctor's remark that Elizabeth seems sad?
  Answer: She "would speak but cannot," and they are separated not only by the length of the room but also in their hearts.
- Why does Elizabeth try so hard to avoid friction? What does this suggest about her relationship with John?
  Answer: Elizabeth is afraid of John's anger. She is afraid of conflict. This suggests that the relationship is fragile; if they were sure of each other they wouldn't hesitate to quarrel.

PROCTOR: It's well seasoned.

ELIZABETH, *blushing with pleasure:* I took great care. She's tender?

PROCTOR: Aye. *He eats. She watches him.* I think we'll see green fields soon. It's warm as blood beneath the clods.

ELIZABETH: That's well.

PROCTOR *eats, then looks up.*

PROCTOR: If the crop is good I'll buy George Jacob's heifer. How would that please you?

❹ **ELIZABETH:** Aye, it would.

PROCTOR, *with a grin:* I mean to please you, Elizabeth.

ELIZABETH—*it is hard to say:* I know it, John.

He gets up, goes to her, kisses her. She receives it. With a certain disappointment, he returns to the table.

PROCTOR, *as gently as he can:* Cider?

ELIZABETH, *with a sense of reprimanding herself for having forgot:* Aye! *She gets up and goes and pours a glass for him. He now arches his back.*

Reading Strategy
Reading Drama What do you learn about Elizabeth's feelings toward her husband from these stage directions?

PROCTOR: This farm's a continent when you go foot by foot droppin' seeds in it.

ELIZABETH, *coming with the cider:* It must be.

PROCTOR, *drinks a long draught, then, putting the glass down:* You ought to bring some flowers in the house.

ELIZABETH: Oh! I forgot! I will tomorrow.

PROCTOR: It's winter in here yet. On Sunday let you come with me, and we'll walk the farm together; I never see such a load of flowers on the earth. *With good feeling he goes and looks up at the sky through the open doorway.* Lilacs have a purple smell. Lilac is the smell of nightfall, I think. Massachusetts is a beauty in the spring!

ELIZABETH: Aye, it is.

There is a pause. She is watching him from the table as he stands there absorbing the night. It is as though she would speak but cannot. Instead, now, she takes up his plate and glass and fork and goes with them to the basin. Her back is turned to him. He turns to her and watches her. A sense of their separation rises.

Reading Strategy
Reading Drama How do these stage directions help prepare you for Proctor's remark that Elizabeth seems sad?

PROCTOR: I think you're sad again. Are you?

ELIZABETH—*she doesn't want friction, and yet she must:* You come so
❺ late I thought you'd gone to Salem this afternoon.

PROCTOR: Why? I have no business in Salem.

ELIZABETH: You did speak of going, earlier this week.

PROCTOR—*he knows what she means:* I thought better of it since.

ELIZABETH: Mary Warren's there today.

PROCTOR: Why'd you let her? You heard me forbid her go to Salem any more!

ELIZABETH: I couldn't stop her.

PROCTOR, *holding back a full condemnation of her:* It is a fault, it is a fault, Elizabeth—you're the mistress here, not Mary Warren.

ELIZABETH: She frightened all my strength away.

PROCTOR: How may that mouse frighten you, Elizabeth? You—

ELIZABETH: It is a mouse no more. I forbid her go, and she raises up her chin like the daughter of a prince and says to me, "I must go to Salem, Goody Proctor; I am an official of the court!"

PROCTOR: Court! What court?

ELIZABETH: Aye, it is a proper court they have now. They've sent four judges out of Boston, she says, weighty magistrates of the General Court, and at the head sits the Deputy Governor of the Province.

PROCTOR, *astonished:* Why, she's mad.

6 **ELIZABETH:** I would to God she were. There be fourteen people in the jail now, she says. PROCTOR *simply looks at her, unable to grasp it.* And they'll be tried, and the court have power to hang them too, she says.

PROCTOR, *scoffing but without conviction:* Ah, they'd never hang—

ELIZABETH: The Deputy Governor promise hangin' if they'll not confess, John. The town's gone wild, I think. She speak of Abigail, and I thought she were a saint, to hear her. Abigail brings the other girls into the court, and where she walks the crowd will part like the sea for Israel.[1] And folks are brought before them, and if they scream and howl and fall to the floor—the person's clapped in the jail for bewitchin' them.

PROCTOR, *wide-eyed:* Oh, it is a black mischief.

ELIZABETH: I think you must go to Salem, John. *He turns to her.* I think so. You must tell them it is a fraud.

PROCTOR, *thinking beyond this:* Aye, it is, it is surely.

ELIZABETH: Let you go to Ezekiel Cheever—he knows you well. And tell him what she said to you last week in her uncle's house. She said it had naught to do with witchcraft, did she not?

PROCTOR, *in thought:* Aye, she did, she did. *Now, a pause.*

7 **ELIZABETH,** *quietly, fearing to anger him by prodding:* God forbid you keep that from the court, John. I think they must be told.

PROCTOR, *quietly, struggling with his thought:* Aye, they must, they must. It is a wonder they do believe her.

ELIZABETH: I would go to Salem now, John—let you go tonight.

PROCTOR: I'll think on it.

ELIZABETH, *with her courage now:* You cannot keep it, John.

PROCTOR, *angering:* I know I cannot keep it. I say I will think on it!

ELIZABETH, *hurt, and very coldly:* Good, then, let you think on it. *She stands and starts to walk out of the room.*

PROCTOR: I am only wondering how I may prove what she told me, Elizabeth. If the girl's a saint now, I think it is not easy to prove she's

1. **part like . . . Israel** In the Bible, God commanded Moses, the leader of the Jews, to part the Red Sea to enable the Jews to escape from the Egyptians into Canaan.

Literary Analysis
Allusion What does Elizabeth's allusion to Moses' parting of the Red Sea reveal about Abigail's new standing in the community?

Reading Strategy
Reading Drama How would you describe Elizabeth's changing emotions as she challenges John?

8 **Reading Check**
What does Elizabeth want John to do?

6 Literary Analysis
Allusion

- Have students read the footnote at the bottom of the page. **Ask** the Literary Analysis question: What does Elizabeth's allusion to Moses' parting of the Red Sea reveal about Abigail's new standing in the community?
  Answer: The comparison between Abigail and Moses suggests that she has become a power in the community. The Israelites looked up to Moses because God spoke to him directly.
- Point out that the allusion to Moses is a simile—"the crowd will part *like* the sea for Israel." Have students find another simile in this passage and discuss its effect.
  Answer: Mary "raises up her chin like the daughter of a prince." This simile lets the audience picture Mary's newfound pride and self-importance.

7 Reading Strategy
Reading Drama

- **Ask** students the Reading Strategy question: How would you describe Elizabeth's changing emotions as she challenges John?
  Answer: She feels frightened, then angry, then hurt.
- **Ask** students why they think Elizabeth feels the way she does.
  Answer: She is probably still upset about John's affair with Abigail. She wants him to prove that he no longer cares for Abigail. When he hesitates, she thinks it is out of love for Abigail.

8 Reading Check

Answer: She wants him to tell the court that Abigail's accusations of witchcraft are lies.

Differentiated Instruction
Solutions for All Learners

Strategy for English Learners
To help students follow the events of the eight days since Act I ended, have students create a K-W-L chart to recall main events and speculate about what will happen next.

What I Know	Many townspeople believe the girls are bewitched.
What I Want To Know	Will the girls' lies be found out?
What I Learned	

Strategy for Gifted/Talented Students
Have students analyze this scene between John and Elizabeth (pp. 1291–1295). Remind them that Elizabeth knows about John's affair with Abigail, but that the affair ended several months ago. Have students consider how John and Elizabeth treat each other in this scene, what motivates them to behave as they do, and what this suggests about their characters. Students can gather for a small-group discussion of their ideas.

❾ Critical Viewing

Answer: John Proctor's adultery with Abigail is likely to cause continued ill-feeling between husband and wife.

❿ Literary Analysis
Allusion

- Have students identify the metaphor Proctor uses in his speeches here. To what official body does he allude?
  Answer: He alludes to a court. He compares Elizabeth to a judge of the court.
- What effect do these allusions have?
  Answer: We see that the Proctors have not resolved the anger resulting from John's affair with Abigail; although he has confessed and repented, John still feels that Elizabeth judges him.

➤ **Monitor Progress Ask** students with which character they sympathize more, John or Elizabeth. Have them explain their answers. Remind them of the historical context in which the Proctors live.
Answer: Students who sympathize with Elizabeth should point out that she is trying to be a good wife in spite of John's infidelity. Those who sympathize with John should point out that he has apologized and broken off the affair.

fraud, and the town gone so silly. She told it to me in a room alone—I have no proof for it.

ELIZABETH: You were alone with her?

PROCTOR, *stubbornly:* For a moment alone, aye.

ELIZABETH: Why, then, it is not as you told me.

PROCTOR, *his anger rising:* For a moment, I say. The others come in soon after.

ELIZABETH, *quietly—she has suddenly lost all faith in him:* Do as you wish, then. *She starts to turn.*

PROCTOR: Woman. *She turns to him.* I'll not have your suspicion any more.

ELIZABETH, *a little loftily:* I have no—

PROCTOR: I'll not have it!

ELIZABETH: Then let you not earn it.

PROCTOR, *with a violent undertone:* You doubt me yet?

ELIZABETH, *with a smile, to keep her dignity:* John, if it were not Abigail that you must go to hurt, would you falter now? I think not.

PROCTOR: Now look you—

ELIZABETH: I see what I see, John.

PROCTOR, *with solemn warning:* You will not judge me more, Elizabeth. I have good reason to think before I charge fraud on Abigail, and I will think on it. Let you look to your own improvement before you go to judge your husband any more. I have forgot Abigail, and—

ELIZABETH: And I.

PROCTOR: Spare me! You forget nothin' and forgive nothin'. Learn charity, woman. I have gone tiptoe in this house all seven month since she is gone. I have not moved from there to there without I think to please you, and still an everlasting funeral marches round your heart. I can-
❿ not speak but I am doubted, every moment judged for lies, as though I come into a court when I come into this house!

ELIZABETH: John, you are not open with me. You saw her with a crowd, you said. Now you—

PROCTOR: I'll plead my honesty no more, Elizabeth.

ELIZABETH *—now she would justify herself:* John, I am only—

PROCTOR: No more! I should have roared you down when first you told me your suspicion. But I wilted, and, like a Christian, I confessed. Confessed! Some dream I had must have mistaken you for God that day. But you're not, you're not, and let you remember it! Let you look sometimes for the goodness in me, and judge me not.

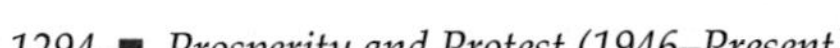

❾ ▲ **Critical Viewing** What aspects of the Proctors' lives early in the play seem likely to have caused the emotional intensity shown on John Proctor's face in this photo? **[Interpret]**

ELIZABETH: I do not judge you. The magistrate sits in your heart that judges you. I never thought you but a good man, John—*with a smile*—only somewhat bewildered.

PROCTOR, *laughing bitterly:* Oh, Elizabeth, your justice would freeze beer! *He turns suddenly toward a sound outside. He starts for the door as* MARY WARREN *enters. As soon as he sees her, he goes directly to her and grabs her by the cloak, furious.* How do you go to Salem when I forbid it? Do you mock me? *Shaking her.* I'll whip you if you dare leave this house again!

Strangely, she doesn't resist him, but hangs limply by his grip.

MARY WARREN: I am sick, I am sick, Mr. Proctor. Pray, pray, hurt me not. *Her strangeness throws him off, and her evident pallor and weakness. He frees her.* My insides are all shuddery; I am in the proceedings all day, sir.

PROCTOR, *with draining anger—his curiosity is draining it:* And what of these proceedings here? When will you proceed to keep this house, as you are paid nine pound a year to do—and my wife not wholly well?

As though to compensate, MARY WARREN *goes to* ELIZABETH *with a small rag doll.*

MARY WARREN: I made a gift for you today, Goody Proctor. I had to sit long hours in a chair, and passed the time with sewing.

ELIZABETH, *perplexed, looking at the doll:* Why, thank you, it's a fair poppet.[2]

MARY WARREN, *with a trembling, decayed voice:* We must all love each other now, Goody Proctor.

ELIZABETH, *amazed at her strangeness:* Aye, indeed we must.

MARY WARREN, *glancing at the room:* I'll get up early in the morning and clean the house. I must sleep now. *She turns and starts off.*

PROCTOR: Mary. *She halts.* Is it true? There be fourteen women arrested?

MARY WARREN: No, sir. There be thirty-nine now— *She suddenly breaks off and sobs and sits down, exhausted.*

ELIZABETH: Why, she's weepin'! What ails you, child?

MARY WARREN: Goody Osburn—will hang!

There is a shocked pause, while she sobs.

PROCTOR: Hang! *He calls into her face.* Hang, y'say?

MARY WARREN, *through her weeping:* Aye.

PROCTOR: The Deputy Governor will permit it?

MARY WARREN: He sentenced her. He must. *To ameliorate it:* But not Sarah Good. For Sarah Good confessed, y'see.

PROCTOR: Confessed! To what?

MARY WARREN: That she—*in horror at the memory*—she sometimes made a compact with Lucifer, and wrote her name in his black book—with

2. **poppet** doll.

Vocabulary Builder
pallor (pal′ ər) *n.* paleness

Reading Strategy
Reading Drama
What do these stage directions clarify?

12 ***Arthur Miller***
Author's Insight
Miller was fully aware that those who participated in the trials had no perspective on their beliefs or actions. He once wrote: "I spent some ten days in the Salem courthouse reading the crudely recorded trials of the 1692 outbreak, and it was striking how totally absent was the least sense of irony, let alone humor."

Vocabulary Builder
ameliorate (ə mēl′ yə rāt′) *v.* make better

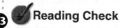

13 **Reading Check**
What are John and Elizabeth Proctor arguing about?

11 Reading Strategy
Reading Drama

- **Ask** students the Reading Strategy question: What do these stage directions clarify?
  Answer: They clarify Mary's physical weakness and John's change from fury to curiosity and pity.
- Ask students to infer why Mary is in such shaky physical condition.
  Answer: She has been in court all day; she has probably heard people condemned and arrested. She probably feels guilty and frightened because of her lies. She says she had to sit "long hours in a chair," which probably tired her out.

12 Author's Insight

- Direct students' attention to Arthur Miller's comment. **Ask** what he means by referring to a lack of a sense of irony or humor.
  Possible response: In his reading, he must have observed that the participants took this situation completely seriously. They believed the accusations without question. They did not appear to consider any possible motives behind the outbursts.
- **Ask** how Miller conveys this lack of irony or humor in the scene on this page.
  Possible response: Neither John nor Elizabeth perceive any irony in Mary's giving Elizabeth a "poppet." Nor do they appear to see any irony in Sarah Good's confession.

13 Reading Check

Answer: They argue about Elizabeth's inability to forgive John and what she sees as his reluctance to cause trouble for Abigail.

Differentiated Instruction
Solutions for All Learners

Strategy for Advanced Readers
The Crucible is filled with figurative language and imaginative comparisons—similes, metaphors, and personification. Point out some examples on these two pages:

- . . . and still an everlasting funeral marches round your heart.
- The magistrate sits in your heart that judges you.
- Oh, Elizabeth, your justice would freeze beer!

As students read the play, have them note especially striking metaphors and similes. When they are finished, ask them how Miller's figurative language contributes to the play.

⓮ The American Experience
Arthur Miller, Joseph McCarthy, and the Blacklist

In October 1947, the House Un-American Activities Committee turned its attention to Hollywood. J. Parnell Thomas, the chairman of the committee, announced that he had a list of 45 names of Hollywood writers and others who were implicated in subversive activities. Many actors, writers, and other artists were called before the committee and questioned.

The "Hollywood Ten" included writers Alvah Bessie, Herbert Biberman, Lester Cole, Edward Dmytryk, Ring Lardner Jr., John Howard Lawson, Albert Maltz, Samuel Ornitz, Adrian Scott, and Dalton Trumbo. All ten were considered "unfriendly" witnesses because they refused to answer the question, "Are you a member of the Communist party?"

In 1950, the Ten were fined $1,000 each and given prison sentences of up to one year. When they returned to Hollywood, they discovered that no major studio would hire them.

Connect to the Literature Review with students the behavior of John Proctor. Then, **ask** the Connect to the Literature question.

Possible response: Miller, like Proctor, refused to be victimized and stood up to his accusers.

⓯ Critical Thinking
Evaluate

- Have students **evaluate** Mary's description of her reaction to Goody Osburn's denials. Do students think Mary really felt these things? Why or why not?
  Answer: Students learned in Act I that Mary is a coward, easily led by the other girls, but that her inclinations are honest. They may say that Mary imagined her coldness and shortness of breath, or they may say that she really felt these things because of the pressure she was under.
- Have students **evaluate** Mary's evidence against Goody Osburn.
  Answer: Students should agree with Proctor that there is no proof against Goody Osburn. She denied witchcraft, and her failure to repeat the commandments should not be enough to condemn her. The fact that Mary fell ill after Goody Osburn's visit is pure coincidence.

her blood—and bound herself to torment Christians till God's thrown down—and we all must worship Hell forevermore.

Pause.

PROCTOR: But—surely you know what a jabberer she is. Did you tell them that?

MARY WARREN: Mr. Proctor, in open court she near to choked us all to death.

PROCTOR: How, choked you?

MARY WARREN: She sent her spirit out.

ELIZABETH: Oh, Mary, Mary, surely you—

MARY WARREN, *with an indignant edge:* She tried to kill me many times, Goody Proctor!

ELIZABETH: Why, I never heard you mention that before.

MARY WARREN: I never knew it before. I never knew anything before. When she come into the court I say to myself, I must not accuse this woman, for she sleep in ditches, and so very old and poor. But then—then she sit there, denying and denying, and I feel a misty coldness climbin' up my back, and the skin on my skull begin to creep, and I feel a clamp around my neck and I cannot breathe air; and then—*entranced*—I hear a voice, a screamin' voice, and it were my voice—and all at once I remembered everything she done to me!

PROCTOR: Why? What did she do to you?

MARY WARREN, *like one awakened to a marvelous secret insight:* So many time, Mr. Proctor, she come to this very door, beggin' bread and a cup of cider—and mark this: whenever I turned her away empty, she *mumbled.*

ELIZABETH: Mumbled! She may mumble if she's hungry.

⓯ **MARY WARREN:** But *what* does she mumble? You must remember, Goody Proctor. Last month—a Monday, I think—she walked away, and I thought my guts would burst for two days after. Do you remember it?

ELIZABETH: Why—I do, I think, but—

MARY WARREN: And so I told that to Judge Hathorne, and he asks her so. "Goody Osburn," says he, "what curse do you mumble that this girl must fall sick after turning you away?" And then she replies—*mimicking an old crone*—"Why, your excellence, no curse at all. I only say my commandments; I hope I may say my commandments," says she!

ELIZABETH: And that's an upright answer.

MARY WARREN: Aye, but then Judge Hathorne say, "Recite for us your commandments!"—*leaning avidly toward them*—and of all the ten she could not say a single one. She never knew no commandments, and they had her in a flat lie!

PROCTOR: And so condemned her?

⓮ *Arthur Miller, Joseph McCarthy, and the Blacklist*

In the late 1940s, the House Un-American Activities Committee developed a "blacklist" of Hollywood screenwriters suspected of being Communists. For many years, film producers used this list to deny employment to these writers.

Arthur Miller himself was called before the House Un-American Activities Committee and asked to name people he had met at a meeting of alleged Communist writers. After refusing, Miller was convicted of contempt; later, he appealed and the contempt charge was overturned.

In 1999, Arthur Miller commented on the relationship between the "Red Scare" and the Salem witch trials. Miller said there were startling similarities in both the rituals of defense and the investigative routines. Three hundred years apart, both prosecutions were alleging membership in a secret, disloyal group.

Connect to the Literature

In what way is Miller like any of the characters in his play in his refusal to answer questions?

Vocabulary Builder

avidly (av′ id lē) *adv.* eagerly

MARY WARREN, *now a little strained, seeing his stubborn doubt:* Why, they must when she condemned herself.

PROCTOR: But the proof, the proof!

MARY WARREN, *with greater impatience with him:* I told you the proof. It's hard proof, hard as rock, the judges said.

PROCTOR, *pauses an instant, then:* You will not go to court again, Mary Warren.

MARY WARREN: I must tell you, sir, I will be gone every day now. I am amazed you do not see what weighty work we do.

PROCTOR: What work you do! It's strange work for a Christian girl to hang old women!

MARY WARREN: But, Mr. Proctor, they will not hang them if they confess. Sarah Good will only sit in jail some time—*recalling*—and here's a wonder for you; think on this. Goody Good is pregnant!

ELIZABETH: Pregnant! Are they mad? The woman's near to sixty!

MARY WARREN: They had Doctor Griggs examine her, and she's full to the brim. And smokin' a pipe all these years, and no husband either! But she's safe, thank God, for they'll not hurt the innocent child. But be that not a marvel? You must see it, sir, it's God's work we do. So I'll be gone every day for some time. I'm—I am an official of the court, they say, and I—*She has been edging toward offstage.*

PROCTOR: I'll official you! *He strides to the mantel, takes down the whip hanging there.*

MARY WARREN, *terrified, but coming erect, striving for her authority:* I'll not stand whipping any more!

ELIZABETH, *hurriedly, as* PROCTOR *approaches:* Mary, promise now you'll stay at home—

MARY WARREN, *backing from him, but keeping her erect posture, striving, striving for her way:* The Devil's loose in Salem, Mr. Proctor; we must discover where he's hiding!

PROCTOR: I'll whip the Devil out of you! *With whip raised he reaches out*
6 *for her, and she streaks away and yells.*

MARY WARREN, *pointing at* ELIZABETH: I saved her life today!

Silence. His whip comes down.

ELIZABETH, *softly:* I am accused?

MARY WARREN, *quaking:* Somewhat mentioned. But I said I never see no sign you ever sent your spirit out to hurt no one, and seeing I do live so closely with you, they dismissed it.

ELIZABETH: Who accused me?

MARY WARREN: I am bound by law, I cannot tell it. *To* PROCTOR: I only hope you'll not be so sarcastical no more. Four judges and the King's deputy sat to dinner with us but an hour ago. I—I would have you speak civilly to me, from this out.

PROCTOR, *in horror, muttering in disgust at her:* Go to bed.

MARY WARREN, *with a stamp of her foot:* I'll not be ordered to bed no more, Mr. Proctor! I am eighteen and a woman, however single!

Reading Strategy
Reading Drama What change has Mary's participation in the court proceedings brought in her attitude toward the Proctors?

17  **Reading Check**
What evidence does Mary Warren use to prove that Goody Osborn is a witch?

16 Reading Strategy
Reading Drama

- **Ask** students the Reading Strategy question: What change has Mary's participation in the court proceedings brought in her attitude toward the Proctors?
  Answer: Mary has acquired a sense of her own importance and will no longer accept being treated as a servant.
- **Ask** students whether this change in Mary is likely to be permanent or temporary, and why.
  Answer: Mary still seems very unsure of herself. She isn't used to standing up for herself. The change is probably temporary.

17 Reading Check

Answer: Mary accuses her of mumbling; Goody can't name the commandments when challenged.

Differentiated Instruction
Solutions for All Learners

Background for Special Needs Students
Help students understand the Proctors' growing anxiety in the face of Mary's news. Proctor says of Abigail, "If the girl's a saint now, I think it is not easy to prove she's fraud, and the town gone so silly." Use this statement to help students think about the use and abuse of power. Discuss the frustration that John and Elizabeth must feel. What are students' experiences with lies? Of what past and present news stories of cover-ups in business or government are students aware?

Enrichment for Gifted/Talented Students
Students probably have a fairly good working knowledge of courtroom procedure and rules from television dramas. Ask them to evaluate Mary's tale of what happens in the Salem courtroom by the modern standards they see depicted on television. How would a modern judge treat a display of screaming such as Mary describes? How would modern lawyers react to the "hard proof" Mary cites?

18 Reading Strategy
Reading Drama

- **Ask** students the Reading Strategy question: How do the stage directions indicating that Proctor speaks "without conviction" affect your understanding of his line?
  Answer: He doesn't really believe what he says.
- Of whom is Elizabeth speaking when she says, "She wants me dead"? How do you know?
  Answer: She believes Abigail is the one who accused her. She knows that Abigail is jealous of her and wants to take her place.
- Why are the stage directions "reasonably" and "conceding" in Elizabeth's speeches enclosed in quotation marks?
  Answer: The quotation marks suggest that she is making an effort to appear reasonable and to appear to concede, when she's actually angry and upset.

PROCTOR: Do you wish to sit up? Then sit up.

MARY WARREN: I wish to go to bed!

PROCTOR, *in anger:* Good night, then!

MARY WARREN: Good night. *Dissatisfied, uncertain of herself, she goes out. Wide-eyed, both* PROCTOR *and* ELIZABETH *stand staring.*

ELIZABETH, *quietly:* Oh, the noose, the noose is up!

PROCTOR: There'll be no noose.

ELIZABETH: She wants me dead. I knew all week it would come to this!

PROCTOR, *without conviction:* They dismissed it. You heard her say—

ELIZABETH: And what of tomorrow? She will cry me out until they take me!

PROCTOR: Sit you down.

ELIZABETH: She wants me dead, John, you know it!

PROCTOR: I say sit down! *She sits, trembling. He speaks quietly, trying to keep his wits.* Now we must be wise, Elizabeth.

ELIZABETH, *with sarcasm, and a sense of being lost:* Oh, indeed, indeed!

PROCTOR: Fear nothing. I'll find Ezekiel Cheever. I'll tell him she said it were all sport.

ELIZABETH: John, with so many in the jail, more than Cheever's help is needed now, I think. Would you favor me with this? Go to Abigail.

PROCTOR, *his soul hardening as he senses . . .:* What have I to say to Abigail?

ELIZABETH, *delicately:* John—grant me this. You have a faulty understanding of young girls. There is a promise made in any bed—

18 **PROCTOR,** *striving against his anger:* What promise!

ELIZABETH: Spoke or silent, a promise is surely made. And she may dote on it now—I am sure she does—and thinks to kill me, then to take my place.

PROCTOR'S *anger is rising; he cannot speak.*

ELIZABETH: It is her dearest hope, John, I know it. There be a thousand names; why does she call mine? There be a certain danger in calling such a name—I am no Goody Good that sleeps in ditches, nor Osburn, drunk and half-witted. She'd dare not call out such a farmer's wife but there be monstrous profit in it. She thinks to take my place, John.

PROCTOR: She cannot think it! *He knows it is true.*

ELIZABETH, *"reasonably":* John, have you ever shown her somewhat of contempt? She cannot pass you in the church but you will blush—

PROCTOR: I may blush for my sin.

ELIZABETH: I think she sees another meaning in that blush.

PROCTOR: And what see you? What see you, Elizabeth?

ELIZABETH, *"conceding":* I think you be somewhat ashamed, for I am there, and she so close.

PROCTOR: When will you know me, woman? Were I stone I would have cracked for shame this seven month!

Reading Strategy
Reading Drama How do the stage directions indicating that Proctor speaks "without conviction" affect your understanding of his line?

Enrichment

The Witch of Blackbird Pond

Elizabeth points out that her social position makes her less vulnerable to an accusation than "Goody Good that sleeps in ditches, nor Osburn, drunk and half-witted." In New England, those who were on the fringes of society were often the easiest targets for accusations of witchcraft.

In her award-winning novel *The Witch of Blackbird Pond,* Elizabeth George Speare tells the story of Hannah Tupper, a peaceful, gentle Quaker widow living just outside the Connecticut town of Wethersfield. Because Hannah is a Quaker, she does not attend religious services with the rest of the town and so no one will have anything to do with her socially. When a spiteful woman accuses Hannah of witchcraft, the community is only too eager to believe in her guilt. Although Hannah escapes with the help of two friends, many actual accused witches were not so fortunate.

ELIZABETH: Then go and tell her she's a whore. Whatever promise she may sense—break it, John, break it.

PROCTOR, *between his teeth:* Good, then. I'll go. *He starts for his rifle.*

ELIZABETH, *trembling, fearfully:* Oh, how unwillingly!

PROCTOR, *turning on her, rifle in hand:* I will curse her hotter than the oldest cinder in hell. But pray, begrudge me not my anger!

ELIZABETH: Your anger! I only ask you—

PROCTOR: Woman, am I so base? Do you truly think me base?

ELIZABETH: I never called you base.

PROCTOR: Then how do you charge me with such a promise? The promise that a stallion gives a mare I gave that girl!

ELIZABETH: Then why do you anger with me when I bid you break it?

PROCTOR: Because it speaks deceit, and I am honest! But I'll plead no more! I see now your spirit twists around the single error of my life, and I will never tear it free!

ELIZABETH, *crying out:* You'll tear it free—when you come to know that I will be your only wife, or no wife at all! She has an arrow in you yet, John Proctor, and you know it well!

Quite suddenly, as though from the air, a figure appears in the doorway. They start slightly. It is MR. HALE. *He is different now—drawn a little, and there is a quality of deference, even of guilt, about his manner now.*

HALE: Good evening.

PROCTOR, *still in his shock:* Why, Mr. Hale! Good evening to you, sir. Come in, come in.

HALE, *to Elizabeth:* I hope I do not startle you.

ELIZABETH: No, no, it's only that I heard no horse—

HALE: You are Goodwife Proctor.

PROCTOR: Aye; Elizabeth.

HALE, *nods, then:* I hope you're not off to bed yet.

PROCTOR, *setting down his gun:* No, no. HALE *comes further into the room. And* PROCTOR, *to explain his nervousness:* We are not used to visitors after dark, but you're welcome here. Will you sit you down, sir?

HALE: I will. *He sits.* Let you sit, Goodwife Proctor.

She does, never letting him out of her sight. There is a pause as HALE *looks about the room.*

PROCTOR, *to break the silence:* Will you drink cider, Mr. Hale?

HALE: No, it rebels my stomach; I have some further traveling yet tonight. Sit you down, sir. PROCTOR *sits.* I will not keep you long, but I have some business with you.

PROCTOR: Business of the court?

HALE: No—no, I come of my own, without the court's authority. Hear me. *He wets his lips.* I know not if you are aware, but your wife's name is—mentioned in the court.

Vocabulary Builder
base (bās) *adj.* low; mean

Vocabulary Builder
deference (def′ ər əns) *n.* courteous regard or respect

Reading Strategy
Reading Drama Why is the silent pause indicated by the stage directions important?

20 

What does Elizabeth fear that Abigail will do to her?

19 Reading Strategy
Reading Drama

- **Ask** students the Reading Strategy question: Why is the silent pause indicated by the stage directions important?
  Answer: The silence allows tension and suspense to build.
- **Ask** students how they reacted to the stage direction, "Quite suddenly, as though from the air, a figure appears in the doorway," before they read farther and learned that the figure was Hale.
  Answer: The figure's sudden appearance from nowhere suggests the supernatural. Given the atmosphere of witchcraft that Miller has created, students may have thought it was a witch, the Devil, or some other supernatural being.
- Once students learn that the figure is Hale, **ask** why they think Miller chooses to have him enter in this manner.
  Answer: Miller links Hale in the reader's mind with a spirit; the reader has to read on to find out whether he is a good or evil spirit.
- **Ask** students why Hale would come to the Proctors without the court's authority, and what the stage directions in the passage suggest about his intentions.
  Answer: He may not agree with the court's judgments so far. He may decide the time has come to rely on his own judgment. He may hope that he can help the Proctors.

20 Reading Check

Answer: She fears that Abigail will denounce her as a witch.

Differentiated Instruction
Solutions for All Learners

Strategy for Gifted/Talented Students
Elizabeth urges John to speak privately to Abigail and convince her to confess her lies. Late in the original Broadway run of the play, Miller inserted a short scene to open Act III in which John fulfills this request. Partners can find Miller's scene and perform it for the class. The whole class can debate on the value of such a scene. Does it add anything essential to the play or to the audience's understanding of Abigail and John? If not, what purpose does it serve? Why do students think Miller decided to add this scene?

㉑ Reading Strategy
Reading Drama

- **Ask** students the Reading Strategy question: What do the stage directions here reveal about Elizabeth's true emotions?
  Answer: Elizabeth knows this is no laughing matter; she is horrified at the danger Rebecca may be in.
- Why is Elizabeth especially shocked on Rebecca's account?
  Answer: Everyone recognizes that Rebecca is a truly good person; Elizabeth probably realizes that if Rebecca isn't safe, then no one is safe, including herself.

㉒ Vocabulary Builder
The Greek Suffix *-logy*

- Call students' attention to the word *theology* and its definition. Tell students that the word is derived from the Greek word *theo,* meaning "God," and the suffix *-logy,* meaning "the science or study of."
- Ask students to **volunteer** any other words they know that contain this suffix.
  Possibilities include: *biology, geology, anthropology, archaeology*

㉓ Literary Analysis
Allusion and Historical Context

- **Ask** students the Literary Analysis question: What do you know about the Puritans and their "plain style" that affects your interpretation of the golden candlesticks?
  Answer: The Puritans scorned material goods, especially in church; their churches were as plain as possible. They rejected the pageantry of Roman Catholicism. An insistence on gold candlesticks was not appropriate for a Puritan.
- Point out that Proctor has been to church roughly once every three weeks in the past year and a half. **Ask** students to evaluate this in terms of historical context.
  Answer: Today, this rate of attendance at church would be considered exemplary. However, according to the Puritans of Salem, who were expected to strictly keep the Sabbath, Proctor's attendance record is not good at all.

PROCTOR: We know it, sir. Our Mary Warren told us. We are entirely amazed.

HALE: I am a stranger here, as you know. And in my ignorance I find it hard to draw a clear opinion of them that come accused before the court. And so this afternoon, and now tonight, I go from house to house—I come now from Rebecca Nurse's house and—

ELIZABETH, *shocked:* Rebecca's charged!

HALE: God forbid such a one be charged. She is, however—mentioned somewhat.

ELIZABETH, *with an attempt at a laugh:* You will never believe, I hope, that Rebecca trafficked with the Devil.

HALE: Woman, it is possible.

PROCTOR, *taken aback:* Surely you cannot think so.

㉑ HALE: This is a strange time, Mister. No man may longer doubt the powers of the dark are gathered in monstrous attack upon this village. There is too much evidence now to deny it. You will agree, sir?

PROCTOR, *evading:* I—have no knowledge in that line. But it's hard to think so pious a woman be secretly a Devil's bitch after seventy year of such good prayer.

HALE: Aye. But the Devil is a wily one, you cannot deny it. However, she is far from accused, and I know she will not be. *Pause.* I thought, sir, to put some questions as to the Christian character of this house, if you'll permit me.

PROCTOR, *coldly, resentful:* Why, we—have no fear of questions, sir.

HALE: Good, then. *He makes himself more comfortable.* In the book of record that Mr. Parris keeps, I note that you are rarely in the church on Sabbath Day.

PROCTOR: No, sir, you are mistaken.

㉒ HALE: Twenty-six time in seventeen month, sir. I must call that rare. Will you tell me why you are so absent?

PROCTOR: Mr. Hale, I never knew I must account to that man for I come to church or stay at home. My wife were sick this winter.

HALE: So I am told. But you, Mister, why could you not come alone?

PROCTOR: I surely did come when I could, and when I could not I prayed in this house.

HALE: Mr. Proctor, your house is not a church; your theology must tell you that.

PROCTOR: It does, sir, it does; and it tells me that a minister may pray to God without he have golden candlesticks upon the altar.

㉓ HALE: What golden candlesticks?

PROCTOR: Since we built the church there were pewter candlesticks upon the altar; Francis Nurse made them y'know, and a sweeter hand never touched the metal. But Parris came, and for twenty week he preach nothin' but golden candlesticks until he had them. I labor the earth from dawn of day to blink of night, and I tell you true, when I look

Reading Strategy
Reading Drama What do the stage directions here reveal about Elizabeth's true emotions?

Vocabulary Builder
theology (thē äl′ ə jē) *n.* the study of religion

Literary Analysis
Allusion and Historical Context What do you know about the Puritans and their "plain style" that affects your interpretation of the golden candlesticks?

Enrichment

Puritan Ministers

Throughout Act I and on these two pages, John Proctor is severely critical of Reverend Parris. Parris resents this because "a minister is the Lord's man in the parish . . . not to be so lightly crossed and contradicted!"

The position of the minister in the parish was a radical innovation of Puritanism. The Roman Catholic view, which had dominated Europe for centuries, was that the Pope was the inheritor of the mantle of St. Peter. His priests were seen as assuming this divine authority. A Catholic priest, therefore, mediated between God and the congregation. A Puritan minister, however, was not believed to have any special authority given by the church, but was believed to have been directly chosen by God to preach his word. He was considered a teacher. Puritan ministers were well educated on doctrine and Scripture but were not considered to be better or holier than their parishioners.

to heaven and see my money glaring at his elbows—it hurt my prayer, sir, it hurt my prayer. I think, sometimes, the man dreams cathedrals, not clapboard meetin' houses.

HALE, *thinks, then:* And yet, Mister, a Christian on Sabbath Day must be in church. *Pause.* Tell me—you have three children?

PROCTOR: Aye. Boys.

HALE: How comes it that only two are baptized?

PROCTOR, *starts to speak, then stops, then, as though unable to restrain this:* I like it not that Mr. Parris should lay his hand upon my baby. I see no light of God in that man. I'll not conceal it.

HALE: I must say it, Mr. Proctor; that is not for you to decide. The man's
24 ordained, therefore the light of God is in him.

PROCTOR, *flushed with resentment but trying to smile:* What's your suspicion, Mr. Hale?

HALE: No, no, I have no—

PROCTOR: I nailed the roof upon the church, I hung the door—

HALE: Oh, did you! That's a good sign, then.

PROCTOR: It may be I have been too quick to bring the man to book, but you cannot think we ever desired the destruction of religion. I think that's in your mind, is it not?

HALE, *not altogether giving way:* I—have—there is a softness in your record, sir, a softness.

ELIZABETH: I think, maybe, we have been too hard with Mr. Parris. I think so. But sure we never loved the Devil here.

HALE, *nods, deliberating this. Then, with the voice of one administering a secret test:* Do you know your Commandments, Elizabeth?

ELIZABETH, *without hesitation, even eagerly:* I surely do. There be no mark of blame upon my life, Mr. Hale. I am a covenanted Christian woman.

HALE: And you, Mister?

PROCTOR, *a trifle unsteadily:* I—am sure I do, sir.

HALE, *glances at her open face, then at* JOHN, *then:* Let you repeat them, if you will.

PROCTOR: The Commandments.

HALE: Aye.

PROCTOR, *looking off, beginning to sweat:* Thou shalt not kill.

HALE: Aye.

PROCTOR, *counting on his fingers:* Thou shalt not steal. Thou shalt not
covet thy neighbor's goods, nor make unto thee any graven image.
Thou shalt not take the name of the Lord in vain; thou shalt have no
other gods before me. *With some hesitation:* Thou shalt remember the
25 Sabbath Day and keep it holy. *Pause. Then:* Thou shalt honor thy
father and mother. Thou shalt not bear false witness. *He is stuck. He counts back on his fingers, knowing one is missing.* Thou shalt not make unto thee any graven image.

Reading Strategy
Reading Drama What does this passage reveal about Proctor's attitude toward Parris as a minister?

26 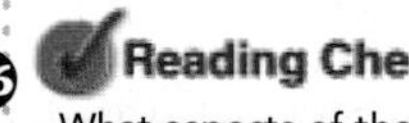

Reading Check

What aspects of the Proctor household does Hale question?

24 Reading Strategy
Reading Drama

- **Ask** students the Reading Strategy question: What does this passage reveal about Proctor's attitude toward Parris as a minister?
  Answer: Proctor believes that Parris does not belong in the clergy. He distrusts Parris's fitness to give the sacraments.
- Have students go back to Act I and review the grounds for Proctor's criticism of Parris.
  Answer: Parris is greedy for the salary and benefits of his position. He summons Hale to the village without calling a meeting. His style of preaching has driven many people away from the church.

25 Critical Thinking
Interpret

- **Ask** students to name the commandment that John has left off the list. Ask why this omission is ironic.
  Answer: He has left out "thou shalt not commit adultery." This is ironic because this is the commandment he has broken.
- Point out the commandment "Thou shalt not bear false witness." **Ask** students to explain the irony of this commandment in view of the present events.
  Answer: The children and other accusers are bearing false witness against the accused, but they are praised for it rather than condemned.
- Tell students that for a Puritan, repeating the commandments in order was as usual as repeating the alphabet in order. Proctor, however, lists the commandments in random order (6, 8, 10, 2, and so on). What might this suggest to Hale?
  Answer: It reinforces Hale's realization that Proctor is not orthodox in his actions or beliefs. It probably prejudices Hale further against him.

26 Reading Check

Answer: He questions whether it is a Christian household.

27 Reading Strategy
Reading Drama

- **Ask** students the Reading Strategy question: How can you tell that Hale is beginning to grow suspicious of the Proctors?
  Answer: Hale is worried over John's failure to name all ten commandments. The stage directions "worried" and "disturbed and evasive" suggest that he doubts the Proctors.
- What does the stage direction "as though a secret arrow had pained his heart" suggest about Proctor? To what might the arrow allude?
  Possible answers: He repents having broken this commandment. He is ashamed.
- What is ironic about Proctor's statement, "I have no witness and cannot prove it, except my word be taken"?
  Answer: The same is true of all the accusations; they are made on people's unsupported word. Proctor is the only one who hesitates to accuse without witnesses, and yet he is the only one speaking the truth.

HALE: You have said that twice, sir.

PROCTOR, *lost:* Aye. *He is flailing for it.*

ELIZABETH, *delicately:* Adultery, John.

PROCTOR, *as though a secret arrow had pained his heart:* Aye. *Trying to grin it away—to* HALE: You see, sir, between the two of us we do know them all. HALE *only looks at* PROCTOR, *deep in his attempt to define this man.* PROCTOR *grows more uneasy.* I think it be a small fault.

HALE: Theology, sir, is a fortress; no crack in a fortress may be accounted small. *He rises; he seems worried now. He paces a little, in deep thought.*

PROCTOR: There be no love for Satan in this house, Mister.

HALE: I pray it, I pray it dearly. *He looks to both of them, an attempt at a smile on his face, but his misgivings are clear.* Well, then—I'll bid you good night.

27 **ELIZABETH,** *unable to restrain herself:* Mr. Hale. *He turns.* I do think you are suspecting me somewhat? Are you not?

HALE, *obviously disturbed—and evasive:* Goody Proctor, I do not judge you. My duty is to add what I may to the godly wisdom of the court. I pray you both good health and good fortune. *To* JOHN: Good night, sir. *He starts out.*

ELIZABETH, *with a note of desperation:* I think you must tell him, John.

HALE: What's that?

ELIZABETH, *restraining a call:* Will you tell him?
Slight pause. HALE *looks questioningly at* JOHN.

PROCTOR, *with difficulty:* I—I have no witness and cannot prove it, except my word be taken. But I know the children's sickness had naught to do with witchcraft.

HALE, *stopped, struck:* Naught to do—?

PROCTOR: Mr. Parris discovered them sportin' in the woods. They were startled and took sick.
Pause.

HALE: Who told you this?

PROCTOR, *hesitates, then:* Abigail Williams.

HALE: Abigail.

PROCTOR: Aye.

HALE, *his eyes wide:* Abigail Williams told you it had naught to do with witchcraft!

PROCTOR: She told me the day you came, sir.

HALE, *suspiciously:* Why—why did you keep this?

PROCTOR: I never knew until tonight that the world is gone daft with this nonsense.

HALE: Nonsense! Mister, I have myself examined Tituba, Sarah Good, and numerous others that have confessed to dealing with the Devil. They have *confessed* it.

Reading Strategy
Reading Drama How can you tell that Hale is beginning to grow suspicious of the Proctors?

Differentiated Instruction
Solutions for All Learners

Strategy for Less Proficient Readers
Help students take a stronger interest in the events of the play by imagining themselves as characters. Have students read the dialogue on this page up to the point where Elizabeth insists that John tell Hale about Abigail. Ask students to imagine that they can advise the Proctors about what to say at this point. What advice would they give John and Elizabeth? Call on volunteers to act out the advice, and continue the scene with improvisation, each student taking a part.

Enrichment for Advanced Readers
Ask students to write essays examining the levels of irony in *The Crucible.* You might start them off with the margin questions above. Have students look at the court proceeding in Act III and think about the irony in the judges' reactions to the testimony of both accusers and accused. Point out that Miller makes the audience or the reader "witnesses" to the proceedings. Ask students whether they think this irony is deliberate.

PROCTOR: And why not, if they must hang for denyin' it? There are them that will swear to anything before they'll hang; have you never thought of that?

HALE: I have. I—I have indeed. *It is his own suspicion, but he resists it. He glances at* ELIZABETH, *then at* JOHN. And you—would you testify to this in court?

PROCTOR: I—had not reckoned with goin' into court. But if I must I will.

HALE: Do you falter here?

PROCTOR: I falter nothing, but I may wonder if my story will be credited in such a court. I do wonder on it, when such a steady-minded minister as you will suspicion such a woman that never lied, and cannot, and the world knows she cannot! I may falter somewhat, Mister; I am no fool.

HALE, *quietly—it has impressed him:* Proctor, let you open with me now, for I have a rumor that troubles me. It's said you hold no belief that there may even be witches in the world. Is that true, sir?

PROCTOR—*he knows this is critical, and is striving against his disgust with* HALE *and with himself for even answering:* I know not what I have said, I may have said it. I have wondered if there be witches in the world—although I cannot believe they come among us now.

HALE: Then you do not believe—

PROCTOR: I have no knowledge of it; the Bible speaks of witches, and I will not deny them.

HALE: And you, woman?

ELIZABETH: I—I cannot believe it.

HALE, *shocked:* You cannot!

PROCTOR: Elizabeth, you bewilder him!

ELIZABETH, *to* HALE: I cannot think the Devil may own a woman's soul, Mr. Hale, when she keeps an upright way, as I have. I am a good woman, I know it; and if you believe I may do only good work in the world, and yet be secretly bound to Satan, then I must tell you, sir, I do not believe it.

HALE: But, woman, you do believe there are witches in—

ELIZABETH: If you think that I am one, then I say there are none.

HALE: You surely do not fly against the Gospel, the Gospel—

PROCTOR: She believe in the Gospel, every word!

ELIZABETH: Question Abigail Williams about the Gospel, not myself!
HALE *stares at her.*

PROCTOR: She do not mean to doubt the Gospel, sir, you cannot think it. This be a Christian house, sir, a Christian house.

HALE: God keep you both; let the third child be quickly baptized, and go you without fail each Sunday to Sabbath prayer; and keep a solemn, quiet way among you. I think—
GILES COREY *appears in doorway.*

GILES: John!

Reading Strategy
Reading Drama In what way do the stage directions help you to understand that Hale wants to believe that the Proctors are good people?

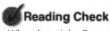

29 
What does John Proctor tell Reverend Hale about Abigail Williams?

28 Reading Strategy
Reading Drama

- **Ask** students the Reading Strategy question: In what way do the stage directions help you to understand that Hale wants to believe that the Proctors are good people?
  Answer: "His own suspicion" agrees with what John says. He is "impressed" with John's reasoning.
- What do the stage directions and dialogue about witches suggest about Proctor's character?
  Answer: He hates hypocrisy but realizes that a little hypocrisy is necessary to keep him out of danger. He doesn't really believe in witches, but he knows it is safer to say that he "will not deny them."
- What do Elizabeth's statements about witches suggest about her character?
  Answer: Her honesty makes her brave enough to speak her mind.

29 Reading Check

Answer: He says that Abigail told him that the children's illness had nothing to do with witchcraft.

30 Literary Analysis
Allusion

- **Ask** students to explain the power of Francis's allusion to the "bricks and mortar of the church."
  Answer: The allusion is a metaphor that compares Rebecca to the church building. The church is the house of God, and the bricks and mortar are both the walls and the substance that holds the walls together. The allusion states directly that Rebecca is a good and holy woman, and states it powerfully by comparing her to the strong, lasting brick walls of the building.
- Have a volunteer read aloud Hale's speech beginning, "Nurse, though our hearts break . . ." **Ask** students to explain in what way the Devil is alive in Salem.
  Answer: The Devil is alive in the false accusations and the sin, envy, and spite that the Putnams, Abigail, and other characters vent on one another.
- **Ask** students the Literary Analysis question: What is the meaning of this allusion to the Devil?
  Answer: Hale compares Rebecca to Lucifer, the archangel who fell from heaven. (If necessary, refer students back to the commentary in Act I.)

PROCTOR: Giles! What's the matter?

GILES: They take my wife.

FRANCIS NURSE *enters.*

GILES: And his Rebecca!

PROCTOR, *to* FRANCIS: Rebecca's in the *jail!*

FRANCIS: Aye, Cheever come and take her in his wagon. We've only now come from the jail, and they'll not even let us in to see them.

ELIZABETH: They've surely gone wild now, Mr. Hale!

FRANCIS, *going to* HALE: Reverend Hale! Can you not speak to the Deputy Governor? I'm sure he mistakes these people—

HALE: Pray calm yourself, Mr. Nurse.

FRANCIS: My wife is the very brick and mortar of the church, Mr. Hale—*indicating* GILES—and Martha Corey, there cannot be a woman closer yet to God than Martha.

HALE: How is Rebecca charged, Mr. Nurse?

FRANCIS, *with a mocking, half-hearted laugh:* For murder, she's charged! *Mockingly quoting the warrant:* "For the marvelous and supernatural murder of Goody Putnam's babies." What am I to do, Mr. Hale?

HALE, *turns from* FRANCIS, *deeply troubled, then:* Believe me, Mr. Nurse, if Rebecca Nurse be tainted, then nothing's left to stop the
30 whole green world from burning. Let you rest upon the justice of the court; the court will send her home. I know it.

FRANCIS: You cannot mean she will be tried in court!

HALE, *pleading:* Nurse, though our hearts break, we cannot flinch; these are new times, sir. There is a misty plot afoot so subtle we should be criminal to cling to old respects and ancient friendships. I have seen too many frightful proofs in court—the Devil is alive in Salem, and we dare not quail to follow wherever the accusing finger points!

PROCTOR, *angered:* How may such a woman murder children?

HALE, *in great pain:* Man, remember, until an hour before the Devil fell, God thought him beautiful in Heaven.

GILES: I never said my wife were a witch, Mr. Hale; I only said she were reading books!

HALE: Mr. Corey, exactly what complaint were made on your wife?

GILES: That bloody mongrel Walcott charge her. Y'see, he buy a pig of my wife four or five year ago, and the pig died soon after. So he come dancin' in for his money back. So my Martha, she says to him, "Walcott, if you haven't the wit to feed a pig properly, you'll not live to own many," she says. Now he goes to court and claims that from that day to this he cannot keep a pig alive for more than four weeks because my Martha bewitch them with her books!

Enter EZEKIEL CHEEVER. *A shocked silence.*

CHEEVER: Good evening to you, Proctor.

PROCTOR: Why, Mr. Cheever. Good evening.

Vocabulary Builder
quail (kwāl) *v.* cringe from

Literary Analysis
Allusion What is the meaning of this allusion to the Devil?

Enrichment

Paradise Lost
Lucifer, an archangel who fell from heaven, is the central figure of *Paradise Lost,* the Renaissance epic by British poet John Milton (1608–1674). Milton was a Protestant, a supporter of Cromwell and the protectorate. His *Paradise Lost,* published in 1667, recounts the creation of hell and the subsequent battle for the soul of man between God and Satan. Some critics have protested that Milton's Satan, who declares that he prefers to reign in hell rather than serve in heaven, is much more appealing than his God. Others have answered that this appeal mirrors the experience of humankind, which finds temptation more attractive than virtue. Still others point to Lucifer's powerful impact as a symbol of the erring human being, who tragically puts self before others or before God.

CHEEVER: Good evening, all. Good evening, Mr. Hale.

PROCTOR: I hope you come not on business of the court.

CHEEVER: I do, Proctor, aye. I am clerk of the court now, y'know.

Enter MARSHAL HERRICK, *a man in his early thirties, who is somewhat shamefaced at the moment.*

GILES: It's a pity, Ezekiel, that an honest tailor might have gone to Heaven must burn in Hell. You'll burn for this, do you know it?

CHEEVER: You know yourself I must do as I'm told. You surely know that, Giles. And I'd as lief[3] you'd not be sending me to Hell. I like not the sound of it, I tell you; I like not the sound of it. *He fears* PROCTOR, *but starts to reach inside his coat.* Now believe me, Proctor, how heavy be the law, all its tonnage I do carry on my back tonight. *He takes out a warrant.* I have a warrant for your wife.

PROCTOR, *to* HALE: You said she were not charged!

HALE: I know nothin' of it. *To* CHEEVER: When were she charged?

CHEEVER: I am given sixteen warrant tonight, sir, and she is one.

PROCTOR: Who charged her?

CHEEVER: Why, Abigail Williams charge her.

PROCTOR: On what proof, what proof?

CHEEVER, *looking about the room:* Mr. Proctor, I have little time. The court bid me search your house, but I like not to search a house. So will you hand me any poppets that your wife may keep here?

PROCTOR: Poppets?

ELIZABETH: I never kept no poppets, not since I were a girl.

CHEEVER, *embarrassed, glancing toward the mantel where sits* MARY WARREN'S *poppet:* I spy a poppet, Goody Proctor.

ELIZABETH: Oh! *Going for it:* Why, this is Mary's.

CHEEVER, *shyly:* Would you please to give it to me?

ELIZABETH, *handing it to him, asks* HALE: Has the court discovered a text in poppets now?

CHEEVER, *carefully holding the poppet:* Do you keep any others in this house?

PROCTOR: No, nor this one either till tonight. What signifies a poppet?

CHEEVER: Why, a poppet—*he gingerly turns the poppet over*—a poppet may signify—Now, woman, will you please to come with me?

PROCTOR: She will not! *To* ELIZABETH: Fetch Mary here.

CHEEVER, *ineptly reaching toward* ELIZABETH: No, no, I am forbid to leave her from my sight.

PROCTOR, *pushing his arm away:* You'll leave her out of sight and out of mind, Mister. Fetch Mary, Elizabeth. ELIZABETH *goes upstairs.*

HALE: What signifies a poppet, Mr. Cheever?

Reading Strategy
Reading Drama
How can you tell that Cheever does not at first believe the charges against Elizabeth?

Vocabulary Builder
gingerly (jin′ jər′ lē) *adv.* cautiously

Reading Check
What turn of events causes Hale to feel he must defend the court?

---

3. **as lief** (as lēf) *adv.* rather.

㉛ Reading Strategy
Reading Drama

- **Ask** students the Reading Strategy question: How can you tell that Cheever does not at first believe the charges against Elizabeth?
  Answer: "Embarrassed," "shyly," "gingerly," and "ineptly" all indicate that he finds his task distasteful.
- **Ask** students what Elizabeth's responses reveal about her state of mind.
  Answer: She seems perfectly calm, even amused. The line, "Has the court discovered a text in poppets now?" has some humor in it. Her attitude suggests that she is innocent.

㉜ Reading Check

Answer: Rebecca's arrest causes Hale to feel he must defend the court.

33 Reading Strategy
Reading Drama

- **Ask** students the Reading Strategy question: What do the stage directions reveal about Hale's true thoughts?
  Answer: Hale is torn between his belief in Elizabeth's goodness and his belief in the evidence of the needle.
- **Ask** students to infer what really happened to Abigail at dinner.
  Answer: Since Mary sewed the doll in court, Abigail probably saw her doing it. She probably saw Mary push the needle into the doll. She knew, therefore, that the doll would be in the Proctors' house with the needle in it. She stabbed herself with a needle to make her accusation match the "evidence."

▶ **Monitor Progress** Have students **evaluate** Abigail's character in light of her accusation of Elizabeth.
Answer: Abigail is desperate to have John even at the cost of having Elizabeth arrested and perhaps hanged.

CHEEVER, *turning the poppet over in his hands:* Why, they say it may signify that she—*he has lifted the poppet's skirt, and his eyes widen in astonished fear.* Why, this, this—

PROCTOR, *reaching for the poppet:* What's there?

CHEEVER: Why—*He draws out a long needle from the poppet*—it is a needle! Herrick, Herrick, it is a needle!

HERRICK *comes toward him.*

PROCTOR, *angrily, bewildered:* And what signifies a needle!

CHEEVER, *his hands shaking:* Why, this go hard with her, Proctor, this—I had my doubts, Proctor, I had my doubts, but here's calamity. *To* HALE, *showing the needle:* You see it, sir, it is a needle!

HALE: Why? What meanin' has it?

CHEEVER, *wide-eyed, trembling:* The girl, the Williams girl, Abigail Williams, sir. She sat to dinner in Reverend Parris's house tonight, and without word nor warnin' she falls to the floor. Like a struck beast, he says, and screamed a scream that a bull would weep to hear. And he goes to save her, and, stuck two inches in the flesh of her belly, he draw a needle out. And demandin' of her how she come to be so stabbed, she—*to* PROCTOR *now*—testify it were your wife's familiar spirit pushed
33 it in.

PROCTOR: Why, she done it herself! *To* HALE: I hope you're not takin' this for proof, Mister!

HALE, *struck by the proof, is silent.*

CHEEVER: 'Tis hard proof! *To* HALE: I find here a poppet Goody Proctor keeps. I have found it, sir. And in the belly of the poppet a needle's stuck. I tell you true, Proctor, I never warranted to see such proof of Hell, and I bid you obstruct me not, for I—

Enter ELIZABETH *with* MARY WARREN. PROCTOR, *seeing* MARY WARREN, *draws her by the arm to* HALE.

PROCTOR: Here now! Mary, how did this poppet come into my house?

MARY WARREN, *frightened for herself, her voice very small:* What poppet's that, sir?

PROCTOR, *impatiently, points at the doll in* CHEEVER'S *hand:* This poppet, this poppet.

MARY WARREN, *evasively, looking at it:* Why, I—I think it is mine.

PROCTOR: It is your poppet, is it not?

MARY WARREN, *not understanding the direction of this:* It—is, sir.

PROCTOR: And how did it come into this house?

MARY WARREN, *glancing about at the avid faces:* Why—I made it in the court, sir, and—give it to Goody Proctor tonight.

PROCTOR, *to* HALE: Now, sir—do you have it?

HALE: Mary Warren, a needle have been found inside this poppet.

MARY WARREN, *bewildered:* Why, I meant no harm by it, sir.

PROCTOR, *quickly:* You stuck that needle in yourself?

Reading Strategy
Reading Drama What do these stage directions reveal about Hale's true thoughts?

MARY WARREN: I—I believe I did, sir, I—

PROCTOR, *to* HALE: What say you now?

HALE, *watching* MARY WARREN *closely:* Child, you are certain this be your natural memory? May it be, perhaps that someone conjures you even now to say this?

MARY WARREN: Conjures me? Why, no, sir, I am entirely myself, I think. Let you ask Susanna Walcott—she saw me sewin' it in court. *Or better still:* Ask Abby, Abby sat beside me when I made it.

PROCTOR, *to* HALE, *of* CHEEVER: Bid him begone. Your mind is surely settled now. Bid him out, Mr. Hale.

ELIZABETH: What signifies a needle?

HALE: Mary—you charge a cold and cruel murder on Abigail.

MARY WARREN: Murder! I charge no—

HALE: Abigail were stabbed tonight; a needle were found stuck into her belly—

ELIZABETH: And she charges me?

HALE: Aye.

ELIZABETH, *her breath knocked out:* Why—! The girl is murder! She must be ripped out of the world!

CHEEVER, *pointing at* ELIZABETH: You've heard that, sir! Ripped out of the world! Herrick, you heard it!

PROCTOR, *suddenly snatching the warrant out of* CHEEVER'S *hands:* Out with you.

CHEEVER: Proctor, you dare not touch the warrant.

PROCTOR, *ripping the warrant:* Out with you!

CHEEVER: You've ripped the Deputy Governor's warrant, man!

PROCTOR: Damn the Deputy Governor! Out of my house!

HALE: Now, Proctor, Proctor!

PROCTOR: Get y'gone with them! You are a broken minister.

HALE: Proctor, if she is innocent, the court—

PROCTOR: If *she* is innocent! Why do you never wonder if Parris be innocent, or Abigail? Is the accuser always holy now? Were they born this morning as clean as God's fingers? I'll tell you what's walking Salem—vengeance is walking Salem. We are what we always were in Salem, but now the little crazy children are jangling the keys of the kingdom, and common vengeance writes the law! This warrant's vengeance! I'll not give my wife to vengeance!

ELIZABETH: I'll go, John—

PROCTOR: You will not go!

HERRICK: I have nine men outside. You cannot keep her. The law binds me, John, I cannot budge.

PROCTOR, *to* HALE, *ready to break him:* Will you see her taken?

HALE: Proctor, the court is just—

Reading Strategy
Reading Drama What do the stage directions and Hale's comment reveal about his trust in Mary Warren?

36 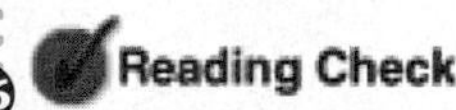

What does Cheever discover in the Proctor's home?

34 Reading Strategy
Reading Drama

- **Ask** students the Reading Strategy question: What do the stage directions and Hale's comment reveal about Hale's trust in Mary Warren?
  Answer: He isn't ready to take her at her word.
- Why is Hale unwilling to trust Mary?
  Answer: Mary is easily persuaded to believe and do what she is told. Hale is a good judge of people and he can see that Mary is the type to lie under pressure.

35 Critical Thinking
Connect

- Have students connect Proctor's speech with the speech Hale makes beginning, "Nurse, though our hearts break . . ." In what way is this speech a response to the previous one?
  Answer: Hale had said that the Devil was in Salem; Proctor identifies the Devil as "vengeance."
- Explain that "the keys of the kingdom" alludes to Jesus' statement to the apostle Peter: "I will give unto thee the keys of the kingdom of heaven" (Matthew 16:19). **Ask** students what connection Proctor makes.
  Answer: St. Peter uses his keys to let souls into heaven. Proctor is saying that by believing their accusations, the court has given the "little crazy children" the power to decide who will be saved and who will be damned.

36 Reading Check

Answer: The evidence he finds supports Abigail's accusation of Elizabeth.

Differentiated Instruction
Solutions for All Learners

Strategy for Less Proficient Readers
Have students make a character web for Reverend Hale at the end of each of the four acts. Students should note changes in his behavior and attitude from each act to the next. Have them use their notes to trace Hale's character development throughout the play.

37 Background

Film

The photographs used to illustrate *The Crucible* are taken from the 1996 Hollywood film of the play, starring Daniel Day-Lewis, Winona Ryder, Joan Allen, and Paul Scofield. Arthur Miller wrote the screenplay for the film. Miller was pleased at the ability of film to "open wide enough to contain a whole society and move in close enough to see into a girl's heart." The film was shot near Salem, only a mile or so away from land once owned by John Proctor. About two hundred local people were used as extras in the film; most claimed descent from the victims of the witchcraft trials.

37

38 **PROCTOR:** Pontius Pilate![4] God will not let you wash your hands of this!

ELIZABETH: John—I think I must go with them. *He cannot bear to look at her.* Mary, there is bread enough for the morning; you will bake, in the afternoon. Help Mr. Proctor as you were his daughter—you owe me that, and much more. *She is fighting her weeping. To* PROCTOR: When the children wake, speak nothing of witchcraft—it will frighten them. *She cannot go on.*

PROCTOR: I will bring you home. I will bring you soon.

ELIZABETH: Oh, John, bring me soon!

PROCTOR: I will fall like an ocean on that court! Fear nothing, Elizabeth.

ELIZABETH, *with great fear:* I will fear nothing. *She looks about the room, as though to fix it in her mind.* Tell the children I have gone to visit someone sick.

She walks out the door, HERRICK *and* CHEEVER *behind her. For a moment,* PROCTOR *watches from the doorway. The clank of chain is heard.*

PROCTOR: Herrick! Herrick, don't chain her! *He rushes out the door. From outside:* Damn you, man, you will not chain her! Off with them! I'll not have it! I will not have her chained!

There are other men's voices against his. HALE, *in a fever of guilt and uncertainty, turns from the door to avoid the sight:* MARY WARREN *bursts into tears and sits weeping.* GILES COREY *calls to* HALE.

GILES: And yet silent, minister? It is fraud, you know it is fraud! What keeps you, man? PROCTOR *is half braced, half pushed into the room by two deputies and* HERRICK.

PROCTOR: I'll pay you, Herrick, I will surely pay you!

HERRICK, *panting:* In God's name, John, I cannot help myself. I must chain them all. Now let you keep inside this house till I am gone! *He goes out with his deputies.*

PROCTOR *stands there, gulping air. Horses and a wagon creaking are heard.*

4. **Pontius** (pän′ shəs) **Pilate** (pī′ lət) Roman leader who condemned Jesus to be crucified.

Literary Analysis
Allusion To what biblical event, key to Puritan belief, does Proctor refer when he alludes to Pontius Pilate?

39 **◀ Critical Viewing**
What thoughts or feelings do the facial expressions of Elizabeth Proctor and the two deputies convey in this photo? **[Interpret]**

40  **Reading Check**
What happens to Elizabeth Proctor?

38 Literary Analysis
Allusion

- Provide some biblical background: Pontius Pilate knew that Jesus had been unjustly convicted, and he offered the people a choice: to crucify either Jesus or the robber Barabbas. The people chose Jesus, and Pilate literally washed his hands before the crowd as a symbol of his refusal to accept responsibility for Jesus' death. The figure of Pilate thus became notorious as an image of hypocritical innocence.
- **Ask** students the Literary Analysis question: To what biblical event, key to Puritan belief, does Proctor refer when he alludes to Pontius Pilate?
  Answer: Proctor refers to the crucifixion of Jesus Christ, particularly Pontius Pilate's role in it.
- **Ask** students to evaluate the allusion. What does it suggest about Hale?
  Answer: It suggests that even though Hale disclaims responsibility, he will knowingly allow the fraud to go forward.

39 Critical Viewing
Answer: They look deeply concerned.

40 Reading Check
Answer: She is arrested and charged with witchcraft.

Differentiated Instruction
Solutions for All Learners

Enrichment for Special Needs Students
Have students make a set of index cards with which to play a matching game. On one side of each card, students can copy a brief quotation from the play. On the other side, students should write the name of the character who speaks these lines. Players can take turns reading the quotations and identifying the characters' names. For bonus points, students can identify the point in the action at which the lines are spoken. Make sure that students choose lines that give some clue as to the speaker. For example, students should guess from the context that the line, "Help Mr. Proctor as you were his daughter—you owe me that, and much more," is spoken by Elizabeth as she makes arrangements with Mary Warren for the household before leaving for the jail.

41 Critical Thinking
Evaluate

- Why is Hale so unwilling to believe that Abigail is guilty of fraud and murder?
  Answer: To condemn so many innocent people to death, Abigail must be profoundly evil. Hale doesn't want to believe this of anyone. He prefers to blame it on the Devil rather than on a person.
- **Ask** students to explain in what way the Devil is involved in the court proceedings.
  Answer: The Devil exists in the evil that people do. Abigail has not literally seen the Devil—and neither has anyone else in Salem Village, for that matter—but she has done things that she knows to be wrong: drinking a charm to kill Elizabeth, having an affair with John, lying about Tituba and many others, and condemning people to death with false testimony.

HALE, *in great uncertainty:* Mr. Proctor—

PROCTOR: Out of my sight!

HALE: Charity, Proctor, charity. What I have heard in her favor, I will not fear to testify in court. God help me, I cannot judge her guilty or innocent—I know not. Only this consider: the world goes mad, and it profit nothing you should lay the cause to the vengeance of a little girl.

PROCTOR: You are a coward! Though you be ordained in God's own tears, you are a coward now!

HALE: Proctor, I cannot think God be provoked so grandly by such a petty cause. The jails are packed—our greatest judges sit in Salem now—and hangin's promised. Man, we must look to cause proportionate. Were there murder done, perhaps, and never brought to light?
41 Abomination? Some secret blasphemy that stinks to Heaven? Think on cause, man, and let you help me to discover it. For there's your way, believe it, there is your only way, when such confusion strikes upon the world. *He goes to* GILES *and* FRANCIS. Let you counsel among yourselves; think on your village and what may have drawn from heaven such thundering wrath upon you all. I shall pray God open up our eyes.

HALE *goes out.*

FRANCIS, *struck by* HALE'S *mood:* I never heard no murder done in Salem.

PROCTOR—*he has been reached by* HALE'S *words:* Leave me, Francis, leave me.

GILES, *shaken:* John—tell me, are we lost?

PROCTOR: Go home now, Giles. We'll speak on it tomorrow.

GILES: Let you think on it. We'll come early, eh?

PROCTOR: Aye. Go now, Giles.

GILES: Good night, then.

GILES COREY *goes out. After a moment:*

MARY WARREN, *in a fearful squeak of a voice:* Mr. Proctor, very likely they'll let her come home once they're given proper evidence.

PROCTOR: You're coming to the court with me, Mary. You will tell it in the court.

MARY WARREN: I cannot charge murder on Abigail.

PROCTOR, *moving menacingly toward her:* You will tell the court how that poppet come here and who stuck the needle in.

MARY WARREN: She'll kill me for sayin' that! PROCTOR *continues toward her.* Abby'll charge lechery[5] on you, Mr. Proctor!

PROCTOR, *halting:* She's told you!

MARY WARREN: I have known it, sir. She'll ruin you with it, I know she will.

Vocabulary Builder

abomination (ə bäm′ ə nā′ shən) *n.* something that causes great horror or disgust

blasphemy (blas′ fə mē′) *n.* sinful act or remark

5. **lechery** (lech′ ər ē) *n.* lust; adultery—a charge almost as serious as witchcraft in this Puritan community.

PROCTOR, *hesitating, and with deep hatred of himself:* Good. Then her saintliness is done with. MARY *backs from him.* We will slide together into our pit; you will tell the court what you know.

MARY WARREN, *in terror:* I cannot, they'll turn on me—

PROCTOR *strides and catches her, and she is repeating, "I cannot, I cannot!"*

PROCTOR: My wife will never die for me! I will bring your guts into your mouth but that goodness will not die for me!

MARY WARREN, *struggling to escape him:* I cannot do it. I cannot!

PROCTOR, *grasping her by the throat as though he would strangle her:* Make your peace with it! Now Hell and Heaven grapple on our backs, and all our pretense is ripped away—make your peace! *He throws her to the floor, where she sobs, "I cannot, I cannot . . ." And now, half to himself, staring, and turning to the open door:* Peace. It is a providence, and no great change; we are only what we always were, but naked now. *He walks as though toward a great horror, facing the open sky.* Aye, naked! And the wind, God's icy wind, will blow!

And she is over and over again sobbing, "I cannot, I cannot, I cannot."

Critical Reading

1. **Respond:** Which character do you find the most intriguing? Why?
2. **(a) Recall:** What does Mary Warren bring home to Elizabeth Proctor? **(b) Interpret:** What is the significance of this gift?
3. **(a) Recall:** What evidence is used to support Abigail Williams's assertion that Elizabeth Proctor is guilty of witchcraft? **(b) Assess:** Do you think the evidence is compelling? Why or why not?
4. **(a) Recall:** What does Sarah Good do to save herself from hanging? **(b) Draw Conclusions:** Why would such an action save her?
5. **(a) Recall:** According to John Proctor, what is "walking Salem" and writing the law in the community? **(b) Support:** What evidence would support Proctor's assertion?
6. **(a) Recall:** Who says the witchcraft trials are "a black mischief"? **(b) Analyze:** What is ironic about that remark?
7. **Analyze:** Why is it surprising that Rebecca Nurse is charged with witchcraft?
8. **Evaluate:** Do you find any irony in the fact that Ezekiel Cheever is the one who arrests Elizabeth Proctor? Why or why not?

For: More about Arthur Miller
Visit: www.PHSchool.com
Web Code: ere-9635

ASSESS

Answers

1. Answers will vary. Ask students to cite speeches or actions that explain their choices.
2. (a) a doll she made for her (b) The gift serves later as evidence that allows the court to arrest Elizabeth.
3. (a) Elizabeth's possession of the doll with a needle stuck through it (b) The evidence is not compelling because Mary made the doll, stuck the needle into it, and gave it to Elizabeth.
4. (a) She confesses. (b) Only the unrepentant are put to death. The court believed that confession was the same as repentance.
5. (a) vengeance (b) Abigail clearly wants to strike back at Elizabeth for firing her and because she loves John; Walcott accuses Martha Corey because of an old quarrel over a pig.
6. (a) Proctor (b) The avowed purpose of the trials is to expose and punish the "black mischief" of witchcraft. Instead, the trials themselves are evil.
7. Everyone in Salem agrees that Rebecca is a good, kind Christian woman.
8. It was to Cheever that Elizabeth urged John to turn with the truth about Abigail. Now it is too late.

Go Online Author Link For additional information about Arthur Miller, have students type in the Web Code, then select *M* from the alphabet, and then select Arthur Miller.

Answers

1. God spoke directly to Moses and gave him the power to part the Red Sea; people believe that Abigail is possessed of special powers, as Moses was.
2. (a) Proctor implies that Hale refuses to take responsibility for his official actions. (b) It suggests that the innocent are being condemned.
3. Students should note that in the play, most often women accuse other women of witchcraft; the question is not simple. Students may feel that the low status of women, and especially of young girls, fuels the anger of accusers such as Abigail and Mary.
4. Proctor risks his social position by refusing to have his son baptized. He also risks his son's immortal soul. This suggests that Proctor's principles are of far greater importance to him than any interest he might have in what people think of him.
5. Since there were no laws against them, searches and arrests were not illegal. It suggests that the society had great faith in the correctness of its judges.
6. Make sure that students choose examples of lines that might be spoken with a variety of tones or emotions.

   Another sample answer can be found on **Reading Strategy Graphic Organizer B**, p. 293, in ***Graphic Organizer Transparencies.***
7. They describe how the actors are meant to move about the stage, how and whether they touch one another, and to whom their lines are addressed.
8. In a modern court, an accusation is not proof. A statement like Abigail's that a spirit is attacking her is not proof. A court official like Hale cannot visit suspects privately. Suspects are entitled to the protection of lawyers.

Go Online Assessment Students may use the **Self-test** to prepare for **Selection Test A** or **Selection Test B.**

Apply the Skills

The Crucible, Act II

Literary Analysis

Allusion

1. What does the biblical **allusion** to Moses and the parting of the Red Sea on page 1293 suggest about how the crowd views Abigail?
2. **(a)** What does John Proctor's allusion to Pontius Pilate on page 1309 imply about Proctor's opinion of Reverend Hale? **(b)** What does the allusion to Pontius Pilate imply about the witchcraft proceedings in Salem?

Connecting Literary Elements

3. In what way do details of **historical context,** including the status of women, explain why women were accused of witchcraft?
4. Knowing that keeping the Sabbath and attending church services were strictly enforced by the Puritans, how do you interpret John Proctor's exchange with Reverend Hale about the baptism of Proctor's sons? Explain.
5. The Puritans lacked laws to protect people from illegal searches and arrests. How does this fact add to your appreciation of the scene in which Elizabeth Proctor is apprehended?

Reading Strategy

Reading Drama

6. Using a chart like the one shown here, cite three examples of dialogue in which a character's attitudes would have been unclear to you if you had not read the stage directions.

Dialogue	Attitude Revealed in Stage Direction

7. In addition to characters' attitudes, what other significant information do the stage directions in Act II reveal to you?

Extend Understanding

8. **Social Studies Connection:** How are legal principles and evidence-gathering procedures different in America today than they were in the time in which the play is set? Explain.

QuickReview

An **allusion** is a brief reference within a literary work to another literary work, a well-known person, a place, or a historical event.

Considering the **historical context** of a literary work can help you better understand key factors about the work's setting, background, and culture.

When you **read drama,** pay close attention to dialogue and stage directions to enrich your understanding of the play's plot, characters, and themes.

For: Self-test
Visit: www.PHSchool.com
Web Code: era-6621

Build Language Skills

1 Vocabulary Lesson

Word Analysis: Greek Suffix *-logy*

The Greek suffix *-logy* means "the science, theory, or study of." When combined with the Greek root *-theo-*, meaning "god," the word *theology* means "the study of religion." For each item below, identify a word that combines a root with the suffix *-logy*.

1. "star" ___*logy*
2. "life" ___*logy*
3. "earth" ___*logy*
4. "social" ___*logy*

Spelling Strategy

For verbs that end in *-er*, add the suffix *-ence* to form nouns. For each of these words, use the suffix *-ence* to generate a noun.

1. differ 2. confer 3. prefer

Vocabulary Builder: Context

Explain why each statement is *true* or *false*.

1. Lying is *base* behavior.
2. To step *gingerly* is to stomp.
3. Someone who watches sports *avidly* probably knows very little about them.
4. Rude youngsters show *deference* to elders.
5. Puritans think witchcraft is an *abomination*.
6. A fearful animal may *quail* at the sight of a whip.
7. A minister is pleased to hear *blasphemy*.
8. A blushing person exhibits *pallor*.
9. The Puritans questioned their *theology*.
10. To *ameliorate* a situation is to make it better.

2 Grammar and Style Lesson

Commas After Introductory Words

Use a **comma** to set off a mild interjection or another interrupter that introduces a sentence.

Examples: *Oh*, you're not done then.
Aye, the farm is seeded.

Practice Add commas to set off introductory words. If a sentence is correct as is, write *Correct*.

1. Hey did you ever see *The Crucible?*
2. Yes I saw a local theater group's production.
3. Well which characters are sympathetic?
4. I must admit I found it unpleasant.
5. Perhaps but the problem could have been with the performance you saw.

Writing Application Write a brief scene using dialogue that involves two or more characters. Use commas to set off at least three introductory words.

WG *Prentice Hall Writing and Grammar Connection: Chapter 27, Section 2*

Extend Your Learning

Writing Imagine that one of the citizens accused of witchcraft has disappeared. In a group, design a **wanted poster** that describes the individual and the reason he or she should be apprehended. **[Group Activity]**

Listening and Speaking Write and perform a **scene** that dramatizes the arrest of Rebecca Nurse. Make the style of your scene consistent with that of the rest of the play. Present the scene to your class.

EXTEND/ASSESS

1 Vocabulary Lesson

Word Analysis

1. astrology
2. biology
3. geology
4. sociology

Spelling

1. difference
2. conference
3. preference

Vocabulary Builder

1. true; *base* means "ignoble"
2. false; *gingerly* means "tentatively"
3. false; *avidly* means "with eager interest"
4. false; *deference* means "respect"
5. true; an *abomination* is evil
6. true; *quail* means "to flinch"
7. false; *blasphemy* is ungodly speech
8. false; *pallor* means "paleness"
9. false; *theology* refers to religious beliefs
10. true; *ameliorate* means "to improve"

2 Grammar and Style Lesson

1. Hey,
2. Yes,
3. Well,
4. correct
5. Perhaps,

Writing Application

Check students' work for commas.

3 Extention Activities

Writing Lesson

- Display students' finished work in the classroom.

Listening and Speaking

- The **Support for Extend Your Learning** page (*Unit 6 Resources*, p. 363) provides guided note-taking opportunities to help students complete the Extend Your Learning activities.

Assessment Practice

Sentence Structure **(For more practice, see *Standardized Test Preparation Workbook*, p.77.)**

Many tests require students to identify correct sentence structure. Use this sample test item.

Elizabeth is frightened, the court clerk and the magistrate enter.

Which is the best way to write this sentence?

A Although Elizabeth is frightened—the court clerk and the magistrate enter.
B Elizabeth being frightened, the court clerk and the magistrate enter.
C Elizabeth becomes frightened when the court clerk and the magistrate enter.
D correct as is

Only choice **C** is grammatically correct and shows the correct cause-and-effect relationship.

Go Online Research Have students type in the Web Code for another research activity.

Meeting Your Standards

Students will

1. **analyze and respond to literary elements.**
   - Literary Analysis: Dramatic and Verbal Irony
2. **read, comprehend, analyze, and critique a drama.**
   - Reading Strategy: Categorizing Characters by Role
   - Reading Check questions
   - Apply the Skills questions
   - Assessment Practice (ATE)
3. **develop vocabulary.**
   - Vocabulary Lesson: Concept Development: Legal Terms
4. **understand and apply written and oral language conventions.**
   - Spelling Strategy
   - Grammar and Style Lesson: Subject and Verb Agreement in Inverted Sentences
5. **develop writing proficiency.**
   - Writing Lesson: Defense of a Character's Actions (After Act IV)
6. **develop writing strategies.**
   - Extend Your Learning: Character Sketch
7. **understand and apply listening and speaking strategies.**
   - Extend Your Learning: Monologue

Block Scheduling: Use one 90-minute class period to preteach the skills and have students read the selection. Use a second 90-minute class period to assess students' mastery of skills, extend their learning, and monitor their progress.

Homework Suggestions

Following are possibilities for homework assignments.

- Support pages from **Unit 6 Resources:**
  Literary Analysis
  Reading Strategy
  Vocabulary Builder
  Grammar and Style
- An Extend Your Learning project and the Writing Lesson for this selection may be completed over several days.

Step-by-Step Teaching Guide	Pacing Guide
PRETEACH	
• Administer Vocabulary and Reading Warm-ups as necessary.	5 min.
• Engage students' interest with the motivation activity.	5 min.
• Read and discuss author and background features. **FT**	10 min.
• Introduce the Literary Analysis skill: Dramatic and Verbal Irony. **FT**	5 min.
• Introduce the Reading Strategy: Categorizing Characters by Role. **FT**	10 min.
• Prepare students to read by teaching the selection vocabulary. **FT**	
TEACH	
• Informally monitor comprehension while students read independently or in groups. **FT**	30 min.
• Monitor students' comprehension with the Reading Check notes.	as students read
• Reinforce vocabulary with Vocabulary Builder notes.	as students read
• Develop students' understanding of dramatic and verbal irony with the Literary Analysis annotations. **FT**	5 min.
• Develop students' ability to categorize characters by role with the Reading Strategy annotations. **FT**	5 min.
ASSESS/EXTEND	
• Assess students' comprehension and mastery of the Literary Analysis and Reading Strategy by having them answer the Apply the Skills questions. **FT**	15 min.
• Have students complete the Vocabulary Lesson and the Grammar and Style Lesson. **FT**	15 min.
• Apply students' understanding by using one or more of the Extend Your Learning activities.	20–90 min. or homework
• Administer Selection Test A or Selection Test B. **FT**	15 min.

Resources

PRINT
Unit 6 Resources
Vocabulary Warm-up Word Lists **[L1, L2, EL]** ....p. 371
Vocabulary Warm-up Practice **[L1, L2, EL]** ....p. 372
Reading Warm-up A **[L1, L2, EL]** ....p. 373
Reading Warm-up B **[L1, L2, L3]** ....p. 374

TRANSPARENCY
Graphic Organizer Transparencies
Literary Analysis Graphic Organizer A **[L3]** ....p. 296
Literary Analysis Graphic Organizer B **[L1, L2, EL]** ....p. 297
Reading Strategy Graphic Organizer A **[L3]** ....p. 294
Reading Strategy Graphic Organizer B **[L1, L2, EL]** ....p. 295

PRINT
Reader's Notebook [L2]
Reader's Notebook: Adapted Version [L1]
Reader's Notebook: English Learner's Version [EL]
Unit 6 Resources
Literary Analysis **[L3]** ....p. 375
Reading Strategy **[L3]** ....p. 376
Vocabulary Builder **[L3]** ....p. 377

PRINT
Unit 6 Resources
Grammar and Style **[L3]** ....p. 378
Support for Extend Your Learning **[L3]** ....p. 379
Enrichment **[L4]** ....p. 380
Selection Test A **[L1, L2, EL]** ....pp. 381–383
Selection Test B **[L3, L4]** ....pp. 384–386

TECHNOLOGY
Go Online: Research **[L3]**
Go Online: Self-test **[L3]**
***ExamView®* Test Bank [L3]**

Choosing Resources for Differentiated Instruction

[L1] Special Needs Students
[L2] Below-Level Students
[L3] All Students
[L4] Advanced Students
[EL] English Learners

For Vocabulary and Reading Warm-ups and for Selection Tests, **A** signifies "less challenging" and **B** "more challenging." For Graphic Organizer transparencies, **A** signifies "not filled in" and **B** "filled in."

FT Fast Track Instruction: To move the lesson more quickly, use the strategies and activities identified with **FT**.

Scaffolding for Less Proficient and Advanced Students

The leveled Critical Thinking questions after selections progress in the levels of thinking required to answer them. To address the needs of your different students, you may use the (a) level questions for your less proficient students and the (b) level questions with your on-level and advanced students. The occasional (c) level questions are appropriate for your advanced students.

PRENTICE HALL **TeacherEXPRESS™** Plan · Teach · Assess Use this complete suite of powerful teaching tools to make lesson planning and testing quicker and easier.

PRENTICE HALL **StudentEXPRESS™** Learn · Study · Succeed Use the interactive textbook (online and on CD-ROM) to make selections and activities come alive with audio and video support and interactive questions.

Go Online Professional Development **For:** Information about Lexiles **Visit:** www.PHSchool.com **Web Code:** eue-1111

PRETEACH

❶ Literary Analysis
Dramatic and Verbal Irony

- Review the definition of irony from Kate Chopin's "The Story of an Hour." Remind students that irony is the difference between expectation and reality.
- List some examples of irony from Acts I and II of *The Crucible.* Have students decide whether these are examples of verbal or dramatic irony.

❷ Reading Strategy
Categorizing Characters by Role

- Work with students to fill in the chart on this page.
- Give students a copy of **Reading Strategy Graphic Organizer A,** p. 294 in ***Graphic Organizer Transparencies.*** Encourage them to reread parts of the play to refresh their memory about each character's role.
- Then, have students suggest other categories into which they can divide the characters. Have them discuss why categorizing characters is helpful.

Vocabulary Builder

- Pronounce each vocabulary word for students, and read the definitions as a class. Have students identify any words with which they are already familiar.

Build Skills *Drama*

The Crucible, Act III

❶ Literary Analysis

Dramatic and Verbal Irony

Irony involves a contrast between what is stated and what is meant, or between what is expected to happen and what actually happens.

- In **dramatic irony,** there is a contradiction between what a character thinks and what the audience knows to be true.
- In **verbal irony,** a character says one thing but means something quite different.

Look for both forms of irony as you read Act III.

Connecting Literary Elements

In this act of the play, Miller challenges audiences to think critically. Beyond maintaining an awareness of irony, the audience must also weigh the logic presented in the court scene. There, Miller introduces a **logical fallacy,** an idea or argument that appears logical though it is based on a completely faulty premise. Judge Danforth explains his reasoning for believing the accusations of witchcraft. Though his thoughts seem logical, read them critically—all are based on a mistaken premise.

❷ Reading Strategy

Categorizing Characters by Role

The introduction of many characters in a drama can become confusing. It may be helpful to **categorize the characters.** One way you can classify characters in *The Crucible* is by the roles they play in the community. Using a chart like the one shown, identify the characters and their positions in Salem Village.

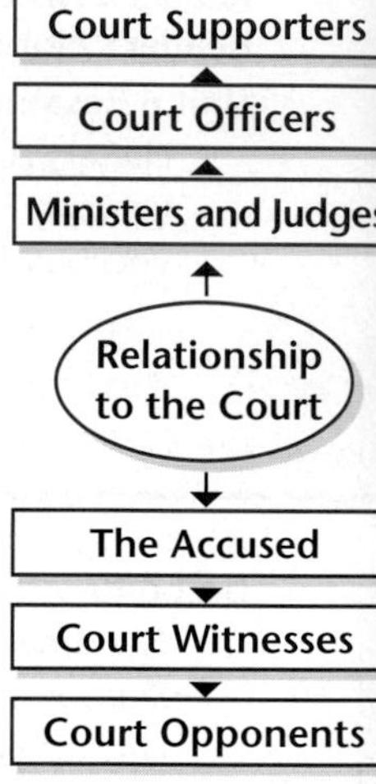

Vocabulary Builder

contentious (kən ten′ shəs) *adj.* argumentative (p. 1316)

deposition (dep′ ə zish′ ən) *n.* the testimony of a witness made under oath but not in open court (p. 1318)

imperceptible (im′ pər sep′ tə bəl) *adj.* barely noticeable (p. 1320)

deferentially (def′ ər en′ shəl lē) *adv.* in a manner that bows to another's wishes; very respectfully (p. 1321)

anonymity (an′ ə nim′ ə tē) *n.* the condition of being unknown (p. 1323)

prodigious (prə dij′ əs) *adj.* of great size, power, or extent (p. 1324)

effrontery (e frunt′ ər ē) *n.* shameless boldness (p. 1324)

confounded (kən found′ id) *v.* confused; dismayed (p. 1325)

incredulously (in krej′ o͞o ləs lē) *adv.* skeptically (p. 1328)

blanched (blancht) *adj.* paled; whitened (p. 1333)

DANFORTH: Let me continue. I understand well, a husband's tenderness may drive him to extravagance in defense of a wife. Are you certain in your conscience, Mister, that your evidence is the truth?

PROCTOR: It is. And you will surely know it.

DANFORTH: And you thought to declare this revelation in the open court before the public?

PROCTOR: I thought I would, aye—with your permission.

DANFORTH, *his eyes narrowing:* Now, sir, what is your purpose in so doing?

PROCTOR: Why, I—I would free my wife, sir.

DANFORTH: There lurks nowhere in your heart, nor hidden in your spirit, any desire to undermine this court?

PROCTOR, *with the faintest faltering:* Why, no, sir.

CHEEVER, *clears his throat, awakening:* I—Your Excellency.

DANFORTH: Mr. Cheever.

CHEEVER: I think it be my duty, sir—*Kindly, to* PROCTOR: You'll not deny it, John. *To* DANFORTH: When we come to take his wife, he damned the court and ripped your warrant.

PARRIS: Now you have it!

DANFORTH: He did that, Mr. Hale?

HALE, *takes a breath:* Aye, he did.

PROCTOR: It were a temper, sir. I knew not what I did.

DANFORTH, *studying him:* Mr. Proctor.

PROCTOR: Aye, sir.

DANFORTH, *straight into his eyes:* Have you ever seen the Devil?

PROCTOR: No, sir.

DANFORTH: You are in all respects a Gospel Christian?

PROCTOR: I am, sir.

PARRIS: Such a Christian that will not come to church but once in a month!

DANFORTH, *restrained—he is curious:* Not come to church?

PROCTOR: I—I have no love for Mr. Parris. It is no secret. But God I surely love.

CHEEVER: He plow on Sunday, sir.

DANFORTH: Plow on Sunday!

CHEEVER, *apologetically:* I think it be evidence, John. I am an official of the court, I cannot keep it.

PROCTOR: I—I have once or twice plowed on Sunday. I have three children, sir, and until last year my land give little.

GILES: You'll find other Christians that do plow on Sunday if the truth be known.

HALE: Your Honor, I cannot think you may judge the man on such evidence.

Reading Strategy
Categorizing Characters by Role Would you classify either Parris or Danforth as a villain? Why or why not?

11 

Reading Check
What new testimony does Mary Warren give?

10 Reading Strategy
Categorizing Characters by Role

- **Ask** students the Reading Strategy question: Would you classify either Parris or Danforth as a villain? Why or why not?
  Answer: Parris is a villain because his hysteria is largely responsible for the trials. Up to this point in the play, students should reserve judgment about Danforth; there is some evidence of an attempt to be just and to hear all sides.
- Which other characters in the play might you characterize as villains? Why?
  Answer: Students may say that Abigail and the Putnams are villains because Abigail's lies and the Putnams' desire to blame others for their misfortunes have led to murder.

11 Reading Check

Answer: She testifies that she and the other girls have lied.

Differentiated Instruction Solutions for All Learners

Background for Advanced Readers
Danforth's line, "We burn a hot fire here; it melts down all concealment", alludes to the play's title. One meaning of the word *crucible* is "a pot in which metals are melted down." Such a pot must be made of earthenware or some other material that can withstand extreme temperatures. Share the Background information at the begining of the selection, or have students look up the definitions of the word *crucible.* Have them analyze the symbolism of the title. Ask them to look for further direct references to fire in the play and to relate these references to the title. You might ask them this question: Which characters are, like crucibles, strong enough to withstand the heat of the court's fire?

⓬ Literary Analysis
Dramatic and Verbal Irony and Logical Fallacy

- What is ironic about Danforth's statement, "I judge nothing"?
  Answer: Danforth is a judge who makes life-and-death decisions.
- **Ask** students the Literary Analysis question: In what way does Danforth's statement represent a logical fallacy?
  Answer: He says he has no reason to suspect deception, but the events he is asked to believe are incredible by nature.
- Share the Enrichment information below with students. Why is Parris's allusion to the story of Cain and Abel illogical?
  Answer: Cain was not an upright man but a deliberate murderer; he killed his brother because he was jealous. Jealousy in this play motivates the accusers, not the victims.

⓬ **DANFORTH:** I judge nothing. *Pause. He keeps watching* PROCTOR, *who tries to meet his gaze.* I tell you straight, Mister—I have seen marvels in this court. I have seen people choked before my eyes by spirits; I have seen them stuck by pins and slashed by daggers. I have until this moment not the slightest reason to suspect that the children may be deceiving me. Do you understand my meaning?

PROCTOR: Excellency, does it not strike upon you that so many of these women have lived so long with such upright reputation, and—

PARRIS: Do you read the Gospel, Mr. Proctor?

PROCTOR: I read the Gospel.

PARRIS: I think not, or you should surely know that Cain were an upright man, and yet he did kill Abel.[2]

PROCTOR: Aye, God tells us that. *To* DANFORTH: But who tells us Rebecca Nurse murdered seven babies by sending out her spirit on them? It is the children only, and this one will swear she lied to you.

DANFORTH *considers, then beckons* HATHORNE *to him.* HATHORNE *leans in, and he speaks in his ear.* HATHORNE *nods.*

HATHORNE: Aye, she's the one.

DANFORTH: Mr. Proctor, this morning, your wife send me a claim in which she states that she is pregnant now.

PROCTOR: My wife pregnant!

DANFORTH: There be no sign of it—we have examined her body.

PROCTOR: But if she say she is pregnant, then she must be! That woman will never lie, Mr. Danforth.

DANFORTH: She will not?

PROCTOR: Never, sir, never.

DANFORTH: We have thought it too convenient to be credited. However, if I should tell you now that I will let her be kept another month; and if she begin to show her natural signs, you shall have her living yet another year until she is delivered—what say you to that? JOHN PROCTOR *is struck silent.* Come now. You say your only purpose is to save your wife. Good, then, she is saved at least this year, and a year is long. What say you, sir? It is done now. *In conflict,* PROCTOR *glances at* FRANCIS *and* GILES. Will you drop this charge?

PROCTOR: I—I think I cannot.

DANFORTH, *now an almost imperceptible hardness in his voice:* Then your purpose is somewhat larger.

PARRIS: He's come to overthrow this court, Your Honor!

PROCTOR: These are my friends. Their wives are also accused—

DANFORTH, *with a sudden briskness of manner:* I judge you not, sir. I am ready to hear your evidence.

PROCTOR: I come not to hurt the court; I only—

Literary Analysis
Dramatic and Verbal Irony and Logical Fallacy
In what way does Danforth's statement represent a logical fallacy?

Vocabulary Builder
imperceptible (im′ pər sep′ tə bəl) *adj.* barely noticeable

2. **Cain . . . Abel** In the Bible, Cain, the oldest son of Adam and Eve, killed his brother, Abel.

Enrichment

Cain and Abel

In the book of Genesis in the Bible, Cain offers God produce from his harvest, while Abel offers lambs from his flock. God accepts Abel's gift but rejects Cain's. Cain kills Abel out of jealousy.

John Steinbeck based his 1952 novel *East of Eden* on this biblical story. Cyrus Trask loves his son Adam, who fears and dislikes him, but is indifferent to Charles, who loves him devotedly. This causes terrible tension between the brothers. In the next generation, the pattern is repeated. Adam loves Aron, who is indifferent to him, but gives little thought to Caleb, who loves him. In their late teens, both boys offer birthday gifts to their father, who accepts Aron's but rejects Cal's. Passion and jealousy drive Cal to commit an act that leads to his brother's death.

DANFORTH, *cutting him off:* Marshal, go into the court and bid Judge Stoughton and Judge Sewall declare recess for one hour. And let them go to the tavern, if they will. All witnesses and prisoners are to be kept in the building.

HERRICK: Aye, sir. *Very deferentially:* If I may say it, sir. I know this man all my life. It is a good man, sir.

DANFORTH—*it is the reflection on himself he resents:* I am sure of it, Marshal. HERRICK *nods, then goes out.* Now, what deposition do you have for us, Mr. Proctor? And I beg you be clear, open as the sky, and
13 honest.

PROCTOR, *as he takes out several papers:* I am no lawyer, so I'll—

DANFORTH: The pure in heart need no lawyers. Proceed as you will.

PROCTOR, *handing* DANFORTH *a paper:* Will you read this first, sir? It's a sort of testament. The people signing it declare their good opinion of Rebecca, and my wife, and Martha Corey.

DANFORTH *looks down at the paper.*

PARRIS, *to enlist* DANFORTH'S *sarcasm:* Their good opinion! *But* DANFORTH *goes on reading, and* PROCTOR *is heartened.*

PROCTOR: These are all landholding farmers, members of the church. *Delicately, trying to point out a paragraph:* If you'll notice, sir—they've known the women many years and never saw no sign they had dealings with the Devil.

PARRIS *nervously moves over and reads over* DANFORTH'S *shoulder.*

DANFORTH, *glancing down a long list:* How many names are here?

FRANCIS: Ninety-one, Your Excellency.

PARRIS, *sweating:* These people should be summoned. DANFORTH *looks up at him questioningly.* For questioning.

FRANCIS. *trembling with anger:* Mr. Danforth, I gave them all my word no harm would come to them for signing this.

PARRIS: This is a clear attack upon the court!

HALE, *to* PARRIS, *trying to contain himself:* Is every defense an attack upon the court? Can no one—?

PARRIS: All innocent and Christian people are happy for the courts in Salem! These people are gloomy for it. *To* DANFORTH *directly:* And I think you will want to know, from each and every one of them, what discon-
14 tents them with you!

HATHORNE: I think they ought to be examined, sir.

DANFORTH: It is not necessarily an attack, I think. Yet—

FRANCIS: These are all covenanted Christians, sir.

DANFORTH: Then I am sure they may have nothing to fear. *Hands* CHEEVER *the paper.* Mr. Cheever, have warrants drawn for all of these—arrest for examination. *To* PROCTOR: Now, Mister, what other information do you have for us? FRANCIS *is still standing, horrified.* You may sit, Mr. Nurse.

FRANCIS: I have brought trouble on these people: I have—

Vocabulary Builder

deferentially (def′ ər en′ shəl lē) *adv.* in a manner that bows to another's wishes; very respectfully

Literary Analysis

Dramatic and Verbal Irony

What makes Danforth's statement about the "pure in heart" an example of verbal irony?

15 

Reading Check

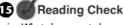

What document does Proctor present to the count?

13 Literary Analysis

Dramatic and Verbal Irony

- **Ask** students the Literary Analysis question: What makes Danforth's statement about "the pure in heart" an example of verbal irony?
  Answer: It suggests that truth always prevails in court, when the audience has already seen innocent people condemned.
- What is ironic about Parris's insistence that the signers of the testament be summoned to court?
  Answer: By signing the testament, these people were trying to tell the truth and help others. Their punishment for this is that they are now all in danger from the court.
- Why is Parris's reaction to the testament ironic?
  Answer: Proctor says that all the signers are members of the church. Therefore, Parris's livelihood depends on these people. He should treat them well rather than suggesting that their actions are suspicious.

14 Critical Thinking

Making Judgments

- Which character is responsible for the arrest of the people on the list? How does he achieve this?
  Answer: Parris is responsible. He appeals to Danforth's pride by suggesting that the signers are not in favor of the court.
- What judgments can you make about both Danforth and Parris, given Danforth's decision to arrest the signers?
  Answer: Parris is manipulative; he will do anything to save himself from blame. Danforth can't stand to have the court criticized, and this affects his judgment.

15 Reading Check

Answer: The document that Proctor presents says that Rebecca, Elizabeth, and Martha are all good Christian women. It is signed by 91 people.

Differentiated Instruction

Solutions for All Learners

Strategy for Less Proficient Readers

One interesting aspect of Miller's play is that most of the characters are not entirely good or evil but a mix of faults and good qualities. Ask students to choose three or four characters and make a word web to describe each one. As students read Act III, they should note personality traits and brief quotations supporting their descriptions on the rays of the webs. Students can use these graphic organizers for a group discussion of the characters. As a follow-up, have them discuss what this mix of good and bad in each character suggests about the play's overall themes. How do the personalities relate to the play's events and outcome?

16 Literary Analysis
Dramatic and Verbal Irony

- Why is Danforth's statement that "a person is either with this court or he must be counted against it" ironic?
  Answer: The court's job is to be impartial, not to assume the guilt of the accused as this court does. Proctor, Corey, and others who try to present actual evidence are ignored, but they are the ones trying to work by the rules of the court. Danforth is on the side of the accusers, ignoring the fact that their unsupported accusations flout the court's rules.
- **Ask** students the Literary Analysis question: In what sense is Proctor's quotation from the Bible ironic?
  Answer: It is ironic because so far in the play, harm has come to several characters who have done nothing but good.

DANFORTH: No, old man, you have not hurt these people if they are of good conscience. But you must understand, sir, that a person is either with this court or he must be counted against it, there be no road between. This is a sharp time, now, a precise time—we live no longer in the dusky afternoon when evil mixed itself with good and befuddled the world. Now, by God's grace, the shining sun is up, and them that fear not light will surely praise it. I hope you will be one of those.

MARY WARREN *suddenly sobs.* She's not hearty, I see.

PROCTOR: No, she's not, sir. *To* MARY, *bending to her, holding her hand, quietly:* Now remember what the angel Raphael said to the boy Tobias.[3] Remember it.

MARY WARREN, *hardly audible:* Aye.

PROCTOR: "Do that which is good, and no harm shall come to thee."

MARY WARREN: Aye.

DANFORTH: Come, man, we wait you.

MARSHAL HERRICK *returns, and takes his post at the door.*

GILES: John, my deposition, give him mine.

PROCTOR: Aye. *He hands* DANFORTH *another paper.* This is Mr. Corey's deposition.

DANFORTH: Oh? *He looks down at it. Now* HATHORNE *comes behind him and reads with him.*

HATHORNE, *suspiciously:* What lawyer drew this, Corey?

GILES: You know I never hired a lawyer in my life, Hathorne.

DANFORTH, *finishing the reading:* It is very well phrased. My compliments. Mr. Parris, if Mr. Putnam is in the court, will you bring him in? HATHORNE *takes the deposition, and walks to the window with it.* PARRIS *goes into the court.* You have no legal training, Mr. Corey?

GILES, *very pleased:* I have the best, sir—I am thirty-three time in court in my life. And always plaintiff, too.

DANFORTH: Oh, then you're much put-upon.

GILES: I am never put-upon; I know my rights, sir, and I will have them. You know, your father tried a case of mine—might be thirty-five year ago, I think.

DANFORTH: Indeed.

GILES: He never spoke to you of it?

DANFORTH: No, I cannot recall it.

GILES: That's strange, he gave me nine pound damages. He were a fair judge, your father. Y'see, I had a white mare that time, and this fellow come to borrow the mare—*Enter* PARRIS *with* THOMAS PUTNAM. *When he*

Literary Analysis
Dramatic and Verbal Irony In what sense is Proctor's quotation from the bible ironic?

3. **Raphael. . . Tobias** In the Bible, Tobias is guided by the archangel Raphael to save two people who have prayed for their deaths. One of the two is Tobias's father, Tobit, who has prayed for his death because he has lost his sight; the other is Sara, a woman who is afflicted by a demon and has killed her seven husbands on their wedding day. With Raphael's assistance, Tobias exorcises the devil from Sara and cures his father of blindness.

sees PUTNAM, GILES' *ease goes; he is hard.* Aye, there he is.

DANFORTH: Mr. Putnam, I have here an accusation by Mr. Corey against you. He states that you coldly prompted your daughter to cry witchery upon George Jacobs that is now in jail.

PUTNAM: It is a lie.

DANFORTH, *turning to* GILES: Mr. Putnam states your charge is a lie. What say you to that?

GILES, *furious, his fists clenched:* A fart on Thomas Putnam, that is what I say to that!

DANFORTH: What proof do you submit for your charge, sir?

GILES: My proof is there! *Pointing to the paper.* If Jacobs hangs for a witch he forfeit up his property—that's law! And there is none but Putnam with the coin to buy so great a piece. This man is killing his neighbors for their land!

DANFORTH: But proof, sir, proof.

GILES, *pointing at his deposition:* The proof is there! I have it from an honest man who heard Putnam say it! The day his daughter cried out on Jacobs, he said she'd given him a fair gift of land.

HATHORNE: And the name of this man?

GILES, *taken aback:* What name?

HATHORNE: The man that give you this information.

GILES, *hesitates, then:* Why, I—I cannot give you his name.

HATHORNE: And why not?

GILES, *hesitates, then bursts out:* You know well why not! He'll lay in jail if I give his name!

HATHORNE: This is contempt of the court, Mr. Danforth!

DANFORTH, *to avoid that:* You will surely tell us the name.

GILES: I will not give you no name. I mentioned my wife's name once and I'll burn in hell long enough for that. I stand mute.

DANFORTH: In that case, I have no choice but to arrest you for contempt of this court, do you know that?

GILES: This is a hearing; you cannot clap me for contempt of a hearing.

DANFORTH: Oh, it is a proper lawyer! Do you wish me to declare the court in full session here? Or will you give me good reply?

GILES, *faltering:* I cannot give you no name, sir, I cannot.

DANFORTH: You are a foolish old man. Mr. Cheever, begin the record. The court is now in session. I ask you, Mr. Corey—

PROCTOR, *breaking in:* Your Honor—he has the story in confidence, sir, and he—

PARRIS: The Devil lives on such confidences! *To* DANFORTH: Without confidences there could be no conspiracy, Your Honor!

HATHORNE: I think it must be broken, sir.

DANFORTH, *to* GILES: Old man, if your informant tells the truth let him come here openly like a decent man. But if he hide in anonymity I

Reading Strategy
Categorizing Characters by Role In which segment of the community would you classify Giles? Why?

18 ***Arthur Miller***
Author's Insight
During the Cultural Revolution in China (1966–1976), Communist party true-believers persecuted intellectuals and artists. Miller wrote how a young Chinese author thought that the courtroom scenes in *The Crucible* were all too familiar: "As she listened to [a production of the play] . . . the interrogations sounded . . . precisely the same as the ones she and others had been subject to by the Cultural Revolutionaries. . . ."

Vocabulary Builder
anonymity (an´ ə nim´ ə tē) *n.* the condition of being unknown

19 **Reading Check**
What is Giles Corey's defense? Explain.

17 Reading Strategy
Categorizing Characters by Role

- **Ask** students the Reading Strategy question: In which segment of the community would you classify Giles? Why?
  Answer: Giles is an opponent of the court. He fears it will condemn innocent people, such as his wife, George Jacobs, and the witness to Mr. Putnam's plan to accuse Jacobs.
- Do Danforth and Hathorne belong in the same category? What differences do you see between them?
  Answer: Hathorne is quicker to condemn. Danforth will do anything to protect the good name of the court, but he has a greater sense of justice than Hathorne. Students would probably still put both in the same category; neither is impartial as a judge should be.

18 Author's Insight

Point out Arthur Miller's comment. **Ask** students what similarities there might be between the techniques of persecution in Salem and in other, contemporary situations.
Possible response: Students might mention that, as in Salem, when one group is intent on persecuting another, evidence and rationality tend to be ignored.

19 Reading Check

Answer: Corey claims that Putnam wanted Jacobs's property and therefore accused him. He mentions a witness to this whom he will not name.

Differentiated Instruction
Solutions for All Learners

Strategy for Gifted/Talented Students

In Act II, John Proctor accuses Elizabeth of judging him harshly: "I cannot speak but I am doubted, every moment judged for lies, as though I come into a court when I come into this house!" Have students compare his conversation with Elizabeth in Act II to the court session that takes place in these pages of Act III. In what way is Elizabeth like the judges in the courtroom? In what way is she different? Remind students that Elizabeth judged John for something he did, while the court judges characters like Rebecca and Martha Corey for things they deny doing. Students can gather in a small group to compare and contrast Elizabeth and the judges.

20 Critical Thinking
Analyzing

- **Ask** students to analyze Danforth's character. What kind of person is he?
  Answer: Danforth is a true Puritan. He believes in the idea of demonic possession and takes it for granted that no one would lie about such a thing. In a way, he is innocent and naive; he thinks it much more likely that a witch would deny being a witch than that a child would make a false accusation. He is impressed by some of what the other characters say, but only up to a point. Above all, he wants to protect the reputation of the court.
- **Ask** students to suggest the motivation for Danforth's feelings about the court.
  Answer: Danforth's own good name is linked to the court's reputation.

must know why. Now sir, the government and central church demand of you the name of him who reported Mr. Thomas Putnam a common murderer.

HALE: Excellency—

DANFORTH: Mr. Hale.

HALE: We cannot blink it more. There is a prodigious fear of this court in the country—

DANFORTH: Then there is a prodigious guilt in the country. Are you afraid to be questioned here?

HALE: I may only fear the Lord, sir, but there is fear in the country nevertheless.

DANFORTH, *angered now:* Reproach me not with the fear in the country; 20 there is fear in the country because there is a moving plot to topple Christ in the country!

HALE: But it does not follow that everyone accused is part of it.

DANFORTH: No uncorrupted man may fear this court, Mr. Hale! None! *To* GILES: You are under arrest in contempt of this court. Now sit you down and take counsel with yourself, or you will be set in the jail until you decide to answer all questions.

GILES COREY *makes a rush for* PUTNAM. PROCTOR *lunges and holds him.*

PROCTOR: No, Giles!

GILES, *over Proctor's shoulder at* PUTNAM: I'll cut your throat, Putnam, I'll kill you yet!

PROCTOR, *forcing him into a chair:* Peace, Giles, peace. *Releasing him.* We'll prove ourselves. Now we will. *He starts to turn to* DANFORTH.

GILES: Say nothin' more, John. *Pointing at* DANFORTH: He's only playin' you! He means to hang us all!

MARY WARREN *bursts into sobs.*

DANFORTH: This is a court of law, Mister. I'll have no effrontery here!

PROCTOR: Forgive him, sir, for his old age. Peace, Giles, we'll prove it all now. *He lifts up* MARY'S *chin.* You cannot weep, Mary. Remember the angel, what he say to the boy. Hold to it, now; there is your rock. MARY *quiets. He takes out a paper, and turns to* DANFORTH. This is Mary Warren's deposition. I—I would ask you remember, sir, while you read it, that until two week ago she were no different than the other children are today. *He is speaking reasonably, restraining all his fears, his anger, his anxiety.* You saw her scream, she howled, she swore familiar spirits choked her; she even testified that Satan, in the form of women now in jail, tried to win her soul away, and then when she refused—

DANFORTH: We know all this.

PROCTOR: Aye, sir. She swears now that she never saw Satan; nor any spirit, vague or clear, that Satan may have sent to hurt her. And she declares her friends are lying now.

PROCTOR *starts to hand* DANFORTH *the deposition, and* HALE *comes up to* DANFORTH *in a trembling state.*

Vocabulary Builder
prodigious (prə dij′ əs) *adj.* of great size, power, or extent

Vocabulary Builder
effrontery (e frunt′ ər ē) *n.* shameless boldness

HALE: Excellency, a moment. I think this goes to the heart of the matter.

DANFORTH, *with deep misgivings:* It surely does.

HALE: I cannot say he is an honest man; I know him little. But in all justice, sir, a claim so weighty cannot be argued by a farmer. In God's name, sir, stop here; send him home and let him come again with a lawyer—

DANFORTH, *patiently:* Now look you, Mr. Hale—

HALE: Excellency, I have signed seventy-two death warrants; I am a minister of the Lord, and I dare not take a life without there be a proof so immaculate no slightest qualm of conscience may doubt it.

DANFORTH: Mr. Hale, you surely do not doubt my justice.

HALE: I have this morning signed away the soul of Rebecca Nurse, Your Honor. I'll not conceal it, my hand shakes yet as with a wound! I pray you, sir, *this* argument let lawyers present to you.

DANFORTH: Mr. Hale, believe me; for a man of such terrible learning you are most bewildered—I hope you will forgive me. I have been thirty-two year at the bar, sir, and I should be confounded were I called upon to defend these people. Let you consider, now—*To* PROCTOR *and the others:* And I bid you all do likewise. In an ordinary crime, how does one defend the accused? One calls up witnesses to prove his innocence.
25 But witchcraft is *ipso facto,*[4] on its face and by its nature, an invisible crime, is it not? Therefore, who may possibly be witness to it? The witch and the victim. None other. Now we cannot hope the witch will accuse herself; granted? Therefore, we must rely upon her victims—and they do testify, the children certainly do testify. As for the witches, none will deny that we are most eager for all their confessions. Therefore, what is left for a lawyer to bring out? I think I have made my point. Have I not?

HALE: But this child claims the girls are not truthful, and if they are not—

DANFORTH: That is precisely what I am about to consider, sir. What more may you ask of me? Unless you doubt my probity?[5]

HALE, *defeated:* I surely do not, sir. Let you consider it, then.

DANFORTH: And let you put your heart to rest. Her deposition, Mr. Proctor.

PROCTOR *hands it to him.* HATHORNE *rises, goes beside* DANFORTH, *and starts reading.* PARRIS *comes to his other side.* DANFORTH *looks at* JOHN PROCTOR, *then proceeds to read.* HALE *gets up, finds position near the judge, reads too.* PROCTOR *glances at* GILES. FRANCIS *prays silently, hands pressed together.* CHEEVER *waits placidly, the sublime official, dutiful.* MARY WARREN *sobs once.* JOHN PROCTOR *touches her head reassuringly. Presently* DANFORTH *lifts his eyes, stands up, takes out a kerchief and blows his nose. The others stand aside as he moves in thought toward the window.*

PARRIS, *hardly able to contain his anger and fear:* I should like to question—

4. **ipso facto** (ip´ sō fak´ tō) "by that very fact"; "therefore" (Latin).
5. **probity** (prō´ bə tē) *n.* complete honesty: integrity.

Vocabulary Builder
confounded (kən fo͝und´ id) *v.* confused; dismayed

Literary Analysis
Dramatic and Verbal Irony and Logical Fallacy In what ways is Danforth's entire argument based on a faulty premise?

Reading Strategy
Categorizing Characters by Role Based on this scene, how would you classify Danforth?

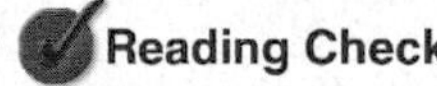
Reading Check
What is Danforth's basic argument about witnesses and witchcraft?

21 Literary Analysis
Dramatic and Verbal Irony and Logical Fallacy

- **Ask** students the Literary Analysis question: In what ways is Danforth's entire argument based on a faulty premise?
  Answer: Danforth does not allow for the possibility that an accused person may be innocent of witchcraft.
- Why is Danforth's insistence that lawyers are unnecessary ironic?
  Answer: Since the court is so unwilling to listen to defenders of the accused or to accept their evidence, they need the legal protection that the court insists no innocent person needs.

22 Reading Strategy
Categorizing Characters by Role

- **Ask** students the Reading Strategy question: Based on this scene, how would you classify Danforth?
  Answer: Students will probably classify Danforth as a villain.
- Does Danforth have any good or admirable qualities?
  Answer: Students should see that Danforth is more inclined to listen to the defenders than any of the other officials, but he allows his judgment to be swayed by Parris, Hathorne, and others.

23 Reading Check

Answer: He argues that witchcraft is a crime with only two witnesses—the witch and the victim.

Differentiated Instruction
Solutions for All Learners

Strategy for Gifted/Talented Students
Ask students to imagine that they are lawyers appointed to represent Proctor, and have them rebut Danforth's argument (given in the speech beginning "Mr. Hale, believe me" on this page). Students should find the logical fallacies in Danforth's argument, point them out, and correct his faulty thinking. Students may want to work together or individually on their speeches. Volunteers can present their speeches to the class. If time allows, have students choose another argument in the play that is based on a logical fallacy. Have them repeat the exercise, sharpening both their written and oral skills of persuasion.

24 Critical Viewing

Answer: Students will probably say that they don't find Danforth sympathetic or understanding.

DANFORTH —*his first real outburst, in which his contempt for* PARRIS *is clear:* Mr. Parris, I bid you be silent! *He stands in silence, looking out the window. Now, having established that he will set the gait:* Mr. Cheever, will you go into the court and bring the children here? CHEEVER *gets up and goes out upstage.* DANFORTH *now turns to* MARY. Mary Warren, how came you to this turnabout? Has Mr. Proctor threatened you for this deposition?

MARY WARREN: No, sir.

DANFORTH: Has he ever threatened you?

MARY WARREN, *weaker:* No, sir.

DANFORTH, *sensing a weakening:* Has he threatened you?

MARY WARREN: No, sir.

DANFORTH: Then you tell me that you sat in my court, callously lying, when you knew that people would hang by your evidence? *She does not answer.* Answer me!

MARY WARREN, *almost inaudibly:* I did, sir.

DANFORTH: How were you instructed in your life? Do you not know that God damns all liars? *She cannot speak.* Or is it now that you lie?

24 ▼ **Critical Viewing** In this movie still, Danforth conveys a feeling of sympathy or understanding for Mary Warren. Compare this portrayal with your own image of Danforth. **[Compare/Contrast]**

Differentiated Instruction
Solutions for All Learners

Support for Less Proficient Readers

Students may have guessed that Mary would have to confront her friends in court. Invite students to consider the conflicts in that meeting. Use the following questions for discussion:

- Ask students whether they can think of a modern, real-life example of a person turning against his or her friends. Invite them to explain what happened.
- Have students predict what Mary's friends will do when they come into the courtroom. What do they predict Mary will do? Make sure they can support their predictions with details about Mary's behavior thus far.

MARY WARREN: No, sir—I am with God now.

DANFORTH: You are with God now.

MARY WARREN: Aye, sir.

DANFORTH, *containing himself:* I will tell you this—you are either lying now, or you were lying in the court, and in either case you have committed perjury and you will go to jail for it. You cannot lightly say you lied, Mary. Do you know that?

MARY WARREN: I cannot lie no more. I am with God, I am with God.

But she breaks into sobs at the thought of it, and the right door opens, and enter SUSANNA WALCOTT, MERCY LEWIS, BETTY PARRIS, *and finally* ABIGAIL. CHEEVER *comes to* DANFORTH.

CHEEVER: Ruth Putnam's not in the court, sir, nor the other children.

25 **DANFORTH:** These will be sufficient. Sit you down, children. *Silently they sit.* Your friend, Mary Warren, has given us a deposition. In which she swears that she never saw familiar spirits, apparitions, nor any manifest of the Devil. She claims as well that none of you have seen these things either. *Slight pause.* Now, children, this is a court of law. The law, based upon the Bible, and the Bible, writ by Almighty God, forbid the practice of witchcraft, and describe death as the penalty thereof. But likewise, children, the law and Bible damn all bearers of false witness. *Slight pause.* Now then. It does not escape me that this deposition may be devised to blind us; it may well be that Mary Warren has been conquered by Satan, who sends her here to distract our sacred purpose. If so, her neck will break for it. But if she speak true, I bid you now drop your guile and confess your pretense, for a quick confession will go easier with you. *Pause.* Abigail Williams, rise. ABIGAIL *slowly rises.* Is there any truth in this?

Literary Analysis
Dramatic and Verbal Irony In what ways are Danforth's statements examples of dramatic irony?

ABIGAIL: No, sir.

DANFORTH, *thinks, glances at* MARY *then back to* ABIGAIL: Children, a very augur bit[6] will now be turned into your souls until your honesty is proved. Will either of you change your positions now, or do you force me to hard questioning?

ABIGAIL: I have naught to change, sir. She lies.

DANFORTH, *to* MARY: You would still go on with this?

MARY WARREN, *faintly:* Aye, sir.

DANFORTH, *turning to* ABIGAIL: A poppet were discovered in Mr. Proctor's house, stabbed by a needle. Mary Warren claims that you sat beside her in the court when she made it, and that you saw her make it and witnessed how she herself stuck her needle into it for safe-keeping. What say you to that?

ABIGAIL, *with a slight note of indignation:* It is a lie, sir.

26 **DANFORTH,** *after a slight pause:* While you worked for Mr. Proctor, did you see poppets in that house?

ABIGAIL: Goody Proctor always kept poppets.

Reading Check
According to Danforth, what is Mary Warren's fate—regardless of what she testifies? Why?

6. **augur bit** sharp point of an augur, a tool used for boring holes.

25 Literary Analysis
Dramatic and Verbal Irony

- **Ask** students the Literary Analysis question: In what ways are Danforth's statements examples of dramatic irony?
  Answer: The play is filled with people who bear false witness against their neighbors.
- Describe the difference between the judge's interrogation of Abigail and his interrogation of the defenders.
  Answer: He takes Abigail's unsupported word as hard evidence, whereas he expects the defenders to bring more proof.

26 Reading Check

Answer: Mary Warren will go to prison for perjury.

Differentiated Instruction
Solutions for All Learners

Strategy for Advanced Readers

Ask students to classify the characters as minor—those who have relatively few lines and play a small part in the action—and major—those who take a prominent part in the action. For instance, John Proctor is a major character; Mercy Lewis is a minor character. Have students consider the significance of the minor characters in *The Crucible.* Is their importance in the proceedings related to the number of lines they speak or their amount of time on stage? Abigail, for instance, appears only in Acts I and III; she might be considered a minor character, but she plays a crucial part in bringing the trials about. How effectively does Miller use these minor characters? How individual are their personalities? Students can write essays analyzing the importance and effectiveness of the play's minor characters.

27 Reading Strategy
Categorizing Characters by Role

- **Ask** students the Reading Strategy question: How might Proctor classify Mary Warren? Why?
  Answer: Proctor feels sorry for her. He might classify her as a victim at this point. He tries to help her.
- What do Parris's questions and comments suggest about his role in the play?
  Answer: He is one of the villains of the play. He continues to try to obscure the truth for his own ends. His questions are misleading and irrelevant.

28 Reading Strategy
Categorizing Characters by Role

- **Ask** students the Reading Strategy question: In what category would you place Hathorne? Explain.
  Answer: Students should classify Hathorne as a villain. He shows no real interest in hearing new evidence.
- Have students **predict** the effect of Mary's testimony on the judges. Have them give reasons for their predictions.
  Answer: Mary is so frightened that she speaks with little conviction. The judges probably won't believe her.

PROCTOR: Your Honor, my wife never kept no poppets. Mary Warren confesses it was her poppet.

CHEEVER: Your Excellency.

DANFORTH: Mr. Cheever.

CHEEVER: When I spoke with Goody Proctor in that house, she said she never kept no poppets. But she said she did keep poppets when she were a girl.

PROCTOR: She has not been a girl these fifteen years, Your Honor.

HATHORNE: But a poppet will keep fifteen years, will it not?

PROCTOR: It will keep if it is kept, but Mary Warren swears she never saw no poppets in my house, nor anyone else.

PARRIS: Why could there not have been poppets hid where no one ever saw them?

27 **PROCTOR,** *furious:* There might also be a dragon with five legs in my house, but no one has ever seen it.

PARRIS: We are here, Your Honor, precisely to discover what no one has ever seen.

PROCTOR: Mr. Danforth, what profit this girl to turn herself about? What may Mary Warren gain but hard questioning and worse?

DANFORTH: You are charging Abigail Williams with a marvelous cool plot to murder, do you understand that?

PROCTOR: I do, sir. I believe she means to murder.

DANFORTH, *pointing at* ABIGAIL, *incredulously:* This child would murder your wife?

PROCTOR: It is not a child. Now hear me, sir. In the sight of the congregation she were twice this year put out of this meetin' house for laughter during prayer.

DANFORTH, *shocked, turning to* ABIGAIL: What's this? Laughter during—!

PARRIS: Excellency, she were under Tituba's power at that time, but she is solemn now.

GILES: Aye, now she is solemn and goes to hang people!

DANFORTH: Quiet, man.

28 **HATHORNE:** Surely it have no bearing on the question, sir. He charges contemplation of murder.

DANFORTH: Aye. *He studies* ABIGAIL *for a moment, then:* Continue, Mr. Proctor.

PROCTOR: Mary. Now tell the Governor how you danced in the woods.

PARRIS, *instantly:* Excellency, since I come to Salem this man is blackening my name. He—

DANFORTH: In a moment, sir. *To* MARY WARREN, *sternly, and surprised.* What is this dancing?

MARY WARREN: I—*She glances at* ABIGAIL, *who is staring down at her remorselessly. Then, appealing to* PROCTOR: Mr. Proctor—

Reading Strategy Categorizing Characters by Role How might Proctor classify Mary Warren? Why?

Vocabulary Builder
incredulously (in krej′ o͞o ləs lē) *adv.* skeptically

Reading Strategy Categorizing Characters by Role In what category would you place Hathorne? Explain.

PROCTOR, *taking it right up:* Abigail leads the girls to the woods, Your Honor, and they have danced there naked—

PARRIS: Your Honor, this—

PROCTOR, *at once:* Mr. Parris discovered them himself in the dead of night! There's the "child" she is!

DANFORTH— *it is growing into a nightmare, and he turns, astonished, to* PARRIS: Mr. Parris—

PARRIS: I can only say, sir, that I never found any of them naked, and this man is—

DANFORTH: But you discovered them dancing in the woods? *Eyes on* PARRIS, *he points at* ABIGAIL. Abigail?

HALE: Excellency, when I first arrived from Beverly, Mr. Parris told me that.

DANFORTH: Do you deny it, Mr. Parris?

PARRIS: I do not, sir, but I never saw any of them naked.

DANFORTH: But she have *danced?*

PARRIS, *unwillingly:* Aye, sir.

DANFORTH, *as though with new eyes, looks at* ABIGAIL.

HATHORNE: Excellency, will you permit me? *He points at* MARY WARREN.

DANFORTH, *with great worry:* Pray, proceed.

HATHORNE: You say you never saw no spirits, Mary, were never threatened or afflicted by any manifest of the Devil or the Devil's agents.

MARY WARREN, *very faintly:* No, sir.

HATHORNE, *with a gleam of victory:* And yet, when people accused of witchery confronted you in court, you would faint, saying their spirits came out of their bodies and choked you—

MARY WARREN: That were pretense, sir.

DANFORTH: I cannot hear you.

MARY WARREN: Pretense, sir.

PARRIS: But you did turn cold, did you not? I myself picked you up many times, and your skin were icy. Mr. Danforth, you—

DANFORTH: I saw that many times.

PROCTOR: She only pretended to faint, Your Excellency. They're all marvelous pretenders.

HATHORNE: Then can she pretend to faint now?

PROCTOR: Now?

PARRIS: Why not? Now there are no spirits attacking her, for none in this room is accused of witchcraft. So let her turn herself cold now, let her pretend she is attacked now, let her faint. *He turns to* MARY WARREN. Faint!

MARY WARREN: Faint?

PARRIS: Aye, faint. Prove to us how you pretended in the court so many times.

Reading Strategy
Categorizing Characters by Role In what category is Parris? Explain your choice.

30 **Reading Check**
What information about Abigail does Danforth find shocking?

29 Reading Strategy
Categorizing Characters by Role

- **Ask** students the Reading Strategy question: In what category is Parris? Explain your choice.
  Answer: Parris will do anything to divert attention from his own role in the fraud.
- **Ask** students: Into what category would you place John Proctor? Explain your answer.
  Answer: Students should classify Proctor as a hero or a good character. Even though Mary's ability to faint at will would help his case enormously, he doesn't berate or abuse her; he tries not to frighten her.

30 Reading Check

Answer: Danforth is shocked that Abigail laughed during church services.

Differentiated Instruction
Solutions for All Learners

Background for Advanced Readers
In an essay called "*The Crucible* in History," Arthur Miller discusses the historical context of his own day and his reasons for writing the play. Have students locate and read this essay (available in a recent anthology of Miller's essays titled *Echoes Down the Corridor*).

Students can discuss their opinions of the essay and its effect on their understanding of the play's historical contexts—both the time in which it is set and the time in which it was written.

31 Literary Analysis
Dramatic and Verbal Irony and Logical Fallacy

- **Ask** students the Literary Analysis question: In what sense does Danforth's question express a logical fallacy?
  Answer: Danforth's question assumes that Mary Warren's ability to faint depends on the presence of spirits.
- Then, **ask** students to speculate about why Mary was able to faint in the past, but cannot do so now.
  Answer: Mary had been stirred up by the frenzy around her—the other girls claimed they were affected by spirits, so Mary did, too.

32 Critical Viewing

Answer: The photograph shows a dramatic moment. Everyone is paying attention to what is happening. Everyone looks alert, intense, or frightened.

MARY WARREN, *looking to* PROCTOR: I—cannot faint now, sir.

PROCTOR, *alarmed, quietly:* Can you not pretend it?

MARY WARREN: I—*She looks about as though searching for the passion to faint.* I—have no *sense* of it now, I—

DANFORTH: Why? What is lacking now?

MARY WARREN: I—cannot tell, sir, I—

31 **DANFORTH:** Might it be that here we have no afflicting spirit loose, but in the court there were some?

MARY WARREN: I never saw no spirits.

PARRIS: Then see no spirits now, and prove to us that you can faint by your own will, as you claim.

MARY WARREN, *stares, searching for the emotion of it, and then shakes her head:* I—cannot do it.

PARRIS: Then you will confess, will you not? It were attacking spirits made you faint!

MARY WARREN: No, sir, I—

PARRIS: Your Excellency, this is a trick to blind the court!

MARY WARREN: It's not a trick! *She stands.* I—I used to faint because I—I thought I saw spirits.

DANFORTH: *Thought* you saw them!

MARY WARREN: But I did not, Your Honor.

HATHORNE: How could you think you saw them unless you saw them?

MARY WARREN: I—I cannot tell how, but I did. I—I heard the other girls screaming, and you, Your Honor, you seemed to believe them, and I—It

Literary Analysis
Dramatic and Verbal Irony and Logical Fallacy
In what sense does Danforth's question express a logical fallacy?

32 **▼Critical Viewing**
In this scene, Parris and Danforth order Mary to pretend to faint. Analyze this movie still and describe the emotions conveyed by Parris, Danforth, Mary, and the girls. **[Analyze]**

were only sport in the beginning, sir, but then the whole world cried spirits, spirits, and I—I promise you, Mr. Danforth, I only thought I saw them but I did not.

DANFORTH *peers at her.*

PARRIS, *smiling, but nervous because* DANFORTH *seems to be struck by* MARY WARREN'S *story:* Surely Your Excellency is not taken by this simple lie.

DANFORTH, *turning worriedly to* ABIGAIL: Abigail. I bid you now search your heart and tell me this—and beware of it, child, to God every soul is precious and His vengeance is terrible on them that take life without cause. Is it possible, child, that the spirits you have seen are illusion only, some deception that may cross your mind when—

ABIGAIL: Why, this—this—is a base question, sir.

DANFORTH: Child, I would have you consider it—

ABIGAIL: I have been hurt, Mr. Danforth; I have seen my blood runnin' out! I have been near to murdered every day because I done my duty pointing out the Devil's people—and this is my reward? To be mistrusted, denied, questioned like a—

DANFORTH, *weakening:* Child, I do not mistrust you—

ABIGAIL, *in an open threat:* Let *you* beware, Mr. Danforth. Think you to be so mighty that the power of Hell may not turn *your* wits? Beware of it! There is—*Suddenly, from an accusatory attitude, her face turns, looking into the air above—it is truly frightened.*

DANFORTH, *apprehensively:* What is it, child?

ABIGAIL, *looking about in the air, clasping her arms about her as though cold:* I—I know not. A wind, a cold wind, has come. *Her eyes fall on* MARY WARREN.

MARY WARREN, *terrified, pleading:* Abby!

MERCY LEWIS, *shivering:* Your Honor, I freeze!

PROCTOR: They're pretending!

HATHORNE, *touching* ABIGAIL'S *hand:* She is cold, Your Honor, touch her!

MERCY LEWIS, *through chattering teeth:* Mary, do you send this shadow on me?

MARY WARREN: Lord, save me!

SUSANNA WALCOTT: I freeze, I freeze!

ABIGAIL, *shivering, visibly:* It is a wind, a wind!

MARY WARREN: Abby, don't do that!

DANFORTH, *himself engaged and entered by* ABIGAIL: Mary Warren, do you witch her? I say to you, do you send your spirit out?

With a hysterical cry MARY WARREN *starts to run.* PROCTOR *catches her.*

MARY WARREN, *almost collapsing:* Let me go, Mr. Proctor, I cannot, I cannot—

ABIGAIL, *crying to Heaven:* Oh, Heavenly Father, take away this shadow!

Without warning or hesitation, PROCTOR *leaps at* ABIGAIL *and, grabbing*

Literary Analysis
Dramatic and Verbal Irony Which kind of irony does Abigail's speech about her "blood runnin' out" demonstrate? Explain.

34  **Reading Check**
What threat does Abigail level at Judge Danforth?

33 Literary Analysis
Dramatic and Verbal Irony

- **Ask** students the Literary Analysis question: Which kind of irony does Abigail's speech about her "blood runnin' out" demonstrate? Explain.
  Answer: Abigail describes herself as a victim when in fact she is the accuser. This is verbal irony.
- Why do Abigail and the others suddenly pretend to be cold and to see spirits?
  Answer: They want to reinforce Danforth's belief in their innocence, and they realize he is beginning to doubt them.

34 Reading Check

Answer: She implies that she may accuse him of witchcraft.

Differentiated Instruction
Solutions for All Learners

Strategy for Less Proficient Readers
Like a short story, a long narrative is made of basic elements—plot, character, setting, and themes. Have students treat each act as a short story. Help them identify the setting and the main characters, summarize the plot, and determine the overall theme. As a follow-up, have students discuss which of these four elements seems to contribute the most to this play.

35 Critical Viewing

Answer: Students may say that the high camera angle, showing the room from the point of view of the bird, is effective.

her by the hair, pulls her to her feet. She screams in pain. DANFORTH, *astonished, cries, "What are you about?" and* HATHORNE *and* PARRIS *call, "Take your hands off her!" and out of it all comes* PROCTOR'S *roaring voice.*

PROCTOR: How do you call Heaven! Whore! Whore!

HERRICK *breaks* PROCTOR *from her.*

HERRICK: John!

35 ▲ **Critical Viewing** Abigail pretends to be under the control of spirits. Does this scene from the movie effectively portray the scene in the play? **[Evaluate]**

Differentiated Instruction Solutions for All Learners

Strategy for Special Needs Students

Ask students to identify the characters pictured in each illustration for *The Crucible*. Have them explain how they were able to identify each character. As a follow-up, have them try to identify lines or passages of dialogue that the photographs illustrate.

Strategy for Less Proficient Readers

Have students discuss the photographs used to illustrate the play. What do these illustrations add to their understanding of the characters and themes? How do the illustrations help draw them into the time and place of the Salem witchcraft trials?

DANFORTH: Man! Man, what do you—

PROCTOR, *breathless and in agony:* It is a whore!

DANFORTH, *dumfounded:* You charge—?

ABIGAIL: Mr. Danforth, he is lying!

PROCTOR: Mark her! Now she'll suck a scream to stab me with, but—

DANFORTH: You will prove this! This will not pass!

PROCTOR, *trembling, his life collapsing about him:* I have known her, sir. I have known her.

DANFORTH: You—you are a lecher?

FRANCIS, *horrified:* John, you cannot say such a—

PROCTOR: Oh, Francis, I wish you had some evil in you that you might know me! *To* DANFORTH: A man will not cast away his good name. You surely know that.

DANFORTH, *dumfounded:* In—in what time? In what place?

PROCTOR, *his voice about to break, and his shame great:* In the proper place—where my beasts are bedded. On the last night of my joy, some eight months past. She used to serve me in my house, sir. *He has to clamp his jaw to keep from weeping.* A man may think God sleeps, but God sees everything. I know it now. I beg you, sir, I beg you—see her what she is. My wife, my dear good wife, took this girl soon after, sir, and put her out on the highroad. And being what she is, a lump of vanity, sir—*He is being overcome.* Excellency, forgive me, forgive me. *Angrily against himself, he turns away from the* GOVERNOR *for a moment. Then, as though to cry out is his only means of speech left:* She thinks to dance with me on my wife's grave! And well she might, for I thought of her softly. God help me, I lusted, and there *is* a promise in such sweat. But it is a whore's vengeance, and you must see it; I set myself entirely in your hands. I know you must see it now.

Reading Strategy
Categorizing Characters by Role Does Proctor's confession cause you to change the category to which you have assigned him? Why or why not?

DANFORTH, *blanched, in horror, turning to* ABIGAIL: You deny every scrap and tittle of this?

Vocabulary Builder
blanched (blancht) *adj.* paled; whitened

ABIGAIL: If I must answer that, I will leave and I will not come back again!

DANFORTH *seems unsteady.*

PROCTOR: I have made a bell of my honor! I have rung the doom of my good name—you will believe me, Mr. Danforth! My wife is innocent, except she knew a whore when she saw one!

ABIGAIL, *stepping up to* DANFORTH: What look do you give me? DANFORTH *cannot speak.* I'll not have such looks! *She turns and starts for the door.*

DANFORTH: You will remain where you are! HERRICK *steps into her path. She comes up short, fire in her eyes.* Mr. Parris, go into the court and bring Goodwife Proctor out.

PARRIS, *objecting:* Your Honor, this is all a—

DANFORTH, *sharply to* PARRIS: Bring her out! And tell her not one word of what's been spoken here. And let you knock before you enter. PARRIS *goes out.* Now we shall touch the bottom of this swamp. *To* PROCTOR:

37 
What does John Proctor reveal about Abigail Williams?

36 Reading Strategy
Categorizing Characters by Role

- **Ask** students the Reading Strategy question: Does Proctor's confession cause you to change the category to which you have assigned him? Why or why not?
  Answer: Students are not likely to change their opinions of Proctor, since his confession is not new information to them and they knew that he planned to denounce Abigail.
- **Ask** students to predict what will happen when Elizabeth comes into the room. Have them give reasons for their predictions.

37 Reading Check

Answer: He reveals that he and Abigail were lovers.

38 Literary Analysis
Dramatic and Verbal Irony

- **Ask** students the Literary Analysis question: Which details in Elizabeth's exchange with Danforth reveal the dramatic irony at work in this scene?
  Answer: Elizabeth believes that defending her husband requires her to lie, but the audience knows that in this case, defending him requires her to tell the truth.
- **Ask** students why Elizabeth hesitates to answer Danforth's questions.
  Answer: She knows that lechery is a crime. She wants to protect John.
- Have students read ahead to Elizabeth's line, "Oh, God!". Have them **analyze** the dramatic irony of the scene.
  Answer: Elizabeth is an honest woman who finds it very difficult to lie. The one time that the truth is most essential is the time she decides she must lie to protect someone. Once again in Salem, lies to the court have hurt the innocent and protected the guilty.

Monitor Progress: Ask students what might have happened if Elizabeth had told the truth.
Answer: The judges would have been much more inclined to doubt Abigail's accusations; she would have been arrested in any case as a harlot. John might also have been arrested, but lechery is not punishable by death.

Your wife, you say, is an honest woman.

PROCTOR: In her life, sir, she have never lied. There are them that cannot sing, and them that cannot weep—my wife cannot lie. I have paid much to learn it, sir.

DANFORTH: And when she put this girl out of your house, she put her out for a harlot?

PROCTOR: Aye, sir.

DANFORTH: And knew her for a harlot?

PROCTOR: Aye, sir, she knew her for a harlot.

DANFORTH: Good then. *To* ABIGAIL: And if she tell me, child, it were for harlotry, may God spread His mercy on you! *There is a knock. He calls to the door.* Hold! *To* ABIGAIL: Turn your back. Turn your back. *To* PROCTOR: Do likewise. *Both turn their backs—*ABIGAIL *with indignant slowness.* Now let neither of you turn to face Goody Proctor. No one in this room is to speak one word, or raise a gesture aye or nay. *He turns toward the door, calls:* Enter! *The door opens.* ELIZABETH *enters with* PARRIS. PARRIS *leaves her. She stands alone, her eyes looking for* PROCTOR. Mr. Cheever, report this testimony in all exactness. Are you ready?

CHEEVER: Ready, sir.

DANFORTH: Come here, woman. ELIZABETH *comes to him, glancing at* PROCTOR'S *back.* Look at me only, not at your husband. In my eyes only.

ELIZABETH, *faintly:* Good, sir.

DANFORTH: We are given to understand that at one time you dismissed your servant, Abigail Williams.

ELIZABETH: That is true, sir.

DANFORTH: For what cause did you dismiss her? *Slight pause. Then* ELIZABETH *tries to glance at* PROCTOR. You will look in my eyes only and not at your husband. The answer is in your memory and you need no help to give it to me. Why did you dismiss Abigail Williams?

ELIZABETH, *not knowing what to say, sensing a situation, wetting her lips to stall for time:* She—dissatisfied me. *Pause.* And my husband.

DANFORTH: In what way dissatisfied you?

ELIZABETH: She were—*She glances at* PROCTOR *for a cue.*

DANFORTH: Woman, look at me? ELIZABETH *does.* Were she slovenly? Lazy? What disturbance did she cause?

ELIZABETH: Your Honor, I—in that time I were sick. And I—My husband is a good and righteous man. He is never drunk as some are, nor wastin' his time at the shovelboard, but always at his work. But in my sickness—you see, sir, I were a long time sick after my last baby, and I thought I saw my husband somewhat turning from me. And this girl—*She turns to* ABIGAIL.

DANFORTH: Look at me.

ELIZABETH: Aye, sir. Abigail Williams—*She breaks off.*

Literary Analysis
Dramatic and Verbal Irony Which details in Elizabeth's exchange with Danforth reveal the dramatic irony at work in this scene?

DANFORTH: What of Abigail Williams?

ELIZABETH: I came to think he fancied her. And so one night I lost my wits, I think, and put her out on the highroad.

DANFORTH: Your husband—did he indeed turn from you?

ELIZABETH, *in agony:* My husband—is a goodly man, sir.

DANFORTH: Then he did not turn from you.

ELIZABETH, *starting to glance at* PROCTOR: He—

39 **DANFORTH,** *reaches out and holds her face, then:* Look at me! To your own knowledge, has John Proctor ever committed the crime of lechery? *In a crisis of indecision she cannot speak.* Answer my question! Is your husband a lecher!

ELIZABETH, *faintly:* No, sir.

DANFORTH: Remove her, Marshal.

PROCTOR: Elizabeth, tell the truth!

DANFORTH: She has spoken. Remove her!

PROCTOR, *crying out:* Elizabeth, I have confessed it!

ELIZABETH: Oh, God! *The door closes behind her.*

PROCTOR: She only thought to save my name!

HALE: Excellency, it is a natural lie to tell; I beg you, stop now before another is condemned! I may shut my conscience to it no more—private vengeance is working through this testimony! From the beginning this man has struck me true. By my oath to Heaven, I believe him now, and I pray you call back his wife before we—

DANFORTH: She spoke nothing of lechery, and this man has lied!

HALE: I believe him! *Pointing at* ABIGAIL: This girl has always struck me false! She has—

ABIGAIL, *with a weird, wild, chilling cry, screams up to the ceiling.*

ABIGAIL: You will not! Begone! Begone, I say!

DANFORTH: What is it, child? *But* ABIGAIL, *pointing with fear, is now raising up her frightened eyes, her awed face, toward the ceiling—the girls are doing the same—and now* HATHORNE, HALE, PUTNAM, CHEEVER, HERRICK, *and* DANFORTH *do the same. What's there? He lowers his eyes* 40 *from the ceiling, and now he is frightened; there is real tension in his voice.* Child! *She is transfixed—with all the girls, she is whimpering, openmouthed, agape at the ceiling.* Girls! Why do you—?

MERCY LEWIS, *pointing:* It's on the beam! Behind the rafter!

DANFORTH, *looking up:* Where!

ABIGAIL: Why—? *She gulps.* Why do you come, yellow bird?

PROCTOR: Where's a bird? I see no bird!

ABIGAIL, *to the ceiling:* My face? My face?

PROCTOR: Mr. Hale—

DANFORTH: Be quiet!

PROCTOR, *to* HALE: Do you see a bird?

Reading Strategy
Categorizing Characters by Role What qualities or characteristics does Elizabeth now demonstrate?

Literary Analysis
Dramatic and Verbal Irony What does the audience know that Danforth does not know?

41  **Reading Check**
In what ways do John and Elizabeth's testimony differ? Why?

39 Reading Strategy
Categorizing Characters by Role

- **Ask** students the Reading Strategy question: What qualities or characteristics does Elizabeth now demonstrate?
  Answer: She shows her love and protective feelings toward her husband.
- **Ask** students whether Elizabeth's action is heroic. If so, in what way?
  Possible answer: Elizabeth has done something that was very hard for her. She has committed the sin of lying in order to protect someone. This makes her action heroic, in spite of its unintended outcome.

40 Literary Analysis
Dramatic and Verbal Irony

- **Ask** students the Literary Analysis question: What does the audience know that Danforth does not know?
  Answer: The audience knows that the girls are pretending.
- Why does Abigail choose this moment to scream?
  Answer: She knows that Danforth may listen to Hale; she needs to distract attention from the conversation about adultery.

41 Reading Check

Answer: John says that Elizabeth knew that Abigail was a harlot; Elizabeth denies it.

Differentiated Instruction
Solutions for All Learners

Strategy for Special Needs Students

Check comprehension and help maintain student interest by having students ask questions of the characters. Have students generate a list of questions they would like to ask these characters at this point in the play:

Mary Warren
Danforth
John Proctor
Abigail
Elizabeth Proctor

Allow students to work in pairs and answer one another's questions, as in the following:
Question: Elizabeth, why did you lie in court?
Answer: I wanted to protect my husband.

42 Literature in Context
Puritans and Nathaniel Hawthorne

The Scarlet Letter tells the story of Hester Prynne, a married woman living alone in Boston. When Hester's pregnancy becomes obvious, she is charged with adultery and condemned to wear the scarlet letter of the title, an A for adultery, on her clothing at all times. Hester accepts her punishment and continues to live in the community. She refuses to name the child's father. As her daughter Pearl grows older, readers realize that Pearl's father is the minister, Arthur Dimmesdale. In the end, Dimmesdale publicly confesses his love for Hester, acknowledges Pearl as his child, and dies. The novel is remarkable because the "fallen woman" is the heroine. Hester is the novel's only sympathetic character, just as Proctor, guilty of the same crime, is one of the few sympathetic characters in *The Crucible.*

Connect to the Literature

Have a volunteer read aloud the Literature in Context note. Then, **ask** the Literature in Context question. **Possible response:** Hathorne's villainous quality and eagerness to condemn probably influenced Hawthorne's vision.

43 Literary Analysis
Dramatic and Verbal Irony

- **Ask** students: Which type of irony do Abigail's words represent? Explain.
  Possible answers: Her words "She sees nothin'" represent verbal irony. They are true, but she intends everyone to think they are a lie.
- **Ask** students why the girls' repetition of Mary's words is ironic.
  Answer: All children play this mimicking game. It is ironic because it is a game played by innocent children, but the children here are not innocent and their actions have gone far beyond playing a game.

DANFORTH: Be quiet!!

ABIGAIL, *to the ceiling, in a genuine conversation with the "bird," as though trying to talk it out of attacking her:* But God made my face; you cannot want to tear my face. Envy is a deadly sin, Mary.

MARY WARREN, *on her feet with a spring, and horrified, pleading:* Abby!

ABIGAIL, *unperturbed, continuing to the "bird":* Oh, Mary, this is a black art to change your shape. No, I cannot, I cannot stop my mouth; it's God's work I do.

MARY WARREN: Abby, I'm *here!*

PROCTOR, *frantically:* They're pretending, Mr. Danforth!

ABIGAIL *—now she takes a backward step, as though in fear the bird will swoop down momentarily:* Oh, please, Mary! Don't come down.

SUSANNA WALCOTT: Her claws, she's stretching her claws!

PROCTOR: Lies, lies.

ABIGAIL, *backing further, eyes still fixed above:* Mary, please don't hurt me!

MARY WARREN, *to* DANFORTH: I'm not hurting her!

DANFORTH, *to* MARY WARREN: Why does she see this vision?

MARY WARREN: She sees nothin'!

43 **ABIGAIL,** *now staring full front as though hypnotized, and mimicking the exact tone of* MARY WARREN'S *cry:* She sees nothin'!

MARY WARREN, *pleading:* Abby, you mustn't!

ABIGAIL AND ALL THE GIRLS, *all transfixed:* Abby, you mustn't!

MARY WARREN, *to all the girls:* I'm here, I'm here!

GIRLS: I'm here, I'm here!

DANFORTH, *horrified:* Mary Warren! Draw back your spirit out of them!

MARY WARREN: Mr. Danforth!

GIRLS, *cutting her off:* Mr. Danforth!

DANFORTH: Have you compacted with the Devil? Have you?

MARY WARREN: Never, never!

GIRLS: Never, never!

DANFORTH, *growing hysterical:* Why can they only repeat you?

PROCTOR: Give me a whip—I'll stop it!

MARY WARREN: They're sporting. They—!

GIRLS: They're sporting!

MARY WARREN, *turning on them all hysterically and stamping her feet:* Abby, stop it!

Literature in Context

42 History Connection

Puritans and Nathaniel Hawthorne

One of the many characters in *The Crucible* who have real historical counterparts is John Hathorne, a judge who took part in the Salem witchcraft trials. Hathorne's most famous descendant is the writer Nathaniel Hawthorne (see page 338), who lived in Salem during the nineteenth century. Hawthorne used the Puritan colonies of his ancestors as the settings for much of his work. In Puritan rigidity and repression he found an expression for his dark vision of the human soul.

Hawthorne's best-known novel, *The Scarlet Letter,* examines the repressive side of Puritanism and the hypocrisy and pain that such an atmosphere produced. His short stories "Young Goodman Brown" and "The Minister's Black Veil" also focus on New England's Puritan communities.

Connect to the Literature

What inspiration for Hawthorne's dark vision may have come from his Salem ancestor?

GIRLS, *stamping their feet:* Abby, stop it!

MARY WARREN: Stop it!

GIRLS: Stop it!

MARY WARREN, *screaming it out at the top of her lungs, and raising her fists:* Stop it!!

GIRLS, *raising their fists:* Stop it!!

44 MARY WARREN, *utterly confounded, and becoming overwhelmed by* ABIGAIL'S*—and the girls'—utter conviction, starts to whimper, hands half raised, powerless, and all the girls begin whimpering exactly as she does.*

DANFORTH: A little while ago you were afflicted. Now it seems you afflict others; where did you find this power?

MARY WARREN, *staring at* ABIGAIL: I—have no power.

GIRLS: I have no power.

PROCTOR: They're gulling[7] you, Mister!

DANFORTH: Why did you turn about this past two weeks? You have seen the Devil, have you not?

HALE, *indicating* ABIGAIL *and the* GIRLS: You cannot believe them!

MARY WARREN: I—

PROCTOR, *sensing her weakening:* Mary, God damns all liars!

DANFORTH, *pounding it into her:* You have seen the Devil, you have made compact with Lucifer, have you not?

PROCTOR: God damns liars, Mary!

MARY *utters something unintelligible, staring at* ABIGAIL, *who keeps watching the "bird" above.*

DANFORTH: I cannot hear you. What do you say? MARY *utters again unintelligibly.* You will confess yourself or you will hang! *He turns her roughly to face him.* Do you know who I am? I say you will hang if you do not open with me!

PROCTOR: Mary, remember the angel Raphael—do that which is good and—

ABIGAIL, *pointing upward:* The wings! Her wings are spreading! Mary, please, don't, don't—!

HALE: I see nothing, Your Honor!

DANFORTH: Do you confess this power! *He is an inch from her face.* Speak!

ABIGAIL: She's going to come down! She's walking the beam!

DANFORTH: Will you speak!

MARY WARREN, *staring in horror:* I cannot!

GIRLS: I cannot!

PARRIS: Cast the Devil out! Look him in the face! Trample him! We'll save you, Mary, only stand fast against him and—

ABIGAIL, *looking up:* Look out! She's coming down!

---

7. gulling fooling.

Literary Analysis
Dramatic and Verbal Irony In what ways does the idea of Abigail's "utter conviction" serve as an ironic statement?

45  **Reading Check**

What do the girls do to undermine Mary Warren's testimony?

44 Literary Analysis
Dramatic and Verbal Irony

- Make sure students understand that Abigail has turned against Mary in order to fool Danforth and protect her own reputation.
- **Ask** students the Literary Analysis question: In what ways does the idea of Abigail's "utter conviction" serve as an ironic statement?
Answer: It is impossible to feel utter conviction about something that one knows is untrue. However, it is Abigail's display of utter conviction that strengthens her case; Mary's hesitance and lack of conviction make her case look weak, though she is telling the truth.

45 Reading Check

Answer: They pretend to see Mary's spirit walking in the rafters and trying to attack them.

Differentiated Instruction
Solutions for All Learners

Strategy for Less Proficient Readers
While they read Act I, students learned to question a character's motivation. Have students discuss Mary's motives for recanting her confession and supporting the other girls' lies. Remind them that Mary knows her actions will lead to the arrests and possibly the deaths of innocent people. Remind students of Abigail's forcefulness and her current popularity in the town, and have them think about situations in which they have been pressured to give in to the demands of classmates. Would students have reacted differently in Mary's situation?

46 Literary Analysis
Dramatic and Verbal Irony

- **Ask** students the Literary Analysis question: Which two words in these stage directions describing Abigail and Mary are an example of verbal irony?
  Answer: The words "infinite charity" are ironic because in feigning "charity," Abigail is once again acting out of self-interest.
- Why is Mary's accusation of Proctor ironic?
  Answer: Proctor is the only person who tried to help her crush the fraud.

Monitor Progress: Have students read Proctor's speech on the next page and analyze its verbal irony.
Answer: Proctor has tried to do the right thing—to show up the fraud—and for this he is condemned to hang for witchcraft. It is ironic that he is falsely condemned.

She and all the girls run to one wall, shielding their eyes. And now, as though cornered, they let out a gigantic scream, and MARY, *as though infected, opens her mouth and screams with them. Gradually* ABIGAIL *and the girls leave off, until only* MARY *is left there, staring up at the "bird," screaming madly. All watch her, horrified by this evident fit.* PROCTOR *strides to her.*

PROCTOR: Mary, tell the Governor what they—*He has hardly got a word out, when, seeing him coming for her, she rushes out of his reach, screaming in horror.*

MARY WARREN: Don't touch me—don't touch me! *At which the girls halt at the door.*

PROCTOR, *astonished:* Mary!

MARY WARREN, *pointing at* PROCTOR: You're the Devil's man!

He is stopped in his tracks.

PARRIS: Praise God!

GIRLS: Praise God!

PROCTOR, *numbed:* Mary, how—?

MARY WARREN: I'll not hang with you! I love God, I love God.

DANFORTH, *to* MARY: He bid you do the Devil's work?

MARY WARREN, *hysterically, indicating* PROCTOR: He come at me by night and every day to sign, to sign, to—

DANFORTH: Sign what?

PARRIS: The Devil's book? He come with a book?

MARY WARREN, *hysterically, pointing at* PROCTOR, *fearful of him:* My name, he want my name. "I'll murder you," he says, "if my wife hangs! We must go and overthrow the court," he says!

DANFORTH'S *head jerks toward* PROCTOR, *shock and horror in his face.*

PROCTOR, *turning, appealing to* HALE: Mr. Hale!

MARY WARREN, *her sobs beginning:* He wake me every night, his eyes were like coals and his fingers claw my neck, and I sign, I sign . . .

HALE: Excellency, this child's gone wild!

PROCTOR, *as* DANFORTH'S *wide eyes pour on him:* Mary, Mary!

46 **MARY WARREN,** *screaming at him:* No, I love God; I go your way no more. I love God, I bless God. *Sobbing, she rushes to* ABIGAIL. Abby, Abby, I'll never hurt you more! *They all watch, as* ABIGAIL, *out of her infinite charity, reaches out and draws the sobbing* MARY *to her, and then looks up to* DANFORTH.

DANFORTH, *to* PROCTOR: What are you? PROCTOR *is beyond speech in his anger.* You are combined with anti-Christ,[8] are you not? I have seen your power; you will not deny it! What say you, Mister?

HALE: Excellency—

Literary Analysis
Dramatic and Verbal Irony Which two words in these stage directions describing Abigail and Mary are an example of verbal irony?

8. **anti-Christ** In the Bible, the great antagonist of Christ expected to spread universal evil.

DANFORTH: I will have nothing from you, Mr. Hale! *To* PROCTOR: Will you confess yourself befouled with Hell, or do you keep that black allegiance yet? What say you?

PROCTOR, *his mind wild, breathless:* I say—I say—God is dead!

PARRIS: Hear it, hear it!

PROCTOR, *laughs insanely, then:* A fire, a fire is burning! I hear the boot of Lucifer, I see his filthy face! And it is my face, and yours, Danforth! For them that quail to bring men out of ignorance, as I have quailed, and as you quail now when you know in all your black hearts that this be fraud—God damns our kind especially, and we will burn, we will burn together.

DANFORTH: Marshal! Take him and Corey with him to the jail!

HALE, *staring across to the door:* I denounce these proceedings!

PROCTOR: You are pulling Heaven down and raising up a whore!

HALE: I denounce these proceedings, I quit this court! *He slams the door to the outside behind him.*

DANFORTH, *calling to him in a fury:* Mr. Hale! Mr. Hale!

Critical Reading

1. **Respond:** Which incident in Act III provoked the strongest emotional response in you? Why?
2. **(a) Recall:** Which three depositions are presented to the judges and on whose behalf? **(b) Analyze:** How do the judges discourage defenses of the accused?
3. **(a) Recall:** What does John Proctor confess to Danforth? **(b) Interpret:** Why does Proctor make this confession? **(c) Infer:** What does his confession reveal about his character?
4. **(a) Recall:** What is the lie Elizabeth Proctor tells Danforth? **(b) Analyze:** What are the consequences of her lie?
5. **(a) Recall:** What truth does Mary Warren reveal about her involvement with "spirits"? **(b) Analyze:** Why does she change her testimony and turn on John Proctor?
6. **(a) Recall:** What does Hale denounce at the end of Act III? **(b) Evaluate:** Do you find Hale sympathetic? Why or why not?
7. **Apply:** Imagine that Elizabeth Proctor had told Danforth the truth. In what way might the outcome of the trials have been different?
8. **Assess:** Who bears the most guilt for the fate of those hanged in the Salem witch trials—the girls who accused innocent people or the judges who sentenced them to death?

For: More about Arthur Miller
Visit: www.PHSchool.com
Web Code: ere-9635

ASSESS

Answers

1. Students may choose Elizabeth's attempt to protect John, Mary Warren's accusation of John, Hale's denunciation of the proceedings, or another incident. Have them explain their answers.
2. (a) The following depositions are presented to the judges: Mary's deposition that the accusations are false; a deposition testifying to the good character of Rebecca, Elizabeth, and Martha; Giles's deposition accusing Putnam. (b) The judges insist that a protest shows contempt of the court.
3. (a) He confesses to his affair with Abigail. (b) He believes that Abigail is a murderess and must be revealed as untrustworthy. Also, he wants to uncover Abigail's motivation for lying. (c) He is willing to sacrifice his good name to save others.
4. (a) She claims ignorance of John's affair with Abigail. (b) John is arrested, and the court's confidence in Abigail is restored.
5. (a) She says she made it all up. (b) The other girls all turn on her, and she is too cowardly to stand up to them.
6. (a) He denounces the court proceedings. (b) Students will probably say yes; Hale has always tried to do what was right.
7. Abigail might have been hanged, and the accused witches might have been pardoned.
8. Answers will vary. Make sure students defend their opinions.

Go Online Author Link For additional information about Arthur Miller, have students type in the Web Code, then select *M* from the alphabet, and then select Arthur Miller.

Answers

1. **Possible answers:** Abigail's cry, "She sees nothin!", is an example of verbal irony; what she says is true, but she intends everyone to believe that it is false. Elizabeth's denial of knowledge of the affair between John and Abigail is an example of dramatic irony; it is a lie, but everyone believes it because of her reputation for honesty.

   Another sample answer can be found on **Literary Analysis Graphic Organizer B**, p. 297, in ***Graphic Organizer Transparencies.***
2. The audience knows that Proctor has confessed to the affair.
3. She achieves the opposite of what she wanted to achieve: Her husband is arrested, and the court's confidence in Abigail is restored.
4. Mary has the power to stop the proceedings by telling the truth.
5. Danforth does not allow for the possibility that an accused person may be innocent.
6. If an accusation is enough to condemn a person, there can be no justice.
7. (a) Parris cares only for the strong social position that the ministry gives him. Everything he does in the play is done only to protect himself. Hale is genuinely interested in theology and tries to do right. (b) Parris is a villain. Hale is a dynamic character who gives the audience hope that those on the side of the accusers may be brought to see reason.
8. (a) All three are easily led and frightened. None seems to have a conscience. (b) Students may sympathize with the girls' fears of punishment in Act I but are not likely to sympathize with their willingness to see innocent people hanged.
9. Elizabeth and Hale are dynamic characters. The others are static characters. Parris has been frightened throughout the play; Abigail has lied throughout; and Proctor has acted according to his conscience throughout.
10. Ask students to explain their answers.

Apply the Skills

The Crucible, Act III

Literary Analysis

Dramatic and Verbal Irony

1. Using a chart like the one shown, list three examples of **dramatic and verbal irony** from Act III. Identify the type of irony and explain what each speaker really means.

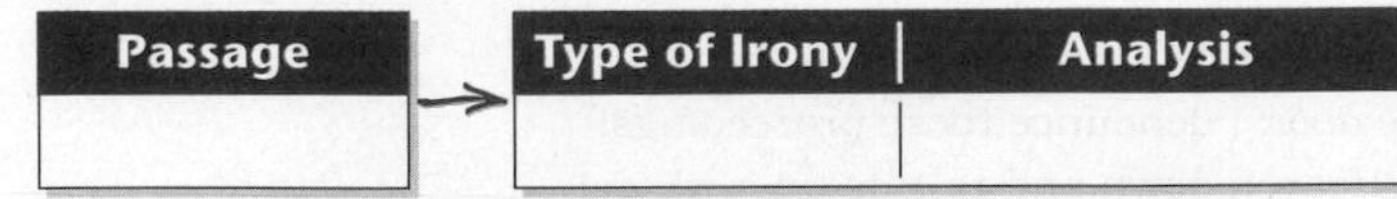

2. What does the audience know that Elizabeth does not know when she testifies about her husband's behavior?
3. Why is the effect of Elizabeth's testimony ironic?
4. What is ironic about Mary Warren's statement, "I—have no power," when she is being interrogated in front of Abigail Williams?

Connecting Literary Elements

5. In Judge Danforth's dramatic exchange with Reverend Hale, what erroneous idea underlies all his reasoning about the legal proceedings? Explain.
6. In what sense does Danforth's **logical fallacy** have ramifications far beyond the conviction of John Proctor?

Reading Strategy

Categorizing Characters by Role

7. **(a)** Compare and contrast Reverend Parris with Reverend Hale. **(b)** How would you **categorize** the effectiveness of each in his role as minister?
8. **(a)** Which character traits would you ascribe to Betty Parris, Sarah Good, and Mercy Lewis? **(b)** Do you have sympathy for them? Why or why not?
9. Which characters would you classify as static (unchanging), and which would you classify as dynamic (changing or growing)? Why?
10. What other categories do you think would be useful for classifying the characters? Explain.

Extend Understanding

11. **Career Connection:** Which qualities of a good judge do you think are lacking in Hathorne and Danforth? Explain.

QuickReview

Dramatic irony occurs when there is a contradiction between what a character thinks and what the audience knows to be true.

Verbal irony occurs when a character says one thing but means something else.

A **logical fallacy** is an argument that appears logical but is based on a faulty premise.

To understand the characters' roles in a play, **categorize the characters** in meaningful ways.

For: Self-test
Visit: www.PHSchool.com
Web Code: era-6622

Answers continued

11. Judges are supposed to be impartial. Both Danforth and Hale assume that those accused must be guilty before they hear any evidence.

Go Online Assessment Students may use the **Self-test** to prepare for **Selection Test A** or **Selection Test B.**

Build Language Skills

❶ Vocabulary Lesson

Concept Development: Legal Terms

The Crucible contains a number of legal terms. For example, a *deposition* is a legal document that contains the written testimony of a witness. Determine the meaning of each of these words from the context in which it appears in Act III. Then, use each word in a sentence.

1. prosecutor **2.** contempt **3.** perjury

Spelling Strategy

When adding an *-ly* suffix to a word that ends in a consonant, do not double or change the consonant. The words *deferentially* and *incredulously* follow this rule. Change each of the following adjectives into adverbs by adding the suffix *-ly:*

1. dubious **2.** bountiful **3.** obvious

Vocabulary Builder: Relationships

Review the vocabulary list on page 1314. Then, for each item below, indicate whether the paired words are synonyms or antonyms.

1. contentious, combative
2. deposition, testimony
3. imperceptible, obvious
4. deferentially, politely
5. anonymity, notoriety
6. prodigious, minuscule
7. effrontery, timidity
8. confounded, puzzled
9. incredulously, disbelievingly
10. blanched, darkened

❷ Grammar and Style Lesson

Subject and Verb Agreement in Inverted Sentences

In most sentences, the subject precedes the verb, but in an **inverted sentence** the verb comes first. Notice how the verb **agrees** in number with the subject of the following inverted sentences.

Plural: Now there are (V) no spirits (S) attacking her.

Practice Complete each sentence by choosing the correct form of the verb in parentheses.

1. There (is, are) a courtroom scene in Act III.
2. In the courtroom (sits, sit) many people.
3. Hearing the case (is, are) Danforth and Hathorne.
4. Here (is, are) Abigail and her cohorts.
5. Under suspicion (is, are) dozens of citizens.

Writing Application As Reverend Hale, write a letter to the editor of the Salem newspaper explaining why you now oppose the court's actions. Use three inverted sentences, and make your subjects and verbs agree in number.

WG Prentice Hall Writing and Grammar Connection: Chapter 23, Section 1

❸ Extend Your Learning

Writing Write a **character sketch** of Mary Warren in which you evaluate her strengths and weaknesses.

Listening and Speaking Draft and perform the **monologue** Elizabeth might give at the moment she learns the effect of her lie in court.

Assessment Practice

Using Commas Correctly

(For more practice, see *Standardized Test Preparation Workbook*, p. 77.)

Many tests require students to identify errors in punctuation. Use this following sample test item.

DANFORTH I will have nothing from you Mr. Hale!

After which word should you insert a comma?

A I
B have
C you
D no comma needed

The name of the person being addressed must be set off with a comma. The correct answer is *C*.

EXTEND/ASSESS

Answers

❶ Vocabulary Lesson

Concept Development

1. attorney: The prosecutor cross-examined the witness.
2. refusal to cooperate: The man was thrown out of court for contempt.
3. false testimony: Perjury is a crime because a witness swears to tell the truth.

Spelling Strategy

1. dubiously
2. bountifully
3. obviously

Vocabulary Builder

1. Synonyms
2. Synonyms
3. Antonyms
4. Synonyms
5. Antonyms
6. Antonyms
7. Antonyms
8. Synonyms
9. Synonyms
10. Antonyms

❷ Grammar and Style Lesson

1. is
2. sit
3. are
4. are
5. are

Writing Application

Check students' paragraphs.

❸ Extension Activities

Writing Lesson

- Make sure that essays accurately reflect Mary's speeches and actions.

Listening and Speaking

- The **Support for Extend Your Learning** page (*Unit 6 Resources,* p. 379) provides guided note-taking opportunities to help students complete the activities.

Go Online Research Have students type in the Web Code for another research activity.

Meeting Your Standards

Students will

1. **analyze and respond to literary elements.**
   - Literary Analysis: Theme
2. **read, comprehend, analyze, and critique a drama.**
   - Reading Strategy: Applying Themes to Contemporary Events
   - Reading Check questions
   - Apply the Skills questions
   - Assessment Practice (ATE)
3. **develop vocabulary.**
   - Vocabulary Lesson: Concept Development: Words From Myths
4. **understand and apply written and oral language conventions.**
   - Spelling Strategy
   - Grammar and Style Lesson: Commonly Confused Words: *raise* and *rise*
5. **develop writing proficiency.**
   - Writing Lesson: Defense of a Character's Actions
6. **develop appropriate research strategies.**
   - Extend Your Learning: Comparison-and-Contrast Chart
7. **understand and apply listening and speaking strategies.**
   - Extend Your Learning: Mock Trial

Block Scheduling: Use one 90-minute class period to preteach the skills and have students read the selection. Use a second 90-minute class period to assess students' mastery of skills, extend their learning, and monitor their progress.

Homework Suggestions

Following are possibilities for homework assignments.

- Support pages from *Unit 6 Resources:*
  Literary Analysis
  Reading Strategy
  Vocabulary Builder
  Grammar and Style
- An Extend Your Learning project and the Writing Lesson for this selection group may be completed over several days.

Step-by-Step Teaching Guide	Pacing Guide
PRETEACH	
• Administer Vocabulary and Reading Warm-ups as necessary.	5 min.
• Engage students' interest with the motivation activity.	5 min.
• Read and discuss author and background features. **FT**	10 min.
• Introduce the Literary Analysis skill: Theme. **FT**	5 min.
• Introduce the Reading Strategy: Applying Themes to Contemporary Events. **FT**	10 min.
• Prepare students to read by teaching the selection vocabulary. **FT**	
TEACH	
• Informally monitor comprehension while students read independently or in groups. **FT**	30 min.
• Monitor students' comprehension with the Reading Check notes.	as students read
• Reinforce vocabulary with Vocabulary Builder notes.	as students read
• Develop students' understanding of theme with the Literary Analysis annotations. **FT**	5 min.
• Develop students' ability to apply themes to contemporary events with the Reading Strategy annotations. **FT**	5 min.
ASSESS/EXTEND	
• Assess students' comprehension and mastery of the Literary Analysis and Reading Strategy by having them answer the Apply the Skills questions. **FT**	15 min.
• Have students complete the Vocabulary Lesson and the Grammar and Style Lesson. **FT**	15 min.
• Apply students' ability to analyze the evidence by using the Writing Lesson. **FT**	45 min. or homework
• Apply students' understanding by using one or more of the Extend Your Learning activities.	20–90 min. or homework
• Administer Selection Test A or Selection Test B. **FT**	15 min.

Resources

PRINT

Unit 6 Resources

Vocabulary Warm-up Word Lists **[L1, L2, EL]** .p. 387
Vocabulary Warm-up Practice **[L1, L2, EL]** . . . . .p. 388
Reading Warm-up A **[L1, L2, EL]** . . . . .p. 389
Reading Warm-up B **[L1, L2, L3]** . . . . .p. 390

TRANSPARENCY

Graphic Organizer Transparencies

Literary Analysis Graphic Organizer A **[L3]** . . . . .pp. 298, 300
Literary Analysis Graphic Organizer B **[L1, L2, EL]** . . . . .pp. 299, 301

PRINT

Reader's Notebook [L2]
Reader's Notebook: Adapted Version [L1]
Reader's Notebook: English Learner's Version [EL]

Unit 6 Resources

Literary Analysis **[L3]** . . . . .p. 391
Reading Strategy **[L3]** . . . . .p. 392
Vocabulary Builder **[L3]** . . . . .p. 393

PRINT

Unit 6 Resources

Grammar and Style **[L3]** . . . . .p. 394
Support for Writing Lesson **[L3]** . . . . .p. 395
Support for Extend Your Learning **[L3]** . . . . .p. 396
Enrichment **[L4]** . . . . .p. 397
Selection Test A **[L1, L2, EL]** . . . . .pp. 398–400
Selection Test B **[L3, L4]** . . . . .pp. 401–403

General Resources

Rubrics for Persuasion: Persuasive Essay **[L3]** . . . . .pp. 45–46
Rubric for Speaking: Delivering a Research Presentation **[L3]** . . . . .p. 92

TECHNOLOGY

Go Online: Research **[L3]**
Go Online: Self-test **[L3]**
***ExamView*® Test Bank [L3]**

Choosing Resources for Differentiated Instruction

[L1] Special Needs Students
[L2] Below-Level Students
[L3] All Students
[L4] Advanced Students
[EL] English Learners

For Vocabulary and Reading Warm-ups and for Selection Tests, **A** signifies "less challenging" and **B** "more challenging." For Graphic Organizer transparencies, **A** signifies "not filled in" and **B** "filled in."

FT Fast Track Instruction: To move the lesson more quickly, use the strategies and activities identified with **FT**.

Scaffolding for Less Proficient and Advanced Students

The leveled Critical Thinking questions after selections progress in the levels of thinking required to answer them. To address the needs of your different students, you may use the (a) level questions for your less proficient students and the (b) level questions with your on-level and advanced students. The occasional (c) level questions are appropriate for your advanced students.

PRENTICE HALL **TeacherEXPRESS**™ Plan · Teach · Assess — Use this complete suite of powerful teaching tools to make lesson planning and testing quicker and easier.

PRENTICE HALL **StudentEXPRESS**™ Learn · Study · Succeed — Use the interactive textbook (online and on CD-ROM) to make selections and activities come alive with audio and video support and interactive questions.

Benchmark

After students have completed Act IV, administer **Benchmark Test 12** (***Unit 6 Resources,*** p. 411). If the Benchmark Test reveals that some students need further work, use the **Interpretation Guide** to determine the appropriate reteaching pages in the **Reading Kit** or on **Success Tracker.**

Go Online Professional Development
For: Information about Lexiles
Visit: www.PHSchool.com
Web Code: eue-1111

PRETEACH

❶ Literary Analysis
Theme

- Explain that a work's theme comprises both main idea and author's purpose. The theme is the concept that a writer most wants the reader to take away and think about. The plot, characters, and setting are all chosen to illustrate the theme. The theme is also the reason the author wrote the work. Miller wrote *The Crucible* because he wanted to express certain beliefs about human nature.
- **Ask** students to name some themes Miller introduced and developed during the first three acts.
  Possible answers: Unresolved conflicts between people can have tragic results; fear and hypocrisy are a deadly combination.

❷ Reading Strategy
Applying Themes to Contemporary Events

- Share the Background information on the McCarthy era.
- Remind students that in this case, "contemporary" does not refer to the present time; it refers to the time in which the play was written.
- Have students share what they know about the political climate in the United States during the years leading up to *The Crucible*. Remind them that during World War II, the enemies of the United States were fascist states. Ask students to notice any anti-fascist messages or themes in the play, such as Cheever's claim that he is only following the orders of the court when he arrests Elizabeth. What do students think this statement would have suggested to this play's contemporary audience?
  Answer: Students may recall that the same defense was offered at the Nuremberg trials by Nazi war criminals.

Vocabulary Builder

- Pronounce each vocabulary word for students, and read the definitions as a class. Have students identify any words with which they are already familiar.

Build Skills *Drama*

The Crucible, Act IV

❶ Literary Analysis
Theme

A **theme** is the central idea or insight into life that a writer strives to convey in a work of literature. Like most longer works, *The Crucible* has several themes. One theme is that fear and suspicion are infectious and can turn into mass hysteria. Miller also touches upon the destructive power of guilt, revenge, and the failure of a judicial system fueled by ideology instead of justice. As you read Act IV, use a chart like the one shown to consider these and other themes that Miller conveys.

Connecting Literary Elements

An **extended metaphor** is a comparison that is developed throughout the course of a literary work. Miller's imagery of the seventeenth-century witch hunt in Salem builds a comparison to the events of the late 1940s and early 1950s in America, a time characterized by these intensified emotions:

- Fear of communism and a widespread hysteria that Communists had infiltrated the State Department.
- Panic based on witch hunt tactics—those who opposed McCarthy's hearings were charged with Communism themselves.

Notice Miller's ability to explore the events of his own era within the parallel context of the Salem witchcraft trials.

❷ Reading Strategy
Applying Themes to Contemporary Events

The parallel between the events in Salem, as Miller depicts them, and ongoing events in Congress at the time Miller wrote the play are clear. As you read Act IV, think about what themes or messages Miller was conveying that specifically related to contemporary events.

Vocabulary Builder

agape (ə gāp′) *adj.* wide open (p. 1346)

conciliatory (kən sil′ ē ə tôr′ ē) *adj.* tending to soothe anger (p. 1348)

beguile (bē gīl′) *v.* trick (p. 1348)

floundering (floun′ də riŋ) *n.* awkward struggling (p. 1348)

retaliation (ri ta′ lē ā′ shən) *n.* act of returning an injury or wrong (p. 1348)

adamant (ad′ ə mənt) *adj.* firm; unyielding (p. 1348)

cleave (klēv) *v.* adhere; cling (p. 1350)

sibilance (sib′ əl əns) *n.* hissing sound (p. 1350)

tantalized (tan′ tə līzd) *adj.* tormented; frustrated (p. 1353)

purged (purjd) *v.* cleansed (p. 1355)

1 ## Review and Anticipate

"Is every defense an attack upon the court?" Hale asks in Act III. Danforth observes, "A person is either with this court or he must be counted against it." Such remarks stress the powerlessness of people like John Proctor and Giles Corey against the mounting injustices in Salem. In pursuing justice, their efforts backfire, and their own names join the list of those accused. What do you think the final outcome will be? Who will survive, and who will perish? Read the final act to see if your predictions are correct.

A cell in Salem jail, that fall.

At the back is a high barred window; near it, a great, heavy door. Along the walls are two benches.

2 *The place is in darkness but for the moonlight seeping through the bars. It appears empty. Presently footsteps are heard coming down a corridor beyond the wall, keys rattle, and the door swings open.* MARSHAL HERRICK *enters with a lantern. He is nearly drunk, and heavy-footed. He goes to a bench and nudges a bundle of rags lying on it.*

HERRICK: Sarah, wake up! Sarah Good! *He then crosses to the other benches.*

SARAH GOOD, *rising in her rags:* Oh, Majesty! Comin',comin'! Tituba, he's here, His Majesty's come!

HERRICK: Go to the north cell; this place is wanted now. *He hangs his lantern on the wall.* TITUBA sits up.

TITUBA: That don't look to me like His Majesty; look to me like the marshal.

HERRICK, *taking out a flask:* Get along with you now, clear this place. *He drinks, and* SARAH GOOD *comes and peers up into his face.*

SARAH GOOD: Oh, is it you, Marshal! I thought sure you be the devil comin' for us. Could I have a sip of cider for me goin'-away?

HERRICK, *handing her the flask:* And where are you off to, Sarah?

TITUBA, *as* SARAH *drinks:* We goin' to Barbados, soon the Devil gits here with the feathers and the wings.

HERRICK: Oh? A happy voyage to you.

SARAH GOOD: A pair of bluebirds wingin' southerly, the two of us! Oh, it be a grand transformation, Marshal! *She raises the flask to drink again.*

HERRICK, *taking the flask from her lips:* You'd best give me that or you'll never rise off the ground. Come along now.

Literary Analysis
Theme In what ways do these stage directions describing an empty cell help to convey a theme?

3 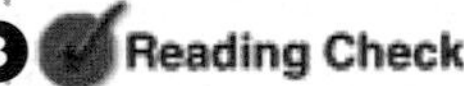

Who is Sarah Good talking about in this scene?

Differentiated Instruction

Solutions for All Learners

Support for Special Needs Students
Have students complete the **Preview** and **Build Skills** pages for Act IV of *The Crucible* in the ***Reader's Notebook: Adapted Version***. These pages provide a selection summary, an abbreviated presentation of the reading and literary skills, and the graphic organizer on the **Build Skills** page in the student book.

Support for Less Proficient Readers
Have students complete the **Preview** and **Build Skills** pages for Act IV of *The Crucible* in the ***Reader's Notebook***. These pages provide a selection summary, an abbreviated presentation of the reading and literary skills, and the graphic organizer on the **Build Skills** page in the student book.

Support for English Learners
Have students complete the **Preview** and **Build Skills** pages for Act IV of *The Crucible* in the ***Reader's Notebook: English Learner's Version***. These pages provide a selection summary, an abbreviated presentation of the reading and literary skills, and the graphic organizer on the **Build Skills** page in the student book.

TEACH

Learning Modalities Logical/ Mathematical Learners

Have students discuss whether John Proctor qualifies as a tragic hero in the classical tradition. Review with them the definition of a tragic hero. Have them reread the play, looking for evidence to support their answers. Students may want to divide into two groups to debate the question.

1 About Act IV

Parris pleads with the judges for a postponement of the hangings; he fears that the town will revolt if residents such as Rebecca Nurse are hanged without having confessed. Danforth agrees to a last attempt to persuade Proctor to confess and thus escape death. Elizabeth has the best chance to persuade him.

Left alone together, the Proctors ask each other's forgiveness. John asks whether he should falsely confess to witchcraft. Elizabeth tells him to do as he thinks best; she believes in his goodness either way.

Proctor confesses to having seen the Devil but refuses to name anyone else. He reluctantly signs his confession, but then tears it up, proclaiming that he prefers hanging to living a lie. The sentence is carried out as the curtain falls.

2 Literary Analysis
Theme

- **Ask** students the Literary Analysis question: In what ways do these stage directions describing an empty cell help to convey a theme?
Answer: This setting reminds the audience of the danger that the condemned prisoners are in.
- **Ask** what Sarah's comments about the devil suggest. Why are these comments ironic?
Answer: Sarah's comments are ironic because she looks on the Devil as a blessed escape. Her comments make it clear that the real Devil is in the court and its false accusations and injustice.

3 Reading Check

Answer: She is talking about the Devil .

❹ Literary Analysis
Theme

- **Ask** students the Literary Analysis question: What theme do you think Herrick's drunkenness on execution day implies?
  Answer: Herrick finds the proceedings too distasteful to face without the numbness of alcohol. This suggests that he, like others, knows injustice is taking place but feels powerless to stop it.
- What theme is implied in Danforth's statement, "There is a prodigious stench in this place"?
  Answer: The stench is of the crimes of the court rather than of the prisoners. The broad theme suggested here is that evil cannot take place without consequences.

TITUBA: I'll speak to him for you, if you desires to come along, Marshal.

HERRICK: I'd not refuse it, Tituba; it's the proper morning to fly into Hell.

TITUBA: Oh, it be no Hell in Barbados. Devil, him be pleasure man in Barbados, him be singin' and dancin' in Barbados. It's you folks—you riles him up 'round here; it be too cold 'round here for that Old Boy. He freeze his soul in Massachusetts, but in Barbados he just as sweet and—*A bellowing cow is heard, and* TITUBA *leaps up and calls to the window:* Aye, sir! That's him, Sarah!

SARAH GOOD: I'm here, Majesty! *They hurriedly pick up their rags as* HOPKINS, *a guard, enters.*

HOPKINS: The Deputy Governor's arrived.

HERRICK, *grabbing* TITUBA: Come along, come along.

TITUBA, *resisting him:* No, he comin' for me. I goin' home!

HERRICK, *pulling her to the door:* That's not Satan, just a poor old cow with a hatful of milk. Come along now, out with you!

TITUBA, *calling to the window:* Take me home, Devil! Take me home!

SARAH GOOD, *following the shouting* TITUBA *out:* Tell him I'm goin', Tituba! Now you tell him Sarah Good is goin' too!

In the corridor outside TITUBA *calls on—"Take me home, Devil: Devil take me home!" and* HOPKINS' *voice orders her to move on.* HERRICK *returns and begins to push old rags and straw into a corner. Hearing footsteps, he turns, and enter* DANFORTH *and* JUDGE HATHORNE. *They are in greatcoats and wear hats against the bitter cold. They are followed in by* CHEEVER, *who carries a dispatch case and a flat wooden box containing his writing materials.*

HERRICK: Good morning, Excellency.

DANFORTH: Where is Mr. Parris?

HERRICK: I'll fetch him. *He starts for the door.*

DANFORTH: Marshal. HERRICK *stops.* When did Reverend Hale arrive?

HERRICK: It were toward midnight, I think.

DANFORTH, *suspiciously:* What is he about here?

HERRICK: He goes among them that will hang, sir. And he prays with them. He sits with Goody Nurse now. And Mr. Parris with him.

DANFORTH: Indeed. That man have no authority to enter here, Marshal. Why have you let him in?

❹ **HERRICK:** Why, Mr. Parris command me, sir. I cannot deny him.

DANFORTH: Are you drunk, Marshal?

HERRICK: No, sir; it is a bitter night, and I have no fire here.

DANFORTH, *containing his anger:* Fetch Mr. Parris.

HERRICK: Aye, sir.

DANFORTH: There is a prodigious stench in this place.

HERRICK: I have only now cleared the people out for you.

DANFORTH: Beware hard drink, Marshal.

Literary Analysis
Theme What theme do you think Herrick's drunkenness on execution day implies?

Differentiated Instruction
Solutions for All Learners

Enrichment for Gifted/Talented Students
Ask students to do some research on Barbados society and culture at the turn of the seventeenth century. How many ethnic groups and nationalities were represented in the population? What were race relations like? Which country ruled Barbados? What was the climate like? Which crops were grown? What were the communities like—villages like Salem, small farms, plantations, bigger cities? Which religions were dominant? What was the relationship between church and society? Have students use these and other questions to find out about Barbados and compare and contrast it with Salem. Ask students how they think the Puritans of Salem would have reacted to Barbados. Remind them that Parris, Betty, and Tituba all come from there. What effect does this contrast have on students' understanding of what happened in the woods?

HERRICK: Aye, sir. *He waits an instant for further orders. But* DANFORTH, *in dissatisfaction, turns his back on him, and* HERRICK *goes out. There is a pause.* DANFORTH *stands in thought.*

HATHORNE: Let you question Hale, Excellency; I should not be surprised he have been preaching in Andover[1] lately.

DANFORTH: We'll come to that; speak nothing of Andover. Parris prays with him. That's strange. *He blows on his hands, moves toward the window, and looks out.*

HATHORNE: Excellency, I wonder if it be wise to let Mr. Parris so continuously with the prisoners. DANFORTH *turns to him, interested.* I think, sometimes, the man has a mad look these days.

DANFORTH: Mad?

HATHORNE: I met him yesterday coming out of his house, and I bid him good morning—and he wept and went his way. I think it is not well the village sees him so unsteady.

DANFORTH: Perhaps he have some sorrow.

CHEEVER, *stamping his feet against the cold:* I think it be the cows, sir.

DANFORTH: Cows?

CHEEVER: There be so many cows wanderin' the highroads, now their masters are in the jails, and much disagreement who they will belong to now. I know Mr. Parris be arguin' with farmers all yesterday—there is great contention, sir, about the cows. Contention make him weep, sir; it were always a man that weep for contention. *He turns, as do* HATHORNE *and* DANFORTH *hearing someone coming up the corridor.* DANFORTH *raises his head as* PARRIS *enters. He is gaunt, frightened, and sweating in his greatcoat.*

PARRIS, *to* DANFORTH , *instantly:* Oh, good morning, sir, thank you for coming. I beg your pardon wakin' you so early. Good morning, Judge Hathorne.

DANFORTH: Reverend Hale have no right to enter this—

PARRIS: Excellency, a moment. *He hurries back and shuts the door.*

HATHORNE: Do you leave him alone with the prisoners?

DANFORTH: What's his business here?

PARRIS, *prayerfully holding up his hands:* Excellency, hear me. It is a providence. Reverend Hale has returned to bring Rebecca Nurse to God.

DANFORTH, *surprised:* He bids her confess?

PARRIS, *sitting:* Hear me. Rebecca have not given me a word this three month since she came. Now she sits with him, and her sister and Martha Corey and two or three others, and he pleads with them, confess their crimes and save their lives.

1. **Andover** During the height of the terror in Salem Village, a similar hysteria broke out in the nearby town of Andover. There, many respected people were accused of practicing witchcraft and confessed to escape death. However, in Andover people soon began questioning the reality of the situation and the hysteria quickly subsided.

Literary Analysis
Theme What theme does Miller convey through Hathorne's description of Parris?

Reading Strategy
Applying Themes to Contemporary Events What warning might the details about changes in Salem convey about the growing anti-Communist fear and suspicion in Miller's own time?

7 

Why are so many cows wandering the roads?

5 Literary Analysis
Theme

- **Ask** students the Literary Analysis question: What theme does Miller convey through Hathorne's description of Parris?
  Answer: Parris has lied from the beginning and bears a great deal of responsibility for the hysteria. Parris is now suffering from guilt and shame of having condemned innocent people to death. Miller suggests that evil will come back to haunt the person who commits it.
- **Ask** students to explain the irony in Danforth's line, "Perhaps he have some sorrow."
  Answer: Parris's sorrow lies in the horror he feels at his own complicity in the trials and executions, but Danforth assumes it is simply a private matter.

6 Reading Strategy
Applying Themes to Contemporary Events

- **Ask** students the Reading Strategy question: What warning might the details about changes in Salem convey about the growing anti-Communist fear and suspicion in Miller's own time?
  Answer: The information about the conflict between Parris and the farmers suggests that Parris and perhaps the other accusers are beginning to lose the prominence they acquired when the trials began. In the same way, as fears about communism faded, McCarthy and his colleagues lost their reputations.
- What do Rebecca's different reported responses to Parris and Hale suggest about her and about the two ministers?
  Answer: Rebecca clearly despises Parris but likes Hale and is willing to listen to him. Her refusal to confess suggests that she is confident in her innocence.
- **Ask** students why Hale is trying to get the prisoners to confess.
  Answer: He wants to save their lives.

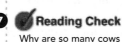

7 Reading Check

Answer: Their owners have been jailed or executed.

Differentiated Instruction
Solutions for All Learners

Strategy for Less Proficient Readers
Have students choose any two characters and make them the subject of a comparison-contrast essay. Possible pairings include Abigail and Elizabeth, Abigail and Mary, Cheever and Herrick, Hathorne and Danforth, Hale and Parris. Students can begin by making a word web for each character that lists his or her characteristics. They can then list the actions each character takes in the play. Finally, they can use these graphic organizers to pinpoint similarities and differences in the two characters. Students' essays should consider the effect of the two characters' differences, how each character serves as a foil for the other, and the thematic importance of the contrast between them.

8 Critical Thinking
Speculate

- **Ask** students why they think Abigail and Mercy have run away. Have them review the footnote about Andover at the bottom of the previous page.
  Possible answers: Abigail is afraid that the tide of opinion in Salem will turn against the accusers, just as has happened in Andover. She doesn't want to stay in Salem when she knows her affair with John is over. She wants to start over somewhere else.
- Have students **consider** why Parris waited so long to tell Danforth of the girls' disappearance.
  Answer: He didn't want to admit that he was a poor guardian or that Abigail had made a fool of him.

9 Critical Viewing

Answer: He may be confessing that his niece has run away.

DANFORTH: Why—this is indeed a providence. And they soften, they soften?

PARRIS: Not yet, not yet. But I thought to summon you, sir, that we might think on whether it be not wise, to—*He dares not say it.* I had thought to put a question, sir, and I hope you will not—

DANFORTH: Mr. Parris, be plain, what troubles you?

PARRIS: There is news, sir, that the court—the court must reckon with. My niece, sir, my niece—I believe she has vanished.

DANFORTH: Vanished!

PARRIS: I had thought to advise you of it earlier in the week, but—

DANFORTH: Why? How long is she gone?

8 **PARRIS:** This be the third night. You see, sir, she told me she would stay a night with Mercy Lewis. And next day, when she does not return, I send to Mr. Lewis to inquire. Mercy told him she would sleep in *my* house for a night.

DANFORTH: They are both gone?!

PARRIS, *in fear of him:* They are, sir.

DANFORTH, *alarmed:* I will send a party for them. Where may they be?

PARRIS: Excellency, I think they be aboard a ship. DANFORTH *stands agape.* My daughter tells me how she heard them speaking of ships last week, and tonight I discover my—my strongbox is broke into. *He presses his fingers against his eyes to keep back tears.*

HATHORNE, *astonished:* She have robbed you?

PARRIS: Thirty-one pound is gone. I am penniless. *He covers his face and sobs.*

DANFORTH: Mr. Parris, you are a brainless man! *He walks in thought, deeply worried.*

PARRIS: Excellency, it profit nothing you should blame me. I cannot think they would run off except they fear to keep in Salem any more. *He is pleading.* Mark it, sir, Abigail had close knowledge of the town, and since the news of Andover has broken here—

DANFORTH: Andover is remedied. The court returns there on Friday, and will resume examinations.

PARRIS: I am sure of it, sir. But the rumor here speaks rebellion in Andover, and it—

DANFORTH: There is no rebellion in Andover!

PARRIS: I tell you what is said here, sir. Andover have thrown out the court, they say, and will have no part of witchcraft. There be a faction here, feeding on that news, and I tell you true, sir, I fear there will be riot here.

HATHORNE: Riot! Why at every execution I have seen naught but high satisfaction in the town.

PARRIS: Judge Hathorne—it were another sort that hanged till now. Rebecca Nurse is no Bridget that lived three year with Bishop before she married him. John Proctor is not Isaac Ward that drank his family

Vocabulary Builder
agape (ə gāp′) *adj.* wide open

9 **Critical Viewing**
In this court scene from execution day what might Parris be saying to Judge Danforth? **[Speculate]**

to ruin. *To* DANFORTH: I would to God it were not so, Excellency, but these people have great weight yet in the town. Let Rebecca stand upon the gibbet[2] and send up some righteous prayer, and I fear she'll wake a vengeance on you.

HATHORNE: Excellency, she is condemned a witch. The court have—

DANFORTH, *in deep concern, raising a hand to* HATHORNE: Pray you. *To* PARRIS: How do you propose, then?

10 **PARRIS:** Excellency, I would postpone these hangin's for a time.

DANFORTH: There will be no postponement.

PARRIS: Now Mr. Hale's returned, there is hope, I think—for if he bring even one of these to God, that confession surely damns the others in the public eye, and none may doubt more that they are all linked to Hell. This way, unconfessed and claiming innocence, doubts are multiplied, many honest people will weep for them, and our good purpose is lost in their tears.

DANFORTH, *after thinking a moment, then going to* CHEEVER: Give me the list.

CHEEVER *opens the dispatch case, searches.*

PARRIS: It cannot be forgot, sir, that when I summoned the congregation for John Proctor's excommunication there were hardly thirty people come to hear it. That speak a discontent, I think, and—

DANFORTH, *studying the list:* There will be no postponement.

PARRIS: Excellency—

DANFORTH: Now, sir—which of these in your opinion may be brought to God? I will myself strive with him till dawn. *He hands the list to* PARRIS, *who merely glances at it.*

2. **gibbet** (jib′ it) *n.* gallows.

Reading Strategy
Applying Themes to Contemporary Events What might have happened if the McCarthy hearings had been postponed?

11 
Reading Check
What has happened to Abigail?

10 Reading Strategy
Applying Themes to Contemporary Events

- **Ask** students the Reading Strategy question: What might have happened if the McCarthy hearings had been postponed?
  Answer: The mood of the country might have changed and McCarthy might have lost his public support.
- Why does Danforth refuse to postpone the hangings?
  Answer: He does not want to risk the court's reputation. He thinks that people will interpret a postponement as weakness or doubt, and he won't let that happen.

11 Reading Check

Answer: Abigail, together with Mercy Lewis, has stolen money from her uncle and run away.

Differentiated Instruction
Solutions for All Learners

Strategy for Less Proficient Readers
Help students to make inferences about Hale, Parris, and Danforth by answering these questions:

- What is each man's hope for the prisoners? (Parris wants the hangings postponed; Hale wants the prisoners to confess; Danforth wants the hangings over with.)
- What is each man's greatest fear? (Parris fears a revolt in the town; Hale fears innocent people will die; Danforth fears others thinking he has put innocent people to death.)

Enrichment for Gifted/Talented Students
Ask students to write and perform a brief scene in which Mercy and Abigail decide to steal Parris's money and run away. Students should consider why the girls run, where they plan to go, and what they plan to do when they arrive. The scene should also discuss Abigail's and Mercy's thoughts about the situation and the people they leave behind.

⓬ Literary Analysis
Theme and Extended Metaphor

- **Ask** students to consider how Danforth's statement about being ready to hang any who might dare to "rise against the law" could be understood as a metaphor for what happened in the McCarthy hearings. How does the dialogue emphasize one of Miller's themes?
Answer: Danforth's dialogue here is ironic, and reinforces Miller's theme of grotesque injustices inflicted on innocent citizens. The McCarthy hearings themselves were illegal, because membership in the Communist party was never illegal in the United States.

PARRIS: There is not sufficient time till dawn.

DANFORTH: I shall do my utmost. Which of them do you have hope for?

PARRIS, *not even glancing at the list now, and in a quavering voice, quietly:* Excellency—a dagger—*He chokes up.*

DANFORTH: What do you say?

PARRIS: Tonight, when I open my door to leave my house—a dagger clattered to the ground. *Silence.* DANFORTH *absorbs this. Now* PARRIS *cries out:* You cannot hang this sort. There is danger for me. I dare not step outside at night!

REVEREND HALE *enters. They look at him for an instant in silence. He is steeped in sorrow, exhausted, and more direct than he ever was.*

DANFORTH: Accept my congratulations, Reverend Hale; we are gladdened to see you returned to your good work.

HALE, *coming to* DANFORTH *now:* You must pardon them. They will not budge.

HERRICK *enters, waits.*

DANFORTH, *conciliatory:* You misunderstand, sir; I cannot pardon these when twelve are already hanged for the same crime. It is not just.

PARRIS, *with failing heart:* Rebecca will not confess?

HALE: The sun will rise in a few minutes. Excellency, I must have more time.

⓬ **DANFORTH:** Now hear me, and beguile yourselves no more. I will not receive a single plea for pardon or postponement. Them that will not confess will hang. Twelve are already executed; the names of these seven are given out, and the village expects to see them die this morning. Postponement now speaks a floundering on my part; reprieve or pardon must cast doubt upon the guilt of them that died till now. While I speak God's law, I will not crack its voice with whimpering. If retaliation is your fear, know this—I should hang ten thousand that dared to rise against the law, and an ocean of salt tears could not melt the resolution of the statutes. Now draw yourselves up like men and help me, as you are bound by Heaven to do. Have you spoken with them all, Mr. Hale?

HALE: All but Proctor. He is in the dungeon.

DANFORTH, *to* HERRICK: What's Proctor's way now?

HERRICK: He sits like some great bird; you'd not know he lived except he will take food from time to time.

DANFORTH, *after thinking a moment:* His wife—his wife must be well on with child now.

HERRICK: She is, sir.

DANFORTH: What think you, Mr. Parris? You have closer knowledge of this man; might her presence soften him?

PARRIS: It is possible, sir. He have not laid eyes on her these three months. I should summon her.

DANFORTH, *to* HERRICK: Is he yet adamant? Has he struck at you again?

Vocabulary Builder

conciliatory (kən sil′ ē ə tôr′ ē) *adj.* tending to soothe anger

beguile (bē gīl′) *v.* trick

floundering (floun′ dər iŋ) *n.* awkward struggling

retaliation (ri tal′ ē ā′ shən) *n.* act of returning an injury or wrong

Vocabulary Builder

adamant (ad′ ə mənt) *adj.* firm; unyielding

HERRICK: He cannot, sir, he is chained to the wall now.

DANFORTH, *after thinking on it:* Fetch Goody Proctor to me. Then let you bring him up.

HERRICK: Aye, sir. HERRICK *goes. There is silence.*

HALE: Excellency, if you postpone a week and publish to the town that you are striving for their confessions, that speak mercy on your part, not faltering.

DANFORTH: Mr. Hale, as God have not empowered me like Joshua to stop this sun from rising,[3] so I cannot withhold from them the perfection of their punishment.

HALE, *harder now:* If you think God wills you to raise rebellion, Mr. Danforth, you are mistaken!

DANFORTH, *instantly:* You have heard rebellion spoken in the town?

13 **HALE:** Excellency, there are orphans wandering from house to house; abandoned cattle bellow on the highroads, the stink of rotting crops hangs everywhere, and no man knows when the harlots' cry will end his life—and you wonder yet if rebellion's spoke? Better you should marvel how they do not burn your province!

DANFORTH: Mr. Hale, have you preached in Andover this month?

HALE: Thank God they have no need of me in Andover.

DANFORTH: You baffle me, sir. Why have you returned here?

HALE: Why, it is all simple. I come to do the Devil's work. I come to counsel Christians they should belie themselves. *His sarcasm collapses.* There is blood on my head! Can you not see the blood on my head!!

PARRIS: Hush! *For he has heard footsteps. They all face the door.* HERRICK *enters with* ELIZABETH. *Her wrists are linked by heavy chain, which* HERRICK *now removes. Her clothes are dirty; her face is pale and gaunt.* HERRICK *goes out.*

DANFORTH, *very politely:* Goody Proctor. *She is silent.* I hope you are hearty?

ELIZABETH, *as a warning reminder:* I am yet six month before my time.

DANFORTH: Pray be at your ease, we come not for your life. We— *uncertain how to plead, for he is not accustomed to it.* Mr. Hale, will you speak with the woman?

HALE: Goody Proctor, your husband is marked to hang this morning *Pause.*

ELIZABETH, *quietly:* I have heard it.

HALE: You know, do you not, that I have no connection with the court? *She seems to doubt it.* I come of my own, Goody Proctor. I would save your husband's life, for if he is taken I count myself his murderer. Do you understand me?

Literary Analysis
Theme What themes do these descriptions of abandonment convey?

14 

Reading Check
Why does Hale say he has returned to Salem?

3. **Joshua . . . rising** In the Bible, Joshua, leader of the Jews after the death of Moses, asks God to make the sun and the moon stand still during a battle, and his request is granted.

13 Literary Analysis
Theme

- **Ask** students the Literary Analysis question: What themes do these descriptions of abandonment convey?
  Answer: Persecution of the innocent destroys the society it claims to be protecting.
- What theme does Danforth's refusal to postpone the hangings suggest?
  Answer: It suggests that unjust people, out of fear, shame, or pride, will perpetuate and defend their mistakes.

Monitor Progress: Hale's line, "Better you should marvel how they do not burn your province," is one of the play's many references to fire. Remind students that the play's title refers to a vessel that sits in the fire and holds molten metals or ores. Have the whole class discuss the themes suggested by the play's title.

14 Reading Check

Answer: He says sarcastically that he comes to do the Devil's work. He has actually come to try to save lives.

Differentiated Instruction
Solutions for All Learners

Support for English Learners
Help students understand Hale's motives at this point in the play. Draw a detail web on the chalkboard. Explain that Hale now wants the accused and condemned prisoners to offer false confessions to save themselves. Write the following in the center of the web: *Hale wants the accused to lie to save themselves.* Ask students to find details from this page and the next page that suggest why Hale wants the prisoners to lie, and add these around the center of the web.

Enrichment for Advanced Readers
As students approach the conclusion of *The Crucible,* have them decide which character in the play is the most compelling and write essays identifying and explaining their choices. Students need not choose a character they like or admire; they should choose the one who seems most fully realized, the character who is the most individual and memorable after they have closed the book. Students should explain what makes the character memorable—language? actions? motivations? other qualities?

15 Literary Analysis
Theme

- **Ask** students the Literary Analysis question: What theme or themes does Reverend Hale state in this speech?
  Answer: Hale suggests no principle is worth taking lives for.
- **Ask** students whether they agree with Hale. Why or why not?
  Answer: Students may say that each individual must make this decision for himself or herself. Proctor, for instance, must weigh his obligations to his family and his knowledge of his innocence against his unwillingness to lie. Remind students that to the Puritans, lying was a sin that could mean eternal damnation. The life after death that Puritans hoped for was considered much more important than life on earth; this was the reason Puritans lived so plainly and poorly.

16 Critical Viewing

Answer: They are concerned for each other; each can see that the other has suffered both mentally and physically. They both may feel some guilt over the situation they have helped to create.

ELIZABETH: What do you want of me?

HALE: Goody Proctor, I have gone this three month like our Lord into the wilderness. I have sought a Christian way, for damnation's doubled on a minister who counsels men to lie.

HATHORNE: It is no lie, you cannot speak of lies.

HALE: It is a lie! They are innocent!

DANFORTH: I'll hear no more of that!

HALE, *continuing to* ELIZABETH: Let you not mistake your duty as I mistook my own. I came into this village like a bridegroom to his beloved, bearing gifts of high religion; the very crowns of holy law I brought, and what I touched with my bright confidence, it died; and where I turned the eye of my great faith, blood flowed up. Beware, Goody Proctor—
15 cleave to no faith when faith brings blood. It is mistaken law that leads you to sacrifice. Life, woman, life is God's most precious gift; no principle, however glorious, may justify the taking of it. I beg you, woman, prevail upon your husband to confess. Let him give his lie. Quail not before God's judgment in this, for it may well be God damns a liar less than he that throws his life away for pride. Will you plead with him? I cannot think he will listen to another.

ELIZABETH, *quietly:* I think that be the Devil's argument.

HALE, *with a climactic desperation:* Woman, before the laws of God we are as swine! We cannot read His will!

ELIZABETH: I cannot dispute with you, sir; I lack learning for it.

DANFORTH, *going to her:* Goody Proctor, you are not summoned here for disputation. Be there no wifely tenderness within you? He will die with the sunrise. Your husband. Do you understand it? *She only looks at him.* What say you? Will you contend with him? *She is silent.* Are you stone? I tell you true, woman, had I no other proof of your unnatural life, your dry eyes now would be sufficient evidence that you delivered up your soul to Hell! A very ape would weep at such calamity! Have the devil dried up any tear of pity in you? *She is silent.* Take her out. It profit nothing she should speak to him!

ELIZABETH, *quietly:* Let me speak with him, Excellency.

PARRIS, *with hope:* You'll strive with him? *She hesitates.*

DANFORTH: Will you plead for his confession or will you not?

ELIZABETH: I promise nothing. Let me speak with him.

A sound—the sibilance of dragging feet on stone. They turn. A pause. HERRICK *enters with* JOHN PROCTOR. *His wrists are chained. He is another man, bearded, filthy, his*

Literary Analysis
Theme What theme or themes does Reverend Hale state in this speech?

Vocabulary Builder
cleave (klēv) *v.* adhere; cling

Vocabulary Builder
sibilance (sib′ əl əns) *n.* hissing sound

16 **▼ Critical Viewing**
From this movie still, what emotions do you imagine that John and Elizabeth Proctor are experiencing at this point? **[Infer]**

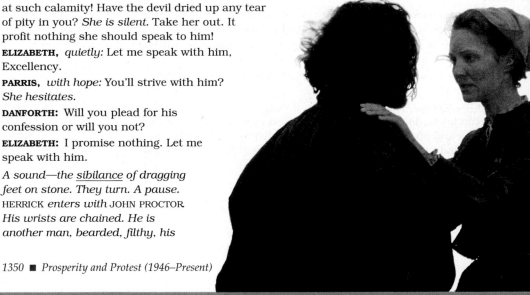

eyes misty as though webs had overgrown them. He halts inside the doorway, his eyes caught by the sight of ELIZABETH. *The emotion flowing between them prevents anyone from speaking for an instant. Now* HALE, *visibly affected, goes to* DANFORTH *and speaks quietly.*

HALE: Pray, leave them Excellency.

DANFORTH, *pressing* HALE *impatiently aside:* Mr. Proctor, you have been notified, have you not? PROCTOR *is silent, staring at* ELIZABETH. I see light in the sky, Mister; let you counsel with your wife, and may God help you turn your back on Hell. PROCTOR *is silent, staring at* ELIZABETH.

HALE, *quietly:* Excellency, let—

DANFORTH *brushes past* HALE *and walks out.* HALE *follows.* CHEEVER *stands and follows,* HATHORNE *behind.* HERRICK *goes.* PARRIS, *from a safe distance, offers:*

PARRIS: If you desire a cup of cider, Mr. Proctor, I am sure I—PROCTOR *turns an icy stare at him, and he breaks off.* PARRIS *raises his palms toward* PROCTOR. God lead you now. PARRIS *goes out.*

Alone, PROCTOR *walks to her, halts. It is as though they stood in a spinning world. It is beyond sorrow, above it. He reaches out his hand as though toward an embodiment not quite real, and as he touches her, a strange soft sound, half laughter, half amazement, comes from his throat. He pats her hand. She covers his hand with hers. And then, weak, he sits. Then she sits, facing him.*

PROCTOR: The child?

ELIZABETH: It grows.

PROCTOR: There is no word of the boys?

ELIZABETH: They're well. Rebecca's Samuel keeps them.

17 **PROCTOR:** You have not seen them?

ELIZABETH: I have not. *She catches a weakening in herself and downs it.*

PROCTOR: You are a—marvel, Elizabeth.

ELIZABETH: You—have been tortured?

PROCTOR: Aye. *Pause. She will not let herself be drowned in the sea that threatens her.* They come for my life now.

ELIZABETH: I know it.

Pause.

PROCTOR: None—have yet confessed?

ELIZABETH: There be many confessed.

PROCTOR: Who are they?

ELIZABETH: There be a hundred or more, they say. Goody Ballard is one; Isaiah Goodkind is one. There be many.

PROCTOR: Rebecca?

ELIZABETH: Not Rebecca. She is one foot in Heaven now; naught may hurt her more.

PROCTOR: And Giles?

ELIZABETH: You have not heard of it?

Literary Analysis
Theme How does Miller's depiction of Elizabeth's attitude and behavior support his theme?

18 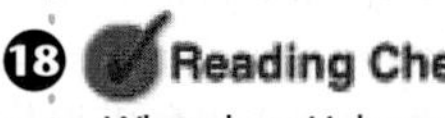
Reading Check
What does Hale urge Elizabeth Proctor to do?

17 Literary Analysis
Theme

- **Ask** students the Literary Analysis question: How does Miller's depiction of Elizabeth's attitude and behavior support his theme?
  Answer: Miller's theme is that honesty and integrity are stronger than any attempt to break them down. Elizabeth shows that she can still triumph over her feelings because she knows herself to be honest.
- Why does John say that Elizabeth is a marvel?
  Answer: He admires her for her self-control given the terrible situation that she is in.

18 Reading Check

Answer: He wants her to persuade John to confess and thus save his own life.

⓳ Literature in Context
Being Abigail Williams

The first film version of *The Crucible* was made in France in 1957 and released the following year in the United States. The film is called *Les sorcieres de Salem* and stars the famous French actors Simone Signoret and Yves Montand as the Proctors. Both actors occasionally appeared in English-language films, notably *Room at the Top* (Signoret won an Academy Award for her performance in this film) and *Grand Prix* (Montand). The French screenplay was written by the philosopher Jean-Paul Sartre.

Connect to the Literature

Ask students their thoughts on the degree of Abigail's malice and how much came from the people around her. Then, **ask** the Connect to the Literature question.

Possible response: Encourage students to give at least two reasons for their answers and then explain each reason.

PROCTOR: I hear nothin', where I am kept.

ELIZABETH: Giles is dead.

He looks at her incredulously.

PROCTOR: When were he hanged?

ELIZABETH, *quietly, factually:* He were not hanged. He would not answer aye or nay to his indictment; for if he denied the charge they'd hang him surely, and auction out his property. So he stand mute, and died Christian under the law. And so his sons will have his farm. It is the law, for he could not be condemned a wizard without he answer the indictment, aye or nay.

PROCTOR: Then how does he die?

ELIZABETH, *gently:* They press him, John.

PROCTOR: Press?

ELIZABETH: Great stones they lay upon his chest until he plead aye or nay. *With a tender smile for the old man:* They say he give them but two words. "More weight," he says. And died.

PROCTOR, *numbed—a thread to weave into his agony:* "More weight."

ELIZABETH: Aye. It were a fearsome man, Giles Corey.

Pause.

PROCTOR, *with great force of will, but not quite looking at her:* I have been thinking I would confess to them, Elizabeth. *She shows nothing.* What say you? If I give them that?

ELIZABETH: I cannot judge you, John.

Pause.

PROCTOR, *simply—a pure question:* What would you have me do?

ELIZABETH: As you will, I would have it. *Slight pause:* I want you living, John. That's sure.

PROCTOR, *pauses, then with a flailing of hope:* Giles' wife? Have she confessed?

ELIZABETH: She will not.

Pause.

PROCTOR: It is a pretense, Elizabeth.

ELIZABETH: What is?

PROCTOR: I cannot mount the gibbet like a saint. It is a fraud. I am not that man. *She is silent.* My honesty is broke, Elizabeth; I am no good man. Nothing's spoiled by giving them this lie that were not rotten long before.

ELIZABETH: And yet you've not confessed till now. That speak goodness in you.

PROCTOR: Spite only keeps me silent. It is hard to give a lie to dogs. *Pause, for the first time he turns directly to her.* I would have your forgiveness, Elizabeth.

Literature in Context

⓳ Media Connection

Being Abigail Williams

For more than four decades, no American film director chose to tackle Arthur Miller's challenging stage drama *The Crucible*. Finally, in 1996, Nicholas Hytner enlisted actors including Winona Ryder, Daniel Day-Lewis, and Joan Allen to star in a film based on a screenplay by Miller himself.

Ryder found playing Abigail Williams engrossing and disturbing. "I've heard Abigail called the villain of the piece, but I'm not so sure," she says. "She's never been given any power. . . . Abigail understands that she could get attention and power, so she goes with it. There's always a part of her that knows she is fooling, but I think she was convinced that spirits were attacking her. I see her as insane in a way, but so is the whole town. It's like a disease."

Connect to the Literature

Do you agree with Ryder's assessment of Abigail? Explain.

Enrichment

Abigail's Explanation

In a scene inserted into *The Crucible* late in its original Broadway run, Abigail explains to Proctor why she will not renounce her testimony:

> It were a fire you walked me through, and all my ignorance were burned away. It were a fire, John, we lay in fire. And from that night no woman dare call me wicked any more but I knew my answer. I used to weep for my sins when the wind lifted up my skirts; and blushed for shame because some old Rebecca called me loose. And then you burned my ignorance away. As bare as some December tree I saw them all—walking like saints to the church, running to feed the sick, and hypocrites in their hearts! And God gave me strength to call them liars, and God made men to listen to me, and by God I will scrub the world clean for the love of Him!

ELIZABETH: It is not for me to give, John, I am—

PROCTOR: I'd have you see some honesty in it. Let them that never lied die now to keep their souls. It is pretense for me, a vanity that will not blind God nor keep my children out of the wind. *Pause.* What say you?

ELIZABETH, *upon a heaving sob that always threatens:* John, it come to naught that I should forgive you, if you'll not forgive yourself. *Now he turns away a little, in great agony.* It is not my soul, John, it is yours. *He stands, as though in physical pain, slowly rising to his feet with a great immortal longing to find his answer. It is difficult to say, and she is on the verge of tears.* Only be sure of this, for I know it now: Whatever you will do, it is a good man does it. *He turns his doubting, searching gaze upon her.* I have read my heart this three month, John. *Pause.* I have sins of my own to count. It needs a cold wife to prompt lechery.

PROCTOR, *in great pain:* Enough, enough—

ELIZABETH, *now pouring out her heart:* Better you should know me!

PROCTOR: I will not hear it! I know you!

ELIZABETH: You take my sins upon you, John—

PROCTOR, *in agony:* No, I take my own, my own!

ELIZABETH: John, I counted myself so plain, so poorly made, no honest love could come to me! Suspicion kissed you when I did; I never knew how I should say my love. It were a cold house I kept! *In fright, she swerves, as* HATHORNE *enters.*

HATHORNE: What say you Proctor? The sun is soon up.

PROCTOR, *his chest heaving, stares, turns to* ELIZABETH. *She comes to him as though to plead, her voice quaking.*

ELIZABETH: Do what you will. But let none be your judge. There be no higher judge under Heaven than Proctor is! Forgive me, forgive me, John—I never knew such goodness in the world! *She covers her face, weeping.*

PROCTOR *turns from her to* HATHORNE*; he is off the earth, his voice hollow.*

PROCTOR: I want my life.

HATHORNE *electrified, surprised:* You'll confess yourself?

PROCTOR: I will have my life.

HATHORNE, *with a mystical tone:* God be praised! It is a providence! *He rushes out the door, and his voice is heard calling down the corridor:* He will confess! Proctor will confess!

PROCTOR, *with a cry, as he strides to the door:* Why do you cry it? *In great pain he turns back to her.* It is evil, is it not? It is evil.

ELIZABETH, *in terror, weeping:* I cannot judge you, John, I cannot!

PROCTOR: Then who will judge me? *Suddenly clasping his hands:* God in Heaven, what is John Proctor, what is John Proctor? *He moves as an animal, and a fury is riding in him, a tantalized search.* I think it is honest, I think so; I am no saint. *As though she had denied this he calls angrily at her:* Let Rebecca go like a saint; for me it is fraud!

Literary Analysis
Theme What theme does Miller convey through John Proctor's statement about honesty?

Vocabulary Builder
tantalized (tan′ tə līzd) *adj.* tormented; frustrated

Reading Check
What sins does Elizabeth think she has committed?

Differentiated Instruction
Solutions for All Learners

Support for Special Needs Students
Help students prepare for the play's climax by reviewing the rise and fall of the play's action. Have students compile lists of the main events of the play, act by act, up to this page. As a class, use the chalkboard to create a graph that shows the rise and fall of the plot. Tell students to write specific examples of events that have led to this crisis. As students read, have them add plot elements that contribute to the denouement, or resolution.

Support for English Learners
Help students understand that this intimate and powerful exchange between John and Elizabeth Proctor leads the audience swiftly toward the play's climax. Help students understand the conflicts faced by the characters. On the chalkboard, draw and label a T-chart headed "What is important to John" and "What is important to Elizabeth." In each column, list an example. Sample: "His wife's forgiveness" and "That John be true to himself." Ask students for additional examples from the play to complete the chart.

20 Literary Analysis
Theme

- Have students paraphrase Proctor's speech (beginning "I'd have you see some honesty . . .").
  Answer: I might as well confess. Even though I would be lying, I have lied before. I need not pretend to be an honest man.
- **Ask** students the Literary Analysis question: What theme does Miller convey through John Proctor's statements about honesty?
  Answer: Miller shows that a man can be a hero in spite of having some flaws. Proctor's integrity is still strong.
- How has Elizabeth changed since her conversation with John in Act II?
  Answer: In Act II, she judged him because of his adultery; now she refuses to judge him. She has learned humility.

21 Vocabulary Builder
Words From Myths

- Draw students' attention to the word *tantalized,* and tell students that words from myths most often are drawn from the names of mythic characters.
- Write the following words on the chalkboard and have students make inferences about their meaning by recalling the myths from which they are derived: *herculean, narcissism, protean.*
  Answers: *Herculean* is an adjective meaning "miraculously strong" and/or "able to accomplish many difficult tasks," as Hercules did in his legendary labors. *Narcissism* is the condition of being preoccupied with the self, like the mythic character Narcissus. *Protean* is an adjective describing things or people who are highly changeable or able to take on many forms or aspects. The word comes from the Greek sea god who could change his shape at will.

22 Reading Check

Answer: She blames herself for coldness toward John.

23 Literature in Context

Comedy and Tragedy In modern times, popular preference seems to be for comedy over tragedy, perhaps as an escape from the terrible events of the world, such as war, poverty, and terrorism. Nevertheless, tragedy on the stage or in film still has the power to provide catharsis—the process in which the viewer or reader becomes emotionally involved and, through the action of the play, is "cleansed" of disturbing emotions.

Connect to the Literature Have students consider what drives the action of *The Crucible* as they answer the question.

Possible responses: *The Crucible* is a tragedy because the major character, who is capable of some degree of greatness, is doomed. John Proctor may be seen as a tragic hero, perhaps because of circumstances beyond his control or perhaps because his pride leads to his death.

24 Literary Analysis
Theme

- **Ask** students the Literary Analysis question: Which details of Rebecca Nurse's character reinforce the theme of courage and personal integrity?
  Answer: her refusal to confess; her pleasure in seeing that Proctor is still alive; her compassion for him when she hears him give a false confession
- Suggest to students that Proctor's confession is doubly ironic; although he believes it to be false, it is actually true. Have them explore this irony and the theme it suggests.
  Answer: Miller suggests throughout the play that the Devil is not a supernatural being; the Devil exists in human beings and is manifested in their pride, avarice, envy, malice, and lies. John has indeed seen the Devil—in Abigail, in the Putnams, in Danforth, and even in himself.

Voices are heard in the hall, speaking together in suppressed excitement.

ELIZABETH: I am not your judge, I cannot be. *As though giving him release:* Do as you will, do as you will!

PROCTOR: Would you give them such a lie? Say it. Would you ever give them this? *She cannot answer.* You would not; if tongs of fire were singeing you you would not! It is evil. Good, then—it is evil, and I do it!

HATHORNE *enters with* DANFORTH, *and, with them,* CHEEVER, PARRIS, *and* HALE. *It is a businesslike, rapid entrance, as though the ice had been broken.*

DANFORTH, *with great relief and gratitude:* Praise to God, man, praise to God; you shall be blessed in Heaven for this. CHEEVER *has hurried to the bench with pen, ink, and paper.* PROCTOR *watches him.* Now then, let us have it. Are you ready, Mr. Cheever?

PROCTOR, *with a cold, cold horror at their efficiency:* Why must it be written?

DANFORTH: Why, for the good instruction of the village, Mister; this we shall post upon the church door! *To* PARRIS, *urgently:* Where is the marshal?

PARRIS, *runs to the door and calls down the corridor:* Marshal! Hurry!

DANFORTH: Now, then, Mister, will you speak slowly, and directly to the point, for Mr. Cheever's sake. *He is on record now, and is really dictating to* CHEEVER, *who writes.* Mr. Proctor, have you seen the Devil in your life? PROCTOR'S *jaws lock.* Come, man, there is light in the sky; the town waits at the scaffold; I would give out this news. Did you see the Devil?

PROCTOR: I did.

PARRIS: Praise God!

DANFORTH: And when he come to you, what were his demand?

PROCTOR *is silent.* DANFORTH *helps.* Did he bid you to do his work upon the earth?

PROCTOR: He did.

DANFORTH: And you bound yourself to his service? DANFORTH *turns, as* REBECCA *Nurse enters, with* HERRICK *helping to support her. She is barely able to walk.* Come in, come in, woman!

REBECCA, *brightening as she sees* PROCTOR: Ah, John! You are well, then, eh?

PROCTOR *turns his face to the wall.*

24 **DANFORTH:** Courage, man, courage—let her witness your good example that she may come to God herself. Now hear it, Goody Nurse! Say on, Mr. Proctor. Did you bind yourself to the Devil's service?

REBECCA, *astonished:* Why, John!

Literature in Context

Comedy and Tragedy

Ever since the development of Western drama in ancient Greece, plays have been divided into two broad categories. A **comedy** is a play that has a happy ending. Comedies often show ordinary characters in conflict with society—conflicts that arise from misunderstandings, deceptions, disapproving parents, or mistaken identities.

A **tragedy** is a play that shows the downfall or death of the main character, or **tragic hero.** In ancient Greek tragedy, the hero is always a noble or outstanding person, such as a king. The tragic hero's downfall is caused by a **tragic flaw:** an error or unwise decision. Sometimes this mistake is the result of an innate character weakness, such as excessive pride. However, the error may instead result from circumstances beyond the hero's control.

In modern tragedy, the main character is usually an ordinary person. The cause of the tragedy might be a character flaw, but it may instead be some weakness or evil in society itself.

Connect to the Literature

Do you think *The Crucible* is a tragedy? If so, who is the tragic hero, and what causes this character's downfall?

Literary Analysis
Theme Which details of Rebecca Nurse's character reinforce the theme of courage and personal integrity?

PROCTOR, *through his teeth, his face turned from* REBECCA: I did.

DANFORTH: Now, woman, you surely see it profit nothin' to keep this conspiracy any further. Will you confess yourself with him?

REBECCA: Oh, John—God send his mercy on you!

DANFORTH: I say, will you confess yourself, Goody Nurse?

REBECCA: Why, it is a lie, it is a lie; how may I damn myself? I cannot, I cannot.

DANFORTH: Mr. Proctor. When the Devil came to you did you see Rebecca Nurse in his company? PROCTOR *is silent.* Come, man, take courage—did you ever see her with the Devil?

PROCTOR, *almost inaudibly:* No.

DANFORTH, *now sensing trouble, glances at* JOHN *and goes to the table, and picks up a sheet—the list of condemned.*

DANFORTH: Did you ever see her sister, Mary Easty, with the Devil?

PROCTOR: No, I did not.

DANFORTH, *his eyes narrow on* PROCTOR: Did you ever see Martha Corey with the Devil?

PROCTOR: I did not.

DANFORTH, *realizing, slowly putting the sheet down:* Did you ever see anyone with the Devil?

PROCTOR: I did not.

DANFORTH: Proctor, you mistake me. I am not empowered to trade your life for a lie. You have most certainly seen some person with the Devil. PROCTOR *is silent.* Mr. Proctor, a score of people have already testified they saw this woman with the Devil.

PROCTOR: Then it is proved. Why must I say it?

DANFORTH: Why "must" you say it! Why, you should rejoice to say it if your soul is truly purged of any love for Hell!

PROCTOR: They think to go like saints. I like not to spoil their names.

DANFORTH, *inquiring, incredulous:* Mr. Proctor, do you think they go like saints?

PROCTOR, *evading:* This woman never thought she done the Devil's work.

DANFORTH: Look you, sir. I think you mistake your duty here. It matter nothing what she thought—she is convicted of the unnatural murder of children, and you for sending your spirit out upon Mary Warren. Your soul alone is the issue here, Mister, and you will prove its whiteness or you cannot live in a Christian country. Will you tell me now what persons conspired with you in the Devil's company? PROCTOR *is silent.* To your knowledge was Rebecca Nurse ever—

25 **PROCTOR:** I speak my own sins; I cannot judge another. *Crying out, with hatred:* I have no tongue for it.

HALE, *quickly to* DANFORTH: Excellency, it is enough he confess himself. Let him sign it, let him sign it.

PARRIS, *feverishly:* It is a great service, sir. It is a weighty name; it will strike the village that Proctor confess. I beg you, let him sign it. The sun is up, Excellency! 26

Vocabulary Builder
purged (purjd) *v.* cleansed

Literary Analysis
Theme and Extended Metaphor How might Proctor's refusal to incriminate others relate to the McCarthy hearings of the 1950s?

Reading Check
What does Danforth want Proctor to do?

25 Literary Analysis
Theme and Extended Metaphor

- **Ask** students the Literary Analysis question: How might Proctor's refusal to incriminate others relate to the McCarthy hearings of the 1950s?
  Answer: Many witnesses for the House Committee on Un-American Activities showed the same courage as Proctor and refused to name others.
- What theme does Proctor's cry, "I cannot judge another," suggest?
  Answer: Miller suggests that judging others is intrinsically wrong, that people should show compassion and understanding and not be quick to condemn. The actual judges in the play are criminals because they condemn the innocent to death.

26 Reading Check

Answer: He wants him to name the people he saw with the Devil and then to sign his confession.

Differentiated Instruction
Solutions for All Learners

Strategy for Advanced Readers
Suggest that students compose position statements—a statement of opinion about an issue—from various characters' points of view, describing the cause of the deaths at Salem. The statement should evince a thorough knowledge of the play, and include relevant, specific supporting details. Suggest that students write in the voice of Elizabeth Proctor to her husband, in John Proctor's voice to the family and friends he leaves behind, or in Hale's voice to church authorities.

Enrichment for Gifted/Talented Students
Have students imagine that they have just been in the audience for a performance of *The Crucible* and have to review it for the next day's paper. Remind them that their reviews should give their opinions of the piece, discuss the ideas and issues it raises, and explain why they do or do not recommend it to theatergoers. Students might enjoy looking up some of the reviews that were published at the time the play first opened on Broadway; these will give them some idea of the kinds of questions they should address.

27 Reading Strategy
Applying Themes to Contemporary Events

- **Ask** students the Reading Strategy question: Which notorious aspect of the McCarthy hearings might Miller be suggesting here? **Answer:** Miller alludes to those who betrayed their friends and acquaintances by naming names to the HUAC.
- Have students continue reading through Proctor's speech beginning "Because it is my name!" on the right-hand page. **Ask** what theme is suggested by his insistence on keeping his name private. **Answer:** Proctor equates his name with himself—with his identity. His name symbolizes who he is. The honor of his name is a deeply personal thing and he is unwilling to betray it.

DANFORTH, *considers; then with dissatisfaction:* Come, then, sign your testimony. *To* CHEEVER: Give it to him. CHEEVER *goes to* PROCTOR, *the confession and a pen in hand.* PROCTOR *does not look at it.* Come, man, sign it.

PROCTOR, *after glancing at the confession:* You have all witnessed it—it is enough.

DANFORTH: You will not sign it?

PROCTOR: You have all witnessed it; what more is needed?

DANFORTH: Do you sport with me? You will sign your name or it is no confession, Mister! *His breast heaving with agonized breathing,* PROCTOR *now lays the paper down and signs his name.*

PARRIS: Praise be to the Lord!

PROCTOR *has just finished signing when* DANFORTH *reaches for the paper. But* PROCTOR *snatches it up, and now a wild terror is rising in him, and a boundless anger.*

DANFORTH, *perplexed, but politely extending his hand:* If you please, sir.

PROCTOR: No.

DANFORTH, *as though* PROCTOR *did not understand:* Mr. Proctor, I must have—

PROCTOR: No, no. I have signed it. You have seen me. It is done! You have no need for this.

PARRIS: Proctor, the village must have proof that—

PROCTOR: Damn the village! I confess to God, and God has seen my name on this! It is enough!

DANFORTH: No, sir, it is—

PROCTOR: You came to save my soul, did you not? Here! I have confessed myself; it is enough!

DANFORTH: You have not con—

PROCTOR: I have confessed myself! Is there no good penitence but it be public? God does not need my name nailed upon the church! God sees my name; God knows how black my sins are! It is enough!

DANFORTH: Mr. Proctor—

PROCTOR: You will not use me! I am no Sarah Good or Tituba, I am John Proctor! You will not use me! It is no part of salvation that you should use me!

DANFORTH: I do not wish to—

27 **PROCTOR:** I have three children—how may I teach them to walk like men in the world, and I sold my friends?

DANFORTH: You have not sold your friends—

PROCTOR: Beguile me not! I blacken all of them when this is nailed to the church the very day they hang for silence!

DANFORTH: Mr. Proctor, I must have good and legal proof that you—

PROCTOR: You are the high court, your word is good enough! Tell them I confessed myself; say Proctor broke his knees and wept like a woman; say what you will, but my name cannot—

Reading Strategy
Applying Themes to Contemporary Events
Which notorious aspect of the McCarthy hearings might Miller be suggesting here?

Enrichment

What Happened Afterward

The following is the text of Miller's brief end note to *The Crucible,* titled "Echoes Down the Corridor."

Not long after the fever died, Parris was voted from office, walked out on the highroad, and was never seen again.

The legend has it that Abigail turned up later as a prostitute in Boston.

Twenty years after the last execution, the government awarded compensation to the victims still living, and to the families of the dead. However, it is evident that some people still were unwilling to admit their total guilt, and also that the factionalism was still alive, for some beneficiaries were actually not victims at all but informers.

(continued on the next page)

DANFORTH, *with suspicion:* It is the same, is it not? If I report it or you sign to it?

PROCTOR *—he knows it is insane:* No, it is not the same! What others say and what I sign to is not the same!

DANFORTH: Why? Do you mean to deny this confession when you are free?

PROCTOR: I mean to deny nothing!

DANFORTH: Then explain to me, Mr. Proctor, why you will not let—

PROCTOR, *with a cry of his whole soul:* Because it is my name! Because I cannot have another in my life! Because I lie and sign myself to lies! Because I am not worth the dust on the feet of them that hang! How may I live without my name? I have given you my soul; leave me my name!

DANFORTH, *pointing at the confession in* PROCTOR'S *hand*: Is that document a lie? If it is a lie I will not accept it! What say you? I will not deal in lies, Mister! PROCTOR *is motionless.* You will give me your honest confession in my hand, or I cannot keep you from the rope. PROCTOR *does not reply.* What way do you go, Mister?

His breast heaving, his eyes staring, PROCTOR *tears the paper and crumples it, and he is weeping in fury, but erect.*

DANFORTH: Marshal!

PARRIS, *hysterically, as though the tearing paper were his life:* Proctor, Proctor!

HALE: Man, you will hang! You cannot!

PROCTOR, *his eyes full of tears:* I can. And there's your first marvel, that I can. You have made your magic now, for now I do think I see some shred of goodness in John Proctor. Not enough to weave a banner with, but white enough to keep it from such dogs. ELIZABETH, *in a burst of terror, rushes to him and weeps against his hand.* Give them no tear! Tears pleasure them! Show honor now, show a stony heart and sink them with it! *He has lifted her, and kisses her now with great passion.*

REBECCA: Let you fear nothing! Another judgment waits us all!

DANFORTH: Hang them high over the town! Who weeps for these, weeps for corruption! *He sweeps out past them.* HERRICK *starts to lead* REBECCA, *who almost collapses, but* PROCTOR *catches her, and she glances up at him apologetically.*

REBECCA: I've had no breakfast.

28  **Critical Viewing** Judge Danforth says, "He who weeps for these weeps for corruption." What do you think the people surrounding the condemned are thinking? **[Analyze]**

Literary Analysis
Theme In what way does Proctor's change of heart reflect the themes of integrity and courage?

30  **Reading Check**
What decision does John Proctor finally make?

28 Critical Viewing

Answer: They look upset. They probably feel guilty, ashamed, and horrified.

29 Literary Analysis

Theme

- Remind students that at the end of Act II, Proctor tore up the warrant for Elizabeth's arrest. Here he repeats the same action. Have students **comment** on this repetition and on the theme it suggests.
  Answer: Students should say that the papers Proctor tears up are not just papers; they have a symbolic power. He tried to destroy the court's power in Act II by ripping up the warrant, but Elizabeth was arrested anyway. Here he tears up the confession and succeeds in destroying its power. The theme suggests that the truth will be revealed and that it is always stronger than the forces that try to destroy it.
- **Ask** students the Literary Analysis question: In what way does Proctor's change of heart reflect the themes of integrity and courage?
  Answer: Proctor agrees to die as an honest man rather than to live as a liar and a traitor to his friends and his conscience.

30 Reading Check

Answer: He decides to go to his death rather than lie.

Enrichment

What Happened Afterward
(continued from previous page)

Elizabeth Proctor married again, four years after Proctor's death.

In solemn meeting, the congregation rescinded the excommunications—this in March, 1712. But they did so upon orders of the government. The jury, however, wrote a statement praying forgiveness of all who had suffered.

Certain farms which had belonged to the victims were left to ruin, and for more than a century no one would buy them or live on them.

To all intents and purposes, the power of theocracy in Massachusetts was broken.

31 Author's Insight

Have students read Arthur Miller's comment. **Ask:** What does his comment imply about his attitude toward the events that inspired *The Crucible*?

Possible response: Although the events were tragic because of the loss of innocent lives, he believes that in a sense they were "absurd." Looking back on the situation now, one can see that many people were simply caught in the hysteria of the situation and took it to absurd lengths.

ASSESS

Answers

1. (a) Students will probably be sad that Proctor dies. (b) Make sure students support their answers.
2. (a) Hale, Parris, and Danforth (b) Hale wants to save their lives; Parris wants them to confess because this will swing the town's sympathies back toward the court; Danforth wants their confessions to justify the entire proceedings.
3. (a) She steals Parris's savings and runs away. (b) She probably realized, like Parris, that the mood of the town no longer supported the court and that she was the most likely to suffer from this reaction since she was the greatest troublemaker.
4. (a) Proctor must choose between death and lying. (b) She wants him to live but knows in her heart that lying would be wrong.
5. (a) for falsely naming others as witches (b) He truly wants to live, but he renounces the confession when he realizes that he doesn't want to live as a dishonored man.
6. She believes that he did the right thing—he dies with honor.
7. Make sure students support their answers.

Go Online Author Link For additional information about Arthur Miller, have students type in the Web Code, then select M from the alphabet, and then select Arthur Miller.

HERRICK: Come, man.

HERRICK *escorts them out,* ATHORNE *and* CHEEVER *behind them.* ELIZABETH *stands staring at the empty doorway.*

PARRIS, *in deadly fear, to* ELIZABETH: Go to him, Goody Proctor! There is yet time!

From outside a drumroll strikes the air. PARRIS *is startled.* ELIZABETH *jerks about toward the window.*

PARRIS: Go to him! *He rushes out the door, as though to hold back his fate.* Proctor! Proctor!

Again, a short burst of drums.

HALE: Woman, plead with him! *He starts to rush out the door, and then goes back to her.* Woman! It is pride, it is vanity. *She avoids his eyes, and moves to the window. He drops to his knees.* Be his helper!—What profit him to bleed? Shall the dust praise him? Shall the worms declare his truth? Go to him, take his shame away! 31

ELIZABETH, *supporting herself against collapse, grips the bars of the window, and with a cry:* He have his goodness now. God forbid I take it from him!

The final drumroll crashes, then heightens violently. HALE *weeps in frantic prayer, and the new sun is pouring in upon her face, and the drums rattle like bones in the morning air.*

THE CURTAIN FALLS

Arthur Miller
Author's Insight
Miller once wrote about how *The Crucible* might have been a different kind of play entirely: "I am glad, of course, that I managed to write *The Crucible*, but looking back I have often wished I'd had the temperament to have done an absurd comedy, since that is what the situation often deserved."

Critical Reading

1. **(a) Respond:** How did you react to the ending of the play? **(b) Extend:** Would you recommend the play to a friend? Why or why not?
2. **(a) Recall:** Who seeks confessions from Rebecca Nurse and other condemned prisoners? **(b) Infer:** What motivates this person—or people—to seek these confessions?
3. **(a) Recall:** What unexpected action does Abigail take in this act? **(b) Draw Conclusions:** Why do you think she does this?
4. **(a) Recall:** What decision torments John Proctor? **(b) Interpret:** What conflict does Elizabeth experience as her husband seeks her guidance?
5. **(a) Recall:** What does John Proctor have "no tongue for"? **(b) Analyze:** Why does Proctor confess and then retract his confession?
6. **Interpret:** Why does Elizabeth say her husband has "his goodness" as he is about to be hanged?
7. **Evaluate:** Do you think John Proctor made the right decision? Why or why not?

For: More about Arthur Miller
Visit: www.PHSchool.com
Web Code: ere-9635

Apply the Skills

The Crucible, Act IV

Literary Analysis

Theme

1. Use evidence from the play to show how Arthur Miller conveys the **theme** that fear and suspicion are infectious and can produce a mass hysteria that destroys public order and rationality.
2. Cite evidence from the play that supports the theme that it is more noble to die with integrity than to live with compromised principles that harm others.
3. **(a)** In what ways do Hale's reactions to events compare to those of the other ministers and court officers? **(b)** What do these differences suggest about the ideas of integrity, pride, and vanity?
4. State and support another theme that you believe is central to the meaning of the play.

Connecting Literary Elements

5. Using a chart like the one shown, cite examples from the text that show how ideas such as witchcraft and "the work of the Devil" function in *The Crucible* as **extended metaphors** for Communism.

Passage From the Text	How It Relates to Communism

6. **(a)** What does the ending of the play suggest about the value of integrity and of holding fast to principles? **(b)** How might this idea relate to the McCarthy era?

Reading Strategy

Applying Themes to Contemporary Events

7. Based on the play's details, what criticisms might Miller be making about the way McCarthy's Senate committee dealt with those it questioned and those who criticized it?
8. What does the play suggest about the motives behind Senator Joseph McCarthy's political "witch hunts"? Explain.

Extend Understanding

9. **Social Studies Connection:** Given the nation's experience with McCarthyism, do you think a tragedy like the Salem witchcraft trials could occur today? Explain.

QuickReview

A **theme** is a central idea or insight about life revealed by a literary work.

An **extended metaphor** is a comparison that is developed through the course of a literary work.

To **apply a theme to a contemporary event,** draw a parallel between the central idea of a story and a current event.

Go Online Assessment

For: Self-test
Visit: www.PHSchool.com
Web Code: era-6623

Students may use the **Self-test** to prepare for **Selection Test A** or **Selection Test B**.

Answers

1. The children feign illness in Act I because they fear punishment. Parris calls in Hale because he fears his enemies. John fails to denounce Abigail because he fears admitting to adultery. The fearful actions of the characters fuel the suspicions of witchcraft that drive events.
2. Rebecca, Giles, and Proctor are the good characters. They are honest, direct, and likable people.
3. (a) Hale's reactions, from Act I when he believes witchcraft to be present in Salem to Act IV when he knows that he has been wrong, are honest. He has no ulterior motives, as do the other men. (b) Although pride and vanity may prompt people to persecute others, even an honest man who makes a mistake can do great harm.
4. Answers will vary. Make sure students support their choice with evidence from the text.
5. **Possible answers: Passage from the Text:** Danforth's questioning of Proctor ("When the Devil came to you did you see Rebecca Nurse in his company? . . . Did you ever see her sister Mary Easty . . . ? Did you ever see Martha Corey . . . ?") **How it Relates to Communism:** During the 1950s, many Americans feared Communism. They saw it as a secret force infiltrating American society. Details about witchcraft and the Devil in *The Crucible* suggest a similar idea of a secret evil engineered to penetrate the very fabric of society.
6. (a) The ending suggests that integrity is more important than any other virtue. (b) It suggests that those who withstood the pressures of the McCarthy era were heroes.
7. Committee members, like the Salem judges, presumed guilt and accepted accusation as proof.
8. McCarthy probably acted out of base motives, just as HUAC did.
9. Students may say no because there are so many journalists and commentators that it is unlikely that something of the kind could continue. Others may say that other "witch hunts" have taken place since the 1950s.

EXTEND/ASSESS

Answers

❶ Vocabulary Lesson

Concept Development

Sample sentences are given.

1. Cereals are made from grains.
2. *Titanic* was the perfect name for the largest, strongest, fastest-moving ship ever built.
3. A narcissistic person's favorite possession is his or her mirror.

Spelling Strategy

1. basting
2. purify
3. serenity

Vocabulary Builder

1. b	6. c
2. a	7. c
3. b	8. a
4. a	9. b
5. c	10. b

❷ Grammar and Style Lesson

1. rose
2. raising
3. raised
4. risen
5. raised

Writing Application

Have students check one another's paragraphs.

WG Writing and Grammar, Ruby Level

Students will find further instruction and practice on commonly confused words in Chapter 21, Section 1.

Build Language Skills

❶ Vocabulary Lesson

Concept Development: Words From Myths

The word *tantalize* comes from the Greek myth about Tantalus a man tormented by the gods. Review the list of mythological figures below. Write a sentence for each, using the word in parentheses.

1. Ceres: The goddess of the harvest (*cereal*)
2. Titan: A race of giants with brute strength (*titanic*)
3. Narcissus: A boy punished by the gods for vanity (*narcissistic*)

Spelling Strategy

When you add a suffix beginning with a vowel to a word that ends in a silent *e*, drop the *e* before adding the suffix. For example, *tantalize* + *-ing* = *tantalizing*. For each word below, add the suffix indicated.

1. baste (*-ing*) **2.** pure (*-ify*) **3.** serene (*-ity*)

Vocabulary Builder: Synonyms

Select the letter of the word that is the closest in meaning to the first word.

1. agape: **(a)** dark, **(b)** open, **(c)** shocking
2. conciliatory: **(a)** soothing, **(b)** rude, **(c)** vengeful
3. beguile: **(a)** plead, **(b)** fool, **(c)** straighten
4. floundering: **(a)** groping, **(b)** jogging, **(c)** smelling
5. retaliation: **(a)** narration, **(b)** restatement, **(c)** revenge
6. adamant: **(a)** calm, **(b)** first, **(c)** stubborn
7. cleave: **(a)** depart, **(b)** grow, **(c)** adhere
8. sibilance: **(a)** hissing, **(b)** humming, **(c)** screaming
9. tantalized: **(a)** freed, **(b)** tempted, **(c)** danced
10. purged: **(a)** soothed, **(b)** washed, **(c)** filled

❷ Grammar and Style Lesson

Commonly Confused Words: *raise* and *rise*

Some words in English sound similar but function differently. For example, to ***raise*** means "to lift up"; it takes a direct object (a noun or pronoun that receives the action of the verb). To ***rise*** means "to go up or get up," and it does not take a direct object.

Verb	Present	Present Participle	Past	Past Participle
raise	raise, raises	raising	raised	(have) raised
rise	rise, rises	rising	rose	(have) risen

Practice Complete each sentence with the correct form of *rise* or *raise* in the tense indicated.

1. All *(past)* when the judge entered.
2. They were *(present participle)* the flag outside the courthouse.
3. Cries of witchcraft *(past)* a ruckus.
4. Spirits were reported to have *(past participle)* to the courtroom ceiling.
5. Citizens had *(past participle)* a rebellion.

Writing Application Write a paragraph in which you use the verbs *raise* and *rise* correctly.

WG Prentice Hall Writing and Grammar Connection: Chapter 21, Section 1

Assessment Practice

Punctuation **(For more practice, see *Standardized Test Preparation Workbook*, p. 70.)**

Many tests require students to identify errors in punctuation. Use this following sample test item.

PROCTOR You have all witnessed it; what more is needed

With which punctuation mark should you end this sentence?

A question mark **C** exclamation mark
B period **D** comma

"What more is needed" is a question; the correct answer is *A*.

3 Writing Lesson

Timed Writing: Defense of a Character's Actions

Write an essay in which you defend the actions of an accused character in *The Crucible.* Like a good trial lawyer, you need not agree with your client's actions, but you must present the best defense possible to prove why he or she should not be found guilty. ***(40 minutes)***

Prewriting *(10 minutes)* Skim the play to decide which character's actions you will defend. Record possible "pros" and "cons" in a two-column chart. You might discuss the character with others to come up with as complete a list of pros and cons as possible.

Model: Analyzing the Evidence

"Pros"	"Cons"
He is honest.	He angers quickly.
He is trustworthy.	He made a mistake.
He is loyal.	He is stubborn.

Drafting *(20 minutes)* Begin by presenting the negative aspects of your character's actions. Then, move on to the positive aspects. In each case, cite specific evidence from the play. Use forceful, persuasive language to explain why the pros outweigh the cons.

Revising *(10 minutes)* Make sure you have effectively refuted the negatives and included enough positive ideas to support the defense. Also, be sure that your word choice is clear, precise, and persuasive.

WG *Prentice Hall Writing and Grammar Connection: Chapter 7, Section 2*

Extend Your Learning

Listening and Speaking Stage a **mock trial** to determine whether Danforth and Hathorne are guilty of murder for their roles in the Salem witch trials. Appoint a prosecutor, a defense attorney, defendants, witnesses, a jury, and a fair judge. Consider the following:

- Select prosecution and defense witnesses.
- Have both the defense attorney and the prosecutor give summations.

Present the trial to the class. **[Group Activity]**

Research and Technology Research the facts of the Salem witchcraft trials. Then, present a **comparison-and-contrast chart,** listing differences between the trials and the events in this play. For each difference, provide reasons Miller might have had for making those changes.

For: An additional research activity
Visit: www.PHSchool.com
Web Code: erd-7619

3 Writing Lesson

You may use this Writing Lesson as timed-writing practice, or you may allow students to develop the essay as a writing assignment over several days.

- Give students the **Support for Writing Lesson,** p. 395 in ***Unit 6 Resources,*** to use as they write their essays.
- Encourage students to try to defend Parris, Abigail, or one of the other less sympathetic or heroic characters.
- Guide students to use the Writing Lesson to complete their essays.
- Use the Persuasion: Persuasive Speech rubrics in ***General Resources,*** pp. 45–46, to evaluate students' essays.

4 Research and Technology

- Remind students that Miller had access to the Salem court records and that, in some places, he quotes verbatim from the transcripts.
- Have students consider why Miller made certain changes. You might tell them, for example, that Miller raised Abigail's age (the real Abigail was probably about 14) and invented the affair between her and John Proctor. How would the removal of this aspect of the play change it?
- Use the rubric for Speaking: Delivering a Research presentation, p. 92 in ***General Resources,*** to evaluate students' work.

The **Support for Extend Your Learning** page (***Unit 6 Resources,*** p. 396) provides guided note-taking opportunities to help students complete the Extend Your Learning activities.

Go Online Research Have students type in the Web Code for another research activity.

Assessment Resources

The following resources can be used to assess students' knowledge and skills.

Unit 6 Resources
- **Selection Test A,** pp. 398–400
- **Selection Test B,** pp. 401–403
- **Benchmark Test 12,** pp. 411–416

General Resources
- **Rubrics for Persuasion: Persuasive Essay,** pp. 45–46
- **Rubric for Speaking: Delivering a Research Presentation,** p. 92

Go Online Assessment Students may use the **Self-test** to prepare for **Selection Test A** or **Selection Test B.**

Benchmark
Administer **Benchmark Test 12.** If the Benchmark Test reveals that some students need further work, use the **Interpretation Guide** to determine the appropriate reteaching pages in the **Reading Kit** or on **Success Tracker.**

Meeting Your Standards

1. understand the connection between a critical review and the work about which it is written.
2. compare and contrast two critical reviews.

See Teacher Express™/Lesson View for a detailed lesson plan for Reading Informational Materials.

About Critical Reviews

- Have students read "About Critical Reviews."
- Encourage students to discuss any critical reviews that they have read. Most likely they have read film and music reviews. Have them describe how the reviews influenced their decisions to view a performance or purchase a product.
- Go over the elements of a critical review. **Ask** which part of a critical review is most important to readers. **Answer:** Students will likely say that the opinions in the review are most important.

Reading Strategy
Comparing and Contrasting Critical Reviews

- Remind students that people will have different opinions about the same performances or products. **Ask** why it is wise to read more than one review of an item. **Answer:** Reading several reviews will supply a range of opinions, which helps readers make more informed decisions.
- Review with students the chart for critical reviews.
- Explain that the chart provides elements of the play that each reviewer commented upon. Students can use the chart to note how each reviewer approached and responded to each element.
- Suggest that students copy the chart onto paper and complete it as they read.

Reading Informational Materials

Critical Reviews

About Critical Reviews

A **critical review** is an analysis and evaluation of a work of literature, art, or culture: a book, play, movie, concert, dance performance, art exhibit, or even a consumer product such as a car or video game. As the name suggests, a critical review usually contains strong opinions about the work it is evaluating. However, the word *critical* can signal either a positive or a negative judgment, and reviews often include a mixture of both. Most critical reviews contain these elements:

- a brief summary of the subject matter, including facts about the work
- carefully thought-out, clearly expressed opinions
- supporting evidence and reasons to back up these opinions

The purpose of a critical review is to persuade readers to accept the validity of the reviewer's opinions. As a result, effective critical reviews feature both strong arguments and powerful, persuasive language.

Reading Strategy

Comparing and Contrasting Critical Reviews

Reviewers and critics often have different opinions about the same work or even the same performance of a work—with convincing reasons to back up their judgments. Whenever possible, read several critical reviews on the same subject, looking for points of agreement and disagreement. Compare the reviews to see where the critics share the same opinions. Then, contrast the reviews to see the ways in which their opinions differ.

Comparing and contrasting critical reviews will help you gain enough insight and objectivity to make your own decisions, rather than accepting one reviewer's evaluation as the only possible perspective.

The writers of the following critical reviews saw the same play, *The Crucible*, by Arthur Miller (page 1257). However, the first reviewer, Brooks Atkinson, saw the original Broadway production in 1953. The second reviewer, Howard Kissel, saw a recent New York revival. Each critic was responding not only to the merits of the play itself, but also to the specific performance he saw. To compare and contrast their overall evaluations, complete a chart like the one shown.

Critical Reviews

Critic	Brooks Atkinson	Howard Kissel
Script		
Leading Actors/Actresses		
Other Actors/Actresses		
Director, Sets, Costumes, Lighting		
Overall Evaluation (+ or –)		

Differentiated Instruction Solutions for All Learners

Reading Support

Give students reading support with the appropriate version of the ***Reader's Notebooks:***

Reader's Notebook [L2, L3]

Reader's Notebook: Adapted Version [L1, L2]

Reader's Notebook: English Learner's Version [EL]

The New York Times

January 23, 1953

The Crucible

By Brooks Atkinson

Arthur Miller has written another powerful play. *The Crucible*, it is called, and it opened at the Martin Beck last evening in an equally powerful performance. Riffling back the pages of American history, he has written the drama of the witch trials and hangings in Salem in 1692. Neither Mr. Miller nor his audiences are unaware of certain similarities between the perversions of justice then and today.

Atkinson begins by presenting his overall opinion of both the play and the performance. He then provides historical content about the play's subject matter.

But Mr. Miller is not pleading a cause in dramatic form. For *The Crucible*, despite its current implications, is a self-contained play about a terrible period in American history. Silly accusations of witchcraft by some mischievous girls in Puritan dress gradually take possession of Salem. Before the play is over good people of pious nature and responsible temper are condemning other good people to the gallows.

Having a sure instinct for dramatic form, Mr. Miller goes bluntly to essential situations. John Proctor and his wife, farm people, are the central characters of the play. At first the idea that Goodie Proctor is a witch is only an absurd rumor. But *The Crucible* carries the Proctors through the whole ordeal—first vague suspicion, then the arrest, the implacable, highly wrought trial in the church vestry, the final opportunity for John Proctor to save his neck by confessing to something he knows is a lie, and finally the baleful roll of the drums at the foot of the gallows.

This paragraph provides a brief plot summary.

Although *The Crucible* is a powerful drama, it stands second to *Death of a Salesman* as a work of art. Mr. Miller has had more trouble with this one, perhaps because he is too conscious of its implications. The literary style is cruder. . . .

Atkinson argues that *The Crucible* is not as good as one of Miller's previous plays.

It may be that Mr. Miller . . . has permitted himself to be concerned more with the technique of the witch hunt than with its humanity. For all its power generated on the surface, *The Crucible* is most moving in the simple, quiet scenes between John Proctor and his wife. By the standards of *Death of a Salesman*, there is too much excitement and not enough emotion in *The Crucible*.

As the director, Jed Harris has given it a driving performance in which the clashes are fierce and clamorous. Inside Boris Aronson's gaunt, pitiless sets of rude buildings, the acting is at a high pitch of bitterness, anger and fear. As the patriarchal deputy Governor, Walter Hampden gives one of his most vivid performances in which righteousness and ferocity are unctuously mated. Fred Stewart as a vindictive parson, E. G. Marshall as a parson who finally rebels at the indiscriminate ruthlessness of the trial, Jean Adair as an aging woman of God . . . all give able performances.

As John Proctor and his wife, Arthur Kennedy and Beatrice Straight have the most attractive roles in the drama. . . . They are superb—Mr. Kennedy clear and resolute, full of fire, searching his own mind; Miss Straight, reserved, detached, above and beyond the contention. Like all the members of the cast, they are dressed in the chaste and lovely costumes Edith Lutyens has designed from old prints of early Massachusetts.

This evaluation of the leading actor and the leading actress is extremely positive.

After the experience of *Death of a Salesman* we probably expect Mr. Miller to write a masterpiece every time. *The Crucible* is not of that stature and it lacks that universality. On a lower level of dramatic history with considerable pertinence for today, it is a powerful play and a genuine contribution to the season.

The reviewer concludes by stating his mixed evaluation of the play.

Reading Critical Reviews

- Tell students that many people use the information in a critical review to decide whether to see a play or a film.
- Have students read the review of *The Crucible* by Brooks Atkinson and the side notes.
- **Ask** students to summarize Atkinson's opinion of the play and its presentation.
  Answer: Atkinson thinks that the play is good but not as good as *Death of a Salesman*. Although *The Crucible* has historical significance, it lacks the earlier play's universality. He thinks that the production itself is worthwhile, but not wonderful.
- Remind students that critical reviews often contain opinions about details. **Ask** students for examples of details about which Atkinson provides an opinion.
  Answers: He evaluates the actors' performances and costumes.

continued on page 1364

Differentiated Instruction

Solutions for All Learners

Strategy for Less Proficient Readers

Students may need help understanding the relationship between an opinion and how it is supported in a review. Have students create an outline or make a chart of the major opinions in each of the reviews. Underneath each opinion, have students summarize the evidence, or support, that the writer includes. Point out that the writer forms an opinion and creates support, using details from the play.

Support for English Learners

Guide students through the first three noted passages, asking them to pause and look at these words that they may find unfamiliar: *crucible, vestry,* and *gallows*. Have students predict what these words mean before writing these definitions on the board. Have students compare their original definitions with the actual definitions. Once they understand the meaning of each word, have them restate the main ideas in their own words. Have students repeat this process with any other words they find unfamiliar.

Reading Critical Reviews (cont.)

- Have students read the review by Howard Kissel and the notes accompanying it.
- Point out that this review was written almost fifty years after the first review, and it tells about a different production of the same play. **Ask** how the passage of time changed the way the reviewer wrote about the politics of the 1950s.
  Answer: The first reviewer may have toned down his opinion of politics so that he would not call attention to himself. When the second review was written, the hunt for Communists was over, so the writer could speak freely about the politics of the 1950s.
- Have students note how much attention is given to individual performances. **Ask** students to summarize Kissel's opinion of the actors' work.
  Answer: Kissel praises most of the actors but seems to disagree with the overt portrayal of evil from the actor playing the judge.
- **Ask** students to summarize Kissel's opinion of the play and the overall production.
  Answer: Like Atkinson, he thinks that the play is not as good as *Death of a Salesman,* but Kissel thinks that the production is "impressive."

March 8, 2002

NEW YORK'S HOMETOWN CONNECTION WWW.NYDAILYNEWS.COM

DAILY NEWS

NEESON & CO. CAST A POWERFUL SPELL

By Howard Kissel

Four years after Arthur Miller wrote a play about a louse—a man who was a failure as a husband, a father and a salesman—he wrote a play about a hero.

> Kissel contrasts Miller's play with one of his previous plays.

The hero was a man in Puritan Massachusetts who redeemed his failures as a husband by his courageous, self-sacrificial commitment to honesty in a world gone berserk.

The louse, of course, was Willy Loman, whose name has become a by word for the failure of the American dream in the mid-20th century.

> The reviewer is referring to Miller's *Death of a Salesman.*

John Proctor, the hero of Miller's 1953 *The Crucible,* should be every bit as emblematic as Loman. If he isn't, it may be because he is rarely played as powerfully as he is by Liam Neeson in the current revival, which also stars Laura Linney.

> Kissel praises the play and the leading actor.

Miller's play about the witch hunts in 17th-century Salem draws much of its power from its subtext. It was written when the country was in the grip of another witch hunt: Congress' attempt to find American Communists in the early years of the Cold War.

> Kissel is more specific than Atkinson in stating the play's political context.

This has given the play a longer life than it might have had on its own.

The Crucible is, after all, a melodrama.

An Honest Family Before the play begins, Proctor had been an upstanding citizen. His one failing was a brief fling with a servant girl, Abigail Williams, whom his wife dismissed when she learned of the affair.

Shortly afterward, Mary Warren, a servant who replaced Abigail, joined a band of girls accusing townspeople of witchcraft, often as a way of settling old scores.

The pivot point of the play comes when Proctor's longsuffering wife is called on to denounce him for adultery. Not knowing that he has already confessed, she refuses to condemn him. She thus unwittingly seals his fate, implying to the court that he has lied. Such plotting would normally be dismissed as quaint and old-fashioned, but here the subtext makes it acceptable.

> This paragraph identifies the turning point in the plot and provides a positive opinion of its effectiveness.

Neeson's haunted, brooding look is perfect for Proctor. Moreover, his easy sensuality brings his difficult past effortlessly onto the stage, making his transformation into a man of unassailable character all the more dramatic and thrilling.

Linney gives a performance of disarming simplicity. She is a woman wronged not only by her husband but by his villainous accusers. But she responds to a mountain of cruel torments with a dignity that is profoundly moving. . . .

> Kissel praises the leading actress.

Jennifer Carpenter gives a wrenching performance as the ultimately disloyal Mary, and Angela Bettis is wonderfully ruthless as Abigail, the leader of the accusing girls. As the judge who brings about the deaths of innocent people, Brian Murray falls into the trap of signaling us that he knows his character is evil, making the melodramatic aspects of the writing too apparent.

Tim Hatley's costumes and sets, beautifully lit by Paul Gallo, have muted colors that suggest a world desperately trying to keep sensuality at bay. Under Richard Eyre's direction, the large cast handles Miller's artful creation of 17th-century language and inflections with great ease.

The Crucible is one of Miller's most-revived plays, but it is seldom as impressive as this.

> Kissel ends with a strongly positive evaluation.

Extend the Lesson

Activity

- Discuss what makes a review credible, or believable. Elicit from students such criteria as the credentials of the writer and the journal that publishes the review.
- **Ask** students whether these reviews should be considered credible.
  Answer: Yes, because they were published in major New York newspapers and were written by well-qualified reviewers.
- **Ask** students what they themselves would be qualified to review.
  Answer: Depending upon students' experiences, they may be qualified to write reviews of music, high school plays, dance productions, software, and consumer electronics.

Monitor Your Progress

Assessment Practice

Reading: Comparing and Contrasting Critical Reviews

Directions: *Choose the letter of the best answer to each question about the critical reviews.*

1. Which of the following is an opinion expressed by both reviewers?
   - **A** *The Crucible* is a powerful play.
   - **B** *The Crucible* is a melodrama.
   - **C** There is not enough emotion in *The Crucible.*
   - **D** The hero of *The Crucible* is more heroic than the hero of *Death of a Salesman.*
2. Which of the following is an opinion expressed by only one of the reviewers?
   - **A** *The Crucible* is Miller's most powerful play.
   - **B** *The Crucible* is not as good a play as Miller's *Death of a Salesman*
   - **C** This production of *The Crucible* features powerful performances by the leads.
   - **D** This production of *The Crucible* does not do justice to the play.
3. Which of the following does only one of the reviewers discuss?
   - **A** the performances of the leading actor and actress
   - **B** the performances of the supporting actors and actresses
   - **C** the costumes and sets
   - **D** the lighting design
4. Which of the following ideas is not expressed in either review?
   - **A** John Proctor's wife unwittingly seals his fate by refusing to condemn him.
   - **B** John Proctor refuses to save himself by confessing to a lie.
   - **C** The theme of the play is no longer relevant to contemporary society.
   - **D** The play connects to political events that occurred when Miller wrote the play.

Reading: Comprehension and Interpretation

Directions: *Write your answers on a separate sheet of paper.*

5. What evidence does Atkinson present to support his opinion about the merits of *The Crucible* compared with *Death of a Salesman*?
6. What reasons does Kissel give to support his opinion about the merits of *The Crucible* compared with *Death of a Salesman*?
7. Which review is more positive in its evaluation of the play and the production the reviewer saw? Cite evidence from both reviews to support your answer?

Timed Writing: Evaluation

Write a critical review of a movie, television show, play, concert, or other performance that you have seen recently. Include a brief description of the plot or the program. Then, present your opinions about the quality of the work and the production. Evaluate a few specific elements such as the script, acting, direction, choreography, costumes, music, or lighting. Be sure to support your opinions with evidence and reasons. **(*30 minutes*)**

ASSESS

Answers

Reading: Comparing and Contrasting Critical Reviews

1. A
2. C
3. D
4. C

Reading: Comprehension and Interpretation

5. Atkinson says that the literary style of *The Crucible* is cruder than the style of *Death of a Salesman* and that motivation and presentation of the theme are weaker.
6. Kissel says that politics of the 1950s gave *The Crucible* a longer life than it would otherwise have had and calls it a "melodrama." He also says that acting makes a difference in how the play is perceived.

Timed Writing

- Tell students that their reviews must include description and well-supported opinions.
- Suggest that students plan their time to give 5 minutes to planning, 20 minutes to writing, and 5 minutes to reviewing and revising. Review the need for support and clearly stated opinions.

Meeting Your Standards

Students will
1. write an essay analyzing literary trends.
2. analyze the ways in which different short stories address the same theme.
3. synthesize analyses of different stories into one argument about a literary trend.
4. use writing strategies to generate ideas, plan, organize, evaluate, and revise writing.

Prewriting

- Explain to students that for this essay, they will need to choose stories that focus on the relationship between the individual and his or her family or community. Instruct students to use a chart like the one on the page to decide which stories in the unit have this focus.
- Instruct students to take careful notes on the details in each story that reveal information about the characters' relationships. Notes should include quotations and page numbers.
- Explain that the thesis should sum up what the stories reveal about the individual within the family or community.
- To guide students in this assignment, give them the **Writing About Literature** support pages in *Unit 6 Resources,* pp. 404–405

Tips for Test Taking

In a timed writing test, students must sacrifice parts of the writing process; they will not be able to write a draft and revise it, nor will they be able to spend much time proofreading and checking for mechanical errors. Therefore, suggest that a student first brainstorm ideas that will lead to a strong and clear thesis. From there, tell them to outline what they will say and then write it. Creators of standardized tests take into consideration time limits, and scorers look for coherence and clarity, more than anything else.

Writing About Literature

Analyze Literary Trends

During the period covered by this unit, issues of identity became a preoccupation in American life and literature. The changing role of women and the awareness that America is home to people of many cultural backgrounds added resonance to this preoccupation. Writers ask questions of identity in very personal ways: Who am I? Where do I come from? What is my role in my family and community?

To explore the variety of ways in which writers have answered these questions, complete the assignment outlined in the yellow box at right.

Assignment: A Question of Identity

Write an analytical essay that examines the fate of the individual within the family and community as it is depicted in at least three pieces of fiction from this unit.

Criteria:
- Analyze elements of plot and characterization from at least three stories.
- Identify larger trends or social forces to which characters are responding.
- Approximate length: 700 words.

Prewriting

Find a focus. Use a chart like the one below to choose the characters and ideas that you want to analyze. Narrow your focus by answering these questions:

- Are the goals of the characters at odds with those of others?
- Are the beliefs of the characters in conflict with those of others?
- Do the actions of the characters reflect personal desires or the desires of others?

Use a self-sticking note to jot down ideas for the focus of your essay.

Possible focus: Explore conflict between materialism (status) and traditional values.

Model: Listing to Find a Focus

Story	Individual Characters	Family and Community	Notes
"The First Seven Years" p. 998	Miriam	Feld; Sobel; Max; aspiration for a better life; how is "better" measured?	Story shows conflict of values between materialism and depth of soul.
"Everyday Use" p. 1090	Dee	Dee is educated, sophisticated. Mother and Maggie are poor, uneducated.	Dee has "escaped" but she is the story's villain.

Gather details. Collect detailed information about the characters, including dialogue and descriptions. Note page numbers for future reference. These details will help you formulate your ideas.

Write a working thesis. A thesis is the focus, or main point, of your essay—the argument that you intend to prove. Your thesis may change as you write, but you need to have an idea of your intentions when you begin. Review your notes and write a thesis sentence.

Read to Write

Reread the texts to identify each character's goals and desires.

Teaching Resources

The following resources can be used to extend or enrich the instruction for Writing About Literature.

Unit 6 Resources
Support for Writing About Literature pp. 404–405

General Resources
Rubrics for Response to Literature pp. 65–66

Graphic Organizer Transparencies
Outline, p. 309

Drafting

Organize. Create an informal outline like the one shown below, and note where you will include quotations from the literature. Like your thesis, your outline may change as you clarify your ideas.

Model: Creating an Informal Outline

I. **Introduction/thesis:** In these stories, those who seek new identities challenge traditional values.

II. **Example:** Feld wants Miriam to have a 'better' life.

III. **Example:** Dee escapes the "backward" life of her family.

IV. **Conclusion:** To Dee, the quilt is an artifact, not something to use every day. In the same way, traditional values become quaint artifacts when abandoned by those seeking status.

Frame your ideas. Write an introduction that will grab the reader's attention. Consider beginning with a compelling quotation or detail. Then, write a strong conclusion that reinforces your main idea.

Write to Learn

Writing is a tool for discovery, a way to figure out what you think and feel. This means that you may change your mind or get new ideas as you work. Allowing for this will improve your final draft.

Revising and Editing

Review content: Revise to ensure a powerful argument. Make sure that your thesis is clearly stated and that you have proved it with evidence from the reading. Underline main ideas in your paper and confirm that each one is supported. Add more proof as needed.

Review style: Revise to cut wordy language. Check that you have found the clearest, simplest way to communicate your ideas. Omit unnecessary words.

Wordy: Miriam is not interested in or attracted to Max, but Feld pushes her to date him because he believes that Max, a college student, will be willing and able to give Miriam a life filled with luxury, wealth, and material comfort.

Revised: Miriam is not interested in the sullen Max, but Feld dreams that the college student will give her a comfortable life.

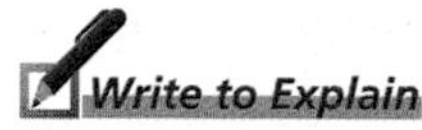

Write to Explain

Do not simply summarize selections. Give examples from the reading to support your ideas.

Publishing and Presenting

Give an oral presentation. Develop a brief talk for your class in which you detail your thesis. After your presentation, ask for questions and comments from your listeners.

WG Prentice Hall Writing and Grammar Connection: Chapter 14

Drafting

Explain to students that an informal outline provides a way to organize the information they have gathered during the prewriting stage.

Revising and Editing

On their drafts, have students underline or highlight their thesis and main points. Then, ask them to make sure that the thesis is clear and that all main points are supported with evidence from the stories. If they need more support, students should refer to their notes.

Publishing and Presenting

Encourage students to make note cards for their presentations. Students can prepare one card each for the introduction and conclusion, and one for each story.

WG Writing and Grammar, Ruby Level

Students will find additional instruction on writing a Response to Literature essay in Chapter 14.

Writing and Grammar Interactive Textbook CD-ROM

Students can use the following tools as they complete their Response to Literature essays.

- Character Trait Word Bin
- Unity and Coherence
- Revising tool

Six Traits Focus

✔	Ideas	✔	Word Choice
✔	Organization	✔	Sentence Fluency
	Voice		Conventions

Assessing the Essay

To evaluate students' essays, use the Response to Literature rubrics, pp. 65–66 in ***General Resources.***

Differentiated Instruction

Solutions for All Learners

Support for Less Proficient Writers

These students may have difficulty synthesizing analyses into one thesis. Encourage them to write their answers to the questions on p. 1366. Then, have students line up the answers for each story. Students should select three stories for which the answers are the same, so they can find one pattern for the thesis.

Support for English Learners

These students may find writing a clear thesis about characters' relationships difficult. If students have trouble finding appropriate words with which to state their arguments, have them use the Character Trait Word Bin on **Writing and Grammar iText CD-ROM.** They should look up any unfamiliar words.

Enrichment for Advanced Writers

Encourage these students to construct more challenging theses. Instead of selecting three stories that treat the theme in the same way, encourage these students to include at least one story that does not match. Their theses should account for the different ways the stories express the theme.

PRETEACH

Writing Workshop

Meeting Your Standards

1. write a résumé for a job portfolio.
2. use writing strategies to generate ideas, plan, organize, evaluate, and revise writing.
3. apply grammar skills.

From the Author's Desk

Arthur Miller

Show students Segment 2 on Arthur Miller on **From the Author's Desk DVD**. Discuss Miller's comments about the differences between journalism and the fictionalized narrative in *The Crucible.*

Writing Genres

Using the Form Point out to students that they will frequently use their job portfolios both in college and in the business world.

- Employment applications for both temporary and permanent work generally require a résumé and a job portfolio.
- Applications for membership in certain clubs or groups or applications for candidacy for elected office may require a résumé.
- Internship or training programs may require applicants to submit résumés and cover letters.

Workplace Writing: Job Portfolio and Résumé

In addition to their writing, the authors in this unit have had a variety of jobs. Many have been teachers; poet William Stafford worked for the U.S. Forest Service; Anne Tyler was a librarian. Today, people seeking these jobs submit a **job portfolio** to prospective employers. A job portfolio usually consists of two main components—the **résumé,** which is a summary of your qualifications and experience, and a **cover letter** that introduces you. Other elements may include a list of references and writing or work samples. Follow the steps outlined in this workshop to write a résumé to show your strengths as a candidate for a job.

Assignment Write a résumé to submit to perspective employers that highlights your qualifications.

What to Include Your résumé should feature the following elements:

- your name, address, and contact information provided in a highly visible format
- emphasis on work history, education, and related experience suited to the type of job you are seeking
- precise, active language
- formal and consistent use of language and format

To preview the criteria on which your job portfolio may be assessed, see the rubric on page 1375.

Using the Form

You may use elements of workplace writing in these types of writing:

- applications
- forms
- cover letters
- memorandums (memos)

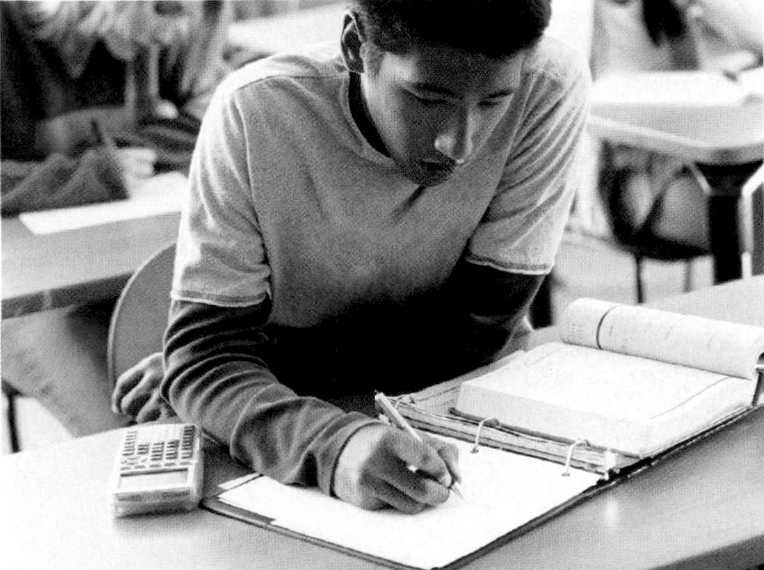

Teaching Resources

The flowing resources can be used to enrich or extend the instruction for the Writing Workshop.

Unit 6 Resources
Writing Workshop: Job Portfolio and Résumé, pp. 406–407

General Resources
Rubrics for Business Letter, pp. 61–62

Graphic Organizer Transparencies
Rubric for Self-Assessment, p. 302
Timeline, p. 314

From the Author's Desk DVD
Arthur Miller, Segments 3 and 4

Prewriting

Gathering Information

Before you write, select facts that showcase your qualifications for employment. Use one of the following strategies:

- **Collect elements.** Compile your personal history by brainstorming for a list that thoroughly represents your work experience, education, honors, hobbies, interests, and extracurricular activities. Include whatever dates you know. As you cut and focus your résumé, you will not include every item, but it is helpful to begin by examining all the possibilities.
- **Select the most appropriate items.** Use a chart like the one shown to assess your list of elements. Place a check beside those that best express your experience and skills. Then, select an appropriate category, such as work experience, activities, or skills, for each item. Note that many high-school students do not have extensive work histories, but you can consider other activities, including experience in school clubs or responsibilities at home, for skills valuable to an employer.

Model: Selecting and Categorizing Experience

Include?	Item	Category
√	Videographer	Work Experience
√	Mock Trial Team	Activities
X	Mow Lawn	Work Experience
√	Speak Hebrew	Skills

Narrowing Your Focus

Review your notes with an eye to how prospective employers will see these details and experiences. They need to know what you have done well so they can take a chance on what you might do for them. Zero in on the accomplishments that make you special.

Organizing Details

Create an event timeline. Using your notes, create a timeline to present your experiences as a progression that shows your growth and maturation. Place each Item on the relevant line, and then circle the most important.

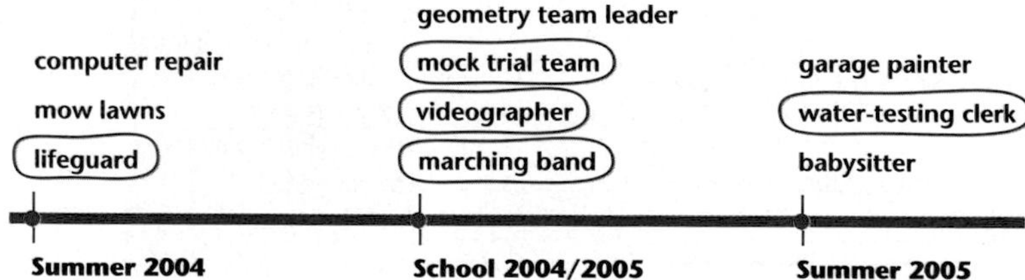

TEACH

Prewriting

- Suggest that students use timelines to help them organize their lists. The timeline can function as an outline for drafting their résumés.
- Assure students that employers or scholarship boards expect them to have little real work experience.
- Tell the class that employers look at high-school students' résumés more for potential success on the job than for relevant experience. Explain that positions of responsibility, well carried out, are important.
- Encourage students to include titles of offices held in school or community groups or clubs and to include any advancements in positions.
- Make sure that students elaborate on their responsibilities. For example, tell students to indicate that they were entrusted with closing the shop on weekend nights or with making dinner for their siblings.
- Have students use their timelines to record their entries and to decide which to place in their résumés. Tell them to include only those in which they played key roles or in which they were active members over a sustained time period. Make sure students avoid submitting a list of random activities.

Six Traits Focus

✔	Ideas		Word Choice
✔	Organization		Sentence Fluency
	Voice		Conventions

Writing and Grammar, Ruby Level

Students will find additional instruction on prewriting for job portfolios in Chapter 16, Section 3.

Writing and Grammar Interactive Textbook CD-ROM

Students can use the following tools as they complete their job portfolios.

- Timeline
- Self-Interview
- Descriptive Word Bin
- Sticky Notes Revising Tool

Tips for Using Rubrics

- Before students begin work on this Assignment, have them preview the Rubric for Self-Assessment (p. 1375) to know what is expected.
- Review the Assessment criteria in Class. Before students use the Rubric for Self-Assessment, work with them to rate the student model by applying one or two criteria to it.
- If you wish to assess students' cover letters with a 4-, 5-, or 6-point scoring rubric, see ***General Resources,*** pp. 61 and 62.

Writing Workshop

Drafting

- Emphasize the importance of maintaining a consistent style and tone throughout the résumé.
- Although students are free to choose between sentence and phrase style, lead them to see that most often the phrase style is more appropriate for busy employers who may have many résumés to read in a limited amount of time.
- In addition, tell students to select an easy-to-read format and to adhere to it throughout. Point out that heads should be in boldface type and details in lightface. Tell them to use bullets for lists and to maintain consistent parallel construction in all entries.
- Remind students that résumés are similar to outlines and timelines and that cover letters are the places to elaborate on their character traits, experience, and responsibilities.
- Help students create a balanced tone that makes them sound competent and responsible; make sure they avoid a tone that sounds boastful or, conversely, self defeating or overly modest.

Six Traits Focus

✔	Ideas		Word Choice
✔	Organization		Sentence Fluency
✔	Voice		Conventions

Writing and Grammar, Ruby Level

Students will find additional instruction on drafting a résumé in Chapter 16, Section 3

Drafting

Shaping Your Résumé

Outline your résumé. Choose and organize headings such as *Education, Work Experience, Life Experience,* and *Skills*.

Select a style. Choose a style with which to convey information and apply it consistently as you draft. For example, use either whole sentences or phrases in your experience descriptions, but do not mix the two.

Sentences: I edit videotapes and add special effects.
Phrases: Edit videotapes; add special effects.

Adhere to standards. As you draft, use a checklist like the one shown to verify that you have included all standard and expected elements. Add any element that you may have overlooked.

Résumé Conventions

- ❑ **Heading** indicates name, address and contact information of the candidate.
- ❑ **Overview or Summary** provides a brief statement about the candidate.
- ❑ **Experience** lists details of work history.
- ❑ **Education** provides history of candidate's schooling and other training.
- ❑ **Skills** notes special abilities, such as computer training or fluency in a foreign language.
- ❑ **Honors/Awards/Activities/Memberships** is a flexible category used to show interests or hobbies.

Providing Elaboration

Put a title on every job. Not every position you have held has a formal title, like salesman or mother's helper. Challenge yourself to give every unnamed job a title. A title sounds official and helps employers see quickly what job you might be able to fill.

Untitled	Titled
took care of an elderly relative	Personal Assistant
carried cameras and lights	Videographer

Play to your strengths. If you, like many high-school students, have had only limited work experience, use your résumé to emphasize academic and life experiences that show your capabilities. For every job or extracurricular experience you list, stress skills that show your ability to assume a leadership role, to share responsibility, and to complete tasks, and skills related to the job for which you are applying.

To read the complete student model, see page 1374.

Student Model: Play to Your Strengths for Maximum Effect

ACTIVITIES
- Marching Band: Alto Sax Section Leader (1 yr)
- Varsity Spring Track
- School Musical: Program Editor, Stage Crew
- National Honor Society

Sports demonstrate fitness, teamwork, and receptivity to coaching, while band and drama show teamwork and leadership in addition to academic achievement.

Tips for Using Technology in Writing

Explain to students that some word-processing programs include résumé formatting tools. Encourage students to investigate these tools, using the Help tool and tutorials.

Even if their programs do not offer a résumé format, students should be able to use such typesetting features as boldfacing, underlining, columns, and bulleted lists. Instruct students to use these features to help organize their résumés, but discourage them from using such features as nonstandard fonts. Students can also use the **Writing and Grammar iText CD-ROM.**

From the Author's Desk
Arthur Miller on Using Historical Facts

In reading the record [of the Salem witchcraft trials], which was taken down verbatim at the trial, I found one recurring note which had a growing effect upon my concept, not only of the phenomenon itself, but of our modern way of thinking about people, and especially of the treatment of evil in contemporary drama. Some critics have taken exception, for instance, to the unrelieved badness of the prosecution in the play [*The Crucible*]. I understand how this is possible, and I plead no mitigation, but I was up against historical facts which were immutable.

Arthur Miller

> *". . . I could not imagine a theatre worth my time that did not want to change the world."*
>
> —— **Arthur Miller**

Professional Model:

From *"the Crucible"*

HALE: Man, you will hang! You cannot!

PROCTOR, *his eyes full of tears*: I can. And there's your first marvel, that I can. You have made your magic now, for now I do think I see some shed of goodness in John Proctor. Not enough to weave a banner with, but white enough to keep it from such dogs.

ELIZABETH, *in a burst of terror, rushes to him and weeps against his hand.* Give them no tear! Tears pleasure them! Show honor now, show a stony heart and sink them with it! *He has lifted her, and kisses her now with great passion.*

REBECCA: Let you fear nothing! Another judgment awaits us all!

DANFORTH: Hang them high over the town! Who weeps for these, weeps for corruption! *He sweeps out past them.*

I do not think that either the record itself or the numerous commentaries upon it reveal any mitigation of the unrelieved, straightforward, and absolute dedication to evil displayed by the judges of these trials and the prosecutors. After days of study it became quite incredible how perfect they were in this respect. . . .
No human weakness could be displayed without the prosecution's stabbing into it with greater fury. The most patent contradictions, almost laughable even in that day, were overridden with warnings not to repeat their mention.

From the Author's Desk
Arthur Miller

- Show students Segment 3 on Arthur Miller on **From the Author's Desk DVD.** Tell students that as a playwright can "make old forms new again," students can make a résumé new and interesting even though it uses a well established form.
- Tell students that like Miller's refusal to gloss over unpleasant historical facts or to change the truth, résumés, too, present factual accuracy.
- Miller says that truth is absolute, that people frequently temporize, or yield to the time, in explaining away certain parts of history. Tell students that their job portfolios, too, should contain absolute truths and should not attempt to rationalize.

Tips for Improving Tone

Remind students that tone is the writer's attitude toward the audience and the subject.

Tell students to choose words that reinforce the image of themselves as reasonable, responsible, proactive, and good at what they do.

Encourage them to choose words with positive connotations and to sound positive rather than passive or exaggerated. Use the following examples:

Passive	Positive	Exaggerated
Babysitter: Summer 2006 Watched three kids on weekdays	Babysitter: Summer 2006 Primary caregiver responsible for three preschoolers, Mondays through Fridays	Babysitter: Summer 2006 Parents entrusted me with sole responsibility for childcare. Acted as surrogate parent.

Revising

- Have students read over the drafts of their résumés. Instruct them to ask themselves the following: Are my categories appropriate? Are they clearly labeled? Is the information in the right categories? Is the résumé organized consistently?
- Give students sufficient time to make notes for correcting their work.
- Then, have students work individually or with a partner to read through their or their partner's résumé as a check. Tell students also to make sure that entries are chronological, starting with the most recent activities or employment and working backwards.

Six Traits Focus

✔	Ideas	✔	Word Choice
✔	Organization		Sentence Fluency
✔	Voice		Conventions

Writing and Grammar, Ruby Level

Students will find additional instruction on revising a résumé in Chapter 16, Section 3.

Writing Workshop

Revising

Revising Your Overall Structure

Make your format consistent. Make sure that you have followed a consistent organizational strategy throughout the résumé.

1. Check that you have labeled your categories clearly and placed your descriptions of experience under the proper sections.
2. Check that all elements of the résumé are uniform. For example, the dates of your activities should be formatted consistently—do not switch back and forth between styles.
3. Make sure that your résumé is only one page long. If it is too long, edit it or revise margins so that it fits on one page.

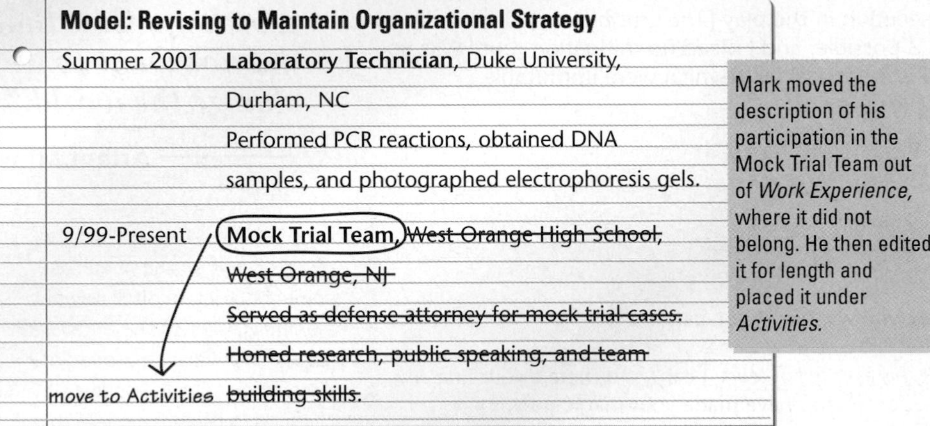
Model: Revising to Maintain Organizational Strategy

Summer 2001 **Laboratory Technician,** Duke University, Durham, NC
Performed PCR reactions, obtained DNA samples, and photographed electrophoresis gels.

9/99-Present Mock Trial Team, ~~West Orange High School, West Orange, NJ~~
~~Served as defense attorney for mock trial cases.~~
~~Honed research, public speaking, and team building skills.~~

Mark moved the description of his participation in the Mock Trial Team out of *Work Experience,* where it did not belong. He then edited it for length and placed it under *Activities.*

Revising Your Word Choice

Use active and specific language. Your résumé has to stand out among many others. The language you use reveals your attitudes and seriousness of purpose. Avoid the use of unspecific, bland, or passive language. Use active verbs and specific descriptions.

Bland: Made brochures for public relations firm.
Specific: Researched, wrote, and edited four-color brochures for public relations firm.
Vague: Watch children at after-school program.
Precise: Lead games and sports activities. Teach Hebrew to students, ages 9–11.

Peer Review: In a small group of classmates, compare your résumés. Note differences in the organization of information and discuss how best to phrase and explain common experiences. Together, work to find the best way to phrase job descriptions and activities.

Tips for Using Technology in Writing

Remind students to set up a folder in which they save their résumé and cover letter. Having the major portion of these texts already written and accessible will enable students to update them easily. If necessary, they can put their folder on a disk and keep it in a handy place.

Suggest that students also keep in that folder a list of the names, addresses, and telephone numbers of the people they have listed as references, updating it as necessary.

Developing Your Style

Active vs. Passive Voice

Using the Active Voice In a résumé, your language should project a tone of all-around competence and initiative. In every part of your résumé, present yourself as an active, take-charge employee, volunteer, or team member who seizes opportunities to make effective contributions. One way you can present yourself in this way is through the words you choose. Use verbs in the active voice rather than the passive.

Voice is the form of a verb that indicates whether the subject of the sentence is performing the action. A verb is **active** when the subject performs the action. A verb is **passive** when the subject receives the action or when the action is performed upon the subject. A passive verb is always a verb phrase made from a form of the verb *be* plus the past participle of another verb.

Passive: Games and activities *were developed* by me.
Active: I *developed* games and activities.

In some passive constructions, the performer of the action is not named.

Passive: Games and activities were developed.

Strong writers use the active voice because it is more direct and forceful. When you present your skills and accomplishments in a résumé, you want to showcase your active role—without exaggerating, of course. Notice the difference between the following two job descriptions:

Passive: I was assigned to help teachers after school.
Active: I assist after-school teachers with children, ages 5–7.

Even if you are using a résumé style that omits the pronoun *I*, you can still word your description in the active rather than the passive voice.

Active: Lead games and sports activities. [*I* is implied.]

Find It in Your Reading Review the Student Model on page 1374.

1. Isolate sentences or phrases that focus attention on Mark. Identify and list all verbs in the active voice.
2. Mentally replace each verb with a verb in the passive voice. Explain the differences in effect.

Apply It to Your Writing Review the draft of your résumé. For the information under each heading, follow these steps:

1. Underline each verb you have used.
2. Determine whether each verb is in the active voice. If a verb is in the passive voice, rewrite the item to make the verb active. If necessary, add the subject to help you, but delete it in your résumé.

WG *Prentice Hall Writing and Grammar Connection: Chapter 21, Section 4*

Developing Your Style

- Tell students that writers rely on active verbs and the active voice to make their writing more energetic and lively.
- Then, remind them that the active voice similarly makes their job portfolios livelier. In addition, it may show them as more active, engaged people rather than passive ones.
- Tell them, too, that another reason for using the active voice is that it cuts down on words by eliminating the wordier passive construction (for example, "I did it" rather than "It was done by me.")
- Ask students to go work with a partner to do **Find It in Your Reading.** Then, have them do the **Try It in Your Writing** activity individually and work with a partner to check each other's use of the active voice.
- **Answers** to **Find It in Your Reading:** 1. Active verbs appear in the WORK EXPERIENCE section. They are *performed, obtained, photographed; videotape, edit, add; assist, lead,* and *teach.* 2. If these were not active verbs (or participles), Mark might seem less active and less responsible, and his work might seem less significant.

WG Writing and Grammar, Ruby Level

Students will find additional instruction on active and passive voice in Chapter 21, Section 4.

Differentiated Instruction
Solutions for All Learners

Support for Less Proficient Writers
These students may have difficulty selecting elements from their initial list to include in their résumés. Help students restate items from their list so that they fit an appropriate category. You can refer students to the Word Bins on **Writing and Grammar iText CD-ROM.**

Support for English Learners
Students who did not grow up in the United States may be unsure about what experiences they should Include in their résumés. Point out that their fluency in their first languages and their familiarity with another culture are skills that many employers value very highly. These experiences should be emphasized in a résumé.

Support for Advanced Writers
These students may be inclined to describe their experiences in too much detail. Discourage them from overwriting. Remind students that their résumé should be only one page long. Explain that their audience wants essential information communicated efficiently in a short space.

Student Model

- Explain that the Student Model is a sample and that résumés may include more information.
- Point out to students that Mark's name is placed so that it is the very first thing a reader sees. **Ask** students: Why might this placement be important?
  Possible answer: It may be important because the name tells a potential employer who Mark is before the résumé tells what experience he has.
- Call students' attention to the headings that Mark has used. Explain that they keep the résumé well organized. **Ask** students what distinguishes the headings from the other text.
  Answer: They are boldfaced and written in capital letters.
- Ask students to review Mark's work experience. Point out that Mark has included clear, readable dates for each of them.
- Finally, call attention to Mark's last heading, Activities. Explain that Mark is a well-rounded, motivated individual. Encourage students to take their own activities seriously and to include them in their résumés.

Writing Genres

Job Portfolios in the Workplace Tell students that job portfolios and résumés may turn out to be the most important step of their careers—the first step. When they enter the job market, each of the students will need to write these documents in order to let prospective employers know who they are and what they can do. Encourage the class to see a résumé as a chance to show the world their very best.

Writing Workshop

Student Model: **Mark Israel Schilsky**
West Orange, New Jersey

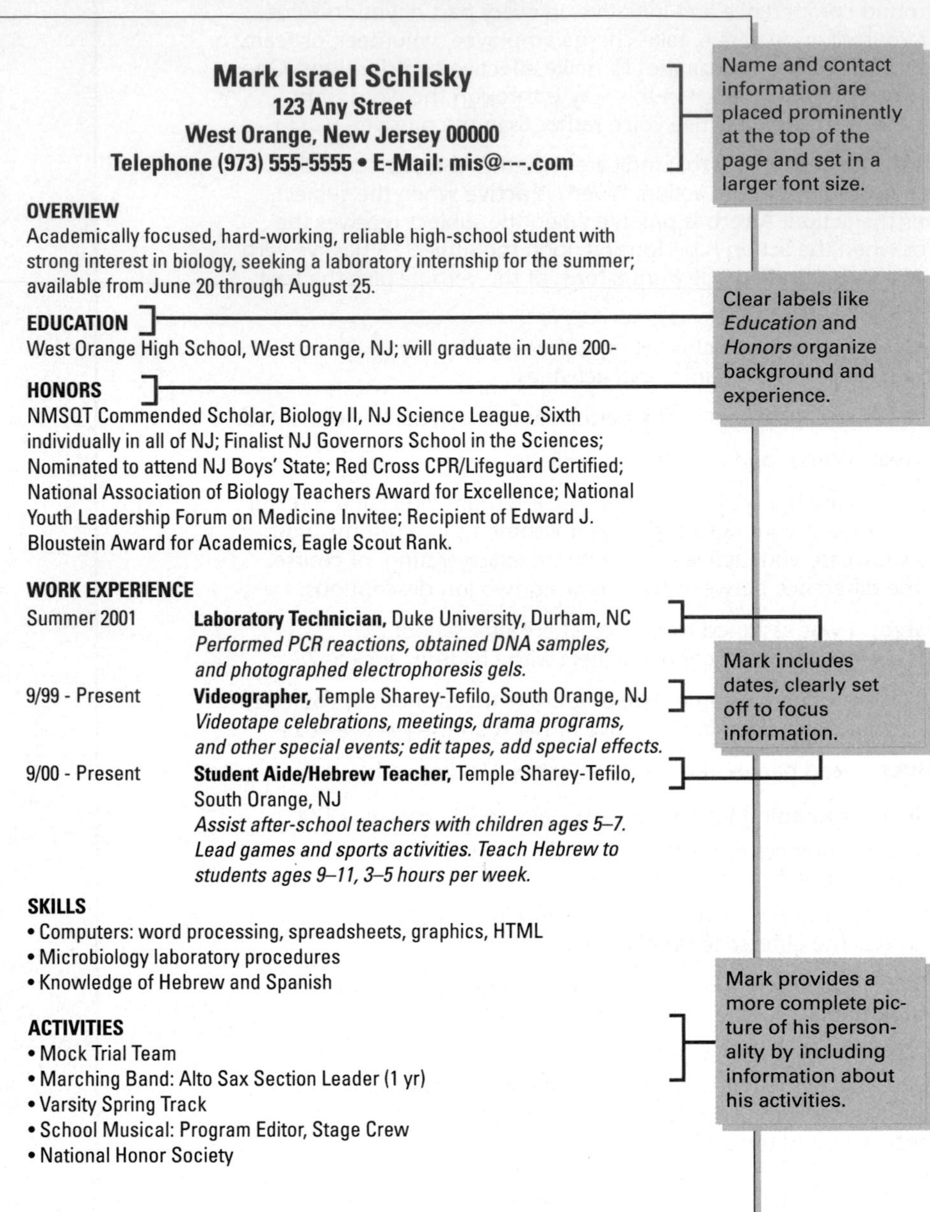

Mark Israel Schilsky
123 Any Street
West Orange, New Jersey 00000
Telephone (973) 555-5555 • E-Mail: mis@---.com

OVERVIEW
Academically focused, hard-working, reliable high-school student with strong interest in biology, seeking a laboratory internship for the summer; available from June 20 through August 25.

EDUCATION
West Orange High School, West Orange, NJ; will graduate in June 200-

HONORS
NMSQT Commended Scholar, Biology II, NJ Science League, Sixth individually in all of NJ; Finalist NJ Governors School in the Sciences; Nominated to attend NJ Boys' State; Red Cross CPR/Lifeguard Certified; National Association of Biology Teachers Award for Excellence; National Youth Leadership Forum on Medicine Invitee; Recipient of Edward J. Bloustein Award for Academics, Eagle Scout Rank.

WORK EXPERIENCE

Summer 2001 — **Laboratory Technician,** Duke University, Durham, NC
Performed PCR reactions, obtained DNA samples, and photographed electrophoresis gels.

9/99 - Present — **Videographer,** Temple Sharey-Tefilo, South Orange, NJ
Videotape celebrations, meetings, drama programs, and other special events; edit tapes, add special effects.

9/00 - Present — **Student Aide/Hebrew Teacher,** Temple Sharey-Tefilo, South Orange, NJ
Assist after-school teachers with children ages 5–7. Lead games and sports activities. Teach Hebrew to students ages 9–11, 3–5 hours per week.

SKILLS
- Computers: word processing, spreadsheets, graphics, HTML
- Microbiology laboratory procedures
- Knowledge of Hebrew and Spanish

ACTIVITIES
- Mock Trial Team
- Marching Band: Alto Sax Section Leader (1 yr)
- Varsity Spring Track
- School Musical: Program Editor, Stage Crew
- National Honor Society

Name and contact information are placed prominently at the top of the page and set in a larger font size.
Clear labels like *Education* and *Honors* organize background and experience.
Mark includes dates, clearly set off to focus information.
Mark provides a more complete picture of his personality by including information about his activities.

Tips for Using Technology in Writing

Suggest to students that when they return to their résumé folders to update their résumés and cover letters, they should not delete the older version of the résumés. Tell them that some of the entries they delete may at some point become important again. Having a copy of the information at hand will help students maintain accurate records and synthesize information.

Suggest, too, that they update their references to include people who know them now rather than two or three years previously. Remind students to check with each person before including his or her name as a reference.

Editing and Proofreading

Review your résumé to make sure it is free from errors in grammar, punctuation, capitalization, and spelling.

Focus on Spelling: Check that you have spelled all words correctly, especially proper names, technical terms, and abbreviations.

Publishing and Presenting

Consider one of the following ways to share your résumé:

Prepare a cover letter. Using business letter format, state your interest in the position and briefly present your qualifications. Address your letter to the person responsible for reviewing applications.

- Follow standard business letter format by including a heading, the inside address, the date, and an appropriate salutation and closing.
- State that your résumé is attached, and request an interview.
- Thank the recipient in advance for his or her consideration.

Build a job portfolio. To complete your job portfolio, attach samples of your work, letters of recommendation, citations, and other information that might help a prospective employer.

Reflecting on Your Writing

Writer's Journal Jot down your thoughts on the experience of creating a job portfolio. Begin by answering these questions:

- What did you learn about the power of active, specific language?
- What discoveries did you make about yourself?

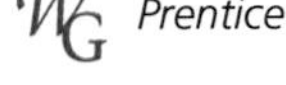 *Prentice Hall Writing and Grammar Connection: Chapter 16*

Rubric for Self-Assessment

Evaluate your résumé *using the following criteria and rating scale, or, with your classmates, determine your own reasonable evaluation criteria.*

Criteria	Rating Scale				
	not very				*very*
Focus: How well does the résumé convey job and life experiences?	1	2	3	4	5
Organization: How well organized is the résumé?	1	2	3	4	5
Support/Elaboration: How appropriate are the specific details of the résumé for the type of work sought?	1	2	3	4	5
Style: How active and precise is your use of language?	1	2	3	4	5
Conventions: How correct is your spelling and grammar?	1	2	3	4	5

Tips for Test Taking

Although it is not likely that students will be asked to write a résumé in a test situation, many tests do require students to work with such workplace documents as résumés and memoranda. Explain to students that familiarity with writing these documents will help them read and answer questions about them on a test.

While workplace documents vary widely in format, nearly all share such characteristics as formal language, clear organization, headings and subheadings, concrete details, correct mechanics, and a focus on conveying information efficiently in as little space as possible.

Editing and Proofreading

- Emphasize that résumés should contain no mistakes in grammar, spelling, or punctuation.
- Remind them that their résumés are not first drafts but finished products that must be perfect. Tell them that although some employers might not notice small errors, others will and may well decide not to grant an interview to or hire the person whose résumé contains a mechanical error.
- **Ask** students why they think an employer might react this way. **Possible answer:** A typographical error or an error of ignorance sends the message that the writer of the résumé or cover letter is either careless or uses English incorrectly. Neither gives a positive impression.
- Remind students that the spell check will help them find typographical errors; it will not distinguish between correct and incorrect words.

Six Traits Focus

	Ideas		Word Choice
	Organization		Sentence Fluency
	Voice	✔	Conventions

ASSESS

Publishing and Presenting

- Give students a copy of the rubrics for Business Letter, pp. 61–62 in ***General Resources.***
- Make sure that students tailor their cover letters to the information in their résumés and that they elaborate on the skills or experiences that make them especially well qualified for the position they are seeking.

Reflecting on Your Writing

- Ask students whether they gained new insights into their characters or marketability.

Writing and Grammar, Ruby Level

Students will find additional guidance for editing and proofreading, publishing and presenting, and reflecting on a job portfolio in Chapter 16, Section 3.

Meeting Your Standards

Students will

1. learn the terms *interpret, evaluate,* and *judge.*
2. apply knowledge of these terms in standardized-test situations.

Know Your Terms: Determining the Value of Texts

Explain that the terms listed under Terms to Learn will be used in standardized-test situations when students are asked to explain and to judge what the writer has said.

Terms to Learn

- Review *interpret* and *interpretation.* Explain that an interpretation is an opinion based on evidence from the text. Most teachers and tests allow students considerable latitude in interpretations when supported by sufficient and plausible material from the text.
- Review *evaluate* and *evaluation.* Explain that these terms require students to go beyond explaining and to decide upon the significance of an action, a thesis, or an argument. Areas that students might explore as they evaluate are characters' motivation and actions.
- Review *judge* and *judgment*. Once they explain and explore the value or importance, they can form an opinion, or judgment.

ASSESS

Answers

1. Miller says that contemporary, industrialized society views the hero as an oddball and that the social system no longer values t ragic" heroism.
2. Students may say that Miller does not provide examples or support for his statements in this excerpt and that they cannot evaluate it unless they rely on their own knowledge.
3. Make sure that students base their answers on information from the text.

Vocabulary Workshop

SAT® PREP ACT

High-Frequency Academic Words

High-frequency academic words are words that appear often in textbooks and on standardized tests. Though you may already know the meaning of many of these words, they usually have a more specific meaning when they are used in textbooks and on tests.

Know Your Terms: Determining the Value of Texts

Each of the words listed is a verb that tells you to explain the significance or merits of the material. The words indicate the kinds of details you should provide in your answer.

Terms to Learn

Interpret Explain the underlying meaning of a phrase, a passage, or an entire work by examining words, images, and events.

Sample test item: ***Interpret*** the theme of *The Crucible.*

Evaluate Determine the value or importance of something.

Sample test item: ***Evaluate*** the writer's main argument.

Judge Assess or form an opinion about something.

Sample test item: ***Judge*** the literary qualities of *The Crucible.*

Practice

Directions: *Read the following passage from Arthur Miller's essay "On Social Plays." Then, on a separate piece of paper, answer questions 1–3.*

Our society—and I am speaking of every industrialized society in the world—is so complex, each person being so specialized an integer, that the moment any individual is dramatically characterized and set forth as a hero, our common sense reduces him to the size of a complainer, a misfit. For deep down we no longer believe in the rules of the tragic contest; we no longer believe that some ultimate sense can in fact be made of social causation, or in the possibility that any individual can, by a heroic effort, make sense of it. Thus the man that is driven to question the moral chaos in which we live ends up in our estimate as a possibly commendable but definitely odd fellow, and probably as a compulsively driven neurotic. In place of a social aim which called an all-around excellence—physical, intellectual, and moral—the ultimate good, we have set up a goal which can best be characterized as "happiness"—namely, staying out of trouble. This concept is the end result of the truce which all of us have made with society. . . .

1. *Interpret* Miller's view of the hero in society, based on this passage.
2. *Evaluate* the support Miller provides for his characterization of the hero.
3. *Judge* the validity of Miller's claim that our goal is "staying out of trouble."

Tips for Test-Taking

Questions requiring students to interpret, evaluate, and judge frequently appear on standardized tests. Tell students that in interpreting, evaluating, and judging, they must focus on the text and the question itself. If the question asks for an opinion, then they can give their opinions; however, if it does not, they should limit their interpretations and judgments to the selection itself.

For: An Interactive Crossword Puzzle
Visit: www.PHSchool.com
Web Code: erj-5601

Critical Reading:
Punctuation, Usage, and Sentence Structure

The writing sections of some tests examine your knowledge of the usage and mechanics of standard written English. Use the following strategies to help you answer test questions regarding punctuation, grammar and usage, and sentence structure:

- You can often identify errors by reading the sentence aloud, as if it were being spoken. Incorrect English usually sounds wrong, and you can learn to hear errors.
- Remember that punctuation marks act as symbols for readers, telling them where to stop, pause, read with a questioning tone, or read with excitement.
- Memorize the rules for specific grammatical structures, such as the use of *its* or *it's* and *who* or *whom,* that are a common source of errors.
- As you read, recognize correct and incorrect grammar—especially subject-verb agreement and pronoun usage.
- Learn to recognize structural errors, such as run-on sentences, sentence fragments, and misplaced modifiers.

Practice

Directions: *Read each item, and then, answer the questions that follow.*

Some automobiles require diesel fuel to run properly, some do not.

1. Which of the following choices is the best revision to the underlined part of the sentence?

A properly; some do not

B properly . . . some do not

C properly: some do not

D Correct as is.

(1) It has been a long and hard-fought campaign the voters were ready to make a choice. (2) With the qualifications of all the candidates in mind, the voters chose Dan O'Neill to be mayor. (3) Voters claimed that they were impressed with the full range of his positive attributes.

2. How would you correct sentence 1?

A campaign, the voters

B campaign; the voters

C campaign The voters

D Correct as is.

Test-Taking Strategies

- Look carefully at all punctuation in each passage.
- Remember that there may be more than one error in each passage.
- Choose the answer that corrects *all* the errors in the passage.

Meeting Your Standards

Students will

1. **identify and correct errors in punctuation, grammar, and usage.**
2. **recognize structural errors, such as run-on sentences, fragments, and misplaced modifiers, in a standardized-test situation.**

Critical Reading

- Explain to students that visualizing the action in their minds, an important reading strategy for fiction, can help them to recognize errors in sentences. If a reader pays close enough attention, errors in punctuation, usage, or sentence structure interrupt visualizing and demand corrections.
- Have students read the Practice sentences and answer the questions.
- Point out that in question 1, the underlined section of the sentence contains a comma splice. A comma splice is an error in which a comma separates two independent clauses.
- Since there is an error, answer choice *D* is incorrect. Answer choice *B* is incorrect because no information is missing from the sentence. Answer choice *C* is incorrect because the sentence after the colon does not summarize or explain the one before it.
- Point out that question 2 contains two independent clauses. Answer choice *B* corrects the punctuation.

ASSESS

Answers

1. A
2. B

Meeting Your Standards

Students will

1. analyze the impact of the media on the news and the democratic process.
2. analyze the explicit ways journalists can influence news coverage and public opinion.
3. analyze the implicit ways media makers can influence news coverage and public opinion.

Analyze Explicit Influence

- Explain that an editorial is an explicit statement of a journalist's view on an issue and one way that journalists and media makers can influence public opinion.
- Add that opinion forums are another explicit influence.
- If possible, show students videotape of a televised editorial and an opinion forum. Tell students to be on the lookout for opinion words such as "views," "thoughts," or "comments."

Analyze Implicit Influence

- Explain that media also influences public opinion implicitly. Have students read the comment on images of leaders. Then **ask:** How do the images of leaders chosen by news media influence public opinion?
Possible response: When media makers broadcast flattering images of a leader, they communicate a positive message; an unflattering image communicates a negative message.
- Explain that the sequence of news stories on a television broadcast influences public opinion by directing audience attention toward the first stories covered.
- Tell students that journalists can also exercise influence by choosing what questions to ask leaders, because this determines what answers leaders can give and what information they can offer the public.

Assess the Activity

To evaluate students' work, use the Analyzing Media rubric, p. 85 in ***General Resources.***

Communications Workshop

Analyze the Impact of the Media

Both print and broadcast media can have a dramatic effect on the unfolding of the democratic process. As a potential voter, you must develop critical listening and viewing skills in order to analyze media activities and evaluate their effects. The strategies outlined below will help you understand some common points of media influence. The form on this page offers a starting point for actual analysis.

Analyze Explicit Influence

Journalists and media makers often hold strong views and sometimes seek to affect the political process by expressing their beliefs. Familiarize yourself with these opinion forums.

Identify editorials. Talk-show hosts and journalists may deliver editorials that are intended to express opinions. Likewise, news shows may host discussions in which a variety of participants express opinions. Be careful to discriminate between factual news coverage and opinion-based journalism. Words such as *views, thoughts,* or *comments* signal an opinion that listeners should evaluate.

Recognize opinion forums. Debate forums in which journalists express opposing views offer you the opportunity to hear many opinions. Note, however, that each speaker hopes to influence you to share a particular view.

Feedback Form for Evaluating Media Influence

Rating System
\+ = Present − = Omitted

Explicit Influence of Reports
Editorial ____________
Opinion Forum ____________
How did these reports exert influence? What signals suggested opinion?

Implicit Influence of Reports
Persuasive images ________
Reporting priorities ________
Questioning priorities ________
Time issues ________

Answer the following question:
How might the media choices or elements that you noted affect the audience or even influence the outcome of a story?

Analyze Implicit Influence

Often, media makers exert indirect influence on elections or public opinion. Pay attention to these avenues of influence.

- **Persuasive Images** When the media shows a candidate looking strong, it sends a positive message about that candidate. If the candidate looks tired or confused, the media presents a negative message. Be alert for images that may be politically or culturally biased or even sterotyped.
- **Reporting priorities** Media makers exert influence through the stories they report *and* the sequence in which they present them. The lead story of a television news show usually gets the largest audience, while stories reported later may reach a tiny audience. The placement of a story in the sequence may affect public perception.
- **Shaping attitudes** When journalists conduct interviews, the questions they ask influence the information you receive. To avoid accepting biased information, compare news sources.

Activity *Listen and Analyze* For a week, analyze the coverage of an important story in at least one form of media. Use the feedback form shown here to analyze the impact of the coverage each day.

Differentiated Instruction
Solutions for All Learners

Support for Special Needs Students
These students may have trouble distinguishing between objective and subjective news. Tell them that presenting opinions is a legitimate function of news media. Explain that explicit opinions are presented in editorials or opinion forums. If a segment on a news program is introduced as an editorial, students can assume it will present an opinion.

Support for Less Proficient Readers
To help these students distinguish between objective and subjective news, show them the front page, editorials, and letters to the editor of a local newspaper. Explain that the front page is objective news, and editorials and letters are subjective. Letters to the editor in a newspaper are similar to opinion forums in television or radio news.

Vocabulary for English Learners
To help these students recognize editorials in audiovisual news media, encourage them to gather a word bank of opinion-oriented words such as "views," "thoughts," and "comments." Have them practice using these words before they try to recognize them in an actual news broadcast.

Suggestions for Further Reading

Featured Titles:

The Joy Luck Club

Amy Tan *Putnam, 1989*

Fiction Organized as a group of sixteen related stories, *The Joy Luck Club* deals with mother-daughter relationships in the Chinese immigrant community of San Francisco. The title refers to the name of a club begun in 1949 by four immigrant Chinese women who meet regularly to play the Chinese game of mah jong. The book is divided into four sections, two in which the mothers speak and two in which their American-raised daughters express themselves.

On Nature: Great Writers on the Great Outdoors

Edited by Lee Gutkind *Most Tarcher/Putnam, 2002*

Nonfiction This book of contemporary nature essays will appeal to those who love outdoor activities as well as to those who prefer mental exercise in an armchair. It features nonfiction by some of America's best contemporary authors: Joyce Carol Oates, Barry Lopez, Mark Doty, Diane Ackerman, John McPhee, and Bill Bryson, among others.

The Left Hand of Darkness

Ursula K. Le Guin

Ace Books, 1991

To begin reading *The Left Hand of Darkness* is to enter a strange world where familiar ideas about gender differences do not apply. This novel tells the story of an ambassador sent to a wayword planet to bring it into the same company as other advanced worlds. When the ambassador arrives, he finds the arctic planet populated by people who are neither men nor women. Instead, a single individual alternates between both genders. In order to accomplish his mission, the ambassador must cast aside his own prejudices and negotiate the complex power relationships of an unfamiliar world.

Nonfiction Readings Across the Curriculum

Prentice Hall *Pearson Prentice Hall, 2000*

Nonfiction These essays by well-known authors provide exciting ways of thinking about many subjects, including literature, science, social studies, mathematics, sports, and the arts. In a memoir, for example, author Beverly Cleary tells how she got started. Football great Joe Namath gives players a pep talk in his how-to essay from *Football for Young Players and Parents*. Readers will find that the enthusiasm of the writers in this volume is contagious.

Work Presented in Unit Six:

If sampling a portion of the following text has built your interest, treat yourself to the full work.

Twentieth-Century American Drama

Prentice Hall *Pearson Prentice Hall, 2000*

***Many of these titles are available in the* Prentice Hall/Penguin Literature Library.**
Consult your teacher before choosing one.

Planning Students' Further Reading

Discussions of literature can raise sensitive and often controversial issues. Before you recommend further reading to your students, consider the values and sensitivities of your community as well as the age, ability, and sophistication of your students. It is also good policy to preview literature before you recommend it to students. The notes below offer some guidance on specific titles.

***The Joy Luck Club,* by Amy Tan**

Multiple narrators discuss life in both the United States and China, touching on such sensitive issues as smoking and drinking, divorce, premarital sex, abortion, families with multiple wives and concubines, the horrors of famine and war, and loss of faith in God. In China, one narrator's mother kills herself by taking poison. The book also contains examples of profane language.

Lexile: 930L

***The Left Hand of Darkness,* by Ursula K. LeGuin**

Sensitive Issues: Le Guin's story presents a culture that is "alien" in more than just its off-world setting. In particular, each Gethenian is sometimes male, sometimes female—a phenomenon that one character describes as "an appalling experience for a Terran."

On Nature: Great Writers on the Great Outdoors
Edited by Lee Gutkind

Sensitive issues in these essays include the trapping and killing of animals, drunkenness, foul language, sexual situation, religion, and descriptions of animal breeding.

Lexile: Appropriate for high school students

Nonfiction Readings Across the Curriculum

Sensitive issues include racial prejudice against Asians and Asian Americans, Native Americans, and African Americans. Other issues include the horrors of war and the Holocaust, as well as their terrible impact on children.

Lexile: Appropriate for high school students

Continued from right column

20th-Century American Drama

Our Town deals directly with death and includes references to one character's suicide. In *The Glass Menagerie,* Tom abuses alcohol; Tom and Laura's father is also remembered as a problem drinker. The play focuses on Laura's physical disabilities and Amanda's belief that the only appropriate goals for Laura are marriage and a family. Also, Jim uses a derogatory term for German Americans. *Death of a Salesman* includes scenes from Willy's adulterous affair with the woman in Boston. There are references to the fact that both Biff and Happy steal things. Finally, the play concludes with Willy's suicide. *The Crucible* deals with people who believed in the literal existence of Satan and witchcraft. The play also includes references to adultery and John Proctor's use of the word *whore.* The play includes the wrongful execution of innocent people.

Lexile: NP

RESOURCES

Reading and Vocabulary Handbook

Literary Handbook

Writing Handbook

Communications Handbook

Test Prep Handbook

Grammar, Usage, and Mechanics Handbook

Indexes

GLOSSARY

High–utility and academic vocabulary words appear in green.

abeyance (ə bā′ əns) *n.* temporary suspension

ablutions (ab lo͞o′ shənz) *n.* cleansing the body as part of a religious rite

abomination (ə bäm′ ə nā′ shən) *n.* something that causes great horror or disgust

abundance (ə bun′ dəns) *n.* a great supply; more than enough

acceded (ak sēd′ id) *v.* yielded (to); agreed

acquiesce (ak′ wē es′) *v.* agree without protest

adamant (ad′ ə mənt) *adj.* firm; unyielding

adversary (ad′ vər ser′ ē) *n.* opponent; enemy

aesthetic (es thet′ ik) *adj.* pertaining to the study or theory of beauty

affliction (ə flik′ shən) *n.* something causing pain or suffering

agape (ə gāp′) *adj.* wide open

aggregation (ag′ grə gā′ shən) *n.* group of distinct objects or individuals

agues (ā′ gyo͞oz) *n.* fits of shivering

alacrity (ə lak′ rə tē) *n.* speed

allegiances (ə lē′ jəns əz) *n.* loyalties

alliance (ə lī′ əns) *n.* union of nations for a specific purpose

ambush (am′ bo͝osh′) *n.* lying in wait to attack by surprise

ameliorate (ə mēl′ yə rāt′) *v.* make better

ammunition (am′ yo͞o nish′ ən) *n.* anything hurled by a weapon or exploded as a weapon

analyze (an′ ə līz′) *v.* break down a topic or issue into parts and explain them

anarchy (an′ ər kē) *n.* absence of government

anathema (ə nath′ ə mə) *n.* curse

anomalous (ə näm′ ə ləs) *adj.* abnormal

anonymity (an′ ə nim′ ə tē) *n.* the condition of being unknown

anthology (an thäl′ ə jē) *n.* collection of poems, stories, and so on

apparition (ap′ ə rish′ ən) *n.* act of appearing or becoming visible

appease (ə pēz′) *v.* satisfy

appellation (ap′ ə lā′ shən) *n.* name or title

appendage (ə pen′ dij) *n.* something added on

apply (ə plī′) *v.* tell how you use information in a specific situation

apprised (ə prīzd′) *v.* informed; notified

arduous (är′ jo͞o əs) *adj.* difficult

arrested (ə res′ tid) *adj.* stopped

aspiration (as′ pə rā′ shən) *n.* strong ambition

asylum (ə sī′ ləm) *n.* place of refuge

audaciously (ô dā′ shəs lē) adv. boldly or daringly

automation (ôt′ ə mā′ shən) *n.* manufacturing conducted with partly or fully self-operating machinery

avarice (av′ ər is) *n.* extreme desire for wealth; greed for riches

aversion (əv ʉr′ zhən) *n.* object arousing an intense dislike

avidly (av′ id lē) adv. eagerly

barometer (bə räm′ ət ər) *n.* instrument for measuring atmospheric pressure

base (bās) *adj.* low; mean

bastions (bas′ chənz) *n.* fortifications

beguile (bē gīl′) *v.* charm or delight; trick

bellicose (bel′ ə kōs) *adj.* quarrelsome

benevolent (bə nev′ ə lənt) *adj.* kindly; charitable

benign (bi nīn′) *adj.* not injurious or malignant; not cancerous

blanched (blancht) *adj.* paled; whitened

blaspheming (blas fēm′ iŋ) *v.* cursing

blasphemy (blas′ fə mē′) *n.* sinful act or remark

blithe (blīth) *adj.* carefree

brazenness (brā′ zən nis) *n.* shamelessness; boldness; impudence

bronchitis (bräŋ kīt′ is) *n.* inflammation of the lining of the major air passageways of the lungs

brooding (bro͞od′ iŋ) *v.* pondering in a troubled or mournful way

brutal (bro͞ot′ əl) *adj.* cruel and without feeling; savage; violent

calligraphy (kə lig′ rə fē) *n.* artistic handwriting

calumny (kal′ əm nē) *n.* false accusation; slander

caper (kā′ pər) *n.* prank

capitulate (kə pich′ ə lāt′) *v.* surrender conditionally

caveat (kā′ vē at′) *n.* formal notice; warning

celestial (sə les′ chəl) *adj.* of the heavens

chaos (kā′ äs′) *n.* disorder of matter and space, supposed to have existed before the ordered universe

circumvent (sʉr′ kəm vent′) *v.* prevent; get around

claustrophobia (klôs′ trə fō′ bē ə) *n.* fear of being in a confined space

cleave (klēv) *v.* adhere; cling

collusion (kə lo͞o′ zhən) *n.* secret agreement; conspiracy

compare (kəm per′) *v.* tell the important similarities and explain why they are important

conceits (kən sētz′) *n.* strange or fanciful ideas

conciliatory (kən sil′ ē ə tôr′ ē) *adj.* tending to soothe anger

conclude (kən klo͞od′) *v.* tell how you use reasoning to reach a decision or opinion based on the information provided

concocted (kən käkt′ əd) *v.* made by combining various ingredients

confederate (kən fed′ ər it) *adj.* united with others for a common purpose

conflagration (kän′ flə grā′ shən) *n.* big, destructive fire

confluence (kän′ flo͞o əns) *n.* a flowing together

confounded (kən found′ id) *v.* confused; dismayed

congenial (kən jēn′ yəl) *adj.* agreeable

conjectural (kən jek′ chər əl) *adj.* based on guesswork

conjectured (kən jek′ chərd) *v.* guessed

conjure (kän′ jər) *v.* summon by magic or as if by magic; call forth

connate (kän′ āt′) *adj.* existing naturally; innate

connivance (kə nī′ vəns) *n.* secret cooperation

consanguinity (kän′ saŋ gwin′ ə tē) *n.* kinship

consecrate (kän′ si krāt′) *v.* cause to be revered or honored

conspicuous (kən spik′ yo͞o əs) *adj.* obvious; easy to see or perceive

consternation (kän′ stər nā′ shən) *n.* great fear or shock that makes one feel helpless or bewildered

contentious (kən ten′ shəs) *adj.* argumentative

contiguous (kən tig′ yo͞o əs) *adj.* bordering; adjacent

contrast (kən trast′) *v.* tell the important differences and explain why they are important

convivial (kən viv′ ē əl) *adj.* fond of good company; sociable

copious (kō′ pē əs) *adj.* plentiful; abundant

cornice (kôr′ nis) *n.* projecting decorative molding along the top of a building

corollary (kôr′ ə ler′ ē) *n.* easily drawn conclusion

cosmopolitan (käz′ mə päl′ ə tən) *adj.* at ease in all countries or places

countenance (koun′ tə nəns) *v.* approve; tolerate

craven (krā′ vən) *adj.* very cowardly

crevices (krev′ is iz) *n.* narrow cracks or splits

cronies (krō′ nēz) *n.* close companions

cunning (kun′ iŋ) *adj.* skillful in deception; crafty; sly

declivity (dē kliv′ ə tē) *n.* downward slope

decorously (dek′ ər əs lē) adv. characterized by or showing decorum and good taste

deduce (dē do͞os) *v.* tell what you figure out by using logic to apply general information to a particular situation

deference (def′ ər əns) *n.* courteous regard or respect; courtesy

deferentially (def′ ər en′ shəl lē) adv. in a manner that bows to another's wishes; very respectfully

define (dē fīn′) *v.* tell the specific qualities or features that make something what it is

degenerate (dē jen′ ər it) *adj.* morally corrupt

deliberation (di lib′ ər ā′ shən) *n.* careful consideration

demarcation (dē′ mär kā′ shən) *n.* separation

demonstrate (dəm′ ən strāt′) *v.* use examples to show that you understand how the information works in a specific situation

deposition (dep′ ə zish′ ən) *n.* the testimony of a witness made under oath but not in open court

depravity (di prav′ ə tē) *n.* corruption; wickedness

deprecated (dep′ rə kāt′ id) *v.* expressed disapproval of

depredations (dep′ rə dā′ shənz) *n.* acts of robbing

derivative (də riv′ ə tiv) *adj.* not original; based on something else

describe (di skrīb′) *v.* show that you know and understand something by explaining it in detail

desolate (des′ ə lit) *adj.* forlorn; wretched

despotic (des pät´ ik) *adj.* harsh; cruel; unjust

despotism (des´ pət iz´ əm) *n.* absolute rule; tyranny

dictum (dik´ təm) *n.* formal statement of fact or opinion

differentiate (dif´ ər en´ shē āt) *v.* identify and explain the qualities that distinguish two items or ideas

digress (dì gres´) *v.* depart temporarily from the main subject

dilapidated (də lap´ ə dāt´ id) *adj.* in disrepair

diligence (dil´ ə jəns) *n.* constant, careful effort; perseverance

din (din) *n.* loud, continuous noise; uproar or clamor

discern (di sʉrn´) *v.* perceive or recognize; make out clearly

disconcerting (dis´ kən sʉrt´ iŋ) *adj.* upsetting

discrimination (di skrim´ in ā´ shən) *n.* show of partiality or prejudice

disdain (dis dān´) *n.* scorn

disdainfully (dis dān´ fəl ē) adv. showing scorn or contempt

dispatched (di spacht´) *v.* sent off on a specific assignment

disposition (dis´ pə zish´ ən) *n.* an inclination or tendency; management

dissembling (di sem´ bliŋ) *n.* disguising one's real nature or motives

dissuade (di swād´) *v.* convince someone not to do something

distinguishing (di stiŋ´ gwish iŋ) *adj.* serving to mark as separate or different

divines (də vìnz´) *n.* clergy

divulge (də vulj´) *v.* reveal

docile (däs´ əl) *adj.* easy to direct or manage; obedient

doctrines (däk´ trinz) *n.* religious beliefs or principles

dogma (dôg´ mə) *n.* authoritative doctrines or beliefs

dolorous (dò´ lər əs) *adj.* sad; mournful

domain (dò mān´) *n.* territory; sphere

dominion (də min´ yən) *n.* power to rule

dusky (dus´ kē) *adj.* dim; shadowy

dyspepsia (dis pep´ shə) *n.* indigestion

efface (ə fās´) *v.* erase; wipe out

effaced (ə fāsd´) *adj.* erased; wiped out

effigies (ef´ i jēz) *n.* likenesses; figures, such as dolls or statues

effrontery (e frunt´ ər ē) *n.* shameless boldness

effuse (e fyo͞oz´) *v.* to pour out

elixir (i liks´ ər) *n.* supposed remedy for all ailments

elusive (ē lo͞o´ siv) *adj.* hard to grasp

embankment (em baŋk´ mənt) *n.* mound of earth or stone built to hold back water or support a roadway

emigrants (em´ i grəntz) *n.* people who leave one area to move to another

eminence (em´ i nəns) *n.* greatness; celebrity

empirical (em pir´ i kəl) *adj.* derived from observation or experiment

encampment (en kamp´ mənt) *n.* place where a person has set up camp

encroached (en kròch´ t) *v.* intruded

engrossed (en gròst´) *adj.* occupied wholly; absorbed

entreated (en trēt´ id) *v.* begged; pleaded

enunciated (ē nun´ sē āt´ əd) *v.* pronounced; stated precisely

epitaph (ep´ ə taf) *n.* inscription on a tombstone or grave marker

equanimity (ek´ wə nim ə tē) *n.* composure

equivocal (i kwiv´ ə kəl) *adj.* having more than one possible interpretation

eradicate (e rad´ i kāt´) *v.* wipe out; destroy

etiquette (et´ i kit) *n.* appropriate behavior and ceremonies

evacuated (ē vak´ yo͞o āt´ id) *v.* to have made empty; withdrawn

evaluate (ē val´ yo͞o āt´) *v.* determine the value or importance of something

evitable (ev´ i tə bəl) *adj.* avoidable

exalted (eg zôlt´ id) *adj.* filled with joy or pride; elated

excavated (eks´ kə vāt´ id) *v.* dug out; made a hole

excluded (eks klo͞od´ id) *v.* kept out

exhaust (eg zôst´) *n.* discharge of used steam or gas from an engine

expatriated (eks pā´ trē āt´ id) *adj.* deported; driven from one's native land

expedient (ek spē´ dē ənt) *n.* resource

exquisite (eks´ kwi zit) *adj.* very beautiful; delicate; carefully wrought

extort (eks tôrt´) *v.* to obtain by threat or violence

extricate (eks´ tri kāt´) *v.* set free

fallowness (fal´ ò nis) *n.* inactivity

fasting (fast´ iŋ) *v.* eating very little or nothing

feigned (fānd) *adj.* pretended; faked

felicity (fə lis´ i tē) *n.* happiness; bliss

finite (fí´ nìt´) *adj.* having measurable or definable limits

flagrant (flā´ grənt) *adj.* glaring, outrageous

flamboyant (flam boi´ ənt) *adj.* too extravagant

floundering (floun´ dər iŋ) *n.* awkward struggling

foppery (fäp´ ər ē) *n.* foolishness

foreboding (fôr bòd´ iŋ) *n.* presentiment

foreknowledge (fôr´ näl´ ij) *n.* awareness of something before it happens or exists

forestall (fôr stôl´) *v.* prevent by acting ahead of time

fortuitous (fôr to͞o´ ə təs) *adj.* fortunate

frippery (frip´ ər ē) *n.* showy display of elegance

furtive (f ʉr´ tiv) *adj.* sneaky; stealthy

garrulous (gar´ ə ləs) *adj.* talking too much

genial (jēn´ yəl) *adj.* promoting life and growth

geography (jē äg´ rə fē) *n.* study of Earth's surface

gingerly (jin´ jər lē) adv. very carefully, cautiously

glade (glād) *n.* open space in a wood or forest

glean (glēn) *v.* collect the remaining grain after reaping

grave (grāv) *adj.* serious; solemn

gravity (grav´ i tē) *n.* seriousness

guffawing (gə fô´ iŋ) *adj.* laughing in a loud, coarse manner

guile (gìl) *n.* craftiness

hallow (hal´ ò) *v.* honor as sacred

harrowing (har´ ò iŋ´) *adj.* disturbing; frightening

heirs (erz) *n.* people who carry on the tradition of predecessors

heritage (her´ i tij´) *n.* something handed down from one's ancestors or from the past

host (hòst) *n.* great number

hysterically (hi ster´ i klē) adv. in a highly emotional manner

identify (ì den´ tə fì) *v.* name or show that you recognize something

illiterate (i lit´ ər it) *adj.* unable to read or write

illustrate (il´ ə strāt´) *v.* give examples that show what information means

immortality (im´môr tal´ i tē) *n.* quality or state of being exempt from death; unending existence

impelled (im peld´) *v.* moved; forced

imperceptible (im´ pər sep´ tə bəl) *adj.* barely noticeable

imperially (im pir´ ē əl ē) adv. majestically

imperious (im pir´ ē əs) *adj.* urgent; imperative

impertinent (im pʉrt´ 'n ənt) *adj.* not showing proper respect

imperviousness (im pur´ vē əs nis) *n.* resistance to being affected

impious (im´ pē əs) *adj.* lacking reverence for God

importunate (im pôr´ chə nit) *adj.* insistent

importunities (im´ pôr to͞on´ i tēz) *n.* persistent requests or demands

imprecations (im´ pri kā´ shənz) *n.* curses

improvident (im präv´ ə dənt) *adj.* short-sighted

inaudibly (in ôd´ə blē) adv. in a manner that cannot be heard

incessant (in ses´ənt) *adj.* constant; continuing or repeating in a way that seems endless

incitement (in sìt´ mənt) *n.* act of urging; encouragement

incongruous (in käŋ´ gro͞o əs) adv. inappropriate

incredulously (in krej´ o͞o ləs lē) adv. skeptically

increment (in´ krə mənt) *n.* increase, as in a series

inculcation (in´ kul kā´ shən) *n.* teaching by repetition and urging

indecorous (in dek´ ə rəs) *adj.* improper

indications (in´ di kā´ shənz) *n.* signs; things that point out or signify

ineffable (in ef´ ə bəl) *adj.* too overwhelming to be spoken; inexpressible

inert (in ʉrt´) *adj.* motionless

inextricable (in eks´ tri kə bəl) *adj.* unable to be separated or extracted from

infallibility (in fal´ ə bil´ ə tē) *n.* inability to be wrong; reliability

infer (in f ʉr´) *v.* show that you have used text details to figure out what it not stated

infidel (in′ fə dəl′) *n.* a person who holds no religious belief
infinity (in fin′ i tē) *n.* endless or unlimited space, time, or distance
ingratiating (in grā′ shē āt′ iŋ) *adj.* charming or flattering
iniquity (i nik′ wi tē) *n.* sin
insatiable (in sā′ shə bəl) *adj.* constantly wanting more
inscrutable (in skro͞ot′ ə bəl) *adj.* not able to be easily understood; impossible to see
insidious (in sid′ ē əs) *adj.* deceitful; secretly treacherous
insurgents (in sur′ jənts) *n.* rebels; those who revolt against authority
integral (in′tə grəl) *adj.* essential
interminable (in tur′ mi nə bəl) *adj.* seeming to last forever
interpret (in tur′ prət) *v.* explain the underlying meaning of a phrase, a passage, or an entire work by examining words, images, and events
intrigues (in′ trēgz′) *n.* secrets
intriguing (in trē′ giŋ) *adj.* interesting or curious
intuitively (in to͞o′ i tiv lē) adv. instinctively
invalided (in′ və lid id) *v.* released because of illness or disability
invective (in vek′ tiv) *n.* verbal attack; strong criticism
jocularity (jäk′ yo͞o lar′ ə tē) *n.* joking good humor
jubilant (jo͞o′ bə lənt) *adj.* joyful and triumphant
judge (juj) *v.* assess or form an opinion about something
label (lā′ bəl) *v.* attach the correct name to something
labyrinth (lab′ ə rinth′) *n.* network of passages; maze
latent (lāt′ ənt) *adj.* present but invisible or inactive
liberty (lib′ ər tē) *n.* condition of being free from control by others
licentious (lī sen′ shəs) *adj.* lacking moral restraint
limber (lim′ bər) *adj.* flexible
listed (list′ id) *v.* tilted; inclined
literalists (lit′ ər əl ists) *n.* those who take words at their exact meaning
liturgy (lit′ ər jē) *n.* public religious ceremonies; religious ritual
loath (lōth) *adj.* reluctant; unwilling
loathsome (lōth′ səm) *adj.* hateful; detestable
lulled (luld) *v.* calmed or soothed by a gentle sound or motion
luminary (lo͞o′ mə ner′ ē) *adj.* giving off light
lye (lī) *n.* strong alkaline solution used in cleaning and making soap
machetes (mə shet′ ēz) *n.* large heavy knives with broad blades
magnanimity (mag′ nə nim′ ə tē) *n.* ability to rise above pettiness or meanness; generosity
maledictions (mal′ ə dik′ shənz) *n.* curses
malevolence (mə lev′ ə ləns) *n.* malice; spitefulness
malice (mal′ is) *n.* ill will; spite
malign (mə līn′) *adj.* malicious; very harmful
malingers (mə liŋ′ gərz) *v.* pretends to be ill
manifest (man′ ə fest′) *adj.* evident; obvious; clear
manifold (man′ ə fōld′) *adv.* in many ways
maverick (mav′ ər ik) *n.* nonconformist
meditate (med′ ə tāt′) *v.* think deeply; ponder
meditation (med′ ə tā′ shən) *n.* deep thought or solemn reflection
meticulous (mə tik′ yo͞o ləs) *adj.* extremely careful about details
mollified (mäl′ ə fīd′) *v.* soothed; calmed
monotonous (mə nät′ ən əs) *adj.* tiresome because unvarying
monotony (mə nät′ ən ē) *n.* tiresome unchanging sameness; lack of variety
morose (mə rōs′) *adj.* gloomy; sullen
mortality (môr tal′ ə tē) *n.* death on a large scale
multifarious (mul′ tə far′ ē əs) *adj.* having many parts; diverse
multitudinous (mul′ tə to͞od′ ′n əs) *adj.* numerous
mundane (mun dān′) *adj.* commonplace; ordinary
munificent (myo͞o nif′ ə sənt) *adj.* generous
muzzle (muz′ əl) *n.* front end of a barrel of a gun; the snout of an animal
myriad (mir′ ē əd) *adj.* countless
nascent (nas′ ənt, nā′ sənt) *adj.* coming into existence; emerging
nomadic (nō mad′ ik) *adj.* wandering; leading the life of a nomad
nonplused (nän′ plüsd′) *adj.* bewildered; perplexed
obeisance (ō bā′ səns) *n.* gesture of respect
obliterated (ə blit′ ər ā td′) *v.* wiped out
oblivious (ə bliv′ ē əs) *adj.* lacking all awareness
obstinacy (äb′ stə nə sē) *n.* stubbornness
obstinate (äb′ stə nət) *adj.* stubborn
obtuse (äb to͞os′) *adj.* slow to understand or perceive
ominous (äm′ ə nəs) *adj.* threatening; sinister
omnipotent (äm nip′ ə tənt) *adj.* all-powerful
oppress (ə pres′) *v.* keep down by cruel or unjust use of power or authority
oppressed (ə prest′) *v.* kept down by cruel or unjust power
oppresses (ə pres′ əz) *v.* weighs heavily on the mind
ornery (ôr′ nər ē) *adj.* having a mean disposition
orthopedic (ôr′ thō pē′ dik) *adj.* correcting posture or other disorders of the skeletal system
oscillation (äs′ ə lā′ shən) *n.* act of swinging back and forth
ostentation (äs′ tən tā′ shən) *n.* boastful display
ostentatious (äs′ tən tā′ shəs) *adj.* intended to attract notice; showy
pacify (pas′ ə fī′) *v.* calm; soothe
palisades (pal′ ə sādz′) *n.* large, pointed stakes set in the ground to form a fence used for defense
pallor (pal′ ər) *n.* paleness
palpable (pal′ pə bəl) *adj.* able to be touched, felt, or handled
parsimony (pär′ sə mō′ nē) *n.* stinginess
paternal (pə tur′ nəl) *adj.* like a father
patriarch (pā′ trē ärk′) *n.* the father and ruler of a family or tribe
pensive (pen′ siv) *adj.* expressing deep thoughtfulness
pensive (pen′ siv) *adj.* thinking deeply or seriously
penury (pen′ yə rē) *n.* lack of money, property, or necessities
perdition (pər dish′ ən) *n.* complete and irreparable loss; ruin
peremptorily (pər emp′ tə rə lē) *adj.* decisively; commandingly
perfidy (pur′ fə dē) *n.* betrayal of trust
peril (per′ əl) *n.* danger
permeated (pur′ mē āt′ id) *adj.* penetrated and spread through
persevere (pur′ sə vir′) *v.* persist; be steadfast in purpose
pertinaciously (pur′ tə nā′ shəs lē) adv. unyieldingly
pervade (pər vād′) *v.* spread throughout
pervading (pər vād iŋ) *adj.* spreading throughout
pestilential (pes′ tə len′ shəl) *adj.* likely to cause disease
petrified (pe′trə fīd′) *adj.* paralyzed as with fear
phantasm (fan′ taz′ əm) *n.* supernatural form or shape; ghost; figment of the mind
philanthropies (fə lan′ thrə pēz) *n.* charitable acts or gifts
piety (pī′ ə tē) *n.* devotion to religious duties
pilfer (pil′ fər) *v.* steal
placid (plas′ id) *adj.* tranquil; calm; quiet
platitude (plat′ ə to͞od′) *n.* statement lacking originality
plight (plīt) *n.* sad or difficult situation
poignant (pɪn′ yənt) *adj.* sharply painful to the feelings
poise (poiz) *n.* balance; stability
posterity (päs ter′ ə tē) *n.* all succeeding generations
precipitate (prē sip′ ə tāt′) *v.* cause to happen before expected or desired
precipitate (prē sip′ ə tit) *adj.* very sudden
preconceptions (prē′ kən sep′ shənz) *n.* ideas formed beforehand
predict (prē dikt′) *v.* tell what you think will happen based on details in the text
predilection (pred′ ə lek′ shən) *n.* preexisting preference
prelude (prel′ yo͞od) *n.* introductory section of a work of music
preposterous (prē päs′ tər əs) *adj.* ridiculous
prescient (presh′ənt) *adj.* having foreknowledge
pristine (pris′ tēn) *adj.* pure; uncorrupted

prodigious (prə dij′ əs) *adj.* of great size, power, or extent
profundity (prò fun′ də tē) *n.* intellectual depth
profusion (prò fyo͞o′ zhən) *n.* abundance; rich supply
propitiation (prə pish′ ē ā′ shən) *n.* action designed to soothe or satisfy a person, a cause, etc.
propitious (prò pish′ əs) *adj.* favorably inclined or disposed
protruded (prò tro͞od′ id) *v.* jutted out
psychology (sì käl′ ə jē) *n.* science dealing with the mind and with mental and emotional processes
pugilistic (pyo͞o′ jəl is′ tik) *adj.* looking for a fight
purged (purjd) *v.* cleansed
quail (kwāl) *v.* cringe from
quandary (kwän′ dä rē) *n.* state of uncertainty; dilemma
querulous (kwer′ ə ləs) *adj.* inclined to find fault
radiant (rā′ dē ənt) *adj.* shining brightly
ravenous (rav′ ə nəs) *adj.* extremely eager
reaping (rēp′ iŋ) *v.* cutting or harvesting grain from a field
recall (ri kôl′) *v.* tell the details as you remember them
recompense (rek′ əm pens′) *n.* reward; repayment; something given or done in return for something else
recumbent (ri kum′ bənt) *adj.* resting
redolent (red′ əl ənt) *adj.* suggestive
redress (ri dres′) *n.* compensation for a wrong done; atonement; rectification
refluent (ref′ lo͞o ənt) *adj.* flowing back
refuge (ref′ yo͞oj) *n.* shelter or protection from danger
refulgent (ri ful′ jənt) *adj.* radiant; shining
rendezvous (rän′dā vo͞o′) *n.* meeting place
replicate (rep′ li kāt) *v.* duplicate
repose (ri pòz′) *n.* state of being at rest
repression (ri presh′ ən) *n.* restraint
repugnant (ri pug′ nənt) *adj.* offensive; disagreeable
retaliation (ri tal′ ē ā′ shən) *n.* act of returning an injury or wrong
revelation (rev′ə lā′ shən) *n.* discovery
revelatory (rev′ ə lə tôr′ ē) *adj.* revealing; disclosing
reverential (rev′ ə ren′ shəl) *adj.* caused by a feeling of deep respect and love
rueful (ro͞o′ fəl) *adj.* feeling or showing someone sorrow or pity
sagacious (sə gā′ shəs) *adj.* shrewd; perceptive
salient (sāl′ yənt) *adj.* standing out from the rest
sallow (sal′ ò) *adj.* sickly; pale yellow
salutary (sal′ yoo ter′ ē) *adj.* beneficial; promoting a good purpose
scepter (sep′ tər) *n.* a rod or staff held by rulers as a symbol of sovereignty
scourge (skurj) *n.* cause of serious trouble or affliction
semantic (sə man′ tik) *adj.* pertaining to meaning in language
semi-somnambulant (sem′ i säm nam′ byo͞o lənt) *adj.* half-sleepwalking
sentience (sen′ shəns) *n.* capacity of feeling
sepulcher (sep′əl kər) *n.* tomb
serenity (sə ren′ ə tē) *n.* calmness
shackles (shak′ əlz) *n.* restraints on freedom of expression or action
shrouded (shroud′ əd) *v.* wrapped
sibilance (sib′ əl əns) *n.* hissing sound
sinuous (sin′ yo͞o əs) *adj.* moving in and out; wavy
slovenly (sluv′ ən lē) *adj.* untidy
smite (smìt) *v.* kill by a powerful blow
somnolent (säm′ nə lənt) *adj.* sleepy; drowsy
specious (spē′ shəs) *adj.* seeming to be good or sound without actually being so
squander (skwän′ dər) *v.* spend or use wastefully
stark (stärk) *adj.* stiff; rigid; severe
statistics (stə tis′ tiks) *n.* science of collecting and arranging facts about a particular subject in the form of numbers
staunch (stônch) *adj.* strong; unyielding
stealthy (stel′ thē) *adj.* avoiding detection
stocky (stäk′ ē) *adj.* solidly built; sturdy
stoically (stò′ i klē) *adv.* done with indifference to pain or pleasure
stringency (strin′ jən sē) *n.* strictness; severity
subjugation (sub′ jə gā′ shən) *n.* the act of conquering
sublime (sə blìm′) *adj.* inspiring admiration; noble; majestic
subsisted (səb sist′ id) *v.* remained alive; were sustained
subsistence (səb sis′ təns) *n.* means of support
subterranean (sub′ tə rā′ nē ən) *adj.* underground
suffice (sə fis′) *v.* be adequate; meet the needs of
suffrage (suf′ rij) *n.* vote or voting
sullen (sul′ ən) *adj.* sulky; glum
summarily (sə mer′ ə lē) adv. promptly and without formality
summarize (sum′ ə rìz′) *v.* briefly state the most important information and ideas in the text
sundry (sun′ drē) *adj.* various; different
superfluous (so͞o pur′ flo͞o əs) *adj.* excessive; not necessary
supple (sup′ əl) *adj.* able to bend and move easily and nimbly
surmised (sər mìzd′) *v.* guessed
tantalized (tan′ tə lìzd) *adj.* tormented; frustrated
tempest (tem′ pist) *n.* violent storm
tempo (tem′ pò) *n.* rate of activity of a sound or motion; pace
tensile (ten′ sil) *adj.* stretchable
terra firma (ter′ ə fur′ mə) *n.* firm earth; solid ground (Latin)
theology (thē äl′ ə jē) *n.* the study of religion
thwarted (thwôrt əd) *v.* blocked; frustrated
timorous (tim′ ər əs) *adj.* full of fear
transcribed (tran skrìbd′) *v.* wrote or typed a copy
transient (tran′ zē ənt) *adj.* not permanent
transparent (trans per′ ənt) *adj.* capable of being seen through
traversed (trə vurst′) *v.* moved over, across, or through
tremulous (trem′ yo͞o ləs) *adj.* characterized by trembling
tremulously (trem′ yo͞o ləs lē) adv. fearfully; timidly
trough (trôf) *n.* a low point of a wave
tumultuous (to͞o mul′ cho͞o əs) *adj.* rough; stormy
tumultuously (to͞o mul′ cho͞o əs lē) *adv.* in an agitated way
tyranny (tir′ ə nē) *n.* oppressive and unjust government
unalienable (un āl′ yən ə bəl) *adj.* not to be taken away
unanimity (yoo′ nə nim′ ə tē) *n.* complete agreement
ungenial (un jēn′ yəl) *adj.* disagreeable; characterized by bad weather
unscrupulous (un skro͞op′ yə ləs) *adj.* unethical; unprincipled
unwonted (un wän′ tid) *adj.* unusual; unfamiliar
usurers (yo͞o′ zhər ərz) *n.* moneylenders who charge very high interest
usurpations (yo͞o′ sər pā′ shənz) *n.* unlawful seizures of rights or privileges
vagary (və ger′ ē) *n.* unpredictable occurrence
vanquished (vaŋ′ kwisht) *v.* thoroughly defeated
venerable (ven′ər ə bəl) *adj.* worthy of respect; commanding respect
vestiges (ves′ tij iz) *n.* traces
vigilance (vij′ ə ləns) *n.* watchfulness
vigilant (vij′ ə lənt) *adj.* alert to danger
vindicated (vin′ də kāt′ əd) *v.* cleared from blame
viper (vì′pər) *n.* type of snake; a malicious person
virulent (vir′ yoo lənt) *v.* extremely hurtful or infectious
visage (viz′ ij) *n.* appearance
vituperative (vì to͞o′ pər ə tiv) *adj.* spoken abusively
vociferation (vò sif′ ər ā′ shən) *n.* loud or vehement shouting
volition (vò lish′ ən) *n.* act of using the will
voluminous (və lo͞om′ ə nəs) *adj.* of enough material to fill volumes
waggery (wag′ ər ē) *n.* mischievous humor
wanton (wän′ tən) *adj.* senseless; unjustified
wily (wì′ lē) *adj.* sly; cunning

TIPS FOR IMPROVING READING FLUENCY

When you were younger, you learned to read. Then, you read to expand your experiences or for pure enjoyment. Now, you are expected to read to learn. As you progress in school, you are given more and more material to read. The tips on these pages will help you improve your reading fluency, or your ability to read easily, smoothly, and expressively. Use these tips as you read daily.

Keeping Your Concentration

One common problem that readers face is the loss of concentration. When you are reading an assignment, you might find yourself rereading the same sentence several times without really understanding it. The first step in changing this behavior is to notice that you do it. Becoming an active, aware reader will help you get the most from your assignments. Practice using these strategies:

- Cover what you have already read with a note card as you go along. Then, you will not be able to reread without noticing that you are doing it.
- Set a purpose for reading beyond just completing the assignment. Then, read actively by pausing to ask yourself questions about the material as you read. Check the accuracy of your answers as you continue to read.
- Use the Reading Strategy instruction and notes that appear with each selection in this textbook.
- Look at any art or illustrations that accompany the reading and use picture clues to help your comprehension.
- Stop reading after a specified period of time (for example, 5 minutes) and summarize what you have read. To help you with this strategy, use the Reading Check questions that appear with each selection in this textbook. Reread to find any answers you do not know.

Reading Phrases

Fluent readers read phrases rather than individual words. Reading this way will speed up your reading and improve your comprehension. Here are some useful ideas:

- Experts recommend rereading as a strategy to increase fluency. Choose a passage of text that is neither too hard nor too easy. Read the same passage aloud several times until you can read it smoothly. When you can read the passage fluently, pick another passage and keep practicing.
- Read aloud into a tape recorder. Then, listen to the recording, noting your accuracy, pacing, and expression. You can also read aloud and share feedback with a partner.
- Use the *Prentice Hall Listening to Literature* audiotapes or CDs to hear the selections read aloud. Read along silently in your textbook, noticing how the reader uses his or her voice and emphasizes certain words and phrases.
- Set a target reading rate. Time yourself as you read and work to increase your speed without sacrificing the level of your comprehension.

Understanding Key Vocabulary

If you do not understand some of the words in an assignment, you may miss out on important concepts. Therefore, it is helpful to keep a dictionary nearby when you are reading. Follow these steps:

- Before you begin reading, scan the text for unfamiliar words or terms. Find out what those words mean before you begin reading.
- Use context—the surrounding words, phrases, and sentences—to help you determine the meanings of unfamiliar words.
- If you are unable to understand the meaning through context, refer to the dictionary.

Paying Attention to Punctuation

When you read, pay attention to punctuation. Commas, periods, exclamation points, semicolons, and colons tell you when to pause or stop. They also indicate relationships between groups of words. When you recognize these relationships you will read with greater understanding and expression. Look at the chart below.

Punctuation Mark	Meaning
comma	brief pause
period	pause at the end of a thought
exclamation point	pause that indicates emphasis
semicolon	pause between related but distinct thoughts
colon	pause before giving explanation or examples

Using the Reading Fluency Checklist

Use the checklist below each time you read a selection in this textbook. In your Language Arts journal or notebook, note which skills you need to work on and chart your progress each week.

Reading Fluency Checklist

- ❑ Preview the text to check for difficult or unfamiliar words.
- ❑ Practice reading aloud.
- ❑ Read according to punctuation.
- ❑ Break down long sentences into the subject and its meaning.
- ❑ Read groups of words for meaning rather than reading single words.
- ❑ Read with expression (change your tone of voice to add meaning to the word).

Reading is a skill that can be improved with practice. The key to improving your fluency is to read. The more you read, the better your reading will become.

HIGH-FREQUENCY ACADEMIC WORDS

Academic vocabulary is the specialized vocabulary that appears frequently throughout academic texts in all content areas, including standardized tests and textbooks. The words on this page are culled from a variety of academic vocabulary word lists, including the work of Averil Coxhead, Jim Burke, and Xue Guoyi and I.S.P. Nation. Words in green are featured in the Vocabulary Workshops in this book.

abstract
affect
alter
analogy
analyze
anticipate
apply
approach
appropriate
approximate
aspects
assemble
assert
assess
assume
brief
category
chart
cite
clarify
code
coherent
compare
compile
complement
conceive
conclude
conduct
confirm
consequence
consist
constant
constitutes
consult
contend
context
contradict
contrast
correlate
correspond
credible
credit
criteria
crucial
debate
deduce
define
demonstrate
derive
describe

detect
devise
differentiate
dimension
diminish
discriminate
domain
draft
edit
elements
emphasize
equivalent
establish
estimate
evaluate
exclude
exhibit
extract
factor
feature
focus
format
formulate
fragment
graph
highlight
hypothesize
identify
illustrate
imply
incorporate
indicate
infer
integrate
interact
interpret
investigate
involve
isolate
judge
label
locate
margin
metaphor
method
modify
monitor
notation
objective
occur

participation
perspective
plot
predict
presume
previous
primary
prior
process
project
quote
reaction
recall
relevant
require
respond
reveal
revise
score
series
significance
source
spatial
specific
speculate
strategy
structure
style
subjective
subsequent
substitute
sum
summarize
summary
survey
technique
theme
thesis
tone
topic
trace
trait
transition
unique
utilize
valid
vary
verify

THE LIFE OF THE ENGLISH LANGUAGE

The life of every language depends on the people who use it. Whenever you use English by asking a question, talking on the phone, going to a movie, reading a magazine, or writing an e-mail, you keep it healthy and valuable.

Using a Dictionary

Use a **dictionary** to find the meaning, the pronunciation, and the part of speech of a word. Consult a dictionary also to trace the word's *etymology,* or its origin. Etymology explains how words change, how they are borrowed from other languages, and how new words are invented.

Here is an entry from a dictionary. Notice what it tells about the word *anthology.*

anthology (an thäl'ə jē) ***n.,*** *pl.* **–gies** [Gr. *anthologia,* a garland, collection of short poems < *anthologos,* gathering flowers < *anthos,* flower + *legein,* to gather] a collection of poems, stories, songs, excerpts, etc., chosen by the compiler

Dictionaries provide the *denotation* of each word, or its objective meaning. The symbol < means "comes from" or "is derived from." In this case, the Greek words for "flower" and "gather" combined to form a Greek word that meant a garland, and then that word became an English word that means a collection of literary flowers—a collection of literature like the one you are reading now.

Using a Thesaurus

Use a **thesaurus** to increase your vocabulary. In a thesaurus, you will find synonyms, or words that have similar meanings, for most words. When you use a thesaurus:

- Do not choose a word just because it sounds interesting or educated. Choose the word that expresses exactly the meaning you intend.
- To avoid errors, look up the word in a dictionary to check its precise meaning and to make sure you are using it properly.

Here is an entry from a thesaurus. Notice what it tells about the word *book.*

book *noun* A printed and bound work: tome, volume. *See* WORDS.

book *verb* **1.** To register in or as if in a book: catalog, enroll, inscribe, list, set down, write down. *See* REMEMBER. **2.** To cause to be set aside, as for one's use, in advance: bespeak, engage, reserve. *See* GET.

If the word can be used as different parts of speech, as *book* can, the thesaurus entry provides synonyms for the word as each part of speech. Many words also have *connotations,* or emotional associations that the word calls to mind. A thesaurus entry also gives specific synonyms for each connotation of the word.

Activity: Look up the words *knight* and *chivalry* in a dictionary. **(a)** What are their etymologies? **(b)** Explain what their etymologies reveal about the development of English.

Then, check the word *chivalry* in a thesaurus. **(c)** What are two synonyms for this word? **(d)** In what way do the connotations of the synonyms differ?

The Origin and Development of English

Old Engish English began about the year 500 when Germanic tribes settled in Britain. The language of these peoples—the Angles, Saxons, and Jutes—combined with Danish and Norse when Vikings attacked Britain and added some Latin elements when Christian missionaries arrived. The result was Old English, which looked like this:

Hwaet! We Gar-Dena   in gear-dagum,
peod-cyninga,   prym gefrunon,
hu da aepelingas   ellen fremedon!

These words are the opening lines of the Old English epic poem *Beowulf,* probably composed in the eighth century. In modern English, they mean: "Listen! We know the ancient glory of the Spear-Danes, and the heroic deeds of those noble kings!"

Middle English The biggest change in English took place after the Norman Conquest of Britain in 1066. The Normans spoke a dialect of Old French, and Old English changed dramatically when the Normans became the new aristocracy. From about 1100 to 1500, the people of Britain spoke what we now call Middle English.

A Knyght ther was, and that a worthy man,
That fro the tyme that he first bigan
To riden out, he loved chivalrie,
Trouthe and honour, fredom and curtesie.

These lines from the opening section of Chaucer's *Canterbury Tales* (c. 1400) are much easier for us to understand than lines from *Beowulf.* They mean: "There was a knight, a worthy man who, from the time he began to ride, loved chivalry, truth, honor, freedom, and courtesy."

Modern English During the Renaissance, with its emphasis on reviving classical culture, Greek and Latin languages exerted a strong influence on the English language. In addition, Shakespeare added about two thousand words to the language. Grammar, spelling, and pronunciation continued to change. Modern English was born.

But soft! What light through yonder window breaks?

It is the East, and Juliet is the sun!

These lines from Shakespeare's *Romeo and Juliet* (c. 1600) need no translation, although it is helpful to know that "soft" means "speak softly." Since Shakespeare's day, conventions of usage and grammar have continued to change. For example, the *th* at the ends of many verbs has become *s.* In Shakespeare's time, it was correct to say "Romeo *hath* fallen in love." In our time, it is right to say "he *has* fallen in love." However, the changes of the past five hundred years are not nearly as drastic as the changes from Old English to Middle English, or from Middle English to Modern English. We still speak Modern English.

Old Words, New Words

Modern English has a larger vocabulary than any other language in the world. The *Oxford English Dictionary* contains about a half million words, and it is estimated that another half million scientific and technical terms do not appear in the dictionary. Here are the main ways that new words enter the language:

- **War**—Conquerors introduce new terms and ideas—and new vocabulary, such as *anger,* from Old Norse.
- **Immigration**—When large groups of people move from one country to another, they bring their languages with them, such as *boycott,* from Ireland.
- **Travel and Trade**—Those who travel to foreign lands and those who do business in faraway places bring new words back with them, such as *shampoo,* from Hindi.
- **Science and Technology**—In our time, the amazing growth of science and technology adds multitudes of new words to English, such as *Internet.*

English is also filled with **borrowings,** words taken directly from other languages. Sometimes borrowed words keep basically the same meanings they have in their original languages: *pajamas* (Hindi), *sauna* (Finnish), *camouflage* (French), *plaza* (Spanish). Sometimes borrowed words take on new meanings. *Sleuth,* for example, an Old Norse word for *trail,* has come to mean the person who follows a trail—a detective.

Mythology contributed to our language too. Some of the days of the week are named after Norse gods—Wednesday was Woden's Day, Thursday was Thor's Day. Greek and Roman myths have given us many words, such as *jovial* (from Jove), *martial* (from Mars), *mercurial* (from Mercury), and *herculean* (from Hercules).

Americanisms are words, phrases, usages, or idioms that originated in American English or that are unique to the way Americans speak. They are expressions of our national character in all its variety: *easy as pie, prairie dog, bamboozle, panhandle, halftime, fringe benefit, bookmobile, jackhammer, southpaw, lickety split.*

Activity: Look up the following words in a dictionary. Describe the ways in which you think these words entered American English.

sabotage *burrito* *moccasin* *mecca* *megabyte*

The Influence of English

English continues to have an effect on world cultures and literature. There are about three hundred million native English speakers, and about the same number who speak English as a second language. Although more people speak Mandarin Chinese, English is the dominant language of trade, tourism, international diplomacy, science, and technology.

Language is a vehicle of both communication and culture, and the cultural influence of English in the twenty-first century is unprecedented in the history of the world's languages. Beyond business and science, English spreads through sports, pop music, Hollywood movies, television, and journalism. A book that is translated into English reaches many more people than it would in its native language alone. Perhaps most significantly, English dominates the Internet. The next time you log on, notice how many websites from around the world also have an English version. The global use of English is the closest the world has ever come to speaking an international language.

Activity: Choose one area of culture—such as sports, fashion, the arts, or technology—and identify three new words that English has recently added to the *world's* vocabulary. **(a)** How do you think non-English speakers feel about the spread of English? **(b)** Do you think English helps to bring people together? Why or why not?

LITERARY TERMS

ALLEGORY An *allegory* is a story or tale with two or more levels of meaning—a literal level and one or more symbolic levels. The events, setting, and characters in an allegory are symbols for ideas or qualities. Many of Nathaniel Hawthorne's short stories, such as "The Minister's Black Veil" (p. 340), are allegories.

ALLITERATION *Alliteration* is the repetition of consonant sounds at the beginning of words or accented syllables. Sara Teasdale uses alliteration in these lines from her poem "Understanding":

> Your spirit's secret hides like gold
> Sunk in a Spanish galleon

ALLUSION An *allusion* is a reference to a well-known person, place, event, literary work, or work of art. Writers often make allusions to stories from the Bible, to Greek and Roman myths, to plays by Shakespeare, to political and historical events, and to other materials with which they can expect their readers to be familiar. In "The Love Song of J. Alfred Prufrock" (p. 716), T. S. Eliot alludes to, among other things, Dante's *Inferno,* Italian artist Michelangelo, Shakespeare's *Hamlet,* and the Bible. By using allusions, writers can suggest complex ideas simply and easily.

AMBIGUITY *Ambiguity* is the effect created when words suggest and support two or more divergent interpretations. Ambiguity may be used in literature to express experiences or truths that are complex or contradictory. Ambiguity often derives from the fact that words have multiple meanings.

See also Irony.

ANALOGY An *analogy* is an extended comparison of relationships. It is based on the idea that the relationship between one pair of things is like the relationship between another pair. Unlike a metaphor, an analogy involves an explicit comparison, often using the words *like* or *as.*

See also Metaphor, Simile.

ANECDOTE An *anecdote* is a brief story about an interesting, amusing, or strange event. An anecdote is told to entertain or to make a point. In the excerpt from *Life on the Mississippi* (p. 576), Mark Twain tells several anecdotes about his experiences on the Mississippi River.

ANTAGONIST An *antagonist* is a character or force in conflict with a main character, or protagonist. In Jack London's "To Build a Fire" (p. 620), the antagonist is neither a person nor an animal but rather the extreme cold. In many stories, the conflict between the antagonist and the protagonist is the basis for the plot.

See also Conflict, Plot, *and* Protagonist.

APHORISM An *aphorism* is a general truth or observation about life, usually stated concisely. Often witty and wise, aphorisms appear in many kinds of works. An essay writer may have an aphoristic style, making many such statements. Ralph Waldo Emerson was famous for his aphoristic style. His essay entitled "Fate" contains the following aphorisms:

> Nature is what you may do.
> So far as a man thinks, he is free.
> A man's fortunes are the fruit of his character.

Used in an essay, an aphorism can be a memorable way to sum up or to reinforce a point or an argument.

APOSTROPHE An *apostrophe* is a figure of speech in which a speaker directly addresses an absent person or a personified quality, object, or idea. Phillis Wheatley uses apostrophe in this line from "To the University of Cambridge, in New England":

> Students, to you 'tis given to scan the heights

See also Figurative Language.

ARCHETYPAL LITERARY ELEMENTS *Archetypal literary elements* are patterns in literature found around the world. For instance, the occurrence of events in threes is an archetypal element of fairy tales. Certain character types, such as mysterious guides, are also archetypal elements of such traditional stories. Archetypal elements make stories easier to remember and retell. In *Moby-Dick* (p. 358), Melville uses the archetype of a whale—like the biblical mammal in conflict with Jonah—to address man's conflict with nature.

ASSONANCE *Assonance* is the repetition of vowel sounds in conjunction with dissimilar consonant sounds. Emily Dickinson uses assonance in the line "The mountain at a given distance." The *i* sound is repeated in *given* and *distance,* in the context of the dissimilar consonant sounds *g–v* and *d–s.*

ATMOSPHERE *See* Mood.

AUTOBIOGRAPHY An *autobiography* is a form of nonfiction in which a person tells his or her own life story. Notable examples of autobiographies include those by Benjamin Franklin and Frederick Douglass. *Memoirs,* first-person accounts of personally or historically significant events in which the writer was a participant or an eyewitness, are a form of autobiographical writing.

See also Biography *and* Journal.

BALLAD A *ballad* is a songlike poem that tells a story, often one dealing with adventure and romance. Most ballads include simple language, four- or six-line stanzas, rhyme, and regular meter.

BIOGRAPHY A *biography* is a form of nonfiction in which a writer tells the life story of another person. Carl Sandburg's *Abe Lincoln Grows Up* is a biography of President Lincoln.

See also Autobiography.

BLANK VERSE *Blank verse* is poetry written in unrhymed iambic pentameter. An iamb is a poetic foot consisting of one weak stress followed by one strong stress. A pentameter line has five poetic feet. Robert Frost's "Birches" (p. 882) is written in blank verse.

CHARACTER A *character* is a person or an animal that takes part in the action of a literary work. The following are some terms used to describe various types of characters:

The *main character* in a literary work is the one on whom the work focuses. *Major characters* in a literary work include the main character and any other characters who play significant roles. A *minor character* is one who does not play a significant role. A *round character* is one who is complex and multifaceted, like a real person. A *flat character* is one who is one-dimensional. A *dynamic character* is one who changes in the course of a work. A *static character* is one who does not change in the course of a work.

See also Characterization *and* Motivation.

CHARACTERIZATION *Characterization* is the act of creating and developing a character. In *direct characterization,* a writer simply states a character's traits, as when F. Scott Fitzgerald writes of the main character in his story "Winter Dreams" (p. 742), "He wanted not association with glittering things and glittering people—he wanted the glittering things themselves." In *indirect characterization*, character is revealed through one of the following means:

1. words, thoughts, or actions of the character
2. descriptions of the character's appearance or background
3. what other characters say about the character
4. the ways in which other characters react to the character

See also Character.

CINQUAIN *See* Stanza.

CLASSICISM *Classicism* is an approach to literature and the other arts that stresses reason, balance, clarity, ideal beauty, and orderly form in imitation of the arts of ancient Greece and Rome. Classicism is often contrasted with *Romanticism,* which stresses imagination, emotion, and individualism. Classicism also differs from *Realism,* which stresses the actual rather than the ideal.

See also Realism *and* Romanticism.

CLIMAX The *climax* is the high point of interest or suspense in a literary work. For example, Jack London's "To Build a Fire" (p. 620) reaches its climax when the man realizes that he is going to freeze to death. The climax generally appears near the end of a story, play, or narrative poem.

See also Plot.

COMEDY A *comedy* is a literary work, especially a play, that has a happy ending.

CONFLICT A *conflict* is a struggle between opposing forces. Sometimes this struggle is internal, or within a character, as in Bernard Malamud's "The First Seven Years" (p. 998). At other times, this struggle is external, or between a character and an outside force, as in Jack London's "To Build a Fire" (p. 620). Conflict is one of the primary elements of narrative literature because most plots develop from conflicts.

See also Antagonist, Plot, *and* Protagonist.

CONNOTATION A *connotation* is an association that a word calls to mind in addition to the dictionary meaning of the word. Many words that are similar in their dictionary meanings, or denotations, are quite different in their connotations. Consider, for example, José García Villa's line, "Be beautiful, noble, like the antique ant." This line would have a very different effect if it were "Be pretty, classy, like the old ant." Poets and other writers choose their words carefully so that the connotations of those words will be appropriate.

See also Denotation.

CONSONANCE *Consonance* is the repetition of similar final consonant sounds at the ends of words or accented syllables. Emily Dickinson uses consonance in these lines:

> But if he ask where you are hid
> Until to-morrow,—happy letter!
> Gesture, coquette, and shake your head!

COUPLET *See* Stanza.

CRISIS In the plot of a narrative, the *crisis* is the turning point for the protagonist—the point at which the protagonist's situation or understanding changes dramatically. In Bernard Malamud's "The First Seven Years" (p. 998), the crisis occurs when Feld recognizes that Sobel loves Miriam.

DENOTATION The *denotation* of a word is its objective meaning, independent of other associations that the word brings to mind.

See also Connotation.

DENOUEMENT *See* Plot.

DESCRIPTION A *description* is a portrayal, in words, of something that can be perceived by the senses. Writers create descriptions by using images, as John Wesley Powell does in this passage from "The Most Sublime Spectacle on Earth," his description of the Grand Canyon (p. 301):

> Clouds creep out of canyons and wind into other canyons. The heavens seem to be alive, not moving as move the heavens over a plain, in one direction with the wind, but following the multiplied courses of these gorges.

See also Image.

DEVELOPMENT *See* Plot.

DIALECT A *dialect* is the form of a language spoken by people in a particular region or group. Writers often use dialect to make their characters seem realistic and to create local color. See, for example, Mark Twain's "The Notorious Jumping Frog of Calaveras County" (p. 581).
See also Local Color.

DIALOGUE A *dialogue* is a conversation between characters. Writers use dialogue to reveal character, to present events, to add variety to narratives, and to arouse their readers' interest.
See also Drama.

DICTION *Diction* is a writer's or speaker's word choice. Diction is part of a writer's style and may be described as formal or informal, plain or ornate, common or technical, abstract or concrete.
See also Style.

DRAMA A *drama* is a story written to be performed by actors. The playwright supplies dialogue for the characters to speak, as well as stage directions that give information about costumes, lighting, scenery, properties, the setting, and the characters' movements and ways of speaking. Dramatic conventions include soliloquies, asides, or the passage of time between acts or scenes.

See also Genre.

DRAMATIC MONOLOGUE A *dramatic monologue* is a poem or speech in which an imaginary character speaks to a silent listener. T. S. Eliot's "The Love Song of J. Alfred Prufrock" (p. 716) is a dramatic monologue.

See also Dramatic Poem *and* Monologue.

DRAMATIC POEM A *dramatic poem* is one that makes use of the conventions of drama. Such poems may be monologues or dialogues or may present the speech of many characters. Robert Frost's "The Death of the Hired Man" is a famous example of a dramatic poem.

See also Dramatic Monologue.

DYNAMIC CHARACTER *See* Character.

EPIGRAM An *epigram* is a brief, pointed statement, in prose or in verse. Benjamin Franklin was famous for his epigrams, which include "Fools make feasts, and wise men eat them," and "A plowman on his legs is higher than a gentleman on his knees."

EPIPHANY An *epiphany* is a sudden revelation or flash of insight. The shoemaker in Bernard Malamud's "The First Seven Years" (p. 998) experiences an epiphany when he suddenly and thoroughly comprehends that the actions of his apprentice, Sobel, are motivated by his secret love for Miriam.

ESSAY An *essay* is a short nonfiction work about a particular subject. Essays can be classified as *formal* or *informal*, *personal* or *impersonal.* They can also be classified according to purpose, such as *analytical* (see the excerpt from *Loneliness . . . An American Malady* on p. 1153), *satirical* (see "Coyote v. Acme" on p. 1148), or *reflective* (see Amy Tan's "Mother Tongue" on p. 1172). Modes of discourse, such as *expository, descriptive, persuasive*, or *narrative*, are other means of classifying essays.

See also Satire, Exposition, Description, Persuasion, *and* Narration.

EXPOSITION *Exposition* is writing or speech that explains, informs, or presents information. The main techniques of expository writing include analysis, classification, comparison and contrast, definition, and exemplification, or illustration. An essay may be primarily expository, as is William Safire's "Onomatopoeia" (p. 1146), or it may use exposition to support another purpose, such as persuasion or argumentation, as in Ian Frazier's satirical essay "Coyote v. Acme" (p. 1148).

In a story or play, the exposition is that part of the plot that introduces the characters, the setting, and the basic situation.
See also Plot.

FALLING ACTION *See* Plot.

FICTION *Fiction* is prose writing that tells about imaginary characters and events. Short stories and novels are works of fiction.

See also Genre, Narrative, Nonfiction, *and* Prose.

FIGURATIVE LANGUAGE *Figurative language* is writing or speech not meant to be taken literally. Writers use figurative language to express ideas in vivid and imaginative ways. For example, Emily Dickinson begins one poem with the following description of snow:

> It sifts from leaden sieves, / It powders all the wood

By describing the snow as if it were flour, Dickinson renders a precise and compelling picture of it.
See also Figure of Speech.

FIGURE OF SPEECH A *figure of speech* is an expression or a word used imaginatively rather than literally.

See also Figurative Language.

FLASHBACK A *flashback* is a section of a literary work that interrupts the chronological presentation of events to relate an event from an earlier time. A writer may present a flashback as a character's memory or recollection, as part of an account or story told by a character, as a dream or a daydream, or simply by having the narrator switch to a time in the past.

FLAT CHARACTER *See* Character.

FOIL A *foil* is a character who provides a contrast to another character. In F. Scott Fitzgerald's "Winter Dreams" (p. 742), Irene Scheerer is a foil for the tantalizing Judy Jones.

FOLK LITERATURE *Folk literature* is the body of stories, legends, myths, ballads, songs, riddles, sayings, and other works arising out of the oral traditions of peoples around the globe. The folk literature traditions of the United States, including those of Native Americans and of the American pioneers, are especially rich.

FOOT *See* Meter.

FORESHADOWING *Foreshadowing* in a literary work is the use of clues to suggest events that have yet to occur.

FREE VERSE *Free verse* is poetry that lacks a regular rhythmical pattern, or meter. A writer of free verse is at liberty to use any rhythms that are appropriate to what he or she is saying. Free verse has been widely used by twentieth-century poets such as Leslie Marmon Silko, who begins "Where Mountain Lion Lay Down With Deer" with these lines:

I climb the black rock mountain
          stepping from day to day
                              silently.

See also Meter.

GENRE A *genre* is a division, or type, of literature. Literature is commonly divided into three major genres: poetry, prose, and drama. Each major genre can in turn be divided into smaller genres. Poetry can be divided into lyric, concrete, dramatic, narrative, and epic poetry. Prose can be divided into fiction and nonfiction. Drama can be divided into serious drama, tragedy, comic drama, melodrama, and farce.

See also Drama, Poetry, *and* Prose.

GOTHIC *Gothic* refers to the use of primitive, medieval, wild, or mysterious elements in literature. Gothic novels feature places like mysterious and gloomy castles, where horrifying, supernatural events take place. Their influence on Edgar Allan Poe is evident in "The Fall of the House of Usher" (p. 312).

GROTESQUE *Grotesque* refers to the use of bizarre, absurd, or fantastic elements in literature. The grotesque is generally characterized by distortions or striking incongruities. *Grotesque characters*, like those in Flannery O'Connor's "The Life You Save May Be Your Own" (p. 982), are characters who have become bizarre through their obsession with an idea or a value or as a result of an emotional problem.

HARLEM RENAISSANCE The *Harlem Renaissance*, which occurred during the 1920s, was a time of African American artistic creativity centered in Harlem, in New York City. Writers of the Harlem Renaissance include Countee Cullen, Claude McKay, Jean Toomer, and Langston Hughes.

HYPERBOLE *Hyperbole* is a deliberate exaggeration or overstatement, often used for comic effect. In Mark Twain's "The Notorious Jumping Frog of Calaveras County" (p. 581), the claim that Jim Smiley would follow a bug as far as Mexico to win a bet is hyperbole.

IAMBIC PENTAMETER *Iambic pentameter* is a line of poetry with five iambic feet, each containing one unstressed syllable followed by one stressed syllable (˘ ´). Iambic pentameter may be rhymed or unrhymed. Unrhymed iambic pentameter is called blank verse. These lines from Anne Bradstreet's "The Author to Her Book" are in iambic pentameter:

Ănd fór thy̆, Móthĕr, shé ălás ĭs póor,
Whĭch cáused hĕr thús tŏ sénd thĕe oút
    ŏf dóor.

See also Blank Verse *and* Meter.

IDYLL An *idyll* is a poem or part of a poem that describes and idealizes country life. John Greenleaf Whittier's "Snowbound" (excerpt on p. 282) is an idyll.

IMAGE An *image* is a word or phrase that appeals to one or more of the five senses—sight, hearing, touch, taste, or smell.

See also Imagery.

IMAGERY *Imagery* is the descriptive or figurative language used in literature to create word pictures for the reader. These pictures, or images, are created by details of sight, sound, taste, touch, smell, or movement.

IMAGISM *Imagism* was a literary movement that flourished between 1912 and 1927. Led by Ezra Pound and Amy Lowell, the Imagist poets rejected nineteenth-century poetic forms and language. Instead, they wrote short poems that used ordinary language and free verse to create sharp, exact, concentrated pictures. Pound's poetry (p. 727) provides examples of Imagism.

IRONY *Irony* is a contrast between what is stated and what is meant, or between what is expected to happen and what actually happens. In *verbal irony*, a word or a phrase is used to suggest the opposite of its usual meaning. In *dramatic irony*, there is a contradiction between what a character thinks and what the reader or audience knows. In *irony of situation*, an event occurs that contradicts the expectations of the characters, of the reader, or of the audience.

JOURNAL A *journal* is a daily autobiographical account of events and personal reactions. For example, Mary Chesnut's journal (p. 550) records events during the Civil War.

LEGEND A *legend* is a traditional story. Usually a legend deals with a particular person—a hero, a saint, or a national leader. Often legends reflect a people's cultural values. American legends include those of the early Native Americans and those about folk heroes such as Davy Crockett.

See also Myth.

LETTER A *letter* is a written message or communication addressed to a reader or readers and is generally sent by mail. Letters may be *private* or *public*, depending on their intended audience. A *public letter*, also called a *literary letter* or *epistle*, is a work of literature written in the form of a personal letter but created for publication. Michel-Guillaume Jean de Crèvecoeur's "Letters From an American Farmer," excerpted on page 220, are public letters.

LOCAL COLOR *Local color* is the use in a literary work of characters and details unique to a particular geographic area. It can be created by the use of dialect and by descriptions of customs, clothing, manners, attitudes, and landscape. Local-color stories were especially popular after the Civil War, bringing readers the West of Bret Harte and the Mississippi River of Mark Twain.

See also Realism *and* Regionalism.

LYRIC POEM A lyric poem is a melodic poem that expresses the observations and feelings of a single speaker. Unlike a narrative poem, a lyric poem focuses on producing a single, unified effect. Types of lyric poems include the *elegy*, the *ode*, and the *sonnet*. Among contemporary American poets, the lyric is the most common poetic form.

MAIN CHARACTER *See* Character.

MEMOIR A *memoir* is a type of nonfiction autobiographical writing that tells about a person's own life, usually focusing on the writer's involvement in historically or culturally significant events—either as a participant or an eyewitness.

METAPHOR A *metaphor* is a figure of speech in which one thing is spoken of as though it were something else. The identification suggests a comparison between the two things that are identified, as in "death is a long sleep."

A *mixed metaphor* occurs when two metaphors are jumbled together. For example, thorns and rain are illogically mixed in "the thorns of life rained down on him." A *dead metaphor* is one that has been overused and has become a common expression, such as "the arm of the chair" or "nightfall."

METER The *meter* of a poem is its rhythmical pattern. This pattern is determined by the number and types of stresses, or beats, in each line. To describe the meter of a poem, you must scan its lines. *Scanning* involves marking the stressed and unstressed syllables, as follows:

> Sóon ăs | thĕ sún | fŏrsóok | thĕ eás|tĕrn máin
> Thĕ péal | ĭng thún | dĕr shóok | thĕ héav'n | ly̆ pláin;
>
> — "An Hymn to the Evening," p. 182

As the example shows, each strong stress is marked with a slanted line (´) and each weak stress with a horseshoe symbol (˘). The weak and strong stresses are then divided by vertical lines (|) into groups called feet. The following types of feet are common in poetry written in English:

1. *Iamb:* a foot with one unstressed syllable followed by one stressed syllable, as in the word "around"
2. *Trochee:* a foot with one stressed syllable followed by one unstressed syllable, as in the word "broken"
3. *Anapest:* a foot with two unstressed syllables followed by one stressed syllable, as in the phrase "in a flash"
4. *Dactyl:* a foot with one stressed syllable followed by two unstressed syllables, as in the word "argument"
5. *Spondee:* a foot with two stressed syllables, as in the word "airship"
6. *Pyrrhic:* a foot with two unstressed syllables, as in the last foot of the word "imag|ining"

Lines of poetry are often described as *iambic*, *trochaic*, *anapestic*, or *dactylic*. Lines are also described in terms of the number of feet that occur in them, as follows:

1. *Monometer:* verse written in one-foot lines

   Évĭl
   Bĕgéts
   Évĭl

   —Anonymous

2. *Dimeter:* verse written in two-foot lines

   Thís ĭs | thĕ tíme
   ŏf thĕ trág|ĭc mán

   —"Visits to St. Elizabeth's," Elizabeth Bishop

3. *Trimeter:* verse written in three-foot lines:

Ó̆ver | the wĭn|tĕr glắciers
Í̆ see | thĕ sŭm|mĕr glów,
Ănd through | thĕ wild-|pĭlĕd snówdrift
Thĕ wárm | rŏsebúds | bĕlów.

—"Beyond Winter," Ralph Waldo Emerson

4. *Tetrameter:* verse written in four-foot lines:

Thĕ sún | thăt brief | Dĕcém|bĕr dáy
Rŏse cheer|lĕss ŏv|ĕr hílls | ŏf gráy

—"Snowbound," p. 282

5. *Pentameter:* verse written in five-foot lines:

Ĭ dóubt | nŏt Gód | ĭs góod, | wĕll-méan|ĭng, kínd,
Ănd díd | Hĕ stóop | tŏ quíb|blĕ cóuld | tĕll whý
Thĕ lít|tlĕ búr|ĭed móle | cŏntín|ŭes blínd

—"Yet Do I Marvel," Countee Cullen

A complete description of the meter of a line tells both how many feet there are in the line and what kind of foot is most common. Thus, the lines from Countee Cullen's poem would be described as *iambic pentameter. Blank verse* is poetry written in unrhymed iambic pentameter. Poetry that does not have a regular meter is called *free verse.*

MONOLOGUE A *monologue* is a speech delivered entirely by one person or character.

See also Dramatic Monologue.

MOOD *Mood,* or atmosphere, is the feeling created in the reader by a literary work or passage. Elements that can influence the mood of a work include its setting, tone, and events.

See also Setting *and* Tone.

MOTIVATION A *motivation* is a reason that explains a character's thoughts, feelings, actions, or speech. Characters are motivated by their values and by their wants, desires, dreams, wishes, and needs. Sometimes the reasons for a character's actions are stated directly, as in Willa Cather's "A Wagner Matinée" (p. 670), when Clark explains his reception of his aunt by saying, "I owed to this woman most of the good that ever came my way in my boyhood." At other times, the writer will just suggest a character's motivation.

MYTH A *myth* is a fictional tale that explains the actions of gods or heroes or the causes of natural phenomena. Myths that explain the origins of earthly life, as do the Onondaga, Najavo, and Modoc myths in this text, are known as origin myths. Other myths express the central values of the people who created them.

NARRATION *Narration* is writing that tells a story. The act of telling a story is also called *narration.* The *narrative,* or story, is told by a storyteller called the *narrator.* A story is usually told chronologically, in the order in which events take place in time, though it may include flashbacks and foreshadowing. Narratives may be true, like the events recorded in Mary Chesnut's journal (p. 550), or fictional, like the events in Flannery O'Connor's "The Life You Save May Be Your Own" (p. 982). Narration is one of the forms of discourse and is used in novels, short stories, plays, narrative poems, anecdotes, autobiographies, biographies, and reports.

See also Narrative Poem *and* Narrator.

NARRATIVE A *narrative* is a story told in fiction, nonfiction, poetry, or drama. Narratives are often classified by their content or purpose. An *exploration narrative* is a firsthand account of an explorer's travels in a new land. Alvar Núñez Cabeza de Vaca's account of his exploration of the wilderness that is now Texas, "A Journey Through Texas," appears on page 42. "The Interesting Narrative of the Life of Olaudah Equiano" (excerpt on p. 160) is a *slave narrative,* an account of the experiences of an enslaved person. A *historical narrative* is a narrative account of significant historical events, such as John Smith's *The General History of Virginia* (p. 70).

See also Narration.

NARRATIVE POEM A *narrative poem* tells a story in verse. Three traditional types of narrative verse are *ballads,* songlike poems that tell stories; *epics,* long poems about the deeds of gods or heroes; and *metrical romances,* poems that tell tales of love and chivalry.

See also Ballad.

NARRATOR A *narrator* is a speaker or character who tells a story. A story or novel may be narrated by a main character, by a minor character, or by someone uninvolved in the story. The narrator may speak in the first person or in the third person. An *omniscient narrator* is all-knowing, while a *limited narrator* knows only what one character does.

See also Point of View.

NATURALISM *Naturalism* was a literary movement among novelists at the end of the nineteenth century and during the early decades of the twentieth century. The Naturalists tended to view people as hapless victims of immutable natural laws. Early exponents of Naturalism included Stephen Crane, Jack London, and Theodore Dreiser.

See also Realism.

NONFICTION *Nonfiction* is prose writing that presents and explains ideas or that tells about real people, places, objects, or events. Essays, biographies, autobiographies, journals, and reports are all examples of nonfiction.

See also Fiction *and* Genre.

NOVEL A *novel* is a long work of fiction. A novel often has a complicated plot, many major and minor characters, a significant theme, and several varied settings. Novels can be classified in many ways, based on the historical periods in which they are written, the subjects and themes that they treat, the techniques that are used in them, and the literary movements that inspired them. Classic nineteenth-century novels include Herman Melville's *Moby-Dick* (p. 358) and Nathaniel Hawthorne's *The Scarlet Letter* (an extended reading suggestion). Well-known twentieth-century novels include F. Scott Fitzgerald's *The Great Gatsby* and Edith Wharton's *Ethan Frome* (recommended selections for extended reading). A *novella* is not as long as a novel but is longer than a short story. Ernest Hemingway's *The Old Man and the Sea* is a novella.

ODE An *ode* is a long, formal lyric poem with a serious theme that may have a traditional stanza structure. Odes often honor people, commemorate events, respond to natural scenes, or consider serious human problems.

See also Lyric Poem.

OMNISCIENT NARRATOR *See* Narrator *and* Point of View.

ONOMATOPOEIA *Onomatopoeia* is the use of words that imitate sounds. Examples of such words are *buzz, hiss, murmur,* and *rustle.*

ORAL TRADITION *Oral tradition* is the passing of songs, stories, and poems from generation to generation by word of mouth. The oral tradition in America has preserved Native American myths and legends, spirituals, folk ballads, and other works originally heard and memorized rather than written down.

See also Ballad, Folk Literature, Legend, Myth, *and* Spiritual.

ORATORY *Oratory* is public speaking that is formal, persuasive, and emotionally appealing. Patrick Henry's "Speech in the Virginia Convention" (p. 202) is an example of oratory.

OXYMORON An *oxymoron* is a figure of speech that combines two opposing or contradictory ideas. An oxymoron, such as "freezing fire," suggests a paradox in just a few words.

See also Figurative Language *and* Paradox.

PARADOX A *paradox* is a statement that seems to be contradictory but that actually presents a truth. Marianne Moore uses paradox in "Nevertheless" when she says, "Victory won't come / to me unless I go / to it." Because a paradox is surprising, it draws the reader's attention to what is being said.

See also Figurative Language *and* Oxymoron.

PARALLELISM *Parallelism* is the repetition of a grammatical structure. Robert Hayden concludes his poem "Astronauts" with these questions in parallel form:

> What do we want of these men?
> What do we want of ourselves?

Parallelism is used in poetry and in other writing to emphasize and to link related ideas.

PARODY A *parody* is a humorous imitation of a literary work, one that exaggerates or distorts the characteristic features of the original.

PASTORAL *Pastoral* poems deal with rural settings, including shepherds and rustic life. Traditionally, pastoral poems have presented idealized views of rural life. In twentieth-century pastorals, however, poets like Robert Frost introduced ethical complexity into an otherwise simple landsape.

PERSONIFICATION *Personification* is a figure of speech in which a nonhuman subject is given human characteristics. In "April Rain Song," Langston Hughes personifies the rain:

> Let the rain sing you a lullaby.

Effective personification of things or ideas makes them seem vital and alive, as if they were human.

See also Figurative Language.

PERSUASION *Persuasion* is writing or speech that attempts to convince a reader to think or act in a particular way. During the Revolutionary War period, leaders such as Patrick Henry, Thomas Paine, and Thomas Jefferson used persuasion in their political arguments. Persuasion is also used in advertising, in editorials, in sermons, and in political speeches.

PLAIN STYLE *Plain style* is a type of writing in which uncomplicated sentences and ordinary words are used to make simple, direct statements. This style was favored by those Puritans who wanted to express themselves clearly, in accordance with their religious beliefs. In the twentieth century, Ernest Hemingway was a master of plain style.

See also Style.

PLOT *Plot* is the sequence of events in a literary work. In most fiction, the plot involves both characters and a central conflict. The plot usually begins with an *exposition* that introduces the setting, the characters, and the basic situation. This is followed by the *inciting incident,* which introduces the central conflict. The conflict then increases during the *development* until it reaches a high point of interest or suspense, the *climax.* The climax is followed by the end, or *resolution,* of the central conflict. Any events that occur after the resolution make up the *denouement.* The events that lead up to the climax make up the *rising action.* The events that follow the climax make up the *falling action.*

See also Conflict.

POETRY *Poetry* is one of the three major types of literature. In poetry, form and content are closely connected, like the two faces of a single coin. Poems are often divided into lines and stanzas and often employ regular rhythmical patterns, or meters. Most poems use highly concise, musical, and emotionally charged language. Many also make use of imagery, figurative language, and special devices such as rhyme.

See also Genre.

POINT OF VIEW *Point of view* is the perspective, or vantage point, from which a story is told. Three commonly used points of view are first person, omniscient third person, and limited third person.

In the *first-person point of view,* the narrator is a character in the story and refers to himself or herself with the first-person pronoun "I." "The Fall of the House of Usher" (p. 312) is told by a first-person narrator.

The two kinds of third-person point of view, limited and omniscient, are called "third person" because the narrator uses third-person pronouns such as "he" and "she" to refer to the characters. There is no "I" telling the story.

In stories told from the *omniscient third-person point of view,* the narrator knows and tells about what each character feels and thinks. "The Devil and Tom Walker" (p. 258) is written from the omniscient third-person point of view.

In stories told from the *limited third-person point of view,* the narrator relates the inner thoughts and feelings of only one character, and everything is viewed from this character's perspective. "An Occurrence at Owl Creek Bridge" (p. 518) is written from the limited third-person point of view.

See also Narrator.

PROSE *Prose* is the ordinary form of written language. Most writing that is not poetry, drama, or song is considered prose. Prose is one of the major genres of literature. It occurs in two forms: fiction and nonfiction.

See also Fiction, Genre, *and* Nonfiction.

PROTAGONIST The *protagonist* is the main character in a literary work. In "The Jilting of Granny Weatherall" (p. 848), the protagonist is the dying grandmother.

See also Antagonist.

QUATRAIN *See* Stanza.

REALISM *Realism* is the presentation in art of the details of actual life. Realism was also a literary movement that began during the nineteenth century and stressed the actual as opposed to the imagined or the fanciful. The Realists tried to write objectively about ordinary characters in ordinary situations. They reacted against Romanticism, rejecting heroic, adventurous, or unfamiliar subjects. Naturalists, who followed the Realists, traced the effects of heredity and environment on people helpless to change their situations.

See also Local Color, Naturalism, *and* Romanticism.

REFRAIN A refrain is a repeated line or group of lines in a poem or song. Most refrains end stanzas, as does "And the tide rises, the tide falls," the refrain in Henry Wadsworth Longfellow's poem (p. 275), or "Coming for to carry me home," the refrain in "Swing Low, Sweet Chariot" (p. 498). Although some refrains are nonsense lines, many increase suspense or emphasize character and theme.

REGIONALISM Regionalism in literature is the tendency among certain authors to write about specific geographical areas. Regional writers, like Willa Cather and William Faulkner, present the distinct culture of an area, including its speech, customs, beliefs, and history. Local-color writing may be considered a type of Regionalism, but Regionalists, like the Southern writers of the 1920s, usually go beyond mere presentation of cultural idiosyncrasies and attempt, instead, a sophisticated sociological or anthropological treatment of the culture of a region.

See also Local Color *and* Setting.

RESOLUTION *See* Plot.

RHYME *Rhyme* is the repetition of sounds at the ends of words. Rhyming words have identical vowel sounds in their final accented syllables. The consonants before the vowels may be different, but any consonants occurring after these vowels are the same, as in *frog* and *bog* or *willow* and *pillow.* End rhyme occurs when rhyming words are repeated at the ends of lines. Internal rhyme occurs when rhyming words fall within a line. *Approximate,* or *slant, rhyme* occurs when the rhyming sounds are similar, but not exact, as in *prove* and *glove.*

See also Rhyme Scheme.

RHYME SCHEME A *rhyme scheme* is a regular pattern of rhyming words in a poem. To describe a rhyme scheme, one uses a letter of the alphabet to represent each rhyming sound in a poem or stanza. Consider how letters are used to represent the *abab* ryhme scheme rhymes in the following example:

> With innocent wide penguin eyes, three — a
> large fledgling mocking-birds below — b
> the pussywillow tree, — a
> stand in a row. — b
>
> —"Bird-Witted," Marianne Moore

See also Rhyme.

RHYTHM *Rhythm* is the pattern of beats, or stresses, in spoken or written language. Prose and free verse are written in the irregular rhythmical patterns of everyday speech. Consider, for example, the rhythmical pattern in the following free-verse lines by Gwendolyn Brooks:

> Life for my child is simple, and is good.
>
> He knows his wish. Yes, but that is not all.
>
> Because I know mine too.

Traditional poetry often follows a regular rhythmical pattern, as in the following lines by America's first great female poet, Anne Bradstreet:

> In critic's hands beware thou dost not come,
>
> And take thy way where yet thou art not known
>
> —"The Author to Her Book"

See also Meter.

RISING ACTION *See* Plot.

ROMANTICISM *Romanticism* was a literary and artistic movement of the nineteenth century that arose in reaction against eighteenth-century Neoclassicism and placed a premium on imagination, emotion, nature, individuality, and exotica. Romantic elements can be found in the works of American writers as diverse as Cooper, Poe, Thoreau, Emerson, Dickinson, Hawthorne, and Melville. Romanticism is particularly evident in the works of the Transcendentalists.

See also Classicism *and* Transcendentalism.

ROUND CHARACTER *See* Character.

SATIRE *Satire* is writing that ridicules or criticizes individuals, ideas, institutions, social conventions, or other works of art or literature. The writer of a satire, the satirist, may use a tolerant, sympathetic tone or an angry, bitter tone. Some satire is written in prose and some, in poetry. Examples of satire in this text include W. H. Auden's "The Unknown Citizen" (p. 777) and Ian Frazier's "Coyote v. Acme" (p. 1148).

SCANSION *Scansion* is the process of analyzing a poem's metrical pattern. When a poem is scanned, its stressed and unstressed syllables are marked to show what poetic feet are used and how many feet appear in each line. The last two lines of Edna St. Vincent Millay's "I Shall Go Back Again to the Bleak Shore" may be scanned as follows:

> But I | shall find | the sul|len rocks | and skies
>
> Unchanged | from what | they were | when I | was young.

See also Meter.

SENSORY LANGUAGE *Sensory language* is writing or speech that appeals to one or more of the five senses.

See also Image.

SETTING The *setting* of a literary work is the time and place of the action. A setting may serve any of a number of functions. It may provide a background for the action. It may be a crucial element in the plot or central conflict. It may also create a certain emotional atmosphere, or mood.

SHORT STORY A *short story* is a brief work of fiction. The short story resembles the novel but generally has a simpler plot and setting. In addition, the short story tends to reveal character at a crucial moment rather than developing it through many incidents. For example, Thomas Wolfe's "The Far and the Near" (p. 784) concentrates on what happens to a train engineer when he visits people who had waved to him every day.

See also Fiction *and* Genre.

SIMILE A *simile* is a figure of speech that makes a direct comparison between two subjects, using either *like* or *as.* Here are two examples of similes:

> The trees looked like pitch forks against the sullen sky.
>
> Her hair was as red as a robin's breast.

See also Figurative Language.

SLANT RHYME *See* Rhyme.

SONNET A *sonnet* is a fourteen-line lyric poem focused on a single theme. Sonnets have many variations but are usually written in iambic pentameter, following one of two traditional patterns: the *Petrarchan*, or *Italian*, *sonnet*, which is divided into two parts, the eight-line octave and the six-line sestet; and the *Shakespearean*, or *English, sonnet*, which consists of three quatrains and a concluding couplet.

See also Lyric Poem.

SPEAKER The *speaker* is the voice of a poem. Although the speaker is often the poet, the speaker may also be a fictional character or even an inanimate object or another type of non-human entity. Interpreting a poem often depends upon recognizing who the speaker is, whom the speaker is addressing, and what the speaker's attitude, or tone, is.

See also Point of View.

SPIRITUAL A *spiritual* is a type of African American folk song dating from the period of slavery and Reconstruction. A typical spiritual deals both with religious freedom and, on an allegorical level, with political and economic freedom. In some spirituals the biblical river Jordan was used as a symbol for the Ohio River, which separated slave states from free states; and the biblical promised land, Canaan, was used as a symbol for the free northern United States. Most spirituals made use of repetition, parallelism, and rhyme. See "Swing Low, Sweet Chariot" (p. 498) and "Go Down, Moses" (p. 500).

STAGE DIRECTIONS *See* Drama.

STANZA A *stanza* is a group of lines in a poem that are considered to be a unit. Many poems are divided into stanzas that are separated by spaces. Stanzas often function just like paragraphs in prose. Each stanza states and develops a single main idea.

Stanzas are commonly named according to the number of lines found in them, as follows:

1. *Couplet:* a two-line stanza
2. *Tercet:* a three-line stanza
3. *Quatrain:* a four-line stanza
4. *Cinquain:* a five-line stanza
5. *Sestet:* a six-line stanza
6. *Heptastich:* a seven-line stanza
7. *Octave:* an eight-line stanza

STATIC CHARACTER *See* Character.

STREAM OF CONSCIOUSNESS *Stream of consciousness* is a narrative technique that presents thoughts as if they were coming directly from a character's mind. Instead of being arranged in chronological order, the events are presented from the character's point of view, mixed in with the character's thoughts just as they might spontaneously occur. Katherine Anne Porter uses this technique in "The Jilting of Granny Weatherall" (p. 848) to capture Granny's dying thoughts and feelings. Ambrose Bierce also uses the stream of consciousness technique in "An Occurrence at Owl Creek Bridge" (p. 518).

See also Point of View.

STYLE A writer's *style* includes word choice, tone, degree of formality, figurative language, rhythm, grammatical structure, sentence length, organization—in short, every feature of a writer's use of language. Ernest Hemingway, for example, is noted for a simple prose style that contrasts with Thomas Paine's aphoristic style and with N. Scott Momaday's reflective style.

See also Diction *and* Plain Style.

SUSPENSE *Suspense* is a feeling of growing uncertainty about the outcome of events. Writers create suspense by raising questions in the minds of their readers. Suspense builds until the climax of the plot, at which point the suspense reaches its peak.

See also Climax *and* Plot.

SYMBOL A *symbol* is anything that stands for or represents something else. A *conventional symbol* is one that is widely known and accepted, such as a voyage symbolizing life or a skull symbolizing death. A *personal symbol* is one developed for a particular work by a particular author. Examples in this textbook include Hawthorne's black veil and Melville's white whale.

SYMBOLISM *Symbolism* was a literary movement during the nineteenth century that influenced poets, including the Imagists and T. S. Eliot. Symbolists turned away from everyday, realistic details to express emotions by using a pattern of symbols.

See also Imagism *and* Realism.

THEME A *theme* is a central message or insight into life revealed by a literary work. An essay's theme is often directly stated in its thesis statement. In most works of fiction, the theme is only indirectly stated: A story, poem, or play most often has an *implied theme.* For example, in "A Worn Path" (p. 820), Eudora Welty does not directly say that Phoenix Jackson's difficult journey shows the power of love, but readers learn this indirectly by the end of the story.

TONE The tone of a literary work is the writer's attitude toward his or her subject, characters, or audience. A writer's tone may be formal or informal, friendly or distant, personal or pompous. For example, William Faulkner's tone in his "Nobel Prize Acceptance Speech" (p. 875) is earnest and serious, whereas James Thurber's tone in "The Night the Ghost Got In" (p. 898) is humorous and ironic.

See also Mood.

TRAGEDY A *tragedy* is a work of literature, especially a play, that shows the downfall or death of the main character, or *tragic hero.*

TRANSCENDENTALISM *Transcendentalism* was an American literary and philosophical movement of the nineteenth century. The Transcendentalists, who were based in New England, believed that intuition and the individual conscience "transcend" experience and thus are better guides to truth than are the senses and logical reason. Influenced by Romanticism, the Transcendentalists respected the individual spirit and the natural world, believing that divinity was present everywhere, in nature and in each person. The Transcendentalists included Ralph Waldo Emerson, Henry David Thoreau, Bronson Alcott, W. H. Channing, Margaret Fuller, and Elizabeth Peabody.

See also Romanticism.

TIPS FOR DISCUSSING LITERATURE

As you read and study literature, discussions with other readers can help you understand, enjoy, and develop interpretations of what you read. Use the following tips to practice good speaking and listening skills in group discussions of literature.

- **Understand the purpose of your discussion.**
  Your purpose when you discuss literature is to broaden your understanding and appreciation of a work by testing your own ideas and hearing the ideas of others. Be sure to stay focused on the literature you are discussing and to keep your comments relevant to that literature. Starting with one focus question will help to keep your discussion on track.

- **Communicate effectively.**
  Effective communication requires thinking before speaking. Plan the points that you want to make and decide how you will express them. Organize these points in logical order and cite details from the work to support your ideas. Jot down informal notes to help keep your ideas focused.
  Remember to speak clearly, pronouncing words slowly and carefully so that your listeners will understand your ideas. Also, keep in mind that some literature touches readers deeply—be aware of the possibility of counterproductive emotional responses and work to control them.

- **Make relevant contributions.**
  Especially when responding to a short story or a novel, avoid simply summarizing the plot. Instead, consider *what* you think might happen next, *why* events take place as they do, or *how* a writer provokes a response in you. Let your ideas inspire deeper thought or discussion about the literature.

- **Consider other ideas and interpretations.**
  A work of literature can generate a wide variety of responses in different readers—and that can make your discussions really exciting. Be open to the idea that many interpretations can be valid. To support your own ideas, point to the events, descriptions, characters, or other literary elements in the work that led to your interpretation. To consider someone else's ideas, decide whether details in the work support the interpretation he or she presents. Be sure to convey your criticism of the ideas of others in a respectful and supportive manner.

- **Ask questions and extend the contributions of others.**
  Get in the habit of asking questions to help you clarify your understanding of another reader's ideas. You can also use questions to call attention to possible areas of confusion, to points that are open to debate, or to errors in the speaker's points.

  In addition, offer elaboration of the points that others make by providing examples and illustrations from the literature. To move a discussion forward, summarize and evaluate tentative conclusions reached by the group members.

  When you meet with a group to discuss literature, use a chart like the one shown to analyze the discussion.

Work Being Discussed:	
Focus Question:	
Your Response:	Another Student's Response:
Supporting Evidence:	Supporting Evidence:
One New Idea That You Considered About the Work During the Discussion:	

TYPES OF WRITING

NARRATION

Whenever writers tell any type of story, they are using **narration.** Although there are many kinds of narration, most narratives share certain elements, such as characters, a setting, a sequence of events, and, often, a theme. Following are some types of narration:

Autobiographical Writing Autobiographical writing tells a true story about an important period, experience, or relationship in the writer's life. An autobiographical narrative can be as simple as a description of a recent car trip or as complex as the entire story of a person's life. Effective autobiographical writing includes

- A series of events that involve the writer as the main character
- Details, thoughts, feelings, and insights from the writer's perspective
- A conflict or an event that affects the writer
- A logical organization that tells the story clearly
- Insights that the writer gained from the experience

A few types of autobiographical writing are autobiographical incidents, personal narratives, autobiographical narratives or sketches, reflective essays, eyewitness accounts, anecdotes, and memoirs.

Short Story A short story is a brief, creative narrative—a retelling of events arranged to hold a reader's attention. Most short stories include

- Details that establish the setting in time and place
- A main character who undergoes a change or learns something during the course of the story
- A conflict or a problem to be introduced, developed, and resolved
- A plot, the series of events that make up the action of the story
- A theme or generalization about life

A few types of short stories are realistic stories, fantasies, historical narratives, mysteries, thrillers, science-fiction stories, and adventure stories.

DESCRIPTION

Descriptive writing is writing that creates a vivid picture of a person, place, thing, or event. Descriptive writing can stand on its own or be part of a longer work, such as a short story. Most descriptive writing includes

- Sensory details—sights, sounds, smells, tastes, and physical sensations
- Vivid, precise language
- Figurative language or comparisons
- Adjectives and adverbs that paint a word picture
- An organization suited to the subject

Some examples of descriptive writing include description of ideas, observations, travel brochures, physical descriptions, functional descriptions, remembrances, and character sketches.

PERSUASION

Persuasion is writing or speaking that attempts to convince people to accept a position or take a desired action. When used effectively, persuasive writing has the power to change people's lives. As a reader and a writer, you will find yourself engaged in many forms of persuasion. Here are a few of them:

Persuasive Essay A persuasive essay presents your position on an issue, urges your readers to accept that position, and may encourage them to take an action. An effective persuasive essay

- Explores an issue of importance to the writer
- Addresses an issue that is arguable
- Uses facts, examples, statistics, or personal experiences to support a position
- Tries to influence the audience through appeals to the readers' knowledge, experiences, or emotions
- Uses clear organization to present a logical argument

Persuasion can take many forms. A few forms of persuasion include editorials, position papers, persuasive speeches, grant proposals, advertisements, and debates.

Advertisements An advertisement is a planned communication meant to be seen, heard, or read. It attempts to persuade an audience to buy a product or service, accept an idea, or support a cause. Advertisements may appear in printed form—in newspapers and magazines, on billboards, or as posters or flyers. They may appear on radio or television, as commercials or public-service announcements. An effective advertisement includes

- A memorable slogan to grab the audience's attention
- A call to action, which tries to rally the audience to do something
- Persuasive and/or informative text
- Striking visual or aural images
- Details that provide such information as price, location, date, and time

Several common types of advertisements are public-service announcements, billboards, merchandise ads, service ads, online ads, product packaging, and political campaign literature.

EXPOSITION

Exposition is writing that informs or explains. The information you include in expository writing is factual or based on fact. Effective expository writing reflects a well-thought-out organization—one that includes a clear introduction, body, and conclusion. The organization should be appropriate for the type of exposition you are writing. Here are some types of exposition:

Comparison-and-Contrast Essay A comparison-and-contrast essay analyzes the similarities and differences between two or more things. You may organize your essay either point by point or subject by subject. An effective comparison-and-contrast essay

- Identifies a purpose for comparison and contrast
- Identifies similarities and differences between two or more things, people, places, or ideas
- Gives factual details about the subjects being compared
- Uses an organizational plan suited to its topic and purpose

Types of comparison-and-contrast essays are product comparisons, essays on economic or historical developments, comparison and contrast of literary works, and plan evaluations.

Cause-and-Effect Essay A cause-and-effect essay examines the relationship between events, explaining how one event or situation causes another. A successful cause-and-effect essay includes

- A discussion of a cause, event, or condition that produces a specific result
- An explanation of an effect, outcome, or result
- Evidence and examples to support the relationship between cause and effect
- A logical organization that makes the explanation clear

Some appropriate subjects for cause-and-effect essays are science reports, current-events articles, health studies, historical accounts, and cause-and-effect investigations.

Problem-and-Solution Essay A problem-and-solution essay describes a problem and offers one or more solutions to it. It describes a clear set of steps to achieve a result. An effective problem-and-solution essay includes

- A clear statement of the problem, with its causes and effects summarized for the reader
- The most important aspects of the problem
- A proposal of at least one realistic solution
- Facts, statistics, data, or expert testimony to support the solution
- Language appropriate to the audience's knowledge and ability levels
- A clear organization that makes the relationship between problem and solution obvious

Some types of issues that might be addressed in a problem-and-solution essay include consumer issues, business issues, time-management issues, and local issues.

RESEARCH WRITING

Research writing is based on information gathered from outside sources, and it gives a writer the power to become an expert on any subject. A research paper—a focused study of a topic—helps writers explore and connect ideas, make discoveries, and share their findings with an audience. Effective research writing

- Focuses on a specific, narrow topic, which is usually summarized in a thesis statement
- Presents relevant information from a wide variety of sources
- Structures the information logically and effectively
- Identifies the sources from which the information was drawn

Besides the formal research report, there are many other specialized types of writing that depend on accurate and insightful research, including multimedia presentations, statistical reports, annotated bibliographies, and experiment journals.

Documented Essay A documented essay uses research gathered from outside sources to support an idea. What distinguishes this essay from other categories of research is the level and intensity of the research. In a documented essay, the writer consults a limited number of sources to elaborate an idea. In contrast, a formal research paper may include many more research sources. An effective documented essay includes

- A well-defined thesis that can be fully discussed in a brief essay
- Facts and details to support each main point
- Expert or informed ideas gathered from interviews and other sources
- A clear, coherent method of organization
- Full internal documentation to show sources of information

Subjects especially suited to the documented essay format include health issues, current events, and cultural trends.

Research Paper A research paper presents and interprets information gathered through an extensive study of a subject. An effective research paper has

- A clearly stated thesis statement
- Convincing factual support from a variety of outside sources, including direct quotations whose sources are credited
- A clear organization that includes an introduction, body, and conclusion
- A bibliography, or works-cited list, that provides a complete listing of research sources

Some research formats you may encounter include lab reports, annotated bibliographies, and multigenre research papers.

RESPONSE TO LITERATURE

When you write a **response-to-literature essay,** you give yourself the opportunity to discover *what, how,* and *why* a piece of writing communicated to you. An effective response

- Contains a reaction to a poem, story, essay, or other work of literature
- Analyzes the content of a literary work, its related ideas, or the work's effect on the reader
- Presents a thesis statement to identify the nature of the response
- Focuses on a single aspect of the work or gives a general overview
- Supports opinion with evidence from the work addressed

The following are just a few of the ways you might respond in writing to a literary work: reader's response journals, character analyses, literary letters, and literary analyses.

WRITING FOR ASSESSMENT

One of the most common types of school **assessment** is the written test. Most often, a written test is announced in advance, allowing you time to study and prepare. When a test includes an essay, you are expected to write a response that includes

- A clearly stated and well-supported thesis or main idea
- Specific information about the topic derived from your reading or from class discussion
- A clear organization

In your school career, you will probably encounter questions that ask you to address each of the following types of writing: explain a process; defend a position; compare, contrast, or categorize; and show cause and effect.

WORKPLACE WRITING

Workplace writing is probably the format you will use most after you finish school. It is used in offices and factories and by workers on the road. Workplace writing includes a variety of formats that share common features. In general, workplace writing is fact-based writing that communicates specific information to readers in a structured format. Effective workplace writing

- Communicates information concisely to make the best use of both the writer's and the reader's time
- Includes a level of detail that provides necessary information and anticipates potential questions
- Reflects the writer's care if it is error-free and neatly presented

Some common types of workplace writing include business letters, memorandums, résumés, forms, and applications.

WRITING PERSONAL LETTERS

A personal letter is a letter to a friend, a family member, or anyone with whom the writer wants to communicate in a personal, friendly way. Most personal or friendly letters are made up of five parts:

- the heading
- the salutation, or greeting
- the body
- the closing
- the signature

The purpose of a personal letter is often one of the following:

- to share personal news and feelings
- to send or to answer an invitation
- to express thanks

Model Personal Letter

In this personal letter, Betsy thanks her grandparents for a birthday present and gives them some news about her life.

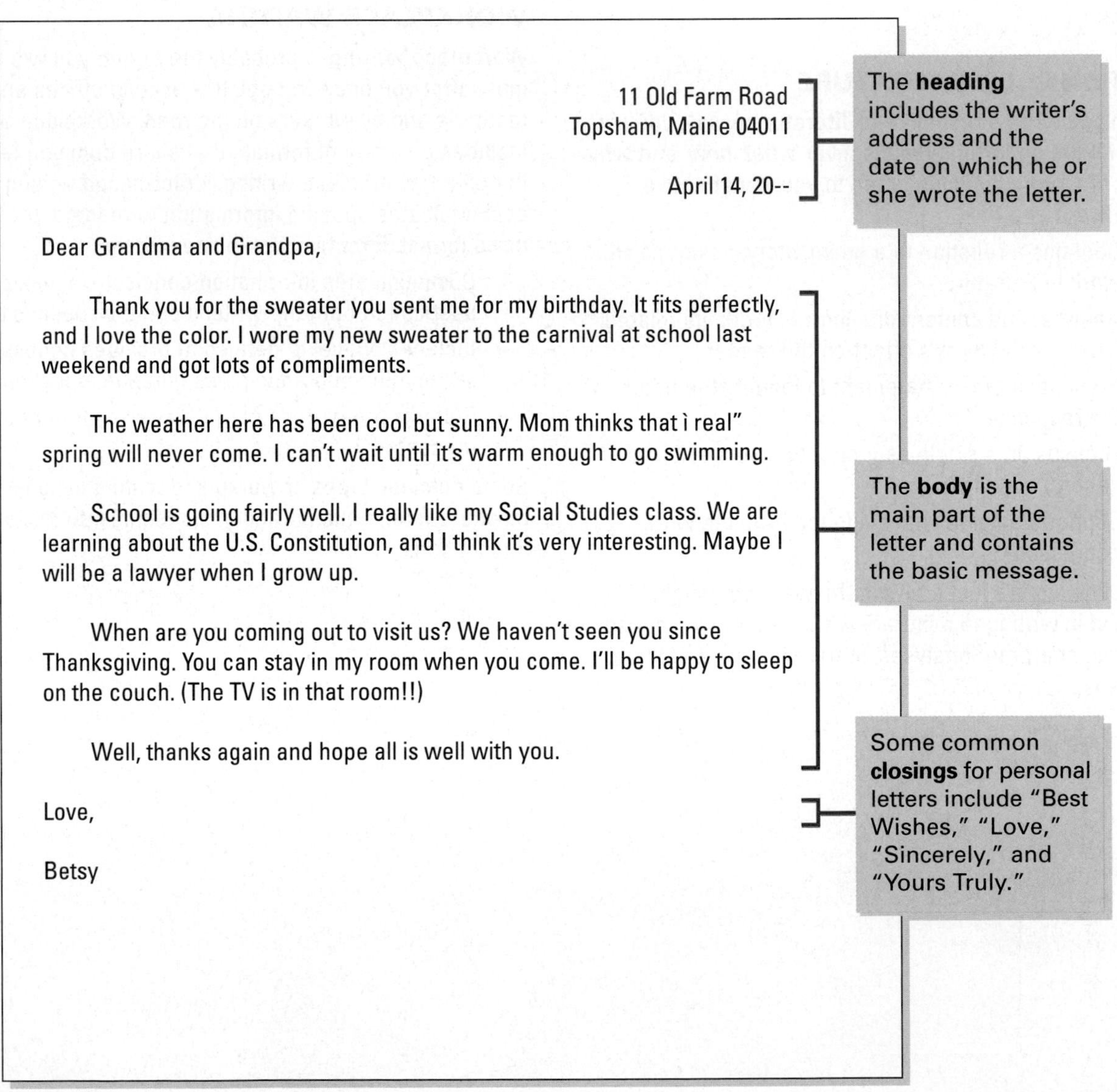

11 Old Farm Road
Topsham, Maine 04011

April 14, 20--

Dear Grandma and Grandpa,

Thank you for the sweater you sent me for my birthday. It fits perfectly, and I love the color. I wore my new sweater to the carnival at school last weekend and got lots of compliments.

The weather here has been cool but sunny. Mom thinks that ì real" spring will never come. I can't wait until it's warm enough to go swimming.

School is going fairly well. I really like my Social Studies class. We are learning about the U.S. Constitution, and I think it's very interesting. Maybe I will be a lawyer when I grow up.

When are you coming out to visit us? We haven't seen you since Thanksgiving. You can stay in my room when you come. I'll be happy to sleep on the couch. (The TV is in that room!!)

Well, thanks again and hope all is well with you.

Love,

Betsy

The **heading** includes the writer's address and the date on which he or she wrote the letter.
The **body** is the main part of the letter and contains the basic message.
Some common **closings** for personal letters include "Best Wishes," "Love," "Sincerely," and "Yours Truly."

WRITING BUSINESS LETTERS

Business letters follow one of several acceptable formats. In **block format** each part of the letter begins at the left margin. A double space is used between paragraphs. In **modified block format,** the headings, the closings, and the signature are indented to the center of the page. No matter which format is used, all letters in business format have a heading, an inside address, a salutation, or greeting, a body, a closing, and a signature. These parts are shown and annotated on the model business letter below, formatted in modified block style.

Model Business Letter

In this letter, Yolanda Dodson uses modified block format to request information.

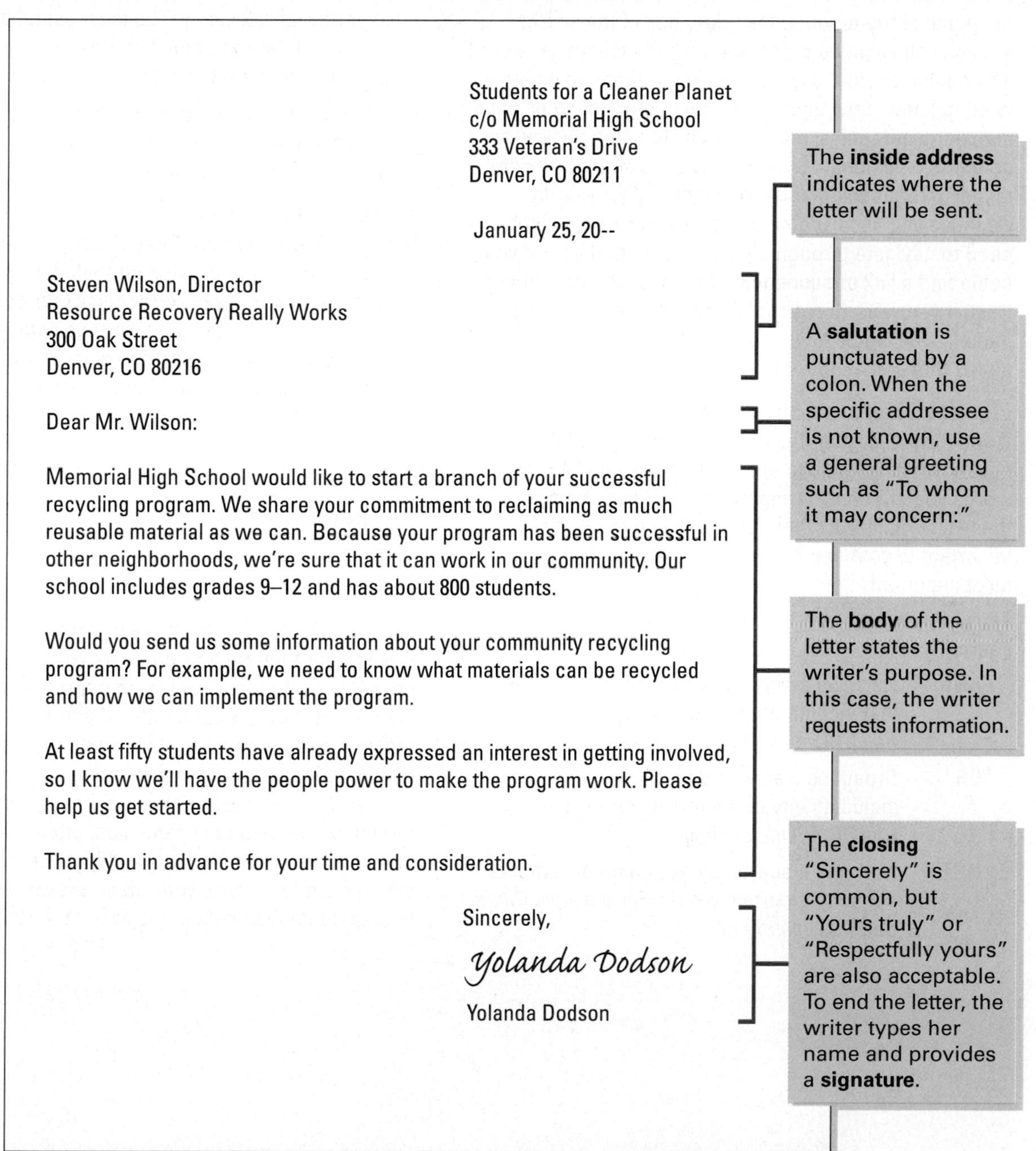

Students for a Cleaner Planet
c/o Memorial High School
333 Veteran's Drive
Denver, CO 80211

January 25, 20--

Steven Wilson, Director
Resource Recovery Really Works
300 Oak Street
Denver, CO 80216

Dear Mr. Wilson:

Memorial High School would like to start a branch of your successful recycling program. We share your commitment to reclaiming as much reusable material as we can. Because your program has been successful in other neighborhoods, we're sure that it can work in our community. Our school includes grades 9–12 and has about 800 students.

Would you send us some information about your community recycling program? For example, we need to know what materials can be recycled and how we can implement the program.

At least fifty students have already expressed an interest in getting involved, so I know we'll have the people power to make the program work. Please help us get started.

Thank you in advance for your time and consideration.

Sincerely,

Yolanda Dodson

Yolanda Dodson

The **inside address** indicates where the letter will be sent.

A **salutation** is punctuated by a colon. When the specific addressee is not known, use a general greeting such as "To whom it may concern:"

The **body** of the letter states the writer's purpose. In this case, the writer requests information.

The **closing** "Sincerely" is common, but "Yours truly" or "Respectfully yours" are also acceptable. To end the letter, the writer types her name and provides a **signature**.

RESEARCH AND TECHNOLOGY GUIDE

Using the Internet for Research

Key Word Search

Before you begin a search, you should identify your specific topic. To make searching easier, narrow your subject to a key word or a group of key words. These are your search terms, and they should be as specific as possible. For example, if you are looking for the latest concert dates for your favorite musical group, you might use the band's name as a key word. However, if you were to enter the name of the group in the query box of the search engine, you might be presented with thousands of links to information about the group that is unrelated to what you want to know. You might locate such information as band member biographies, the group's history, fan reviews of concerts, and hundreds of sites with related names containing information that is irrelevant to your search. Because you used such a broad key word, you might need to navigate through all that information before you could find a link or subheading for concert dates. In contrast, if you were to type in "Duplex Arena and [band name]," you would have a better chance of locating pages that contain this information.

How to Narrow Your Search

If you have a large group of key words and still do not know which ones to use, write out a list of all the words you are considering. Once you have completed the list, scrutinize it. Then, delete the words that are least important to your search, and highlight those that are most important.

These **key search connectors** can help you fine-tune your search:

AND: Narrows a search by retrieving documents that include both terms. For example: *baseball* AND *playoffs*

OR: Broadens a search by retrieving documents including any of the terms. For example: *playoffs* OR *championships*

NOT: Narrows a search by excluding documents containing certain words. For example: *baseball* NOT *history of*

Tips for an Effective Search

1. Remember that search engines can be case-sensitive. If your first attempt at searching fails, check your search terms for misspellings and try again.
2. If you are entering a group of key words, present them in order from the most important to the least important key word.
3. Avoid opening the link to every single page in your results list. Search engines present pages in descending order of relevancy. The most useful pages will be located at the top of the list. However, read the description of each link before you open the page.
4. Some search engines provide helpful tips for specializing your search. Take the opportunity to learn more about effective searching.

Other Ways to Search

Using Online Reference Sites How you search should be tailored to what you are hoping to find. If you are looking for data and facts, use reference sites before you jump onto a simple search engine. For example, you can find reference sites to provide definitions of words, statistics about almost any subject, biographies, maps, and concise information on many topics. Here are some useful online reference sites:

Online libraries

Online periodicals

Almanacs

Encyclopedias

You can find these sources using subject searches.

Conducting Subject Searches As you prepare to go online, consider your subject and the best way to find information to suit your needs. If you are looking for general information on a topic and you want your search results to be extensive, consider the subject search indexes on most search engines. These indexes, in the form of category and subject lists, often appear on the first page of a search engine. When you click on a specific highlighted word, you will be presented with a new screen containing subcategories of the topic you chose.

Evaluating the Reliability of Internet Resources

Just as you would evaluate the quality, bias, and validity of any other research material you locate, check the source of information you find online. Compare these two sites containing information about the poet and writer Langston Hughes:

Site A is a personal Web site constructed by a college student. It contains no bibliographic information or links to sites that he used. Included on the site are several poems by Langston Hughes and a student essay about the poet's use of symbolism. It has not been updated in more than six months.

Site B is a Web site constructed and maintained by the English Department of a major university. Information on Hughes is presented in a scholarly format, with a bibliography and credits for the writer. The site includes links to other sites and indicates new features that are added weekly.

For your own research, consider the information you find on Site B to be more reliable and accurate than that on Site A. Because it is maintained by experts in their field who are held accountable for their work, the university site will be a better research tool than the student-generated one.

Tips for Evaluating Internet Sources

1. Consider who constructed and who now maintains the Web page. Determine whether this author is a reputable source. Often, the URL endings indicate a source.
   - Sites ending in *.edu* are maintained by educational institutions.
   - Sites ending in *.gov* are maintained by government agencies (federal, state, or local).
   - Sites ending in *.org* are normally maintained by non-profit organizations and agencies.
   - Sites ending in *.com* are commercially or personally maintained.
2. Skim the official and trademarked Web pages first. It is safe to assume that the information you draw from Web pages of reputable institutions, online encyclopedias, online versions of major daily newspapers, or government-owned sites produce information as reliable as the material you would find in print. In contrast, unbranded sites or those generated by individuals tend to borrow information from other sources without providing documentation. As information travels from one source to another, it could have been muddled, misinterpreted, edited, or revised.
3. You can still find valuable information in the less "official" sites. Check for the writer's credentials, and then consider these factors:
   - Do not be misled by official-looking graphics or presentations.
   - Make sure that the information is updated enough to suit your needs. Many Web pages will indicate how recently they have been updated.
   - If the information is borrowed, notice whether you can trace it back to its original source.

Respecting Copyrighted Material

Because the Internet is a relatively new and quickly growing medium, issues of copyright and ownership arise almost daily. As laws begin to govern the use and reuse of material posted online, they may change the way that people can access or reprint material.

Text, photographs, music, and fine art printed online may not be reproduced without acknowledged permission of the copyright owner.

CITING SOURCES AND PREPARING MANUSCRIPT

In research writing, cite your sources. In the body of your paper, provide a footnote, an endnote, or an internal citation, identifying the sources of facts, opinions, or quotations. At the end of your paper, provide a bibliography or a Works Cited list, a list of all the sources you cite. Follow an established format, such as Modern Language Association (MLA) Style or American Psychological Association (APA) Style.

Works Cited List (MLA Style)

A Works Cited list must contain accurate information sufficient to enable a reader to locate each source you cite. The basic components of an entry are as follows:

- Name of the author, editor, translator, or group responsible for the work
- Title
- Place and date of publication
- Publisher

For print materials, the information required for a citation generally appears on the copyright and title pages of a work. For the format of Works Cited list entries, consult the examples at right and in the chart on page R29.

Parenthetical Citations (MLA Style)

A parenthetical citation briefly identifies the source from which you have taken a specific quotation, factual claim, or opinion. It refers the reader to one of the entries on your Works Cited list. A parenthetical citation has the following features:

- It appears in parentheses.
- It identifies the source by the last name of the author, editor, or translator.
- It gives a page reference, identifying the page of the source on which the information cited can be found.

Punctuation A parenthetical citation generally falls outside a closing quotation mark but within the final punctuation of a clause or sentence. For a long quotation set off from the rest of your text, place the citation at the end of the excerpt without any punctuation following.

Special Cases

- If the author is an organization, use the organization's name, in a shortened version if necessary.
- If you cite more than one work by the same author, add the title or a shortened version of the title.

Sample Works Cited Lists

Carwardine, Mark, Erich Hoyt, R. Ewan Fordyce, and Peter Gill. *The Nature Company Guides: Whales, Dolphins, and Porpoises.* New York: Time-Life Books, 1998.

Whales in Danger. "Discovering Whales." 18 Oct 1999. <http://whales.magna.com.au/DISCOVER>

Neruda, Pablo. *"Ode to Spring." Odes to Opposites.* Trans. Ken Krabbenhoft. Ed. and illus. Ferris Cook. Boston: Little, Brown and Company, 1995.

The Saga of the Volsungs. Trans. Jesse L. Byock. London: Penguin Books, 1990.

List an anonymous work by title.

List both the title of the work and the collection in which it is found.

Sample Parenthetical Citations

It makes sense that baleen whales such as the blue whale, the bowhead whale, the humpback whale, and the sei whale (to name just a few) grow to immense sizes (Carwardine, Hoyt, and Fordyce 19–21). The blue whale has grooves running from under its chin to partway along the length of its underbelly. As in some other whales, these grooves expand and allow even more food and water to be taken in (Ellis 18–21).

Author's last name

Page numbers where information can be found

MLA Style for Listing Sources

Book with one author	Pyles, Thomas. *The Origins and Development of the English Language.* 2nd ed. New York: Harcourt Brace Jovanovich, Inc., 1971.
Book with two or three authors	McCrum, Robert, William Cran, and Robert MacNeil. *The Story of English.* New York: Penguin Books, 1987.
Book with an editor	Truth, Sojourner. *Narrative of Sojourner Truth.* Ed. Margaret Washington. New York: Vintage Books, 1993.
Book with more than three authors or editors	Donald, Robert B., et al. *Writing Clear Essays.* Upper Saddle River, NJ: Prentice Hall, Inc., 1996.
Single work from an anthology	Hawthorne, Nathaniel. "Young Goodman Brown." *Literature: An Introduction to Reading and Writing.* Ed. Edgar V. Roberts and Henry E. Jacobs. Upper Saddle River, NJ: Prentice-Hall, Inc., 1998. 376–385. [Indicate pages for the entire selection.]
Introduction in a published edition	Washington, Margaret. Introduction. *Narrative of Sojourner Truth.* By Sojourner Truth. New York: Vintage Books, 1993, pp. v–xi.
Signed article in a weekly magazine	Wallace, Charles. "A Vodacious Deal." *Time* 14 Feb. 2000: 63.
Signed article in a monthly magazine	Gustaitis, Joseph. "The Sticky History of Chewing Gum." *American History* Oct. 1998: 30–38.
Unsigned editorial or story	"Selective Silence." Editorial. *Wall Street Journal* 11 Feb. 2000: A14. [If the editorial or story is signed, begin with the author's name.]
Signed pamphlet or brochure	[Treat the pamphlet as though it were a book.]
Pamphlet with no author, publisher, or date	*Are You at Risk of Heart Attack?* n.p. n.d. [n.p. n.d. indicates that there is no known publisher or date.]
Filmstrips, slide programs, videotape, DVDs, and other audiovisual material	*The Diary of Anne Frank.* Dir. George Stevens. Perf. Millie Perkins, Shelly Winters, Joseph Schildkraut, Lou Jacobi, and Richard Beymer. Twentieth Century Fox, 1959.
Radio or television program transcript	"Nobel for Literature." Narr. Rick Korr. *All Things Considered.* National Public Radio. WNYC, New York. 10 Oct. 2002. Transcript.
Internet	*National Association of Chewing Gum Manufacturers.* 19 Dec. 1999 <http://www.nacgm.org/consumer/funfacts.html> [Indicate the date you accessed the information. Content and addresses at Web sites change frequently.]
Newspaper	Thurow, Roger. "South Africans Who Fought for Sanctions Now Scrap for Investors." *Wall Street Journal* 11 Feb. 2000: A1+ [For a multipage article, write only the first page number on which it appears, followed by a plus sign.]
Personal interview	Smith, Jane. Personal interview. 10 Feb. 2000.
CD (with multiple publishers)	Simms, James, ed. *Romeo and Juliet.* By William Shakespeare. CD-ROM. Oxford: Attica Cybernetics Ltd.; London: BBC Education; London: HarperCollins Publishers, 1995.
Signed article from an encyclopedia	Askeland, Donald R. "Welding." *World Book Encyclopedia.* 1991 ed.

Writing Criticism

Like all solid writing, a work of criticism presents a thesis (a central idea) and supports it with arguments and evidence. Follow the strategies below to develop a critical thesis and gather support for it.

Formulate a Working Thesis

Once you have chosen a work or works on which to write, formulate a working thesis. First, ask yourself questions like these:

- What strikes you most about the work or the writer that your paper will address? What puzzles you most?
- In what ways is the work unlike others you have read?
- What makes the techniques used by the writer so well-suited to (or so poorly chosen for) conveying the theme of the work?

Jot down notes answering your questions. Then, reread passages that illustrate your answers, jotting down notes about what each passage contributes to the work. Review your notes, and write a sentence that draws a conclusion about the work.

Gather Support

Taking Notes From the Work Once you have a working thesis, take notes on passages in the work that confirm it. To aid your search for support, consider the type of support suited to your thesis, as in the chart.

If your thesis concerns . . .	look for support in the form of . . .
Character	• dialogue • character's actions • writer's descriptions of the character • other characters' reactions to the character
Theme	• fate of characters • patterns and contrasts of imagery, character, or events • mood • writer's attitude toward the action
Style	• memorable descriptions, observations • passages that "sound like" the writer • examples of rhetorical devices, such as exaggeration and irony
Historical Context	• references to historical events and personalities • evidence of social or political pressures on characters • socially significant contrasts between characters (for example, between the rich and the poor)
Literary Influences	• writer's chosen form or genre • passages that "sound like" another writer • events or situations that resemble those in other works • evidence of an outlook similar to that of another writer

Conducting Additional Research If you are writing biographical or historical criticism, you will need to consult sources on the writer's life and era. Even if you are writing a close analysis of a poem, you should consider consulting the works of critics to benefit from their insights and understanding. For a more detailed explanation of the research process, see pages 684–693.

Take Notes

Consider recording notes from the works you are analyzing, as well as from any critical works you consult, on a set of note cards. A good set of note cards enables you to recall details accurately, to organize your ideas effectively, and to see connections between ideas.

One Card, One Idea If you use note cards while researching, record each key passage, theme, critical opinion, or fact on a separate note card. A good note card includes a brief quotation or summary of an idea and a record of the source, including the page number, in which you found the information. When copying a sentence from a work, use quotation marks and check to make sure you have copied it correctly.

Coding Sources Keep a working bibliography, a list of all works you consult, as you conduct research. Assign a code, such as a letter, to each work on the list. For each note you take, include the code for the source.

Coding Cards Organize your note cards by labeling each with the subtopic it concerns.

Present Support Appropriately

As you draft, consider how much support you need for each point and the form that support should take. You can provide support in the following forms:

- **Summaries** are short accounts in your own words of important elements of the work, such as events, a character's traits, or the writer's ideas. They are appropriate for background information.
- **Paraphrases** are restatements of passages from a work in your own words. They are appropriate for background and for information incidental to your main point.
- **Quotations of key passages** are direct transcriptions of the writer's words, enclosed in quotation marks or, if longer than three lines, set as indented text. If a passage is crucial to your thesis, you should quote it directly and at whatever length is necessary.

Quotations of multiple examples are required to support claims about general features of a work, such as a claim about the writer's ironic style or use of cartoonlike characters.

Stage of the Writing Process	The Developing Thesis Statement
Prewriting: A student rereads Sarte's story "The Wall" to find passages that support her thesis.	**First formulation:** "In his short story 'The Wall,' Sartre illustrates the belief that human life is ruled by inescapable fate."
Drafting: As the student summarizes the story's ending, she is struck by the fact that the narrator's final act has exactly the opposite effect from what he intended. She revises her thesis statement.	**Second formulation:** "In his short story 'The Wall,' Sartre demonstrates the power of fate by showing how the effects of a person's actions can completely contradict the person's intentions."
Revising: As the student rereads her first draft, she grows dissatisfied with her explanation of the story's ending. Why does the writer spend so much time showing the narrator's resignation to fate, only to to have fate strike unexpectedly? She reworks her paper to support a new thesis statement.	**Final formulation:** "In his short story 'The Wall,' Sartre shows that 'fate' is a myth: However hard we try to resign ourselves to fate, we can never eliminate our responsibility for our own actions."

Revise Ideas as You Draft

When writing criticism, do not be afraid to revise your early ideas based on what you learn as you research or write further. As you draft, allow the insights—or the difficulties—that emerge to guide you back to the writer's works or other sources for clarification or support. What you discover may lead you to modify your thesis.

The chart above presents an example of the way this circular process can work.

DO's and DON'T's of Academic Writing

Avoid gender and cultural bias. Certain terms and usages reflect the bias of past generations. To eliminate bias in any academic work you do, edit with the following rules in mind:

- **Pronoun usage** When referring to an unspecified individual in a case in which his or her gender is irrelevant, use forms of the pronoun phrase *he or she.* Example: "A lawyer is trained to use his or her mind."
- **"Culture-centric" terms** Replace terms that reflect a bias toward one culture with more generally accepted synonyms. For instance, replace terms such as *primitive* (used of hunting-gathering peoples), *the Orient* (used to refer to Asia), and *Indians* (used of Native Americans), all of which suggest a view of the world centered in Western European culture.

Avoid plagiarism. Presenting someone else's ideas, research, or exact words as your own is plagiarism, the equivalent of stealing or fraud. Laws protect the rights of writers and researchers in cases of commercial plagiarism. Academic standards protect their rights in cases of academic plagiarism.

To avoid plagiarism, follow these practices:

- Read from several sources.
- Synthesize what you learn.
- Let the ideas of experts help you draw your own conclusions.
- Always credit your sources properly when using someone else's ideas to support your view.

By following these guidelines, you will also push yourself to think independently.

GUIDE TO RUBRICS

What is a rubric?

A rubric is a tool, often in the form of a chart or a grid, that helps you assess your work. Rubrics are particularly helpful for writing and speaking assignments.

To help you or others assess, or evaluate, your work, a rubric offers several specific criteria to be applied to your work. Then the rubric helps you or an evaluator indicate your range of success or failure according to those specific criteria. Rubrics are often used to evaluate writing for standardized tests.

Using a rubric will save you time, focus your learning, and improve the work you do. When you know what the rubric will be before you begin writing a persuasive essay, for example, you will be aware as you write of specific criteria that are important in that kind of an essay. As you evaluate the essay before giving it to your teacher, you will focus on the specific areas that your teacher wants you to master—or on areas that you know present challenges for you. Instead of searching through your work randomly for any way to improve it or correct its errors, you will have a clear and helpful focus on specific criteria.

How are rubrics constructed?

Rubrics can be constructed in several ways.

- Your teacher may assign a rubric for a specific assignment.
- Your teacher may direct you to a rubric in your textbook.
- Your teacher and your class may construct a rubric for a particular assignment together.
- You and your classmates may construct a rubric together.
- You may create your own rubric with criteria you want to evaluate in your work.

How will a rubric help me?

A rubric will help you assess your work on a scale. Scales vary from rubric to rubric but usually range from 6 to 1, 5 to 1, or 4 to 1, with 6, 5, or 4 being the highest score and 1 being the lowest. If someone else is using the rubric to assess your work, the rubric will give your evaluator a clear range within which to place your work. If you are using the rubric yourself, it will help you make improvements to your work.

What are the types of rubrics?

- A **holistic rubric** has general criteria that can apply to a variety of assignments. See p. R36 for an example of a holistic rubric.
- An **analytic rubric** is specific to a particular assignment. The criteria for evaluation address the specific issues important in that assignment. See p. R35 for examples of analytic rubrics.

Sample Analytic Rubrics

Rubric With a 4-point Scale

The following analytic rubric is an example of a rubric to assess a persuasive essay. It will help you evaluate focus, organization, support/elaboration, and style/convention.

	Focus	Organization	Support/Elaboration	Style/Convention
4	Demonstrates highly effective word choice; clearly focused on task.	Uses clear, consistent organizational strategy.	Provides convincing, well-elaborated reasons to support the position.	Incorporates transitions; includes very few mechanical errors.
3	Demonstrates good word choice; stays focused on persuasive task.	Uses clear organizational strategy with occasional inconsistencies.	Provides two or more moderately elaborated reasons to support the position.	Incorporates some transitions; includes few mechanical errors.
2	Shows some good word choices; minimally stays focused on persuasive task.	Uses inconsistent organizational strategy; presentation is not logical.	Provides several reasons, but few are elaborated; only one elaborated reason.	Incorporates few transitions; includes many mechanical errors.
1	Shows lack of attention to persuasive task.	Demonstrates lack of organizational strategy.	Provides no specific reasons or does not elaborate.	Does not connect ideas; includes many mechanical errors.

Rubric With a 6-point Scale

The following analytic rubric is an example of a rubric to assess a persuasive essay. It will help you evaluate presentation, position, evidence, and arguments.

	Presentation	Position	Evidence	Arguments
6	Essay clearly and effectively addresses an issue with more than one side.	Essay clearly states a supportable position on the issue.	All evidence is logically organized, well presented, and supports the position.	All reader concerns and counterarguments are effectively addressed.
5	Most of essay addresses an issue that has more than one side.	Essay clearly states a position on the issue.	Most evidence is logically organized, well presented, and supports the position.	Most reader concerns and counterarguments are effectively addressed.
4	Essay adequately addresses issue that has more than one side.	Essay adequately states a position on the issue.	Many parts of evidence support the position; some evidence is out of order.	Many reader concerns and counterarguments are adequately addressed.
3	Essay addresses issue with two sides but does not present second side clearly.	Essay states a position on the issue, but the position is difficult to support.	Some evidence supports the position, but some evidence is out of order.	Some reader concerns and counterarguments are addressed.
2	Essay addresses issue with two sides but does not present second side.	Essay states a position on the issue, but the position is not supportable.	Not much evidence supports the position, and what is included is out of order.	A few reader concerns and counterarguments are addressed.
1	Essay does not address issue with more than one side.	Essay does not state a position on the issue.	No evidence supports the position.	No reader concerns or counterarguments are addressed.

Sample Holistic Rubric

Holistic rubrics such as this one are sometimes used to assess writing assignments on standardized tests. Notice that the criteria for evaluation are focus, organization, support, and use of conventions.

Points	Criteria
6 Points	• The writing is strongly focused and shows fresh insight into the writing task. • The writing is marked by a sense of completeness and coherence and is organized with a logical progression of ideas. • A main idea is fully developed, and support is specific and substantial. • A mature command of the language is evident, and the writing may employ characteristic creative writing strategies. • Sentence structure is varied, and writing is free of all but purposefully used fragments. • Virtually no errors in writing conventions appear.
5 Points	• The writing is clearly focused on the task. • The writing is well organized and has a logical progression of ideas, though there may be occasional lapses. • A main idea is well developed and supported with relevant detail. • Sentence structure is varied, and the writing is free of fragments, except when used purposefully. • Writing conventions are followed correctly.
4 Points	• The writing is clearly focused on the task, but extraneous material may intrude at times. • Clear organizational pattern is present, though lapses may occur. • A main idea is adequately supported, but development may be uneven. • Sentence structure is generally fragment free but shows little variation. • Writing conventions are generally followed correctly.
3 Points	• Writing is generally focused on the task, but extraneous material may intrude at times. • An organizational pattern is evident, but writing may lack a logical progression of ideas. • Support for the main idea is generally present but is sometimes illogical. • Sentence structure is generally free of fragments, but there is almost no variation. • The work generally demonstrates a knowledge of writing conventions, with occasional misspellings.
2 Points	• The writing is related to the task but generally lacks focus. • There is little evidence of organizational pattern, and there is little sense of cohesion. • Support for the main idea is generally inadequate, illogical, or absent. • Sentence structure is unvaried, and serious errors may occur. • Errors in writing conventions and spellings are frequent.
1 Point	• The writing may have little connection to the task and is generally unfocused. • There has been little attempt at organization or development. • The paper seems fragmented, with no clear main idea. • Sentence structure is unvaried, and serious errors appear. • Poor word choice and poor command of the language obscure meaning. • Errors in writing conventions and spelling are frequent.
Unscorable	The paper is considered unscorable if: • The response is unrelated to the task or is simply a rewording of the prompt. • The response has been copied from a published work. • The student did not write a response. • The response is illegible. • The words in the response are arranged with no meaning. • There is an insufficient amount of writing to score.

Student Model

Persuasive Writing

This persuasive letter, which would receive a top score according to a persuasive rubric, is a response to the following writing prompt, or assignment:

Write a letter to a government official strongly supporting an environmental issue that is important to you and urging the official to take a specific action that supports your cause.

Dear Secretary of the Interior:

It's a normal carefree day in the forest. The birds are singing and all of the animals are relaxing under the refreshing glow of the sun. But suddenly the thunderous sound of a chainsaw echoes throughout the woodlands, and trees fall violently. The creatures of the forest run in terror. Many of these beautiful creatures will starve to death slowly and painfully as their homes are destroyed, and this precious ecosystem will not be able to regrow to its previous greatness for many years to come.

A descriptive and interesting introduction grabs the reader's attention and shows a persuasive focus.

This sad story is a true one in many places around the globe. We must slow deforestation and replant trees immediately to save our breathable air, fertile soil, and fragile ecosystems.

If entire forests continue to be obliterated, less oxygen will be produced and more CO_2 emitted. In fact, deforestation accounts for a quarter of the CO_2 released into the atmosphere each year: about 1–2 billion tons. Forests provide the majority of the oxygen on earth, and if these forests disappear our air will soon be unbreathable.

Second, deforestation results in a loss of topsoil. Many of the companies who are involved in deforestation claim that the land is needed for farms, but deforestation makes the land much less fertile because it accelerates the process of erosion. According to the UN Food and Agriculture Organization, deforestation has damaged almost 6 million square kilometers of soil.

Finally, if cutting doesn't slow, many species will die off and many ecosystems will be destroyed. The 2000 UN Global Environment Outlook says that forests and rain forests have the most diverse plant and animal life in the world. The GEO also notes that there are more than 1,000 threatened species living in the world's forests. Imagine someone destroying all the houses in your neighborhood and leaving all of the residents homeless. This is how it is for the organisms that live in the forests.

The writer supports the argument with facts and evidence, and also uses the persuasive technique to the reader's emotions.

In conclusion, deforestation must slow down and trees must be replanted immediately, or we will lose clean air, topsoil, and many precious organisms. Furthermore, a loss in forests will result in a generation that knows very little about nature. So, to prevent the chaotic disturbance of peace in the forests, please do whatever you can to prevent deforestation. Vote YES on any UN bills that would help the condition of our world's forests.

The conclusion restates the argument and presents a call to action.

Sincerely Yours,
Jamil Khouri

COLLEGE APPLICATION ESSAY

If you are applying for admission to a college, you will probably need to submit an essay as part of your application. This essay is your introduction to a college applications committee. It will help committee members get a sense of you as a person and as a student. Review the chart at right for general strategies, and then follow the guidelines below to ensure that your college application essay does the best job presenting you.

Strategies for Writing an Effective College Application Essay

- **Choose the right topic.** If you have a choice of essay topics, choose the one that interests you.
- **Organize.** Use a strong organization that carries the reader from introduction to conclusion.
- **Begin with a bang.** Open with an introduction that has a good chance of sparking the reader's interest.
- **Elaborate.** Be sure to explain why the experiences you discuss are important to you or what you learned from them.
- **Show style.** Bring life to your essay through vivid descriptions, precise word choice, and sophisticated sentence structure, such as parallelism. Consider including dialogue where appropriate.
- **Close with a clincher.** Write a conclusion that effectively sums up your ideas.
- **Do a clean job.** Proofread your essay carefully to ensure that it is error-free.

Selecting a Topic

Read the essay question on the application form with care. Mark key criteria and direction words such as *describe* and *explain.* After you have written a first draft, check to make sure you have met all of the requirements of the question. Your essay has a better chance of succeeding if it meets the requirements exactly.

General Questions About You

The essay question on a college application may be as general as "Describe a significant experience or event in your life and explain its consequences for you." To choose the right topic for such a question, think of an event or experience that truly is meaningful to you—a camping trip, a volunteer event, a family reunion. Test the subject by drafting a letter about it to a good friend or relative. If you find that your enthusiasm for the subject grows as you write, and if your discussion reveals something about your growth or your outlook on life, the topic may be the right one for your essay.

Directed Questions

The essay question on an application may be more directed than a simple "tell us about yourself." For instance, you may be asked to select three figures from history you would like to meet and to explain your choices.

In such cases, do not give an answer just because you think it will please reviewers. Instead, consult your own interests and instincts. Your most convincing writing will come from genuine interest in the subject. You might discover the best topic by jotting down a diary entry or a letter to a friend in which you discuss possible subjects.

Style

Though an essay is a chance to tell something about yourself, it is also a formal document addressed to strangers. Use a formal to semiformal style. Avoid incomplete sentences and slang unless you are using them for clear stylistic effect. Use words with precision, selecting one or two accurate words for what you mean, rather than piling up words in the hope that one of them will hit the mark.

Format

Most applications limit the length of essays. Do not exceed the allowed space or number of words. Your college application essay should be neatly typed or printed, using adequate margins. Proofread your final draft carefully. If you submit a separate copy of the essay (rather than writing on the application form), number the pages and include your name and contact information on each page.

Reusing Your Essay

Most students apply to a number of different colleges in order to ensure their admission to a school for the next semester. Once you have written a strong essay for one application, you should consider adapting it for others.

Do not submit a single essay to several schools blindly. Always read the application essay question carefully to ensure that the essay you submit fulfills all of its requirements.

CRITICAL COMMUNICATION SKILLS

You use communication every day in writing, speaking, listening, and viewing. Having strong communication skills will benefit you both in and out of school. Many of the assignments accompanying the literature in this textbook involve speaking, listening, and viewing. This handbook identifies some of the terminology related to the oral and visual communication you experience every day and the assignments you may do in conjunction with the literature in this book.

You use speaking and listening skills every day. When you talk with your friends, teachers, or parents, or when you interact with store clerks, you are communicating orally. In addition to everyday conversation, oral communication includes class discussions, speeches, interviews, presentations, debates, and performances. When you communicate, you usually use more than your voice to get your message across. For example, you use one set of skills in face-to-face communication and another set of skills in a telephone conversation. In all types of communication, be sure to be polite, accept praise graciously, and say thank you as necessary.

The following terms will give you a better understanding of the many elements that are part of communication and help you eliminate barriers to listening by managing any distractions.

BODY LANGUAGE refers to the use of facial expressions, eye contact, gestures, posture, and movement to communicate a feeling or an idea.

CONNOTATION is the set of associations a word calls to mind. The connotations of the words you choose influence the message you send. For example, most people respond more favorably to being described as "slim" rather than as "skinny." The connotation of *slim* is more appealing than that of *skinny.*

EYE CONTACT is direct visual contact with another person's eyes.

FEEDBACK is the set of verbal and nonverbal reactions that indicate to a speaker that a message has been received and understood.

GESTURES are the movements made with arms, hands, face and fingers to communicate.

LISTENING is understanding and interpreting sound in a meaningful way. You listen differently for different purposes.

Listening for key information: For example, when a teacher gives an assignment, or when someone gives you directions to a place, you listen for key information.

Listening for main points: In a classroom exchange of ideas or information, or while watching a television documentary, you listen for main points.

Listening critically: When you evaluate a performance, song, or a persuasive or political speech, you listen critically, questioning and judging the speaker's message.

MEDIUM is the material or technique used to present a visual image. Common media include paint, clay, and film.

NONVERBAL COMMUNICATION is communication without the use of words. People communicate nonverbally through gestures, facial expressions, posture, and body movements. Sign language is an entire language based on nonverbal communication. Be aware of your nonverbal communication and make sure that your gestures and facial expressions do not conflict with your words.

PROJECTION is speaking in such a way that the voice carries clearly to an audience. It's important to project your voice when speaking in a large space like a classroom or an auditorium.

VIEWING is observing, understanding, analyzing, and evaluating information presented through visual means. You might use the following questions to help you interpret what you view:

- What subject is presented?
- What is communicated about the subject?
- Which parts are factual? Which are opinion?
- What mood, attitude, or opinion is conveyed?
- What is your emotional response?

VOCAL DELIVERY is the way in which you present a message. Your vocal delivery involves all of the following elements:

Volume: the loudness or quietness of your voice

Pitch: the high or low quality of your voice

Rate: the speed at which you speak; also called pace

Stress: the amount of emphasis placed on different syllables in a word or on different words in a sentence

All of these elements individually, and the way in which they are combined, contribute to the meaning of a spoken message.

Speaking, Listening, and Viewing Situations

Here are some of the many types of situations in which you apply speaking, listening, and viewing skills:

AUDIENCE Your audience in any situation refers to the person or people to whom you direct your message. An audience can be a group of people observing a performance or just one person. When preparing for any speaking situation, it's useful to analyze your audience, so that you can tailor your message to them.

CHARTS AND GRAPHS are visual representations of statistical information. For example, a pie chart might indicate how the average dollar is spent by government, and a bar graph might compare populations in cities over time.

DEBATE A debate is a formal public-speaking situation in which participants prepare and present arguments on opposing sides of a question, states as a **proposition.**

The two sides in a debate are the *affirmative* (pro) and the *negative* (con). The affirmative side argues in favor of the proposition, while the negative side argues against it. Each side has an opportunity for *rebuttal,* in which they may challenge or question the other side's argument.

DOCUMENTARIES are nonfiction films that analyze news events or other focused subjects. You can watch a documentary for the information on its subject.

GRAPHIC ORGANIZERS summarize and present information in ways that can help you understand the information. Graphic organizers include charts, outlines, webs, maps, lists, and diagrams. For example, a graphic organizer for a history chapter might be an outline. A Venn diagram is intersecting circles that display information showing how concepts are alike and different.

GROUP DISCUSSION results when three or more people meet to solve a common problem, arrive at a decision, or answer a question of mutual interest. Group discussion is one of the most widely used forms or interpersonal communication in modern society.

INTERVIEW An interview is a form of interaction in which one person, the interviewer, asks questions of another person, the interviewee. Interviews may take place for many purposes: to obtain information, to discover a person's suitability for a job or a college, or to inform the public of a notable person's opinions.

MAPS are visual representations of Earth's surface. Maps may show political boundaries and physical features and provide information on a variety of other topics. A map's titles and its key identify the content of the map.

ORAL INTERPRETATION is the reading or speaking of a work of literature aloud for an audience. Oral interpretation involves giving expression to the ideas, meaning, or even the structure of a work of literature. The speaker interprets the work through his or her vocal delivery. **Storytelling,** in which a speaker reads or tells a story expressively, is a form of oral interpretation.

PANEL DISCUSSION is a group discussion on a topic of interest common to all members of a panel and to a listening audience. A panel is usually composed of four to six experts on a particular topic who are brought together to share information and opinions.

PANTOMIME is a form of nonverbal communication in which an idea or a story is communicated completely through the use of gesture, body language, and facial expressions, without any words at all.

POLITICAL CARTOONS are drawings that comment on important political or social issues. Often, these cartoons use humor to convey a message about their subject. Viewers use their own knowledge of events to evaluate the cartoonist's opinion.

READERS THEATRE is a dramatic reading of a work of literature in which participants take parts from a story or play and read them aloud in expressive voices. Unlike a play, however, sets and costumes are not part of the performance, and the participants remain seated as they deliver their lines.

ROLE PLAY To role-play is to take the role of a person or character and act out a given situation, speaking, acting, and responding in the manner of the character.

SPEECH A speech is a talk or address given to an audience. A speech may be **impromptu** or **extemporaneous**—delivered on the spur of the moment with no preparation—or formally prepared and delivered for a specific purpose or occasion.

- ***Purposes:*** the most common purposes of speeches are to persuade, to entertain, to explain, and to inform.
- ***Occasions:*** Different occasions call for different types of speeches. Speeches given on these occasions could be persuasive, entertaining, or informative, as appropriate.

VISUAL REPRESENTATION refers to informative texts, such as newspapers and advertisements, and entertaining texts, such as magazines. Visual representations use elements of design—such as texture and color, shapes, drawings, and photographs—to convey the meaning, message, or theme.

PREPARING FOR COLLEGE ENTRANCE, THE NEW SAT, AND AP™ EXAMS

College Entrance Exams

College entrance exams are called "high-stakes tests" because they provide important information for college admission boards. AP tests are also "high-stakes" because a good score can let you opt out of basic classes in college. Preparation for these tests ranges from years of tutoring to a quick review of testing tips and depends not only on your comfort level when you are taking tests, but also on your target score. Luckily, you have had a lot of practice taking this type of test. Yearly standardized tests, graduation requirement tests, and end-of-course tests all prepare you to do well on tests for college admission.

Aptitude Tests for College Admission	
PSAT/ NMSQT	Preliminary Scholastic Aptitude Test / National Merit Scholarship Qualifying Test **General Description** An eighty-minute version of the SAT, covering verbal and math skills and including a writing multiple-choice section. **Why Take It** Most often taken by juniors to prepare for the SAT, to make contact with colleges, and to qualify for the National Merit Scholarship.
SAT	Scholastic Aptitude Test **General Description** An aptitude test of vocabulary, math, and reasoning skills. Mostly multiple-choice questions. **Why Take It** Most colleges require that applicants submit either SAT or ACT scores. **Sections** Critical Reading—two 25-minute sections and one 20-minute section. Math—two 25-minute sections and one 20-minute section. Writing—one 35-minute multiple-choice section and one 25-minute essay.
ACT	American College Test **General Description** An aptitude test of English, math, and science reasoning skills. More content-based than the SAT. Multiple-choice questions only. Optional writing test. **Why Take It** Most colleges require that applicants submit either SAT or ACT scores. **Sections** One English section—75 questions; 45 minutes. One Math section—60 questions; 60 minutes. One Reading section—40 questions; 35 minutes. One Science Reasoning section—40 questions; 35 minutes.

Types of Tests

There are two types of national college entrance exams, the SAT and the ACT. The SAT is considered a prediction of how well you will do with college level material. It tests not the content that you have learned in high school, but the skills in reading, writing, math, and thinking that you have acquired. The ACT, on the other hand, tests your aptitude and your ability to apply specific skills to subject material. Individual colleges determine which test or combination of tests they will accept.

Preparing for the Test

To decide which tests you will take, identify the colleges of your choice. Find out what tests are required and which tests they prefer. Be certain to schedule testing dates so that you can take a test more than once. Consult with your guidance counselor, and use testing Web sites or library resources to determine the registration date, the deadlines, any fees, and the testing locations. You can register for tests on-line, through the mail, or by phone.

Familiarize Yourself With the Test

Each testing company has a Web site that provides information about the test along with sample questions. Use those resources. There are also many publications with sample tests and helpful test-taking hints.

As of 2005, the new SAT verbal section contains these elements:

- Critical Reading passages with questions linked to the passages
- Sentence Completions that test vocabulary in context
- Writing/Editing multiple-choice questions that test your knowledge of standard grammar and sentence structure
- Timed Writing that tests your ability to write an essay based on a prompt

The ACT has these three sections dealing with language arts:

- English that tests your knowledge of standard grammar and usage
- Reading that consists of passages with questions linked to those passages
- Science Reasoning and Reading that tests your ability to understand and apply information gathered from reading.

Study for the Test

Take a practice exam and then honestly evaluate your strengths and weaknesses. If you read slowly, you should practice to increase your reading speed. If you labor over your writing, you should train yourself to organize and express your ideas faster. Time is a critical factor on these tests, and the more practice you have in working within the set time frames, the more comfortable you will be with the actual test.

Subject-Area Tests for College Placement

SAT II	**General Description** Disipline-specific tests measuring command of a subject **Why Take It** Some colleges may require SAT IIs for admission. Others use the scores to place students appropriately. **Specifics** All SAT II tests except the Writing test are multiple choice. Each takes an hour. the SAT II: Literature test divides 60 questions among 6 to 8 reading passages, covering poetry and prose from a broad range of periods
AP exams	**General Description** Discipline-specific tests measuring command of a subject **Why Take It** Participating colleges will award students college credit for achieving or bettering a given score. **Specifics** Formats vary with subject. The AP English Literature and Composition test traditionally features 50 to 55 multiple-choice questions divided among 4 to 5 reading passages (60 minutes) and 3 essay questions (120 minutes total). Passages cover poetry and prose from a broad range of periods. The English Language and Composition Test has the same basic format but concentrates on the way language is used.

Know Your Style

Knowing how you best approach material is critical in timed test situations. You should try several techniques to determine the one that works best for you. Here are some options:

Some students focus their reading by pre-reading the questions. Other students find this technique slows them down. Try both methods.

Mark the reading passage. Read with your pencil in your hand. Underline, star, or bracket important points as you read. This process saves time when you are looking for ideas.

There are two general methods of answering sentence completions. The first is to "substitute" a word in the blank and then look for a synonym of that word in the answer choices. The second is to eliminate answers by substituting them in the sentence and determining if they make sense.

Practice skimming a passage and then going back to answer the questions. For some students this is an effective method; others find they lose their reading focus.

Practice

Determine the parts that are difficult for you. Those are the parts that you should concentrate on for the majority of your study time.

Review the format of the test. Each section will have a specific time. Practice using that timing.

Monitor your pacing. Practice leaving problem questions blank, putting a mark next to them, and returning to them after you have answered the other questions. This technique will help you learn to pace yourself.

Keep your focus. To read effectively, you must first motivate yourself. Although *beets* may not be a subject that grabs your interest, if that is the subject of the passage, developing a disciplined focus for the subject helps. You do not need to understand everything in the passage. However, you do need to follow the main idea as it is developed. If you find your mind wandering—your eyes just running down the page without absorbing information—stop. Focus your attention and keep reading.

Know the scoring rules. Determine whether you can leave a question blank. The way the test is scored will determine whether you should guess on an answer or leave it blank.

Review several historical events and literary works. This preparation will be helpful in writing your essay.

Read the sample essays. Most tests provide samples of essays that received high scores. Look for the characteristics of those essays. Underline those characteristics in your own practice essays and make a list of the points you should work to include.

Know the key words. Questions for reading will ask for vocabulary in context, passage details, main ideas, inferences, tone, and style. Each type of question has a specific vocabulary with which you should be familiar. Questions for subject reading also have specific "key words" that tell you exactly what is required.

Practice prolonged focus. One of the most difficult parts of a standardized test is the length of the test. Practice sitting and working for the length of time of the entire test. Take no more than one five-minute break each hour.

Practice writing legibly under pressure. Try writing essays in pencil if you will hand write your essay on the test. Your handwriting must be legible to the graders.

Schedule a routine review time. Set aside a specific time each day to study. It is difficult to be consistent with long-term studying and a routine is helpful.

Taking the Test

The night before a standardized test you should gather everything you need: calculator, pencils, watch, etc.

On the day of the test, give yourself plenty of time to get to the testing site. Rushing makes most students nervous and does not help you perform to the best of your ability.

Manage Your Time

Flip through the test section. You can work on questions in the order that is most comfortable to you. It is generally best to work on the hardest questions first and those that are easier for you last.

Pace Yourself

Follow these steps to be sure you have enough time to finish the test:

- Periodically check your time. Adjust your speed accordingly.
- Do not be concerned if other students appear to be finished. Everyone works at a different pace.
- Always go back to the passage to verify your answer. The SAT asks you for information only from the reading passage. The ACT asks for information from both the provided passage and your own background.
- Determine which type of reading question is the hardest for you. Save those questions for last. All of the questions in a section are worth the same point value. Therefore, answer the questions you are fairly certain of before those that you struggle to answer.

Strategies for Essay Questions

Follow these steps for the writing portion of a test:

- Adapt your thesis from the question. The materials for the thesis of an essay question are in the test question, or prompt. Read the question carefully. Jot down a thesis statement that mirrors the question.
- In the body of your essay, use specific details from literature, history, and your own experiences.
- Be certain that the topic sentences of paragraphs have clear ties to your thesis.

Strategies for AP tests

AP tests evaluate specific knowledge. You cannot really study for standardized tests, but you can study for specific AP questions.

Review your notes and major tests from the AP class. It is important that you are comfortable with the literary and rhetorical terms that are used.

Use the structure of the test to your advantage.

Understanding the test will help you prepare for it. For instance, the AP English Literature and Composition test traditionally asks you to choose a work to comment on from a fairly broad list of works.To prepare for this question, you should be thoroughly comfortable with the plot, characters, setting, and themes of two classic works and two more modern works. Read any papers you have written pertaining to this literature to review your ideas.

Practice your writing using the prompts posted on the AP Web site or found in AP test-preparation books, which often contain old tests that you can use to prepare.

GRAMMAR, USAGE, AND MECHANICS HANDBOOK

Summary of Grammar

Nouns A **noun** names a person, place, or thing. A **common noun** names any one of a class of people, places, or things. A **proper noun** names a specific person, place, or thing.

Common Nouns	*Proper Nouns*
essayist	William Safire
city	New Orleans

Pronouns A **pronoun** is a word that stands for a noun or for words that take the place of a noun.

A **personal pronoun** refers to (1) the person speaking, (2) the person spoken to, or (3) the person, place, or thing spoken about.

	Singular	*Plural*
First Person	I, me, my, mine	we, us, our, ours
Second Person	you, your, yours	you, your, yours
Third Person	he, him, his, she, her, hers, it, its	they, them, their, theirs

A **reflexive pronoun** ends in *-self* or *-selves* and adds information to a sentence by pointing back to a noun or pronoun in the sentence.

> . . . They click upon *themselves*
> As the breeze rises, . . .Frost, p. 882

An **intensive pronoun** ends in *-self* or *-selves* and simply adds emphasis to a noun or pronoun in the same sentence.

> The United States *themselves* are essentially the greatest poem. . . .Whitman, p. 441

Demonstrative pronouns (*this, these, that,* and *those*) direct attention to a specific person, place, or thing.

this hat *these* coats *that* frame

A **relative pronoun** begins a subordinate (relative) clause and connects it to another idea in the sentence.

> The brave men, living and dead, *who* struggled here, have consecrated it . . . Lincoln, p. 532

> I made a little book, in *which* I allotted a page for each of the virtues. . . . Franklin, p. 144

An **indefinite pronoun** refers to a noun or pronoun that is not specifically named.

> *Few* could refrain from twisting their heads towards the door; *many* stood upright, and turned directly about; . . . Hawthorne, p. 342

Verbs A **verb** is a word or group of words that expresses time while showing an action, a condition, or the fact that something exists.

An **action verb** is a verb that tells what action someone or something is performing.

> The sun that brief December day
> *Rose* cheerless over hills of gray, . . .
> Whittier, p. 283

A **linking verb** is a verb that connects its subject with a word generally found near the end of the sentence. All linking verbs are intransitive.

> Her name *was* Phoenix Jackson. . . .Welty, p. 821

A **helping verb** is a verb that can be added to another verb to make a single verb phrase.

> Sir, we *have* done everything that could be done to avert the storm which is now coming on.
> Henry, p. 204

Adjectives An **adjective** is a word used to describe a noun or pronoun or to give a noun or pronoun a more specific meaning. Adjectives answer these questions:

What kind?	*green* leaf, *tall* chimney
Which one?	*this* clock, *those* pictures
How many?	*six* days, *several* concerts
How much?	*more* effort, *enough* applause
Whose?	*Kennedy's* address, *my* name

The articles *the, a,* and *an* are adjectives. *An* is used before a word beginning with a vowel sound.

A noun or pronoun may sometimes be used as an adjective.

diamond necklace *summer* vacation

Adverbs An **adverb** is a word that modifies a verb, an adjective, or another adverb. Adverbs answer the questions *where, when, in what way,* or *to what extent.*

> She came *yesterday.* (modifies verb *came*)

> They were *completely* unaware. (modifies adjective *unaware*)

> It rained *rather* often. (modifies adverb *often*)

Prepositions A **preposition** is a word that relates a noun or pronoun that appears with it to another word in the sentence. Prepositions are almost always followed by nouns or pronouns.

aboard the train *among* us *below* our plane

Conjunctions A **conjunction** is a word used to connect other words or groups of words.

A **coordinating conjunction** connects similar kinds or groups of words.

dogs *and* cats friendly *but* dignified

Correlative conjunctions are used in pairs to connect similar words or groups of words.

both Prem *and* Sanjay *neither* she *nor* I

A **subordinating conjunction** connects two complete ideas by placing one idea below the other in rank or importance.

Even before I asked, you knew . . .

A **conjunctive adverb** is an adverb used as a conjunction to connect complete ideas.

O'Connor portrayed social outcasts; *however,* she addresses society as a whole.

Interjections An **interjection** is a word that expresses feeling or emotion and functions independently of a sentence.

Oh, woe is me!

Subject and Verb Agreement To make a subject and verb agree, make sure that both are singular or both are plural.

He reads Hemingway. *We read* Thoreau.

Phrases A **phrase** is a group of words, without a subject and verb, that functions in a sentence as one part of speech.

A **prepositional phrase** is a group of words that includes a preposition and a noun or pronoun.

beyond the horizon inside the corral

An **adjective phrase** is a prepositional phrase that modifies a noun or pronoun by telling *what kind* or *which one.*

the book *on the table* the size *of the classroom*

An **adverb phrase** is a prepositional phrase that modifies a verb, an adjective, or an adverb by pointing out *where, when, in what way,* or *to what extent.*

During the intermission before the second half of the concert, I questioned my aunt and found that the "Prize Song" was not new to her.
Cather, p. 677

An **appositive phrase** is a noun or pronoun with modifiers, placed next to a noun or pronoun to add information and details.

Miss Toshiko Sasaki, *a clerk in the personnel department of the East Asia Tin Works,* had just sat down . . .
Hersey, p. 1199

A **participial phrase** is a participle that is modified by an adjective or adverb phrase or that has a complement. The entire phrase acts as an adjective.

Two or three men, *conversing earnestly together,* ceased as he approached, . . . Harte, p. 593

A **nominative absolute** is a noun or pronoun followed by a participle or participial phrase that functions independently of the rest of the sentence.

The preparations being complete, the two private soldiers stepped aside and each drew away the plank upon which he had been standing.
Bierce, p. 519

An **infinitive phrase** is an infinitive ' modifiers, complements, or a subject, all acting together as a single part of speech.

. . . some set *to mow,* others *to bind thatch,* some *to build houses,* others *to thatch them* . . .
Smith, p. 72

Clauses A **clause** is a group of words with its own subject and verb.

An **independent clause** can stand by itself as a complete sentence. A **subordinate clause** cannot stand by itself as a complete sentence; it can only be part of a sentence.

An **adjective clause** is a subordinate clause that modifies a noun or pronoun by telling *what kind* or *which one.*

In compliance with the request of a friend of mine, *who wrote me from the East,* I called on good-natured, garrulous old Simon Wheeler . . .
Twain, p. 581

A **subordinate adverb clause** modifies a verb, an adjective, an adverb, or a verbal by telling *where, when, in what way, to what extent, under what condition,* or *why.*

Whenever you like, please visit.

A **noun clause** is a subordinate clause that acts as a noun.

As I knew, or thought I knew, *what was right and wrong,* I did not see why I might not always do the one and avoid the other. . . . Franklin, p. 143

Summary of Capitalization and Punctuation

Capitalization

Capitalize the first word in sentences, interjections, and incomplete questions. Also, capitalize the first word in a quotation if the quotation is a complete sentence.

And then I said in perfect English, "Yes, I'm getting rather concerned." . . . Tan, p. 1174

Capitalize all proper nouns and adjectives.

T. S. Eliot Mississippi River Harvard University
Turkish November Puerto Rican

Capitalize a person's title when it is followed by the person's name or when it is used in direct address.

Rev. Leonidas W. Smiley General Robert E. Lee

Capitalize titles showing family relationships when they refer to a specific person, unless they are preceded by a possessive noun or pronoun.

Granny Weatherall my grandfather Mammedaty

Capitalize the first word and all other key words in the titles of books, periodicals, poems, stories, plays, paintings, and other works of art.

The Crucible "Anecdote of the Jar"

Capitalize the first word and all nouns in letter salutations and the first word in letter closings.

Dear Henry, Yours truly,

Punctuation

End Marks Use a **period** to end a declarative sentence, a mild imperative sentence, an indirect question, and most abbreviations.

Pile the bodies high at Austerlitz and Waterloo.
Sandburg, p. 842

Use a **question mark** to end an interrogative sentence, an incomplete question, or a statement that is intended as a question.

Was it even Kentucky or Tennessee?
Warren, p. 1051

Use an **exclamation mark** after an exclamatory sentence, a forceful imperative sentence, or an interjection expressing strong emotion.

"Don't let him, sister!" . . . Frost, p. 889

Commas Use a comma before the conjunction to separate two independent clauses in a compound sentence.

From my mother's sleep I fell into the State,
And I hunched in its belly till my wet fur froze.
Jarrell, p. 1210

Use commas to separate three or more words, phrases, or clauses in a series.

I spun, I wove, I kept the house, I nursed the sick, . . . Masters, p. 663

Use commas to separate adjectives of equal rank. Do not use commas to separate adjectives that must stay in a specific order.

She carried a thin, small cane made from an umbrella . . . Welty, p. 821

Use a comma after an introductory word, phrase, or clause.

Finding Tom so squeamish on this point, he did not insist upon it, . . . Irving, p. 265

Use commas to set off parenthetical and nonessential expressions.

My poor aunt's figure, however, would have presented astonishing difficulties to any dressmaker. Cather, p. 673

Use commas with places, dates, and titles.

Boston, Massachusetts November 17, 1915

Dr. Martin Luther King, Jr.

Use commas after items in addresses, after the salutation in a personal letter, after the closing in all letters, and in numbers of more than three digits.

Linden Lane, Princeton, N.J. Dear Marian,

Affectionately yours, 6,778

Use a comma to indicate words left out of an elliptical sentence and to set off a direct quotation.

In T. S. Eliot's poetry, allusions are perhaps the most prominent device; in Ezra Pound's, images.

"Well, Granny," he said, "you must be a hundred years old and scared of nothing." . . . Welty, p. 825

Semicolons Use a semicolon to join independent clauses that are not already joined by a conjunction.

The old woman didn't change her position until he was almost into her yard; then she rose with one hand fisted on her hip. . . .O'Connor, p. 983

Use semicolons to avoid confusion when independent clauses or items in a series already contain commas.

Before these events, the day was glorious with expectancy; after them, the day was a dead and empty thing. . . .Twain, p. 577

Colons Use a colon before a list of items following an independent clause.

Great literature provides us with many things: entertainment, enrichment, and inspiration.

Use a colon to introduce a formal or a lengthy quotation.

In *The Member of the Wedding*, the lonely twelve-year-old girl, Frankie Addams, articulates this universal need: "The trouble with me is that for a long time I have just been an *I* person." . . .
McCullers, p. 1154

Quotation Marks A **direct quotation** represents a person's exact speech and is enclosed in quotation marks.

"Good," he said. "You will be able to play football again better than ever." . . . Hemingway, p. 810

An **indirect quotation** reports only the general meaning of what a person said and does not require quotation marks.

One day I had said that Italian seemed such an easy language to me . . . Hemingway, p. 812

Always place a comma or a period inside the final quotation mark.

"Well, Missy, excuse me," Doctor Harry patted her cheek. . . . Porter, p. 848

Place a question mark or an exclamation mark inside the final quotation mark if the end mark is part of the quotation; if it is not part of the quotation, place it outside the final quotation mark.

"Cornelia! Cornelia!" No footsteps, but a sudden hand on her cheek. "Bless you, where have you been?" . . .Porter, p. 851

Use single quotation marks for a quotation within a quotation.

"'All right,' I say, 'I can't afford to pay
Any fixed wages, though I wish I could.'
'Someone else can.' 'Then someone else will
have to.'" . . . "The Death of the Hired Man," Robert
Frost

Underline or italicize the titles of long written works, movies, television and radio shows, lengthy works of music, paintings, and sculpture.

The Great Gatsby *Mary Poppins* Aida

Use quotation marks around the titles of short written works, episodes in a series, songs, and titles of works mentioned as parts of a collection.

"Winter Dreams" "Go Down, Moses"

Dashes Use dashes to indicate an abrupt change of thought, a dramatic interrupting idea, or a summary statement.

She'd had moments herself of picturing some kind of
evil gene in her husband's ordinary, stocky body—a
dark little egg like a black jelly bean, she imagined it. . . .
Tyler, p. 1065

Use dashes to set off a nonessential appositive or modifier when it is long, when it is already punctuated, or when you want to be dramatic.

. . . for some reason he was not completely sure of—it
may have been the cold and his fatigue—he decided
not to insist on seeing him. . . .
Malamud, p. 1002

Hyphens Use a hyphen with certain numbers, after certain prefixes, with two or more words used as one word, with a compound modifier coming before a noun, and within a word when a combination of letters might otherwise be confusing.

fifty-four daughter-in-law up-to-date report

Apostrophes Add an apostrophe and *-s* to show the possessive case of most singular nouns.

Taylor's poetry a poet's career

Add an apostrophe to show the possessive case of plural nouns ending in *-s* and *-es.*

the boys' ambition the Cruzes' house

Add an apostrophe and *-s* to show the possessive case of plural nouns that do not end in *-s* or *-es.*

the men's suits the deer's antlers

Use an apostrophe in a contraction to indicate the position of the missing letter or letters.

"You look like a saint, Doctor Harry, and I vow that's as
near as you'll ever come to it."
Porter, p. 855

Glossary of Common Usage

adapt, adopt

Adapt is a verb meaning "to change." *Adopt* is a verb meaning "to take as one's own."

Washington Irving *adapted* many characters and situations from folk tales for his short stories.

Ezra Pound's followers *adopted* a spare style.

advice, advise

Advice is a noun meaning "an opinion." *Advise* is a verb meaning "to give an opinion."

The man ignores the *advice* of the old-timer.

How might you *advise* the younger generation?

affect, effect

Affect is almost always a verb meaning "to influence." *Effect* is usually a noun meaning "result." *Effect* can also be a verb meaning "to bring about" or "to cause."

An understanding of T. S. Eliot's multiple allusions can *affect* one's appreciation of his poetry.

In Cather's story, the concert has a profound *effect* on Aunt Georgiana.

The aim of persuasive writing is often to *effect* a change in the attitudes of the audience.

among, between

Among is usually used with three or more items. *Between* is generally used with only two items.

Among the writers of the Harlem Renaissance, Langston Hughes stands out.

In Frost's "Mending Wall," the speaker reports a conversation *between* himself and his neighbor.

as, because, like, as to

The word *as* has several meanings and can function as several parts of speech. To avoid confusion, use *because* rather than *as* when you want to indicate cause and effect.

Because Jonathan Edwards believed that his listeners' souls were in danger, he wanted them to repent.

Do not use the preposition *like* to introduce a clause that requires the conjunction *as.*

The Puritans reacted to music and dancing *as* one might expect: They considered that such entertainments were dangerous occasions for sin.

The use of *as to* for *about* is awkward and should be avoided.

Captain Ahab's bitter vehemence *about* the white whale must seem puzzling to the crew.

bad, badly

Use the predicate adjective *bad* after linking verbs such as *feel, look*, and *seem*. Use *badly* whenever an adverb is required.

Although Granny Weatherall looks *bad*, she is not at all happy to see Doctor Harry.

Elizabeth is *badly* shaken when Mr. Hooper refuses to remove the black veil.

because of, due to

Use *due to* if it can logically replace the phrase *caused by*. In introductory phrases, however, *because of* is better usage than *due to*.

Farquhar's failure to recognize the scout's trap may be *due to* his eagerness to aid a cause.

Because of Masters's ability to sketch characters accurately, his work became popular.

being as, being that

Avoid using the expressions *being as* and *being that*. Use *because* or *since* instead.

Because Whitman believed that new styles were needed in American poetry, he broke with traditional forms.

Since Shiftlet is more interested in the car than in Lucynell, it is hardly surprising that he abandons her.

beside, besides

Beside is a preposition meaning "at the side of" or "close to." Do not confuse *beside* with *besides*, which means "in addition to." *Besides* can be a preposition or an adverb.

When Clark sits *beside* Georgiana, he tries to imagine her emotions as she hears the music.

Besides Mr. Oakhurst, which other characters are run out of town?

Thomas Jefferson was the third president of the United States; he was a gifted architect, *besides*.

can, may

The verb *can* generally refers to the ability to do something. The verb *may* generally refers to being allowed or permitted to do something.

One of Ralph Waldo Emerson's major themes is that human beings *can* acquire from nature a sense of their own potential and autonomy.

May I borrow your copy of *The Grapes of Wrath*?

different from, different than

The preferred usage is *different from*.

In her powerful exploration of women's consciousness, Kate Chopin was *different from* the vast majority of her contemporaries.

due to the fact that

Replace this awkward expression with *because* or *since*.

Because Dexter Green cherishes his memories of the glamourous Judy Jones, it is not surprising that he is saddened by the knowledge that her youth and beauty have faded.

farther, further

Use *farther* when you refer to distance. Use *further* when you mean "to a greater degree."

The *farther* Phoenix Jackson travels in Eudora Welty's story "A Worn Path," the more her determination to reach her goal grows.

In his speech, Patrick Henry urges his countrymen to trust the British no *further*.

fewer, less

Use *fewer* for things that can be counted. Use *less* for amounts or quantities that cannot be counted.

The poem "The Red Wheelbarrow" uses *fewer* words than many other poems.

The train engineer felt *less* anticipation with each step.

good, well

Use the predicate adjective *good* after linking verbs such as *feel, look, smell, taste*, and *seem*. Use *well* whenever you need an adverb.

At the end of "Winter Dreams," Devon implies that Judy does not look as *good* as she used to.

Anne Tyler writes especially *well* about ordinary people and family relationships.

hopefully

You should not loosely attach this adverb to a sentence, as in "Hopefully, the rain will stop by noon." Rewrite the sentence so that *hopefully* modifies a specific verb. Other possible ways of revising such sentences include using the adjective *hopeful* or a phrase such as *everyone hopes that*.

William Faulkner wrote *hopefully* about mankind's ability to endure and prevail.

Mai was *hopeful* that she could locate some more biographical information about Jean Toomer.

Everyone hopes that Diane will win the essay contest.

its, it's

Do not confuse the possessive pronoun *its* with the contraction *it's*, standing for "it is" or "it has."

Perhaps the most memorable line in Emerson's poem "The Rhodora" is "Beauty is *its* own excuse for being."

Wallace Stevens's "Anecdote of the Jar" suggests that *it's* impossible to mediate completely between the wilderness and the world of civilization.

kind of, sort of

In formal writing, you should not use these colloquial expressions. Instead, use a word such as *rather* or *somewhat.*

Robert Lowell's train of thought in "Hawthorne" is *rather* difficult to follow.

Mary Chesnut is accurate but *somewhat* emotional.

lay, lie

Do not confuse these verbs. *Lay* is a transitive verb meaning "to set or put something down." Its principal parts are *lay, laying, laid, laid. Lie* is an intransitive verb meaning "to recline." Its principal parts are *lie, lying, lay, lain.*

Stream-of-consciousness narration *lays* a special responsibility on the reader.

The speaker of "I heard a Fly buzz—when I died—" *lies* in a silent room as her life slips away.

many, much

Use *many* to refer to a specific quantity. Use *much* for an indefinite amount or for an abstract concept.

Many of William Faulkner's novels deal with the themes of pride, guilt, and the search for identity.

Much of Mark Twain's fiction was influenced by his boyhood along the Mississippi.

may be, maybe

Be careful not to confuse the verb phrase *may be* with the adverb *maybe* (meaning "perhaps").

The speaker *may be* the poet herself; in others, the speaker is clearly a different persona.

The most memorable, and *maybe* the most ineffectual, character in T. S. Eliot's poetry is Prufrock.

plurals that do not end in *-s*

The plurals of certain nouns from Greek and Latin are formed as they were in their original language. Words such as *criteria, media,* and *phenomena* are plural and should not be treated as if they were singular (*criterion, medium, phenomenon*).

In "Ars Poetica," Archibald MacLeish seems to deny that meaning is the most important *criterion* for the evaluation of poetry.

The *phenomena* discussed by the "learn'd astronomer" in Whitman's poem may have included planetary orbits and the influence of the moon on the tides.

raise, rise

Raise is a transitive verb that usually takes a direct object. *Rise* is intransitive and never takes a direct object.

Suspense *raises* readers' expectations.

Flannery O'Connor published a collection entitled *Everything That Rises Must Converge.*

set, sit

Do not confuse these verbs. *Set* is a transitive verb meaning "to put (something) in a certain place." Its principal parts are *set, setting, set, set. Sit* is an intransitive verb meaning "to be seated." Its principal parts are *sit, sitting, sat, sat.*

Phillis Wheatley's poem is so complimentary to Washington that it seems to *set* him on a pedestal.

As Mrs. Mallard *sits* upstairs alone, she contemplates the death of her husband.

that, which, who

Use the relative pronoun *that* to refer to things or people. Use *which* only for things and *who* only for people.

The poet *that* Lee liked best was Sylvia Plath.

The Romantic movement, *which* emphasized emotions, took place during the early 1800s.

The poet *who* was the first to read his work at a presidential inauguration was Robert Frost.

unique

Because *unique* means "one of a kind," you should not use it carelessly instead of the words "interesting" or "unusual." Avoid such illogical expressions as "most unique," "very unique," and "extremely unique."

Some critics have argued that its themes make Herman Melville's *Moby-Dick unique* in literary history.

who, whom

In formal writing, use *who* only as a subject in clauses and sentences and *whom* only as an object.

Walt Whitman, *who* grieved Lincoln's assassination, wrote a tribute to the slain president.

F. Scott Fitzgerald, *whom* many have heralded as the voice of the Jazz Age, wrote *The Great Gatsby.*

INDEX OF AUTHORS AND TITLES

Note: Nonfiction selections and informational text appear in red. Page numbers in italic text refer to background or biographical information.

L

M

N

O

P

Q

R

S

T

U

W

INDEX OF SKILLS

Note: Page numbers in **boldface** refer to pages where terms are defined.

Literary Analysis

Reading Strategies

Critical Viewing

Writing

Listening and Speaking

Research and Technology

INDEX OF FEATURES

Maps

Reading Informational Materials

Research and Technology Guide

Unit Introductions

Vocabulary Workshop

Writing About Literature

Writing Workshop

ACKNOWLEDGMENTS (continued)

Diana Chang Herrmann "from Most Satisfied by Snow" by Diana Chang. Copyrighted and reprinted by permission of Diana Chang. **The Barbara Hogenson Agency** "The Night the Ghost Got In" from *My Life and Hard Times* by James Thurber. Copyright © 1933, 1961 by James Thurber. Reprinted by arrangement with Rosemary Thurber and The Barbara Hogenson Agency, Inc. All rights reserved. **Henry Holt and Company** "The Gift Outright" from *The Poetry of Robert Frost.* Copyright © 1942 by Robert Frost, © 1970 by Lesley Frost Ballantine, © 1969 by Henry Holt and Company. "Stopping by Woods on a Snowy Evening" from *The Poetry of Robert Frost,* edited by Edward Connery Lathem. Copyright © 1951 by Robert Frost, © 1923, 1969 by Henry Holt and Company. "Acquainted with the Night" from *The Poetry of Robert Frost* edited by Edward Connery Lathem. Copyright © 1956 by Robert Frost, © 1928, 1969 by Henry Holt and Company. Reprinted by permission of Henry Holt and Company, LLC. **Houghton Mifflin Company** "Ambush" from *The Things They Carried* by Tim O'Brien. Copyright © 1990 by Tim O'Brien. "Loneliness... An American Malady", from *The Mortgaged Heart* by Carson McCullers. Copyright 1940, 1941, 1942, 1945, 1948, 1949, 1953, © 1956, 1959, 1963, 1971 by Floria V. Lasky, Executrix of the Estate of Carson McCullers. "Ars Poetica" from *Collected Poems 1917–1982* by Arachibald MacLeish. Copyright © 1985 by The Estate of Archibald MacLeish. Reprinted by permission of Houghton Mifflin Company. All rights reserved. **International African Institute** "African Proverbs: Liberia: The Jabo: "Children are the wisdom . . ."" by Anonymous from *Jabo Proverbs From Liberia: Maxims In The Life Of A Native Tribe.* "African Proverbs: Liberia: The Jabo: "One who cannot pick up an ant . . ."" by Anonymous from *Jabo Proverbs From Liberia: Maxims In The Life Of A Native Tribe.* "African Proverbs: Liberia: The Jabo: "Daring talk . . ."" by Anonymous from *Jabo Proverbs From Liberia: Maxims In The Life Of A Native Tribe.* "African Proverbs: Liberia: The Jabo: "A man's ways are good . . ."" by Anonymous from *Jabo Proverbs From Liberia: Maxims In The Life Of A Native Tribe.* "African Proverbs: Liberia: The Jabo: "The one who listens . . ."" by Anonymous from *Jabo Proverbs From Liberia: Maxims In The Life Of A Native Tribe.* "African Proverbs: Liberia: The Jabo: "The butterfly that flies among . . ."" by Anonymous from *Jabo Proverbs From Liberia: Maxims In The Life Of A Native Tribe.* Published from the International Institute of African Languages & Cultures by Oxford University Press, London: Humphrey Milford, 1936. **International Creative Management, Inc.** "One Day, Now Broken in Two" by Anna Quindlen. Copyright © 2002 by Anna Quindlen. First appeared in *Newsweek.* Reprinted by permission of International Creative Management, Inc. **Johnson Publishing Company** "From My Bondage and My Freedom" by Frederick Douglass from *My Bondage and My Freedom.* Reprinted by permission. **Estate of Martin Luther King, Jr. c/o Writers House as agent for the proprietor** "Letter from Birmingham City Jail (Why We Can't Wait)" by Martin Luther King, Jr. Copyright 1963 Martin Luther King, Jr. renewed 1991 by Coretta Scott King. **Alfred A. Knopf, a division of Random House, Inc.** "I, Too" from *The Selected Poems of Langston Hughes* by Langston Hughes, copyright © 1994 by the Estate of Langston Hughes. "Anecdote of the Jar" copyright 1923 and renewed 1951 by Wallace Stevens from *The Collected Poems of Wallace Stevens* by Wallace Stevens. "Of Modern Poetry" copyright 1942 by Wallace Stevens and renewed 1970 by Holly Stevens from *The Collected Poems of Wallace Stevens by Wallace Stevens.* "Dream Variations" by Langston Hughes from *Selected Poems of Langston Hughes.* Copyright © 1926 by Alfred A. Knopf, Inc. and renewed 1954 by Langston Hughes. "Refugee in America" copyright © 1943 by The Curtis Publishing Company. "The Negro Speaks of Rivers" copyright © 1926 by Alfred A. Knopf, Inc. and renewed 1954 by Langston Hughes, from *Selected Poems of Langston Hughes.* Used by permission of Alfred A. Knopf, a division of Random House, Inc. From *Hiroshima* by John Hersey, copyright 1946 and renewed 1974 by John Hersey. From "The Woman Warrior" by Maxine Hong Kingston, copyright © 1975, 1976 by Maxine Hong Kingston. **Little, Brown and Company, Inc.** "Aliceville" by Tony Earley from *Here We Are In Paradise.* Copyright © 1994 by Tony Earley. All rights reserved. **Liveright Publishing Corporation** "Runagate Runagate" by Robert Hayden Copyright © 1966 by Robert Hayden, from *Collected Poems of Robert Hayden* by Robert Hayden, edited by Frederick Glaysher. "Frederick Douglass" Copyright © 1966 by Robert Hayden, from *Collected Poems of Robert Hayden,* edited by Frederick Glaysher. "anyone lived in a pretty how town" copyright 1940, © 1968, 1991, by the Trustees for the E. E. Cummings Trust, from *Complete Poems: 1904–1962* by E. E. Cummings, edited by George J. Firmage. "old age sticks" Copyright © 1958, 1986, 1991 by the Trustees for the E. E. Cummings Trust, from *Complete Poems: 1904–1962* by E. E. Cummings, edited by George J. Firmage. Used by permission of Liveright Publishing Corporation. **The Estate of Edgar Lee Masters** "Lucinda Matlock" from *Spoon River Anthology* by Edgar Lee Masters. Originally published by the Macmillan Company. Used by permission of Hilary Masters. **Mekko Productions** "Suspended" by Joy Harjo from *In Short: A Collection of Brief Nonfiction.* Used by permission of Joy Harjo. **Milkweed Editions** "Museum Indians" by Susan Power from *Roofwalker.* Copyright © 2002 by Susan Power. Reprinted with permission from Milkweed Editions. **Navarre Scott Momaday** From "The Names" by N. Scott Momaday. Used by permission of N. Scott Momaday. **William Morris Agency** "Gold Glade" by Robert Penn Warren from *Selected Poems.* **Jonathan Musere** "African Proverbs: Uganda: The Bagada: "A small deed out of friendship . . ."", "African Proverbs: Uganda: The Bagada: "One who loves you, warns you . . ."", "African Proverbs: Uganda: The Bagada: "Words are easy, but friendship is difficult . . ."", "African Proverbs: Uganda: The Bagada: "Where there are no dogs . . ."", "African Proverbs: Uganda: The Bagada: "The one who has not made the journey . . ."" by Anonymous from *African Proverbs And Proverbial Names.* Copyright © 1999 by Ariko Publications. Used by permission. **New Directions Publishing Corporation** "Heat, part II of Garden" and "Pear Tree" by HD (Hilda Doolittle), from *Collected Poems, 1912–1944,* copyright © 1982 by The Estate of Hilda Doolittle. "Fern Hill" by Dylan Thomas, from *The Poems of Dylan Thomas.* Copyright © 1945 by The Trustees for the Copyrights of Dylan Thomas. "from A Few Don'ts (A Retrospect)" by Ezra Pound, from *The Literary Essays of Ezra Pound.* Copyright © 1935 by Ezra Pound. "The Red Wheelbarrow," "The is Just to Say" and "The Great Figure" by William Carlos Williams, from *Collected Poems: 1909–1939,* Volume I, copyright © 1938 by New Directions Publishing Corp. "In a Station of the Metro" and "The River-Merchant's Wife: A Letter" by Ezra Pound, from *Personae,* copyright © 1926 by Ezra Pound. Reprinted by permission of New Directions Publishing Corp. **The New York Times Agency** "Onomatopoeia" originally titled "Zapmanship" by William Safire from *You Could Look It Up.* Copyright © 1964. Reprinted by permission of The New York Times. **W. W. Norton & Company, Inc.** "Who Burns for the Perfection of Paper" from *City Of Coughing And Dead Radiators* by Martin Espada. Copyright © 1993 by Martin Espada. "Water Names" from *Hunger* by Lan Samantha Chang. Copyright © 1998 by Lan Samantha Chang. "In a Classroom" by Adrienne Rich. Copyright © 2002, 1989 by Adrienne Rich from *The Fact of a Doorframe: Selected Poems 1950–2001.* Used by permission of the author and W. W. Norton & Company, Inc. "from Civil Disobedience" by Henry David Thoreau from *Walden and Civil Disobedience.* Copyright © 1966. Used by permission of of W. W. Norton & Company, Inc. **Naomi Shihab Nye** "Mint Snowball" by Naomi Shihab Nye from. Reprinted by permission of the author. **Harold Ober Associates, Inc.** "A Black Man Talks of Reaping" by Arna Bontemps from *American Negro Poetry.* Copyright © 1963 by Arna Bontemps. Reprinted by permission of Harold Ober Associates Incorporated. **Simon Ortiz** "Hunger in New York City" by Simon Ortiz from *Going For The Rain.* Published by Harper & Row 1976. Copyright © 1976 by Simon J. Ortiz. **Penguin Books Ltd., London** From "The Rig Veda: Creation Hymn" and from "The Rig Veda: Night" translated by Wendy Doniger O'Flaherty from *The Rig Veda: An Anthology.* Copyright © 1981 Wendy Doniger O'Flaherty. **Peter Pauper Press, Inc.** "African Proverbs: Ghana: The Ashanti: "If you are in hiding . . ."", "African Proverbs: Ghana: The Ashanti: "No one tests the depth of a river . . ."", "African Proverbs: Nigeria: The Yoruba: "The day on which one starts out . . ."", "African Proverbs: Nigeria: The Yoruba: "He who is being carried does not realize . . ."", "African Proverbs: Nigeria: The Yoruba: "Little is better than nothing."", "African Proverbs: Ghana: The Ashanti: "Rain beats a leopard skin . . ."", "African Proverbs: Tanzania and Kenya: The Masai: "Do not say the first thing . . ."", "African Proverbs: Nigeria: The Yoruba: "Time destroys all things."", "African Proverbs: Ghana: The Ashanti: "One falsehood . . ."" from *African Proverbs.* Copyright © 1962 by the Peter Pauper Press, Inc. Used by permission. **Plimoth Plantation** "Plimoth Plantation" by Staff from *www.plimoth.org/index.html.* Used by permission of Plimoth Plantation, Inc. www.plimoth.org. **Princeton University Press** From *Walden* by Henry David Thoreau. Copyright © 1971 by Princeton University Press. 1999 copyright renewed by PUP, 1989 paperback edition. Reprinted by permission of Princeton University Press. **Random House, Inc.** "A Rose for Emily" by William Faulkner from *Collected Stories Of William Faulkner.* Copyright © 1930 and renewed 1958 by William Faulkner. "The Unknown Citizen" copyright 1940 and renewed 1968 by W. H. Auden. From *Collected Poems* by W. H. Auden. Used by permission of Random House, Inc. **Russell & Volkening, Inc.** "Average Waves in Unprotected Waters" by Anne Tyler from *The New Yorker.* Copyright © 1977 by Anne Tyler. This story originally appeared in The New Yorker, February 28th, 1977. Reproduced by permission of Russell & Volkening as agents for the author. **The Schomburg Center for Research in Black Culture** "The Tropics of New York" by Claude McKay from *The Poems of Clause McKay.* Courtesy of the Literary Representative for the Works of Claude McKay, Schomburg Center for Research in Black Culture, The New York Public Library, Astor, Lenox and Tilden Foundations. Used by permission. **Scribner, a division of Simon & Schuster** "The Far and the Near, from *Death to Morning* by Thomas Wolfe. Copyright 1925 by Charles Scribner's Sons; copyright renewed © 1963 by Paul Gitlin." Reprinted with the permission of Scribner, a division of Simon & Schuster. **Scribner, an imprint of Simon & Schuster Adult Publishing Group** "In Another Country" from *Men Without Women* by Ernest Hemingway. Copyright © 1927 by Charles Scribner's Sons. Copyright renewed 1955 by Ernest Hemingway. "Poetry" from the *Collected Poems of Marianne Moore.* Copyright © 1935 by Marianne Moore; copyright renewed © 1963 by Marianne Moore and T.S. Eliot. Reprinted with the permission of Scribner, an imprint of Simon & Schuster Adult Publishing Group. **Don D. Stanford** "Huswifery" from *The Poems of Edward Taylor* by

Edward Taylor. Copyright © 1960, renewed 1988 by Donald E. Stanford; University of North Carolina Press, 1989. Used by permission of Don D. Stanford. **Sterling Lord Literistic, Inc.** "The Crisis, Number 1" by Thomas Paine from *Citizen Tom Paine*. Copyright by Howard Fast. Used by permission of Sterling Lord Literistic, Inc. **Syracuse University Press** "The Iroquois Constitution" from *Parker on the Iroquois: Iroquois Uses of Maize and Other Food Plants; The Code of Handsome Lake; The Seneca Prophet; The Constitution of the Five Nations* by Arthur C. Parker, edited by William N. Fenton (Syracuse University Press, Syracuse, NY, 1981). Copyright © 1968 by Syracuse University Press. **Thompson and Thompson** From "The Dark Tower" by Countee Cullen from *Copper Sun*. Copyright 1927 by Harper & Bros, NY. Renewed in 1954 by Ida M. Culllen. Reprinted with permission of Thompson and Thompson. **University of Nebraska Press** "Crossing the Great Divide" by Meriweather Lewis. Reprinted from *The Journals of the Lewis and Clark Expedition, volume 5*, edited by Gary E. Moulton by permission of the University of Nebraska Press. Copyright © 1988 by the University of Nebraska Press. **University of North Carolina Press** "To His Excellency, General Washington" by Phillis Wheatley from *The Poems Of Phillis Wheatley*. "An Hymn to the Evening" by Phillis Wheatley from *The Poems Of Phillis Wheatley*. **University of Texas Press** "Sonnet 71" and "Sonnet 49" by Pablo Neruda translated by Stephen Tapscott from *100 Love Sonnets: Cien Sonetos De Amor*. Copyright © Pablo Neruda, 1959. Copyright © 1986 by the University of Texas Press. All rights reserved. Originally published as *Cien sonetos de amor* © Editorial Losada, S.A., Buenos Aires, 1960. **Viking Penguin, Inc.** From *The Crucible* by Arthur Miller, copyright 1952, 1953, 1954, renewed © 1980, 1981, 1982 by Arthur Miller. CAUTION: Professionals and amateurs are hereby warned that *The Crucible*, being fully protected under the copyright Laws of the United States of America, the British Empire, including the Dominion of Canada, and all other countries of the Universal Copyright and Berne Conventions, are subject to royalty. All rights, including professional, amateur, motion picture, recitation, lecturing, public reading, radio and television broadcasting, and the rights of translation into foreign languages, are strictly reserved. Particular emphasis is laid on the question of readings, permission for which must be secured in writing. All inquiries for *The Crucible* should be addressed to Viking Penguin, 375 Hudson Street, NY, NY 10014. "The Turtle (Chapter 3)" from *The Grapes of Wrath* by John Steinbeck, copyright 1939, renewed © 1967 by John Steinbeck. Used by permission of Viking Penguin, a division of Penguin Group (USA) Inc. **Wesleyan University Press** "What For" by Garrett Kaoru Hongo from *Yellow Light*. Copyright © 1982 by Karrett Kaoru Hongo. "Camouflaging the Chimera" by Yusef Komunyakaa from *Dien Cai Dau* Copyright © 1988 by Yusef Komunyakaa. "For My Children" by Colleen McElroy from *What Madness Brought Me Here*. Copyright © 1990 by Coleen McElory. Reprinted by permission of Wesleyan University Press. **Witwatersrand University Press** "African Proverbs: South Africa: The Zulu: "Do not speak of rhinoceros . . ."", "African Proverbs: South Africa: The Zulu: "Eyes do not see all."", "African Proverbs: South Africa: The Zulu: "No dew ever competed . . ."", "African Proverbs: South Africa: The Zulu: "What has happened before . . ."", "African Proverbs: South Africa: The Zulu: "It never dawns in the same way."", "African Proverbs: South Africa: The Zulu: "The one offended never forgets . . ."", "African Proverbs: South Africa: The Zulu: "You cannot chase two gazelles."", "African Proverbs: South Africa: The Zulu: "There is no foot . . ."" and "African Proverbs: South Africa: The Zulu: "Look as you fell a tree."" from Zulu Proverbs. Copyright © 1954 by Witwatersrand University Press. **Yale University Press** Excerpt from "Sinners in the Hands of an Angry God" *from The Sermons of Jonathan Edwards: A Reader* published by Yale University Press. Copyright © 1999 by Yale University Press. From "Mary Chesnut's Civil War, edited by C. Vann Woodward. Copyright © 1981 by C. Vann Woodward, Sally Bland Metts, Barbara G. Carpenter, Sally Bland Johnson, and Katherine W. Herbert. Reprinted with permission of Yale University Press.

Note: Every effort has been made to locate the copyright owner of material reproduced on this component. Omissions brought to our attention will be corrected in subsequent editions.

CREDITS

Cover: *Flag on Orange Field,* 1957, oil on canvas, Johns, Jasper (b.1930)/Ludwig Museum, Cologne, Germany, Lauros/Giraudon/www.bridgeman.co.uk/Cover art © Jasper Johns/Licensed by VAGA, New York, NY **iv: (t.):** Photo by Rebecca Dallinger; Courtesy of Susan Power **iv: (m.):** Prentice Hall **iv: (b.):** Prentice Hall **v: (t.):** ©Elisheba Johnson **v: (m.t.):** Prentice Hall **v: (m.b.):** Prentice Hall **v: (b.):** ©Sophie Bassouls/CORBIS Sygma **vii:** John Chase/Dorling Kindersley. © Museum of London **viii:** Photo by Rebecca Dallinger; Courtesy of Susan Power **ix:** Corel Professional Photos CD-ROM™ **x:** Prentice Hall **xi:** Francis G. Mayer/CORBIS **xii:** Prentice Hall **xiv:** Prentice Hall **xvi:** Prentice Hall **xvii:** Dewitt Jones/Woodfin Camp & Associates **xviii:** Martial Columb/Getty Images **xix:** ©Sophie Bassouls/CORBIS Sygma **xx:** *Passion of Paints*, Bob Peters, Exclusively represented by Applejack Licensing International **1:** *World Map,* 1630, Jan Jansson, The Huntington Library, Art Collections and Botanical Gardens, San Marino, CA **2: (m.):** Photo by Rebecca Dallinger; Courtesy of Susan Power **2: (b.):** Marilyn "Angel" Wynn/Nativestock.com **2: (t.):** Astrolabe, Museum fur Kunst und Gewerbe, Hamburg **4: (m.t.):** *John Smith* (detail), National Portrait Gallery, Smithsonian Institution, Washington, D.C./Art Resource, NY **4: (r.):** The Granger Collection, New York **4: (l.):** Bettmann/CORBIS **4: (b.):** Victoria & Albert Museum, London/Art Resource, NY **4: (t.l.):** Astrolabe, Museum fur Kunst und Gewerbe, Hamburg **5: (b.):** Corel Professional Photos CD-ROM™ **5: (t.r.):** The Granger Collection, New York **5: (t.l.):** North Wind Picture Archives **6:** Astrolabe, Museum fur Kunst und Gewerbe, Hamburg **7:** North Wind Picture Archives **8: (b.):** Colonial Williamsburg Foundation **8: (t.):** Astrolabe, Museum fur Kunst und Gewerbe, Hamburg **10: (b.):** The Granger Collection, New York **10: (t.):** Astrolabe, Museum fur Kunst und Gewerbe, Hamburg **11:** The Bettmann Archive **12: (t.):** Astrolabe, Museum fur Kunst und Gewerbe, Hamburg **12: (b.):** Corel Professional Photos CD-ROM™ **13: (t.):** North Wind Picture Archives **13: (b.):** Corel Professional Photos CD-ROM™ **15:** *Oneida Chieftain Shikellamy*, Unknown American, c.1820, 45 1/2" x 32", oil on canvas, Philadelphia Museum of Art. The Collection of Edgar William and Bernice Chrysler Garbisch **16:** Silver Burdett Ginn **18:** Nicole Galeazzi/Omni-Photo Communications, Inc. **22:** *Dreamwalker*, Nancy Wood Taber, colored pencil, Courtesy of the artist **27:** *Red Jacket,* George Catlin, From the Collection of Gilcrease Museum, Tulsa **32: (b.):** Viviane Moos/CORBIS **32: (t.):** Photo by Rebecca Dallinger; Courtesy of Susan Power **34:** Marilyn "Angel" Wynn/Nativestock.com **35: (inset):** Courtesy of the Library of Congress **36:** Joseph Sohm; Visions of America/CORBIS **37:** *The Old Guitarist*, 1903, Pablo Picasso, Spanish, 1881–1973, oil on panel 122.9 x 82.6 cm, Helen Birch Bartlett Memorial Collection, 1926.253. Reproduction, The Art Institute of Chicago, ©2004Estate of Pablo Picasso/Artists Rights Society (ARS), New York; **38:** Buffalo Bill Historical Center; Cody, Wyoming; Gift of Hon. and Mrs. William Henry Harrison; NA. 202.70 **42–43:** Corel Professional Photos CD-ROM™ **44:** Painting of Cabeza de Vaca, Esteban and their companions among various Texas Indian tribes, Tom Mirrat, The Institute of Texan Cultures, San Antonio, Texas **47:** Jeff Greenberg/Photo Researchers, Inc. **52–53:** © Matthias Kulka/CORBIS **54:** © Otto Rogge/Stock Photos/CORBIS **55:** The Bridgeman Art Library, London/New York **56:** John Chase/Dorling Kindersley. © Museum of London **58:** Erich Lessing/Art Resource, NY **60:** Astrolabe, Museum fur Kunst und Gewerbe, Hamburg **61:** Bettmann/CORBIS **66:** Peabody Museum of Archaeology and Ethnology, Harvard University **66: (t.):** Astrolabe, Museum fur Kunst und Gewerbe, Hamburg **67:** The Rosenbach Museum & Library **68: (l.):** John Smith (detail), National Portrait Gallery, Smithsonian Institution, Washington, D.C./Art Resource, NY; **68: (r.):** Bettmann/CORBIS **70:** The First Day at Jamestown, 14th May 1607, from "The Romance and Tragedy of Pioneer Life" by Augustus L. Mason, 1883, William Ludlow Sheppard/Bridgeman Art Library, London/New York **72:** Print Collection, Miriam and Ira D. Wallach Division of Art, Prints and Photographs, The New York Public Library, Astor, Lenox and Tilden Foundations **74:** Architect of the Capitol **77:** *The Coming of the Mayflower*, N.C. Wyeth, from the Collection of Metropolitan Life Insurance Company, New York City, photograph by Malcolm Varon **78:** *The Mayflower in Plymouth Harbor*, William Halsall, Burstein Collection/CORBIS **81:** Cary Wolinsky/Stock, Boston **82:** The Granger Collection, New York **91:** *Pilgrims Going to Church*, George Henry Boughton, Collection of The New-York Historical Society **91: (t.r.):** istockphoto.com **92:** *Anne Bradstreet , The Tenth Muse Lately Sprung Up in America,* Ladonna Gulley Warrick, Courtesy of the artist **94:** Crewel Work Chair Seat Cover, Gift of Samuel Bradstreet, Courtesy, Museum of Fine Arts, Boston. Reproduced with permission. ©2002 Museum of Fine Arts, Boston. All Rights Reserved. 19.602 **100:** Bettmann/CORBIS **103:** *The Puritan*, c. 1898, Frank E. Schoonover, Oil on canvas, Collection of The Brandywine River Museum, Gift of Mr. and Mrs. Jacob J. Foster, 1981. ©2002 Brandywine Conservancy **112:** istockphoto.com **115:** Photo by Rebecca Dallinger; Courtesy of Susan Power **124–125:** *Washington Crossing the Delaware* (copy after the Emmanuel Leutze painting), Eastman Johnson, Private Collection/Art Resource, NY **126: (b.):** Prentice Hall **126: (t.):** Astrolabe, Museum fur Kunst und Gewerbe, Hamburg **127:** Bettmann/CORBIS **128: (m.r.):** The Granger Collection, New York **128: (m.l.):** The Granger Collection, New York **128: (b.):** Independence National Historical Park **128: (m.m.):** The Granger Collection, New York **128: (t.):** Astrolabe, Museum fur Kunst und Gewerbe, Hamburg **129: (t.):** The Granger Collection, New York **129: (m.):** The Granger Collection, New York **129: (b.):** The Granger Collection, New York **130:** Astrolabe, Museum fur Kunst und Gewerbe, Hamburg **131:** Courtesy, American Antiquarian Society **132: (b.):** Corel Professional Photos CD-ROM™ **132: (t.):** Astrolabe, Museum fur Kunst und Gewerbe, Hamburg **133:** ©Archive Photos **134: (b.):** Corel Professional Photos CD-ROM™ **134: (t.):** Astrolabe, Museum fur Kunst und Gewerbe, Hamburg **135:** Courtesy of the Library of Congress **136:** Astrolabe, Museum fur Kunst und Gewerbe, Hamburg **137: (b.):** *George Washington* (Vaughan Portrait), Gilbert Stuart, Photograph ©Board of Trustees, National Gallery of Art, Washington, Andrew Mellon Collection **137: (t.):** Corel Professional Photos CD-ROM™ **138:** ©Archive Photos **139:** Miss Liberty, Abby Aldrich Rockefeller Folk Art Center, Williamsburg, VA **139:** backgroundCourtesy of the Library of Congress **139:** backgroundCorel Professional Photos CD-ROM™ **140:** *Benjamin Franklin* (detail), c.1790, Pierre Michel Alix, National Portrait Gallery, Smithsonian Institution, Washington, D.C./Art Resource, New York **142:** *Quaker Meeting*, Unidentified Artist, Courtesy, Museum of Fine Arts, Boston. Reproduced with permission. ©2002 Museum of Fine Arts, Boston. All Rights Reserved. 64.456 **144:** ©British Museum **146:** The Granger Collection, New York **148:** The Granger Collection, New York **154: (b.):** ©Bettmann/CORBIS **154: (t.):** Astrolabe, Museum fur Kunst und Gewerbe, Hamburg **156:** Prentice Hall **157:** The Art Archive/Maritime Museum Kronborg Castle Denmark/Dagli Orti **158:** Royal Albert Memorial Museum, Exeter, Devon, UK/The Bridgeman Art Library, London/New York **160:** National Maritime Museum, London **162:** Courtesy of the Library of Congress **168: (r.):** The Granger Collection, New York **168: (l.):** The Granger Collection, New York **170:** Corel Professional Photos CD-ROM™ **171:** Yale University Art Gallery **172: (r.):** Ron Watts/CORBIS **172: (l.):** Corel Professional Photos CD-ROM™ **174:** *Recruiting for the Continental Army*, William T. Ranney, Munson-Williams-Proctor Institute Museum of Art, Utica, New York **180:** Bettmann/CORBIS **182–183:** Corel Professional Photos CD-ROM™ **184:** *Liberty and Washington*, New York State Historical Association, Cooperstown **191:** istockphoto.com **192:** istockphoto.com **194:** Werner Forman/Art Resource, NY **197:** *George Washington, standing on the platform*, Penn State Capitol, Harrisburg, Photo: Brian K. Foster. Courtesy Senate Communications **199:** Bettmann/CORBIS **200: (l.):** *Patrick Henry* (detail), c.1835, James Barton Longacre after Lawrence Sully, The National Portrait Gallery, Smithsonian Institution, Washington, D.C./Art Resource, New York **200: (r.):** Bettmann/CORBIS **202:** *Patrick Henry Before the Virginia House of Burgesses 1851*, Peter F. Rothermel, Red Hill, The Patrick Henry National Memorial, Brookneal, Virginia **205:** Courtesy of the Library of Congress **207:** Courtesy National Archives and Records Administration, College Park, Maryland, photo no. ( ) **208:** *Benjamin Franklin (1706-90) - Overseeing the Printing of Poor Richard's Almanack,* Norman Rockwell, Lawrence Steigrad Fine Arts, New York/The Bridgeman Art Library, London/New York **213:** 18th c. New England needlework, Colonial Williamsburg Foundation **214: (l.):** The Granger Collection, New York **214: (r.):** The Granger Collection, New York **216:** *Building the First White House,* 1930, N.C. Wyeth, Copyrighted © by the White House Historical Association, photo by the National Geographical Society **220:** *Independence (Squire Jack Porter),* 1858, Frank Blackwell Mayer, National Museum of American Art, Smithsonian Institution, Bequest of Harriet Lane Johnson, Art Resource, New York **228:** Cleve Bryant/PhotoEdit Inc. **231:** Prentice Hall **240–241:** *Niagara Falls*, Hippolyte Victor Valentin Sebron, Musee des Beaux-Arts, Rouen, France. Lauros/Giraudon/The Bridgeman Art Library, London/New York **242: (m.):** Prentice Hall **242: (b.):** Ansel Adams Publishing Rights Trust/CORBIS **242: (t.):** Astrolabe, Museum fur Kunst und Gewerbe, Hamburg **244: (m.l.):** Seltzer, Lewis' *First Glimpse of the Rockies*, The Thomas Gilcrease Institute of Art Tulsa, Oklahoma **244: (b.l.):** Giraudon/Art Resource, NY **244: (m.r.):** Samuel S. Spaulding Collection, Buffalo and Erie County Historcal Society **244: (m.m.):** The Granger Collection, New York **244: (b.r.):** Adam Woolfit/CORBIS **244: (t.):** Astrolabe, Museum fur Kunst und Gewerbe, Hamburg **245: (b.):** Christie's Images/SuperStock **245: (t.l.):** Image Select/Art Resource, NY **245: (t.m.):** The Granger Collection, New York **245: (t.l.):** Bettmann/CORBIS **246: (t.):** Astrolabe, Museum fur Kunst und Gewerbe, Hamburg **247:** Corel Professional Photos CD-ROM™ **248: (r.):** The Granger Collection, New York **248: (l.):** Astrolabe, Museum fur Kunst und Gewerbe, Hamburg **249:** Corel Professional Photos CD-ROM™ **250: (r.):** The National Portrait Gallery, Smithsonian Institution/Art Resource, NY **250: (l.):** Astrolabe, Museum fur Kunst und Gewerbe, Hamburg **251:** Corel Professional Photos CD-ROM™ **252:** Astrolabe, Museum fur Kunst und Gewerbe, Hamburg **253:** American Steel Foundries **254:** Copyrighted by the White House Historical Association; Photograph by the National Geographic Society **255:** *Fredericksburg Refugee Family at Campfire*, D.E. Henderson, Gettysburg National Military Park Museum **256:** *Washington Irving* (detail): Daniel Huntington, National Portrait Gallery, Smithsonian Institution, Washington, D.C./Art Resource, New York **261:** John Quidor, American, 1801–1881, *The Devil and Tom Walker,* 1856. Oil on canvas, 68.8cm x 86.6cm. © The Cleveland Museum of Art, 2002. Mr. and Mrs. William H. Marlatt Fund, 1967.18 **262:** Walking stick, King Georges County, Virginia, 1846, carved wood with ink decoration, 37 x 2 inches in diameter, Abby Aldrich Rockefeller Folk Art Center, Williamsburg VA **263:** Yale University Art Gallery, New Haven. The Mabel Brady Garvan Collection **264:** Leonard Lee Rue III/Stock, Boston **266:** Index Stock Photography, Inc. **267: (r.):** Ron Watts/CORBIS **267: (l.):** Corel Professional Photos CD-ROM™ **272: (t.l.):** *Henry Wadsworth Longfellow* (detail), Thomas B. Read, The National Portrait Gallery, Smithsonian Institution, Washington, D.C./Art Resource, New York **272: (b.):** The Granger Collection, New York **272: (t.r.):** Samuel F.B. Morse *William Cullen Bryant*, 1828-1829 Oil on Canvas, 29 1/2 x 34 3/4 in. National Academy Museum, New York (892-P) **273: (b.):** The Granger Collection, New York **273: (t.):** *John Greenleaf Whittier* (detail), 1881, William Notman, The National Portrait Gallery, Smithsonian Institution, Washington, D.C./Art Resource, New York; **275:** *Seashore in Normandy*, 1893, Maximilien Luce, Erich Lessing/Art Resource, NY **276:** *Seashore in Normandy,*(detail) 1893, Maximilien Luce, Erich Lessing/Art Resource, NY **277:** *Kindred*

Spirits, Asher B. Durand, New York Public Library, Astor, Lenox and Tilden Foundations **280:** Charles Krups/AP/Wide World Photos **282–283:** *Old Holley House, Cos Cob*, John Henry Twachtman, Cincinnati Art Museum, John J. Emery Endowment **284–285:** Martial Columb/Getty Images **296: (l.):** The Granger Collection, New York **296: (r.):** *John Wesley Powell* (detail), Edmund Clarence Messer, National Portrait Gallery, Smithsonian Institution, Washington, D.C./Art Resource, NY **298: (r.):** *Draught of the Falls and Portage of the Missouri River (Clark's map of the Missouri River),* Missouri Historical Society, Clark Papers, Voorhis #1, 2 July 1805, ink on paper, L/A 464b. **298: (l.):** *Lewis and Clark with Sacajawea at the Great Falls of the Missouri*, Olaf Seltzer, #0137.871. The Thomas Gilcrease Institute of Art, Tulsa, Oklahoma; **299:** *White Salmon Trout*, ink on paper (Clark's drawing of salmon from his journal) Missouri Historical Society MHS Archives, entry before 17 March 1806. L/A #407b **301:** Corel Professional Photos CD-ROM™ **303:** *Grand Canyon with Rainbow*, 1912, Thomas Moran, oil on canvas, 25x30" (63.5 x 76.3cm) Collection of the Fine Arts Museums of San Francisco, Gift of Mr. and Mrs. Robert Gill through the Patrons of Art and Music, (1981.89) **309:** Cummer Museum of Art & Gardens, Jacksonville, FL/SuperStock **310:** Bettmann/CORBIS **313:** "I at length...," Edgar Allen Poe's Tales of Mystery and Imagination (London: George G. Harrap, 1935), Arthur Rackham, Print Collection, Miriam and Ira D. Wallach Division of Art, Prints and Photographs, The New York Public Library; Astor, Lenox and Tilden Foundations **316: (r.):** Ron Watts/CORBIS **316: (l.):** Corel Professional Photos CD-ROM™ **320–321:** Steve Mohlenkamp/Index Stock Photography, Inc. **327:** ©2000 The Munch Museum/The Munch-Ellingsen Group/Artists Rights Society (ARS), New York **332:** *The Raven,* 1845, Edmund Dulac, The Granger Collection, New York **338:** *Nathaniel Hawthorne* (detail), 1862, Emanuel Gottlieb Leutze, The National Portrait Gallery, Smithsonian Institution, Washington, D.C./Art Resource, New York **341:** New York State Historical Association, Cooperstown, New York **344: (r.):** Ron Watts/CORBIS **344: (l.):** Corel Professional Photos CD-ROM™ **348:** *Cemetery*, Peter McIntyre, Courtesy of the artist **356:** The Granger Collection, New York **360:** *Captain Ahab on the deck of the Pequod,* 1930, pen and ink drawing, The Granger Collection, New York **361:** Stock Newport, Inc. **363:** CORBIS **365:** *Moby-Dick,* 1930, pen and ink drawing, The Granger Collection, New York **366:** The Whaling Museum **368:** *Moby-Dick,* 1930, pen and ink drawing, The Granger Collection, New York **373:** Culver Pictures, Inc. **379:** *A View of Chamonix and Mt. Blanc,* Ludwig Ferdinand Schnorr von Carolsfeld, Austrian Gallery, Vienna **382:** *Mary Shelley* (detail), c.1840, Richard Rothwell, by courtesy of the National Portrait Gallery, London **383:** *Early Morning at Cold Spring,* 1850, oil on canvas, 60 x 48" Asher B. Durand, Collection of the Montclair Art Museum, Montclair New Jersey **384: (b.):** ©Lee Snider; Lee Snider/CORBIS **385: (t.):** Hulton-Deutsch Collection/CORBIS **385: (b.):** Courtesy of the Library of Congress **386:** ©Elisheba Johnson **387:** Bettmann/CORBIS **388:** *Ralph Waldo Emerson* (detail), Frederick Gutekunst/National Portrait Gallery, Smithsonian Institution, Washington, D.C./Art Resource, NY **391:** *Sunset,* Frederick Edwin Church, Munson-Williams-Proctor Institute Museum of Art, Utica, New York **393:** Tom Bean/CORBIS **395:** Leonard Harris/Stock, Boston **396–397:** Frank Whitney/Getty Images **402: (b.):** Courtesy Concord Free Public Library, Concord Massachusetts **402: (t.):** Prentice Hall **404:** Getty Images **406:** Owen Franken/PNI **411:** Burstein Collection/CORBIS **412:** ©The Stock Market/Dan McCoy **414:** ©Lee Snider; Lee Snider/CORBIS **421:** *Walden Pond Revisited,* 1942, N.C. Wyeth, tempera, possibly mixed with other media on panel, 42x48" Collection of the Brandywine River Museum, Bequest of Miss Carolyn Wyeth, 1996. ©2002 Brandywine Conservancy **424:** Amherst College Archives and Special Collections, by permission of the Trustees of Amherst College **426:** *Waiting Outside No. 12,* Anonymous, Crane Kalman Gallery **428:** *Room With a Balcony,* Adolph von Menzel, Staatliche Museen Preubischer Kulturbesitz, Nationgalerie, Berlin **430:** eStock Photography, LLC **432:** Frederic Edwin Church, American, 1826–1900. *Twilight in the Wilderness,* 1860. Oil on canvas, 101.6 x 162.6 cm. © The Cleveland Museum of Art, 2002, Mr. and Mrs. William H. Marlett Fund, 1965.233 **434:** Darrell Gulin/Getty Images **438:** The Granger Collection, New York **442:** Courtesy of the Library of Congress **446:** *The Lawrence Tree,* 1929, Georgia O'Keeffe, Wadsworth Atheneum, Hartford, CT. The Ella Gallup Sumner and Mary Catlin Sumner Collection, ©1998 The Georgia O'Keeffe Foundation/Artists Rights Society (ARS), New York **449:** *The Reaper,* c.1881, Louis C. Tiffany, oil on canvas, National Academy of Design, New York City **456:** Cleve Bryant/PhotoEdit Inc. **459:** Prentice Hall **468–469:** Currier & Ives/SuperStock **469: (t.r.):** Photo Researchers, Inc. **469: (b.r.):** Bettmann/CORBIS **470: (b.):** Prentice Hall **470: (t.):** Astrolabe, Museum fur Kunst und Gewerbe, Hamburg **471:** Bettmann/CORBIS **472: (b.l.):** The Granger Collection, New York **472: (b.m.):** The Granger Collection, New York **472: (b.r.):** The Granger Collection, New York **472: (t.):** Astrolabe, Museum fur Kunst und Gewerbe, Hamburg **473: (b.):** Bettmann/CORBIS **473: (t.l.):** The Granger Collection, New York **473: (m.):** The Granger Collection, New York **473: (t.r.):** The Granger Collection, New York **474: (b.):** CORBIS-Bettmann **474: (t.):** Astrolabe, Museum fur Kunst und Gewerbe, Hamburg **475: (r.):** Courtesy of the Library of Congress **475: (l.):** Courtesy of the Library of Congress **476: (t.):** Astrolabe, Museum fur Kunst und Gewerbe, Hamburg **476: (b.):** Corel Professional Photos CD-ROM™ **477:** Nebraska State Historical Society **478:** Astrolabe, Museum fur Kunst und Gewerbe, Hamburg **479:** Corel Professional Photos CD-ROM™ **480:** Astrolabe, Museum fur Kunst und Gewerbe, Hamburg **481: (r.):** *Six O'Clock, Winter,* 1912, John Sloan, The Phillips Collection **481: (l.):** Corel Professional Photos CD-ROM™ **482: (b.):** *Samuel Longhorne Clemens (Mark Twain),* (detail), 1935, Frank Edwin Larson, National Portrait Gallery, Smithsonian Institution, Washington, D.C./Art Resource, New York **483: (inset):** *Fight for the Standard*, oil on canvas, H 26 3/4 inches, W 21 1/2 inches, Wadsworth Atheneum, Hartford, CT. The Ella Gallup Sumner and Mary Catlin Sumner Collection Fund **483:** backgroundCourtesy of the Library of Congress **484: (l.):** Bettmann/CORBIS **484: (r.):** Center for American Music. Stephen Foster Memorial, University of Pittsburgh **486:** Courtesy of the Library of Congress **489:** Courtesy National Archives **490:** Museum of the Confederacy, Richmond, Virginia **491:** *Young Soldier: Separate Study of a Soldier Giving Water to a Wounded Companion,* (detail) 1861, Winslow Homer, Oil, gouache, black crayon on canvas, 36 x 17.5 cm., United States, 1836–1910, Cooper-Hewitt, National Museum of Design, Smithsonian Institution, Gift of Charles Savage Homer, Jr., 1912-12-110, Photo by Ken Pelka, Courtesy of Art Resource, New York **498:** Courtesy of the Library of Congress **504:** *Frederick Douglass* (detail), c.1844, Attributed to Elisha Hammond, The National Portrait Gallery, Smithsonian Institution, Washington, D.C./Art Resource, New York **506:** *The Chimney Corner,* 1863, Eastman Johnson, oil on cardboard, 15 1/2 x 13 in., Munson-Williams-Proctor Institute Museum of Art, Utica, New York; Gift of Edmund G. Munson, Jr. **508:** *A Home on the Mississippi,* 1871, Currier & Ives, The Museum of the City of New York, Harry T. Peters Collection **510: (r.):** Ron Watts/CORBIS **510: (l.):** Corel Professional Photos CD-ROM™ **516:** Bettmann/CORBIS **518:** Superstock **519:** The Kobal Collection **530: (r.):** *Robert E. Lee* (detail), 1864–1865, Edward Caledon Bruce, The National Portrait Gallery, Smithsonian Institution, Washington, D.C./Art Resource, New York **530: (l.):** *Portrait of Abraham Lincoln* (detail), William Willard, National Portrait Gallery, Smithsonian Institution, Washington, D.C./Art Resource, New York **533:** CORBIS **535:** Buddy Mays/CORBIS **542: (t.):** Courtesy of the Library of Congress **542: (b.):** Courtesy of the Library of Congress **543: (inset):** *Newspapers in the Trenches*' 64, William Ludwell Sheppard, Museum of the Confederacy, Richmond, Virginia, Photography by Katherine Wetzel **543:** backgroundCourtesy of the Library of Congress **544:** Comstock Images/Alamy Images **546: (b.):** Getty Images **546: (t.):** Prentice Hall **548:** Courtesy of the Library of Congress **551:** Courtesy of the Library of Congress **553: (r.):** Ron Watts/CORBIS **553: (l.):** Corel Professional Photos CD-ROM™ **556:** Andre Jenny/Focus Group/PictureQuest **558:** The Granger Collection, New York **560:** The Granger Collection, New York **561:** Bettmann/CORBIS **566:** CORBIS **567:** *A Star Shell*, exh. 1916, Christopher R.W. Nevinson, © Tate Gallery, London 2004/Art Resource, NY **568:** *Italian Soldiers*, Karl Fahringer, Heeresgeschichtliches Museum, Vienna, Austria **569:** Burstein Collection/CORBIS **570:** Luigi Pirandello, Primo Conti, Giraudon/Art Resource, New York; **571:** Corel Professional Photos CD-ROM™ **572: (b.):** Corel Professional Photos CD-ROM™ **572: (m.):** Courtesy National Archives **572: (t.):** Astrolabe, Museum fur Kunst und Gewerbe, Hamburg **573:** ©Bettmann/CORBIS **574:** *Samuel Longhorne Clemens* (Mark Twain), (detail), 1935, Frank Edwin Larson, National Portrait Gallery, Smithsonian Institution, Washington, D.C./Art Resource, New York **576:** *Paddle Steamboat Mississippi*, Shelburne Museum, Shelburne, Vermont, Photo by Ken Burris **578:** Courtesy of the Library of Congress **581:** *Mark Twain (Samuel L. Clemens) Riding the Celebrated Jumping Frog* – an English caricature, 1872, Frederic Waddy, The Granger Collection, New York **583:** The Granger Collection, New York **584:** ©Craig K. Lorenz/Photo Researchers, Inc. **590:** The Granger Collection, New York **592:** *Edge of Town,* Charles Ephraim Burchfield, The Nelson-Atkins Museum of Art, Kansas City, Missouri **594:** Corel Professional Photos CD-ROM™ **596: (r.):** Ron Watts/CORBIS **596: (l.):** Corel Professional Photos CD-ROM™ **598:** Esbin/Anderson/Omni-Photo Communications, Inc. **606:** *Chief Joseph* (detail), 1878, Cyrenius Hall, National Portrait Gallery, Smithsonian Institution, Washington, D.C./Art Resource, New York; **608:** Kansas State Historical Society **611: (r.):** Ron Watts/CORBIS **611: (l.):** Corel Professional Photos CD-ROM™ **612:** Kansas State Historical Society **614:** National Museum of American History, Smithsonian Institution **618:** Bettmann/CORBIS **620:** Wayne Lynch/DRK Photo **623:** Corel Professional Photos CD-ROM™ **626:** Corel Professional Photos CD-ROM™ **629:** Annie Griffiths/DRK Photo **630–631:** CORBIS **632:** Niebrugge Images **639:** *Channel to the Mills,* 1913, Edwin M. Dawes, oil on canvas, 51 x 39 1/2 in. Minneapolis Institute of Arts, anonymous gift. **640:** Photograph courtesy Newberry Library, Chicago **642–643:** *Afternoon in Piedmont, (Elsie at the Window),* c.1911, Xavier Martínez, Collection of The Oakland Museum of California, Gift of Dr. William S. Porter **644:** Corel Professional Photos CD-ROM™ **650:** The Granger Collection, New York **652:** Stock Montage, Inc. **658: (r.):** *Edgar Lee Masters* (detail), 1946, Francis J. Quirk, National Portrait Gallery, Smithsonian Institution, Washington, D.C./Art Resource, New York **658: (l.):** *Edwin Arlington Robinson* (detail), 1933, Thomas Richard Hood, National Portrait Gallery, Smithsonian Institution, Washington, D.C./Art Resource, New York **660:** Horst Oesterwinter/International Stock Photography, Ltd. **662:** *The Thinker* (Portrait of Louis N. Kenton, 1900), Thomas Eakins, The Metropolitan Museum of Art, John Stewart Kennedy Fund, 1917. (17.172) Photograph © 2001 The Metropolitan Museum of Art **664:** Joel Greenstein/Omni-Photo Communications, Inc. **668:** Bettmann/CORBIS **670:** George Schreiber (1904–1977), *From Arkansas*, 1939, oil on canvas, Sheldon Swope Art Museum, Terre Haute, Indiana; **674:** Robbie Jack/CORBIS **676:** The Granger Collection, New York **684:** Jonathan Nourok/PhotoEdit Inc. **687:** Prentice Hall **698–699:** Pam Ingalls/CORBIS **700: (b.):** Prentice Hall **700: (t.):** Astrolabe, Museum fur Kunst und Gewerbe, Hamburg **701:** Getty Images **702: (m.r.):** The Granger Collection, New York **702: (m.l.):** Bettmann/CORBIS **702: (m.m.):** Bettmann/CORBIS **702: (b.):** National Archives **702: (t.):** Astrolabe, Museum fur Kunst und Gewerbe, Hamburg **703: (t.m.):** The Granger Collection, New York **703: (t.l.):** SuperStock **703: (t.r.):** Alfred Eisenstaedt, Life Magazine © Time Warner **703: (b)** *The Persistence of Memory,* 1931, Salvador Dali, The Museum of Modern Art, New York. Given anonymously. Digital Image © The Museum of Modern Art/Licensed by SCALA/Art Resource, NY, ©2003 Salvador Dali, Gala-Salvador Dali Foundation/Artists Rights Society (ARS), New York **704: (b.):** Culver Pictures, Inc. **704: (t.):** Astrolabe, Museum fur Kunst und Gewerbe, Hamburg **705: (r.):** Museum of Connecticut History **705: (l.):** Corel Professional Photos CD-ROM™ **706: (b.):** Culver Pictures, Inc. **706: (t.):** Astrolabe,

Museum fur Kunst und Gewerbe, Hamburg **707:** Corel Professional Photos CD-ROM™ **708: (b.):** Courtesy of the Library of Congress **708: (t.):** Astrolabe, Museum fur Kunst und Gewerbe, Hamburg **710:** Photograps and Prints Division, Schomburg Center for Research in Black Culture, The New York Public Library, Astor, Lenox and Tilden Foundations **711:** Corel Professional Photos CD-ROM™ **712:** Historical Pictures Collection/Stock Montage, Inc. **713: (inset):** *No Place to Go*, 1935, Maynard Dixon, Oil on canvas, 25 x 30 inches. The Herald Clark Memorial Collection, Courtesy of Brigham Young University Museum of Fine Arts. All Rights Reserved. Photo by David W. Hawkinson **713:** backgroundCourtesy of the Library of Congress **714:** *T. S. Elliot* (detail), 1888–1965, Sir Gerald Kelly, National Portrait Gallery, Smithsonian Institution, Art Resource, New York **718:** Corel Professional Photos CD-ROM™ **724: (l.):** The Granger Collection, New York **724: (r.):** *William Carlos Williams* (detail), The National Portrait Gallery, Smithsonian Institution, Washington, D.C./Art Resource, NY **725:** Bettmann/CORBIS **728:** The Granger Collection, New York **731:** Zha Shibiao, Chinese, 1615–1698, Qing dynasty. *Shibiao Waiting for the Moon from Landscape Album in Various Styles*, 1684. Album of twelve leaves, ink or ink and color on paper; each 29.9 x 39.4 cm. © The Cleveland Museum of Art, 2002, Gift of Mr. and Mrs. Severance A. Millikin, 1955.37 **733:** *The Figure 5 in Gold*, 1928, Charles Demuth, oil on composition board. H. 36 in. W. 29-3/4 in. (91.4 x 75.6 cm) Signed (lower left): C.D. Inscribed (bottom center): W.C.W. (William Carlos Williams), The Metropolitan Museum of Art, Alfred Steiglitz Collection, 1949. (49.59.1). Photograph © 1986 The Metropolitan Museum of Art **735:** Adam Jones/Photo Researchers, Inc. **736:** *Overhanging Cloud in July*, Charles Burchfield, Collection of Whitney Museum of American Art. Purchase, with funds from the Friends of the Whitney Museum of American Art (60.23). Photography Copyright © 2000: Whitney Museum of American Art **740:** *F. Scott Fitzgerald* (detail), David Silvette, The National Portrait Gallery, Smithsonian Institution, Washington, D.C./Art Resource, New York **742:** Corel Professional Photos CD-ROM™ **746–747:** *Golf Course-California*, 1917, George Wesley Bellows, Oil on canvas, 30 x 38 inches, Collection Cincinnati Art Museum, The Edwin and Virginia Irwin Memorial, 1966.6 **748:** Getty Images **752:** *The Morning Sun*, c. 1920, o/c, 50 x 40 ins., Pauline Palmer, Collection Rockford Art Museum, Gift of the Friends of American Art, 1922 **754:** Bettmann/CORBIS **756:** Getty Images **758: (r.):** Ron Watts/CORBIS **758: (l.):** Corel Professional Photos CD-ROM™ **764:** Bettmann/CORBIS **766:** ©The Stock Market/Milt/Patti Putnam **772: (r.):** Bettmann/CORBIS **772: (l.):** Courtesy of the Library of Congress **774–775:** *Remember Now the Days of Thy Youth*, 1950, Paul Starrett Sample, Oil on canvas, 34 x 48 inches, Hood Museum of Art, Dartmouth College, Hanover, NH; Gift of Frank L. Harrington, class of 1954 **777:** *The Turret Lathe Operator (J.G. Cherry series)*, 1925, Grant Wood, oil on canvas 18" x 24" Cedar Rapids Museum of Art, Cedar Rapids, Iowa, Gift of the Cherry Burrell Charitable Foundation Collection. 75.5.8, ©Estate of Grant Wood/Licensed by VAGA, New York, NY **782:** Bettmann/CORBIS **784:** *Stone City, Iowa*, 1930, Grant Wood, Joslyn Art Museum, Omaha, Nebraska, ©Estate of Grant Wood/Licensed by VAGA, New York, NY **787: (r.):** Ron Watts/CORBIS **787: (l.):** Corel Professional Photos CD-ROM™ **792: (t.l.):** The Granger Collection, New York **792: (t.r.):** Bettmann/CORBIS **792: (b.):** AP/Wide World Photos **795:** Silver Burdett Ginn **796:** Index Stock Photography, Inc. **797:** Index Stock Photography, Inc. **798:** *Untitled*, 1964, Alexander Calder, (one of seven lithographs in series), 19 1/2 x 25 1/2" Solomon R. Guggenheim Museum, New York, Gift of the artist, 1965, Photo by David Heald, © The Solomon R. Guggenheim Foundation, New York, ©1998 Estate of Alexander Calder/Artists Rights Society (ARS), New York **803:** *Do It Yourself Landscape*, 1962, Andy Warhol, Museum Ludwig, Cologne, photo courtesy of Rheinisches Bildarchiv Köln. ©1998 Andy Warhol Foundation for the Visual Arts/ARS, New York **806: (l.):** Larry Burrows/Life Magazine © Time Warner Inc. **806: (r.):** Bettmann/CORBIS **807:** Thomas Victor **809:** American Red Cross **811:** Verlog Suddeutscher-Bilderdienst **812:** ©FPG International LLC **813:** American Red Cross **815: (l.):** David Toase/Getty Images **816:** Ryan Beyer/Getty Images **820:** *Miz Emily*, Joseph Holston, 24" x 16", Courtesy of Joseph Holston (www.holstonart. com) **824:** *Georgia Red Clay*, 1946, Nell Choate Jones, oil on canvas, 25 x 30 inches, 1989.01.094, Morris Museum of Art, Augusta, Georgia **832: (b.):** Prentice Hall **833:** AP/Wide World Photos **834–835:** P.J. Griffiths/Magnum Photos, Inc. **837:** *The Tower*, 1920, Charles Demuth, Tempera on pasteboard, 23 1/4 x 19 1/2 in. (58.4 x 49.4 cm) Initialed and inscribed in pencil on reverse: After Christopher Wren (?) Provincetown, Mass./1BO (?) – CD, Columbus Museum of Art, Ohio; Gift of Ferdinarnd Howald, 31.146 **838:** Time Life Pictures/Getty Images **840:** Stock Montage, Inc. **842:** Corel Professional Photos CD-ROM™ **846:** Getty Images **849:** *Garden of Memories*, 1917, Charles Burchfield, The Museum of Modern Art, New York. Gift of Abby Aldrich Rockefeller (by exchange). Digital Image © The Museum of Modern Art/Licensed by SCALA/Art Resource, NY **850:** ©Bettmann/CORBIS **854:** ©1993 J. Fishkin. All Rights Reserved. **860:** Time Life Pictures/Getty Images **864:** Collection of the Prentice and Paul Sack Photographic Trust of the San Francisco Museum of Modern Art **865: (r.):** Ron Watts/CORBIS **865: (l.):** Corel Professional Photos CD-ROM™ **867:** *Woman by a Window*, Gustav Vermehren Snark/Art Resource, NY **868:** 66.1522 Thomas Eakins, *Mrs. Thomas Eakins*, ca. 1899. Oil on Canvas 20 1/8 x 16 1/8 Hirshhorn Museum/Smithsonian Institution. **871:** Elizabeth A. Whiting; Elizabeth Whiting & Associates/CORBIS **872:** Markus Amon/Getty Images **873:** Elizabeth Barakah Hodges/SuperStock **880:** CORBIS **882-883:** Corel Professional Photos CD-ROM™ **885:** Corel Professional Photos CD-ROM™ **886:** Dewitt Jones/Woodfin Camp & Associates **888:** Corel Professional Photos CD-ROM™ **890:** Bettmann/CORBIS **892:** Ellis Herwig/PNI **896: (r.):** AP/Wide World Photos **896: (l.):** Bettmann/CORBIS **898:** My Life and Hard Times Copyright ©1933 by James Thurber. Copyright © renewed 1961 by James Thurber. Reprinted by arrangement with Rosemary A. Thurber and The Barbara Hogenson Agency. **900:** My Life and Hard Times Copyright ©1933 by James Thurber. Copyright © renewed 1961 by James Thurber. Reprinted by arrangement with Rosemary A. Thurber and The Barbara Hogenson Agency. **901:** My Life and Hard Times Copyright ©1933 by James Thurber. Copyright © renewed 1961 by James Thurber. Reprinted by arrangement with Rosemary A. Thurber and The Barbara Hogenson Agency. **903:** Culver Pictures, Inc. **910: (b.):** Bettmann/CORBIS **910: (t.):** Astrolabe, Museum fur Kunst und Gewerbe, Hamburg **911:** *Zora and Langston*, Phoebe Beasley, Bettmann/CORBIS **912:** Courtesy of the Estate of Carl Van Vechten, Joseph Solomon, EXECUTOR, The National Portrait Gallery, Smithsonian Institution, Washington, D.C./Art Resource, New York **914:** ©Hulton Getty/Archive Photos **917:** *School Bell Time*, 1978 From the Profile/Part I: The Twenties series (Mecklenburg County), Romare Bearden, 29 1/4 x 41" Collection: Kingsborough Community College, The City University of New York; ©Romare Bearden Foundation/Licensed by VAGA, New York, NY **919: (l.):** Corel Professional Photos CD-ROM™ **919: (r.):** Ron Watts/CORBIS **924: (l.):** *Langston Hughes* (detail), c.1925, Winold Reiss, The National Portrait Gallery, Smithsonian Institution, Washington, D.C./Art Resource, New York **924: (r.):** The Granger Collection, New York **927:** Aaron Douglas, *Into Bondage*, 1936, 60 3/8 x 60 1/2, oil on canvas. In the collection of the Corcoran Gallery of Art, Washington, DC. Museum Purchase and Partial Gift of Thurlow Tibbs Jr., The Evans-Tibbs Collection. 1996.9 **928:** *Nobody Around Here Calls Me Citizen*, 1943, Robert Gwathmey, oil on canvas, H. 14-1/4" x W. 17" Collection Frederick R. Weisman Art Museum at the University of Minnesota, Minneapolis, Bequest of Hudson Walker from the Ione and Hudson Walker Collection. ©Estate of Robert Gwathmey/Licensed by VAGA, New York, NY **930:** *Girls Skipping*, 1949, Hale Woodruff, oil on canvas, 24" x 32" , Private Collection. Courtesy of Michael Rosenfeld Gallery, New York **932:** Michael Skott/Getty Images **936:** Bettmann/CORBIS **936: (t.):** *Countee Cullen* (detail), c.1925, Winold Reiss, The National Portrait Gallery, Smithsonian Institution, Washington, D.C./Art Resource, New York **936: (m.):** *Jean Toomer* (detail), c.1925, Winold Reiss, Gift of Laurence A. Fleischman and Howard Garfinkle with a matching grant from the National Endowment of the Arts, National Portrait Gallery, Smithsonian Institution, Washington, D.C./Art Resource, New York **939:** *Hoeing*, 1934, Robert Gwathmey, Oil on canvas, 40 by 60 1/4 (101.6 by 153), Carnegie Institute Museum of Art, Pittsburgh, Pennsylvania, Patrons Art Fund, 44.3. Photograph by Richard Stoner, ©Estate of Robert Gwathmey/Licensed by VAGA, New York, NY **940:** Corel Professional Photos CD-ROM™ **948:** James P. Blair/Getty Images **949:** Bettmann/CORBIS **952:** David Young-Wolff/PhotoEdit Inc. **955:** Prentice Hall **964–965:** Dale Kennington/SuperStock **966: (m.):** ©Sophie Bassouls/CORBIS Sygma **966: (b.):** Adam Woolfitt/CORBIS **966: (t.):** Astrolabe, Museum fur Kunst und Gewerbe, Hamburg **968: (m.m.):** Jay Leviton/Black Star **968: (t.r.):** The Granger Collection, New York **968: (m.r.):** Peter Garfield/Folio, Inc **968: (m.l.):** Nancy Crampton **968: (b.):** Bettmann/CORBIS **968: (t.):** Astrolabe, Museum fur Kunst und Gewerbe, Hamburg **969: (t.):** ©Larry Downing/Woodfin Camp & Associates **969: (m.):** ©1985 Peter Marlow/Magnum Photots, Inc. **969: (r.):** ©Dan Groshong/CORBIS Sygma **970: (b.):** The Granger Collection, New York **970: (t.):** Astrolabe, Museum fur Kunst und Gewerbe, Hamburg **971:** Corel Professional Photos CD-ROM™ **972:** Astrolabe, Museum fur Kunst und Gewerbe, Hamburg **974:** Astrolabe, Museum fur Kunst und Gewerbe, Hamburg **975: (r.):** *Down 18th Street*, 1980, Wayne Thiebaud, Hirshorn Museum and Sculpture Garden, Smithsonian Institution, Museum Purchase with Funds Donated by Edward R. Downe, Jr., 1980. Photography by Ricardo Blanc **975: (l.):** Corel Professional Photos CD-ROM™ **976: (t.):** Astrolabe, Museum fur Kunst und Gewerbe, Hamburg **976: (b.):** Corel Professional Photos CD-ROM™ **977:** ©Mark Bolster/International Stock Photography, Ltd. **978: (b.):** Getty Images **979: (inset):** *Television Moon*, 1978-79, Alfred Leslie, oil on canvas, Wichita Art Museum, gift of Virginia and George Ablah **979:** backgroundPearson Education **980:** Flannery O'Connor Collection, Ina Dillard Russel Library, Georgia College **982:** *Deep Fork Overlook*, Joan Marron-LaRue, Courtesy of the artist **987:** *Black Walnuts*, Joseph Pollet, Collection of Whitney Museum of American Art. Purchase and gift of Gertrude Vanderbilt Whitney, by exchange (52.30). Photograph Copyright © 2000: Whitney Museum of American Art **991: (r.):** Ron Watts/CORBIS **991: (l.):** Corel Professional Photos CD-ROM™ **996:** Nancy Crampton **998:** Culver Pictures, Inc. **1002: (r.):** Ron Watts/CORBIS **1002: (l.):** Corel Professional Photos CD-ROM™ **1004:** ©The Stock Market/Shiki **1010:** Courtesy of Eugenia Collier **1012:** ©age/fotostock/SuperStock **1014:** CORBIS **1016: (t)** Getty Images **1016–1017:** CORBIS **1018: (t.):** Courtesy National Archives and Records Administration, College Park, Maryland **1018: (b.):** CORBIS **1021:** Courtesy of the Library of Congress **1022:** SuperStock **1023:** Karl J. Kuerner III/SuperStock **1024:** ©Darlene Bordwell/www.darbaby.net **1028:** Miriam Berkley/Authorpix **1030:** *Sunrise. Pinkfeet Against the Cumbrian Hills*, 1994, Julian Novrol/Private Collection/The Bridgeman Art Library, London/New York **1032–1033:** The State Russian Museum/CORBIS **1034:** Getty Images **1037:** Courtesy of the Library of Congress **1038–1039:** CORBIS **1040–1041:** Private Collection, David Findlay, Jr. Fine Art, NYC/The Bridgeman Art Library, London/New York **1043:** *Pinkfooted Geese Over the Roost*, 2000, Julian Novrol/Private Collection/The Bridgeman Art Library, London/New York **1044:** *Sunrise. Pinkfeet against the Cumbrian Hills*, 1994, (detail) Julian Novrol/Private Collection/The Bridgeman Art Library, London/New York **1048: (t.):** *Robert Penn Warren* (detail), 1935, Conrad A. Albrizio, The National Portrait Gallery, Smithsonian Institution, Washington, D.C./Art Resource, New York **1048: (b.):** AP/Wide World Photos **1048: (m.):** Kit Stafford **1050:** Corel Professional Photos CD-ROM™ **1052:** Corel Professional Photos CD-ROM™ **1053:** Tim Lynch/Stock, Boston **1058:** ©Wolfgang Kaehler/CORBIS **1059:** Getty Images **1060:** Diana Walker **1062:** Fred Charles/Getty Images **1069:** *Girl Looking at Landscape*, 1957, Richard Diebenkorn, oil on canvas, 59 x 60 3/8 inches, (149.9 x 153.4 cm), Gift of Mr. and Mrs. Alan H. Temple, 61.49, Collection of Whitney Museum of American Art, photograph by Geoffrey Clements, N.Y., Photograph copyright (c) 1997: Whitney Museum of American Art **1074: (t.):** Thomas Victor **1074: (b.):** Photo by Michael Nye **1074: (m.):** Photo by

Paul Abdoo **1077:** *Passion of Paints*, Bob Peters, Exclusively represented by Applejack Licensing International **1079:** Museo de Santa Cruz/Bridgeman Art Library, London/New York **1081:** Culver Pictures, Inc. **1083:** *Getting Down*, Joseph Holston, 14" x 14", Courtesy of Joseph Holston (www.holstonart.com) **1088:** Thomas Victor **1090:** Jeff Greenberg/Omni-Photo Communications, Inc. **1095:** Museum of English Rural Life/© Dorling Kindersley **1096:** Lee Russell/CORBIS **1097:** Jeff Greenberg/Omni-Photo Communications, Inc. **1102:** ©Anthony Barboza/Life Magazine **1104:** AP/Wide World Photos **1107: (r.):** Ron Watts/CORBIS **1107: (l.):** Corel Professional Photos CD-ROM™ **1108–1109:** Matt Lambert/Getty Images **1114:** Prentice Hall **1116:** *Fruit Vendor*, 1951, Olga Costa, Museo de Arte Moderno, Mexico. © Olga Costa - SOMAAP, Mexico, 1999 **1121:** Richard Bickel/CORBIS **1124:** Andre Jenny/Focus Group/PictureQuest **1130: (t.r.):** Marlene Fostor **1130: (b.l.):** Rollie McKenna **1130: (t.l.):** Shelley Rotner/Omni-Photo Communications, Inc. **1130: (b.r.):** Photo courtesy of Garrett Gongo **1132:** Arlene Collins **1133:** Corel Professional Photos CD-ROM™ **1134:** Mitchell Funk/Getty Images **1135:** Animals Animals/©John Lemker **1141: (inset):** *My Mother's Book of Life*, 1987, Lee Lawson, Courtesy of the artist **1142:** Images.com/CORBIS **1144: (b.r.):** John Barrett/Globe Photos **1144: (b.l.):** © 1996 Sigrid Estrada **1144: (t.r.):** The Granger Collection, New York **1144: (t.l.):** AP/Wide World Photos **1146:** *Blam*, 1962,© Roy Lichtenstein, oil on canvas, 68 x 80 in. **1149:** Warner Bros./Photofest **1150:** Warner Bros./Photofest **1153:** Paul Edmondson/Getty Images **1157:** Reuters/CORBIS **1162: (b.):** Robert Severi/Getty Images **1162: (t.):** AP/Wide World Photos **1162: (m.):** Frank Capri/Getty Images **1165:** *Biography*, 1988, Marina Gutierrez, Courtesy of the artist **1169:** Andrew Ward/Getty Images **1172:** Jim McHugh **1175:** Gary Gay/Getty Images **1181: (inset):** *Choke*, 1964, Robert Rauschenberg, Oil and screenprint on canvas, 60" x 48", Washington University Gallery of Art, St. Louis, Gift of Mr. and Mrs. Richard K. Weil, 1972, ©Robert Rauschenberg/Licensed by VAGA, New York, NY **1181:** backgroundCourtesy of the Library of Congress **1182:** Thomas Victor **1184:** *Push to Walk*, collage 48" x 48"Phoebe Beasley **1189:** ©Telegraph Colour Library 1998/FPG International LLC **1196: (l.):** AP/Wide World Photos **1196: (r.):** Rollie McKenna **1198:** FPG International Corp. **1200:** ©CORBIS **1202:** FPG International Corp. **1204–1205:** Courtesy National Archives **1206: (r.):** Ron Watts/CORBIS **1206: (l.):** Corel Professional Photos CD-ROM™ **1209:** Stock Montage, Inc. **1210:** Stock Montage, Inc. **1214: (b.r.):** Bettmann/CORBIS **1214: (b.l.):** Thomas Victor **1214: (t.l.):** AP/Wide World Photos **1214: (t.r.):** ©Nancy Crampton **1216:** *Mirror II*, George Tooker, (1920–1938), Egg tempera on gesso panel, 20 x 20 in., 1968.4, Gift of R. H. Donnelley Erdman (PA 1956), ©Addison Gallery of American Art, Phillips Academy, Andover, Massachusetts. All Rights Reserved. **1219:** *Part II, The Free Man, No. 30, The Frederick Douglass Series*, Jacob Lawrence, Hampton University Museum, Hampton, Virginia, ©Gwendolyn Knight Lawrence, courtesy of the Jacob and Gwendolyn Lawrence Foundation **1221:** © Pekka Parviainen/Science Photo Library/Photo Researchers, Inc. **1226: (r.):** Bettmann/CORBIS **1226: (l.):** AP/Wide World Photos **1230:** *Retroactive I*, Robert Rauschenberg, 1964, Wadsworth Atheneum, Hartford, CT, Gift of Susan Morse Hilles, ©Robert Rauschenberg/Licensed by VAGA, New York, NY **1233:** Bettmann/CORBIS **1238: (b.):** Thomas Victor **1238: (m.):** Photo by Mandy Sayer **1238: (t.):** Nihad Becirovic **1240:** *The Madonna And Child*, 1990, Momodou Ceesay, Dialogue Systems, Inc. **1243:** *Winter*, Ozz Franca , Oil, 24 x 18", Edition of 1999 s/n, Courtesy of The Hadley Companies **1245:** Brian Parker/Tom Stack & Associates **1250: (b.):** Courtesy of the Library of Congress **1250: (m.):** ©Bettmann/CORBIS **1250: (t.):** Astrolabe, Museum fur Kunst und Gewerbe, Hamburg **1251:** Oscar White/CORBIS **1252:** ©Sophie Bassouls/CORBIS Sygma **1253:** Mark Peterson/CORBIS **1254:** AP/Wide World Photos **1255:** *The Trial of Two "Witches" at Salem, Massachusetts, in 1662*, Howard Pyle, The Granger Collection, New York **1258:** James Cotier/Getty Images **1260:** *The Execution of the Reverend Stephen Burroughs for Witchcraft at Salem Massachusetts, in 1692*, 19th century engraving, The Granger Collection, New York; **1264:** AP/Wide World Photos **1266:** Photofest **1268:** Photofest **1272:** Photofest **1277:** Musee Conde, Chantilly, France/Bridgeman Art Library, London/New York **1278:** Steve Cole/Getty Images **1283:** Photofest **1291:** James Cotier/Getty Images **1294:** Photofest **1296: (r.):** Ron Watts/CORBIS **1296: (l.):** Corel Professional Photos CD-ROM™ **1304:** Pocumtuck Valley Memorial Association, Memorial Hall Museum, Deerfield, Massachusetts **1308:** Photofest **1315:** James Cotier/Getty Images **1319:** © Joe Sohm/Stone **1326:** Photofest **1330:** Photofest **1332:** Photofest **1334:** Playbill, is a registered trademark of Playbill, Inc. All rights reserved. Used by permission. **1336:** Penguin USA **1343:** James Cotier/Getty Images **1347:** Photofest **1350:** Photofest **1352:** ©Reuters/Brad Rickerby/Archive Photos **1357:** Photofest **1368:** IT Stock/PictureQuest **1371:** ©Sophie Bassouls/CORBIS Sygma

Map and Art Credits: All graphic organizers: In-House Pros; All maps by Mapping Specialist, except where noted

Staff Credits: Ernie Albanese, Diane Alimena, **Rosalyn Arcilla,** Jasjit Arneja, Penny Baker, **Nancy Barker, Amy Baron,** Rachel Beckman, Betsy Bostwick, **Ellen Bowler,** Jennifer Brady, Nikki Bruno, Evonne Burgess, Pradeep Byram, Rui Camarinha, **Pam Carey,** Lisa Carrillo, Anathea Chartand, Jaime Cohen, Allison Cook, **Irene Ehrmann,** Leanne Esterly, Libby Forsyth, Steve Frankel, Philip Fried, **Maggie Fritz,** Michael Ginsberg, **Elaine Goldman,** Patricia Hade, **Monduane Harris, Martha Heller,** Beth Hyslip, Vicki A. Kane, Kimon Kirk, **Kate Krimsky,** Mary Sue Langan, Monica Lehmann, **Mary Luthi, George Lychock,** Gregory Lynch, John McClure, Jim McDonough, Kathleen Mercandetti, Kerrie Miller, Karyl Murray, Ken Myett, Michael O'Donnell, Kim Ortell, Carolyn Pallof, Sal Pisano, Jackie Regan, Erin Rehill-Seker, Bruce Rolff, **Laura Ross,** Carolyn Sapontzis, Donna Schindler, Mildred Schulte, **Melissa Shustyk, Robert Siek, Rita Sullivan, Cynthia Summers,** Patrice Titterington, **Elizabeth Torjussen,** Jane S. Traulsen, Daniela Velez

Additional Credits: Susan C. Ball, William Bingham, Andrea Brescia, Donna Chappelle, Jennifer Ciccone, Jason Cuoco, Florrie Gadson, Judith Gaelick, Phillip Gagler, James Garratt, Allen Gold, Kristan Hoskins, Lisa Iozzia, Mohamed Kaptan, Barbara Kehr, Terry Kim, Stuart Kirschenbaum, Linda Latino, Julian Liby, Ginidir Marshall, Bill McAllister, Patrick J. McCarthy, Caroline McDonnell, Michael McLaughlin, Meg Montgomery, Gita Nadas, Karen Mancinelli Paige, Lesley Pierson, Maureen Raymond, Rachel Ross, Lloyd Sabin, James Savakis, Debi Taffet, Ryan Vaarsi, Alfred Voto, Gina M. Wangrycht, Lindsay White

Gary Blackwood
Richard Mühlberger
Zlata Filipovic
Cornelius Eady
Pat Mora
John Phillip Santos
Erik Weihenmayer
Joao Magueijo
Anita Desai
Frank Kermode
Walter Dean Myers
Gary Soto
Julius Lester
Dean Smith
Coleman Barks
Marilyn Nelson
Patricia McKissack
James Berry
Jean Craighead George
William L. Andrews
John Kilgo
Richard Rodriguez
Laurence Yep
Judith Ortiz Cofer
Pat Mora
Susan Power
Gretel Ehrlich
David Mamet
Jane Yolen
Richard Peck
Jon Scieszka
Jamaica Kincaid
Burton Raffel
Royall Tyler
Susan Vreeland
Jacqueline Woodson
Wayson Choy
Charles Johnson
Andrew Mishkin
Cherie Bennett
David Henry Hwang
Nell Irvin Painter
Walter Dean Myers
Chinua Achebe
Elizabeth McCracken
Frank Kermode
Anita Desai
C.J. Cherryh
Patricia McKissack
Zlata Filipovic
Elizabeth McCracken
Gary Blackwood
Jean Craighead George
Jon Scieszka
Walter Dean Myers
Julius Lester
Dean Smith
Richard Mühlberger
Pat Mora
Jamaica Kincaid
Gretel Ehrlich
Arthur Miller
Rebecca Walker
Gretel Ehrlich
James Berry
Seamus Heaney
Joseph Bruchac
Lan Samantha Chang
Wendy Doniger
Tim O'Brien
Cornelius Eady
Arthur Miller